LITERATURE
FOR OUR TIME

REVISED EDITION

LITERATURE FOR OUR TIME

An Anthology for College Students

REVISED EDITION

Edited by

HARLOW O. WAITE
Syracuse University

BENJAMIN P. ATKINSON
Hobart College

HENRY HOLT AND COMPANY · NEW YORK

PREFACE TO THE REVISED EDITION

THIS ANTHOLOGY represents an extensive revision of our first collection of modern writing, published in 1947. In place of the arrangement by themes used in the first edition we have chosen to organize the readings according to the types of literature they exemplify. We are certain that we have thereby provided not only for better illustration of literary forms but also for a broader treatment of contemporary issues. We have also taken this opportunity to eliminate readings which proved to have a limited appeal and we have added many new readings. Some of the added selections are by authors more recent than those included in the first edition and some are by older figures, famous in literary history. We have thus not allowed ourselves to be hampered by a strict definition of "modern" when we set out to represent both the chief kinds of current writing and the most illuminating views on contemporary problems. In making these changes we have held to our standards for the first edition: to offer a selection for the modern reader of the best literature in drama, essay, short story, poetry—and through these and other art forms to stimulate interest in the significant ideas and attitudes, the problems and concerns, of the twentieth century.

The design of the first edition of *Literature for Our Time* was centrally concerned with "the consequences to human society of the release of atomic energy." If some may claim that, since August 6, 1945, men have learned to live—albeit uneasily—with the fruits of atomic research, they will also admit that their attempts to deal with the "consequences" are still unsatisfactory. In presenting this revision, we still feel, as we wrote in 1946, that "the problem of our time is how modern man can learn to live in harmony with his neighbors. He can more easily achieve that harmony if he understands his world, with all its political, social, moral, ethical, and spiritual puzzles. This book shows him how some of the writers of our time have endeavored to solve the puzzles."

We have made many changes in the readings. In response to numerous requests we have added essays by Emerson, Whitman, and Turner. Prose selections by George Orwell, J. W. N. Sullivan, Lincoln Barnett, E. M. Forster, and others have further enlarged this section. In drama Tennessee Williams replaces Čapek. In poetry we have added Emerson, Dickinson, Whitman,

Dylan Thomas, and increased the number of poems by Robinson, Yeats, Eliot, Jeffers, and Auden. We have broadened the short story section with the work of Eudora Welty, Lionel Trilling, D. H. Lawrence, F. Scott Fitzgerald, and Ernest Hemingway. New reproductions of paintings and drawings by Picasso, March Avery, Peter Blume, Luigi Lucioni, Marsden Hartley, and Edward Hopper will also be found. These, along with many photographs and cartoons, are placed in the collection to emphasize for the reader the relationships among various forms of art in our time.

Within each section of the anthology we have intended a particular purpose or plan, which selection and arrangement make clear. This is most apparent in Part I, where painter, poet, dramatist, short story writer and essayist deal with the theme of "Coming-of-Age in Our Time" in their differing ways. This opening section is meant to suggest to the reader how the selections that follow may be used in exploring themes and viewpoints through various types of literature and art. Part II, "How Writing Is Written," presents the writer on his own art and emphasizes the sense of craft which the modern reader needs in order to share fully in literary experience. Here, for example, will be found Thomas Wolfe on the novel, Maugham on prose, Miller and Anderson on tragedy.

Parts III, IV, V, and VI bring together varying examples of the literary types—Story, Drama, Poetry, Prose. Within each of these Parts, the selections are arranged to help the reader, by taking him from the easy to the difficult (as in the story), or by offering him the older and more familiar as an introduction to the newer and more complex (as in the poetry), or by keeping his attention on a number of recurrent ideas (as in the prose). The Appendix includes listings of modern novels and of recordings by contemporary poets, the biographies of the authors, and an index of titles and contributors.

We wish to express our thanks to Donald Dike of Syracuse University and John Lydenberg of Hobart and William Smith Colleges for their many suggestions.

We regret that Leonard Brown, of Syracuse University, our co-editor on the first edition, found it necessary to withdraw from this revision because of other publishing commitments.

Syracuse University H. O. W.
Hobart and William Smith Colleges B. P. A.
March 24, 1953

CONTENTS

[vii]

Contents

Contents

Part IV: DRAMA

Part V: POETRY

Contents

Contents

Contents

Contents

PART I · COMING-OF-AGE IN OUR TIME

THIS IS an introductory section intended to show how various types of literature deal with a universal theme. Here, in poem, story, play, prose, and picture are some of our finest creative artists dealing with certain problems posed by coming of age.

We often forget that none of us is one individual; we are several or many, at different times and at different ages. One way of seeing this is to watch the individual grow up. The following selections proceed through several of the ages of man, from the bright springtime of his childhood, through the wondering awkwardness of adolescence, the worldly assurance of young manhood, and the uncertainties of maturity. The Cummings and MacLeish poems show us children who "belong," who feel themselves part of things; Wolfe's "lost boy" discovers that something he once clung to has gone from his life, and the advice that follows recognizes this as a condition of youth. In these and the other stories are presented the discovery of moral values, the reluctant acceptance of what has to be, and with this discovery and acceptance are developed the flexibilities which any being must possess to survive. As the characters become aware of their own fragility in a harsh natural and social world, they have glimpses—and sometimes experiences—of something unbreakable and immutable that may be theirs in time. And this is ultimately as true of the springtime in Cummings' poem and the summer of "Sophistication" as it is of Anderson's *Winterset*.

The last few selections in this section are concerned with what can and what cannot be said to the young in the form of advice; they suggest that there is more to a man's life than the process of existing through several stages of growth.

YEARS OF THE MODERN

by WALT WHITMAN

Years of the modern! years of the unperform'd!
Your horizon rises, I see it parting away for more august dramas,
I see not America only, not only Liberty's nation but other nations preparing,
I see tremendous entrances and exits, new combinations, the solidarity of races,
I see that force advancing with irresistible power on the world's stage,
(Have the old forces, the old wars, played their parts? are the acts suitable to them
    closed?)
I see Freedom, completely arm'd and victorious and very haughty, with Law on
    one side and Peace on the other,
A stupendous trio all issuing forth against the idea of caste;
What historic denouements are these we so rapidly approach?
I see men marching and countermarching by swift millions,
I see the frontiers and boundaries of the old aristocracies broken,
I see the landmarks of European kings removed,
I see this day the People beginning their landmarks, (all others give way);
Never were such sharp questions ask'd as this day,
Never was average man, his soul, more energetic, more like a God,
Lo, how he urges and urges, leaving the masses no rest!
His daring foot is on land and sea everywhere, he colonizes the Pacific, the archi-
    pelagoes,
With the steamship, the electric telegraph, the newspaper, the wholesale engines
    of war,
With these and the world-spreading factories he interlinks all geography, all lands;
What whispers are these O lands, running ahead of you, passing under the seas?
Are all nations communing? is there going to be but one heart to the globe?
Is humanity forming en-masse? for lo, tyrants tremble, crowns grow dim,
The earth, restive, confronts a new era, perhaps a general divine war,
No one knows what will happen next, such portents fill the days and nights;
Years prophetical! the space ahead as I walk, as I vainly try to pierce it, is full of
    phantoms,
Unborn deeds, things soon to be, project their shapes around me,
This incredible rush and heat, this strange ecstatic fever of dreams O years!
Your dreams O years, how they penetrate through me! (I know not whether I
    sleep or wake;)
The perform'd America and Europe grow dim, retiring in shadow behind me,
The unperform'd, more gigantic than ever, advance, advance, upon me.

From *Leaves of Grass* by Walt Whitman. With permission from Doubleday and Company, Inc.

. . . all the men and women merely players:
They have their exits and their entrances;
And one man in his time plays many parts,
His acts being seven ages.

                              —As You Like It

IN JUST-SPRING

by E. E. CUMMINGS

in Just-
spring   when the world is mud-
luscious the little
lame balloonman

whistles   far   and wee

and eddieandbill come
running from marbles and
piracies and it's
spring

when the world is puddle-wonderful

the queer
old balloonman whistles
far   and   wee
and bettyandisabel come dancing

from hop-scotch and jump-rope and

it's
spring
and
        the

              goat-footed

balloonman   whistles
far
and
wee

[3]

ELEVEN

by ARCHIBALD MacLEISH

And summer mornings the mute child, rebellious,
Stupid, hating the words, the meanings, hating
The Think now, Think, the O but Think! would leave
On tiptoe the three chairs on the verandah
And crossing tree by tree the empty lawn
Push back the shed door and upon the sill
Stand pressing out the sunlight from his eyes
And enter and with outstretched fingers feel
The grindstone and behind it the bare wall
And turn and in the corner on the cool
Hard earth sit listening. And one by one,
Out of the dazzled shadow in the room
The shapes would gather, the brown plowshare, spades,
Mattocks, the polished helves of picks, a scythe
Hung from the rafters, shovels, slender tines
Glinting across the curve of sickles—shapes
Older than men were, the wise tools, the iron
Friendly with earth. And sit there quiet, breathing
The harsh dry smell of withered bulbs, the faint
Odor of dung, the silence. And outside
Beyond the half-shut door the blind leaves
And the corn moving. And at noon would come,
Up from the garden, his hard crooked hands
Gentle with earth, his knees still earth-stained, smelling
Of sun, of summer, the old gardener, like
A priest, like an interpreter, and bend
Over his baskets.   And they would not speak:
They would say nothing. And the child would sit there
Happy as though he had no name, as though
He had been no one: like a leaf, a stem,
Like a root growing—

The selection from Archibald MacLeish *Poems 1924-1933* is used by permission of the publishers, Houghton Mifflin Company.

Youth

Pablo Picasso. 1905

From the Collection of Edward M. M. Warburg, New York. Photograph, courtesy the Museum of Modern Art, New York.

THE RED PONY ✓

by JOHN STEINBECK

Part I. The Gift

AT DAYBREAK Billy Buck emerged from the bunkhouse and stood for a moment on the porch looking up at the sky. He was a broad, bandy-legged little man with a walrus mustache, with square hands, puffed and muscled on the palms. His eyes were a contemplative, watery gray and the hair which protruded from under his Stetson hat was spiky and weathered. Billy was still stuffing his shirt into his blue jeans as he stood on the porch. He unbuckled his belt and tightened it again. The belt showed, by the worn shiny places opposite each hole, the gradual increase of Billy's middle over a period of years. When he had seen to the weather, Billy cleared each nostril by holding its mate closed with his forefinger and blowing fiercely. Then he walked down to the barn, rubbing his hands together. He curried and brushed two saddle horses in the stalls, talking quietly to them all the time; and he had hardly finished when the iron triangle started ringing at the ranch house. Billy stuck the brush and currycomb together and laid them on the rail, and went up to breakfast. His action had been so deliberate and yet so wasteless of time that he came to the house while Mrs. Tiflin was still ringing the triangle. She nodded her gray head to him and withdrew into the kitchen. Billy Buck sat down on the steps, because he was a cow-hand, and it wouldn't be fitting that he should go first into the dining-room. He heard Mr. Tiflin in the house, stamping his feet into his boots.

The high jangling note of the triangle put the boy Jody in motion. He was only a little boy, ten years old, with hair like dusty yellow grass and with shy polite gray eyes, and with a mouth that worked when he thought. The triangle picked him up out of sleep. It didn't occur to him to disobey the harsh note. He never had: no one he knew ever had. He brushed the tangled hair out of his eyes and skinned his nightgown off. In a moment he was dressed—blue chambray shirt and overalls. It was late in the summer, so of course there were no shoes to bother with. In the kitchen he waited until his mother got from in front of the sink and went back to the stove. Then he washed himself and brushed back his wet hair with his fingers. His mother turned sharply on him as he left the sink. Jody looked shyly away.

"I've got to cut your hair before long," his mother said. "Breakfast's on the table. Go on in, so Billy can come."

Jody sat at the long table which was covered with white oilcloth washed through to the fabric in some places. The fried eggs lay in rows on their platter. Jody took three eggs on his plate and followed with three thick slices of crisp bacon. He carefully scraped a spot of blood from one of the egg yolks.

Billy Buck clumped in. "That won't hurt you," Billy explained. "That's only a sign the rooster leaves."

Jody's tall stern father came in then and Jody knew from the noise on the floor that he was wearing boots, but he looked under the table anyway, to make sure. His father turned off the oil lamp over the table, for plenty of morning light now came through the windows.

Jody did not ask where his father and Billy Buck were riding that day, but he wished he might go along. His father was a disciplinarian. Jody obeyed him in everything without questions of any kind. Now, Carl Tiflin sat down and reached for the egg platter.

"Got the cows ready to go, Billy?" he asked.

"In the lower corral," Billy said. "I could just as well take them in alone."

"Sure you could. But a man needs company. Besides your throat gets pretty dry." Carl Tiflin was jovial this morning.

Jody's mother put her head in the door. "What time do you think to be back. Carl?"

"I can't tell. I've got to see some men in Salinas. Might be gone till dark."

The eggs and coffee and big biscuits disappeared rapidly. Jody followed the two men out of the house. He watched them mount their horses and drive six old milk cows out of the corral and start over the hill toward Salinas. They were going to sell the old cows to the butcher.

When they had disappeared over the crown of the ridge Jody walked up the hill in back of the house. The dogs trotted around the house corner hunching their shoulders and grinning horribly with pleasure. Jody patted their heads—Doubletree Mutt with the big thick tail and yellow eyes, and Smasher, the shepherd, who had killed a coyote and lost an ear in doing it. Smasher's one good ear stood up higher than a collie's ear should. Billy Buck said that always happened. After the frenzied greeting the dogs lowered their noses to the ground in a business-like way and went ahead, looking back now and then to make sure that the boy was coming. They walked up through the chicken yard and saw the quail eating with the chickens. Smasher chased the chickens a little to keep in practice in case there should ever be sheep to herd. Jody continued on through the large vegetable patch where the green corn was higher than his head. The cow-pumpkins were green and small yet. He went on to the sagebrush line where the cold spring ran out of its pipe and fell into a round wooden tub. He leaned over and drank close to the green mossy wood where the water tasted best. Then he turned and looked back on the ranch, on the low, whitewashed house girded with red geraniums, and on the long bunkhouse by the cypress tree where Billy Buck lived alone. Jody could see the great black kettle under the cypress tree. That was where the pigs were scalded. The sun was coming over the ridge now, glaring on the whitewash of the houses and barns,

making the wet grass blaze softly. Behind him, in the tall sagebrush, the birds were scampering on the ground, making a great noise among the dry leaves; the squirrels piped shrilly on the side-hills. Jody looked along at the farm buildings. He felt an uncertainty in the air, a feeling of change and of loss and of the gain of new and unfamiliar things. Over the hillside two big black buzzards sailed low to the ground and their shadows slipped smoothly and quickly ahead of them. Some animal had died in the vicinity. Jody knew it. It might be a cow or it might be the remains of a rabbit. The buzzards overlooked nothing. Jody hated them as all decent things hate them, but they could not be hurt because they made away with carrion.

After a while the boy sauntered down hill again. The dogs had long ago given him up and gone into the brush to do things in their own way. Back through the vegetable garden he went, and he paused for a moment to smash a green muskmelon with his heel, but he was not happy about it. It was a bad thing to do, he knew perfectly well. He kicked dirt over the ruined melon to conceal it.

Back at the house his mother bent over his rough hands, inspecting his fingers and nails. It did little good to start him clean to school for too many things could happen on the way. She sighed over the black cracks on his fingers, and then gave him his books and his lunch and started him on the mile walk to school. She noticed that his mouth was working a good deal this morning.

Jody started his journey. He filled his pockets with little pieces of white quartz that lay in the road, and every so often he took a shot at a bird or at some rabbit that had stayed sunning itself in the road too long. At the crossroads over the bridge he met two friends and the three of them walked to school together, making ridiculous strides and being rather silly. School had just opened two weeks before. There was still a spirit of revolt among the pupils.

It was four o'clock in the afternoon when Jody topped the hill and looked down on the ranch again. He looked for the saddle horses, but the corral was empty. His father was not back yet. He went slowly, then, toward the afternoon chores. At the ranch house, he found his mother sitting on the porch, mending socks.

"There's two doughnuts in the kitchen for you," she said. Jody slid to the kitchen, and returned with half of one of the doughnuts already eaten and his mouth full. His mother asked him what he had learned in school that day, but she didn't listen to his doughnut-muffled answer. She interrupted, "Jody, tonight see you fill the wood-box clear full. Last night you crossed the sticks and it wasn't only about half full. Lay the sticks flat tonight. And Jody, some of the hens are hiding eggs, or else the dogs are eating them. Look about in the grass and see if you can find any nests."

Jody, still eating, went out and did his chores. He saw the quail come down to eat with the chickens when he threw out the grain. For some reason his father was proud to have them come. He never allowed any shooting near the house for fear the quail might go away.

When the wood-box was full, Jody took his twenty-two rifle up to the cold spring at the brush line. He drank again and then aimed the gun at all manner of things, at rocks, at birds on the wing, at the big black pig kettle under the cypress tree, but he didn't shoot for he had no cartridges and wouldn't have until he was twelve. If his father had seen him aim the rifle in the direction of the house he would have put the cartridges off another year. Jody remembered this and did not point the rifle down the hill again. Two years was enough to wait for cartridges. Nearly all of his father's presents were given with reservations which hampered their value somewhat. It was good discipline.

The supper waited until dark for his father to return. When at last he came in with Billy Buck, Jody could smell the delicious brandy on their breaths. Inwardly he rejoiced, for his father sometimes talked to him when he smelled of brandy, sometimes even told things he had done in the wild days when he was a boy.

After supper, Jody sat by the fireplace and his shy polite eyes sought the room corners, and he waited for his father to tell what it was he contained, for Jody knew he had news of some sort. But he was disappointed. His father pointed a stern finger at him.

"You'd better go to bed, Jody. I'm going to need you in the morning."

That wasn't so bad. Jody liked to do the things he had to do as long as they weren't routine things. He looked at the floor and his mouth worked out a question before he spoke it. "What are we going to do in the morning, kill a pig?" he asked softly.

"Never you mind. You better get to bed."

When the door was closed behind him, Jody heard his father and Billy Buck chuckling and he knew it was a joke of some kind. And later, when he lay in bed, trying to make words out of the murmurs in the other room, he heard his father protest, "But, Ruth, I didn't give much for him."

Jody heard the hoot-owls hunting mice down by the barn, and he heard a fruit tree limb tap-tapping against the house. A cow was lowing when he went to sleep.

When the triangle sounded in the morning, Jody dressed more quickly even than usual. In the kitchen, while he washed his face and combed back his hair, his mother addressed him irritably. "Don't you go out until you get a good breakfast in you."

He went into the dining-room and sat at the long white table. He took a steaming hotcake from the platter, arranged two fried eggs on it, covered them with another hotcake and squashed the whole thing with his fork.

His father and Billy Buck came in. Jody knew from the sound on the floor that both of them were wearing flat-heeled shoes, but he peered under the table to make sure. His father turned off the oil lamp, for the day had arrived, and he looked stern and disciplinary, but Billy Buck didn't look at Jody at all. He avoided the shy questioning eyes of the boy and soaked a whole piece of toast in his coffee.

Carl Tiflin said crossly, "You come with us after breakfast!"

Jody had trouble with his food then, for he felt a kind of doom in the air. After Billy had tilted his saucer and drained the coffee which had slopped into it, and had wiped his hands on his jeans, the two men stood up from the table and went out into the morning light together, and Jody respectfully followed a little behind them. He tried to keep his mind from running ahead, tried to keep it absolutely motionless.

His mother called, "Carl! Don't you let it keep him from school."

They marched past the cypress, where a singletree hung from a limb to butcher the pigs on, and past the black iron kettle, so it was not a pig killing. The sun shone over the hill and threw long, dark shadows of the trees and buildings. They crossed a stubble-field to shortcut to the barn. Jody's father unhooked the door and they went in. They had been walking toward the sun on the way down. The barn was black as night in contrast and warm from the hay and from the beasts. Jody's father moved over toward the one box stall. "Come here!" he ordered. Jody could begin to see things now. He looked into the box stall and then stepped back quickly.

A red pony colt was looking at him out of the stall. Its tense ears were forward and a light of disobedience was in its eyes. Its coat was rough and thick as an airedale's fur and its mane was long and tangled. Jody's throat collapsed in on itself and cut his breath short.

"He needs a good currying," his father said, "and if I ever hear of you not feeding him or leaving his stall dirty, I'll sell him off in a minute."

Jody couldn't bear to look at the pony's eyes any more. He gazed down at his hands for a moment, and he asked very shyly, "Mine?" No one answered him. He put his hand out toward the pony. Its gray nose came close, sniffing loudly, and then the lips drew back and the strong teeth closed on Jody's fingers. The pony shook its head up and down and seemed to laugh with amusement. Jody regarded his bruised fingers. "Well," he said with pride—"Well, I guess he can bite all right." The two men laughed, somewhat in relief. Carl Tiflin went out of the barn and walked up a side-hill to be by himself, for he was embarrassed, but Billy Buck stayed. It was easier to talk to Billy Buck. Jody asked again—"Mine?"

Billy became professional in tone. "Sure! That is, if you look out for him and break him right. I'll show you how. He's just a colt. You can't ride him for some time."

Jody put out his bruised hand again, and this time the red pony let his nose be rubbed. "I ought to have a carrot," Jody said. "Where'd we get him, Billy?"

"Bought him at a sheriff's auction," Billy explained. "A show went broke in Salinas and had debts. The sheriff was selling off their stuff."

The pony stretched out his nose and shook the forelock from his wild eyes. Jody stroked the nose a little. He said softly, "There isn't a—saddle?"

Billy Buck laughed. "I'd forgot. Come along."

In the harness room he lifted down a little saddle of red morocco leather. "It's just a show saddle," Billy Buck said disparagingly. "It isn't practical for the brush, but it was cheap at the sale."

Jody couldn't trust himself to look at the saddle either, and he couldn't speak at all. He brushed the shining red leather with his fingertips, and after a long time he said, "It'll look pretty on him though." He thought of the grandest and prettiest things he knew. "If he hasn't a name already, I think I'll call him Gabilan Mountains," he said.

Billy Buck knew how he felt. "It's a pretty long name. Why don't you just call him Gabilan? That means hawk. That would be a fine name for him." Billy felt glad. "If you will collect tail hair, I might be able to make a hair rope for you sometime. You could use it for a hackamore."

Jody wanted to go back to the box stall. "Could I lead him to school, do you think —to show the kids?"

But Billy shook his head. "He's not even halter-broke yet. We had a time getting him here. Had to almost drag him. You better be starting for school though."

"I'll bring the kids to see him here this afternoon," Jody said.

Six boys came over the hill half an hour early that afternoon, running hard, their heads down, their forearms working, their breath whistling. They swept by the house and cut across the stubble-field to the barn. And then they stood self-consciously before the pony, and then they looked at Jody with eyes in which there was a new admiration and a new respect. Before today Jody had been a boy, dressed in overalls and a blue shirt—quieter than most, even suspected of being a little cowardly. And now he was different. Out of a thousand centuries they drew the ancient admiration of the footman for the horseman. They knew instinctively that a man on a horse is spiritually as well as physically bigger than a man on foot. They knew that Jody had been miraculously lifted out of equality with them, and had been placed over them. Gabilan put his head out of the stall and sniffed them.

"Why'n't you ride him?" the boys cried. "Why'n't you braid his tail with ribbons like in the fair?" "When you going to ride him?"

Jody's courage was up. He too felt the superiority of the horseman. "He's not old enough. Nobody can ride him for a long time. I'm going to train him on the long halter. Billy Buck is going to show me how."

"Well, can't we even lead him around a little?"

"He isn't even halter-broke," Jody said. He wanted to be completely alone when

[10]

he took the pony out the first time. "Come and see the saddle."

They were speechless at the red morocco saddle, completely shocked out of comment. "It isn't much use in the brush," Jody explained. "It'll look pretty on him though. Maybe I'll ride bareback when I go into the brush."

"How you going to rope a cow without a saddle horn?"

"Maybe I'll get another saddle for every day. My father might want me to help him with the stock." He let them feel the red saddle, and showed them the brass chain throat-latch on the bridle and the big brass buttons at each temple where the headstall and brow band crossed. The whole thing was too wonderful. They had to go away after a little while, and each boy, in his mind, searched among his possessions for a bribe worthy of offering in return for a ride on the red pony when the time should come.

Jody was glad when they had gone. He took brush and currycomb from the wall, took down the barrier of the box stall and stepped cautiously in. The pony's eyes glittered, and he edged around into kicking position. But Jody touched him on the shoulder and rubbed his high arched neck as he had always seen Billy Buck do, and he crooned, "So-o-o Boy," in a deep voice. The pony gradually relaxed his tenseness. Jody curried and brushed until a pile of dead hair lay in the stall and until the pony's coat had taken on a deep red shine. Each time he finished he thought it might have been done better. He braided the mane into a dozen little pigtails, and he braided the forelock, and then he undid them and brushed the hair out straight again.

Jody did not hear his mother enter the barn. She was angry when she came, but when she looked in at the pony and at Jody working over him, she felt a curious pride rise up in her. "Have you forgot the wood-box?" she asked gently. "It's not far off from dark and there's not a stick of wood in the house, and the chickens aren't fed."

Jody quickly put up his tools. "I forgot, ma'am."

"Well, after this do your chores first. Then you won't forget. I expect you'll forget lots of things now if I don't keep an eye on you."

"Can I have carrots from the garden for him, ma'am?"

She had to think about that. "Oh—I guess so, if you only take the big tough ones."

"Carrots keep the coat good," he said, and again she felt the curious rush of pride.

Jody never waited for the triangle to get him out of bed after the coming of the pony. It became his habit to creep out of bed even before his mother was awake, to slip into his clothes and to go quietly down to the barn to see Gabilan. In the gray quiet mornings when the land and the brush and the houses and the trees were silver-gray and black like a photograph negative, he stole toward the barn, past the sleeping stones and the sleeping cypress tree. The turkeys, roosting in the tree out of coyotes' reach, clicked drowsily. The fields glowed with a gray frost-like light and in the dew the tracks of rabbits and of field mice stood out sharply. The good dogs came stiffly out of their little houses, hackles up and deep growls in their throats. Then they caught Jody's scent, and their stiff tails rose up and waved a greeting—Doubletree Mutt with the big thick tail, and Smasher, the incipient shepherd—then went lazily back to their warm beds.

It was a strange time and a mysterious journey, to Jody—an extension of a dream. When he first had the pony he liked to torture himself during the trip by thinking Gabilan would not be in his stall, and worse, would never have been there. And he had other delicious little self-induced pains. He thought how the rats had gnawed ragged holes in the red saddle, and how the mice had nibbled Gabilan's tail until it was stringy and thin. He usually ran the last little way to the barn. He unlatched the rusty hasp of the barn door and stepped in, and no matter how quietly he opened the door, Gabilan was always looking at him over the barrier of the box stall and Gabilan whinnied softly and stamped his front foot, and his eyes had big sparks of red fire in them like oakwood embers.

Sometimes, if the work horses were to be used that day, Jody found Billy Buck in the barn harnessing and currying. Billy stood with him and looked long at Gabilan and he told Jody a great many things about horses. He explained that they were terribly afraid for their feet, so that one must make a practice of lifting the legs and patting the hooves and ankles to remove their terror. He told Jody how horses love conversation. He must talk to the pony all the time, and tell him the reasons for everything. Billy wasn't sure a horse could understand everything that was said to him, but it was impossible to say how much was understood. A horse never kicked up a fuss if someone he liked explained things to him. Billy could give examples, too. He had known, for instance, a horse nearly dead beat with fatigue to perk up when told it was only a little farther to his destination. And he had known a horse paralyzed with fright to come out of it when his rider told him what it was that was frightening him. While he talked in the mornings, Billy Buck cut twenty or thirty straws into neat three-inch lengths and stuck them into his hatband. Then during the whole day, if he wanted to pick his teeth or merely to chew on something, he had only to reach up for one of them.

Jody listened carefully, for he knew and the whole country knew that Billy Buck was a fine hand with horses. Billy's own horse was a stringy cayuse with a hammer head, but he nearly always won the first prizes at the stock trials. Billy could rope a steer, take a double half-hitch about the horn with his riata, and dismount, and his horse would play the steer as an angler plays a fish, keeping a tight rope until the steer was down or beaten.

Every morning, after Jody had curried and brushed the pony, he let down the barrier of the stall, and Gabilan thrust past him and raced down the barn and into the corral. Around and around he galloped, and sometimes he jumped forward and landed on stiff legs. He stood quivering, stiff ears forward, eyes rolling so that the whites showed, pretending to be frightened. At last he walked snorting to the water-trough and buried his nose in the water up to the nostrils. Jody was proud then, for he knew that was the way to judge a horse. Poor horses only touched their lips to the water, but a fine spirited beast put his whole nose and mouth under, and only left room to breathe.

Then Jody stood and watched the pony, and he saw things he had never noticed about any other horse, the sleek, sliding flank muscles and the cords of the buttocks, which flexed like a closing fist, and the shine the sun put on the red coat. Having seen horses all his life, Jody had never looked at them very closely before. But now he noticed the moving ears which gave expression and even inflection of expression to the face. The pony talked with his ears. You could tell exactly how he felt about everything by the way his ears pointed. Sometimes they were stiff and upright and sometimes lax and sagging. They went back when he was angry or fearful, and forward when he was anxious and curious and pleased; and their exact position indicated which emotion he had.

Billy Buck kept his word. In the early fall the training began. First there was the halter-breaking, and that was the hardest because it was the first thing. Jody held a carrot and coaxed and promised and pulled on the rope. The pony set his feet like a burro when he felt the strain. But before long he learned. Jody walked all over the ranch leading him. Gradually he took to dropping the rope until the pony followed him unled wherever he went.

And then came the training on the long halter. That was slower work. Jody stood in the middle of a circle, holding the long halter. He clucked with his tongue and the pony started to walk in a big circle, held in by the long rope. He clucked again to make the pony trot, and again to make him gallop. Around and around Gabilan went thundering and enjoying it immensely. Then he called, "Whoa," and the pony stopped. It was not long until Gabilan was perfect at it. But in many ways he was a bad pony. He bit Jody in the pants and stomped on Jody's feet. Now and then his ears went back and he aimed a tremendous kick at the boy. Every time he did one of these bad things, Gabilan settled back and seemed to laugh to himself.

Billy Buck worked at the hair rope in the evenings before the fireplace. Jody collected tail hair in a bag, and he sat and watched Billy slowly constructing the rope, twisting a few hairs to make a string and rolling two strings together for a cord, and then braiding a number of cords to make the rope. Billy rolled the finished rope on the floor under his foot to make it round and hard.

The long halter work rapidly approached perfection. Jody's father, watching the pony stop and start and trot and gallop, was a little bothered by it.

"He's getting to be almost a trick pony," he complained. "I don't like trick horses. It takes all the—dignity out of a horse to make him do tricks. Why, a trick horse is kind of like an actor—no dignity, no character of his own." And his father said, "I guess you better be getting him used to the saddle pretty soon."

Jody rushed for the harness-room. For some time he had been riding the saddle on a sawhorse. He changed the stirrup length over and over, and could never get it just right. Sometimes, mounted on the sawhorse in the harness-room, with collars and hames and tugs hung all about him, Jody rode out beyond the room. He carried his rifle across the pommel. He saw the fields go flying by, and he heard the beat of the galloping hoofs.

It was a ticklish job, saddling the pony the first time. Gabilan hunched and reared and threw the saddle off before the cinch could be tightened. It had to be replaced again and again until at last the pony let it stay. And the cinching was difficult, too. Day by day Jody tightened the girth a little more until at last the pony didn't mind the saddle at all.

Then there was the bridle. Billy explained how to use a stick of licorice for a bit until Gabilan was used to having something in his mouth. Billy explained, "Of course we could force-break him to everything, but he wouldn't be as good a horse if we did. He'd always be a little bit afraid, and he wouldn't mind because he wanted to."

The first time the pony wore the bridle he whipped his head about and worked his tongue against the bit until the blood oozed from the corners of his mouth. He tried to rub the headstall off on the manger. His ears pivoted about and his eyes turned red with fear and with general rambunctiousness. Jody rejoiced, for he knew that only a mean-souled horse does not resent training.

And Jody trembled when he thought of the time when he would first sit in the saddle. The pony would probably throw him off. There was no disgrace in that. The disgrace would come if he did not get right up and mount again. Sometimes he dreamed that he lay in the dirt and cried and couldn't make himself mount again. The shame of the dream lasted until the middle of the day.

Gabilan was growing fast. Already he had lost the long-leggedness of the colt; his mane was getting longer and blacker. Under the constant currying and brushing his coat lay as smooth and gleaming as orange-red lacquer. Jody oiled the hoofs and kept them carefully trimmed so they would not crack.

The hair rope was nearly finished. Jody's father gave him an old pair of spurs and bent in the side bars and cut down the strap and took up the chainlets until they fitted. And then one day Carl Tiflin said:

"The pony's growing faster than I thought. I guess you can ride him by Thanksgiving. Think you can stick on?"

"I don't know," Jody said shyly. Thanksgiving was only three weeks off. He hoped it wouldn't rain, for rain would spot the red saddle.

Gabilan knew and liked Jody by now. He nickered when Jody came across the stubble-field, and in the pasture he came running when his master whistled for him. There was always a carrot for him every time.

Billy Buck gave him riding instructions over and over. "Now when you get up there, just grab tight with your knees and keep your hands away from the saddle, and if you get throwed, don't let that stop you. No matter how good a man is, there's always some horse can pitch him. You just climb up again before he gets to feeling smart about it. Pretty soon, he won't throw you no more, and pretty soon he *can't* throw you no more. That's the way to do it."

"I hope it don't rain before," Jody said.

"Why not? Don't want to get throwed in the mud?"

That was partly it, and also he was afraid that in the flurry of bucking Gabilan might slip and fall on him and break his leg or his hip. He had seen that happen to men before, had seen how they writhed on the ground like squashed bugs, and he was afraid of it.

He practiced on the sawhorse how he would hold the reins in his left hand and a hat in his right hand. If he kept his hands thus busy, he couldn't grab the horn if he felt himself going off. He didn't like to think of what would happen if he did grab the horn. Perhaps his father and Billy Buck would never speak to him again, they would be so ashamed. The news would get about and his mother would be ashamed too. And in the school yard—it was too awful to contemplate.

He began putting his weight in a stirrup when Gabilan was saddled, but he didn't throw his leg over the pony's back. That was forbidden until Thanksgiving.

Every afternoon he put the red saddle on the pony and cinched it tight. The pony was learning already to fill his stomach out unnaturally large while the cinching was going on, and then to let it down when the straps were fixed. Sometimes Jody led him up to the brush line and let him drink from the round green tub, and sometimes he led him up through the stubble-field to the hilltop from which it was possible to see the white town of Salinas and the geometric fields of the great valley, and the oak trees clipped by the sheep. Now and then they broke through the brush and came to little cleared circles so hedged in that the world was gone and only the sky and the circle of brush were left from the old life. Gabilan liked these trips and showed it by keeping his head very high and by quivering his nostrils with interest. When the two came back from an expedition they smelled of the sweet sage they had forced through.

Time dragged on toward Thanksgiving, but winter came fast. The clouds swept down and hung all day over the land and brushed the hilltops, and the winds blew shrilly at night. All day the dry oak leaves drifted down from the trees until they covered the ground, and yet the trees were unchanged.

Jody had wished it might not rain before Thanksgiving, but it did. The brown earth turned dark and the trees glistened. The cut ends of the stubble turned black with mildew; the haystacks grayed from exposure to the damp, and on the roofs the moss, which had been all summer as gray as lizards, turned a brilliant yellow-green. During the week of rain, Jody kept the pony in the box stall out of the dampness, except for a little time after school when he took him out for exercise and to drink at the water-trough in the upper corral. Not once did Gabilan get wet.

The wet weather continued until little new grass appeared. Jody walked to school dressed in a slicker and short rubber boots. At length one morning the sun came out brightly. Jody, at his work in the box stall, said to Billy Buck, "Maybe I'll leave Gabilan in the corral when I go to school today."

"Be good for him to be out in the sun," Billy assured him. "No animal likes to be cooped up too long. Your father and me are going back on the hill to clean the leaves out of the spring." Billy nodded and picked his teeth with one of his little straws.

"If the rain comes, though—" Jody suggested.

"Not likely to rain today. She's rained herself out." Billy pulled up his sleeves and snapped his arm bands. "If it comes on to rain—why a little rain don't hurt a horse."

"Well, if it does come on to rain, you put him in, will you, Billy? I'm scared he might get cold so I couldn't ride him when the time comes."

"Oh sure! I'll watch out for him if we get back in time. But it won't rain today."

And so Jody, when he went to school left Gabilan standing out in the corral.

Billy Buck wasn't wrong about many things. He couldn't be. But he was wrong about the weather that day, for a little after noon the clouds pushed over the hills and the rain began to pour down. Jody heard it start on the schoolhouse roof. He considered holding up one finger for permission to go to the outhouse and, once outside, running for home to put the pony in. Punishment would be prompt both at school and at home. He gave it up and took ease from Billy's assurance that rain couldn't hurt a horse. When school was finally out, he hurried home through the dark rain. The banks at the sides of the road spouted little jets of muddy water. The rain slanted and swirled under a cold and gusty wind. Jody dog-trotted home, slopping through the gravelly mud of the road.

From the top of the ridge he could see Gabilan standing miserably in the corral. The red coat was almost black, and streaked with water. He stood head down with his rump to the rain and wind. Jody arrived running and threw open the barn door and led the wet pony in by his fore-lock. Then he found a gunny sack and rubbed the soaked hair and rubbed the legs and ankles. Gabilan stood patiently, but he trembled in gusts like the wind.

When he had dried the pony as well as he could, Jody went up to the house and brought hot water down to the barn and soaked the grain in it. Gabilan was not very hungry. He nibbled at the hot mash, but he was not very much interested in it, and he still shivered now and then. A little steam rose from his damp back.

It was almost dark when Billy Buck and Carl Tiflin came home. "When the rain started we put up at Ben Herche's place, and the rain never let up all afternoon," Carl Tiflin explained. Jody looked reproachfully at Billy Buck and Billy felt guilty.

"You said it wouldn't rain," Jody accused him.

Billy looked away. "It's hard to tell, this time of year," he said, but his excuse was

lame. He had no right to be fallible, and he knew it.

"The pony got wet, got soaked through."

"Did you dry him off?"

"I rubbed him with a sack and I gave him hot grain."

Billy nodded in agreement.

"Do you think he'll take cold, Billy?"

"A little rain never hurt anything," Billy assured him.

Jody's father joined the conversation then and lectured the boy a little. "A horse," he said, "isn't any lap-dog kind of thing." Carl Tiflin hated weakness and sickness, and he held a violent contempt for helplessness.

Jody's mother put a platter of steaks on the table and boiled potatoes and boiled squash, which clouded the room with their steam. They sat down to eat. Carl Tiflin still grumbled about weakness put into animals and men by too much coddling.

Billy Buck felt bad about his mistake. "Did you blanket him?" he asked.

"No. I couldn't find any blanket. I laid some sacks over his back."

"We'll go down and cover him up after we eat, then." Billy felt better about it then. When Jody's father had gone in to the fire and his mother was washing dishes, Billy found and lighted a lantern. He and Jody walked through the mud to the barn. The barn was dark and warm and sweet. The horses still munched their evening hay. "You hold the lantern!" Billy ordered. And he felt the pony's legs and tested the heat of the flanks. He put his cheek against the pony's gray muzzle and then he rolled up the eyelids to look at the eyeballs and he lifted the lips to see the gums, and he put his fingers inside the ears. "He don't seem so chipper," Billy said. "I'll give him a rub-down."

Then Billy found a sack and rubbed the pony's legs violently and he rubbed the chest and the withers. Gabilan was strangely spiritless. He submitted patiently to the rubbing. At last Billy brought an old cotton comforter from the saddle-room, and threw it over the pony's back and tied it at neck and chest with string.

"Now he'll be all right in the morning," Billy said.

Jody's mother looked up when he got back to the house. "You're late up from bed," she said. She held his chin in her hard hand and brushed the tangled hair out of his eyes and she said, "Don't worry about the pony. He'll be all right. Billy's as good as any horse doctor in the country."

Jody hadn't known she could see his worry. He pulled gently away from her and knelt down in front of the fireplace until it burned his stomach. He scorched himself through and then went in to bed, but it was a hard thing to go to sleep. He awakened after what seemed a long time. The room was dark but there was a grayness in the window like that which precedes the dawn. He got up and found his overalls and searched for the legs, and then the clock in the other room struck two. He laid his clothes down and got back into bed. It was broad daylight when he awakened again. For the first time he had slept through the ringing of the triangle. He leaped up, flung on his clothes and went out of the door still buttoning his shirt. His mother looked after him for a moment and then went quietly back to her work. Her eyes were brooding and kind. Now and then her mouth smiled a little but without changing her eyes at all.

Jody ran on toward the barn. Halfway there he heard the sound he dreaded, the hollow rasping cough of a horse. He broke into a sprint then. In the barn he found Billy Buck with the pony. Billy was rubbing its legs with his strong thick hands. He looked up and smiled gaily. "He just took a little cold," Billy said. "We'll have him out of it in a couple of days."

Jody looked at the pony's face. The eyes were half closed and the lids thick and dry. In the eye corners a crust of hard mucus stuck. Gabilan's ears hung loosely sideways and his head was low. Jody put out his hand, but the pony did not move close to it. He coughed again and his whole body constricted with the effort. A little stream of thin fluid ran from his nostrils.

Jody looked back at Billy Buck. "He's awful sick, Billy."

"Just a little cold, like I said," Billy insisted. "You go get some breakfast and then go back to school. I'll take care of him."

"But you might have to do something else. You might leave him."

"No, I won't. I won't leave him at all. Tomorrow's Saturday. Then you can stay with him all day." Billy had failed again, and he felt badly about it. He had to cure the pony now.

Jody walked up to the house and took his place listlessly at the table. The eggs and bacon were cold and greasy, but he didn't notice it. He ate his usual amount. He didn't even ask to stay home from school. His mother pushed his hair back when she took his plate. "Billy'll take care of the pony," she assured him.

He moped through the whole day at school. He couldn't answer any questions nor read any words. He couldn't even tell anyone the pony was sick, for that might make him sicker. And when school was finally out he started home in dread. He walked slowly and let the other boys leave him. He wished he might continue walking and never arrive at the ranch.

Billy was in the barn, as he had promised, and the pony was worse. His eyes were almost closed now, and his breath whistled shrilly past an obstruction in his nose. A film covered that part of the eyes that was visible at all. It was doubtful whether the pony could see any more. Now and then he snorted, to clear his nose, and by the action seemed to plug it tighter. Jody looked dispiritedly at the pony's coat. The hair lay rough and unkempt and seemed to have lost all of its old luster. Billy stood quietly beside the stall. Jody hated to ask, but he had to know.

"Billy, is he—is he going to get well?"

Billy put his fingers between the bars under the pony's jaw and felt about. "Feel here," he said and he guided Jody's fingers to a large lump under the jaw. "When that gets bigger, I'll open it up and then he'll get better."

Jody looked quickly away, for he had heard about that lump. "What is it the matter with him?"

Billy didn't want to answer, but he had to. He couldn't be wrong three times. "Strangles," he said shortly, "but don't you worry about that. I'll pull him out of it. I've seen them get well when they were worse than Gabilan is. I'm going to steam him now. You can help."

"Yes," Jody said miserably. He followed Billy into the grain room and watched him make the steaming bag ready. It was a long canvas nose bag with straps to go over a horse's ears. Billy filled it one-third full of bran and then he added a couple of handfuls of dried hops. On top of the dry substance he poured a little carbolic acid and a little turpentine. "I'll be mixing it all

up while you run to the house for a kettle of boiling water," Billy said.

When Jody came back with the steaming kettle, Billy buckled the straps over Gabilan's head and fitted the bag tightly around his nose. Then through a little hole in the side of the bag he poured the boiling water on the mixture. The pony started away as a cloud of strong steam rose up, but then the soothing fumes crept through his nose and into his lungs, and the sharp steam began to clear out the nasal passages. He breathed loudly. His legs trembled in an ague, and his eyes closed against the biting cloud. Billy poured in more water and kept the steam rising for fifteen minutes. At last he set down the kettle and took the bag from Gabilan's nose. The pony looked better. He breathed freely, and his eyes were open wider than they had been.

"See how good it makes him feel," Billy said. "Now we'll wrap him up in the blanket again. Maybe he'll be nearly well by morning."

"I'll stay with him tonight," Jody suggested.

"No. Don't you do it. I'll bring my blankets down here and put them in the hay. You can stay tomorrow and steam him if he needs it."

The evening was falling when they went to the house for their supper. Jody didn't even realize that someone else had fed the chickens and filled the wood-box. He walked up past the house to the dark brush line and took a drink of water from the tub. The spring water was so cold that it stung his mouth and drove a shiver through him. The sky above the hills was still light. He saw a hawk flying so high that it caught the sun on its breast and shone like a spark. Two blackbirds were driving him down the sky, glittering as they attacked their enemy. In the west, the clouds were moving in to rain again.

Jody's father didn't speak at all while the family ate supper, but after Billy Buck had taken his blankets and gone to sleep in the barn, Carl Tiflin built a high fire in the fireplace and told stories. He told about the wild man who ran naked through the country and had a tail and ears like a horse, and he told about the rabbit-cats of Moro Cojo that hopped into the trees for birds. He revived the famous Maxwell brothers who found a vein of gold and hid the traces of it so carefully that they could never find it again.

Jody sat with his chin in his hands; his mouth worked nervously, and his father gradually became aware that he wasn't listening very carefully. "Isn't that funny?" he asked.

Jody laughed politely and said, "Yes, sir." His father was angry and hurt, then. He didn't tell any more stories. After a while, Jody took a lantern and went down to the barn. Billy Buck was asleep in the hay, and, except that his breath rasped a little in his lungs, the pony seemed to be much better. Jody stayed a little while, running his fingers over the red rough coat, and then he took up the lantern and went back to the house. When he was in bed, his mother came into the room.

"Have you enough covers on? It's getting winter."

"Yes, ma'am."

"Well, get some rest tonight." She hesitated to go out, stood uncertainly. "The pony will be all right," she said.

Jody was tired. He went to sleep quickly and didn't awaken until dawn. The triangle sounded, and Billy Buck came up from the barn before Jody could get out of the house.

"How is he?" Jody demanded.

Billy always wolfed his breakfast. "Pretty good. I'm going to open that lump this morning. Then he'll be better maybe."

After breakfast, Billy got out his best knife, one with a needle point. He whetted the shining blade a long time on a little carborundum stone. He tried the point and the blade again and again on his calloused thumb-ball, and at last he tried it on his upper lip.

On the way to the barn, Jody noticed how the young grass was up and how the stubble was melting day by day into the new green crop of volunteer. It was a cold sunny morning.

As soon as he saw the pony, Jody knew he was worse. His eyes were closed and sealed shut with dried mucus. His head hung so low that his nose almost touched the straw of his bed. There was a little groan in each breath, a deep-seated, patient groan.

Billy lifted the weak head and made a quick slash with the knife. Jody saw the yellow pus run out. He held up the head while Billy swabbed out the wound with weak carbolic acid salve.

"Now he'll feel better," Billy assured him. "That yellow poison is what makes him sick."

Jody looked unbelieving at Billy Buck. "He's awful sick."

Billy thought a long time what to say. He nearly tossed off a careless assurance, but he saved himself in time. "Yes, he's pretty sick," he said at last. "I've seen worse ones get well. If he doesn't get pneumonia, we'll pull him through. You stay with him. If he gets worse, you can come and get me."

For a long time after Billy went away, Jody stood beside the pony, stroking him behind the ears. The pony didn't flip his head the way he had done when he was well. The groaning in his breathing was becoming more hollow.

Doubletree Mutt looked into the barn, his big tail waving provocatively, and Jody was so incensed at his health that he found a hard black clod on the floor and deliberately threw it. Doubletree Mutt went yelping away to nurse a bruised paw.

In the middle of the morning, Billy Buck came back and made another steam bag. Jody watched to see whether the pony improved this time as he had before. His breathing eased a little, but he did not raise his head.

The Saturday dragged on. Late in the afternoon Jody went to the house and brought his bedding down and made up a place to sleep in the hay. He didn't ask permission. He knew from the way his mother looked at him that she would let him do almost anything. That night he left a lantern burning on a wire over the box stall. Billy had told him to rub the pony's legs every little while.

At nine o'clock the wind sprang up and howled around the barn. And in spite of his worry, Jody grew sleepy. He got into his blankets and went to sleep, but the breathy groans of the pony sounded in his dreams. And in his sleep he heard a crashing noise which went on and on until it awakened him. The wind was rushing through the barn. He sprang up and looked down the lane of stalls. The barn door had blown open, and the pony was gone.

He caught the lantern and ran outside into the gale, and he saw Gabilan weakly shambling away into the darkness, head down, legs working slowly and mechanically. When Jody ran up and caught him by the forelock, he allowed himself to be led back and put into his stall. His groans were louder, and a fierce whistling came from his nose. Jody didn't sleep any more then. The hissing of the pony's breath grew louder and sharper.

He was glad when Billy Buck came in at dawn. Billy looked for a time at the pony as though he had never seen him before. He felt the ears and flanks. "Jody," he said, "I've got to do something you won't want to see. You run up to the house for a while."

Jody grabbed him fiercely by the forearm. "You're not going to shoot him?"

Billy patted his hand. "No. I'm going to open a little hole in his windpipe so he can breathe. His nose is filled up. When he gets well, we'll put a little brass button in the hole for him to breathe through."

Jody couldn't have gone away if he had wanted to. It was awful to see the red hide cut, but infinitely more terrible to know it was being cut and not to see it. "I'll stay right here," he said bitterly. "You sure you got to?"

"Yes. I'm sure. If you stay, you can hold his head. If it doesn't make you sick, that is."

The fine knife came out again and was whetted again just as carefully as it had been the first time. Jody held the pony's head up and the throat taut, while Billy felt up and down for the right place. Jody sobbed once as the bright knife point disappeared into the throat. The pony plunged weakly away and then stood still, trembling violently. The blood ran thickly out and up the knife and across Billy's hand and into his shirtsleeve. The sure square hand sawed out a round hole in the flesh, and the breath came bursting out of the hole, throwing a fine spray of blood. With the rush of oxygen, the pony took a sudden strength. He lashed out with his hind feet and tried to rear, but Jody held his head down while Billy mopped the new wound with carbolic salve. It was a good job. The blood stopped flowing and the air puffed out the hole and sucked it in regularly with a little bubbling noise.

The rain brought in by the night wind began to fall on the barn roof. Then the triangle rang for breakfast. "You go up and eat while I wait," Billy said. "We've got to keep this hole from plugging up."

Jody walked slowly out of the barn. He was too dispirited to tell Billy how the barn door had blown open and let the pony out. He emerged into the wet gray morning and sloshed up to the house, taking a perverse pleasure in splashing through all the puddles. His mother fed him and put dry clothes on. She didn't question him. She seemed to know he couldn't answer questions. But when he was ready to go back to the barn she brought him a pan of steaming meal. "Give him this," she said.

But Jody did not take the pan. He said, "He won't eat anything," and ran out of the house. At the barn, Billy showed him how to fix a ball of cotton on a stick, with which to swab out the breathing hole when it became clogged with mucus.

Jody's father walked into the barn and stood with them in front of the stall. At length he turned to the boy. "Hadn't you better come with me? I'm going to drive over the hill." Jody shook his head. "You better come on, out of this," his father insisted.

Billy turned on him angrily. "Let him alone. It's his pony, isn't it?"

Carl Tiflin walked away without saying another word. His feelings were badly hurt.

All morning Jody kept the wound open and the air passing in and out freely. At noon the pony lay wearily down on his side and stretched his nose out.

Billy came back. "If you're going to stay with him tonight, you better take a little nap," he said. Jody went absently out of the barn. The sky had cleared to a hard thin blue. Everywhere the birds were busy with worms that had come to the damp surface of the ground.

Jody walked to the brush line and sat on the edge of the mossy tub. He looked down at the house and at the old bunk-house and at the dark cypress tree. The place was familiar, but curiously changed. It wasn't itself any more, but a frame for things that were happening. A cold wind blew out of the east now, signifying that the rain was over for a little while. At his feet Jody could see the little arms of new weeds spreading out over the ground. In the mud about the spring were thousands of quail tracks.

Doubletree Mutt came sideways and embarrassed up through the vegetable patch, and Jody, remembering how he had thrown the clod, put his arm about the dog's neck and kissed him on his wide black nose. Doubletree Mutt sat still, as though he knew some solemn thing was happening. His big tail slapped the ground gravely. Jody pulled a swollen tick out of Mutt's neck and popped it dead between his thumb-nails. It was a nasty thing. He washed his hands in the cold spring water.

Except for the steady swish of the wind, the farm was very quiet. Jody knew his mother wouldn't mind if he didn't go in to eat his lunch. After a little while he went slowly back to the barn. Mutt crept into his own little house and whined softly to himself for a long time.

Billy Buck stood up from the box and surrendered the cotton swab. The pony still lay on his side and the wound in his throat bellowsed in and out. When Jody saw how dry and dead the hair looked, he knew at last that there was no hope for the pony. He had seen the dead hair before on dogs and on cows, and it was a sure sign. He sat heavily on the box and let down the barrier of the box stall. For a long time he kept his eyes on the moving wound, and at last he dozed, and the afternoon passed quickly. Just before dark his mother brought a deep dish of stew and left it for him and went away. Jody ate a little of it, and, when it was dark, he set the lantern on the floor by the pony's head so he could watch the wound and keep it open. And he dozed again until the night chill awakened him. The wind was blowing fiercely, bringing the north cold with it. Jody brought a blanket from his bed in the hay and wrapped himself in it. Gabilan's breathing was quiet at last; the hole in his throat moved gently. The owls flew through the hayloft, shrieking and looking for mice. Jody put his hands down on his head and slept. In his sleep he was aware that the wind had increased. He heard it slamming about the barn.

It was daylight when he awakened. The barn door had swung open. The pony was gone. He sprang up and ran out into the morning light.

The pony's tracks were plain enough, dragging through the frostlike dew on the young grass, tired tracks with little lines between them where the hoofs had dragged. They headed for the brush line halfway up the ridge. Jody broke into a run and followed them. The sun shone on the sharp white quartz that stuck through the ground here and there. As he followed the plain trail, a shadow cut across in front of him. He looked up and saw a high circle of black buzzards, and the slowly revolving circle dropped lower and lower. The solemn birds soon disappeared over the ridge. Jody ran faster then, forced on by panic and rage. The trail entered the brush at last and followed a winding route among the tall sage bushes.

At the top of the ridge Jody was winded. He paused, puffing noisily. The blood pounded in his ears. Then he saw what he was looking for. Below, in one of the little clearings in the brush, lay the red pony. In the distance, Jody could see the legs moving slowly and convulsively. And in a circle around him stood the buzzards, waiting for the moment of death they know so well.

Jody leaped forward and plunged down the hill. The wet ground muffled his steps and the brush hid him. When he arrived, it was all over. The first buzzard sat on the pony's head and its beak had just risen dripping with dark eye fluid. Jody plunged into the circle like a cat. The black brotherhood arose in a cloud, but the big one on the pony's head was too late. As it hopped along to take off, Jody caught its wing tip and pulled it down. It was nearly as big as he was. The free wing crashed into his face with the force of a club, but he hung on. The claws fastened on his leg and the wing elbows battered his head on either side. Jody groped blindly with his free hand. His fingers found the neck of the struggling bird. The red eyes looked into his face, calm and fearless and fierce; the naked head turned from side to side. Then the beak opened and vomited a stream of putrefied fluid. Jody brought up his knee and fell on the great bird. He held the neck to the ground with one hand while his other found a piece of sharp white quartz. The first blow broke the beak sideways and black blood spurted from the twisted, leathery mouth corners. He struck again and missed. The red fearless eyes still looked at him, impersonal and unafraid and detached. He struck again and again, until the buzzard lay dead, until its head was a red pulp. He was still beating the dead bird when Billy Buck pulled him off and held him tightly to calm his shaking.

Carl Tiflin wiped the blood from the boy's face with a red bandana. Jody was limp and quiet now. His father moved the buzzard with his toe. "Jody," he explained, "the buzzard didn't kill the pony. Don't you know that?"

"I know it," Jody said wearily.

It was Billy Buck who was angry. He had lifted Jody in his arms, and had turned to carry him home. But he turned back on Carl Tiflin. "'Course he knows it," Billy said furiously, "Jesus Christ! man, can't you see how he'd feel about it?"

YOUNG ARCHIMEDES ✓

by ALDOUS HUXLEY

MEN CANNOT LIVE at ease except where they have mastered their surroundings and where their accumulated lives outnumber and outweigh the vegetative lives about them. Stripped of its dark woods, planted, terraced, and tilled almost to the mountain tops, the Tuscan landscape is humanized and safe. Sometimes upon those who live in the midst of it there comes a longing for some place that is solitary, inhuman, lifeless, or peopled only with alien life. But the longing is soon satisfied, and one is glad to return to the civilized and submissive scene.

I found that house on the hilltop the ideal dwelling-place. For there, safe in the midst of a humanized landscape, one was yet alone; one could be as solitary as one liked. Neighbors whom one never sees at close quarters are the ideal and perfect neighbors.

Our nearest neighbors, in terms of physical proximity, lived very near. We had two sets of them, as a matter of fact, almost in the same house with us. One was the peasant family, who lived in a long, low building, part dwelling-house, part stables, storerooms and cowsheds, adjoining the villa. Our other neighbors—intermittent neighbors, however, for they only ventured out of town every now and then, during the most flawless weather—were the owners of the villa, who had reserved for themselves the smaller wing of the huge L-shaped house—a mere dozen rooms or so—leaving the remaining eighteen or twenty to us.

They were a curious couple, our proprietors. An old husband, gray, listless, tottering, seventy at least; and a signora of about forty, short, very plump, with tiny fat hands and feet and a pair of very large, very dark black eyes, which she used with all the skill of a born comedian. Her vitality, if you could have harnessed it and made it do some useful work, would have supplied a whole town with electric light. The physicists talk of deriving energy from the atom; they would be more profitably employed nearer home—in discovering some way of tapping those enormous stores of vital energy which accumulate in unemployed women of sanguine temperament and which, in the present imperfect state of social and scientific organization, vent themselves in ways that are generally so deplorable: in interfering with other people's affairs, in working up emotional scenes, in thinking about love and making it, and in bothering men till they cannot get on with their work.

Signora Bondi got rid of her superfluous energy, among other ways, by "doing in" her tenants. The old gentleman, who was a retired merchant with a reputation for the most perfect rectitude, was allowed to have no dealings with us. When we came to see the house, it was the wife who showed us round. It was she who, with a lavish display of charm, with irresistible rollings of the eyes, expatiated on the merits of the place, sang the praises of the electric pump, glorified the bathroom (considering which, she insisted, the rent was remarkably moderate), and when we suggested calling in a surveyor to look over the house, earnestly begged us, as though our well-being were her only consideration, not to waste our money unnecessarily in doing anything so superfluous. "After all," she said, "we are honest people. I wouldn't dream of letting you the house except in perfect condition. Have confidence." And she looked at me with an appealing, pained expression in her magnificent eyes, as though begging me not to insult her by my coarse suspiciousness. And leaving us no time to pursue the subject of surveyors any further, she began assuring us that our little boy was the most beautiful angel she had ever seen. By the time our interview with

Signora Bondi was at an end, we had definitely decided to take the house.

"Charming woman," I said, as we left the house. But I think that Elizabeth was not quite so certain of it as I.

Then the pump episode began.

On the evening of our arrival in the house we switched on the electricity. The pump made a very professional whirring noise; but no water came out of the taps in the bathroom. We looked at one another doubtfully.

"Charming woman?" Elizabeth raised her eyebrows.

We asked for interviews; but somehow the old gentleman could never see us, and the Signora was invariably out or indisposed. We left notes; they were never answered. In the end, we found that the only method of communicating with our landlords, who were living in the same house with us, was to go down into Florence and send a registered express letter to them. For this they had to sign two separate receipts and even, if we chose to pay forty centimes more, a third incriminating document, which was then returned to us. There could be no pretending, as there always was with ordinary letters or notes, that the communication had never been received. We began at last to get answers to our complaints. The Signora, who wrote all the letters, started by telling us that, naturally, the pump didn't work, as the cisterns were empty, owing to the long drought. I had to walk three miles to the post office in order to register my letter reminding her that there had been a violent thunderstorm only last Wednesday, and that the tanks were consequently more than half full. The answer came back: bath water had not been guaranteed in the contract; and if I wanted it, why hadn't I had the pump looked at before I took the house? Another walk into town to ask the Signora next door whether she remembered her adjurations to us to have confidence in her, and to inform her that the existence in a house of a bathroom was in itself an implicit guarantee of bath water. The reply to that was that the Signora couldn't continue to have communications with people who wrote so rudely to her. After that I put the matter into the hands of a lawyer. Two months later the pump was actually replaced. But we had to serve a writ on the lady before she gave in. And the costs were considerable.

One day, towards the end of the episode, I met the old gentleman in the road, taking his big maremman dog for a walk—or being taken, rather, for a walk by the dog. For where the dog pulled the old gentleman had perforce to follow. And when it stopped to smell, or scratch the ground, or leave against a gatepost its visiting-card or an offensive challenge, patiently, at his end of the leash, the old man had to wait. I passed him standing at the side of the road, a few hundred yards below our house. The dog was sniffing at the roots of one of the twin cypresses which grew one on either side of the entry to a farm; I heard the beast growling indignantly to itself, as though it scented an intolerable insult. Old Signor Bondi, leashed to his dog, was waiting. The knees inside the tubular gray trousers were slightly bent. Leaning on his cane, he stood gazing mournfully and vacantly at the view. The whites of his old eyes were discolored, like ancient billiard balls. In the gray, deeply wrinkled face, his nose was dyspeptically red. His white moustache, ragged and yellowing at the fringes, drooped in a melancholy curve. In his black tie he wore a very large diamond;

perhaps that was what Signora Bondi had found so attractive about him.

I took off my hat as I approached. The old man stared at me absently, and it was only when I was already almost past him that he recollected who I was.

"Wait," he called after me, "wait!" And he hastened down the road in pursuit. Taken utterly by surprise and at a disadvantage—for it was engaged in retorting to the affront imprinted on the cypress roots—the dog permitted itself to be jerked after him. Too much astonished to be anything but obedient, it followed its master. "Wait!"

I waited.

"My dear sir," said the old gentleman, catching me by the lapel of my coat and blowing most disagreeably in my face, "I want to apologize." He looked around him, as though afraid that even here he might be overheard. "I want to apologize," he went on, "about that wretched pump business. I assure you that, if it had been only my affair, I'd have put the thing right as soon as you asked. You were quite right: a bathroom is an implicit guarantee of bath water. I saw from the first that we should have no chance if it came to court. And besides, I think one ought to treat one's tenants as handsomely as one can afford to. But my wife"—he lowered his voice—"the fact is that she likes this sort of thing, even when she knows that she's in the wrong and must lose. And besides, she hoped, I dare say, that you'd get tired of asking and have the job done yourself. I told her from the first that we ought to give in; but she wouldn't listen. You see, she enjoys it. Still, now she sees that it must be done. In the course of the next two or three days you'll be having your bath water. But I thought I'd just like to tell you how . . ." But the Maremmano, which had recovered by this time from its surprise of a moment since, suddenly bounded, growling, up the road. The old gentleman tried to hold the beast, strained at the leash, tottered unsteadily, then gave way and allowed himself to be dragged off. ". . . how sorry I am," he went on, as he receded from me, "that this little misunderstanding . . ." But it was no use. "Good-bye." He smiled politely, made a little deprecating gesture, as though he had suddenly remembered a pressing engagement, and had no time to explain what it was. "Good-bye." He took off his hat and abandoned himself completely to the dog.

A week later the water really did begin to flow, and the day after our first bath Signora Bondi, dressed in dove-gray satin and wearing all her pearls, came to call.

"Is it peace now?" she asked, with a charming frankness, as she shook hands.

We assured her that, so far as we were concerned, it certainly was.

"But why *did* you write me such dreadfully rude letters?" she said, turning on me a reproachful glance that ought to have moved the most ruthless malefactor to contrition. "And then that writ. How *could* you? To a lady . . ."

I mumbled something about the pump and our wanting baths.

"But how could you expect me to listen to you while you were in that mood? Why didn't you set about it differently—politely, charmingly?" She smiled at me and dropped her fluttering eyelids.

I thought it best to change the conversation. It is disagreeable, when one is in the right, to be made to appear in the wrong.

A few weeks later we had a letter—duly registered and by express messenger—in which the Signora asked us whether we proposed to renew our lease (which was only for six months), and notifying us that, if we did, the rent would be raised 25 per cent, in consideration of the improvements which had been carried out. We thought ourselves lucky, at the end of much bargaining, to get the lease renewed for a whole year with an increase in the rent of only 15 per cent.

It was chiefly for the sake of the view that we put up with these intolerable extortions. But we had found other reasons, after a few days' residence, for liking the house. Of these, the most cogent was that, in the peasant's youngest child, we had discovered what seemed the perfect playfellow for our own small boy. Between little Guido—for that was his name—and the youngest of his brothers and sisters there was a gap of six or seven years. His two elder brothers worked with their father in the fields; since the time of the mother's death, two or three years before we knew them, the eldest sister had ruled the house, and the younger, who had just left school, helped her and in betweenwhiles kept an eye on Guido, who by this time, however, needed very little looking after; for he was between six and seven years old and as precocious, self-assured, and responsible as the children of the poor, left as they are to themselves almost from the time they can walk, generally are.

Though fully two and a half years older than little Robin—and at that age thirty months are crammed with half a lifetime's experience—Guido took no undue advantage of his superior intelligence and strength. I have never seen a child more patient, tolerant, and untyrannical. He never laughed at Robin for his clumsy efforts to imitate his own prodigious feats; he did not tease or bully, but helped his small companion when he was in difficulties and explained when he could not understand. In return, Robin adored him, regarded him as the model and perfect Big Boy, and slavishly imitated him in every way he could.

These attempts of Robin's to imitate his companion were often exceedingly ludicrous. For by an obscure psychological law, words and actions in themselves quite serious become comic as soon as they are copied; and the more accurately, if the imitation is a deliberate parody, the funnier—for an overloaded imitation of someone we know does not make us laugh so much as one that is almost indistinguishably like the original. The bad imitation is only ludicrous when it is a piece of sincere and earnest flattery which does not quite come off. Robin's imitations were mostly of this kind. His heroic and unsuccessful attempts to perform the feats of strength and skill, which Guido could do with ease, were exquisitely comic. And his careful, long-drawn imitations of Guido's habits and mannerisms were no less amusing. Most ludicrous of all, because most earnestly undertaken and most incongruous in the imitator, were Robin's impersonations of Guido in the pensive mood. Guido was a thoughtful child, given to brooding and sudden abstractions. One would find him sitting in a corner by himself, chin in hand, elbow on knee, plunged, to all appearances, in the profoundest meditation. And sometimes, even in the midst of his play, he would suddenly break off, to stand, his hands behind his back, frowning and staring at the ground. When this happened Robin became overawed and a little disquieted. In a puzzled silence he looked at his companion. "Guido," he would say softly, "Guido." But Guido was generally too much preoccupied to answer; and Robin, not venturing to insist, would creep near him, and throwing himself as nearly as possible into Guido's attitude—standing Napoleonically, his hands clasped behind him, or sitting in the posture of Michelangelo's Lorenzo the Magnificent—would try to meditate too. Every few seconds he would turn his bright blue eyes towards the elder child to see whether he was doing it quite right. But at the end of a minute he began to grow impatient; meditation wasn't his strong point. "Guido," he called again and, louder, "Guido!" And he would take him by the hand and try to pull him away. Sometimes Guido roused himself from his reverie and went back to the interrupted game. Sometimes he paid no attention. Melancholy, perplexed, Robin had to take himself off to play by himself. And Guido would go on sitting or standing there, quite still; and his eyes, if one looked into them, were beautiful in their grave and pensive calm.

They were large eyes, set far apart and, what was strange in a dark-haired Italian child, of a luminous pale blue-gray color. They were not always grave and calm, as in these pensive moments. When he was playing, when he talked or laughed, they lit up; and the surface of those clear, pale lakes of thought seemed, as it were, to be shaken into brilliant sun-flashing ripples. Above those eyes was a beautiful forehead, high and steep and domed in a curve that was like the subtle curve of a rose petal. The nose was straight, the chin small and rather pointed, the mouth drooped a little sadly at the corners.

I have a snapshot of the two children sitting together on the parapet of the terrace. Guido sits almost facing the camera, but looking a little to one side and downwards; his hands are crossed in his lap and his expression, his attitude are thoughtful, grave, and meditative. It is Guido in one of those moods of abstraction into which he would pass even at the height of laughter and play—quite suddenly and completely, as though he had all at once taken it into his head to go away and had left the silent and beautiful body behind, like an empty house, to wait for his return. And by his side sits little Robin, turning to look up at him, his face half averted from the camera, but the curve of his cheek showing that he is laughing; one little raised hand is caught at the top of a gesture, the other clutches at Guido's sleeve as though he were urging him to come away and play. And the legs dangling from the parapet have been seen by the blinking instrument in the midst of an impatient wriggle; he is on the point of slipping down and running off to play hide-and-seek in the garden. All the essential characteristics of both the children are in that little snapshot.

"If Robin were not Robin," Elizabeth used to say, "I could almost wish he were Guido."

And even at that time, when I took no particular interest in the child, I agreed with her. Guido seemed to me one of the most charming little boys I had ever seen.

We were not alone in admiring him. Signora Bondi when, in those cordial intervals between our quarrels, she came to call, was constantly speaking of him. "Such a beautiful, beautiful child!" she would exclaim with enthusiasm. "It's really a waste that he should belong to peasants who can't afford to dress him properly. If he were mine, I should put him into black velvet; or little white knickers and a white knitted silk jersey with a red line at the collar and cuffs! or perhaps a white sailor suit would be pretty. And in winter a little fur coat,

with a squirrel skin cap, and possibly Russian boots . . ." Her imagination was running away with her. "And I'd let his hair grow, like a page's, and have it just curled up a little at the tips. And a straight fringe across his forehead. Everyone would turn round and stare after us if I took him out with me in Via Tornabuoni."

What you want, I should have liked to tell her, is not a child; it's a clock-work doll or a performing monkey. But I did not say so—partly because I could not think of the Italian for a clock-work doll and partly because I did not want to risk having the rent raised another 15 per cent.

"Ah, if only I had a little boy like that!" She sighed and modestly dropped her eyelids. "I adore children. I sometimes think of adopting one—that is, if my husband would allow it."

I thought of the poor old gentleman being dragged along at the heels of his big white dog and inwardly smiled.

"But I don't know if he would," the Signora was continuing, "I don't know if he would." She was silent for a moment, as though considering a new idea.

A few days later, when we were sitting in the garden after luncheon, drinking our coffee, Guido's father, instead of passing with a nod and the usual cheerful good-day, halted in front of us and began to talk. He was a fine handsome man, not very tall, but well-proportioned, quick and elastic in his movements, and full of life. He had a thin brown face, featured like a Roman's and lit by a pair of the most intelligent-looking gray eyes I ever saw. They exhibited almost too much intelligence when, as not infrequently happened, he was trying, with an assumption of perfect frankness and a childlike innocence, to take one in or get something out of one. Delighting in itself, the intelligence shone there mischievously. The face might be ingenuous, impassive, almost imbecile in its expression; but the eyes on these occasions gave him completely away. One knew, when they glittered like that, that one would have to be careful.

Today, however, there was no dangerous light in them. He wanted nothing out of us, nothing of any value—only advice, which is a commodity, he knew, that most people are only too happy to part with. But he wanted advice on what was, for us, rather a delicate subject: on Signora Bondi. Carlo had often complained to us about her. The old man is good, he told us, very good and kind indeed. Which meant, I dare say, among other things, that he could easily be swindled. But his wife . . . Well, the woman was a beast. And he would tell us stories of her insatiable rapacity: she was always claiming more than the half of the produce which, by the laws of the metayage[1] system, was the proprietor's due. He complained of her suspiciousness: she was forever accusing him of sharp practices, of downright stealing—him, he struck his breast, the soul of honesty. He complained of her short-sighted avarice: she wouldn't spend enough on manure, wouldn't buy him another cow, wouldn't have electric light installed in the stables. And we had sympathized, but cautiously, without expressing too strong an opinion on the subject. The Italians are wonderfully noncommittal in their speech; they will give nothing away to an interested person until they are quite certain that it is right and necessary and, above all, safe to do so. We had lived long enough among them to imitate their caution. What we said to Carlo would be sure, sooner or later, to get back to Signora

Bondi. There was nothing to be gained by unnecessarily embittering our relations with the lady—only another 15 per cent, very likely, to be lost.

Today he wasn't so much complaining as feeling perplexed. The Signora had sent for him, it seemed, and asked him how he would like it if she were to make an offer—it was all very hypothetical in the cautious Italian style—to adopt little Guido. Carlo's first instinct had been to say that he wouldn't like it at all. But an answer like that would have been too coarsely committal. He had preferred to say that he would think about it. And now he was asking for our advice.

Do what you think best, was what in effect we replied. But we gave it distantly but distinctly to be understood that we didn't think that Signora Bondi would make a very good foster-mother for the child. And Carlo was inclined to agree. Besides, he was very fond of the boy.

"But the thing is," he concluded rather gloomily, "that if she has really set her heart on getting hold of the child, there's nothing she won't do to get him—nothing."

He too, I could see, would have liked the physicists to start on unemployed childless women of sanguine temperament before they tried to tackle the atom. Still, I reflected, as I watched him striding away along the terrace, singing powerfully from a brazen gullet as he went, there was force there, there was life enough in those elastic limbs, behind those bright gray eyes, to put up a good fight even against the accumulated vital energies of Signora Bondi.

It was a few days after this that my gramophone and two or three boxes of records arrived from England. They were

[1] share-cropping.

a great comfort to us on the hilltop, providing as they did the only thing in which that spiritually fertile solitude—otherwise a perfect Swiss Family Robinson's island—was lacking: music. There is not much music to be heard nowadays in Florence. The times when Dr. Burney could tour through Italy, listening to an unending succession of new operas, symphonies, quartets, cantatas, are gone. Gone are the days when a learned musician, inferior only to the Reverend Father Martini of Bologna, could admire what the peasants sang and the strolling players thrummed and scraped on their instruments. I have traveled for weeks through the peninsula and hardly heard a note that was not "Salome" or the Fascists' song. Rich in nothing else that makes life agreeable or even supportable, the northern metropolises are rich in music. That is perhaps the only inducement that a reasonable man can find for living there. The other attractions—organized gaiety, people, miscellaneous conversation, the social pleasures—what are those, after all, but an expense of spirit that buys nothing in return? And then the cold, the darkness, the mouldering dirt, the damp and squalor. . . . No, where there is no necessity that retains, music can be the only inducement. And that, thanks to the ingenious Edison, can now be taken about in a box and unpacked in whatever solitude one chooses to visit. One can live at Benin, or Nuneaton, or Tozeur in the Sahara, and still hear Mozart quartets, and selections from the Well-Tempered Clavichord, and the Fifth Symphony, and the Brahms clarinet quintet, and motets by Palestrina.

Carlo, who had gone down to the station with his mule and cart to fetch the packing-case, was vastly interested in the machine.

"One will hear some music again," he said, as he watched me unpacking the gramophone and the disks. "It is difficult to do much oneself."

Still, I reflected, he managed to do a good deal. On warm nights we used to hear him, where he sat at the door of his house, playing his guitar and softly singing; the eldest boy shrilled out the melody on the mandolin, and sometimes the whole family would join in, and the darkness would be filled with their passionate, throaty singing. Piedigrotta[2] songs they mostly sang; and the voices drooped slurringly from note to note, lazily climbed or jerked themselves with sudden sobbing emphases from one tone to another. At a distance and under the stars the effect was not unpleasing.

"Before the war," he went on, "in normal times" (and Carlo had a hope, even a belief, that the normal times were coming back and that life would soon be as cheap and easy as it had been in the days before the flood), "I used to go and listen to the operas at the Politeama. Ah, they were magnificent. But it costs five lire now to get in."

"Too much," I agreed.

"Have you got *Trovatore?*" he asked.

I shook my head.

"Rigoletto?"

"I'm afraid not."

"Bohème? Fanciulla del West? Pagliacci?"

I had to go on disappointing him.

"Not even *Norma?* Or the *Barbiere?*"

I put on Battistini in "La ci darem" out of *Don Giovanni.* He agreed that the singing was good; but I could see that he

[2] popular songs of Naples.

didn't much like the music. Why not? He found it difficult to explain.

"It's not like *Pagliacci*," he said at last.

"Not palpitating?" I suggested, using a word with which I was sure he would be familiar; for it occurs in every Italian political speech and patriotic leading article.

"Not palpitating," he agreed.

And I reflected that it is precisely by the difference between *Pagliacci* and *Don Giovanni,* between the palpitating and the nonpalpitating, that modern musical taste is separated from the old. The corruption of the best, I thought, is the worst. Beethoven taught music to palpitate with his intellectual and spiritual passion. It has gone on palpitating ever since, but with the passion of inferior men. Indirectly, I thought, Beethoven is responsible for *Parsifal, Pagliacci,* and the *Poem of Fire;* still more indirectly for *Samson and Delilah* and "Ivy, cling to me." Mozart's melodies may be brilliant, memorable, infectious; but they don't palpitate, don't catch you between wind and water, don't send the listener off into erotic ecstasies.

Carlo and his elder children found my gramophone, I am afraid, rather a disappointment. They were too polite, however, to say so openly; they merely ceased, after the first day or two, to take any interest in the machine and the music it played. They preferred the guitar and their own singing.

Guido, on the other hand, was immensely interested. And he liked, not the cheerful dance tunes, to whose sharp rhythms our little Robin loved to go stamping round and round the room, pretending that he was a whole regiment of soldiers, but the genuine stuff. The first record he heard, I remember, was that of the slow movement of Bach's Concerto in D Minor for two violins. That was the disk I put on the turntable as soon as Carlo had left me. It seemed to me, so to speak, the most musical piece of music with which I could refresh my long-parched mind—the coolest and clearest of all draughts. The movement had just got under way and was beginning to unfold its pure and melancholy beauties in accordance with the laws of the most exacting intellectual logic, when the two children, Guido in front and little Robin breathlessly following, came clattering into the room from the loggia.

Guido came to a halt in front of the gramophone and stood there, motionless, listening. His pale blue-gray eyes opened themselves wide; making a little nervous gesture that I had often noticed in him before, he plucked at his lower lip with his thumb and forefinger. He must have taken a deep breath; for I noticed that, after listening for a few seconds, he sharply expired and drew in a fresh gulp of air. For an instant he looked at me—a questioning, astonished, rapturous look—gave a little laugh that ended in a kind of nervous shudder, and turned back towards the source of the incredible sounds. Slavishly imitating his elder comrade, Robin had also taken up his stand in front of the gramophone, and in exactly the same position, glancing at Guido from time to time to make sure that he was doing everything, down to plucking at his lip, in the correct way. But after a minute or so he became bored.

"Soldiers," he said, turning to me; "I want soldiers. Like in London." He remembered the rag-time and the jolly marches round and round the room.

I put my fingers to my lips. "Afterwards," I whispered.

Robin managed to remain silent and still for perhaps another twenty seconds.

Then he seized Guido by the arm, shouting, "Vieni, Guido! Soldiers. Soldati. Vieni giuocare soldati!"

It was then, for the first time, that I saw Guido impatient. "Vai!" he whispered angrily, slapped at Robin's clutching hand and pushed him roughly away. And he leaned a little closer to the instrument, as though to make up by yet intenser listening for what the interruption had caused him to miss.

Robin looked at him, astonished. Such a thing had never happened before. Then he burst out crying and came to me for consolation.

When the quarrel was made up—and Guido was sincerely repentant, was as nice as he knew how to be when the music had stopped and his mind was free to think of Robin once more—I asked him how he liked the music. He said he thought it was beautiful. But *bello* in Italian is too vague a word, too easily and frequently uttered, to mean very much.

"What did you like best?" I insisted. For he had seemed to enjoy it so much that I was curious to find out what had really impressed him.

He was silent for a moment, pensively frowning. "Well," he said at last, "I liked the bit that went like this." And he hummed a long phrase. "And then there's the other thing singing at the same time—but what are those things," he interrupted himself, "that sing like that?"

"They're called violins," I said.

"Violins." He nodded. "Well, the other violin goes like this." He hummed again. "Why can't one sing both at once? And what is in that box? What makes it make that noise?" The child poured out his questions.

I answered him as best I could, showing him the little spirals on the disk, the needle, the diaphragm. I told him to remember how the string of the guitar trembled when one plucked it; sound is a shaking in the air, I told him, and I tried to explain how those shakings get printed on the black disk. Guido listened to me very gravely, nodding from time to time. I had the impression that he understood perfectly well everything I was saying.

By this time, however, poor Robin was so dreadfully bored that in pity for him I had to send the two children out into the garden to play. Guido went obediently; but I could see that he would have preferred to stay indoors and listen to more music. A little while later, when I looked out, he was hiding in the dark recesses of the big bay tree, roaring like a lion, and Robin, laughing, but a little nervously, as though he were afraid that the horrible noise might possibly turn out, after all, to be the roaring of a real lion, was beating the bush with a stick, and shouting, "Come out, come out! I want to shoot you."

After lunch, when Robin had gone upstairs for his afternoon sleep, he reappeared. "May I listen to the music now?" he asked. And for an hour he sat there in front of the instrument, his head cocked slightly on one side, listening while I put on one disk after another.

Thenceforward he came every afternoon. Very soon he knew all my library of records, had his preferences and dislikes, and could ask for what he wanted by humming the principal theme.

"I don't like that one," he said of Strauss's *Till Eulenspiegel*. "It's like what we sing in our house. Not really like, you know. But somehow rather like, all the same. You understand?" He looked at us perplexedly and appealingly, as though begging us to understand what he meant and so save him from going on explaining. We nodded. Guido went on. "And then," he said, "the end doesn't seem to come properly out of the beginning. It's not like the one you played the first time." He hummed a bar or two from the slow movement of Bach's D Minor Concerto.

"It isn't," I suggested, "like saying: All little boys like playing. Guido is a little boy. Therefore Guido likes playing."

He frowned. "Yes, perhaps that's it," he said at last. "The one you played first is more like that. But, you know," he added, with an excessive regard for truth, "I don't like playing as much as Robin does."

Wagner was among his dislikes; so was Debussy. When I played the record of one of Debussy's Arabesques, he said, "Why does he say the same thing over and over again? He ought to say something new, or go on, or make the thing grow. Can't he think of anything different?" But he was less censorious about the "Après-Midi d'un Faune." "The things have beautiful voices," he said.

Mozart overwhelmed him with delight. The duet from *Don Giovanni,* which his father had found insufficiently palpitating, enchanted Guido. But he preferred the quartets and the orchestral pieces.

"I like music," he said, "better than singing."

Most people, I reflected, like singing better than music; are more interested in the executant than in what he executes, and find the impersonal orchestra less moving than the soloist. The touch of the pianist is the human touch, and the soprano's high C is the personal note. It is for the sake of this touch, that note, that audiences fill the concert halls.

Guido, however, preferred music. True,

he liked "La ci darem"; he liked "Deh vieni alla finestra"; he thought "Che soave zefiretto" so lovely that almost all our concerts had to begin with it. But he preferred the other things. The *Figaro* overture was one of his favorites. There is a passage not far from the beginning of the piece, where the first violins suddenly go rocketing up into the heights of loveliness; as the music approached that point, I used always to see a smile developing and gradually brightening on Guido's face, and when, punctually, the thing happened, he clapped his hands and laughed aloud with pleasure.

On the other side of the same disk, it happened, was recorded Beethoven's *Egmont* overture. He liked that almost better than *Figaro.*

"It has more voices," he explained. And I was delighted by the acuteness of the criticism; for it is precisely in the richness of its orchestration that *Egmont* goes beyond *Figaro.*

But what stirred him almost more than anything was the *Coriolan* overture. The third movement of the Fifth Symphony, the second movement of the Seventh, the slow movement of the Emperor Concerto —all these things ran it pretty close. But none excited him so much as *Coriolan.* One day he made me play it three or four times in succession; then he put it away.

"I don't think I want to hear that any more," he said.

"Why not?"

"It's too . . . too . . ." he hesitated, "too big," he said at last. "I don't really understand it. Play me the one that goes like this." He hummed the phrase from the D Minor Concerto.

"Do you like that one better?" I asked.

He shook his head. "No, it's not that exactly. But it's easier."

"Easier?" It seemed to me rather a queer word to apply to Bach.

"I understand it better."

One afternoon, while we were in the middle of our concert, Signora Bondi was ushered in. She began at once to be overwhelmingly affectionate towards the child; kissed him, patted his head, paid him the most outrageous compliments on his appearance. Guido edged away from her.

"And do you like music?" she asked.

The child nodded.

"I think he has a gift," I said. "At any rate, he has a wonderful ear and a power of listening and criticising such as I've never met with in a child of that age. We're thinking of hiring a piano for him to learn on."

A moment later I was cursing myself for my undue frankness in praising the boy. For Signora Bondi began immediately to protest that, if she could have the upbringing of the child, she would give him the best masters, bring out his talent, make an accomplished maestro of him—and, on the way, an infant prodigy. And at that moment, I am sure, she saw herself sitting maternally, in pearls and black satin, in the lee of the huge Steinway, while an angelic Guido, dressed like little Lord Fauntleroy, rattled out Liszt and Chopin, to the loud delight of a thronged auditorium. She saw the bouquets and all the elaborate floral tributes, heard the clapping and the few well-chosen words with which the veteran maestri, touched almost to tears, would hail the coming of the little genius. It became more than ever important for her to acquire the child.

"You've sent her away fairly ravening," said Elizabeth, when Signora Bondi had gone. "Better tell her next time that you made a mistake, and that the boy's got no musical talent whatever."

In due course, the piano arrived. After giving him the minimum of preliminary instruction, I let Guido loose on it. He began by picking out for himself the melodies he had heard, reconstructing the harmonies in which they were embedded. After a few lessons, he understood the rudiments of musical notation and could read a simple passage at sight, albeit very slowly. The whole process of reading was still strange to him; he had picked up his letters somehow, but nobody had yet taught him to read whole words and sentences.

I took occasion, next time I saw Signora Bondi, to assure her that Guido had disappointed me. There was nothing in his musical talent, really. She professed to be very sorry to hear it; but I could see that she didn't for a moment believe me. Probably she thought that we were after the child too, and wanted to bag the infant prodigy for ourselves, before she could get in her claim, thus depriving her of what she regarded almost as her feudal right. For, after all, weren't they her peasants? If anyone was to profit by adopting the child it ought to be herself.

Tactfully, diplomatically, she renewed her negotiations with Carlo. The boy, she put it to him, had genius. It was the foreign gentleman who had told her so, and he was the sort of man, clearly, who knew about such things. If Carlo would let her adopt the child, she'd have him trained. He'd become a great maestro and get engagements in the Argentine and the United States, in Paris and London. He'd earn millions and millions. Think of Caruso, for example. Part of the millions, she explained, would of course come to Carlo. But before they began to roll in, those millions, the boy would have to be trained. But training was very expensive.

In his own interest, as well as in that of his son, he ought to let her take charge of the child. Carlo said he would think it over, and again applied to us for advice. We suggested that it would be best in any case to wait a little and see what progress the boy made.

He made, in spite of my assertions to Signora Bondi, excellent progress. Every afternoon, while Robin was asleep, he came for his concert and his lesson. He was getting along famously with his reading; his small fingers were acquiring strength and agility. But what to me was more interesting was that he had begun to make up little pieces on his own account. A few of them I took down as he played them and I have them still. Most of them, strangely enough, as I thought then, are canons. He had a passion for canons. When I explained to him the principles of the form he was enchanted.

"It is beautiful," he said, with admiration. "Beautiful, beautiful. And so easy!"

Again the word surprised me. The canon is not, after all, so conspicuously simple. Thenceforward he spent most of his time at the piano in working out little canons for his own amusement. They were often remarkably ingenious. But in the invention of other kinds of music he did not show himself so fertile as I had hoped. He composed and harmonized one or two solemn little airs like hymn tunes, with a few sprightlier pieces in the spirit of the military march. They were extraordinary, of course, as being the inventions of a child. But a great many children can do extraordinary things; we are all geniuses up to the age of ten. But I had hoped that Guido was a child who was going to be a genius at forty; in which case what was extraordinary for an ordinary child was not extraordinary enough

for him. "He's hardly a Mozart," we agreed, as we played his little pieces over. I felt, it must be confessed, almost aggrieved. Anything less than a Mozart, it seemed to me, was hardly worth thinking about.

He was not a Mozart. No. But he was somebody, as I was to find out, quite as extraordinary. It was one morning in the early summer that I made the discovery. I was sitting in the warm shade of our westward-facing balcony, working. Guido and Robin were playing in the little enclosed garden below. Absorbed in my work, it was only, I suppose, after the silence had prolonged itself a considerable time that I became aware that the children were making remarkably little noise. There was no shouting, no running about; only a quiet talking. Knowing by experience that when children are quiet it generally means that they are absorbed in some delicious mischief, I got up from my chair and looked over the balustrade to see what they were doing. I expected to catch them dabbling in water, making a bonfire, covering themselves with tar. But what I actually saw was Guido, with a burnt stick in his hand, demonstrating on the smooth paving-stones of the path, that the square on the hypotenuse of a right-angled triangle is equal to the sum of the squares on the other two sides.

Kneeling on the floor, he was drawing with the point of his blackened stick on the flagstones. And Robin, kneeling imitatively beside him, was growing, I could see, rather impatient with this very slow game.

"Guido," he said. But Guido paid no attention. Pensively frowning, he went on with his diagram. "Guido!" The younger child bent down and then craned round his neck so as to look up into Guido's face. "Why don't you draw a train?"

"Afterwards," said Guido. "But I just want to show you this first. It's *so* beautiful," he added cajolingly.

"But I want a train," Robin persisted.

"In a moment. Do just wait a moment." The tone was almost imploring. Robin armed himself with renewed patience. A minute later Guido had finished both his diagrams.

"There!" he said triumphantly, and straightened himself up to look at them. "Now I'll explain."

And he proceeded to prove the theorem of Pythagoras—not in Euclid's way, but by the simpler and more satisfying method which was, in all probability, employed by Pythagoras himself. He had drawn a square and dissected it, by a pair of crossed perpendiculars, into two squares and two equal rectangles. The equal rectangles he divided up by their diagonals into four equal right-angled triangles. The two squares are then seen to be the squares on the two sides of any one of these triangles other than the hypotenuse. So much for the first diagram. In the next he took the four right-angled triangles into which the rectangles had been divided and rearranged them round the original square so that their right angles filled the corners of the square, the hypotenuses looked inwards and the greater and less sides of the triangles were in continuation along the sides of the square (which are each equal to the sum of these sides). In this way the original square is redissected into four right-angled triangles and the square on the hypotenuse. The four triangles are equal to the two rectangles of the original dissection. Therefore the square on the hypotenuse is equal to the sum of the two squares—the squares on

the other two sides—into which, with the rectangles, the original square was first dissected.

In very untechnical language, but clearly and with a relentless logic, Guido expounded his proof. Robin listened, with an expression on his bright, freckled face of perfect incomprehension.

"Treno," he repeated from time to time. "Treno. Make a train."

"In a moment," Guido implored. "Wait a moment. But do just look at this. *Do.*" He coaxed and cajoled. "It's so beautiful. It's so easy."

So easy. . . . The theorem of Pythagoras seemed to explain for me Guido's musical predilections. It was not an infant Mozart we had been cherishing; it was a little Archimedes with, like most of his kind, an incidental musical twist.

"Treno, treno!" shouted Robin, growing more and more restless as the exposition went on. And when Guido insisted on going on with his proof, he lost his temper. "Cattivo Guido," he shouted, and began to hit out at him with his fists.

"All right," said Guido resignedly. "I'll make a train." And with his stick of charcoal he began to scribble on the stones.

I looked on for a moment in silence. It was not a very good train. Guido might be able to invent for himself and prove the theorem of Pythagoras; but he was not much of a draughtsman.

"Guido!" I called. The two children turned and looked up. "Who taught you to draw those squares?" It was conceivable, of course, that somebody might have taught him.

"Nobody." He shook his head. Then, rather anxiously, as though he were afraid there might be something wrong about drawing squares, he went on to apologize and explain. "You see," he said, "it seemed to me so beautiful. Because those squares" —he pointed at the two small squares in the first figure—"are just as big as this one." And, indicating the square on the hypotenuse in the second diagram, he looked up at me with a deprecating smile.

I nodded. "Yes, it's very beautiful," I said—"it's very beautiful indeed."

An expression of delighted relief appeared on his face; he laughed with pleasure. "You see, it's like this," he went on, eager to initiate me into the glorious secret he had discovered. "You cut these two long squares"—he meant the rectangles— "into two slices. And then there are four slices, all just the same, because, because —oh, I ought to have said that before— because these long squares are the same, because those lines, you see . . ."

"But I want a train," protested Robin.

Leaning on the rail of the balcony, I watched the children below. I thought of the extraordinary thing I had just seen and of what it meant.

I thought of the vast differences between human beings. We classify men by the color of their eyes and hair, the shape of their skulls. Would it not be more sensible to divide them up into intellectual species? There would be even wider gulfs between the extreme mental types than between a Bushman and a Scandinavian. This child, I thought, when he grows up, will be to me, intellectually, what a man is to a dog. And there are other men and women who are, perhaps, almost as dogs to me.

Perhaps the men of genius are the only true men. In all the history of the race there have been only a few thousand real men. And the rest of us—what are we? Teachable animals. Without the help of the real men, we should have found out almost nothing at all. Almost all the ideas with which we are familiar could never have occurred to minds like ours. Plant the seeds there and they will grow; but our minds could never spontaneously have generated them.

There have been whole nations of dogs, I thought; whole epochs in which no Man was born. From the dull Egyptians the Greeks took crude experience and rules of thumb and made sciences. More than a thousand years passed before Archimedes had a comparable successor. There has been only one Buddha, one Jesus, only one Bach that we know of, one Michelangelo.

Is it by a mere chance, I wondered, that a Man is born from time to time? What causes a whole constellation of them to come contemporaneously into being and from out of a single people? Taine thought that Leonardo, Michelangelo, and Raphael were born when they were because the time was ripe for great painters and the Italian scene congenial. In the mouth of a rationalizing nineteenth-century Frenchman the doctrine is strangely mystical; it may be none the less true for that. But what of those born out of time? Blake, for example. What of those?

This child, I thought, has had the fortune to be born at a time when he will be able to make good use of his capacities. He will find the most elaborate analytical methods lying ready to his hand; he will have a prodigious experience behind him. Suppose him born while Stonehenge was building; he might have spent a lifetime discovering the rudiments, guessing darkly where now he might have had a chance of proving. Born at the time of the Norman Conquest, he would have had to wrestle with all the preliminary difficulties created by an inadequate symbolism; it would have taken him long years, for example, to learn the art of dividing MMMCCCCLXXXVIII by MCMXIX. In five years, nowadays, he will learn what it took generations of Men to discover.

And I thought of the fate of all the men born so hopelessly out of time that they could achieve little or nothing of value. Beethoven born in Greece, I thought, would have had to be content to play thin melodies on the flute or lyre; in those intellectual surroundings it would hardly have been possible for him to imagine the nature of harmony.

From drawing trains, the children in the garden below had gone on to playing trains. They were trotting round and round; with blown round cheeks and pouting mouth, like the cherubic symbol of a wind, Robin puff-puffed, and Guido, holding the skirt of his smock, shuffled behind him, tooting. They ran forward, backed, stopped at imaginary stations, shunted, roared over bridges, crashed through tunnels, met with occasional collisions and derailments. The young Archimedes seemed to be just as happy as the little tow-headed barbarian. A few minutes ago he had been busy with the theorem of Pythagoras. Now, tooting indefatigably along imaginary rails, he was perfectly content to shuffle backwards and forwards among the flower-beds, between the pillars of the loggia, in and out of the dark tunnels of the laurel tree. The fact that one is going to be Archimedes does not prevent one from being an ordinary cheerful child meanwhile. I thought of this strange talent distinct and separate from the rest of the mind, independent, almost, of experience. The typical child-prodigies are musical and mathematical; the other talents ripen slowly under the influence of emotional experience and growth. Till he was thirty Balzac gave

proof of nothing but ineptitude; but at four the young Mozart was already a musician, and some of Pascal's most brilliant work was done before he was out of his teens.

In the weeks that followed, I alternated the daily piano lessons with lessons in mathematics. Hints rather than lessons they were; for I only made suggestions, indicated methods, and left the child himself to work out the ideas in detail. Thus I introduced him to algebra by showing him another proof of the theorem of Pythagoras. In this proof one drops a perpendicular from the right angle on to the hypotenuse, and arguing from the fact that the two triangles thus created are similar to one another and to the original triangle, and that the proportions which their corresponding sides bear to one another are therefore equal, one can show in algebraical form that $c^2 + d^2$ (the squares on the other two sides) are equal to $a^2 + b^2$ (the squares on the two segments of the hypotenuse) $+ 2ab$; which last, it is easy to show geometrically, is equal to $(a + b)^2$, or the square on the hypotenuse. Guido was as much enchanted by the rudiments of algebra as he would have been if I had given him an engine worked by steam, with a methylated spirit lamp to heat the boiler; more enchanted, perhaps—for the engine would have got broken, and remaining always itself, would in any case have lost its charm, while the rudiments of algebra continued to grow and blossom in his mind with an unfailing luxuriance. Every day he made the discovery of something which seemed to him exquisitely beautiful; the new toy was inexhaustible in its potentialities.

In the intervals of applying algebra to the second book of Euclid, we experimented with circles; we stuck bamboos into the parched earth, measured their shadows at different hours of the day, and drew exciting conclusions from our observations. Sometimes, for fun, we cut and folded sheets of paper so as to make cubes and pyramids. One afternoon Guido arrived carrying carefully between his small and rather grubby hands a flimsy dodecahedron.

"E tanto bello!" he said, as he showed us his paper crystal; and when I asked him how he managed to make it, he merely smiled and said it had been so easy. I looked at Elizabeth and laughed. But it would have been more symbolically to the point, I felt, if I had gone down on all fours, wagged the spiritual outgrowth of my *os coccyx,* and barked my astonished admiration.

It was an uncommonly hot summer. By the beginning of July our little Robin, unaccustomed to these high temperatures, began to look pale and tired; he was listless, had lost his appetite and energy. The doctor advised mountain air. We decided to spend the next ten or twelve weeks in Switzerland. My parting gift to Guido was the first six books of Euclid in Italian. He turned over the pages, looked ecstatically at the figures.

"If only I knew how to read properly," he said. "I'm so stupid. But now I shall really try to learn."

From our hotel near Grindelwald we sent the child, in Robin's name, various post cards of cows, Alp-horns, Swiss chalets, edelweiss, and the like. We received no answers to these cards; but then we did not expect answers. Guido could not write, and there was no reason why his father or his sisters should take the trouble to write for him. No news, we took it,

was good news. And then one day, early in September, there arrived at the hotel a strange letter. The manager had it stuck up on the glass-fronted notice-board in the hall, so that all the guests might see it, and whoever conscientiously thought that it belonged to him might claim it. Passing the board on the way in to lunch, Elizabeth stopped to look at it.

"But it must be from Guido," she said.

I came and looked at the envelope over her shoulder. It was unstamped and black with postmarks. Traced out in pencil, the big uncertain capital letters sprawled across its face. In the first line was written: AL BABBO DI ROBIN, and there followed a travestied version of the name of the hotel and the place. Round the address bewildered postal officials had scrawled suggested emendations. The letter had wandered for a fortnight at least, back and forth across the face of Europe.

"Al Babbo di Robin. To Robin's father." I laughed. "Pretty smart of the postmen to have got it here at all." I went to the manager's office, set forth the justice of my claim to the letter and, having paid the fifty-centime surcharge for the missing stamp, had the case unlocked and the letter given me. We went in to lunch.

"The writing's magnificent," we agreed, laughing, as we examined the address at close quarters. "Thanks to Euclid," I added. "That's what comes of pandering to the ruling passion."

But when I opened the envelope and looked at its contents I no longer laughed. The letter was brief and almost telegraphical in style. "SONO DALLA PADRONA," it ran, "NON MI PIACE HA RUBATO IL MIO LIBRO NON VOGLIO SUONARE PIU VOGLIO TORNARE A CASA VENGA SUBITO GUIDO." [3]

[3] I am at the Padrona's—I don't like it—she has stolen my book—I don't want to play [the piano] any more—I want to return home—come quickly—Guido.

"What is it?"

I handed Elizabeth the letter. "That blasted woman's got hold of him," I said.

Busts of men in Homburg hats, angels bathed in marble tears extinguishing torches, statues of little girls, cherubs, veiled figures, allegories and ruthless realisms—the strangest and most diverse idols beckoned and gesticulated as we passed. Printed indelibly on tin and embedded in the living rock, the brown photographs looked out, under glass, from the humbler crosses, headstones, and broken pillars. Dead ladies in the cubistic geometrical fashions of thirty years ago—two cones of black satin meeting point to point at the waist, and the arms: a sphere to the elbow, a polished cylinder below—smiled mournfully out of their marble frames; the smiling faces, the white hands, were the only recognizably human things that emerged from the solid geometry of their clothes. Men with black mustaches, men with white beards, young clean-shaven men, stared or averted their gaze to show a Roman profile. Children in their stiff best opened wide their eyes, smiled hopefully in anticipation of the little bird that was to issue from the camera's muzzle, smiled skeptically in the knowledge that it wouldn't, smiled laboriously and obediently because they had been told to. In spiky Gothic cottages of marble the richer dead privately reposed; through grilled doors one caught a glimpse of pale Inconsolables weeping, of distraught Geniuses guarding the secret of the tomb. The less prosperous sections of the majority slept in communities, close-crowded but elegantly housed under smooth continuous marble floors, whose every flagstone was the mouth of a separate grave.

These continental cemeteries, I thought, as Carlo and I made our way among the dead, are more frightful than ours, because these people pay more attention to their dead than we do. That primordial cult of corpses, that tender solicitude for their material well-being, which led the ancients to house their dead in stone, while they themselves lived between wattles and under thatch, still lingers here; persists, I thought, more vigorously than with us. There are a hundred gesticulating statues here for every one in an English graveyard. There are more family vaults, more "luxuriously appointed" (as they say of liners and hotels) than one would find at home. And embedded in every tombstone there are photographs to remind the powdered bones within what form they will have to resume on the Day of Judgment; beside each are little hanging lamps to burn optimistically on All Souls' Day. To the Man who built the Pyramids they are nearer, I thought, than we.

"If I had known," Carlo kept repeating, "if only I had known." His voice came to me through my reflections as though from a distance. "At the time he didn't mind at all. How should I have known that he would take it so much to heart afterwards? And she deceived me, she lied to me."

I assured him yet once more that it wasn't his fault. Though, of course, it was, in part. It was mine too, in part; I ought to have thought of the possibility and somehow guarded against it. And he shouldn't have let the child go, even temporarily and on trial, even though the woman was bringing pressure to bear on him. And the pressure had been considerable. They had worked on the same holding for more than a hundred years, the men of Carlo's family; and now she had made the old man threaten to turn him out. It would be a dreadful thing to leave the place; and besides, another place wasn't so easy to find. It was made quite plain, however, that he could stay if he let her have the child. Only for a little to begin with; just to see how he got on. There would be no compulsion whatever on him to stay if he didn't like it. And it would be all to Guido's advantage; and to his father's, too, in the end. All that the Englishman had said about his not being such a good musician as he had thought at first was obviously untrue—mere jealousy and little-mindedness: the man wanted to take credit for Guido himself, that was all. And the boy, it was obvious, would learn nothing from him. What he needed was a real good professional master.

All the energy that, if the physicists had known their business, would have been driving dynamos, went into this campaign. It began the moment we were out of the house, intensively. She would have more chance of success, the Signora doubtless thought, if we weren't there. And besides, it was essential to take the opportunity when it offered itself and get hold of the child before we could make our bid—for it was obvious to her that we wanted Guido just as much as she did.

Day after day she renewed the assault. At the end of a week she sent her husband to complain about the state of the vines: they were in a shocking condition; he had decided, or very nearly decided, to give Carlo notice. Meekly, shamefacedly, in obedience to higher orders, the old gentleman uttered his threats. Next day Signora Bondi returned to the attack. The padrone, she declared, had been in a towering passion; but she'd do her best, her

very best, to mollify him. And after a significant pause she went on to talk about Guido.

In the end Carlo gave in. The woman was too persistent and she held too many trump cards. The child could go and stay with her for a month or two on trial. After that, if he really expressed a desire to remain with her, she could formally adopt him.

At the idea of going for a holiday to the seaside—and it was to the seaside, Signora Bondi told him, that they were going— Guido was pleased and excited. He had heard a lot about the sea from Robin. "Tanta acqua!" It had sounded almost too good to be true. And now he was actually to go and see this marvel. It was very cheerfully that he parted from his family.

But after the holiday by the sea was over, and Signora Bondi had brought him back to her town house in Florence, he began to be homesick. The Signora, it was true, treated him exceedingly kindly, bought him new clothes, took him out to tea in the Via Tornabuoni and filled him up with cakes, iced strawberryade, whipped cream, and chocolates. But she made him practice the piano more than he liked, and what was worse, she took away his Euclid, on the score that he wasted too much time with it. And when he said that he wanted to go home, she put him off with promises and excuses and downright lies. She told him that she couldn't take him at once, but that next week, if he were good and worked hard at his piano meanwhile, next week . . . And when the time came she told him that his father didn't want him back. And she redoubled her petting, gave him expensive presents, and stuffed him with yet unhealthier foods. To no purpose. Guido didn't like his new life, didn't want to practice scales, pined for his book, and longed to be back with his brothers and sisters. Signora Bondi, meanwhile, continued to hope that time and chocolates would eventually make the child hers; and to keep his family at a distance, she wrote to Carlo every few days letters which still purported to come from the seaside (she took the trouble to send them to a friend, who posted them back again to Florence), and in which she painted the most charming picture of Guido's happiness.

It was then that Guido wrote his letter to me. Abandoned, as he supposed, by his family—for that they shouldn't take the trouble to come to see him when they were so near was only to be explained on the hypothesis that they really had given him up—he must have looked to me as his last and only hope. And the letter, with its fantastic address, had been nearly a fortnight on its way. A fortnight—it must have seemed hundreds of years; and as the centuries succeeded one another, gradually, no doubt, the poor child became convinced that I too had abandoned him. There was no hope left.

"Here we are," said Carlo.

I looked up and found myself confronted by an enormous monument. In a kind of grotto hollowed in the flanks of a monolith of gray sandstone, Sacred Love, in bronze, was embracing a funerary urn. And in bronze letters riveted into the stone was a long legend to the effect that the inconsolable Ernesto Bondi had raised this monument to the memory of his beloved wife, Annunziata, as a token of his undying love for one whom, snatched from him by a premature death, he hoped very soon to join beneath this stone. The first Signora Bondi had died in 1912. I thought of the old man leashed to his white dog; he must always, I reflected, have been a most uxorious husband.

"They buried him here."

We stood there for a long time in silence. I felt the tears coming into my eyes as I thought of the poor child lying there underground. I thought of those luminous grave eyes, and the curve of that beautiful forehead, the droop of the melancholy mouth, of the expression of delight which illumined his face when he learned of some new idea that pleased him, when he heard a piece of music that he liked. And this beautiful small being was dead; and the spirit that inhabited this form, the amazing spirit, that too had been destroyed almost before it had begun to exist.

And the unhappiness that must have preceded the final act, the child's despair, the conviction of his utter abandonment—those were terrible to think of, terrible.

"I think we had better come away now," I said at last, and touched Carlo on the arm. He was standing there like a blind man, his eyes shut, his face slightly lifted towards the light; from between his closed eyelids the tears welled out, hung for a moment, and trickled down his cheeks. His lips trembled and I could see that he was making an effort to keep them still. "Come away," I repeated.

The face which had been still in its sorrow, was suddenly convulsed; he opened his eyes, and through the tears they were bright with a violent anger. "I shall kill her," he said, "I shall kill her. When I think of him throwing himself out, falling through the air . . ." With his two hands he made a violent gesture, bringing them down from over his head and arresting them with a sudden jerk when they were on a level with his breast. "And then crash." He shuddered. "She's as much responsible as though she had pushed him down herself. I shall kill her." He clenched his teeth.

To be angry is easier than to be sad, less painful. It is comforting to think of revenge. "Don't talk like that," I said. "It's no good. It's stupid. And what would be the point?" He had had those fits before, when grief became too painful and he had tried to escape from it. Anger had been the easiest way of escape. I had had, before this, to persuade him back into the harder path of grief. "It's stupid to talk like that," I repeated, and I led him away through the ghastly labyrinth of tombs, where death seemed more terrible even than it is.

By the time we had left the cemetery, and were walking down from San Miniato towards the Piazzale Michelangelo be-low, he had become calmer. His anger had subsided again into sorrow from which it had derived all its strength and its bitterness. In the Piazzale we halted for a moment to look down at the city in the valley below us. It was a day of floating clouds—great shapes, white, golden, and gray; and between them patches of a thin, transparent blue. Its lantern level, almost, with our eyes, the dome of the cathedral revealed itself in all its grandiose lightness, its vastness and aerial strength. On the innumerable brown and rosy roofs of the city the afternoon sunlight lay softly, sumptuously, and the towers were as though varnished and enameled with an old gold. I thought of all the Men who had lived here and left the visible traces of their spirit and conceived extraordinary things, I thought of the dead child.

ARABY

by JAMES JOYCE

NORTH RICHMOND STREET, being blind, was a quiet street except at the hour when the Christian Brothers' School set the boys free. An uninhabited house of two stories stood at the blind end, detached from its neighbors in a square ground. The other houses of the street, conscious of decent lives within them, gazed at one another with brown imperturbable faces.

The former tenant of our house, a priest, had died in the back drawing room. Air, musty from having been long enclosed, hung in all the rooms, and the waste room behind the kitchen was littered with old useless papers. Among these I found a few paper-covered books, the pages of which were curled and damp: *The Abbot,* by Walter Scott, *The Devout Communicant,* and *The Memoirs of Vidocq.* I liked the last best because its leaves were yellow. The wild garden behind the house contained a central apple tree and a few straggling bushes under one of which I found the late tenant's rusty bicycle pump. He had been a very charitable priest; in his will he had left all his money to institutions and the furniture of his house to his sister.

When the short days of winter came dusk fell before we had well eaten our dinners. When we met in the street the houses had grown somber. The space of

From *Dubliners* by James Joyce. By permission of The Viking Press, Inc., New York.

sky above us was the color of ever-changing violet and towards it the lamps of the street lifted their feeble lanterns. The cold air stung us and we played till our bodies glowed. Our shouts echoed in the silent street. The career of our play brought us through the dark muddy lanes behind the houses where we ran the gauntlet of the rough tribes from the cottages, to the back doors of the dark dripping gardens where odors arose from the ashpits, to the dark odorous stables where a coachman smoothed and combed the horse or shook music from the buckled harness. When we returned to the street, light from the kitchen windows had filled the areas. If my uncle was seen turning the corner we hid in the shadow until we had seen him safely housed. Or if Mangan's sister came out on the doorstep to call her brother in to his tea we watched her from our shadow peer up and down the street. We waited to see whether she would remain or go in and, if she remained, we left our shadow and walked up to Mangan's steps resignedly. She was waiting for us, her figure defined by the light from the half-opened door. Her brother always teased her before he obeyed and I stood by the railings looking at her. Her dress swung as she moved her body and the soft rope of her hair tossed from side to side.

Every morning I lay on the floor in the front parlor watching her door. The blind was pulled down to within an inch of the sash so that I could not be seen. When she came out on the doorstep my heart leaped. I ran to the hall, seized my books and followed her. I kept her brown figure always in my eye and, when we came near the point at which our ways diverged, I quickened my pace and passed her. This happened morning after morning. I had never spoken to her, except for a few casual words, and yet her name was like a summons to all my foolish blood.

Her image accompanied me even in places the most hostile to romance. On Saturday evenings when my aunt went marketing I had to go to carry some of the parcels. We walked through the flaring streets, jostled by drunken men and bargaining women, amid the curses of laborers, the shrill litanies of shop boys who stood on guard by the barrels of pigs' cheeks, the nasal chanting of street singers, who sang a *come-all-you* about O'Donovan Rossa, or a ballad about the troubles in our native land. These noises converged in a single sensation of life for me: I imagined that I bore my chalice safely through a throng of foes. Her name sprang to my lips at moments in strange prayers and praises which I myself did not understand. My eyes were often full of tears (I could not tell why) and at times a flood from my heart seemed to pour itself out into my bosom. I thought little of the future. I did not know whether I would ever speak to her or not or, if I spoke to her, how I could tell her of my confused adoration. But my body was like a harp and her words and gestures were like fingers running upon the wires.

One evening I went into the back drawing room in which the priest had died. It was a dark rainy evening and there was no sound in the house. Through one of the broken panes I heard the rain impinge upon the earth, the fine incessant needles of water playing in the sodden beds. Some distant lamp or lighted window gleamed below me. I was thankful that I could see so little. All my senses seemed to desire to veil themselves and, feeling that I was about to slip from them, I pressed the palms of my hands together until they trembled, murmuring: *"O love! O love!"* many times.

At last she spoke to me. When she addressed the first words to me I was so confused that I did not know what to answer. She asked me was I going to *Araby*. I forgot whether I answered yes or no. It would be a splendid bazaar, she said; she would love to go.

"And why can't you?" I asked.

While she spoke she turned a silver bracelet round and round her wrist. She could not go, she said, because there would be a retreat that week in her convent. Her brother and two other boys were fighting for their caps and I was alone at the railings. She held one of the spikes, bowing her head towards me. The light from the lamp opposite our door caught the white curve of her neck, lit up her hair that rested there and, falling, lit up the hand upon the railing. It fell over one side of her dress and caught the white border of a petticoat, just visible as she stood at ease.

"It's well for you," she said.

"If I go," I said, "I will bring you something."

What innumerable follies laid waste my waking and sleeping thoughts after that evening! I wished to annihilate the tedious intervening days. I chafed against the work of school. At night in my bedroom and by day in the classroom her image came between me and the page I strove to read. The syllables of the word *Araby* were called to me through the silence in which my soul luxuriated and cast an Eastern enchantment over me. I asked for leave to go to the bazaar on Saturday night. My aunt was surprised and hoped it was not some Freemason affair. I answered few questions in class. I watched my master's face pass from amiability to sternness; he hoped I was not beginning to idle. I could not call my wandering thoughts together. I had hardly any patience with the serious work of life which, now that it stood between me and my desire, seemed to me child's play, ugly monotonous child's play.

On Saturday morning I reminded my uncle that I wished to go to the bazaar in the evening. He was fussing at the hall stand, looking for the hat brush, and answered me curtly:

"Yes, boy, I know."

As he was in the hall I could not go into the front parlor and lie at the window. I left the house in bad humor and walked slowly towards the school. The air was pitilessly raw and already my heart misgave me.

When I came home to dinner my uncle had not yet been home. Still it was early. I sat staring at the clock for some time and, when its ticking began to irritate me, I left the room. I mounted the staircase and gained the upper part of the house. The high cold empty gloomy rooms liberated me and I went from room to room singing. From the front window I saw my companions playing below in the street. Their cries reached me weakened and indistinct and, leaning my forehead against the cool glass, I looked over at the dark house where she lived. I may have stood there for an hour, seeing nothing but the brown-clad figure cast by my imagination, touched discreetly by the lamplight at the curved neck, at the hand upon the railings and at the border below the dress.

When I came downstairs again I found Mrs. Mercer sitting at the fire. She was an old garrulous woman, a pawnbroker's widow, who collected used stamps for some pious purpose. I had to endure the gossip of the tea table. The meal was prolonged beyond an hour and still my uncle did not come. Mrs. Mercer stood up to go: she was sorry she couldn't wait any longer, but it was after eight o'clock and she did not like to be out late, as the night air was bad for her. When she had gone I began to walk up and down the room, clenching my fists. My aunt said:

"I'm afraid you may put off your bazaar for this night of Our Lord."

At nine o'clock I heard my uncle's latch-key in the hall door. I heard him talking to himself and heard the hall stand rocking when it had received the weight of his overcoat. I could interpret these signs. When he was midway through his dinner I asked him to give me the money to go to the bazaar. He had forgotten.

"The people are in bed and after their first sleep now," he said.

I did not smile. My aunt said to him energetically:

"Can't you give him the money and let him go? You've kept him late enough as it is."

My uncle said he was very sorry he had forgotten. He said he believed in the old saying: "All work and no play makes Jack a dull boy." He asked me where I was going and, when I had told him a second time he asked me did I know *The Arab's Farewell to His Steed*. When I left the kitchen he was about to recite the opening lines of the piece to my aunt.

I held a florin tightly in my hand as I strode down Buckingham Street towards the station. The sight of the streets thronged with buyers and glaring with gas recalled to me the purpose of my journey. I took my seat in a third-class carriage of a deserted train. After an intolerable delay the train moved out of the station slowly. It crept onward among ruinous houses and over the twinkling river. At Westland Row Station a crowd of people pressed to the carriage doors; but the porters moved them back, saying that it was a special train for the bazaar. I remained alone in the bare carriage. In a few minutes the train drew up beside an improvised wooden platform. I passed out on to the road and saw by the lighted dial of a clock that it was ten minutes to ten. In front of me was a large building which displayed the magical name.

I could not find any sixpenny entrance and, fearing that the bazaar would be closed, I passed in quickly through a turnstile, handing a shilling to a weary-looking man. I found myself in a big hall girdled at half its height by a gallery. Nearly all the stalls were closed and the greater part of the hall was in darkness. I recognized a silence like that which pervades a church after a service. I walked into the center of the bazaar timidly. A few people were gathered about the stalls which were still open. Before a curtain, over which the words *Café Chantant* were written in colored lamps, two men were counting money on a salver. I listened to the fall of the coins.

Remembering with difficulty why I had come I went over to one of the stalls and examined porcelain vases and flowered tea sets. At the door of the stall a young lady was talking and laughing with two young gentlemen. I remarked their English accents and listened vaguely to their conversation.

"O, I never said such a thing!"

"O, but you did!"

"O, but I didn't!"

"Didn't she say that?"

"Yes. I heard her."

"O, there's a . . . fib!"

Observing me, the young lady came over and asked me did I wish to buy anything. The tone of her voice was not encouraging; she seemed to have spoken to me out of a sense of duty. I looked humbly at the great jars that stood like eastern guards at either side of the dark entrance to the stall and murmured:

"No, thank you."

The young lady changed the position of one of the vases and went back to the two young men. They began to talk of the same subject. Once or twice the young lady glanced at me over her shoulder.

I lingered before her stall, though I knew my stay was useless, to make my interest in her wares seem the more real. Then I turned away slowly and walked down the middle of the bazaar. I allowed the two pennies to fall against the sixpence in my pocket. I heard a voice call from one end of the gallery that the light was out. The upper part of the hall was now completely dark.

Gazing up into the darkness I saw myself as a creature driven and derided by vanity; and my eyes burned with anguish and anger.

SOPHISTICATION

by Sherwood Anderson

It was early evening of a day in the late fall and the Winesburg County Fair had brought crowds of country people into town. The day had been clear and the night came on warm and pleasant. On the Trunion Pike, where the road after it left town stretched away between berry fields now covered with dry brown leaves, the dust from passing wagons arose in clouds. Children, curled into little balls, slept on the straw scattered on wagon beds. Their hair was full of dust and their fingers black and sticky. The dust rolled away over the fields and the departing sun set it ablaze with colors.

In the main street of Winesburg crowds filled the stores and the sidewalks. Night came on, horses whinnied, the clerks in the stores ran madly about, children became lost and cried lustily, an American town worked terribly at the task of amusing itself.

Pushing his way through the crowds in Main Streeet, young George Willard concealed himself in the stairway leading to Doctor Reefy's office and looked at the people. With feverish eyes he watched the faces drifting past under the store lights. Thoughts kept coming into his head and he did not want to think. He stamped impatiently on the wooden steps and looked sharply about. "Well, is she going to stay with him all day? Have I done all this waiting for nothing?" he muttered.

George Willard, the Ohio village boy, was fast growing into manhood and new thoughts had been coming into his mind. All that day, amid the jam of people at the Fair, he had gone about feeling lonely. He was about to leave Winesburg to go away to some city where he hoped to get work on a city newspaper and he felt grown up. The mood that had taken possession of him was a thing known to men and unknown to boys. He felt old and a little tired. Memories awoke in him. To his mind his new sense of maturity set him apart, made of him a half-tragic figure. He wanted someone to understand the feeling that had taken possession of him after his mother's death.

There is a time in the life of every boy when he for the first time takes the backward view of life. Perhaps that is the moment when he crosses the line into manhood. The boy is walking through the street of his town. He is thinking of the future and of the figure he will cut in the world. Ambitions and regrets awake within him. Suddenly something happens; he stops under a tree and waits as for a voice calling his name. Ghosts of old things creep into his consciousness; the voices outside of himself whisper a message concerning the limitations of life. From being quite sure of himself and his future he becomes not at all sure. If he be an imaginative boy a door is torn open and for the first time he looks out upon the world, seeing, as though they marched in procession before him, the countless figures of men who before his time have come out of nothingness into the world, lived their lives and again disappeared into nothingness. The sadness of sophistication has come to the boy. With a little gasp he sees himself as merely a leaf blown by the wind through the streets of his village. He knows that in spite of all the stout talk of his fellows he must live and die in uncertainty, a thing blown by the winds, a thing destined like corn to wilt in the sun. He shivers and looks

eagerly about. The eighteen years he has lived seem but a moment, a breathing space in the long march of humanity. Already he hears death calling. With all his heart he wants to come close to some other human, touch someone with his hands, be touched by the hand of another. If he prefers that the other be a woman, that is because he believes that a woman will be gentle, that she will understand. He wants, most of all, understanding.

When the moment of sophistication came to George Willard, his mind turned to Helen White, the Winesburg banker's daughter. Always he had been conscious of the girl growing into womanhood as he grew into manhood. Once on a summer night when he was eighteen, he had walked with her on a country road and in her presence had given way to an impulse to boast, to make himself appear big and significant in her eyes. Now he wanted to see her for another purpose. He wanted to tell her of the new impulses that had come to him. He had tried to make her think of him as a man when he knew nothing of manhood and now he wanted to be with her and to try to make her feel the change he believed had taken place in his nature.

As for Helen White, she also had come to a period of change. What George felt, she in her young woman's way felt also. She was no longer a girl and hungered to reach into the grace and beauty of womanhood. She had come home from Cleveland, where she was attending college, to spend a day at the Fair. She also had begun to have memories. During the day she sat in the grandstand with a young man, one of the instructors from the college, who was a guest of her mother's. The young man was of a pedantic turn of mind and she felt at once he would not do for her purpose. At the Fair she was glad to be seen in his company as he was well dressed and a stranger. She knew that the fact of his presence would create an impression. During the day she was happy, but when night came on she began to grow restless. She wanted to drive the instructor away, to get out of his presence. While they sat together in the grandstand and while the eyes of former schoolmates were upon them, she paid so much attention to her escort that he grew interested. "A scholar needs money. I should marry a woman with money," he mused.

Helen White was thinking of George Willard even as he wandered gloomily through the crowds thinking of her. She remembered the summer evening when they had walked together and wanted to walk with him again. She thought that the months she had spent in the city, the going to theaters and the seeing of great crowds wandering in lighted thoroughfares, had changed her profoundly. She wanted him to feel and be conscious of the change in her nature.

The summer evening together that had left its mark on the memory of both the young man and woman had, when looked at quite sensibly, been rather stupidly spent. They had walked out of town along a country road. Then they had stopped by a fence near a field of young corn and George had taken off his coat and let it hang on his arm. "Well, I've stayed here in Winesburg—yes—I've not yet gone away but I'm growing up," he said. "I've been reading books and I've been thinking. I'm going to try to amount to something in life.

"Well," he explained, "that isn't the point. Perhaps I'd better quit talking."

The confused boy put his hand on the girl's arm. His voice trembled. The two started to walk back along the road to town. In his desperation George boasted, "I'm going to be a big man, the biggest that ever lived here in Winesburg," he declared. "I want you to do something, I don't know what. Perhaps it is none of my business. I want you to try to be different from other women. You see the point. It's none of my business I tell you. I want you to be a beautiful woman. You see what I want."

The boy's voice failed and in silence the two came back into town and went along the street to Helen White's house. At the gate he tried to say something impressive. Speeches he had thought out came into his head, but they seemed utterly pointless. "I thought—I used to think—I had it in my mind you would marry Seth Richmond. Now I know you won't," was all he could find to say as she went through the gate and toward the door of her house.

On the warm fall evening as he stood in the stairway and looked at the crowd drifting through Main Street, George thought of the talk beside the field of young corn and was ashamed of the figure he had made of himself. In the street the people surged up and down like cattle confined in a pen. Buggies and wagons almost filled the narrow thoroughfare. A band played and small boys raced along the sidewalk, diving between the legs of men. Young men with shining red faces walked awkwardly about with girls on their arms. In a room above one of the stores, where a dance was to be held, the fiddlers tuned their instruments. The broken sounds floated down through an open window and out across the murmur of voices and the loud blare of the horns of the band.

The medley of sounds got on young Willard's nerves. Everywhere, on all sides, the sense of crowding, moving life closed in about him. He wanted to run away by himself and think. "If she wants to stay with that fellow she may. Why should I care? What difference does it make to me?" he growled and went along Main Street and through Hern's grocery into a side street.

George felt so utterly lonely and dejected that he wanted to weep but pride made him walk rapidly along, swinging his arms. He came to Westley Moyer's livery barn and stopped in the shadows to listen to a group of men who talked of a race Westley's stallion, Tony Tip, had won at the Fair during the afternoon. A crowd had gathered in front of the barn and before the crowd walked Westley, prancing up and down and boasting. He held a whip in his hand and kept tapping the ground. Little puffs of dust arose in the lamplight. "Hell, quit your talking," Westley exclaimed. "I wasn't afraid, I knew I had 'em beat all the time. I wasn't afraid."

Ordinarily George Willard would have been intensely interested in the boasting of Moyer, the horseman. Now it made him angry. He turned and hurried away along the street. "Old windbag," he sputtered. "Why does he want to be bragging? Why don't he shut up?"

George went into a vacant lot and as he hurried along, fell over a pile of rubbish. A nail protruding from an empty barrel tore his trousers. He sat down on the ground and swore. With a pin he mended the torn place and then arose and went on. "I'll go to Helen White's house, that's what I'll do. I'll walk right in. I'll say that I want to see her. I'll walk right in and sit down, that's what I'll do," he declared, climbing over a fence and beginning to run.

On the veranda of Banker White's house Helen was restless and distraught. The instructor sat between the mother and daughter. His talk wearied the girl. Although he had also been raised in an Ohio town, the instructor began to put on the airs of the city. He wanted to appear cosmopolitan. "I like the chance you have given me to study the background out of which most of our girls come," he declared. "It was good of you, Mrs. White, to have me down for the day." He turned to Helen and laughed. "Your life is still bound up with the life of this town?" he asked. "There are people here in whom you are interested?" To the girl his voice sounded pompous and heavy.

Helen arose and went into the house. At the door leading to a garden at the back she stopped and stood listening. Her mother began to talk. "There is no one here fit to associate with a girl of Helen's breeding," she said.

Helen ran down a flight of stairs at the back of the house and into the garden. In the darkness she stopped and stood trembling. It seemed to her that the world was full of meaningless people saying words. Afire with eagerness she ran through a garden gate and turning a corner by the banker's barn, went into a little side street. "George! Where are you, George?" she cried, filled with nervous excitement. She stopped running, and leaned against a tree to laugh hysterically. Along the dark little street came George Willard, still saying words. "I'm going to walk right into her house. I'll go right in and sit down," he declared as he came up to her. He stopped and stared stupidly. "Come on," he said and took hold of her hand. With hanging heads they walked away along the street under the trees. Dry leaves rustled under foot. Now that he had found her George wondered what he had better do and say.

At the upper end of the fair ground, in Winesburg, there is a half decayed old grandstand. It has never been painted and the boards are all warped out of shape. The fair ground stands on top of a low hill rising out of the valley of Wine Creek and from the grandstand one can see at night, over a cornfield, the lights of the town reflected against the sky.

George and Helen climbed the hill to the fair ground, coming by the path past Waterworks Pond. The feeling of loneliness and isolation that had come to the young man in the crowded streets of his town was both broken and intensified by the presence of Helen. What he felt was reflected in her.

In youth there are always two forces fighting in people. The warm unthinking little animal struggles against the thing that reflects and remembers, and the older, the more sophisticated thing had possession of George Willard. Sensing his mood, Helen walked beside him filled with respect. When they got to the grandstand they climbed up under the roof and sat down on one of the long bench-like seats.

There is something memorable in the experience to be had by going into a fair ground that stands at the edge of a Middle Western town on a night after the annual fair has been held. The sensation is one never to be forgotten. On all sides are ghosts, not of the dead, but of living people. Here, during the day just passed, have come the people pouring in from the town and the country around. Farmers with their wives and children and all the people from the hundreds of little frame houses have gathered within these board walls. Young girls have laughed and men with beards have talked of the affairs of their lives. The place has been filled to overflowing with life. It has itched and squirmed with life and now it is night and the life has all gone away. The silence is almost terrifying. One conceals oneself standing silently beside the trunk of a tree and what there is of a reflective tendency in his nature is intensified. One shudders at the thought of the meaninglessness of life while at the same instant, and if the people of the town are his people, one loves life so intensely that tears come into the eyes.

In the darkness under the roof of the grandstand, George Willard sat beside Helen White and felt very keenly his own insignificance in the scheme of existence. Now that he had come out of town where the presence of the people stirring about, busy with a multitude of affairs, had been so irritating the irritation was all gone. The presence of Helen renewed and refreshed him. It was as though her woman's hand was assisting him to make some minute readjustment of the machinery of his life. He began to think of the people in the town where he had always lived with something like reverence. He had reverence for Helen. He wanted to love and to be loved by her, but he did not want at the moment to be confused by her womanhood. In the darkness he took hold of her hand and when she crept close put a hand on her shoulder. A wind began to blow and he shivered. With all his strength he tried to hold and to understand the mood that had come upon him. In that high place in the darkness the two oddly sensitive human atoms held each other tightly and waited. In the mind of each was that same thought. "I have come to this lonely place and here is this other," was the substance of the thing felt.

In Winesburg the crowded day had run itself out into the long night of the late fall. Farm horses jogged away along lonely country roads pulling their portion of weary people. Clerks began to bring samples of goods in off the sidewalk and lock the doors of stores. In the Opera House a crowd had gathered to see a show and further down Main Street the fiddlers, their instruments tuned, sweated and worked to keep the feet of youth flying over a dance floor.

In the darkness of the grandstand Helen White and George Willard remained silent. Now and then the spell that held them was broken and they turned and tried in the dim light to see into each other's eyes. They kissed but that impulse did not last. At the upper end of the fair ground a half dozen men worked over horses that had raced during the afternoon. The men had built a fire and were heating kettles of water. Only their legs could be seen as they passed back and forth in the light. When the wind blew the little flames of the fire danced crazily about.

George and Helen arose and walked away into the darkness. They went along a path past a field of corn that had not yet been cut. The wind whispered among the dry corn blades. For a moment during the walk back into town the spell that held them was broken. When they had come to the crest of Waterworks Hill they stopped by a tree and George again put his hands on the girl's shoulders. She embraced him eagerly and then again they drew quickly back from that impulse. They stopped kissing and stood a little apart. Mutual respect grew big in them. They were both embarrassed and to relieve their embarrassment dropped into the animalism of youth. They laughed and began to pull and haul at each other. In some way chastened and purified by the mood they had been in they became, not man and woman, not boy and girl, but excited little animals.

It was so they went down the hill. In the darkness they played like two splendid young things in a young world. Once, running swiftly forward, Helen tripped George and he fell. He squirmed and shouted. Shaking with laughter, he rolled down the hill. Helen ran after him. For just a moment she stopped in the darkness. There is no way of knowing what woman's thoughts went through her mind but, when the bottom of the hill was reached and she came up to the boy, she took his arm and walked beside him in dignified silence. For some reason they could not have explained they had both got from their silent evening together the thing needed. Man or boy, woman or girl, they had for a moment taken hold of the thing that makes the mature life of men and women in the modern world possible.

THE LOST BOY

by THOMAS WOLFE

I

LIGHT CAME and went and came again, the booming strokes of three o'clock beat out across the town in thronging bronze from the courthouse bell, light winds of April blew the fountain out in rainbow sheets, until the plume returned and pulsed, as Grover turned into the Square. He was a child, dark-eyed and grave, birthmarked upon his neck—a berry of warm brown—and with a gentle face, too quiet and too listening for his years. The scuffed boy's shoes, the thick-ribbed stockings gartered at the knees, the short knee pants cut straight with three small useless buttons at the side, the sailor blouse, the old cap battered out of shape, perched sideways up on top of the raven head, the old soiled canvas bag slung from the shoulder, empty now, but waiting for the crisp sheets of the afternoon—these friendly, shabby garments, shaped by Grover, uttered him. He turned and passed along the north side of the Square and in that moment saw the union of Forever and of Now.

Light came and went and came again, the great plume of the fountain pulsed and winds of April sheeted it across the Square in a rainbow gossamer of spray. The fire department horses drummed on the floors with wooden stomp, most casually, and with dry whiskings of their clean, coarse tails. The street cars ground into the Square from every portion of the compass and halted briefly like wound toys in their familiar quarter-hourly formula. A dray, hauled by a boneyard nag, rattled across the cobbles on the other side before his father's shop. The courthouse bell boomed out its solemn warning of immediate three, and everything was just the same as it had always been.

He saw that haggis of vexed shapes with quiet eyes—that hodgepodge of ill-sorted architectures that made up the Square, and he did not feel lost. For "Here," thought Grover, "here is the Square as it has always been—and papa's shop, the fire department and the City Hall, the fountain pulsing with its plume, the street cars coming in and halting at the quarter hour, the hardware store on the corner there, the row of old brick buildings on this side of the street, the people passing and the light that comes and changes and that always will come back again, and everything that comes and goes and changes in the Square, and yet will be the same again. And here," the boy thought, "is Grover with his paper bag. Here is old Grover, almost twelve years old. Here is the month of April, 1904. Here is the courthouse bell and three o'clock. Here is Grover on the Square that never changes. Here is Grover, caught upon this point of time."

It seemed to him that the Square, itself the accidental masonry of many years, the chance agglomeration of time and of disrupted strivings, was the center of the universe. It was for him, in his soul's picture, the earth's pivot, the granite core of changelessness, the eternal place where all things came and passed, and yet abode forever and would never change.

He passed the old shack on the corner —the wooden fire-trap where S. Goldberg ran his wiener stand. Then he passed the Singer place next door, with its gleaming display of new machines. He saw them and admired them, but he felt no joy. They brought back to him the busy hum of housework and of women sewing, the intricacy of stitch and weave, the mystery of style and pattern, the memory of women bending over flashing needles, the pedaled tread, the busy whir. It was women's work: it filled him with unknown associations of dullness and of vague depression. And always, also, with a moment's twinge of horror, for his dark eye would always travel toward that needle stitching up and down so fast the eye could never follow it. And then he would remember how his mother once had told him she had driven the needle through her finger, and always, when he passed this place, he would remember it and for a moment crane his neck and turn his head away.

He passed on then, but had to stop again next door before the music store. He always had to stop by places that had shining perfect things in them. He loved hardware stores and windows full of accurate geometric tools. He loved windows full of hammers, saws, and planing boards. He liked windows full of strong new rakes and hoes, with unworn handles, of white perfect wood, stamped hard and vivid with the maker's seal. He loved to see such things as these in the windows of hardware stores. And he would fairly gloat upon them and think that some day he would own a set himself.

Also, he always stopped before the music and piano store. It was a splendid store. And in the window was a small white dog upon his haunches, with head cocked gravely to one side, a small white dog that never moved, that never barked,

that listened attentively at the flaring funnel of a horn to hear "His Master's Voice" —a horn forever silent, and a voice that never spoke. And within were many rich and shining shapes of great pianos, an air of splendor and of wealth.

And now, indeed, he *was* caught, held suspended. A waft of air, warm, chocolate-laden, filled his nostrils. He tried to pass the white front of the little eight-foot shop; he paused, struggling with conscience; he could not go on. It was the little candy shop run by old Crocker and his wife. And Grover could not pass.

"Old stingy Crockers!" he thought scornfully. "I'll not go there any more. But—" as the maddening fragrance of rich cooking chocolate touched him once again—"I'll just look in the window and see what they've got." He paused a moment, looking with his dark and quiet eyes into the window of the little candy shop. The window, spotlessly clean, was filled with trays of fresh-made candy. His eyes rested on a tray of chocolate drops. Unconsciously he licked his lips. Put one of them upon your tongue and it just melted there, like honeydew. And then the trays full of rich home-made fudge. He gazed longingly at the deep body of the chocolate fudge, reflectively at maple walnut, more critically, yet with longing, at the mints, the nougatines, and all the other dainties.

"Old stingy Crockers!" Grover muttered once again, and turned to go. "I wouldn't go in *there* again."

And yet he did not go away. "Old stingy Crockers" they might be; still, they did make the best candy in town, the best, in fact, that he had ever tasted.

He looked through the window back into the little shop and saw Mrs. Crocker there. A customer had gone in and had made a purchase, and as Grover looked he saw Mrs. Crocker, with her little wrenny face, her pinched features, lean over and peer primly at the scales. She had a piece of fudge in her clean, bony, little fingers, and as Grover looked, she broke it, primly, in her little bony hands. She dropped a morsel down into the scales. They weighted down alarmingly, and her thin lips tightened. She snatched the piece of fudge out of the scales and broke it carefully once again. This time the scales wavered, went down very slowly, and came back again. Mrs. Crocker carefully put the reclaimed piece of fudge back in the tray, dumped the remainder in a paper bag, folded it and gave it to the customer, counted the money carefully and doled it out into the till, the pennies in one place, the nickels in another.

Grover stood there, looking scornfully. "Old stingy Crocker—afraid that she might give a crumb away!"

He grunted scornfully and again he turned to go. But now Mr. Crocker came out from the little partitioned place where they made all their candy, bearing a tray of fresh-made fudge in his skinny hands. Old Man Crocker rocked along the counter to the front and put it down. He really rocked along. He was a cripple. And like his wife, he was a wrenny, wizened little creature, with bony hands, thin lips, a pinched and meager face. One leg was inches shorter than the other, and on this leg there was an enormous thick-soled boot, with a kind of wooden, rocker-like arrangement, six inches high at least, to make up for the deficiency. On this wooden cradle Mr. Crocker rocked along, with a prim and apprehensive little smile, as if he were afraid he was going to lose something.

"Old stingy Crocker!" muttered Grover.

"Humph! He wouldn't give you anything!"

And yet—he did not go away. He hung there curiously, peering through the window, with his dark and gentle face now focused and intent, alert and curious, flattening his nose against the glass. Unconsciously he scratched the thick-ribbed fabric of one stockinged leg with the scuffed and worn toe of his old shoe. The fresh, warm odor of the new-made fudge was delicious. It was a little maddening. Half consciously he began to fumble in one trouser pocket, and pulled out his purse, a shabby worn old black one with a twisted clasp. He opened it and prowled about inside.

What he found was not inspiring—a nickel and two pennies and—he had forgotten them—the stamps. He took the stamps out and unfolded them. There were five twos, eight ones, all that remained of the dollar-sixty-cents' worth which Reed, the pharmacist, had given him for running errands a week or two before.

"Old Crocker," Grover thought, and looked somberly at the grotesque little form as it rocked back into the shop again, around the counter, and up the other side. "Well—" again he looked indefinitely at the stamps in his hand—"he's had all the rest of them. He might as well take these."

So, soothing conscience with this sop of scorn, he went into the shop and stood looking at the trays in the glass case and finally decided. Pointing with a slightly grimy finger at the fresh-made tray of chocolate fudge, he said, "I'll take fifteen cents' worth of this, Mr. Crocker." He paused a moment, fighting with embarrassment, then he lifted his dark face and said quietly, "And please, I'll have to give you stamps again."

Mr. Crocker made no answer. He did not look at Grover. He pressed his lips together primly. He went rocking away and got the candy scoop, came back, slid open the door of the glass case, put fudge into the scoop, and, rocking to the scales, began to weigh the candy out. Grover watched him as he peered and squinted, he watched him purse and press his lips together, he saw him take a piece of fudge and break it in two parts. And then old Crocker broke two parts in two again. He weighed, he squinted, and he hovered, until it seemed to Grover that by calling *Mrs.* Crocker stingy he had been guilty of a rank injustice. But finally, to his vast relief, the job was over, the scales hung there, quivering apprehensively, upon the very hair-line of nervous balance, as if even the scales were afraid that one more move from Old Man Crocker and they would be undone.

Mr. Crocker took the candy then and dumped it in a paper bag and, rocking back along the counter toward the boy, he dryly said: "Where are the stamps?" Grover gave them to him. Mr. Crocker relinquished his claw-like hold upon the bag and set it down upon the counter. Grover took the bag and dropped it in his canvas sack, and then remembered. "Mr. Crocker—" again he felt the old embarrassment that was almost like strong pain— "I gave you too much," Grover said. "There were eighteen cents in stamps. You—you can just give me three ones back."

Mr. Crocker did not answer. He was busy with his bony little hands, unfolding the stamps and flattening them out on top of the glass counter. When he had done so, he peered at them sharply for a moment, thrusting his scrawny neck forward and running his eye up and down, like a bookkeeper who totes up rows of figures.

When he had finished, he said tartly: "I don't like this kind of business. If you want candy, you should have the money for it. I'm not a post office. The next time you come in here and want anything, you'll have to pay me money for it."

Hot anger rose in Grover's throat. His olive face suffused with angry color. His tarry eyes got black and bright. He was on the verge of saying: "Then why did you take my other stamps? Why do you tell me now, when you have taken all the stamps I had, that you don't want them?"

But he was a boy, a boy of eleven years, a quiet, gentle, gravely thoughtful boy, and he had been taught how to respect his elders. So he just stood there looking with his tar-black eyes. Old Man Crocker, pursing at the mouth a little, without meeting Grover's gaze, took the stamps up in his thin, parched fingers and, turning, rocked away with them down to the till.

He took the twos and folded them and laid them in one rounded scallop, then took the ones and folded them and put them in the one next to it. Then he closed the till and started to rock off, down toward the other end. Grover, his face now quiet and grave, kept looking at him, but Mr. Crocker did not look at Grover. Instead he began to take some stamped cardboard shapes and fold them into boxes.

In a moment Grover said, "Mr. Crocker, will you give me the three ones, please?"

Mr. Crocker did not answer. He kept folding boxes, and he compressed his thin lips quickly as he did so. But Mrs. Crocker, back turned to her spouse, also folding boxes with her birdlike hands, muttered: "Hm! *I'd* give him nothing!"

Mr. Crocker looked up, looked at

Grover, said, "What are you waiting for?"

"Will you give me the three ones, please?" Grover said.

"I'll give you nothing," Mr. Crocker said.

He left his work and came rocking forward along the counter. "Now you get out of here! Don't you come in here with any more of those stamps," said Mr. Crocker.

"I should like to know where he gets them—that's what *I* should like to know," said Mrs. Crocker.

She did not look up as she said these words. She inclined her head a little to the side, in Mr. Crocker's direction, and continued to fold the boxes with her bony fingers.

"You get out of here!" said Mr. Crocker. "And don't you come back here with any stamps. . . . Where did you get those stamps?" he said.

"That's just what *I've* been thinking," Mrs. Crocker said. "*I've* been thinking all along."

"You've been coming in here for the last two weeks with those stamps," said Mr. Crocker. "I don't like the look of it. Where did you get those stamps?" he said.

"That's what *I've* been thinking," said Mrs. Crocker, for a second time.

Grover had got white underneath his olive skin. His eyes had lost their luster. They looked like dull, stunned balls of tar. "From Mr. Reed," he said. "I got the stamps from Mr. Reed." Then he burst out desperately. "Mr. Crocker—Mr. Reed will tell you how I got the stamps. I did some work for Mr. Reed, he gave me those stamps two weeks ago."

"Mr. Reed," said Mrs. Crocker acidly. She did not turn her head. "I call it mighty funny."

"Mr. Crocker," Grover said, "if you'll just let me have three ones—"

"You get out of here!" cried Mr. Crocker, and he began rocking forward toward Grover. "Now don't you come in here again, boy! There's something funny about this whole business! I don't like the look of it," said Mr. Crocker. "If you can't pay as other people do, then I don't want your trade."

"Mr. Crocker," Grover said again, and underneath the olive skin his face was gray, "if you'll just let me have those three—"

"You get out of here!" Mr. Crocker cried, rocking down toward the counter's end. "If you don't get out, boy—"

"*I'd* call a policeman, that's what I'd do," Mrs. Crocker said.

Mr. Crocker rocked around the lower end of the counter. He came rocking up to Grover. "You get out," he said.

He took the boy and pushed him with his bony little hands, and Grover was sick and gray down to the hollow pit of his stomach.

"You've got to give me those three ones," he said.

"You get out of here!" shrilled Mr. Crocker. He seized the screen door, pulled it open, and pushed Grover out. "Don't you come back in here," he said, pausing for a moment, and working thinly at the lips. He turned and rocked back in the shop again. The screen door slammed behind him. Grover stood there on the pavement. And light came and went and came again into the Square.

The boy stood there, and a wagon rattled past. There were some people passing by, but Grover did not notice them. He stood there blindly, in the watches of the sun, feeling this was Time, this was the center of the universe, the granite core of changelessness, and feeling, this is Grover, this the Square, this is Now.

But something had gone out of day. He felt the overwhelming, soul-sickening guilt that all the children, all the good men of the earth, have felt since Time began. And even anger had died down, had been drowned out, in this swelling tide of guilt, and "This is the Square"— thought Grover as before—"This is Now. There is my father's shop. And all of it is as it has always been—save I."

And the Square reeled drunkenly around him, light went in blind gray motes before his eyes, the fountain sheeted out to rainbow iridescence and returned to its proud, pulsing plume again. But all the brightness had gone out of day, and "Here is the Square, and here is permanence, and here is Time—and all of it the same as it has always been, save I."

The scuffed boots of the lost boy moved and stumbled blindly. The numb feet crossed the pavement—reached the cobbled street, reached the plotted central square—the grass plots, and the flower beds, so soon to be packed with red geraniums.

"I want to be alone," thought Grover, "where I cannot go near him. . . . Oh God, I hope he never hears, that no one ever tells him—"

The plume blew out, the iridescent sheet of spray blew over him. He passed through, found the other side and crossed the street, and— "Oh God, if papa ever hears!" thought Grover, as his numb feet started up the steps into his father's shop.

He found and felt the steps—the width and thickness of old lumber twenty feet in length. He saw it all—the iron columns on his father's porch, painted with the dull anomalous black-green that all such columns in this land and weather come

to; two angels, fly-specked, and the waiting stones. Beyond and all around, in the stonecutter's shop, cold shapes of white and marble, rounded stone, the languid angel with strong marble hands of love.

He went on down the aisle, the white shapes stood around him. He went on to the back of the workroom. This he knew —the little cast-iron stove in left-hand corner, caked, brown, heat-blistered, and the elbow of the long stack running out across the shop; the high and dirty window looking down across the Market Square toward Niggertown; the rude old shelves, plank-boarded, thick, the wood not smooth but pulpy, like the strong hair of an animal; upon the shelves the chisels of all sizes and a layer of stone dust; an emery wheel with pump tread; and a door that let out on the alleyway, yet the alleyway twelve feet below. Here in the room, two trestles of this coarse spiked wood upon which rested gravestones, and at one, his father at work.

The boy looked, saw the name was Creasman: saw the carved analysis of John, the symmetry of the s, the fine sentiment that was being polished off beneath the name and date: "John Creasman, November 7, 1903."

Gant looked up. He was a man of fifty-three, gaunt-visaged, mustache cropped, immensely long and tall and gaunt. He wore good dark clothes—heavy, massive— save he had no coat. He worked in shirt-sleeves with his vest on, a strong watch chain stretching across his vest, wing collar and black tie, Adam's apple, bony forehead, bony nose, light eyes, gray-green, undeep and cold, and, somehow, lonely-looking, a striped apron going up around his shoulders and starched cuffs. And in one hand a tremendous rounded wooden mallet like a butcher's bole; and in his other hand, a strong cold chisel.

"How are you, son?"

He did not look up as he spoke. He spoke quietly, absently. He worked upon the chisel and the wooden mallet, as a jeweler might work on a watch, except that in the man and in the wooden mallet there was power too.

"What is it, son?" he said.

He moved around the table from the head, started up on "J" once again.

"Papa, I never stole the stamps," said Grover.

Gant put down the mallet, laid the chisel down. He came around the trestle.

"What?" he said.

As Grover winked his tar-black eyes, they brightened, the hot tears shot out. "I never stole the stamps," he said.

"Hey? What is this?" his father said. "What stamps?"

"That Mr. Reed gave me, when the other boy was sick and I worked there for three days. . . . And Old Man Crocker," Grover said, "he took all the stamps. And I told him Mr. Reed had given them to me. And now he owes me three ones—and Old Man Crocker says he don't believe that they were mine. He says—he says—that I must have taken them somewhere," Grover blurted out.

"The stamps that Reed gave you—hey?" the stonecutter said. "The stamps you had—" He wet his thumb upon his lips, threw back his head and slowly swung his gaze around the ceiling, then turned and strode quickly from his workshop out into the storeroom.

Almost at once he came back again, and as he passed the old gray painted-board partition of his office he cleared his throat and wet his thumb and said, "Now, I tell you—"

Then he turned and strode up toward the front again and cleared his throat and said, "I tell you now—" He wheeled about and started back, and as he came along the aisle between the marshaled rows of gravestones he said beneath his breath, "By God, now—"

He took Grover by the hand and they went out flying. Down the aisle they went by all the gravestones, past the fly-specked angels waiting there, and down the wooden steps and across the Square. The fountain pulsed, the plume blew out in sheeted iridescence, and it swept across them; an old gray horse, with a peaceful look about his torn lips, swucked up the cool mountain water from the trough as Grover and his father went across the Square, but they did not notice it.

They crossed swiftly to the other side in a direct line to the candy shop. Gant was still dressed in his long striped apron, and he was still holding Grover by the hand. He opened the screen door and stepped inside.

"Give him the stamps," Gant said.

Mr. Crocker came rocking forward behind the counter, with the prim and careful look that now was somewhat like a smile. "It was just—" he said.

"Give him the stamps," Gant said, and threw some coins down on the counter.

Mr. Crocker rocked away and got the stamps. He came rocking back. "I just didn't know—" he said.

The stonecutter took the stamps and gave them to the boy. And Mr. Crocker took the coins.

"It was just that—" Mr. Crocker began again, and smiled.

Gant cleared his throat: "You never were a father," he said. "You never knew the feelings of a father, or understood the feelings of a child; and that is why you acted as you did. But a judgment is upon you. God has cursed you. He has afflicted you. He has made you lame and childless as you are—and lame and childless, miserable as you are, you will go to your grave and be forgotten!"

And Crocker's wife kept kneading her bony little hands and said, imploringly, "Oh, no—oh don't say that, please don't say that."

The stonecutter, the breath still hoarse in him, left the store, still holding the boy tightly by the hand. Light came again into the day.

"Well, son," he said, and laid his hand on the boy's back. "Well, son," he said, "now don't you mind."

They walked across the Square, the sheeted spray of iridescent light swept out on them, the horse swizzled at the watertrough, and "Well, son," the stonecutter said.

And the old horse sloped down, ringing with his hoofs upon the cobblestones.

"Well, son," said the stonecutter once again, "be a good boy."

And he trod his own steps then with his great stride and went back again into his shop.

The lost boy stood upon the Square, hard by the porch of his father's shop.

"This is Time," thought Grover. "Here is the Square, here is my father's shop, and here am I."

And light came and went and came again—but now not quite the same as it had done before. The boy saw the pattern of familiar shapes and knew that they were just the same as they had always been. But something had gone out of day, and something had come in again. Out of the vision of those quiet eyes some brightness had gone, and into their vision had come some deeper color. He could not say, he did not know through what transforming shadows life had passed within that quarter hour. He only knew that something had been lost—something forever gained.

Just then a buggy curved out through the Square, and fastened to the rear end was a poster, and it said "St. Louis" and "Excursion" and "The Fair."

II—*The Mother*

As we went down through Indiana— you were too young, child, to remember it —but I always think of all of you the way you looked that morning, when we went down through Indiana, going to the Fair. All of the apple trees were coming out, and it was April; it was the beginning of spring in southern Indiana and everything was getting green. Of course we don't have farms at home like those in Indiana. The childern had never seen such farms as those, and I reckon, kidlike, they had to take it in.

So all of them kept running up and down the aisle—well, no, except for you and Grover. *You* were too young, Eugene. You were just three, I kept you with me. As for Grover—well, I'm going to tell you about that.

But the rest of them kept running up and down the aisle and from one window to another. They kept calling out and hollering to each other every time they saw something new. They kept trying to look out on all sides, in every way at once, as if they wished they had eyes at the back of their heads. It was the first time any of them had ever been in Indiana, and I reckon that it all seemed strange and new.

And so it seemed they couldn't get enough. It seemed they never could be still. They kept running up and down and back and forth, hollering and shouting to each other, until—"I'll vow! You childern! I never saw the beat of you!" I said. "The way that you keep running up and down and back and forth and never can be quiet for a minute beats all I ever saw," I said.

You see, they were excited about going to St. Louis, and so curious over everything they saw. They couldn't help it, and they wanted to see everything. But— "I'll vow!" I said. "If you childern don't sit down and rest you'll be worn to a frazzle before we ever get to see St. Louis and the Fair!"

Except for Grover! He—no, sir! not him. Now, boy, I want to tell you—I've raised the lot of you—and if I do say so, there wasn't a numbskull in the lot. But *Grover!* Well, you've all grown up now, all of you have gone away, and none of you are childern any more. . . . And of course, I hope that, as the fellow says, you have reached the dignity of man's estate. I suppose you have the judgment of grown men. . . . But *Grover! Grover* had it even then!

Oh, even as a child, you know—at a time when I was almost afraid to trust the rest of you out of my sight—I could depend on Grover. He could go anywhere, I could send him anywhere, and I'd always know he'd get back safe, and do exactly what I told him to!

Why, I didn't even have to tell him. You could send that child to market and tell him what you wanted, and he'd come home with *twice* as much as you could get yourself for the same money!

Now you know, I've always been consid-

ered a good trader. But *Grover!*—why, it got so finally that I wouldn't even tell him. Your papa said to me: "You'd be better off if you'd just tell him what you want and leave the rest to him. For," your papa says, "damned if I don't believe he's a better trader than you are. He gets more for the money than anyone I ever saw."

Well, I had to admit it, you know. I had to own up then. Grover, even as a child, was a far better trader than I was. . . . Why, yes, they told it on him all over town, you know. They said all of the market men, all of the farmers, knew him. They'd begin to laugh when they saw him coming—they'd say: "Look out! Here's Grover! Here's one trader you're not going to fool!"

And they were right! *That* child! I'd say, "Grover, suppose you run uptown and see if they've got anything good to *eat* today"—and I'd just wink at him, you know, but he'd know what I meant. I wouldn't let on that I *wanted* anything exactly, but I'd say, "Now it just occurs to me that some good fresh stuff may be coming in from the country, so suppose you take this dollar and just see what you can do with it."

Well, sir, that was all that was needed. The minute you told that child that you depended on his judgment, he'd have gone to the ends of the earth for you—and, let me tell you something, he wouldn't *miss*, either!

His eyes would get as black as coals— oh! the way that child would look at you, the intelligence and sense in his expression. He'd say: "Yes, *ma'am!* Now don't you worry, mama. You leave it all to me— and I'll do *good!*" said Grover.

And he'd be off like a streak of lightning and—oh Lord! As your father said to me, "I've been living in this town for almost thirty years," he said—"I've seen it grow up from a crossroads village, and I thought I knew everything there was to know about it—but that child—" your papa says—"he knows places that I never heard of!" . . . Oh, he'd go right down there to that place below your papa's shop where the draymen and the country people used to park their wagons—or he'd go down there to those old lots on Concord Street where the farmers used to keep their wagons. And, child that he was, he'd go right in among them, sir—*Grover* would!—go right in and barter with them like a grown man!

And he'd come home with things he'd bought that would make your eyes stick out. . . . Here he comes one time with another boy, dragging a great bushel basket full of ripe termaters between them. "Why, Grover!" I says. "How on earth are we ever going to use them? Why they'll go bad on us before we're half way through with them." "Well, mama," he says, "I know—" oh, just as solemn as a judge—"but they were the last the man had," he says, "and he wanted to go home, and so I got them for ten cents," he says. "They were so cheap," said Grover, "I thought it was a shame to let 'em go, and I figgered that what we couldn't eat—why," says Grover, "you could *put up!*" Well, the way he said it—so earnest and so serious—I had to laugh. "But I'll vow!" I said. "If you don't beat all!" . . . But that was *Grover!*—the way he was in *those* days! As everyone said, boy that he was, he had the sense and judgment of a grown man. . . . Child, child, I've seen you all grow up, and all of you were bright enough. There were no half-wits in *my* family. But for all-round intelligence, judgment, and general ability, Grover surpassed the whole crowd. I've never seen his equal, and everyone who knew him as a child will say the same.

So that's what I tell them now when they ask me about all of you. I have to tell the truth. I always said that *you* were smart enough, Eugene—but when they come around and brag to me about you, and about how you have got on and have a kind of name—I don't let on, you know. I just sit there and let them talk. I don't brag on you—if *they* want to brag on you, that's *their* business. I never bragged on one of my own children in my life. When father raised us up, we were all brought up to believe that it was not good breeding to brag about your kin. "If the others want to do it," father said, "well, let *them* do it. Don't ever let on by a word or sign that you know what they are talking about. Just let *them* do the talking, and say nothing."

So when they come around and tell me all about the things *you've* done—I don't let on to them, I never say a word. Why yes!—why, here, you know—oh, along about a month or so ago, this feller comes —a well-dressed man, you know—he looked intelligent, a good substantial sort of person. He said he came from New Jersey, or somewhere up in that part of the country, and he began to ask me all sorts of questions—what you were like when you were a boy, and all such stuff as that.

I just pretended to study it all over and then I said, "Well, yes"—real serious-like, you know—"well, yes—I reckon I ought to know a little something about him. Eugene was my child, just the same as all the others were. I brought him up just the way I brought up all the others. And," I says—oh, just as solemn as you please—

"he wasn't a *bad* sort of a boy. Why," I says, "up to the time that he was twelve years old he was just about the same as any other boy—a good, average, normal sort of fellow."

"Oh," he says, "But didn't you notice something? Wasn't there something kind of strange?" he says—"something different from what you noticed in the other childern?"

I didn't let on, you know—I just took it all in and looked as solemn as an owl—I just pretended to study it all over, just as serious as you please.

"Why no," I says, real slow-like, after I'd studied it all over. "As I remember it, he was a good, ordinary, normal sort of boy, just like all the others."

"Yes," he says—oh, all excited-like, you know— "But didn't you notice how brilliant he was? Eugene must have been more brilliant than the rest!"

"Well, now," I says, and pretended to study that all over too. "Now let me see. . . . Yes," I says—I just looked him in the eye, as solemn as you please—"he did pretty well. . . . Well, yes," I says, "I guess he was a fairly bright sort of a boy. I never had no complaints to make of him on that score. He was bright enough," I says. "The only trouble with him was that he was lazy."

"Lazy!" he says—oh, you should have seen the look upon his face, you know—he jumped like someone had stuck a pin in him. "Lazy!" he says. "Why, you don't mean to tell me—"

"Yes," I says—oh, I never cracked a smile— "I was telling him the same thing myself the last time that I saw him. I told him it was a mighty lucky thing for him that he had the gift of gab. Of course, he went off to college and read a lot of books, and I reckon that's where he got this flow

of language they say he has. But as I said to him the last time that I saw him: 'Now look a-here,' I said. 'If you can earn your living doing a light, easy class of work like this you do,' I says, 'you're mighty lucky, because none of the rest of your people,' I says, 'had any such luck as that. They had to work hard for a living.'"

Oh, I told him, you know. I came right out with it. I made no bones about it. And I tell you what—I wish you could have seen his face. It was a study.

"Well," he says, at last, "you've got to admit this, haven't you—he was the brightest boy you had, now wasn't he?"

I just looked at him a moment. I had to tell the truth. I couldn't fool him any longer. "No," I says. "He was a good, bright boy—I got no complaint to make about him on that score—but the brightest boy I had, the one that surpassed all the rest of them in sense, and understanding, and in judgment—the best boy I had—the smartest boy I ever saw—was—well, it wasn't Eugene," I said. "It was another one."

He looked at me a moment, then he said, "Which boy was that?"

Well, I just looked at him, and smiled. I shook my head, you know. I wouldn't tell him. "I never brag about my own," I said. "You'll have to find out for yourself."

But—I'll have to tell *you*—and you know yourself, I brought the whole crowd up, I knew you all. And you can take my word for it—the best one of the lot was—*Grover!*

And when I think of Grover as he was along about that time, I always see him sitting there, so grave and earnest-like, with his nose pressed to the window, as we went down through Indiana in the morning, to the Fair.

All through that morning we were going down along beside the Wabash River —the Wabash River flows through Indiana, it is the river that they wrote the song about—so all that morning we were going down along the river. And I sat with all you childern gathered about me as we went down through Indiana, going to St. Louis, to the Fair.

And Grover sat there, so still and earnest-like, looking out the window, and he didn't move. He sat there like a man. He was just eleven and a half years old, but he had more sense, more judgment, and more understanding than any child I ever saw.

So here he sat beside this gentleman and looked out the window. I never knew the man—I never asked his name—but I tell you what! He was certainly a fine-looking, well-dressed, good, substantial sort of man, and I could see that he had taken a great liking to Grover. And Grover sat there looking out, and then turned to this gentleman, as grave and earnest as a grown-up man, and says, "What kind of crops grow here, sir?" Well, this gentleman threw his head back and just hah-hahed. "Well, I'll see if I can tell you," says this gentleman, and then, you know, he talked to him, they talked together, and Grover took it all in, as solemn as you please, and asked this gentleman every sort of question—what the trees were, what was growing there, how big the farms were—all sorts of questions, which

this gentleman would answer, until I said: "Why, I'll vow, Grover! You shouldn't ask so many questions. You'll bother the very life out of this gentleman."

The gentleman threw his head back and laughed right out. "Now you leave that boy alone. He's all right," he said. "He doesn't bother me a bit, and if I know the answers to his questions I will answer him. And if I don't know, why, then, I'll tell him so. But he's *all right*," he said, and put his arm round Grover's shoulders. "You leave him alone. He doesn't bother me a bit."

And I can still remember how he looked that morning, with his black eyes, his black hair, and with the birthmark on his neck—so grave, so serious, so earnest-like—as he sat by the train window and watched the apple trees, the farms, the barns, the houses, and the orchards, taking it all in, I reckon, because it was strange and new to him.

It was so long ago, but when I think of it, it all comes back, as if it happened yesterday. Now all of you have either died or grown up and gone away, and nothing is the same as it was then. But all of you were there with me that morning and I guess I should remember how the others looked, but somehow I don't. Yet I can still see Grover just the way he was, the way he looked that morning when we went down through Indiana, by the river, to the Fair.

III—*The Sister*

Can you remember, Eugene, how Grover used to look? I mean the birthmark, the black eyes, the olive skin. The birthmark always showed because of those open sailor blouses kids used to wear. But

I guess you must have been too young when Grover died. . . . I was looking at that old photograph the other day. You know the one I mean—that picture showing mama and papa and all of us children before the house on Woodson Street. *You* weren't there, Eugene. *You* didn't get in. *You* hadn't arrived when that was taken. . . . You remember how mad you used to get when we'd tell you that you were only a dishrag hanging out in Heaven when something happened?

You were the baby. That's what you get for being the baby. You don't get in the picture, do you? . . . I was looking at that old picture just the other day. There we were. And, my God, what is it all about? I mean, when you see the way we were—Daisy and Ben and Grover, Steve and all of us—and then how everyone either dies or grows up and goes away— and then—look at us now! Do you ever get to feeling funny? You know what I mean—do you ever get to feeling *queer*— when you try to figure these things out? You've been to college and you ought to know the answer—and I wish you'd tell me if you know.

My Lord, when I think sometimes of the way I used to be—the dreams I used to have. Playing the piano, practicing seven hours a day, thinking that some day I would be a great pianist. Taking singing lessons from Aunt Nell because I felt that some day I was going to have a great career in opera. . . . Can you beat it now? Can you imagine it? *Me!* In grand opera! . . . Now I want to ask you. I'd like to know.

My Lord! When I go uptown and walk down the street and see all these funny-looking little boys and girls hanging around the drug store—do you suppose any of them have ambitions the way we did? Do you suppose any of these funny-looking little girls are thinking about a big career in opera? . . . Didn't you ever see that picture of us? I was looking at it just the other day. It was made before the old house down on Woodson Street, with papa standing there in his swallow-tail, and mama there beside him—and Grover, and Ben, and Steve, and Daisy, and myself, with our feet upon our bicycles. Luke, poor kid, was only four or five. *He* didn't have a bicycle like us. But there he was. And there were all of us together.

Well, there I was, and my poor old skinny legs and long white dress, and two pigtails hanging down my back. And all the funny-looking clothes we wore, with the doo-lolley business on them. . . . But I guess you can't remember. You weren't born.

But, well, we were a right nice-looking set of people, if I do say so. And there was "86" the way it used to be, with the front porch, the grape vines, and the flower beds before the house—and "Miss Eliza" standing there by papa, with a watch charm pinned upon her waist. . . . I shouldn't laugh, but "Miss Eliza"—well, mama was a pretty woman then. Do you know what I mean? "Miss Eliza" was a right good-looking woman, and papa in his swallow-tail was a good-looking man. Do you remember how he used to get dressed up on Sunday? And how grand we thought he was? And how he let me take his money out and count it? And how rich we all thought he was? And how wonderful that dinkey little shop on the Square looked to us? . . . Can you beat it, now? Why we thought that papa was the biggest man in town and—oh, you can't tell me! You can't tell me! He had his faults, but papa was a wonderful man. You know he was!

And there was Steve and Ben and Grover, Daisy, Luke, and me lined up there before the house with one foot on our bicycles. And I got to thinking back about it all. It all came back.

Do you remember anything about St. Louis? You were only three or four years old then, but you must remember something. . . . Do you remember how you used to bawl when I would scrub you? How you'd bawl for Grover? Poor kid, you used to yell for Grover every time I'd get you in the tub. . . . He was a sweet kid and he was crazy about you—he almost brought you up.

That year Grover was working at the Inside Inn out on the Fair Grounds. Do you remember the old Inside Inn? That big old wooden thing inside the Fair? And how I used to take you there to wait for Grover when he got through working? And old fat Billy Pelham at the newsstand—how he always used to give you a stick of chewing gum?

They were all crazy about Grover. Everybody liked him. . . . And how proud Grover was of you! Don't you remember how he used to show you off? How he used to take you around and make you talk to Billy Pelham? And Mr. Curtis at the desk? And how Grover would try to make you talk and get you to say "Grover"? And you couldn't say it—you couldn't pronounce the "r." You'd say "Gova." Have you forgotten that? You shouldn't forget *that,* because—you were a *cute* kid, then—Ho-ho-ho-ho-ho— I don't know where it's gone to, but you were a big hit in those days. . . . I tell you, boy, you were Somebody back in those days.

And I was thinking of it all the other day when I was looking at that photograph. How we used to go and meet Grover there, and how he'd take us to the Midway. Do you remember the Midway? The Snake-Eater and the Living Skeleton, the Fat Woman and the Chute-the-chute, the Scenic Railway and the Ferris Wheel?

How you bawled the night we took you up on the Ferris Wheel? You yelled your head off—I tried to laugh it off, but I tell you, I was scared myself. Back in those days, that was Something. And how Grover laughed at us and told us there was no danger. . . . My Lord! poor little Grover. He wasn't quite twelve years old at the time, but he seemed so grown up to us. I was two years older, but I thought he knew it all.

It was always that way with him. Looking back now, it sometimes seems that it was Grover who brought us up. He was always looking after us, telling us what to do, bringing us something—some ice cream or some candy, something he had bought out of the poor little money he'd gotten at the Inn.

Then I got to thinking of the afternoon we sneaked away from home. Mama had gone out somewhere. And Grover and I got on the street car and went downtown. And my Lord, we thought that we were going Somewhere. In those days, that was what we called a *trip.* A ride in the street car was something to write home about in those days. . . . I hear that it's all built up around there now.

So we got on the car and rode the whole way down into the business section of St. Louis. We got out on Washington Street and walked up and down. And I tell you, boy, we thought that that was Something. Grover took me into a drug store and set me up to soda water. Then we came out and walked around some more, down to the Union Station and clear over to the river. And both of us half scared to death at what we'd done and wondering what mama would say if she found out.

We stayed down there till it was getting dark, and we passed by a lunchroom—an old one-armed joint with one-armed chairs and people sitting on stools and eating at the counter. We read all the signs to see what they had to eat and how much it cost, and I guess nothing on the menu was more than fifteen cents, but it couldn't have looked grander to us if it had been Delmonico's. So we stood there with our noses pressed against the window, looking in. Two skinny little kids, both of us scared half to death, getting the thrill of a lifetime out of it. You know what I mean? And smelling everything with all our might and thinking how good it all smelled. . . . Then Grover turned to me and whispered: "Come on, Helen. Let's go in. It says fifteen cents for pork and beans. And I've got the money," Grover said. "I've got sixty cents."

I was so scared I couldn't speak. I'd never been in a place like that before. But I kept thinking, "Oh Lord, if mama should find out!" I felt as if we were committing some big crime. . . . Don't you know how it is when you're a kid? It was the thrill of a lifetime. . . . I couldn't resist. So we both went in and sat down on those high stools before the counter and ordered pork and beans and a cup of coffee. I suppose we were too frightened at what we'd done really to enjoy anything. We just gobbled it all up in a hurry, and gulped our coffee down. And I don't know whether it was the excitement—I guess the poor kid was already sick when we came in there and didn't know it. But I turned and looked at him, and he was white as death. . . . And when I asked him what was the matter, he wouldn't tell me. He was too proud. He said he was all right, but I could see that he was sick as a dog. . . . So he paid the bill. It came to forty cents—I'll never forget *that* as long as I live. . . . And sure enough, we no more than got out the door—he hardly had

time to reach the curb—before it all came up.

And the poor kid was so scared and so ashamed. And what scared him so was not that he had gotten sick, but that he had spent all that money and it had come to nothing. And mama would find out. . . . Poor kid, he just stood there looking at me and he whispered: "Oh Helen, don't tell mama. She'll be mad if she finds out." Then we hurried home, and he was still white as a sheet when we got there.

Mama was waiting for us. She looked at us—you know how "Miss Eliza" looks at you when she thinks you've been doing something that you shouldn't. Mama said, "Why, where on earth have you two children been?" I guess she was all set to lay us out. Then she took one look at Grover's face. That was enough for her. She said, "Why, child, what in the world!" She was white as a sheet herself. . . . And all that Grover said was— "Mama, I feel sick."

He was sick as a dog. He fell over on the bed, and we undressed him and mama put her hand upon his forehead and came out in the hall—she was so white you could have made a black mark on her face with chalk—and whispered to me, "Go get the doctor quick, he's burning up."

And I went chasing up the street, my pigtails flying, to Dr. Packer's house. I brought him back with me. When he came out of Grover's room he told mama what to do but I don't know if she even heard him.

Her face was white as a sheet. She looked at me and looked right through me. She never saw me. And oh, my Lord, I'll never forget the way she looked, the way my heart stopped and came up in my throat. I was only a skinny little kid of fourteen. But she looked as if she was dying right before my eyes. And I knew that if anything happened to him, she'd never get over it if she lived to be a hundred.

Poor old mama. You know, he always was her eyeballs—you know that, don't you?—not the rest of us!—no, sir! I know what I'm talking about. It always has been Grover—she always thought more of him than she did of any of the others. And—poor kid!—he was a sweet kid. I can still see him lying there, and remember how sick he was, and how scared I was! I don't know why I was so scared. All we'd done had been to sneak away from home and go into a lunchroom—but I felt guilty about the whole thing, as if it was my fault.

It all came back to me the other day when I was looking at that picture, and I thought, my God, we were two kids together, and I was only two years older than Grover was, and now I'm forty-six. . . . Can you believe it? Can you figure it out—the way we grow up and change and go away? . . . And my Lord, Grover seemed so grown-up to me. He was such a quiet kid—I guess that's why he seemed older than the rest of us.

I wonder what Grover would say now if he could see that picture. All my hopes and dreams and big ambitions have come to nothing, and it's all so long ago, as if it happened in another world. Then it comes back, as if it happened yesterday. . . . Sometimes I lie awake at night and think of all the people who have come and gone, and how everything is different from the way we thought that it would be. Then I go out on the street next day and see the faces of the people that I pass. . . . Don't they look strange to you? Don't you see something funny in people's eyes, as if all of them were puzzled about something? As if they were wondering what had happened to them since they were kids? Wondering what it is that they have lost? . . .

Now am I crazy, or do you know what I mean? You've been to college, Gene, and I want you to tell me if you know the answer. Now do they look that way to you? I never noticed that look in people's eyes when I was a kid—did you?

My God, I wish I knew the answer to these things. I'd like to find out what is wrong—what has changed since then—and if we have the same queer look in our eyes, too. Does it happen to us all, to everyone? . . . Grover and Ben, Steve, Daisy, Luke, and me—all standing there before that house on Woodson Street in Altamont—there we are, and you see the way we were—and how it all gets lost. What is it, anyway, that people lose?

How is it that nothing turns out the way we thought it would be? It all gets lost until it seems that it has never happened—that it is something we dreamed somewhere. . . . You see what I mean? . . . It seems that it must be something we heard somewhere—that it happened to someone else. And then it all comes back again.

And suddenly you remember just how it was, and see again those two funny, frightened, skinny little kids with their noses pressed against the dirty window of that lunchroom thirty years ago. You remember the way it felt, the way it smelled, even the strange smell in the old pantry in that house we lived in then. And the steps before the house, the way the rooms looked. And those two little boys in sailor suits who used to ride up and down before the house on tricycles. . . . And the birthmark on Grover's neck. . . . The Inside Inn. . . . St. Louis and the Fair.

It all comes back as if it happened yesterday. And then it goes away again, and seems farther off and stranger than if it happened in a dream.

IV—*The Brother*

"*This* is King's Highway," the man said.

And then Eugene looked and saw that it was just a street. There were some big new buildings, a large hotel, some restaurants and "bar-grill" places of the modern kind, the livid monotone of neon lights, the ceaseless traffic of motor cars—all this was new, but it was just a street. And he knew that it had always been just a street and nothing more—but somehow—well, he stood there looking at it, wondering what else he had expected to find.

The man kept looking at him with inquiry in his eyes, and Eugene asked him if the Fair had not been out this way.

"Sure, the Fair was out beyond here," the man said. "Out where the park is now. But this street you're looking for—don't you remember the name of it or nothing?" the man said.

Eugene said he thought the name of the street was Edgemont, but that he wasn't sure. Anyhow it was something like that. And he said the house was on the corner of that street and of another street.

Then the man said: "What was that other street?"

Eugene said he did not know, but that King's Highway was a block or so away, and that an interurban line ran past about half a block from where he once had lived.

"What line was this?" the man said, and stared at him.

"The interurban line," Eugene said.

Then the man stared at him again, and finally, "I don't know no interurban line," he said.

Eugene said it was a line that ran behind some houses, and that there were board fences there and grass beside the tracks. But somehow he could not say that it was summer in those days and that you could smell the ties, a wooden, tarry smell, and feel a kind of absence in the afternoon after the car had gone. He only said the interurban line was back behind somewhere between the backyards of some houses and some old board fences, and that King's Highway was a block or two away.

He did not say that King's Highway had not been a street in those days but a kind of road that wound from magic out of some dim and haunted land, and that along the way it had got mixed in with Tom the Piper's son, with hot cross buns, with all the light that came and went, and with coming down through Indiana in the morning, and the smell of engine smoke, the Union Station, and most of all with voices lost and far and long ago that said "King's Highway."

He did not say these things about King's Highway because he looked about him and he saw what King's Highway was. All he could say was that the street was near King's Highway, and was on the corner, and that the interurban trolley line was close to there. He said it was a stone house, and that there were stone steps before it, and a strip of grass. He said he thought the house had had a turret at one corner, he could not be sure.

The man looked at him again, and said, "This is King's Highway, but I never heard of any street like that."

Eugene left him then, and went on till he found the place. And so at last he turned into the street, finding the place where the two corners met, the huddled block, the turret, and the steps, and paused a moment, looking back, as if the street were Time.

For a moment he stood there, waiting—for a word, and for a door to open, for the child to come. He waited but no words were spoken; no one came.

Yet all of it was just as it had always been, except that the steps were lower, the porch less high, the strip of grass less wide, than he had thought. All the rest of it was as he had known it would be. A graystone front, three-storied, with a slant slate roof, the side red brick and windowed, still with the old arched entrance in the center for the doctor's use.

There was a tree in front, and a lamp post; and behind and to the side, more trees than he had known there would be. And all the slatey turret gables, all the slatey window gables, going into points, and the two arched windows, in strong stone, in the front room.

It was all so strong, so solid, and so ugly—and all so enduring and so good, the way he had remembered it, except he did not smell the tar, the hot and caulky dryness of the old cracked ties, the boards of backyard fences and the coarse and sultry grass, and absence in the afternoon when the street car had gone, and the twins, sharp-visaged in their sailor suits, pumping with furious shrillness on tricycles up and down before the house, and the feel of the hot afternoon, and the sense that everyone was absent at the Fair.

Except for this, it all was just the same; except for this and for King's Highway, which was now a street; except for this, and for the child that did not come.

It was a hot day. Darkness had come. The heat rose up and hung and sweltered like a sodden blanket in St. Louis. It was wet heat, and one knew that there would be no relief or coolness in the night. And when one tried to think of the time when the heat would go away, one said: "It can-not last. It's bound to go away," as we always say it in America. But one did not believe it when he said it. The heat soaked down and men sweltered in it; the faces of the people were pale and greasy with the heat. And in their faces was a patient wretchedness, and one felt the kind of desolation that one feels at the end of a hot day in a great city in America—when one's home is far away, across the continent, and he thinks of all that distance, all that heat, and feels, "Oh God! but it's a big country!"

And he feels nothing but absence, absence, and the desolation of America, the loneliness and sadness of the high, hot skies, and evening coming on across the Middle West, across the sweltering and heat-sunken land, across all the lonely little towns, the farms, the fields, the oven swelter of Ohio, Kansas, Iowa, and Indiana at the close of day, and voices, casual in the heat, voices at the little stations, quiet, casual, somehow faded into that enormous vacancy and weariness of heat, of space, and of the immense, the sorrowful, the most high and awful skies.

Then he hears the engine and the wheel again, the wailing whistle and the bell, the sound of shifting in the sweltering yard, and walks the street, and walks the street, beneath the clusters of hard lights, and by the people with sagged faces, and is drowned in desolation and in no belief.

He feels the way one feels when one comes back, and knows that he should not have come, and when he sees that, after all, King's Highway is—a street; and St. Louis—the enchanted name—a big, hot, common town upon the river, sweltering in wet, dreary heat, and not quite South, and nothing else enough to make it better.

It had not been like this before. He could remember how it would get hot, and how good the heat was, and how he would lie out in the backyard on an airing mattress, and how the mattress would get hot and dry and smell like a hot mattress full of sun, and how the sun would make him want to sleep, and how, sometimes, he would go down into the basement to feel coolness, and how the cellar smelled as cellars always smell—a cool, stale smell, the smell of cobwebs and of grimy bottles. And he could remember, when you opened the door upstairs, the smell of the cellar would come up to you —cool, musty, stale and dank and dark— and how the thought of the dark cellar always filled him with a kind of numb excitement, a kind of visceral expectancy.

He could remember how it got hot in the afternoons, and how he would feel a sense of absence and vague sadness in the afternoons, when everyone had gone away. The house would seem so lonely, and sometimes he would sit inside, on the second step of the hall stairs, and listen to the sound of silence and of absence in the afternoon. He could smell the oil upon the floor and on the stairs, and see the sliding doors with their brown varnish and the beady chains across the door, and thrust his hands among the beady chains, and gather them together in his arms, and let them clash, and swish with light beady swishings all around him. He could feel darkness, absence, varnished darkness, and stained light within the house, through the stained glass of the window on the stairs, through the small stained glasses by the door, stained light and absence, silence and the smell of floor oil and vague sadness in the house on a hot mid-afternoon. And all these things themselves would have a kind of life: would seem to wait attentively, to be most living and most still.

He would sit there and listen. He could hear the girl next door practice her piano lessons in the afternoon, and hear the street car coming by between the backyard fences, half a block away, and smell the dry and sultry smell of backyard fences, the smell of coarse hot grasses by the car tracks in the afternoon, the smell of tar, of dry caulked ties, the smell of bright worn flanges, and feel the loneliness of backyards in the afternoon and the sense of absence when the car was gone.

Then he would long for evening and return, the slant of light, and feet along the street, the sharp-faced twins in sailor suits upon their tricycles, the smell of supper and the sound of voices in the house again, and Grover coming from the Fair.

That is how it was when he came into the street, and found the place where the two corners met, and turned at last to see if Time was there. He passed the house: some lights were burning, the door was open, and a woman sat upon the porch. And presently he turned, came back, and stopped before the house again. The corner light fell blank upon the house. He stood looking at it, and put his foot upon the step.

Then he said to the woman who was sitting on the porch: "This house—excuse me—but could you tell me, please, who lives here in this house?"

He knew his words were strange and hollow, and he had not said what he wished to say. She stared at him a moment, puzzled.

Then she said: "I live here. Who are you looking for?"

He said, "Why, I am looking for—"

And then he stopped, because he knew he could not tell her what it was that he was looking for.

"There used to be a house—" he said.

The woman was now staring at him hard.

[71]

He said, "I think I used to live here."

She said nothing.

In a moment he continued, "I used to live here in this house," he said, "when I was a little boy."

She was silent, looking at him, then she said: "Oh. Are you sure this was the house? Do you remember the address?"

"I have forgotten the address," he said, "but it was Edgemont Street, and it was on the corner. And I know this is the house."

"This isn't Edgemont Street," the woman said. "The name is Bates."

"Well, then, they changed the name of the street," he said, "but this is the same house. It hasn't changed."

She was silent a moment, then she nodded: "Yes. They did change the name of the street. I remember when I was a child they called it something else," she said. "But that was a long time ago. When was it that you lived here?"

"In 1904."

Again she was silent, looking at him. Then presently: "Oh. That was the year of the Fair. You were here then?"

"Yes." He now spoke rapidly, with more confidence. "My mother had the house, and we were here for seven months. And the house belonged to Dr. Packer," he went on. "We rented it from him."

"Yes," the woman said, and nodded, "this was Dr. Packer's house. He's dead now, he's been dead for many years. But this was the Packer house, all right."

"That entrance on the side," he said, "where the steps go up, that was for Dr. Packer's patients. That was the entrance to his office."

"Oh," the woman said, "I didn't know that. I've often wondered what it was. I didn't know what it was for."

"And this big room in front here," he continued, "that was the office. And there were sliding doors, and next to it, a kind of alcove for his patients—"

"Yes, the alcove is still there, only all of it has been made into one room now—and I never knew just what the alcove was for."

"And there were sliding doors on this side, too, that opened on the hall—and a stairway going up upon this side. And halfway up the stairway, at the landing, a little window of colored glass—and across the sliding doors here in the hall, a kind of curtain made of strings of beads."

She nodded, smiling. "Yes, it's just the same—we still have the sliding doors and the stained glass window on the stairs. There's no bead curtain any more," she said, "but I remember when people had them. I know what you mean."

"When we were here," he said, "we used the doctor's office for a parlor—except later on—the last month or two—and then we used it for—a bedroom."

"It is a bedroom now," she said. "I run the house—I rent rooms—all of the rooms upstairs are rented—but I have two brothers and they sleep in this front room."

Both of them were silent for a moment, then Eugene said, "My brother stayed there too."

"In the front room?" the woman said.

He answered, "Yes."

She paused, then said: "Won't you come in? I don't believe it's changed much. Would you like to see?"

He thanked her and said he would, and he went up the steps. She opened the screen door to let him in.

Inside it was just the same—the stairs, the hallway, the sliding doors, the window of stained glass upon the stairs. And all of it was just the same, except for absence, the stained light of absence in the afternoon, and the child who once had sat there, waiting on the stairs.

It was all the same except that as a child he had sat there feeling things were *Somewhere*—and now he *knew*. He had sat there feeling that a vast and sultry river was somewhere—and now he knew! He had sat there wondering what King's Highway was, where it began, and where it ended—now he knew! He had sat there haunted by the magic word "downtown" —now he knew!—and by the street car, after it had gone—and by all things that came and went and came again, like the cloud shadows passing in a wood, that never could be captured.

And he felt that if he could only sit there on the stairs once more, in solitude and absence in the afternoon, he would be able to get it back again. Then would he be able to remember all that he had seen and been—the brief sum of himself, the universe of his four years, with all the light of Time upon it—that universe which was so short to measure, and yet so far, so endless, to remember. Then would he be able to see his own small face again, pooled in the dark mirror of the hall, and peer once more into the grave eyes of the child that he had been, and discover there in his quiet three-years' self the lone integrity of "I," knowing: "Here is the House, and here House listening; here is Absence, Absence in the afternoon; and here in this House, this Absence, is my core, my kernel—here am I!"

But as he thought it, he knew that even if he could sit here alone and get it back again, it would be gone as soon as seized, just as it had been then—first coming like the vast and drowsy rumors of the distant and enchanted Fair, then fading like cloud shadows on a hill, going like faces in a dream—coming, going, coming, possessed and held but never captured, like lost voices in the mountains long ago—and like the dark eyes and quiet face of the dark, lost boy, his brother, who, in the mysterious rhythms of his life and work, used to come into this house, then go, and return again.

The woman took Eugene back into the house and through the hall. He told her of the pantry, told her where it was and pointed to the place, but now it was no longer there. And he told her of the backyard, and of the old board fence around the yard. But the old board fence was gone. And he told her of the carriage house, and told her it was painted red. But now there was a small garage. And the backyard was still there, but smaller than he thought, and now there was a tree.

"I did not know there was a tree," he said. "I do not remember any tree."

"Perhaps it was not there," she said. "A tree could grow in thirty years." And then they came back through the house again and paused at the sliding doors.

"And could I see this room?" he said.

She slid the doors back. They slid open smoothly, with a rolling heaviness, as they used to do. And then he saw the room again. It was the same. There was a window at the side, the two arched windows at the front, the alcove and the sliding doors, the fireplace with the tiles of mottled green, the mantel of dark mission wood, the mantel posts, a dresser and a bed, just where the dresser and the bed had been so long ago.

"Is this the room?" the woman said. "It hasn't changed?"

He told her that it was the same.

"And your brother slept here where my brothers sleep?"

"This is his room," he said.

They were silent. He turned to go, and said, "Well, thank you. I appreciate your showing me."

She said that she was glad and that it was no trouble. "And when you see your family, you can tell them that you saw the house," she said. "My name is Mrs. Bell. You can tell your mother that a Mrs. Bell has the house now. And when you see your brother, you can tell him that you saw the room he slept in, and that you found it just the same."

He told her then that his brother was dead.

The woman was silent for a moment. Then she looked at him and said: "He died here, didn't he? In this room?"

He told her that it was so.

"Well, then," she said, "I knew it. I don't know how. But when you told me he was here, I knew it."

He said nothing. In a moment the woman said, "What did he die of?"

"Typhoid."

She looked shocked and troubled, and said involuntarily, "My two brothers—"

"That was a long time ago," he said. "I don't think you need to worry now."

"Oh, I wasn't thinking about that," she said. "It was just hearing that a little boy—your brother—was—was in this room that my two brothers sleep in now—"

"Well, maybe I shouldn't have told you then. But he was a good boy—and if you'd known him you wouldn't mind."

She said nothing, and he added quickly: "Besides, he didn't stay here long. This wasn't really his room—but the night he came back with my sister he was so sick—they didn't move him."

"Oh," the woman said, "I see." And then: "Are you going to tell your mother you were here?"

"I don't think so."

"I—I wonder how she feels about this room."

"I don't know. She never speaks of it."

"Oh. . . . How old was he?"

"He was twelve."

"You must have been pretty young yourself."

"I was not quite four."

"And—you just wanted to see the room, didn't you? That's why you came back."

"Yes."

"Well—" indefinitely—"I guess you've seen it now."

"Yes, thank you."

"I guess you don't remember much about him, do you? I shouldn't think you would."

"No, not much."

The years dropped off like fallen leaves: the face came back again—the soft dark oval, the dark eyes, the soft brown berry on the neck, the raven hair, all bending down, approaching—the whole appearing to him ghostwise, intent and instant.

"Now say it—*Grover!*"

"Gova."

"No—not Gova.—*Grover!* . . . Say it!"

"Gova."

"Ah-h—you didn't say it. You said Gova. *Grover*—now say it!"

"Gova."

"Look, I tell you what I'll do if you say it right. Would you like to go down to King's Highway? Would you like Grover to set you up? All right, then. If you say Grover and say it right, I'll take you to King's Highway and set you up to ice cream. Now say it right—*Grover!*"

"Gova."

"Ah-h, you-u. You're the craziest little old boy I ever did see. Can't you even say Grover?"

"Gova."

"Ah-h, you-u. Old Tongue-Tie, that's what you are. . . . Well, come on, then, I'll set you up anyway."

It all came back, and faded, and was

lost again. Eugene turned to go, and thanked the woman and said good-by.

"Well, then, good-by," the woman said, and they shook hands. "I'm glad if I could show you. I'm glad if—" She did not finish, and at length she said: "Well, then, that was a long time ago. You'll find everything changed now, I guess. It's all built up around here now—and way out beyond here, out beyond where the Fair Grounds used to be. I guess you'll find it changed."

They had nothing more to say. They just stood there for a moment on the steps, and then shook hands once more.

"Well, good-by."

And again he was in the street, and found the place where the corners met, and for the last time turned to see where Time had gone.

And he knew that he would never come again, and that lost magic would not come again. Lost now was all of it—the street, the heat, King's Highway, and Tom the Piper's son, all mixed in with the vast and drowsy murmur of the Fair, and with the sense of absence in the afternoon, and the house that waited, and the child that dreamed. And out of the enchanted wood, that thicket of man's memory, Eugene knew that the dark eye and the quiet face of his friend and brother—poor child, life's stranger, and life's exile, lost like all of us, a cipher in blind mazes, long ago—the lost boy was gone forever, and would not return.

Winterset   Jo Mielziner

Used with the permission of Jo Mielziner.
Photograph by Peter A. Guley and Son.

WINTERSET

by MAXWELL ANDERSON

CHARACTERS

TROCK	HERMAN
SHADOW	LUCIA
GARTH	PINY
MIRIAMNE	A SAILOR
ESDRAS	STREET URCHIN
THE HOBO	POLICEMAN
1ST GIRL	RADICAL
2ND GIRL	SERGEANT
JUDGE GAUNT	*Non-speaking*
MIO	URCHINS
CARR	TWO MEN IN BLUE SERGE

ACT I

SCENE I

[*The scene is the bank of a river under a bridgehead. A gigantic span starts from the rear of the stage and appears to lift over the heads of the audience and out to the left. At the right rear is a wall of solid supporting masonry. To the left an apartment building abuts against the bridge and forms the left wall of the stage with a dark basement window and a door in the brick wall. To the right, and in the foreground, an outcropping of original rock makes a barricade behind which one may enter through a cleft. To the rear, against the masonry, two sheds have been built by waifs and strays for shelter. The river bank, in the foreground, is black rock worn smooth by years of trampling. There is room for exit and entrance to the left around the apartment house, also around the rock to the right. A single street lamp is seen at the left—and a glimmer of apartment lights in the back-ground beyond. It is an early, dark December morning.*

TWO YOUNG MEN IN SERGE lean against the masonry, matching bills. TROCK and SHADOW come in from the left.]

TROCK. Go back and watch the car.

[*The* TWO YOUNG MEN *go out.* TROCK *walks to the corner and looks toward the city.*]

You roost of punks and gulls! Sleep, sleep
   it off,
whatever you had last night, get down in
   warm,
one big ham-fat against another—sleep,
cling, sleep and rot! Rot out your pasty
   guts
with diddling, you had no brain to begin.
   If you had
there'd be no need for us to sleep on iron
who had too much brains for you.

SHADOW. Now look, Trock, look,
what would the warden say to talk like
   that?

TROCK. May they die as I die!

By God, what life they've left me
they shall keep me well! I'll have that out
    of them—
these pismires that walk like men!
    SHADOW. Because, look, chief,
it's all against science and penology
for you to get out and begin to cuss that
    way
before your prison vittles are out of you.
    Hell,
you're supposed to leave the pen full of
    high thought,
kind of noble-like, loving toward all man-
    kind,
ready to kiss their feet—or whatever parts
they stick out toward you. Look at me!
    TROCK. I see you.
And even you may not live as long as you
    think.
You think too many things are funny.
    Well, laugh.
But it's not so funny.
    SHADOW. Come on, Trock, you know
    me.
Anything you say goes, but give me leave
to kid a little.
    TROCK. Then laugh at somebody else!
It's a lot safer! They've soaked me once
    too often
in that vat of poisoned hell they keep up-
    state
to soak men in, and I'm rotten inside,
    I'm all
one liquid puke inside where I had lungs
once, like yourself! And now they want
    to get me
and stir me in again—and that'd kill me—
and that's fine for them. But before that
    happens to me
a lot of these healthy boys'll know what
    it's like
when you try to breathe and have no place
    to put air—
they'll learn it from me!

SHADOW. They've got nothing on you,
    chief.
    TROCK. I don't know yet. That's what
    I'm here to find out.
If they've got what they might have
It's not a year this time—
no, nor ten. It's screwed down under a
    lid.—
I can die quick enough, without help.
    SHADOW. You're the skinny kind
that lives forever.
    TROCK. He gave me a half a year,
the doc at the gate.
    SHADOW. Jesus.
    TROCK. Six months I get,
and the rest's dirt, six feet.
[LUCIA, *the street-piano man, comes in*
    right from behind the rock and goes
    to the shed where he keeps his piano.
    PINY, *the apple-woman, follows and*
    stands in the entrance. LUCIA *speaks*
    to ESTRELLA, *who still stands facing*
    SHADOW.]
    LUCIA. Morning.
[TROCK *and* SHADOW *go out round the*
    apartment house without speaking.]
    PINY. Now what would you call them?
    LUCIA. Maybe something da river
washed up.
    PINY. Nothing ever washed him—that
black one.
    LUCIA. Maybe not, maybe so. More like
his pa and ma raise-a heem in da cellar.
[*He wheels out the piano.*]
    PINY. He certainly gave me a turn. [*She*
lays a hand on the rock.]
    LUCIA. You don' live-a right, ol' gal.
Take heem easy. Look on da bright-a
side. Never say-a die. Me, every day in
every way I getta be da regular heller.
[*He starts out.*]

        CURTAIN

[77]

SCENE 2

[*A cellar apartment under the apartment building, floored with cement and roofed with huge boa constrictor pipes that run slantwise from left to right, dwarfing the room. An outside door opens to the left and a door at the right rear leads to the interior of the place. A low squat window to the left. A table at the rear and a few chairs and books make up the furniture.* GARTH, *son of* ESDRAS, *sits alone, holding a violin upside down to inspect a crack at its base. He lays the bow on the floor and runs his fingers over the joint.* MIRIAMNE *enters from the rear, a girl of fifteen.* GARTH *looks up, then down again.*]

MIRIAMNE. Garth—

GARTH. The glue lets go. It's the steam, I guess.

It splits the hair on your head.

MIRIAMNE. It can't be mended?

GARTH. I can't mend it.

No doubt there are fellows somewhere who'd mend it for a dollar—and glad to do it.

That is if I had a dollar.—Got a dollar?

No, I thought not.

MIRIAMNE. Garth, you've sat at home here

three days now. You haven't gone out at all.

Something frightens you.

GARTH. Yes?

MIRIAMNE. And father's frightened.

He reads without knowing where. When a shadow falls

across the page he waits for a blow to follow

after the shadow. Then in a little while he puts his book down softly and goes out to see who passed.

GARTH. A bill collector, maybe.

We haven't paid the rent.

MIRIAMNE. No.

GARTH. You're a bright girl, sis.—

You see too much. You run along and cook.

Why don't you go to school?

MIRIAMNE. I don't like school.

They whisper behind my back.

GARTH. Yes? about what?

MIRIAMNE. What did the lawyer mean

that wrote to you?

GARTH [*rising*]. What lawyer?

MIRIAMNE. I found a letter

on the floor of your room. He said, "Don't get me wrong,

but stay in out of the rain the next few days,

just for instance."

GARTH. I thought I burned that letter.

MIRIAMNE. Afterward you did. And then what was printed

about the Estrella gang—you hid it from me,

you and father. What is it—about this murder—?

GARTH. Will you shut up, you fool!

MIRIAMNE. But if you know

why don't you tell them, Garth?

If it's true—what they say—

you knew all the time Romagna wasn't guilty,

and could have said so—

GARTH. Everybody knew

Romagna wasn't guilty! But they weren't listening

to evidence in his favor. They didn't want it.

They don't want it now.

MIRIAMNE. But was that why

they never called on you?—

GARTH. So far as I know

they never'd heard of me—and I can assure you

I knew nothing about it—
MIRIAMNE. But something's wrong—
and it worries father—
GARTH. What could be wrong?
MIRIAMNE. I don't know. [*A pause.*]
GARTH. And I don't know. You're a
good kid, Miriamne,
but you see too many movies. I wasn't
mixed up
in any murder, and I don't mean to be.
If I had a dollar to get my fiddle fixed
and another to hire a hall, by God I'd
fiddle
some of the prodigies back into Sunday
School
where they belong, but I won't get either,
and so
I sit here and bite my nails—but if you
hoped
I had some criminal romantic past
you'll have to look again!
MIRIAMNE. Oh, Garth, forgive me—
But I want you to be so far above such
things
nothing could frighten you. When you
seem to shrink
and be afraid, and you're the brother I
love,
I want to run there and cry, if there's any
question
they care to ask, you'll be quick and glad
to answer,
for there's nothing to conceal!
GARTH. And that's all true—
MIRIAMNE. But then I remember—
how you dim the lights—
and we go early to bed—and speak in
whispers—
and I could think there's a death somewhere behind us—
an evil death—
GARTH [*hearing a step*].
Now for God's sake, be quiet!
[ESDRAS, *an old rabbi with a kindly face,*

*enters from the outside. He is hur-
ried and troubled.*]
ESDRAS. I wish to speak alone with some-
one here
if I may have this room. Miriamne—
MIRIAMNE [*turning to go*]. Yes, father.
[*The outer door is suddenly thrown open.*
TROCK *appears.*]
TROCK [*after a pause*].
You'll excuse me for not knocking.
[SHADOW *follows* TROCK *in.*]
Sometimes it's best to come in quiet. Some-
times
it's a good way to go out. Garth's home, I
see.
He might not have been here if I made a
point
of knocking at doors.
GARTH. How are you, Trock?
TROCK. I guess
you can see how I am. [*To* MIRIAMNE.]
Stay here. Stay where you are.
We'd like to make your acquaintance.
—If you want the facts
I'm no better than usual, thanks. Not
enough sun,
my physician tells me. Too much close
confinement.
A lack of exercise and an overplus
of beans in the diet. You've done well, no
doubt?
GARTH. I don't know what makes you
think so.
TROCK. Who's the family?
GARTH. My father and my sister.
TROCK. Happy to meet you.
Step inside a minute. The boy and I have
something to talk about.
ESDRAS. No, no—he's said nothing—
nothing, sir, nothing!
TROCK. When I say go out, you go—
ESDRAS [*pointing to the door*]. Miri-
amne—
GARTH. Go on out, both of you!

Esdras. Oh, sir—I'm old—
old and unhappy—
Garth. Go on!
[Miriamne *and* Esdras *go inside.*]
Trock. And if you listen
I'll riddle that door!
[Shadow *shuts the door behind them and*
stands against it.]
I just got out, you see,
and I pay my first call on you.
Garth. Maybe you think
I'm not in the same jam you are.
Trock. That's what I do think.
Who started looking this up?
Garth. I wish I knew,
and I wish he was in hell! Some damned
professor
with nothing else to do. If you saw his
stuff
you know as much as I do.
Trock. It wasn't you
turning state's evidence?
Garth. Hell, Trock, use your brain!
The case was closed. They burned Romagna for it
and that finished it. Why should I look
for trouble
and maybe get burned myself?
Trock. Boy, I don't know,
but I just thought I'd find out.
Garth. I'm going straight, Trock.
I can play this thing, and I'm trying to
make a living.
I haven't talked and nobody's talked to
me.
Christ—it's the last thing I'd want!
Trock. Your old man knows.
Garth. That's where I got the money
that last time
when you needed it. He had a little saved
up,
but I had to tell him to get it. He's as
safe
as Shadow there.

Trock [*looking at* Shadow].
There could be people safer
than that son-of-a-bitch.
Shadow. Who?
Trock. You'd be safer dead
along with some other gorillas.
Shadow. It's beginning to look
as if you'd feel safer with everybody dead,
the whole god-damn world.
Trock. I would. These Jesus-bitten
professors! Looking up their half-ass cases!
We've got enough without that.
Garth. There's no evidence
to reopen the thing.
Trock. And suppose they called on you
and asked you to testify?
Garth. Why then I'd tell 'em
that all I know is what I read in the
papers.
And I'd stick to that.
Trock. How much does your sister
know?
Garth. I'm honest with you, Trock. She
read my name
in the professor's pamphlet, and she was
scared
the way anybody would be. She got nothing
from me, and anyway she'd go to the
chair
herself before she'd send me there.
Trock. Like hell.
Garth. Besides, who wants to go to
trial again
except the radicals?—You and I won't spill
and unless we did there's nothing to take
to court
as far as I know. Let the radicals go on
howling
about getting a dirty deal. They always
howl
and nobody gives a damn. This professor's
red—
everybody knows it.

TROCK. You're forgetting the judge.
Where's the damn judge?

GARTH. What judge?

TROCK. Read the morning papers.
It says Judge Gaunt's gone off his nut.
He's got
that damn trial on his mind, and been
going round
proving to everybody he was right all the
time
and the radicals were guilty—stopping
people
in the street to prove it—and now he's
nuts entirely
and nobody knows where he is.

GARTH. Why don't they know?

TROCK. Because he's on the loose somewhere! They've got
the police of three cities looking for him.

GARTH. Judge Gaunt?

TROCK. Yes. Judge Gaunt.

SHADOW. Why should that worry you?
He's crazy, ain't he? And even if he
wasn't
he's arguing on your side. You're jittery,
chief.
God, all the judges are looney. You've got
the jitters,
and you'll damn well give yourself away
some time
peeing yourself in public.

[TROCK *half turns toward* SHADOW *in
anger.*]

Don't jump the gun now,
I've got pockets in my clothes, too.

[*His hand is in his coat pocket.*]

TROCK. All right. Take it easy.

[*He takes his hand from his pocket, and*
SHADOW *does the same. To* GARTH.]

Maybe you're lying to me and maybe
you're not.
Stay at home a few days.

GARTH. Sure thing. Why not?

TROCK. And when I say stay home I
mean stay home.

If I have to go looking for you you'll stay
a long time
wherever I find you.

[*To* SHADOW.] Come on. We'll get out of
here.

[*To* GARTH.] Be seeing you.

[SHADOW *and* TROCK *go out. After a pause*
GARTH *walks over to his chair and
picks up the violin. Then he puts it
down and goes to the inside door,
which he opens.*]

GARTH. He's gone.

[MIRIAMNE *enters,* ESDRAS *behind her.*]

MIRIAMNE [*going up to* GARTH].
Let's not stay here.

[*She puts her hands on his arms.*]

I thought he'd come for something—horrible.
Is he coming back?

GARTH. I don't know.

MIRIAMNE. Who is he, Garth?

GARTH. He'd kill me if I told you who
he is,
that is, if he knew.

MIRIAMNE. Then don't say it—

GARTH. Yes, and I'll say it! I was with a
gang one time
that robbed a pay roll. I saw a murder
done
and Trock Estrella did it. If that got out
I'd go to the chair and so would he—
that's why
he was here today—

MIRIAMNE. But that's not true—

ESDRAS. He says it
to frighten you, child.

GARTH. Oh, no I don't! I say it
because I've held it in too long! I'm
damned
if I sit here forever and look at the door,
waiting for Trock with his submachine
gun, waiting
for police with a warrant!—I say I'm
damned, and I am,
no matter what I do! These piddling scales

on a violin—first position, third, fifth,
arpeggios in E—and what I'm thinking
is Romagna dead for the murder—dead
    while I sat here
dying inside—dead for the thing Trock did
while I looked on—and I could have saved
    him, yes—
but I sat here and let him die instead of
    me
because I wanted to live! Well, it's no life,
and it doesn't matter who I tell, because
I mean to get it over!

    MIRIAMNE. Garth, it's not true!

    GARTH. I'd take some scum down with
    me if I died—
that'd be one good deed—

    ESDRAS. Son, son, you're mad—
someone will hear—

    GARTH. Then let them hear! I've lived
with ghosts too long, and lied too long.
    God damn you
if you keep me from the truth!—
[*He turns away.*] Oh, God damn the
    world!
I don't want to die!

    ESDRAS. I should have known.
I thought you hard and sullen,
Garth, my son. And you were a child,
    and hurt
with a wound that might be healed.
—All men have crimes,
and most of them are hidden, and many
    are heavy
as yours must be to you.
[GARTH *sobs.*]
They walk the streets
to buy and sell, but a spreading crimson
    stain
tinges the inner vestments, touches flesh,
and burns the quick. You're not alone.

    GARTH. I'm alone
in this

    ESDRAS. Yes, if you hold with the world
    that only

those who die suddenly should be re
    venged.
But those whose hearts are cancered, drop
    by drop
in small ways, little by little, till they've
    borne
all they can bear, and die—these deaths
    will go
unpunished now as always. When we're
    young
we have faith in what is seen, but when
    we're old
we know that what is seen is traced in air
and built on water. There's no guilt under
    heaven,
just as there's no heaven, till men believe
    it—
no earth, till men have seen it, and have a
    word
to say this is the earth.

    GARTH. Well, I say there's an earth,
and I say I'm guilty on it, guilty as hell.

    ESDRAS. Yet till it's known you bear no
    guilt at all—
unless you wish. The days go by like
    film,
like a long written scroll, a figured veil
unrolling out of darkness into fire
and utterly consumed. And on this veil,
running in sounds and symbols of men's
    minds
reflected back, life flickers and is shadow
going toward flame. Only what men can
    see
exists in that shadow. Why must you rise
    and cry out:
That was I, there in the ravelled tapestry,
there, in that pistol flash, when the man
    was killed.
I was there, and was one, and am blood-
    stained!
Let the wind
and fire take that hour to ashes out of
    time

and out of mind! This thing that men
call justice,
this blind snake that strikes men down
in the dark,
mindless with fury, keep your hand back
from it,
pass by in silence—let it be forgotten, forgotten!—
Oh, my son, my son—have pity!
MIRIAMNE. But if it was true
and someone died—then it was more than
shadow—
and it doesn't blow away—
GARTH. Well, it was true.
ESDRAS. Say it if you must. If you have
heart to die,
say it, and let them take what's left—
there was little
to keep, even before—
GARTH. Oh, I'm a coward—
I always was. I'll be quiet and live. I'll
live
even if I have to crawl. I know.
[*He gets up and goes into the inner
room.*]
MIRIAMNE. Is it better
to tell a lie and live?
ESDRAS. Yes, child. It's better.
MIRIAMNE. But if I had to do it—
I think I'd die.
ESDRAS. Yes, child. Because you're young.
MIRIAMNE. Is that the only reason?
ESDRAS. The only reason.

CURTAIN

SCENE 3

[*Under the bridge, evening of the same
day. When the curtain rises* MIRIAMNE *is
sitting alone on the ledge at the rear of
the apartment house. A spray of light falls
on her from a street lamp above. She shivers a little in her thin coat, but sits still as
if heedless of the weather. Through the*

rocks on the other side a TRAMP *comes
down to the river bank, hunting a place
to sleep. He goes softly to the apple-
woman's hut and looks in, then turns
away, evidently not daring to pre-empt it.
He looks at* MIRIAMNE *doubtfully. The
door of the street-piano man is shut. The
vagabond passes it and picks carefully
among some rags and shavings to the
right.* MIRIAMNE *looks up and sees him
but makes no sign. She looks down again,
and the man curls himself up in a make-
shift bed in the corner, pulling a piece of
sacking over his shoulders.* TWO GIRLS
come in round the apartment house.]

1ST GIRL. Honest, I never heard of anything so romantic. Because you never liked
him.
2ND GIRL. I certainly never did.
1ST GIRL. You've got to tell me how it
happened. You've got to.
2ND GIRL. I couldn't. As long as I live
I couldn't. Honest, it was terrible. It was
terrible.
1ST GIRL. What was so terrible?
2ND GIRL. The way it happened.
1ST GIRL. Oh, please—not to a soul,
never.
2ND GIRL. Well, you know how I hated
him because he had such a big mouth. So
he reached over and grabbed me, and I
began all falling to pieces inside, the way
you do—and I said, "Oh no you don't mister," and started screaming and kicked a
hole through the windshield and lost a
shoe, and he let go and was cursing and
growling because he borrowed the car and
didn't have money to pay for the windshield, and he started to cry, and I got so
sorry for him I let him, and now he wants
to marry me.
1ST GIRL. Honest, I never heard of anything so romantic! [*She sees the sleeping*

TRAMP.] My God, what you won't see! [*They give the* TRAMP *a wide berth, and go out right. The* TRAMP *sits up looking about him.* JUDGE GAUNT, *an elderly, quiet man, well dressed but in clothes that have seen some weather, comes in uncertainly from the left. He holds a small clipping in his hand and goes up to the* HOBO.]

GAUNT [*tentatively*]. Your pardon, sir. Your pardon, but perhaps you can tell me the name of this street.

HOBO. Huh?

GAUNT. The name of this street?

HOBO. This ain't no street.

GAUNT. There, where the street lamps are.

HOBO. That's the alley.

GAUNT. Thank you. It has a name, no doubt?

HOBO. That's the alley.

GAUNT. I see. I won't trouble you. You wonder why I ask, I daresay.—I'm a stranger.—Why do you look at me? [*He steps back.*] I—I'm not the man you think. You've mistaken me, sir.

HOBO. Huh?

GAUNT. Perhaps misled by a resemblance. But you're mistaken—I had an errand in this city. It's only by accident that I'm here—

HOBO [*muttering*]. You go to hell.

GAUNT [*going nearer to him, bending over him*]. Yet why should I deceive you? Before God, I held the proofs in my hands. I hold them still. I tell you the defense was cunning beyond belief, and unscrupulous in its use of propaganda—they gagged at nothing—not even—[*He rises.*] No, no— I'm sorry—this will hardly interest you. I'm sorry. I have an errand.

[*He looks toward the street.* ESDRAS *enters from the basement and goes to* MIRIAMNE. *The* JUDGE *steps back into the shadows.*]

ESDRAS. Come in, my daughter. You'll be cold here.

MIRIAMNE. After a while.

ESDRAS. You'll be cold. There's a storm coming.

MIRIAMNE. I didn't want him to see me crying. That was all.

ESDRAS. I know.

MIRIAMNE. I'll come soon.

[ESDRAS *turns reluctantly and goes out the way he came.* MIRIAMNE *rises to go in, pausing to dry her eyes.* MIO *and* CARR, *road boys of seventeen or so, come round the apartment house. The* JUDGE *has disappeared.*]

CARR. Thought you said you were never coming east again.

MIO. Yeah, but—I heard something changed my mind.

CARR. Same old business?

MIO. Yes. Just as soon not talk about it.

CARR. Where did you go from Portland?

MIO. Fishing—I went fishing. God's truth.

CARR. Right after I left?

MIO. Fell in with a fisherman's family on the coast and went after the beautiful mackerel fish that swim in the beautiful sea. Family of Greeks—Aristides Marinos was his lovely name. He sang while he fished. Made the pea-green Pacific ring with his bastard Greek chanties. Then I went to Hollywood High School for a while.

CARR. I'll bet that's a seat of learning.

MIO. It's the hind end of all wisdom. They kicked me out after a time.

CARR. For cause?

MIO. Because I had no permanent address, you see. That means nobody's paying school taxes for you, so out you go. [*To* MIRIAMNE.] What's the matter, Kid?

MIRIAMNE. Nothing. [*She looks up at him, and they pause for a moment.*] Nothing.

Mio. I'm sorry.

Miriamne. It's all right. [*She withdraws her eyes from his and goes out past him. He turns and looks after her.*]

Carr. Control your chivalry.

Mio. A pretty kid.

Carr. A baby.

Mio. Wait for me.

Carr. Be a long wait? [Mio *steps swiftly out after* Miriamne, *then returns.*] Yeah?

Mio. She's gone.

Carr. Think of that.

Mio. No, but I mean—vanished. Presto —into nothing—prodigioso.

Carr. Damn good thing, if you ask me. The homely ones are bad enough, but the lookers are fatal.

Mio. You exaggerate, Carr.

Carr. I doubt it.

Mio. Well, let her go. This river bank's loaded with typhus rats, too. Might as well die one death as another.

Carr. They say chronic alcoholism is nice but expensive. You can always starve to death.

Mio. Not always. I tried it. After the second day I walked thirty miles to Niagara Falls and made a tour of the plant to get the sample of shredded wheat biscuit on the way out.

Carr. Last time I saw you you couldn't think of anything you wanted to do except curse God and pass out. Still feeling low?

Mio. Not much different. [*He turns away, then comes back.*] Talk about the lost generation, I'm the only one fits that title. When the State executes your father, and your mother dies of grief, and you know damn well he was innocent, and the authorities of your home town politely inform you they'd consider it a favor if you lived somewhere else—that cuts you off from the world—with a meat-axe.

Carr. They asked you to move?

Mio. It came to that.

Carr. God, that was white of them.

Mio. It probably gave them a headache just to see me after all that agitation. They knew as well as I did my father never staged a holdup. Anyway, I've got a new interest in life now.

Carr. Yes—I saw her.

Mio. I don't mean the skirt.—No, I got wind of something, out west, some college professor investigating the trial and turning up new evidence. Couldn't find anything he'd written out there, so I beat it east and arrived on this blessed island just in time to find the bums holing up in the public library for the winter. I know now what the unemployed have been doing since the depression started. They've been catching up on their reading in the main reference room. Man, what a stench! Maybe I stank, too, but a hobo has the stench of ten because his shoes are poor.

Carr. Tennyson.

Mio. Right. Jeez, I'm glad we met up again! Never knew anybody else that could track me through the driven snow of Victorian literature.

Carr. Now you're cribbing from some half-forgotten criticism of Ben Jonson's Roman plagiarisms.

Mio. Where did you get your education, sap?

Carr. Not in the public library, sap. My father kept a news-stand.

Mio. Well, you're right again. [*There is a faint rumble of thunder.*] What's that? Winter thunder?

Carr. Or Mister God, beating on His little tocsin. Maybe announcing the advent of a new social order.

Mio. Or maybe it's going to rain coffee and doughnuts.

Carr. Or maybe it's going to rain.

Mio. Seems more likely. [*Lowering his*

voice.] Anyhow, I found Professor Hobhouse's discussion of the Romagna case. I think he has something. It occurred to me I might follow it up by doing a little sleuthing on my own account.

CARR. Yes?

MIO. I have done a little. And it leads me to somewhere in that tenement house that backs up against the bridge. That's how I happen to be here.

CARR. They'll never let you get anywhere with it, Mio. I told you that before.

MIO. I know you did.

CARR. The State can't afford to admit it was wrong, you see. Not when there's been that much of a row kicked up over it. So for all practical purposes the State was right and your father robbed the pay roll.

MIO. There's still such a thing as evidence.

CARR. It's something you can buy. In fact, at the moment I don't think of anything you can't buy, including life, honor, virtue, glory, public office, conjugal affection and all kinds of justice, from the traffic court to the immortal nine. Go out and make yourself a pot of money and you can buy all the justice you want. Convictions obtained, convictions averted. Lowest rates in years.

MIO. I know all that.

CARR. Sure.

MIO. This thing didn't happen to you. They've left you your name
and whatever place you can take. For my heritage
They've left me one thing only, and that's to be
my father's voice crying up out of the earth
and quicklime where they stuck him. Electrocution

doesn't kill, you know. They eviscerate them
with a turn of the knife in the dissecting room.
The blood spurts out. The man was alive. Then into
the lime pit, leave no trace. Make it short shrift
and chemical dissolution. That's what they thought
of the man that was my father. Then my mother—
I tell you these county burials are swift
and cheap and run for profit! Out of the house
and into the ground, you wife of a dead dog. Wait,
here's some Romagna spawn left.
Something crawls here—
something they called a son. Why couldn't he die
along with his mother? Well, ease him out of town,
ease him out, boys, and see you're not too gentle.
He might come back. And, by their own living Jesus,
I will go back, and hang the carrion
around their necks that made it!
Maybe I can sleep then.
Or even live.

CARR. You have to try it?

MIO. Yes.
Yes. It won't let me alone. I've tried to live
and forget it—but I was birthmarked with hot iron
into the entrails. I've got to find out who did it
and make them see it till it scalds their eyes
and make them admit it till their tongues are blistered
with saying how black they lied!

[HERMAN, *a gawky shoe salesman, enters from the left.*]

HERMAN. Hello. Did you see a couple of girls go this way?

CARR. Couple of girls? Did we see a couple of girls?

MIO. No.

CARR. No. No girls.

[HERMAN *hesitates, then goes out right. LUCIA comes in from the left, trundling his piano. PINY follows him, weeping.*]

PINY. They've got no right to do it—

LUCIA. All right, hell what, no matter, I got to put him away, I got to put him away, that's what the hell! [*Two* STREET URCHINS *follow him in.*]

PINY. They want everybody on the relief rolls and nobody making a living?

LUCIA. The cops, they do what the big boss say. The big boss, that's the mayor, he says he heard it once too often, the sextette—

PINY. They want graft, that's all. It's a new way to get graft—

LUCIA. Oh, no, no, no! He's a good man, the mayor. He's just don't care for music, that's all.

PINY. Why shouldn't you make a living on the street? The National Biscuit Company ropes off Eighth Avenue—and does the mayor do anything? No, the police hit you over the head if you try to go through!

LUCIA. You got the big dough, you get the pull, fine. No big dough, no pull, what the hell, get off the city property! Tomorrow I start cooking chestnuts . . . [*He strokes the piano fondly. The* TWO GIRLS *and* HERMAN *come back from the right.*] She's a good little machine, this baby. Cost plenty—and two new records I only played twice. See this one. [*He starts turning the crank, talking while he plays.*] Two weeks since they play this one

in a picture house. [*A* SAILOR *wanders in from the left. One of the* STREET URCHINS *begins suddenly to dance a wild rumba, the others watch.*] Good boy—see, it's a lulu—it itches in the feet!

[HERMAN, *standing with his girl, tosses the boy a penny. He bows and goes on dancing; the other* URCHIN *joins him. The* SAILOR *tosses a coin.*]

SAILOR. Go it, Cuba! Go it!

[LUCIA *turns the crank, beaming.*]

2ND GIRL. Oh, Herman! [*She throws her arms round* HERMAN *and they dance.*]

1ST URCHIN. Hey, pipe the professionals!

1ST GIRL. Do your glide, Shirley! Do your glide!

LUCIA. Maybe we can't play in front, maybe we can play behind! [*The* HOBO *gets up from his nest and comes over to watch. A* YOUNG RADICAL *wanders in.*] Maybe you don't know, folks! Tonight we play good-bye to the piano! Good-bye forever! No more piano on the streets! No more music! No more money for the music-man! Last time, folks! Good-bye to the piano—good-bye forever! [MIRIAMNE *comes out the rear door of the apartment and stands watching. The* SAILOR *goes over to the* 1ST GIRL *and they dance together.*] Maybe you don't know, folks! Tomorrow will be sad as hell, tonight we dance! Tomorrow no more Verdi, no more rumba, no more good time! Tonight we play good-bye to the piano, good-bye forever! [*The* RADICAL *edges up to* MIRIAMNE *and asks her to dance. She shakes her head and he goes to* PINY, *who dances with him. The* HOBO *begins to do a few lonely curvets on the side above.*] Hoy! Hoy! Pick 'em up and take 'em around! Use the head, use the feet! Last time forever! [*He begins to sing to the air.*]

MIO. Wait for me, will you?

CARR. Now's your chance.

[Mio *goes over to* Miriamne *and holds out a hand, smiling. She stands for a moment uncertain, then dances with him.* Esdras *comes out to watch.* Judge Gaunt *comes in from the left. There is a rumble of thunder.*]

Lucia. Hoy! Hoy! Maybe it rains to-night, maybe it snows tomorrow! Tonight we dance good-bye. [*He sings the air lustily. A* Policeman *comes in from the left and looks on.* Two or Three Pedestrians *follow him.*]

Policeman. Hey you! [Lucia *goes on singing.*] Hey, you!

Lucia [*still playing*]. What you want?

Policeman. Sign off!

Lucia. What you mean? I get off the street!

Policeman. Sign off!

Lucia [*still playing*]. What you mean? [*The* Policeman *walks over to him.* Lucia *stops playing and the* Dancers *pause.*]

Policeman. Cut it.

Lucia. Is this a street?

Policeman. I say cut it out.

[*The* Hobo *goes back to his nest and sits in it, watching.*]

Lucia. It's the last time. We dance good-bye to the piano.

Policeman. You'll dance good-bye to something else if I catch you cranking that thing again.

Lucia. All right.

Piny. I'll bet you don't say that to the National Biscuit Company!

Policeman. Lady, you've been selling apples on my beat for some time now, and I said nothing about it—

Piny. Selling apples is allowed—

Policeman. You watch yourself—[*He takes a short walk around the place and comes upon the* Hobo.] What are you doing here? [*The* Hobo *opens his mouth,*

points to it, and shakes his head.*] Oh, you are, are you? [*He comes back to* Lucia.] So you trundle your so-called musical instrument to wherever you keep it, and don't let me hear it again.

[*The* Radical *leaps on the base of the rock at right. The* 1st Girl *turns away from the* Sailor *toward the* 2nd Girl *and* Herman.]

Sailor. Hey, captain, what's the matter with the music?

Policeman. Not a thing, admiral.

Sailor. Well, we had a little party going here—

Policeman. I'll say you did.

2nd Girl. Please, officer, we want to dance.

Policeman. Go ahead. Dance.

2nd Girl. But we want music!

Policeman [*turning to go*]. Sorry. Can't help you.

Radical. And there you see it, the perfect example of capitalistic oppression! In a land where music should be free as air and the arts should be encouraged, a uniformed minion of the rich, a guardian myrmidon of the Park Avenue pleasure hunters, steps in and puts a limit on the innocent enjoyments of the poor! We don't go to theaters! Why not? We can't afford it! We don't go to night clubs, where women dance naked and the music drips from saxophones and leaks out of Rudy Vallee—we can't afford that either! —But we might at least dance on the river bank to the strains of a barrel organ—! [Garth *comes out of the apartment and listens.*]

Policeman. It's against the law!

Radical. What law? I challenge you to tell me what law of God or man—what ordinance—is violated by this spontaneous diversion? None! I say none! An official whim of the masters who should be our servants!—

POLICEMAN. Get down! Get down and shut up!

RADICAL. By what law, by what ordinance do you order me to be quiet?

POLICEMAN. Speaking without a flag. You know it.

RADICAL [*pulling out a small American flag*]. There's my flag! There's the flag of this United States which used to guarantee the rights of man—the rights of man now violated by every statute of the commonweal—

POLICEMAN. Don't try to pull tricks on me! I've seen you before! You're not making any speech, and you're climbing down—

GAUNT [*who has come quietly forward*]. One moment, officer. There is some difference of opinion even on the bench as to the elasticity of police power when applied in minor emergencies to preserve civil order. But the weight of authority would certainly favor the defendant in any equable court, and he would be upheld in his demand to be heard.

POLICEMAN. Who are you?

GAUNT. Sir, I am not accustomed to answer that question.

POLICEMAN. I don't know you.

GAUNT. I am a judge of some standing, not in your city but in another with similar statutes. You are aware, of course, that the Bill of Rights is not to be set aside lightly by the officers of any municipality—

POLICEMAN [*looking over* GAUNT's *somewhat bedraggled costume*]. Maybe they understand you better in the town you come from, but I don't get your drift.— [*To the* RADICAL.] I don't want any trouble, but if you ask for it you'll get plenty. Get down!

RADICAL. I'm not asking for trouble, but I'm staying right here. [*The* POLICEMAN *moves towards him.*]

GAUNT [*taking the* POLICEMAN's *arm, but shaken off roughly*]. I ask this for yourself, truly, not for the dignity of the law nor the maintenance of precedent. Be gentle with them when their threats are childish—be tolerant while you can—for your least harsh word will return on you in the night—return in a storm of cries!—[*He takes the* POLICEMAN's *arm again.*] Whatever they may have said or done, let them disperse in peace! It is better that they go softly, lest when they are dead you see their eyes pleading, and their outstretched hands touch you, fingering cold on your heart!—I have been harsher than you. I have sent men down that long corridor into blinding light and blind darkness! [*He suddenly draws himself erect and speaks defiantly.*] And it was well that I did so! I have been an upright judge! They are all liars! Liars!

POLICEMAN [*shaking* GAUNT *off so that he falls*]. Why, you fool, you're crazy!

GAUNT. Yes, and there are liars on the force! They came to me with their shifty lies! [*He catches at the* POLICEMAN, *who pushes him away with his foot.*]

POLICEMAN. You think I've got nothing better to do than listen to a crazy fool?

1ST GIRL. Shame, shame!

POLICEMAN. What have I got to be ashamed of? And what's going on here, anyway? Where in hell did you all come from?

RADICAL. Tread on him! That's right! Tread down the poor and the innocent! [*There is a protesting murmur in the crowd.*]

SAILOR [*moving in a little*]. Say, big boy, you don't have to step on the guy.

POLICEMAN [*facing them, stepping back*].
What's the matter with you! I haven't
stepped on anybody!
MIO [*at the right, across from the
POLICEMAN*].
Listen now, fellows, give the badge a
chance.
He's doing his job, what he gets paid to
do,
the same as any of you. They're all picked
men,
these metropolitan police, hand picked
for loyalty and a fine up-standing pair
of shoulders on their legs—it's not so easy
to represent the law. Think what he does
for all of us, stamping out crime!
Do you want to be robbed and murdered
in your beds?
SAILOR. What's eating you?
RADICAL. He must be a capitalist.
MIO. They pluck them fresh,
from Ireland, and a paucity of head-piece
is a prime prerequisite. You from Ireland,
buddy?
POLICEMAN [*surly*].
Where are you from?
MIO. Buddy, I tell you flat
I wish I was from Ireland, and could boast
some Tammany connections. There's only
one drawback
about working on the force. It infects the
brain,
it eats the cerebrum. There've been cases
known,
fine specimens of manhood, too, where
autopsies,
conducted in approved scientific fashion,
revealed conditions quite incredible
in policemen's upper layers. In some, a
trace,
in others, when they've swung a stick too
long,
there was nothing there!—but nothing!

Oh, my friends,
this fine athletic figure of a man
that stands so grim before us, what will
they find
when they saw his skull for the last inspection?
I fear me a little puffball dust will blow
away
rejoining earth, our mother—and this
same dust,
this smoke, this ash on the wind, will
represent
all he had left to think with!
THE HOBO. Hooray!
[*The* POLICEMAN *turns on his heel and
looks hard at the* HOBO, *who slinks
away.*]
POLICEMAN. Oh, yeah?
MIO. My theme
gives ears to the deaf and voice to the
dumb! But now
forgive me if I say you were most unkind
in troubling the officer. He's a simple man
of simple tastes, and easily confused
when faced with complex issues. He may
reflect
on returning home, that is, so far as he
is capable of reflection, and conclude
that he was kidded out of his uniform
pants,
and in his fury when this dawns on him
may smack his wife down!
POLICEMAN. That'll be about enough
from you, too, professor!
MIO. May I say that I think you have
managed this whole situation rather badly,
from the beginning?—
POLICEMAN. You may not!
[TROCK *slips in from the background. The*
TWO YOUNG MEN IN SERGE *come with
him.*]
MIO. Oh, but your pardon, sir! It's apparent to the least competent among us

that you should have gone about your task more subtly—the glove of velvet, the hand of iron, and all that sort of thing—

POLICEMAN. Shut that hole in your face!

MIO. Sir, for that remark I shall be satisfied with nothing less than an unconditional apology! I have an old score to settle with policemen, brother, because they're fools and fat-heads, and you're one of the most fatuous fat-heads that ever walked his feet flat collecting graft! Tell that to your sergeant back in the booby-hatch.

POLICEMAN. Oh, you want an apology, do you? You'll get an apology out of the other side of your mouth! [*He steps toward* MIO. CARR *suddenly stands in his path.*] Get out of my way! [*He pauses and looks round him; the crowd looks less and less friendly. He lays a hand on his gun and backs to a position where there is nobody behind him.*] Get out of here, all of you! Get out! What are you trying to do—start a riot?

MIO. There now, that's better! That's in the best police tradition. Incite a riot yourself and then accuse the crowd.

POLICEMAN. It won't be pleasant if I decide to let somebody have it! Get out! [*The onlookers begin to melt away. The* SAILOR *goes out left with the* GIRLS *and* HERMAN. CARR *and* MIO *go out right,* CARR *whistling "The Star Spangled Banner." The* HOBO *follows them. The* RADICAL *walks past with his head in the air.* PINY *and* LUCIA *leave the piano where it stands and slip away to the left. At the end the* POLICEMAN *is left standing in the center, the* JUDGE *near him.* ESDRAS *stands in the doorway.* MIRIAMNE *is left sitting half in shadow and unseen by* ESDRAS.]

GAUNT [*to the* POLICEMAN]. Yes, but should a man die, should it be necessary that one man die for the good of many, make not yourself the instrument of death, lest you sleep to wake sobbing! Nay, it avails nothing that you are the law—this delicate ganglion that is the brain, it will not bear these things—!

[*The* POLICEMAN *gives the* JUDGE *the once-over, shrugs, decides to leave him there and starts out left.* GARTH *goes to his father—a fine sleet begins to fall through the street lights.* TROCK *is still visible.*]

GARTH. Get him in here, quick.

ESDRAS. Who, son?

GARTH. The Judge, damn him!

ESDRAS. Is it Judge Gaunt?

GARTH. Who did you think it was? He's crazy as a bedbug and telling the world. Get him inside! [*He looks round.*]

ESDRAS [*going up to* GAUNT]. Will you come in, sir?

GAUNT. You will understand, sir. We old men know how softly we must proceed with these things.

ESDRAS. Yes, surely, sir.

GAUNT. It was always my practice—always. They will tell you that of me where I am known. Yet even I am not free of regret—even I. Would you believe it?

ESDRAS. I believe we are none of us free of regret.

GAUNT. None of us? I would it were true. I would I thought it were true.

ESDRAS. Shall we go in, sir? This is sleet that's falling.

GAUNT. Yes. Let us go in.

[ESDRAS, GAUNT *and* GARTH *enter the basement and shut the door.* TROCK *goes out with his men. After a pause* MIO *comes back from the right, alone. He*

[91]

stands at a little distance from Miriamne.]

Mio. Looks like rain. [*She is silent.*]
You live around here? [*She nods
gravely.*] I guess
you thought I meant it—about waiting
here to meet me. [*She nods again.*]
I'd forgotten about it till I got that winter
across the face. You'd better go inside.
I'm not your kind. I'm nobody's kind but
my own.
I'm waiting for this to blow over.
[*She rises.*]
I lied. I meant it—
I meant it when I said it—but there's too
much black
whirling inside me—for any girl to know.
So go on in. You're somebody's angel child
and they're waiting for you.

Miriamne. Yes. I'll go. [*She turns.*]
Mio. And tell them
when you get inside where it's warm,
And you love each other,
and mother comes to kiss her darling, tell,
them
to hang on to it while they can, believe
while they can
it's a warm safe world, and Jesus finds
his lambs
and carries them in his bosom.—I've seen
some lambs
that Jesus missed. If they ever want the
truth
tell them that nothing's guaranteed in
this climate
except it gets cold in winter, nor on this
earth
except you die sometime.
[*He turns away.*]

Miriamne. I have no mother.
And my people are Jews.
Mio. Then you know something about it.
Miriamne. Yes.
Mio. Do you have enough to eat?

Miriamne. Not always.
Mio. What do you believe in?
Miriamne. Nothing.
Mio. Why?
Miriamne. How can one?
Mio. It's easy if you're a fool. You see
the words
in books. Honor, it says there, chivalry,
freedom,
heroism, enduring love—and these
are words on paper. It's something to have
them there.
You'll get them nowhere else.
Miriamne. What hurts you?
Mio. Just that.
You'll get them nowhere else.
Miriamne. Why should you want them?
Mio. I'm alone, that's why. You see
those lights,
along the river, cutting across the rain—?
those are the hearths of Brooklyn, and up
this way
the love-nests of Manhattan—they turn
their points
like knives against me—outcast of the
world,
snake in the streets.—I don't want a hand-
out.
I sleep and eat.
Miriamne. Do you want me to go with
you?
Mio. Where?
Miriamne. Where you go.
[*A pause. He goes nearer to her.*]
Mio. Why, you god-damned little fool
—what made you say that?
Miriamne. I don't know.
Mio. If you have a home
stay in it. I ask for nothing. I've schooled
myself
to ask for nothing, and take what I can get,
and get along. If I fell for you, that's my
look-out,
and I'll starve it down.

[92]

MIRIAMNE. Wherever you go, I'd go.

MIO. What do you know about loving?
How could you know?
Have you ever had a man?

MIRIAMNE [*after a slight pause*]. No.
But I know.
Tell me your name.

MIO. Mio. What's yours?

MIRIAMNE. Miriamne.

MIO. There's no such name.

MIRIAMNE. But there's no such name as
Mio!

M.I.O. It's no name.

MIO. It's for Bartolomeo.

MIRIAMNE. My mother's name was
Miriam,
so they called me Miriamne.

MIO. Meaning little Miriam?

MIRIAMNE. Yes.

MIO. So now little Miriamne will go in
and take up quietly where she dropped
them all
her small housewifely cares.—When I first
saw you,
not a half-hour ago, I heard myself saying,
this is the face that launches ships for
me—
and if I owned a dream—yes, half a
dream—
we'd share it. But I have no dream. This
earth
came tumbling down from chaos, fire and
rock,
and bred up worms, blind worms that
sting each other
here in the dark. These blind worms of
the earth
took out my father—and killed him, and
set a sign
on me—the heir of the serpent—and he
was a man
such as men might be if the gods were
men—

but they killed him—
as they'll kill all others like him
till the sun cools down to the stabler molecules,
yes, till men spin their tent-worm webs to
the stars
and what they think is done, even in the
thinking,
and they are the gods, and immortal, and
constellations
turn for them all like mill wheels—still as
they are
they will be, worms and blind. Enduring
love,
oh gods and worms, what mockery!—And
yet
I have blood enough in my veins. It goes
like music,
singing, because you're here. My body
turns
as if you were the sun, and warm. This
men called love
in happier times, before the Freudians
taught us
to blame it on the glands. Only go in
before you breathe too much of my atmosphere
and catch death from me.

MIRIAMNE. I will take my hands
and weave them to a little house, and there
you shall keep a dream—

MIO. God knows I could use a dream
and even a house.

MIRIAMNE. You're laughing at me, Mio!

MIO. The worms are laughing.
I tell you there's death about me
and you're a child! And I'm alone and
half mad
with hate and longing. I shall let you love
me
and love you in return, and then, why
then
God knows what happens!

[93]

MIRIAMNE. Something most unpleasant?

MIO. Love in a box car—love among the children.

I've seen too much of it. Are we to live

in this same house you make with your two hands

mystically, out of air?

MIRIAMNE. No roof, no mortgage!

Well, I shall marry a baker out in Flatbush,

it gives hot bread in the morning! Oh, Mio, Mio,

in all the unwanted places and waste lands

that roll up into the darkness out of sun

and into sun out of dark, there should be one empty

for you and me.

MIO. No.

MIRIAMNE. Then go now and leave me.

I'm only a girl you saw in the tenements,

and there's been nothing said.

MIO. Miriamne.

[*She takes a step toward him.*]

MIRIAMNE. Yes. [*He kisses her lips lightly.*]

MIO. Why, girl, the transfiguration on the mount

was nothing to your face. It lights from within—

a white chalice holding fire, a flower in flame,

this is your face.

MIRIAMNE. And you shall drink the flame

and never lessen it. And round your head

the aureole shall burn that burns there now,

forever. This I can give you. And so forever

the Freudians are wrong.

MIO. They're well-forgotten

at any rate.

MIRIAMNE. Why did you speak to me

when you first saw me?

MIO. I knew then.

MIRIAMNE. And I came back

because I must see you again. And we danced together

and my heart hurt me. Never, never, never,

though they should bind me down and tear out my eyes,

would I ever hurt you now. Take me with you, Mio,

let them look for us, whoever there is to look,

but we'll be away.

[MIO *turns away toward the tenement.*]

MIO. When I was four years old

we climbed through an iron gate, my mother and I,

to see my father in prison. He stood in the death-cell

and put his hand through the bars and said, My Mio,

I have only this to leave you, that I love you,

and will love you after I die. Love me then, Mio,

when this hard thing comes on you, that you must live

a man despised for your father. That night the guards,

walking in flood-lights brighter than high noon,

led him between them with his trousers slit

and a shaven head for the cathodes. This sleet and rain

that I feel cold here on my face and hands

will find him under thirteen years of clay

in prison ground. Lie still and rest, my father,

for I have not forgotten. When I forget

may I lie blind as you. No other love,

time passing, nor the spaced light-years of suns

shall blur your voice, or tempt me from the path

that clears your name—

till I have these rats in my grip
or sleep deep where you sleep.
[*To* Miriamne.] I have no house,
nor home, nor love of life, nor fear of
    death,
nor care for what I eat, or who I sleep
    with,
or what color of calcimine the Govern-
    ment
will wash itself this year or next to lure
the sheep and feed the wolves. Love some-
    where else,
and get your children in some other image
more acceptable to the State! This face
    of mine
is stamped for sewage!
[*She steps back, surmising.*]
    Miriamne. Mio—
Mio. My road is cut
in rock, and leads to one end. If I hurt
    you, I'm sorry.
One gets over hurts.
    Miriamne. What was his name—
your father's name?
    Mio. Bartolomeo Romagna.
I'm not ashamed of it.
    Miriamne. Why are you here?
    Mio. For the reason
I've never had a home. Because I'm a cry
out of a shallow grave, and all roads are
    mine
that might revenge him!
    Miriamne. But Mio—why here—why
here?
    Mio. I can't tell you that.
    Miriamne. No—but—there's someone
lives here—lives not far—and you mean to
    see him—
you mean to ask him—[*She pauses.*]
    Mio. Who told you that?
    Miriamne. His name
is Garth—Garth Esdras—
    Mio [*after a pause, coming nearer*].
Who are you, then? You seem

to know a good deal about me.—Were
    you sent
to say this?
    Miriamne. You said there was death
        about you! Yes,
but nearer than you think! Let it be as
    it is—
let it all be as it is, never see this place
nor think of it—forget the streets you
    came
when you're away and safe! Go before
    you're seen
or spoken to!
    Mio. Will you tell me why?
    Miriamne. As I love you
I can't tell you—and I can never see you—
    Mio. I walk where I please—
    Miriamne. Do you think it's easy for
        me to send you away? [*She steps back
        as if to go.*]
    Mio. Where will I find you then
if I should want to see you?
    Miriamne. Never—I tell you
I'd bring you death! Even now. Listen!
[Shadow *and* Trock *enter between the
    bridge and the tenement house.* Miri-
    amne *pulls* Mio *back into the shadow
    of the rock to avoid being seen.*]
    Trock. Why, fine.
    Shadow. You watch it now—just for the
        record, Trock—
you're going to thank me for staying away
    from it
and keeping you out. I've seen men get
    that way,
thinking they had to plug a couple of
    guys
and then a few more to cover it up, and
    then
maybe a dozen more. You can't own all
and territory adjacent, and you can't
slough all the witnesses, because every
    man
you put away has friends—

TROCK. I said all right.
I said fine.

SHADOW. They're going to find this
judge,
and if they find him dead it's just too bad,
and I don't want to know anything about
it—
and you don't either.

TROCK. You all through?

SHADOW. Why sure.

TROCK. All right.
We're through, too, you know.

SHADOW. Yeah? [*He becomes wary.*]

TROCK. Yeah, we're through.

SHADOW. I've heard that said before, and
afterwards
somebody died.
[*TROCK is silent.*] Is that what you mean?

TROCK. You can go.
I don't want to see you.

SHADOW. Sure, I'll go.
Maybe you won't mind if I just find out
what you've got on you. Before I turn my
back
I'd like to know.
[*Silently and expertly he touches TROCK's
pockets, extracting a gun.*]
Not that I'd distrust you,
but you know how it is. [*He pockets the
gun.*]
So long, Trock.

TROCK. So long.

SHADOW. I won't talk.
You can be sure of that.

TROCK. I know you won't.
[*SHADOW turns and goes out right, past
the rock and along the bank. As he
goes the* TWO YOUNG MEN IN BLUE
SERGE *enter from the left and walk
slowly after SHADOW. They look toward TROCK as they enter and he motions with his thumb in the direction
taken by SHADOW. They follow
SHADOW out without haste. TROCK*

*watches them disappear, then slips out
the way he came. MIO comes a step
forward, looking after the two men.
Two or three shots are heard, then
silence. MIO starts to run after
SHADOW.*]

MIRIAMNE. Mio!

MIO. What do you know about this?

MIRIAMNE. The other way,
Mio—quick!
[*CARR slips in from the right, in haste.*]

CARR. Look, somebody's just been shot.
He fell in the river. The guys that did
the shooting
ran up the bank.

MIO. Come on.
[*MIO and CARR run out right. MIRIAMNE
watches uncertainly, then slowly turns
and walks to the rear door of the tenement. She stands there a moment,
looking after MIO, then goes in, closing the door. CARR and MIO return.*]

CARR. There's a rip tide past the point.
You'd never find him.

MIO. No.

CARR. You know a man really ought to
carry insurance living around here.—God,
it's easy, putting a fellow away. I never
saw it done before.

MIO [*looking at the place where MIRI-
AMNE stood*]. They have it all worked out.

CARR. What are you doing now?

MIO. I have a little business to transact
in this neighborhood.

CARR. You'd better forget it.

MIO. No.

CARR. Need any help?

MIO. Well, if I did I'd ask you first. But
I don't see how it would do any good. So
you keep out of it and take care of yourself.

CARR. So long, then.

MIO. So long, Carr.

CARR [*looking down-stream*]. He was drifting face up. Must be halfway to the island the way the tide runs. [*He shivers.*] God, it's cold here. Well—

[*He goes out to the left.* MIO *sits on the edge of the rock.* LUCIA *comes stealthily back from between the bridge and the tenement, goes to the street-piano and wheels it away.* PINY *comes in. They take a look at* MIO, *but say nothing.* LUCIA *goes into his shelter and* PINY *into hers.* MIO *rises, looks up at the tenement, and goes out to the left.*]

CURTAIN

ACT II

[*The basement as in Scene Two of Act I. The same evening.* ESDRAS *sits at the table reading,* MIRIAMNE *is seated at the left, listening and intent. The door of the inner room is half open and* GARTH's *violin is heard. He is playing the theme from the third movement of Beethoven's Archduke Trio.* ESDRAS *looks up.*]

ESDRAS. I remember when I came to the end
of all the Talmud said, and the commentaries,
then I was fifty years old—and it was time
to ask what I had learned. I asked this question
and gave myself the answer. In all the Talmud
there was nothing to find but the names of things,
set down that we might call them by those names
and walk without fear among things known. Since then
I have had twenty years to read on and on
and end with Ecclesiastes. Names of names,
evanid days, evanid nights and days
and words that shift their meaning. Space is time,
that which was is now—the men of to-morrow
live, and this is their yesterday. All things
that were and are and will be, have their being
then and now and to come. If this means little
when you are young, remember it. It will return
to mean more when you are old.

MIRIAMNE. I'm sorry—I
was listening for something.

ESDRAS. It doesn't matter.
It's a useless wisdom. It's all I have,
but useless. It may be there is no time,
but we grow old. Do you know his name?

MIRIAMNE. Whose name?

ESDRAS. Why, when we're young and listen for a step
the step should have a name—

[MIRIAMNE, *not hearing, rises and goes to the window.* GARTH *enters from within, carrying his violin and carefully closing the door.*]

GARTH [*as* ESDRAS *looks at him*]. Asleep.

ESDRAS. He may
sleep on through the whole night—then in the morning
we can let them know.

GARTH. We'd be wiser to say nothing—
let him find his own way back.

ESDRAS. How did he come here?

GARTH. He's not too crazy for that. If he wakes again
we'll keep him quiet and shift him off to-morrow.
Somebody'd pick him up.

ESDRAS. How have I come
to this sunken end of a street, at a life's
    end—?
    GARTH. It was cheaper here—not to be
    transcendental—
So—we say nothing—?
    ESDRAS. Nothing.
    MIRIAMNE. Garth, there's no place
in this whole city—not one—
where you would be safer
than here—tonight—or tomorrow.
    GARTH [*bitterly*]. Well, that may be.
What of it?
    MIRIAMNE. If you slipped away and took
a place somewhere where Trock couldn't
    find you—
    GARTH. Yes—
using what for money? and why do you
    think
I've sat here so far—because I love my home
so much? No, but if I stepped round the
    corner
it'd be my last corner and my last step.
    MIRIAMNE. And yet—
if you're here—they'll find you here—
Trock will come again—
and there's worse to follow—
    GARTH. Do you want to get me killed?
    MIRIAMNE. No.
    GARTH. There's no way out of it. We'll
    wait
and take what they send us.
    ESDRAS. Hush! You'll wake him.
    GARTH. I've done it.
I hear him stirring now.
[*They wait quietly.* JUDGE GAUNT *opens
    the door and enters.*]
    GAUNT [*in the doorway*]. I beg your
    pardon—
no, no, be seated—keep your place—I've
    made
your evening difficult enough, I fear;
and I must thank you doubly for your
    kindness,
for I've been ill—I know it.

ESDRAS. You're better, sir?
    GAUNT. Quite recovered, thank you.
    Able, I hope,
to manage nicely now. You'll be rewarded
for your hospitality—though at this moment
[*He smiles.*] I'm low in funds.
[*He inspects his billfold.*] Sir, my embar-
    rassment
is great indeed—and more than monetary,
for I must own my recollection's vague
of how I came here—how we came to-
    gether—
and what we may have said. My name is
    Gaunt,
Judge Gaunt, a name long known in the
    criminal courts,
and not unhonored there.
    ESDRAS. My name is Esdras—
and this is Garth, my son. And Miriamne,
the daughter of my old age.
    GAUNT. I'm glad to meet you.
Esdras. Garth Esdras.
[*He passes a hand over his eyes.*]
It's not a usual name.
Of late it's been connected with a case—
a case I knew. But this is hardly the man.
Though it's not a usual name.
[*They are silent.*] Sir, how I came here,
as I have said, I don't well know. Such
    things
are sometimes not quite accident.
    ESDRAS. We found you
outside our door and brought you in.
    GAUNT. The brain
can be overworked, and weary, even when
    the man
would swear to his good health. Sir, on
    my word
I don't know why I came here, nor how,
    nor when,
nor what would explain it. Shall we say
    the machine
begins to wear? I felt no twinge of it.—
You will imagine how much more than
    galling

I feel it, to ask my way home—and where
  I am—
but I do ask you that.

ESDRAS. This is New York City—
or part of it.

GAUNT. Not the best part, I presume?
[*He smiles grimly.*] No, not the best.

ESDRAS. Not typical, no.

GAUNT. And you—[*To* GARTH.]
you are Garth Esdras?

GARTH. That's my name.

GAUNT. Well, sir, [*To* ESDRAS.]
I shall lie under the deepest obligation
if you will set an old man on his path,
for I lack the homing instinct, if the truth
were known. North, east and south mean
  nothing to me
here in this room.

ESDRAS. I can put you in your way.

GARTH. Only you'd be wiser to wait a
  while—
if I'm any judge.—

GAUNT. It happens I'm the judge—
[*With stiff humor.*]
in more ways than one. You'll forgive me
  if I say
I find this place and my predicament
somewhat distasteful.
[*He looks round him.*]

GARTH. I don't doubt you do;
but you're better off here.

GAUNT. Nor will you find it wise
to cross my word as lightly as you seem
inclined to do. You've seen me ill and
  shaken—
and you presume on that.

GARTH. Have it your way.

GAUNT. Doubtless what information is
  required
we'll find nearby.

ESDRAS. Yes, sir—the terminal,—
if you could walk so far.

GAUNT. I've done some walking—
to look at my shoes.

[*He looks down, then puts out a hand to
  steady himself.*] That—that was why
  I came—
never mind—it was there—and it's gone.
[*To* GARTH.] Professor Hobhouse—
that's the name—he wrote some trash
  about you
and printed it in a broadside.
—Since I'm here I can tell you
it's a pure fabrication—lacking facts
and legal import. Senseless and impudent,
written with bias—with malicious intent
to undermine the public confidence
in justice and the courts. I knew it then—
all he brings out about this testimony
you might have given. It's true I could
  have called you,
but the case was clear—Romagna was
  known guilty,
and there was nothing to add. If I've endured
some hours of torture over their attacks
upon my probity—and in this torture
have wandered from my place, wandered
  perhaps
in mind and body—and found my way to
  face you—
why, yes, it is so—I know it—I beg of
  you
say nothing. It's not easy to give up
a fair name after a full half century
of service to a state. It may well rock
the surest reason. Therefore I ask of you
say nothing of this visit.

GARTH. I'll say nothing.

ESDRAS. Nor any of us.

GAUNT. Why, no—for you'd lose, too.
You'd have nothing to gain.

ESDRAS. Indeed we know it.

GAUNT. I'll remember you kindly. When
  I've returned,
there may be some mystery made of where
  I was—
we'll leave it a mystery?

GARTH. Anything you say.

GAUNT. Why, now I go with much
more peace of mind—if I can call you
friends.

ESDRAS. We shall be grateful
for silence on your part, Your Honor.

GAUNT. Sir—
if there were any just end to be served
by speaking out, I'd speak! There is none.
No—
bear that in mind!

ESDRAS. We will, Your Honor.

GAUNT. Then—
I'm in some haste. If you can be my guide,
we'll set out now.

ESDRAS. Yes, surely.

[*There is a knock at the door. The four
look at each other with some apprehension.* MIRIAMNE *rises.*]
I'll answer it.

MIRIAMNE. Yes.

[*She goes into the inner room and closes
the door.* ESDRAS *goes to the outer
door. The knock is repeated. He opens
the door.* MIO *is there.*]

ESDRAS. Yes, sir.

MIO. May I come in?

ESDRAS. Will you state your business, sir?
It's late—and I'm not at liberty—

MIO. Why, I might say
that I was trying to earn my tuition fees
by peddling magazines. I could say that,
or collecting old newspapers—paying
cash—
highest rates—no questions asked—
[*He looks round sharply.*]

GARTH. We've nothing to sell.
What do you want?

MIO. Your pardon, gentlemen.
My business is not of an ordinary kind,
and I felt the need of this slight introduction
while I might get my bearings. Your name
is Esdras,
or they told me so outside.

GARTH. What do you want?

MIO. Is that the name?

GARTH. Yes.

MIO. I'll be quick and brief.
I'm the son of a man who died many
years ago
for a pay roll robbery in New England.
You
should be Garth Esdras, by what I've
heard. You have
some knowledge of the crime, if one can
believe
what he reads in the public prints, and
it might be
that your testimony, if given, would clear
my father
of any share in the murder. You may not
care
whether he was guilty or not. You may
not know.
But I do care—and care deeply, and I've
come
to ask you face to face.

GARTH. To ask me what?

MIO. What do you know of it?

ESDRAS. This man Romagna,
did he have a son?

MIO. Yes, sir, this man Romagna,
as you choose to call him, had a son, and I
am that son, and proud.

ESDRAS. Forgive me.

MIO. Had you known him,
and heard him speak, you'd know why
I'm proud, and why
he was no malefactor.

ESDRAS. I quite believe you.
If my son can help he will. But at this
moment,
as I told you—could you, I wonder, come
tomorrow,
at your own hour?

MIO. Yes.

ESDRAS. By coincidence

we too of late have had this thing in
    mind—
there have been comments printed, and
    much discussion
which we could hardly avoid.
    Mio. Could you tell me then
in a word?—What you know—
is it for him or against him?—
that's all I need.
    Esdras. My son knows nothing.
    Garth. No.
The picture-papers lash themselves to a
    fury
over any rumor—make them up when
    they're short
of bedroom slops.—This is what hap-
    pened. I
had known a few members of a gang one
    time
up there—and after the murder they
    picked me up
because I looked like someone that was
    seen
in what they called the murder car. They
    held me
a little while, but they couldn't identify
    me
for the most excellent reason I wasn't
    there
when the thing occurred. A dozen years
    later now
a professor comes across this, and sees red
and asks why I wasn't called on as a wit-
    ness
and yips so loud they syndicate his picture
in all the rotos. That's all I know about it.
I wish I could tell you more.
    Esdras. Let me say too
that I have read some words your father
    said,
and you were a son fortunate in your
    father,
whatever the verdict of the world.

Mio. There are few
who think so, but it's true, and I thank
    you. Then—
that's the whole story?
    Garth. All I know of it.
    Mio. They cover their tracks well, the
    inner ring
that distributes murder. I came three
    thousand miles
to this dead end.
    Esdras. If he was innocent
and you know him so, believe it, and let
    the others
believe as they like.
    Mio. Will you tell me how a man's
to live, and face his life, if he can't believe
that truth's like a fire,
and will burn through and be seen
though it takes all the years there are?
While I stand up and have breath in my
    lungs
I shall be one flame of that fire;
it's all the life I have.
    Esdras. Then you must live so.
One must live as he can.
    Mio. It's the only way
of life my father left me.
    Esdras. Yes? Yet it's true
the ground we walk on is impacted down
and hard with blood and bones of those
    who died
unjustly. There's not one title to land or
    life,
even your own, but was built on rape and
    murder,
back a few years. It would take a fire in-
    deed
to burn out all this terror.
    Mio. Then let it burn down,
all of it!
    Esdras. We ask a great deal of the world
at first—then less—and then less.
We ask for truth

and justice. But this truth's a thing unknown
in the lightest, smallest matter—and as for
justice,
who has once seen it done? You loved
your father,
and I could have loved him, for every
word he spoke
in his trial was sweet and tolerant, but
the weight
of what men are and have, rests heavy on
the graves of those who lost. They'll not
rise again,
and their causes lie there with them.

GAUNT. If you mean to say
that Bartolomeo Romagna was innocent,
you are wrong. He was guilty.
There may have been injustice
from time to time, by regrettable chance,
in our courts,
but not in that case, I assure you.

MIO. Oh, you assure me!
You lie in your scrag teeth, whoever you
are!
My father was murdered!

GAUNT. Romagna was found guilty
by all due process of law, and given his
chance
to prove his innocence.

MIO. What chance? When a court
panders to mob hysterics, and the jury
comes in loaded to soak an anarchist
and a foreigner, it may be due process of
law
but it's also murder!

GAUNT. He should have thought of that
before he spilled blood.

MIO. He?

GAUNT. Sir, I know too well
that he was guilty.

MIO. Who are you? How do you know?
I've searched the records through, the trial
and what

came after, and in all that million words
I found not one unbiased argument
to fix the crime on him.

GAUNT. And you yourself,
were you unprejudiced?

MIO. Who are you?

ESDRAS. Sir,
this gentleman is here, as you are here,
to ask my son, as you have asked, what
ground
there might be for this talk of new evidence
in your father's case. We gave him the
same answer
we've given you.

MIO. I'm sorry. I'd supposed
his cause forgotten except by myself.
There's still
a defense committee then?

GAUNT. There may be. I
am not connected with it.

ESDRAS. He is my guest,
and asks to remain unknown.

MIO [*after a pause, looking at* GAUNT].
The judge at the trial
was younger, but he had your face. Can
it be
that you're the man?—Yes—Yes.—The
jury charge—
I sat there as a child and heard your voice,
and watched that Brahminical mouth. I
knew even then
you meant no good to him. And now
you're here
to winnow out truth and justice—the
fountain-head
of the lies that slew him! Are you Judge
Gaunt?

GAUNT. I am.

MIO. Then tell me what damnation to
what inferno
would fit the toad that sat in robes and
lied

when he gave the charge, and knew he
    lied! Judge that,
and then go to your place in that hell!
    GAUNT. I know and have known
what bitterness can rise against a court
when it must say, putting aside all weak-
    ness,
that a man's to die. I can forgive you that,
for you are your father's son, and you
    think of him
as a son thinks of his father. Certain laws
seem cruel in their operation; it's neces-
    sary
that we be cruel to uphold them. This
    cruelty
is kindness to those I serve.
    MIO. I don't doubt that.
I know who it is you serve.
    GAUNT. Would I have chosen
to rack myself with other men's despairs,
stop my ears, harden my heart, and listen
    only
to the voice of law and light, if I had
    hoped
some private gain for serving? In all my
    years
on the bench of a long-established com-
    monwealth
not once has my decision been in question
save in this case. Not once before or since.
For hope of heaven or place on earth, or
    power
or gold, no man has had my voice, nor
    will
while I still keep the trust that's laid on
    me
to sentence and define.
    MIO. Then why are you here?
    GAUNT. My record's clean. I've kept it
    so. But suppose
with the best intent, among the myriad
    tongues
that come to testify, I had missed my way

and followed a perjured tale to a lethal
    end
till a man was forsworn to death? Could
    I rest or sleep
while there was doubt of this,
even while there was question in a lay-
    man's mind?
For always, night and day,
there lies on my brain like a weight, the
    admonition:
see truly, let nothing sway you; among all
    functions
there's but one godlike, to judge. Then
    see to it
you judge as a god would judge, with
    clarity,
with truth, with what mercy is found con-
    sonant
with order and law. Without law men are
    beasts,
and it's a judge's task to lift and hold
    them
above themselves. Let a judge be once mis-
    taken
or step aside for a friend, and a gap is
    , made
in the dykes that hold back anarchy and
    chaos,
and leave men bond but free.
    MIO. Then the gap's been made,
and you made it.
    GAUNT. I feared that too. May you be a
    judge
sometime, and know in what fear,
through what nights long
in fear, I scanned and verified and com-
    pared
the transcripts of the trial.
    MIO. Without prejudice,
no doubt. It was never in your mind to
    prove
that you'd been right.
    GAUNT. And conscious of that, too—

that that might be my purpose—watchful
of that,
and jealous as his own lawyer of the rights
that should hedge the defendant!
And still I found no error,
shook not one staple of the bolts that
linked
the doer to the deed! Still following on
from step to step, I watched all modern
comment,
and saw it centered finally on one fact—
Garth Esdras was not called. This is Garth
Esdras,
and you have heard him. Would his depo-
sition
have justified a new trial?
    Mio. No. It would not.
    Gaunt. And there I come, myself. If the
man were still
in his cell, and waiting, I'd have no faint
excuse
for another hearing.
    Mio. I've told you that I read
the trial from beginning to end. Every
word you spoke
was balanced carefully to keep the letter
of the law and still convict—convict, by
Christ,
if it tore the seven veils! You stand here
now
running cascades of casuistry, to prove
to yourself and me that no judge of rank
and breeding
could burn a man out of hate! But that's
what you did
under all your varnish!
    Gaunt. I've sought for evidence,
and you have sought. Have you found it?
Can you cite
one fresh word in defence?
    Mio. The trial itself
was shot full of legerdemain, prearranged
to lead
the jury astray—

    Gaunt. Could you prove that?
    Mio. Yes!
    Gaunt. And if
the jury were led astray, remember it's
the jury, by our Anglo-Saxon custom,
that finds for guilt or innocence. The
judge
is powerless in that matter.
    Mio. Not you! Your charge
misled the jury more than the evidence,
accepted every biased meaning, distilled
the poison for them!
    Gaunt. But if that were so
I'd be the first, I swear it, to step down
among all men, and hold out both my
hands
for manacles—yes, publish it in the streets,
that all I've held most sacred was defiled
by my own act. A judge's brain becomes
a delicate instrument to weigh men's lives
for good and ill—too delicate to bear
much tampering. If he should push aside
the weights and throw the beam, and say,
this once
the man is guilty, and I will have it so
though his mouth cry out from the
ground,
and all the world
revoke my word, he'd have a short way
to go
to madness. I think you'd find him in the
squares,
stopping the passers-by with arguments,—
see, I was right, the man was guilty
there—
this was brought in against him, this—
and this—
and I was left no choice! It's no light thing
when a long life's been dedicate to one
end
to wrench the mind awry!
    Mio. By your own thesis
you should be mad, and no doubt you
are.

GAUNT. But my madness
is only this—that I would fain look back
on a life well spent—without one stain—
one breath
of stain to flaw the glass—not in men's
minds
nor in my own. I take my God as witness
I meant to earn that clearness, and believe
that I have earned it. Yet my name is
clouded
with the blackest, fiercest scandal of our
age
that's touched a judge. What I can do to
wipe
that smutch from my fame I will. I think
you know
how deeply I've been hated, for no cause
that I can find there. Can it not be—and
I ask this
quite honestly—that the great injustice lies
on your side and not mine? Time and
time again
men have come before me perfect in their
lives,
loved by all who knew them, loved at
home,
gentle, not vicious, yet caught so ripe red-
handed
in some dark violence there was no denying
where the onus lay.
    MIO. That was not so with my father!
    GAUNT. And yet it seemed so to me. To
other men
who sat in judgment on him. Can you be
sure—
I ask this in humility—that you,
who were touched closest by the tragedy,
may not have lost perspective—may have
brooded
day and night on one theme—till your
eyes are tranced
and show you one side only?

MIO. I see well enough.
    GAUNT. And would that not be part of
the malady—
to look quite steadily at the drift of things
but see there what you wish—not what is
there—
not what another man to whom the story
was fresh would say is there?
    MIO. You think I'm crazy.
Is that what you meant to say?
    GAUNT. I've seen it happen
with the best and wisest men. I but ask
the question.
I can't speak for you. Is it not true wherever
you walk, through the little town where
you knew him well,
or flying from it, inland or by the sea,
still walking at your side, and sleeping
only
when you too sleep, a shadow not your
own
follows, pleading and holding out its
hands
to be delivered from shame?
    MIO. How you know that
by God I don't know.
    GAUNT. Because one spectre haunted
you and me—
and haunts you still, but for me it's laid
to rest
now that my mind is satisfied. He died
justly and not by error. [*A pause.*]
    MIO [*stepping forward*]. Do you care to
know
you've come so near to death it's miracle
that pulse still beats in your splotchy
throat?
Do you know
there's murder in me?
    GAUNT. There was murder in your sire,
and it's to be expected! I say he died
justly, and he deserved it!
    MIO. Yes, you'd like too well

[105]

to have me kill you! That would prove
your case
and clear your name, and dip my father's
name
in stench forever! You'll not get that from
me!
Go home and die in bed, get it under
cover,
your lux-et-lex putrefaction of the right
thing,
you man that walks like a god!
　　GAUNT. Have I made you angry
by coming too near the truth?
　　MIO. This sets him up,
this venomous slug, this sets him up in a
gown,
deciding who's to walk above the earth
and who's to lie beneath! And giving reasons!
The cobra giving reasons; I'm a god,
by Buddha, holy and worshipful my fang,
and can I sink it in!
[*He pauses, turns as if to go, then sits.*]
This is no good.
This won't help much.
[*The* JUDGE *and* ESDRAS *look at each
other.*]
　　GAUNT. We should be going.
　　ESDRAS. Yes. [*They prepare to go.*]
I'll lend you my coat.
　　GAUNT [*looking at it with distaste*].
No, keep it. A little rain
shouldn't matter to me.
　　ESDRAS. It freezes as it falls,
and you've a long way to go.
　　GAUNT. I'll manage, thank you.
[GAUNT *and* ESDRAS *go out,* ESDRAS *ob-
sequious, closing the door.*]
　　GARTH [*looking at* MIO's *back*]. Well?
　　MIO [*not moving*]. Let me sit here a
moment.
[GARTH *shrugs his shoulders and goes to-
ward the inner door.* MIRIAMNE *opens
it and comes out.* GARTH *looks at her,*

then at MIO, *then lays his fingers on
his lips. She nods.* GARTH *goes out.*
MIRIAMNE *sits and watches* MIO. *After
a little he turns and sees her.*]
　　MIO. How did you come here?
　　MIRIAMNE. I live here.
　　MIO. Here?
　　MIRIAMNE. My name is Esdras. Garth
is my brother. The walls are thin.
I heard what was said.
　　MIO [*stirring wearily*]. I'm going. This
is no place for me.
　　MIRIAMNE. What place
would be better?
　　MIO. None. Only it's better to go.
Just to go.
[*She comes over to him, puts her arm
around him and kisses his forehead.*]
　　MIRIAMNE. Mio.
　　MIO. What do you want?
Your kisses burn me—and your arms.
Don't offer
what I'm never to have! I can have nothing. They say
they'll cross the void sometime to the other
planets
and men will breathe in that air.
Well, I could breathe there,
but not here now. Not on this ball of
mud.
I don't want it.
　　MIRIAMNE. They can take away so little
with all their words. For you're a king
among them.
I heard you, and loved your voice.
　　MIO. I thought I'd fallen
so low there was no further, and now a pit
opens beneath. It was bad enough that he
should have died innocent, but if he were
guilty—
then what's my life—what have I left to
do—?
The son of a felon—and what they spat
on me

[106]

was earned—and I'm drenched with the
stuff.
Here on my hands
and cheeks, their spittle hanging! I liked
my hands
because they were like his. I tell you I've
lived
by his innocence, lived to see it flash
and blind them all—

MIRIAMNE. Never believe them, Mio,
never. [*She looks toward the inner door.*]

MIO. But it was truth I wanted, truth—
not the lies you'd tell yourself, or tell a
woman,
or a woman tells you! The judge with his
cobra mouth
may have spat truth—and I may be mad!
For me—
your hands are too clean to touch me. I'm
to have
the scraps from hotel kitchens—and instead of love
those mottled bodies that hitch themselves
through alleys
to sell for dimes or nickels. Go, keep yourself chaste
for the baker bridegroom—baker and son
of a baker,
let him get his baker's dozen on you!

MIRIAMNE. No—
say once you love me—say it once; I'll
never
ask to hear it twice, nor for any kindness,
and you shall take all I have!

[GARTH *opens the inner door and comes
out.*]

GARTH. I interrupt.
a love scene, I believe. We can do without
your adolescent mawkishness.
[*To* MIRIAMNE.] You're a child.
You'll both remember that.

MIRIAMNE. I've said nothing to harm
you—
and will say nothing.

GARTH. You're my sister, though,
and I take a certain interest in you. Where
have you two met?

MIRIAMNE. We danced together.

GARTH. Then
the dance is over, I think.

MIRIAMNE. I've always loved you
and tried to help you, Garth. And you've
been kind.
Don't spoil it now.

GARTH. Spoil it how?

MIRIAMNE. Because I love him.
I didn't know it would happen. We
danced together.
And the world's all changed. I see you
through a mist,
and our father, too. If you brought this to
nothing
I'd want to die.

GARTH [*to* MIO]. You'd better go.

MIO. Yes, I know.
[*He rises. There is a trembling knock at
the door.* MIRIAMNE *goes to it. The*
HOBO *is there shivering.*]

HOBO. Miss, could I sleep under the
pipes tonight, miss?
Could I, please?

MIRIAMNE. I think—not tonight.

HOBO. There won't be any more nights—
if I don't get warm, miss.

MIRIAMNE. Come in.
[*The* HOBO *comes in, looks round deprecatingly, then goes to a corner beneath
a huge heating pipe, which he crawls
under as if he'd been there before.*]

HOBO. Yes, miss, thank you.

GARTH. Must we put up with that?

MIRIAMNE. Father let him sleep there—
last winter.

GARTH. Yes, God, yes.

MIO. Well, good night.

MIRIAMNE. Where will you go?

MIO. Yes, where? As if it mattered.

GARTH. Oh, sleep here, too.

We'll have a row of you under the pipes.
MIO. No, thanks.
    MIRIAMNE. Mio, I've saved a little
    money. It's only
some pennies, but you must take it.
[*She shakes some coins out of a box into
    her hand.*]
    MIO. No, thanks.
    MIRIAMNE. And I love you.
You've never said you love me.
    MIO. Why wouldn't I love you
when you're clean and sweet,
and I've seen nothing sweet or clean
this last ten years? I love you. I leave you
    that
for what good it may do you. It's none to
    me.
    MIRIAMNE. Then kiss me.
    MIO [*looking at* GARTH].
With that scowling over us? No.
When it rains, some spring
on the planet Mercury, where the spring
    comes often,
I'll meet you there, let's say. We'll wait
    for that.
It may be some time till then.
[*The outside door opens and* ESDRAS *en-
    ters with* JUDGE GAUNT, *then, after a
    slight interval,* TROCK *follows.* TROCK
    *surveys the interior and its occupants
    one by one, carefully.*]
    TROCK. I wouldn't want to cause you in-
    convenience,
any of you, and especially the Judge.
I think you know that. You've all got
    things to do—
trains to catch, and so on. But trains can
    wait.
Hell, nearly anything can wait, you'll
    find,
only I can't. I'm the only one that can't
because I've got no time. Who's all this
    here?
Who's that? [*He points to the* HOBO.]

ESDRAS. He's a poor half-wit, sir,
that sometimes sleeps there.
    TROCK. Come out. I say come out,
whoever you are.
[*The* HOBO *stirs and looks up.*]
Yes, I mean you. Come out.
[*The* HOBO *emerges.*]
What's your name?
    HOBO. They mostly call me Oke.
    TROCK. What do you know?
    HOBO. No, sir.
    TROCK. Where are you from?
    HOBO. I got a piece of bread.
[*He brings it out, trembling.*]
    TROCK. Get back in there!
[*The* HOBO *crawls back into his corner.*]
Maybe you want to know why I'm doing
    this.
Well, I've been robbed, that's why—
robbed five or six times;
the police can't find a thing—so I'm out
    for myself—
if you want to know.
[*To* MIO.] Who are you?
    MIO. Oh, I'm a half-wit,
came in here by mistake. The difference
    is
I've got no piece of bread.
    TROCK. What's your name?
    MIO. My name?
Theophrastus Such. That's respectable.
You'll find it all the way from here to the
    coast
on the best police blotters.
Only the truth is we're a little touched in
    the head,
Oke and me. You'd better ask somebody
    else.
    TROCK. Who is he?
    ESDRAS. His name's Romagna. He's the
son.
    TROCK. Then what's he doing here?
You said you were on the level.
    GARTH. He just walked in. On account

[108]

of the stuff in the papers. We didn't ask him.

TROCK. God, we are a gathering. Now if we had Shadow we'd be all here, huh? Only I guess we won't see Shadow. No, that's too much to ask.

MIO. Who's Shadow?

TROCK. Now you're putting questions. Shadow was just nobody, you see. He blew away. It might happen to anyone. [*He looks at* GARTH.] Yes, anyone at all.

MIO. Why do you keep your hand in your pocket, friend?

TROCK. Because I'm cold, punk. Because I've been outside and it's cold as the tomb of Christ. [*To* GARTH.] Listen, there's a car waiting up at the street to take the Judge home. We'll take him to the car.

GARTH. That's not necessary.

ESDRAS. No.

TROCK. I say it is, see? You wouldn't want to let the Judge walk, would you? The Judge is going to ride where he's going, with a couple of chauffeurs, and everything done in style. Don't you worry about the Judge. He'll be taken care of. For good.

GARTH. I want no hand in it.

TROCK. Anything happens to me happens to you too, musician.

GARTH. I know that.

TROCK. Keep your mouth out of it then. And you'd better keep the punk here tonight, just for luck. [*He turns toward the door. There is a brilliant lightning flash through the windows, followed slowly by dying thunder.* TROCK *opens the door. The rain begins to pour in sheets.*] Jesus, somebody tipped it over again! [*A cough racks him.*] Wait till it's over. It takes ten days off me every time I step into it. [*He closes the door.*] Sit down and wait.

[*Lightning flashes again. The thunder is fainter.* ESDRAS, GARTH *and the* JUDGE *sit down.*]

GAUNT. We were born too early. Even you who are young
are not of the elect. In a hundred years
man will put his finger on life itself, and then
he will live as long as he likes. For you and me
we shall die soon—one day, one year more or less,
when or where, it's no matter. It's what we call
an indeterminate sentence. I'm hungry.

[GARTH *looks at* MIRIAMNE.]

MIRIAMNE. There was nothing left tonight.

HOBO. I've got a piece of bread.

[*He breaks his bread in two and hands half to the* JUDGE.]

GAUNT. I thank you, sir. [*He eats.*]
This is not good bread. [*He rises.*] Sir, I am used
to other company. Not better, perhaps, but their clothes
were different. These are what it's the fashion to call
the underprivileged.

TROCK. Oh, hell!

[*He turns toward the door.*]

MIO [*to* TROCK]. It would seem that you and the Judge know each other. [TROCK *faces him.*]

TROCK. I've been around.

MIO. Maybe you've met before.

TROCK. Maybe we have.

MIO. Will you tell me where?

TROCK. How long do you want to live?

MIO. How long? Oh, I've got big ideas about that.

TROCK. I thought so. Well, so far I've got nothing against you but your name, see? You keep it that way.

[*He opens the door. The rain still falls in torrents. He closes the door. As he turns from it, it opens again, and* SHADOW, *white, bloodstained and drip-*

ping, stands in the doorway. GARTH
rises. TROCK *turns.*]

GAUNT [*to the* HOBO]. Yet if one were
careful of his health, ate sparingly, drank
not at all, used himself wisely, it might be
that even an old man could live to touch
immortality. They may come on the secret
sooner than we dare hope. You see? It
does no harm to try.

TROCK [*backing away from* SHADOW].
By God, he's out of his grave!

SHADOW [*leaning against the doorway
holding a gun in his hands*]. Keep your
hands where they belong, Trock.
You know me.

TROCK. Don't! Don't! I had nothing to
do with it! [*He backs to the opposite
wall.*]

SHADOW. You said the doctor gave you
six months to live—well, I don't give you
that much. That's what you had, six
months, and so you start bumping off your
friends to make sure of your damn six
months. I got it from you.
I know where I got it.
Because I wouldn't give it to the Judge.
So he wouldn't talk.

TROCK. Honest to God—

SHADOW. What God?
The one that let you put three holes in me
when I was your friend? Well, He let me
  get up again
and walk till I could find you. That's as
  as far as I get,
but I got there, by God! And I can hear
  you
even if I can't see!
[*He takes a staggering step forward.*]
  A man needs blood
to keep going.—I got this far.—And now
  I can't see!
It runs out too fast—too fast—
when you've got three slugs
clean through you.

Show me where he is, you fools! He's here!
I got here! [*He drops the gun.*]
Help me! Help me! Oh, God! Oh, God!
I'm going to die! Where does a man lie
  down?
I want to lie down!
[MIRIAMNE *starts toward* SHADOW. GARTH
and ESDRAS *help him into the next
room,* MIRIAMNE *following.* TROCK
*squats in his corner, breathing hard,
looking at the door.* MIO *stands,
watching* TROCK. GARTH *returns, wiping his hand with a handkerchief.*
MIO *picks up and pockets the gun.*
MIRIAMNE *comes back and leans
against the door jamb.*]

GAUNT. You will hear it said that an
old man makes a good judge, being calm,
clear-eyed, without passion. But this is not
true. Only the young love truth and justice. The old are savage, wary, violent,
swayed by maniac desires, cynical of
friendship or love, open to bribery and
the temptations of lust, corrupt and das-
tardly to the heart. I know these old men.
What have they left to believe, what have
they left to lose? Whorers of daughters,
lickers of girls' shoes, contrivers of nasti-
ness in the night, purveyors of perversion,
worshippers of possession! Death is the
only radical. He comes late, but he comes
at last to put away the old men and give
the young their places. It was time. [*He
leers.*] Here's one I heard yesterday:
  Marmaduke behind the barn
    got his sister in a fix;
  he says damn instead of darn;
    ain't he cute? He's only six!

THE HOBO. He, he, he!

GAUNT.
  And the hoot-owl hoots all night,
    and the cuckoo cooks all day,
  and what with a minimum grace of
    God
    we pass the time away.

[110]

THE HOBO. He, he, he—I got ya! [*He makes a sign with his thumb.*]

GAUNT [*sings*].
And he led her all around
and laid her on the ground
and he ruffled up the feathers of
her cuckoo's nest!

HOBO. Ho, ho, ho!

GAUNT. I am not taken with the way you laugh. You should cultivate restraint. [ESDRAS *re-enters.*]

TROCK. Shut the door.

ESDRAS. He won't come back again.

TROCK. I want the door shut! He was dead, I tell you! [ESDRAS *closes the door.*] And Romagna was dead, too, once! Can't they keep a man under ground?

MIO. No. No more! They don't stay under ground any more, and they don't stay under water! Why did you have him killed?

TROCK. Stay away from me! I know you!

MIO. Who am I, then?

TROCK. I know you, damn you! Your name's Romagna!

MIO. Yes! And Romagna was dead, too, and Shadow was dead, but the time's come when you can't keep them down, these dead men! They won't stay down! They come in with their heads shot off and their entrails dragging! Hundreds of them! One by one—all you ever killed! Watch the door! See!—It moves!

TROCK [*looking, fascinated, at the door*]. Let me out of here! [*He tries to rise.*]

MIO [*the gun in his hand*]. Oh, no! You'll sit there and wait for them! One by one they'll come through that door, pulling their heads out of the gunny-sacks where you tied them—glauming over you with their rotten hands! They'll see without eyes and crawl over you—Shadow and the paymaster and all the rest of them

—putrescent bones without eyes! Now! Look! Look! For I'm first among them!

TROCK. I've done for better men than you! And I'll do for you!

GAUNT [*rapping on the table*]. Order, gentlemen, order! The witness will remember that a certain decorum is essential in the court-room!

MIO. By God, he'll answer me!

GAUNT [*thundering*]. Silence! Silence! Let me remind you of courtesy toward the witness! What case is this you try?

MIO. The case of the state against Bartolomeo Romagna for the murder of the paymaster!

GAUNT. Sir, that was disposed of long ago!

MIO. Never disposed of, never, not while I live!

GAUNT. Then we'll have done with it now! I deny the appeal! I have denied the appeal before and I do so again!

HOBO. He, he!—He thinks he's in the moving pictures! [*A flash of lightning.*]

GAUNT. Who set that flash! Bailiff, clear the court! This is not Flemington, gentlemen! We are not conducting this case to make a journalistic holiday! [*The thunder rumbles faintly.* GARTH *opens the outside door and faces a solid wall of rain.*] Stop that man! He's one of the defendants! [GARTH *closes the door.*]

MIO. Then put him on the stand!

GARTH. What do you think you're doing?

MIO. Have you any objection?

GAUNT. The objection is not sustained. We will hear the new evidence. Call your witness.

MIO. Garth Esdras!

GAUNT. He will take the stand!

GARTH. If you want me to say what I said before I'll say it!

MIO. Call Trock Estrella then!

GAUNT. Trock Estrella to the stand!

TROCK. No, by God!

MIO. Call Shadow, then! He'll talk! You thought he was dead, but he'll get up again and talk!

TROCK [*screaming*]. What do you want of me?

MIO. You killed the paymaster! You!

TROCK. You lie! It was Shadow killed him!

MIO. And now I know! Now I know!

GAUNT. Again I remind you of courtesy toward the witness!

MIO. I know them now!
Let me remind you of courtesy toward the dead!
He says that Shadow killed him! If Shadow were here
he'd say it was Trock! There were three men involved
in the new version of the crime for which
my father died! Shadow and Trock Estrella
as principals in the murder—Garth as witness!—
Why are they here together?—and you—the Judge—
why are you here? Why, because you were all afraid
and you drew together out of that fear to arrange
a story you could tell! And Trock killed Shadow
and meant to kill the Judge out of that same fear—
to keep them quiet! This is the thing I've hunted
over the earth to find out, and I'd be blind indeed if I missed it now!
[*To* GAUNT.] You heard what he said:
It was Shadow killed him! Now let the night conspire
with the sperm of hell! It's plain beyond denial
even to this fox of justice—and all his words

are curses on the wind! You lied! You lied!
You knew this too!

GAUNT [*low*]. Let me go. Let me go!

MIO. Then why
did you let my father die?

GAUNT. Suppose it known,
but there are things a judge must not believe
though they should head and fester underneath
and press in on his brain. Justice once rendered
in a clear burst of anger, righteously,
upon a very common laborer,
confessed an anarchist, the verdict found
and the precise machinery of law
invoked to know him guilty—think what furor
would rock the state if the court then flatly said:
all this was lies—must be reversed? It's better,
as any judge can tell you, in such cases,
holding the common good to be worth more
than small injustice, to let the record stand,
let one man die. For justice, in the main,
is governed by opinion. Communities
will have what they will have, and it's quite as well,
after all, to be rid of anarchists. Our rights
as citizens can be maintained as rights
only while we are held to be the peers
of those who live about us. A vendor of fish
is not protected as a man might be
who kept a market. I own I've sometimes wished
this was not so, but it is. The man you defend
was unfortunate—and his misfortune bore
almost as heavily on me.—I'm broken—
broken across. You're much too young to know

how bitter it is when a worn connection chars
and you can't remember—can't remember.
[*He steps forward.*] You
will not repeat this? It will go no further?
  Mio. No.
No further than the moon takes the tides
    —no further
than the news went when he died—
when you found him guilty
and they flashed that round the earth.
    Wherever men
still breathe and think, and know what's
    done to them
by the powers above, they'll know. That's
    all I ask.
That'll be enough.
[Trock *has risen and looks darkly at* Mio.]
  Gaunt. Thank you. For I've said some
    things
a judge should never say.
  Trock. Go right on talking.
Both of you. It won't get far, I guess.
  Mio. Oh, you'll see to that?
  Trock. I'll see to it. Me and some others.
Maybe I lost my grip there just for a
    minute.
That's all right.
  Mio. Then see to it! Let it rain!
What can you do to me now when the
    night's on fire
with this thing I know? Now I could al-
    most wish
there was a god somewhere—I could al-
    most think
there was a god—and he somehow brought
    me here
and set you down before me here in the
    rain
where I could wring this out of you! For
    it's said,
and I've heard it, and I'm free! He was
    as I thought him,
true and noble and upright, even when
    he went

to a death contrived because he was as
    he was
and not your kind! Let it rain! Let the
    night speak fire
and the city go out with the tide, for he
    was a man
and I know you now, and I have my day!
[*There is a heavy knock at the outside
    door.* Miriamne *opens it, at a glance
    from* Garth. *The* Policeman *is there
    in oilskins.*]
  Policeman. Evening. [*He steps in, fol-
lowed by a* Sergeant, *similarly dressed.*]
We're looking for someone
might be here. Seen an old man around
acting a little off?
[*To* Esdras.] You know the one
I mean. You saw him out there. Jeez!
    You've got
a funny crowd here!
[*He looks round. The* Hobo *shrinks into
    his corner.*] That's the one I saw.
What do you think?
  Sergeant. That's him. You mean to say
you didn't know him by his pictures?
[*He goes to* Gaunt.] Come on, old man.
You're going home.
  Gaunt. Yes, sir. I've lost my way.
I think I've lost my way.
  Sergeant. I'll say you have.
About three hundred miles. Now don't
    you worry.
We'll get you back.
  Gaunt. I'm a person of some rank
in my own city.
  Sergeant. We know that. One look at
    you
and we'd know that.
  Gaunt. Yes, sir.
  Policeman. If it isn't Trock!
Trock Estrella. How are you, Trock?
  Trock. Pretty good,
Thanks.
  Policeman. Got out yesterday again, I
hear?

TROCK. That's right.

SERGEANT. Hi'ye, Trock?

TROCK. O. K.

SERGEANT. You know we got orders
to watch you pretty close. Be good now, baby,
or back you go. Don't try to pull anything,
not in my district.

TROCK. No, sir.

SERGEANT. No bumping off.
If you want my advice quit carrying a gun.
Try earning your living for once.

TROCK. Yeah.

SERGEANT. That's an idea.
Because if we find any stiffs on the river bank
we'll know who to look for.

MIO. Then look in the other room!
I accuse that man of murder! Trock Estrella!
He's a murderer!

POLICEMAN. Hello. I remember you.

SERGEANT. Well, what murder?

MIO. It was Trock Estrella
that robbed the pay roll thirteen years ago
and did the killing my father died for! You know
the Romagna case! Romagna was innocent,
and Trock Estrella guilty!

SERGEANT [*disgusted*]. Oh, what the hell!
That's old stuff—the Romagna case.

POLICEMAN. Hey, Sarge!
[*The* SERGEANT *and* POLICEMAN *come closer together.*]
The boy's a professional kidder. He took me over
about half an hour ago. He kids the police
and then ducks out!

SERGEANT. Oh, yeah?

MIO. I'm not kidding now.
You'll find a dead man there in the next room
and Estrella killed him!

SERGEANT. Thirteen years ago?
And nobody smelled him yet?

MIO [*pointing*]. I accuse this man
of two murders! He killed the paymaster long ago
and had Shadow killed tonight. Look, look for yourself!
He's there all right!

POLICEMAN. Look boy. You stood out there
and put the booby sign on the dumb police
because they're fresh out of Ireland. Don't try it twice.

SERGEANT [*to* GARTH]. Any corpses here?

GARTH. Not that I know of.

SERGEANT. I thought so. [MIO *looks at* MIRIAMNE.]
[*To* MIO.] Think up a better one.

MIO. Have I got to drag him
out here where you can see him?
[*He goes toward the inner door.*] Can't you scent a murder
when it's under your nose? Look in!

MIRIAMNE. No, no—there's no one— there's no one there!

SERGEANT [*looking at* MIRIAMNE]. Take a look inside.

POLICEMAN. Yes, sir. [*He goes into the inside room. The* SERGEANT *goes up to the door. The* POLICEMAN *returns.*]
He's kidding, Sarge. If there's a cadaver
in here I don't see it.

MIO. You're blind then!
[*He goes into the room, the* SERGEANT *following him.*]

SERGEANT. What do you mean?
[*He comes out,* MIO *following him.*]
When you make a charge of murder it's better to have
the corpus delicti, son. You're the kind puts in
fire alarms to see the engine!

MIO. By God, he was there!
He went in there to die.

SERGEANT. I'll bet he did.
And I'm Haile Selassie's aunt! What's
  your name?
MIO. Romagna. [*To* GARTH.] What have
  you done with him?
GARTH. I don't know what you mean.
SERGEANT [*to* GARTH]. What's he talking
  about?
GARTH. I wish I could tell you.
I don't know.
SERGEANT. He must have seen something.
POLICEMAN. He's got
the Romagna case on the brain. You watch
  yourself,
chump, or you'll get run in.
MIO. Then they're in it together!
All of them!
[*To* MIRIAMNE.] Yes, and you!
GARTH. He's nuts, I say.
MIRIAMNE [*gently*].
You have dreamed something—isn't it
  true?
You've dreamed—
But truly, there was no one—
[MIO *looks at her comprehendingly.*]
MIO. You want me to say it. [*He
pauses.*] Yes, by God, I was dreaming.
SERGEANT [*to* POLICEMAN]. I guess you're
  right.
We'd better be going. Haven't you got a
  coat?
GAUNT. No, sir.
SERGEANT. I guess I'll have to lend you
mine. [*He puts his oilskins on* GAUNT.]
Come on, now. It's getting late. [GAUNT,
the POLICEMAN *and the* SERGEANT *go out.*]
TROCK. They're welcome to him.
His fuse is damp. Where is that walking
  fool
with the three slugs in him?
ESDRAS. He fell in the hall beyond
and we left him there.
TROCK. That's lucky for some of us. Is

he out this time
or is he still butting around?
ESDRAS. He's dead.
TROCK. That's perfect.
[*To* MIO.] Don't try using your firearms,
  amigo baby,
the Sarge is outside. [*He turns to go.*]
Better ship that carrion
back in the river! The one that walks
  when he's dead;
maybe he'll walk the distance for you.
GARTH. Coming back?
TROCK. Well, if I come back
you'll see me. If I don't, you won't. Let
  the punk
go far as he likes. Turn him loose and
  let him go.
And may you all rot in hell.
[*He pulls his coat around him and goes
  to left.* MIRIAMNE *climbs up to look
  out a window.*]
MIRIAMNE. He's climbing up to the
street, along the bridgehead. [*She turns.*]
Quick, Mio! It's safe now! Quick!
GARTH. Let him do as he likes.
MIRIAMNE. What do you mean? Garth!
  He means to kill him!
You know that!
GARTH. I've no doubt Master Romagna
can run his own campaign.
MIRIAMNE. But he'll be killed!
MIO. Why did you lie about Shadow?
[*There is a pause.* GARTH *shrugs, walks
across the room, and sits.*] You were one
of the gang!
GARTH. I can take a death if I have to!
  Go tell your story,
only watch your step, for I warn you,
  Trock's out gunning
and you may not walk very far. Oh, I
  could defend it
but it's hardly worth while.
If they get Trock they get me too.
Go tell them. You owe me nothing.

ESDRAS. This Trock you saw,
no one defends him. He's earned his death
     so often
there's nobody to regret it. But his crime,
his same crime that has dogged you,
     dogged us down
from what little we had, to live here
     among the drains,
where the waterbugs break out like a
     scrofula
on what we eat—and if there's lower to go
we'll go there when you've told your
     story. And more
that I haven't heart to speak—
MIO [*to* GARTH]. My father died
in your place. And you could have saved
     him!
You were one of the gang!
     GARTH. Why, there you are.
You certainly owe me nothing.
     MIRIAMNE [*moaning*]. I want to die.
I want to go away.
     MIO. Yes, and you lied!
And trapped me into it!
     MIRIAMNE. But Mio, he's my brother.
I couldn't give them my brother.
     MIO. No. You couldn't.
You were quite right. The gods were
     damned ironic
tonight, and they've worked it out.
     ESDRAS. What will be changed
if it comes to trial again? More blood
     poured out
to a mythical justice, but your father lying
     still
where he lies now.
     MIO. The bright, ironical gods!
What fun they have in heaven! When a
     man prays hard
for any gift, they give it, and then one
     more
to boot that makes it useless.
[*To* MIRIAMNE.] You might have picked

some other stranger to dance with!
     MIRIAMNE. I know.
     MIO. Or chosen
some other evening to sit outside in the
     rain.
But no, it had to be this. All my life long
I've wanted only one thing, to say to the
     world
and prove it: the man you killed was clean
     and true
and full of love as the twelve-year-old that
     stood
and taught in the temple. I can say that
     now
and give my proofs—and now you stick
     a girl's face
between me and the rites I've sworn the
     dead
shall have of me! You ask too much! Your
     brother
can take his chance! He was ready enough
     to let
an innocent man take certainty for him
to pay for the years he's had. That parts
     us, then,
but we're parted anyway, by the same
     dark wind
that blew us together. I shall say what I
     have to say.
[*He steps back.*] And I'm not welcome
     here.
     MIRIAMNE. But don't go now! You've
     stayed
too long! He'll be waiting!
     MIO. Well, is this any safer?
Let the winds blow, the four winds of the
     world,
and take us to the four winds.
[*The three are silent before him. He turns
     and goes out.*]

CURTAIN

ACT III

[*The river bank outside the tenement, a little before the close of the previous act. The rain still falls through the street lamps. The* Two Natty Young Men in Serge and Gray *are leaning against the masonry in a ray of light, concentrating on a game of chance. Each holds in his hand a packet of ten or fifteen crisp bills. They compare the numbers on the top notes and immediately a bill changes hands. This goes on with varying fortune until the tide begins to run toward the* 1st Gunman, *who has accumulated nearly the whole supply. They play on in complete silence, evidently not wishing to make any noise. Occasionally they raise their heads slightly to look carefully about. Luck begins to favor the* 2nd Gunman, *and the notes come his way. Neither evinces the slightest interest in how the game goes. They merely play on, bored, half-absorbed. There is a slight noise at the tenement door. They put the bills away and watch.* Trock *comes out, pulls the door shut and comes over to them. He says a few words too low to be heard, and without changing expression the* Young Men *saunter toward the right.* Trock *goes out to the left, and the* 2nd Player, *catching that out of the corner of his eye, lingers in a glimmer of light to go on with the game. The* 1st, *with an eye on the tenement door, begins to play without ado, and the bills again shift back and forth, then concentrate in the hands of the* 1st Gunman. *The* 2nd *shrugs his shoulders, searches his pockets, finds one bill, and playing with it begins to win heavily. They hear the door opening, and putting the notes away, slip out in front of the rock.* Mio *emerges, closes the door, looks around him and walks to the left. Near the corner of the tenement he pauses, reaches out his hand to try the rain, looks up toward the street, and stands uncertainly a moment. He returns and leans against the tenement wall.* Miriamne *comes out.* Mio *continues to look off into space as if unaware of her. She looks away.*]

Mio. This rather takes one off his high horse.—What I mean, tough weather for a hegira. You see, this is my sleeping suit, and if I get it wet—basta!

Miriamne. If you could only hide here.

Mio. Hide?

Miriamne. Lucia would take you in. The street-piano man.

Mio. At the moment I'm afflicted with claustrophobia. I prefer to die in the open, seeking air.

Miriamne. But you could stay there till daylight.

Mio. You're concerned about me.

Miriamne. Shall I ask him?

Mio. No. On the other hand there's a certain reason in your concern. I looked up the street and our old friend Trock hunches patiently under the warehouse eaves.

Miriamne. I was sure of that.

Mio. And here I am, a young man on a cold night, waiting the end of the rain. Being read my lesson by a boy, a blind boy—you know the one I mean. Knee-deep in the salt-marsh, Miriamne, bitten from within, fought.

Miriamne. Wouldn't it be better if you came back in the house?

Mio. You forget my claustrophobia.

Miriamne. Let me walk with you, then. Please. If I stay beside you he wouldn't dare.

Mio. And then again he might.—We

don't speak the same language, Miriamne.

MIRIAMNE. I betrayed you. Forgive me.

MIO. I wish I knew this region. There's probably a path along the bank.

MIRIAMNE. Yes. Shadow went that way.

MIO. That's true, too. So here I am, a young man on a wet night, and blind in my weather eye. Stay and talk to me.

MIRIAMNE. If it happens—it's my fault.

MIO. Not at all, sweet. You warned me to keep away. But I would have it. Now I have to find a way out. It's like a chess game. If you think long enough there's always a way out.—For one or the other. —I wonder why white always wins and black always loses in the problems. White to move and mate in three moves. But what if white were to lose—ah, what then? Why, in that case, obviously black would be white and white would be black.—As it often is.—As we often are.—Might makes white. Losers turn black. Do you think I'd have time to draw a gun?

MIRIAMNE. No.

MIO. I'm a fair shot. Also I'm fair game. [*The door of the tenement opens and* GARTH *comes out to look about quickly. Seeing only* MIO *and* MIRIAMNE *he goes in and comes out again almost immediately carrying one end of a door on which a body lies covered with a cloth. The* HOBO *carries the other end. They go to the right with their burden.*]

This is the burial of Shadow, then;

feet first he dips, and leaves the haunts of men.

Let us make mourn for Shadow, wetly lying,

in elegiac stanzas and sweet crying.

Be gentle with him, little cold waves and fishes;

nibble him not, respect his skin and tissues—

MIRIAMNE. Must you say such things?

MIO. My dear, some requiem is fitting over the dead, even for Shadow. But the last rhyme was bad.

Whittle him not, respect his dying wishes.

That's better. And then to conclude:

His aromatic virtues, slowly rising

will circumnamb the isle, beyond disguising.

He clung to life beyond the wont of men.

Time and his silence drink us all. Amen.

How I hate these identicals. The French allow them, but the French have no principles anyway. You know, Miriamne, there's really nothing mysterious about human life. It's purely mechanical, like an electric appliance. Stop the engine that runs the generator and the current's broken. When we think the brain gives off a small electrical discharge—quite measurable, and constant within limits. But that's not what makes your hair stand up when frightened.

MIRIAMNE. I think it's a mystery.

MIO. Human life? We'll have to wear veils if we're to keep it a mystery much longer. Now if Shadow and I were made up into sausages we'd probably make very good sausages.

MIRIAMNE. Don't—

MIO. I'm sorry. I speak from a high place, far off, long ago, looking down. The cortège returns. [GARTH *and the* HOBO *return, carrying the door, the cloth lying loosely over it.*] I hope you placed an obol in his mouth to pay the ferryman? Even among the Greeks a little money was prerequisite to Elysium. [GARTH *and the* HOBO *go inside, silent.*] No? It's grim to think of Shadow lingering among lesser shades on the hither side. For lack of a small gratuity.

[ESDRAS *comes out the open door and closes it behind him.*]

ESDRAS. You must wait here, Mio, or go inside. I know
you don't trust me, and I haven't earned your trust.
You're young enough to seek truth—
and there is no truth;
and I know that—
but I shall call the police and see that you get safely off.

MIO. It's a little late for that.

ESDRAS. I shall try.

MIO. And your terms? For I daresay you make terms?

ESDRAS. No.

MIO. Then let me remind you what will happen.
The police will ask some questions.
When they're answered
they'll ask more, and before they're done with it
your son will be implicated.

ESDRAS. Must he be?

MIO. I shall not keep quiet. [*A pause.*]

ESDRAS. Still, I'll go.

MIO. I don't ask help, remember. I make no truce.
He's not on my conscience, and I'm not on yours.

ESDRAS. But you
could make it easier, so easily.
He's my only son. Let him live.

MIO. His chance of survival's
better than mine, I'd say.

ESDRAS. I'll go.

MIO. I don't urge it.

ESDRAS. No. I put my son's life in your hands.
When you're gone,
that may come to your mind.

MIO. Don't count on it.

ESDRAS. Oh,
I count on nothing.

[*He turns to go.* MIRIAMNE *runs over to him and silently kisses his hands.*]
Not mine, not mine, my daughter!
They're guilty hands.
[*He goes out left.* GARTH'S *violin is heard within.*]

MIO. There was a war in heaven
once, all the angels on one side, and all
the devils on the other, and since that time
disputes have raged among the learned, concerning
whether the demons won, or the angels. Maybe
the angels won, after all.

MIRIAMNE. And again, perhaps
there are no demons or angels.

MIO. Oh, there are none.
But I could love your father.

MIRIAMNE. I love him. You see,
he's afraid because he's old. The less one has
to lose the more he's afraid.

MIO. Suppose one had
only a short stub end of life, or held
a flashlight with the batteries run down
till the bulb was dim, and knew that he could live
while the glow lasted. Or suppose one knew
that while he stood in a little shelter of time
under a bridgehead, say, he could live, and then,
from then on, nothing. Then to lie and turn
with the earth and sun, and regard them not in the least
when the bulb was extinguished or he stepped beyond
his circle into the cold? How could he live
that last dim quarter-hour, before he went,
minus all recollection, to grow in grass
between cobblestones?

MIRIAMNE. Let me put my arms round
  you, Mio.
Then if anything comes, it's for me, too.
[*She puts both arms round him.*]
  Mio. Only suppose
this circle's charmed! To be safe until he
  steps
from this lighted space into dark! Time
  pauses here
and high eternity grows in one quarter-
  hour
in which to live.
  MIRIAMNE. Let me see if anyone's
  there—
there in the shadows.
[*She looks toward the right.*]
  Mio. It might blast our eternity—
blow it to bits. No, don't go. This is forever,
here where we stand. And I ask you,
  Miriamne,
how does one spend a forever?
  MIRIAMNE. You're frightened?
  Mio. Yes.
So much that time stands still.
  MIRIAMNE. Why didn't I speak—
tell them—when the officers were here? I
  failed you
in that one moment!
  Mio. His life for mine? Oh, no.
I wouldn't want it, and you couldn't
  give it.
And if I should go on living we're cut
  apart
by that brother of yours.
  MIRIAMNE. Are we?
  Mio. Well, think about it.
A body lies between us, buried in quick-
  lime.
Your allegiance is on the other side of
  that grave
and not to me.
  MIRIAMNE. No, Mio! Mio, I love you!

Mio. I love you, too, but in case my life
  went on
beyond that barrier of dark—then Garth
would run his risk of dying.
  MIRIAMNE. He's punished, Mio.
His life's been torment to him. Let him
  go,
for my sake, Mio.
  Mio. I wish I could. I wish
I'd never seen him—or you. I've steeped
  too long
in this thing. It's in my teeth and bones.
  I can't
let go or forget. And I'll not add my lie
to the lies that cumber his ground. We
  live our days
in a storm of lies that drifts the truth too
  deep
for path or shovel; but I've set my foot on
  a truth
for once, and I'll trail it down!
[*A silence.* MIRIAMNE *looks out to the
  right.*]
  MIRIAMNE. There's someone there—
I heard—
[CARR *comes in from the right.*]
  Mio. It's Carr.
  CARR. That's right. No doubt about it.
Excuse me.
  Mio. Glad to see you. This is Miriamne.
Carr's a friend of mine.
  CARR. You're better employed
than when I saw you last.
  Mio. Bow to the gentleman,
Miriamne. That's meant for you.
  MIRIAMNE. Thank you, I'm sure.
Should I leave you, Mio? You want to
  talk?
  Mio. Oh, no,
we've done our talking.
  MIRIAMNE. But—
  CARR. I'm the one's out of place—
I wandered back because I got worried
  about you,

that's the truth.—Oh—those two fellows
with the hats
down this way, you know, the ones that
ran
after we heard the shooting—they're back
again,
lingering or malingering down the bank,
revisiting the crime, I guess. They may
mean well.
    Mio. I'll try to avoid them.
    Carr. I didn't care
for the way they looked at me.—No luck,
    I suppose,
with that case history? The investigation
you had on hand?
    Mio. I can't say. By the way,
the stiff that fell in the water and we saw
swirling
down the eddy, he came trudging up,
later on,
long enough to tell his name. His name
was Shadow
but he's back in the water now. It's all in
an evening.
These things happen here.
    Carr. Good God!
    Mio. I know.
I wouldn't believe it if you told it.
    Carr. But—
the man was alive?
    Mio. Oh, not for long! He's dunked
for good this time. That's all that's happened.
    Carr. Well,
if you don't need me—
    Miriamne. You had a message to send—
have you forgotten—?
    Mio. I?—Yes, I had a message—
but I won't send it—not now.
    Miriamne. Then I will—!
    Mio. No.
Let it go the way it is! It's all arranged
another way. You've been a good scout,
    Carr,

the best I ever knew on the road.
    Carr. That sounds
like making your will.
    Mio. Not yet, but when I do
I've thought of something to leave you. It's
the view
of Mt. Rainier from the Seattle jail,
snow over cloud. And the rusty chain in
my pocket
from a pair of handcuffs my father wore.
    That's all
the worldly goods I'm seized of.
    Carr. Look, Mio—hell—
if you're in trouble—
    Mio. I'm not. Not at all. I have
a genius that attends me where I go,
and guards me now. I'm fine.
    Carr. Well, that's good news.
He'll have his work cut out.
    Mio. Oh, he's a genius.
    Carr. I'll see you then.
I'll be at the Grand Street place. I'm lucky
tonight,
and I can pay. I could even pay for two.
    Mio. Thanks, I may take you up.
    Carr. Good night.
    Mio. Right, Carr.
    Carr [*to* Miriamne]. Good night.
    Miriamne [*after a pause*]. Good night.
    [Carr *goes out to the left.*]
Why did you do that? He's your genius,
    Mio,
and you let him go.
    Mio. I couldn't help it.
    Miriamne. Call him.
Run after him and call him!
    Mio. I tried to say it
and it strangled in my throat. I might
have known
you'd win in the end.
    Miriamne. Is it for me?
    Mio. For you?
It stuck in my throat, that's all I know.
    Miriamne. Oh, Mio,

I never asked for that! I only hoped
Garth could go clear.
  Mio. Well, now he will.
  Miriamne. But you—
It was your chance!
  Mio. I've lost
my taste for revenge if it falls on you. Oh,
  God,
deliver me from the body of this death
I've dragged behind me all these years!
  Miriamne!
Miriamne!
  Miriamne. Yes!
  Mio. Miriamne, if you love me
teach me a treason to what I am, and have
  been,
till I learn to live like a man! I think I'm
  waking
from a long trauma of hate and fear and
  death
that's hemmed me from my birth—and
  glimpse a life
to be lived in hope—but it's young in me
  yet, I can't
get free, or forgive! But teach me how to
  live
and forget to hate!
  Miriamne. He would have forgiven.
  Mio. He?
  Miriamne. Your father. [*A pause.*]
  Mio. Yes. [*Another pause.*]
You'll think it strange, but I've never
remembered that.
  Miriamne. How can I help you?
  Mio. You have.
  Miriamne. If I were a little older—if I
 • knew
the things to say! I can only put out my
  hands
and give you back the faith you bring to
  me
by being what you are. Because to me
you are all hope and beauty and brightness drawn

across what's black and mean!
  Mio. He'd have forgiven—
Then there's no more to say—I've groped
  long enough
through this everglades of old revenges—
  here
the road ends.—Miriamne, Miriamne,
the iron I wore so long—it's eaten through
and fallen from me. Let me have your
  arms.
They'll say we're children—Well—the
  world's made up of children.
  Miriamne. Yes.
  Mio. But it's too late for me.
  Miriamne. No.
[*She goes into his arms, and they kiss for
the first time.*]
Then we'll meet again?
  Mio. Yes.
  Miriamne. Where?
  Mio. I'll write—
or send Carr to you.
  Miriamne. You won't forget?
  Mio. Forget?
Whatever streets I walk, you'll walk them,
  too,
from now on, and whatever roof or stars
I have to house me, you shall share my
  roof
and stars and morning. I shall not forget.
  Miriamne. God keep you!
  Mio. And keep you. And this to re-
  member!
if I should die, Miriamne, this half-hour
is our eternity. I came here seeking
light in darkness, running from the dawn,
and stumbled on a morning.
[*One of the* Young Men in Serge *strolls
in casually from the right, looks up
and down without expression, then,
seemingly having forgotten something, retraces his steps and goes out.
Esdras comes in slowly from the left.
He has lost his hat, and his face is*]

bleeding from a slight cut on the temple. He stands abjectly near the tenement.]

MIRIAMNE. Father—what is it? [*She goes toward* ESDRAS.]

ESDRAS. Let me alone. [*He goes nearer to* MIO.]
He wouldn't let me pass.
The street's so icy up along the bridge
I had to crawl on my knees—he kicked me back
three times—and then he held me there—I swear
what I could do I did! I swear to you
I'd save you if I could.

MIO. What makes you think
that I need saving?

ESDRAS. Child, save yourself if you can!
He's waiting for you.

MIO. Well, we knew that before.

ESDRAS. He won't wait much longer.
He'll come here—
he told me so. Those damned six months of his—
he wants them all—and you're to die—you'd spread
his guilt—I had to listen to it—

MIO. Wait—
[*He walks forward and looks casually to the right, then returns.*]
There must be some way up through the house and out
across the roof—

ESDRAS. He's watching that. But come in—
and let me look.—

MIO. I'll stay here, thanks. Once in
and I'm a rat in a deadfall—I'll stay here—
look for me if you don't mind.

ESDRAS. Then watch for me—
I'll be on the roof—
[*He goes in hurriedly.*]

MIO [*looking up*]. Now all you silent powers

that make the sleet and dark, and never yet
have spoken, give us a sign, let the throw be ours
this once, on this longest night, when the winter sets
his foot on the threshold leading up to spring
and enters with remembered cold—let fall
some mercy with the rain. We are two lovers
here in your night, and we wish to live.

MIRIAMNE. Oh, Mio—
if you pray that way, nothing good will come!
You're bitter, Mio.

MIO. How many floors has this building?

MIRIAMNE. Five or six. It's not as high as the bridge.

MIO. No, I thought not. How many pomegranate seeds
did you eat, Persephone?

MIRIAMNE. Oh, darling, darling,
if you die, don't die alone.

MIO. I'm afraid I'm damned
to hell, and you're not damned at all. Good God,
how long he takes to climb!

MIRIAMNE. The stairs are steep.
[*A slight pause.*]

MIO. I'll follow him.

MIRIAMNE. He's there—at the window—now.
He waves you to go back, not to go in.
Mio, see, that path between the rocks—
they're not watching that—they're out at the river—
I can see them there—they can't watch both—
it leads to a street above.

MIO. I'll try it, then.
Kiss me. You'll hear. But if you never hear—

then I'm the king of hell, Persephone,
and I'll expect you.

MIRIAMNE. Oh, lover, keep safe.

MIO. Good-by.

[*He slips out quickly between the rocks.
There is a quick machine gun rat-tat.
The violin stops.* MIRIAMNE *runs toward the path.* MIO *comes back
slowly, a hand pressed under his
heart.*]

It seems you were mistaken.

MIRIAMNE. Oh, God, forgive me! [*She
puts an arm around him. He sinks to
his knees.*]

Where is it, Mio? Let me help you in!
Quick, quick,
let me help you!

MIO. I hadn't thought to choose—this—
ground—
but it will do. [*He slips down.*]

MIRIAMNE. Oh, God, forgive me!

MIO. Yes?

The king of hell was not forgiven then,
Dis is his name and Hades is his home—
and he goes alone—

MIRIAMNE. Why does he bleed so? Mio,
if you go
I shall go with you.

MIO. It's better to stay alive.
I wanted to stay alive—because of you—
I leave you that—and what he said to me
dying:
I love you, and will love you after I die.
Tomorrow, I shall still love you, as I've
loved
the stars I'll never see, and all the mornings
that might have been yours and mine. Oh,
Miriamne,
you taught me this.

MIRIAMNE. If only I'd never seen you
then you could live—

MIO. That's blasphemy—Oh, God,
there might have been some easier way
of it.

You didn't want me to die, did you,
Miriamne—?
You didn't send me away—?

MIRIAMNE. Oh, never, never—

MIO. Forgive me—kiss me—I've got
blood on your lips—
I'm sorry—it doesn't matter—I'm sorry—

[ESDRAS *and* GARTH *come out.*]

MIRIAMNE. Mio—
I'd have gone to die myself—you must
hear this, Mio,
I'd have died to help you—you must listen, sweet,
you must hear it—[*She rises.*]
I can die, too, see! You! There!
You in the shadows!—You killed him to
silence him!

[*She walks toward the path.*]

But I'm not silenced! All that he knew I
know,
and I'll tell it tonight! Tonight—
tell it and scream it
through all the streets—that Trock's a
murderer
and he hired you for this murder!
Your work's not done—
and you won't live long! Do you hear?
You're murderers, and I know who you
are!

[*The machine gun speaks again. She sinks
to her knees.* GARTH *runs to her.*]

GARTH. You little fool! [*He tries to lift
her.*]

MIRIAMNE. Don't touch me! [*She crawls
toward* MIO.]

Look, Mio! They killed me, too. Oh, you
can believe me
now, Mio. You can believe I wouldn't hurt
you,
because I'm dying! Why doesn't he answer me?
Oh, now he'll never know!

[*She sinks down, her hand over her
mouth, choking.* GARTH *kneels beside
her, then rises, shuddering. The* HOBO

comes out. LUCIA *and* PINY *look out.*]

ESDRAS. It lacked only this.

GARTH. Yes. [ESDRAS *bends over* MIRI-
AMNE, *then rises slowly.*]

Why was the bastard born? Why did he
come here?

ESDRAS. Miriamne—Miriamne—yes, and
Mio,

one breath shall call you now—forgive us
both—

forgive the ancient evil of the earth

that brought you here—

GARTH. Why must she be a fool?

ESDRAS. Well, they were wiser than you
and I. To die

when you are young and untouched, that's
beggary

to a miser of years, but the devils locked
in synod

shake and are daunted when men set their
lives

at hazard for the heart's love, and lose.
And these,

who were yet children, will weigh more
than all

a city's elders when the experiment

is reckoned up in the end. Oh, Miriamne,

and Mio—Mio, my son—know this where
you lie,

this is the glory of earth-born men and
women,

not to cringe, never to yield, but standing,

take defeat implacable and defiant,

die unsubmitting. I wish that I'd died so,

long ago; before you're old you'll wish

that you had died as they have. On this
star,

in this hard star-adventure, knowing not

what the fires mean to right and left, nor
whether

a meaning was intended or presumed,

man can stand up, and look out blind, and
say:

in all these turning lights I find no clue,

only a masterless night, and in my blood

no certain answer, yet is my mind my
own,

yet is my heart a cry toward something
dim

in distance, which is higher than I am

and makes me emperor of the endless
dark

even in seeking! What odds and ends of
life

men may live otherwise, let them live, and
then

go out, as I shall go, and you. Our part

is only to bury them. Come, take her up.

They must not lie here.

[LUCIA *and* PINY *come near to help.* ES-
DRAS *and* GARTH *stoop to carry* MIRI-
AMNE.]   CURTAIN

POLONIUS TO LAERTES

And these few precepts in thy memory
Look thou character. Give thy thoughts no tongue,
Nor any unproportion'd thought his act.
Be thou familiar, but by no means vulgar.
Those friends thou hast, and their adoption tried,
Grapple them to thy soul with hoops of steel,
But do not dull thy palm with entertainment

[125]

Of each new-hatch'd unfledged comrade. Beware
Of entrance to a quarrel; but being in,
Bear 't that the opposed may beware of thee. . . .
This above all: to thine own self be true.

F. SCOTT FITZGERALD TO HIS DAUGHTER

August 8, 1933
La Paix, Rodgers' Forge,
Towson, Maryland

Dear Pie:

I feel very strongly about you doing duty. Would you give me a little more documentation about your reading in French? I am glad you are happy—but I never believe much in happiness. I never believe in misery either. Those are things you see on the stage or the screen or the printed page, they never really happen to you in life.

All I believe in in life is the rewards for virtue (according to your talents) and the *punishments* for not fulfilling your duties, which are doubly costly. If there is such a volume in the camp library, will you ask Mrs. Tyson to let you look up a sonnet of Shakespeare's in which the line occurs *Lilies that fester smell far worse than weeds.*

Have had no thoughts today, life seems composed of getting up a *Saturday Evening Post* story. I think of you, and always pleasantly; but if you call me "Pappy" again I am going to take the White Cat out and beat his bottom *hard, six times for every time you are impertinent.* Do you react to that?

I will arrange the camp bill.

Half-wit, I will conclude. Things to worry about:

Worry about courage

Worry about cleanliness
Worry about efficiency
Worry about horsemanship . . .
 Things not to worry about:
Don't worry about popular opinion
Don't worry about dolls
Don't worry about the past
Don't worry about the future
Don't worry about growing up
Don't worry about anybody getting ahead of you
Don't worry about triumph
Don't worry about failure unless it comes through your own fault
Don't worry about mosquitoes
Don't worry about flies
Don't worry about insects in general
Don't worry about parents
Don't worry about boys
Don't worry about disappointments
Don't worry about pleasures
Don't worry about satisfactions
 Things to think about:
What am I really aiming at?
How good am I really in comparison to my contemporaries in regard to:
 (a) Scholarship
 (b) Do I really understand about people and am I able to get along with them?
 (c) Am I trying to make my body a useful instrument or am I neglecting it?

 With dearest love,

A PRAYER FOR MY DAUGHTER

by WILLIAM BUTLER YEATS

Once more the storm is howling, and half
    hid
Under this cradle-hood and coverlid
My child sleeps on. There is no obstacle
But Gregory's wood and one bare hill
Whereby the haystack- and roof-leveling
    wind,
Bred on the Atlantic, can be stayed;
And for an hour I have walked and prayed
Because of the great gloom that is in my
    mind.

I have walked and prayed for this young
    child an hour
And heard the sea-wind scream upon the
    tower,
And under the arches of the bridge, and
    scream
In the elms above the flooded stream;
Imagining in excited reverie
That the future years had come,
Dancing to a frenzied drum,
Out of the murderous innocence of the
    sea.

May she be granted beauty, and yet not
Beauty to make a stranger's eye distraught,
Or hers before a looking-glass, for such,
Being made beautiful overmuch,
Consider beauty a sufficient end,
Lose natural kindness and maybe
The heart-revealing intimacy
That chooses right, and never find a friend.

Helen being chosen found life flat and dull
And later had much trouble from a fool,
While that great Queen, that rose out of
    the spray,
Being fatherless could have her way

Yet chose a bandy-leggèd smith for man.
It's certain that fine women eat
A crazy salad with their meat
Whereby the Horn of Plenty is undone.

In courtesy I'd have her chiefly learned;
Hearts are not had as a gift but hearts are
    earned
By those that are not entirely beautiful;
Yet many, that have played the fool
For beauty's very self, has charm made
    wise,
And many a poor man that has roved,
Loved and thought himself beloved,
From a glad kindness cannot take his eyes.

May she become a flourishing hidden tree
That all her thoughts may like the linnet
    be,
And have no business but dispensing
    round
Their magnanimities of sound,
Nor but in merriment begin a chase,
Nor but in merriment a quarrel.
Oh, may she live like some green laurel
Rooted in one dear perpetual place.

My mind, because the minds that I have
    loved,
The sort of beauty that I have approved,
Prosper but little, has dried up of late,
Yet knows that to be choked with hate
May well be of all evil chances chief.
If there's no hatred in a mind
Assault and battery of the wind
Can never tear the linnet from the leaf.

An intellectual hatred is the worst,
So let her think opinions are accursed.

From W. B. Yeats, *Collected Poems*. By permission of The Macmillan Company, publishers.

Have I not seen the loveliest woman born
Out of the mouth of Plenty's horn,
Because of her opinionated mind
Barter that horn and every good
By quiet natures understood
For an old bellows full of angry wind?

Considering that, all hatred driven hence,
The soul recovers radical innocence
And learns at last that it is self-delighting,
Self-appeasing, self-affrighting,
And that its own sweet will is Heaven's
    will;

She can, though every face should scowl
And every windy quarter howl
Or every bellows burst, be happy still.

And may her bridegroom bring her to a
    house
Where all's accustomed, ceremonious;
For arrogance and hatred are the wares
Peddled in the thoroughfares.
How but in custom and in ceremony
Are innocence and beauty born?
Ceremony's a name for the rich horn,
And custom for the spreading laurel tree.

from THE PEOPLE, YES

by CARL SANDBURG

9

A father sees a son nearing manhood.
What shall he tell that son?
"Life is hard; be steel; be a rock."
And this might stand him for the storms
and serve him for humdrum and monotony
and guide him amid sudden betrayals
and tighten him for slack moments.
"Life is a soft loam; be gentle; go easy."
And this too might serve him.
Brutes have been gentled where lashes failed.
The growth of a frail flower in a path up
has sometimes shattered and split a rock.
A tough will counts. So does desire.
So does a rich soft wanting.
Without rich wanting nothing arrives.
Tell him too much money has killed men
and left them dead years before burial:
the quest of lucre beyond a few easy needs
has twisted good enough men
sometimes into dry thwarted worms.
Tell him time as a stuff can be wasted.

Tell him to be a fool every so often
and to have no shame over having been a fool
yet learning something out of every folly
hoping to repeat none of the cheap follies
thus arriving at intimate understanding
of a world numbering many fools.
Tell him to be alone often and get at himself
and above all tell himself no lies about himself
whatever the white lies and protective fronts
he may use amongst other people.
Tell him solitude is creative if he is strong
and the final decisions are made in silent rooms.
Tell him to be different from other people
if it comes natural and easy being different.
Let him have lazy days seeking his deeper motives.
Let him seek deep for where he is a born natural.
Then he may understand Shakespeare
and the Wright brothers, Pasteur, Pavlov,
Michael Faraday and free imaginations
bringing changes into a world resenting change.
He will be lonely enough
to have time for the work
he knows as his own.

ANY MAN'S ADVICE TO HIS SON

by KENNETH FEARING

If you have lost the radio beam, then guide yourself by the sun or the stars.
(By the North Star at night, and in daytime by the compass and the sun.)
Should the sky be overcast and there are neither stars nor a sun, then steer by dead
    reckoning.
If the wind and direction and speed are not known, then trust to your wits and
    your luck.

Do you follow me? Do you understand? Or is this too difficult to learn?
But you must and you will, it is important that you do,
Because there may be troubles even greater than these that I have said.

Because, remember this: Trust no man fully.
Remember: If you must shoot at another man squeeze, do not jerk the trigger.
    Otherwise you may miss and die, yourself, at the hand of some other man's son.

And remember: In all this world there is nothing so easily squandered, or once gone,
    so completely lost as life.

I tell you this because I remember you when you were small,
And because I remember all your monstrous infant boasts and lies,
And the way you smiled, and how you ran and climbed, as no one else quite did,
    and how you fell and were bruised,
And because there is no other person, anywhere on earth, who remembers these
    things as clearly as I do now.

from NOT SO WILD A DREAM

by ERIC SEVAREID

THE UNIVERSITY OF MINNESOTA sprawls over its many acres between the cities of Minneapolis and Saint Paul. It is an excellent center of learning, as mass-production institutions go, and has produced in profusion football players and poets, scientists and embalmers, vast numbers of politicians, businessmen, farmers, dentists, and writers of advertising copy. It is a miniature of American life, faithfully accommodating the taxpayers of the state in all their ideas of what their children and their civilization should grow up to be. With a flick of the wrist you can turn the index of its catalogues and locate Plato or the latest manual on disassembling the Garand rifle. It is a city in itself, which like most American cities has grown by accretion without symmetry or plan, so that the visitor wanders in a kind of architectural Wonderland, passing in a few steps from a red-brick Victorian monstrosity to a functionally sleek structure of glass and steel. Some time back it became evident that the university would continue to grow, and some kind of pattern was required. The decision was obviously in favor of a compromise between factory and academic cloister, for the dominant theme is now that of massive, warehouse-like buildings with Greek pillars attached to the front.

Students came from all the northwest states, and some came from distant nations seeking to profit by our excellence in special matters like dentistry or journalism. Regularly, once a week—on Thursday, as I remember—a noted speaker addressed thousands of students who sat with their books in their laps within the softly lighted Northrop Auditorium. Local political candidates stirred us up, and there were frequent academic or scientific conventions, but the highest pitch of general passion was generated by the Saturday afternoon football games. In my period at the school, our brawny Swedes and Poles and Germans developed a habit of winning every game, and our fame spread far and wide. These behemoths of the gridiron became national figures, and it was an honor to sit beside one of them in a class and to awaken him when the class was ended. This matter of sporting fame eventually began to get out of hand—the "downtown" sports writers seemed to have acquired as much authority over the university's policies as the regents—and I well remember the university president confessing that he prayed secretly for a football defeat.

There were a few pleasant knolls and bowers for the summertime, but the odor of automobile exhaust was likely to have predominance over that of lilacs; and in the winter students and professors alike were obliged to fortify themselves against the blasts that blew across the adjacent Mississippi by resorting to long under-wear, stocking caps, mackinaws, and ski pants. One's eyes streamed with the cold, and the powder on the faces of the girls crystallized into ragged patches in a way that the editors of *Mademoiselle* would have to politely ignore. A railroad ran along the river's edge, and the tramps who established their "jungle" there used frequently to lie in the bushes for hours, peering toward the established nooks in the hope of observing a physical manifes-tation of undergraduate romance.

It was, all in all, an excellent school for those who were not wealthy; and most of us certainly were not—the records then showed that two thirds of the men were obliged to work part time in order to pay the very reasonable charges. Most of us came with firm and serious intent, and those who did not usually drifted out after a few terms. I came, like others, in the quest for first principles. Like most, I did not possess the exceptional intuitive powers by which some men can grasp the interrelation of contemporary phe-nomena and thus construct an ordered view of society without the discipline of organized study. Like all average brains, mine required the impulse that cannot be planned—a stray book, a disturbing remark, or the challenge of a great teacher who deliberately kicks at the self-starter

with which every mental engine is pre-sumably equipped.

I was twenty and, like most of my class-mates of twenty, knew nothing. I strayed one day into a class on political first prin-ciples conducted by a young man named Benjamin Lippincott, disciple of the Greeks and of another, more articulate disciple, Harold Laski of London. Lippin-cott would survey us with darting eyes, a tinge of sardonic humor in his soft, mo-bile face. His method was new to most of us. He would throw an idea into our midst and watch us struggle with it. In the Socratic manner he would challenge and play one of us off against the other.

"What is the State?"

Somebody would grope for a definition.

"All right—if that's the State, then what is the Government?

"What is Freedom? Do you consider yourself a free man, Mr. Smith? Suppose you are very tired and lie down on the sidewalk in Nicollet Avenue. A police-man makes you get up. Has he inter-fered with your freedom? All right, the law does say so, but you didn't have a thing to do with making that law, did you? But you obey the law anyway—a law somebody made without asking whether you would agree. Does that make you a slave? And if not, why not?

"Ah, Mr. Jones, if the government can't tell a man where and how he has to work, that's freedom, is it? But suppose the man has to work in Mr. Ford's factory because there's no other job to be found and he doesn't want to starve. Is he still a free man?

"What is Equality? When everybody has an equal vote, you say? Well, now, Mr. Adams, why *should* everybody have an equal vote? Why should Mr. Ford, who employs thousands of people, who has properties all over America, have no more vote than a tramp, who has no responsibilities except to his own stomach?

"What is Anarchy? Is it the same thing as Socialism, or as Communism? Your answer, Mr. Smith, sounds as if Anarchy were more like Capitalism. Would you say this is a country of Anarchy?

"What is democracy? A republican form of government? But England does not have a republican form of government. Would you say then that England is not a democracy?"

So he would begin. At first, most of us were not only confused, but angry and resentful. Some did not come back to his classes. For those of us who stayed it was not an easy time, but it was wonderful. We were just discovering the exciting world of Ideas, the world of Theory and of Principle. Not having the capacity to work backward from phenomena and discover first principles, the only way I could ever understand my times was by going back to the political Genesis, the Greeks, and working my passage home. It was a long trip. We sailed and tacked through the Romans, the Churchmen of the Middle Ages, through Locke, Hume, Roger Williams, Jefferson, Tom Paine, Adam Smith, Rousseau, Voltaire, Burke, Hegel, Marx, Spencer, Marshall, Lenin, and Trotsky. The wide channel dividing Washington from Lincoln became understandable; we were able to pin Woodrow Wilson and Herbert Hoover to their proper points on the chart; we knew where Norman Thomas was and how he got there, and it became no trouble at all to distinguish between a Roosevelt and a Churchill or a Chamberlain. (The last two are so much alike at bottom!) Five thousand miles removed from it in space, we lived in angry intimacy with Fascism because it is a thing, first of all, of the mind. To change the metaphor, it was like learning

a foreign language after one is grown. For a long time the words and phrases beat without effect upon the brain—then suddenly one day they all drop into place; one can understand, and he can speak.

But he continues to make mistakes, sometimes very grave mistakes. We did, my very articulate college generation of political liberals. We made some frightful mistakes, and the story of that is an integral part of the story of those last, dwindling years in America between the two great wars. The new war, when it came, was for us not merely a crisis in our physical lives but an intellectual and moral purgatory.

2

Now, when I read a novel of American campus life, or see a Hollywood version with its fair maidens in lovers' lane, dreamy-eyed youths in white flannels lolling under leafy boughs or lustily singing, arms about one another's shoulders, of their school's immortal glories and their own undying loyalty—when I come across all this I am astonished and unbelieving, or I have a faint twinge of nostalgia for a beautiful something I never knew. I remember only struggle, not so much the struggle of "working my way through" as the battle, in deadly earnest, with other students of different persuasion or of no persuasion, with the university authorities, with the American society of that time. I remember emotional exhaustion, not from singing about the "dear old college" but from public debate. I remember exhilarating triumphs and the most acute bitterness of my life. A class reunion is something I have never experienced. I would know few of the members of my class. Our loyalties were not defined by such simple categories. I remember only a small group of all the classes, of various ages, some from the college of liberal arts, others from law or medicine or agriculture—the small, intense group of my friends, cohesive by political conviction and solidified by struggle.

It would be possible, no doubt, and in an accepted tradition, to write of this university period with the humorous superiority of tolerant adulthood, to regard it as a natural manifestation of the naïve idealism of youth. It would be easier, but it would be an error of judgment in considering the recent history of America, for with my college generation a new thing developed: the "student movement," long a serious political factor in China and many European countries, became for the first time a reality in American affairs. We had a definite effect upon our times.

We were in revolt. Not in the manner of many preceding academic generations, not in any bohemian, individualistic sense of hating the smugness of middle-class life and mores. We sought no escape for our personal souls in new art forms or in any new concepts of emotional or sexual freedom. Those were minor matters to us. We believed passionately in freedom for men and in the integrity of the human personality, but we sought these ends, not by changing the individual, but by changing his environment, the way society—meaning chiefly economic society—was organized. For us there was no question of seeking new geographical frontiers, as our struggling forebears had done in their revolt. Even were that physically possible, to us it would have been mere escapism. We sought neither wealth nor fame, nor did we expect security and serenity in the end. The key to life in our times, we thought, was the relationship of a man to society in general and what a man did about it. To be otherwise was to be only

half alive. We reasoned in reverse, compared with our fathers—not from ourselves to society, but from society to ourselves. We had to help change society and let private life take care of itself, and we knew that what we sought, the "good life" of the philosophers, would hardly be found in our lifetime. Nevertheless, viewing our fellows who concentrated solely on the narrow technique of their chosen professions, we had no neurotic sense of martyrdom. We did not feel sorry for ourselves; we felt sorry for the others.

If we were reformers, it was not in the old-fashioned, Lincoln Steffens sense. The reformation of local government, the putting of "honesty" into public affairs, seemed an outdated, fruitless, and inconsequential matter to us. We were concerned with the whole underlying motivation of public affairs, on national and world scales, with the forces that produced the phenomena we observed. The methods would have to be the methods of election and legislation, of large-scale organization, of mass meeting and strike and protest parade. The methods of the Christian Church in worldly matters we wrote off very early as ineffectual, and we had nothing but contempt for approaches such as that of the Oxford Movement, which would deal with dictatorship by improving the dictators and with capitalism by making capitalists better men. No one ever got our vote for a public-office holder by proving the man's personal sincerity. Hitler was sincere enough. What mattered was the force, the movement, the set of ideas the man represented.

To a degree, no doubt, we were sentimentalists, as so many liberals are. The man who labored with his hands became in our minds a more precious human entity, endowed—by us—with greater personal virtues. Had we ourselves been born among industrial workers we would have escaped this illusion. Still, this sensation showed that we had bridged a psychological gulf which the great majority of people never cross, for it is generally true, in all countries, that members of one social class are quite unable to feel personal sympathy for the pains of members of another class. This is true of capitalists toward workmen and vice versa. As our small group began to have obvious effect on the life of this enormous university, we were explained, our behavior was rationalized in various ways. To the psychologist it was a simple pattern—we suffered from hidden inferiority complexes and were trying to compensate by taking it out on a society that frightened us. This would not serve, since nearly all of us, certainly all the members of our exclusive "Jacobin Club," had won high academic laurels in the competition of our classrooms, we had athletic heroes among us, and we knew perfectly well that we could compete successfully in the professional worlds most of us were preparing to enter. If anything, we suffered from a superiority complex. To a tolerant businessman like my own father it was a simple phenomenon of growth: "If a man isn't a socialist at twenty and a conservative at forty, there's something wrong with him"—a phrase that particularly maddened me. To the conservative students of law who dabbled in politics for reasons of professional advancement, we were simply fellow-travelers of the university and downtown Communists and were really dancing on the end of their invisible wires. But we knew the Communists well enough—much better than our critics did —and understood their methods clearly; and, while we frequently worked with them, we never worked under them. We disbelieved their methods and program because we understood far more about the

peculiar nature of American society than they did. It just would not work in this country. Furthermore, with two or three exceptions it was hard to like them personally. They were—most of them—obvious examples of the inferiority complex. Either by nature or as a fetish, they were uncleanly. They were definitely antisocial in a personal sense, quite humorless, and complete bores. We did not adhere to the strict line of any party allegiance. Philosophically and in our contemplation of the economic riddle, we were socialists; in state politics, we would vote Farmer-Labor; and nationally we supported Roosevelt. We were opportunists in the sense that we would use any lawful means, however diverse, to achieve a cohesive end.

It was true that Minnesota, politically speaking, was an exceptional state. It had a long third-party tradition, antedating most of the Progressive movement next door in Wisconsin, beginning far back in Civil War times with that truly remarkable agrarian revolter and scholar, Ignatius Donnelly, who organized farmers' revolts against the railroad and milling trusts one year and lectured at Oxford and Cambridge on Shakespeare the next. One of the great personalities of American history, now buried in oblivion. In the tradition was the elder Lindbergh, who was hated by "the interests," persecuted by the St. Paul and Minneapolis press, and stoned by mobs when he attempted to speak against American entry into the First World War. The contemporary successor of these men, the inheritor of the mantle, was Floyd B. Olson, three times governor of the state, a towering, fearless, extraordinarily able man with a hard eye, a tough manner, and traces of bitterness remaining from an impoverished childhood, but a man who loved people and devoted his life to the defense of the poor. He was almost certainly America's greatest political orator of that time, not excepting Franklin Roosevelt. To his office we as students always had access. He hated the stuffed shirts of the university as much as he hated them anywhere, and he gave us public as well as private support. His conservative opponents, incapable of understanding that ideals are a reality with some men, accused him of lining his own pockets as governor. He died very young of cancer, quite penniless, just as he was about to go to the United States Senate. He was our particular hero.

Doubtless we had absorbed by propinquity some of this purely local nonconformism, but state affairs were really a secondary matter for us, merely an accessible theater in which to perform the roles we had learned in the great books and by our own analysis of economic society, then so clearly in a state of collapse all around us. We were part of a nationwide student revolt.

These were the years of the tragic Depression, produced in part by the first war and removed, as it was to happen, only by the imperatives of the next. We observed bread lines from the street car as we went to school carrying the books that described the good society. We duly listened to lectures on orthodox economics, which explained the "natural laws" of capitalist competition, which would, if not interfered with, ultimately produce the general good by permitting everyone to pursue his selfish ends unhindered. And every day the headlines spoke of riots, of millions thrown out of work, of mass migrations by the desperate. All this was happening in the richest country on earth, a country that possessed all the political rights and instruments by which free men could change their condition—and still they could not prevent this. Meanwhile the ex-

perts on orthodoxy droned away: "The mobility and immobility of labor"—"The price of labor." Labor, under the competitive conception, was merely a budgetary item, to be added and subtracted, moved around like machine tools or money capital. The whole fabrication had a dreamlike quality about it; it had no connection with the painful reality we could see out of the classroom windows.

Fellow Jacobin Sherman Dryer would raise an indignant finger. "But, sir, it wouldn't work, to do it that way. There would be revolution."

Professor Garver (co-author of *The Principles of Economics,* studied in all languages including the Scandinavian) would peer over his glasses. "We are not concerned with other forces, including the political, Mr. Dryer. We are concerned only with the basic laws of economics."

It simply made no sense to us. There were no immutable "laws"—or damned few—about it. Economics was not a "science" at all; it was fruitless to treat it as such, and to study it as a special, exclusive field. It was all mixed up with politics, with sociology, with geography and a good many other things. Clearly the "economic laws" of competition were a fantastic delusion, merely an elaborate effort to justify things as they were by the invention of supposedly unchangeable forces which men mustn't attempt to interfere with. It seemed to us as much of a hoax as the medieval scholars' explanation of kingly authority as something derived from God. The system did not work, and if it did not work in America it certainly would not work anywhere. We knew from the history books that even in the famously "prosperous" times of the Victorian era, millions in England and elsewhere labored under insecurity and the most abject conditions of life. We believed the system had worked with passable success in the United States partly because the frontiers were constantly expanding; but even in those days it had frequently collapsed, and once had been rescued by the invention of the automobile which made a basic change in our pattern of living. But the frontiers were gone, and it was senseless to rely on mere chance.

When a Republican candidate for governor spoke to the Student Forum and declared with pride: "Why, the United States has gone through *fifty-two* economic depressions!" we screamed with delight at his unintentional indictment of the system.

No, it was clear that the system contained a basic flaw which invalidated the whole thing. The matter of production, we could see, was solved. Capitalism could produce overwhelmingly; but periodically, at the height of its production, it collapsed because it provided no certain, continuing method for getting the product into the hands of the mass of people. It could not *direct* its efforts to any channel, nor switch its accumulation of capital investment toward anything except that which happened at the moment to be profitable. That might be the manufacture of "Rendezvous" perfume instead of shoes, regardless of the fact that millions needed shoes and didn't care how they smelled. And thus came periodically the drive for export markets, the sending of machinery and whole factories after consumer goods, the political control necessary to safeguard the capital investments—in other words, Imperialism as an escape from domestic crisis that the system could not solve. Then the collision of expanding and competing empires, and thus war—all wars, we thought.

At the moment crops were being plowed under, and millions suffered from malnutrition. Doctors were impoverished, and hundreds of thousands lacked proper medical care. Teachers were on the breadlines, and vast sections of the country were populated by illiterates. To us, it was all a mess. We refused to accept it as inevitable, untouchable. Men were *not,* regardless of all the determinists, the helpless victims of uncontrollable forces. We did not live in an age of superstition, worshipping the mysteries. Men could take hold of the system and direct it. But they had to be taught to understand it, encouraged to organize, and they had to be led. We didn't like the leaders we observed in political life, and we didn't like the university authorities, who we thought were merely serving the system and not the cause of truth. (I fear we did them a little less than justice.)

The university was in a state of intellectual ferment, and we were fortunate to be students at this particular moment. The gaunt brick structures with their fake Grecian façades did not even look like ivory towers on the outside. The place was a kind of fortress for us, and periodically we sallied forth to do battle with evil. We enjoyed the privilege of having little to lose. Before we had even studied much about the function of the American labor movement, many of us had trudged around factories bearing strike placards to the mystified annoyance of the employers who couldn't see what the hell we had to do with it. In the summer of 1934 the two cities were thrown into uproar by the famous truck drivers' strike, led by the Dunne brothers, Trotskyists, who organized the strike as none had been organized before in American labor history. They had patrol cars of their own, stopping trucks entering or leaving the city, a daily strike newspaper, loud-speaker broadcasts, a commissary, and medical and ambulance services for their wounded. When they put on a funeral procession for one of their fallen, the life of the business district came to a stop on the streets.

I went to work as reporter for the Minneapolis *Star* to cover the strike. Some of the boys from the Greek fraternities on the campus joined the police and Citizens' Alliance forces with baseball bats on their shoulders, in defense of what they regarded as law and order. Some of my little crowd joined the strikers, in noncombative functions. Most of us, be it confessed, were not of the type that is willing to fight for its beliefs with brickbat or club. Fellow Jacobin Dick Scammon, son of the medical dean, was different; he was of the stuff from which true leaders are made. He was six feet four, weighed two hundred and sixty pounds, ate, drank, and sang with rabelaisian gusto, and belonged to thirteen political organizations before he could vote; he had a prodigious memory and thought so much faster and more incisively than his classmates that he could sleep through most of his courses. (Harold Laski told me in London during the blitz that he regarded Scammon as the ablest American student he ever had.) Dick could swing a club, if he were convinced there was no other resort. We were all morally courageous, but he had physical courage.

The whole city divided in its sympathies. The *Star* was reasonably fair in its running account of what became a minor civil war, but the other newspapers were not. The police chief also worked on behalf of the employers, believing with them that "order" meant tranquillity no matter what kind of order it was. So the police took measures more lawless than those of the strikers to enforce their conception of order. There were fights every day, and mostly the victims were strikers. When a prominent businessman, who had gone into the streets with a club, was himself struck down by a picketer's club, the conservative newspapers went wild. Strikers could get hurt, and so could policemen, but *this* could not happen. This extraordinary reaction disturbed me very much. Why was this man with his white collar a human reality to a big section of the community while the truck drivers in blue shirts were not? Had class allegiance got so deeply into the blood of democratic America?

The police set a deliberate trap one day. The truck drivers walked squarely into it, and fifty or more of them were shot down with buckshot. According to the *Journal* the police had been "literally fighting for their lives." The results showed that one policeman had been hurt, while the nurses at the city hospital that night demonstrated to me that nearly all the injured strikers had wounds in the backs of their heads, arms, legs, and shoulders: they had been shot while trying to run out of the ambush. Suddenly I knew, I understood deep in my bones and blood what Fascism was. I had learned the lesson in such a way that I could never forget it, and I had learned it in the precise area which is psychologically the most removed from the troubles of Europe—in the heart of the Middle West. I went home, as close to becoming a practising revolutionary as one of my noncombative instincts could ever get.

My father sat on the screened porch, staring at the newspaper headline. His face was pale. "This—this—is *revolution!*" he said to me.

"Well," I flung out recklessly, "if it is, maybe we'd better make the most of it."

To my consternation, he let the paper slip from his fingers, put his leonine head in his hands, and in a husky, uncertain voice said: "I did not ever think that one of my sons would become a revolutionary." I had never seen him so deeply shaken

[137]

since the day, years before, when Duff Aaker died. I had not understood that to some people like my father, the institutions of public order, no matter what kind of social system they reinforced, were endowed with a religious sanctity.

. . . . .

4

We tried to apply our general ideas about human society to the specific world of the university. I doubt if our families and the public ever realized the deadly earnestness of "campus politics" and the appalling amount of time and energy students put into its practice. As in most state universities the authorities encouraged a modicum of "student government" as a kind of harmless training, always making sure to retain final control themselves. Hitherto, the machinery of student elections to various organizations and the organizations themselves had been the special preserve of the permanent fraternities and sororities, whose real leaders were frequently found among senior students in the law school. A small group of these men usually controlled all nominations by the dominant "party," which was essentially conservative, never dreaming of seriously challenging the university authorities on any real issue. They parceled out the elective honors to the Greek houses as a reward for party loyalty, arbitrarily deciding the class officers, for example, and which girls would have the honors of which places in line for the "grand march" of the class proms and balls. The award of these prerogatives was cause for endless conniving, bitter animosities, and the most acute heartburning imaginable. The most successful exponent of campus politics in years was a law student named Harold

Stassen, who had been graduated two or three years previously and whose name was still a byword for political skill. But the coming of the new academic era with its intense concern over economic reform, over the issue of military preparedness and peace, edged our wooden swords with steel, and the battle seemed very real indeed. The Greek houses suddenly discovered that while they had been immersed in such matters as the class proms, other students by some diabolical and mysterious means had overreached them and were controlling the really vital instruments— the daily newspaper, the literary review, the law review, the board of publications, the student council, and so on. At the bottom of all this was the Jacobin Club, formed by ten or twelve of us who were in general revolt against things as they were. The Greek houses first learned of our organized existence when we were included with the regular fraternities in the quarterly list of academic standings, and they found us at the top of the list with a scholastic average higher than any fraternity had established in thirty years. We became suspect among the conventional conformists and very quickly feared by the university administration. We very nearly succeeded—we thought—in making student government truly that, and did succeed in abolishing compulsory military training, the most important issue of all. In the midst of this campaign, the authorities were forced to throw over all pretense of being disinterested advisors of student affairs and clamped a censorship on the daily newspaper. They sent their young stooges from the publications board down to our printery, and the editorial column of the paper carried the heading: "These editorials have been approved by the board of publications." Then followed a series of mock essays on the joys of springtime, the desirability of sprinklers that would throw water in squares instead of circles, and the like. The embarrassed president and the dean of men gave up this form of control, and tried other means, including personal intimidation; but it was too late. We had the Governor of the state on our side, he controlled some appointments to the board of regents, and sixty years of compulsory military training came to an end at that university.

This battle and many others went on, however, and the next year the editor of the paper also was a member of the Jacobin Club. I was to follow him, by right of seniority and general agreement, as editor in my senior year. But the habit of success had relaxed our vigilance. As the election to the editorship drew near, the authorities worked steadily behind us. They had found a weak spot in the wavering convictions of my fellow Jacobin, the incumbent editor. They turned his head with a great deal of flattering attention— the president would call him in for "advice" very frequently—and convinced him that it was his duty to stand again for election and for the good of the university prevent Sevareid from taking over the paper, even though this meant that the boy would have to change his life plan and enter the law school in order to remain on the campus. It was a miniature example of a recognizable political pattern: the liberal, softened by success and propinquity with the rich and powerful, renouncing his comrades in revolt "for the good of all." When we discovered that this lad was "doing a Ramsay MacDonald" on us, the fight became intense and bitter. My friends pleaded with the boy for hours at a time, warning him that his victory would turn to ashes because not only

would he lose all his friends but his sponsors would despise him as their tool. It was too late. The military officers, we found, had been working for months on two or three members of the publications board to prevent my election, and the president did something he had never stooped to before—he ordered his own faculty representative on the board to vote as he desired regardless of that gentleman's convictions. After all, he had to keep his job. In sum, the administration in its own behavior betrayed all the principles of political uprightness that it insisted we be taught in our classes. As I later learned from my friends, some of the men and women in the Greek houses, who saw their chance to begin breaking down the power of the Jacobins, deliberately spread a rumor that I needed the editor's salary because I was in trouble and "had to get married." (I was engaged to a girl in the law school, an influential nonconformist herself.) The ferocity and vindictiveness of the campaign reached unbelievable heights. In the election by the board I lost by one vote. Tammany methods, when thus applied, were unbeatable.

Loevinger, who was president of the publications board, broke the news to me in the law review office next morning, and I was stunned. I had worked three years for this position and honor, and by every rule was entitled to it. I had never hidden anything nor worked behind anyone's back. I had assumed the opposition felt as we did: that controversy was controversy, that a man's opinions were his own, and that, however anyone opposed them, he did not resort to calumny nor twist the very lives of his friendly enemies. I was the naïve liberal, still feeling somehow that truth could defeat a Hitler. Dimly I began to perceive the realities of political life. I was unable to speak and walked down the stairs. Sherman Dryer caught up with me, put his arm over my shoulder, and solemnly said: "This changes my whole philosophy."

When the news got out there was an uproar. Although I was doing my major studies in political science and not in the journalism department, all the members of the journalism faculty protested the decision, and about twenty-five of the thirty or so students on the newspaper staff signed an objection. They offered to strike, to refuse to publish, but—still clinging to the liberal's characteristic belief that the persuasion of truth would somehow suffice —I refused this drastic move. A second election was forced, but after an exhausting all-night battle, the board confirmed its vote and we gave up. I became a minor hero and martyr; my opponent was expelled from the Jacobin Club, formally censured for "conduct unbecoming a gentleman" by the journalistic honorary society of which I was president, and continued as editor, a friendless, lonely boy. The pattern of power politics was carried out to its final orthodox step: I was called into the dean's office and with much flattery informed I had been chosen for membership in the senior honor society. This corresponded to a knighthood for an influential but defeated opponent of the ruling system, which uses the glamorous apparatus of royal orders as a political weapon.

After that I buried myself in my books, earning bread and board by rising at five each morning and working in the university post office before classes, handling and distributing bundles of the newspaper which I had cherished and lost. It was many months before the pangs of bitterness left me. I had one last fling. Every four years the students staged a mock political convention, of all parties instead of one, to nominate their choice for the presidency of the United States. As comic relief, I made a nominating speech for one Bernarr MacFadden, elderly exponent of vitamins and setting-up exercises, at that time (1936) seriously trying to get the Republican nomination. I hired a bugler, a girl acrobatic dancer with a fulsome bust, and a football hero with sizable biceps, and paraded with them to the stand carrying a banner that depicted a muscular arm wielding a dumbbell. The speech began: "Fellow Americans, are we men or mice?" and argued the need for a Strong Man in the White House. I was making a sarcastic attack on the preparedness program and warned with mock rhetoric of the imminent danger of the Japanese "invading the California coast in bathing suits." The mass of students in the field house screamed their delight. Sherman, with glittering eye, made an impassioned attack on Governor Landon, "who would sacrifice the youth of the land on the altar of the balanced budget." We nominated Floyd B. Olson. The downtown political writers complimented us on our oratorical mastery and wondered in print why this level of platform brilliance was unattained in state politics.

With this speech, with this message to my fellow students, I ended my university career. It was one year before the battle of Shanghai, two years before the *Anschluss*.

PART II · HOW WRITING IS WRITTEN

ALL WRITING, as Thomas Mann has said, is autobiographical. It is the work of the whole man, the way he takes himself becoming what is called his style. The selections which follow will show how the writer takes himself and afford a number of clues to why he writes the way he does. Some of them will give aid toward better writing and some toward improvement in reading.

The writer in our time has been faced with a number of difficulties, both technical and personal. He has often felt alone, at cross currents with the flow of the times, yet in his desire to put down what he sees he has also reflected the world in which he finds himself. He has often had to invent new manners and methods to express the strange, new and intractable experiences of his world, but he has also felt the need to arrange and clarify those experiences for his readers.

The writer is here posed as the representative individual, whose values lie in honesty to his knowledge and fidelity to his beliefs. The emphasis is on a man's need to know himself and his world before he can act.

If the writing itself is an act both enjoyable and meaningful, so much the better. Some of the writers here leave no doubt that it was so with them, and they echo the attitude Byron expressed in *Childe Harold's Pilgrimage:*

> 'T is to create, and in creating live
> A being more intense that we endow
> With form our fancy, gaining as we give
> The life we image, even as I do now.
> What am I? Nothing: but not so art thou,
> Soul of my thought! with whom I traverse earth,
> Invisible but gazing, as I glow
> Mix'd with thy spirit, blended with thy birth,
> And feeling still with thee in my crush'd feelings' dearth.
> —Canto III, Stanza VI

Inspiration

From It's a long way to Heaven, *copyright, 1945, by Abner Dean, and reproduced by permission of Rinehart & Company, Inc., Publishers.*

[143]

Preface to the first edition of THE DARING YOUNG MAN ON THE FLYING TRAPEZE

by WILLIAM SAROYAN

I AM writing this preface of the first edition so that in the event that this book is issued in a second edition I will be able to write a preface to the second edition, explaining what I said in the preface to the first edition and adding a few remarks about what I have been doing in the meantime, and so on.

In the event that the book reaches a third edition, it is my plan to write a preface to the third edition, covering all that I said in the prefaces to the first and second editions, and it is my plan to go on writing prefaces for new editions of this book until I die. After that I hope there will be children and grandchildren to keep up the good work.

In this early preface, when I have no idea how many copies of the book are going to be sold, the only thing I can do is talk about how I came to write these stories.

Years ago when I was getting a thorough grammar-school education in my home town I found out that stories were something very odd that some sort of men had been turning out (for some odd reason) for hundreds of years, and that there were rules governing the writing of stories.

I immediately began to study all the classic rules, including Ring Lardner's, and in the end I discovered that the rules were wrong.

The trouble was, they had been leaving me out, and as far as I could tell I was the most important element in the matter, so I made some new rules.

I wrote rule Number One when I was eleven and had just been sent home from the fourth grade for having talked out of turn and meant it.

Do not pay any attention to the rules other people make, I wrote. They make them for their own protection, and to hell with them. (I was pretty sore that day.)

Several months later I discovered rule Number Two, which caused a sensation. At any rate, it was a sensation with me. This rule was: Forget Edgar Allan Poe and O. Henry and write the kind of stories you feel like writing. Forget everybody who ever wrote anything.

Since that time I have added four other rules and I have found this number to be enough. Sometimes I do not have to bother about rules at all, and I just sit down and write. Now and then I stand and write.

My third rule was: Learn to typewrite, so you can turn out stories as fast as Zane Grey.

It is one of my best rules.

But rules without a system are, as every good writer will tell you, utterly inadequate. You can leave out "utterly" and the sentence will mean the same thing, but it is always nicer to throw in an "utterly" whenever possible. All successful writers believe that one word by itself hasn't enough meaning and that it is best to emphasize the meaning of one word with the help of another. Some writers will go so far as to help an innocent word with as many as four and five other words, and at times they will kill an innocent word by charity and it will take years and years for some ignorant writer who doesn't know adjectives at all to resurrect the word that was killed by kindness.

Anyway, these stories are the result of a method of composition.

I call it the Festival or Fascist method of composition, and it works this way:

Someone who isn't a writer begins to want to be a writer and he keeps on wantting to be one for ten years, and by that time he has convinced all his relatives and friends and even himself that he *is* a writer, but he hasn't written a thing and he is no longer a boy, so he is getting worried. All he needs now is a system. Some authorities claim there are as many as fifteen systems, but actually there are only two: (1) you can decide to write like Anatole France or Alexandre Dumas or somebody else, or (2) you can decide to forget that you are a writer at all and you can decide to sit down at your typewriter and put words on paper, one at a time, in the best fashion you know how—which brings me to the matter of style.

The matter of style is one that always excites controversy, but to me it is as simple as A B C, if not simpler.

A writer can have, ultimately, one of two styles: he can write in a manner that implies that death in inevitable, or he can write in a manner that implies that death is *not* inevitable. Every style ever employed by a writer has been influenced by one or another of these attitudes toward death.

If you write as if you believe that ultimately you and everyone else alive will be dead, there is a chance that you will write in a pretty earnest style. Otherwise you are apt to be either pompous or soft. On the other hand, in order not to be a fool, you must believe that as much as death is inevitable life is inevitable. That is, the earth is inevitable, and people and other living things on it are inevitable, but that no man can remain on the earth very long. You do not have to be melodramatically tragic about this. As a matter of fact, you can be as amusing as you like about it. It is really one of the basically humorous things, and it has all sorts of possibilities for laughter. If you will remember that living people are as good as dead, you will be able to perceive much that is very funny in their conduct that you perhaps might never have thought of perceiving if you did not believe that they were as good as dead.

The most solid advice, though, for a writer is this, I think: Try to learn to breathe deeply, really to taste food when you eat, and when you sleep, really to sleep. Try as much as possible to be wholly alive, with all your might, and when you laugh, laugh like hell, and when you get angry, get good and angry. Try to be alive. You will be dead soon enough.

WRITING PROSE

by W. Somerset Maugham

I HAVE NEVER had more than two English lessons in my life, for though I wrote essays at school, I do not remember that I ever received any instruction on how to put sentences together. The two lessons I have had were given me so late in life that I am afraid I cannot hope greatly to profit by them. The first was only a few years ago. I was spending some weeks in London and had engaged as temporary secretary a young woman. She was shy, rather pretty, and absorbed in a love affair with a married man. I had written a book called *Cakes and Ale,* and, the typescript arriving one Saturday morning, I asked her if she would be good enough to take it home and correct it over the weekend. I meant her only to make a note of mistakes in spelling that the typist might have made and point out errors occasioned by a handwriting that is not always easy to decipher. But she was a conscientious young·person and she took me more literally than I intended. When she brought back the typescript on Monday morning it was accompanied by four foolscap sheets of corrections. I must confess that at the first glance I was a trifle vexed; but then I thought that it would be silly of me not to profit, if I could, by the trouble she had taken and so sat me down to examine them. I suppose the young woman had taken a course at a secretarial college and she had gone through my novel in the same methodical way as her masters had gone through her essays. The remarks that filled the four neat pages of foolscap were incisive and severe. I could not but surmise that the professor of English at the secretarial college did not mince matters. He took a marked line, there could be no doubt about that; and he did not allow that there might be two opinions about anything. His apt pupil would have nothing to do with a preposition at the end of a sentence. A mark of exclamation betokened her disapproval of a colloquial phrase. She had a feeling that you must not use the same word twice on a page and she was ready every time with a synonym to put in its place. If I had indulged myself in the luxury of a sentence of ten lines, she wrote: "Clarify this. Better break

it up into two or more periods." When I had availed myself of the pleasant pause that is indicated by a semicolon, she noted: "A full stop"; and if I had ventured upon a colon she remarked stingingly: "Obsolete." But the harshest stroke of all was her comment on what I thought was rather a good joke: "Are you sure of your facts?" Taking it all in all I am bound to conclude that the professor at her college would not have given me very high marks.

The second lesson I had was given me by a don, both intelligent and charming, who happened to be staying with me when I was myself correcting the typescript of another book. He was good enough to offer to read it. I hesitated, because I knew that he judged from a standpoint of excellence that is hard to attain; and though I was aware that he had a profound knowledge of Elizabethan literature, his inordinate admiration for *Esther Waters* made me doubtful of his discernment in the productions of our own day: no one could attach so great a value to that work who had an intimate knowledge of the French novel during the nineteenth century. But I was anxious to make my book as good as I could and I hoped to benefit by his criticisms. They were in point of fact lenient. They interested me peculiarly because I inferred that this was the way in which he dealt with the compositions of undergraduates. My don had, I think, a natural gift for language, which it has been his business to cultivate; his taste appeared to me faultless. I was much struck by his insistence on the force of individual words. He liked the stronger word rather than the euphonious. To give an example, I had written that a statue would be placed in a certain square and he suggested that I should write: the statue will stand. I had not done that because my ear was offended by the alliteration. I noticed also that he had a feeling that words should be used not only to balance a sentence but to balance an idea. This is sound, for an idea may lose its effect if it is delivered abruptly; but it is a matter of delicacy, since it may well lead to verbiage. Here a knowledge of stage dialogue should help. An actor will sometimes say to an author: "Couldn't you give me a word or two more in this speech? It seems to take away all the point of my line if I have nothing else to say." As I listened to my don's remarks I could not but think how much better I should write now if in my youth I had had the advantage of such sensible, broadminded and kindly advice.

As it is, I have had to teach myself. I have looked at the stories I wrote when I was very young in order to discover what natural aptitude I had, my original stock-in-trade, before I developed it by taking thought. The manner had a superciliousness that perhaps my years excused and an irascibility that was a defect of nature; but I am speaking now only of the way in which I expressed myself. It seems to me that I had a natural lucidity and a knack for writing easy dialogue.

When Henry Arthur Jones, then a well-known playwright, read my first novel, he told a friend that in due course I should be one of the most successful dramatists of the day. I suppose he saw in it directness and an effective way of presenting a scene that suggested a sense of the theater. My language was commonplace, my vocabulary limited, my grammar shaky, and my phrases hackneyed. But to write was an instinct that seemed as natural to me as to breathe, and I did not stop to consider if I wrote well or badly. It was not till some years later that it dawned upon me that it was a delicate art that must be painfully acquired. The discovery was forced upon me by the difficulty I found in getting my meaning down on paper. I wrote dialogue fluently, but when it came to a page of description I found myself entangled in all sorts of quandaries. I would struggle for a couple of hours over two or three sentences that I could in no way manage to straighten out. I made up my mind to teach myself how to write. Unfortunately I had no one to help me. I made many mistakes. If I had had someone to guide me like the charming don of whom I spoke just now, I might have been saved much time. Such a one might have told me that such gifts as I had lay in one direction and that they must be cultivated in that direction; it was useless to try to do something for which I had no aptitude. But at that time a florid prose was admired. Richness of texture was sought by means of a jeweled phrase and sentences stiff with exotic epithets; the ideal was a brocade so heavy with gold that it stood up by itself. The intelligent young read Walter Pater with enthusiasm. My common sense suggested to me that it was anemic stuff; behind those elaborate, gracious periods I was conscious of a tired, wan personality. I was young, lusty, and energetic; I wanted fresh air, action, violence, and I found it hard to breathe that dead, heavily scented atmosphere and sit in those hushed rooms in which it was indecorous to speak above a whisper. But I would not listen to my common sense. I persuaded myself that this was the height of culture and turned a scornful shoulder on the outside world where men shouted and swore, played the fool, wenched and got drunk. I read *Intentions* and *The Picture of Dorian Gray*. I was intoxicated by the color and rareness of the fantastic words that thickly stud the pages of *Salome*. Shocked by the poverty of my own vocabulary, I went to the British Museum with pencil and paper and noted down the names of curious jewels, the Byzantine hues of old enamels, the sensual feel of textiles, and made elaborate sentences to bring them in. Fortunately I could never find an opportunity to use them and they lie there yet in an old notebook ready for anyone who has a mind to write nonsense. It was generally thought then that the Authorized Version of the Bible was the greatest piece of prose that the English language has produced. I read it diligently, especially the Song of Solomon, jotting down for future use turns of phrase that struck me and making lists of unusual or beautiful words. I studied Jeremy Taylor's *Holy Dying*. In order to assimilate his style I copied out passages and then tried to write them down from memory.

The first fruit of this labor was a little book about Andalusia called *The Land of the Blessed Virgin*. I had occasion to read parts of it the other day. I know Andalusia a great deal better now than I knew it then, and I have changed my mind about a good many things of which I wrote. Since it has continued in America to have a small sale, it occurred to me that it might be worth while to revise it. I soon saw that this was impossible. The book was written by someone I have completely forgotten. It bored me to distraction. But what I am concerned with is the prose, for it was as an exercise in style that I wrote it. It is wistful, allusive, and elaborate. It has neither ease nor spontaneity. It smells of hothouse plants and Sunday dinner like the air in the greenhouse that leads out of the dining-room of a big house in Bayswater. There are a great many melodious adjectives. The vocabulary is sentimental. It does not remind one of an Italian brocade, with its rich pattern of gold, but of a curtain material designed by Burne-Jones and reproduced by Morris.

I do not know whether it was a subconscious feeling that this sort of writing was contrary to my bent or a naturally methodical cast of mind that led me then to turn my attention to the writers of the Augustan Period. The prose of Swift enchanted me. I made up my mind that this was the perfect way to write and I started to work on him in the same way as I had done with Jeremy Taylor. I chose *The Tale of a Tub*. It is said that when the Dean re-read it in his old age he cried: "What genius I had then!" To my mind his genius was better shown in other works. It is a tiresome allegory and the irony is facile. But the style is admirable. I cannot imagine that English can be better written. Here are no flowery periods, fantastic turns of phrase or high-flown images. It is a civilized prose, natural, discreet, and pointed. There is no attempt to surprise by an extravagant vocabulary. It looks as though Swift made do with the first word that came to hand, but since he had an acute and logical brain it was always the right one, and he put it in the right place. The strength and balance of his sentences are due to an exquisite taste. As I had done before I copied passages and then tried to write them out again from memory. I tried altering words or the order in which they were set. I found that the only possible words were those Swift had used and that the order in which he had placed them was the only possible order. It is an impeccable prose.

But perfection has one grave defect: it is apt to be dull. Swift's prose is like a French canal, bordered with poplars, that runs through a gracious and undulating country. Its tranquil charm fills you with satisfaction, but it neither excites the emotions nor stimulates the imagination. You go on and on and presently you are a trifle bored. So, much as you may admire Swift's wonderful lucidity, his terseness, his naturalness, his lack of affectation, you find your attention wandering after a while unless his matter peculiarly interests you. I think if I had my time over again I would give to the prose of Dryden the close study I gave to that of Swift. I did not come across it till I had lost the inclination to take so much pains. The prose of Dryden is delicious. It has not the perfection of Swift nor the easy elegance of Addison, but it has a springtime gaiety, a conversational ease, a blithe spontaneousness that are enchanting. Dryden was a very good poet, but it is not the general opinion that he had a lyrical quality; it is strange that it is just this that sings in his softly sparkling prose. Prose had never been written in England like that before; it has seldom been written like that since. Dryden flourished at a happy moment. He had in his bones the sonorous periods and the baroque massiveness of Jacobean language and under the influence of the nimble and well-bred felicity that he learnt from the French he turned it into an instrument that was fit not only for solemn themes but also to express the light thought of the passing moment. He was the first of the rococo artists. If Swift reminds you of a French canal Dryden recalls an English river winding its cheerful way round hills, through quietly busy towns and by nestling villages, pausing now in a noble reach and then running powerfully through a woodland country. It is alive, varied, windswept; and it has the pleasant open-air smell of England.

The work I did was certainly very good for me. I began to write better; I did not write well. I wrote stiffly and self-con-

sciously. I tried to get a pattern into my sentences, but did not see that the pattern was evident. I took care how I placed my words, but did not reflect that an order that was natural at the beginning of the eighteenth century was most unnatural at the beginning of ours. My attempt to write in the manner of Swift made it impossible for me to achieve the effect of inevitable rightness that was just what I so much admired in him. I then wrote a number of plays and ceased to occupy myself with anything but dialogue. It was not till five years had passed that I set out again to write a novel. By then I no longer had any ambition to be a stylist; I put aside all thought of fine writing. I wanted to write without any frills of language, in as bare and unaffected a manner as I could. I had so much to say that I could afford to waste no words. I wanted merely to set down the facts. I began with the impossible aim of using no adjectives at all. I thought that if you could find the exact term a qualifying epithet could be dispensed with. As I saw it in my mind's eye my book would have the appearance of an immensely long telegram in which for economy's sake you had left out every word that was not necessary to make the sense clear. I have not read it since I corrected the proofs and do not know how near I came to doing what I tried. My impression is that it is written at least more naturally than anything I had written before; but I am sure that it is often slipshod and I daresay there are in it a good many mistakes in grammar.

Since then I have written many other books; and though ceasing my methodical study of the old masters (for though the spirit is willing, the flesh is weak), I have continued with increasing assiduity to try to write better. I discovered my limitations and it seemed to me that the only sensible thing was to aim at what excellence I could within them. I knew that I had no lyrical quality. I had a small vocabulary and no efforts that I could make to enlarge it much availed me. I had little gift of metaphor; the original and striking simile seldom occurred to me. Poetic flights and the great imaginative sweep were beyond my powers. I could admire them in others as I could admire their far-fetched tropes and the unusual but suggestive language in which they clothed their thoughts, but my own invention never presented me with such embellishments; and I was tired of trying to do what did not come easily to me. On the other hand, I had an acute power of observation and it seemed to me that I could see a great many things that other people missed. I could put down in clear terms what I saw. I had a logical sense, and if no great feeling for the richness and strangeness of words, at all events a lively appreciation of their sound. I knew that I should never write as well as I could wish, but I thought with pains I could arrive at writing as well as my natural defects allowed. On taking thought it seemed to me that I must aim at lucidity, simplicity and euphony. I have put these three qualities in the order of the importance I assigned to them.

I have never had much patience with the writers who claim from the reader an effort to understand their meaning. You have only to go to the great philosophers to see that it is possible to express with lucidity the most subtle reflections. You may find it difficult to understand the thought of Hume, and if you have no philosophical training its implications will doubtless escape you; but no one with any education at all can fail to understand exactly what the meaning of each sentence is. Few people have written English with more grace than Berkeley. There are two sorts of obscurity that you find in writers. One is due to negligence and the other to willfulness. People often write obscurely because they have never taken the trouble to learn to write clearly. This sort of obscurity you find too often in modern philosophers, in men of science, and even in literary critics. Here it is indeed strange. You would have thought that men who passed their lives in the study of the great masters of literature would be sufficiently sensitive to the beauty of language to write if not beautifully at least with perspicuity. Yet you will find in their works sentence after sentence that you must read twice to discover the sense. Often you can only guess at it, for the writers have evidently not said what they intended.

Another cause of obscurity is that the writer is himself not quite sure of his meaning. He has a vague impression of what he wants to say, but has not, either from lack of mental power or from laziness, exactly formulated it in his mind and it is natural enough that he should not find a precise expression for a confused idea. This is due largely to the fact that many writers think, not before, but as they write. The pen originates the thought. The disadvantage of this, and indeed it is a danger against which the author must be always on his guard, is that there is a sort of magic in the written word. The idea acquires substance by taking on a visible nature, and then stands in the way of its own clarification. But this sort of obscurity merges very easily into the willful. Some writers who do not think clearly are inclined to suppose that their thoughts have a significance greater than at first sight appears. It is flattering to believe that they are too profound to be expressed so clearly that all who run may read, and very naturally it does not occur to such writers that the fault is with their own minds which have not the faculty of precise reflection. Here again the magic of the written word obtains. It is very easy to persuade oneself that a phrase that one does not quite understand may mean a great deal more than one realizes. From this there is only a little way to go to fall into the habit of setting down one's impressions in all their original vagueness. Fools can always be found to discover a hidden sense in them. There is another form of willful obscurity that masquerades as aristocratic exclusiveness. The author wraps his meaning in mystery so that the vulgar shall not participate in it. His soul is a secret garden into which the elect may penetrate only after overcoming a number of perilous obstacles. But this kind of obscurity is not only pretentious; it is shortsighted. For time plays it an odd trick. If the sense is meager, time reduces it to a meaningless verbiage that no one thinks of reading. This is the fate that has befallen the lucubrations of those French writers who were seduced by the example of Guillaume Apollinaire. But occasionally it throws a sharp cold light on what had seemed profound and thus discloses the fact that these contortions of language disguised very commonplace notions. There are few of Mallarmé's poems now that are not clear; one cannot fail to notice that his thought singularly lacked originality. Some of his phrases were beautiful; the materials of his verse were the poetic platitudes of his day.

Simplicity is not such an obvious merit as lucidity. I have aimed at it because I have no gift for richness. Within limits I admire richness in others, though I find it difficult to digest in quantity. I can read one page of Ruskin with delight, but twenty only with weariness. The rolling period, the stately epithet, the noun rich in poetic associations, the subordinate clauses that give the sentence weight and magnificence, the grandeur like that of wave following wave in the open sea; there is no doubt that in all this there is something inspiring. Words thus strung together fall on the ear like music. The appeal is sensuous rather than intellectual, and the beauty of the sound leads you easily to conclude that you need not bother about the meaning. But words are tyrannical things, they exist for their meanings, and if you will not pay attention to these, you cannot pay attention at all. Your mind wanders. This kind of writing demands a subject that will suit it. It is surely out of place to write in the grand style of inconsiderable things. No one wrote in this manner with greater success than Sir Thomas Browne, but even he did not always escape this pitfall. In the last chapter of *Hydriotaphia* the matter, which is the destiny of man, wonderfully fits the baroque splendor of the language, and here the Norwich doctor produced a piece of prose that has never been surpassed in our literature; but when he describes the finding of his urns in the same splendid manner the effect (at least to my taste) is less happy.

But if richness needs gifts with which everyone is not endowed, simplicity by no means comes by nature. To achieve it needs rigid discipline. So far as I know ours is the only language in which it has been found necessary to give a name to the piece of prose which is described as the purple patch; it would not have been necessary to do so unless it were characteristic. English prose is elaborate rather than simple. It was not always so. Nothing could be more racy, straightforward and alive than the prose of Shakespeare; but it must be remembered that this was dialogue written to be spoken. We do not know how he would have written if like Corneille he had composed prefaces to his plays. It may be that they would have been as euphuistic as the letters of Queen Elizabeth. But earlier prose, the prose of Sir Thomas More, for instance, is neither ponderous, flowery nor oratorical. It smacks of the English soil. To my mind King James's Bible has been a very harmful influence on English prose. I am not so stupid as to deny its great beauty. It is majestical. But the Bible is an oriental book. Its alien imagery has nothing to do with us. Those hyperboles, those luscious metaphors, are foreign to our genius. I cannot but think that not the least of the misfortunes that the Secession from Rome brought upon the spiritual life of our country is that this work for so long a period became the daily, and with many the only, reading of our people. Those rhythms, that powerful vocabulary, that grandiloquence, became part and parcel of the national sensibility. The plain, honest English speech was overwhelmed with ornament. Blunt Englishmen twisted their tongues to speak like Hebrew prophets. There was evidently something in the English temper to which this was congenial, perhaps a native lack of precision in thought, perhaps a naive delight in fine words for their own sake, an innate eccentricity and love of embroidery, I do not know; but the fact remains that ever since, English prose has had to struggle against the tendency to luxuriance. When from time to time the spirit of the language has reasserted itself, as it did with Dryden and the writers of Queen Anne,

it was only to be submerged once more by the pompousities of Gibbon and Dr. Johnson. When English prose recovered simplicity with Hazlitt, the Shelley of the letters, and Charles Lamb at his best, it lost it again with De Quincey, Carlyle, Meredith, and Walter Pater. It is obvious that the grand style is more striking than the plain. Indeed many people think that a style that does not attract notice is not style. They will admire Walter Pater's, but will read an essay by Matthew Arnold without giving a moment's attention to the elegance, distinction and sobriety with which he set down what he had to say.

The dictum that the style is the man is well known. It is one of those aphorisms that say too much to mean a great deal. Where is the man in Goethe, in his bird-like lyrics or in his clumsy prose? And Hazlitt? But I suppose that if a man has a confused mind he will write in a confused way, if his temper is capricious his prose will be fantastical, and if he has a quick, darting intelligence that is reminded by the matter in hand of a hundred things, he will, unless he has great self-control, load his pages with metaphor and simile. There is a great difference between the magniloquence of the Jacobean writers, who were intoxicated with the new wealth that had lately been brought into the language, and the turgidity of Gibbon and Dr. Johnson, who were the victims of bad theories. I can read every word that Dr. Johnson wrote with delight, for he had good sense, charm and wit. No one could have written better if he had not willfully set himself to write in the grand style. He knew good English when he saw it. No critic has praised Dryden's prose more aptly. He said of him that he appeared to have no art other than that of expressing with clearness what he thought with vigor. And one of his *Lives* he finished with the words: "Whoever wishes to attain an English style, familiar but not coarse, and elegant but not ostentatious, must give his days and nights to the volumes of Addison." But when he himself sat down to write, it was with a very different aim. He mistook the orotund for the dignified. He had not the good breeding to see that simplicity and naturalness are the truest marks of distinction.

Whether you ascribe importance to euphony, the last of the three characteristics that I mentioned, must depend on the sensitiveness of your ear. A great many readers, and many admirable writers, are devoid of this quality. Poets as we know have always made a great use of alliteration. They are persuaded that the repetition of a sound gives an effect of beauty. I do not think it does so in prose. It seems to me that in prose alliteration should be used only for a special reason; when used by accident it falls on the ear very disagreeably. But its accidental use is so common that one can only suppose that the sound of it is not universally offensive. Many writers without distress will put two rhyming words together, join a monstrous long adjective to a monstrous long noun, or between the end of one word and the beginning of another have a conjunction of consonants that almost breaks your jaw. These are trivial and obvious instances. I mention them only to prove that if careful writers can do such things, it is only because they have no ear. Words have weight, sound, and appearance; it is only by considering these that you can write a sentence that is good to look at and good to listen to.

If you could write lucidly, simply, euphoniously and yet with liveliness you would write perfectly: you would write like Voltaire. And yet we know how fatal the pursuit of liveliness may be: it may result in the tiresome acrobatics of Meredith. Macaulay and Carlyle were in their different ways arresting; but at the heavy cost of naturalness. Their flashy effects distract the mind. They destroy their persuasiveness; you would not believe a man was very intent on plowing a furrow if he carried a hoop with him and jumped through it at every other step. A good style should show no sign of effort. What is written should seem a happy accident. I think no one in France now writes more admirably than Colette, and such is the ease of her expression that you cannot bring yourself to believe that she takes any trouble over it. I am told that there are pianists who have a natural technique so that they can play in a manner that most executants can achieve only as the result of unremitting toil, and I am willing to believe that there are writers who are equally fortunate. Among them I was much inclined to place Colette. I asked her. I was exceedingly surprised to hear that she wrote everything over and over again. She told me that she would often spend a whole morning working upon a single page. But it does not matter how one gets the effect of ease. For my part, if I get it at all, it is only by strenuous effort. Nature seldom provides me with the word, the turn of phrase, that is appropriate without being far-fetched or commonplace.

I have read that Anatole France tried to use only the constructions and the vocabulary of the writers of the seventeenth century whom he so greatly admired. I do not know if it is true. If so, it may explain why there is some lack of vitality in his beautiful and simple French. But simplicity is false when you do not say a thing that you should say because you cannot say it in a certain way. One should write in the manner of one's period. The language is alive and constantly changing; to try to write like the authors of a distant past can only give rise to artificiality. I should not hesitate to use the common phrases of the day, knowing that their vogue was ephemeral, or slang, though aware that in ten years it might be incomprehensible, if they gave vividness and actuality. If the style has a classical form it can support the discreet use of a phraseology that has only a local and temporary aptness. I would sooner a writer were vulgar than mincing; for life is vulgar, and it is life he seeks.

I think that we English authors have much to learn from our fellow authors in America. For American writing has escaped the tyranny of King James's Bible and American writers have been less affected by the old masters whose mode of writing is part of our culture. They have formed their style, unconsciously perhaps, more directly from the living speech that surrounds them; and at its best it has a directness, a vitality, and a drive that give our more urbane manner an air of languor. It has been an advantage to American writers, many of whom at one time or another have been reporters, that their journalism has been written in a more trenchant, nervous, graphic English than ours. For we read the newspaper as our ancestors read the Bible. Not without profit either; for the newspaper, especially when it is of the popular sort, offers us a part of experience that we writers cannot afford to miss. It is raw material straight from the knacker's yard, and we are stupid if we turn up our noses because it smells of blood and sweat. We cannot,

however willingly we would, escape the influence of this workaday prose. But the journalism of a period has very much the same style; it might all have been written by the same hand; it is impersonal. It is well to counteract its effect by reading of another kind. One can do this only by keeping constantly in touch with the writing of an age not too remote from one's own. So can one have a standard by which to test one's own style and an ideal which in one's modern way one can aim at. For my part the two writers I have found most useful to study for this purpose are Hazlitt and Cardinal Newman. I would try to imitate neither. Hazlitt can be unduly rhetorical; and sometimes his decoration is as fussy as Victorian Gothic. Newman can be a trifle flowery. But at their best both are admirable. Time has little touched their style; it is almost contemporary. Hazlitt is vivid, bracing, and energetic; he has strength and liveliness. You feel the man in his phrases, not the mean, querulous, disagreeable man that he appeared to the world that knew him, but the man within of his own ideal vision. (And the man within us is as true in reality as the man, pitiful and halting, of our outward seeming.) Newman had an exquisite grace, music, playful sometimes and sometimes grave, a woodland beauty of phrase, dignity and mellowness. Both wrote with extreme lucidity. Neither is quite as simple as the purest taste demands. Here I think Matthew Arnold excels them. Both had a wonderful balance of phrase and both knew how to write sentences pleasing to the eye. Both had an ear of extreme sensitiveness.

If anyone could combine their merits in the manner of writing of the present day, he would write as well as it is possible for anyone to write.

Nigger of the Narcissus

Language most shows a man: Speak, that I may see thee. It springs out of the most retired and inmost parts of us, and is the image of the parent of it, the mind. No glass renders a man's form or likeness so true as his speech. Nay, it is likened to a man; and as we consider feature and composition in a man, so words in language; in the greatness, aptness, sound, structure, and harmony of it.

—Ben Jonson in *Timber, or Discoveries Made Upon Men and Matter*

Preface to NIGGER OF THE NARCISSUS

by Joseph Conrad

A WORK that aspires, however humbly, to the condition of art should carry its justification in every line. And art itself may be defined as a single-minded attempt to render the highest kind of justice to the visible universe, by bringing to light the truth, manifold and one, underlying its every aspect. It is an attempt to find in its forms, in its colors, in its light, in its shadows, in the aspects of matter and in the facts of life what of each is fundamental, what is enduring and essential—their one illuminating and convincing quality —the very truth of their existence. The artist, then, like the thinker or the scientist, seeks the truth and makes his appeal. Impressed by the aspect of the world the thinker plunges into ideas, the scientist into facts—whence, presently, emerging they make their appeal to those qualities of our being that fit us best for the hazardous enterprise of living. They speak authoritatively to our common-sense, to our intelligence, to our desire of peace or to our desire of unrest; not seldom to our

prejudices, sometimes to our fears, often to our egoism—but always to our credulity. And their words are heard with reverence, for their concern is with weighty matters: with the cultivation of our minds and the proper care of our bodies, with the attainment of our ambitions, with the perfection of the means and the glorification of our precious aims.

It is otherwise with the artist.

Confronted by the same enigmatical spectacle the artist descends within himself, and in that lonely region of stress and strife, if he be deserving and fortunate, he finds the terms of his appeal. His appeal is made to our less obvious capacities: to that part of our nature which, because of the warlike conditions of existence, is necessarily kept out of sight within the more resisting and hard qualities—like the vulnerable body within a steel armor. His appeal is less loud, more profound, less distinct, more stirring—and sooner forgotten. Yet its effect endures forever. The changing wisdom of successive generations discards ideas, questions facts, demolishes theories. But the artist appeals to that part of our being which is not dependent on wisdom; to that in us which is a gift and not an acquisition—and, therefore, more permanently enduring. He speaks to our capacity for delight and wonder, to the sense of mystery surrounding our lives; to our sense of pity, and beauty, and pain; to the latent feeling of fellowship with all creation—and to the subtle but invincible conviction of solidarity that knits together the loneliness of innumerable hearts, to the solidarity in dreams, in joy, in sorrow, in aspirations, in illusions, in hope, in fear, which binds men to each other, which binds together all humanity—the dead to the living and the living to the unborn.

It is only some such train of thought, or rather of feeling, that can in a measure explain the aim of the attempt, made in the tale which follows, to present an unrestful episode in the obscure lives of a few individuals out of all the disregarded multitude of the bewildered, the simple and the voiceless. For, if any part of truth dwells in the belief confessed above, it becomes evident that there is not a place of splendor or a dark corner of the earth that does not deserve, if only a passing glance of wonder and pity. The motive then, may be held to justify the matter of the work; but this preface, which is simply an avowal of endeavor, cannot end here —for the avowal is not yet complete.

Fiction—if it at all aspires to be art— appeals to temperament. And in truth it must be, like painting, like music, like all art, the appeal of one temperament to all the other innumerable temperaments whose subtle and resistless power endows passing events with their true meaning, and creates the moral, the emotional atmosphere of the place and time. Such an appeal to be effective must be an impression conveyed through the senses; and, in fact, it cannot be made in any other way, because temperament, whether individual or collective, is not amenable to persuasion. All art, therefore, appeals primarily to the senses, and the artistic aim when expressing itself in written words must also make its appeal through the senses, if its high desire is to reach the secret spring of responsive emotions. It must strenuously aspire to the plasticity of sculpture, to the color of painting, and to the magic suggestiveness of music—which is the art of arts. And it is only through complete, unswerving devotion to the perfect blending of form and substance; it is only through an unremitting never-discouraged care for the shape and ring of sentences that an approach can be made to plasticity, to color, and that the light of magic suggestiveness may be brought to play for an evanescent instant over the commonplace surface of words: of the old, old words, worn thin, defaced by ages of careless usage.

The sincere endeavor to accomplish that creative task, to go as far on that road as his strength will carry him, to go undeterred by faltering, weariness or reproach, is the only valid justification for the worker in prose. And if his conscience is clear, his answer to those who in the fullness of a wisdom which looks for immediate profit, demand specifically to be edified, consoled, amused; who demand to be promptly improved, or encouraged, or frightened, or shocked, or charmed, must run thus:—My task which I am trying to achieve is, by the power of the written word to make you hear, to make you feel —it is, before all, to make you *see*. That —and no more, and it is everything. If I succeed, you shall find there, according to your deserts: encouragement, consolation, fear, charm—all you demand—and, perhaps, also that glimpse of truth for which you have forgotten to ask.

To snatch in a moment of courage, from the remorseless rush of time, a passing phase of life, is only the beginning of the task. The task approached in tenderness and faith is to hold up unquestioningly, without choice and without fear, the rescued fragment before all eyes in the light of a sincere mood. It is to show its vibration, its color, its form; and through its movement, its form, and its color, reveal the substance of its truth—disclose its inspiring secret: the stress and passion within the core of each convincing moment. In a single-minded attempt of that kind, if one be deserving and fortunate, one may perchance attain to such clearness of sincerity that at last the presented vision of regret or pity, of terror or birth, shall awaken in the hearts of the beholders that feeling of unavoidable solidarity; of the solidarity in mysterious origin, in toil, in joy, in hope, in uncertain fate, which binds men to each other and all mankind to the visible world.

It is evident that he who, rightly or wrongly, holds by the convictions expressed above cannot be faithful to any one of the temporary formulas of his craft. The enduring part of them—the truth which each only imperfectly veils—should abide with him as the most precious of his possessions, but they all: Realism, Romanticism, Naturalism, even the unofficial sentimentalism (which like the poor, is exceedingly difficult to get rid of), all these gods must, after a short period of fellowship, abandon him—even on the very threshold of the temple—to the stammerings of his conscience and to the outspoken consciousness of the difficulties of his work. In that uneasy solitude the supreme cry of Art for Art itself, loses the exciting ring of its apparent immorality. It sounds far off. It has ceased to be a cry, and is heard only as a whisper, often incomprehensible, but at times and faintly encouraging.

Sometimes, stretched at ease in the shade of a roadside tree, we watch the motions of a laborer in a distant field, and after a time, begin to wonder languidly as to what the fellow may be at. We watch the movements of his body, the waving of his arms, we see him bend down, stand up, hesitate, begin again. It may add to the charm of an idle hour to be told the purpose of his exertions. If we know he is trying to lift a stone, to dig a ditch, to uproot a stump, we look with a more real interest at his efforts; we are disposed to condone the jar of his agitation upon the restfulness of the landscape; and even, if in a brotherly frame of mind, we may bring ourselves to forgive his failure. We understood his object, and, after all, the fellow has tried, and perhaps he had not the strength—and perhaps he had not the knowledge. We forgive, go on our way—and forget.

And so it is with the workman of art. Art is long and life is short, and success is very far off. And thus, doubtful of strength to travel so far, we talk a little about the aim—the aim of art, which, like life itself, is inspiring, difficult—obscured by mists. It is not in the clear logic of a triumphant conclusion; it is not in the unveiling of one of those heartless secrets which are called the Laws of Nature. It is not less great, but only more difficult.

To arrest, for the space of a breath, the hands busy about the work of the earth, and compel men entranced by the sight of distant goals to glance for a moment at the surrounding vision of form and color, of sunshine and shadows; to make them pause for a look, for a sigh, for a smile—such is the aim, difficult and evanescent, and reserved only for a few to achieve. But sometimes, by the deserving and the fortunate, even that task is accomplished. And when it is accomplished—behold!—all the truth of life is there: a moment of vision, a sigh, a smile—and the return to an eternal rest.

LITERATURE AS EQUIPMENT FOR LIVING

by KENNETH BURKE

HERE I shall put down as briefly as possible a statement in behalf of what might be catalogued, with a fair degree of accuracy, as a *sociological* criticism of literature. Sociological criticism in itself is certainly not new. I shall here try to suggest what partially new elements or emphasis I think should be added to this old approach. And to make the "way in" as easy as possible, I shall begin with a discussion of proverbs.

I

Examine random specimens in *The Oxford Dictionary of English Proverbs*. You will note, I think, that there is no "pure" literature here. Everything is "medicine." Proverbs are designed for consolation or vengeance, for admonition or exhortation, for foretelling.

Or they name typical, recurrent situations. That is, people find a certain social relationship recurring so frequently that they must "have a word for it." The Eskimos have special names for many different kinds of snow (fifteen, if I remember rightly) because variations in the quality of snow greatly affect their living. Hence, they must "size up" snow much more accurately than we do. And the same is true of social phenomena. Social structures give rise to "type" situations, subtle subdi-

visions of the relationships involved in competitive and co-operative acts. Many proverbs seek to chart, in more or less homey and picturesque ways, these "type" situations. I submit that such naming is done, not for the sheer glory of the thing, but because of its bearing upon human welfare. A different name for snow implies a different kind of hunt. Some names for snow imply that one should not hunt at all. And similarly, the names for typical, recurrent social situations are not developed out of "disinterested curiosity," but because the names imply a command (what to expect, what to look out for).

To illustrate with a few representative examples:

Proverbs designed for consolation: "The sun does not shine on both sides of the hedge at once." "Think of ease, but work on." "Little troubles the eye, but far less the soul." "The worst luck now, the better another time." "The wind in one's face makes one wise." "He that hath lands hath quarrels." "He knows how to carry the dead cock home." "He is not poor that hath little, but he that desireth much."

For vengeance: "At length the fox is brought to the furrier." "Shod in the cradle, barefoot in the stubble." "Sue a beggar and get a louse." "The higher the ape goes, the more he shows his tail." "The

From Kenneth Burke, *The Philosophy of Literary Form*, Louisiana State University Press.

moon does not heed the barking of dogs." "He measures another's corn by his own bushel." "He shuns the man who knows him well." "Fools tie knots and wise men loose them."

Proverbs that have to do with foretelling: (The most obvious are those to do with the weather.) "Sow peas and beans in the wane of the moon, Who soweth them sooner, he soweth too soon." "When the wind's in the north, the skillful fisher goes not forth." "When the sloe tree is as white as a sheet, sow your barley whether it be dry or wet." "When the sun sets bright and clear, An easterly wind you need not fear. When the sun sets in a bank, A westerly wind we shall not want."

In short: "Keep your weather eye open": be realistic about sizing up today's weather, because your accuracy has bearing upon tomorrow's weather. And forecast not only the meteorological weather, but also the social weather: "When the moon's in the full, then wit's in the wane." "Straws show which way the wind blows." "When the fish is caught, the net is laid aside." "Remove an old tree, and it will wither to death." "The wolf may lose his teeth, but never his nature." "He that bites on every weed must needs light on poison." "Whether the pitcher strikes the stone, or the stone the pitcher, it is bad for the pitcher." "Eagles catch no flies." "The more laws, the more offenders."

In this foretelling category we might also include the recipes for wise living, sometimes moral, sometimes technical: "First thrive, and then wive." "Think with the wise but talk with the vulgar." "When the fox preacheth, then beware your geese." "Venture a small fish to catch a great one." "Respect a man, he will do the more."

In the class of "typical, recurrent situations" we might put such proverbs and

proverbial expressions as: "Sweet appears sour when we pay." "The treason is loved but the traitor is hated." "The wine in the bottle does not quench thirst." "The sun is never the worse for shining on a dunghill." "The lion kicked by an ass." "The lion's share." "To catch one napping." "To smell a rat." "To cool one's heels."

By all means, I do not wish to suggest that this is the only way in which the proverbs could be classified. For instance, I have listed in the "foretelling" group the proverb, "When the fox preacheth, then beware your geese." But it could obviously be "taken over" for vindictive purposes. Or consider a proverb like, "Virtue flies from the heart of a mercenary man." A poor man might obviously use it either to console himself for being poor (the implication being, "Because I am poor in money I am rich in virtue") or to strike at another (the implication being, "When he got money, what else could you expect of him but deterioration?"). In fact, we could even say that such symbolic vengeance would itself be an aspect of solace. And a proverb like "The sun is never the worse for shining on a dung-hill" (which I have listed under "typical recurrent situations") might as well be put in the vindictive category.

The point of issue is not to find categories that "place" the proverbs once and for all. What I want is categories that suggest their active nature. Here there is no "realism for its own sake." There is realism for promise, admonition, solace, vengeance, foretelling, instruction, charting, all for the direct bearing that such acts have upon matters of welfare.

2

Step two: Why not extend such analysis of proverbs to encompass the whole field of literature? Could the most complex and sophisticated works of art legitimately be considered somewhat as "proverbs writ large"? Such leads, if held admissible, should help us to discover important facts about literary organization (thus satisfying the requirements of technical criticism). And the kind of observation from this perspective should apply beyond literature to life in general (thus helping to take literature out of its separate bin and give it a place in a general "sociological" picture).

The point of view might be phrased in this way: Proverbs are *strategies* for dealing with *situations*. In so far as situations are typical and recurrent in a given social structure, people develop names for them and strategies for handling them. Another name for strategies might be *attitudes*.

People have often commented on the fact that there are contrary *proverbs*. But I believe that the above approach to proverbs suggests a necessary modification of that comment. The apparent contradictions depend upon differences in *attitude*, involving a correspondingly different choice of *strategy*. Consider, for instance, the *apparently* opposite pair: "Repentance comes too late" and "Never too late to mend." The first is admonitory. It says in effect: "You'd better look out, or you'll get yourself too far into this business." The second is consolatory, saying in effect: "Buck up, old man, you can still pull out of this."

Some critics have quarreled with me about my selection of the word "strategy" as the name for this process. I have asked them to suggest an alternative term, so far without profit. The only one I can think of is "method." But if "strategy" errs in suggesting to some people an overly *conscious* procedure, "method" errs in suggesting an overly *methodical* one. Anyhow, let's look at the documents:

Concise Oxford Dictionary: "Strategy: Movement of an army or armies in a campaign, art of so moving or disposing troops or ships as to impose upon the enemy the place and time and conditions for fighting preferred by oneself" (from a Greek word that refers to the leading of an army).

New English Dictionary: "Strategy: The art of projecting and directing the larger military movements and operations of a campaign."

André Cheron, *Traité Complet d'Echecs:* "*On entend par stratégie les manoeuvres qui ont pour but la sortie et le bon arrangement des pièces.*"

Looking at these definitions, I gain courage. For surely, the most highly alembicated and sophisticated work of art, arising in complex civilizations, could be considered as designed to organize and command the army of one's thoughts and images, and to so organize them that one "imposes upon the enemy the time and place and conditions for fighting preferred by oneself." One seeks to "direct the larger movements and operations" in one's campaign of living. One "maneuvers," and the maneuvering is an "art."

Are not the final results one's "strategy"? One tries, as far as possible, to develop a strategy whereby one "can't lose." One tries to change the rules of the game until they fit his own necessities. Does the artist encounter disaster? He will "make capital" of it. If one is a victim of competition, for instance, if one is elbowed out, if one is willy-nilly more jockeyed against than jockeying, one can by the solace and vengeance of art convert this very "liability" into an "asset." One tries to fight on his own terms, developing a strategy for imposing the proper "time, place, and conditions."

But one must also, to develop a full

strategy, be *realistic*. One must *size things up* properly. One cannot accurately know how things *will be,* what is promising and what is menacing, unless he accurately knows how things *are.* So the wise strategist will not be content with strategies of merely a self-gratifying sort. He will "keep his weather eye open." He will not too eagerly "read into" a scene an attitude that is irrelevant to it. He won't sit on the side of an active volcano and "see" it as a dormant plain.

Often, alas, he will. The great allurement in our present popular "inspirational literature," for instance, may be largely of this sort. It is a strategy for easy consolation. It "fills a need," since there is always a need for easy consolation—and in an era of confusion like our own the need is especially keen. So people are only too willing to "meet a man halfway" who will *play down* the realistic naming of our situation and *play up* such strategies as make solace cheap. However, I should propose a reservation here. We usually take it for granted that people who consume our current output of books on "How to Buy Friends and Bamboozle Oneself and Other People" are reading as *students* who will attempt applying the recipes given. Nothing of the sort. *The reading of a book on the attaining of success is in itself the symbolic attaining of that success.* It is *while they read* that these readers are "succeeding." I'll wager that, in by far the great majority of cases, such readers make no serious attempt to apply the book's recipes. The lure of the book resides in the fact that the reader, while reading it, is then living in the aura of success. What he wants is *easy* success; and he gets it in symbolic form by mere reading itself. To attempt applying such stuff in real life would be very difficult, full of many disillusioning difficulties.

Sometimes a different strategy may arise. The author may remain realistic, avoiding too easy a form of solace—yet he may get as far off the track in his own way. Forgetting that realism is an aspect for foretelling, he may take it as an end in itself. He is tempted to do this by two factors: (1) an *ill-digested* philosophy of science, leading him mistakenly to assume that "relentless" naturalistic "truthfulness" is a proper end in itself, and (2) a merely *competitive* desire to outstrip other writers by being "more realistic" than they. Works thus made "efficient" by tests of competition internal to the book trade are a kind of academicism not so named (the writer usually thinks of it as the *opposite* of academicism). Realism thus stepped up competitively might be distinguished from the proper sort by the name of "naturalism." As a way of "sizing things up," the naturalistic tradition tends to become as inaccurate as the "inspirational" strategy, though at the opposite extreme.

Anyhow, the main point is this: A work like *Madame Bovary* (or its homely American translation, *Babbitt*) is the strategic naming of a situation. It singles out a pattern of experience that is sufficiently representative of our social structure, that recurs sufficiently often *mutandis mutatis,* for people to "need a word for it" and to adopt an attitude towards it. Each work of art is the addition of a word to an informal dictionary (or, in the case of purely derivative artists, the addition of a subsidiary meaning to a word already given by some originating artist). As for *Madame Bovary,* the French critic Jules de Gaultier proposed to add it to our formal dictionary by coining the word "Bovarysme" and writing a whole book to say what he meant by it.

Mencken's book on *The American Language,* I hate to say, is splendid. I console myself with the reminder that Mencken didn't write it. Many millions of people wrote it, and Mencken was merely the amanuensis who took it down from their dictation. He found a true "vehicle" (that is, a book that could be greater than the author who wrote it). He gets the royalties, but the job was done by a collectivity. As you read that book, you see a people who were up against a new set of typical recurrent situations, situations typical of their business, their politics, their criminal organizations, their sports. Either there were no words for these in standard English, or people didn't know them, or they didn't "sound right." So a new vocabulary arose, to "give us a word for it." I see no reason for believing that Americans are unusually fertile in word-coinage. American slang was not developed out of some exceptional gift. It was developed out of the fact that new typical situations had arisen and people needed names for them. They had to "size things up." They had to console and strike, to promise and admonish. They had to describe for purposes of forecasting. And "slang" was the result. It is, by this analysis, simply *proverbs not so named,* a kind of "folk criticism."

3

With what, then, would "sociological criticism" along these lines be concerned? It would seek to codify the various strategies which artists have developed with relation to the naming of situation. In a sense, much of it would even be "timeless," for many of the "typical, recurrent situations" are not peculiar to our civilization at all. The situation and strategies framed in Aesop's Fables, for instance, apply to human relations now just as fully as they applied in ancient Greece. They are, like philosophy, sufficiently "generalized"

to extend far beyond the particular combination of events named by them in any one instance. They name an "essence." Or, as Korzybski might say, they are on a "high level of abstraction." One doesn't usually think of them as "abstract," since they are usually so concrete in their stylistic expression. But they invariably aim to discern the "general behind the particular" (which would suggest that they are good Goethe).

The attempt to treat literature from the standpoint of situations and strategies suggests a variant of Spengler's notion of the "contemporaneous." By "contemporaneity" he meant corresponding stages of different cultures. For instance, if modern New York is much like decadent Rome, then we are "contemporaneous" with decadent Rome, or with some corresponding decadent city among the Mayas, etc. It is in this sense that situations are "timeless," "non-historical," "contemporaneous." A given human relationship may be at one time named in terms of foxes and lions, if there are foxes and lions about; or it may now be named in terms of salesmanship, advertising, the tactics of politicians, etc. But beneath the change in particulars, we may often discern the naming of the one situation.

So sociological criticism, as here understood, would seek to assemble and codify this lore. It might occasionally lead us to outrage good taste, as we sometimes found exemplified in some great sermon or tragedy or abstruse work of philosophy the same strategy as we found exemplified in a dirty joke. At this point we'd put the sermon and the dirty joke together, thus "grouping by situation" and showing the range of possible particularizations. In his exceptionally discerning essay, "A Critic's Job of Work," R. P. Blackmur says, "I think on the whole his [Burke's] method could be applied with equal fruitfulness to Shakespeare, Dashiell Hammett, or Miss Marie Corelli." When I got through wincing, I had to admit that Blackmur was right. This article is an attempt to say for the method what can be said. As a matter of fact, I'll go a step further and maintain: You can't properly put Marie Corelli and Shakespeare apart until you have first put them together. First genus, then differentia. The strategy in common is the genus. The *range* or *scale* or *spectrum* of particularizations is the differentia.

Anyhow, that's what I'm driving at. And that's why reviewers sometime find in my work "intuitive" leaps that are dubious as "science." They are not "leaps" at all. They are classifications, groupings, made on the basis of some strategic element common to the ideas grouped. They are neither more nor less "intuitive" than *any* grouping or classification of social events. Apples can be grouped with bananas as fruits, and they can be grouped with tennis balls as round. I am simply proposing, in the social sphere, a method of classification with reference to *strategies*.

The method has these things to be said in its favor: It gives definite insight into the organization of literary works; and it automatically breaks down the barriers erected about literature as a specialized pursuit. People can classify novels by reference to three kinds, eight kinds, seventeen kinds. It doesn't matter. Students patiently copy down the professor's classification and pass examinations on it, because the range of possible academic classifications is endless. Sociological classification, as herein suggested, would derive its relevance from the fact that it should apply both to works of art and to social situations outside of art.

It would, I admit, violate current pieties, break down current categories, and thereby "outrage good taste." But "good taste" has become *inert*. The classifications I am proposing would be *active*. I think that what we need is active categories.

These categories will lie on the bias across the categories of modern specialization. The new alignment will outrage in particular those persons who take the division of faculties in our universities to be an exact replica of the way God himself divided up the universe. We have had the Philosophy of the Being; and we have had the Philosophy of the Becoming. In contemporary specialization, we have been getting the Philosophy of the Bin. Each of these mental localities has had its own peculiar way of life, its own values, even its own special idiom for seeing, thinking, and "proving." Among other things, a sociological approach should attempt to provide a reintegrative point of view, a broader empire of investigation encompassing the lot.

What would such sociological categories be like? They would consider works of art, I think, as strategies for selecting enemies and allies, for socializing losses, for warding off evil eye, for purification, propitiation, and desanctification, consolation and vengeance, admonition and exhortation, implicit commands or instructions of one sort or another. Art forms like "tragedy" or "comedy" or "satire" would be treated as *equipments for living*, that size up situations in various ways and in keeping with correspondingly various attitudes. The typical ingredients of such forms would be sought. Their relation to typical situations would be stressed. Their comparative values would be considered, with the intention of formulating a "strategy of strategies," the "over-all" strategy obtained by inspection of the lot.

March Avery '51

From The New Generation, *Summer 1952.*
The New Generation, Inc., Geneva, New York.

from THE PATTERN-MAKERS

by WILLIAM McFEE

The encouragement a young writer wants is mainly the inspiration of masterpieces, and when he learns a trade he can be forever bringing those masterpieces to the touchstone of reality. Better than any rumble-bumble of philosophy and theory is the ring of steel on an anvil, the clean finish of a finely made pattern. The pattern is a symbol of what he is to do in the future. For what a man writes is no more than a pattern fashioned in the workshop of his soul, and goes out thence to be cast and cunningly fashioned for the public eye. He must allow for shrinkage and the passage of time. He must make it so all parts fit truly yet will draw from the mold with ease and smoothness. Above all, he must take heed never to use words that have no meaning, any more than he would put fillets and beadings on a pattern no workman in the foundry could understand, and he will use clean, dry scantling, keeping his tools very sharp, so that part fits into part as I have shown, and his work will hold together, year after year, without shake or bind.

THE LANGUAGE OF REPORTS

by S. I. HAYAKAWA

To put it briefly, in human speech, different sounds have different meanings. To study this co-ordination of certain sounds with certain meanings is to study language. This co-ordination makes it possible for man to interact with great precision. When we tell someone, for instance, the address of a house he has never seen, we are doing something which no animal can do.

LEONARD BLOOMFIELD

Vague and insignificant forms of speech, and abuse of language, have so long passed for mysteries of science; and hard or misapplied words with little or no meaning have, by prescription, such a right to be mistaken for deep learning and height of speculation, that it will not be easy to persuade either those who speak or those who hear them, that they are but the covers of ignorance and hindrance of true knowledge.

JOHN LOCKE

FOR THE PURPOSES of the interchange of information, the basic symbolic act is the *report* of what we have seen, heard, or felt: "There is a ditch on each side of the road." "You can get those at Smith's hardware store for $2.75." "There aren't any fish on that side of the lake, but there are on this side." Then there are reports of reports: "The longest waterfall in the world is Victoria Falls in Rhodesia." "The Battle of Hastings took place in 1066." "The papers say that there was a big smash-up on Highway 41 near Evansville." Reports adhere to the following rules: first, they are *capable of verification;* second, they *exclude,* as far as possible, *inferences* and *judgments.* (These terms will be defined later.)

Verifiability

Reports are verifiable. We may not always be able to verify them ourselves, since we cannot track down the evidence for every piece of history we know, nor can we all go to Evansville to see the remains of the smash-up before they are cleared away. But if we are roughly agreed on the names of things, on what constitutes a "foot," "yard," "bushel," and so on, and on how to measure time, there is relatively little danger of our misunderstanding each other. Even in a world such as we have today, in which everybody seems to be quarreling with everybody else, *we still to a surprising degree trust each other's reports.* We ask directions of total strangers when we are traveling. We follow directions on road signs without being suspicious of the people who put them up. We read books of information about science, mathematics, automotive engineering, travel, geography, the history of costume, and other such factual matters, and we usually assume that the author is doing his best to tell us as truly as he can what he knows. And we are safe in so assuming most of the time. With the emphasis that is being given today to the discussion of biased newspapers, propagandists, and the general untrustworthiness of many of the communications we receive, we are likely to forget that we still have an enormous amount of reliable information available and that deliberate misinformation, except in warfare, still is more the exception than the rule. The desire for self-preservation that compelled men to evolve means for the exchange of information also compels them to regard the giving of false information as profoundly reprehensible.

At its highest development, the langauge of reports is the language of science. By "highest development" we mean greatest general usefulness. Presbyterian and Catholic, workingman and capitalist, German and Englishman, *agree* on the meanings of such symbols as $2 \times 2 = 4$, $100°$ *C.*, HNO_3, *3:35* A.M., *1940* A.D., *5000 r.p.m.*, *1000 kilowatts, pulex irritans,* and so on. But how, it may be asked, can there be agreement about even this much among people who are at each other's throats about practically everything else: political philosophies, ethical ideas, religious beliefs, and the survival of my business *versus* the survival of yours? The answer is that circumstances *compel men to agree,* whether they wish to or not. If, for example, there were a dozen different religious sects in the United States, each insisting on its own way of naming the time of the day and the days of the year, the mere necessity of having a dozen different calendars, a dozen different kinds of watches, and a dozen sets of schedules for business hours, trains, and radio programs, to say nothing of the effort that would be required for translating terms from one nomenclature to another, would make life as we know it impossible.[1]

The language of reports, then, including the more accurate reports of science, is "map" language, and because it gives us reasonably accurate representations of the "territory," it enables us to get work done. Such language may often be what is commonly termed "dull" or "uninteresting" reading: one does not usually read logarithmic tables or telephone directories for entertainment. But we could not get along without it. There are numberless occasions in the talking and writing we do in everyday life that *require that we state things in such a way that everybody will agree with our formulation.*

Inferences

The reader will find that practice in writing reports is a quick means of increasing his linguistic awareness. It is an exercise which will constantly provide him with his own examples of the principles of language and interpretation under discussion. The reports should be about firsthand experience—scenes the reader has witnessed himself, meetings and social events he has taken part in, people he knows well. They should be of such a nature that they can be verified and agreed upon. For the purpose of this exercise, inferences will be excluded.

Not that inferences are not important— we rely in everyday life and in science as

[1] According to information supplied by the Association of American Railroads, "Before 1883 there were nearly 100 different time zones in the United States. It wasn't until November 18 of that year that . . . a system of standard time was adopted here and in Canada. Before then there was nothing but local or 'solar' time. . . . The Pennsylvania Railroad in the East used Philadelphia time, which was five minutes slower than New York time and five minutes faster than Baltimore time. The Baltimore & Ohio used Baltimore time for trains running out of Baltimore, Columbus time for Ohio, Vincennes (Indiana) time for those going out of Cincinnati. . . . When it was noon in Chicago, it was 12:31 in Pittsburgh; 12:24 in Cleveland; 12:17 in Toledo; 12:13 in Cincinnati; 12:09 in Louisville; 12:07 in Indianapolis; 11:50 in St. Louis; 11:48 in Dubuque; 11:39 in St. Paul, and 11:27 in Omaha. There were 27 local time zones in Michigan alone. . . . A person traveling from Eastport, Maine, to San Francisco, if he wanted always to have the right railroad time and get off at the right place, had to twist the hands of his watch 20 times en route." Chicago *Daily News,* September 29, 1948.

much on *inferences* as on reports—in some areas of thought, for example, geology, paleontology, and nuclear physics, reports are the foundations, but inferences (and inferences upon inferences) are the main body of the science. An inference, as we shall use the term, is *a statement about the unknown made on the basis of the known.* We may *infer* from the handsomeness of a woman's clothes her wealth or social position; we may *infer* from the character of the ruins the origin of the· fire that destroyed the building; we may *infer* from a man's calloused hands the nature of his occupation; we may *infer* from a senator's vote on an armaments bill his attitude toward Russia; we may *infer* from the structure of the land the path of a prehistoric glacier; we may *infer* from a halo on an unexposed photographic plate that it has been in the vicinity of radioactive materials; we may *infer* from the noise an engine makes the condition of its connecting rods. Inferences may be carelessly or carefully made. They may be made on the basis of a great background of previous experience with the subject-matter, or no experience at all. For example, the inferences a good mechanic can make about the internal condition of a motor by listening to it are often startlingly accurate, while the inferences made by an amateur (if he tries to make any) may be entirely wrong. But the common characteristic of inferences is that they are statements about matters which are not directly known, made on the basis of what has been observed.

The avoidance of inferences in our suggested practice in report-writing requires that we make no guesses as to what is going on in other people's minds. When we say, "He was angry," we are not reporting; we are making an inference from such observ-

able facts as the following: "He pounded his fist on the table; he swore; he threw the telephone directory at his stenographer." In this particular example, the inference appears to be fairly safe; nevertheless, it is important to remember, especially for the purposes of training oneself, that it is an inference. Such expressions as "He thought a lot of himself," "He was scared of girls," "He has an inferiority complex," made on the basis of casual social observation, and "What Russia really wants to do is to establish a world communist dictatorship," made on the basis of casual newspaper reading, are highly inferential. One should keep in mind their inferential character and, in our suggested exercises, should substitute for them such statements as "He rarely spoke to subordinates in the plant," I saw him at a party, and he never danced except when one of the girls asked him to," "He wouldn't apply for the scholarship although I believe he could have won it easily," and "The Russian delegation to the United Nations has asked for A, B, and C. Last year they voted against M and N, and voted for X and Y. On the basis of facts such as these, the newspaper I read makes the inference that what Russia really wants is to establish a world communist dictatorship. I tend to agree."

Judgments

In our suggested writing exercise, judgments are also to be excluded. By judgments, we shall mean *all expressions of the writer's approval or disapproval of the occurrences, persons, or objects he is describing.* For example, a report cannot say, "It was a wonderful car," but must say something like this: "It has been driven 50,000 miles and has never required any repairs." Again statements like "Jack lied to us" must be suppressed in favor of the more verifiable statement, "Jack told us he didn't have the keys to his car with him. However, when he pulled a handkerchief out of his pocket a few minutes later, a bunch of car keys fell out." Also a report may not say, "The senator was stubborn, defiant, and unco-operative," or "The senator courageously stood by his principles"; it must say instead, "The senator's vote was the only one against the bill."

Many people regard statements like the following as statements of "fact": "Jack *lied* to us," "Jerry is a *thief*," "Tommy is *clever*." As ordinarily employed, however, the word "lied" involves first an inference (that Jack knew otherwise and deliberately misstated the facts) and secondly a judgment (that the speaker disapproves of what he has inferred that Jack did). In the other two instances, we may substitute such expressions as, "Jerry was convicted of theft and served two years at Waupun," and "Tommy plays the violin, leads his class in school, and is captain of the debating team." After all, to say of a man that he is a "thief" is to say in effect, "He has stolen *and will steal again*"—which is more of a prediction than a report. Even to say, "He has stolen," is to make an inference (and simultaneously to pass a judgment) on an act about which there may be difference of opinion among those who have examined the evidence upon which the conviction was obtained. But to say that he was "convicted of theft" is to make a statement capable of being agreed upon through verification in court and prison records.

Scientific verifiability rests upon the external observation of facts, not upon the heaping up of judgments. If one person says, "Peter is a deadbeat," and another

says, "I think so too," the statement has not been verified. In court cases, considerable trouble is sometimes caused by witnesses who cannot distinguish their judgments from the facts upon which those judgments are based. Cross-examinations under these circumstances go something like this:

WITNESS: That dirty double-crosser Jacobs ratted on me.

DEFENSE ATTORNEY: Your honor, I object.

JUDGE: Objection sustained. (Witness's remark is stricken from the record.) Now, try to tell the court exactly what happened.

WITNESS: He double-crossed me, the dirty, lying rat!

DEFENSE ATTORNEY: Your honor, I object!

JUDGE: Objection sustained. (Witness's remark is again stricken from the record.) Will the witness try to stick to the facts.

WITNESS: But I'm telling you the facts, your honor. He did double-cross me.

This can continue indefinitely unless the cross-examiner exercises some ingenuity in order to get at the facts behind the judgment. To the witness it is a "fact" that he was "double-crossed." Often hours of patient questioning are required before the factual bases of the judgment are revealed.

Many words, of course, simultaneously convey a report and a judgment on the fact reported, as will be discussed more fully in a later chapter. For the purposes of a report as here defined, these should be avoided. Instead of "sneaked in," one might say "entered quietly"; instead of "politicians," "congressmen," or "aldermen," or "candidates for office"; instead of "bureaucrat," "public official"; instead of "tramp," "homeless unemployed"; instead of "dictatorial set-up," "centralized authority"; instead of "crackpots," "holders of uncommon views." A newspaper reporter, for example, is not permitted to write, "A crowd of suckers came to listen to Senator Smith last evening in that rickety firetrap and ex-dive that disfigures the south edge of town." Instead he says, "Between seventy-five and a hundred people heard an address last evening by Senator Smith at the Evergreen Gardens near the South Side city limits."

Snarl-Words and Purr-Words

Throughout this book, it is important to remember that we are considering language not as an isolated phenomenon, but language in action—language in the full context of the nonlinguistic events which are its setting. The making of noises with the vocal organs is a muscular activity, and like other muscular activities, often involuntary. Our responses to powerful stimuli, such as to something that makes us very angry, are a complex of muscular and physiological events: the contracting of fighting muscles, the increase of blood pressure, change in body chemistry, clutching one's hair, and so on, *and* the making of noises, such as growls and snarls. We are a little too dignified, perhaps, to growl like dogs, but we do the next best thing and substitute series of words, such as "You dirty double-crosser!" "The filthy scum!" Similarly, if we are pleasurably agitated, we may, instead of purring or wagging the tail, say things like "She's the sweetest girl in all the world!"

Speeches such as these are, as direct expressions of approval or disapproval, judgments in their simplest form. They may be said to be human equivalents of snarling and purring. "She's the sweetest girl in all the world" is not a statement about the girl; it is a purr. This seems to be a fairly obvious fact; nevertheless, it is surprising how often, when such a statement is made, both the speaker and the hearer feel that something has been said about the girl. This error is especially common in the interpretation of utterances of orators and editorialists in some of their more excited denunciations of "Reds," "greedy monopolists," "Wall Street," "radicals," "foreign ideologies," and in their more fulsome dithyrambs about "our way of life." Constantly, because of the impressive sound of the words, the elaborate structure of the sentences, and the appearance of intellectual progression, we get the feeling that something is being said about something. On closer examination, however, we discover that these utterances merely say, "What I hate ('Reds,' 'Wall Street,' or whatever) I hate very, very much," and "What I like ('our way of life') I like very, very much." We may call such utterances "snarl-words" and "purr-words." They are not reports describing conditions in the extensional world in any way.

To call these judgments "snarl-words" and "purr-words" does not mean that we should simply shrug them off. It means that we should be careful to *allocate the meaning correctly*—placing such a statement as "She's the sweetest girl in the world" as a revelation of the speaker's state of mind, and not as a revelation of facts about the girl. If the "snarl-words" about "Reds," or "greedy monopolists" are accompanied by verifiable reports (which would also mean that we have previously agreed as to who, specifically, is meant by the terms "Reds" or "greedy monopolists"), we might find reason to be just as disturbed as the speaker. If the "purr-words" about the sweetest girl in the world are accompanied by verifiable reports about her appearance, manners, skill in cooking, and so on, we might find reason to admire her too. But "snarl-words" and "purr-words" as such, unaccompanied by reports, offer nothing further to discuss, except possibly the question, "Why do you feel as you do?"

It is usually fruitless to debate such questions as "Was President Roosevelt a great statesman or merely a skillful politician?" "Is the music of Wagner the greatest music of all time or is it merely hysterical screeching?" "Which is the finer sport, tennis or baseball?" "Could Joe Louis in his prime have licked Bob Fitzsimmons in his prime?" To take sides on such issues of conflicting judgments is to reduce oneself to the same level of stubborn imbecility as one's opponents. But to ask questions of the form, "Why do you like (or dislike) Roosevelt (or Wagner, or tennis, or Joe Louis)?" is to learn something about one's friends and neighbors. After listening to their opinions and their reasons for them, we may leave the discussion slightly wiser, slightly better informed, and perhaps slightly less one-sided than we were before the discussion began.

How Judgments Stop Thought

A judgment ("He is a fine boy," "It was a beautiful service," "Baseball is a healthful sport," "She is an awful bore") is a conclusion, summing up a large number of previously observed facts. The reader is probably familiar with the fact that students almost always have difficulty in writing themes of the required length because their ideas give out after a paragraph or two. The reason for this is that those early paragraphs contain so many judgments that there is little left to be said. When the conclusions are carefully excluded, however, and observed facts are given in-

stead, there is never any trouble about the length of papers; in fact, they tend to become too long, since inexperienced writers, when told to give facts, often give far more than are necessary, because they lack discrimination between the important and the trivial.

Still another consequence of judgments early in the course of a written exercise —and this applies also to hasty judgments in everyday thought—is the temporary blindness they induce. When, for example, an essay starts with the words, "He was a real Wall Street executive," or "She was a typical cute little co-ed," if we continue writing at all, we must make all our later statements consistent with those judgments. The result is that all the individual characteristics of this particular "executive" or this particular "co-ed" are lost sight of entirely; and the rest of the essay is likely to deal not with observed facts, but with the writer's private notion (based on previously read stories, movies, pictures, and so forth) of what "Wall Street executives" or "typical co-eds" look like. The premature judgment, that is, often prevents us from seeing what is directly in front of us. Even if the writer feels sure at the beginning of a written exercise that the man he is describing is a "loafer" or that the scene he is describing is a "beautiful residential suburb," he will conscientiously keep such notions out of his head, lest his vision be obstructed.

Slanting

In the course of writing reports of personal experiences, it will be found that in spite of all endeavors to keep judgments out, some will creep in. An account of a man, for example, may go like this: "He had apparently not shaved for several days, and his face and hands were covered with grime. His shoes were torn, and his coat, which was several sizes too small for him, was spotted with dried clay." Now, in spite of the fact that no judgment has been stated, a very obvious one is implied. Let us contrast this with another description of the same man. "Although his face was bearded and neglected, his eyes were clear, and he looked straight ahead as he walked rapidly down the road. He looked very tall; perhaps the fact that his coat was too small for him emphasized that impression. He was carrying a book under his left arm, and a small terrier ran at his heels." In this example, the impression about the same man is considerably changed, simply by the inclusion of new details and the subordination of unfavorable ones. Even if explicit judgments are kept out of one's writing, implied judgments will get in.

How, then, can we ever give an impartial report? The answer is, of course, that we cannot attain complete impartiality while we use the language of everyday life. Even with the very impersonal language of science, the task is sometimes difficult. Nevertheless, we can, by being aware of the favorable or unfavorable feelings that certain words and facts can arouse, attain enough impartiality for practical purposes. Such awareness enables us to balance the implied favorable and unfavorable judgments against each other. To learn to do this, it is a good idea to write two essays at a time on the same subject, both strict reports, to be read side by side: the first to contain facts and details likely to prejudice the reader in favor of the subject, the second to contain those likely to prejudice the reader against it. For example:

FOR	AGAINST
He had white teeth.	His teeth were uneven.
His eyes were blue, his hair blond and abundant.	He rarely looked people straight in the eye.
He had on a clean blue shirt.	His shirt was frayed at the cuffs.
He often helped his wife with the dishes.	He rarely got through drying dishes without breaking a few.
His pastor spoke very highly of him.	His grocer said he was always slow about paying his bills.

Slanting Both Ways at Once

This process of selecting details favorable or unfavorable to the subject being described may be termed slanting. Slanting gives no explicit judgments, but it differs from reporting in that it deliberately makes certain judgments inescapable. The writer striving for impartiality will, therefore, take care to slant both for and against his subject, trying as conscientiously as he can to keep the balance even. The next stage of the exercise, then, should be to rewrite the parallel essays into a single coherent essay in which details on both sides are included.

His teeth were white, but uneven; his eyes were blue, his hair blond and abundant. He did not often look people straight in the eye. His shirt was slightly frayed at the cuffs, but it was clean. He frequently helped his wife with the dishes, but he broke many of them. Opinion about him in the community was divided. His grocer said he was slow about paying his bills, but his pastor spoke very highly of him.

This example is, of course, oversimplified and admittedly not very graceful. But practice in writing such essays will first of all help to prevent one from slipping unconsciously from observable facts to judgments; that is, from "He was a member of the Ku Klux Klan" to "the dirty scoundrel!" Next, it will reveal how little we really want to be impartial anyway, especially about our best friends, our parents, our alma mater, our own children, our country, the company we work for, the product we sell, our competitor's product, or anything else in which our interests are deeply involved. Finally, we will discover that, even if we have no wish to be impartial, we write more clearly, more forcefully, and more convincingly by this process of sticking as close as possible to observable facts. There will be, as someone once remarked, more horsepower and less exhaust.

A few weeks of practice in writing reports, slanted reports, and reports slanted both ways will improve powers of observation, as well as ability to recognize soundness of observation in the writings of others. A sharpened sense for the distinction between facts and judgments, facts and inferences, will reduce susceptibility to the flurries of frenzied public opinion which certain people find it to their interest to arouse. Alarming judgments and inferences can be made to appear inevitable by means of skillfully slanted reports. A reader who is aware of the technique of slanting, however, is relatively difficult to stampede by such methods. He knows too well that there may be other relevant facts which have been left out.

Discovering One's Bias

Here, however, a caution is necessary. When a newspaper tells a story in a way that we dislike, leaving out facts we think important and playing up unimportant facts in ways that we think unfair, we are often tempted to say, "Look how they've slanted the story! What a dirty trick!" In making such a statement we are, of course, making an inference about the newspaper's editors. We are assuming that what seems important or unimportant to us seems equally important or unimportant to them, and on the basis of that assumption we are inferring that the editors "deliberately" gave the story a misleading emphasis. Is this necessarily the case? Can the reader, as an outsider, say whether a story assumes a given form because the editors "deliberately slanted it that way" or because that was the way the events appeared to them?

The point is that, by the process of selection and abstraction imposed on us by our own interests and background, experience comes to all of us (including newspaper editors) already "slanted." If you happen to be pro-CIO, pro-Catholic, and a midget-auto racing fan, your ideas of what is important or unimportant will of necessity be different from those of a man who happens to be indifferent to all three of your favorite interests. If, then, some newspapers often seem to side with the big businessman on public issues, the reason is less a matter of "deliberate" slanting than the fact that publishers are often, in enterprises as large as modern urban newspapers, big businessmen themselves, accustomed both in work and in social life to associating with other big businessmen. Nevertheless, the best newspapers, whether owned by "big businessmen" or not, often do try to tell us as accurately as possible what is going on in the world, because they are run by newspapermen who conceive it to be part of their professional responsibility to present fairly the conflicting points of view in controversial issues. Such newspapermen are *reporters* indeed.

But to get back to our exercises—the importance of trying to "slant both ways" lies not in the hope of achieving a godlike impartiality in one's thinking and writing —which is manifestly an impossible goal. It lies in discovering what poor reporters most of us really are—in other words, how little we see of the world since we of necessity see it from our own point of view. To discover one's own biases is the beginning of wisdom.

If one man says, "Co-operatives will be the salvation of America," and another replies, "Co-operatives are un-American," they might as well stop talking right there.

If, however, one says, "Co-operatives seem to me, *from where I sit,* to offer a solution to our problems," and the other says, *"From where I sit,* they look like a pretty vicious institution," the possibility of further communication between the two remains. "Whenever agreement or assent is arrived at in human affairs . . . this agreement is reached by linguistic processes, or else it is not reached." To be aware of one's own "slant" and to be able to make allowances for it is to remain capable of continuing those linguistic processes that may eventually lead to agreement.

POLITICS AND THE ENGLISH LANGUAGE
by GEORGE ORWELL

MOST PEOPLE who bother with the matter at all would admit that the English language is in a bad way, but it is generally assumed that we cannot by conscious action do anything about it. Our civilization is decadent, and our language—so the argument runs—must inevitably share in the general collapse. It follows that any struggle against the abuse of language is a sentimental archaism, like preferring candles to electric light or hansom cabs to aeroplanes. Underneath this lies the half-conscious belief that language is a natural growth and not an instrument which we shape for our own purposes.

Now, it is clear that the decline of a language must ultimately have political and economic causes: it is not due simply to the bad influence of this or that individual writer. But an effect can become a cause, reinforcing the original cause and producing the same effect in an intensified form, and so on indefinitely. A man may take to drink because he feels himself to be a failure, and then fail all the more completely because he drinks. It is rather the same thing that is happening to the English language. It becomes ugly and inaccurate because our thoughts are foolish, but the slovenliness of our language makes it easier for us to have foolish thoughts. The point is that the process is reversible. Modern English, especially written English, is full of bad habits which spread by imitation and which can be avoided if one is willing to take the necessary trouble. If one gets rid of these habits one can think more clearly, and to think clearly is a necessary first step towards political regeneration: so that the fight against bad English is not frivolous and is not the exclusive concern of professional writers. I will come back to this presently, and I hope that by that time the meaning of what I have said here will have become clearer. Meanwhile, here are five specimens of the English language as it is now habitually written.

These five passages have not been picked out because they are especially bad—I could have quoted far worse if I had chosen—but because they illustrate various of the mental vices from which we now suffer. They are a little below the average, but are fairly representative samples. I number them so that I can refer back to them when necessary:

(1) I am not, indeed, sure whether it is not true to say that the Milton who once seemed not unlike a seventeenth-century Shelley had not become, out of an experience ever more bitter in each year, more alien (*sic*) to the founder of that Jesuit sect which nothing could induce him to tolerate.

PROFESSOR HAROLD LASKI
(Essay in Freedom of Expression).

(2) Above all, we cannot play ducks and drakes with a native battery of idioms which prescribes such egregious collocations of vocables as the Basic *put up with* for *tolerate* or *put at a loss* for *bewilder*.

PROFESSOR LANCELOT HOGBEN
(Interglossa).

(3) On the one side we have the free personality: by definition it is not neurotic, for it has neither conflict nor dream. Its desires, such as they are, are transparent, for they are just what institutional approval keeps in the forefront of consciousness; another institutional pattern would alter their number and intensity; there is little in them that is natural, irreducible, or culturally dangerous. But *on the other side,* the social bond itself is nothing but the mutual reflection of these self-secure integrities. Recall the definition of love. Is not this the very picture of a small academic? Where is there a place in this hall of mirrors for either personality or fraternity?

Essay on psychology
in Politics (New York).

(4) All the "best people" from the gentlemen's clubs, and all the frantic fascist captains, united in common hatred of Socialism and bestial horror of the rising tide of the mass revolutionary movement, have turned to acts of provocation, to foul incendiarism, to medieval legends of poisoned wells, to legalize their own destruction of proletarian organizations, and rouse the agitated petty-bourgeoisie to chauvinistic fervour on behalf of the fight against the revolutionary way out of the crisis.

Communist pamphlet.

(5) If a new spirit *is* to be infused into this old country, there is one thorny and contentious reform which must be tackled, and that is the humanization and galvanization of the B.B.C. Timidity here will bespeak canker and atrophy of the soul. The heart of Britain may be sound and of strong beat, for instance, but the British lion's roar at present is like that of Bottom in Shakespeare's *Midsummer Night's Dream*—as gentle as any sucking dove. A virile new Britain cannot continue indefinitely to be traduced in the eyes, or rather ears, of the world by the effete languors of Langham Place, brazenly masquerading as "standard English." When the Voice of Britain is heard at nine o'clock, better far and infinitely less ludicrous to hear aitches honestly dropped than the present priggish, inflated, inhibited, school-ma'amish arch braying of blameless bashful mewing maidens!

Letter in Tribune.

Each of these passages has faults of its own, but, quite apart from avoidable ugliness, two qualities are common to all of them. The first is staleness of imagery: the other is lack of precision. The writer either has a meaning and cannot express it, or he inadvertently says something else, or he is almost indifferent as to whether his words mean anything or not. This mixture of vagueness and sheer incompetence is the most marked characteristic of modern

English prose, and especially of any kind of political writing. As soon as certain topics are raised, the concrete melts into the abstract and no one seems able to think of turns of speech that are not hackneyed: prose consists less and less of *words* chosen for the sake of their meaning, and more and more of *phrases* tacked together like the sections of a prefabricated hen-house. I list below, with notes and examples, various of the tricks by means of which the work of prose-construction is habitually dodged:

Dying metaphors. A newly invented metaphor assists thought by evoking a visual image, while on the other hand a metaphor which is technically "dead" (e.g. *iron resolution*) has in effect reverted to being an ordinary word and can generally be used without loss of vividness. But in between these two classes there is a huge dump of worn-out metaphors which have lost all evocative power and are merely used because they save people the trouble of inventing phrases for themselves. Examples are: *Ring the changes on, take up the cudgels for, toe the line, ride rough-shod over, stand shoulder to shoulder with, play into the hands of, no axe to grind, grist to the mill, fishing in troubled waters, on the order of the day, Achilles' heel, swan song, hotbed.* Many of these are used without knowledge of their meaning (what is a "rift," for instance?), and incompatible metaphors are frequently mixed, a sure sign that the writer is not interested in what he is saying. Some metaphors now current have been twisted out of their original meaning without those who use them even being aware of the fact. For example, *toe the line* is sometimes written *tow the line*. Another example is *the hammer and the anvil*, now always used with the implication that the anvil

gets the worst of it. In real life it is always the anvil that breaks the hammer, never the other way about: a writer who stopped to think what he was saying would be aware of this, and would avoid perverting the original phrase.

Operators, or *verbal false limbs.* These save the trouble of picking out appropriate verbs and nouns, and at the same time pad each sentence with extra syllables which give it an appearance of symmetry. Characteristic phrases are: *render inoperative, militate against, prove unacceptable, make contact with, be subjected to, give rise to, give grounds for, have the effect of, play a leading part (role) in, make itself felt, take effect, exhibit a tendency to, serve the purpose of,* etc., etc. The keynote is the elimination of simple verbs. Instead of being a single word, such as *break, stop, spoil, mend, kill,* a verb becomes a *phrase,* made up of a noun or adjective tacked on to some general-purpose verb such as *prove, serve, form, play, render.* In addition, the passive voice is wherever possible used in preference to the active, and noun constructions are used instead of gerunds (*by examination of* instead of *by examining*). The range of verbs is further cut down by means of the *-ize* and *de-* formations, and banal statements are given an appearance of profundity by means of the *not un-* formation. Simple conjunctions and prepositions are replaced by such phrases as *with respect to, having regard to, the fact that, by dint of, in view of, in the interests of, on the hypothesis that;* and the ends of sentences are saved from anti-climax by such resounding commonplaces as *greatly to be desired, cannot be left out of account, a development to be expected in the near future, deserving of serious consideration, brought to a satisfactory conclusion,* and so on and so forth.

Pretentious diction. Words like *phenomenon, element, individual* (as noun), *objective, categorical, effective, virtual, basic, primary, promote, constitute, exhibit, exploit, utilize, eliminate, liquidate,* are used to dress up simple statement and give an air of scientific impartiality to biased judgements. Adjectives like *epoch-making, epic, historic, unforgettable, triumphant, age-old, inevitable, inexorable, veritable,* are used to dignify the sordid processes of international politics, while writing that aims at glorifying war usually takes on an archaic colour, its characteristic words being: *realm, throne, chariot, mailed fist, trident, sword, shield, buckler, banner, jackboot, clarion.* Foreign words and expressions such as *cul de sac, ancien régime, deus ex machina, mutatis mutandis, status quo, gleichschaltung, weltanschauung,* are used to give an air of culture and elegance. Except for the useful abbreviations *i.e., e.g.,* and *etc.,* there is no real need for any of the hundreds of foreign phrases now current in English. Bad writers, and especially scientific, political and sociological writers, are nearly always haunted by the notion that Latin or Greek words are grander than Saxon ones, and unnecessary words like *expedite, ameliorate, predict, extraneous, deracinated, clandestine, subaqueous* and hundreds of others constantly gain ground from their Anglo-Saxon opposite numbers.[1] The jargon peculiar to Marxist writing (*hyena, hangman, cannibal, petty bourgeois, these gentry, lacquey, flunkey, mad dog, White Guard,* etc.) consists largely of words and phrases translated from Russian, German or French; but the normal way of coining a new word is to use a Latin or Greek root with the appropriate affix and, where necessary, the -ize formation. It is often easier to make up words of this kind (*deregionalize, impermissible, extramarital, non-fragmentary,* and so forth) than to think up the English words that will cover one's meaning. The result, in general, is an increase in slovenliness and vagueness.

Meaningless words. In certain kinds of writing, particularly in art criticism and literary criticism, it is normal to come across long passages which are almost completely lacking in meaning.[2] Words like *romantic, plastic, values, human, dead, sentimental, natural, vitality,* as used in art criticism, are strictly meaningless, in the sense that they not only do not point to any discoverable object, but are hardly even expected to do so by the reader. When one critic writes, "The outstanding feature of Mr. X's work is its living quality," while another writes, "The immediately striking thing about Mr. X's work is its peculiar deadness," the reader accepts this as a simple difference of opinion. If words like *black* and *white* were involved, instead of the jargon words *dead* and *living,* he would see at once that language was being used in an improper way. Many

[1] An interesting illustration of this is the way in which the English flower names which were in use till very recently are being ousted by Greek ones, *snapdragon* becoming *antirrhinum,* *forget-me-not* becoming *myosotis,* etc. It is hard to see any practical reason for this change of fashion: it is probably due to an instinctive turning-away from the more homely word and a vague feeling that the Greek word is scientific.

[2] Example: "Comfort's catholicity of perception and image, strangely Whitmanesque in range, almost the exact opposite in aesthetic compulsion, continues to evoke that trembling atmospheric accumulative hinting at a cruel, an inexorably serene timelessness . . . Wrey Gardiner scores by aiming at simple bullseyes with precision. Only they are not so simple, and through this contented sadness runs more than the surface bitter-sweet of resignation." (*Poetry Quarterly.*)

political words are similarly abused. The word *Fascism* has now no meaning except in so far as it signifies "something not desirable." The words *democracy, socialism, freedom, patriotic, realistic, justice,* have each of them several different meanings which cannot be reconciled with one another. In the case of a word like *democracy,* not only is there no agreed definition, but the attempt to make one is resisted from all sides. It is almost universally felt that when we call a country democratic we are praising it: consequently the defenders of every kind of régime claim that it is a democracy, and fear that they might have to stop using the word if it were tied down to any one meaning. Words of this kind are often used in a consciously dishonest way. That is, the person who uses them has his own private definition, but allows his hearer to think he means something quite different. Statements like *Marshal Pétain was a true patriot, The Soviet Press is the freest in the world, The Catholic Church is opposed to persecution,* are almost always made with intent to deceive. Other words used in variable meanings, in most cases more or less dishonestly, are: *class, totalitarian, science, progressive, reactionary, bourgeois, equality.*

Now that I have made this catalogue of swindles and perversions, let me give another example of the kind of writing that they lead to. This time it must of its nature be an imaginary one. I am going to translate a passage of good English into modern English of the worst sort. Here is a well-known verse from *Ecclesiastes:*

I returned, and saw under the sun, that the race is not to the swift, nor the battle to the strong, neither yet bread to the wise, nor yet riches to men of understanding, nor yet favour to men of skill; but time and chance happeneth to them all.

Here it is in modern English:

Objective consideration of contemporary phenomena compels the conclusion that success or failure in competitive activities exhibits no tendency to be commensurate with innate capacity, but that a considerable element of the unpredictable must invariably be taken into account.

This is a parody, but not a very gross one. Exhibit (3), above, for instance, contains several patches of the same kind of English. It will be seen that I have not made a full translation. The beginning and ending of the sentence follow the original meaning fairly closely, but in the middle the concrete illustrations—race, battle, bread—dissolve into the vague phrase "success or failure in competitive activities." This had to be so, because no modern writer of the kind I am discussing—no one capable of using phrases like "objective consideration of contemporary phenomena"—would ever tabulate his thoughts in that precise and detailed way. The whole tendency of modern prose is away from concreteness. Now analyse these two sentences a little more closely. The first contains 49 words but only 60 syllables, and all its words are those of everyday life. The second contains 38 words of 90 syllables: 18 of its words are from Latin roots, and one from Greek. The first sentence contains six vivid images, and only one phrase ("time and chance") that could be called vague. The second contains not a single fresh, arresting phrase, and in spite of its 90 syllables it gives only a shortened version of the meaning contained in the first. Yet without a doubt it is the second kind of sentence that is gaining ground in modern English. I do not want to exaggerate. This kind of writing is not yet universal, and outcrops of simplicity will occur here and there in the worst-written page. Still, if you or I were told to write a few lines on the uncertainty of human fortunes, we should probably come much nearer to my imaginary sentence than to the one from *Ecclesiastes*.

As I have tried to show, modern writing at its worst does not consist in picking out words for the sake of their meaning and inventing images in order to make the meaning clearer. It consists in gumming together long strips of words which have already been set in order by someone else, and making the results presentable by sheer humbug. The attraction of this way of writing is that it is easy. It is easier—even quicker, once you have the habit—to say *In my opinion it is a not unjustifiable assumption that* than to say *I think*. If you use ready-made phrases, you not only don't have to hunt about for words; you also don't have to bother with the rhythms of your sentences, since these phrases are generally so arranged as to be more or less euphonious. When you are composing in a hurry—when you are dictating to a stenographer, for instance, or making a public speech—it is natural to fall into a pretentious, Latinized style. Tags like *a consideration which we should do well to bear in mind* or *a conclusion to which all of us would readily assent* will save many a sentence from coming down with a bump. By using stale metaphors, similes and idioms, you save much mental effort, at the cost of leaving your meaning vague, not only for your reader but for yourself. This is the significance of mixed metaphors. The sole aim of a metaphor is to call up a visual image. When these images clash—as in *The Fascist octopus has sung its swan song, the jackboot is thrown into the melting pot*—it can be taken as certain that the writer is not seeing a mental image of the objects he is naming; in other words he is not really thinking. Look again at the examples I gave at the beginning of this essay. Professor Laski (1) uses five negatives in 53 words. One of these is superfluous, making nonsense of the whole passage, and in addition there is the slip *alien* for akin, making further nonsense, and several avoidable pieces of clumsiness which increase the general vagueness. Professor Hogben (2) plays ducks and drakes with a battery which is able to write prescriptions, and, while disapproving of the everyday phrase *put up with,* is unwilling to look *egregious* up in the dictionary and see what it means. (3), If one takes an uncharitable attitude towards it, is simply meaningless: probably one could work out its intended meaning by reading the whole of the article in which it occurs. In (4), the writer knows more or less what he wants to say, but an accumulation of stale phrases chokes him like tea leaves blocking a sink. In (5), words and meaning have almost parted company. People who write in this manner usually have a general emotional meaning—they dislike one thing and want to express solidarity with another—but they are not interested in the detail of what they are saying. A scrupulous writer, in every sentence that he writes, will ask himself at least four questions, thus: What am I trying to say? What words will express it? What image or idiom will make it clearer? Is this image fresh enough to have an effect? And he will probably ask himself two more: Could I put it more shortly? Have I said anything that is avoidably ugly? But you are not obliged to go to all this trouble. You can shirk it by simply throwing your mind open and letting the ready-made phrases come crowding in. They will construct your sentences for you—even think your thoughts for you, to a certain extent—

and at need they will perform the important service of partially concealing your meaning even from yourself. It is at this point that the special connection between politics and the debasement of language becomes clear.

In our time it is broadly true that political writing is bad writing. Where it is not true, it will generally be found that the writer is some kind of rebel, expressing his private opinions and not a "party line." Orthodoxy, of whatever colour, seems to demand a lifeless, imitative style. The political dialects to be found in pamphlets, leading articles, manifestoes, White Papers and the speeches of under-secretaries do, of course, vary from party to party, but they are all alike in that one almost never finds in them a fresh, vivid, home-made turn of speech. When one watches some tired hack on the platform mechanically repeating the familiar phrases —*bestial atrocities, iron heel, bloodstained tyranny, free peoples of the world, stand shoulder to shoulder*—one often has a curious feeling that one is not watching a live human being but some kind of dummy: a feeling which suddenly becomes stronger at moments when the light catches the speaker's spectacles and turns them into blank discs which seem to have no eyes behind them. And this is not altogether fanciful. A speaker who uses that kind of phraseology has gone some distance towards turning himself into a machine. The appropriate noises are coming out of his larynx, but his brain is not involved as it would be if he were choosing his words for himself. If the speech he is making is one that he is accustomed to make over and over again, he may be almost unconscious of what he is saying, as one is when one utters the responses in church. And this reduced state of consciousness, if

not indispensable, is at any rate favourable to political conformity.

In our time, political speech and writing are largely the defence of the indefensible. Things like the continuance of British rule in India, the Russian purges and deportations, the dropping of the atom bombs on Japan, can indeed be defended, but only by arguments which are too brutal for most people to face, and which do not square with the professed aims of political parties. Thus political language has to consist largely of euphemism, question-begging and sheer cloudy vagueness. Defenceless villages are bombarded from the air, the inhabitants driven out into the countryside, the cattle machine-gunned, the huts set on fire with incendiary bullets: this is called *pacification*. Millions of peasants are robbed of their farms and sent trudging along the roads with no more than they can carry: this is called *transfer of population* or *rectification of frontiers*. People are imprisoned for years without trial, or shot in the back of the neck or sent to die of scurvy in Arctic lumber camps: this is called *elimination of unreliable elements*. Such phraseology is needed if one wants to name things without calling up mental pictures of them. Consider for instance some comfortable English professor defending Russian totalitarianism. He cannot say outright, "I believe in killing off your opponents when you can get good results by doing so." Probably, therefore, he will say something like this:

While freely conceding that the Soviet régime exhibits certain features which the humanitarian may be inclined to deplore, we must, I think, agree that a certain curtailment of the right to political opposition is an unavoidable concomitant of transitional periods, and that the rigours which the Russian people have been called upon to undergo have been amply justified in the sphere of concrete achievement.

The inflated style is itself a kind of euphemism. A mass of Latin words falls upon the facts like soft snow, blurring the outlines and covering up all the details. The great enemy of clear language is insincerity. When there is a gap between one's real and one's declared aims, one turns as it were instinctively to long words and exhausted idioms, like a cuttlefish squirting out ink. In our age there is no such thing as "keeping out of politics." All issues are political issues, and politics itself is a mass of lies, evasions, folly, hatred and schizophrenia. When the general atmosphere is bad, language must suffer. I should expect to find—this is a guess which I have not sufficient knowledge to verify—that the German, Russian and Italian languages have all deteriorated in the last ten or fifteen years, as a result of dictatorship.

But if thought corrupts language, language can also corrupt thought. A bad usage can spread by tradition and imitation, even among people who should and do know better. The debased language that I have been discussing is in some ways very convenient. Phrases like *a not unjustifiable assumption, leaves much to be desired, would serve no good purpose, a consideration which we should do well to bear in mind,* are a continuous temptation, a packet of aspirins always at one's elbow. Look back through this essay, and for certain you will find that I have again and again committed the very faults I am protesting against. By this morning's post I have received a pamphlet dealing with conditions in Germany. The author tells me that he "felt impelled" to write it. I open it at random, and here is almost the first sentence that I see: "(The Allies) have an opportunity not only of achieving a radical transformation of Germany's social and political structure in such a way as to avoid a nationalistic reaction in Germany itself, but at the same time of laying the foundations of a co-operative and unified Europe." You see, he "feels impelled" to write—feels, presumably, that he has something new to say—and yet his words, like cavalry horses answering the bugle, group themselves automatically into the familiar dreary pattern. This invasion of one's mind by ready-made phrases (*lay the foundations, achieve a radical transformation*) can only be prevented if one is constantly on guard against them, and every such phrase anaesthetizes a portion of one's brain.

I said earlier that the decadence of our language is probably curable. Those who deny this would argue, if they produced an argument at all, that language merely reflects existing social conditions, and that we cannot influence its development by any direct tinkering with words and constructions. So far as the general tone or spirit of a language goes, this may be true, but it is not true in detail. Silly words and expressions have often disappeared, not through any evolutionary process but owing to the conscious action of a minority. Two recent examples were *explore every avenue* and *leave no stone unturned,* which were killed by the jeers of a few journalists. There is a long list of flyblown metaphors which could similarly be got rid of if enough people would interest themselves in the job; and it should also be possible to laugh the *not un-* formation out of existence,[3] to reduce the amount of Latin and Greek in the average sentence, to drive out foreign phrases and strayed scientific words, and, in general, to make preten-

[3] One can cure oneself of the *not un-* formation by memorizing this sentence: *A not unblack dog was chasing a not unsmall rabbit across a not ungreen field.*

tiousness unfashionable. But all these are minor points. The defence of the English language implies more than this, and perhaps it is best to start by saying what it does *not* imply.

To begin with, it has nothing to do with archaism, with the salvaging of obsolete words and turns of speech, or with the setting-up of a "standard English" which must never be departed from. On the contrary, it is especially concerned with the scrapping of every word or idiom which has outworn its usefulness. It has nothing to do with correct grammar and syntax, which are of no importance so long as one makes one's meaning clear, or with the avoidance of Americanisms, or with having what is called a "good prose style." On the other hand it is not concerned with fake simplicity and the attempt to make written English colloquial. Nor does it even imply in every case preferring the Saxon word to the Latin one, though it does imply using the fewest and shortest words that will cover one's meaning. What is above all needed is to let the meaning choose the word, and not the other way about. In prose, the worst thing one can do with words is to surrender to them. When you think of a concrete object, you think wordlessly, and then, if you want to describe the thing you have been visualizing, you probably hunt about till you find the exact words that seem to fit it. When you think of something abstract you are more inclined to use words from the start, and unless you make a conscious effort to prevent it, the existing dialect will come rushing in and do the job for you, at the expense of blurring or even changing your meaning. Probably it is better to put off using words as long as possible and get one's meaning as clear as one can through pictures or sensations. Afterwards one can choose—not simply *accept*—the phrases

that will best cover the meaning, and then switch round and decide what impression one's words are likely to make on another person. This last effort of the mind cuts out all stale or mixed images, all prefabricated phrases, needless repetitions, and humbug and vagueness generally. But one can often be in doubt about the effect of a word or a phrase, and one needs rules that one can rely on when instinct fails. I think the following rules will cover most cases:

(i) Never use a metaphor, simile or other figure of speech which you are used to seeing in print.

(ii) Never use a long word where a short one will do.

(iii) If it is possible to cut a word out, always cut it out.

(iv) Never use the passive where you can use the active.

(v) Never use a foreign phrase, a scientific word or a jargon word if you can think of an everyday English equivalent.

(vi) Break any of these rules sooner than say anything outright barbarous.

These rules sound elementary, and so they are, but they demand a deep change of attitude in anyone who has grown used to writing in the style now fashionable. One could keep all of them and still write bad English, but one could not write the kind of stuff that I quoted in those five specimens at the beginning of this article.

I have not here been considering the literary use of language, but merely language as an instrument for expressing and not for concealing or preventing thought. Stuart Chase and others have come near to claiming that all abstract words are meaningless, and have used this as a pretext for advocating a kind of political quietism. Since you don't know what Fascism is, how can you struggle against Fascism? One need not swallow such absurdities as this, but one ought to recognize that the present political chaos is connected with the decay of language, and that one can probably bring about some improvement by starting at the verbal end. If you simplify your English, you are freed from the worst follies of orthodoxy. You cannot speak any of the necessary dialects, and when you make a stupid remark its stupidity will be obvious, even to yourself. Political language—and with variations this is true of all political parties, **from**

Conservatives to Anarchists—is designed to make lies sound truthful and murder respectable, and to give an appearance of solidity to pure wind. One cannot change this all in a moment, but one can at least change one's own habits, and from time to time one can even, if one jeers loudly enough, send some worn-out and useless phrase—some *jackboot, Achilles' heel, hotbed, melting pot, acid test, veritable inferno* or other lump of verbal refuse—into the dustbin where it belongs.

from THE STORY OF A NOVEL
by THOMAS WOLFE

I DON'T KNOW how I became a writer, but I think it was because of a certain force in me that had to write and that finally burst through and found a channel. My people were of the working class of people. My father, a stonecutter, was a man with a great respect and veneration for literature. He had a tremendous memory, and he loved poetry, and the poetry that he loved best was naturally of the rhetorical kind that such a man would like. Nevertheless it was good poetry, Hamlet's Soliloquy, "Macbeth," Mark Antony's Funeral Oration, Grey's "Elegy," and all the rest of it. I heard it all as a child; I memorized and learned it all.

He sent me to college to the state university. The desire to write, which had been strong during all my days in high school, grew stronger still. I was editor of the college paper, the college magazine, etc., and in my last year or two I was a member of a course in playwriting which had just been established there. I wrote several little one-act plays, still thinking I would become a lawyer or a newspaper

man, never daring to believe I could seriously become a writer. Then I went to Harvard, wrote some more plays there, became obsessed with the idea that I had to be a playwright, left Harvard, had my plays rejected, and finally in the autumn of 1926, how, why, or in what manner I have never exactly been able to determine, but probably because the force in me that had to write at length sought out its channel, I began to write my first book in London. I was living all alone at that time. I had two rooms—a bedroom and a sitting room—in a little square in Chelsea in which all the houses had that familiar, smoked brick and cream-yellow-plaster look of London houses. They looked exactly alike.

As I say, I was living alone at that time and in a foreign country. I did not know why I was there or what the direction of my life should be, and that was the way I began to write my book. I think that is one of the hardest times a writer goes through. There is no standard, no outward judgment, by which he can measure what he has done. By day I would write for hours in big ledgers which I had bought for the purpose; then at night I would lie in bed and fold my hands behind my head and think of what I had done that day and hear the solid, leather footbeat of the London bobby as he came by my window, and remember that I was born in North Carolina and wonder why the hell I was now in London lying in the darkened bed, and thinking about words I had that day put down on paper. I would get a great, hollow, utterly futile feeling inside me, and then I would get up and switch on the light and read the words I had written that day, and then I would wonder: why am I here now? why have I come?

By day there would be the great, dull roar of London, the gold, yellow, foggy light you have there in October. The man-swarmed and old, weblike, smoky London! And I loved the place, and I loathed it and abhorred it. I knew no one there, and I had been a child in North Carolina long ago, and I was living there in two rooms in the huge octopal and illimitable web of that overwhelming city. I did not know why I had come, why I was there.

I worked there every day with such feelings as I have described, and came back to America in the winter and worked here. I would teach all day and write all night, and finally about two and a half years after I had begun the book in London, I finished it in New York.

My book was what is often referred to as an autobiographical novel. I protested against this term in a preface to the book upon the grounds that any serious work of creation is of necessity autobiographical and that few more autobiographical works than *Gulliver's Travels* have ever been written.

My conviction is that all serious crea-tive work must be at bottom autobio-graphical, and that a man must use the material and experience of his own life if he is to create anything that has sub-stantial value. But I also believe now that the young writer is often led through inex-perience to a use of the materials of life which are, perhaps, somewhat too naked and direct for the purpose of a work of art. The thing a young writer is likely to do is to confuse the limits between actual-ity and reality. He tends unconciously to describe an event in such a way because it actually happened that way, and from an artistic point of view, I can now see that this is wrong. It is not, for example, im-portant that one remembers a beautiful woman of easy virtue as having come from the state of Kentucky in the year 1907. She could perfectly well have come from Idaho or Texas or Nova Scotia. The important thing really is only to express as well as possible the character and quality of the beautiful woman of easy virtue. But the young writer, chained to fact and to his own inexperience, as yet unliberated by maturity, is likely to argue, "she must be described as coming from Kentucky be-cause that is where she actually did come from."

In spite of this, it is impossible for a man who has the stuff of creation in him to make a literal transcription of his own ex-perience. Everything in a work of art is changed and transfigured by the personal-ity of the artist. And as far as my own first book is concerned, I can truthfully say that I do not believe that there is a single page of it that is true to fact. And from this cir-cumstance, also, I learned another curious thing about writing. For although my book was not true to fact, it was true to the gen-eral experience of the town I came from and I hope, of course, to the general ex-perience of all men living. The best way I can describe the situation is this: it was as if I were a sculptor who had found a certain kind of clay with which to model. Now a farmer who knew well the neighborhood from which this clay had come might pass by and find the sculptor at his work and say to him, "I know the farm from which you got that clay." But it would be unfair of him to say, "I know the figure, too." Now I think what happened in my native town is that having seen the clay, they became immediately convinced that they recognized the figure, too, and the results of this misconception were so painful and ludicrous that the telling of it is almost past belief.

It was my experience to be assured by people from my native town not only that they remembered incidents and characters in my first book, which may have had some basis in actuality, but also that they remembered incidents which so far as I know had no historical basis whatever. For example, there was one scene in the book in which a stonecutter is represented as selling to a notorious woman of the town a statue of a marble angel which he has treasured for many years. So far as I know, there was no basis in fact for this story, and yet I was informed by several people later that they not only remembered the incident perfectly, but had actually been witnesses to the transaction. Nor was this the end of the story. I heard that one of the newspapers sent a reporter and a photographer to the cemetery and a photograph was printed in the paper with a statement to the effect that the angel was the now famous angel which had stood upon the stonecutter's porch for so many years and had given the title to my book. The unfortunate part of this proceeding was that I had never seen or heard of this angel before, and that this angel was, in fact, erected over the grave of a well-

known Methodist lady who had died a few years before and that her indignant family had immediately written the paper to demand a retraction of its story, saying that their mother had been in no way connected with the infamous book or the infamous angel which had given the infamous book its name. Such, then, were some of the unforeseen difficulties with which I was confronted after the publication of my first book.

Month was passing into month; I had had a success. The way was opened to me. There was only one thing for me to do and that was work, and I was spending my time consuming myself with anger, grief, and useless passion about the reception the book had had in my native town, or wasting myself again in exuberant elation because of the critics' and the readers' praise, or in anguish and bitterness because of their ridicule. For the first time, I realized the nature of one of the artist's greatest conflicts, and was faced with the need of meeting it. For the first time I saw not only that the artist must live and sweat and love and suffer and enjoy as other men, but that the artist must also work as other men and that furthermore, he must work even while these common events of life are going on. It seems a simple and banal assertion, but I learned it hardly, and in one of the worst moments of my life. There is no such thing as an artistic vacuum; there is no such thing as a time when the artist may work in a delightful atmosphere, free of agony that other men must know, or if the artist ever does find such a time, it is something not to be hoped for, something not to be sought for indefinitely.

At any rate, while my life and energy were absorbed in the emotional vortex which my first book had created, I was getting almost no work done on the second. And now I was faced with another fundamental problem which every young writer must meet squarely if he is to continue. How is a man to get his writing done? How long should he work at writing, and how often? What kind of method, if any, must he find in following his work? I suddenly found myself face to face with the grim necessity of constant, daily work. And as simple as this discovery may seem to everyone, I was not prepared for it. A young writer without a public does not feel the sense of necessity, the pressure of time, as does a writer who has been published and who must now begin to think of time schedules, publishing seasons, the completion of his next book. I realized suddenly with a sense of definite shock that I had let six months go by since the publication of my first book and that, save for a great many notes and fragments, I had done nothing. Meanwhile, the book continued to sell slowly but steadily, and in February 1930, about five months after its publication, I found it possible to resign from the faculty of New York University and devote my full time to the preparation of a second book. That spring I was also fortunate enough to be awarded the Guggenheim Fellowship which would enable me to live and work abroad for a year. And accordingly at the beginning of May, I went abroad again.

I was in Paris for a couple of months, until the middle of July, and although I now compelled myself to work for four or five hours a day, my effort at composition was still confused and broken, and there was nothing yet that had the structural form and unity of a book. The life of the great city fascinated me as it had always done, but also aroused all the old feelings of naked homelessness, rootlessness, and loneliness which I have always felt there.

It was, and has always remained for me, at least, the most homesick city in the world; the place where I have felt mostly an alien and a stranger, and certainly for me as fascinating and seductive as the city is, it has never been a good place to work. But here I would like to say something about places to work because that is another problem which causes young writers a great deal of doubt, uncertainty, and confusion, and I think, uselessly.

I had gone through the whole experience and now I was almost done with it. I had come to Paris first six years before, a youth of twenty-four, filled with all the romantic faith and foolishness which many young men at that time felt when they saw Paris. I had come there that first time, so I told myself, to work, and so glamorous was the magic name of Paris at that time, that I really thought one could work far better there than anywhere on earth; that it was a place where the very air was impregnated with the energies of art; where the artist was bound to find a more fortunate and happy life than he could possibly find in America. Now I had come to see that this was wrong. I had come to understand very plainly that what many of us were doing in those years when we fled from our own country and sought refuge abroad was not really looking for a place to work, but looking for a place where we could escape from work; that what we were really fleeing from in those years was not the Philistinism, the materialism, and ugliness in American life which we said we were fleeing from, but from the necessity of grappling squarely with ourselves and the necessity of finding in ourselves, somehow, the stuff to live by, to get from our own lives and our own experience the substance of our art which every man who ever wrote a living thing has had to get out of himself and without which he is lost.

The place to work! Yes, the place to work *was* Paris; it *was* Spain; it *was* Italy and Capri and Majorca, but great God, it was also Keokuk, and Portland, Maine, and Denver, Colorado, and Yancey County, North Carolina, and wherever we might be, if work was there within us at the time. If this was all that I had learned from these voyages to Europe, if the price of all this wandering had been just this simple lesson, it would have been worth the price, but that was not all. I had found out during these years that the way to discover one's own country was to leave it; that the way to find America was to find it in one's heart, one's memory, and one's spirit, and in a foreign land.

I think I may say that I discovered America during these years abroad out of my very need of her. The huge gain of this discovery seemed to come directly from my sense of loss. I had been to Europe five times now; each time I had come with delight, with maddening eagerness to return, and each time how, where, and in what way I did not know, I had felt the bitter ache of homelessness, a desperate longing for America, an overwhelming desire to return.

During that summer in Paris, I think I felt this great homesickness more than ever before, and I really believe that from this emotion, this constant and almost intolerable effort of memory and desire, the material and the structure of the books I now began to write were derived.

The quality of my memory is characterized, I believe, in a more than ordinary degree by the intensity of its sense impressions, its power to evoke and bring back the odors, sounds, colors, shapes, and feel of things with concrete vividness. Now my memory was at work night and day, in a way that I could at first neither check nor control and that swarmed unbidden in a stream of blazing pageantry across my mind, with the million forms and substances of the life that I had left, which was my own, America. I would be sitting, for example, on the terrace of a café watching the flash and play of life before me on the Avenue de l'Opéra and suddenly I would remember the iron railing that goes along the boardwalk at Atlantic City. I could see it instantly just the way it was, the heavy iron pipe; its raw, galvanized look; the way the joints were fitted together. It was all so vivid and concrete that I could feel my hand upon it and know the exact dimensions, its size and weight and shape. And suddenly I would realize that I had never seen any railing that looked like this in Europe. And this utterly familiar, common thing would suddenly be revealed to me with all the wonder with which we discover a thing which we have seen all our life and yet have never known before. Or again, it would be a bridge, the look of an old iron bridge across an American river, the sound the train makes as it goes across it; the spoke-and-hollow rumble of the ties below; the look of the muddy banks; the slow, thick, yellow wash of an American river; an old flat-bottomed boat half filled with water stogged in the muddy bank; or it would be, most lonely and haunting of all the sounds I know, the sound of a milk wagon as it entered an American street just at the first gray of the morning, the slow and lonely clopping of the hoof upon the street, the jink of bottles, the sudden rattle of a battered old milk can, the swift and hurried footsteps of the milkman, and again the jink of bottles, a low word spoken to his horse, and then the great, slow, clopping hoof receding into silence, and then quietness and a bird song rising in the street again. Or it would be a little wooden shed out in the country two miles from my home town where people waited for the street car, and I could see and feel again the dull and rusty color of the old green paint and see and feel all of the initials that had been carved out with jackknives on the planks and benches within the shed, and smell the warm and sultry smell so resinous and so thrilling, so filled with a strange and nameless excitement of an unknown joy, a coming prophecy, and hear the street car as it came to a stop, the moment of brooding, drowsing silence; a hot thrum and drowsy stitch at three o'clock; the smell of grass and hot sweet clover; and then the sudden sense of absence, loneliness and departure when the street car had gone and there was nothing but the hot and drowsy stitch at three o'clock again.

Or again, it would be an American street with all its jumble of a thousand ugly architectures. It would be Montague Street or Fulton Street in Brooklyn, or Eleventh Street in New York, or other streets where I had lived; and suddenly I would see the gaunt and savage webbing of the elevated structure along Fulton Street, and how the light swarmed through in dusty, broken bars, and I could remember the old, familiar rusty color, that incomparable rusty color that gets into so many things here in America. And this also would be like something I had seen a million times and lived with all my life.

I would sit there, looking out upon the Avenue de l'Opéra and my life would ache with the whole memory of it; the desire to see it again; somehow to find a word for it; a language that would tell its shape, its color, the way we have all known and felt and seen it. And when I understood this thing, I saw that I must find for my-self the tongue to utter what I knew but could not say. And from the moment of that discovery, the line and purpose of my life was shaped. The end toward which every energy of my life and talent would be henceforth directed was in such a way as this defined. It was as if I had discovered a whole new universe of chemical elements and had begun to see certain relations between some of them but had by no means begun to organize the whole series into a harmonious and coherent union. From this time on, I think my efforts might be described as the effort to complete that organization, to discover that articulation for which I strove, to bring about that final coherent union. I know that I have failed thus far in doing so, but I believe I understand pretty thoroughly just where the nature of my failure lies, and of course my deepest and most earnest hope is that the time will come when I shall not fail.

At any rate, from this time on the general progress of the three books which I was to write in the next four and a half years could be fairly described in somewhat this way. It was a progress that began in a whirling vortex and a creative chaos and that proceeded slowly at the expense of infinite confusion, toil, and error toward clarification and the articulation of an ordered and formal structure. An extraordinary image remains to me from that year, the year I spent abroad when the material of these books first began to take on an articulate form. It seemed that I had inside me, swelling and gathering all the time, a huge black cloud, and that this cloud was loaded with electricity, pregnant, crested, with a kind of hurricane violence that could not be held in check much longer; that the moment was approaching fast when it must break.

Well, all I can say is that the storm did break. It broke that summer while I was in Switzerland. It came in torrents, and it is not over yet.

The life of the artist at any epoch of man's history has not been an easy one. And here in America, it has often seemed to me, it may well be the hardest life that man has ever known. I am not speaking of some frustration in our native life, some barrenness of spirit, some arid Philistinism which contends against the artist's life and which prevents his growth. I do not speak of these things because I do not put the same belief in them that I once did. I am speaking as I have tried to speak from first to last in the concrete terms of the artist's actual experience, of the nature of the physical task before him. It seems to me that the task is one whose physical proportions are vaster and more difficult here than in any other nation on the earth. It is not merely that in the cultures of Europe and of the Orient the American artist can find no antecedent scheme, no structural plan, no body of tradition that can give his own work the validity and truth that it must have. It is not merely that he must make somehow a new tradition for himself, derived from his own life and from the enormous space and energy of American life, the structure of his own design; it is not merely that he is confronted by these problems; it is even more than this, that the labor of a complete and whole articulation, the discovery of an entire universe and of a complete language, is the task that lies before him.

Such is the nature of the struggle to which henceforth our lives must be devoted. Out of the billion forms of America, out of the savage violence and the dense complexity of all its swarming life; from the unique and single substance of this land and life of ours, must we draw the power and energy of our own life, the articulation of our speech, the substance of our art.

For here it seems to me in hard and honest ways like these we may find the tongue, the language, and the conscience that as men and artists we have got to have. Here, too, perhaps, must we who have no more than what we have, who know no more than what we know, who are no more than what we are, find our America. Here, at this present hour and moment of my life, I seek for mine.

UNTRAGIC AMERICA

AFTER 12 YEARS of silence, a new drama by our No. 1 playwright, Eugene O'Neill, is an event. But this one, *The Iceman Cometh,* prompts the reflection that no first-rate American tragedy has ever been written, not even by O'Neill. This despite the fact that the world has been steeped in tragedy for many years and despite the fact that all the characters in *The Iceman* are miserable specimens indeed. Instead of the ennobling effect that tragedy is supposed to give, *The Iceman* is more like a cosmic bellyache. And O'Neill's best plays, as a writer in *Theatre Arts* magazine has pointed out, are not so much real tragedies as "dramatizations of the tragic fact that man has lost sight of his own greatness."

America's failure to create first-rate tragedies may not seem like a national disaster. Yet dramatic tragedy has been the chosen medium of history's greatest art-

From *Life,* December 2, 1946. Reprinted by permission of *Life,* New York. Copyright 1946.

ists, and our failure in it may betoken some deeper failure in the American character or scene. A people who cannot witness great reminders of the tragic aspect of their own existence are not getting the most out of life and perhaps cannot be ranked among the greatest civilizations. The people of Athens and of Shakespeare's England were able to suffer vicariously with their tragic heroes in an emotional workout that left them wiser and more serene. That, said Aristotle, is the purpose of tragedy—to purge the emotions through pity and fear. But Americans disapprove of fear and want to free the world of it. Are we an essentially untragic people?

What Is Tragedy?

First, a few definitions, necessarily dogmatic. According to Aristotle, the first authority on the subject, tragedy must be "serious, complete and of a certain magnitude," to which Webster's dictionary adds that the hero "is by some passion or limitation brought to a catastrophe," the action as a whole working out as "a manifestation of fate." Strictly speaking, first-rate tragedy has been written in only two eras, by only four men: by Aeschylus, Sophocles and Euripedes in the 5th Century B.C. and by Shakespeare. Grade B tragedy (still very fine stuff) has been achieved by Corneille, Racine, Goethe, Ibsen and others, including composers of 19th Century opera; and you can grade it on down from there. But high tragedy must not be confused with pathos, gloom or a mere unhappy ending.

A key word in Aristotle's definition is "magnitude." The Greek and Shakespearean heroes were princes, kings or generals at least, outsize characters whose fate involved the fate of whole cities or nations with their own. Compare King Oedipus or King Lear with what passes for a tragic hero on the American stage— the clerk-hero of Elmer Rice's *Adding Machine,* significantly named Mr. Zero, or the moronic Lennie in Steinbeck's *Of Mice and Men.* Our heroes appeal not to our awe but to our power of sympathetic identification. Aided by naturalistic settings and dialog, we are above all made to feel at home, among equals or inferiors. The characters on our stage and screen may be rich and admirable, but we are always reminded of their humble origin, their warts or some other comfortable and exceedingly nontragic flaw. *The Iceman* carries this democratic snobbism about as far as it can be carried: the characters all start out as a bunch of drunken bums and finish the same.

The requirement of "magnitude," which our drama fails to meet, suggests that great tragedy may be incompatible with American democracy. Except at the Sinatra-fan level, we don't really believe in heroes, and when they appear among us anyway we unfit them for tragedy by cutting them down to size. Just as we reacted to the phenomenon of Hitler by singing *Der Führer's Face,* so we debunk our own heroes, good or bad. American fiction has produced a few characters, such as Ahab in *Moby Dick,* who are of truly tragic magnitude. But the typical American reader tries to get around Ahab by dubbing him a fanatic.

One reason for the greatness of Ahab and for the high seriousness of much Victorian literature in comparison with our own was that our forebears shared a deep Christian sense of sin. This sense of sin was related to a sense of man's cosmic importance, which we seem to have lost. To a Greek, also, man was the center of the universe; his very gods had manlike attributes and were constantly involving themselves in man's affairs, whether guiding him in battle or making love to his wife. But modern man has moved from the center of the universe and reduced himself to a trivial biological specimen. He cannot esteem himself highly enough for high tragedy. He can appraise, analyze, respect and belittle himself, but he cannot regard himself with awe.

Without awe, tragedy cannot achieve its greatest impact. And it may be that our belief that all men are equal, our refusal to admit the very concept of aristocracy, debars us from ever feeling the awe that the Athenians felt toward Oedipus or the Elizabethan groundlings toward Lear. In that case our failure to produce great tragedy may be a virtue, or at least a fair price to pay for our democracy. Maybe we are more like the Romans, who also had great political gifts and never produced any great tragedy either.

Yet democracy does produce heroes, and our history is replete with tragic themes. These themes and heroes may make great American tragedy if we get over our belittling habit and admit to ourselves that the average man is not the measure of all things. But even that won't be enough. For while great tragedy is not necessarily incompatible with democracy, it is incompatible with another habit that lies deep in the American grain.

The Idea of Progress

This habit is an optimistic faith in progress. Professor J. B. Bury, who wrote a history of *The Idea of Progress,* defines it to mean "that civilization has moved, is moving and will move in a desirable direction." This idea is only about as old as modern science, stemming from Bacon and Descartes. But it has as firm a grip on the modern world as the expectation of Judgment Day had on the medieval world. And except among Russian Communists (for Marx swallowed it whole) the idea of progress has nowhere taken deeper root than in America.

Now why is this idea incompatible with high tragedy? Because we have let it replace the old convictions on which tragedy depends, that man is finite (or sinful) and that his destiny does not lie wholly in his own hands. The idea of progress grew from the observable fact of science's increasing conquest of material nature. But Darwin, Herbert Spencer and others stretched this observable fact into certain unprovable assumptions: namely, that "all environments [Darwin's words] will tend to progress toward perfection," that man himself is perfectible through scientific self-knowledge and that evil is not a permanent necessity in the world. Even devout men like Tennyson, whose *Locksley Hall* is the battle hymn of progress, could promote the new faith by assuming God was on its side.

As indeed He may be. But there is increasing evidence to the contrary. There is also evidence that the underpinnings of our faith in progress may be weakening, for the scientists themselves are no longer so sure. The leading physicists have long since regained an almost primitive awe of the universe, and H. G. Wells repudiated a lifelong worship of progress before he left a world for which his final epithet was "doomed formicary." Bury's book was written a generation before the atomic bomb, but the bomb gives these words of his a new point: "If there were good cause for believing that the earth would be uninhabitable in A.D. 2000 or 2100, the doctrine of Progress would lose its meaning and would automatically disappear."

Reversal of Values

To gain a sense of tragedy, Americans must therefore virtually reverse two of their dearest values: on the one hand, we must recover our awareness of evil, uncertainty and fear; on the other, we must gain a sense of man's occasional greatness (which is quite a different thing from "the dignity of the common man"). For tragedy, in essence, is the spectacle of a great man confronting his own finiteness and being punished for letting his reach exceed his grasp. The Greeks had two words for this—*hybris,* pride, and *moira,* fate—which told them that subtle dangers lurk in all human achievements and that the bigger they are the harder they fall. But if Americans believe that there are no insoluble questions, they can't ask tragic questions. And if they believe that punishment is only for ignorance or inadequate effort, they can't give tragic answers. They can't have the tragic sense.

That sense is to feel a due humility before the forces that are able to humble us, without wishing to avoid the contest where the humbling may take place. We will be a more civilized people when we get it.

THE ESSENCE OF TRAGEDY

by MAXWELL ANDERSON

ANYBODY WHO DARES to discuss the making of tragedy lays himself open to critical assault and general barrage, for the theorists have been hunting for the essence of tragedy since Aristotle without entire success. There is no doubt that playwrights have occasionally written tragedy successfully, from Aeschylus on, and there is no doubt that Aristotle came very close to a definition of what tragedy is in his famous passage on catharsis. But why the performance of tragedy should have a cleansing effect on the audience, why an audience is willing to listen to tragedy, why tragedy has a place in the education of men, has never, to my knowledge, been convincingly stated. I must begin by saying that I have not solved the Sphinx's riddle which fifty generations of skillful brains have left in shadow. But I have one suggestion which I think might lead to a solution if it were put to laboratory tests by those who know something about philosophical analysis and dialectic.

There seems no way to get at this suggestion except through a reference to my own adventures in playwriting, so I ask your tolerance while I use myself as an instance. A man who has written successful plays is usually supposed to know something about the theory of playwriting, and perhaps he usually does. In my own case, however, I must confess that I came into the theater unexpectedly, without preparation, and stayed in it because I had a certain amount of rather accidental success. It was not until after I had fumbled my way through a good many successes and an appalling number of failures that I began to doubt the sufficiency of dramatic instinct and to wonder whether or not there were general laws governing dramatic structure which so poor a head for theory as my own might grasp and use. I had read the *Poetics* long before I tried playwriting, and I had looked doubtfully into a few well-known handbooks on dramatic structure, but the maxims and theories propounded always drifted by me in a luminous haze—brilliant, true, profound in context, yet quite without meaning for me when I considered the plan for a play or tried to clarify an emotion in dialogue. So far as I could make out every play was a new problem, and the old rules were inapplicable. There were so many rules, so many landmarks, so many pitfalls, so many essential reckonings, that it seemed impossible to find your way through the jungle except by plunging ahead, trusting to your sense of direction and keeping your wits about you as you went.

But as the seasons went by and my failures fell as regularly as the leaves in autumn I began to search again among the theorists of the past for a word of wisdom that might take some of the gamble out of playwriting. What I needed most of all, I felt, was a working definition of what a play is, or perhaps a formula which would include all the elements necessary to a play structure. A play is almost always, probably, an attempt to recapture a vision for the stage. But when you are working in the theater it's most unsatisfactory to follow the gleam without a compass, quite risky to trust "the light that never was on sea or land" without making sure beforehand that you are not being led straight into a slough of despond. In other words you must make a choice among visions, and you must check your chosen vision carefully before assuming that it will make a play. But by what rules, what maps, what fields of reference can you check so intangible a substance as a revelation, a dream, an inspiration, or any

similar nudge from the subconscious mind?

I shan't trouble you with the details of my search for a criterion, partly because I can't remember it in detail. But I reread Aristotle's *Poetics* in the light of some bitter experience, and one of his observations led me to a comparison of ancient and modern playwriting methods. In discussing construction he made a point of *the recognition scene* as essential to tragedy. The recognition scene, as Aristotle isolated it in the tragedies of the Greeks, was generally an artificial device, a central scene in which the leading character saw through a disguise, recognized as a friend or as an enemy, perhaps as a lover or a member of his own family, some person whose identity had been hidden. Iphigeneia, for example, acting as priestess in an alien country, receives a victim for sacrifice and then recognizes her own brother in this victim. There is an instant and profound emotional reaction, instantly her direction in the play is altered. But occasionally, in the greatest of the plays, the recognition turned on a situation far more convincing, though no less contrived. Oedipus, hunting savagely for the criminal who has brought the plague upon Thebes, discovers that he is himself that criminal—and since this is a discovery that affects not only the physical well-being and happiness of the hero, but the whole structure of his life, the effect on him and on the direction of the story is incalculably greater than could result from the more superficial revelation made to Iphigeneia.

Now scenes of exactly this sort are rare in the modern drama except in detective stories adapted for the stage. But when I probed a little more deeply into the memorable pieces of Shakespeare's theater and our own I began to see that though modern recognition scenes are subtler and harder to find, they are none the less present in the plays we choose to remember. They seldom have to do with anything so naïve as disguise or the unveiling of a personal identity. But the element of discovery is just as important as ever. For the mainspring in the mechanism of a modern play is almost invariably a discovery by the hero of some element in his environment or in his own soul of which he has not been aware—or which he has not taken sufficiently into account. Moreover, nearly every teacher of playwriting has had some inkling of this, though it was not until after I had worked out my own theory that what they said on this point took on accurate meaning for me. I still think that the rule which I formulated for my own guidance is more concise than any other, and so I give it here: A play should lead up to and away from a central crisis, and this crisis should consist in a discovery by the leading character which has an indelible effect on his thought and emotion and completely alters his course of action. The leading character, let me say again, must make the discovery; it must affect him emotionally; and it must alter his direction in the play.

Try that formula on any play you think worthy of study, and you will find that, with few exceptions, it follows this pattern or some variation of this pattern. The turning point of *The Green Pastures,* for example, is the discovery by God, who is the leading character, that a God who is to endure must conform to the laws of change. The turning point of *Hamlet* is Hamlet's discovery, in the play scene, that his uncle was unquestionably the murderer of his father. In *Abe Lincoln in Illinois* Lincoln's discovery is that he has been a coward, that he has stayed out of the fight for the Union because he was afraid. In each case, you will note, the discovery

has a profound emotional effect on the hero, and gives an entirely new direction to his action in the play.

I'm not writing a disquisition on playwriting and wouldn't be competent to write one, but I do want to make a point of the superlative usefulness of this one touchstone for play structure. When a man sets out to write a play his first problem is his subject and the possibilities of that subject as a story to be projected from the stage. His choice of subject matter is his personal problem, and one that takes its answer from his personal relation to his times. But if he wants to know a possible play subject when he finds it, if he wants to know how to mold the subject into play form after he has found it, I doubt that he'll ever discover another standard as satisfactory as the modern version of Aristotle which I have suggested. If the plot he has in mind does not contain a playable episode in which the hero or heroine makes an emotional discovery, a discovery that practically dictates the end of the story, then such an episode must be inserted—and if no place can be found for it the subject is almost certainly a poor one for the theater. If this emotional discovery is contained in the story, but is not central, then it must be made central, and the whole action must revolve around it. In a three-act play it should fall near the end of the second act, though it may be delayed till the last; in a five-act play it will usually be found near the end of the third, though here also it can be delayed. Everything else in the play should be subordinated to this one episode—should lead up to or away from it.

Now this prime rule has a corollary which is just as important as the rule itself. The hero who is to make the central discovery in a play must not be a perfect man. He must have some variation of what

Aristotle calls a tragic fault; and the reason he must have it is that when he makes his discovery he must change both in himself and in his action—and he must change for the better. The fault can be a very simple one—a mere unawareness, for example—but if he has no fault he cannot change for the better, but only for the worse, and for a reason which I shall discuss later, it is necessary that he must become more admirable, and not less so, at the end of the play. In other words, a hero must pass through an experience which opens his eyes to an error of his own. He must learn through suffering. In a tragedy he suffers death itself as a consequence of his fault or his attempt to correct it, but before he dies he has become a nobler person because of his recognition of his fault and the consequent alteration of his course of action. In a serious play which does not end in death he suffers a lesser punishment, but the pattern remains the same. In both forms he has a fault to begin with, he discovers that fault during the course of the action, and he does what he can to rectify it at the end. In *The Green Pastures* God's fault was that he believed himself perfect. He discovered that he was not perfect, that he had been in error and must make amends. Hamlet's fault was that he could not make up his mind to act. He offers many excuses for his indecision until he discovers that there is no real reason for hesitation and that he has delayed out of cowardice. Lincoln, in *Abe Lincoln in Illinois,* has exactly the same difficulty. In the climactic scene it is revealed to him that he had hesitated to take sides through fear of the consequences to himself, and he then chooses to go ahead without regard for what may be in store for him. From the point of view of the playwright, then, the essence of a tragedy, or even of a serious play, is the spiritual awakening, or regeneration, of his hero.

When a playwright attempts to reverse the formula, when his hero makes a discovery which has an evil effect, or one which the audience interprets as evil, on his character, the play is inevitably a failure on the stage. In *Troilus and Cressida* Troilus discovers that Cressida is a light woman. He draws from her defection the inference that all women are faithless—that faith in woman is the possession of fools. As a consequence he turns away from life and seeks death in a cause as empty as the love he has given up, the cause of the strumpet Helen. All the glory of Shakespeare's verse cannot rescue the play for an audience, and save in *Macbeth* Shakespeare nowhere wrote so richly, so wisely, or with such a flow of brilliant metaphor.

For the audience will always insist that the alteration in the hero be for the better —or for what it believes to be the better. As audiences change the standards of good and evil change, though slowly and unpredictably, and the meanings of plays change with the centuries. One thing only is certain: that an audience watching a play will go along with it only when the leading character responds in the end to what it considers a higher moral impulse than moved him at the beginning of the story, though the audience will of course define morality as it pleases and in the terms of its own day. It may be that there is no absolute up or down in this world, but the race believes that there is, and will not hear of any denial.

And now at last I come to the point toward which I've been struggling so laboriously. Why does the audience come to the theater to look on while an imaginary hero is put to an imaginary trial and comes out of it with credit to the race and to himself? It was this question that prompted my essay, and unless I've been led astray by my own predilections there is a very possible answer in the rules for playwriting which I have just cited. The theater originated in two complementary religious ceremonies, one celebrating the animal in man and one celebrating the god. Old Greek Comedy was dedicated to the spirits of lust and riot and earth, spirits which are certainly necessary to the health and continuance of the race. Greek tragedy was dedicated to man's aspiration, to his kinship with the gods, to his unending, blind attempt to lift himself above his lusts and his pure animalism into a world where there are other values than pleasure and survival. However unaware of it we may be, our theater has followed the Greek patterns with no change in essence, from Aristophanes and Euripides to our own day. Our more ribald musical comedies are simply our approximation of the Bacchic rites of Old Comedy. In the rest of our theater we sometimes follow Sophocles, whose tragedy is always an exaltation of the human spirit, sometimes Euripides, whose tragicomedy follows the same pattern of an excellence achieved through suffering. The forms of both tragedy and comedy have changed a good deal in non-essentials, but in essentials—and especially in the core of meaning which they must have for audiences—they are in the main the same religious rites which grew up around the altars of Attica long ago.

It is for this reason that when you write for the theater you must choose between your version of a phallic revel and your vision of what mankind may or should become. Your vision may be faulty, or shallow, or sentimental, but it must conform to some aspiration in the audience, or the audience will reject it. Old Comedy, the celebration of the animal in us, still has a

place in our theater, as it had in Athens, but here, as there, that part of the theater which celebrated man's virtue and his regeneration in hours of crisis is accepted as having the more important function. Our comedy is largely the Greek New Comedy, which grew out of Euripides' tragicomedy, and is separated from tragedy only in that it presents a happier scene and puts its protagonist through an ordeal which is less than lethal.

And since our plays, aside from those which are basically Old Comedy, are exaltations of the human spirit, since that is what an audience expects when it comes to the theater, the playwright gradually discovers, as he puts plays before audiences, that he must follow the ancient Aristotelian rule: he must build his plot around a scene wherein his hero discovers some mortal frailty or stupidity in himself and faces life armed with a new wisdom. He must so arrange his story that it will prove to the audience that men pass through suffering purified, that, animal though we are, despicable though we are in many ways, there is in us all some divine, incalculable fire that urges us to be better than we are.

It could be argued that what the audience demands of a hero is only conformity to race morality, to the code which seems to the spectators most likely to make for race survival. In many cases, especially in comedy, and obviously in the comedy of Molière, this is true. But in the majority of ancient and modern plays it seems to me that what the audience wants to believe is that men have a desire to break the molds of earth which encase them and claim a kinship with a higher morality than that which hems them in. The rebellion of Antigone, who breaks the laws of men through adherence to a higher law of affection, the rebellion of Prometheus, who breaks the law of the gods to bring fire to men, the rebellion of God in *The Green Pastures* against the rigid doctrine of the Old Testament, the rebellion of Tony in *They Knew What They Wanted* against the convention that called on him to repudiate his cuckold child, the rebellion of Liliom against the heavenly law which asked him to betray his own integrity and make a hypocrisy of his affection, even the repudiation of the old forms and the affirmation of new by the heroes of Ibsen and Shaw, these are all instances to me of the groping of men toward an excellence

dimly apprehended, seldom possible of definition. They are evidence to me that the theater at its best is a religious affirmation, an age-old rite restating and reassuring man's belief in his own destiny and his ultimate hope. The theater is much older than the doctrine of evolution, but its one faith, asseverated again and again for every age and every year, is a faith in evolution, in the reaching and the climb of men toward distant goals, glimpsed but never seen, perhaps never achieved, or achieved only to be passed impatiently on the way to a more distant horizon.

TRAGEDY AND THE COMMON MAN

by ARTHUR MILLER

IN THIS AGE few tragedies are written. It has often been held that the lack is due to a paucity of heroes among us, or else that modern man has had the blood drawn out of his organs of belief by the skepticism of science, and the heroic attack on life cannot feed on an attitude of reserve and circumspection. For one reason or another, we are often held to be below tragedy—or tragedy above us. The inevitable conclusion is, of course, that the tragic mode is archaic, fit only for the very highly placed, the kings or the kingly, and where this admission is not made in so many words it is most often implied.

I believe that the common man is as apt a subject for tragedy in its highest sense as kings were. On the face of it this ought to be obvious in the light of modern psychiatry, which bases its analysis upon classific formulations, such as the Oedipus and Orestes complexes, for instances, which were enacted by royal beings, but which

apply to everyone in similar emotional situations.

Not Exclusive

More simply, when the question of tragedy in art is not at issue, we never hesitate to attribute to the well-placed and the exalted the very same mental processes as the lowly. And finally, if the exaltation of tragic action were truly a property of the high-bred character alone, it is inconceivable that the mass of mankind should cherish tragedy above all other forms, let alone be capable of understanding it.

As a general rule, to which there may be exceptions unknown to me, I think the tragic feeling is evoked in us when we are in the presence of a character who is ready to lay down his life, if need be, to secure one thing—his sense of personal dignity. From Orestes to Hamlet, Medea to Macbeth, the underlying struggle is that of the individual attempting to gain his "rightful" position in his society.

Sometimes he is one who has been displaced from it, sometimes one who seeks to attain it for the first time, but the fateful wound from which the inevitable events spiral is the wound of indignity, and its dominant force is indignation. Tragedy, then, is the consequence of a man's total compulsion to evaluate himself justly.

In the sense of having been initiated by the hero himself, the tale always reveals what has been called his "tragic flaw," a failing that is not peculiar to grand or elevated characters. Nor is it necessarily a weakness. The flaw, or crack in the character, is really nothing—and need be nothing, but his inherent unwillingness to remain passive in the face of what he conceives to be a challenge to his dignity, his image of his rightful status. Only the passive, only those who accept their lot without active retaliation, are "flawless." Most of us are in that category.

But there are among us today, as there always have been, those who act against the scheme of things that degrades them, and in the process of action everything we have accepted out of fear or insensitivity or ignorance is shaken before us and examined, and from this total onslaught by an individual against the seemingly stable cosmos surrounding us—from this total examination of the "unchangeable" environment—comes the terror and the fear that is classically associated with tragedy.

More important, from this total questioning of what has previously been unquestioned, we learn. And such a process is not beyond the common man. In revolutions around the world, these past thirty years, he has demonstrated again and again this inner dynamic of all tragedy.

Insistence upon the rank of the tragic hero, or the so-called nobility of his character, is really but a clinging to the outward forms of tragedy. If rank or nobility of character was indispensable, then it would follow that the problems of those with rank were the particular problems of tragedy. But surely the right of one monarch to capture the domain from another no longer raises our passions, nor are our concepts of justice what they were to the mind of an Elizabethan king.

What It Is

The quality in such plays that does shake us, however, derives from the underlying fear of being displaced, the disaster inherent in being torn away from our chosen image of what and who we are in this world. Among us today this fear is as strong, and perhaps stronger, than it ever was. In fact, it is the common man who knows this fear best.

Now, if it is true that tragedy is the consequence of a man's total compulsion to evaluate himself justly, his destruction in the attempt posits a wrong or an evil in his environment. And this is precisely the morality of tragedy and its lesson. The discovery of the moral law, which is what the enlightenment of tragedy consists of, is not the discovery of some abstract or metaphysical quantity.

The tragic right is a condition of life, a condition in which the human personality is able to flower and realize itself. The wrong is the condition which suppresses man, perverts the flowing out of his love and creative instinct. Tragedy enlightens—and it must, in that it points the heroic finger at the enemy of man's freedom. The thrust for freedom is the quality in tragedy which exalts. The revolutionary questioning of the stable environment is what terrifies. In no way is the common man debarred from such thoughts or such actions.

Seen in this light, our lack of tragedy may be partially accounted for by the turn which modern literature has taken toward the purely psychiatric view of life, or the purely sociological. If all our miseries, our indignities, are born and bred within our minds, then all action, let alone the heroic action, is obviously impossible.

And if society alone is responsible for the cramping of our lives, then the protagonist must needs be so pure and faultless as to force us to deny his validity as a character. From neither of these views can tragedy derive, simply because neither represents a balanced concept of life. Above all else, tragedy requires the finest appreciation by the writer of cause and effect.

No tragedy can therefore come about when its author fears to question absolutely everything, when he regards any institution, habit or custom as being either everlasting, immutable or inevitable. In the tragic view the need of man to wholly realize himself is the only fixed star, and whatever it is that hedges his nature and lowers it is ripe for attack and examination. Which is not to say that tragedy must preach revolution.

Gaining "Size"

The Greeks could probe the very heavenly origin of their ways and return to confirm the rightness of laws. And Job could face God in anger, demanding his right and end in submission. But for a moment everything is in suspension, nothing is accepted, and in this stretching and tearing apart of the cosmos, in the very action of so doing, the character gains "size," the tragic stature which is spuriously attached to the royal or the high born in our minds. The commonest of men may take on that stature to the extent of his willingness to throw all he has into the contest, the battle to secure his rightful place in his world.

There is a misconception of tragedy with which I have been struck in review after review, and in many conversations with writers and readers alike. It is the idea that tragedy is of necessity allied to pessimism. Even the dictionary says nothing more about the word than that it means a story with a sad or unhappy ending. This impression is so firmly fixed that I almost hesitate to claim that in truth tragedy implies more optimism in its author than does comedy, and that its final result ought to be the reinforcement of the onlooker's brightest opinions of the human animal.

For, if it is true to say that in essence the tragic hero is intent upon claiming his whole due as a personality, and if this struggle must be total and without reservation, then it automatically demonstrates the indestructible will of man to achieve his humanity.

The possibility of victory must be there in tragedy. Where pathos rules, where pathos is finally derived, a character has fought a battle he could not possibly have won. The pathetic is achieved when the protagonist is, by virtue of his witlessness, his insensitivity, or the very air he gives off, incapable of grappling with a much superior force.

Nicer Balance

Pathos truly is the mode for the pessimist. But tragedy requires a nicer balance between what is possible and what is impossible. And it is curious, although edifying, that the plays we revere, century after century, are the tragedies. In them, and in them alone, lies the belief—optimistic, if you will, in the perfectibility of man.

It is time, I think, that we who are with-out kings, took up this bright thread of our history and followed it to the only place it can possibly lead in our time—the heart and spirit of the average man.

THE NEW WAY OF WRITING
by Bonamy Dobrée

Can we say that there is, definitely, 'a new way of writing'? Is there such a thing as *modern* prose, with characteristics the older prose does not possess?[1] It may seem at first sight that the question can-not reasonably be put, for if we are agreed that style is the personal voice—which pierces through even the 'impersonal' man-ner—and that the voice is the man; and if we assume, as we plausibly can, that man does not alter except over very long peri-ods, can we talk of a modern as opposed to an old-fashioned style?

One can make two answers to this. The first is, that though time may not change man physically, nor perhaps mentally, leaving his vocal cords and what he wants to do with them still the same, two things do change: the social being, and with him the method of speech he must use to be effective with other social beings. Man as a social animal alters in tune with what we call, since a better term is lacking, 'the spirit of the age,' which we gauge by the different approaches men make to the external universe, and, more important perhaps, to their own emotions. Man may be fundamentally unchanged, but in the social process of his time, different facets

are polished, unfamiliar aspects emerge. To take a simple example: How would a fourteenth-century man react if he were asked to think of 'the wonders of the deep' compared with the way a twentieth-century man would react? To-day we should at once let our minds turn to what we might roughly call 'scientific marvels,' that is to various detailed manifestations of fish life, or of corals. The fourteenth-century man would shudder deliciously at a vision of leviathans, appallingly, even incredibly shaped, of mermaids, of ghostly inhabitants. Not only, then, will men of various ages wish to *ex*press different things, but they will wish to *im*press men differently. What would be the good, for instance, of a member of the House of Lords rising up and saying:

> My Lords, this ruinous and ignominious situation, where we cannot act with success nor suffer with honour, calls upon us to remonstrate in the strongest and loudest lan-guage of truth, to rescue the ears of majesty from the delusions which surround it.

We can imagine a peer having similar feelings about, perhaps, the situation in India, but such language, used by Chat-

From Bonamy Dobrée, *Modern Prose Style,* Oxford, 1934. Reprinted by permission of The Clarendon Press, Oxford.

[1] I may suggest to begin with, that had I been writing thirty years ago, I would probably have felt constrained to write 'with characteristics *which* the older . . .'

ham in 1777, would have no result whatever now, though in its way it is splendid, and in its own age was no doubt very effective indeed. Our second answer arises out of the first: since the needs of the voice have changed, the instrument has been altered: we no longer use the same tool as our ancestors did to move other people. And there is still another consideration. If we use a different tool it is that our emotions have changed, or at any rate, if our emotions do not change, our attitude towards them differs with the age in which we live. These things, however, interact upon each other. We know, as once we did not know, that our emotions vary with the language we use in describing them: the spirit of an age may not only be reflected in its prose, it may be, indeed it is, to some extent conditioned by it. This, however, is an issue which would take us too far outside the bounds of our subject; nor am I qualified to pursue it.

Let us now take two passages, dealing with much the same range of ideas, written by men who were each in their day stylists. We have already done something of the sort in the Introduction, but we can use another example to reinforce the argument of the first. This time one writer is Sir Thomas Browne, the other William James, and I am taking Browne at his most straightforward.

Let thy studies be free as thy thoughts and contemplations: but fly not only upon the wings of imagination; join sense unto reason, and experiment unto speculation, and so give life unto embryon truths, and verities yet in their chaos. There is nothing more acceptable unto the ingenious world, than this noble eluctation of truth; wherein, against the tenacity of prejudice and prescription, this century now prevaileth.

That is from *Christian Morals:* now let us take this from *The Will to Believe:*

On the whole, then, we must conclude that no philosophy of ethics is possible in the old-fashioned absolute sense of the term. Everywhere the ethical philosopher must wait on facts. The thinkers who create the ideals come he knows not whence, their sensibilities are evolved he knows not how; and the question as to which of two conflicting ideals will give the best universe then and there, can be answered by him only through the aid of the experience of other men.

I take it that anybody, even neglecting Browne's obsolete forms, would at once recognize the first passage as belonging to the seventeenth century, and the second to our own time. Can we put our finger on where exactly the difference lies?

It is pretty obvious that the difference lies in the rhythm, but that is too easy a thing to say: and as a matter of fact, if we analyse these two passages into 'prose rhythms' in the way that Saintsbury did in his fascinating book, they are not, prosodically speaking at least, so different after all. Are not such cadences as

$$\text{embry\u{o}n/truths, a\u{n}d/verit\u{i}es/yet \u{i}n their/cha\u{o}s,}$$

and

$$\text{old-fashioned/absolute/sense of the/term,}$$

of much the same order? Both are, in a sense, dactylic. What is different is the way the metres are used. In modern writing there is far less insistence on the rhythms; the unit into which the rhythms are woven, that is to say the phrase, is far more flexible, on the whole longer. The antithetical balance has gone. But what is more significant is that the written language to-day is much nearer the spoken language, with implications we shall follow up in a moment. But first I must dispose of two possible objections. The first and lesser one is that for the seventeenth-century example we have a very conscious stylist. That is true, but Jeremy Taylor or Milton will give much the same result. Why do we remember, except for its insistence on rhythm, Milton's 'rousing herself like a strong man after sleep, and shaking her invincible locks'? But how do I know, it will be asked in the second place, that the older people did not speak as they wrote? The suggestion is often made, most notably by Mr. Gordon Bottomley, that in the seventeenth century, especially in Shakespeare's time, the rhythms of everyday speech were more accentuated, approached even those of blank verse, or of obviously cadenced speech. Let us look at something from a contemporary of Sir Thomas Browne's:

Up, and by water, stopping at Michell's, and there saw Betty, but could have no discourse with her, but there drank. To White Hall, and there walked to St. James's, where I find the Court mighty full, it being the Duke of York's birthday; and he mighty fine, and all the musick, one after another, to my great content.

Pepys, you see at once, was not writing literary English: he was setting down his doings as he might have chatted about them to his wife—if, of course, he had been a brave enough man to do so.

It is fairly certain, I think, that the written language of the seventeenth century was farther from the spoken language than the written language of to-day is from our conversation, a division which probably began with Caxton. John Donne, one can be sure, never spoke at home in the way that he thundered from the pulpit. The proof is to be found in the correspondence of the time, much of which has been collected by Professor Wyld in his *History of Modern Colloquial English,* largely for this purpose; and what comes out is that the language of the Elizabethans was not essentially unlike our own. Here, for one example, is Sir Philip Sidney writing to Edward Molyneux:

Few words are best. My letters to my father have come to the eyes of some. Neither can I condemn any but you for it. If it be so you have played the very knave with me; and so I will make you know if I have good proof of it. But that for so much as is past. For that is to come, I assure you before God, that if ever I know you do so much as read any letter I write to my father, without his commandment, or my consent, I will thrust my dagger into you. And trust to it, for I speak it in earnest. In the mean time, farewell.

The sentiments of this prose (we trust) are not ours, and the forms are not quite so, but the ring of it is. If we were to say that sort of thing, we should say it in that kind of way. Sidney's prose here, we see, is altogether different from what he wrote for the press, his 'Sidneyan showers of sweet discourse.' Here is another example; and making allowance for stage speech, does it sound very quaint or old-fashioned, or very heavily rhythmed?

Thou are so fat-witted, with drinking of old sack, and unbuttoning thee after supper, and sleeping upon benches after noon, that thou hast forgotten to demand that truly which thou wouldst truly know. What a devil hast thou to do with the time of the day. . . .

Prince Hal probably spoke fairly current English; and the journalists of the time, Nashe, Greene, Dekker, wrote much in the way Prince Hal spoke, for they were not labouring after fine style, but trying to write as men talked. What appears to have happened is that in the seventeenth century a profound division developed between the spoken and the written language, a division bridged by the journalists and the comic writers. What seems to have occurred afterwards was, to cut a long story short, that the journalists, forgetting Dryden, deserted to the written side: one has only to think of Addison, and then of Dr. Johnson, who, far from trying to write as he naturally spoke, did his best to model his conversation on his writing. Everybody remembers how he let slip the remark about *The Rehearsal* not having wit enough to keep it sweet, and then, recoiling in horror from so natural an expression, hurriedly amended the phrase to 'has not vitality enough to preserve it from corruption.' The stylists of the eighteenth century seem to have taken their writing farther and farther away from their speech—Gibbon, Burke, Smollett. This process went on through the nineteenth century; we have only to think of Carlyle or Pater, though it is true that some people all the while kept up the spoken tradition, Defoe, Sterne, and even Lamb, for though Lamb's style is artificial as regards words, his rhythms are those of his talk, or at any rate of his possible talk. What I think is going on at the present day is a return to speech rhythms: the conscious stylists are, so to speak, ridding themselves of 'style': not 'style,' but *a* style is what they are aiming at, a style that will faithfully reflect their mind as it

utters itself naturally. What is curious is that now it is the leading authors who write naturally, style, so-called, being left to the journalists. I take the opening sentence of the first leading article of *The Times* of the day on which I happened to be taking notes for this chapter (19 August 1933): 'As soon as it was announced, on the morrow of Parliament's rising. . . .' One need not go on. Who would dream of *saying* 'on the morrow of Parliament's rising'? It is jargon. What we would probably say is, 'the day after Parliament rose.' Not that this *pompier* 'style' is confined to the august heights of journalism: it runs all through, and not long ago *The Daily Worker* printed with regard to certain prisons: 'No sound comes from out those walls.' Does the man who wrote those words habitually say 'from out'? Why does this happen? Why do people write forms which are dead, which they would never utter? In both the examples quoted one is tempted to diagnose insincerity of thought, or at least mental laziness.

Does it not seem, then, that the modern prosewriter, in returning to the rhythms of everyday speech, is trying to be more honest with himself than if he used, as is too wreckingly easy, the forms and terms already published as the expression of other people's minds? 'Style . . . is not an ornament; it is not an exercise, not a caper, nor complication of any sort. It is the sense of one's self, the knowledge of what one wants to say, and the saying of it in the most fitting words.' [2] And that is why it is extremely hard to achieve *a* style, for all these three things are very difficult to attain. Take only the last task, the saying of what one wants to say in the most fitting words. It seems almost impossible, for

[2] Introduction to *The London Book of English Prose,* by Herbert Read and Bonamy Dobrée, Eyre and Spottiswoode, 1931.

every time we speak we have virtually to re-create the instrument if we want to be faithful to our idea or feeling. Everywhere the words and phrasing of past generations interpose themselves between us and the reality. 'It is . . . a true and lamentable fact that, in ultimate analysis, one cannot speak about anything without altering it to some extent.'[3] It is the realization of this, a realization possibly new in our day, which impels authors to try to write as they speak in ordinary life on ordinary physical matters, for it is only in this way that one can achieve fidelity to one's self: otherwise the language and style of the literary tradition assert themselves. But the modern writer must not think of style: the man who thinks first of style is lost: the primary thing to do—this is an old observation—is to think clearly. As M. Jean Cocteau says, writing for modern authors: 'Style cannot be a starting point: it happens. What is style? For a great many people it is a complicated way of saying very simple things. From our point of view it is a very simple way of saying complicated things.'[4] How does a modern writer tackle this problem? Here, I think, is a good example:

I had great ambitions. I have none now—and have not even the fear of failing. What matters to me and to many of the survivors of my generation is only that which is common to us all, our fear for our children. If it were not for that, I should know how to act in what remains of my life—that would be to withdraw as far as possible from the little world of writing and talking about books which is a microcosm of the whole, its values no finer than those accepted by the rest of the world, and only valid on the as-

sumption that to a writer success means precisely what it means to a stockbroker or a multiple grocer. That is, material wealth, and the respect paid to it. This seems to me a denial of all the writer, the 'clerk,' should stand for, but I can do nothing to alter it, and therefore I ought to run away for my life.

After all that turbulence of desire and ambitions it seems strange I should believe now that very little in me is real except the absolute need, intellectual and spiritual, for withdrawal, for resolving to satisfy in my life only the simple wants. It is as strange as that I am only just learning to write and don't care to.

There are days when I retract all this, and think how queer I shall grow if I live alone, and think too that what is needed is some effort to create cells inside the body social, groups of angry, last-minute saints. That would be no good. I should weary in a week of the company of persons who thought and felt no differently from myself.[5]

That, as prose, is simple, easy, fluent, and flexible; what is important, however, is that it is written, apparently, in the *tones* of every day, though here and there we can detect traces of literary forms—'only that which' instead of 'only what': 'how to act' instead of 'what to do': it is extraordinarily difficult to rid one's self of terms of that kind. But to show how new the tone is, here is a passage from another autobiography written, one always thought, in a natural, confidential manner:

There were perhaps twenty boys in the school at most, and often fewer. I made the excursion between home and school four times a day; if I walked fast, the transit might take five minutes, and, as there were several objects of interest on the way, it

[3] *The Theory of Speech and Language*, by A. H. Gardiner, Oxford, 1932.
[4] *A Call to Order*, Allen and Unwin, trs. 1933.
[5] From *No Time Like the Present*, by Storm Jameson, Cassell, 1933.

might be spread over an hour. In fine weather the going to and from school was very delightful, and small as the scope was, it could be varied almost indefinitely.[6]

There are, we see immediately, one or two obvious 'literary' turns in that passage: 'I made the excursion between home and school,' instead of 'I went to and from school': 'If I walked fast, the transit might take five minutes,' instead of 'I could get there or back (or do the journey) in five minutes': 'objects of interest,' with others of the same sort. And the general run, which is the important thing, though simple and easy, and we might perhaps admit fluent, is not flexible. Each sentence contains an idea and completes it. The mind comes to a full stop at the end of each phrase. But our minds in life do not work in that way; they are always ready to frame the next sentence, carried on by the impetus of the last. Gosse, in common with the older writers, was concerned, not to follow the movements of his mind, but to present something concrete.

To say, then, that the hall-mark of good modern prose style is an essential fidelity does not imply that writers of previous generations were charlatans and liars, only that they owed fidelity to other things. And it is here that the spirit of our age imposes itself upon our style. All the previous ages whose writers have been quoted or referred to here had something they could take for granted, and it never occurred to the older writers that they could not take themselves for granted. We can be sure of nothing; our civilization is threatened, even the simplest things we live by: we are on the verge of amazing changes. In our present confusion our only hope is to be scrupulously honest with ourselves, so

honest as to doubt our own minds and the conclusions they arrive at. Most of us have ceased to believe, except provisionally, in truths, and we feel that what is important is not so much truth as the way our minds move towards truths. Therefore, to quote M. Cocteau again, 'Form must be the form of the mind. Not a way of saying things, but of thinking them.' Perhaps that is why we nowadays instinctively mistrust any one who pontificates: and, as a matter of experience, if we examine the writings of the pontificators, people skilled in 'a way of saying things,' we invariably find that their style is bad, that falsity has crept in somewhere. The writer is not being faithful to the movement of his mind; he is taking things for granted, and he fills us of to-day with uneasiness.

We have, then, to judge of the integrity of a modern writer by this sense of himself that we feel he has. If we are to respond, he must (we suppose) be aware of himself as something a little uncertain in this shifting universe: he also is part of the material which he has to treat with respect: he must listen to himself, so to speak, to hear what he has to say. He must not prejudge, or force an issue: we must be able to imagine that he is talking to himself. In no other way can he achieve *a* style, which is the sound of his voice, which is the man himself.

It is not so simple as it sounds for a man to watch his own mind; it is as difficult as writing in the way you ordinarily talk: literary habits continually get in the way. Nor must a man write as he might lazily talk, and it is more important than ever for him to reject the dead metaphor which can never be more than an approximation, to choose the exact, the expressive word,

[6] From *Father and Son,* by Edmund Gosse, Heinemann, 1907.

to rid his style of fat, to make it athletic. What he must really do, as the first essential, is to keep his awareness athletic, especially his awareness of himself. And he must not watch his mind idly; he must watch it as he might a delicate piece of machinery doing its work, and he must watch it, not flickering about in every direction, as an active mind does, but only in the direction he wants it to go. Otherwise the result may be disastrous. Even the following extremely clever attempt seems to me an object-lesson:

The problem from this time on became more definite.

It was all so nearly alike it must be different and it is different, it is natural that if everything is used and there is a continuous present and a beginning again and again if it is all so alike it must be simply different and everything simply different was the natural way of creating it then.

In this natural way of creating it then that it was simply different everything being alike it was simply different, this kept on leading one to lists. Lists naturally for a while and by lists I mean a series. More and more in going back over what was done at this time I find that I naturally kept simply different as an intention. Whether there was or whether there was not a continuous present did not then any longer trouble me there was or there was, and using everything no longer troubled me if everything is alike using everything could no longer trouble me and beginning again and again could no longer trouble me because if lists were inevitable if series were inevitable and the whole of it was inevitable beginning again and again could not trouble me so then with nothing to trouble me I very completely began naturally since everything is alike making it as simply different naturally as simply different as possible. I began doing natural phenomena what I call natural phenomena

and natural phenonema naturally everything being alike natural phenomena are making things be naturally simply different. This found its culmination later, in the beginning it began in a center confused with lists with series with geography with returning portraits and with particularly often four and three and often with five and four. It is easy to see that in the beginning such a conception as everything being naturally different would be very inarticulate and very slowly it began to emerge and take the form of anything, and then naturally if anything that is simply different is simply different what follows will follow.[7]

One cannot say whether Miss Stein's mind really moves like that: possibly it does, and possibly most of our minds move more like that than we are aware of, or at any rate are prepared to admit. What is clear is that the mere following of the mind, its echoes and repetitions, does not really give its shape; and this makes us realize that to write naturally as the mind would wish to utter, is just as much an art—or an artifice—as to write in what we call an artificial style, say that of a Pater or Meredith. What has happened is that the modern writer is faced with new material, and what he has to do is to discover the new form that this material requires.

But because this new form can only be an adaptation of the old, it takes consummate art to prevent literature interposing itself between us and life. The problem, no doubt, has always existed, but if it has been realized the solution has rarely, if ever, been hit on. Yet there is Sterne, and what Mrs. Woolf has to say about him is illuminating:

. . . With the first words—They order, said I, this matter better in France—we are in the world of *Tristram Shandy*. It is a

[7] From *Composition as Explanation,* by Gertrude Stein, Hogarth Press, 1926.

world in which anything may happen. We hardly know what jest, what jibe, what flash of poetry is not going to glance suddenly through the gap which this astonishingly agile pen has cut in the thick-set hedge of English prose. Is Sterne himself responsible? Does he know what he is going to say next for all his resolve to be on his best behaviour this time? The jerky disconnected sentences are as rapid and it would seem as little under control as the phrases that fall from the lips of a brilliant talker. The very punctuation is that of speech, not writing, and brings the sounds and associations of the speaking voice in with it. The order of the ideas, their suddenness and irrelevancy, is more true to life than to literature. . . . Under the influence of this extraordinary style the book becomes semi-transparent. The usual ceremonies and conventions which keep reader and writer at arm's length disappear. We are as close to life as we can be.[8]

That passage is not quoted as being characteristic of Mrs. Woolf: to hear her real voice one must go to the novels: it is quoted as an aid to my argument. And it serves it in two ways, because of what it says, and because of the way it says it, for if the prose is not markedly Mrs. Woolf's, it is obviously modern: the voice that is speaking is a voice of to-day: I shall not be misunderstood, I hope, if I say that any one might have written it. Now let us compare this with the way Bagehot wrote about Sterne in the *National Review* in 1864:

But here the great excellence of Sterne ends as well as begins. In *Tristram Shandy* especially there are several defects which, while we are reading it, tease and disgust us so much that we are scarcely willing even to admire as we ought to admire the refined pictures of human emotion. The first of

these, and perhaps the worst, is the fantastic disorder of the form. It is an imperative law of the writing art, that a book should go straight on. A great writer should be able to tell a great meaning as coherently as a small writer tells a small meaning. . . .

and so it goes on. That is typical nineteenth-century prose: we get something very like it in Matthew Arnold, or Huxley, and in its way it is excellent. But the rhythms and inflexions are quite different from those of to-day: it consists, not of thoughts closely followed, not of ideas suggested, but of utterances, of pronouncements. Again, as with Gosse, we have the end-stopped phrase: there is a door banged at the end of each, and we feel as though we were on parade receiving orders.

What seems to us to be lacking in the older prose is the sense of the uninterrupted flow of the mind: Bagehot, for example, appears to cut off this continuum, shall we call it, into arbitrary lengths, as we slice chunks off a cucumber. This is to force on our minds a logic that is not of their own making; and though it may be true that, as T. E. Hulme said, 'All styles are only means of subduing the reader,' we must not feel that our minds are being forced, and therefore distorted. Perhaps it was George Moore's principal achievement to give this sense of flow: there is hardly an instant's pause in his mental processes. His style is very distinctive; all the time one hears a voice, a personal utterance, though pursued to the lengths to which he took it, or allowed it to carry him, it becomes in the end monotonous. The mind runs on too much; it has no form but that of a stream: no solid shape emerges. But the sort of flow we are talking about can, and sometimes does, take form. Here is an extract from Henry

[8] *The Common Reader*, ii, Hogarth Press, 1932.

James, whose whole being was directed to following the movement of his mind, and who gave form to this movement, not indeed in a language natural to us, but one which seems to have been natural to him, a way which he could not have escaped from even if he had wanted to:

Momentary side-winds—things of no real authority—break in every now and then to put their inferior little questions to me; but I come back, I come back, as I say, I all throbbingly and yearningly and passionately, oh mon bon come back to this way that is clearly the only one in which I can do anything now, and that will open out to me more and more, and that has overwhelming reasons pleading all beautifully in its breast. What really happens is that the closer I get to the problem of the application of it in any particular case, the more I get *into* that application, so that the more doubts and torments fall away from me, the more I know where I am, the more everything spreads and shines and draws me on and I'm justified in my logic and my passion. . . . Causons, causons, mon bon—oh celestial, soothing, sanctifying process, with all the high sane forces of the sacred time fighting, through it, on my side! Let me fumble it gently and patiently out—with fever and fidget laid to rest—as in all the old enchanted months! It only looms, it only shines and shimmers, *too* beautiful and too interesting, it only hangs there too rich and too full and with too much to give and to pay; it only presents itself too admirably and too vividly, too straight and square and vivid, as a little organic and effective Action.[9]

We may think that artificial, but we do not feel, complicated as it is, that this is a literary language. It is the language of Henry James's speech; it reflects his mind accurately, a mind with a very definite form. James, if you like, had a tortuous

way of thinking, but he had broken down the barriers between his mind and the expression of it.

What we look for, however, is a style which shall be as free and individual as in that passage, but which smacks less of idiosyncrasy, for something we might all use, though, no doubt, not so well as our model, for something which does not give us, as some recent prose does, the uneasy effect of submitting us to a laboratory experiment. Perhaps this is what we want:

The trouble with her ship was that it would *not* sail. It rode water-logged in the rotting port of home. All very well to have wild, reckless moods of irony and independence, if you have to pay for them by withering dustily on the shelf.

Alvina fell again into humility and fear: she began to show symptoms of her mother's heart trouble. For day followed day, month followed month, season after season went by, and she grubbed away like a housemaid in Manchester House, she hurried round doing the shopping, she sang in the choir on Sundays, she attended the various chapel events, she went out to visit friends, and laughed and talked and played games. But all the time, what was there actually in her life? Not much. She was withering towards old-maiddom. Already in her twenty-eighth year, she spent her days grubbing in the house, whilst her father became an elderly, frail man still too lively in mind and spirit. Miss Pinnegar began to grow grey and elderly too, money became scarcer and scarcer, there was a black day ahead when her father would die and the home be broken up, and she would have to tackle life as a worker.

There lay the only alternative: in work. She might slave her days away teaching the piano, as Miss Frost had done: she might find a subordinate post as nurse: she might sit in the cash-desk of some shop. Some

[9] *Letters,* Macmillan.

work of some sort would be found for her. And she would sink into the routine of her job, as did so many women, and grow old and die, chattering and fluttering. She would have what is called her independence. But, seriously faced with that treasure, and without the option of refusing it, strange how hideous she found it.

Work!—a job! More even than she rebelled against the Withams did she rebel against a job. . . .[10]

It is clear, I imagine, that that could not have been written in the last century; it speaks with the authentic voice of this. It has the ring of what we hear around us every day: it has no air of 'style,' yet it is extremely expressive. Certain liberties are taken, such as leaving out 'It is . . .' before 'all very well . . .' in the first paragraph. Here and there we feel just a touch of literary formulas, and we wish they were not there: 'as did so many women' instead of 'as so many women did,' but these things are very rare in Lawrence. We feel that he is nearly always completely free of 'literature' and can be himself. We follow his mind working—and he speaks as it works. Or, at least, that is the impression we get. It is not true, of course: but at least he is using his material (part of which is his mind) with complete freedom, and finding a form which will make it tell.

Suppose that, before we go on to discuss experiments, we try to prophesy what direction our prose will take. We might perhaps say that it will be in that of greater flexibility and a more curious following of our mental processes, with, sometimes, violence offered to our old notions of syntax wherever we find them distorting or cumbrous. One would like to think that all of us will come to the stage of refusing to write what we would not, indeed could not, say, though that, of course, is not to limit our writing to what we actually do say. This is not to claim for a moment that by writing as we speak we shall achieve a style; before we do that we must go through at least three fundamental disciplines. First there is that of fidelity to thought, the extremely difficult task of complete honesty; we must not, as is so easy, allow language to condition our thought: then there is the labour of finding the exact words and the exact inflexion of phrase to carry the whole sense, the emotional colour, of the words; and thirdly, it is over and above these things that we have to model our prose to give it what seems to be the run and structure of our usual speaking. That is where the artifice comes in, and that is where we can achieve the art.

[10] From *The Lost Girl*, by D. H. Lawrence, Secker, 1920.

Speed photograph of a tennis player, 1939. Edgerton.

Used with the permission of H. E. Edgerton and publisher. From Siegfried Giedion, Space, Time and Architecture, *Harvard University Press.*

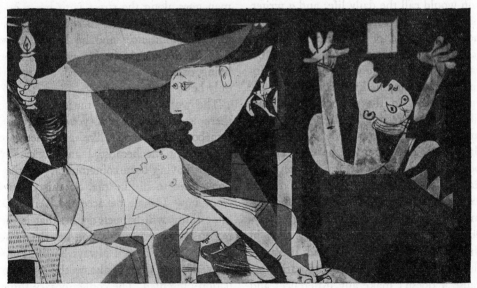

Guernica. 1937. Detail. Pablo Picasso.

Lent by the artist to the Museum of Modern Art, New York.

Many people today as in former days look at pictures for what they say rather than for what they are. Then, stories and sentiments were read; today, the reading is of formal relations. The authenticity in one case may be no greater than in the other.*

* From *Appreciation: Painting, Poetry and Prose* by Leo Stein, copyright 1947 by Leo Stein, used by permission of Crown Publishers, Inc.

HOW WRITING IS WRITTEN

by Gertrude Stein

What i want to talk about to you is just the general subject of how writing is written. The beginning of it is what everybody has to know: everybody is contemporary with his period. A very bad painter once said to a very great painter, 'Do what you like, you cannot get rid of the fact that we are contemporaries.' That is what goes on in writing. The whole crowd of you are contemporary to each other, and the whole business of writing is the question of living in the contemporariness. Each generation has to live in that. The thing that is important is that nobody knows what the contemporariness is. In other words, they don't know where they are going, but they are on their way.

Each generation has to do with what you would call the daily life: and a writer, painter, or any sort of creative artist, is not at all ahead of his time. He is contemporary. He can't live in the past, because it is gone. He can't live in the future, because no one knows what it is. He can live only in the present of his daily life. He is expressing the thing that is being expressed by everybody else in their daily lives. The thing you have to remember is that everybody lives a contemporary daily life. The writer lives it, too, and expresses it imperceptibly. The fact remains that in the act of living, everybody has to live contemporarily. But in the things concerning art and literature they don't have to live contemporarily, because it doesn't make any difference; and they live about forty years behind their time. And that is the real explanation of why the artist or painter is not recognized by his contemporaries. He is expressing the time-sense of his contemporaries, but nobody is really interested. After the new generation has come, after the grandchildren, so to speak, then the opposition dies out: because after all there is then a new contemporary expression to oppose.

That is really the fact about contemporariness. As I see the whole crowd of you, if there are any of you who are going to express yourselves contemporarily, you will do something which most people won't want to look at. Most of you will be so busy living the contemporary life that it will be like the tired business man: in the things of the mind you will want the things you know. And too, if you don't live contemporarily, you are a nuisance. That is why we live contemporarily. If a man goes along the street with horse and carriage in New York in the snow, that man is a nuisance; and he knows it, so now he doesn't do it. He would not be living, or acting, contemporarily: he would only be in the way, a drag.

The world can accept me now because there is coming out of *your* generation somebody they won't like, and therefore they accept me because I am sufficiently past in having been contemporary so they don't have to dislike me. So thirty years from now I shall be accepted. And the same thing will happen again: that is the reason why every generation has the same thing happen. It will always be the same story, because there is always the same situation presented. The contemporary thing in art and literature is the thing which doesn't make enough difference to the people of that generation so that they can accept it or reject it.

Most of you know that in a funny kind of way you are nearer your grandparents than your parents. Since this contemporariness is always there, nobody realizes that you cannot follow it up. That is the reason people discover—those interested in the activities of other people—that they cannot understand their contemporaries. If you kids started in to write, I wouldn't be a good judge of you, because I am of the third generation. What you are going to do I don't know any more than anyone else. But I created a movement of which you are the grandchildren. The contemporary thing is the thing you can't get away from. That is the fundamental thing in all writing.

Another thing you have to remember is that each period of time not only has its contemporary quality, but it has a time-sense. Things move more quickly, slowly, or differently, from one generation to another. Take the Nineteenth Century. The Nineteenth Century was roughly the Englishman's Century. And their method, as they themselves, in their worst moments, speak of it, is that of 'muddling through.' They begin at one end and hope to come out at the other: their grammar, parts of speech, methods of talk, go with this fashion. The United States began a different phase when, after the Civil War, they discovered and created out of their inner need a different way of life. They created the Twentieth Century. The United States, instead of having the feeling of beginning at one end and ending at another, had the conception of assembling the whole thing out of its parts, the whole thing which made the Twentieth Century productive. The Twentieth Century conceived an automobile as a whole, so to speak, and then created it, built it up out of its parts. It was an entirely different point of view

from the Nineteenth Century's. The Nineteenth Century would have seen the parts, and worked towards the automobile through them.

Now in a funny sort of way this expresses, in different terms the difference between the literature of the Nineteenth Century and the literature of the Twentieth. Think of your reading. If you look at it from the days of Chaucer, you will see that what you might call the 'internal history' of a country always affects its use of writing. It makes a difference in the expression, in the vocabulary, even in the handling of grammar. In an amusing story in your *Literary Magazine,* when the author speaks of the fact that he is tired of using quotation marks and isn't going to use them any more, with him that is a joke; but when I began writing, the whole question of punctuation was a vital question. You see, I had this new conception: I had this conception of the whole paragraph, and in *The Making of Americans* I had this idea of a whole thing. But if you think of contemporary English writers, it doesn't work like that at all. They conceive of it as pieces put together to make a whole, and I conceived it as a whole made up of its parts. I didn't know what I was doing any more than you know, but in response to the need of my period I was doing this thing. That is why I came in contact with people who were unconsciously doing the same thing. They had the Twentieth Century conception of a whole. So the element of punctuation was very vital. The comma was just a nuisance. If you got the thing as a whole, the comma kept irritating you all along the line. If you think of a thing as a whole, and the comma keeps sticking out, it gets on your nerves; because, after all, it destroys the reality of the whole. So I got rid more and more of commas. Not because I had any prejudice against commas; but the comma was a stumbling-block. When you were conceiving a sentence, the comma stopped you. That is the illustration of the question of grammar and parts of speech, as part of the daily life as we live it.

The other thing which I accomplished was the getting rid of nouns. In the Twentieth Century you feel like movement. The Nineteenth Century didn't feel that way. The element of movement was not the predominating thing that they felt. You know that in your lives movement is the thing that occupies you most—you feel movement all the time. And the United States had the first instance of what I call Twentieth Century writing. You see it first in Walt Whitman. He was the beginning of movement. He didn't see it very clearly, but there was a sense of movement that the European was much influenced by, because the Twentieth Century has become the American Century. That is what I mean when I say that each generation has its own literature.

There is a third element. You see, everybody in this generation has his sense of time which belongs to his crowd. But then, you always have the memory of what you were brought up with. In most people that makes a double time, which makes confusion. When one is beginning to write he is always under the shadow of the thing that is just past. And that is the reason why the creative person always has the appearance of ugliness. There is this persistent drag of the habits that belong to you. And in struggling away from this thing there is always an ugliness. That is the other reason why the contemporary writer is always refused. It is the effort of escaping from the thing which is a drag upon you that is so strong that the result is an apparent ugliness; and the world always says of the new writer, 'It is so ugly!' And they are right, because it *is* ugly. If you disagree with your parents, there is an ugliness in the relation. There is a double resistance that makes the essence of this thing ugly.

You always have in your writing the resistance outside of you and inside of you, a shadow upon you, and the thing which you must express. In the beginning of your writing, this struggle is so tremendous that that result is ugly; and that is the reason why the followers are always accepted before the person who made the revolution. The person who has made the fight probably makes it seem ugly, although the struggle has the much greater beauty. But the followers die out; and the man who made the struggle and the quality of beauty remains in the intensity of the fight. Eventually it comes out all right, and so you have this very queer situation which always happens with the followers: the original person has to have in him a certain element of ugliness. You know that is what happens over and over again: the statement made that it is ugly—the statement made against me for the last twenty years. And they are quite right, because it *is* ugly. But the essence of that ugliness is the thing which will always make it beautiful. I myself think it is much more interesting when it seems ugly, because in it you see the element of the fight. The literature of one hundred years ago is perfectly easy to see, because the sediment of ugliness has settled down and you got the solemnity of its beauty. But to a person of my temperament, it is much more amusing when it has the vitality of the struggle.

In my own case, the Twentieth Century,

which America created after the Civil War, and which had certain elements, had a definite influence on me. And in *The Making of Americans,* which is a book I would like to talk about, I gradually and slowly found out that there were two things I had to think about; the fact that knowledge is acquired, so to speak, by memory; but that when you know anything, memory doesn't come in. At any moment that you are conscious of knowing anything, memory plays no part. When any of you feels anybody else, memory doesn't come into it. You have the sense of the immediate. Remember that my immediate forebears were people like Meredith, Thomas Hardy, and so forth, and you will see what a struggle it was to do this thing. This was one of my first efforts to give the appearance of one time-knowledge, and not to make it a narrative story. This is what I mean by immediacy of description: you will find it in *The Making of Americans:* 'It happens very often that a man has it in him, that a man does something, that he does very often that he does many things, when he is a young man when he is an old man, when he is an older man.' Do you see what I mean? And here is a description of a thing that is very interesting: 'One of such of these kind of them had a little boy and this one, the little son wanted to make a collection of butterflies and beetles and it was all exciting to him and it was all arranged then and then the father said to the son you are certain this is not a cruel thing that you are wanting to be doing, killing things to make collections of them, and the son was very disturbed then and they talked about it together the two of them and more and more they talked about it then and then at last the boy was convinced it was a cruel thing and he said he would not do it and the father said the little boy was a noble boy to give up pleasure when it was a cruel one. The boy went to bed then and then the father when he got up in the early morning saw a wonderfully beautiful moth in the room and he caught him and he killed him and he pinned him and he woke up his son then and showed it to him and he said to him "see what a good father I am to have caught and killed this one," the boy was all mixed up inside him and then he said he would go on with his collecting and that was all there was then of discussing and this is a little description of something that happened once and it is very interesting.'

I was trying to get this present immediacy without trying to drag in anything else. I had to use present participles, new constructions of grammar. The grammar-constructions are correct, but they are changed, in order to get this immediacy. In short, from that time I have been trying in every possible way to get the sense of immediacy, and practically all the work I have done has been in that direction.

In *The Making of Americans* I had an idea that I could get a sense of immediacy if I made a description of every kind of human being that existed, the rules for resemblances and all the other things, until really I had made a description of every human being—I found this out when I was at Harvard working under William James.

Did you ever see that article that came out in *The Atlantic Monthly* a year or two ago, about my experiments with automatic writing? It was very amusing. The experiment that I did was to take a lot of people in moments of fatigue and rest and activity of various kinds, and see if they could do anything with automatic writing.

I found they could not do anything with automatic writing, but I found out a great deal about how people act. I found there a certain kind of human being who acted in a certain way, and another kind who acted in another kind of way, and their resemblances and their differences. And then I wanted to find out if you could make a history of the whole world, if you could know the whole life history of everyone in the world, their slight resemblances and lack of resemblances. I made enormous charts, and I tried to carry these charts out. You start in and you take everyone that you know, and then when you see anybody who has a certain expression or turn of the face that reminds you of some one, you find out where he agrees or disagrees with the character, until you build up the whole scheme. I got to the place where I didn't know whether I knew people or not. I made so many charts that when I used to go down the streets of Paris I wondered whether they were people I knew or ones I didn't. That is what *The Making of Americans* was intended to be. I was to make a description of every kind of human being until I could know by these variations how everybody was to be known. Then I got very much interested in this thing, and I wrote about nine hundred pages, and I came to a logical conclusion that this thing could be done. Anybody who has patience enough could literally and entirely make of the whole world a history of human nature. When I found it could be done, I lost interest in it. As soon as I found definitely and clearly and completely that I could do it, I stopped writing the long book. It didn't interest me any longer. In doing the thing, I found out this question of resemblances, and I found in making these analyses that the resemblances were not of memory. I

had to remember what person looked like the other person. Then I found this contradiction: that the resemblances were a matter of memory. There were two prime elements involved, the element of memory and the other of immediacy.

The element of memory was a perfectly feasible thing, so then I gave it up. I then started a book which I called *A Long Gay Book* to see if I could work the thing up to a faster tempo. I wanted to see if I could make that a more complete vision. I wanted to see if I could hold it in the frame. Ordinarily the novels of the Nineteenth Century live by association; they are wont to call up other pictures than the one they present to you. I didn't want, when I said 'water,' to have you think of running water. Therefore I began limiting my vocabulary, because I wanted to get rid of anything except the picture within the frame. While I was writing I didn't want, when I used one word, to make it carry with it too many associations. I wanted as far as possible to make it exact, as exact as mathematics; that is to say, for example, if one and one make two, I wanted to get words to have as much exactness as that. When I put them down they were to have this quality. The whole history of my work, from *The Making of Americans,* has been a history of that. I made a great many discoveries, but the thing that I was always trying to do was this thing.

One thing which came to me is that the Twentieth Century gives of itself a feeling of movement, and has in its way no feeling for events. To the Twentieth Century events are not important. You must know that. Events are not exciting. Events have lost their interest for people. You read them more like a soothing syrup, and if you listen over the radio you don't get very excited. The thing has got to this place, that events are so wonderful that they are not exciting. Now you have to remember that the business of an artist is to be exciting. If the thing has its proper vitality, the result must be exciting. I was struck with it during the War: the average dough-boy standing on a street corner doing nothing—(they say, at the end of their doing nothing, 'I guess I'll go home')—was much more exciting to people than when the soldiers went over the top. The populace were passionately interested in their standing on the street corners, more so than in the St. Mihiel drive. And it is a perfectly natural thing. Events had got so continuous that the fact that events were taking place no longer stimulated anybody. To see three men, strangers, standing, expressed their personality to the European man so much more than anything else they could do. That thing impressed me very much. But the novel which tells about what happens is of no interest to anybody. It is quite characteristic that in *The Making of Americans,* Proust, *Ulysses,* nothing much happens. People are interested in existence. Newspapers excite people very little. Sometimes a personality breaks through the newspapers—Lindbergh, Dillinger,—when the personality has vitality. It wasn't what Dillinger *did* that excited anybody. The feeling is perfectly simple. You can see it in my *Four Saints.* Saints shouldn't do anything. The fact that a saint is there is enough for anybody. The *Four Saints* was written about as static as I could make it. The saints conversed a little, and it all did something. It did something more than the theater which has tried to make events has done. For our purposes, for our contemporary purposes, events have no im-

portance. I merely say that for the last thirty years events are of no importance. They may make a great many people unhappy, they may cause convulsions in history, but from the standpoint of excitement, the kind of excitement the Nineteenth Century got out of events doesn't exist.

And so what I am trying to make you understand is that every contemporary writer has to find out what is the inner time-sense of his contemporariness. The writer or painter, or what not, feels this thing more vibrantly, and he has a passionate need of putting it down; and that is what creativeness does. He spends his life in putting down this thing which he doesn't know is a contemporary thing. If he doesn't put down the contemporary thing, he isn't a great writer, for he has to live in the past. That is what I mean by 'everything is contemporary.' The minor poets of the period, or the precious poets of the period, are all people who are under the shadow of the past. A man who is making a revolution has to be contemporary. A minor person can live in the imagination. That tells the story pretty completely.

The question of repetition is very important. It is important because there is no such thing as repetition. Everybody tells every story in about the same way. You know perfectly well that when you and your roommates tell something, you are telling the same story in about the same way. But the point about it is this. Everybody is telling the story in the same way. But if you listen carefully, you will see that not all the story is the same. There is always a slight variation. Somebody comes in, and you tell the story over again. Every time you tell that story it is told slightly differently. All my early work was a careful listening to all the people telling their story, and I conceived the idea which is, funnily enough, the same as the idea of the cinema. The cinema goes on the same principle: each picture is just infinitesimally different from the one before. If you listen carefully, you say something, the other person says something; but each time it changes just a little, until finally you come to the point where you convince him or you don't convince him. I used to listen very carefully to people talking. I had a passion for knowing just what I call their 'insides.' And in *The Making of Americans* I did this thing; but of course to my mind there is no repetition. For instance, in these early 'Portraits,' and in a whole lot of them in this book (*Portraits and Prayers*) you will see that every time a statement is made about someone being somewhere, that statement is different. If I had repeated, nobody would listen. Nobody could be in the room with a person who said the same thing over and over. He would drive everybody mad. There has to be a very slight change. Really listen to the way you talk, and every time you change it a little bit. That change, to me, was a very important thing to find out. You will see that when I kept on saying something was something or somebody was somebody, I changed it just a little bit until I got a whole portrait. I conceived the idea of building this thing up. It was all based upon this thing of everybody's slightly building this thing up. What I was after was this immediacy. A single photograph doesn't give it. I was trying for this thing, and so to my mind there is no repetition. The only thing that is repetition is when somebody tells you what he has learned.

No matter how you say it, you say it differently. It was this that led me in all that early work.

You see, finally, after I got this thing as completely as I could, then, of course, it being my nature, I wanted to tear it down. I attacked the problem from another way. I listened to people. I condensed it in about three words. There again, if you read those later 'Portraits,' you will see that I used three or four words instead of making a cinema of it. I wanted to condense it as much as possible and change it around, until you could get the movement of a human being. If I wanted to make a picture of you as you sit there, I would wait until I got a picture of you as individuals and then I'd change them until I got a picture of you as a whole.

I did these 'Portraits,' and then I got the idea of doing plays. I had the 'Portraits' so much in my head that I would almost know how you differ one from the other. I got this idea of the play, and put it down in a few words. I wanted to put them down in that way, and I began writing plays and I wrote a great many of them. The Nineteenth Century wrote a great many plays, and none of them are now read, because the Nineteenth Century wanted to put their novels on the stage. The better the play the more static. The minute you try to make a play a novel, it doesn't work. That is the reason I got interested in doing these plays.

When you get to that point there is no essential difference between prose and poetry. This is essentially the problem with which your generation will have to wrestle. The thing has got to the point where poetry and prose have to concern themselves with the static thing. That is up to you.

PART III · STORIES

A PIECE OF FICTION is both a design of experience and somebody's truth about life. It must stand by itself as well as carry more than its own weight of meaning. This section opens with three examples of semi-fiction. In them the beginnings of the fictional method are easily discerned because we know, or can find out, more facts and details about the subjects than the author tells us. The section closes with stories where material and method have been merged, and we need to know little more than the overwhelming number of details the author has formed into his narrative.

In theme, the selections from Huxley's and Saroyan's novels ring theoretical and human changes on Sherwood Anderson's insight into one aspect of modern life, while the pieces from Forster and Thurber remind us that such a situation is neither improbable nor unenjoyable. Katherine Anne Porter brings us realistically back to the everyday life, where the desire to escape routine may appear funny or pathetic, with the help of Thurber, or may involve an ignorance that is fundamentally tragic, as for Eudora Welty's salesman. Four stories of learning and losing the values the world offers, of acceptance and rejection, follow, with glimpses here and there of some value that can be won, if men but knew how. These stories lead almost logically to the last two, where the need to assert life in death and the desire to maintain identity in separateness appear as the central problems of human existence.

The last few stories are a fair test of the art of reading fiction. If the reader has gone carefully through the other stories, leaving no relevant question unanswered and allowing no uncontrolled play of the fancy, he will come to know the persons, places and things out of which, in these last stories, the authors have created their special worlds for the truth's sake. He will then be learning that the imagination makes legitimate use of facts, that imagination and knowledge are mingled in the truth, and finally that fiction is truth.

THE CAMPERS AT KITTY HAWK

by JOHN DOS PASSOS

ON DECEMBER SEVENTEENTH, nineteen hundred and three, Bishop Wright of the United Brethren onetime editor of the *Religious Telescope* received in his frame house on Hawthorn Street in Dayton, Ohio, a telegram from his boys Wilbur and Orville who'd gotten it into their heads to spend their vacations in a little camp out on the dunes of the North Carolina coast tinkering with a homemade glider they'd knocked together themselves. The telegram read:

SUCCESS FOUR FLIGHTS THURSDAY MORNING ALL AGAINST TWENTYONE MILE WIND STARTED FROM LEVEL WITH ENGINEPOWER ALONE AVERAGE SPEED THROUGH AIR THIRTYONE MILES LONGEST FIFTYSEVEN SECONDS INFORM PRESS HOME CHRISTMAS

The figures were a little wrong because the telegraph operator misread Orville's hasty penciled scrawl
but the fact remains
that a couple of young bicycle mechanics from Dayton, Ohio
had designed constructed and flown
for the first time ever a practical airplane.

After running the motor a few minutes to heat it up I released the wire that held the machine to the track and the machine started forward into the wind. Wilbur ran at the side of the machine holding the wing to balance it on the track. Unlike the start on the 14th made in a calm the machine facing a 27 mile wind started very slowly. . . . Wilbur was able to stay with it until it lifted from the track after a forty-foot run. One of the lifesaving men snapped the camera for us taking a picture just as it reached the end of the track and the machine had risen to a height of about two feet. . . . The course of the flight up and down was extremely erratic, partly due to the irregularities of the air, partly to lack of experience in handling this machine. A sudden dart when a little over a hundred and twenty feet from the point at which it rose in the air ended the flight. . . . This flight lasted only 12 seconds but it was nevertheless the first in the history of the world in which a machine carrying a man had raised itself by its own power into the air in full flight, had sailed forward without reduction of speed and had finally landed at a point as high as that from which it started.

A little later in the day the machine was caught in a gust of wind and turned over and smashed, almost killing the coastguardsman who tried to hold it down;
it was too bad
but the Wright brothers were too happy to care
they'd proved that the damn thing flew.

When these points had been definitely established we at once packed our goods and returned home knowing that the age of the flying machine had come at last.

They were home for Christmas in Dayton, Ohio, where they'd been born in the seventies of a family who had been settled west of the Alleghenies since eighteen fourteen, in Dayton, Ohio, where they'd been to grammarschool and highschool and joined their father's church and played baseball and hockey and worked out on the parallel bars and the flying swing and sold newspapers and built themselves a printingpress out of odds and ends from the junkheap and flown kites and tinkered with mechanical contraptions and gone around town as boys doing odd jobs to turn an honest penny.

The folks claimed it was the bishop's bringing home a helicopter, a fiftycent mechanical toy made of two fans worked by elastic bands that was supposed to hover in the air, that had got his youngest boys hipped on the subject of flight

so that they stayed home instead of marrying the way the other boys did, and puttered all day about the house picking up a living with jobprinting,

bicyclerepair work

sitting up late nights reading books on aerodynamics.

Still they were sincere churchmembers, their bicycle business was prosperous, a man could rely on their word. They were popular in Dayton.

In those days flyingmachines were the big laugh of all the crackerbarrel philosophers. Langley's and Chanute's unsuccessful experiments had been jeered down with an I-told-you-so that rang from coast to coast. The Wrights' big problem was to find a place secluded enough to carry on their experiments without being the horselaugh of the countryside. Then they had no money to spend;

they were practical mechanics; when they needed anything they built it themselves.

They hit on Kitty Hawk,

on the great dunes and sandy banks that stretch south towards Hatteras seaward of Albemarle Sound,

a vast stretch of seabeach

empty except for a coastguard station, a few fishermen's shacks and the swarms of mosquitoes and the ticks and chiggers in the crabgrass behind the dunes

and overhead the gulls and swooping terns, in the evening fishhawks and cranes flapping across the saltmarshes, occasionally eagles

that the Wright brothers followed soaring with their eyes

as Leonardo watched them centuries before

straining his sharp eyes to apprehend the laws of flight.

Four miles across the loose sand from the scattering of shacks, the Wright brothers built themselves a camp and a shed for their gliders. It was a long way to pack their groceries, their tools, anything they happened to need; in summer it was hot as blazes, the mosquitoes were hell;

but they were alone there

and they figured out that the loose sand was as soft as anything they could find to fall in.

There with a glider made of two planes and a tail in which they lay flat on their bellies and controlled the warp of the planes by shimmying their hips, taking off again and again all day from a big dune named Kill Devil Hill,

they learned to fly.

Once they'd managed to hover for a few seconds

and soar ever so slightly on a rising aircurrent

they decided the time had come

to put a motor in their biplane

Back in the shop in Dayton, Ohio, they built an airtunnel, which is their first great contribution to the science of flying, and tried out model planes in it.

They couldn't interest any builders of gasoline engines so they had to build their own motor.

It worked; after that Christmas of nineteen three the Wright brothers weren't doing it for fun any more; they gave up their bicycle business, got the use of a big old cowpasture belonging to the local banker for practice flights, spent all the time when they weren't working on their machine in promotion, worrying about patents, infringements, spies, trying to interest government officials, to make sense out of the smooth involved heartbreaking remarks of lawyers.

In two years they had a plane that would cover twentyfour miles at a stretch round and round the cowpasture.

People on the interurban car used to crane their necks out of the windows when they passed along the edge of the field, startled by the clattering pop pop of the old Wright motor and the sight of the white biplane like a pair of ironing-boards one on top of the other chugging along a good fifty feet in the air. The cows soon got used to it.

As the flights got longer
The Wright brothers got backers,
engaged in lawsuits,
lay in their beds at night sleepless with the whine of phantom millions, worse than the mosquitoes at Kitty Hawk.

In nineteen seven they went to Paris,
allowed themselves to be togged out in dress suits and silk hats,
learned to tip waiters
talked with government experts, got used to gold braid and postponements

and vandyke beards and the outspread palms of politicos. For amusement
they played diabolo in the Tuileries gardens.

They gave publicized flights at Fort Myers, where they had their first fatal crackup, St. Petersburg, Paris, Berlin; at Pau they were all the rage,
such an attraction that the hotelkeeper wouldn't charge them for their room.
Alfonso of Spain shook hands with them and was photographed sitting in the machine,
King Edward watched a flight,
the Crown Prince insisted on being taken up,
the rain of medals began.

They were congratulated by the Czar
and the King of Italy and the amateurs of sport, and the society climbers and the papal titles,
and decorated by a society for universal peace.

Aeronautics became the sport of the day.
The Wrights don't seem to have been very much impressed by the upholstery and the braid and the gold medals and the parades of plush horses,
they remained practical mechanics
and insisted on doing all their own work themselves,
even to filling the gasolinetank.

In nineteen eleven they were back on the dunes
at Kitty Hawk with a new glider.
Orville stayed up in the air for nine and a half minutes, which remained a long time the record for motorless flight.
The same year Wilbur died of typhoidfever in Dayton.

In the rush of new names: Farman, Blériot, Curtiss, Ferber, Esnault-Peltrie, Delagrange;

in the sporting impact of bombs and the whine and rattle of shrapnel and the sudden stutter of machineguns after the motor's been shut off overhead,

and we flatten into the mud

and make ourselves small cowering in the corners of ruined walls,

the Wright brothers passed out of the headlines

but not even headlines or the bitter smear of newsprint or the choke of smokescreen and gas or chatter of brokers on the stockmarket or barking of phantom millions or oratory of brasshats laying wreaths on new monuments

can blur the memory

of the chilly December day

two shivering bicycle mechanics from Dayton, Ohio,

first felt their homemade contraption whittled out of hickory sticks,

gummed together with Arnstein's bicycle cement,

stretched with muslin they'd sewn on their sister's sewingmachine in their own backyard on Hawthorn Street in Dayton, Ohio,

soar into the air

above the dunes and the wide beach at Kitty Hawk.

PROTEUS

by JOHN DOS PASSOS

STEINMETZ was a hunchback, son of a hunchback lithographer.

He was born in Breslau in eighteen sixtyfive, graduated with highest honors at seventeen from the Breslau Gymnasium, went to the University of Breslau to study mathematics;

mathematics to Steinmetz was muscular strength and long walks over the hills and the kiss of a girl in love and big evenings spent swilling beer with your friends;

on his broken back he felt the topheavy weight of society the way workingmen felt it on their straight backs, the way poor students felt it, was a member of a socialist club, editor of a paper called *The People's Voice*.

Bismarck was sitting in Berlin like a big paperweight to keep the new Germany feudal, to hold down the empire for his bosses the Hohenzollerns.

Steinmetz had to run off to Zurich for fear of going to jail; at Zurich his mathematics woke up all the professors at the Polytechnic;

but Europe in the eighties was no place for a penniless German student with a broken back and a big head filled with symbolic calculus and wonder about electricity that is mathematics made power

and a socialist at that.

With a Danish friend he sailed for America steerage on an old French line boat *La Champagne,*

lived in Brooklyn at first and commuted to Yonkers where he had a twelvedollar a week job with Rudolph Eichemeyer who was a German exile from fortyeight an inventor and electrician and owner of a factory where he made hatmaking machinery and electrical generators.

In Yonkers he worked out the theory of the Third Harmonics

and the law of hysteresis which states in a formula the hundredfold relations between the metallic heat, density, frequency when the poles change places in the core of a magnet under an alternating current.

It is Steinmetz's law of hysteresis that makes possible all the transformers that crouch in little boxes and gableroofed houses in all the hightension lines all over everywhere. The mathematical symbols of Steinmetz's law are the patterns of all transformers everywhere.

In eighteen ninetytwo when Eichemeyer sold out to the corporation that was to form General Electric, Steinmetz was entered in the contract along with other valuable apparatus. All his life Steinmetz was a piece of apparatus belonging to General Electric.

First his laboratory was at Lynn, then it was moved and the little hunchback with it to Schenectady, the electric city.

General Electric humored him, let him be a socialist, let him keep a greenhouseful of cactuses lit up by mercury lights, let him have alligators, talking crows and a gila monster for pets and the publicity department talked up the wizard, the medicine man who knew the symbols that opened up the doors of Ali Baba's cave.

Steinmetz jotted a formula on his cuff and next morning a thousand new powerplants had sprung up and the dynamos sang dollars and the silence of the transformers was all dollars,

and the publicity department poured oily stories into the ears of the American public every Sunday and Steinmetz became the little parlor magician,

who made a toy thunderstorm in his laboratory and made all the toy trains run on time and the meat stay cold in the icebox and the lamp in the parlor and the great lighthouses and the searchlights and the revolving beams of light that guide airplanes at night towards Chicago, New York, St. Louis, Los Angeles,

and they let him be a socialist and believe that human society could be improved the way you can improve a dynamo and they let him be pro-German and write a letter offering his services to Lenin because mathematicians are so impractical who make up formulas by which you can build powerplants, factories, subway systems, light, heat, air, sunshine but not human relations that affect the stockholders' money and the directors' salaries.

Steinmetz was a famous magician and he talked to Edison tapping with the Morse code on Edison's knee

because Edison was so very deaf

and he went out West

to make speeches that nobody understood

and he talked to Bryan about God on a railroad train

and all the reporters stood round while he and Einstein

met face to face,

but they couldn't catch what they said

and Steinmetz was the most valuable piece of apparatus General Electric had

until he wore out and died.

"Sometimes I ask myself, 'Where will it ever end?'"

LIFT UP THINE EYES

by SHERWOOD ANDERSON

IT IS a big assembling plant in a city of
the Northwest. They assemble there the
Bogel car. It is a car that sells in large
numbers and at a low price. The parts
are made in one great central plant and
shipped to the places where they are to

Sherwood Anderson, "Lift Up Thine Eyes," *The Nation*, May 28, 1930. By permission of
The Nation.

be assembled. There is little or no manufacturing done in the assembling plant itself. The parts come in. These great companies have learned to use the railroad cars for storage.

At the central plant everything is done on schedule. As soon as the parts are made they go into railroad cars. They are on their way to the assembling plants scattered all over the United States and they arrive on schedule.

The assembling plant assembles cars for a certain territory. A careful survey has been made. This territory can afford to buy so and so many cars per day.

"But suppose the people do not want the cars?"

"What has that to do with it?"

People, American people, no longer buy cars. They do not buy newspapers, books, foods, pictures, clothes. Things are sold to people now. If a territory can take so and so many Bogel cars, find men who can make them take the cars. That is the way things are done now.

In the assembling plant everyone works "on the belt." This is a big steel conveyor, a kind of moving sidewalk, waist-high. It is a great river running down through the plant. Various tributary streams come into the main stream, the main belt. They bring tires, they bring headlights, horns, bumpers for cars. They flow into the main stream. The main stream has its source at the freight cars, where the parts are unloaded, and it flows out to the other end of the factory and into other freight cars.

The finished automobiles go into the freight cars at the delivery end of the belt. The assembly plant is a place of peculiar tension. You feel it when you go in. It never lets up. Men here work always on tension. There is no let-up to the tension. If you can't stand it, get out.

It is the belt. The belt is boss. It moves always forward. Now the chassis goes on the belt. A hoist lifts it up and places it just so. There is a man at each corner. The chassis is deposited on the belt and it begins to move. Not too rapidly. There are things to be done.

How nicely everything is calculated. Scientific men have done this. They have watched men work. They have stood looking, watch in hand. There is care taken about everything. Look up. Lift up thine eyes. Hoists are bringing engines, bodies, wheels, fenders. These come out of side streams flowing into the main stream. They move at a pace very nicely calculated. They will arrive at the main stream at just a certain place at just a certain time.

In this shop there is no question of wages to be wrangled about. The men work but eight hours a day and are well paid. They are, almost without exception, young, strong men. It is, however, possible that eight hours a day in this place may be much longer than twelve or even sixteen hours in the old carelessly run plants.

They can get better pay here than at any other shop in town. Although I am a man wanting a good many minor comforts in life, I could live well enough on the wages made by the workers in this place. Sixty cents an hour to begin and then, after a probation period of sixty days, if I can stand the pace, seventy cents or more.

To stand the pace is the real test. Special skill is not required. It is all perfectly timed, perfectly calculated. If you are a body upholsterer, so many tacks driven per second. Not too many. If a man hurries too much too many tacks drop on the floor. If a man gets too hurried he is not efficient. Let an expert take a month, two months, to find out just how many tacks the average good man can drive per second.

There must be a certain standard maintained in the finished product. Remember that. It must pass inspection after inspection.

Do not crowd too hard.

Crowd all you can.

Keep crowding.

There are fifteen, twenty, thirty, perhaps fifty such assembling plants, all over the country, each serving its own section. Wires pass back and forth daily. The central office—from which all the parts come —at Jointville is the nerve center. Wires come in and go out of Jointville. In so and so many hours Williamsburg, with so and so many men, produced so and so many cars.

Now Burkesville is ahead. It stays ahead. What is up at Burkesville? An expert flies there.

The man at Burkesville was a major in the army. He is the manager there. He is a cold, rather severe, rather formal man. He has found out something. He is a real Bogel man, an ideal Bogel man. There is no foolishness about him. He watches the belt. He does not say foolishly to himself, "I am the boss here." He knows the belt is boss.

He says there is a lot of foolishness talked about the belt. The experts are too expert, he says. He has found out that the belt can be made to move just a little faster than the experts say. He has tried it. He knows. Go and look for yourself. There are the men out there on the belt, swarming along the belt, each in his place. They are all right, aren't they?

Can you see anything wrong?

Just a trifle more speed in every man. Shove the pace up just a little, not much.

With the same number of men, in the same number of hours, six more cars a day.

That's the way a major gets to be a colonel, a colonel a general. Watch that fellow at Burkesville, the man with the military stride, the cold steady voice. He'll go far.

Everything is nicely, perfectly calculated in all the Bogel assembling plants. There are white marks on the floor everywhere. Everything is immaculately clean. No one smokes, no one chews tobacco, no one spits. There are white bands on the cement floor along which the men walk. As they work, sweepers follow them. Tacks dropped on the floor are at once swept up. You can tell by the sweepings in a plant where there is too much waste, too much carelessness. Sweep everything carefully and frequently. Weigh the sweepings. Have an expert examine the sweepings. Report to Jointville.

Jointville says: "Too many upholsterers' tacks wasted in the plant at Port Smith. Belleville produced one hundred and eleven cars a day, with seven hundred and forty-nine men, wasting only nine hundred and six tacks."

It is a good thing to go through the plant now and then, select one man from all the others, give him a new and bigger job, just like that, offhand. If he doesn't make good, fire him.

It is a good thing to go through the plant occasionally, pick out some man, working apparently just as the others are, fire him.

If he asks why, just say to him, "You know."

He'll know why all right. He'll imagine why.

The thing is to build up Jointville. This country needs a religion. You have got to build up the sense of a mysterious central thing, a thing working outside your knowledge.

Let the notion grow and grow that there is something superhuman at the core of all this.

Lift up thine eyes, lift up thine eyes.

The central office reaches down into your secret thoughts. It knows, it knows.

Jointville knows.

Do not ask questions of Jointville. Keep up the pace.

Get the cars out.

Get the cars out.

Get the cars out.

The pace can be accelerated a little this year. The men have all got tuned into the old pace now.

Step it up a little, just a little.

They have got a special policeman in all the Bogel assembling plants. They have got a special doctor there. A man hurts his finger a little. It bleeds a little, a mere scratch. The doctor reaches down for him. The finger is fixed. Jointville wants no blood poisonings, no infections.

The doctor puts men who want jobs through a physical examination, as in the army. Try his nerve reactions. We want only the best men here, the youngest, the fastest.

Why not?

We pay the best wages, don't we?

The policeman in the plant has a special job. That's queer. It is like this. Now and then the big boss passes through. He selects a man off the belt.

"You're fired."

"Why?"

"You know."

Now and then a man goes off his nut. He goes fantoed. He howls and shouts. He grabs up a hammer.

A stream of crazy profanity comes from his lips.

There is Jointville. That is the central thing. That controls the belt.

The belt controls me.

It moves.

It moves.

It moves.

I've tried to keep up.

I tell you I have been keeping up.

Jointville is God.

Jointville controls the belt.

The belt is God.

God has rejected me.

You're fired.

Sometimes a man, fired like that, goes nutty. He gets dangerous. A strong policeman on hand knocks him down, takes him out.

You walk within certain definite white lines.

It is calculated that a man, rubbing automobile bodies with pumice, makes thirty thousand and twenty-one arm strokes per day. The difference between thirty thousand and twenty-one and twenty-eight thousand and four will tell a vital story of profits or loss at Jointville.

Do you think things are settled at Jointville, or at the assembling plants of the Bogel car scattered all over America? Do you think men know how fast the belt can be made to move, what the ultimate, the final pace will be, can be?

Certainly not.

There are experts studying the nerves of men, the movements of men. They are watching, watching. Calculations are always going on. The thing is to produce goods and more goods at less cost. Keep the standard up. Increase the pace a little.

Stop waste.

Calculate everything.

A man walking to and from his work

between white lines saves steps. There is a tremendous science of lost motion not perfectly calculated yet.

More goods at less cost.

Increase the pace.

Keep up standards.

It is so you advance civilization.

In the Bogel assembling plants, as at Jointville itself, there isn't any laughter. No one stops work to play. No one fools around or throws things, as they used to do in the old factories. That is why Bogel is able to put the old-fashioned factories, one by one, out of business.

It is all a matter of calculation. You feel it when you go in. You feel rigid lines. You feel movement. You feel a strange tension in the air. There is a quiet terrible intensity.

The belt moves. It keeps moving. The day I was there a number of young boys had come in. They had been sent by a Bogel car dealer, away back somewhere in the country. They had driven in during the night and were to drive Bogel cars back over country roads to some dealer. A good many Bogel cars go out to dealers from the assembling plants, driven out by boys like that.

Such boys, driving all night, fooling along the road, getting no sleep.

They have a place for them to wait for the cars in the Bogel assembling plants. You have been at dog shows and have seen how prize dogs are exhibited, each in his nice clean cage. They have nice clean cages like that for country boys who drive in to Bogel assembling plants to get cars.

The boys come in. There is a place to lie down in there. It is clean. After the boy goes into his cage a gate is closed. He is fastened in.

If a country boy, sleepy like that, waiting for his car, wandered about in a plant he might get hurt.

There might be damage suits, all sorts of things.

Better to calculate everything. Be careful. Be exact.

Jointville thought of that. Jointville thinks of everything. It is the center of power, the new mystery.

Every year in America Jointville comes nearer and nearer being the new center. Men nowadays do not look to Washington. They look to Jointville.

Lift up thine eyes, lift up thine eyes.

EDUCATION IN THE WORLD STATE

by Aldous Huxley

Mr. Foster was left in the decanting room. The D.H.C. and his students stepped into the nearest lift and were carried up to the fifth floor.

Infant Nurseries. Neo-Pavlovian Conditioning Rooms, announced the notice board.

The Director opened a door. They were

From *Brave New World*, by Aldous Huxley. Harper & Brothers. Copyright, 1932, by Aldous Huxley.

in a large bare room, very bright and sunny; for the whole of the southern wall was a single window. Half a dozen nurses, trousered and jacketed in the regulation white viscose-linen uniform, their hair aseptically hidden under white caps, were engaged in setting out bowls of roses in a long row across the floor. Big bowls, packed tight with blossom. Thousands of petals, ripe-blown and silkily smooth, like the cheeks of innumerable little cherubs, but of cherubs, in that bright light, not exclusively pink and Aryan, but also luminously Chinese, also Mexican, also apoplectic with too much blowing of celestial trumpets, also pale as death, pale with the posthumous whiteness of marble.

The nurses stiffened to attention as the D.H.C. came in.

"Set out the books," he said curtly.

In silence the nurses obeyed his command. Between the rose bowls the books were duly set out—a row of nursery quartos opened invitingly each at some gaily colored image of beast or fish or bird.

"Now bring in the children."

They hurried out of the room and returned in a minute or two, each pushing a kind of tall dumbwaiter laden, on all its four wire-netted shelves, with eight-month-old babies, all exactly alike (a Bokanovsky Group, it was evident) and all (since their caste was Delta) dressed in khaki.

"Put them down on the floor."

The infants were unloaded.

"Now turn them so that they can see the flowers and books."

Turned, the babies at once fell silent, then began to crawl towards those clusters of sleek colors, those shapes so gay and brilliant on the white pages. As they approached, the sun came out of a momentary eclipse behind a cloud. The roses flamed up as though with a sudden passion from within; a new and profound significance seemed to suffuse the shining pages of the books. From the ranks of the crawling babies came little squeals of excitement, gurgles and twitterings of pleasure.

The Director rubbed his hands. "Excellent!" he said. "It might almost have been done on purpose."

The swiftest crawlers were already at their goal. Small hands reached out uncertainly, touched, grasped, unpetaling the transfigured roses, crumpling the illuminated pages of the books. The Director waited until all were happily busy. Then, "Watch carefully," he said. And, lifting his hand, he gave the signal.

The Head Nurse, who was standing by a switchboard at the other end of the room, pressed down a little lever.

There was a violent explosion. Shriller and even shriller, a siren shrieked. Alarm bells maddeningly sounded.

The children started, screamed: their faces were distorted with terror.

"And now," the Director shouted (for the noise was deafening), "now we proceed to rub in the lesson with a mild electric shock."

He waved his hand again, and the Head Nurse pressed a second lever. The screaming of the babies suddenly changed its tone. There was something desperate, almost insane, about the sharp spasmodic yelps to which they now gave utterance. Their little bodies twitched and stiffened; their limbs moved jerkily as if to the tug of unseen wires.

"We can electrify that whole strip of floor," bawled the Director in explanation. "But that's enough," he signaled to the nurse.

The explosions ceased, the bells stopped

ringing, the shriek of the siren died down from tone to tone into silence. The stiffly twitching bodies relaxed, and what had become the sob and yelp of infant maniacs broadened out once more into a normal howl of ordinary terror.

"Offer them the flowers and the books again."

The nurses obeyed; but at the approach of the roses, at the mere sight of those gaily-colored images of pussy and cock-a-doodle-doo and baa-baa black sheep, the infants shrank away in horror; the volume of their howling suddenly increased.

"Observe," said the Director triumphantly, "observe."

Books and loud noises, flowers and electric shocks—already in the infant mind these couples were compromisingly linked; and after two hundred repetitions of the same or a similar lesson would be wedded indissolubly. What man has joined, nature is powerless to put asunder.

"They'll grow up with what the psychologists used to call an 'instinctive' hatred of books and flowers. Reflexes unalterably conditioned. They'll be safe from books and botany all their lives." The Director turned to his nurses. "Take them away again."

Still yelling, the khaki babies were loaded on to their dumbwaiters and wheeled out, leaving behind them the smell of sour milk and a most welcome silence.

One of the students held up his hand; and though he could see quite well why you couldn't have lower-caste people wasting the Community's time over books, and that there was always the risk of their reading something which might undesirably decondition one of their reflexes, yet . . . well, he couldn't understand about the flowers. Why go to the trouble of making it psychologically impossible for Deltas to like flowers?

Patiently the D.H.C. explained. If the children were made to scream at the sight of a rose, that was on grounds of high economic policy. Not so very long ago (a century or thereabouts), Gammas, Deltas, even Epsilons, had been conditioned to like flowers—flowers in particular and wild nature in general. The idea was to make them want to be going out into the country at every available opportunity, and so compel them to consume transport.

"And didn't they consume transport?" asked the student.

"Quite a lot," the D.H.C. replied. "But nothing else."

Primroses and landscapes, he pointed out, have one grave defect: they are gratuitous. A love of nature keeps no factories busy. It was decided to abolish the love of nature, at any rate among the lower classes: to abolish the love of nature, but *not* the tendency to consume transport. For of course it was essential that they should keep on going to the country, even though they hated it. The problem was to find an economically sounder reason for consuming transport than a mere affection for primroses and landscapes. It was duly found.

"We condition the masses to hate the country," concluded the Director. "But simultaneously we condition them to love all country sports. At the same time, we see to it that all country sports shall entail the use of elaborate apparatus. So that they consume manufactured articles as well as transport. Hence those electric shocks."

"I see," said the student, and was silent, lost in admiration.

There was a silence; then, clearing his throat, "Once upon a time," the Director began, "while our Ford was still on earth, there was a little boy called Reuben Rabinovitch. Reuben was the child of Polish speaking parents." The Director interrupted himself. "You know what Polish is, I suppose?"

"A dead language."

"Like French and German," added another student, officiously showing off his learning.

"And 'parent'?" questioned the D.H.C.

There was an uneasy silence. Several of the boys blushed. They had not yet learned to draw the significant but often very fine distinction between smut and pure science. One, at least, had the courage to raise a hand.

"Human beings used to be . . ." he hesitated; the blood rushed to his cheeks. "Well, they used to be viviparous."

"Quite right." The Director nodded approvingly.

"And when the babies were decanted . . ."

"'Born,'" came the correction.

"Well, then they were the parents—I mean, not the babies, of course; the other ones." The poor boy was overwhelmed with confusion.

"In brief," the Director summed up, "the parents were the father and the mother." The smut that was really science fell with a crash into the boys' eye-avoiding silence. "Mother," he repeated loudly, rubbing in the science; and, leaning back in his chair, "These," he said gravely, "are unpleasant facts; I know it. But then most historical facts *are* unpleasant."

He returned to Little Reuben—to Little Reuben, in whose room, one evening, by an oversight, his father and mother (crash, crash!) happened to leave the radio turned on.

("For you must remember that in those days of gross viviparous reproduction, children were always brought up by their parents and not in State Conditioning Centers.")

While the child was asleep, a broadcast program from London suddenly started to come through; and the next morning, to the astonishment of his crash and crash (the more daring of the boys ventured to grin at one another), Little Reuben woke up repeating word for word a long lecture by that curious old writer ("one of the very few whose works have been permitted to come down to us"), George Bernard Shaw, who was speaking, according to a well-authenticated tradition, about his own genius. To Little Reuben's wink and snigger, this lecture was, of course, perfectly incomprehensible and, imagining that their child had suddenly gone mad, they sent for a doctor. He, fortunately, understood English, recognized the discourse as that which Shaw had broadcasted the previous evening, realized the significance of what had happened, and sent a letter to the medical press about it.

"The principle of sleep-teaching, or hypnopaedia, had been discovered." The D.H.C. made an impressive pause.

The principle had been discovered; but many, many years were to elapse before that principle was usefully applied.

"The case of Little Reuben occurred only twenty-three years after Our Ford's first T-Model was put on the market." (Here the Director made a sign of the T on his stomach and all the students reverently followed suit.) "And yet . . ."

Furiously the students scribbled. *"Hypnopaedia, first used officially in A.F. 214. Why not before? Two reasons. (a) . . ."*

"These early experimenters," the D.H.C. was saying, "were on the wrong track. They thought that hypnopaedia could be made an instrument of intellectual education . . ."

(A small boy asleep on his right side, the right arm stuck out, the right hand hanging limp over the edge of the bed. Through a round grating in the side of a box a voice speaks softly.

"The Nile is the longest river in Africa and the second in length of all the rivers of the globe. Although falling short of the length of the Mississippi-Missouri, the Nile is at the head of all rivers as regards the length of its basin, which extends through 35 degrees of latitude . . ."

At breakfast the next morning, "Tommy" someone says, "do you know which is the longest river in Africa?" A shaking of the head. "But don't you remember something that begins: The Nile is the . . ."

"The-Nile-is-the-longest-river-in-Africa-and-the-second-in-length-of-all-the-rivers-of-the-globe . . ." The words come rushing out. "Although-falling-short-of . . ."

"Well, now, which is the longest river in Africa?"

The eyes are blank. "I don't know."

"But the Nile, Tommy."

"The-Nile-is-the-longest-river-in-Africa-and-second . . ."

"Then which river is the longest, Tommy?"

Tommy bursts into tears. "I don't know," he howls.)

That howl, the Director made it plain, discouraged the earliest investigators. The experiments were abandoned. No further attempt was made to teach children the length of the Nile in their sleep. Quite rightly. You can't learn a science unless you know what it's all about.

"Whereas, if they'd only started on *moral* education," said the Director, leading the way towards the door. The stu-dents followed him, desperately scribbling as they walked and all the way up in the lift. "Moral education, which ought never, in any circumstance, to be rational."

"Silence, silence," whispered a loud speaker as they stepped out at the four-teenth floor, and "Silence, silence," the trumpet mouths indefatigably repeated at intervals down every corridor. The stu-dents and even the Director himself rose automatically to the tips of their toes. They were Alphas, of course; but even Alphas have been well conditioned. "Silence, si-lence." All the air of the fourteenth floor was sibilant with the categorical impera-tive.

Fifty yards of tiptoeing brought them to a door which the Director cautiously opened. They stepped over the threshold into the twilight of a shuttered dormitory. Eighty cots stood in a row against the wall. There was a sound of light regular breathing and a continuous murmur, as of very faint voices remotely whispering.

A nurse rose as they entered and came to attention before the Director.

"What's the lesson this afternoon?" he asked.

"We had Elementary Sex for the first forty minutes," she answered. "But now it's switched over to Elementary Class Con-sciousness."

The Director walked slowly down the long line of cots. Rosy and relaxed with sleep, eighty little boys and girls lay softly breathing. There was a whisper under every pillow. The D.H.C. halted and, bending over one of the little beds, lis-tened attentively.

"Elementary Class Consciousness, did you say? Let's have it repeated a little louder by the trumpet."

At the end of the room a loud speaker projected from the wall. The Director walked up to it and pressed a switch.

". . . all wear green," said a soft but very distinct voice, beginning in the middle of a sentence, "and Delta children wear khaki. Oh, no, I don't want to play with Delta children. And Epsilons are still worse. They're too stupid to be able to read or write. Besides they wear black, which is such a beastly color. I'm *so* glad I'm a Beta."

There was a pause; then the voice began again.

"Alpha children wear gray. They work much harder than we do, because they're so frightfully clever. I'm really awfully glad I'm a Beta, because I don't work so hard. And then we are much better than the Gammas and Deltas. Gammas are stupid. They all wear green, and Delta children wear khaki. Oh, no, I *don't* want to play with Delta children. And Epsilons are still worse. They're too stupid to be able . . ."

The Director pushed back the switch. The voice was silent. Only its thin ghost continued to mutter from beneath the eighty pillows.

"They'll have that repeated forty or fifty times more before they wake; then again on Thursday, and again on Saturday. A hundred and twenty times three times a week for thirty months. After which they go on to a more advanced lesson."

Roses and electric shocks, the khaki of Deltas and a whiff of asafoetida—welded indissolubly before the child can speak. But wordless conditioning is crude and wholesale; cannot bring home the finer distinctions, cannot inculcate the more complex courses of behavior. For that there must be words, but words without reason. In brief, hypnopaedia.

"The greatest moralizing and socializing force of all time."

The students took it down in their little books. Straight from the horse's mouth.

Once more the Director touched the switch.

". . . so frightfully clever," the soft, insinuating, indefatigable voice was saying. "I'm really awfully glad I'm a Beta, because . . ."

Not so much like drops of water, though water, it is true, can wear holes in the hardest granite; rather, drops of liquid sealing-wax, drops that adhere, incrust, incorporate themselves with what they fall on, till finally the rock is all one scarlet blob.

"Till at last the child's mind *is* these suggestions, and the sum of the suggestions *is* the child's mind. And not the child's mind only. The adult's mind too—all his life long. The mind that judges and desires and decides—made up of these suggestions. But all these suggestions are *our* suggestions!" The Director almost shouted in his triumph. "Suggestions from the State." He banged the nearest table. "It therefore follows . . ."

A noise made him turn round.

"Oh, Ford!" he said in another tone, "I've gone and woken the children."

*"Ed Ricketts says that when he was little he was in trouble all
the time until he suddenly realized that adults were crazy. Then,
when he knew that, everything was all right and he could be nice to
them. He says he has never found occasion to revise that opinion."*
—from a letter by JOHN STEINBECK.

MR. MECHANO

by WILLIAM SAROYAN

AFTER THEIR ADVENTURE in the public library, Lionel and Ulysses continued to explore Ithaca. At sundown they found themselves standing at the very front of a small crowd of idlers and passers-by, watching a man in the window of a third-rate drug store. The man moved like a piece of machinery, although he *was* a human being. He looked, however, as if he had been made of wax instead of flesh. He seemed inhuman and in fact he looked like nothing so much as an upright, unburied corpse still capable of moving. The man was the most incredible thing Ulysses had seen in all of his four years of life in the world. No light came out of the man's eyes. His lips were set as if they would never part.

The man was engaged in advertising *Dr. Bradford's Tonic*. He worked between two easels. On one easel was a sign on which this message had been printed: "Mr. Mechano—The Machine Man—Half Machine, Half Human. More Dead Than Alive. $50 if you can make him smile. $500 if you can make him laugh." On the other easel Mr. Mechano placed pasteboard cards which he took in an extremely mechanical fashion from the small table in front of the easel. On these cards were printed various messages urging people to buy the patent medicine which Dr. Brad-

ford had invented and thereby to become more alive. After each new card had been placed on the easel Mr. Mechano pointed at each word of the message on the card with a pointer. When all ten of the cards had been placed on the easel, Mr. Mechano removed them all and put them back on the table and began the procedure all over again.

"It's a man, Ulysses," Lionel said to his friend. "I can see him. It's not a machine, Ulysses. It's a man! See his eyes? He's alive. See him?"

The card Mr. Mechano had just placed on the easel read: "Don't drag yourself around half dead. Enjoy life. Take Dr. Bradford's Tonic and feel like a new man."

"There's another card," Lionel said. "It says something on that card." Suddenly he was weary and eager to get home. "Come on, Ulysses," he said, "let's go. We've seen him go through all the cards three times. Let's go home. It's almost night now." He took his friend by the hand, but Ulysses drew his hand away.

"Come on, Ulysses!" Lionel said. "I've got to go home now. I'm hungry." But Ulysses did not want to go. It seemed that he did not even *hear* Lionel's words.

"I'm going, Ulysses," Lionel challenged. He waited for Ulysses to turn and go with him, but the boy did not budge. A little hurt and amazed by this betrayal of friendship, Lionel began to walk home, turning every three or four steps to see if his friend was not going to join him after all. But no, Ulysses wanted to stay and watch Mr. Mechano. Lionel felt deeply wounded as he continued his journey home. "I thought he was my best friend in the whole world," he said.

Ulysses stood among the handful of people watching Mr. Mechano until at last only he and an old man were left. Mr. Mechano went right on picking up the cards and putting them on the easel. He went right on pointing to each word on each card. Soon the old man went away too, and then only Ulysses stood on the sidewalk looking up at the strange human being in the window of the drug store. It was growing dark now. When the street lights came on, Ulysses came out of the trance of fascination into which the vision of Mr. Mechano had placed him. It was almost as if he had become hypnotized by the sight of the man. Now, out of the trance, he looked around. Day had ended and everybody had gone— The only thing left anywhere was something for which he had no word—Death.

The small boy looked back suddenly at the mechanical man. It seemed then that the man was looking at *him*. There was swift and fierce terror in the boy. Suddenly he was running away. The few people he saw in the streets now seemed full of death, too, like Mr. Mechano. They seemed suddenly ugly, not beautiful, as they had always seemed before. Ulysses ran until he was almost exhausted. He stopped, breathing hard and almost crying. He looked around, feeling a deep silent steady horror in all things—the horror of Mr. Mechano—Death! He had

never before known fear of *any* kind, let alone fear such as this, and it was the most difficult thing in the world for him to know what to do. His poise was all gone—scattered by the fear of the horror catching up with *him,* and he began to run again. This time as he ran he said to himself, almost crying, "Papa, Mama, Marcus, Bess, Homer! Papa, Mama, Marcus, Bess, Homer!"

The world was surely wonderful and it was surely full of good things to be seen again and again, but now the world was a thing to escape, only he could think of no direction to take. He wanted swiftly to reach somebody of his family. He stood panic-stricken, and then began moving a few steps in one direction and then a few in another, feeling all around him a presence of incredible disaster, a disaster he could escape only by reaching his father, his mother, one of his brothers, or his sister. And then, instead of reaching one of these, he saw far down the street the leader of the neighborhood gang, August Gottlieb. The newsboy was standing on a deserted street corner, calling out the headline as if the area around him were full of people who must be told what had happened that day in the world. Hollering headlines had always seemed slightly ridiculous to August Gottlieb because, for one thing, the headlines were always about murder of one sort or another and, for another, because it seemed somehow a thing of bad taste to go about among people in the streets of Ithaca lifting his voice. Consequently, the newsboy felt pleased when at last he discovered that the streets were deserted. Without even knowing that he was doing such a thing, whenever the streets had become empty of the people of Ithaca, August Gottlieb, as if grateful for his almost solitary inhabitance of the city, lifted his voice more powerfully than ever, calling out the day's miserable news. What could a man do about the news—sell a paper, and make a few pennies? Is that what he could do about it? Wasn't it foolish for him to cry out the daily message of mistake as if it were glad tidings? Wasn't it shameful for the people to be so steadily unimpressed with the nature of every day's news? Sometimes even in his sleep the newsboy dreamed of calling out the headlines of the world's news, but there, in that inner area of experience, he felt mockery and contempt for the nature of the news, and when he shouted, it was always from a great height, and beneath him always were multitudes engaged in activities of error and crime. But the minute they heard his roaring voice, they stopped in their tracks to look up at him, and then he always shouted, "Now go back, go back where you belong! Stop your murder! Plant trees instead!" He had always loved the idea of planting a tree.

When Ulysses saw August Gottlieb on the street corner, much of the terror in his heart passed away and he began to feel that it would not be years and years before he might again find goodness and love in the world. The little boy wanted to shout out to August Gottlieb, but he couldn't make a sound. Instead, he ran with all his might to the newsboy and flung himself upon him in an embrace so forceful that it almost knocked Auggie down.

"Ulysses!" the newsboy said. "What's the matter? What are you crying about?"

Ulysses looked up into the eyes of the newsboy, but still he could not speak.

"You're scared, Ulysses," Auggie said. "Well, don't be scared—there's nothing to be scared of. Now don't cry, Ulysses. You don't have to be scared." But still the boy could not stop sobbing. "Now don't cry

any more," Auggie said, and waited for Ulysses to stop. Ulysses tried very hard not to cry and soon the sobs came at infrequent intervals, each sob like a hiccup. Then Auggie said, "Come on, Ulysses, we'll go to Homer."

At the sound of that name, the name of his brother, Ulysses smiled, and then hiccuped another sob. "Homer?" he said.

"Sure," Auggie said. "Your brother. Come on."

It was almost too wonderful for the little boy to believe. "Going to see Homer?" he said.

"Sure," Auggie said. "The telegraph office is just around the corner."

August Gottlieb and Ulysses Macauley walked around the corner to the telegraph office. They found Homer seated at the delivery desk. When Ulysses saw his brother, a wonderful thing happened to his face. All the terror left his eyes, because now he was home.

When Homer saw his brother, he got up and went to the boy and lifted him in his arms. He turned to Auggie. "What's the matter?" he said. "What's Ulysses doing in town at this hour?"

"He got lost, I guess," Auggie said. "He was crying."

"Crying?" Homer said, and then hugged his brother, just as Ulysses hiccuped another sob. "All right, Ulysses," he said. "Don't cry any more. I'll take you home on my bike. Now, don't cry."

From his desk the manager of the telegraph office, Thomas Spangler, watched the three boys, and the old telegraph operator, William Grogan, stopped his work to watch them, too. They looked at one another several times. Homer put his brother down. He knew the boy was all right again when Ulysses went to the delivery desk to look at things there. Ulysses was always all right if he was interested in things, and now he was interested again. Homer put his arm around August and said, "Thanks, Auggie. It would have been terrible if he didn't find you."

Spangler got up and went to the two boys. "Hello, Auggie," he said. "Let me have a paper."

"Yes, sir," Auggie said, and began to go through the routine of folding the paper and making the sale, but Spangler stopped him so that he could hold the paper up before him. The manager of the telegraph office glanced at the headline, and then threw the paper into the wastebasket. "How's it going, Auggie?" he said.

"Not bad, Mr. Spangler," Auggie said. "I've made fifty-five cents so far today, but I started selling papers at one o'clock this afternoon. When I make seventy-five cents I'm going home."

"Why?" Spangler said. "Why do you want to make seventy-five cents?"

"I don't know," Auggie said. "I just thought I ought to make seventy-five cents on a Saturday. There's nobody in town hardly, but I think I can sell the rest of my papers in another hour or two. Pretty soon people start coming back to town after supper—the movie crowd."

"Well," Spangler said, "to hell with the movie crowd. You give me the rest of your papers and go on home *now*. Here's a quarter."

Even though the newsboy felt deeply grateful to the manager of the telegraph office for this gesture, somehow it didn't seem right to him. You had to sell papers one at a time and each one to a different person, and you had to stand on a street corner and holler the headline and make the people *want* to read the news. But even so, he was tired, and he wanted to get home to supper, and he never did know anybody like Spangler before, and maybe Spangler wanting to buy all his pa-

pers at once to throw into the wastebasket was the best news of the whole day anyway. It just didn't seem right that it should be a good man like Spangler, though, instead of the riffraff of the streets —well, maybe not exactly riffraff, but whatever they were. The newsboy felt that he would have to protest a sale of this sort. "I don't want to make a quarter from *you*, Mr. Spangler," he said.

"Never mind," Spangler said. "Give me the papers and go home."

"Yes, sir," Auggie said. "But maybe you'll let me do something for you to make up for this quarter some day."

"Sure, sure," Spangler said, and threw the papers into the wastebasket.

Auggie turned to Ulysses who was now studying the call box on the delivery desk. "Ulysses got lost," Auggie said to Mr. Spangler.

"Well," Spangler said, "he's not lost now. Ulysses!" he called out to the boy, and Ulysses turned to look at the manager of the telegraph office. After a moment, finding nothing appropriate to say to the boy, Spangler said, "How are you?" And after a moment, Ulysses, finding nothing appropriate to say in reply to this question said, "O.K." Each of them knew that something else had been meant.

Homer said, knowing it was the wrong thing, "He's O.K." And then Auggie, purely out of confusion, repeated these two words, as if he meant a whole new wonderful bright meaning. They all felt awkward, but very happy, especially Spangler.

William Grogan, the telegraph operator, after this exchange of ideas, brought out his bottle, unscrewed the cap, and took a good long swig.

Auggie turned to go home, but Homer stopped him. "Wait a minute, Auggie," he said, "I'll hike you home. Is it all right,

Mr. Spangler? I've got a pickup at Ithaca Wine, and it's on the way home. So if it's all right, I'll hike Ulysses and Auggie home and then go and get the pickup at Ithaca Wine. Is it all right?"

"Sure, sure," Spangler said, and went back to his desk. He picked up the hard-boiled egg which he believed brought him good luck—or at least kept away anything like extremely bad luck.

"No," Auggie said to Homer. "You don't need to hike me home. Hiking two people at once on a bike is too much, Homer. I can walk it in no time."

"I'll hike you home," Homer said. "You can't walk it in no time. It's almost three miles. I can hike both of you very easily. You can sit on the frame and Ulysses can sit on the handlebars. Now come on."

The three boys went out to Homer's bicycle. The load was a heavy one, especially for a man with one bad leg, but Homer got his passengers home all right. They stopped first at the little house next door to Ara's Market—Auggie's house. Ara himself was standing in front of his store, holding the hand of his little boy. They were looking up into the sky. Down the street, next to the empty lot, Mrs. Macauley stood in the yard under the old walnut tree, taking clothes off the line. Mary and Bess were in the parlor playing and singing, and the sound of the piano and Mary's voice could be heard faintly.

Auggie got off the bicycle and went into his house. Homer stood a moment in the street, holding the bike and looking up at the sky and over at the Macauley house. Then, Auggie came out of the house and went up to Ara, the grocer.

"Did you do a lot of business today, Mr. Ara?" Auggie said to the grocer.

"Thank you, Auggie," the grocer said. "I am satisfied."

"I've got seventy-five cents I want to spend," Auggie said. "I want to get a lot of things for tomorrow."

"All right, Auggie," the grocer said, but before turning to go back into the store he pointed to the clouds in the sky and then looked at his son. "See, John?" he said. "Nighttime come now—pretty soon we get in our beds, go to sleep. Sleep all night. When daytime come, we get up again. New day."

The grocer and his son and the neighbor boy went into the store. In the meantime, Ulysses, sitting on the handlebars of his brother's bicycle, was watching his mother. Now Homer got back onto the bicycle and began to ride toward the house.

"Mama," Ulysses said to his brother, turning to look up into his face.

"Sure," Homer said. "That's Mama right over there in the yard under the tree. See her?"

As they came closer to the woman in the yard under the tree, the little brother's face grew full of a smiling light, but at the same time there was now a deep sadness in that face and in the face of the brother who held the handlebars, almost embracing him.

Homer rode straight across the empty lot into the backyard, under the walnut tree. He got off the bicycle and set Ulysses down on his feet. Ulysses stood looking at his mother. Gone from him now almost as if forever was the terror that had come from Mr. Mechano.

"He got lost, Ma," Homer said. "Auggie found him and brought him to the telegraph office. I can't stay, but I'll go in and say hello to Bess and Mary."

Homer went into the house and stood in the dark dining room, listening to his sister and the girl his brother loved. When the song was over, he moved into the parlor. "Hello," he said.

The two girls turned. "Hello, Homer," Mary said, and then very swiftly, with great happiness, "I got a letter from Marcus today."

"Did you, Mary?" Homer said. "How is he?"

"Just fine," Mary said. "They're going away soon, but they don't know where. He says not to worry if we don't get any more letters for a while."

"He wrote to all of us," Bess said, "to Mama, and me, and even to Ulysses."

"Did he?" Homer said. He waited a moment for the announcement of the arrival of *his* letter, afraid there might not be any such announcement. At last he said very quietly, "Didn't he send *me* a letter, too?"

"Oh, of course," Mary said. "Yours is the biggest letter of all. I thought you would know that if he wrote to all of us, he would write to you, too."

Homer's sister lifted a letter off the table and handed it to him. Homer looked at the letter a long time and then his sister said, "Well, why don't you open it and read it? Read it to us."

"No, Bess," Homer said. "I've got to go now. I'll take it to the office and read it there tonight when I've got a lot of time."

"We spent the whole day looking for a job," Bess said, "but we didn't find one."

"We had a lot of fun just the same, Bess," Mary said. "It was a lot of fun just going in and asking."

"Well, fun or no fun," Homer said, "I'm glad you didn't find a job. Never mind a job. I make all the money we need, and Mary's father's got a good job at Ithaca Wine. You two don't need to go looking for a job."

"Yes, we do, Homer," Bess said. "Sure we do. And one of these days we're going to find ourselves a job. Two places asked us to come back."

"Never mind finding a job," Homer said. He was angry now. "You don't have to find a job, Bess, or you, Mary. Any work that has to be done around here, men can do. Girls belong in homes, taking care of men, that's all—just play the piano and sing and look pretty for a fellow to see when he comes home. That's all you need to do." He stopped a moment and when he spoke again he spoke gently, turning to Mary. "When Marcus comes home," he said, "you two can rent a little house of your own and start bringing up a family, the way you want to." He turned to Bess. "And one of these days, Bess, you'll find a guy you like. That's the only job you ought to be thinking about. Just because there happens to be a war in the world isn't a reason for everybody to go out of their heads. Just stay home where you belong and help Mama, and you help your father, Mary."

He was so bossy, his sister Bess was almost proud of him, because never before had she seen him so concerned about *anything*.

"And don't forget it," Homer said to his sister and to the neighbor girl. "Now," he said, "play another song before I go."

"What song would you like to hear?" Bess said.

"Any song," Homer said.

Homer's sister Bess began to play a song and soon Mary began to sing. The messenger stood in the dark of the parlor listening and before the song was half finished he went quietly out of the house. Now, in the yard, he found Ulysses standing over the hen nest looking down at one egg.

"Ma," Homer said. His mother turned to him. "Tomorrow be sure we all go to church. All of us together—and Mary."

"Why, what do you mean, Homer?" Mrs. Macauley said. "We go to church almost *every* Sunday, and Mary is almost *always* with us."

"I know," Homer said almost impatiently. "But tomorrow, for *sure*. And with Mary, for sure." He turned to his brother and said, "What have you got there in your hand, Ulysses?"

"Egg," Ulysses said as if the word were also the word for God.

Homer got onto his bicycle and began riding toward Ithaca Wine.

THE MACHINE STOPS

by E. M. Forster

Part I

The Air-ship

Imagine, if you can, a small room, hexagonal in shape, like the cell of a bee. It is lighted neither by window nor by lamp, yet it is filled with a soft radiance. There are no apertures for ventilation, yet the air is fresh. There are no musical instruments, and yet, at the moment that my meditation opens, this room is throbbing with melodious sounds. An arm-chair is in the center, by its side a reading-desk—that is all the furniture. And in the arm-chair there sits a swaddled lump of flesh—a woman, about five feet high, with a face as white as a fungus. It is to her that the little room belongs.

An electric bell rang.

The woman touched a switch and the music was silent.

"I suppose I must see who it is," she thought, and set her chair in motion. The chair, like the music, was worked by machinery, and it rolled her to the other side of the room, where the bell still rang importunately.

"Who is it?" she called. Her voice was irritable, for she had been interrupted often since the music began. She knew several thousand people; in certain directions human intercourse had advanced enormously.

But when she listened into the receiver, her white face wrinkled into smiles, and she said:

"Very well. Let us talk, I will isolate myself. I do not expect anything important will happen for the next five minutes—for I can give you fully five minutes, Kuno.

Then I must deliver my lecture on 'Music during the Australian Period.'"

She touched the isolation knob, so that no one else could speak to her. Then she touched the lighting apparatus, and the little room was plunged into darkness.

"Be quick!" she called, her irritation returning. "Be quick, Kuno; here I am in the dark wasting my time."

But it was fully fifteen seconds before the round plate that she held in her hands began to glow. A faint blue light shot across it, darkening to purple, and presently she could see the image of her son, who lived on the other side of the earth, and he could see her.

"Kuno, how slow you are."

He smiled gravely.

"I really believe you enjoy dawdling."

"I have called you before, mother, but you were always busy or isolated. I have something particular to say."

"What is it, dearest boy? Be quick. Why could you not send it by pneumatic post?"

"Because I prefer saying such a thing. I want—"

"Well?"

"I want you to come and see me."

Vashti watched his face in the blue plate.

"But I can see you!" she exclaimed. "What more do you want?"

"I want to see you not through the Machine," said Kuno. "I want to speak to you not through the wearisome Machine."

"Oh, hush!" said his mother, vaguely shocked. "You mustn't say anything against the Machine."

"Why not?"

"One mustn't."

"You talk as if a god had made the Machine," cried the other. "I believe that you pray to it when you are unhappy. Men made it, do not forget that. Great men, but men. The Machine is much, but it is not everything. I see something like you in this plate, but I do not see you. I hear something like you through this telephone, but I do not hear you. That is why I want you to come. Come and stop with me. Pay me a visit, so that we can meet face to face, and talk about the hopes that are in my mind."

She replied that she could scarcely spare the time for a visit.

"The air-ship barely takes two days to fly between me and you."

"I dislike air-ships."

"Why?"

"I dislike seeing the horrible brown earth, and the sea, and the stars when it is dark. I get no ideas in an air-ship."

"I do not get them anywhere else."

"What kind of ideas can the air give you?"

He paused for an instant.

"Do you not know four big stars that form an oblong, and three stars close together in the middle of the oblong, and hanging from these stars, three other stars?"

"No, I do not. I dislike the stars. But did they give you an idea? How interesting; tell me."

"I had an idea that they were like a man."

"I do not understand."

"The four big stars are the man's shoulders and his knees. The three stars in the middle are like the belts that men wore once, and the three stars hanging are like a sword."

"A sword?"

"Men carried swords about with them, to kill animals and other men."

"It does not strike me as a very good idea, but it is certainly original. When did it come to you first?"

"In the air-ship—" He broke off, and she fancied that he looked sad. She could not be sure, for the Machine did not transmit *nuances* of expression. It only gave a general idea of people—an idea that was good enough for all practical purposes, Vashti thought. The imponderable bloom, declared by a discredited philosophy to be the actual essence of intercourse, was rightly ignored by the Machine, just as the imponderable bloom of the grape was ignored by the manufacturers of artificial fruit. Something "good enough" had long since been accepted by our race.

"The truth is," he continued, "that I want to see these stars again. They are curious stars. I want to see them not from the air-ship, but from the surface of the earth, as our ancestors did, thousands of years ago. I want to visit the surface of the earth."

She was shocked again.

"Mother, you must come, if only to explain to me what is the harm of visiting the surface of the earth."

"No harm," she replied, controlling herself. "But no advantage. The surface of the earth is only dust and mud, no life remains on it, and you would need a respirator, or the cold of the outer air would kill you. One dies immediately in the outer air."

"I know; of course I shall take all precautions."

"And besides—"

"Well?"

She considered, and chose her words with care. Her son had a queer temper, and she wished to dissuade him from the expedition.

"It is contrary to the spirit of the age," she asserted.

"Do you mean by that, contrary to the Machine?"

"In a sense, but—"

His image in the blue plate faded.

"Kuno!"

He had isolated himself.

For a moment Vashti felt lonely.

Then she generated the light, and the sight of her room, flooded with radiance and studded with electric buttons, revived her. There were buttons and switches everywhere—buttons to call for food, for music, for clothing. There was the hot-bath button, by pressure of which a basin of (imitation) marble rose out of the floor, filled to the brim with a warm deodorized liquid. There was the cold-bath button. There was the button that produced literature. And there were of course the buttons by which she communicated with her friends. The room, though it contained nothing, was in touch with all that she cared for in the world.

Vashti's next move was to turn off the isolation-switch, and all the accumulations of the last three minutes burst upon her. The room was filled with the noise of bells, and speaking-tubes. What was the new food like? Could she recommend it? Had she had any ideas lately? Might one tell her one's own ideas? Would she make an engagement to visit the public nurseries at an early date?—say this day month.

To most of these questions she replied with irritation—a growing quality in that accelerated age. She said that the new food was horrible. That she could not visit the public nurseries through press of engagements. That she had no ideas of her own but had just been told one—that four stars and three in the middle were like a man: she doubted there was much in it. Then she switched off her correspondents, for it was time to deliver her lecture on Australian music.

The clumsy system of public gatherings

had been long since abandoned; neither Vashti nor her audience stirred from their rooms. Seated in her arm-chair she spoke, while they in their arm-chairs heard her, fairly well, and saw her, fairly well. She opened with a humorous account of music in the pre-Mongolian epoch, and went on to describe the great outburst of song that followed the Chinese conquest. Remote and primeval as were the methods of I-San-So and the Brisbane school, she yet felt (she said) that study of them might repay the musician of today: they had freshness; they had, above all, ideas.

Her lecture, which lasted ten minutes, was well received, and at its conclusion she and many of her audience listened to a lecture on the sea; there were ideas to be got from the sea; the speaker had donned a respirator and visited it lately. Then she fed, talked to many friends, had a bath, talked again, and summoned her bed.

The bed was not to her liking. It was too large, and she had a feeling for a small bed. Complaint was useless, for beds were of the same dimension all over the world, and to have had an alternative size would have involved vast alterations in the Machine. Vashti isolated herself—it was necessary, for neither day nor night existed under the ground—and reviewed all that had happened since she had summoned the bed last. Ideas? Scarcely any. Events— was Kuno's invitation an event?

By her side, on the little reading-desk, was a survival from the ages of litter—one book. This was the Book of the Machine. In it were instructions against every possible contingency. If she was hot or cold or dyspeptic or at loss for a word, she went to the Book, and it told her which button to press. The Central Committee published it. In accordance with a growing habit, it was richly bound.

Sitting up in the bed, she took it reverently in her hands. She glanced round the glowing room as if some one might be watching her. Then, half ashamed, half joyful, she murmured, "O Machine! O Machine!" and raised the volume to her lips. Thrice she kissed it, thrice inclined her head, thrice she felt the delirium of acquiescence. Her ritual performed, she turned to page 1367, which gave the times of the departure of the air-ships from the island in the southern hemisphere, under whose soil she lived, to the island in the northern hemisphere, whereunder lived her son.

She thought, "I have not the time."

She made the room dark and slept; she awoke and made the room light; she ate and exchanged ideas with her friends, and listened to music and attended lectures; she made the room dark and slept. Above her, beneath her, and around her, the Machine hummed eternally; she did not notice the noise, for she had been born with it in her ears. The earth, carrying her, hummed as it sped through silence, turning her now to the invisible sun, now to the invisible stars. She awoke and made the room light.

"Kuno!"

"I will not talk to you," he answered, "until you come."

"Have you been on the surface of the earth since we spoke last?"

His image faded.

Again she consulted the Book. She became very nervous and lay back in her chair palpitating. Think of her as without teeth or hair. Presently she directed the chair to the wall, and pressed an unfamiliar button. The wall swung apart slowly. Through the opening she saw a tunnel that curved slightly, so that its goal was not visible. Should she go to see her

son, here was the beginning of the journey.

Of course she knew all about the communication-system. There was nothing mysterious in it. She would summon a car and it would fly with her down the tunnel until it reached the lift that communicated with the air-ship station: the system had been in use for many, many years, long before the universal establishment of the Machine. And of course she had studied the civilization that had immediately preceded her own—the civilization that had mistaken the functions of the system, and had used it for bringing people to things, instead of for bringing things to people. Those funny old days, when men went for change of air instead of changing the air in their rooms! And yet—she was frightened of the tunnel: she had not seen it since her last child was born. It curved—but not quite as she remembered; it was brilliant—but not quite as brilliant as a lecturer had suggested. Vashti was seized with the terrors of direct experience. She shrank back into the room, and the wall closed up again.

"Kuno," she said, "I cannot come to see you. I am not well."

Immediately an enormous apparatus fell on to her out of the ceiling, a thermometer was automatically inserted between her lips, a stethoscope was automatically laid upon her heart. She lay powerless. Cool pads soothed her forehead. Kuno had telegraphed to her doctor.

So the human passions still blundered up and down in the Machine. Vashti drank the medicine that the doctor projected into her mouth, and the machinery retired into the ceiling. The voice of Kuno was heard asking how she felt.

"Better." Then with irritation: "But why do you not come to me instead?"

"Because I cannot leave this place."

"Why?"

"Because, any moment, something tremendous may happen."

"Have you been on the surface of the earth yet?"

"Not yet."

"Then what is it?"

"I will not tell you through the Machine."

She resumed her life.

But she thought of Kuno as a baby, his birth, his removal to the public nurseries, her one visit to him there, his visits to her —visits which stopped when the Machine had assigned him a room on the other side of the earth. "Parents, duties of," said the Book of the Machine, "cease at the moment of birth. P. 422327483." True, but there was something special about Kuno— indeed there had been something special about all her children—and, after all, she must brave the journey if he desired it. And "something tremendous might happen." What did that mean? The nonsense of a youthful man, no doubt, but she must go. Again she pressed the unfamiliar button, again the wall swung back, and she saw the tunnel that curved out of sight. Clasping the Book, she rose, tottered onto the platform, and summoned the car. Her room closed behind her: the journey to the northern hemisphere had begun.

Of course it was perfectly easy. The car approached and in it she found arm-chairs exactly like her own. When she signaled, it stopped, and she tottered into the lift. One other passenger was in the lift, the first fellow creature she had seen face to face for months. Few traveled in these days, for, thanks to the advance of science, the earth was exactly alike all over. Rapid intercourse, from which the previous civilization had hoped so much, had ended by defeating itself. What was the good of going to Pekin when it was just like Shrewsbury? Why return to Shrewsbury when it would be just like Pekin? Men seldom moved their bodies; all unrest was concentrated in the soul.

The air-ship service was a relic from the former age. It was kept up, because it was easier to keep it up than to stop it or to diminish it, but it now far exceeded the wants of the population. Vessel after vessel would rise from the vomitories of Rye or of Christchurch (I use the antique names), would sail into the crowded sky, and would draw up at the wharves of the south—empty. So nicely adjusted was the system, so independent of meteorology, that the sky, whether calm or cloudy, resembled a vast kaleidoscope whereon the same patterns periodically recurred. The ship on which Vashti sailed started now at sunset, now at dawn. But always, as it passed above Rheims, it would neighbor the ship that served between Helsingfors and the Brazils, and, every third time it surmounted the Alps, the fleet of Palermo would cross its track behind. Night and day, wind and storm, tide and earthquake, impeded man no longer. He had harnessed Leviathan. All the old literature, with its praise of Nature, and its fear of Nature, rang false as the prattle of a child.

Yet as Vashti saw the vast flank of the ship, stained with exposure to the outer air, her horror of direct experience returned. It was not quite like the air-ship in the cinematophote. For one thing it smelt—not strongly or unpleasantly, but it did smell, and with her eyes shut she should have known that a new thing was close to her. Then she had to walk to it from the lift, had to submit to glances from the other passengers. The man in front dropped his Book—no great matter, but it disquieted them all. In the rooms, if the Book was dropped, the floor raised it mechanically, but the gangway to the air-ship was not so prepared, and the sacred volume lay motionless. They stopped —the thing was unforeseen—and the man, instead of picking up his property, felt the muscles of his arm to see how they had failed him. Then someone actually said with direct utterance: "We shall be late"— and they trooped on board, Vashti treading on the pages as she did so.

Inside, her anxiety increased. The arrangements were old-fashioned and rough. There was even a female attendant, to whom she would have to announce her wants during the voyage. Of course a revolving platform ran the length of the boat, but she was expected to walk from it to her cabin. Some cabins were better than others, and she did not get the best. She thought the attendant had been unfair, and spasms of rage shook her. The glass valves had closed, she could not go back. She saw, at the end of the vestibule, the lift in which she had ascended going quietly up and down, empty. Beneath those corridors of shining tiles were rooms, tier below tier, reaching far into the earth, and in each room there sat a human being, eating, or sleeping, or producing ideas. And buried deep in the hive was her own room. Vashti was afraid.

"O Machine! O Machine!" she murmured, and caressed her Book, and was comforted.

Then the sides of the vestibule seemed to melt together, as do the passages that we see in dreams, the lift vanished, the Book that had been dropped slid to the left and vanished, polished tiles rushed by like a stream of water, there was a slight jar, and the air-ship, issuing from its tunnel, soared above the waters of a tropical ocean.

It was night. For a moment she saw the coast of Sumatra edged by the phosphorescence of waves, and crowned by lighthouses, still sending forth their disregarded beams. They also vanished, and only the stars distracted her. They were not motionless, but swayed to and fro above her head, thronging out of one skylight into another, as if the universe and not the air-ship was careening. And, as often happens on clear nights, they seemed now to be in perspective, now on a plane; now piled tier beyond tier into the infinite heavens, now concealing infinity, a roof limiting for ever the visions of men. In either case they seemed intolerable. "Are we to travel in the dark?" called the passengers angrily, and the attendant, who had been careless, generated the light, and pulled down the blinds of pliable metal. When the air-ships had been built, the desire to look direct at things still lingered in the world. Hence the extraordinary number of skylights and windows, and the proportionate discomfort to those who were civilized and refined. Even in Vashti's cabin one star peeped through a flaw in the blind, and after a few hours' uneasy slumber, she was disturbed by an unfamiliar glow, which was the dawn.

Quick as the ship had sped westwards, the earth had rolled eastwards quicker still, and had dragged back Vashti and her companions towards the sun. Science could prolong the night, but only for a little, and those high hopes of neutralizing the earth's diurnal revolution had passed, together with hopes that were possibly higher. To "keep pace with the sun," or even to outstrip it, had been the aim of the civilization preceding this. Racing aeroplanes had been built for the purpose, capable of enormous speed, and steered by the greatest intellects of the epoch. Round the globe they went, round and round, westward, westward, round and round, amidst humanity's applause. In vain. The globe went eastward quicker still, horrible accidents occurred, and the Committee of the Machine, at the time rising into prominence, declared the pursuit illegal, unmechanical, and punishable by Homelessness.

Of Homelessness more will be said later.

Doubtless the Committee was right. Yet the attempt to "defeat the sun" aroused the last common interest that our race experienced about the heavenly bodies, or indeed about anything. It was the last time that men were compacted by thinking of a power outside the world. The sun had conquered, yet it was the end of his spiritual dominion. Dawn, midday, twilight, the zodiacal path, touched neither men's lives nor their hearts, and science retreated into the ground, to concentrate herself upon problems that she was certain of solving.

So when Vashti found her cabin invaded by a rosy finger of light, she was annoyed, and tried to adjust the blind. But the blind flew up altogether, and she saw through the skylight small pink clouds, swaying against a background of blue, and as the sun crept higher, its radiance entered direct, brimming down the wall, like a golden sea. It rose and fell with the air-ship's motion, just as waves rise and fall, but it advanced steadily, as a tide advances. Unless she was careful, it would strike her face. A spasm of horror shook her and she rang for the attendant. The attendant too was horrified, but she could do nothing; it was not her place to mend the blind. She could only suggest that the lady should change her cabin, which she accordingly prepared to do.

People were almost exactly alike all over the world, but the attendant of the airship, perhaps owing to her exceptional duties, had grown a little out of the common. She had often to address passengers with direct speech, and this had given her a certain roughness and originality of manner. When Vashti swerved away from the sunbeams with a cry, she behaved barbarically—she put out her hand to steady her.

"How dare you!" exclaimed the passenger. "You forget yourself!"

The woman was confused, and apologized for not having let her fall. People never touched one another. The custom had become obsolete, owing to the Machine.

"Where are we now?" asked Vashti haughtily.

"We are over Asia," said the attendant, anxious to be polite.

"Asia?"

"You must excuse my common way of speaking. I have got into the habit of calling places over which I pass by their unmechanical names."

"Oh, I remember Asia. The Mongols came from it."

"Beneath us, in the open air, stood a city that was once called Simla."

"Have you ever heard of the Mongols and of the Brisbane school?"

"No."

"Brisbane also stood in the open air."

"Those mountains to the right—let me show you them." She pushed back a metal blind. The main chain of the Himalayas was revealed. "They were once called the Roof of the World, those mountains."

"What a foolish name!"

"You must remember that, before the dawn of civilization, they seemed to be an impenetrable wall that touched the stars. It was supposed that no one but the gods could exist above their summits. How we have advanced, thanks to the Machine!"

"How we have advanced, thanks to the Machine!" said Vashti.

"How we have advanced, thanks to the Machine!" echoed the passenger who had dropped his Book the night before, and who was standing in the passage.

"And that white stuff in the cracks?— what is it?"

"I have forgotten its name."

"Cover the window, please. These mountains give me no ideas."

The northern aspect of the Himalayas was in deep shadow: on the Indian slope the sun had just prevailed. The forests had been destroyed during the literature epoch for the purpose of making newspaper-pulp, but the snows were awakening to their morning glory, and clouds still hung on the breasts of Kinchinjunga. In the plain were seen the ruins of cities, with diminished rivers creeping by their walls, and by the sides of these were sometimes the signs of vomitories, marking the cities of today. Over the whole prospect airships rushed, crossing and intercrossing with incredible aplomb, and rising nonchalantly when they desired to escape the perturbations of the lower atmosphere and to traverse the Roof of the World.

"We have indeed advanced, thanks to the Machine," repeated the attendant, and hid the Himalayas behind a metal blind.

The day dragged wearily forward. The passengers sat each in his cabin, avoiding one another with an almost physical repulsion and longing to be once more under the surface of the earth. There were eight or ten of them, mostly young males, sent out from the public nurseries to inhabit the rooms of those who had died in various parts of the earth. The man who had dropped his Book was on the homeward journey. He had been sent to Sumatra for the purpose of propagating the race. Vashti alone was traveling by her private will.

At midday she took a second glance at the earth. The air-ship was crossing another range of mountains, but she could see little, owing to clouds. Masses of black rock hovered below her, and merged indistinctly into gray. Their shapes were fantastic; one of them resembled a prostrate man.

"No ideas here," murmured Vashti, and hid the Caucasus behind a metal blind.

In the evening she looked again. They were crossing a golden sea, in which lay many small islands and one peninsula.

She repeated, "No ideas here," and hid Greece behind a metal blind.

Part II

The Mending Apparatus

By a vestibule, by a lift, by a tubular railway, by a platform, by a sliding door—by reversing all the steps of her departure did Vashti arrive at her son's room, which exactly resembled her own. She might well declare that the visit was superfluous. The buttons, the knobs, the reading-desk with the Book, the temperature, the atmosphere, the illumination—all were exactly the same. And if Kuno himself, flesh of her flesh, stood close beside her at last, what profit was there in that? She was too well-bred to shake him by the hand.

Averting her eyes, she spoke as follows:

"Here I am. I have had the most terrible journey and greatly retarded the development of my soul. It is not worth it, Kuno, it is not worth it. My time is too precious. The sunlight almost touched me, and I have met with the rudest people. I can only stop a few minutes. Say what you want to say, and then I must return."

"I have been threatened with Homelessness," said Kuno.

She looked at him now.

"I have been threatened with Homelessness, and I could not tell you such a thing through the Machine."

Homelessness means death. The victim is exposed to the air, which kills him.

"I have been outside since I spoke to you last. The tremendous thing has happened, and they have discovered me."

"But why shouldn't you go outside!" she exclaimed. "It is perfectly legal, perfectly mechanical, to visit the surface of the earth. I have lately been to a lecture on the sea; there is no objection to that; one simply summons a respirator and gets an Egression-permit. It is not the kind of thing that spiritually-minded people do, and I begged you not to do it, but there is no legal objection to it."

"I did not get an Egression-permit."

"Then how did you get out?"

"I found out a way of my own."

The phrase conveyed no meaning to her, and he had to repeat it.

"A way of your own?" she whispered. "But that would be wrong."

"Why?"

The question shocked her beyond measure.

"You are beginning to worship the Machine," he said coldly. "You think it irreligious of me to have found out a way of my own. It was just what the Committee thought, when they threatened me with Homelessness."

At this she grew angry. "I worship nothing!" she cried. "I am most advanced. I don't think you irreligious, for there is no such thing as religion left. All the fear and the superstition that existed once have been destroyed by the Machine. I only meant that to find out a way of your own was— Besides, there is no new way out."

"So it is always supposed."

"Except through the vomitories, for which one must have an Egression-permit, it is impossible to get out. The Book says so."

"Well, the Book's wrong, for I have been out on my feet."

For Kuno was possessed of a certain physical strength.

By these days it was a demerit to be muscular. Each infant was examined at birth, and all who promised undue strength were destroyed. Humanitarians may protest, but it would have been no true kindness to let an athlete live; he would never have been happy in that state of life to which the Machine had called him; he would have yearned for trees to climb, rivers to bathe in, meadows and hills against which he might measure his body. Man must be adapted to his surroundings, must he not? In the dawn of the world our weakly must be exposed on Mount Taygetus, in its twilight our strong will suffer Euthanasia, that the Machine may progress, that the Machine may progress, that the Machine may progress eternally.

"You know that we have lost the sense of space. We say 'space is annihilated,' but we have annihilated not space, but the sense thereof. We have lost a part of ourselves. I determined to recover it, and I began by walking up and down the platform of the railway outside my room. Up and down, until I was tired, and so did recapture the meaning of 'Near' and 'Far.' 'Near' is a place to which I can get quickly *on my feet,* not a place to which the train or the air-ship will take me quickly. 'Far' is a place to which I cannot get quickly on my feet; the vomitory is 'far,' though I could be there in thirty-eight seconds by summoning the train. Man is the measure. That was my first lesson. Man's feet are the measure for distance, his hands are the measure for ownership, his body is the measure for all that is lovable and desirable and strong. Then I went further: it was then that I called to you for the first time, and you would not come.

"This city, as you know, is built deep beneath the surface of the earth, with only the vomitories protruding. Having paced the platform outside my own room, I took the lift to the next platform and paced that also, and so with each in turn, until I came to the topmost, above which begins the earth. All the platforms were exactly alike, and all that I gained by visiting them was to develop my sense of space and my muscles. I think I should have been content with this—it is not a little thing—but as I walked and brooded, it occurred to me that our cities had been built in the days when men still breathed the outer air, and that there had been ventilation shafts for the workmen. I could think of nothing but these ventilation shafts. Had they been destroyed by all the food-tubes and medicine-tubes and music-tubes that the Machine has evolved lately? Or did traces of them remain? One thing was certain. If I came upon them anywhere, it would be in the railway-tunnels of the topmost story. Everywhere else, all space was accounted for.

"I am telling my story quickly, but don't think that I was not a coward or that your answers never depressed me. It is not the proper thing, it is not mechanical, it is not decent to walk along a railway-tunnel. I did not fear that I might tread upon a live rail and be killed. I feared something far more intangible—doing what was not contemplated by the Machine. Then I said to myself, 'Man is the measure,' and I went, and after many visits I found an opening.

"The tunnels, of course, were lighted. Everything is light, artificial light; darkness is the exception. So when I saw a black gap in the tiles, I knew that it was an exception, and rejoiced. I put in my arm—I could put in no more at first—and waved it round and round in ecstasy. I loosened another tile, and put in my head, and shouted into the darkness: 'I am coming, I shall do it yet,' and my voice reverberated down endless passages. I seemed to hear the spirits of those dead workmen who had returned each evening to the starlight and to their wives, and all the generations who had lived in the open air called back to me, 'You will do it yet, you are coming.'"

He paused, and, absurd as he was, his last words moved her. For Kuno had lately asked to be a father, and his request had been refused by the Committee. His was not a type that the Machine desired to hand on.

"Then a train passed. It brushed by me, but I thrust my head and arms into the hole. I had done enough for one day, so I crawled back to the platform, went down in the lift, and summoned my bed. Ah, what dreams! And again I called you, and again you refused."

She shook her head and said:

"Don't. Don't talk of these terrible things. You make me miserable. You are throwing civilization away."

"But I had got back the sense of space and a man cannot rest then. I determined to get in at the hole and climb the shaft. And so I exercised my arms. Day after day I went through ridiculous movements, until my flesh ached, and I could hang by my hands and hold the pillow of my bed outstretched for many minutes. Then I summoned a respirator, and started.

"It was easy at first. The mortar had somehow rotted, and I soon pushed some more tiles in, and clambered after them into the darkness, and the spirits of the dead comforted me. I don't know what I mean by that. I just say what I felt. I felt, for the first time, that a protest had been lodged against corruption, and that even as the dead were comforting me, so I was comforting the unborn. I felt that humanity existed, and that it existed without clothes. How can I possibly explain this? It was naked, humanity seemed naked, and all these tubes and buttons and machineries neither came into the world with us, nor will they follow us out, nor do they matter supremely while we are here. Had I been strong, I would have torn off every garment I had, and gone out into the outer air unswaddled. But this is not for me, nor perhaps for my generation. I climbed with my respirator and my hygienic clothes and my dietetic tabloids! Better thus than not at all.

"There was a ladder, made of some primeval metal. The light from the railway fell upon its lowest rungs, and I saw that it led straight upwards out of the rubble at the bottom of the shaft. Perhaps our ancestors ran up and down it a dozen times daily, in their building. As I climbed, the rough edges cut through my gloves so that my hands bled. The light helped me for a little, and then came darkness and, worse still, silence which pierced my ears like a sword. The Machine hums! Did you know that? Its hum penetrates our blood, and may even guide our thoughts. Who knows! I was getting beyond its power. Then I thought: 'This silence means that I am doing wrong.' But I heard voices in the silence, and again they strengthened me." He laughed. "I had need of them. The next moment I cracked my head against something."

She sighed.

"I had reached one of those pneumatic stoppers that defend us from the outer air. You may have noticed them on the airship. Pitch dark, my feet on the rungs of an invisible ladder, my hands cut; I cannot explain how I lived through this part, but the voices still comforted me, and I felt for fastenings. The stopper, I suppose, was about eight feet across. I passed my hand over it as far as I could reach. It was perfectly smooth. I felt it almost to the center. Not quite to the center, for my arm was too short. Then the voice said: 'Jump. It is worth it. There may be a handle in the center, and you may catch hold of it and so come to us your own way. And if there is no handle, so that you may fall and are dashed to pieces—it is still worth it: you will still come to us your own way.' So I jumped. There was a handle, and—"

He paused. Tears gathered in his mother's eyes. She knew that he was fated. If he did not die today he would die tomorrow. There was not room for such a person in the world. And with her pity disgust mingled. She was ashamed at having borne such a son, she who had always been so respectable and so full of ideas. Was he really the little boy to whom she

had taught the use of his stops and buttons, and to whom she had given his first lessons in the Book? The very hair that disfigured his lip showed that he was reverting to some savage type. On atavism the Machine can have no mercy.

"There was a handle, and I did catch it. I hung tranced over the darkness and heard the hum of these workings as the last whisper in a dying dream. All the things I had cared about and all the people I had spoken to through tubes appeared infinitely little. Meanwhile the handle revolved. My weight had set something in motion and I span slowly, and then—

"I cannot describe it. I was lying with my face to the sunshine. Blood poured from my nose and ears and I heard a tremendous roaring. The stopper, with me clinging to it, had simply been blown out of the earth, and the air that we make down here was escaping through the vent into the air above. It burst up like a fountain. I crawled back to it—for the upper air hurts—and, as it were, I took great sips from the edge. My respirator had flown goodness knows where, my clothes were torn. I just lay with my lips close to the hole, and I sipped until the bleeding stopped. You can imagine nothing so curious. This hollow in the grass—I will speak of it in a minute,—the sun shining into it, not brilliantly but through marbled clouds,—the peace, the nonchalance, the sense of space, and, brushing my cheek, the roaring fountain of our artificial air! Soon I spied my respirator, bobbing up and down in the current high above my head, and higher still were many air-ships. But no one ever looks out of air-ships, and in my case they could not have picked me up. There I was, stranded. The sun shone a little way down the shaft, and revealed the topmost rung of the ladder, but it was hopeless trying to reach it. I should either have been tossed up again by the escape, or else have fallen in, and died. I could only lie on the grass, sipping and sipping, and from time to time glancing around me.

"I knew that I was in Wessex, for I had taken care to go to a lecture on the subject before starting. Wessex lies above the room in which we are talking now. It was once an important state. Its kings held all the southern coast from the Andredswald to Cornwall, while the Wansdyke protected them on the north, running over the high ground. The lecturer was only concerned with the rise of Wessex, so I do not know how long it remained an international power, nor would the knowledge have assisted me. To tell the truth I could do nothing but laugh, during this part. There was I, with a pneumatic stopper by my side and a respirator bobbing over my head, imprisoned, all three of us, in a grass-grown hollow that was edged with fern."

Then he grew grave again.

"Lucky for me that it was a hollow. For the air began to fall back into it and to fill it as water fills a bowl. I could crawl about. Presently I stood. I breathed a mixture, in which the air that hurts predominated whenever I tried to climb the sides. This was not so bad. I had not lost my tabloids and remained ridiculously cheerful, and as for the Machine, I forgot about it altogether. My one aim now was to get to the top, where the ferns were, and to view whatever objects lay beyond.

"I rushed the slope. The new air was still too bitter for me and I came rolling back, after a momentary vision of something gray. The sun grew very feeble, and

I remembered that he was in Scorpio—I had been to a lecture on that too. If the sun is in Scorpio and you are in Wessex, it means that you must be as quick as you can, or it will get too dark. (This is the first bit of useful information I have ever got from a lecture, and I expect it will be the last.) It made me try frantically to breathe the new air, and to advance as far as I dared out of my pond. The hollow filled so slowly. At times I thought that the fountain played with less vigor. My respirator seemed to dance nearer the earth; the roar was decreasing."

He broke off.

"I don't think this is interesting you. The rest will interest you even less. There are no ideas in it, and I wish that I had not troubled you to come. We are too different, mother."

She told him to continue.

"It was evening before I climbed the bank. The sun had very nearly slipped out of the sky by this time, and I could not get a good view. You, who have just crossed the Roof of the World, will not want to hear an account of the little hills that I saw—low colorless hills. But to me they were living and the turf that covered them was a skin, under which their muscles rippled, and I felt that those hills had called with incalculable force to men in the past, and that men had loved them. Now they sleep—perhaps forever. They commune with humanity in dreams. Happy the man, happy the woman, who awakes the hills of Wessex. For though they sleep, they will never die."

His voice rose passionately.

"Cannot you see, cannot all your lecturers see, that it is we who are dying, and that down here the only thing that really lives is the Machine? We created the

Machine, to do our will, but we cannot make it do our will now. It has robbed us of the sense of space and of the sense of touch, it has blurred every human relation and narrowed down love to a carnal act, it has paralyzed our bodies and our wills, and now it compels us to worship it. The Machine develops—but not on our lines. The Machine proceeds—but not to our goal. We only exist as the blood corpuscles that course through its arteries, and if it could work without us, it would let us die. Oh, I have no remedy—or, at least, only one—to tell men again and again that I have seen the hills of Wessex as Aelfrid saw them when he overthrew the Danes.

"So the sun set. I forgot to mention that a belt of mist lay between my hill and other hills, and that it was the color of pearl."

He broke off for the second time.

"Go on," said his mother wearily.

He shook his head.

"Go on. Nothing that you say can distress me now. I am hardened."

"I had meant to tell you the rest, but I cannot: I know that I cannot: good-by."

Vashti stood irresolute. All her nerves were tingling with his blasphemies. But she was also inquisitive.

"This is unfair," she complained. "You have called me across the world to hear your story, and hear it I will. Tell me—as briefly as possible, for this is a disastrous waste of time—tell me how you returned to civilization."

"Oh,—that!" he said, starting. "You would like to hear about civilization. Certainly. Had I got to where my respirator fell down?"

"No—but I understand everything now. You put on your respirator, and managed

to walk along the surface of the earth to a vomitory, and there your conduct was reported to the Central Committee."

"By no means."

He passed his hand over his forehead, as if dispelling some strong impression. Then, resuming his narrative, he warmed to it again.

"My respirator fell about sunset. I had mentioned that the fountain seemed feebler, had I not?"

"Yes."

"About sunset, it let the respirator fall. As I said, I had entirely forgotten about the Machine, and I paid no great attention at the time, being occupied with other things. I had my pool of air, into which I could dip when the outer keenness became intolerable, and which would possibly remain for days, provided that no wind sprang up to disperse it. Not until it was too late, did I realize what the stoppage of the escape implied. You see—the gap in the tunnel had been mended; the Mending Apparatus, the Mending Apparatus, was after me.

"One other warning I had, but I neglected it. The sky at night was clearer than it had been in the day, and the moon, which was about half the sky behind the sun, shone into the dell at moments quite brightly. I was in my usual place—on the boundary between the two atmospheres—when I thought I saw something dark move across the bottom of the dell, and vanish into the shaft. In my folly, I ran down. I bent over and listened, and I thought I heard a faint scraping noise in the depths.

"At this—but it was too late—I took alarm. I determined to put on my respirator and to walk right out of the dell. But my respirator had gone. I knew exactly where it had fallen—between the stopper and the aperture—and I could even feel the mark that it had made in the turf. It had gone, and I realized that something evil was at work, and I had better escape to the other air, and, if I must die, die running towards the cloud that had been the color of a pearl. I never started. Out of the shaft—it is too horrible. A worm, a long white worm, had crawled out of the shaft and was gliding over the moon-lit grass.

"I screamed. I did everything that I should not have done, I stamped upon the creature instead of flying from it, and it at once curled round the ankle. Then we fought. The worm let me run all over the dell, but edged up my leg as I ran. 'Help!' I cried. (That part is too awful. It belongs to the part that you will never know.) 'Help!' I cried. (Why cannot we suffer in silence?) 'Help!' I cried. Then my feet were wound together, I fell, I was dragged away from the dear ferns and the living hills, and past the great metal stopper (I can tell you this part), and I thought it might save me again if I caught hold of the handle. It also was enwrapped, it also. Oh, the whole dell was full of the things. They were searching it in all directions, they were denuding it, and the white snouts of others peeped out of the hole, ready if needed. Everything that could be moved they brought—brush-wood, bundles of fern, everything, and down we all went intertwined into hell. The last things that I saw, ere the stopper closed after us, were certain stars, and I felt that a man of my sort lived in the sky. For I did fight, I fought till the very end, and it was only my head hitting against the ladder that quieted me. I woke up in this room. The worms had van-ished. I was surrounded by artificial air, artificial light, artificial peace, and my friends were calling to me down speaking-tubes to know whether I had come across any new ideas lately."

Here his story ended. Discussion of it was impossible, and Vashti turned to go.

"It will end in Homelessness," she said quietly.

"I wish it would," retorted Kuno.

"The Machine has been most merciful."

"I prefer the mercy of God."

"By that superstitious phrase, do you mean that you could live in the outer air?"

"Yes."

"Have you ever seen, round the vomi-tories, the bones of those who were ex-truded after the Great Rebellion?"

"Yes."

"They were left where they perished for our edification. A few crawled away, but they perished, too—who can doubt it? And so with the Homeless of our own day. The surface of the earth supports life no longer."

"Indeed."

"Ferns and a little grass may survive, but all higher forms have perished. Has any air-ship detected them?"

"No."

"Has any lecturer dealt with them?"

"No."

"Then why this obstinacy?"

"Because I have seen them," he exploded.

"Seen *what?*"

"Because I have seen her in the twilight —because she came to my help when I called—because she, too, was entangled by the worms, and, luckier than I, was killed by one of them piercing her throat."

He was mad. Vashti departed, nor, in the troubles that followed, did she ever see his face again.

Part III

The Homeless

During the years that followed Kuno's escapade, two important developments took place in the Machine. On the surface they were revolutionary, but in either case men's minds had been prepared beforehand, and they did but express tendencies that were latent already.

The first of these was the abolition of respirators.

Advanced thinkers, like Vashti, had always held it foolish to visit the surface of the earth. Air-ships might be necessary, but what was the good of going out for mere curiosity and crawling along for a mile or two in a terrestrial motor? The habit was vulgar and perhaps faintly improper: it was unproductive of ideas, and had no connection with the habits that really mattered. So respirators were abolished, and with them, of course, the terrestrial motors, and except for a few lecturers, who complained that they were debarred access to their subject-matter, the development was accepted quietly. Those who still wanted to know what the earth was like had after all only to listen to some gramophone, or to look into some cinematophote. And even the lecturers acquiesced when they found that a lecture on the sea was none the less stimulating when compiled out of other lectures that had already been delivered on the same subject. "Beware of first-hand ideas!" exclaimed one of the most advanced of them. "First-hand ideas do not really exist. They are but the physical impressions produced by love and fear, and on this gross foundation who could erect a philosophy? Let your ideas be second-hand, and if possible tenth-hand, for then they will be far removed from that disturbing element—direct observation. Do not learn anything about this subject of mine—the French Revolution. Learn instead what I think that Enicharmon thought Urizen thought Gutch thought Ho-Yung thought Chi-Bo-Sing thought Lafcadio Hearn thought Carlyle thought Mirabeau said about the French Revolution. Through the medium of these eight great minds, the blood that was shed at Paris and the windows that were broken at Versailles will be clarified to an idea which you may employ most profitably in your daily lives. But be sure that the intermediates are many and varied, for in history one authority exists to counteract another. Urizen must counteract the skepticism of Ho-Yung and Enicharmon, I must myself counteract the impetuosity of Gutch. You who listen to me are in a better position to judge about the French Revolution than I am. Your descendants will be even in a better position than you, for they will learn what you think I think, and yet another intermediate will be added to the chain. And in time"—his voice rose—"there will come a generation that has got beyond facts, beyond impressions, a generation absolutely colorless, a generation

> seraphically free
> From taint of personality,

which will see the French Revolution not as it happened, nor as they would like it to have happened, but as it would have happened, had it taken place in the days of the Machine."

Tremendous applause greeted this lecture, which did but voice a feeling already latent in the minds of men—a feeling that terrestrial facts must be ignored, and that the abolition of respirators was a positive gain. It was even suggested that air-ships should be abolished too. This was not done, because air-ships had somehow worked themselves into the Machine's system. But year by year they were used less, and mentioned less by thoughtful men.

The second great development was the re-establishment of religion.

This, too, had been voiced in the celebrated lecture. No one could mistake the reverent tone in which the peroration had concluded, and it awakened a responsive echo in the heart of each. Those who had long worshiped silently, now began to talk. They described the strange feeling of peace that came over them when they handled the Book of the Machine, the pleasure that it was to repeat certain numerals out of it, however little meaning those numerals conveyed to the outward ear, the ecstasy of touching a button, however unimportant, or of ringing an electric bell, however superfluously.

"The Machine," they exclaimed, "feeds us and clothes us and houses us; through it we speak to one another, through it we see one another, in it we have our being. The Machine is the friend of ideas and the enemy of superstition: the Machine is omnipotent, eternal; blessed is the Machine." And before long this allocution was printed on the first page of the Book, and in subsequent editions the ritual swelled into a complicated system of praise and prayer. The word "religion" was sedulously avoided, and in theory the Machine was still the creation and the implement of man. But in practice all, save a few retrogrades, worshiped it as divine. Nor was it worshiped in unity. One believer would be chiefly impressed by the blue optic plates, through which he saw other believers; another by the Mending

Apparatus, which sinful Kuno had compared to worms; another by the lifts, another by the Book. And each would pray to this or to that, and ask it to intercede for him with the Machine as a whole. Persecution—that also was present. It did not break out, for reasons that will be set forward shortly. But it was latent, and all who did not accept the minimum known as "undenominational Mechanism" lived in danger of Homelessness, which means death, as we know.

To attribute these two great developments to the Central Committee, is to take a very narrow view of civilization. The Central Committee announced the developments, it is true, but they were no more the cause of them than were the kings of the imperialistic period the cause of war. Rather did they yield to some invincible pressure, which came no one knew whither, and which, when gratified, was succeeded by some new pressure equally invincible. To such a state of affairs it is convenient to give the name of progress. No one confessed the Machine was out of hand. Year by year it was served with increased efficiency and decreased intelligence. The better a man knew his own duties upon it, the less he understood the duties of his neighbor, and in all the world there was not one who understood the monster as a whole. Those master brains had perished. They had left full directions, it is true, and their successors had each of them mastered a portion of those directions. But Humanity, in its desire for comfort, had over-reached itself. It had exploited the riches of nature too far. Quietly and complacently, it was sinking into decadence, and progress had come to mean the progress of the Machine.

As for Vashti, her life went peacefully forward until the final disaster. She made her room dark and slept; she awoke and made the room light. She lectured and attended lectures. She exchanged ideas with her innumerable friends and believed she was growing more spiritual. At times a friend was granted Euthanasia, and left his or her room for the homelessness that is beyond all human conception. Vashti did not much mind. After an unsuccessful lecture, she would sometimes ask for Euthanasia herself. But the death-rate was not permitted to exceed the birth-rate, and the Machine had hitherto refused it to her.

The troubles began quietly, long before she was conscious of them.

One day she was astonished at receiving a message from her son. They never communicated, having nothing in common, and she had only heard indirectly that he was still alive, and had been transferred from the northern hemisphere, where he had behaved so mischievously, to the southern—indeed, to a room not far from her own.

"Does he want me to visit him?" she thought. "Never again, never. And I have not the time."

No, it was madness of another kind.

He refused to visualize his face upon the blue plate, and speaking out of the darkness with solemnity said:

"The Machine stops."

"What do you say?"

"The Machine is stopping, I know it, I know the signs."

She burst into a peal of laughter. He heard her and was angry, and they spoke no more.

"Can you imagine anything more absurd?" she cried to a friend. "A man who was my son believes that the Machine is stopping. It would be impious if it was not mad."

"The Machine is stopping?" her friend replied. "What does that mean? The phrase conveys nothing to me."

"Nor to me."

"He does not refer, I suppose, to the trouble there has been lately with the music?"

"Oh, no, of course not. Let us talk about music."

"Have you complained to the authorities?"

"Yes, and they say it wants mending, and referred me to the Committee of the Mending Apparatus. I complained of those curious gasping sighs that disfigure the symphonies of the Brisbane school. They sound like someone in pain. The Committee of the Mending Apparatus say that it shall be remedied shortly."

Obscurely worried, she resumed her life. For one thing, the defect in the music irritated her. For another thing, she could not forget Kuno's speech. If he had known that the music was out of repair—he could not know it, for he detested music—if he had known that it was wrong, "the Machine stops" was exactly the venomous sort of remark he would have made. Of course he had made it at a venture, but the coincidence annoyed her, and she spoke with some petulance to the Committee of the Mending Apparatus.

They replied, as before, that the defect would be set right shortly.

"Shortly! At once!" she retorted. "Why should I be worried by imperfect music? Things are always put right at once. If you do not mend it at once, I shall complain to the Central Committee."

"No personal complaints are received by the Central Committee," the Committee of the Mending Apparatus replied.

"Through whom am I to make my complaint, then?"

"Through us."

"I complain then."

"Your complaint shall be forwarded in its turn."

"Have others complained?"

This question was unmechanical, and the Committee of the Mending Apparatus refused to answer it.

"It is too bad!" she exclaimed to another of her friends. "There never was such an unfortunate woman as myself. I can never be sure of my music now. It gets worse and worse each time I summon it."

"I too have my troubles," the friend replied. "Sometimes my ideas are interrupted by a slight jarring noise."

"What is it?"

"I do not know whether it is inside my head, or inside the wall."

"Complain, in either case."

"I have complained, and my complaint will be forwarded in its turn to the Central Committee."

Time passed, and they resented the defects no longer. The defects had not been remedied, but the human tissues in that latter day had become so subservient, that they readily adapted themselves to every caprice of the Machine. The sigh at the crisis of the Brisbane symphony no longer irritated Vashti; she accepted it as part of the melody. The jarring noise, whether in the head or in the wall, was no longer resented by her friend. And so with the moldy artificial fruit, so with the bath water that began to stink, so with the defective rhymes that the poetry machine had taken to emit. All were bitterly complained of at first, and then acquiesced in and forgotten. Things went from bad to worse unchallenged.

It was otherwise with the failure of the sleeping apparatus. That was a more serious stoppage. There came a day when over the whole world—in Sumatra, in Wessex, in the innumerable cities of Courland and Brazil—the beds, when summoned by their tired owners, failed to appear. It may seem a ludicrous matter, but from it we may date the collapse of humanity. The Committee responsible for the failure was assailed by complainants, whom it referred, as usual, to the Committee of the Mending Apparatus, who in its turn assured them that their complaints would be forwarded to the Central Committee. But the discontent grew, for mankind was not yet sufficiently adaptable to do without sleeping.

"Someone is meddling with the Machine—" they began.

"Someone is trying to make himself king, to reintroduce the personal element."

"Punish that man with Homelessness."

"To the rescue! Avenge the Machine! Avenge the Machine!"

"War! Kill the man!"

But the Committee of the Mending Apparatus now came forward, and allayed the panic with well-chosen words. It confessed that the Mending Apparatus was itself in need of repair.

The effect of this frank confession was admirable.

"Of course," said a famous lecturer—he of the French Revolution, who gilded each new decay with splendor—"of course we shall not press our complaints now. The Mending Apparatus has treated us so well in the past that we all sympathize with it, and will wait patiently for its recovery. In its own good time it will resume its duties. Meanwhile let us do without our beds, our tabloids, our other little wants. Such, I feel sure, would be the wish of the Machine."

Thousands of miles away his audience applauded. The Machine still linked them. Under the sea, beneath the roots of the mountains, ran the wires through which they saw and heard, the enormous eyes and ears that were their heritage, and the hum of many workings clothed their thoughts in one garment of subserviency. Only the old and the sick remained ungrateful, for it was rumored that Euthanasia, too, was out of order, and that pain had reappeared among men.

It became difficult to read. A blight entered the atmosphere and dulled its luminosity. At times Vashti could scarcely see across her room. The air, too, was foul. Loud were the complaints, impotent the remedies, heroic the tone of the lecturer as he cried: "Courage, courage! What matter so long as the Machine goes on? To it the darkness and the light are one." And though things improved again after a time, the old brilliancy was never recaptured, and humanity never recovered from its entrance into twilight. There was an hysterical talk of "measures," of "provisional dictatorship," and the inhabitants of Sumatra were asked to familiarize themselves with the workings of the central power station, the said power station being situated in France. But for the most part panic reigned, and men spent their strength praying to their Books, tangible proofs of the Machine's omnipotence. There were gradations of terror—at times came rumors of hope—the Mending Apparatus was almost mended—the enemies of the Machine had been got under—new "nerve-centers" were evolving which would do the work even more magnificently than before. But there came a day when, without the slightest warning, without any previous hint of feebleness, the entire communication-system broke down, all over the world, and the world, as they understood it, ended.

Vashti was lecturing at the time and her earlier remarks had been punctuated with applause. As she proceeded the audience became silent, and at the conclusion there was no sound. Somewhat displeased, she called to a friend who was a specialist in sympathy. No sound: doubtless the friend was sleeping. And so with the next friend whom she tried to summon, and so with the next, until she remembered Kuno's cryptic remark, "The Machine stops."

The phrase still conveyed nothing. If Eternity was stopping it would of course be set going shortly.

For example, there was still a little light and air—the atmosphere had improved a few hours previously. There was still the Book, and while there was the Book there was security.

Then she broke down, for with the cessation of activity came an unexpected terror—silence.

She had never known silence, and the coming of it nearly killed her—it did kill many thousands of people outright. Ever since her birth she had been surrounded by the steady hum. It was to the ear what artificial air was to the lungs, and agonizing pains shot across her head. And scarcely knowing what she did, she stumbled forward and pressed the unfamiliar button, the one that opened the door of her cell.

Now the door of the cell worked on a simple hinge of its own. It was not connected with the central power station, dying far away in France. It opened, rousing immoderate hopes in Vashti, for she thought that the Machine had been mended. It opened, and she saw the dim tunnel that curved far away towards freedom. One look, and then she shrank back. For the tunnel was full of people—she was almost the last in that city to have taken alarm.

People at any time repelled her, and these were nightmares from her worst dreams. People were crawling about, people were screaming, whimpering, gasping for breath, touching each other, vanishing in the dark, and ever and anon being pushed off the platform onto the live rail. Some were fighting round the electric bells, trying to summon trains which could not be summoned. Others were yelling for Euthanasia or for respirators, or blaspheming the Machine. Others stood at the doors of their cells fearing, like herself, either to stop in them or to leave them. And behind all the uproar was silence—the silence which is the voice of the earth and of the generations who have gone.

No—it was worse than solitude. She closed the door again and sat down to wait for the end. The disintegration went on, accompanied by horrible cracks and rumbling. The valves that restrained the Medical Apparatus must have been weakened, for it ruptured and hung hideously from the ceiling. The floor heaved and fell and flung her from her chair. A tube oozed towards her serpent fashion. And at last the final horror approached—light began to ebb, and she knew that civilization's long day was closing.

She whirled round, praying to be saved from this, at any rate, kissing the Book, pressing button after button. The uproar outside was increasing, and even penetrated the wall. Slowly the brilliancy of her cell was dimmed, the reflections faded from her metal switches. Now she could not see the reading-stand, now not the Book, though she held it in her hand. Light followed the flight of sound, air was following light, and the original void returned to the cavern from which it had been so long excluded. Vashti continued to whirl, like the devotees of an earlier religion, screaming, praying, striking at the buttons with bleeding hands.

It was thus that she opened her prison and escaped—escaped in the spirit: at least so it seems to me, ere my meditation closes. That she escapes in the body—I cannot perceive that. She struck, by chance, the switch that released the door, and the rush of foul air on her skin, the loud throbbing whispers in her ears, told her that she was facing the tunnel again, and that tremendous platform on which she had seen men fighting. They were not fighting now. Only the whispers remained, and the little whimpering groans. They were dying by hundreds out in the dark.

She burst into tears.

Tears answered her.

They wept for humanity, those two, not for themselves. They could not bear that this should be the end. Ere silence was completed their hearts were opened, and they knew what had been important on the earth. Man, the flower of all flesh, the noblest of all creatures visible, man who had once made god in his image, and had mirrored his strength on the constellations, beautiful naked man was dying, strangled in the garments that he had woven. Century after century had he toiled, and here was his reward. Truly the garment had seemed heavenly at first, shot with the colors of culture, sewn with the threads of self-denial. And heavenly it had been so long as it was a garment and no more, so long as man could shed it at will and live by the essence that is his soul, and the essence, equally divine, that is his body. The sin against the body—it was for that they wept in chief; the centuries of wrong against the muscles and the nerves, and those five portals by which we can alone apprehend—glozing it over with talk of evolution, until the body was white pap, the home of ideas as colorless, last sloshy stirrings of a spirit that had grasped the stars.

"Where are you?" she sobbed.

His voice in the darkness said, "Here."

"Is there any hope, Kuno?"

"None for us."

"Where are you?"

She crawled towards him over the bodies of the dead. His blood spurted over her hands.

"Quicker," he gasped, "I am dying—but we touch, we talk, not through the Machine."

He kissed her.

"We have come back to our own. We die, but we have recaptured life, as it was in Wessex, when Aelfrid overthrew the Danes. We know what they know outside, they who dwelt in the cloud that is the color of a pearl."

"But, Kuno, is it true? Are there still men on the surface of the earth? Is this—this tunnel, this poisoned darkness—really not the end?"

He replied:

"I have seen them, spoken to them, loved them. They are hiding in the mist and the ferns until our civilization stops. Today they are the Homeless—tomorrow—"

"Oh, tomorrow—some fool will start the Machine again, tomorrow."

"Never," said Kuno, "never. Humanity has learnt its lesson."

As he spoke, the whole city was broken like a honeycomb. An air-ship had sailed in through the vomitory into a ruined wharf. It crashed downwards, exploding as it went, rending gallery after gallery with its wings of steel. For a moment they saw the nations of the dead, and, before they joined them, scraps of the untainted sky.

THE DAY THE DAM BROKE

by JAMES THURBER

MY MEMORIES of what my family and I went through during the 1913 flood in Ohio I would gladly forget. And yet neither the hardships we endured nor the turmoil and confusion we experienced can alter my feeling toward my native state and city. I am having a fine time now and wish Columbus were here, but if anyone ever wished a city was in hell it was during that frightful and perilous afternoon in 1913 when the dam broke, or, to be more exact, when everybody in town thought that the dam broke. We were both ennobled and demoralized by the experience. Grandfather especially rose to magnificent heights which can never lose their splendor for me, even though his reactions to the flood were based upon a profound misconception, namely, that Nathan Bedford Forrest's cavalry was the menace we were called upon to face. The only possible means of escape for us was to flee the house, a step which grandfather sternly forbade, brandishing his old army saber in his hand. "Let the sons —— come!" he roared.

From *My Life and Hard Times,* by James Thurber. Harper & Brothers. Originally appeared in *The New Yorker.* Copyright, 1933, by James Thurber and reprinted with his permission.

Meanwhile hundreds of people were streaming by our house in wild panic, screaming "Go east! Go east!" We had to stun grandfather with the ironing board. Impeded as we were by the inert form of the old gentleman—he was taller than six feet and weighed almost a hundred and seventy pounds—we were passed, in the first half-mile, by practically everybody else in the city. Had grandfather not come to, at the corner of Parsons Avenue and Town Street, we would unquestionably have been overtaken and engulfed by the roaring waters—that is, if there had *been* any roaring waters. Later, when the panic had died down and people had gone rather sheepishly back to their homes and their offices, minimizing the distances they had run and offering various reasons for running, city engineers pointed out that even if the dam had broken, the water level would not have risen more than two additional inches in the West Side. The West Side was, at the time of the dam scare, under thirty feet of water—as, indeed, were all Ohio river towns during the great spring floods of twenty years ago. The East Side (where we lived and where all the running occurred) had never been in any danger at all. Only a rise of some ninety-five feet could have caused the flood waters to flow over High Street—the thoroughfare that divided the east side of town from the west—and engulf the East Side.

The fact that we were all as safe as kittens under a cookstove did not, however, assuage in the least the fine despair and the grotesque desperation which seized upon the residents of the East Side when the cry spread like a grass fire that the dam had given way. Some of the most dignified, staid, cynical, and clear-thinking men in town abandoned their wives, stenographers, homes, and offices and ran

east. There are few alarms in the world more terrifying than "The dam has broken!" There are few persons capable of stopping to reason when that clarion cry strikes upon their ears, even persons who live in towns no nearer than five hundred miles to a dam.

The Columbus, Ohio, broken-dam rumor began, as I recall it, about noon of March 12, 1913. High Street, the main canyon of trade, was loud with the placid hum of business and the buzzing of placid businessmen arguing, computing, wheedling, offering, refusing, compromising. Darius Conningway, one of the foremost corporation lawyers in the Middle-West, was telling the Public Utilities Commission in the language of Julius Caesar that they might as well try to move the Northern star as to move him. Other men were making their little boasts and their little gestures. Suddenly somebody began to run. It may be that he had simply remembered, all of a moment, an engagement to meet his wife, for which he was now frightfully late. Whatever it was, he ran east on Broad Street (probably toward the Maramor Restaurant, a favorite place for a man to meet his wife). Somebody else began to run, perhaps a newsboy in high spirits. Another man, a portly gentleman of affairs, broke into a trot. Inside of ten minutes, everybody on High Street, from the Union Depot to the Courthouse was running. A loud mumble gradually crystallized into the dread word "dam." "The dam has broke!" The fear was put into words by a little old lady in an electric, or by a traffic cop, or by a small boy: nobody knows who, nor does it now really matter. Two thousand people were abruptly in full flight. "Go east!" was the cry that arose—east away from the river, east to safety. "Go east! Go east! Go east!"

Black streams of people flowed eastward down all the streets leading in that direction; these streams, whose headwaters were in the drygoods stores, office buildings, harness shops, movie theaters, were fed by trickles of housewives, children, cripples, servants, dogs, and cats, slipping out of the houses past which the main streams flowed, shouting and screaming. People ran out leaving fires burning and food cooking and doors wide open. I remember, however, that my mother turned out all the fires and that she took with her a dozen eggs and two loaves of bread. It was her plan to make Memorial Hall, just two blocks away, and take refuge somewhere in the top of it, in one of the dusty rooms where war veterans met and where old battle flags and stage scenery were stored. But the seething throngs, shouting "Go east!" drew her along and the rest of us with her. When grandfather regained full consciousness, at Parsons Avenue, he turned upon the retreating mob like a vengeful prophet and exhorted the men to form ranks and stand off the Rebel dogs, but at length he, too, got the idea that the dam had broken and, roaring "Go east!" in his powerful voice, he caught up in one arm a small child and in the other a slight clerkish man of perhaps forty-two and we slowly began to gain on those ahead of us.

A scattering of firemen, policemen, and army officers in dress uniforms—there had been a review at Fort Hayes, in the northern part of town—added color to the surging billows of people. "Go east!" cried a little child in a piping voice, as she ran past a porch on which drowsed a lieutenant-colonel of infantry. Used to quick decisions, trained to immediate obedience, the officer bounded off the porch and, running at full tilt, soon passed the child, bawling "Go east!" The two of them emptied rapidly the houses of the little street they were on. "What is it? What is it?" demanded a fat, waddling man who intercepted the colonel. The officer dropped behind and asked the little child what it was. "The dam has broke!" gasped the girl. "The dam has broke!" roared the colonel. "Go east! Go east!" He was soon leading, with the exhausted child in his arms, a fleeing company of three hundred persons who had gathered around him from living-rooms, shops, garages, backyards, and basements.

Nobody has ever been able to compute with any exactness how many people took part in the great rout of 1913, for the panic, which extended from the Winslow Bottling Works in the south end to Clintonville, six miles north, ended as abruptly as it began and the bobtail and ragtag and velvet-gowned groups of refugees melted away and slunk home, leaving the streets peaceful and deserted. The shouting, weeping, tangled evacuation of the city lasted not more than two hours in all. Some few people got as far east as Reynoldsburg, twelve miles away; fifty or more reached the Country Club, eight miles away; most of the others gave up, exhausted, or climbed trees in Franklin Park, four miles out. Order was restored and fear dispelled finally by means of militiamen riding about in motor lorries bawling through megaphones: "The dam has *not* broken!" At first this tended only to add to the confusion and increase the panic, for many stampeders thought the soldiers were bellowing "The dam has now broken!", thus setting an official seal of authentication on the calamity.

All the time, the sun shone quietly and

there was nowhere any sign of oncoming waters. A visitor in an airplane, looking down on the straggling, agitated masses of people below, would have been hard put to it to divine a reason for the phenomenon. It must have inspired, in such an observer, a peculiar kind of terror, like the sight of the *Marie Celeste,* abandoned at sea, its galley fires peacefully burning, its tranquil decks bright in the sunlight.

An aunt of mine, Aunt Edith Taylor, was in a movie theater on High Street when, over and above the sound of the piano in the pit (a W. S. Hart picture was being shown), there rose the steadily increasing tromp of running feet. Persistent shouts rose above the tromping. An elderly man, sitting near my aunt, mumbled something, got out of his seat, and went up the aisle at a dogtrot. This started everybody. In an instant the audience was jamming the aisles. "Fire!" shouted a woman who always expected to be burned up in a theater; but now the shouts outside were louder and coherent. "The dam has broke!" cried somebody. "Go east!" screamed a small woman in front of my aunt. And east they went, emerging finally into the street, torn and sprawling. Inside the theater, Bill Hart was calmly calling some desperado's bluff and the brave girl at the piano played "Row! Row! Row!" loudly and then "In My Harem." Outside, men were streaming across the Statehouse yard, others were climbing trees, a woman managed to get up onto the "These Are My Jewels" statue, whose bronze figures of Sherman, Stanton, Grant, and Sheridan watched with cold unconcern the going to pieces of the capital city.

"I ran south to State Street, east on State to Third, south on Third to Town, and out east on Town," my aunt Edith has written me. "A tall spare woman with grim eyes and a determined chin ran past me down the middle of the street. I was still uncertain as to what was the matter, in spite of all the shouting. I drew up alongside the woman with some effort, for although she was in her late fifties, she had a beautiful easy running form and seemed to be in excellent condition. 'What is it?' I puffed. She gave me a quick glance and then looked ahead again, stepping up her pace a trifle. 'Don't ask me, ask God!' she said.

"When I reached Grant Avenue, I was so spent that Dr. H. R. Mallory—you remember Dr. Mallory, the man with the white beard who looks like Robert Browning?—well, Dr. Mallory, whom I had drawn away from at the corner of Fifth and Town, passed me. 'It's got us!' he shouted, and I felt sure that whatever it was *did* have us, for you know what conviction Dr. Mallory's statements always carried. I didn't know at the time what he meant, but I found out later. There was a boy behind him on roller skates, and Dr. Mallory mistook the swishing of the skates for the sound of rushing water. He eventually reached the Columbus School for Girls, at the corner of Parsons Avenue and Town Street, where he collapsed, expecting the cold frothing waters of the Scioto to sweep him into oblivion. The boy on the skates swirled past him and Dr. Mallory realized for the first time what he had been running from. Looking back up the street, he could see no signs of water, but nevertheless, after resting a few minutes, he jogged east again. He caught up with me at Ohio Avenue, where we rested together. I should say that about seven hundred people passed us. A funny thing was that all of them were on foot. Nobody seemed to have had the courage to stop and start his car; but, as I remember it, all cars had to be cranked in those days, which is probably the reason."

The next day, the city went about its business as if nothing had happened, but there was no joking. It was two years or more before you dared treat the breaking of the dam lightly. And even now, twenty years after, there are a few persons, like Dr. Mallory, who will shut up like a clam if you mention the Afternoon of the Great Run.

A DAY'S WORK
by KATHERINE ANNE PORTER

THE DULL SCRAMBLING like a giant rat in the wall meant the dumb-waiter was on its way up, the janitress below hauling on the cable. Mrs. Halloran paused, thumped her iron on the board, and said, "There it is. Late. You could have put on your shoes and gone around the corner and brought the things an hour ago. I can't do everything."

Mr. Halloran pulled himself out of the chair, clutching the arms and heaving to his feet slowly, looking around as if he hoped to find crutches standing near. "Wearing out your socks, too," added Mrs. Halloran. "You ought either go barefoot outright or wear your shoes over your socks as God intended," she said. "Sock feet. What's the good of it, I'd like to know? Neither one thing nor the other."

She unrolled a salmon-colored chiffon nightgown with cream-colored lace and broad ribbons on it, gave it a light flirt in the air, and spread it on the board. "God's mercy, look at that indecent thing," she said. She thumped the iron again and pushed it back and forth over the rumpled cloth. "You might just set the things in the cupboard," she said, "and not leave them around on the floor. You might just."

Mr. Halloran took a sack of potatoes from the dumb-waiter and started for the cupboard in the corner next the icebox. "You might as well take a load," said Mrs. Halloran. "There's no need on earth making a half-dozen trips back and forth. I'd think the poorest sort of man could well carry more than five pounds of potatoes at one time. But maybe not."

Her voice tapped on Mr. Halloran's ears like wood on wood. "Mind your business, will you?" he asked, not speaking to her directly. He carried on the argument with himself. "Oh, I couldn't do that, Mister Honey," he answered in a dull falsetto. "Don't ever ask me to think of such a thing, even. It wouldn't be right," he said, standing still with his knees bent, glaring bitterly over the potato sack at the scrawny strange woman he had never liked, that one standing there ironing clothes with a dirty look on her whole face like a suffering saint. "I may not be much good any more," he told her in his own voice, "but I still have got wits enough to take groceries off a dumb-waiter, mind you."

"That's a miracle," said Mrs. Halloran. "I'm thankful for that much."

"There's the telephone," said Mr. Halloran, sitting in the armchair again and taking his pipe out of his shirt pocket.

"I heard it as well," said Mrs. Halloran,

sliding the iron up and down over the salmon-colored chiffon.

"It's for you, I've no further business in this world," said Mr. Halloran. His little greenish eyes glittered; he exposed his two sharp dogteeth in a grin.

"You could answer it. It could be the wrong number again or for somebody downstairs," said Mrs. Halloran, her flat voice going flatter, even.

"Let it go in any case," decided Mr. Halloran, "for my own part, that is." He struck a match on the arm of his chair, touched off his pipe, and drew in his first puff while the telephone went on with its nagging.

"It might be Maggie again," said Mrs. Halloran.

"Let her ring, then," said Mr. Halloran, settling back and crossing his legs.

"God help a man who won't answer the telephone when his own daughter calls up for a word," commented Mrs. Halloran to the ceiling. "And she in deep trouble, too, with her husband treating her like a dog about the money, and sitting out late nights in saloons with that crowd from the Little Tammany Association. He's getting into politics now with the McCorkery gang. No good will come of it, and I told her as much."

"She's no troubles at all, her man's a sharp fellow who will get ahead if she'll let him alone," said Mr. Halloran. "She's nothing to complain of, I could tell her. But what's a father?" Mr. Halloran cocked his head toward the window that opened on the brick-paved areaway and crowed like a rooster, "What's a father these days and who would heed his advice?"

"You needn't tell the neighbors, there's disgrace enough already," said Mrs. Halloran. She set the iron back on the gas ring and stepped out to the telephone on the first stair landing. Mr. Halloran leaned forward, his thin, red-haired hands hanging loosely between his knees, his warm pipe sending up its good decent smell right into his nose. The woman hated the pipe and the smell; she was a woman born to make any man miserable. Before the depression, while he still had a good job and prospects of a raise, before he went on relief, before she took in fancy washing and ironing, in the Good Days Before, God's pity, she didn't exactly keep her mouth shut, there wasn't a word known to man she couldn't find an answer for, but she knew which side her bread was buttered on, and put up with it. Now she was, you might say, buttering her own bread and she never forgot it for a minute. And it's her own fault we're not riding round today in a limousine with ash trays and a speaking tube and a cut-glass vase for flowers in it. It's what a man gets for marrying one of these holy women. Gerald McCorkery had told him as much, in the beginning.

"There's a girl will spend her time holding you down," Gerald had told him. "You're putting your head in a noose will strangle the life out of you. Heed the advice of one who wishes you well," said Gerald McCorkery. This was after he had barely set eyes on Lacey Mahaffy one Sunday morning in Coney Island. It was like McCorkery to see that in a flash, born judge of human nature that he was. He could look a man over, size him up, and there was an end to it. And if the man didn't pass muster, McCorkery could ease him out in a way that man would never know how it happened. It was the secret of McCorkery's success in the world.

"This is Rosie, herself," said Gerald that Sunday in Coney Island. "Meet the future Mrs. Gerald J. McCorkery." Lacey Mahaffy's narrow face had gone sour as whey under her big straw hat. She barely nodded to Rosie, who gave Mr. Halloran a look that fairly undressed him right there. Mr. Halloran had thought, too, that McCorkery was picking a strange one; she was good-looking all right, but she had the smell of a regular little Fourteenth Street hustler if Halloran knew anything about women. "Come on," said McCorkery, his arm around Rosie's waist, "let's all go on the roller coaster." But Lacey would not. She said, "No, thank you. We didn't plan to stay, and we must go now." On the way home Mr. Halloran said, "Lacey, you judge too harshly. Maybe that's a nice girl at heart; hasn't had your opportunities." Lacey had turned upon him a face ugly as an angry cat's, and said, "She's a loose, low woman, and 'twas an insult to introduce her to me." It was a good while before the pretty fresh face that Mr. Halloran had fallen in love with returned to her.

Next day in Billy's Place, after three drinks each, McCorkery said, "Watch your step, Halloran; think of your future. There's a straight good girl I don't doubt, but she's no sort of mixer. A man getting into politics needs a wife who can meet all kinds. A man needs a woman knows how to loosen her corsets and sit easy."

Mrs. Halloran's voice was going on in the hall, a steady dry rattle like old newspapers blowing on a park bench. "I told you before it's no good coming to me with your troubles now. I warned you in time but you wouldn't listen. . . . I told you just how it would be, I tried my best. . . . No, you couldn't listen, you always knew better than your mother. . . . So now all you've got to do is stand by your married vows and make the best of it. . . . Now listen to me, if you want him-

self to do right you have to do right first. The woman has to do right first, and then if the man won't do right in turn it's no fault of hers. You do right whether he does wrong or no, just because he does wrong is no excuse for you."

"Ah, will you hear that?" Mr. Halloran asked the areaway in an awed voice. "There's a holy terror of a saint for you."

". . . the woman has to do right first, I'm telling you," said Mrs. Halloran into the telephone, "and then if he's a devil in spite of it, why she has to do right without any help from him." Her voice rose so the neighbors could get an earful if they wanted. "I know you from old, you're just like your father. You must be doing something wrong yourself or you wouldn't be in this fix. You're doing wrong this minute, calling over the telephone when you ought to be getting your work done. I've got an iron on, working over the dirty nightgowns of a kind of woman I wouldn't soil my foot on if I'd had a man to take care of me. So now you do up your housework and dress yourself and take a walk in the fresh air. . . ."

"A little fresh air never hurt anybody," commented Mr. Halloran loudly through the open window. "It's the gas gets a man down."

"Now listen to me, Maggie, that's not the way to talk over the public wires. Now you stop that crying and go and do your duty and don't be worrying me any more. And stop saying you're going to leave your husband, because where will you go, for one thing? Do you want to walk the streets or set up a laundry in your kitchen? You can't come back here, you'll stay with your husband where you belong. Don't be a fool, Maggie. You've got your living, and that's more than many a woman better than you has got. Yes, your father's all right. No, he's just sitting here, the same. God knows what's to become of us. But you know how he is, little he cares. . . . Now remember this, Maggie, if anything goes wrong with your married life it's your own fault and you needn't come here for sympathy. . . . I can't waste any more time on it. Good-by."

Mr. Halloran, his ears standing up for fear of missing a word, thought how Gerald J. McCorkery had gone straight on up the ladder with Rosie; and for every step the McCorkerys took upward, he, Michael Halloran, had taken a step downward with Lacey Mahaffy. They had started as greenhorns with the same chances at the same time and the same friends, but McCorkery had seized all his opportunities as they came, getting in steadily with the Big Shots in ward politics, one good thing leading to another. Rosie had known how to back him up and push him onward. The McCorkerys for years had invited him and Lacey to come over to the house and be sociable with the crowd, but Lacey would not.

"You can't run with that fast set and drink and stay out nights and hold your job," said Lacey, "and you should know better than to ask your wife to associate with that woman." Mr. Halloran had got into the habit of dropping around by himself, now and again, for McCorkery still liked him, was still willing to give him a foothold in the right places, still asked him for favors at election time. There was always a good lively crowd at the McCorkerys, wherever they were; for they moved ever so often to a better place, with more furniture. Rosie helped hand around the drinks, taking a few herself with a gay word for everybody. The player piano or the victrola would be going full blast, with everybody dancing, all looking like

ready money and a bright future. He would get home late these evenings, back to the same little cold-water walk-up flat, because Lacey would not spend a dollar for show. It must all go into savings against old age, she said. He would be full of good food and drink, and find Lacey, in a bungalow apron, warming up the fried potatoes once more, cross and bitterly silent, hanging her head and frowning at the smell of liquor on his breath. "You might at least eat the potatoes when I've fried them and waited all this time," she would say. "Ah, eat them yourself, they're none of mine," he would snarl in his disappointment with her, and with the life she was leading him.

He had believed with all his heart for years that he would one day be manager of one of the G. and I. chain grocery stores he worked for, and when that hope gave out there was still his pension when they retired him. But two years before it was due they fired him, on account of the depression, they said. Overnight he was on the sidewalk, with no place to go with the news but home. "Jesus," said Mr. Halloran, still remembering that day after nearly seven years of idleness.

The depression hadn't touched McCorkery. He went on and on up the ladder, giving beefsteaks and beanfests and beer parties for the boys in Billy's Place, standing in with the right men and never missing a trick. At last the Gerald J. McCorkery Club chartered a whole boat for a big excursion up the river. It was a great day, with Lacey sitting at home sulking. After election Rosie had her picture in the papers, smiling at McCorkery; not fat exactly, just a fine figure of a woman with flowers pinned on her spotted fur coat, her teeth as good as ever. Oh, God, there was a girl for any man's money. Mr. Halloran saw out of his eye-corner the bony stooped back of Lacey Mahaffy, standing on one foot to rest the other like a tired old horse, leaning on her hands waiting for the iron to heat.

"That was Maggie, with her woes," she said.

"I hope you gave her some good advice," said Mr. Halloran. "I hope you told her to take up her hat and walk out on him."

Mrs. Halloran suspended the iron over a pair of pink satin panties. "I told her to do right and leave wrong-doing to the men," she said, in her voice like a phonograph record running down. "I told her to bear with the trouble God sends as her mother did before her."

Mr. Halloran gave a loud groan and knocked out his pipe on the chair arm. "You would ruin the world, woman, if you could, with your wicked soul, treating a new-married girl as if she had no home and no parents to come to. But she's no daughter of mine if she sits there peeling potatoes, letting a man run over her. No daughter of mine and I'll tell her so if she—"

"You know well she's your daughter, so hold your tongue," said Mrs. Halloran, "and if she heeded you she'd be walking the streets this minute. I brought her up an honest girl, and an honest woman she's going to be or I'll take her over my knee as I did when she was little. So there you are, Halloran."

Mr. Halloran leaned far back in his chair and felt along the shelf above his head until his fingers touched a half-dollar he had noticed there. His hand closed over it, he got up instantly and looked about for his hat.

"Keep your daughter, Lacey Mahaffy," he said, "she's none of mine but the fruits of your long sinning with the Holy Ghost. And now I'm off for a little round and a couple of beers to keep my mind from dissolving entirely."

"You can't have that dollar you just now sneaked off the shelf," said Mrs. Halloran. "So you think I'm blind besides? Put it back where you found it. That's for our daily bread."

"I'm sick of bread daily," said Mr. Halloran, "I need beer. It was not a dollar, but a half-dollar as you know well."

"Whatever it was," said Mrs. Halloran, "it stands instead of a dollar to me. So just drop it."

"You've got tomorrow's potatoes sewed up in your pocket this minute, and God knows what sums in that black box wherever you hide it, besides the life savings," said Mr. Halloran. "I earned this half-dollar on relief, and it's going to be spent properly. And I'll not be back for supper, so you'll save on that, too. So long, Lacey Mahaffy, I'm off."

"If you never come back, it will be all the same," said Mrs. Halloran, not looking up.

"If I came back with a pocket full of money, you'd be glad to see me," said Mr. Halloran.

"It would want to be a great sum," said Mrs. Halloran.

Mr. Halloran shut the door behind him with a fine slam.

He strolled out into the clear fall weather, a late afternoon sun warming his neck and brightening the old red-brick, high-stooped houses of Perry Street. He would go after all these years to Billy's Place, he might find some luck there. He took his time, though, speaking to the neighbors as he went. "Good afternoon, Mr. Halloran." "Good afternoon to you, Missis Caffery.". . . "It's fine weather for the time of year, Mr. Gogarty." "It is indeed, Mr. Halloran." Mr. Halloran thrived on these civilities, he loved to flourish his hat and give a hearty good day like a man who has nothing on his mind. Ah, there was the young man from the G. and I. store around the corner. He knew what kind of job Mr. Halloran once held there. "Good day, Mr. Halloran." "Good day to you, Mr. McInerny, how's business holding up with you?" "Good for the times, Mr. Halloran, that's the best I can say." "Things are not getting any better, Mr. McInerny." "It's the truth we are all hanging on by the teeth now, Mr. Halloran."

Soothed by this acknowledgment of man's common misfortune Mr. Halloran greeted the young cop at the corner. The cop, with his quick eyesight, was snatching a read from a newspaper on the stand across the sidewalk. "How do you do, Young O'Fallon," asked Mr. Halloran, "is your business lively these days?"

"Quiet as the tomb itself on this block," said Young O'Fallon. "But that's a sad thing about Connolly, now." His eyes motioned toward the newspaper.

"Is he dead?" asked Mr. Halloran. "I haven't been out until now, I didn't see the papers."

"Ah, not yet," said Young O'Fallon, "but the G-men are after him, it looks they'll get him surely this time."

"Connolly in bad with the G-men? Holy Jesus," said Mr. Halloran, "who will they go after next? The meddlers."

"It's that numbers racket," said the cop. "What's the harm, I'd like to know? A man must get his money from somewhere when he's in politics. They oughta give him a chance."

"Connolly's a great fellow, God bless him, I hope he gives them the slip," said Mr. Halloran, "I hope he goes right

through their hands like a greased pig."

"He's smart," said the cop. "That Connolly's a smooth one. He'll come out of it."

Ah, will he though? Mr. Halloran asked himself. Who is safe if Connolly goes under? Wait till I give Lacey Mahaffy the news about Connolly, I'll like seeing her face the first time in twenty years. Lacey kept saying, "A man is a downright fool must be a crook to get rich. Plenty of the best people get rich and do no harm by it. Look at the Connollys now, good practical Catholics with nine children and more to come if God sends them, and Mass every day, and they're rolling in wealth richer than your McCorkerys with all their wickedness." So there you are, Lacey Mahaffy, wrong again, and welcome to your pious Connollys. Still and all it was Connolly who had given Gerald McCorkery his start in the world; McCorkery had been publicity man and then campaign manager for Connolly, in the days when Connolly had Tammany in the palm of his hand and the sky was the limit. And McCorkery had begun at the beginning, God knows. He was running a little basement place first, rent almost nothing, where the boys of the Connolly Club and the Little Tammany Association, just the mere fringe of the district, you might say, could drop in for quiet evenings for a game and a drink along with the talk. Nothing low, nothing but what was customary, with the house taking a cut on the winnings and a fine profit on the liquor, and holding the crowd together. Many was the big plan hatched there came out well for everybody. For everybody but myself, and why was that? And when McCorkery says to me, "You can take over now and run the place for the McCorkery Club," ah, there was my chance and Lacey Mahaffy wouldn't hear of it, and with Maggie coming on just then it wouldn't do to excite her.

Mr. Halloran went on, following his feet that knew the way to Billy's Place, head down, not speaking to passers-by any more, but talking it out with himself again, again. What a track to go over seeing clearly one by one the crossroads where he might have taken a different turn that would have changed all his fortunes; but no, he had gone the other way and now it was too late. She wouldn't say a thing but "It's not right and you know it, Halloran," so what could a man do in all? Ah, you could have gone on with your rightful affairs like any other man, Halloran, it's not the woman's place to decide such things; she'd have come round once she saw the money, or a good whack on the backsides would have put her in her place. Never had mortal woman needed a good walloping worse than Lacey Mahaffy, but he could never find it in his heart to give it to her for her own good. That was just another of your many mistakes, Halloran. But there was always the life-long job with the G. and I. and peace in the house more or less. Many a man envied me in those days I remember, and I was resting easy on the savings and knowing with that and the pension I could finish out my life with some little business of my own. "What came of that?" Mr. Halloran inquired in a low voice, looking around him. Nobody answered. You know well what came of it, Halloran. You were fired out like a delivery boy, two years before your time was out. Why did you sit there watching the trick being played on others before you, knowing well it could happen to you and never quite believing what you saw with your own eyes? G. and I. gave me my start, when I was green in this country, and they were my own kind or I thought so. Well, it's done now. Yes, it's done now, but there was all the years you could have cashed in on the numbers game with the best of them, helping collect the protection money and taking your cut. You could have had a fortune by now in Lacey's name, safe in the bank. It was good quiet profit and none the wiser. But they're wiser now, Halloran, don't forget; still it's a lump of grief and disappointment to swallow all the same. The game's up with Connolly, maybe; Lacey Mahaffy had said, "Numbers is just another way of stealing from the poor, and you weren't born to be a thief like that McCorkery." Ah, God no, Halloran, you were born to rot on relief and maybe that's honest enough for her. That Lacey— A fortune in her name would have been no good to me whatever. She's got all the savings tied up, such as they are, she'll pinch and she'll starve, she'll wash dirty clothes first, she won't give up a penny to live on. She has stood in my way, McCorkery, like a skeleton rattling its bones, and you were right about her, she has been my ruin. "Ah, it's not too late yet, Halloran," said McCorkery, appearing plain as day inside Mr. Halloran's head with the same old face and way with him. "Never say die, Halloran. Elections are coming on again, it's a busy time for all, there's work to be done and you're the very man I'm looking for. Why didn't you come to me sooner, you know I never forget an old friend. You don't deserve your ill fortune, Halloran," McCorkery told him; "I said so to others and I say it now to your face, never did man deserve more of the world than you, Halloran, but the truth is, there's not always enough good luck to go round; but it's your turn now, and I've got a job for you up to your abilities at last. For a man like you, there's nothing to it at all, you can toss it off with one hand tied, Halloran, and good money in it. Organization work, just among your own neighbors, where you're known and respected for a man of your word and an old friend of Gerald McCorkery. Now look, Halloran," said Gerald McCorkery, tipping him the wink, "do I need to say more? It's voters in large numbers we're after, Halloran, and you're to bring them in, alive or dead. Keep your eye on the situation at all times and get in touch with me when necessary. And name your figure in the way of money. And come up to the house sometimes, Halloran, why don't you? Rosie has asked me a hundred times, 'Whatever went with Halloran, the life of the party?' That's the way you stand with Rosie, Halloran. We're in a two-story flat now with green velvet curtains and carpets you can sink to your shoetops in, and there's no reason at all why you shouldn't have the same kind of place if you want it. With your gifts, you were never meant to be a poor man."

Ah, but Lacey Mahaffy wouldn't have it, maybe. "Then get yourself another sort of woman, Halloran, you're a good man still, find yourself a woman like Rosie to snuggle down with at night." Yes, but McCorkery, you forget that Lacey Mahaffy had legs and hair and eyes and a complexion fit for a chorus girl. But would she do anything with them? Never. Would you believe there was a woman wouldn't take off all her clothes at once even to bathe herself? What a hateful thing she was with her evil mind thinking everything was a sin, and never giving a man a chance to show himself a man in any way. But she's faded away now, her mean soul shows out all over her,

she's ugly as sin itself now, McCorkery. "It's what I told you would happen," said McCorkery, "but now with the job and the money you can go your ways and let Lacey Mahaffy go hers." I'll do it, McCorkery. "And forget about Connolly. Just remember I'm my own man and always was. Connolly's finished, but I'm not. Stronger than ever, Halloran, with Connolly out of the way. I saw this coming long ever ago, Halloran, I got clear of it. They don't catch McCorkery with his pants down, Halloran. And I almost forgot . . . Here's something for the running expenses to start. Take this for the present, and there's more to come. . . ."

Mr. Halloran stopped short, a familiar smell floated under his nose: the warm beer-and-beefsteak smell of Billy's Place, sawdust and onions, like any other bar maybe, but with something of its own besides. The talk within him stopped also as if a hand had been laid on his mind. He drew his fist out of his pocket almost expecting to find green money in it. The half-dollar was in his palm. "I'll stay while it lasts and hope McCorkery will come in."

The moment he stepped inside his eye lighted on McCorkery standing at the bar pouring his own drink from the bottle before him. Billy was mopping the bar before him idly, and his eye, swimming toward Halloran, looked like an oyster in its own juice. McCorkery saw him too. "Well, blow me down," he said, in a voice that had almost lost its old County Mayo ring, "if it ain't my old sidekick from the G. and I. Step right up, Halloran," he said, his poker face as good as ever, no man ever saw Gerald McCorkery surprised at anything. "Step up and name your choice."

Mr. Halloran glowed suddenly with the

warmth around the heart he always had at the sight of McCorkery, he couldn't put a name on it, but there was something about the man. Ah, it was Gerald all right, the same, who never forgot a friend and never seemed to care whether a man was rich or poor, with his face of granite and his eyes like blue agates in his head, a rock of a man surely. There he was, saying "Step right up," as if they had parted only yesterday; portly and solid in his expensive-looking clothes, as always; his hat a darker gray than his suit, with a devil-may-care roll to the brim, but nothing sporting, mind you. All first-rate, well made, and the right thing for him, more power to him. Mr. Halloran said, "Ah, McCorkery, you're the one man on this round earth I hoped to see today, but I says to myself, maybe he doesn't come round to Billy's Place so much nowadays."

"And why not?" asked McCorkery. "I've been coming around to Billy's Place for twenty-five years now, it's still head-quarters for the old guard of the Mc-Corkery Club, Halloran." He took in Mr. Halloran from head to foot in a flash of a glance and turned toward the bottle.

"I was going to have a beer," said Mr. Halloran, "but the smell of that whiskey changes my mind for me." McCorkery poured a second glass, they lifted the drinks with an identical crook of the elbow, a flick of the wrist at each other.

"Here's to crime," said McCorkery, and "Here's looking at you," said Mr. Halloran, merrily. Ah, to hell with it, he was back where he belonged, in good company. He put his foot on the rail and snapped down his whiskey, and no sooner was his glass on the bar than McCorkery was filling it again. "Just time for a few quick ones," he said, "before the boys get here." Mr. Halloran downed that one, too,

before he noticed that McCorkery hadn't filled his own glass. "I'm ahead of you," said McCorkery, "I'll skip this one."

There was a short pause, a silence fell around them that seemed to ooze like a fog from somewhere deep in McCorkery, it was suddenly as if he had not really been there at all, or hadn't uttered a word. Then he said outright: "Well, Halloran, let's have it. What's on your mind?" And he poured two more drinks. That was McCorkery all over, reading your thoughts and coming straight to the point.

Mr. Halloran closed his hand round his glass and peered into the little pool of whiskey. "Maybe we could sit down," he said, feeling weak-kneed all at once. Mc-Corkery took the bottle and moved over to the nearest table. He sat facing the door, his look straying there now and then, but he had a set, listening face as if he was ready to hear anything.

"You know what I've had at home all these years," began Mr. Halloran, solemnly, and paused.

"Oh, God, yes," said McCorkery with simple good-fellowship. "How is herself these days?"

"Worse than ever," said Mr. Halloran, "but that's not it."

"What is it, then, Halloran?" asked Mc-Corkery, pouring drinks. "You know well you can speak out your mind to me. Is it a loan?"

"No," said Mr. Halloran. "It's a job."

"Now that's a different matter," said McCorkery. "What kind of a job?"

Mr. Halloran, his head sunk between his shoulders, saw McCorkery wave a hand and nod at half a dozen men who came in and ranged themselves along the bar. "Some of the boys," said McCorkery. "Go on." His face was tougher, and quieter, as if the drink gave him a firm hold on himself. Mr. Halloran said what he had planned to say, had said already on the way down, and it still sounded reasonable and right to him. McCorkery waited until he had finished, and got up, putting a hand on Mr. Halloran's shoulder. "Stay where you are, and help yourself," he said, giving the bottle a little push, "and anything else you want, Halloran, order it on me. I'll be back in a few minutes, and you know I'll help you out if I can."

Halloran understood everything but it was through a soft warm fog, and he hardly noticed when McCorkery passed him again with the men, all in that creepy quiet way like footpads on a dark street. They went into the back room, the door opened on a bright light and closed again, and Mr. Halloran reached for the bottle to help himself wait until McCorkery should come again bringing the good word. He felt comfortable and easy as if he hadn't a bone or muscle in him, but his elbow slipped off the table once or twice and he upset his drink on his sleeve. Ah, McCorkery, is it the whole family you're taking on with the jobs? For my Maggie's husband is in now with the Little Tammany Association. "There's a bright lad will go far and I've got my eye on him, Halloran," said the friendly voice of McCorkery in his mind, and the brown face, softer than he remembered it, came up clearly behind his closed eyes.

"Ah, well, it's like myself beginning all over again in him," said Mr. Halloran, aloud, "besides my own job that I might have had all this time if I'd just come to see you sooner."

"True for you," said McCorkery in a merry County Mayo voice, inside Mr. Halloran's head, "and now let's drink to the gay future for old times' sake and be

damned to Lacey Mahaffy." Mr. Halloran reached for the bottle but it skipped sideways, rolled out of reach like a creature, and exploded at his feet. When he stood up the chair fell backward from under him. He leaned on the table and it folded up under his hands like cardboard.

"Wait now, take it easy," said McCorkery, and there he was, real enough, holding Mr. Halloran braced on the one side, motioning with his hand to the boys in the back room, who came out quietly and took hold of Mr. Halloran, some of them, on the other side. Their faces were all Irish, but not an Irishman Mr. Halloran knew in the lot, and he did not like any face he saw. "Let me be," he said with dignity, "I came here to see Gerald J. McCorkery, a friend of mine from old times, and let not a thug among you lay a finger upon me."

"Come on, Big Shot," said one of the younger men, in a voice like a file grating, "come on now, it's time to go."

"That's a fine low lot you've picked to run with, McCorkery," said Mr. Halloran, bracing his heels against the slow weight they put upon him toward the door, "I wouldn't trust one of them far as I could throw him by the tail."

"All right, all right, Halloran," said McCorkery. "Come on with me. Lay off him, Finnegan." He was leaning over Mr. Halloran and pressing something into his right hand. It was money, a neat little roll of it, good smooth thick money, no other feel like it in the world, you couldn't mistake it. Ah, he'd have an argument to show Lacey Mahaffy would knock her off her feet. Honest money with a job to back it up. "You'll stand by your given word, McCorkery, as ever?" he asked, peering into the rock-colored face above him, his feet weaving a dance under him, his heart ready to break with gratitude.

"Ah, sure, sure," said McCorkery in a loud hearty voice with a kind of curse in it. "Crisakes, get on with him, do." Mr. Halloran found himself eased into a taxicab at the curb, with McCorkery speaking to the driver and giving him money. "So long, Big Shot," said one of the thug faces, and the taxicab door thumped to. Mr. Halloran bobbed about on the seat for a while, trying to think. He leaned forward and spoke to the driver. "Take me to my friend Gerald J. McCorkery's house," he said, "I've got important business. Don't pay any attention to what he said. Take me to his house."

"Yeah?" said the driver, without turning his head. "Well, here's where you get out, see? Right here." He reached back and opened the door. And sure enough, Mr. Halloran was standing on the sidewalk in front of the flat in Perry Street, alone except for the rows of garbage cans, the taxicab hooting its way around the corner, and a cop coming toward him, plainly to be seen under the street light.

"You should cast your vote for McCorkery, the poor man's friend," Mr. Halloran told the cop, "McCorkery's the man who will get us all off the spot. Stands by his old friends like a maniac. Got a wife named Rosie. Vote for McCorkery," said Mr. Halloran, working hard at his job, "and you'll be Chief of the Force when Halloran says the word."

"To hell with McCorkery, that stooge," said the cop, his mouth square and sour with the things he said and the things he saw and did every night on that beat. "There you are drunk again, Halloran, shame to you, with Lacey Mahaffy working her heart out over the washboard to buy your beer."

"It wasn't beer and she didn't buy it, mind you," said Mr. Halloran, "and what do you know about Lacey Mahaffy?"

"I knew her from old when I used to run errands for St. Veronica's Altar Society," said the cop, "and she was a great one, even then. Nothing good enough."

"It's the same today," said Mr. Halloran, almost sober for a moment.

"Well, go on up now and stay up till you're fit to be seen," said the cop, censoriously.

"You're Johnny Maginnis," said Mr. Halloran, "I know you well."

"You should know me by now," said the cop.

Mr. Halloran worked his way upstairs partly on his hands and knees, but once at his own door he stood up, gave a great blow on the panel with his fist, turned the knob and surged in like a wave after the door itself, holding out the money toward Mrs. Halloran, who had finished ironing and was at her mending.

She got up very slowly, her bony hand over her mouth, her eyes starting out at what she saw. "Ah, did you steal it?" she asked. "Did you kill somebody for that?" the words grated up from her throat in a dark whisper. Mr. Halloran glared back at her in fear.

"Suffering Saints, Lacey Mahaffy," he shouted until the whole houseful could hear him, "haven't ye any mind at all that you can't see your husband has had a turn of fortune and a job and times are changed from tonight? Stealing, is it? That's for your great friends the Connollys with their religion. Connolly steals, but Halloran is an honest man with a job in the McCorkery Club, and money in pocket."

"McCorkery, is it?" said Mrs. Halloran, loudly too. "Ah, so there's the whole family, young and old, wicked and innocent, taking their bread from McCorkery, at last. Well, it's no bread of mine, I'll earn my own as I have, you can keep your dirty money to yourself, Halloran, mind you I mean it."

"Great God, woman," moaned Mr. Halloran, and he tottered from the door to the table, to the ironing board, and stood there, ready to weep with rage, "haven't you a soul even that you won't come along with your husband when he's riding to riches and glory on the Tiger's back itself, with everything for the taking and no questions asked?"

"Yes, I have a soul," cried Mrs. Halloran, clenching her fists, her hair flying. "Surely I have a soul and I'll save it yet in spite of you. . . ."

She was standing there before him in a kind of faded gingham winding sheet, with her dead hands upraised, her dead eyes blind but fixed upon him, her voice coming up hollow from the deep tomb, her throat thick with grave damp. The ghost of Lacey Mahaffy was threatening him, it came nearer, growing taller as it came, the face changing to a demon's face with a fixed glassy grin. "It's all that drink on an empty stomach," said the ghost, in a hoarse growl. Mr. Halloran fetched a yellow horror right out of his very boots, and seized the flatiron from the board. "Ah, God damn you, Lacey Mahaffy, you devil, keep away, keep away," he howled, but she advanced on air, grinning and growling. He raised the flatiron and hurled it without aiming, and the specter, whoever it was, whatever it was, sank and was gone. He did not look, but broke out of the room and was back on the sidewalk before he knew he had meant to go there. Maginnis came up at once. "Hey there now, Halloran," he said, "I mean

business this time. You get back upstairs or I'll run you in. Come along now, I'll help you get there this time, and that's the last of it. On relief the way you are, and drinking your head off."

Mr. Halloran suddenly felt calm, collected; he would take Maginnis up and show him just what had happened. "I'm not on relief any more, and if you want any trouble, just call on my friend, McCorkery. He'll tell you who I am."

"McCorkery can't tell me anything about you I don't know already," said Maginnis. "Stand up there now." For Halloran wanted to go up again on his hands and knees.

"Let a man be," said Mr. Halloran, trying to sit on the cop's feet. "I killed Lacey Mahaffy at last, you'll be pleased to hear," he said, looking up into the cop's face. "It was high time and past. But I did not steal the money."

"Well, ain't that just too bad," said the cop, hauling him up under the arms. "Chees, why'n't you make a good job while you had the chance? Stand up now. Ah, hell with it, stand up or I'll sock you one."

Mr. Halloran said, "Well, you don't believe it so wait and see."

At that moment they both glanced upward and saw Mrs. Halloran coming downstairs. She was holding to the rail, and even in the speckled hall-light they could see a great lumpy clout of flesh standing out on her forehead, all colors. She stopped, and seemed not at all surprised.

"So there you are, Officer Maginnis," she said. "Bring him up."

"That's a fine welt you've got over your eye this time, Mrs. Halloran," commented Officer Maginnis, politely.

"I fell and hit my head on the ironing

board," said Mrs. Halloran. "It comes of overwork and worry, day and night. A dead faint, Officer Maginnis. Watch your big feet there, you thriving, natural fool," she added to Mr. Halloran. "He's got a job now, you mightn't believe it, Officer Maginnis, but it's true. Bring him on up, and thank you."

She went ahead of them, opened the door, and led the way to the bedroom through the kitchen, turned back the covers, and Officer Maginnis dumped Mr. Halloran among the quilts and pillows. Mr. Halloran rolled over with a deep groan and shut his eyes.

"Many thanks to you, Officer Maginnis," said Mrs. Halloran.

"Don't mention it, Mrs. Halloran," said Officer Maginnis.

When the door was shut and locked, Mrs. Halloran went and dipped a large bath towel under the kitchen tap. She wrung it out and tied several good hard knots in one end and tried it out with a whack on the edge of the table. She walked in and stood over the bed and brought the knotted towel down in Mr. Halloran's face with all her might. He stirred and muttered, ill at ease. "That's for the flatiron, Halloran," she told him, in a cautious voice as if she were talking to herself, and whack, down came the towel again. "That's for the half-dollar," she said, and whack, "that's for your drunkenness—" Her arm swung around regularly, ending with a heavy thud on the face that was beginning to squirm, gasp, lift itself from the pillow and fall back again, in a puzzled kind of torment. "For your sock feet," Mrs. Halloran told him, whack, "and your laziness, and this is for missing Mass and"—here she swung half a dozen times—"that is for your daughter and your part in her. . . ."

She stood back breathless, the lump on her forehead burning in its furious colors. When Mr. Halloran attempted to rise, shielding his head with his arms, she gave him a push and he fell back again. "Stay there and don't give me a word," said Mrs. Halloran. He pulled the pillow over his face and subsided again, this time for good.

Mrs. Halloran moved about very deliberately. She tied the wet towel around her head, the knotted end hanging over her shoulder. Her hand ran into her apron pocket and came out again with the money. There was a five-dollar bill with three one-dollar bills rolled in it, and the half-dollar she had thought spent long since. "A poor start, but something," she said, and opened the cupboard door with a long key. Reaching in, she pulled a loosely fitted board out of the wall, and removed a black-painted metal box. She unlocked this, took out one five-cent piece from a welter of notes and coins. She then placed the new money in the box, locked it, put it away, replaced the board, shut the cupboard door and locked that. She went out to the telephone, dropped the nickel in the slot, asked for a number, and waited.

"Is that you, Maggie? Well, are things any better with you now? I'm glad to hear it. It's late to be calling, but there's news about your father. No, no, nothing of that kind, he's got a job. I said a *job*. Yes, at last, after all my urging him onward. . . . I've got him bedded down to sleep it off so he'll be ready for work tomorrow. . . . Yes, it's political work, toward the election time, with Gerald McCorkery. But that's no harm, getting votes and all, he'll be in the open air and it doesn't mean I'll have to associate with low people, now or ever. It's clean enough work, with good pay; if it's not just what I prayed for, still it beats nothing, Maggie. After all my trying . . . it's like a miracle. You see what can be done with patience and doing your duty, Maggie. Now mind you do as well by your own husband."

Parade, 1930   Peter Blume

Collection of the Museum of Modern Art, New York. Gift of Mrs. John D. Rockefeller, Jr. Used with permission.

THE SECRET LIFE OF WALTER MITTY

by James Thurber

"WE'RE GOING THROUGH!" The Commander's voice was like thin ice breaking. He wore his full-dress uniform, with the heavily braided white cap pulled down rakishly over one cold gray eye. "We can't make it, sir. It's spoiling for a hurricane, if you ask me." "I'm not asking you, Lieutenant Berg," said the Commander. "Throw on the power lights! Rev her up to 8,500! We're going through!" The pounding of the cylinders increased: ta-pocketa-pocketa-pocketa-*pocketa-pocketa*. The Commander stared at the ice forming on the pilot window. He walked over and twisted a row of complicated dials. "Switch on No. 8 auxiliary!" he shouted. "Switch on No. 8 auxiliary!" repeated Lieutenant Berg. "Full strength in No. 3 turret!" shouted the Commander. "Full strength in No. 3 turret!" The crew, bending to their various tasks in the huge, hurtling eight-engined Navy hydroplane, looked at each other and grinned. "The Old Man'll get us through," they said to one another. "The Old Man ain't afraid of Hell!" . . .

"Not so fast! You're driving too fast!" said Mrs. Mitty. "What are you driving so fast for?"

"Hmm?" said Walter Mitty. He looked at his wife, in the seat beside him, with shocked astonishment. She seemed grossly unfamiliar, like a strange woman who had yelled at him in a crowd. "You were up to fifty-five," she said. "You know I don't like to go more than forty. You were up to fifty-five." Walter Mitty drove on toward Waterbury in silence, the roaring of the SN202 through the worst storm in twenty years of Navy flying fading in the remote, intimate airways of his mind. "You're tensed up again," said Mrs. Mitty. "It's one of your days. I wish you'd let Dr. Renshaw look you over."

Walter Mitty stopped the car in front of the building where his wife went to have her hair done. "Remember to get those overshoes while I'm having my hair done," she said. "I don't need overshoes," said Mitty. She put her mirror back into her bag. "We've been all through that,"

she said, getting out of the car. "You're not a young man any longer." He raced the engine a little. "Why don't you wear your gloves? Have you lost your gloves?" Walter Mitty reached in a pocket and brought out the gloves. He put them on, but after she had turned and gone into the building and he had driven on to a red light, he took them off again. "Pick it up, brother!" snapped a cop as the light changed, and Mitty hastily pulled on his gloves and lurched ahead. He drove around the streets aimlessly for a time, and then he drove past the hospital on his way to the parking lot.

. . . "It's the millionaire banker, Wellington McMillan," said the pretty nurse. "Yes?" said Walter Mitty, removing his gloves slowly. "Who has the case?" "Dr. Renshaw and Dr. Benbow, but there are two specialists here, Dr. Remington from New York and Dr. Pritchard-Mitford from London. He flew over." A door opened down a long, cool corridor and Dr. Renshaw came out. He looked distraught and haggard. "Hello, Mitty," he said. "We're having the devil's own time with McMillan, the millionaire banker and close personal friend of Roosevelt. Obstreosis of the ductal tract. Tertiary. Wish you'd take a look at him." "Glad to," said Mitty.

In the operating room there were whispered introductions: "Dr. Remington, Dr. Mitty, Dr. Pritchard-Mitford, Dr. Mitty." "I've read your book on streptothricosis," said Pritchard-Mitford, shaking hands. "A brilliant performance, sir." "Thank you," said Walter Mitty. "Didn't know you were in the States, Mitty," grumbled Remington. "Coals to Newcastle, bringing Mitford and me up here for a tertiary." "You are very kind," said Mitty. A huge, complicated machine, connected to the operating table, with many tubes and wires, began at this moment to go pocketa-pocketa-pocketa. "The new anesthetizer is giving way!" shouted an interne. "There is no one in the East who knows how to fix it!" "Quiet, man!" said Mitty, in a low, cool voice. He sprang to the machine, which was now going pocketa-pocketa-queep-pocketa-queep. He began fingering delicately a row of glistening dials. "Give me a fountain pen!" he snapped. Someone handed him a fountain pen. He pulled a faulty piston out of the machine and inserted the pen in its place. "That will hold for ten minutes," he said. "Get on with the operation." A nurse hurried over and whispered to Renshaw, and Mitty saw the man turn pale. "Coreopsis has set in," said Renshaw nervously. "If you would take over, Mitty?" Mitty looked at him and at the craven figure of Benbow, who drank, and at the grave, uncertain faces of the two great specialists. "If you wish," he said. They slipped a white gown on him; he adjusted a mask and drew on thin gloves; nurses handed him shining . . .

"Back it up, Mac! Look out for that Buick!" Walter Mitty jammed on the brakes. "Wrong lane, Mac," said the parking-lot attendant, looking at Mitty closely. "Gee. Yeh," muttered Mitty. He began cautiously to back out of the lane marked "Exit Only." "Leave her sit there," said the attendant. "I'll put her away." Mitty got out of the car. "Hey, better leave the key." "Oh," said Mitty, handing the man the ignition key. The attendant vaulted into the car, backed it up with insolent skill, and put it where it belonged.

They're so damn cocky, thought Walter Mitty, walking along Main Street; they think they know everything. Once he had tried to take his chains off, outside New Milford, and he had got them wound around the axles. A man had had to come out in a wrecking car and unwind them,

a young, grinning garageman. Since then Mrs. Mitty always made him drive to a garage to have the chains taken off. The next time, he thought, I'll wear my right arm in a sling; they won't grin at me then. I'll have my right arm in a sling and they'll see I couldn't possibly take the chains off myself. He kicked at the slush on the sidewalk. "Overshoes," he said to himself, and he began looking for a shoe store.

When he came out into the street again, with the overshoes in a box under his arm, Walter Mitty began to wonder what the other thing was his wife had told him to get. She had told him twice before they set out from their house for Waterbury. In a way he hated these weekly trips to town—he was always getting something wrong. Kleenex, he thought, Squibb's, razor blades? No. Toothpaste, toothbrush, bicarbonate, carborundum, initiative and referendum? He gave it up. But she would remember it. "Where's the what's-its-name?" she would ask. "Don't tell me you forgot the what's-its-name." A newsboy went by shouting something about the Waterbury trial.

. . . "Perhaps this will refresh your memory." The District Attorney suddenly thrust a heavy automatic at the quiet figure on the witness stand. "Have you ever seen this before?" Walter Mitty took the gun and examined it expertly. "This is my Webley-Vickers 50.80," he said calmly. An excited buzz ran around the courtroom. The Judge rapped for order. "You are a crack shot with any sort of firearms, I believe?" said the District Attorney, insinuatingly. "Objection!" shouted Mitty's attorney. "We have shown that the defendant could not have fired the shot. We have shown that he wore his right arm in a sling on the night of the fourteenth of July." Walter Mitty raised his hand briefly and the bickering attorneys were stilled. "With any known make of gun," he said evenly, "I could have killed Gregory Fitzhurst at three hundred feet *with my left hand.*" Pandemonium broke loose in the courtroom. A woman's scream rose above the bedlam and suddenly a lovely, dark-haired girl was in Walter Mitty's arms. The District Attorney struck at her savagely. Without rising from his chair, Mitty let the man have it on the point of the chin. "You miserable cur!" . . .

"Puppy biscuit," said Walter Mitty. He stopped walking and the buildings of Waterbury rose up out of the misty courtroom and surrounded him again. A woman who was passing laughed. "He said 'Puppy biscuit,'" she said to her companion. "That man said 'Puppy biscuit' to himself." Walter Mitty hurried on. He went into an A. & P., not the first one he came to but a smaller one farther up the street. "I want some biscuit for small, young dogs," he said to the clerk. "Any special brand, sir?" The greatest pistol shot in the world thought a moment. "It says 'Puppies Bark for It' on the box," said Walter Mitty.

His wife would be through at the hair-dresser's in fifteen minutes, Mitty saw in looking at his watch, unless they had trouble drying it; sometimes they had trouble drying it. She didn't like to get to the hotel first; she would want him to be there waiting for her as usual. He found a big leather chair in the lobby, facing a window, and he put the overshoes and the puppy biscuit on the floor beside it. He picked up an old copy of *Liberty* and sank down into the chair. "Can Germany Conquer the World Through the Air?" Walter Mitty looked at the pictures of bombing planes and of ruined streets.

. . . "The cannonading has got the

wind up in young Raleigh, sir," said the sergeant. Captain Mitty looked up at him through tousled hair. "Get him to bed," he said wearily, "with the others. I'll fly alone." "But you can't, sir," said the sergeant anxiously. "It takes two men to handle that bomber and the Archies are pounding hell out of the air. Von Richtman's circus is between here and Saulier." "Somebody's got to get that ammunition dump," said Mitty. "I'm going over. Spot of brandy?" He poured a drink for the sergeant and one for himself. War thundered and whined around the dugout and battered at the door. There was a rending of wood, and splinters flew through the room. "A bit of a near thing," said Captain Mitty carelessly. "The box barrage is closing in," said the sergeant. "We only live once, Sergeant," said Mitty, with his faint, fleeting smile. "Or do we?" He poured another brandy and tossed it off. "I never see a man could hold his brandy like you, sir," said the sergeant. "Begging your pardon, sir." Captain Mitty stood up and strapped on his huge Webley-Vickers automatic. "It's forty kilometers through hell, sir," said the sergeant. Mitty finished one last brandy. "After all," he said softly, "what isn't?" The pounding of the cannon increased; there was the rat-tat-tatting of machine guns, and from somewhere came the menacing pocketa-pocketa-pocketa of the new flame-throwers. Walter Mitty walked to the door of the dugout humming "Auprès de Ma Blonde." He turned and waved to the sergeant. "Cheerio!" he said. . . .

Something struck his shoulder. "I've been looking all over this hotel for you," said Mrs. Mitty. "Why do you have to hide in this old chair? How did you expect me to find you?" "Things close in," said Walter Mitty vaguely. "What?" Mrs. Mitty said. "Did you get the what's-its-name? The puppy biscuit? What's in that box?" "Overshoes," said Mitty. "Couldn't you have put them on in the store?" "I was thinking," said Walter Mitty. "Does it ever occur to you that I am sometimes thinking?" She looked at him. "I'm going to take your temperature when I get you home," she said.

They went out through the revolving doors that made a faintly derisive whistling sound when you pushed them. It was two blocks to the parking lot. At the drugstore on the corner she said, "Wait here for me. I forgot something. I won't

be a minute." She was more than a minute. Walter Mitty lighted a cigarette. It began to rain, rain with sleet in it. He stood up against the wall of the drugstore, smoking. . . . He put his shoulders back and his heels together. "To hell with the handkerchief," said Walter Mitty scornfully. He took one last drag on his cigarette and snapped it away. Then, with that faint, fleeting smile playing about his lips, he faced the firing squad; erect and motionless, proud and disdainful, Walter Mitty the Undefeated, inscrutable to the last.

Home

DEATH OF A TRAVELLING SALESMAN

by Eudora Welty

R. J. Bowman, who for fourteen years had travelled for a shoe company through Mississippi, drove his Ford along a rutted dirt path. It was a long day! The time did not seem to clear the noon hurdle and settle into soft afternoon. The sun, keeping its strength here even in winter, stayed at the top of the sky, and every time Bowman stuck his head out of the dusty car to stare up the road, it seemed to reach a long arm down and push against the top of his head, right through his hat—like the practical joke of an old drummer, long on the road. It made him feel all the more angry and helpless. He was feverish, and he was not quite sure of the way.

This was his first day back on the road after a long siege of influenza. He had had very high fever, and dreams, and had become weakened and pale, enough to tell the difference in the mirror, and he could not think clearly. . . . All afternoon, in the midst of his anger, and for no reason, he had thought of his dead grandmother. She had been a comfortable soul. Once more Bowman wished he could fall into the big feather bed that had been in her room. . . . Then he forgot her again.

This desolate hill country! And he seemed to be going the wrong way—it was as if he were going back, far back. There was not a house in sight. . . . There was no use wishing he were back in bed, though. By paying the hotel doctor his bill he had proved his recovery. He had not even been sorry when the pretty trained nurse said good-bye. He did not like ill-ness, he distrusted it, as he distrusted the road without signposts. It angered him. He had given the nurse a really expensive bracelet, just because she was packing up her bag and leaving.

But now—what if in fourteen years on the road he had never been ill before and never had an accident? His record was broken, and he had even begun almost to question it. . . . He had gradually put up at better hotels, in the bigger towns, but weren't they all, eternally, stuffy in summer and draughty in winter? Women? He could only remember little rooms within little rooms, like a nest of Chinese paper boxes, and if he thought of one woman he saw the worn loneliness that the furniture of that room seemed built of. And he himself—he was a man who always wore rather wide-brimmed black hats, and in the wavy hotel mirrors had looked something like a bull-fighter, as he paused for that inevitable instant on the landing, walking downstairs to supper. . . . He leaned out of the car again, and once more the sun pushed at his head.

Bowman had wanted to reach Beulah by dark, to go to bed and sleep off his fatigue. As he remembered, Beulah was fifty miles away from the last town, on a gravelled road. This was only a cow trail. How had he ever come to such a place? One hand wiped the sweat from his face, and he drove on.

He had made the Beulah trip before. But he had never seen this hill or this petering-out path before—or that cloud, he thought shyly, looking up and then down quickly—any more than he had seen this day before. Why did he not admit he was simply lost and had been for miles? . . . He was not in the habit of asking the way of strangers, and these people never knew where the very roads they lived on went to; but then he had not even been close enough to anyone to call out. People standing in the fields now and then, or on top of the haystacks, had been too far away, looking like leaning sticks or weeds, turning a little at the solitary rattle of his car across their countryside, watching the pale sobered winter dust where it chunked out behind like big squashes down the road. The stares of these distant people had followed him solidly like a wall, impenetrable, behind which they turned back after he had passed.

The cloud floated there to one side like the bolster on his grandmother's bed. It went over a cabin on the edge of a hill, where two bare chinaberry trees clutched at the sky. He drove through a heap of dead oak leaves, his wheels stirring their weightless sides to make a silvery melancholy whistle as the car passed through their bed. No car had been along this way ahead of him. Then he saw that he was on the edge of a ravine that fell away, a red erosion, and that this was indeed the road's end.

He pulled the brake. But it did not hold, though he put all his strength into it. The car, tipped toward the edge, rolled a little. Without doubt, it was going over the bank.

He got out quietly, as though some mischief had been done him and he had his dignity to remember. He lifted his bag and sample case out, set them down, and stood back and watched the car roll over the edge. He heard something—not the crash he was listening for, but a slow un-uproarious crackle. Rather distastefully he went to look over, and he saw that his car had fallen into a tangle of immense grape vines as thick as his arm, which caught it and held it, rocked it like a grotesque child in a dark cradle, and then, as he watched, concerned somehow that he was not still inside it, released it gently to the ground.

He sighed.

Where am I? he wondered with a shock. Why didn't I do something? All his anger seemed to have drifted away from him. There was the house, back on the hill. He took a bag in each hand and with almost childlike willingness went toward it. But his breathing came with difficulty, and he had to stop to rest.

It was a shotgun house, two rooms and an open passage between, perched on the hill. The whole cabin slanted a little under the heavy heaped-up vine that covered the roof, light and green, as though forgotten from summer. A woman stood in the passage.

He stopped still. Then all of a sudden his heart began to behave strangely. Like a rocket set off, it began to leap and expand into uneven patterns of beats which showered into his brain, and he could not think. But in scattering and falling it made no noise. It shot up with great power, almost elation, and fell gently, like acrobats into nets. It began to pound profoundly, then waited irresponsibly, hitting in some sort of inward mockery first at his ribs, then against his eyes, then under his shoulder blades, and against the roof of his mouth when he tried to say, "Good afternoon, madam." But he could not hear his heart—it was as quiet as ashes falling. This was rather comforting; still, it was shocking to Bowman to feel his heart beating at all.

Stockstill in his confusion, he dropped his bags, which seemed to drift in slow bulks gracefully through the air and to cushion themselves on the grey prostrate grass near the doorstep.

As for the woman standing there, he saw at once that she was old. Since she could not possibly hear his heart, he ignored the pounding and now looked at her carefully, and yet in his distraction dreamily, with his mouth open.

She had been cleaning the lamp, and held it, half blackened, half clear, in front of her. He saw her with the dark passage behind her. She was a big woman with a weather-beaten but unwrinkled face; her lips were held tightly together, and her eyes looked with a curious dulled brightness into his. He looked at her shoes, which were like bundles. If it were summer she would be barefoot. . . . Bowman, who automatically judged a woman's age on sight, set her age at fifty. She wore a formless garment of some grey coarse material, rough-dried from a washing, from which her arms appeared pink and unexpectedly round. When she never said a word, and sustained her quiet pose of holding the lamp, he was convinced of the strength in her body.

"Good afternoon, madam," he said.

She stared on, whether at him or at the air around him he could not tell, but after a moment she lowered her eyes to show that she would listen to whatever he had to say.

"I wonder if you would be interested—" He tried once more. "An accident—my car . . ."

Her voice emerged low and remote, like a sound across a lake. "Sonny he ain't here."

"Sonny?"

"Sonny ain't here now."

Her son—a fellow able to bring my car up, he decided in blurred relief. He pointed down the hill. "My car's in the bottom of the ditch. I'll need help."

"Sonny ain't here, but he'll be here."

She was becoming clearer to him and her voice stronger, and Bowman saw that she was stupid.

He was hardly surprised at the deepening postponement and tedium of his journey. He took a breath, and heard his voice speaking over the silent blows of his heart. "I was sick. I am not strong yet. . . . May I come in?"

He stooped and laid his big black hat over the handle on his bag. It was a humble motion, almost a bow, that instantly struck him as absurd and betraying of all his weakness. He looked up at the woman, the wind blowing his hair. He might have continued for a long time in this unfamiliar attitude; he had never been a patient man, but when he was sick he had learned to sink submissively into the pillows, to wait for his medicine. He waited on the woman.

Then she, looking at him with blue eyes, turned and held open the door, and after a moment Bowman, as if convinced in his action, stood erect and followed her in.

Inside, the darkness of the house touched him like a professional hand, the doctor's. The woman set the half-cleaned lamp on a table in the center of the room and pointed, also like a professional person, a guide, to a chair with a yellow cowhide seat. She herself crouched on the hearth, drawing her knees up under the shapeless dress.

At first he felt hopefully secure. His heart was quieter. The room was enclosed in the gloom of yellow pine boards. He could see the other room, with the foot of an iron bed showing, across the passage. The bed had been made up with a red-and-yellow pieced quilt that looked like a map or a picture, a little like his grandmother's girlhood painting of Rome burning.

He had ached for coolness, but in this room it was cold. He stared at the hearth with dead coals lying on it and iron pots in the corners. The hearth and smoked chimney were of the stone he had seen ribbing the hills, mostly slate. Why is there no fire? he wondered.

And it was so still. The silence of the fields seemed to enter and move familiarly through the house. The wind used the open hall. He felt that he was in a mysterious, quiet, cool danger. It was necessary to do what? . . . To talk.

"I have a nice line of women's low-priced shoes . . ." he said.

But the woman answered, "Sonny'll be here. He's strong. Sonny'll move your car."

"Where is he now?"

"Farms for Mr. Redmond."

Mr. Redmond. Mr. Redmond. That was someone he would never have to encounter, and he was glad. Somehow the name did not appeal to him. . . . In a flare of touchiness and anxiety, Bowman wished to avoid even mention of unknown men and their unknown farms.

"Do you two live here alone?" He was surprised to hear his old voice, chatty, confidential, inflected for selling shoes, asking a question like that—a thing he did not even want to know.

"Yes. We are alone."

He was surprised at the way she answered. She had taken a long time to say that. She had nodded her head in a deep way too. Had she wished to affect him with some sort of premonition? he wondered unhappily. Or was it only that she would not help him, after all, by talking with him? For he was not strong enough to receive the impact of unfamiliar things without a little talk to break their fall. He had lived a month in which nothing had happened except in his head and his body —an almost inaudible life of heartbeats and dreams that came back, a life of fever and privacy, a delicate life which had left him weak to the point of—what? Of begging. The pulse in his palm leapt like a trout in a brook.

He wondered over and over why the woman did not go ahead with cleaning the lamp. What prompted her to stay there across the room, silently bestowing her presence upon him? He saw that with her it was not a time for doing little tasks. Her face was grave; she was feeling how right she was. Perhaps it was only politeness. In docility he held his eyes stiffly wide; they fixed themselves on the woman's clasped hands as though she held the cord they were strung on.

Then, "Sonny's coming," she said.

He himself had not heard anything, but there came a man passing the window and then plunging in at the door, with two hounds beside him. Sonny was a big enough man, with his belt slung low about his hips. He looked at least thirty. He had a hot, red face that was yet full of silence. He wore muddy blue pants and an old military coat stained and patched. World War? Bowman wondered. Great God, it was a Confederate coat. On the back of his light hair he had a wide filthy black hat which seemed to insult Bowman's own. He pushed down the dogs from his chest.

He was strong with dignity and heaviness in his way of moving. . . . There was the resemblance to his mother.

They stood side by side. . . . He must account again for his presence here.

"Sonny, this man, he had his car to run off over the prec'pice an' wants to know if you will git it out for him," the woman said after a few minutes.

Bowman could not even state his case.

Sonny's eyes lay upon him.

He knew he should offer explanations and show money—at least appear either penitent or authoritative. But all he could do was to shrug slightly.

Sonny brushed by him going to the window, followed by the eager dogs, and looked out. There was effort even in the way he was looking, as if he could throw his sight out like a rope. Without turning Bowman felt that his own eyes could have seen nothing: it was too far.

"Got me a mule out there an' got me a block an' tackle," said Sonny meaningfully. "I *could* catch me my mule an' git me my ropes, an' before long I'd git your car out the ravine."

He looked completely round the room, as if in meditation, his eyes roving in their own distance. Then he pressed his lips firmly and yet shyly together, and with the dogs ahead of him this time, he lowered his head and strode out. The hard earth sounded, cupping to his powerful way of walking—almost a stagger.

Mischievously, at the suggestion of those sounds, Bowman's heart leapt again. It seemed to walk about inside him.

"Sonny's goin' to do it," the woman said. She said it again, singing it almost, like a song. She was sitting in her place by the hearth.

Without looking out, he heard some shouts and the dogs barking and the pounding of hoofs in short runs on the hill. In a few minutes Sonny passed under the window with a rope, and there was a brown mule with quivering, shining, purple-looking ears. The mule actually looked in the window. Under its eyelashes it turned target-like eyes into his. Bowman averted his head and saw the woman looking serenely back at the mule, with only satisfaction in her face.

She sang a little more, under her breath. It occurred to him, and it seemed quite marvellous, that she was not really talking to him, but rather following the thing that came about with words that were unconscious and part of her looking.

So he said nothing, and this time when he did not reply he felt a curious and strong emotion, not fear, rise up in him.

This time, when his heart leapt, something—his soul—seemed to leap too, like a little colt invited out of a pen. He stared at the woman while the frantic nimbleness of his feeling made his head sway. He could not move; there was nothing he could do, unless perhaps he might embrace this woman who sat there growing old and shapeless before him.

But he wanted to leap up, to say to her, I have been sick and I found out then, only then, how lonely I am. Is it too late? My heart puts up a struggle inside me, and you may have heard it, protesting against emptiness. . . . It should be full, he would rush on to tell her, thinking of his heart now as a deep lake, it should be holding love like other hearts. It should be flooded with love. There would be a warm spring day . . . Come and stand in my heart, whoever you are, and a whole river would cover your feet and rise higher and take your knees in whirlpools, and draw you down to itself, your whole body, your heart too.

But he moved a trembling hand across his eyes, and looked at the placid crouching woman across the room. She was still as a statue. He felt ashamed and exhausted by the thought that he might, in one more moment, have tried by simple words and embraces to communicate some strange thing—something which seemed always to have just escaped him . . .

Sunlight touched the farthest pot on the hearth. It was late afternoon. This time to-morrow he would be somewhere on a good gravelled road, driving his car past things that happened to people, quicker than their happening. Seeing ahead to the next day, he was glad, and knew that this was no time to embrace an old woman. He could feel in his pounding temples the readying of his blood for motion and for hurrying away.

"Sonny's hitched up your car by now," said the woman. "He'll git it out the ravine right shortly."

"Fine!" he cried with his customary enthusiasm.

Yet it seemed a long time that they waited. It began to get dark. Bowman was cramped in his chair. Any man should know enough to get up and walk around while he waited. There was something like guilt in such stillness and silence.

But instead of getting up, he listened. . . . His breathing restrained, his eyes powerless in the growing dark, he listened uneasily for a warning sound, forgetting in wariness what it would be. Before long he heard something—soft, continuous, in-sinuating.

"What's the noise?" he asked, his voice jumping into the dark. Then wildly he was afraid it would be his heart beating so plainly in the quiet room, and she would tell him so.

"You might hear the stream," she said grudgingly.

Her voice was closer. She was standing by the table. He wondered why she did not light the lamp. She stood there in the dark and did not light it.

Bowman would never speak to her now, for the time was past. I'll sleep in the dark, he thought, in his bewilderment pitying himself.

Heavily she moved on to the window. Her arm, vaguely white, rose straight from her full side and she pointed out into the darkness.

"That white speck's Sonny," she said, talking to herself.

He turned unwillingly and peered over her shoulder; he hesitated to rise and stand beside her. His eyes searched the dusky air. The white speck floated smoothly toward her finger, like a leaf on a river, growing whiter in the dark. It was as if she had shown him something secret, part of her life, but had offered no explanation. He looked away. He was moved almost to tears, feeling for no reason that she had made a silent declaration equivalent to his own. His hand waited upon his chest.

Then a step shook the house, and Sonny was in the room. Bowman felt how the woman left him there and went to the other man's side.

"I done got your car out, mister," said Sonny's voice in the dark. "She's settin' a-waitin' in the road, turned to go back where she come from."

"Fine!" said Bowman, projecting his own voice to loudness. "I'm surely much obliged—I could never have done it my-self—I was sick. . . ."

"I could do it easy," said Sonny.

Bowman could feel them both waiting in the dark, and he could hear the dogs panting out in the yard, waiting to bark when he should go. He felt strangely help-less and resentful. Now that he could go, he longed to stay. From what was he be-ing deprived? His chest was rudely shaken by the violence of his heart. These people cherished something here that he could not see, they withheld some ancient promise of food and warmth and light. Between them they had a conspiracy. He thought of the way she had moved away from him and gone to Sonny, she had flowed toward him. He was shaking with cold, he was tired, and it was not fair. Humbly and yet angrily he stuck his hand into his pocket.

"Of course I'm going to pay you for everything—"

"We don't take money for such," said Sonny's voice belligerently.

"I want to pay. But do something more . . . Let me stay—to-night. . . ." He took another step toward them. If only they could see him, they would know his sincerity, his real need! His voice went on, "I'm not very strong yet, I'm not able to walk far, even back to my car, maybe, I don't know—I don't know exactly where I am—"

He stopped. He felt as if he might burst into tears. What would they think of him!

Sonny came over and put his hands on him. Bowman felt them pass (they were professional too) across his chest, over his hips. He could feel Sonny's eyes upon him in the dark.

"You ain't no revenuer come sneakin' here, mister, ain't got no gun?"

To this end of nowhere! And yet *he* had come. He made a grave answer. "No."

"You can stay."

"Sonny," said the woman, "you'll have to borry some fire."

"I'll go git it from Redmond's," said Sonny.

"What?" Bowman strained to hear their words to each other.

"Our fire, it's out, and Sonny's got to borry some, because it's dark an' cold," she said.

"But matches—I have matches—"

"We don't have no need for 'em," she said proudly. "Sonny's goin' after his own fire."

"I'm goin' to Redmond's," said Sonny with an air of importance, and he went out.

After they had waited a while, Bowman looked out the window and saw a light moving over the hill. It spread itself out like a little fan. It zigzagged along the field, darting and swift, not like Sonny at all. . . . Soon enough, Sonny staggered in, holding a burning stick behind him in tongs, fire flowing in his wake, blazing light into the corners of the room.

"We'll make a fire now," the woman said, taking the brand.

When that was done she lit the lamp. It showed its dark and light. The whole room turned golden-yellow like some sort of flower, and the walls smelled of it and seemed to tremble with the quiet rushing of the fire and the waving of the burning lampwick in its funnel of light.

The woman moved among the iron pots. With the tongs she dropped hot coals on top of the iron lids. They made a set of soft vibrations, like the sound of a bell far away.

She looked up and over at Bowman, but he could not answer. He was trembling. . . .

"Have a drink, mister?" Sonny asked. He had brought in a chair from the other room and sat astride it with his folded arms across the back. Now we are all visible to one another, Bowman thought, and cried, "Yes, sir, you bet, thanks!"

"Come after me and do just what I do," said Sonny.

It was another excursion into the dark. They went through the hall, out to the back of the house, past a shed and a hooded well. They came to a wilderness of thicket.

"Down on your knees," said Sonny.

"What?" Sweat broke out on his forehead.

He understood when Sonny began to crawl through a sort of tunnel that the bushes made over the ground. He followed, startled in spite of himself when a twig or a thorn touched him gently without making a sound, clinging to him and finally letting him go.

Sonny stopped crawling and, crouched on his knees, began to dig with both his hands into the dirt. Bowman shyly struck matches and made a light. In a few minutes Sonny pulled up a jug. He poured out some of the whisky into a bottle from his coat pocket, and buried the jug again. "You never know who's liable to knock at your door," he said, and laughed. "Start back," he said, almost formally. "Ain't no need for us to drink outdoors, like hogs."

At the table by the fire, sitting opposite each other in their chairs, Sonny and Bowman took drinks out of the bottle, passing it across. The dogs slept; one of them was having a dream.

"This is good," said Bowman. "That is what I needed." It was just as though he were drinking the fire off the hearth.

"He makes it," said the woman with quiet pride.

She was pushing the coals off the pots, and the smells of corn bread and coffee circled the room. She set everything on the table before the men, with a bone-handled knife stuck into one of the potatoes, splitting out its golden fibre. Then she stood for a minute looking at them, tall and full above them where they sat. She leaned a little toward them.

"You-all can eat now," she said, and suddenly smiled.

Bowman had just happened to be looking at her. He set his cup back on the table in unbelieving protest. A pain pressed at his eyes. He saw that she was not an old woman. She was young, still young. He could think of no number of years for her. She was the same age as Sonny, and she belonged to him. She stood with the deep dark corner of the room behind her, the shifting yellow light scattering over her head and her grey formless dress, trembling over her tall body when it bent over them in its sudden communication. She was young. Her teeth were shining and her eyes glowed. She turned and walked slowly and heavily out of the room, and he heard her sit down on the cot and then lie down. The pattern on the quilt moved.

"She goin' to have a baby," said Sonny, popping a bite into his mouth.

Bowman could not speak. He was shocked with knowing what was really in this house. A marriage, a fruitful marriage. That simple thing. Anyone could have had that.

Somehow he felt unable to be indignant or protest, although some sort of joke had certainly been played upon him. There was nothing remote or mysterious here— only something private. The only secret was the ancient communication between two people. But the memory of the woman's waiting silently by the cold hearth, of the man's stubborn journey a mile away to get fire, and how they finally brought out their food and drink and filled the room proudly with all they had to show, was suddenly too clear and too enormous within him for response. . . .

"You ain't as hungry as you look," said Sonny.

The woman came out of the bedroom as soon as the men had finished, and ate her supper while her husband stared peacefully into the fire.

Then they put the dogs out, with the food that was left.

"I think I'd better sleep here by the fire, on the floor," said Bowman.

He felt that he had been cheated, and that he could afford now to be generous. Ill though he was, he was not going to ask them for their bed. He was through with asking favours in this house, now that he understood what was there.

"Sure, mister."

But he had not known yet how slowly he understood. They had not meant to give him their bed. After a little interval they both rose and looking at him gravely went into the other room.

He lay stretched by the fire until it grew low and dying. He watched every tongue of blaze lick out and vanish. "There will be special reduced prices on all footwear during the month of January," he found himself repeating quietly, and then he lay with his lips tight shut.

How many noises the night had! He heard the stream running, the fire dying, and he was sure now that he heard his heart beating, too, the sound it made under his ribs. He heard breathing, round and deep, of the man and his wife in the room across the passage. And that was all. But emotion swelled patiently within him, and he wished that the child were his.

He must get back to where he had been before. He stood weakly before the red coals, and put on his overcoat. It felt too heavy on his shoulders. As he started out he looked and saw that the woman had never got through with cleaning the lamp. On some impulse he put all the money from his billfold under its fluted glass base, almost ostentatiously.

Ashamed, shrugging a little, and then shivering, he took his bags and went out. The cold of the air seemed to lift him bodily. The moon was in the sky.

On the slope he began to run, he could not help it. Just as he reached the road, where his car seemed to sit in the moonlight like a boat, his heart began to give off tremendous explosions like a rifle, bang bang bang.

He sank in fright on to the road, his bags falling about him. He felt as if all this had happened before. He covered his heart with both hands to keep anyone from hearing the noise it made.

But nobody heard it.

THE ROCKING-HORSE WINNER

by D. H. LAWRENCE

THERE WAS a woman who was beautiful, who started with all the advantages, yet she had no luck. She married for love, and the love turned to dust. She had bonny children, yet she felt they had been thrust upon her, and she could not love them. They looked at her coldly, as if they were finding fault with her. And hurriedly she felt she must cover up some fault in herself. Yet what it was that she must cover up she never knew. Nevertheless, when her children were present, she always felt the centre of her heart go hard. This troubled her, and in her manner she was all the more gentle and anxious for her children, as if she loved them very much. Only she herself knew that at the centre of her heart was a hard little place that could not feel love, no, not for anybody. Everybody else said of her: "She is such a good mother. She adores her children." Only she herself, and her children themselves, knew it was not so. They read it in each other's eyes.

There were a boy and two little girls. They lived in a pleasant house, with a garden, and they had discreet servants, and felt themselves superior to anyone in the neighbourhood.

Although they lived in style, they felt always an anxiety in the house. There was never enough money. The mother had a small income, and the father had a small income, but not nearly enough for the social position which they had to keep up. The father went into town to some office. But though he had good prospects, these prospects never materialized. There was always the grinding sense of the shortage of money, though the style was always kept up.

At last the mother said: "I will see if I can't make something." But she did not know where to begin. She racked her brains, and tried this thing and the other, but could not find anything successful. The failure made deep lines come into her face. Her children were growing up, they would have to go to school. There must be more money, there must be more money. The father, who was always very handsome and expensive in his tastes, seemed as if he never would be able to do anything worth doing. And the mother, who had a great belief in herself, did not succeed any better, and her tastes were just as expensive.

And so the house came to be haunted by the unspoken phrase: There must be more money! There must be more money! The children could hear it all the time, though nobody said it aloud. They heard it at Christmas, when the expensive and splendid toys filled the nursery. Behind the shining modern rocking-horse, behind the smart doll's-house, a voice would start whispering: "There must be more money! There must be more money!" And the children would stop playing, to listen for a moment. They would look into each other's eyes, to see if they had all heard. And each one saw in the eyes of the other two that they too had heard. "There must be more money! There must be more money!"

It came whispering from the springs of the still-swaying rocking-horse, and even the horse, bending his wooden, champing head, heard it. The big doll, sitting so pink and smirking in her new pram, could hear it quite plainly, and seemed to be smirking all the more self-consciously because of it. The foolish puppy, too, that took the place of the teddy-bear, he was looking so extraordinarily foolish for no other reason but that he heard the secret whisper all over the house: "There must be more money!"

Yet nobody ever said it aloud. The whisper was everywhere, and therefore no one spoke it. Just as no one ever says: "We are breathing!" in spite of the fact that breath is coming and going all the time.

"Mother," said the boy Paul one day, "why don't we keep a car of our own? Why do we always use uncle's, or else a taxi?"

"Because we're the poor members of the family," said the mother.

"But why are we, mother?"

"Well—I suppose," she said slowly and bitterly, "it's because your father has no luck."

The boy was silent for some time.

"Is luck money, mother?" he asked, rather timidly.

"No, Paul. Not quite. It's what causes you to have money."

"Oh!" said Paul vaguely. "I thought when Uncle Oscar said filthy lucker, it meant money."

"Filthy lucre does mean money," said the mother. "But it's lucre, not luck."

"Oh!" said the boy. "Then what is luck, mother?"

"It's what causes you to have money. If you're lucky you have money. That's why it's better to be born lucky than rich. If you're rich, you may lose your money. But if you're lucky, you will always get more money."

"Oh! Will you? And is father not lucky?"

"Very unlucky, I should say," she said bitterly.

The boy watched her with unsure eyes.

"Why?" he asked.

"I don't know. Nobody ever knows why one person is lucky and another unlucky."

"Don't they? Nobody at all? Does nobody know?"

"Perhaps God. But He never tells."

"He ought to, then. And aren't you lucky either, mother?"

"I can't be, if I married an unlucky husband."

"But by yourself, aren't you?"

"I used to think I was, before I married. Now I think I am very unlucky indeed."

"Why?"

"Well—never mind! Perhaps I'm not really," she said.

The child looked at her, to see if she meant it. But he saw, by the lines of her mouth, that she was only trying to hide something from him.

"Well, anyhow," he said stoutly, "I'm a lucky person."

"Why?" said his mother, with a sudden laugh.

He stared at her. He didn't even know why he had said it.

"God told me," he asserted, brazening it out.

"I hope He did, dear!" she said, again with a laugh, but rather bitter.

"He did, mother!"

"Excellent!" said the mother, using one of her husband's exclamations.

The boy saw she did not believe him; or, rather, that she paid no attention to his assertion. This angered him somewhat, and made him want to compel her attention.

He went off by himself, vaguely, in a childish way, seeking for the clue to "luck." Absorbed, taking no heed of other people, he went about with a sort of stealth, seeking inwardly for luck. He wanted luck, he wanted it, he wanted it. When the two girls were playing dolls in the nursery, he would sit on his big rocking-horse, charging madly into space, with a frenzy that made the little girls peer at him uneasily. Wildly the horse careered, the waving dark hair of the boy tossed, his eyes had a strange glare in them. The little girls dared not speak to him.

When he had ridden to the end of his mad little journey, he climbed down and stood in front of his rocking-horse, staring fixedly into its lowered face. Its red mouth was slightly open, its big eye was wide and glassy-bright.

"Now!" he would silently command the snorting steed. "Now, take me to where there is luck! Now take me!"

And he would slash the horse on the neck with the little whip he had asked Uncle Oscar for. He knew the horse could take him to where there was luck, if only he forced it. So he would mount again, and start on his furious ride, hoping at last to get there. He knew he could get there.

"You'll break your horse, Paul!" said the nurse.

"He's always riding like that! I wish he'd leave off!" said his elder sister Joan.

But he only glared down on them in silence. Nurse gave him up. She could make nothing of him. Anyhow he was growing beyond her.

One day his mother and his Uncle Oscar came in when he was on one of his furious rides. He did not speak to them.

"Hallo, you young jockey! Riding a winner?" said his uncle.

"Aren't you growing too big for a rocking-horse? You're not a very little boy any longer, you know," said his mother.

But Paul only gave a blue glare from his big, rather close-set eyes. He would speak to nobody when he was in full tilt. His mother watched him with an anxious expression on her face.

At last he suddenly stopped forcing his horse into the mechanical gallop, and slid down.

"Well, I got there!" he announced fiercely, his blue eyes still flaring, and his sturdy long legs straddling apart.

"Where did you get to?" asked his mother.

"Where I wanted to go," he flared back at her.

"That's right, son!" said Uncle Oscar. "Don't you stop till you get there. What's the horse's name?"

"He doesn't have a name," said the boy.

"Gets on without all right?" asked the uncle.

"Well, he has different names. He was called Sansovino last week."

"Sansovino, eh? Won the Ascot. How did you know his name?"

"He always talks about horse-races with Bassett," said Joan.

The uncle was delighted to find that his small nephew was posted with all the racing news. Bassett, the young gardener, who had been wounded in the left foot in the war and had got his present job through Oscar Cresswell, whose batman he had been, was a perfect blade of the "turf." He lived in the racing events, and the small boy lived with him.

Oscar Cresswell got it all from Bassett.

"Master Paul comes and asks me, so I can't do more than tell him, sir," said Bassett, his face terribly serious, as if he were speaking of religious matters.

"And does he ever put anything on a horse he fancies?"

"Well—I don't want to give him away— he's a young sport, a fine sport, sir. Would you mind asking him yourself? He sort of takes a pleasure in it, and perhaps he'd feel I was giving him away, sir, if you don't mind."

Bassett was serious as a church.

The uncle went back to his nephew, and took him off for a ride in the car.

"Say, Paul, old man, do you ever put anything on a horse?" the uncle asked.

The boy watched the handsome man closely.

"Why, do you think I oughtn't to?" he parried.

"Not a bit of it! I thought perhaps you might give me a tip for the Lincoln."

The car sped on into the country, going down to Uncle Oscar's place in Hampshire.

"Honour bright?" said the nephew.

"Honour bright, son!" said the uncle.

"Well, then, Daffodil."

"Daffodil! I doubt it, sonny. What about Mirza?"

"I only know the winner," said the boy. "That's Daffodil."

"Daffodil, eh?"

There was a pause. Daffodil was an obscure horse comparatively.

"Uncle!"

"Yes, son?"

"You won't let it go any further, will you? I promised Bassett."

"Bassett be damned, old man! What's he got to do with it?"

"We're partners. We've been partners from the first. Uncle, he lent me my first five shillings, which I lost. I promised him, honour bright, it was only between me and him; only you gave me that ten-shilling note I started winning with, so I thought you were lucky. You won't let it go any further, will you?"

The boy gazed at his uncle from those big, hot, blue eyes, set rather close together. The uncle stirred and laughed uneasily.

"Right you are, son! I'll keep your tip private. Daffodil, eh? How much are you putting on him?"

"All except twenty pounds," said the boy. "I keep that in reserve."

The uncle thought it a good joke.

"You keep twenty pounds in reserve, do you, you young romancer? What are you betting, then?"

"I'm betting three hundred," said the boy gravely. "But it's between you and me, Uncle Oscar! Honour bright?"

The uncle burst into a roar of laughter.

"It's between you and me all right, you young Nat Gould," he said, laughing. "But where's your three hundred?"

"Bassett keeps it for me. We're partners."

"You are, are you? And what is Bassett putting on Daffodil?"

"He won't go quite as high as I do, I expect. Perhaps he'll go a hundred and fifty."

"What, pennies?" laughed the uncle.

"Pounds," said the child, with a surprised look at his uncle. "Bassett keeps a bigger reserve than I do."

Between wonder and amusement Uncle Oscar was silent. He pursued the matter no further, but he determined to take his nephew with him to the Lincoln races.

"Now, son," he said, "I'm putting twenty on Mirza, and I'll put five for you on any horse you fancy. What's your pick?"

"Daffodil, uncle."

"No, not the fiver on Daffodil!"

"I should if it was my own fiver," said the child.

"Good! Good! Right you are! A fiver for me and a fiver for you on Daffodil."

The child had never been to a race-meeting before, and his eyes were blue fire. He pursed his mouth tight, and watched. A Frenchman just in front had put his money on Lancelot. Wild with excitement, he flayed his arms up and down, yelling "Lancelot! Lancelot!" in his French accent.

Daffodil came in first, Lancelot second, Mirza third. The child, flushed and with eyes blazing, was curiously serene. His uncle brought him four five-pound notes, four to one.

"What am I to do with these?" he cried, waving them before the boy's eyes.

"I suppose we'll talk to Bassett," said the boy. "I expect I have fifteen hundred now; and twenty in reserve; and this twenty."

His uncle studied him for some moments.

"Look here, son!" he said. "You're not serious about Bassett and that fifteen hundred, are you?"

"Yes, I am. But it's between you and me, uncle. Honour bright!"

"Honour bright all right, son! But I must talk to Bassett."

"If you'd like to be a partner, uncle, with Bassett and me, we could all be partners. Only, you'd have to promise, honour bright, uncle, not to let it go beyond us three. Bassett and I are lucky, and you must be lucky, because it was your ten shillings I started winning with. . . ."

Uncle Oscar took both Bassett and Paul into Richmond Park for an afternoon, and there they talked.

"It's like this, you see, sir," Bassett said. "Master Paul would get me talking about racing events, spinning yarns, you know, sir. And he was always keen on knowing if I'd made or if I'd lost. It's about a year since, now, that I put five shillings on Blush of Dawn for him—and we lost. Then the luck turned, with that ten shillings he had from you, that we put on Singhalese. And since that time, it's been pretty steady, all things considering. What do you say, Master Paul?"

"We're all right when we're sure," said Paul. "It's when we're not quite sure that we go down."

"Oh, but we're careful then," said Bassett.

"But when are you sure?" smiled Uncle Oscar.

"It's Master Paul, sir," said Bassett, in a secret, religious voice. "It's as if he had it from heaven. Like Daffodil, now, for the Lincoln. That was as sure as eggs."

"Did you put anything on Daffodil?" asked Oscar Cresswell.

"Yes, sir. I made my bit."

"And my nephew?"

Bassett was obstinately silent, looking at Paul.

"I made twelve hundred, didn't I, Bassett? I told uncle I was putting three hundred on Daffodil."

"That's right," said Bassett, nodding.

"But where's the money?" asked the uncle.

"I keep it safe locked up, sir. Master Paul he can have it any minute he likes to ask for it."

"What, fifteen hundred pounds?"

"And twenty! And forty, that is, with the twenty he made on the course."

"It's amazing!" said the uncle.

"If Master Paul offers you to be partners, sir, I would, if I were you; if you'll excuse me," said Bassett.

Oscar Cresswell thought about it.

"I'll see the money," he said.

They drove home again, and sure enough, Bassett came round to the garden-house with fifteen hundred pounds in notes. The twenty pounds reserve was left with Joe Glee, in the Turf Commission deposit.

"You see, it's all right, uncle, when I'm sure! Then we go strong, for all we're worth. Don't we, Bassett?"

"We do that, Master Paul."

"And when are you sure?" said the uncle, laughing.

"Oh, well, sometimes I'm absolutely sure, like about Daffodil," said the boy; "and sometimes I have an idea; and sometimes I haven't even an idea, have I, Bassett? Then we're careful, because we mostly go down."

"You do, do you! And when you're sure, like about Daffodil, what makes you sure, sonny?"

"Oh, well, I don't know," said the boy uneasily. "I'm sure, you know, uncle; that's all."

"It's as if he had it from heaven, sir," Bassett reiterated.

"I should say so!" said the uncle.

But he became a partner. And when the Leger was coming on, Paul was "sure" about Lively Spark, which was a quite inconsiderable horse. The boy insisted on putting a thousand on the horse, Bassett went for five hundred, and Oscar Cresswell two hundred. Lively Spark came in first, and the betting had been ten to one against him. Paul had made ten thousand.

"You see," he said. "I was absolutely sure of him."

Even Oscar Cresswell had cleared two thousand.

"Look here, son," he said, "this sort of thing makes me nervous."

"It needn't, uncle! Perhaps I shan't be sure again for a long time."

"But what are you going to do with your money?" asked the uncle.

"Of course," said the boy, "I started it for mother. She said she had no luck, because father is unlucky, so I thought if I was lucky, it might stop whispering."

"What might stop whispering?"

"Our house. I hate our house for whispering."

"What does it whisper?"

"Why—why"—the boy fidgeted—"why, I don't know. But it's always short of money, you know, uncle."

"I know it, son, I know it."

"You know people send mother writs, don't you, uncle?"

"I'm afraid I do," said the uncle.

"And then the house whispers, like people laughing at you behind your back. It's awful, that is! I thought if I was lucky . . ."

"You might stop it," added the uncle.

The boy watched him with big blue eyes that had an uncanny cold fire in them, and he said never a word.

"Well, then!" said the uncle. "What are we doing?"

"I shouldn't like mother to know I was lucky," said the boy.

"Why not, son?"

"She'd stop me."

"I don't think she would."

"Oh!"—and the boy writhed in an odd way—"I don't want her to know, uncle."

"All right, son! We'll manage it without her knowing."

They managed it very easily. Paul, at the other's suggestion, handed over five thousand pounds to his uncle, who deposited it with the family lawyer, who was then to inform Paul's mother that a relative had put five thousand pounds into his hands, which sum was to be paid out a thousand pounds at a time, on the mother's birthday, for the next five years.

"So she'll have a birthday present of a thousand pounds for five successive years," said Uncle Oscar. "I hope it won't make it all the harder for her later."

Paul's mother had her birthday in November. The house had been "whispering" worse than ever lately, and, even in spite of his luck, Paul could not bear up against it. He was very anxious to see the effect of the birthday letter, telling his mother about the thousand pounds.

When there were no visitors, Paul now took his meals with his parents, as he was beyond the nursery control. His mother went into town nearly every day. She had discovered that she had an odd knack of sketching furs and dress materials, so she worked secretly in the studio of a friend who was the chief "artist" for the leading drapers. She drew the figures of ladies in furs and ladies in silk and sequins for the newspaper advertisements. This young woman artist earned several thousand pounds a year, but Paul's mother only made several hundreds, and she was again dissatisfied. She so wanted to be first in something, and she did not succeed, even in making sketches for drapery advertisements.

She was down to breakfast on the morning of her birthday. Paul watched her face as she read her letters. He knew the lawyer's letter. As his mother read it, her face hardened and became more expressionless. Then a cold, determined look came on her mouth. She hid the letter under the pile of others, and said not a word about it.

"Didn't you have anything nice in the post for your birthday, mother?" said Paul.

"Quite moderately nice," she said, her voice cold and absent.

She went away to town without saying more.

But in the afternoon Uncle Oscar appeared. He said Paul's mother had had a long interview with the lawyer, asking if the whole five thousand could be advanced at once, as she was in debt.

"What do you think, uncle?" said the boy.

"I leave it to you, son."

"Oh, let her have it, then! We can get some more with the other," said the boy.

"A bird in the hand is worth two in the bush, laddie!" said Uncle Oscar.

"But I'm sure to know for the Grand National; or the Lincolnshire; or else the Derby. I'm sure to know for one of them," said Paul.

So Uncle Oscar signed the agreement, and Paul's mother touched the whole five thousand. Then something very curious happened. The voices in the house suddenly went mad, like a chorus of frogs on a spring evening. There were certain new furnishings, and Paul had a tutor. He was really going to Eton, his father's school, in the following autumn. There were flowers in the winter, and a blossoming of the luxury Paul's mother had been used to. And yet the voices in the house, behind the sprays of mimosa and almond blossom, and from under the piles of iridescent cushions, simply trilled and screamed in a sort of ecstasy: "There must be more money! Oh-h-h, there must be more money. Oh, now, now-w! Now-w-w —there must be more money!—more than ever! More than ever!"

It frightened Paul terribly. He studied away at his Latin and Greek with his tutors. But his intense hours were spent with Bassett. The Grand National had gone by: he had not "known," and had lost a hundred pounds. Summer was at hand. He was in agony for the Lincoln. But even for the Lincoln he didn't "know" and he lost fifty pounds. He became wild-eyed and strange, as if something were going to explode in him.

"Let it alone, son! Don't you bother about it!" urged Uncle Oscar. But it was as if the boy couldn't really hear what his uncle was saying.

"I've got to know for the Derby! I've got to know for the Derby!" the child reiterated, his big blue eyes blazing with a sort of madness.

His mother noticed how overwrought he was.

"You'd better go to the seaside. Wouldn't you like to go now to the seaside, instead of waiting? I think you'd better," she said, looking down at him anxiously, her heart curiously heavy because of him.

But the child lifted his uncanny blue eyes.

"I couldn't possibly go before the Derby, mother!" he said. "I couldn't possibly!"

"Why not?" she said, her voice becoming heavy when she was opposed. "Why not? You can still go from the seaside to see the Derby with your Uncle Oscar, if that's what you wish. No need for you to wait here. Besides, I think you care too much about these races. It's a bad sign. My family has been a gambling family, and you won't know till you grow up how much damage it has done. But it has done damage. I shall have to send Bassett away, and ask Uncle Oscar not to talk racing to you, unless you promise to be reasonable about it; go away to the seaside and forget it. You're all nerves!"

"I'll do what you like, mother, so long as you don't send me away till after the Derby," the boy said.

"Send you away from where? Just from this house?"

"Yes," he said, gazing at her.

"Why, you curious child, what makes you care about this house so much, suddenly? I never knew you loved it."

He gazed at her without speaking. He had a secret within a secret, something he had not divulged, even to Bassett or to his Uncle Oscar.

But his mother, after standing undecided and a little bit sullen for some moments, said:

"Very well, then! Don't go to the seaside till after the Derby, if you don't wish it. But promise me you won't let your nerves go to pieces. Promise you won't think so much about horse-racing and events, as you call them!"

"Oh, no," said the boy casually. "I won't think much about them, mother. You needn't worry. I wouldn't worry, mother, if I were you."

"If you were me and I were you," said his mother, "I wonder what we should do!"

"But you know you needn't worry, mother, don't you?" the boy repeated.

"I should be awfully glad to know it," she said wearily.

"Oh, well, you can, you know. I mean, you ought to know you needn't worry," he insisted.

"Ought I? Then I'll see about it," she said.

Paul's secret of secrets was his wooden horse, that which had no name. Since he was emancipated from a nurse and a nursery-governess, he had had his rocking-horse removed to his own bedroom at the top of the house.

"Surely, you're too big for a rocking-horse!" his mother had remonstrated.

"Well, you see, mother, till I can have a real horse, I like to have some sort of animal about," had been his quaint answer.

"Do you feel he keeps you company?" she laughed.

"Oh, yes! He's very good, he always keeps me company, when I'm there," said Paul.

So the horse, rather shabby, stood in an arrested prance in the boy's bedroom.

The Derby was drawing near, and the boy grew more and more tense. He hardly heard what was spoken to him, he was very frail, and his eyes were really uncanny. His mother had sudden seizures of uneasiness about him. Sometimes, for half-an-hour, she would feel a sudden anxiety about him that was almost anguish. She wanted to rush to him at once, and know he was safe.

Two nights before the Derby, she was at a big party in town, when one of her rushes of anxiety about her boy, her first-born, gripped her heart till she could hardly speak. She fought with the feeling, might and main, for she believed in common sense. But it was too strong. She had to leave the dance and go downstairs to telephone to the country. The children's nursery-governess was terribly surprised and startled at being rung up in the night.

"Are the children all right, Miss Wilmot?"

"Oh, yes, they are quite all right."

"Master Paul? Is he all right?"

"He went to bed as right as a trivet. Shall I run up and look at him?"

"No," said Paul's mother reluctantly. "No! Don't trouble. It's all right. Don't sit up. We shall be home fairly soon." She did not want her son's privacy intruded upon.

"Very good," said the governess.

It was about one o'clock when Paul's mother and father drove up to their house. All was still. Paul's mother went to her room and slipped off her white fur cloak. She had told her maid not to wait up for her. She heard her husband downstairs, mixing a whisky-and-soda.

And then, because of the strange anxiety at her heart, she stole upstairs to her son's room. Noiselessly she went along the upper corridor. Was there a faint noise. What was it?

She stood, with arrested muscles, outside his door, listening. There was a strange, heavy, and yet not loud noise. Her heart stood still. It was a soundless noise, yet rushing and powerful. Something huge, in violent, hushed motion. What was it? What in God's name was it? She ought to know. She felt that she knew the noise. She knew what it was.

Yet she could not place it. She couldn't say what it was. And on and on it went, like a madness.

Softly, frozen with anxiety and fear, she turned the door-handle.

The room was dark. Yet in the space near the window, she heard and saw something plunging to and fro. She gazed in fear and amazement.

Then suddenly she switched on the light, and saw her son, in his green pyjamas, madly surging on the rocking-horse. The blaze of light suddenly lit him up, as he urged the wooden horse, and lit her up, as she stood, blonde, in her dress of pale green and crystal, in the doorway.

"Paul!" she cried. "Whatever are you doing?"

"It's Malabar!" he screamed, in a powerful, strange voice. "It's Malabar."

His eyes blazed at her for one strange and senseless second, as he ceased urging his wooden horse. Then he fell with a crash to the ground, and she, all her tormented motherhood flooding upon her, rushed to gather him up.

But he was unconscious, and unconscious he remained, with some brainfever. He talked and tossed, and his mother sat stonily by his side.

"Malabar! It's Malabar! Bassett, Bassett, I know! It's Malabar!"

So the child tried, trying to get up and urge the rocking-horse that gave him his inspiration.

"What does he mean by Malabar?" asked the heart-frozen mother.

"I don't know," said the father stonily.

"What does he mean by Malabar?" she asked her brother Oscar.

"It's one of the horses running for the Derby," was the answer.

And, in spite of himself, Oscar Cresswell spoke to Bassett, and himself put a thousand on Malabar: at fourteen to one.

The third day of the illness was critical: they were waiting for a change. The boy, with his rather long, curly hair, was tossing ceaselessly on the pillow. He neither slept nor regained consciousness, and his eyes were like blue stones. His mother sat, feeling her heart had gone, turned actually into a stone.

In the evening, Oscar Cresswell did not come, but Bassett sent a message, saying could he come up for one moment, just one moment? Paul's mother was very angry at the intrusion, but on second thought she agreed. The boy was the same. Perhaps Bassett might bring him to consciousness.

The gardener, a shortish fellow with a little brown moustache, and sharp little brown eyes, tiptoed into the room, touched his imaginary cap to Paul's mother, and stole to the bedside, staring with glittering, smallish eyes, at the tossing, dying child.

"Master Paul!" he whispered. "Master Paul! Malabar come in first all right, a clean win. I did as you told me. You've made over seventy thousand pounds, you have; you've got over eighty thousand. Malabar came in all right, Master Paul!"

"Malabar! Malabar! Did I say Malabar, mother? Did I say Malabar? Do you think I'm lucky, mother? I knew Malabar, didn't I? Over eighty thousand pounds! I call that lucky, don't you, mother? Over eighty thousand pounds! I knew, didn't I know I knew? Malabar came in all right. If I ride my horse till I'm sure, then I tell you, Bassett, you can go as high as you like. Did you go for all you were worth, Bassett?"

"I went a thousand on it, Master Paul."

"I never told you, mother, that if I can ride my horse, and get there, then I'm absolutely sure—oh, absolutely! Mother, did I ever tell you? I am lucky."

"No, you never did," said the mother.

But the boy died in the night.

And even as he lay dead, his mother heard her brother's voice saying to her: "My God, Hester, you're eighty-odd thousand to the good and a poor devil of a son to the bad. But, poor devil, poor devil, he's best gone out of a life where he rides his rocking-horse to find a winner."

OF THIS TIME, OF THAT PLACE

by LIONEL TRILLING

IT WAS a fine September day. By noon it would be summer again, but now it was true autumn with a touch of chill in the air. As Joseph Howe stood on the porch of the house in which he lodged, ready to leave for his first class of the year, he thought with pleasure of the long indoor days that were coming. It was a moment when he could feel glad of his profession.

On the lawn the peach tree was still in fruit and young Hilda Aiken was taking a picture of it. She held the camera tight against her chest. She wanted the sun behind her, but she did not want her own long morning shadow in the foreground. She raised the camera, but that did not help, and she lowered it, but that made things worse. She twisted her body to the left, then to the right. In the end she had to step out of the direct line of the sun.

At last she snapped the shutter and wound the film with intense care.

Howe, watching her from the porch, waited for her to finish and called good morning. She turned, startled, and almost sullenly lowered her glance. In the year Howe had lived at the Aikens', Hilda had accepted him as one of her family, but since his absence of the summer she had grown shy. Then suddenly she lifted her head and smiled at him, and the humorous smile confirmed his pleasure in the day. She picked up her bookbag and set off for school.

The handsome houses on the streets to the college were not yet fully awake, but they looked very friendly. Howe went by the Bradby house where he would be a guest this evening at the first dinner party of the year. When he had gone the length of the picket fence, the whitest in town, he turned back. Along the path there was a fine row of asters and he went through the gate and picked one for his button-hole. The Bradbys would be pleased if they happened to see him invading their lawn and the knowledge of this made him even more comfortable.

He reached the campus as the hour was striking. The students were hurrying to their classes. He himself was in no hurry. He stopped at his dim cubicle of an office and lit a cigarette. The prospect of facing his class had suddenly presented itself to him and his hands were cold; the lawful seizure of power he was about to make seemed momentous. Waiting did not help. He put out his cigarette, picked up a pad of theme paper, and went to his class-room.

As he entered, the rattle of voices ceased, and the twenty-odd freshmen settled themselves and looked at him apprais-ingly. Their faces seemed gross, his heart sank at their massed impassivity, but he spoke briskly.

'My name is Howe,' he said, and turned and wrote it on the blackboard. The care-lessness of the scrawl confirmed his au-thority. He went on, 'My office is 412 Slemp Hall, and my office-hours are Mon-day, Wednesday and Friday from eleven-thirty to twelve-thirty.'

He wrote, 'M., W., F., 11:30-12:30.' He said, 'I'll be very glad to see any of you at that time. Or if you can't come then, you can arrange with me for some other time.'

He turned again to the blackboard and spoke over his shoulder. 'The text for the course is Jarman's *Modern Plays,* revised edition. The Co-op has it in stock.' He wrote the name, underlined 'revised edi-tion' and waited for it to be taken down in the new notebooks.

When the bent heads were raised again he began his speech of prospectus. 'It is hard to explain—' he said, and paused as they composed themselves. 'It is hard to explain what a course like this is intended to do. We are going to try to learn some-thing about modern literature and some-thing about prose composition.'

As he spoke, his hands warmed and he was able to look directly at the class. Last year on the first day the faces had seemed just as cloddish, but as the term wore on they became gradually alive and quite likable. It did not seem possible that the same thing could happen again.

'I shall not lecture in this course,' he continued. 'Our work will be carried on by discussion and we will try to learn by an exchange of opinion. But you will soon recognize that my opinion is worth more than anyone else's here.'

He remained grave as he said it, but two boys understood and laughed. The rest took permission from them and laughed too. All Howe's private ironies protested the vulgarity of the joke, but the laughter made him feel benign and powerful.

When the little speech was finished, Howe picked up the pad of paper he had brought. He announced that they would write an extemporaneous theme. Its sub-ject was traditional, 'Who I am and why I came to Dwight College.' By now the class was more at ease and it gave a ritu-alistic groan of protest. Then there was a stir as fountain pens were brought out and the writing-arms of the chairs were cleared, and the paper was passed about. At last, all the heads bent to work, and the room became still.

Howe sat idly at his desk. The sun shone through the tall clumsy windows. The cool of the morning was already passing. There was a scent of autumn and of varnish and the stillness of the room was deep and oddly touching. Now and then a student's head was raised and scratched in the old, elaborate students' pantomime that calls the teacher to witness honest intellectual effort.

Suddenly a tall boy stood within the frame of the open door. 'Is this,' he said, and thrust a large nose into a college catalogue, 'is this the meeting place of English 1A? The section instructed by Dr. Joseph Howe?'

He stood on the very sill of the door, as if refusing to enter until he was perfectly sure of all his rights. The class looked up from work, found him absurd and gave a low mocking cheer.

The teacher and the new student, with equal pointedness, ignored the disturbance. Howe nodded to the boy, who pushed his head forward and then jerked it back in a wide elaborate arc to clear his brow of a heavy lock of hair. He advanced into the room and halted before Howe, almost at attention. In a loud, clear voice he announced, 'I am Tertan, Ferdinand R., reporting at the direction of Head of Department Vincent.'

The heraldic formality of this statement brought forth another cheer. Howe looked at the class with a sternness he could not really feel, for there was indeed something ridiculous about this boy. Under his displeased regard the rows of heads dropped to work again. Then he touched Tertan's elbow, led him up to the desk and stood so as to shield their conversation from the class.

'We are writing an extemporaneous theme,' he said. 'The subject is, "Who I am and why I came to Dwight College."'

He stripped a few sheets from the pad and offered them to the boy. Tertan hesitated and then took the paper, but he held it only tentatively. As if with the effort

of making something clear, he gulped, and a slow smile fixed itself on his face. It was at once knowing and shy.

'Professor,' he said, 'to be perfectly fair to my classmates'—he made a large gesture over the room—'and to you'—he inclined his head to Howe—'this would not be for me an extemporaneous subject.'

Howe tried to understand. 'You mean you've already thought about it—you've heard we always give the same subject? That doesn't matter.'

Again the boy ducked his head and gulped. It was the gesture of one who wishes to make a difficult explanation with perfect candor. 'Sir,' he said, and made the distinction with great care, 'the topic I did not expect, but I have given much ratiocination to the subject.'

Howe smiled and said, 'I don't think that's an unfair advantage. Just go ahead and write.'

Tertan narrowed his eyes and glanced sidewise at Howe. His strange mouth smiled. Then in quizzical acceptance, he ducked his head, threw back the heavy, dank lock, dropped into a seat with a great loose noise and began to write rapidly.

The room fell silent again and Howe resumed his idleness. When the bell rang, the students who had groaned when the task had been set now groaned again because they had not finished. Howe took up the papers, and held the class while he made the first assignment. When he dismissed it, Tertan bore down on him, his slack mouth held ready for speech.

'Some professors,' he said, 'are pedants. They are Dryasdusts. However, some professors are free souls and creative spirits. Kant, Hegel and Nietzsche were all professors.' With this pronouncement he paused. 'It is my opinion,' he continued, 'that you occupy the second category.'

Howe looked at the boy in surprise and said with good-natured irony, 'With Kant, Hegel and Nietzsche?'

Not only Tertan's hand and head but his whole awkward body waved away the stupidity. 'It is the kind and not the quantity of the kind,' he said sternly.

Rebuked, Howe said as simply and seriously as he could, 'It would be nice to think so.' He added, 'Of course I am not a professor.'

This was clearly a disappointment but Tertan met it. 'In the French sense,' he said with composure. 'Generically, a teacher.'

Suddenly he bowed. It was such a bow, Howe fancied, as a stage-director might teach an actor playing a medieval student who takes leave of Abelard—stiff, solemn, with elbows close to the body and feet together. Then, quite as suddenly, he turned and left.

A queer fish, and as soon as Howe reached his office, he sifted through the batch of themes and drew out Tertan's. The boy had filled many sheets with his unformed headlong scrawl. 'Who am I?' he had begun. 'Here, in a mundane, not to say commercialized academe, is asked the question which from time long immemorably out of mind has accreted doubts and thoughts in the psyche of man to pester him as a nuisance. Whether in St. Augustine (or Austin as sometimes called) or Miss Bashkirtsieff or Frederic Amiel or Empedocles, or in less lights than these, this posed question has been ineluctable.'

Howe took out his pencil. He circled 'academe' and wrote 'vocab.' in the margin. He underlined 'time long immemorably out of mind' and wrote 'Diction!' But this seemed inadequate for what was wrong. He put down his pencil and read ahead to discover the principle of error

in the theme. 'Today as ever, in spite of gloomy prophets of the dismal science (economics) the question is uninvalidated. Out of the starry depths of heaven hurtles this spear of query demanding to be caught on the shield of the mind ere it pierces the skull and the limbs be unstrung.'

Baffled but quite caught, Howe read on. 'Materialism, by which is meant the philosophic concept and not the moral idea, provides no aegis against the question which lies beyond the tangible (metaphysics). Existence without alloy is the question presented. Environment and heredity relegated aside, the rags and old clothes of practical life discarded, the name and the instrumentality of livelihood do not, as the prophets of the dismal science insist on in this connection, give solution to the interrogation which not from the professor merely but veritably from the cosmos is given. I think, therefore I am (cogito etc.) but who am I? Tertan I am, but what is Tertan? Of this time, of that place, of some parentage, what does it matter?'

Existence without alloy: the phrase established itself. Howe put aside Tertan's paper and at random picked up another. 'I am Arthur J. Casebeer, Jr.,' he read. 'My father is Arthur J. Casebeer and my grandfather was Arthur J. Casebeer before him. My mother is Nina Wimble Casebeer. Both of them are college graduates and my father is in insurance. I was born in St. Louis eighteen years ago and we still make our residence there.'

Arthur J. Casebeer, who knew who he was, was less interesting than Tertan, but more coherent. Howe picked up Tertan's paper again. It was clear that none of the routine marginal comments, no 'sent. str.' or 'punct.' or 'vocab.' could cope with this torrential rhetoric. He read ahead, contenting himself with underscoring the errors against the time when he should have the necessary 'conference' with Tertan.

It was a busy and official day of cards and sheets, arrangements and small decisions, and it gave Howe pleasure. Even when it was time to attend the first of the weekly Convocations he felt the charm of the beginning of things when intention is still innocent and uncorrupted by effort. He sat among the young instructors on the platform, and joined in their humorous complaints at having to assist at the ceremony, but actually he got a clear satisfaction from the ritual of prayer and prosy speech, and even from wearing his academic gown. And when the Convocation was over the pleasure continued as he crossed the campus, exchanging greetings with men he had not seen since the spring. They were people who did not yet, and perhaps never would, mean much to him, but in a year they had grown amiably to be part of his life. They were his fellow-townsmen.

The day had cooled again at sunset, and there was a bright chill in the September twilight. Howe carried his voluminous gown over his arm, he swung his doctoral hood by its purple neckpiece, and on his head he wore his mortarboard with its heavy gold tassel bobbing just over his eye. These were the weighty and absurd symbols of his new profession and they pleased him. At twenty-six Joseph Howe had discovered that he was neither so well off nor so bohemian as he had once thought. A small income, adequate when supplemented by a sizable cash legacy, was genteel poverty when the cash was all spent. And the literary life—the room at the Lafayette, or the small apartment without a lease, the long summers on the Cape, the long afternoons and the social

evenings—began to weary him. His writing filled his mornings and should perhaps have filled his life, yet it did not. To the amusement of his friends, and with a certain sense that he was betraying his own freedom, he had used the last of his legacy for a year at Harvard. The small but respectable reputation of his two volumes of verse had proved useful— he continued at Harvard on a fellowship and when he emerged as Doctor Howe he received an excellent appointment, with prospects, at Dwight.

He had his moments of fear when all that had ever been said of the dangers of the academic life had occurred to him. But after a year in which he had tested every possibility of corruption and seduction he was ready to rest easy. His third volume of verse, most of it written in his first years of teaching, was not only ampler but, he thought, better than its predecessors.

There was a clear hour before the Bradby dinner party, and Howe looked forward to it. But he was not to enjoy it, for lying with his mail on the hall table was a copy of this quarter's issue of *Life and Letters,* to which his landlord subscribed. Its severe cover announced that its editor, Frederic Woolley, had this month contributed an essay called 'Two Poets,' and Howe, picking it up, curious to see who the two poets might be, felt his own name start out at him with cabalistic power—Joseph Howe. As he continued to turn the pages his hand trembled.

Standing in the dark hall, holding the neat little magazine, Howe knew that his literary contempt for Frederic Woolley meant nothing, for he suddenly understood how he respected Woolley in the way of the world. He knew this by the trembling of his hand. And of the little world as well as the great, for although the literary groups of New York might dismiss Woolley, his name carried high authority in the academic world. At Dwight it was even a revered name, for it had been here at the college that Frederic Woolley had made the distinguished scholarly career from which he had gone on to literary journalism. In middle life he had been induced to take the editorship of *Life and Letters,* a literary monthly not widely read but heavily endowed, and in its pages he had carried on the defense of what he sometimes called the older values. He was not without wit, he had great knowledge and considerable taste, and even in the full movement of the 'new' literature he had won a certain respect for his refusal to accept it. In France, even in England, he would have been connected with a more robust tradition of conservatism, but America gave him an audience not much better than genteel. It was known in the college that to the subsidy of *Life and Letters* the Bradbys contributed a great part.

As Howe read, he saw that he was involved in nothing less than an event. When the Fifth Series of *Studies in Order and Value* came to be collected, this latest of Frederic Woolley's essays would not be merely another step in the old direction. Clearly and unmistakably, it was a turning point. All his literary life Woolley had been concerned with the relation of literature to morality, religion, and the private and delicate pieties, and he had been unalterably opposed to all that he had called 'inhuman humanitarianism.' But here, suddenly, dramatically late, he had made an about-face, turning to the public life and to the humanitarian politics he had so long despised. This was the kind of incident the histories of literature make much of. Frederic Woolley was opening for himself a new career and

winning a kind of new youth. He contrasted the two poets, Thomas Wormser, who was admirable, Joseph Howe, who was almost dangerous. He spoke of the 'precious subjectivism' of Howe's verse. 'In times like ours,' he wrote, 'with millions facing penury and want, one feels that the qualities of the *tour d'ivoire* are well-nigh inhuman, nearly insulting. The *tour d'ivoire* becomes the *tour d'ivresse,* and it is not self-intoxicated poets that our people need.' The essay said more: 'The problem is one of meaning. I am not ignorant that the creed of the esoteric poets declares that a poem does not and should not *mean* anything, that it *is* something. But poetry is what the poet makes it, and if he is a true poet he makes what his society needs. And what is needed now is the tradition in which Mr. Wormser writes, the true tradition of poetry. The Howes do no harm, but they do no good when positive good is demanded of all responsible men. Or do the Howes indeed do no harm? Perhaps Plato would have said they do, that in some ways theirs is the Phrygian music that turns men's minds from the struggle. Certainly it is true that Thomas Wormser writes in the lucid Dorian mode which sends men into battle with evil.'

It was easy to understand why Woolley had chosen to praise Thomas Wormser. The long, lilting lines of *Corn Under Willows* hymned, as Woolley put it, the struggle for wheat in the Iowa fields, and expressed the real lives of real people. But why out of the dozen more notable examples he had chosen Howe's little volume as the example of 'precious subjectivism' was hard to guess. In a way it was funny, this multiplication of himself into 'the Howes.' And yet this becoming the multiform political symbol by whose creation Frederic Woolley gave the sign of a sudden new life, this use of him as a sacrifice whose blood was necessary for the rites of rejuvenation, made him feel oddly unclean.

Nor could Howe get rid of a certain practical resentment. As a poet he had a special and respectable place in the college life. But it might be another thing to be marked as the poet of a wilful and selfish obscurity.

As he walked to the Bradbys', Howe was a little tense and defensive. It seemed to him that all the world knew of the 'attack' and agreed with it. And, indeed, the Bradbys had read the essay but Professor Bradby, a kind and pretentious man, said, 'I see my old friend knocked you about a bit, my boy,' and his wife Eugenia looked at Howe with her child-like blue eyes and said, 'I shall *scold* Frederic for the untrue things he wrote about you. You aren't the least obscure.' They beamed at him. In their genial snobbery they seemed to feel that he had distinguished himself. He was the leader of Howeism. He enjoyed the dinner party as much as he had thought he would.

And in the following days, as he was more preoccupied with his duties, the incident was forgotten. His classes had ceased to be mere groups. Student after student detached himself from the mass and required or claimed a place in Howe's awareness. Of them all it was Tertan who first and most violently signaled his separate existence. A week after classes had begun Howe saw his silhouette on the frosted glass of his office door. It was motionless for a long time, perhaps stopped by the problem of whether or not to knock before entering. Howe called, 'Come in!' and Tertan entered with his shambling stride.

He stood beside the desk, silent and at attention. When Howe asked him to sit down, he responded with a gesture of head and hand, as if to say that such amenities were beside the point. Nevertheless, he did take the chair. He put his ragged, crammed briefcase between his legs. His face, which Howe now observed fully for the first time, was confusing, for it was made up of florid curves, the nose arched in the bone and voluted in the nostril, the mouth loose and soft and rather moist. Yet the face was so thin and narrow as to seem the very type of asceticism. Lashes of unusual length veiled the eyes and, indeed, it seemed as if there were a veil over the whole countenance. Before the words actually came, the face screwed itself into an attitude of preparation for them.

'You can confer with me now?' Tertan said.

'Yes, I'd be glad to. There are several things in your two themes I want to talk to you about.' Howe reached for the packet of themes on his desk and sought for Tertan's. But the boy was waving them away.

'These are done perforce,' he said. 'Under the pressure of your requirement. They are not significant; mere duties.' Again his great hand flapped vaguely to dismiss his themes. He leaned forward and gazed at his teacher.

'You are,' he said, 'a man of letters? You are a poet?' It was more declaration than question.

'I should like to think so,' Howe said.

At first Tertan accepted the answer with a show of appreciation, as though the understatement made a secret between himself and Howe. Then he chose to misunderstand. With his shrewd and disconcerting control of expression, he presented to Howe a puzzled grimace. 'What does that mean?' he said.

Howe retracted the irony. 'Yes. I am a poet.' It sounded strange to say.

'That,' Tertan said, 'is a wonder.' He corrected himself with his ducking head. 'I mean that is wonderful.'

Suddenly, he dived at the miserable briefcase between his legs, put it on his knees, and began to fumble with the catch, all intent on the difficulty it presented. Howe noted that his suit was worn thin, his shirt almost unclean. He became aware, even, of a vague and musty odor of garments worn too long in unaired rooms. Tertan conquered the lock and began to concentrate upon a search into the interior. At last he held in his hand what he was after, a torn and crumpled copy of *Life and Letters.*

'I learned it from here,' he said, holding it out.

Howe looked at him sharply, his hackles a little up. But the boy's face was not only perfectly innocent, it even shone with a conscious admiration. Apparently nothing of the import of the essay had touched him except the wonderful fact that his teacher was a 'man of letters.' Yet this seemed too stupid, and Howe, to test it, said, 'The man who wrote that doesn't think it's wonderful.'

Tertan made a moist hissing sound as he cleared his mouth of saliva. His head, oddly loose on his neck, wove a pattern of contempt in the air. 'A critic,' he said, 'who admits *prima facie* that he does not understand.' Then he said grandly, 'It is the inevitable fate.'

It was absurd, yet Howe was not only aware of the absurdity but of a tension suddenly and wonderfully relaxed. Now that the 'attack' was on the table between himself and this strange boy, and subject to the boy's funny and absolutely certain contempt, the hidden force of his feeling was revealed to him in the very moment that it vanished. All unsuspected, there had been a film over the world, a transparent but discoloring haze of danger. But he had no time to stop over the brightened aspect of things. Tertan was going on. 'I also am a man of letters. Putative.'

'You have written a good deal?' Howe meant to be no more than polite, and he was surprised at the tenderness he heard in his words.

Solemnly the boy nodded, threw back the dank lock, and sucked in a deep, anticipatory breath. 'First, a work of homiletics, which is a defense of the principles of religious optimism against the pessimism of Schopenhauer and the humanism of Nietzsche.'

'Humanism? Why do you call it humanism?'

'It is my nomenclature for making a deity of man,' Tertan replied negligently. 'Then three fictional works, novels. And numerous essays in science, combating materialism. Is it your duty to read these if I bring them to you?'

Howe answered simply, 'No, it isn't exactly my duty, but I shall be happy to read them.'

Tertan stood up and remained silent. He rested his bag on the chair. With a certain compunction—for it did not seem entirely proper that, of two men of letters, one should have the right to blue-pencil the other, to grade him or to question the quality of his 'sentence structure'—Howe reached for Tertan's papers. But before he could take them up, the boy suddenly made his bow-to-Abelard, the stiff inclination of the body with the hands seeming to emerge from the scholar's gown. Then he was gone.

But after his departure something was still left of him. The timbre of his curious sentences, the downright finality of so quaint a phrase as 'It is the inevitable fate' still rang in the air. Howe gave the warmth of his feeling to the new visitor who stood at the door announcing himself with a genteel clearing of the throat.

'Doctor Howe, I believe?' the student said. A large hand advanced into the room and grasped Howe's hand. 'Blackburn, sir, Theodore Blackburn, vice-president of the Student Council. A great pleasure, sir.'

Out of a pair of ruddy cheeks a pair of small eyes twinkled good-naturedly. The large face, the large body were not so much fat as beefy and suggested something 'typical'—monk, politician, or innkeeper.

Blackburn took the seat beside Howe's desk. 'I may have seemed to introduce myself in my public capacity, sir,' he said. 'But it is really as an individual that I came to see you. That is to say, as one of your students to be.'

He spoke with an English intonation and he went on, 'I was once an English major, sir.'

For a moment Howe was startled, for the roast-beef look of the boy and the manner of his speech gave a second's credibility to one sense of his statement. Then the collegiate meaning of the phrase asserted itself, but some perversity made Howe say what was not really in good taste even with so forward a student, 'Indeed? What regiment?'

Blackburn stared and then gave a little pouf-pouf of laughter. He waved the misapprehension away. '*Very* good, sir. It certainly is an ambiguous term.' He chuckled in appreciation of Howe's joke, then cleared his throat to put it aside. 'I look forward to taking your course in the romantic poets, sir,' he said earnestly. 'To me the romantic poets are the very crown of English literature.'

Howe made a dry sound, and the boy, catching some meaning in it, said, 'Little

as I know them, of course. But even Shakespeare who is so dear to us of the Anglo-Saxon tradition is in a sense but the preparation for Shelley, Keats and Byron. And Wadsworth.'

Almost sorry for him, Howe dropped his eyes. With some embarrassment, for the boy was not actually his student, he said softly, 'Wordsworth.'

'Sir?'

'Wordsworth, not Wadsworth. You said Wadsworth.'

'Did I, sir?' Gravely he shook his head to rebuke himself for the error. 'Wordsworth, of course—slip of the tongue.' Then, quite in command again, he went on. 'I have a favor to ask of you, Doctor Howe. You see, I began my college course as an English major,'—he smiled—'as I said.'

'Yes?'

'But after my first year I shifted. I shifted to the social sciences. Sociology and government—I find them stimulating and very *real*.' He paused, out of respect for reality. 'But now I find that perhaps I have neglected the other side.'

'The other side?' Howe said.

'Imagination, fancy, culture. A well-rounded man.' He trailed off as if there were perfect understanding between them. 'And so, sir, I have decided to end my senior year with your course in the romantic poets.'

His voice was filled with an indulgence which Howe ignored as he said flatly and gravely, 'But that course isn't given until the spring term.'

'Yes, sir, and that is where the favor comes in. Would you let me take your romantic prose course? I can't take it for credit, sir, my program is full, but just for background it seems to me that I ought to take it. I do hope,' he concluded in a manly way, 'that you will consent.'

'Well, it's no great favor, Mr. Blackburn. You can come if you wish, though there's not much point in it if you don't do the reading.'

The bell rang for the hour and Howe got up.

'May I begin with this class, sir?' Blackburn's smile was candid and boyish.

Howe nodded carelessly and together, silently, they walked to the classroom down the hall. When they reached the door Howe stood back to let his student enter, but Blackburn moved adroitly behind him and grasped him by the arm to urge him over the threshold. They entered together with Blackburn's hand firmly on Howe's biceps, the student inducting the teacher into his own room. Howe felt a surge of temper rise in him and almost violently he disengaged his arm and walked to the desk, while Blackburn found a seat in the front row and smiled at him.

II

The question was, At whose door must the tragedy be laid?

All night the snow had fallen heavily and only now was abating in sparse little flurries. The windows were valanced high with white. It was very quiet; something of the quiet of the world had reached the class, and Howe found that everyone was glad to talk or listen. In the room there was a comfortable sense of pleasure in being human.

Casebeer believed that the blame for the tragedy rested with heredity. Picking up the book he read, 'The sins of the fathers are visited on their children.' This opinion was received with general favor. Nevertheless, Johnson ventured to say that the fault was all Pastor Manders' because the Pastor had made Mrs. Alving go back to her husband and was always hiding the truth. To this Hibbard objected with logic enough, 'Well then, it was really all her husband's fault. He *did* all the bad things.' De Witt, his face bright with an impatient idea, said that the fault was all society's. 'By society I don't mean upper-crust society,' he said. He looked around a little defiantly, taking in any members of the class who might be members of upper-crust society. 'Not in that sense. I mean the social unit.'

Howe nodded and said, 'Yes, of course.'

'If the society of the time had progressed far enough in science,' De Witt went on, 'then there would be no problem for Mr. Ibsen to write about. Captain Alving plays around a little, gives way to perfectly natural biological urges, and he gets a social disease, a venereal disease. If the disease is cured, no problem. Invent salvarsan and the disease is cured. The problem of heredity disappears and li'l Oswald just doesn't get paresis. No paresis, no problem—no problem, no play.'

This was carrying the ark into battle, and the class looked at De Witt with respectful curiosity. It was his usual way and on the whole they were sympathetic with his struggle to prove to Howe that science was better than literature. Still, there was something in his reckless manner that alienated them a little.

'Or take birth-control, for instance,' De Witt went on. 'If Mrs. Alving had some knowledge of contraception, she wouldn't have had to have li'l Oswald at all. No li'l Oswald, no play.'

The class was suddenly quieter. In the back row Stettenhover swung his great football shoulders in a righteous sulking gesture, first to the right, then to the left. He puckered his mouth ostentatiously. Intellect was always ending up by talking dirty.

Tertan's hand went up, and Howe said, 'Mr. Tertan.' The boy shambled to his feet and began his long characteristic gulp. Howe made a motion with his fingers, as small as possible, and Tertan ducked his head and smiled in apology. He sat down. The class laughed. With more than half the term gone, Tertan had not been able to remember that one did not rise to speak. He seemed unable to carry on the life of the intellect without this mark of respect for it. To Howe the boy's habit of rising seemed to accord with the formal shabbiness of his dress. He never wore the casual sweaters and jackets of his classmates. Into the free and comfortable air of the college classroom he brought the stuffy sordid strictness of some crowded, metropolitan high school.

'Speaking from one sense,' Tertan began slowly, 'there is no blame ascribable. From the sense of determinism, who can say where the blame lies? The preordained is the preordained and it cannot be said without rebellion against the universe, a palpable absurdity.'

In the back row Stettenhover slumped suddenly in his seat, his heels held out before him, making a loud, dry, disgusted sound. His body sank until his neck rested on the back of his chair. He folded his hands across his belly and looked significantly out of the window, exasperated not only with Tertan, but with Howe, with the class, with the whole system designed to encourage this kind of thing. There was a certain insolence in the movement and Howe flushed. As Tertan continued to speak, Howe stalked casually toward the window and placed himself in the line of Stettenhover's vision. He stared at the great fellow, who pretended not to see him. There was so much power in the big body, so much contempt in the Greek-athlete face under the crisp Greek-athlete

curls, that Howe felt almost physical fear. But at last Stettenhover admitted him to focus and under his disapproving gaze sat up with slow indifference. His eyebrows raised high in resignation, he began to examine his hands. Howe relaxed and turned his attention back to Tertan.

'Flux of existence,' Tertan was saying, 'produces all things, so that judgment wavers. Beyond the phenomena, what? But phenomena are adumbrated and to them we are limited.'

Howe saw it for a moment as perhaps it existed in the boy's mind—the world of shadows which are cast by a great light upon a hidden reality as in the old myth of the Cave. But the little brush with Stettenhover had tired him, and he said irritably, 'But come to the point, Mr. Tertan.'

He said it so sharply that some of the class looked at him curiously. For three months he had gently carried Tertan through his verbosities, to the vaguely respectful surprise of the other students, who seemed to conceive that there existed between this strange classmate and their teacher some special understanding from which they were content to be excluded. Tertan looked at him mildly, and at once came brilliantly to the point. 'This is the summation of the play,' he said and took up his book and read, ' "Your poor father never found any outlet for the overmastering joy of life that was in him. And I brought no holiday into his home, either. Everything seemed to turn upon duty and I am afraid I made your poor father's home unbearable to him, Oswald." Spoken by Mrs. Alving.'

Yes that was surely the 'summation' of the play and Tertan had hit it, as he hit, deviously and eventually, the literary point of almost everything. But now, as always, he was wrapping it away from sight. 'For most mortals,' he said, 'there are only joys of biological urgings, gross and crass, such as the sensuous Captain Alving. For certain few there are the transmutations beyond these to a contemplation of the utter whole.'

Oh, the boy was mad. And suddenly the word, used in hyperbole, intended almost for the expression of exasperated admiration, became literal. Now that the word was used, it became simply apparent to Howe that Tertan was mad.

It was a monstrous word and stood like a bestial thing in the room. Yet it so completely comprehended everything that had puzzled Howe, it so arranged and explained what for three months had been perplexing him that almost at once its horror became domesticated. With this word Howe was able to understand why he had never been able to communicate to Tertan the value of a single criticism or correction of his wild, verbose themes. Their conferences had been frequent and long but had done nothing to reduce to order the splendid confusion of the boy's ideas. Yet, impossible though its expression was, Tertan's incandescent mind could always strike for a moment into some dark corner of thought.

And now it was suddenly apparent that it was not a faulty rhetoric that Howe had to contend with. With his new knowledge he looked at Tertan's face and wondered how he could have so long deceived himself. Tertan was still talking, and the class had lapsed into a kind of patient unconsciousness, a coma of respect for words which, for all that most of them knew, might be profound. Almost with a suffusion of shame, Howe believed that in some dim way the class had long ago had some intimation of Tertan's madness. He reached out as decisively as he could to

seize the thread of Tertan's discourse before it should be entangled further.

'Mr. Tertan says that the blame must be put upon whoever kills the joy of living in another. We have been assuming that Captain Alving was a wholly bad man, but what if we assume that he became bad only because Mrs. Alving, when they were first married, acted toward him in the prudish way she says she did?'

It was a ticklish idea to advance to freshmen and perhaps not profitable. Not all of them were following.

'That would put the blame on Mrs. Alving herself, whom most of you admire. And she herself seems to think so.' He glanced at his watch. The hour was nearly over. 'What do you think, Mr. De Witt?'

De Witt rose to the idea; he wanted to know if society couldn't be blamed for educating Mrs. Alving's temperament in the wrong way. Casebeer was puzzled, Stettenhover continued to look at his hands until the bell rang.

Tertan, his brows louring in thought, was making as always for a private word. Howe gathered his books and papers to leave quickly. At this moment of his discovery and with the knowledge still raw, he could not engage himself with Tertan. Tertan sucked in his breath to prepare for speech and Howe made ready for the pain and confusion. But at that moment Casebeer detached himself from the group with which he had been conferring and which he seemed to represent. His constituency remained at a tactful distance. The mission involved the time of an assigned essay. Casebeer's presentation of the plea—it was based on the freshmen's heavy duties at the fraternities during Carnival Week— cut across Tertan's preparations for speech. 'And so some of us fellows thought,' Casebeer concluded with heavy solemnity, 'that we could do a better job, give our minds to it more, if we had more time.'

Tertan regarded Casebeer with mingled curiosity and revulsion. Howe not only said that he would postpone the assignment but went on to talk about the Carnival, and even drew the waiting constituency into the conversation. He was conscious of Tertan's stern and astonished stare, then of his sudden departure.

Now that the fact was clear, Howe knew that he must act on it. His course was simple enough. He must lay the case before the Dean. Yet he hesitated. His feeling for Tertan must now, certainly, be in some way invalidated. Yet could he, because of a word, hurry to assign to official and reasonable solicitude what had been, until this moment, so various and warm? He could at least delay and, by moving slowly, lend a poor grace to the necessary, ugly act of making his report.

It was with some notion of keeping the matter in his own hands that he went to the Dean's office to look up Tertan's records. In the outer office the Dean's secretary greeted him brightly, and at his request brought him the manila folder with the small identifying photograph pasted in the corner. She laughed. 'He was looking for the birdie in the wrong place,' she said.

Howe leaned over her shoulder to look at the picture. It was as bad as all the Dean's-office photographs were, but it differed from all that Howe had ever seen. Tertan, instead of looking into the camera, as no doubt he had been bidden, had, at the moment of exposure, turned his eyes upward. His mouth, as though conscious of the trick played on the photographer, had the sly superior look that Howe knew.

The secretary was fascinated by the picture. 'What a funny boy,' she said. 'He looks like Tartuffe!'

And so he did, with the absurd piety of the eyes and the conscious slyness of the mouth and the whole face bloated by the bad lens.

'Is he *like* that?' the secretary said.

'Like Tartuffe? No.'

From the photograph there was little enough comfort to be had. The records themselves gave no clue to madness, though they suggested sadness enough. Howe read of a father, Stanislaus Tertan, born in Budapest and trained in engineering in Berlin, once employed by the Hercules Chemical Corporation—this was one of the factories that dominated the sound end of the town—but now without employment. He read of a mother Erminie (Youngfellow) Tertan, born in Manchester, educated at a Normal School at Leeds, now housewife by profession. The family lived on Greenbriar Street which Howe knew as a row of once elegant homes near what was now the factory district. The old mansion had long ago been divided into small and primitive apartments. Of Ferdinand himself there was little to learn. He lived with his parents, had attended a Detroit high school and had transferred to the local school in his last year. His rating for intelligence, as expressed in numbers, was high, his scholastic record was remarkable, he held a college scholarship for his tuition.

Howe laid the folder on the secretary's desk. 'Did you find what you wanted to know?' she asked.

The phrases from Tertan's momentous first theme came back to him. 'Tertan I am, but what is Tertan? Of this time, of that place, of some parentage, what does it matter?'

'No, I didn't find it,' he said.

Now that he had consulted the sad, half-meaningless record he knew all the more firmly that he must not give the matter out of his own hands. He must not release Tertan to authority. Not that he anticipated from the Dean anything but the greatest kindness for Tertan. The Dean would have the experience and skill which he himself could not have. One way or another the Dean could answer the question, 'What is Tertan?' Yet this was precisely what he feared. He alone could keep alive—not forever but for a somehow important time—the question, 'What is Tertan?' He alone could keep it still a question. Some sure instinct told him that he must not surrender the question to a clean official desk in a clear official light to be dealt with, settled and closed.

He heard himself saying, 'Is the Dean busy at the moment? I'd like to see him.'

His request came thus unbidden, even forbidden, and it was one of the surprising and startling incidents of his life. Later when he reviewed the events, so disconnected in themselves, or so merely odd, of the story that unfolded for him that year, it was over this moment, on its face the least notable, that he paused longest. It was frequently to be with fear and never without a certainty of its meaning in his own knowledge of himself that he would recall this simple, routine request, and the feeling of shame and freedom it gave him as he sent everything down the official chute. In the end, of course, no matter what he did to 'protect' Tertan, he would have had to make the same request and lay the matter on the Dean's clean desk. But it would always be a landmark of his life that, at the very moment when he was rejecting the official way, he had been, without will or intention, so gladly drawn to it.

After the storm's last delicate flurry, the sun had come out. Reflected by the new snow, it filled the office with a golden light which was almost musical in the way it made all the commonplace objects of efficiency shine with a sudden sad and noble significance. And the light, now that he noticed it, made the utterance of his perverse and unwanted request even more momentous.

The secretary consulted the engagement pad. 'He'll be free any minute. Don't you want to wait in the parlor?'

She threw open the door of the large and pleasant room in which the Dean held his Committee meetings, and in which his visitors waited. It was designed with a homely elegance on the masculine side of the eighteenth-century manner. There was a small coal fire in the grate and the handsome mahogany table was strewn with books and magazines. The large windows gave on the snowy lawn, and there was such a fine width of window that the white casements and walls seemed at this moment but a continuation of the snow, the snow but an extension of casement and walls. The outdoors seemed taken in and made safe, the indoors seemed luxuriously freshened and expanded.

Howe sat down by the fire and lighted a cigarette. The room had its intended effect upon him. He felt comfortable and relaxed, yet nicely organized, some young diplomatic agent of the eighteenth century, the newly fledged Swift carrying out Sir William Temple's business. The rawness of Tertan's case quite vanished. He crossed his legs and reached for a magazine.

It was that famous issue of *Life and Letters* that his idle hand had found and his blood raced as he sifted through it, and the shape of his own name, Joseph Howe, sprang out at him, still cabalistic in its power. He tossed the magazine back on the table as the door of the Dean's office opened and the Dean ushered out Theodore Blackburn.

'Ah, Joseph!' the Dean said.

Blackburn said, 'Good morning, Doctor.' Howe winced at the title and caught the flicker of amusement over the Dean's face. The Dean stood with his hand high on the door-jamb and Blackburn, still in the doorway, remained standing almost under the long arm.

Howe nodded briefly to Blackburn, snubbing his eager deference. 'Can you give me a few minutes?' he said to the Dean.

'All the time you want. Come in.' Before the two men could enter the office, Blackburn claimed their attention with a long full 'er.' As they turned to him, Blackburn said, 'Can *you* give *me* a few minutes, Doctor Howe?' His eyes sparkled at the little audacity he had committed, the slightly impudent play with hierarchy. Of the three of them Blackburn kept himself the lowest, but he reminded Howe of his subaltern relation to the Dean.

'I mean, of course,' Blackburn went on easily, 'when you've finished with the Dean.'

'I'll be in my office shortly,' Howe said, turned his back on the ready 'Thank you, sir,' and followed the Dean into the inner room.

'Energetic boy,' said the Dean. 'A bit beyond himself but very energetic. Sit down.'

The Dean lighted a cigarette, leaned back in his chair, sat easy and silent for a moment, giving Howe no signal to go ahead with business. He was a young Dean, not much beyond forty, a tall handsome man with sad, ambitious eyes. He had been a Rhodes scholar. His friends looked for great things from him, and it was generally said that he had notions of education which he was not yet ready to try to put into practice.

His relaxed silence was meant as a compliment to Howe. He smiled and said, 'What's the business, Joseph?'

'Do you know Tertan—Ferdinand Tertan, a freshman?'

The Dean's cigarette was in his mouth and his hands were clasped behind his head. He did not seem to search his memory for the name. He said, 'What about him?'

Clearly the Dean knew something, and he was waiting for Howe to tell him more. Howe moved only tentatively. Now that he was doing what he had resolved not to do, he felt more guilty at having been so long deceived by Tertan and more need to be loyal to his error.

'He's a strange fellow,' he ventured. He said stubbornly, 'In a strange way he's very brilliant.' He concluded, 'But very strange.'

The springs of the Dean's swivel chair creaked as he came out of his sprawl and leaned forward to Howe. 'Do you mean he's so strange that it's something you could give a name to?'

Howe looked at him stupidly. 'What do you mean?' he said.

'What's his trouble?' the Dean said more neutrally.

'He's very brilliant, in a way. I looked him up and he has a top intelligence rating. But somehow, and it's hard to explain just how, what he says is always on the edge of sense and doesn't quite make it.'

The Dean looked at him and Howe flushed up. The Dean had surely read Woolley on the subject of 'the Howes' and the *tour d'ivresse*. Was that quick glance ironical?

The Dean picked up some papers from his desk, and Howe could see that they were in Tertan's impatient scrawl. Perhaps the little gleam in the Dean's glance had come only from putting facts together.

'He sent me this yesterday,' the Dean said. 'After an interview I had with him. I haven't been able to do more than glance at it. When you said what you did, I realized there was something wrong.'

Twisting his mouth, the Dean looked over the letter. 'You seem to be involved,' he said without looking up. 'By the way, what did you give him at mid-term?'

Flushing, setting his shoulders, Howe said firmly, 'I gave him A-minus.'

The Dean chuckled. 'Might be a good idea if some of our nicer boys went crazy —just a little.' He said, 'Well,' to conclude the matter and handed the papers to Howe. 'See if this is the same thing you've been finding. Then we can go into the matter again.'

Before the fire in the parlor, in the chair that Howe had been occupying, sat Blackburn. He sprang to his feet as Howe entered.

'I said my office, Mr. Blackburn.' Howe's voice was sharp. Then he was almost sorry for the rebuke, so clearly and naively did Blackburn seem to relish his stay in the parlor, close to authority.

'I'm in a bit of a hurry, sir,' he said, 'and I did want to be sure to speak to you, sir.'

He was really absurd, yet fifteen years from now he would have grown up to himself, to the assurance and mature beefiness. In banks, in consular offices, in brokerage firms, on the bench, more seriously affable, a little sterner, he would make use of his ability to be administered by his job. It was almost reassuring. Now he was exercising his too-great skill on Howe. 'I owe you an apology, sir,' he said.

Howe knew that he did, but he showed surprise.

'I mean, Doctor, after your having been

so kind about letting me attend your class, I stopped coming.' He smiled in deprecation. 'Extracurricular activities take up so much of my time. I'm afraid I undertook more than I could perform.'

Howe had noticed the absence and had been a little irritated by it after Blackburn's elaborate plea. It was an absence that might be interpreted as a comment on the teacher. But there was only one way for him to answer. 'You've no need to apologize,' he said. 'It's wholly your affair.'

Blackburn beamed. 'I'm so glad you feel that way about it, sir. I was worried you might think I had stayed away because I was influenced by—' he stopped and lowered his eyes.

Astonished, Howe said, 'Influenced by what?'

'Well, by—' Blackburn hesitated and for answer pointed to the table on which lay the copy of *Life and Letters*. Without looking at it, he knew where to direct his hand. 'By the unfavorable publicity, sir.' He hurried on. 'And that brings me to another point, sir. I am secretary of Quill and Scroll, sir, the student literary society, and I wonder if you would address us. You could read your own poetry, sir, and defend your own point of view. It would be very interesting.'

It was truly amazing. Howe looked long and cruelly into Blackburn's face, trying to catch the secret of the mind that could have conceived this way of manipulating him, this way so daring and inept— but not entirely inept—with its malice so without malignity. The face did not yield its secret. Howe smiled broadly and said, 'Of course I don't think you were influenced by the unfavorable publicity.'

'I'm still going to take—regularly, for credit—your romantic poets course next term,' Blackburn said.

'Don't worry, my dear fellow, don't worry about it.'

Howe started to leave and Blackburn stopped him with, 'But about Quill, sir?'

'Suppose we wait until next term? I'll be less busy then.'

And Blackburn said, 'Very good, sir, and thank you.'

In his office the little encounter seemed less funny to Howe, was even in some indeterminate way disturbing. He made an effort to put it from his mind by turning to what was sure to disturb him more, the Tertan letter read in the new interpretation. He found what he had always found, the same florid leaps beyond fact and meaning, the same headlong certainty. But as his eye passed over the familiar scrawl it caught his own name, and for the second time that hour he felt the race of his blood.

'The Paraclete,' Tertan had written to the Dean, 'from a Greek word meaning to stand in place of, but going beyond the primitive idea to mean traditionally the helper, the one who comforts and assists, cannot without fundamental loss be jettisoned. Even if taken no longer in the supernatural sense, the concept remains deeply in the human consciousness inevitably. Humanitarianism is no reply, for not every man stands in the place of every other man for this other comrade's comfort. But certain are chosen out of the human race to be the consoler of some other. Of these, for example, is Joseph Barker Howe, Ph.D. Of intellects not the first yet of true intellect and lambent instructions, given to that which is intuitive and irrational, not to what is logical in the strict word, what is judged by him is of the heart and not the head. Here is one chosen, in that he chooses himself to stand in the place of another for comfort and consolation. To him more than another I

give my gratitude, with all respect to our Dean who reads this, a noble man, but merely dedicated, not consecrated. But not in the aspect of the Paraclete only is Dr. Joseph Barker Howe established, for he must be the Paraclete to another aspect of himself, that which is driven and persecuted by the lack of understanding in the world at large, so that he in himself embodies the full history of man's tribulations and, overflowing upon others, notably the present writer, is the ultimate end.'

This was love. There was no escape from it. Try as Howe might to remember that Tertan was mad and all his emotions invalidated, he could not destroy the effect upon him of his student's stern, affectionate regard. He had betrayed not only a power of mind but a power of love. And, however firmly he held before his attention the fact of Tertan's madness, he could do nothing to banish the physical sensation of gratitude he felt. He had never thought of himself as 'driven and persecuted' and he did not now. But, still he could not make meaningless his sensation of gratitude. The pitiable Tertan sternly pitied him, and comfort came from Tertan's never-to-be-comforted mind.

III

In an academic community, even an efficient one, official matters move slowly. The term drew to a close with no action in the case of Tertan, and Joseph Howe had to confront a curious problem. How should he grade his strange student, Tertan?

Tertan's final examination had been no different from all his other writing, and what did one 'give' such a student? De Witt must have his A, that was clear. Johnson would get a B. With Casebeer it was a question of a B-minus or a C-plus, and Stettenhover, who had been crammed by the team tutor to fill half a blue-book with his thin feminine scrawl, would have his C-minus which he would accept with mingled indifference and resentment. But with Tertan it was not so easy.

The boy was still in the college process and his name could not be omitted from the grade sheet. Yet what should a mind under suspicion of madness be graded? Until the medical verdict was given, it was for Howe to continue as Tertan's teacher and to keep his judgment pedagogical. Impossible to give him an F: he had not failed. B was for Johnson's stolid mediocrity. He could not be put on the edge of passing with Stettenhover, for he exactly did not pass. In energy and richness of intellect he was perhaps even De Witte's superior, and Howe toyed grimly with the notion of giving him an A, but that would lower the value of the A De Witt had won with his beautiful and clear, if still arrogant, mind. There was a notation which the Registrar recognized—Inc., for Incomplete, and in the horrible comedy of the situation, Howe considered that. But really only a mark of M for Mad would serve.

In his perplexity, Howe sought the Dean, but the Dean was out of town. In the end, he decided to maintain the A-minus he had given Tertan at mid-term. After all, there had been no falling away from that quality. He entered it on the grade sheet with something like bravado.

Academic time moves quickly. A college year is not really a year, lacking as it does three months. And it is endlessly divided into units which, at their beginning, appear larger than they are—terms, half-terms, months, weeks. And the ultimate unit, the hour, is not really an hour, lacking as it does ten minutes. And so the new term advanced rapidly, and one day the

fields about the town were all brown, cleared of even the few thin patches of snow which had lingered so long.

Howe, as he lectured on the romantic poets, became conscious of Blackburn emanating wrath. Blackburn did it well, did it with enormous dignity. He did not stir in his seat, he kept his eyes fixed on Howe in perfect attention, but he abstained from using his notebook, there was no mistaking what he proposed to himself as an attitude. His elbow on the writing-wing of the chair, his chin on the curled fingers of his hand, he was the embodiment of intellectual indignation. He was thinking his own thoughts, would give no public offense, yet would claim his due, was not to be intimidated. Howe knew that he would present himself at the end of the hour.

Blackburn entered the office without invitation. He did not smile; there was no cajolery about him. Without invitation he sat down beside Howe's desk. He did not speak until he had taken the blue-book from his pocket. He said, 'What does this mean, sir?'

It was a sound and conservative student tactic. Said in the usual way it meant, 'How could you have so misunderstood me?' or 'What does this mean for my future in the course?' But there were none of the humbler tones in Blackburn's way of saying it.

Howe made the established reply, 'I think that's for you to tell me.'

Blackburn continued icy. 'I'm sure I can't, sir.'

There was a silence between them. Both dropped their eyes to the blue-book on the desk. On its cover Howe had penciled: 'F. This is very poor work.'

Howe picked up the blue-book. There was always the possibility of injustice. The teacher may be bored by the mass of papers and not wholly attentive. A phrase, even the student's handwriting, may irritate him unreasonably. 'Well,' said Howe, 'Let's go through it.'

He opened the first page. 'Now here: you write, "In *The Ancient Mariner,* Coleridge lives in and transports us to a honey-sweet world where all is rich and strange, a world of charm to which we can escape from the humdrum existence of our daily lives, the world of romance. Here, in this warm and honey-sweet land of charming dreams we can relax and enjoy ourselves." '

Howe lowered the paper and waited with a neutral look for Blackburn to speak. Blackburn returned the look boldly, did not speak, sat stolid and lofty. At last Howe said, speaking gently, 'Did you mean that, or were you just at a loss for something to say?'

'You imply that I was just "bluffing"?' The quotation marks hung palpable in the air about the word.

'I'd like to know. I'd prefer believing that you were bluffing to believing that you really thought this.'

Blackburn's eyebrows went up. From the height of a great and firm-based idea he looked at his teacher. He clasped the crags for a moment and then pounced, craftily, suavely. 'Do you mean, Doctor Howe, that there aren't two opinions possible?'

It was superbly done in its air of putting all of Howe's intellectual life into the balance. Howe remained patient and simple. 'Yes, many opinions are possible, but not this one. Whatever anyone believes of *The Ancient Mariner,* no one can in reason believe that it represents a—a honey-sweet world in which we can relax.'

'But that is what I *feel,* sir.'

This was well-done, too. Howe said, 'Look, Mr. Blackburn. Do you really relax with hunger and thirst, the heat and the sea-serpents, the dead men with staring eyes, Life in Death and the skeletons? Come now, Mr. Blackburn.'

Blackburn made no answer, and Howe pressed forward. 'Now, you say of Wordsworth, "Of peasant stock himself, he turned from the effete life of the salons and found in the peasant the hope of a flaming revolution which would sweep away all the old ideas. This is the subject of his best poems." '

Beaming at his teacher with youthful eagerness, Blackburn said, 'Yes, sir, a rebel, a bringer of light to suffering mankind. I see him as a kind of Prothemeus.'

'A kind of what?'

'Prothemeus, sir.'

'Think, Mr. Blackburn. We were talking about him only today and I mentioned his name a dozen times. You don't mean Prothemeus. You mean—' Howe waited, but there was no response.

'You mean Prometheus.'

Blackburn gave no assent, and Howe took the reins. 'You've done a bad job here, Mr. Blackburn, about as bad as could be done.' He saw Blackburn stiffen and his genial face harden again. 'It shows either a lack of preparation or a complete lack of understanding.' He saw Blackburn's face begin to go to pieces and he stopped.

'Oh, sir,' Blackburn burst out, 'I've never had a mark like this before, never anything below a B, never. A thing like this has never happened to me before.'

It must be true, it was a statement too easily verified. Could it be that other instructors accepted such flaunting nonsense? Howe wanted to end the interview. 'I'll set it down to lack of preparation,' he said. 'I know you're busy. That's not an excuse, but it's an explanation. Now, suppose you really prepare, and then take another quiz in two weeks. We'll forget this one and count the other.'

Blackburn squirmed with pleasure and gratitude. 'Thank you, sir. You're really very kind, very kind.'

Howe rose to conclude the visit. 'All right, then—in two weeks.'

It was that day that the Dean imparted to Howe the conclusion of the case of Tertan. It was simple and a little anti-climactic. A physician had been called in, and had said the word, given the name.

'A classic case, he called it,' the Dean said. 'Not a doubt in the world,' he said. His eyes were full of miserable pity, and he clutched at a word. 'A classic case, a classic case.' To his aid and to Howe's there came the Parthenon and the form of the Greek drama, the Aristotelian logic, Racine and the Well-Tempered Clavichord, the blueness of the Aegean and its clear sky. Classic—that is to say, without a doubt, perfect in its way, a veritable model, and, as the Dean had been told, sure to take a perfectly predictable and inevitable course to a foreknown conclusion.

It was not only pity that stood in the Dean's eyes. For a moment there was fear too. 'Terrible,' he said, 'it is simply terrible.'

Then he went on briskly. 'Naturally, we've told the boy nothing. And, naturally, we won't. His tuition's paid by his scholarship, and we'll continue him on the rolls until the end of the year. That will be kindest. After that the matter will be out of our control. We'll see, of course, that he gets into the proper hands. I'm told there will be no change, he'll go on like this, be as good as this, for four to six months. And so we'll just go along as usual.'

So Tertan continued to sit in Section 5 of English 1A, to his classmates still a figure of curiously dignified fun, symbol to most

of them of the respectable but absurd intellectual life. But to his teacher he was now very different. He had not changed—he was still the greyhound casting for the scent of ideas, and Howe could see that he was still the same Tertan, but he could not feel it. What he felt as he looked at the boy sitting in his accustomed place was the hard blank of a fact. The fact itself was formidable and depressing. But what Howe was chiefly aware of was that he had permitted the metamorphosis of Tertan from person to fact.

As much as possible he avoided seeing Tertan's upraised hand and eager eye. But the fact did not know of its mere factuality, it continued its existence as if it were Tertan, hand up and eye questioning, and one day it appeared in Howe's office with a document.

'Even the spirit who lives egregiously, above the herd, must have its relations with the fellowman,' Tertan declared. He laid the document on Howe's desk. It was headed 'Quill and Scroll Society of Dwight College. Application for Membership.'

'In most ways these are crass minds,' Tertan said, touching the paper. 'Yet as a whole, bound together in their common love of letters, they transcend their intellectual lacks since it is not a paradox that the whole is greater than the sum of its parts.'

'When are the elections?' Howe asked.

'They take place tomorrow.'

'I certainly hope you will be successful.'

'Thank you. Would you wish to implement that hope?' A rather dirty finger pointed to the bottom of the sheet. 'A faculty recommender is necessary,' Tertan said stiffly, and waited.

'And you wish me to recommend you?'

'It would be an honor.'

'You may use my name.'

Tertan's finger pointed again. 'It must be a written sponsorship, signed by the sponsor.' There was a large blank space on the form under the heading, 'Opinion of Faculty Sponsor.'

This was almost another thing and Howe hesitated. Yet there was nothing else to do and he took out his fountain pen. He wrote, 'Mr. Ferdinand Tertan is marked by his intense devotion to letters and by his exceptional love of all things of the mind.' To this he signed his name, which looked bold and assertive on the white page. It disturbed him, the strange affirming power of a name. With a businesslike air, Tertan whipped up the paper, folding it with decision, and put it into his pocket. He bowed and took his departure, leaving Howe with the sense of having done something oddly momentous.

And so much now seemed odd and momentous to Howe that should not have seemed so. It was odd and momentous, he felt, when he sat with Blackburn's second quiz before him, and wrote in an excessively firm hand the grade of C-minus. The paper was a clear, an indisputable failure. He was carefully and consciously committing a cowardice. Blackburn had told the truth when he had pleaded his past record. Howe had consulted it in the Dean's office. It showed no grade lower than a B-minus. A canvass of some of Blackburn's previous instructors had brought vague attestations to the adequate powers of a student imperfectly remembered, and sometimes surprise that his abilities could be questioned at all.

As he wrote the grade, Howe told himself that his cowardice sprang from an unwillingness to have more dealings with a student he disliked. He knew it was simpler than that. He knew he feared Blackburn: that was the absurd truth. And

cowardice did not solve the matter after all. Blackburn, flushed with a first success, attacked at once. The minimal passing grade had not assuaged his feelings and he sat at Howe's desk and again the blue-book lay between them. Blackburn said nothing. With an enormous impudence, he was waiting for Howe to speak and explain himself.

At last Howe said sharply and rudely, 'Well?' His throat was tense and the blood was hammering in his head. His mouth was tight with anger at himself for his disturbance.

Blackburn's glance was almost baleful. 'This is impossible, sir.'

'But there it is,' Howe answered.

'Sir?' Blackburn had not caught the meaning but his tone was still haughty.

Impatiently Howe said, 'There it is, plain as day. Are you here to complain again?'

'Indeed I am, sir.' There was surprise in Blackburn's voice that Howe should ask the question.

'I shouldn't complain if I were you. You did a thoroughly bad job on your first quiz. This one is a little, only a very little, better.' This was not true. If anything, it was worse.

'That might be a matter of opinion, sir.'

'It is a matter of opinion. Of my opinion.'

'Another opinion might be different, sir.'

'You really believe that?' Howe said.

'Yes.' The omission of the 'sir' was monumental.

'Whose, for example?'

'The Dean's, for example.' Then the fleshy jaw came forward a little. 'Or a certain literary critic's, for example.'

It was colossal and almost too much for Blackburn himself to handle. The solidity of his face almost crumpled under it. But he withstood his own audacity and went on. 'And the Dean's opinion might be guided by the knowledge that the person who gave me this mark is the man whom a famous critic, the most eminent judge of literature in this country, called a drunken man. The Dean might think twice about whether such a man is fit to teach Dwight students.'

Howe said in quiet admonition, 'Blackburn, you're mad,' meaning no more than to check the boy's extravagance.

But Blackburn paid no heed. He had another shot in the locker. 'And the Dean might be guided by the information, of which I have evidence, documentary evidence,'—he slapped his breast pocket twice —'that this same person personally recommended to the college literary society, the oldest in the country, that he personally recommended a student who is crazy, who threw the meeting into an uproar—a psychiatric case. The Dean might take that into account.'

Howe was never to learn the details of that 'uproar.' He had always to content himself with the dim but passionate picture which at that moment sprang into his mind, of Tertan standing on some abstract height and madly denouncing the multitude of Quill and Scroll who howled him down.

He sat quiet a moment and looked at Blackburn. The ferocity had entirely gone from the student's face. He sat regarding his teacher almost benevolently. He had played a good card and now, scarcely at all unfriendly, he was waiting to see the effect. Howe took up the blue-book and negligently sifted through it. He read a page, closed the book, struck out the C-minus and wrote an F.

'Now you may take the paper to the Dean,' he said. 'You may tell him that after reconsidering it, I lowered the grade.'

The gasp was audible. 'Oh, sir!' Blackburn cried. 'Please!' His face was agonized. 'It means my graduation, my livelihood, my future. Don't do this to me.'

'It's done already.'

Blackburn stood up. 'I spoke rashly, sir, hastily. I had no intention, no real intention, of seeing the Dean. it rests with you —entirely, entirely. I *hope* you will restore the first mark.'

'Take the matter to the Dean or not, just as you choose. The grade is what you deserve and it stands.'

Blackburn's head dropped. 'And will I be failed at mid-term, sir?'

'Of course.'

From deep out of Blackburn's great chest rose a cry of anguish. 'Oh, sir, if you want me to go down on my knees to you, I will, I will.'

Howe looked at him in amazement.

'I will, I will. On my knees, sir. This mustn't, mustn't happen.'

He spoke so literally, meaning so very truly that his knees and exactly his knees were involved and seeming to think that he was offering something of tangible value to his teacher, that Howe, whose head had become icy clear in the nonsensical drama, thought, 'The boy is mad,' and began to speculate fantastically whether something in himself attracted or developed aberration. He could see himself standing absurdly before the Dean and saying, 'I've found another. This time it's the vice-president of the Council, the manager of the debating team and secretary of Quill and Scroll.'

One more such discovery, he thought, and he himself would be discovered! And there, suddenly, Blackburn was on his knees with a thump, his huge thighs straining his trousers, his hand outstretched in a great gesture of supplication.

With a cry, Howe shoved back his swivel chair and it rolled away on its casters half across the little room. Blackburn knelt for a moment to nothing at all, then got to his feet.

Howe rose abruptly. He said, 'Blackburn, you will stop acting like an idiot. Dust your knees off, take your paper and get out. You've behaved like a fool and a malicious person. You have half a term to do a decent job. Keep your silly mouth shut and try to do it. Now get out.'

Blackburn's head was low. He raised it and there was a pious light in his eyes. 'Will you shake hands, sir?' he said. He thrust out his hand.

'I will not,' Howe said.

Head and hand sank together. Blackburn picked up his blue-book and walked to the door. He turned and said, 'Thank you, sir.' His back, as he departed, was heavy with tragedy and stateliness.

IV

After years of bad luck with the weather, the College had a perfect day for Commencement. It was wonderfully bright, the air so transparent, the wind so brisk that no one could resist talking about it.

As Howe set out for the campus he heard Hilda calling from the back yard. She called, 'Professor, professor,' and came running to him.

Howe said, 'What's this "professor" business?'

'Mother told me,' Hilda said. 'You've been promoted. And I want to take your picture.'

'Next year,' said Howe. 'I won't be a professor until next year. And you know better than to call anybody "professor."'

'It was just in fun,' Hilda said. She seemed disappointed.

'But you can take my picture if you want. I won't look much different next year.' Still, it was frightening. It might mean that he was to stay in this town all his life.

Hilda brightened. 'Can I take it in this?' she said, and touched the gown he carried over his arm.

Howe laughed. 'Yes, you can take it in this.'

'I'll get my things and meet you in front of Otis,' Hilda said. 'I have the background all picked out.'

On the campus the Commencement crowd was already large. It stood about in eager, nervous little family groups. As he crossed, Howe was greeted by a student, capped and gowned, glad of the chance to make an event for his parents by introducing one of his teachers. It was while Howe stood there chatting that he saw Tertan.

He had never seen anyone quite so alone, as though a circle had been woven about him to separate him from the gay crowd on the campus. Not that Tertan was not gay, he was the gayest of all. Three weeks had passed since Howe had last seen him, the weeks of examination, the lazy week before Commencement, and this was now a different Tertan. On his head he wore a panama hat, broad-brimmed and fine, of the shape associated with South American planters. He wore a suit of raw silk, luxurious, but yellowed with age and much too tight, and he sported a whangee cane. He walked sedately, the hat tilted at a devastating angle, the stick coming up and down in time to his measured tread. He had, Howe guessed, outfitted himself to greet the day in the clothes of that ruined father whose existence was on record in the Dean's office. Gravely and arrogantly he surveyed the scene—in it, his whole bearing seemed to say, but not of it. With his haughty step, with his flashing eye, Tertan was coming nearer. Howe did not wish to be seen. He shifted his position slightly. When he looked again, Tertan was not in sight.

The chapel clock struck the quarter hour. Howe detached himself from his chat and hurried to Otis Hall at the far end of the campus. Hilda had not yet come. He went up into the high portico and, using the glass of the door for a mirror, put on his gown, adjusted the hood on his shoulders and set the mortarboard on his head. When he came down the steps, Hilda had arrived.

Nothing could have told him more forcibly that a year had passed than the development of Hilda's photographic possessions from the box camera of the previous fall. By a strap about her neck was hung a leather case, so thick and strong, so carefully stitched and so molded to its contents that it could only hold a costly camera. The appearance was deceptive, Howe knew, for he had been present at the Aikens' pre-Christmas conference about its purchase. It was only a fairly good domestic camera. Still, it looked very impressive. Hilda carried another leather case from which she drew a collapsible tripod. Decisively she extended each of its gleaming legs and set it up on the path. She removed the camera from its case and fixed it to the tripod. In its compact efficiency the camera almost had a life of its own, but Hilda treated it with easy familiarity, looked into its eye, glanced casually at its gauges. Then from a pocket she took still another leather case and drew from it a small instrument through which she looked first at Howe, who began to feel inanimate and lost, and then at the sky. She made some adjustment on the instrument, then some adjustment on the camera. She swept the scene with her eye, found a spot and pointed the camera in its direction. She walked to the spot, stood on it and beckoned to Howe. With each new leather case, with each new instrument, and with each new adjustment she had grown in ease and now she said, 'Joe, will you stand here?'

Obediently Howe stood where he was bidden. She had yet another instrument. She took out a tape-measure on a mechanical spool. Kneeling down before Howe, she put the little metal ring of the tape under the tip of his shoe. At her request, Howe pressed it with his toe. When she had measured her distance, she nodded to Howe who released the tape. At a touch, it sprang back into the spool. 'You have to be careful if you're going to get what you want,' Hilda said. 'I don't believe in all this snap-snap-snapping,' she remarked loftily. Howe nodded in agreement, although he was beginning to think Hilda's care excessive.

Now at last the moment had come. Hilda squinted into the camera, moved the tripod slightly. She stood to the side, holding the plunger of the shutter-cable. 'Ready,' she said. 'Will you relax, Joseph, please?' Howe realized that he was standing frozen. Hilda stood poised and precise as a setter, one hand holding the little cable, the other extended with curled dainty fingers like a dancer's, as if expressing to her subject the precarious delicacy of the moment. She pressed the plunger and there was the click. At once she stirred to action, got behind the camera, turned a new exposure. 'Thank you,' she said. 'Would you stand under that tree and let me do a character study with light and shade?'

[323]

The childish absurdity of the remark restored Howe's ease. He went to the little tree. The pattern the leaves made on his gown was what Hilda was after. He had just taken a satisfactory position when he heard in the unmistakable voice, 'Ah, Doctor! Having your picture taken?'

Howe gave up the pose and turned to Blackburn who stood on the walk, his hands behind his back, a little too large for his bachelor's gown. Annoyed that Blackburn should see him posing for a character study in light and shade, Howe said irritably, 'Yes, having my picture taken.'

Blackburn beamed at Hilda. 'And the little photographer?' he said. Hilda fixed her eyes on the ground and stood closer to her brilliant and aggressive camera. Blackburn, teetering on his heels, his hands behind his back, wholly prelatical and benignly patient, was not abashed at the silence. At last Howe said, 'If you'll excuse us, Mr. Blackburn, we'll go on with the picture.'

'Go right ahead, sir. I'm running along.' But he only came closer. 'Doctor Howe,' he said fervently, 'I want to tell you how glad I am that I was able to satisfy your standards at last.'

Howe was surprised at the hard, insulting brightness of his own voice, and even Hilda looked up curiously as he said, 'Nothing you have ever done has satisfied me, and nothing you could ever do would satisfy me, Blackburn.'

With a glance at Hilda, Blackburn made a gesture as if to hush Howe—as though all his former bold malice had taken for granted a kind of understanding between himself and his teacher, a secret which must not be betrayed to a third person. 'I only meant, sir,' he said, 'that I was able to pass your course after all.'

Howe said, 'You didn't pass my course. I passed you out of my course. I passed you without even reading your paper. I wanted to be sure the college would be rid of you. And when all the grades were in and I did read your paper, I saw I was right not to have read it first.'

Blackburn presented a stricken face. 'It was very bad, sir?'

But Howe had turned away. The paper had been fantastic. The paper had been, if he wished to see it so, mad. It was at this moment that the Dean came up behind Howe and caught his arm. 'Hello, Joseph,' he said. 'We'd better be getting along, it's almost late.'

He was not a familiar man, but when he saw Blackburn, who approached to greet him, he took Blackburn's arm, too. 'Hello, Theodore,' he said. Leaning forward on Howe's arm and on Blackburn's, he said, 'Hello, Hilda dear.' Hilda replied quietly, 'Hello, Uncle George.'

Still clinging to their arms, still linking Howe and Blackburn, the Dean said, 'Another year gone, Joe, and we've turned out another crop. After you've been here a few years, you'll find it reasonably upsetting—you wonder how there can be so many graduating classes while you stay the same. But of course you don't stay the same.' Then he said, 'Well,' sharply, to dismiss the thought. He pulled Blackburn's arm and swung him around to Howe. 'Have you heard about Teddy Blackburn?' he asked. 'He has a job already, before graduation—the first man of his class to be placed.' Expectant of congratulations, Blackburn beamed at Howe. Howe remained silent.

'Isn't that good?' the Dean said. Still Howe did not answer and the Dean, puzzled and put out, turned to Hilda. 'That's a very fine-looking camera, Hilda.' She touched it with affectionate pride.

'Instruments of precision,' said a voice. 'Instruments of precision.' Of the three with joined arms, Howe was the nearest to Tertan, whose gaze took in all the scene except the smile and the nod which Howe gave him. The boy leaned on his cane. The broad-brimmed hat, canting jauntily over his eye, confused the image of his face that Howe had established, suppressed the rigid lines of the ascetic and brought out the baroque curves. It made an effect of perverse majesty.

'Instruments of precision,' said Tertan for the last time, addressing no one, making a casual comment to the universe. And it occurred to Howe that Tertan might not be referring to Hilda's equipment. The sense of the thrice-woven circle of the boy's loneliness smote him fiercely. Tertan stood in majestic jauntiness, superior to all the scene, but his isolation made Howe ache with a pity of which Tertan was more the cause than the object, so general and indiscriminate was it.

Whether in his sorrow he made some unintended movement toward Tertan which the Dean checked, or whether the suddenly tightened grip on his arm was the Dean's own sorrow and fear, he did not know. Tertan watched them in the incurious way people watch a photograph being taken, and suddenly the thought that, to the boy, it must seem that the three were posing for a picture together made Howe detach himself almost rudely from the Dean's grasp.

'I promised Hilda another picture,' he announced—needlessly, for Tertan was no longer there, he had vanished in the last sudden flux of visitors who, now that the band had struck up, were rushing nervously to find seats.

'You'd better hurry,' the Dean said. 'I'll go along, it's getting late for me.' He departed and Blackburn walked stately by his side.

Howe again took his position under the little tree which cast its shadow over his face and gown. 'Just hurry, Hilda, won't you?' he said. Hilda held the cable at arm's length, her other arm crooked and her fingers crisped. She rose on her toes and said 'Ready,' and pressed the release. 'Thank you,' she said gravely and began to dismantle her camera as he hurried off to join the procession.

THE RICH BOY

by F. Scott Fitzgerald

BEGIN WITH AN INDIVIDUAL, and before you know it you find that you have created a type; begin with a type, and you find that you have created—nothing. That is because we are all queer fish, queerer behind our faces and voices than we want anyone to know or than we know ourselves. When I hear a man proclaiming himself an "average, honest, open fellow," I feel pretty sure that he has some definite and perhaps terrible abnormality which he has agreed to conceal—and his protestation of being average and honest and open is his way of reminding himself of his misprision.

There are no types, no plurals. There is

a rich boy, and this is his and not his brothers' story. All my life I have lived among his brothers but this one has been my friend. Besides, if I wrote about his brothers I should have to begin by attacking all the lies that the poor have told about the rich and the rich have told about themselves—such a wild structure they have erected that when we pick up a book about the rich, some instinct prepares us for unreality. Even the intelligent and impassioned reporters of life have made the country of the rich as unreal as fairyland.

Let me tell you about the very rich. They are different from you and me. They possess and enjoy early, and it does something to them, makes them soft where we are hard, and cynical where we are trustful, in a way that, unless you were born rich, it is difficult to understand. They think, deep in their hearts, that they are better than we are because we had to discover the compensations and refuges of life for ourselves. Even when they enter deep into our world or sink below us, they still think that they are better than we are. They are different. The only way I can describe young Anson Hunter is to approach him as if he were a foreigner and cling stubbornly to my point of view. If I accept his for a moment I am lost—I have nothing to show but a preposterous movie.

II

Anson was the eldest of six children who would some day divide a fortune of fifteen million dollars, and he reached the age of reason—is it seven?—at the beginning of the century when daring young women were already gliding along Fifth Avenue in electric "mobiles." In those days he and his brother had an English governess who spoke the language very clearly and crisply and well, so that the two boys grew to speak as she did—their words and sentences were all crisp and clear and not run together as ours are. They didn't talk exactly like English children but acquired an accent that is peculiar to fashionable people in the city of New York.

In the summer the six children were moved from the house on 71st Street to a big estate in northern Connecticut. It was not a fashionable locality—Anson's father wanted to delay as long as possible his children's knowledge of that side of life. He was a man somewhat superior to his class, which composed New York society, and to his period, which was the snobbish and formalized vulgarity of the Gilded Age, and he wanted his sons to learn habits of concentration and have sound constitutions and grow up into right-living and successful men. He and his wife kept an eye on them as well as they were able until the two older boys went away to school, but in huge establishments this is difficult—it was much simpler in the series of small and medium-sized houses in which my own youth was spent—I was never far out of the reach of my mother's voice, of the sense of her presence, her approval or disapproval.

Anson's first sense of his superiority came to him when he realized the half-grudging American deference that was paid to him in the Connecticut village. The parents of the boys he played with always inquired after his father and mother, and were vaguely excited when their own children were asked to the Hunters' house. He accepted this as the natural state of things, and a sort of impatience with all groups of which he was not the center—in money, in position, in authority—remained with him for the rest of his life. He disdained to struggle with other boys for precedence—he expected it to be given him freely, and when it wasn't he withdrew into his family. His family was sufficient, for in the East money is still a somewhat feudal thing, a clan-forming thing. In the snobbish West, money separates families to form "sets."

At eighteen, when he went to New Haven, Anson was tall and thick-set, with a clear complexion and a healthy color from the ordered life he had led in school. His hair was yellow and grew in a funny way on his head, his nose was beaked—these two things kept him from being handsome—but he had a confident charm and a certain brusque style, and the upper-class men who passed him on the street knew without being told that he was a rich boy and had gone to one of the best schools. Nevertheless, his very superiority kept him from being a success in college—the independence was mistaken for egotism, and the refusal to accept Yale standards with the proper awe seemed to belittle all those who had. So, long before he graduated, he began to shift the center of his life to New York.

He was at home in New York—there was his own house with "the kind of servants you can't get any more"—and his own family, of which, because of his good humor and a certain ability to make things go, he was rapidly becoming the center, and the débutante parties, and the correct manly world of the men's clubs, and the occasional wild spree with the gallant girls whom New Haven only knew from the fifth row. His aspirations were conventional enough—they included even the irreproachable shadow he would some day marry, but they differed from the aspirations of the majority of young men in that there was no mist over them, none of that quality which is variously known as "idealism" or "illusion." Anson accepted without reservation the world of high finance and high extravagance, of divorce and dis-

sipation, of snobbery and of privilege. Most of our lives end as a compromise—it was as a compromise that his life began.

He and I first met in the late summer of 1917 when he was just out of Yale, and, like the rest of us, was swept up into the systematized hysteria of the war. In the blue-green uniform of the naval aviation he came down to Pensacola, where the hotel orchestras played *I'm Sorry, Dear,* and we young officers danced with the girls. Everyone liked him, and though he ran with the drinkers and wasn't an especially good pilot, even the instructors treated him with a certain respect. He was always having long talks with them in his confident, logical voice—talks which ended by his getting himself, or, more frequently, another officer, out of some impending trouble. He was convivial, bawdy, robustly avid for pleasure, and we were all surprised when he fell in love with a conservative and rather proper girl.

Her name was Paula Legendre, a dark, serious beauty from somewhere in California. Her family kept a winter residence just outside of town, and in spite of her primness she was enormously popular; there is a large class of men whose egotism can't endure humor in a woman. But Anson wasn't that sort, and I couldn't understand the attraction of her "sincerity"—that was the thing to say about her—for his keen and somewhat sardonic mind.

Nevertheless, they fell in love—and on her terms. He no longer joined the twilight gathering at the De Soto bar, and whenever they were seen together they were engaged in a long, serious dialogue, which must have gone on several weeks. Long afterward he told me that it was not about anything in particular but was composed on both sides of immature and even meaningless statements—the emotional content that gradually came to fill it grew up not out of the words but out of its enormous seriousness. It was a sort of hypnosis. Often it was interrupted, giving way to that emasculated humor we call fun; when they were alone it was resumed again, solemn, low-keyed, and pitched so as to give each other a sense of unity in feeling and thought. They came to resent any interruptions of it, to be unresponsible to facetiousness about life, even to the mild cynicism of their contemporaries. They were only happy when the dialogue was going on, and its seriousness bathed them like the amber glow of an open fire. Toward the end there came an interruption they did not resent—it began to be interrupted by passion.

Oddly enough, Anson was as engrossed in the dialogue as she was and as profoundly affected by it, yet at the same time aware that on his side much was insincere, and on hers much was merely simple. At first, too, he despised her emotional simplicity as well, but with his love her nature deepened and blossomed, and he could despise it no longer. He felt that if he could enter into Paula's warm safe life he would be happy. The long preparation of the dialogue removed any constraint—he taught her some of what he had learned from more adventurous women, and she responded with a rapt holy intensity. One evening after a dance they agreed to marry, and he wrote a long letter about her to his mother. The next day Paula told him that she was rich, that she had a personal fortune of nearly a million dollars.

III

It was exactly as if they could say "Neither of us has anything: we shall be poor together"—just as delightful that they should be rich instead. It gave them the same communion of adventure. Yet when Anson got leave in April, and Paula and her mother accompanied him North, she was impressed with the standing of his family in New York and with the scale on which they lived. Alone with Anson for the first time in the rooms where he had played as a boy, she was filled with a comfortable emotion, as though she was pre-eminently safe and taken care of. The pictures of Anson in a skull cap at his first school, of Anson on horseback with the sweetheart of a mysterious forgotten summer, of Anson in a gay group of ushers and bridesmaids at a wedding, made her jealous of his life apart from her in the past, and so completely did his authoritative person seem to sum up and typify these possessions of his that she was inspired with the idea of being married immediately and returning to Pensacola as his wife.

But an immediate marriage wasn't discussed—even the engagement was to be secret until after the war. When she realized that only two days of his leave remained, her dissatisfaction crystallized in the intention of making him as unwilling to wait as she was. They were driving to the country for dinner and she determined to force the issue that night.

Now a cousin of Paula's was staying with them at the Ritz, a severe, bitter girl who loved Paula but was somewhat jealous of her impressive engagement, and as Paula was late in dressing, the cousin, who wasn't going to the party, received Anson in the parlor of the suite.

Anson had met friends at five o'clock and drunk freely and indiscreetly with them for an hour. He left the Yale Club at a proper time, and his mother's chauffeur drove him to the Ritz, but his usual capacity was not in evidence, and the impact of the steam-heated sitting-room made him suddenly dizzy. He knew it, and he was both amused and sorry.

Paula's cousin was twenty-five, but she was exceptionally naïve, and at first failed to realize what was up. She had never met Anson before, and she was surprised when he mumbled strange information and nearly fell off his chair, but until Paula appeared it didn't occur to her that what she had taken for the odor of a dry-cleaned uniform was really whiskey. But Paula understood as soon as she appeared; her only thought was to get Anson away before her mother saw him, and at the look in her eyes the cousin understood too.

When Paula and Anson descended to the limousine they found two men inside, both asleep; they were the men with whom he had been drinking at the Yale Club, and they were also going to the party. He had entirely forgotten their presence in the car. On the way to Hempstead they awoke and sang. Some of the songs were rough, and though Paula tried to reconcile herself to the fact that Anson had few verbal inhibitions, her lips tightened with shame and distaste.

Back at the hotel the cousin, confused and agitated, considered the incident, and then walked into Mrs. Legendre's bedroom, saying: "Isn't he funny?"

"Who is funny?"

"Why—Mr. Hunter. He seemed so funny."

Mrs. Legendre looked at her sharply.

"How is he funny?"

"Why, he said he was French. I didn't know he was French."

"That's absurd. You must have misunderstood." She smiled: "It was a joke."

The cousin shook her head stubbornly.

"No. He said he was brought up in France. He said he couldn't speak any English, and that's why he couldn't talk to me. And he couldn't!"

Mrs. Legendre looked away with impatience just as the cousin added thoughtfully, "Perhaps it was because he was so drunk," and walked out of the room.

This curious report was true. Anson, finding his voice thick and uncontrollable, had taken the unusual refuge of announcing that he spoke no English. Years afterward he used to tell that part of the story, and he invariably communicated the uproarious laughter which the memory aroused in him.

Five times in the next hour Mrs. Legendre tried to get Hempstead on the phone. When she succeeded, there was a ten-minute delay before she heard Paula's voice on the wire.

"Cousin Jo told me Anson was intoxicated."

"Oh, no. . . ."

"Oh, yes. Cousin Jo says he was intoxicated. He told her he was French, and fell off his chair and behaved as if he was very intoxicated. I don't want you to come home with him."

"Mother, he's all right! Please don't worry about—"

"But I do worry. I think it's dreadful. I want you to promise me not to come home with him."

"I'll take care of it, mother. . . ."

"I don't want you to come home with him."

"All right, mother. Good-by."

"Be sure now, Paula. Ask some one to bring you."

Deliberately Paula took the receiver from her ear and hung it up. Her face was flushed with helpless annoyance. Anson was stretched out asleep in a bedroom upstairs, while the dinner-party below was proceeding lamely toward conclusion.

The hour's drive had sobered him somewhat—his arrival was merely hilarious—and Paula hoped that the evening was not

spoiled, after all, but two imprudent cocktails before dinner completed the disaster.
He talked boisterously and somewhat of-
fensively to the party at large for fifteen
minutes, and then slid silently under the
table; like a man in an old print—but, unlike an old print, it was rather horrible
without being at all quaint. None of the
young girls present remarked upon the incident—it seemed to merit only silence.
His uncle and two other men carried him
upstairs, and it was just after this that
Paula was called to the phone.

An hour later Anson awoke in a fog of
nervous agony, through which he perceived after a moment the figure of his
Uncle Robert standing by the door.

". . . I said are you better?"

"What?"

"Do you feel better, old man?"

"Terrible," said Anson.

"I'm going to try you on another bromo-
seltzer. If you can hold it down, it'll do
you good to sleep."

With an effort Anson slid his legs from
the bed and stood up.

"I'm all right," he said dully.

"Take it easy."

"I thin' if you gave me a glassbrandy I
could go downstairs."

"Oh, no—"

"Yes, that's the only thin'. I'm all right
now. . . . I suppose I'm in Dutch dow'
there."

"They know you're a little under the
weather," said his uncle deprecatingly.
"But don't worry about it. Schuyler didn't
even get here. He passed away in the
locker-room over at the Links."

Indifferent to any opinion, except
Paula's, Anson was nevertheless determined to save the débris of the evening,
but when after a cold bath he made his
appearance most of the party had already
left. Paula got up immediately to go home.

In the limousine the old serious dialogue
began. She had known that he drank, she
admitted, but she had never expected anything like this—it seemed to her that perhaps they were not suited to each other,
after all. Their ideas about life were too
different, and so forth. When she finished
speaking, Anson spoke in turn, very soberly. Then Paula said she'd have to think
it over; she wouldn't decide tonight; she
was not angry but she was terribly sorry.
Nor would she let him come into the
hotel with her, but just before she got out
of the car she leaned and kissed him unhappily on the cheek.

The next afternoon Anson had a long
talk with Mrs. Legendre while Paula sat
listening in silence. It was agreed that
Paula was to brood over the incident for a
proper period and then, if mother and
daughter thought it best, they would follow Anson to Pensacola. On his part he
apologized with sincerity and dignity—
that was all; with every card in her hand
Mrs. Legendre was unable to establish
any advantage over him. He made no
promises, showed no humility, only delivered a few serious comments on life which
brought him off with rather a moral
superiority at the end. When they came
South three weeks later, neither Anson in
his satisfaction nor Paula in her relief at
the reunion realized that the psychological
moment had passed forever.

IV

He dominated and attracted her, and at
the same time filled her with anxiety. Confused by his mixture of solidity and self-
indulgence, of sentiment and cynicism—
incongruities which her gentle mind was
unable to resolve—Paula grew to think of
him as two alternating personalities. When
she saw him alone, or at a formal

party, or with his casual inferiors, she felt a tremendous pride in his strong, attractive presence, the paternal, understanding stature of his mind. In other company she became uneasy when what had been a fine imperviousness to mere gentility showed its other face. The other face was gross, humorous, reckless of everything but pleasure. It startled her mind temporarily away from him, even led her into a short covert experiment with an old beau, but it was no use—after four months of Anson's enveloping vitality there was an anæmic pallor in all other men.

In July he was ordered abroad, and their tenderness and desire reached a crescendo. Paula considered a last-minute marriage— decided against it only because there were always cocktails on his breath now, but the parting itself made her physically ill with grief. After his departure she wrote him long letters of regret for the days of love they had missed by waiting. In August Anson's plane slipped down into the North Sea. He was pulled onto a destroyer after a night in the water and sent to hospital with pneumonia; the Armistice was signed before he was finally sent home.

Then, with every opportunity given back to them, with no material obstacle to overcome, the secret weavings of their temperaments came between them, drying up their kisses and their tears, making their voices less loud to one another, muffling the intimate chatter of their hearts until the old communication was only possible by letters, from far away. One afternoon a society reporter waited for two hours in the Hunters' home for a confirmation of their engagement. Anson denied it; nevertheless an early issue carried the report as a leading paragraph—they were "constantly seen together at Southampton, Hot Springs, and Tuxedo Park." But the serious dialogue had turned a cor-

ner into a long-sustained quarrel, and the affair was almost played out. Anson got drunk flagrantly and missed an engagement with her, whereupon Paula made certain behavioristic demands. His despair was helpless before his pride and his knowledge of himself: the engagement was definitely broken.

"Dearest," said their letters now, "Dearest, Dearest, when I wake up in the middle of the night and realize that after all it was not to be, I feel that I want to die. I can't go on living any more. Perhaps when we meet this summer we may talk things over and decide differently—we were so excited and sad that day, and I don't feel that I can live all my life without you. You speak of other people. Don't you know there are no other people for me, but only you. . . ."

But as Paula drifted here and there around the East she would sometimes mention her gaieties to make him wonder. Anson was too acute to wonder. When he saw a man's name in her letters he felt more sure of her and a little disdainful— he was always superior to such things. But he still hoped that they would some day marry.

Meanwhile he plunged vigorously into all the movements and glitter of post-bellum New York, entering a brokerage house, joining half a dozen clubs, dancing late, and moving in three worlds—his own world, the world of young Yale graduates, and that section of the half-world which rests one end on Broadway. But there was always a thorough and infrangible eight hours devoted to his work in Wall Street, where the combination of his influential family connection, his sharp intelligence, and his abundance of sheer physical energy brought him almost immediately forward. He had one of those invaluable minds with partitions in it;

sometimes he appeared at his office refreshed by less than an hour's sleep, but
such occurrences were rare. So early as
1920 his income in salary and commissions exceeded twelve thousand dollars.

As the Yale tradition slipped into the
past he became more and more of a popular figure among his classmates in New
York, more popular than he had ever been
in college. He lived in a great house, and
had the means of introducing young men
into other great houses. Moreover, his life
already seemed secure, while theirs, for
the most part, had arrived again at precarious beginnings. They commenced to
turn to him for amusement and escape,
and Anson responded readily, taking
pleasure in helping people and arranging
their affairs.

There were no men in Paula's letters
now, but a note of tenderness ran through
them that had not been there before. From
several sources he heard that she had "a
heavy beau," Lowell Thayer, a Bostonian
of wealth and position, and though he was
sure she still loved him, it made him uneasy to think that he might lose her, after
all. Save for one unsatisfactory day she
had not been in New York for almost five
months, and as the rumors multiplied he
became increasingly anxious to see her. In
February he took his vacation and went
down to Florida.

Palm Beach sprawled plump and opu-
lent between the sparkling sapphire of
Lake Worth, flawed here and there by
house-boats at anchor, and the great tur-
quoise bar of the Atlantic Ocean. The
huge bulks of the Breakers and the Royal
Poinciana rose as twin paunches from the
bright level of the sand, and around them
clustered the Dancing Glade, Bradley's
House of Chance, and a dozen modistes
and milliners with goods at triple prices
from New York. Upon the trellissed ve-

randa of the Breakers two hundred women
stepped right, stepped left, wheeled, and
slid in that then celebrated calisthenic
known as the double-shuffle, while in half-
time to the music two thousand bracelets
clicked up and down on two hundred
arms.

At the Everglades Club after dark Paula
and Lowell Thayer and Anson and a casual fourth played bridge with hot cards.
It seemed to Anson that her kind, serious
face was wan and tired—she had been
around now for four, five, years. He had
known her for three.

"Two spades."

"Cigarette? . . . Oh, I beg your pardon.
By me."

"By."

"I'll double three spades."

There were a dozen tables of bridge in
the room, which was filling up with
smoke. Anson's eyes met Paula's, held
them persistently even when Thayer's
glance fell between them. . . .

"What was bid?" he asked abstractedly.

"Rose of Washington Square"

sang the young people in the corners:

"I'm withering there
In basement air—"

The smoke banked like fog, and the
opening of a door filled the room with
blown swirls of ectoplasm. Little Bright
Eyes streaked past the tables seeking Mr.
Conan Doyle among the Englishmen who
were posing as Englishmen about the
lobby.

"You could cut it with a knife."

". . . cut it with a knife."

". . . a knife."

At the end of the rubber Paula suddenly
got up and spoke to Anson in a tense, low
voice. With scarcely a glance at Lowell
Thayer, they walked out the door and descended a long flight of stone steps—in a

moment they were walking hand in hand along the moonlit beach.

"Darling, darling. . . ." They embraced recklessly, passionately, in a shadow. . . . Then Paula drew back her face to let his lips say what she wanted to hear—she could feel the words forming as they kissed again. . . . Again she broke away, listening, but as he pulled her close once more she realized that he had said nothing —only *"Darling! Darling!"* in that deep, sad whisper that always made her cry. Humbly, obediently, her emotion yielded to him and the tears streamed down her face, but her heart kept on crying: "Ask me—oh, Anson, dearest, ask me!"

"Paula. . . . *Paula!"*

The words wrung her heart like hands, and Anson, feeling her tremble, knew that emotion was enough. He need say no more, commit their destinies to no practical enigma. Why should he, when he might hold her so, biding his own time, for another year—forever? He was considering them both, her more than himself. For a moment, when she said suddenly that she must go back to her hotel, he hesitated, thinking, first, "This is the moment, after all," and then: "No, let it wait—she is mine. . . ."

He had forgotten that Paula too was worn away inside with the strain of three years. Her mood passed forever in the night.

He went back to New York next morning filled with a certain restless dissatisfaction. Late in April, without warning, he received a telegram from Bar Harbor in which Paula told him that she was engaged to Lowell Thayer, and that they would be married immediately in Boston. What he had never really believed could happen had happened at last.

Anson filled himself with whiskey that morning, and going to the office, carried

on his work without a break—rather with a fear of what would happen if he stopped. In the evening he went out as usual, saying nothing of what had occurred; he was cordial, humorous, unabstracted. But one thing he could not help—for three days in any place, in any company, he would suddenly bend his head into his hands and cry like a child.

v

In 1922 when Anson went abroad with the junior partner to investigate some London loans, the journey intimated that he was to be taken into the firm. He was twenty-seven now, a little heavy without being definitely stout, and with a manner older than his years. Old people and young people liked him and trusted him, and mothers felt safe when their daughters were in his charge, for he had a way, when he came into a room, of putting himself on a footing with the oldest and most conservative people there. "You and I," he seemed to say, "we're solid. We understand."

He had an instinctive and rather charitable knowledge of the weaknesses of men and women, and, like a priest, it made him the more concerned for the maintenance of outward forms. It was typical of him that every Sunday morning he taught in a fashionable Episcopal Sunday-school—even though a cold shower and a quick change into a cutaway coat were all that separated him from the wild night before.

After his father's death he was the political head of his family, and, in effect, guided the destinies of the younger children. Through a complication his authority did not extend to his father's estate, which was administrated by his Uncle Robert, who was the horsey member of that set which centers about Wheatley Hills.

Uncle Robert and his wife, Edna, had been great friends of Anson's youth, and the former was disappointed when his nephew's superiority failed to take a horsey form. He backed him for a city club which was the most difficult in America to enter—one could only join if one's family had "helped to build up New York" (or, in other words, were rich before 1880)—and when Anson, after his election, neglected it for the Yale Club, Uncle Robert gave him a little talk on the subject. But when on top of that Anson declined to enter Robert Hunter's own conservative and somewhat neglected brokerage house, his manner grew cooler. Like a primary teacher who has taught all he knew, he slipped out of Anson's life.

There were so many friends in Anson's life—scarcely one for whom he had not done some unusual kindness and scarcely one whom he did not occasionally embarrass by his bursts of rough conversation or his habit of getting drunk whenever and however he liked. It annoyed him when anyone else blundered in that regard—about his own lapses he was always humorous. Odd things happened to him and he told them with infectious laughter.

I was working in New York that spring, and I used to lunch with him at the Yale Club, which my university was sharing until the completion of our own. I had read of Paula's marriage, and one afternoon, when I asked him about her, something moved him to tell me the story. After that he frequently invited me to family dinners at his house and behaved as though there was a special relation between us, as though with his confidence a little of that consuming memory had passed into me.

I found that despite the trusting mothers, his attitude toward girls was not indis-criminately protective. It was up to the girl—if she showed any inclination toward looseness, she must take care of herself, even with him.

"Life," he would explain sometimes, "has made a cynic of me."

By life he meant Paula. Sometimes, especially when he was drinking, it became a little twisted in his mind, and he thought that she had callously thrown him over.

This "cynicism," or rather his realization that naturally fast girls were not worth sparing, led to his affair with Dolly Karger. It wasn't his only affair in those years, but it came nearest to touching him deeply, and it had a profound effect upon his attitude toward life.

Dolly was the daughter of a notorious "publicist" who had married into society. She herself grew up into the Junior League, came out at the Plaza, and went to the Assembly; and only a few old families like the Hunters could question whether or not she "belonged," for her picture was often in the papers, and she had more enviable attention than many girls who undoubtedly did. She was dark-haired, with carmine lips and a high, lovely color, which she concealed under pinkish-gray powder all through the first year out, because high color was unfashionable—Victorian-pale was the thing to be. She wore black, severe suits and stood with her hands in her pockets leaning a little forward, with a humorous restraint on her face. She danced exquisitely—better than anything she liked to dance—better than anything except making love. Since she was ten she had always been in love, and, usually, with some boy who didn't respond to her. Those who did—and there were many—bored her after a brief encounter, but for her failures she reserved the warmest spot in her heart. When she met them she would always try once more —sometimes she succeeded, more often she failed.

It never occurred to this gypsy of the unattainable that there was a certain resemblance in those who refused to love her—they shared a hard intuition that saw through to her weakness, not a weakness of emotion but a weakness of rudder. Anson perceived this when he first met her, less than a month after Paula's marriage. He was drinking rather heavily, and he pretended for a week that he was falling in love with her. Then he dropped her abruptly and forgot—immediately he took up the commanding position in her heart.

Like so many girls of that day Dolly was slackly and indiscreetly wild. The unconventionality of a slightly older generation had been simply one facet of a postwar movement to discredit obsolete manners—Dolly's was both older and shabbier, and she saw in Anson the two extremes which the emotionally shiftless woman seeks, an abandon to indulgence alternating with a protective strength. In his character she felt both the sybarite and the solid rock, and these two satisfied every need of her nature.

She felt that it was going to be difficult, but she mistook the reason—she thought that Anson and his family expected a more spectacular marriage, but she guessed immediately that her advantage lay in his tendency to drink.

They met at the large débutante dances, but as her infatuation increased they managed to be more and more together. Like most mothers, Mrs. Karger believed that Anson was exceptionally reliable, so she allowed Dolly to go with him to distant country clubs and suburban houses without inquiring closely into their activities or questioning her explanations when they came in late. At first these explana-

tions might have been accurate, but Dolly's worldly ideas of capturing Anson were soon engulfed in the rising sweep of her emotion. Kisses in the back of taxis and motorcars were no longer enough; they did a curious thing:

They dropped out of their world for a while and made another world just beneath it where Anson's tippling and Dolly's irregular hours would be less noticed and commented on. It was composed, this world, of varying elements—several of Anson's Yale friends and their wives, two or three young brokers and bond salesmen and a handful of unattached men, fresh from college, with money and a propensity to dissipation. What this world lacked in spaciousness and scale it made up for by allowing them a liberty that it scarcely permitted itself. Moreover, it centered around them and permitted Dolly the pleasure of a faint condescension —a pleasure which Anson, whose whole life was a condescension from the certitudes of his childhood, was unable to share.

He was not in love with her, and in the long feverish winter of their affair he frequently told her so. In the spring he was weary—he wanted to renew his life at some other source—moreover, he saw that either he must break with her now or accept the responsibility of a definite seduction. Her family's encouraging attitude precipitated his decision—one evening when Mr. Karger knocked discreetly at the library door to announce that he had left a bottle of old brandy in the dining-room, Anson felt that life was hemming him in. That night he wrote her a short letter in which he told her that he was going on his vacation, and that in view of all the circumstances they had better meet no more.

It was June. His family had closed up

the house and gone to the country, so he was living temporarily at the Yale Club. I had heard about his affair with Dolly as it developed—accounts salted with humor, for he despised unstable women, and granted them no place in the social edifice in which he believed—and when he told me that night that he was definitely breaking with her I was glad. I had seen Dolly here and there, and each time with a feeling of pity at the hopelessness of her struggle, and of shame at knowing so much about her that I had no right to know. She was what is known as "a pretty little thing," but there was a certain recklessness which rather fascinated me. Her dedication to the goddess of waste would have been less obvious had she been less spirited —she would most certainly throw herself away, but I was glad when I heard that the sacrifice would not be consummated in my sight.

Anson was going to leave the letter of farewell at her house next morning. It was one of the few houses left open in the Fifth Avenue district, and he knew that the Kargers, acting upon erroneous information from Dolly, had foregone a trip abroad to give their daughter her chance. As he stepped out the door of the Yale Club into Madison Avenue the postman passed him, and he followed back inside. The first letter that caught his eye was in Dolly's hand.

He knew what it would be—a lonely and tragic monologue, full of the reproaches he knew, the invoked memories, the "I wonder if's"—all the immemorial intimacies that he had communicated to Paula Legendre in what seemed another age. Thumbing over some bills, he brought it on top again and opened it. To his surprise it was a short, somewhat formal note, which said that Dolly would be unable to go to the country with him for the week-end, because Perry Hull from Chicago had unexpectedly come to town. It added that Anson had brought this on himself: "—if I felt that you loved me as I loved you I would go with you at any time, any place, but Perry is so nice, and he so much wants me to marry him—"

Anson smiled contemptuously—he had had experience with such decoy epistles. Moreover he knew how Dolly had labored over this plan, probably sent for the faithful Perry and calculated the time of his arrival—even labored over the note so that it would make him jealous without driving him away. Like most compromises, it had neither force nor vitality but only a timorous despair.

Suddenly he was angry. He sat down in the lobby and read it again. Then he went to the phone, called Dolly and told her in his clear, compelling voice that he had received her note and would call for her at five o'clock as they had previously planned. Scarcely waiting for the pretended uncertainty of her "Perhaps I can see you for an hour," he hung up the receiver and went down to his office. On the way he tore his own letter into bits and dropped it in the street.

He was not jealous—she meant nothing to him—but at her pathetic ruse everything stubborn and self-indulgent in him came to the surface. It was a presumption from a mental inferior and it could not be overlooked. If she wanted to know to whom she belonged she would see.

He was on the doorstep at quarter past five. Dolly was dressed for the street, and he listened in silence to the paragraph of "I can only see you for an hour," which she had begun on the phone.

"Put on your hat, Dolly," he said, "we'll take a walk."

They strolled up Madison Avenue and over to Fifth while Anson's shirt dampened upon his portly body in the deep heat. He talked little, scolding her, making no love to her, but before they had walked six blocks she was his again, apologizing for the note, offering not to see Perry at all as an atonement, offering anything. She thought that he had come because he was beginning to love her.

"I'm hot," he said when they reached 71st Street. "This is a winter suit. If I stop by the house and change, would you mind waiting for me downstairs? I'll only be a minute."

She was happy; the intimacy of his being hot, of any physical fact about him, thrilled her. When they came to the iron-grated door and Anson took out his key she experienced a sort of delight.

Downstairs it was dark, and after he ascended in the lift Dolly raised a curtain and looked out through opaque lace at the houses over the way. She heard the lift machinery stop, and with the notion of teasing him pressed the button that brought it down. Then on what was more than an impulse she got into it and sent it up to what she guessed was his floor.

"Anson," she called, laughing a little.

"Just a minute," he answered from his bedroom . . . then after a brief delay: "Now you can come in."

He had changed and was buttoning his vest. "This is my room," he said lightly. "How do you like it?"

She caught sight of Paula's picture on the wall and stared at it in fascination, just as Paula had stared at the pictures of Anson's childish sweethearts five years before. She knew something about Paula—sometimes she tortured herself with fragments of the story.

Suddenly she came close to Anson, raising her arms. They embraced. Outside the area window a soft artificial twilight already hovered, though the sun was still bright on a back roof across the way. In half an hour the room would be quite dark. The uncalculated opportunity overwhelmed them, made them both breathless, and they clung more closely. It was imminent, inevitable. Still holding one another, they raised their heads—their eyes fell together upon Paula's picture, staring down at them from the wall.

Suddenly Anson dropped his arms, and sitting down at his desk tried the drawer with a bunch of keys.

"Like a drink?" he asked in a gruff voice.

"No, Anson."

He poured himself half a tumbler of whiskey, swallowed it, and then opened the door into the hall.

"Come on," he said.

Dolly hesitated.

"Anson—I'm going to the country with you tonight, after all. You understand that, don't you?"

"Of course," he answered brusquely.

In Dolly's car they rode on to Long Island, closer in their emotions than they had ever been before. They knew what would happen—not with Paula's face to remind them that something was lacking, but when they were alone in the still, hot Long Island night they did not care.

The estate in Port Washington where they were to spend the week-end belonged to a cousin of Anson's who had married a Montana copper operator. An interminable drive began at the lodge and twisted under imported poplar saplings toward a huge, pink, Spanish house. Anson had often visited there before.

After dinner they danced at the Linx Club. About midnight Anson assured himself that his cousins would not leave before two—then he explained that Dolly was tired; he would take her home and return to the dance later. Trembling a little with excitement, they got into a borrowed car together and drove to Port Washington. As they reached the lodge he stopped and spoke to the night-watchman.

"When are you making a round, Carl?"

"Right away."

"Then you'll be here till everybody's in?"

"Yes, sir."

"All right. Listen: if any automobile, no matter whose it is, turns in at this gate, I want you to phone the house immediately." He put a five-dollar bill into Carl's hand. "Is that clear?"

"Yes, Mr. Anson." Being of the Old World, he neither winked nor smiled. Yet Dolly sat with her face turned slightly away.

Anson had a key. Once inside he poured a drink for both of them—Dolly left hers untouched—then he ascertained definitely the location of the phone, and found that it was within easy hearing distance of their rooms, both of which were on the first floor.

Five minutes later he knocked at the door of Dolly's room.

"Anson?" He went in, closing the door behind him. She was in bed, leaning up anxiously with elbows on the pillow; sitting beside her he took her in his arms.

"Anson, darling."

He didn't answer.

"Anson. . . . Anson! I love you. . . . Say you love me. Say it now—can't you say it now? Even if you don't mean it?"

He did not listen. Over her head he perceived that the picture of Paula was hanging here upon this wall.

He got up and went close to it. The frame gleamed faintly with thrice-reflected moonlight—within was a blurred shadow of a face that he saw he did not know. Almost sobbing, he turned around and stared with abomination at the little figure on the bed.

"This is all foolishness," he said thickly. "I don't know what I was thinking about. I don't love you and you'd better wait for somebody that loves you. I don't love you a bit, can't you understand?"

His voice broke, and he went hurriedly out. Back in the salon he was pouring himself a drink with uneasy fingers, when the front door opened suddenly, and his cousin came in.

"Why, Anson, I hear Dolly's sick," she began solicitously. "I hear she's sick. . . ."

"It was nothing," he interrupted, raising his voice so that it would carry into Dolly's room. "She was a little tired. She went to bed."

For a long time afterward Anson believed that a protective God sometimes interfered in human affairs. But Dolly Karger, lying awake and staring at the ceiling, never again believed in anything at all.

VI

When Dolly married during the following autumn, Anson was in London on business. Like Paula's marriage, it was sudden, but it affected him in a different way. At first he felt that it was funny, and had an inclination to laugh when he thought of it. Later it depressed him—it made him feel old.

There was something repetitive about it —why, Paula and Dolly had belonged to different generations. He had a foretaste of the sensation of a man of forty who hears that the daughter of an old flame has married. He wired congratulations and, as was not the case with Paula, they were sincere—he had never really hoped that Paula would be happy.

When he returned to New York, he was made a partner in the firm, and, as his responsibilities increased, he had less time on his hands. The refusal of a life-insurance company to issue him a policy made such an impression on him that he stopped drinking for a year, and claimed that he felt better physically, though I think he missed the convivial recounting of those Celliniesque adventures which, in his early twenties, had played such a part in his life. But he never abandoned the Yale Club. He was a figure there, a personality, and the tendency of his class, who were now seven years out of college, to drift away to more sober haunts was checked by his presence.

His day was never too full nor his mind too weary to give any sort of aid to any one who asked it. What had been done at first through pride and superiority had become a habit and a passion. And there was always something—a younger brother in trouble at New Haven, a quarrel to be patched up between a friend and his wife, a position to be found for this man, an investment for that. But his specialty was the solving of problems for young married people. Young married people fascinated him and their apartments were almost sacred to him—he knew the story of their love-affair, advised them where to live and how, and remembered their babies' names. Toward young wives his attitude was circumspect: he never abused the trust which their husbands—strangely enough in view of his unconcealed irregularities—invariably reposed in him.

He came to take a vicarious pleasure in happy marriages, and to be inspired to an almost equally pleasant melancholy by those that went astray. Not a season passed that he did not witness the collapse of an affair that perhaps he himself had fathered. When Paula was divorced and almost immediately remarried to another

Bostonian, he talked about her to me all one afternoon. He would never love any one as he had loved Paula, but he insisted that he no longer cared.

"I'll never marry," he came to say; "I've seen too much of it, and I know a happy marriage is a very rare thing. Besides, I'm too old."

But he did believe in marriage. Like all men who spring from a happy and successful marriage, he believed in it passionately—nothing he had seen would change his belief, his cynicism dissolved upon it like air. But he did really believe he was too old. At twenty-eight he began to accept with equanimity the prospect of marrying without romantic love; he resolutely chose a New York girl of his own class, pretty, intelligent, congenial, above reproach—and set about falling in love with her. The things he had said to Paula with sincerity, to other girls with grace, he could no longer say at all without smiling, or with the force necessary to convince.

"When I'm forty," he told his friends, "I'll be ripe. I'll fall for some chorus girl like the rest."

Nevertheless, he persisted in his attempt. His mother wanted to see him married, and he could now well afford it—he had a seat on the Stock Exchange, and his earned income came to twenty-five thousand a year. The idea was agreeable: when his friends—he spent most of his time with the set he and Dolly had evolved —closed themselves in behind domestic doors at night, he no longer rejoiced in his freedom. He even wondered if he should have married Dolly. Not even Paula had loved him more, and he was learning the rarity, in a single life, of encountering true emotion.

Just as this mood began to creep over him a disquieting story reached his ear.

His aunt Edna, a woman just this side of forty, was carrying on an open intrigue with a dissolute, hard-drinking young man named Cary Sloane. Every one knew of it except Anson's Uncle Robert, who for fifteen years had talked long in clubs and taken his wife for granted.

Anson heard the story again and again with increasing annoyance. Something of his old feeling for his uncle came back to him, a feeling that was more than personal, a reversion toward that family solidarity on which he had based his pride. His intuition singled out the essential point of the affair, which was that his uncle shouldn't be hurt. It was his first experiment in unsolicited meddling, but with his knowledge of Edna's character he felt that he could handle the matter better than a district judge or his uncle.

His uncle was in Hot Springs. Anson traced down the sources of the scandal so that there should be no possibility of mistake and then he called Edna and asked her to lunch with him at the Plaza next day. Something in his tone must have frightened her, for she was reluctant, but he insisted, putting off the date until she had no excuse for refusing.

She met him at the appointed time in the Plaza lobby, a lovely, faded, gray-eyed blond in a coat of Russian sable. Five great rings, cold with diamonds and emeralds, sparkled on her slender hands. It occurred to Anson that it was his father's intelligence and not his uncle's that had earned the fur and the stones, the rich brilliance that buoyed up her passing beauty.

Though Edna scented his hostility, she was unprepared for the directness of his approach.

"Edna, I'm astonished at the way you've been acting," he said in a strong, frank voice. "At first I couldn't believe it."

"Believe what?" she demanded sharply.

"You needn't pretend with me, Edna. I'm talking about Cary Sloane. Aside from any other consideration, I didn't think you could treat Uncle Robert—"

"Now look here, Anson—" she began angrily, but his peremptory voice broke through hers:

"—and your children in such a way. You've been married eighteen years, and you're old enough to know better."

"You can't talk to me like that! You—"

"Yes, I can. Uncle Robert has always been my best friend." He was tremendously moved. He felt a real distress about his uncle, about his three young cousins.

Edna stood up, leaving her crab-flake cocktail untasted.

"This is the silliest thing—"

"Very well, if you won't listen to me I'll go to Uncle Robert and tell him the whole story—he's bound to hear it sooner or later. And afterward I'll go to old Moses Sloane."

Edna faltered back into her chair.

"Don't talk so loud," she begged him. Her eyes blurred with tears. "You have no idea how your voice carries. You might have chosen a less public place to make all these crazy accusations."

He didn't answer.

"Oh, you never liked me, I know," she went on. "You're just taking advantage of some silly gossip to try and break up the only interesting friendship I've ever had. What did I ever do to make you hate me so?"

Still Anson waited. There would be the appeal to his chivalry, then to his pity, finally to his superior sophistication—when he had shouldered his way through all these there would be admissions, and he could come to grips with her. By being silent, by being impervious, by returning constantly to his main weapon, which was his own true emotion, he bullied her into frantic despair as the luncheon hour slipped away. At two o'clock she took out a mirror and a handkerchief, shined away the marks of her tears and powdered the slight hollows where they had lain. She had agreed to meet him at her own house at five.

When he arrived she was stretched on a *chaise-longue* which was covered with cretonne for the summer, and the tears he had called up at luncheon seemed still to be standing in her eyes. Then he was aware of Cary Sloane's dark anxious presence upon the cold hearth.

"What's this idea of yours?" broke out Sloane immediately. "I understand you invited Edna to lunch and then threatened, her on the basis of some cheap scandal."

Anson sat down.

"I have no reason to think it's only scandal."

"I hear you're going to take it to Robert Hunter, and to my father."

Anson nodded.

"Either you break it off—or I will," he said.

"What God damned business is it of yours, Hunter?"

"Don't lose your temper, Cary," said Edna nervously. "It's only a question of showing him how absurd—"

"For one thing, it's my name that's being handed around," interrupted Anson. "That's all that concerns you, Cary."

"Edna isn't a member of your family."

"She most certainly is!" His anger mounted. "Why—she owes this house and the rings on her fingers to my father's brains. When Uncle Robert married her she didn't have a penny."

They all looked at the rings as if they had a significant bearing on the situation.

Edna made a gesture to take them from her hand.

"I guess they're not the only rings in the world," said Sloane.

"Oh, this is absurd," cried Edna. "Anson, will you listen to me? I've found out how the silly story started. It was a maid I discharged who went right to the Chilicheffs—all these Russians pump things out of their servants and then put a false meaning on them." She brought down her fist angrily on the table: "And after Tom lent them the limousine for a whole month when we were South last winter—"

"Do you see?" demanded Sloane eagerly. "This maid got hold of the wrong end of the thing. She knew that Edna and I were friends, and she carried it to the Chilicheffs. In Russia they assume that if a man and a woman—"

He enlarged the theme to a disquisition upon social relations in the Caucasus.

"If that's the case it better be explained to Uncle Robert," said Anson dryly, "so that when the rumors do reach him he'll know they're not true."

Adopting the method he had followed with Edna at luncheon he let them explain it all away. He knew that they were guilty and that presently they would cross the line from explanation into justification and convict themselves more definitely than he could ever do. By seven they had taken the desperate step of telling him the truth—Robert Hunter's neglect, Edna's empty life, the casual dalliance that had flamed up into passion—but like so many true stories it had the misfortune of being old, and its enfeebled body beat helplessly against the armor of Anson's will. The threat to go to Sloane's father sealed their helplessness, for the latter, a retired cotton broker out of Alabama, was a notorious fundamentalist who controlled his son by a rigid allowance and the promise that at his next vagary the allowance would stop forever.

They dined at a small French restaurant, and the discussion continued—at one time Sloane resorted to physical threats, a little later they were both imploring him to give them time. But Anson was obdurate. He saw that Edna was breaking up, and that her spirit must not be refreshed by any renewal of their passion.

At two o'clock in a small night-club on 53d Street, Edna's nerves suddenly collapsed, and she cried to go home. Sloane had been drinking heavily all evening, and he was faintly maudlin, leaning on the table and weeping a little with his face in his hands. Quickly Anson gave them his terms. Sloane was to leave town for six months, and he must be gone within forty-eight hours. When he returned there was to be no resumption of the affair, but at the end of a year Edna might, if she wished, tell Robert Hunter that she wanted a divorce and go about it in the usual way.

He paused, gaining confidence from their faces for his final word.

"Or there's another thing you can do," he said slowly, "if Edna wants to leave her children, there's nothing I can do to prevent your running off together."

"I want to go home!" cried Edna again. "Oh, haven't you done enough to us for one day?"

Outside it was dark, save for a blurred glow from Sixth Avenue down the street. In that light those two who had been lovers looked for the last time into each other's faces, realizing that between them there was not enough youth and strength to avert their eternal parting. Sloane walked suddenly off down the street and Anson tapped a dozing taxi-driver on the arm.

It was almost four; there was a patient flow of cleaning water along the ghostly pavement of Fifth Avenue, and the shadows of two night women flitted over the dark façade of St. Thomas's church. Then the desolate shrubbery of Central Park where Anson had often played as a child, and the mounting numbers, significant as names, of the marching streets. This was his city, he thought, where his name had flourished through five generations. No change could alter the permanence of its place here, for change itself was the essential substratum by which he and those of his name identified themselves with the spirit of New York. Resourcefulness and a powerful will—for his threats in weaker hands would have been less than nothing—had beaten the gathering dust from his uncle's name, from the name of his family, from even this shivering figure that sat beside him in the car.

Cary Sloane's body was found next morning on the lower shelf of a pillar of Queensboro Bridge. In the darkness and in his excitement he had thought that it was the water flowing black beneath him, but in less than a second it made no possible difference—unless he had planned to think one last thought of Edna, and call out her name as he struggled feebly in the water.

VII

Anson never blamed himself for his part in this affair—the situation which brought it about had not been of his making. But the just suffer with the unjust, and he found that his oldest and somehow his most precious friendship was over. He never knew what distorted story Edna told, but he was welcome in his uncle's house no longer.

Just before Christmas Mrs. Hunter retired to a select Episcopal heaven, and Anson became the responsible head of his family. An unmarried aunt who had lived with them for years ran the house, and attempted with helpless inefficiency to chaperone the younger girls. All the children were less self-reliant than Anson, more conventional both in their virtues and in their shortcomings. Mrs. Hunter's death had postponed the début of one daughter and the wedding of another. Also it had taken something deeply material from all of them, for with her passing the quiet, expensive superiority of the Hunters came to an end.

For one thing, the estate, considerably diminished by two inheritance taxes and soon to be divided among six children, was not a notable fortune any more. Anson saw a tendency in his youngest sisters to speak rather respectfully of families that hadn't "existed" twenty years ago. His own feeling of precedence was not echoed in them —sometimes they were conventionally snobbish, that was all. For another thing, this was the last summer they would spend on the Connecticut estate; the clamor against it was too loud: "Who wants to waste the best months of the year shut up in that dead old town?" Reluctantly he yielded—the house would go into the market in the fall, and next summer they would rent a smaller place in Westchester County. It was a step down from the expensive simplicity of his father's idea, and, while he symphathized with the revolt, it also annoyed him; during his mother's lifetime he had gone up there at least every other week-end—even in the gayest summers.

Yet he himself was part of this change, and his strong instinct for life had turned him in his twenties from the hollow obsequies of that abortive leisure class. He did not see this clearly—he still felt that there

was a norm, a standard of society. But there was no norm, it was doubtful if there had ever been a true norm in New York. The few who still paid and fought to enter a particular set succeeded only to find that as a society it scarcely functioned—or, what was more alarming, that the Bohemia from which they fled sat above them at table.

At twenty-nine Anson's chief concern was his own growing loneliness. He was sure now that he would never marry. The number of weddings at which he had officiated as best man or usher was past all counting—there was a drawer at home that bulged with the official neckties of this or that wedding-party, neckties standing for romances that had not endured a year, for couples who had passed completely from his life. Scarfpins, gold pencils, cuff-buttons, presents from a generation of grooms had passed through his jewel-box and been lost—and with every ceremony he was less and less able to imagine himself in the groom's place. Under his hearty good-will toward all those marriages there was despair about his own.

And as he neared thirty he became not a little depressed at the inroads that marriage, especially lately, had made upon his friendships. Groups of people had a disconcerting tendency to dissolve and disappear. The men from his own college—and it was upon them he had expended the most time and affection—were the most elusive of all. Most of them were drawn deep into domesticity, two were dead, one lived abroad, one was in Hollywood writing continuities for pictures that Anson went faithfully to see.

Most of them, however, were permanent commuters with an intricate family life centering around. some suburban country club, and it was from these that he felt his estrangement most keenly.

In the early days of their married life they had all needed him; he gave them advice about their slim finances, he exorcised their doubts about the advisability of bringing a baby into two rooms and a bath, especially he stood for the great world outside. But now their financial troubles were in the past and the fearfully expected child had evolved into an absorbing family. They were always glad to see old Anson, but they dressed up for him and tried to impress him with their present importance, and kept their troubles to themselves. They needed him no longer.

A few weeks before his thirtieth birthday the last of his early and intimate friends was married. Anson acted in his usual rôle of best man, gave his usual silver tea-service, and went down to the usual *Homeric* to say good-by. It was a hot Friday afternoon in May, and as he walked from the pier he realized that Saturday closing had begun and he was free until Monday morning.

"Go where?" he asked himself.

The Yale Club, of course; bridge until dinner, then four or five raw cocktails in somebody's room and a pleasant confused evening. He regretted that this afternoon's groom wouldn't be along—they had always been able to cram so much into such nights: they knew how to attach women and how to get rid of them, how much consideration any girl deserved from their intelligent hedonism. A party was an adjusted thing—you took certain girls to certain places and spent just so much on their amusement; you drank a little, not much, more than you ought to drink, and at a certain time in the morning you stood up and said you were going home. You avoided college boys, sponges, future engagements, fights, sentiment, and indiscretions. That was the way it was done. All the rest was dissipation.

In the morning you were never violently sorry—you made no resolutions, but if you had overdone it and your heart was slightly out of order, you went on the wagon for a few days without saying anything about it, and waited until an accumulation of nervous boredom projected you into another party.

The lobby of the Yale Club was unpopulated. In the bar three very young alumni looked up at him, momentarily and without curiosity.

"Hello there, Oscar," he said to the bartender. "Mr. Cahill been around this afternoon?"

"Mr. Cahill's gone to New Haven."

"Oh . . . that so?"

"Gone to the ball game. Lot of men gone up."

Anson looked once again into the lobby, considered for a moment, and then walked out and over to Fifth Avenue. From the broad window of one of his clubs—one that he had scarcely visited in five years—a gray man with watery eyes stared down at him. Anson looked quickly away—that figure sitting in vacant resignation, in supercilious solitude, depressed him. He stopped and, retracing his steps, started over 47th Street toward Teak Warden's apartment. Teak and his wife had once been his most familiar friends —it was a household where he and Dolly Karger had been used to go in the days of their affair. But Teak had taken to drink, and his wife had remarked publicly that Anson was a bad influence on him. The remark reached Anson in an exaggerated form—when it was finally cleared up, the delicate spell of intimacy was broken, never to be renewed.

"Is Mr. Warden at home?" he inquired.

"They've gone to the country."

The fact unexpectedly cut at him. They were gone to the country and he hadn't known. Two years before he would have known the date, the hour, come up at the last moment for a final drink, and planned his first visit to them. Now they had gone without a word.

Anson looked at his watch and considered a week-end with his family, but the only train was a local that would jolt through the aggressive heat for three hours. And tomorrow in the country, and Sunday—he was in no mood for porch-bridge with polite undergraduates, and dancing after dinner at a rural roadhouse, a diminutive of gaiety which his father had estimated too well.

"Oh, no," he said to himself. . . . "No."

He was a dignified, impressive young man, rather stout now, but otherwise unmarked by dissipation. He could have been cast for a pillar of something—at times you were sure it was not society, at others nothing else—for the law, for the church. He stood for a few minutes motionless on the sidewalk in front of a 47th Street apartment-house; for almost the first time in his life he had nothing whatever to do.

Then he began to walk briskly up Fifth Avenue, as if he had just been reminded of an important engagement there. The necessity of dissimulation is one of the few characteristics that we share with dogs, and I think of Anson on that day as some well-bred specimen who had been disappointed at a familiar back door. He was going to see Nick, once a fashionable bartender in demand at all private dances, and now employed in cooling non-alcoholic champagne among the labyrinthine cellars of the Plaza Hotel.

"Nick," he said, "what's happened to everything?"

"Dead," Nick said.

"Make me a whiskey sour." Anson handed a pint bottle over the counter. "Nick, the girls are different; I had a little girl in Brooklyn and she got married last week without letting me know."

"That a fact? Ha-ha-ha," responded Nick diplomatically. "Slipped it over on you."

"Absolutely," said Anson. "And I was not with her the night before."

"Ha-ha-ha," said Nick, "ha-ha-ha!"

"Do you remember the wedding, Nick, in Hot Springs where I had the waiters and the musicians singing 'God save the King'?"

"Now where was that, Mr. Hunter?" Nick concentrated doubtfully. "Seems to me that was—"

"Next time they were back for more, and I began to wonder how much I'd paid them," continued Anson.

"—seems to me that was at Mr. Trenholm's wedding."

"Don't know him," said Anson decisively. He was offended that a strange name should intrude upon his reminiscences; Nick perceived this.

"Naw—aw—" he admitted, "I ought to know that. It was one of your crowd—Brakins . . . Baker—"

"Bicker Baker," said Anson responsively. "They put me in a hearse after it was over and covered me up with flowers and drove me away."

"Ha-ha-ha," said Nick. "Ha-ha-ha."

Nick's simulation of the old family servant paled presently and Anson went upstairs to the lobby. He looked around—his eyes met the glance of an unfamiliar clerk at the desk, then fell upon a flower from the morning's marriage hesitating in the mouth of a brass cuspidor. He went out and walked slowly toward the blood-red sun over Columbus Circle. Suddenly he turned around and, retracing his steps to the Plaza, immured himself in a tele-phone-booth.

Later he said that he tried to get me three times that afternoon, that he tried everyone who might be in New York—men and girls he had not seen for years, an artist's model of his college days whose faded number was still in his address book—Central told him that even the exchange existed no longer. At length his quest roved into the country, and he held brief disappointing conversations with emphatic butlers and maids. So-and-so was out, rid-ing, swimming, playing golf, sailed to Europe last week. Who shall I say phoned?

It was intolerable that he should pass the evening alone—the private reckonings which one plans for a moment of leisure lose every charm when the solitude is en-forced. There were always women of a sort, but the ones he knew had temporarily vanished, and to pass a New York evening in the hired company of a stranger never occurred to him—he would have consid-ered that that was something shameful and secret, the diversion of a travelling salesman in a strange town.

Anson paid the telephone bill—the girl tried unsuccessfully to joke with him about its size—and for the second time that after-noon started to leave the Plaza and go he knew not where. Near the revolving door the figure of a woman, obviously with child, stood sideways to the light—a sheer beige cape fluttered at her shoulders when the door turned and, each time, she looked impatiently toward it as if she were weary of waiting. At the first sight of her a strong nervous thrill of familiarity went over him, but not until he was within five feet of her did he realize that it was Paula.

"Why, Anson Hunter!"

His heart turned over.

"Why, Paula—"

"Why, this is wonderful. I can't believe it, *Anson!*"

She took both his hands, and he saw in the freedom of the gesture that the mem-ory of him had lost poignancy to her. But not to him—he felt that old mood that she evoked in him stealing over his brain, that gentleness with which he had always met her optimism as if afraid to mar its surface.

"We're at Rye for the summer. Pete had to come East on business—you know of course I'm Mrs. Peter Hagerty now—so we brought the children and took a house. You've got to come out and see us."

"Can I?" he asked directly. "When?"

"When you like. Here's Pete." The re-volving door functioned, giving up a fine tall man of thirty with a tanned face and a trim mustache. His immaculate fitness made a sharp contrast with Anson's in-creasing bulk, which was obvious under the faintly tight cutaway coat.

"You oughtn't to be standing," said Hagerty to his wife. "Let's sit down here." He indicated lobby chairs, but Paula hesi-tated.

"I've got to go right home," she said. "Anson, why don't you—why don't you come out and have dinner with us to-night? We're just getting settled, but if you can stand that—"

Hagerty confirmed the invitation cordi-ally.

"Come out for the night."

Their car waited in front of the hotel, and Paula with a tired gesture sank back against silk cushions in the corner.

"There's so much I want to talk to you about," she said, "it seems hopeless."

"I want to hear about you."

"Well"—she smiled at Hagerty—"that would take a long time too. I have three children—by my first marriage. The oldest is five, then four, then three." She smiled again. "I didn't waste much time having them, did I?"

"Boys?"

"A boy and two girls. Then—oh, a lot of things happened, and I got a divorce in Paris a year ago and married Pete. That's all—except that I'm awfully happy."

In Rye they drove up to a large house near the Beach Club, from which there issued presently three dark, slim children who broke from an English governess and approached them with an esoteric cry. Abstractedly and with difficulty Paula took each one into her arms, a caress which they accepted stiffly, as they had evidently been told not to bump into Mummy. Even against their fresh faces Paula's skin showed scarcely any weariness—for all her physical languor she seemed younger than when he had last seen her at Palm Beach seven years ago.

At dinner she was preoccupied, and afterward, during the homage to the radio, she lay with closed eyes on the sofa, until Anson wondered if his presence at this time were not an intrusion. But at nine o'clock, when Hagerty rose and said pleasantly that he was going to leave them by themselves for a while, she began to talk slowly about herself and the past.

"My first baby," she said—"the one we call Darling, the biggest little girl—I wanted to die when I knew I was going to have her, because Lowell was like a stranger to me. It didn't seem as though she could be my own. I wrote you a letter and tore it up. Oh, you were so bad to me, Anson."

It was the dialogue again, rising and falling. Anson felt a sudden quickening of memory.

"Weren't you engaged once?" she asked —"a girl named Dolly something?"

"I wasn't ever engaged. I tried to be en-gaged, but I never loved anybody but you, Paula."

"Oh," she said. Then after a moment: "This baby is the first one I ever really wanted. You see, I'm in love now—at last."

He didn't answer, shocked at the treachery of her remembrance. She must have seen that the "at last" bruised him, for she continued:

"I was infatuated with you, Anson—you could make me do anything you liked. But we wouldn't have been happy. I'm not smart enough for you. I don't like things to be complicated like you do." She paused. "You'll never settle down," she said.

The phrase struck at him from behind —it was an accusation that of all accusations he had never merited.

"I could settle down if women were different," he said. "If I didn't understand so much about them, if women didn't spoil you for other women, if they had only a little pride. If I could go to sleep for a while and wake up into a home that was really mine—why, that's what I'm made for, Paula, that's what women have seen in me and liked in me. It's only that I can't get through the preliminaries any more."

Hagerty came in a little before eleven; after a whiskey Paula stood up and announced that she was going to bed. She went over and stood by her husband.

"Where did you go, dearest?" she demanded.

"I had a drink with Ed Saunders."

"I was worried. I thought maybe you'd run away."

She rested her head against his coat.

"He's sweet, isn't he, Anson?" she demanded.

"Absolutely," said Anson, laughing.

She raised her face to her husband.

"Well, I'm ready," she said. She turned

to Anson: "Do you want to see our family gymnastic stunt?"

"Yes," he said in an interested voice.

"All right. Here we go!"

Hagerty picked her up easily in his arms.

"This is called the family acrobatic stunt," said Paula. "He carries me upstairs. Isn't it sweet of him?"

"Yes," said Anson.

Hagerty bent his head slightly until his face touched Paula's.

"And I love him," she said. "I've just been telling you, haven't I, Anson?"

"Yes," he said.

"He's the dearest thing that ever lived in this world; aren't you, darling? . . . Well, good night. Here we go. Isn't he strong?"

"Yes," Anson said.

"You'll find a pair of Pete's pajamas laid out for you. Sweet dreams—see you at breakfast."

"Yes," Anson said.

VIII

The older members of the firm insisted that Anson should go abroad for the summer. He had scarcely had a vacation in seven years, they said. He was stale and needed a change. Anson resisted.

"If I go," he declared, "I won't come back any more."

"That's absurd, old man. You'll be back in three months with all this depression gone. Fit as ever."

"No." He shook his head stubbornly. "If I stop, I won't go back to work. If I stop, that means I've given up—I'm through."

"We'll take a chance on that. Stay six months if you like—we're not afraid you'll leave us. Why, you'd be miserable if you didn't work."

They arranged his passage for him.

They liked Anson—every one liked Anson—and the change that had been coming over him cast a sort of pall over the office. The enthusiasm that had invariably signalled up business, the consideration toward his equals and his inferiors, the lift of his vital presence—within the past four months his intense nervousness had melted down these qualities into the fussy pessimism of a man of forty. On every transaction in which he was involved he acted as a drag and a strain.

"If I go I'll never come back," he said.

Three days before he sailed Paula Legendre Hagerty died in childbirth. I was with him a great deal then, for we were crossing together, but for the first time in our friendship he told me not a word of how he felt, nor did I see the slightest sign of emotion. His chief preoccupation was with the fact that he was thirty years old —he would turn the conversation to the point where he could remind you of it and then fall silent, as if he assumed that the statement would start a chain of thought sufficient to itself. Like his partners, I was amazed at the change in him, and I was glad when the *Paris* moved off into the wet space between the worlds, leaving his principality behind.

"How about a drink?" he suggested.

We walked into the bar with that defiant feeling that characterizes the day of departure and ordered four Martinis. After one cocktail a change came over him —he suddenly reached across and slapped my knee with the first joviality I had seen him exhibit for months.

"Did you see that girl in the red tam?" he demanded, "the one with the high color who had the two police dogs down to bid her good-by."

"She's pretty," I agreed.

"I looked her up in the purser's office and found out that she's alone. I'm going down to see the steward in a few minutes. We'll have dinner with her tonight."

After a while he left me, and within an hour he was walking up and down the deck with her, talking to her in his strong, clear voice. Her red tam was a bright spot of color against the steel-green sea, and from time to time she looked up with a flashing bob of her head, and smiled with amusement and interest, and anticipation. At dinner we had champagne, and were very joyous—afterward Anson ran the pool with infectious gusto, and several people who had seen me with him asked me his name. He and the girl were talking and laughing together on a lounge in the bar when I went to bed.

I saw less of him on the trip than I had hoped. He wanted to arrange a foursome, but there was no one available, so I saw him only at meals. Sometimes, though, he would have a cocktail in the bar, and he told me about the girl in the red tam, and his adventures with her, making them all bizarre and amusing, as he had a way of doing, and I was glad he was himself again, or at least the self that I knew, and with which I felt at home. I don't think he was ever happy unless someone was in love with him, responding to him like filings to a magnet, helping him to explain himself, promising him something. What it was I do not know. Perhaps they promised that there would always be women in the world who would spend their brightest, freshest, rarest hours to nurse and protect that superiority he cherished in his heart.

THE BEAR

by WILLIAM FAULKNER

HE WAS TEN. But it had already begun, long before that day when at last he wrote his age in two figures and he saw for the first time the camp where his father and Major de Spain and old General Compson and the others spent two weeks each November and two weeks again each June. He had already inherited then, without ever having seen it, the tremendous bear with one trap-ruined foot which, in an area almost a hundred miles deep, had earned for itself a name, a definite designation like a living man.

He had listened to it for years: the long legend of corncribs rifled, of shotes and grown pigs and even calves carried bodily into the woods and devoured, of traps and deadfalls overthrown and dogs mangled and slain, and shotgun and even rifle charges delivered at point-blank range and with no more effect than so many peas blown through a tube by a boy—a corridor of wreckage and destruction beginning back before he was born, through which sped, not fast but rather with the ruthless and irresistible deliberation of a locomotive, the shaggy tremendous shape.

It ran in his knowledge before he ever saw it. It looked and towered in his dreams before he even saw the unaxed woods where it left its crooked print, shaggy, huge, red-eyed, not malevolent but just big—too big for the dogs which tried to bay it, for the horses which tried to ride it down, for the men and the bullets they fired into it, too big for the very country which was its constricting scope. He seemed to see it entire with a child's complete divination before he ever laid eyes on either—the doomed wilderness whose edges were being constantly and punily gnawed at by men with axes and plows who feared it because it was wilderness, men myriad and nameless even to one another in the land where the old bear had earned a name, through which ran not even a mortal animal but an anachronism, indomitable and invincible, out of an old dead time, a phantom, epitome and apotheosis of the old wild life at which the puny humans swarmed and hacked in a fury of abhorrence and fear, like pygmies about the ankles of a drowsing elephant; the old bear solitary, indomitable and alone, widowered, childless and absolved of mortality—old Priam reft of his old wife and having outlived all his sons.

Until he was ten, each November he would watch the wagon containing the dogs and the bedding and food and guns and his father and Tennie's Jim, the Negro, and Sam Fathers, the Indian, son of a slave woman and a Chickasaw chief, depart on the road to town, to Jefferson, where Major de Spain and the others would join them. To the boy, at seven and eight and nine, they were not going into the Big Bottom to hunt bear and deer, but to keep yearly rendezvous with the bear which they did not even intend to kill. Two weeks later they would return, with no trophy, no head and skin. He had not expected it. He had not even been afraid it would be in the wagon. He believed that even after he was ten and his father would let him go too, for those two November weeks, he would merely make another one, along with his father and Major de Spain and General Compson and the others, the dogs which feared to bay it and the rifles and shotguns which

failed even to bleed it, in the yearly pageant of the old bear's furious immortality.

Then he heard the dogs. It was in the second week of his first time in the camp. He stood with Sam Fathers against a big oak beside the faint crossing where they had stood each dawn for nine days now, hearing the dogs. He had heard them once before, one morning last week—a murmur, sourceless, echoing through the wet woods, swelling presently into separate voices which he could recognize and call by name. He had raised and cocked the gun as Sam told him and stood motionless again while the uproar, the invisible course, swept up and past and faded; it seemed to him that he could actually see the deer, the buck, blond, smoke-colored, elongated with speed, fleeing, vanishing, the woods, the gray solitude, still ringing even when the cries of the dogs had died away.

"Now let the hammers down," Sam said.

"You knew they were not coming here too," he said.

"Yes," Sam said. "I want you to learn how to do when you didn't shoot. It's after the chance for the bear or the deer has done already come and gone that men and dogs get killed."

"Anyway," he said, "it was just a deer."

Then on the tenth morning he heard the dogs again. And he readied the too-long, too-heavy gun as Sam had taught him, before Sam even spoke. But this time it was no deer, no ringing chorus of dogs running strong on a free scent, but a moiling yapping an octave too high, with something more than indecision and even abjectness in it, not even moving very fast, taking a long time to pass completely out of hearing, leaving even then somewhere in the air that echo, thin, slightly hysterical, abject, almost grieving, with no sense of a fleeing, unseen, smoke-colored, grass-eating shape ahead of it, and Sam, who had taught him first of all to cock the gun and take position where he could see everywhere and then never move again, had himself moved up beside him; he could hear Sam breathing at his shoulder and he could see the arched curve of the old man's inhaling nostrils.

"Hah," Sam said. "Not even running. Walking."

"Old Ben!" the boy said. "But up here!" he cried. "Way up here!"

"He do it every year," Sam said. "Once. Maybe to see who in camp this time, if he can shoot or not. Whether we got the dog yet that can bay and hold him. He'll take them to the river, then he'll send them back home. We may as well go back, too; see how they look when they come back to camp."

When they reached the camp the hounds were already there, ten of them crouching back under the kitchen, the boy and Sam squatting to peer back into the obscurity where they huddled, quiet, the eyes luminous, glowing at them and vanishing, and no sound, only that effluvium of something more than dog, stronger than dog and not just animal, just beast, because still there had been nothing in front of that abject and almost painful yapping save the solitude, the wilderness, so that when the eleventh hound came in at noon and with all the others watching—even old Uncle Ash, who called himself first a cook—Sam daubed the tattered ear and the raked shoulder with turpentine and axle grease, to the boy it was still no living creature, but the wilderness which, leaning for the moment down, had patted lightly once the hound's temerity.

"Just like a man," Sam said. "Just like folks. Put off as long as she could having to be brave, knowing all the time that sooner or later she would have to be brave once to keep on living with herself, and knowing all the time beforehand what was going to happen to her when she done it."

That afternoon, himself on the one-eyed wagon mule which did not mind the smell of blood nor, as they told him, of bear, and with Sam on the other one, they rode for more than three hours through the rapid, shortening winter day. They followed no path, no trail even that he could see; almost at once they were in a country which he had never seen before. Then he knew why Sam had made him ride the mule which would not spook. The sound one stopped short and tried to whirl and bolt even as Sam got down, blowing its breath, jerking and wrenching at the rein while Sam held it, coaxing it forward with his voice, since he could not risk tying it, drawing it forward while the boy got down from the marred one.

Then, standing beside Sam in the gloom of the dying afternoon, he looked down at the rotted overturned log, gutted and scored with claw marks and, in the wet earth beside it, the print of the enormous warped two-toed foot. He knew now what he had smelled when he peered under the kitchen where the dogs huddled. He realized for the first time that the bear which had run in his listening and loomed in his dreams since before he could remember to the contrary, and which, therefore, must have existed in the listening and dreams of his father and Major de Spain and even old General Compson, too, before they began to remember in their turn, was a mortal animal, and that if they had departed for the camp each November without any actual hope of bringing its trophy back, it was not because it could not be slain, but because so far they had had no actual hope to.

"Tomorrow," he said.

"We'll try tomorrow," Sam said. "We ain't got the dog yet."

"We've got eleven. They ran him this morning."

"It won't need but one," Sam said. "He ain't here. Maybe he ain't nowhere. The only other way will be for him to run by accident over somebody that has a gun."

"That wouldn't be me," the boy said. "It will be Walter or Major or—"

"It might," Sam said. "You watch close in the morning. Because he's smart. That's how come he has lived this long. If he gets hemmed up and has to pick out somebody to run over, he will pick out you."

"How?" the boy said. "How will he know—" He ceased. "You mean he already knows me, that I ain't never been here before, ain't had time to find out yet whether I—" He ceased again, looking at Sam, the old man whose face revealed nothing until it smiled. He said humbly, not even amazed, "It was me he was watching. I don't reckon he did need to come but once."

The next morning they left the camp three hours before daylight. They rode this time because it was too far to walk, even the dogs in the wagon; again the first gray light found him in a place which he had never seen before, where Sam had placed him and told him to stay and then departed. With the gun which was too big for him, which did not even belong to him, but to Major de Spain, and which he had fired only once—at a stump on the first day, to learn the recoil and how to reload it—he stood against a gum tree beside a little bayou whose black still water

crept without movement out of a cane-brake and crossed a small clearing and into cane again, where, invisible, a bird—the big woodpecker called Lord-to-God by Negroes—clattered at a dead limb.

It was a stand like any other, dissimilar only in incidentals to the one where he had stood each morning for ten days; a territory new to him, yet no less familiar than that other one which, after almost two weeks, he had come to believe he knew a little—the same solitude, the same loneliness through which human beings had merely passed without altering it, leaving no mark, no scar, which looked exactly as it must have looked when the first ancestor of Sam Fathers' Chickasaw predecessors crept into it and looked about, club or stone ax or bone arrow drawn and poised; different only because, squatting at the edge of the kitchen, he smelled the hounds huddled and cringing beneath it and saw the raked ear and shoulder of the one who, Sam said, had had to be brave once in order to live with herself, and saw yesterday in the earth beside the gutted log the print of the living foot.

He heard no dogs at all. He never did hear them. He only heard the drumming of the woodpecker stop short off and knew that the bear was looking at him. He never saw it. He did not know whether it was in front of him or behind him. He did not move, holding the useless gun, which he had not even had warning to cock and which even now he did not cock, tasting in his saliva that taint as of brass which he knew now because he had smelled it when he peered under the kitchen at the huddled dogs.

Then it was gone. As abruptly as it had ceased, the woodpecker's dry, monotonous clatter set up again, and after a while he even believed he could hear the dogs—a murmur, scarce a sound even, which he had probably been hearing for some time before he even remarked it, drifting into hearing and then out again, dying away. They came nowhere near him. If it was a bear they ran, it was another bear. It was Sam himself who came out of the cane and crossed the bayou, followed by the injured bitch of yesterday. She was almost at heel, like a bird dog, making no sound. She came and crouched against his leg, trembling, staring off into the cane.

"I didn't see him," he said. "I didn't, Sam!"

"I know it," Sam said. "He done the looking. You didn't hear him neither, did you?"

"No," the boy said. "I—"

"He's smart," Sam said. "Too smart." He looked down at the hound, trembling faintly and steadily against the boy's knee. From the raked shoulder a few drops of fresh blood oozed and clung. "Too big. We ain't got the dog yet. But maybe some-day. Maybe not next time. But someday."

So I must see him, he thought. *I must look at him.* Otherwise, it seemed to him that it would go on like this forever, as it had gone on with his father and Major de Spain, who was older than his father, and even with old General Compson, who had been old enough to be a brigade com-mander in 1865. Otherwise, it would go on so forever, next time and next time, after and after and after. It seemed to him that he could see the two of them, him-self and the bear, shadowy in the limbo from which time emerged, becoming time; the old bear absolved of mortality and himself partaking, sharing a little of it, enough of it. And he knew now what he had smelled in the huddled dogs and tasted in his saliva. He recognized fear.

So I will have to see him, he thought, without dread or even hope. *I will have to look at him.*

It was in June of the next year. He was eleven. They were in camp again, cele-brating Major de Spain's and General Compson's birthdays. Although the one had been born in September and the other in the depth of winter and in another decade, they had met for two weeks to fish and shoot squirrels and turkey and run coons and wildcats with the dogs at night. That is, he and Boon Hoggenbeck and the Negroes fished and shot squirrels and ran the coons and cats, because the proved hunters, not only Major de Spain and old General Compson, who spent those two weeks sitting in a rocking chair before a tremendous iron pot of Bruns-wick stew, stirring and tasting, with old Ash to quarrel with about how he was making it and Tennie's Jim to pour whisky from the demijohn into the tin dipper from which he drank it, but even the boy's father and Walter Ewell, who were still young enough, scorned such, other than shooting the wild gobblers with pistols for wagers on their marksmanship.

Or, that is, his father and the others believed he was hunting squirrels. Until the third day he thought that Sam Fathers believed that too. Each morning he would leave the camp right after breakfast. He had his own gun now, a Christmas pres-ent. He went back to the tree beside the little bayou where he had stood that morn-ing. Using the compass which old Gen-eral Compson had given him, he ranged from that point; he was teaching himself to be a better-than-fair woodsman with-out knowing he was doing it. On the sec-ond day he even found the gutted log where he had first seen the crooked print. It was almost completely crumbled now, healing with unbelievable speed, a passionate and almost visible relinquishment, back into the earth from which the tree had grown.

He ranged the summer woods now, green with gloom; if anything, actually dimmer than in November's gray dissolution, where, even at noon, the sun fell only in intermittent dappling upon the earth, which never completely dried out and which crawled with snakes—moccasins and water snakes and rattlers, themselves the color of the dappled gloom, so that he would not always see them until they moved, returning later and later, first day, second day, passing in the twilight of the third evening the little log pen enclosing the log stable where Sam was putting up the horses for the night.

"You ain't looked right yet," Sam said.

He stopped. For a moment he didn't answer. Then he said peacefully, in a peaceful rushing burst as when a boy's miniature dam in a little brook gives way, "All right. But how? I went to the bayou. I even found that log again. I—"

"I reckon that was all right. Likely he's been watching you. You never saw his foot?"

"I," the boy said—"I didn't—I never thought—"

"It's the gun," Sam said. He stood beside the fence, motionless—the old man, the Indian, in the battered faded overalls and the frayed five-cent straw hat which in the Negro's race had been the badge of his enslavement and was now the regalia of his freedom. The camp—the clearing, the house, the barn and its tiny lot with which Major de Spain in his turn had scratched punily and evanescently at the wilderness—faded in the dusk, back into the immemorial darkness of the woods. *The gun,* the boy thought. *The gun.*

"Be scared," Sam said. "You can't help that. But don't be afraid. Ain't nothing in the woods going to hurt you unless you corner it, or it smells that you are afraid. A bear or a deer, too, has got to be scared of a coward the same as a brave man has got to be."

The gun, the boy thought.

"You will have to choose," Sam said.

He left the camp before daylight, long before Uncle Ash would wake in his quilts on the kitchen floor and start the fire for breakfast. He had only the compass and a stick for snakes. He could go almost a mile before he would begin to need the compass. He sat on a log, the invisible compass in his invisible hand, while the secret night sounds, fallen still at his movements, scurried again and then ceased for good, and the owls ceased and gave over to the waking of day birds, and he could see the compass. Then he went fast yet still quietly; he was becoming better and better as a woodsman, still without having yet realized it.

He jumped a doe and a fawn at sunrise, walked them out of the bed, close enough to see them—the crash of undergrowth, the white scut, the fawn scudding behind her faster than he had believed it could run. He was hunting right, upwind, as Sam had taught him; not that it mattered now. He had left the gun; of his own will and relinquishment he had accepted not a gambit, not a choice, but a condition in which not only the bear's heretofore inviolable anonymity but all the old rules and balances of hunter and hunted had been abrogated. He would not even be afraid, not even in the moment when the fear would take him completely—blood, skin, bowels, bones, memory from the long time before it became his memory—all save that thin, clear, quenchless, immortal lucidity which alone differed him from this bear and from all the other bear and deer he would ever kill in the humility and pride of his skill and endurance, to which Sam had spoken when he leaned in the twilight on the lot fence yesterday.

By noon he was far beyond the little bayou, farther into the new and alien country than he had ever been. He was traveling now not only by the compass but by the old, heavy, biscuit-thick silver watch which had belonged to his grandfather. When he stopped at last, it was for the first time since he had risen from the log at dawn when he could see the compass. It was far enough. He had left the camp nine hours ago; nine hours from now, dark would have already been an hour old. But he didn't think that. He thought, *All right. Yes. But what?* and stood for a moment, alien and small in the green and topless solitude, answering his own question before it had formed and ceased. It was the watch, the compass, the stick—the three lifeless mechanicals with which for nine hours he had fended the wilderness off; he hung the watch and compass carefully on a bush and leaned the stick beside them and relinquished completely to it.

He had not been going very fast for the last two or three hours. He went no faster now, since distance would not matter even if he could have gone fast. And he was trying to keep a bearing on the tree where he had left the compass, trying to complete a circle which would bring him back to it or at least intersect itself, since direction would not matter now either. But the tree was not there, and he did as Sam had schooled him—made the next circle in the opposite direction, so that the two patterns would bisect somewhere, but crossing no print of his own feet, finding the tree at last, but in the wrong place—no bush, no compass, no watch—and the tree not even the tree, because there was a down log beside it and he did what Sam Fathers had told him was the next thing and the last.

As he sat down on the log he saw the crooked print—the warped, tremendous, two-toed indentation which, even as he watched it, filled with water. As he looked up, the wilderness coalesced, solidified—the glade, the tree he sought, the bush, the watch and the compass glinting where a ray of sunlight touched them. Then he saw the bear. It did not emerge, appear; it was just there, immobile, solid, fixed in the hot dappling of the green and windless noon, not as big as he had dreamed it, but as big as he had expected it, bigger, dimensionless against the dappled obscurity, looking at him where he sat quietly on the log and looked back at it.

Then it moved. It made no sound. It did not hurry. It crossed the glade, walking for an instant into the full glare of the sun; when it reached the other side it stopped again and looked back at him across one shoulder while his quiet breathing inhaled and exhaled three times.

Then it was gone. It didn't walk into the woods, the undergrowth. It faded, sank back into the wilderness as he had watched a fish, a huge old bass, sink and vanish back into the dark depths of its pool without even any movement of its fins.

He thought, *It will be next fall.* But it was not next fall, nor the next nor the next. He was fourteen then. He had killed his buck, and Sam Fathers had marked his face with the hot blood, and in the next year he killed a bear. But even before that accolade he had become as competent in the woods as many grown men with the same experience; by his fourteenth year he was a better woodsman than most grown men with more. There was no territory within thirty miles of the camp that he did not know—bayou, ridge, brake, landmark tree and path. He could have led anyone to any point in it without deviation, and brought them out again. He knew game trails that even Sam Fathers did not know; in his thirteenth year he found a buck's bedding place, and unbeknown to his father he borrowed Walter Ewell's rifle and lay in wait at dawn and killed the buck when it walked back to the bed, as Sam had told him how the old Chickasaw fathers did.

But not the old bear, although by now he knew its footprint better than he did his own, and not only the crooked one. He could see any one of the three sound ones and distinguish it from any other, and not only by its size. There were other bears within those thirty miles which left tracks almost as large, but this was more than that. If Sam Fathers had been his mentor and the back-yard rabbits and squirrels at home his kindergarten, then the wilderness the old bear ran was his college, the old male bear itself, so long unwifed and childless as to have become its own ungendered progenitor, was his alma mater. But he never saw it.

He could find the crooked print now almost whenever he liked, fifteen or ten or five miles, or sometimes nearer the camp than that. Twice while on stand during the three years he heard the dogs strike its trail by accident; on the second time they jumped it seemingly, the voices high, abject, almost human in hysteria, as on that first morning two years ago.

But not the bear itself. He would remember that noon three years ago, the glade, himself and the bear fixed during that moment in the windless and dappled blaze, and it would seem to him that it had never happened, that he had dreamed that too. But it had happened. They had looked at each other, they had emerged from the wilderness old as earth, synchronized to that instant by something more than the blood that moved the flesh and bones which bore them, and touched, pledged something, affirmed something more lasting than the frail web of bones and flesh which any accident could obliterate.

Then he saw it again. Because of the very fact that he thought of nothing else, he had forgotten to look for it. He was still-hunting with Walter Ewell's rifle. He saw it cross the end of a long blowdown, a corridor where a tornado had swept, rushing through rather than over the tangle of trunks and branches as a locomotive would have, faster than he had ever believed it could move, almost as fast as a deer even, because a deer would have spent most of that time in the air, faster than he could bring the rifle sights up to it, so that he believed the reason he never let off the shot was that he was still behind it, had never caught up with it. And now he knew what had been wrong during all the three years. He sat on a log, shaking and trembling as if he had never seen the woods before nor anything that ran them, wondering with incredulous amazement how he could have forgotten the very thing which Sam Fathers had told him and which the bear itself had proved the next day and had now returned after three years to reaffirm.

And he now knew what Sam Fathers had meant about the right dog, a dog in which size would mean less than nothing. So when he returned alone in April—school was out then, so that the sons of farmers could help with the land's planting, and at last his father had granted him permission, on his promise to be back in four days—he had the dog. It was his own, a mongrel of the sort called by Negroes a fyce, a ratter, itself not much bigger than a rat and possessing that bravery which had long since stopped being courage and had become foolhardiness.

It did not take four days. Alone again, he found the trail on the first morning. It was not a stalk; it was an ambush. He timed the meeting almost as if it were an appointment with a human being. Himself holding the fyce muffled in a feed sack and Sam Fathers with two of the hounds on a piece of plowline rope, they lay down wind of the trail at dawn of the second morning. They were so close that the bear turned without even running, as if in surprised amazement at the shrill and frantic uproar of the released fyce, turning at bay against the trunk of a tree, on its hind feet; it seemed to the boy that it would never stop rising, taller and taller, and even the two hounds seemed to take a sort of desperate and despairing courage from the fyce, following it as it went in.

Then he realized that the fyce was actually not going to stop. He flung, threw the gun away, and ran; when he overtook and grasped the frantically pinwheeling little dog, it seemed to him that he was directly under the bear.

He could smell it, strong and hot and rank. Sprawling, he looked up to where it loomed and towered over him like a cloudburst and colored like a thunderclap, quite familiar, peacefully and even lucidly familiar, until he remembered:

This was the way he had used to dream about it. Then it was gone. He didn't see it go. He knelt, holding the frantic fyce with both hands, hearing the abased wailing of the hounds drawing farther and farther away, until Sam came up. He carried the gun. He laid it down quietly beside the boy and stood looking down at him.

"You've done seed him twice now with a gun in your hands," he said. "This time you couldn't have missed him."

The boy rose. He still held the fyce. Even in his arms and clear of the ground, it yapped frantically, straining and surging after the fading uproar of the two hounds like a tangle of wire springs. He was panting a little, but he was neither shaking nor trembling now.

"Neither could you!" he said. "You had the gun! Neither did you!"

"And you didn't shoot," his father said. "How close were you?"

"I don't know, sir," he said. "There was a big wood tick inside his right hind leg. I saw that. But I didn't have the gun then."

"But you didn't shoot when you had the gun," his father said. "Why?"

But he didn't answer, and his father didn't wait for him to, rising and crossing the room, across the pelt of the bear which the boy had killed two years ago and the larger one which his father had killed before he was born, to the bookcase beneath the mounted head of the boy's first buck. It was the room which his father called the office, from which all the plantation business was transacted; in it for the fourteen years of his life he had heard the best of all talking. Major de Spain would be there and sometimes old General Compson, and Walter Ewell and Boon Hoggenbeck and Sam Fathers and Tennie's Jim, too, because they, too, were hunters, knew the woods and what ran them.

He would hear it, not talking himself but listening—the wilderness, the big woods, bigger and older than any recorded document of white man fatuous enough to believe he had bought any fragment of it or Indian ruthless enough to pretend that any fragment of it had been his to convey. It was of the men, not white nor black nor red, but men, hunters with the will and hardihood to endure and the humility and skill to survive, and the dogs and the bear and deer juxtaposed and re-liefed against it, ordered and compelled by and within the wilderness in the ancient and unremitting contest by the ancient and immitigable rules which voided all regrets and brooked no quarter, the voices quiet and weighty and deliberate for retro-spection and recollection and exact re-membering, while he squatted in the blaz-ing firelight as Tennie's Jim squatted, who stirred only to put more wood on the fire and to pass the bottle from one glass to another. Because the bottle was always present, so that after a while it seemed to him that those fierce instants of heart and brain and courage and wiliness and speed were concentrated and distilled into that brown liquor which not women, not boys and children, but only hunters drank, drinking not of the blood they had spilled but some condensation of the wild im-mortal spirit, drinking it moderately, hum-bly even, not with the pagan's base hope of acquiring thereby the virtues of cun-ning and strength and speed, but in salute to them.

His father returned with the book and sat down again and opened it. "Listen," he said. He read the five stanzas aloud, his voice quiet and deliberate in the room where there was no fire now because it was already spring. Then he looked up. The boy watched him. "All right," his father said. "Listen." He read again, but only the second stanza this time, to the end of it, the last two lines, and closed the book and put it on the table beside him. "'She cannot fade, though thou hast not thy bliss, for ever wilt thou love, and she be fair,'" he said.

"He's talking about a girl," the boy said.

"He had to talk about something," his father said. Then he said, "He was talking about truth. Truth doesn't change. Truth is one thing. It covers all things which touch the heart—honor and pride and pity and justice and courage and love. Do you see now?"

He didn't know. Somehow it was sim-pler than that. There was an old bear, fierce and ruthless, not merely just to stay alive, but with the fierce pride of liberty and freedom, proud enough of that lib-erty and freedom to see it threatened with-out fear or even alarm; nay, who at times even seemed deliberately to put that free-dom and liberty in jeopardy in order to savor them, to remind his old strong bones and flesh to keep supple and quick to defend and preserve them. There was an old man, son of a Negro slave and an Indian king, inheritor on the one side of the long chronicle of a people who had learned humility through suffering, and pride through the endurance which sur-vived the suffering and injustice, and on the other side, the chronicle of a people even longer in the land than the first, yet who no longer existed in the land at all save in the solitary brotherhood of an old Negro's alien blood and the wild and invincible spirit of an old bear. There was a boy who wished to learn humility and pride in order to become skillful and worthy in the woods, who suddenly found himself becoming so skillful so rapidly that he feared he would never become worthy because he had not learned humility and pride, although he had tried to, until one day and as suddenly he discovered that an old man who could not have defined either had led him, as though by the hand, to that point where an old bear and a little mongrel dog showed him that, by possessing one thing other, he would possess them both.

And a little dog, nameless and mongrel and many-fathered, grown, yet weighing less than six pounds, saying as if to itself, "I can't be dangerous, because there's nothing much smaller than I am; I can't be fierce, because they would call it just noise; I can't be humble, because I'm already too close to the ground to genuflect; I can't be proud, because I wouldn't be near enough to it for anyone to know who was casting that shadow, and I don't even know that I'm not going to heaven, because they have already decided that I don't possess an immortal soul. So all I can be is brave. But it's all right. I can be that, even if they still call it just noise."

That was all. It was simple, much simpler than somebody talking in a book about a youth and a girl he would never need to grieve over, because he could never approach any nearer her and would never have to get any farther away. He had heard about a bear, and finally got big enough to trail it, and he trailed it four years and at last met it with a gun in his hands and he didn't shoot. Because a little dog— But he could have shot long before the little dog covered the twenty yards to where the bear waited, and Sam Fathers could have shot at any time during that interminable minute while Old Ben stood on his hind feet over them. He stopped. His father was watching him gravely across the spring-rife twilight of the room; when he spoke, his words were as quiet as the twilight, too, not loud, because they did not need to be, because they would last: "Courage, and honor, and pride," his father said, "and pity, and love of justice and of liberty. They all touch the heart, and what the heart holds to becomes truth, as far as we know truth. Do you see now?"

Sam, and Old Ben, and Nip, he thought. And himself too. He had been all right too. His father had said so. "Yes, sir," he said.

Mt. Kilimanjaro, in Tanganyika, called "House of God" by the Masai people

THE SNOWS OF KILIMANJARO

by ERNEST HEMINGWAY

Kilimanjaro is a snow-covered mountain 19,710 feet high, and is said to be the highest mountain in Africa. Its western summit is called the Masai "Ngàje Ngài," the House of God. Close to the western summit there is the dried and frozen carcass of a leopard. No one has explained what the leopard was seeking at that altitude.

"THE MARVELLOUS THING is that it's painless," he said. "That's how you know when it starts."

"Is it really?"

"Absolutely. I'm awfully sorry about the odor, though. That must bother you."

"Don't! Please don't."

"Look at them," he said. "Now is it sight or is it scent that brings them like that?"

The cot the man lay on was in the wide shade of a mimosa tree and as he looked out past the shade onto the glare of the plain there were three of the big birds squatted obscenely, while in the sky a dozen more sailed, making quiet moving shadows as they passed.

"They've been there since the day the truck broke down," he said. "Today's the first time any have lit on the ground. I watched the way they sailed very carefully at first in case I ever wanted to use them in a story. That's funny now."

"I wish you wouldn't," she said.

"I'm only talking," he said. "It's much easier if I talk. But I don't want to bother you."

"You know it doesn't bother me," she said. "It's that I've gotten so very nervous not being able to do anything. I think we might make it as easy as we can until the plane comes."

"Or until the plane doesn't come."

"Please tell me what I can do. There must be something I can do."

"You can take the leg off and that might stop it, though I doubt it. Or you can shoot me. You're a good shot now. I taught you to shoot, didn't I?"

"Please don't talk that way. Couldn't I read to you?"

"Read what?"

"Anything in the book bag that we haven't read."

"I can't listen to it," he said. "Talking is the easiest. We quarrel and that makes the time pass."

"I don't quarrel. I never want to quarrel. Let's not quarrel any more. No matter how nervous we get. Maybe they will be back with another truck today. Maybe the plane will come."

"I don't want to move," the man said. "There is no sense in moving now except to make it easier for you."

"That's cowardly."

"Can't you let a man die as comfortably as he can without calling him names? What's the use of slanging me?"

"You're not going to die."

"Don't be silly. I'm dying now. Ask those bastards." He looked over to where the huge, filthy birds sat, their naked heads sunk in the hunched feathers. A fourth planed down, to run quick-legged and then waddle slowly toward the others.

"They are around every camp. You never notice them. You can't die if you don't give up."

"Where did you read that? You're such a bloody fool."

"You might think about someone else."

"For Christ's sake," he said, "that's been my trade."

He lay then and was quiet for a while and looked across the heat shimmer of the plain to the edge of the bush. There were a few Tommies that showed minute and white against the yellow and, far off, he saw a herd of zebra, white against the green of the bush. This was a pleasant camp under big trees against a hill, with good water, and close by, a nearly dry waterhole where sand grouse flighted in the mornings.

"Wouldn't you like me to read?" she asked. She was sitting on a canvas chair beside his cot. "There's a breeze coming up."

"No, thanks."

"Maybe the truck will come."

"I don't give a damn about the truck."

"I do."

"You give a damn about so many things that I don't."

"Not so many, Harry."

"What about a drink?"

"It's supposed to be bad for you. It said in Black's to avoid all alcohol. You shouldn't drink."

"Molo!" he shouted.

"Yes, Bwana."

"Bring whiskey-soda."

"Yes, Bwana."

"You shouldn't," she said. "That's what I mean by giving up. It says it's bad for you. I know it's bad for you."

"No," he said. "It's good for me."

So now it was all over, he thought. So now he would never have a chance to finish it. So this was the way it ended in a bickering over a drink. Since the gangrene started in his right leg, he had no pain and with the pain the horror had gone, and all he felt now was a great tiredness and anger that this was the end of it. For this, that now was coming, he had very little curiosity. For years it had obsessed him; but now it meant nothing in itself. It was strange how easy being tired enough made it.

Now he would never write the things that he had saved to write until he knew enough to write them well. Well, he would not have to fail at trying to write them either. Maybe you could never write them, and that was why you put them off and delayed the starting. Well, he would never know, now.

"I wish we'd never come," the woman said. She was looking at him holding the glass and biting her lip. "You never would have gotten anything like this in Paris. You always said you loved Paris. We could have stayed in Paris or gone anywhere. I'd have gone anywhere. I said I'd go anywhere you wanted. If you wanted to shoot, we could have gone shooting in Hungary and been comfortable."

"Your bloody money," he said.

"That's not fair," she said. "It was always yours as much as mine. I left everything and I went wherever you wanted to go and I've done what you wanted to do. But I wish we'd never come here."

"You said you loved it."

"I did when you were all right. But now I hate it. I don't see why that had to happen to your leg. What have we done to have that happen to us?"

"I suppose what I did was to forget to put iodine on it when I first scratched it. Then I didn't pay any attention to it because I never infect. Then, later, when it got bad, it was probably using that weak carbolic solution when the other antiseptics ran out that paralyzed the minute blood vessels and started the gangrene." He looked at her, "What else?"

"I don't mean that."

"If we would have hired a good mechanic instead of a half-baked kikuyu driver, he would have checked the oil and never burned out that bearing in the truck."

"I don't mean that."

"If you hadn't left your own people, your goddamned Old Westbury, Saratoga, Palm Beach people to take me on—"

"Why, I loved you. That's not fair. I love you now. I'll always love you. Don't you love me?"

"No," said the man. "I don't think so. I never have."

"Harry, what are you saying? You're out of your head."

"No. I haven't any head to go out of."

"Don't drink that," she said. "Darling, please don't drink that. We have to do everything we can."

"You do it," he said. "I'm tired."

Now in his mind he saw a railway station at Karagatch and he was standing with his pack and that was the headlight of the Simplon-Orient cutting the dark now and he was leaving Thrace then after the retreat. That was one of the things he had saved to write, with, in the morning at breakfast, looking out the window and seeing snow on the mountains in Bulgaria and Nansen's Secretary asking the old man if it were snow and the old man looking at it and saying, No, that's not snow. It's too early for snow. And the Secretary repeating to the other girls, No, you see. It's not snow and them all saying, It's not snow we were mistaken. But it was the snow all right and he sent them on into it when he evolved exchange of populations.

And it was snow they tramped along in until they died that winter.

It was snow too that fell all Christmas week that year up in the Gauertal, that year they lived in the wood-cutter's house with the big square porcelain stove that filled half the room, and they slept on mattresses filled with beech leaves, the time the deserter came with his feet bloody in the snow. He said the police were right behind him and they gave him woolen socks and held the gendarmes talking until the tracks had drifted over.

In Schrunz, on Christmas day, the snow was so bright it hurt your eyes when you looked out from the Weinstube and saw every one coming home from church. That was where they walked up the sleigh-smoothed urine-yellowed road along the river with the steep pine hills, skis heavy on the shoulder, and where they ran that great run down the glacier above the Madlener-Haus, the snow as smooth to see as cake frosting and as light as powder and he remembered the noiseless rush the speed made as you dropped down like a bird.

They were snow-bound a week in the Madlener-Haus that time in the blizzard playing cards in the smoke by the lantern light and the stakes were higher all the time as Herr Lent lost more. Finally he lost it all. Everything, the skischule money and all the season's profit and then his capital. He could see him with his long nose, picking up the cards and then opening, "Sans Voir." There was always gambling then. When there was no snow you gambled and when there was too much you gambled. He thought of all the time in his life he had spent gambling.

But he had never written a line of that, nor of that cold, bright Christmas day with the mountains showing across the plain that Barker had flown across the lines to bomb the Austrian officers' leave train, machine-gunning them as they scattered and ran. He remembered Barker afterwards coming into the mess and starting to tell about it. And how quiet it got and then somebody saying, "You bloody murderous bastard."

Those were the same Austrians they killed then that he skied with later. No not the same. Hans, that he skied with all that year, had been in the Kaiser-Jägers and when they went hunting hares together up the little valley above the sawmill they had talked of the fighting on Pasubio and of the attack on Pertica and Asalone and he had never written a word of that. Nor of Monte Corno, nor the Siete Commum, nor of Arsiedo.

How many winters had he lived in the Voralberg and the Arlberg? It was four and then he remembered the man who had the fox to sell when they had walked into Bludenz, that time to buy presents, and the cherry-pit taste of good kirsch, the fast-slipping rush of running powder-snow on crust, singing "Hi! Ho! said Rolly!" as you ran down the last stretch to the steep drop, taking it straight, then running the orchard in three turns and out across the ditch and onto the icy road behind the inn. Knocking your bindings loose, kicking the skis free and leaning them up against the wooden wall of the inn, the lamplight coming from the window, where inside, in the smoky, new-wine smelling warmth, they were playing the accordion.

"Where did we stay in Paris?" he asked the woman who was sitting by him in a canvas chair, now, in Africa.

"At the Crillon. You know that."

"Why do I know that?"

"That's where we always stayed."

"No. Not always."

"There and at the Pavillon Henri-Quatre in St. Germain. You said you loved it there."

"Love is a dunghill," said Harry. "And I'm the cock that gets on it to crow."

"If you have to go away," she said, "is it absolutely necessary to kill off everything you leave behind? I mean do you have to take away everything? Do you have to kill your horse, and your wife, and burn your saddle and your armour?"

"Yes," he said. "Your damned money was my armour. My Swift and my Armour."

"Don't."

"All right. I'll stop that. I don't want to hurt you."

"It's a little bit late now."

"All right, then. I'll go on hurting you. It's more amusing. The only thing I ever really liked to do with you I can't do now."

"No, that's not true. You liked to do many things and everything you wanted to do I did."

"Oh, for Christ sake stop bragging, will you?"

He looked at her and saw her crying.

"Listen," he said. "Do you think that it is fun to do this? I don't know why I'm doing it. It's trying to kill to keep yourself alive, I imagine. I was all right when we started talking. I didn't mean to start this, and now I'm crazy as a coot and being as cruel to you as I can be. Don't pay any attention, darling, to what I say. I love you, really. You know I love you. I've never loved any one else the way I love you."

He slipped into the familiar lie he made his bread and butter by.

"You're sweet to me."

"You bitch," he said. "You rich bitch. That's poetry. I'm full of poetry now. Rot and poetry. Rotten poetry."

"Stop it. Harry, why do you have to turn into a devil now?"

"I don't like to leave anything," the man said. "I don't like to leave things behind."

It was evening now and he had been asleep. The sun was gone behind the hill and there was a shadow all across the plain and the small animals were feeding close to camp; quick-dropping heads and switching tails, he watched them keeping well out away from the bush now. The birds no longer waited on the ground. They were all perched heavily in a tree. There were many more of them. His personal boy was sitting by the bed.

"Memsahib's gone to shoot," the boy said. "Does Bwana want?"

"Nothing."

She had gone to kill a piece of meat and, knowing how he liked to watch the game, she had gone well away so she would not disturb this little pocket of the plain that he could see. She was always thoughtful, he thought. On anything she knew about, or had read, or that she had ever heard.

It was not her fault that when he went to her he was already over. How could a woman know that you meant nothing that you said; that you spoke only from habit and to be comfortable? After he no longer meant what he said, his lies were more successful with women than when he had told them the truth.

It was not so much that he lied as that there was no truth to tell. He had had his life and it was over and then he went on living it again with different people and more money, with the best of the same places, and some new ones.

You kept from thinking and it was all marvellous. You were equipped with good insides so that you did not go to pieces that way, the way most of them had, and you made an attitude that you cared noth-ing for the work you used to do, now that you could no longer do it. But, in yourself, you said that you would write about these people; about the very rich; that you were really not of them but a spy in their country; that you would leave it and write of it and for once it would be written by someone who knew what he was writing of. But he would never do it, because each day of not writing, of comfort, of being that which he despised, dulled his ability and softened his will to work so that, finally, he did no work at all. The people he knew now were all much more comfortable when he did not work. Africa was where he had been happiest in the good time of his life, so he had come out here to start again. They had made this safari with the minimum of comfort. There was no hardship; but there was no luxury and he had thought that he could get back into training that way. That in some way he could work the fat off his soul the way a fighter went into the mountains to work and train in order to burn it out of his body.

She had liked it. She said she loved it. She loved anything that was exciting, that involved a change of scene, where there were new people and where things were pleasant. And he had felt the illusion of returning strength of will to work. Now if this was how it ended, and he knew it was, he must not turn like some snake biting itself because its back was broken. It wasn't this woman's fault. If it had not been she, it would have been another. If he lived by a lie, he should try to die by it. He heard a shot beyond the hill.

She shot very well, this good, this rich bitch, this kindly caretaker and destroyer of his talent. Nonsense. He had destroyed his talent himself. Why should he blame this woman because she kept him well? He had destroyed his talent by not using it, by betrayals of himself and what he believed in, by drinking so much that he blunted the edge of his perceptions, by laziness, by sloth, and by snobbery, by pride and by prejudice, by hook and by crook. What was this? A catalogue of old books? What was his talent anyway? It was a talent all right, but instead of using it, he had traded on it. It was never what he had done, but always what he could do. And he had chosen to make his living with something else instead of a pen or a pencil. It was strange, too, wasn't it, that when he fell in love with another woman, that woman should always have more money than the last one? But when he no longer was in love, when he was only lying, as to this woman, now, who had the most money of all, who had all the money there was, who had had a husband and children, who had taken lovers and been dissatisfied with them, and who loved him dearly as a writer, as a man, as a companion, and as a proud possession; it was strange that, when he did not love her at all and was lying, he should be able to give her more for her money than when he had really loved.

We must all be cut out for what we do, he thought. However you make your living is where your talent lies. He had sold vitality, in one form or another, all his life, and when your affections are not too involved you give much better value for the money. He had found that out, but he would never write that, now, either. No, he would not write that, although it was well worth writing.

Now she came in sight, walking across the open toward the camp. She was wearing jodhpurs and carrying her rifle. The two boys had a Tommy slung and they were coming along behind her. She was still a good-looking woman, he thought, and she had a pleasant body. She had a

great talent and appreciation for the bed, she was not pretty, but he liked her face, she read enormously, liked to ride and shoot and, certainly, she drank too much. Her husband had died when she was still a comparatively young woman and for a while she had devoted herself to her two just-grown children, who did not need her and were embarrassed at having her about, to her stable of horses, to books, and to bottles. She liked to read in the evening before dinner and she drank Scotch-and-soda while she read. By dinner she was fairly drunk and after a bottle of wine at dinner she was usually drunk enough to sleep.

That was before the lovers. After she had the lovers, she did not drink so much because she did not have to be drunk to sleep. But the lovers bored her. She had been married to a man who had never bored her and these people bored her very much.

Then one of her two children was killed in a plane crash and after that was over she did not want the lovers, and drink being no anaesthetic she had to make another life. Suddenly, she had been acutely frightened of being alone. But she wanted someone that she respected with her.

It had begun very simply. She liked what he wrote and she had always envied the life he led. She thought he did exactly what he wanted to. The steps by which she had acquired him and the way in which she had finally fallen in love with him were all part of a regular progression in which she had built herself a new life and he had traded away what remained of his old life.

He had traded it for security, for comfort, too, there was no denying that, and for what else? He did not know. She would have bought him anything he wanted. He knew that. She was a damned nice woman too. He would as soon be in bed with her as anyone; rather with her, because she was richer, because she was very pleasant and appreciative, and because she never made scenes. And now this life that she had built again was coming to a term because he had not used iodine two weeks ago when a thorn had scratched his knee as they moved forward trying to photograph a herd of water-buck standing, their heads up, peering while their nostrils searched the air, their ears spread wide to hear the first noise that would send them rushing into the bush. They had bolted, too, before he got the picture.

Here she came now.

He turned his head on the cot to look toward her. "Hello," he said.

"I shot a Tommy ram," she told him. "He'll make you good broth and I'll have them mash some potatoes with the Klim. How do you feel?"

"Much better."

"Isn't that lovely? You know I thought perhaps you would. You were sleeping when I left."

"I had a good sleep. Did you walk far?"

"No. Just around behind the hill. I made quite a good shot on the Tommy."

"You shoot marvellously, you know."

"I love it. I've loved Africa. Really. If *you're* all right it's the most fun that I've ever had. You don't know the fun it's been to shoot with you. I've loved the country."

"I love it too."

"Darling, you don't know how marvellous it is to see you feeling better. I couldn't stand it when you felt that way. You won't talk to me like that again, will you? Promise me?"

"No," he said. "I don't remember what I said."

"You don't have to destroy me. Do you? I'm only a middle-aged woman who loves you and wants to do what you want to do. I've been destroyed two or three times already. You wouldn't want to destroy me again, would you?"

"I'd like to destroy you a few times in bed," he said.

"Yes. That's the good destruction. That's the way we're made to be destroyed. The plane will be here tomorrow."

"How do you know?"

"I'm sure. It's bound to come. The boys have the wood all ready and the grass to make the smudge. I went down and looked at it again today. There's plenty of room to land and we have the smudges ready at both ends."

"What makes you think it will come tomorrow?"

"I'm sure it will. It's overdue now. Then, in town, they will fix up your leg and then we will have some good destruction. Not that dreadful talking kind."

"Should we have a drink? The sun is down."

"Do you think you should?"

"I'm having one."

"We'll have one together. *Molo, letti dui whiskey-soda!*" she called.

"You'd better put on your mosquito boots," he told her.

"I'll wait till I bathe . . ."

While it grew dark they drank and just before it was dark and there was no longer enough light to shoot, a hyena crossed the open on his way around the hill.

"That bastard crosses there every night," the man said. "Every night for two weeks."

"He's the one makes the noise at night. I don't mind it. They're a filthy animal, though."

Drinking together, with no pain now except the discomfort of lying in the one position, the boys lighting a fire, its shadow jumping on the tents, he could feel the return of acquiescence in this life of pleasant surrender. She *was* very good to him. He had been cruel and unjust in the afternoon. She was a fine woman, marvelous really. And just then it occured to him that he was going to die.

It came with a rush; not as a rush of water nor of wind; but of a sudden evil-smelling emptiness and the odd thing was that the hyena slipped lightly along the edge of it.

"What is it, Harry?" she asked him.

"Nothing," he said. "You had better move over to the other side. To windward."

"Did Molo change the dressing?"

"Yes. I'm just using the boric now."

"How do you feel?"

"A little wobbly."

"I'm going in to bathe," she said. "I'll be right out. I'll eat with you and then we'll put the cot in."

So, he said to himself, we did well to stop the quarreling. He had never quarreled much with this woman, while with the women that he loved he had quarreled so much they had finally, always, with the corrosion of the quarreling, killed what they had together. He had loved too much, demanded too much, and he wore it all out.

He thought about alone in Constantinople that time, having quarreled in Paris before he had gone out. He had whored the whole time and then, when that was over, and he had failed to kill his loneliness, but only made it worse, he had written her, the first one, the one who left him, a letter telling her how he had never been able to kill it. . . . How when he thought he saw her outside the Régence one time it made him go all faint and sick inside, and that he would follow a woman who looked like her in some way, along

the Boulevard, afraid to see it was not she, afraid to lose the feeling it gave him. How everyone he had slept with had only made him miss her more. How what she had done could never matter since he knew he could not cure himself of loving her. He wrote this letter at the Club, cold sober, and mailed it to New York asking her to write him at the office in Paris. That seemed safe. And that night, missing her so much it made him feel hollow sick inside, he wandered up past Taxim's, picked a girl up and took her out to supper. He had gone to a place to dance with her afterward, she danced badly, and left her for a hot Armenian slut, that swung her belly against him so it almost scalded. He took her away from a British gunner subaltern after a row. The gunner asked him outside and they fought in the street on the cobbles in the dark. He'd hit him twice, hard, on the side of the jaw and when he didn't go down he knew he was in for a fight. The gunner hit him in the body, then beside his eye. He swung with his left again and landed and the gunner fell on him and grabbed his coat and tore the sleeve off and he clubbed him twice behind the ear and then smashed him with his right as he pushed him away. When the gunner went down his head hit first and he ran with the girl because they heard the M.P.'s coming. They got into a taxi and drove out to Rimmily Hissa along the Bosphorus, and around, and back in the cool night and went to bed and she felt as overripe as she looked but smooth, rose-petal, syrupy, smooth-bellied, big-breasted, and needed no pillow under her buttocks, and he left her before she was awake looking blowzy enough in the first daylight and turned up at the Pera Palace with a black eye, carrying his coat because one sleeve was missing.

That same night he left for Anatolia and he remembered, later on that trip, riding all day through fields of the poppies that they raised for opium and how strange it made you feel, finally, and all the distances seemed wrong, to where they had made the attack with the newly arrived Constantine officers, that did not know a goddamned thing, and the artillery had fired into the troops and the British observer had cried like a child.

That was the day he'd first seen dead men wearing white ballet skirts and upturned shoes with pompons on them. The Turks had come steadily and lumpily and he had seen the skirted men running and the officers shooting into them and running then themselves, and he and the British observer had run, too, until his lungs ached and his mouth was full of the taste of pennies, and they stopped behind some rocks and there were the Turks coming as lumpily as ever. Later he had seen the things that he could never think of and later still he had seen much worse. So when he got back to Paris that time he could not talk about it or stand to have it mentioned. And there in the café as he passed was that American poet with a pile of saucers in front of him and a stupid look on his potato face talking about the Dada movement with a Roumanian who said his name was Tristan Tzara, who always wore a monocle and had a headache, and, back at the apartment with his wife that now he loved again, the quarrel all over, the madness all over, glad to be home, the office sent his mail up to the flat. So then the letter in answer to the one he'd written came in on a platter one morning and when he saw the handwriting he went cold all over and tried to slip the letter underneath another. But his wife said, "Who is that letter from, dear?"

and that was the end of the beginning of that.

He remembered the good times with them all, and the quarrels. They always picked the finest places to have the quarrels. And why had they always quarreled when he was feeling best? He had never written any of that because, at first, he never wanted to hurt anyone and then it seemed as though there was enough to write without it. But he had always thought that he would write it finally. There was so much to write. He had seen the world change; not just the events; although he had seen many of them and had watched the people, but he had seen the subtler change and he could remember how the people were at different times. He had been in it and he had watched it and it was his duty to write of it; but now he never would.

"How do you feel?" she said. She had come out from the tent now after her bath.

"All right."

"Could you eat now?" He saw Molo behind her with the folding table and the other boy with the dishes.

"I want to write," he said.

"You ought to take some broth to keep your strength up."

"I'm going to die tonight," he said. "I don't need my strength up."

"Don't be melodramatic, Harry, please," she said.

"Why don't you use your nose? I'm rotted halfway up my thigh now. What the hell should I fool with broth for? Molo bring whiskey-soda."

"Please take the broth," she said gently.

"All right."

The broth was too hot. He had to hold it in the cup until it cooled enough to take it and then he just got it down without gagging.

"You're a fine woman," he said. "Don't pay any attention to me."

She looked at him with her well-known, well-loved face from *Spur* and *Town and Country,* only a little the worse for drink, only a little the worse for bed, but *Town and Country* never showed those good breasts and those useful thighs and those lightly small-of-back-caressing hands, and as he looked and saw her well-known pleasant smile, he felt death come again. This time there was no rush. It was a puff, as of a wind that makes a candle flicker and the flame go tall.

"They can bring my net out later and hang it from the tree and build the fire up. I'm not going in the tent tonight. It's not worth moving. It's a clear night. There won't be any rain."

So this was how you died, in whispers that you did not hear. Well, there would be no more quarreling. He could promise that. The one experience that he had never had he was not going to spoil now. He probably would. You spoiled everything. But perhaps he wouldn't.

"You can't take dictation, can you?"

"I never learned," she told him.

"That's all right."

There wasn't time, of course, although it seemed as though it telescoped so that you might put it all into one paragraph if you could get it right.

There was a log house, chinked white with mortar, on a hill above the lake. There was a bell on a pole by the door to call the people in to meals. Behind the house were fields and behind the fields was the timber. A line of Lombardy poplars ran from the house to the dock. Other poplars ran along the point. A road went up to the hills along the edge of the timber and along that road he picked blackberries. Then that log house was burned down and all the guns that had been on deer foot racks above the open fire place were burned and afterwards their barrels, with the lead melted in the magazines, and the stocks burned away, lay out on the heap of ashes that were used to make lye for the big iron soap kettles, and you asked Grandfather if you could have them to play with, and he said, no. You see they were his guns still and he never bought any others. Nor did he hunt any more. The house was rebuilt in the same place out of lumber now and painted white and from its porch you saw the poplars and the lake beyond; but there were never any more guns. The barrels of the guns that had hung on the deer feet on the wall of the log house lay out there on the heap of ashes and no one ever touched them.

In the Black Forest, after the war, we rented a trout stream and there were two ways to walk to it. One was down the valley from Triberg and around the valley road in the shade of the trees that bordered the white road, and then up a side road that went up through the hills past many small farms, with the big Schwarzwald houses, until that road crossed the stream. That was where our fishing began.

The other way was to climb steeply up to the edge of the woods and then go across the top of the hills through the pine woods, and then out to the edge of a meadow and down across this meadow to the bridge. There were birches along the stream and it was not big, but narrow, clear and fast, with pools where it had cut under the roots of the birches. At the hotel in Triberg the proprietor had a fine season. It was very pleasant and we were all great friends. The next year came the inflation and the money he had made the year before was not enough to buy sup-

plies to open the hotel and he hanged himself.

You could dictate that, but you could not dictate the Place Contrescarpe where the flower sellers dyed their flowers in the street and the dye ran over the paving where the autobus started and the old men and the women, always drunk on wine and bad marc; and the children with their noses running in the cold; the smell of dirty sweat and poverty and drunkenness at the Café des Amateurs and the whores at the Bal Musette they lived above. The Concierge who entertained the trooper of the Garde Républicaine in her loge, his horsehair plumed helmet on a chair. The locataire across the hall whose husband was a bicycle racer and her joy that morning at the Crémerie when she had opened L'Auto and seen where he placed third in Paris-Tours, his first big race. She had blushed and laughed and then gone upstairs crying with the yellow sporting paper in her hand. The husband of the woman who ran the Bal Musette drove a taxi, and when he, Harry, had to take an early plane the husband knocked upon the door to wake him and they each drank a glass of white wine at the zinc of the bar before they started. He knew his neighbors in that quarter then because they all were poor.

Around that Place there were two kinds; the drunkards and the sportifs. The drunkards killed their poverty that way; the sportifs took it out in exercise. They were the descendants of the Communards and it was no struggle for them to know their politics. They knew who had shot their fathers, their relatives, their brothers, and their friends when the Versailles troops came in and took the town after the Commune and executed anyone they could catch with calloused hands, or who wore a cap, or carried any other sign he was a workingman. And in that poverty, and in that quarter across the street from a Boucherie Chevaline and a wine co-operative, he had written the start of all he was to do. There never was another part of Paris that he loved like that, the sprawling trees, the old white plastered houses painted brown below, the long green of the autobus in that round square, the purple flower dye upon the paving, the sudden drop down the hill of the rue Cardinal Lemoine to the river, and the other way the narrow crowded world of the rue Mouffetard. The street that ran up toward the Pantheon and the other that he always took with the bicycle, the only asphalted street in all that quarter, smooth under the tires, with the high narrow houses and the cheap tall hotel where Paul Verlaine had died. There were only two rooms in the apartments where they lived and he had a room on the top floor of that hotel that cost him sixty francs a month where he did his writing, and from it he could see the roofs and chimney pots and all the hills of Paris.

From the apartment you could only see the wood and coal man's place. He sold wine too, bad wine. The golden horse's head outside the Boucherie Chevaline where the carcasses hung yellow gold and red in the open window, and the green painted co-operative where they bought their wine; good wine and cheap. The rest was plaster walls and the windows of the neighbors. The neighbors who, at night, when some one lay drunk in the street, moaning and groaning in that typical French ivresse that you were propaganded to believe did not exist, would open their windows and then the murmur of talk.

"Where is the policeman? When you don't want him the bugger is always there. He's sleeping with some concierge. Get *the* Agent." *Till some one threw a bucket of water from a window and the moaning stopped.* "*What's that? Water. Ah, that's intelligent.*" *And the windows shutting. Marie, his femme de ménage, protesting against the eight-hour day saying,* "*If a husband works until six he gets only a little drunk on the way home and does not waste too much. If he works only until five he is drunk every night and one has no money. It is the wife of the working-man who suffers from this shortening of hours.*"

"Wouldn't you like some more broth?" the woman asked him now.

"No, thank you very much. It is awfully good."

"Try just a little."

"I would like a whiskey-soda."

"It's not good for you."

"No. It's bad for me. Cole Porter wrote the words and the music. This knowledge that you're going mad for me."

"You know I like you to drink."

"Oh, yes. Only it's bad for me."

When she goes, he thought, I'll have all I want. Not all I want, but all there is. Ayee, he was tired. Too tired. He was going to sleep a little while. He lay still and death was not there. It must have gone around another street. It went in pairs, on bicycles, and moved absolutely silently on the pavements.

No, he had never written about Paris. Not the Paris that he cared about. But what about the rest that he had never written?

What about the ranch and the silvered gray of the sage brush, the quick, clear water in the irrigation ditches, and the heavy green of the alfalfa? The trail went up into the hills and the cattle in the summer were shy as deer. The bawling and *the steady noise and slow moving mass raising a dust as you brought them down in the fall. And behind the mountains, the clear sharpness of the peak in the evening light and, riding down along the trail in the moonlight, bright across the valley. Now he remembered coming down through the timber in the dark holding the horse's tail when you could not see and all the stories that he meant to write.*

About the half-wit chore boy who was left at the ranch that time and told not to let any one get any hay, and that old bastard from the Forks who had beaten the boy when he had worked for him stopping to get some feed. The boy refusing and the old man saying he would beat him again. The boy got the rifle from the kitchen and shot him when he tried to come into the barn and when they came back to the ranch he'd been dead a week, frozen in the corral, and the dogs had eaten part of him. But what was left you packed on a sled wrapped in a blanket and roped on and you got the boy to help you haul it, and the two of you took it out over the road on skis, and sixty miles down to town to turn the boy over. He having no idea that he would be arrested. Thinking he had done his duty and that you were his friend and he would be rewarded. He'd helped to haul the old man in so everybody could know how bad the old man had been and how he'd tried to steal some feed that didn't belong to him, and when the sheriff put the handcuffs on the boy he couldn't believe it. Then he'd started to cry. That was one story he had saved to write. He knew at least twenty good stories from out there and he had never written one. Why?

"You tell them why," he said.

"Why what, dear?"

"Why nothing."

She didn't drink so much, now, since she had him. But if he lived he would never write about her, he knew that now. Nor about any of them. The rich were dull and they drank too much, or they played too much backgammon. They were dull and they were repetitious. He remembered poor Julian and his romantic awe of them and how he had started a story once that began, "The very rich are different from you and me." And how someone had said to Julian, Yes, they have more money. But that was not humorous to Julian. He thought they were a special glamorous race and when he found they weren't it wrecked him just as much as any other thing that wrecked him.

He had been contemptuous of those who wrecked. You did not have to like it because you understood it. He could bear anything, he thought, because nothing could hurt him if he did not care.

All right. Now he would not care for death. One thing he had always dreaded was the pain. He could stand pain as well as any man, until it went on too long, and wore him out, but here he had something that had hurt frightfully and just when he had felt it breaking him, the pain had stopped.

He remembered long ago when Williamson, the bombing officer, had been hit by a stick bomb someone in a German patrol had thrown as he was coming in through the wire that night and, screaming, had begged everyone to kill him. He was a fat man, very brave, and a good officer, although addicted to fantastic shows. But that night he was caught in the wire, with a flare lighting him up and his bowels spilled out into the wire, so when they brought him in, alive, they had to cut him loose. Shoot me, Harry. For Christ sake, shoot me. They had had

an argument one time about our Lord never sending you anything you could not bear and someone's theory had been that meant that at a certain time the pain passed you out automatically. But he had always remembered Williamson, that night. Nothing passed out Williamson until he gave him all his morphine tablets that he had always saved to use himself and then they did not work right away.

Still this now, that he had, was very easy; and if it was no worse as it went on there was nothing to worry about. Except that he would rather be in better company.

He thought a little about the company that he would like to have.

No, he thought, when everything you do, you do too long, and do too late, you can't expect to find the people still there. The people all are gone. The party's over and you are with your hostess now.

I'm getting as bored with dying as with everything else, he thought.

"It's a bore," he said out loud.

"What is, my dear?"

"Anything you do too bloody long."

He looked at her face between him and the fire. She was leaning back in the chair and the firelight shone on her pleasantly lined face and he could see that she was sleepy. He heard the hyena make a noise just outside the range of the fire.

"I've been writing," he said. "But I got tired."

"Do you think you will be able to sleep?"

"Pretty sure. Why don't you turn in?"

"I like to sit here with you."

"Do you feel anything strange?" he asked her.

"No. Just a little sleepy."

"I do," he said.

He had just felt death come by again.

"You know the only thing I've never lost is curiosity," he said to her.

"You've never lost anything. You're the most complete man I've ever known."

"Christ," he said. "How little a woman knows. What is that? Your intuition?"

Because, just then, death had come and rested its head on the foot of the cot and he could smell its breath.

"Never believe any of that about a scythe and a skull," he told her. "It can be two bicycle policemen as easily or be a bird. Or it can have a wide snout like a hyena."

It had moved up on him now, but it had no shape any more. It simply occupied space.

"Tell it to go away."

It did not go away, but moved a little closer.

"You've got a hell of a breath," he told it. "You stinking bastard."

It moved up closer to him still, and now he could not speak to it, and when it saw he could not speak, it came a little closer, and now he tried to send it away without speaking, but it moved in on him so its weight was all upon his chest, and while it crouched there and he could not move, or speak, he heard the woman say, "Bwana is asleep now. Take the cot up very gently and carry it into the tent."

He could not speak to tell her to make it go away and it crouched now, heavier, so he could not breathe. And then, while they lifted the cot, suddenly it was all right and the weight went from his chest.

It was morning and had been morning for some time and he heard the plane. It showed very tiny and then made a wide circle and the boys ran out and lit the fires, using kerosene, and piled on grass so there were two big smudges at each end of the level place and the morning breeze blew them toward the camp and the plane circled twice more, low this time, and then glided down and leveled off and landed smoothly and, coming walking toward him, was old Compton in slacks, a tweed jacket, and a brown felt hat.

"What's the matter, old cock?" Compton said.

"Bad leg," he told him. "Will you have some breakfast?"

"Thanks. I'll just have some tea. It's the Puss Moth, you know. I won't be able to take the Memsahib. There's only room for one. Your lorry is on the way."

Helen had taken Compton aside and was speaking to him. Compton came back more cheery than ever.

"We'll get you right in," he said. "I'll be back for the Mem. Now I'm afraid I'll have to stop at Arusha to refuel. We'd better get going."

"What about the tea?"

"I don't really care about it, you know."

The boys had picked up the cot and carried it around the green tents and down along the rock and out onto the plain and along past the smudges that were burning brightly now, the grass all consumed, and the wind fanning the fire, to the little plane. It was difficult getting him in, but once in he lay back in the leather seat, and the leg was stuck straight out to one side of the seat where Compton sat. Compton started the motor and got in. He waved to Helen and to the boys and, as the clatter moved into the old familiar roar, they swung around with Compie watching for wart-hog holes and roared, bumping, along the stretch between the fires and with the last bump rose and he saw them all standing below, waving, and the camp beside the hill, flattening now, and the plain spreading, clumps of trees, and the bush flattening, while the game trails ran now smoothly to the dry waterholes, and there was a new water that he had never known of. The zebra, small rounded backs now, and the wildebeeste, big headed dots seeming to climb as they moved in long fingers across the plain, now scattering as the shadow came toward them, they were tiny now, and the movement had no gallop, and the plain as far as you could see, gray-yellow now and ahead old Compie's tweed back and the brown felt hat. Then they were over the first hills and the wildebeeste were trailing up them, and then they were over mountains with sudden depths of green-rising forest and the solid bamboo slopes, and then the heavy forest again, sculptured into peaks and hollows until they crossed, and hills sloped down and then another plain, hot now, and purple brown, bumpy with heat and Compie looking back to see how he was riding. Then there were other mountains dark ahead.

And then instead of going on to Arusha they turned left, he evidently figured that they had the gas, and looking down he saw a pink sifting cloud, moving over the ground, and in the air, like the first snow in a blizzard, that comes from nowhere, and he knew the locusts were coming up from the south. Then they began to climb and they were going to the east it seemed, and then it darkened and they were in a storm, the rain so thick it seemed like flying through a waterfall, and then they were out and Compie turned his head and grinned and pointed and there, ahead, all he could see, as wide as all the world, great, high, and unbelievably white in the sun, was the square top of Kilimanjaro. And then he knew that there was where he was going.

Just then the hyena stopped whimpering in the night and started to make a strange, human, almost crying sound. The woman heard it and stirred uneasily. She did not wake. In her dream she was at the house on Long Island and it was the night before her daughter's début. Somehow her father was there and he had been very rude. Then the noise the hyena made was so loud she woke and for a moment she did not know where she was and she was very afraid. Then she took the flashlight and shone it on the other cot that they had carried in after Harry had gone to sleep. She could see his bulk under the mosquito bar, but somehow he had gotten his leg out and it hung down alongside the cot. The dressings had all come down and she could not look at it.

"Molo," she called, "Molo! Molo!"

Then she said, "Harry, Harry!" Then her voice rising, "Harry! Please! Oh Harry!"

There was no answer and she could not hear him breathing.

Outside the tent the hyena made the same strange noise that had awakened her. But she did not hear him for the beating of her heart.

THE SECRET SHARER

by Joseph Conrad

On my right hand there were lines of fishing-stakes resembling a mysterious system of half-submerged bamboo fences, incomprehensible in its division of the domain of tropical fishes, and crazy of aspect as if abandoned forever by some nomad tribe of fishermen now gone to the other end of the ocean; for there was no sign of human habitation as far as the eye could reach. To the left a group of barren islets, suggesting ruins of stone walls, towers, and blockhouses, had its foundations set in a blue sea that itself looked solid, so still and stable did it lie below my feet; even the track of light from the westering sun shone smoothly, without that animated glitter which tells of an imperceptible ripple. And when I turned my head to take a parting glance at the tug which had just left us anchored outside the bar, I saw the straight line of the flat shore joined to the stable sea, edge to edge, with a perfect and unmarked closeness, in one leveled floor half brown, half blue under the enormous dome of the sky. Corresponding in their insignificance to the islets of the sea, two small clumps of trees, one on each side of the only fault in the impeccable joint, marked the mouth of the river Meinam we had just left on the first preparatory stage of our homeward journey; and, far back on the inland level, a larger and loftier mass, the grove surrounding the great Paknam pagoda, was the only thing on which the eye could rest from the vain task of exploring the monotonous sweep of the horizon. Here and there gleams as of a few scattered pieces of silver marked the windings of the great river; and on the nearest of them, just within the bar, the tug steaming right into the land became lost to my sight, hull and funnel and masts, as though the impassive earth had swallowed her up without an effort, without a tremor. My eye followed the light cloud of her smoke, now here, now there, above the plain, according to the devious curves of the stream, but always fainter and farther away, till I lost it at last behind the miter-shaped hill of the great pagoda. And then I was left alone with my ship, anchored at the head of the Gulf of Siam.

She floated at the starting-point of a long journey, very still in an immense stillness, the shadows of her spars flung far to the eastward by the setting sun. At that moment I was alone on her decks. There was not a sound in her—and around us nothing moved, nothing lived, not a canoe on the water, not a bird in the air, not a cloud in the sky. In this breathless pause at the threshold of a long passage we seemed to be measuring our fitness for a long and arduous enterprise, the appointed task of both our existences to be carried out, far from all human eyes, with only sky and sea for spectators and for judges.

There must have been some glare in the air to interfere with one's sight, because it was only just before the sun left us that my roaming eyes made out beyond the highest ridge of the principal islet of the group something which did away with the solemnity of perfect solitude. The tide of darkness flowed on swiftly; and with tropical suddenness, a swarm of stars came out above the shadowy earth, while I lingered yet, my hand resting lightly on my ship's rail as if on the shoulder of a trusted friend. But, with all that multitude of celestial bodies staring down at one, the comfort of quiet communion with her was gone for good. And there were also disturbing sounds by this time—voices, footsteps forward; the steward flitted along the main-deck, a busily ministering spirit; a hand-bell tinkled urgently under the poop-deck. . . .

I found my two officers waiting for me near the supper table, in the lighted cuddy. We sat down at once, and as I helped the chief mate, I said:

"Are you aware that there is a ship anchored inside the islands? I saw her mastheads above the ridge as the sun went down."

He raised sharply his simple face, overcharged by a terrible growth of whisker, and emitted his usual ejaculations: "Bless my soul, sir! You don't say so!"

My second mate was a round-cheeked, silent young man, grave beyond his years, I thought; but as our eyes happened to meet I detected a slight quiver on his lips. I looked down at once. It was not my part to encourage sneering on board my ship. It must be said, too, that I knew very little of my officers. In consequence of certain events of no particular significance, except to myself, I had been appointed to the command only a fortnight before. Neither did I know much of the hands forward. All these people had been together for eighteen months or so, and my position was that of the only stranger on board. I mention this because it has some bearing on what is to follow. But what I felt most was my being a stranger to the ship; and if all the truth must be told, I was somewhat of a stranger to myself. The youngest man on board (barring the second mate), and untried as yet by a position of the fullest responsibility, I was willing to take the adequacy of the others for granted. They had simply to be equal to their tasks; but I wondered how far I should turn out faithful to that ideal conception of one's own personality every man sets up for himself secretly.

Meantime the chief mate, with an almost visible effect of collaboration on the part of his round eyes and frightful whiskers, was trying to evolve a theory of the anchored ship. His dominant trait was to take all things into earnest consideration. He was of a painstaking turn of mind. As he used to say, he "liked to account to himself" for practically everything that came in his way, down to a miserable scorpion he had found in his cabin a week before. The why and the wherefore of that scorpion—how it got on board and came to select his room rather than the pantry (which was a dark place and more what a scorpion would be partial to), and how on earth it managed to drown itself in the inkwell of his writing-desk—had exercised him infinitely. The ship within the islands was much more easily accounted for; and just as we were about to rise from table he made his pronouncement.

She was, he doubted not, a ship from home lately arrived. Probably she drew too much water to cross the bar except at the top of spring tides. Therefore she went into that natural harbor to wait for a few days in preference to remaining in an open roadstead.

"That's so," confirmed the second mate, suddenly, in his slightly hoarse voice. "She draws over twenty feet. She's the Liverpool ship *Sephora* with a cargo of coal. Hundred and twenty-three days from Cardiff."

We looked at him in surprise.

"The tugboat skipper told me when he came on board for your letters, sir," explained the young man. "He expects to take her up the river the day after tomorrow."

After thus overwhelming us with the extent of his information he slipped out of the cabin. The mate observed regretfully that he "could not account for that young fellow's whims." What prevented him telling us all about it at once, he wanted to know.

I detained him as he was making a move. For the last two days the crew had had plenty of hard work, and the night before they had very little sleep. I felt painfully that I—a stranger—was doing something unusual when I directed him to let all hands turn in without setting an anchor-watch. I proposed to keep on deck myself till one o'clock or thereabouts. I would get the second mate to relieve me at that hour.

"He will turn out the cook and the steward at four," I concluded, "and then give you a call. Of course at the slightest sign of any sort of wind we'll have the hands up and make a start at once."

He concealed his astonishment. "Very well, sir." Outside the cuddy he put his head in the second mate's door to inform him of my unheard-of caprice to take a five hours' anchor-watch on myself. I heard the other raise his voice incredulously—"What? The Captain himself?" Then a few more murmurs, a door closed, then another. A few moments later I went on deck.

My strangeness, which had made me sleepless, had prompted that unconventional arrangement, as if I had expected in those solitary hours of the night to get on terms with the ship of which I knew nothing, manned by men of whom I knew very little more. Fast alongside a wharf, littered like any ship in port with a tangle of unrelated things, invaded by unrelated shore people, I had hardly seen her yet properly. Now, as she lay cleared for sea, the stretch of her main-deck seemed to me very fine under the stars. Very fine, very roomy for her size, and very inviting. I descended the poop and paced the waist, my mind picturing to myself the coming passage through the Malay Archipelago, down the Indian Ocean, and up the Atlantic. All its phases were familiar enough to me, every characteristic, all the alternatives which were likely to face me on the high seas—everything! . . . except the novel responsibility of command. But I took heart from the reasonable thought that the ship was like other ships, the men like other men, and that the sea was not likely to keep any special surprises expressly for my discomfiture.

Arrived at that comforting conclusion, I bethought myself of a cigar and went below to get it. All was still down there. Everybody at the after end of the ship was sleeping profoundly. I came out again on the quarter-deck, agreeably at ease in my sleeping-suit on that warm breathless night, barefooted, a glowing cigar in my teeth, and, going forward, I was met by the profound silence of the fore end of the ship. Only as I passed the door of the forecastle I heard a deep, quiet, trustful sigh of some sleeper inside. And suddenly I rejoiced in the great security of the sea as compared with the unrest of the land, in my choice of that untempted life presenting no disquieting problems, invested with an elementary moral beauty by the absolute straightforwardness of its appeal and by the singleness of its purpose.

The riding-light in the fore-rigging burned with a clear, untroubled, as if symbolic, flame, confident and bright in the mysterious shades of the night. Passing on my way aft along the other side of the ship, I observed that the rope side-ladder, put over, no doubt, for the master of the tug when he came to fetch away our letters, had not been hauled in as it should have been. I became annoyed at this, for exactitude in small matters is the very soul of discipline. Then I reflected that I had myself peremptorily dismissed my officers from duty, and by my own act had prevented the anchor-watch being formally set and things properly attended to. I asked myself whether it was wise ever to interfere with the established routine of duties even from the kindest of motives. My action might have made me appear eccentric. Goodness only knew how that absurdly whiskered mate would "account" for my conduct, and what the whole ship thought of that informality of their new captain. I was vexed with myself.

Not from compunction certainly, but, as it were mechanically, I proceeded to get the ladder in myself. Now a side-ladder of that sort is a light affair and comes in easily, yet my vigorous tug, which should have brought it flying on board, merely recoiled upon my body in a totally un-expected jerk. What the devil! . . . I was so astounded by the immovableness of that ladder that I remained stock-still, trying to account for it to myself like that imbecile mate of mine. In the end, of course, I put my head over the rail.

The side of the ship made an opaque belt of shadow on the darkling glassy shimmer of the sea. But I saw at once something elongated and pale floating very close to the ladder. Before I could form a guess a faint flash of phosphorescent light, which seemed to issue suddenly from the naked body of a man, flickered in the sleeping water with the elusive, silent play of summer lightning in a night sky. With a gasp I saw revealed to my stare a pair of feet, the long legs, a broad livid back immersed right up to the neck in a greenish cadaverous glow. One hand, awash, clutched the bottom rung of the ladder. He was complete but for the head. A headless corpse! The cigar dropped out of my gaping mouth with a tiny plop and a short hiss quite audible in the absolute stillness of all things under heaven. At that I suppose he raised up his face, a dimly pale oval in the shadow of the ship's side. But even then I could only barely make out down there the shape of his black-haired head. However, it was enough for the horrid, frost-bound sensation which had gripped me about the chest to pass off. The moment of vain exclamations was past, too. I only climbed on the spare spar and leaned over the rail as far as I could, to bring my eyes nearer to that mystery floating alongside.

As he hung by the ladder, like a resting swimmer, the sea-lightning played about his limbs at every stir; and he appeared in it ghastly, silvery, fish-like. He remained as mute as a fish, too. He made no motion to get out of the water, either.

It was inconceivable that he should not attempt to come on board, and strangely troubling to suspect that perhaps he did not want to. And my first words were prompted by just that troubled incertitude.

"What's the matter?" I asked in my ordinary tone, speaking down to the face upturned exactly under mine.

"Cramp," it answered, no louder. Then slightly anxious, "I say, no need to call anyone."

"I was not going to," I said.

"Are you alone on deck?"

"Yes."

I had somehow the impression that he was on the point of letting go the ladder to swim away beyond my ken—mysterious as he came. But, for the moment, this being appearing as if he had risen from the bottom of the sea (it was certainly the nearest land to the ship) wanted only to know the time. I told him. And he, down there, tentatively:

"I suppose your captain's turned in?"

"I am sure he isn't," I said.

He seemed to struggle with himself, for I heard something like the low, bitter murmur of doubt. "What's the good?" His next words came out with a hesitating effort.

"Look here, my man. Could you call him out quietly?"

I thought the time had come to declare myself.

"*I* am the captain."

I heard a "By Jove!" whispered at the level of the water. The phosphorescence flashed in the swirl of the water all about his limbs, his other hand seized the ladder.

"My name's Leggatt."

The voice was calm and resolute. A good voice. The self-possession of that man had somehow induced a correspond-ing state in myself. It was very quietly that I remarked:

"You must be a good swimmer."

"Yes. I've been in the water practically since nine o'clock. The question for me now is whether I am to let go this ladder and go on swimming till I sink from exhaustion, or—to come on board here."

I felt this was no mere formula of desperate speech, but a real alternative in the view of a strong soul. I should have gathered from this that he was young; indeed, it is only the young who are ever confronted by such clear issues. But at the time it was pure intuition on my part. A mysterious communication was established already between us two—in the face of that silent, darkened tropical sea. I was young, too; young enough to make no comment. The man in the water began suddenly to climb up the ladder, and I hastened away from the rail to fetch some clothes.

Before entering the cabin I stood still, listening in the lobby at the foot of the stairs. A faint snore came through the closed door of the chief mate's room. The second mate's door was on the hook, but the darkness in there was absolutely soundless. He, too, was young and could sleep like a stone. Remained the steward, but he was not likely to wake up before he was called. I got a sleeping-suit out of my room and, coming back on deck, saw the naked man from the sea sitting on the main-hatch, glimmering white in the darkness, his elbows on his knees and his head in his hands. In a moment he had concealed his damp body in a sleeping-suit of the same gray-stripe pattern as the one I was wearing and followed me like my double on the poop. Together we moved right aft, barefooted, silent.

"What is it?" I asked in a deadened

voice, taking the lighted lamp out of the binnacle, and raising it to his face.

"An ugly business."

He had rather regular features; a good mouth; light eyes under somewhat heavy, dark eyebrows; a smooth, square forehead; no growth on his cheeks; a small, brown mustache, and a well-shaped, round chin. His expression was concentrated, meditative, under the inspecting light of the lamp I held up to his face; such as a man thinking hard in solitude might wear. My sleeping-suit was just right for his size. A well-knit young fellow of twenty-five at most. He caught his lower lip with the edge of white, even teeth.

"Yes," I said, replacing the lamp in the binnacle. The warm, heavy tropical night closed upon his head again.

"There's a ship over there," he murmured.

"Yes, I know. The *Sephora*. Did you know of us?"

"Hadn't the slightest idea. I am the mate of her—" He paused and corrected himself. "I should say I *was*."

"Aha! Something wrong?"

"Yes. Very wrong indeed. I've killed a man."

"What do you mean? Just now?"

"No, on the passage. Weeks ago. Thirty-nine south. When I say a man—"

"Fit of temper," I suggested, confidently.

The shadowy, dark head, like mine, seemed to nod imperceptibly above the ghostly gray of my sleeping-suit. It was, in the night, as though I had been faced by my own reflection in the depths of a somber and immense mirror.

"A pretty thing to have to own up to for a Conway boy," murmured my double, distinctly.

"You're a Conway boy?"

"I am," he said, as if startled. Then, slowly . . . "Perhaps you too—"

It was so; but being a couple of years older I had left before he joined. After a quick interchange of dates a silence fell; and I thought suddenly of my absurd mate with his terrific whiskers and the "Bless my soul—you don't say so" type of intellect. My double gave me an inkling of his thoughts by saying: "My father's a parson in Norfolk. Do you see me before a judge and jury on that charge? For myself I can't see the necessity. There are fellows that an angel from heaven— And I am not that. He was one of those creatures that are just simmering all the time with a silly sort of wickedness. Miserable devils that have no business to live at all. He wouldn't do his duty and wouldn't let anybody else do theirs. But what's the good of talking! You know well enough the sort of ill-conditioned snarling cur—"

He appealed to me as if our experiences had been as identical as our clothes. And I knew well enough the pestiferous danger of such a character where there are no means of legal repression. And I knew well enough also that my double there was no homicidal ruffian. I did not think of asking him for details, and he told me the story roughly in brusque, disconnected sentences. I needed no more. I saw it all going on as though I were myself inside that other sleeping-suit.

"It happened while we were setting a reefed foresail, at dusk. Reefed foresail! You understand the sort of weather. The only sail we had left to keep the ship running; so you may guess what it had been like for days. Anxious sort of job, that. He gave me some of his cursed insolence at the sheet. I tell you I was overdone with this terrific weather that seemed to have no end to it. Terrific, I tell you—

and a deep ship. I believe the fellow himself was half crazed with funk. It was no time for gentlemanly reproof, so I turned round and felled him like an ox. He up and at me. We closed just as an awful sea made for the ship. All hands saw it coming and took to the rigging, but I had him by the throat, and went on shaking him like a rat, the men above us yelling, 'Look out! look out!' Then a crash as if the sky had fallen on my head. They say that for over ten minutes hardly anything was to be seen of the ship—just the three masts and a bit of the forecastle head and of the poop all awash driving along in a smother of foam. It was a miracle that they found us, jammed together behind the forebitts. It's clear that I meant business, because I was holding him by the throat still when they picked us up. He was black in the face. It was too much for them. It seems they rushed us aft together, gripped as we were, screaming 'Murder!' like a lot of lunatics, and broke into the cuddy. And the ship running for her life, touch and go all the time, any minute her last in a sea fit to turn your hair gray only a-looking at it. I understand that the skipper, too, started raving like the rest of them. The man had been deprived of sleep for more than a week, and to have this sprung on him at the height of a furious gale nearly drove him out of his mind. I wonder they didn't fling me overboard after getting the carcass of their precious ship-mate out of my fingers. They had rather a job to separate us, I've been told. A sufficiently fierce story to make an old judge and a respectable jury sit up a bit. The first thing I heard when I came to myself was the maddening howling of that endless gale, and on that the voice of the old man. He was hanging on to my bunk, staring into my face out of his sou'wester.

"'Mr. Leggatt, you have killed a man. You can act no longer as chief mate of this ship.'"

His care to subdue his voice made it sound monotonous. He rested a hand on the end of the skylight to steady himself with, and all that time did not stir a limb, so far as I could see. "Nice little tale for a quiet tea-party," he concluded in the same tone.

One of my hands, too, rested on the end of the skylight; neither did I stir a limb, so far as I knew. We stood less than a foot from each other. It occurred to me that if old "Bless my soul—you don't say so" were to put his head up the companion and catch sight of us, he would think he was seeing double, or imagine himself come upon a scene of weird witchcraft; the strange captain having a quiet confabulation by the wheel with his own gray ghost. I became very much concerned to prevent anything of the sort. I heard the other's soothing undertone.

"My father's a parson in Norfolk," it said. Evidently he had forgotten he had told me this important fact before. Truly a nice little tale.

"You had better slip down into my state-room now," I said, moving off stealthily. My double followed my movements; our bare feet made no sound; I let him in, closed the door with care, and, after giving a call to the second mate, returned on deck for my relief.

"Not much sign of any wind yet," I remarked when he approached.

"No, sir. Not much," he assented, sleepily, in his hoarse voice, with just enough deference, no more, and barely suppressing a yawn.

"Well, that's all you have to look out for. You have got your orders."

"Yes, sir."

I paced a turn or two on the poop and saw him take up his position face forward with his elbow in the ratlines of the mizzen-rigging before I went below. The mate's faint snoring was still going on peacefully. The cuddy lamp was burning over the table on which stood a vase with flowers, a polite attention from the ship's provision merchant—the last flowers we should see for the next three months at the very least. Two bunches of bananas hung from the beam symmetrically, one on each side of the rudder-casing. Everything was as before in the ship—except that two of her captain's sleeping-suits were simultaneously in use, one motionless in the cuddy, the other keeping very still in the captain's stateroom.

It must be explained here that my cabin had the form of the capital letter L, the door being within the angle and opening into the short part of the letter. A couch was to the left, the bed-place to the right; my writing-desk and the chronometers' table faced the door. But anyone opening it, unless he stepped right inside, had no view of what I call the long (or vertical) part of the letter. It contained some lockers surmounted by a bookcase; and a few clothes, a thick jacket or two, caps, oilskin coat, and such like, hung on books. There was at the bottom of that part a door opening into my bath-room, which could be entered also directly from the saloon. But that way was never used.

The mysterious arrival had discovered the advantage of this particular shape. Entering my room, lighted strongly by a big bulkhead lamp swung on gimbals above my writing-desk, I did not see him anywhere till he stepped out quietly from behind the coats hung in the recessed part.

"I heard somebody moving about, and went in there at once," he whispered.

I, too, spoke under my breath.

"Nobody is likely to come in here without knocking and getting permission."

He nodded. His face was thin and the sunburn faded, as though he had been ill. And no wonder. He had been, I heard presently, kept under arrest in his cabin for nearly seven weeks. But there was nothing sickly in his eyes or in his expression. He was not a bit like me, really; yet, as we stood leaning over my bed-place, whispering side by side, with our dark heads together and our backs to the door, anybody bold enough to open it stealthily would have been treated to the uncanny sight of a double captain busy talking in whispers with his other self.

"But all this doesn't tell me how you came to hang on to our side-ladder," I inquired, in the hardly audible murmurs we used, after he had told me something more of the proceedings on board the *Sephora* once the bad weather was over.

"When we sighted Java Head I had had time to think all those matters out several times over. I had six weeks of doing nothing else, and with only an hour or so every evening for a tramp on the quarter-deck."

He whispered, his arms folded on the side of my bed-place, staring through the open port. And I could imagine perfectly the manner of this thinking out—a stubborn if not a steadfast operation; something of which I should have been perfectly incapable.

"I reckoned it would be dark before we closed with the land," he continued, so low that I had to strain my hearing, near as we were to each other, shoulder touching shoulder almost. "So I asked to speak to the old man. He always seemed very sick when he came to see me—as if he could not look me in the face. You know, that foresail saved the ship. She was too deep to have run long under bare poles. And it was I that managed to set it for him. Anyway, he came. When I had him in my cabin—he stood by the door looking at me as if I had the halter round my neck already—I asked him right away to leave my cabin door unlocked at night while the ship was going through Sunda Straits. There would be the Java coast within two or three miles, off Angier Point. I wanted nothing more. I've had a prize for swimming my second year in the Conway."

"I can believe it," I breathed out.

"God only knows why they locked me in every night. To see some of their faces you'd have thought they were afraid I'd go about at night strangling people. Am I a murdering brute? Do I look it? By Jove! if I had been he wouldn't have trusted himself like that into my room. You'll say I might have chucked him aside and bolted out, there and then—it was dark already. Well, no. And for the same reason I wouldn't think of trying to smash the door. There would have been a rush to stop me at the noise, and I did not mean to get into a confounded scrimmage. Somebody else might have got killed—for I would not have broken out only to get chucked back, and I did not want any more of that work. He refused, looking more sick than ever. He was afraid of the men, and also of that old second mate of his who had been sailing with him for years—a gray-headed old humbug; and his steward, too, had been with him devil knows how long—seventeen years or more —a dogmatic sort of loafer who hated me like poison, just because I was the chief mate. No chief mate ever made more than one voyage in the *Sephora*, you know. Those two old chaps ran the ship. Devil only knows what the skipper wasn't afraid of (all his nerve went to pieces altogether in that hellish spell of bad weather we had)—of what the law would do to him —of his wife, perhaps. Oh, yes! she's on board. Though I don't think she would have meddled. She would have been only too glad to have me out of the ship in any way. The 'brand of Cain' business, don't you see. That's all right. I was ready enough to go off wandering on the face of the earth—and that was price enough to pay for an Abel of that sort. Anyhow, he wouldn't listen to me. 'This thing must take its course. I represent the law here.' He was shaking like a leaf. 'So you won't?' 'No!' 'Then I hope you will be able to sleep on that,' I said, and turned my back on him. 'I wonder that *you* can,' cries he, and locks the door.

"Well, after that, I couldn't. Not very well. That was three weeks ago. We have had a slow passage through the Java Sea; drifted about Carimata for ten days. When we anchored here they thought, I suppose, it was all right. The nearest land (and that's five miles) is the ship's destination; the consul would soon set about catching me; and there would have been no object in bolting to these islets there. I don't suppose there's a drop of water on them. I don't know how it was, but tonight that steward, after bringing me my supper, went out to let me eat it, and left the door unlocked. And I ate it—all there was, too. After I had finished I strolled out on the quarter-deck. I don't know that I meant to do anything. A breath of fresh air was all I wanted, I believe. Then a sudden temptation came over me. I kicked off my slippers and was in the water before I had made up my mind fairly. Somebody heard the splash and they raised an awful hullabaloo. 'He's gone! Lower the boats! He's committed suicide! No, he's swimming.' Certainly I was swimming. It's not so easy for a swimmer like me to commit suicide by drowning. I landed on the nearest islet before the boat left the ship's side. I heard them pulling about in the dark, hailing, and so on, but after a bit they gave up. Everything quieted down and the anchorage became as still as death. I sat down on a stone and began to think. I felt certain they would start searching for me at daylight. There was no place to hide on those stony things—and if there had been, what would have been the good? But now I was clear of that ship, I was not going back. So after a while I took off all my clothes, tied them up in a bundle with a stone inside, and dropped them in the deep water on the outer side of that islet. That was suicide enough for me. Let them think what they liked, but I didn't mean to drown myself. I meant to swim till I sank—but that's not the same thing. I struck out for another of these little islands, and it was from that one that I first saw your riding-light. Something to swim for. I went on easily, and on the way I came upon a flat rock a foot or two above water. In the daytime, I dare say, you might make it out with a glass from your poop. I scrambled up on it and rested myself for a bit. Then I made another start. That last spell must have been over a mile."

His whisper was getting fainter and fainter, and all the time he stared straight out through the port-hole, in which there was not even a star to be seen. I had not interrupted him. There was something that made comment impossible in his narrative, or perhaps in himself; a sort of feeling, a quality, which I can't find a name for. And when he ceased, all I found was a futile whisper: "So you swam for our light?"

"Yes—straight for it. It was something to swim for. I couldn't see any stars low down because the coast was in the way, and I couldn't see the land, either. The water was like glass. One might have been swimming in a confounded thousand-feet-deep cistern with no place for scrambling out anywhere; but what I didn't like was the notion of swimming round and round like a crazed bullock before I gave out; and as I didn't mean to go back . . . No. Do you see me being hauled back, stark naked, off one of these little islands by the scruff of the neck and fighting like a wild beast? Somebody would have got killed for certain, and I did not want any of that. So I went on. Then your ladder—"

"Why didn't you hail the ship?" I asked, a little louder.

He touched my shoulder lightly. Lazy footsteps came right over our heads and stopped. The second mate had crossed from the other side of the poop and might have been hanging over the rail, for all we knew.

"He couldn't hear us talking—could he?" My double breathed into my very ear, anxiously.

His anxiety was an answer, a sufficient answer, to the question I had put to him. An answer containing all the difficulty of that situation. I closed the port-hole quietly, to make sure. A louder word might have been overheard.

"Who's that?" he whispered then.

"My second mate. But I don't know much more of the fellow than you do."

And I told him a little about myself. I had been appointed to take charge while

I least expected anything of the sort, not quite a fortnight ago. I didn't know either the ship or the people. Hadn't had the time in port to look about me or size anybody up. And as to the crew, all they knew was that I was appointed to take the ship home. For the rest, I was almost as much of a stranger on board as himself, I said. And at the moment I felt it most acutely. I felt that it would take very little to make me a suspect person in the eyes of the ship's company.

He had turned about meantime; and we, the two strangers in the ship, faced each other in identical attitudes.

"Your ladder—" he murmured, after a silence. "Who'd have thought of finding a ladder hanging over at night in a ship anchored out here! I felt just then a very unpleasant faintness. After the life I've been leading for nine weeks, anybody would have got out of condition. I wasn't capable of swimming round as far as your rudder-chains. And, lo and behold; there was a ladder to get hold of. After I gripped it I said to myself, 'What's the good?' When I saw a man's head looking over I thought I would swim away presently and leave him shouting—in whatever language it was. I didn't mind being looked at. I—I liked it. And then you speaking to me so quietly—as if you had expected me—made me hold on a little longer. It had been a confounded lonely time—I don't mean while swimming. I was glad to talk a little to somebody that didn't belong to the *Sephora*. As to asking for the captain, that was a mere impulse. It could have been no use, with all the ship knowing about me and the other people pretty certain to be round here in the morning. I don't know— I wanted to be seen, to talk with somebody, before I went on. I don't know what I would have said.

. . . 'Fine night, isn't it?' or something of the sort."

"Do you think they will be round here presently?" I asked with some incredulity.

"Quite likely," he said, faintly.

He looked extremely haggard all of a sudden. His head rolled on his shoulders.

"H'm. We shall see then. Meantime get into that bed," I whispered. "Want help? There."

It was a rather high bed-place with a set of drawers underneath. This amazing swimmer really needed the lift I gave him by seizing his leg. He tumbled in, rolled over on his back, and flung one arm across his eyes. And then, with his face nearly hidden, he must have looked exactly as I used to look in that bed. I gazed upon my other self for a while before drawing across carefully the two green serge curtains which ran on a brass rod. I thought for a moment of pinning them together for greater safety, but I sat down on the couch, and once there I felt unwilling to rise and hunt for a pin. I would do it in a moment. I was extremely tired, in a peculiarly intimate way, by the strain of stealthiness, by the effort of whispering and the general secrecy of this excitement. It was three o'clock by now and I had been on my feet since nine, but I was not sleepy; I could not have gone to sleep. I sat there, fagged out, looking at the curtains, trying to clear my mind of the confused sensation of being in two places at once, and greatly bothered by an exasperating knocking in my head. It was a relief to discover suddenly that it was not in my head at all, but on the outside of the door. Before I could collect myself the words "Come in" were out of my mouth, and the steward entered with a tray, bringing in my morning coffee. I had slept, after all, and I was so frightened that I shouted, "This way! I am here, steward," as though he had been miles away. He put down the tray on the table next the couch and only then said, very quietly, "I can see you are here, sir." I felt him give me a keen look, but I dared not meet his eyes just then. He must have wondered why I had drawn the curtains of my bed before going to sleep on the couch. He went out, hooking the door open as usual.

I heard the crew washing decks above me. I knew I would have been told at once if there had been any wind. Calm, I thought, and I was doubly vexed. Indeed, I felt dual more than ever. The steward reappeared suddenly in the doorway. I jumped up from the couch so quickly that he gave a start.

"What do you want here?"

"Close your port, sir—they are washing decks."

"It is closed," I said, reddening.

"Very well, sir." But he did not move from the doorway and returned my stare in an extraordinary, equivocal manner for a time. Then his eyes wavered, all his expression changed, and in a voice unusually gentle, almost coaxingly:

"May I come in to take the empty cup away, sir?"

"Of course!" I turned my back on him while he popped in and out. Then I unhooked and closed the door and even pushed the bolt. This sort of thing could not go on very long. The cabin was as hot as an oven, too. I took a peep at my double, and discovered that he had not moved, his arm was still over his eyes; but his chest heaved; his hair was wet; his chin glistened with perspiration. I reached over him and opened the port.

"I must show myself on deck," I reflected.

Of course, theoretically, I could do what I liked, with no one to say nay to me within the whole circle of the horizon; but to lock my cabin door and take the key away I did not dare. Directly I put my head out of the companion I saw the group of my two officers, the second mate barefooted, the chief mate in long india-rubber boots, near the break of the poop, and the steward half-way down the poop-ladder talking to them eagerly. He happened to catch sight of me and dived, the second ran down on the main-deck shouting some order or other, and the chief mate came to meet me, touching his cap.

There was a sort of curiosity in his eye that I did not like. I don't know whether the steward had told them that I was "queer" only, or downright drunk, but I know the man meant to have a good look at me. I watched him coming with a smile which, as he got into point-blank range, took effect and froze his very whiskers. I did not give him time to open his lips.

"Square the yards by lifts and braces before the hands go to breakfast."

It was the first particular order I had given on board that ship; and I stayed on deck to see it executed, too. I had felt the need of asserting myself without loss of time. That sneering young cub got taken down a peg or two on that occasion, and I also seized the opportunity of having a good look at the face of every foremast man as they filed past me to go to the after braces. At breakfast time, eating nothing myself, I presided with such frigid dignity that the two mates were only too glad to escape from the cabin as soon as decency permitted; and all the time the dual working of my mind distracted me almost to the point of insanity. I was constantly watching myself, my secret self, as dependent on my actions as my own personality, sleeping in that bed, behind that door which faced me as I sat at the head of the table. It was very much like being mad, only it was worse because one was aware of it.

I had to shake him for a solid minute, but when at last he opened his eyes it was in the full possession of his senses, with an inquiring look.

"All's well so far," I whispered. "Now you must vanish into the bath-room."

He did so, as noiseless as a ghost, and then I rang for the steward, and facing him boldly, directed him to tidy up my stateroom while I was having my bath—"and be quick about it." As my tone admitted of no excuses, he said, "Yes, sir," and ran off to fetch his dust-pan and brushes. I took a bath and did most of my dressing, splashing, and whistling softly for the steward's edification, while the secret sharer of my life stood drawn up bolt upright in that little space, his face looking very sunken in daylight, his eyelids lowered under the stern, dark line of his eyebrows drawn together by a slight frown.

When I left him there to go back to my room the steward was finishing dusting. I sent for the mate and engaged him in some insignificant conversation. It was, as it were, trifling with the terrific character of his whiskers; but my object was to give him an opportunity for a good look at my cabin. And then I could at last shut, with a clear conscience, the door of my stateroom and get my double back into the recessed part. There was nothing else for it. He had to sit still on a small folding stool, half smothered by the heavy coats hanging there. We listened to the steward going into the bath-room out of the saloon, filling the water-bottles there, scrubbing the bath, setting things to rights, whisk, bang, clatter—out again into the saloon—turn the key—click. Such was my scheme for keeping my second self invisible. Nothing better could be contrived under the circumstances. And there we sat; I at my writing-desk ready to appear busy with some papers, he behind me out of sight of the door. It would not have been prudent to talk in daytime; and I could not have stood the excitement of that queer sense of whispering to myself. Now and then, glancing over my shoulder, I saw him far back there, sitting rigidly on the low stool, his bare feet close together, his arms folded, his head hanging on his breast—and perfectly still. Anybody would have taken him for me.

I was fascinated by it myself. Every moment I had to glance over my shoulder. I was looking at him when a voice outside the door said:

"Beg pardon, sir."

"Well!" . . . I kept my eyes on him, and so when the voice outside the door announced, "There's a ship's boat coming our way, sir," I saw him give a start—the first movement he had made for hours. But he did not raise his bowed head.

"All right. Get the ladder over."

I hesitated. Should I whisper something to him? But what? His immobility seemed to have been never disturbed. What could I tell him he did not know already? . . . Finally I went on deck.

II

The skipper of the *Sephora* had a thin red whisker all round his face, and the sort of complexion that goes with hair of that color; also the particular, rather smeary shade of blue in the eyes. He was not exactly a showy figure; his shoulders were high, his stature but middling—one leg slightly more bandy than the other. He shook hands, looking vaguely around. A spiritless tenacity was his main characteristic, I judged. I behaved with a politeness which seemed to disconcert him. Perhaps he was shy. He mumbled to me as if he were ashamed of what he was saying; gave his name (it was something like Archbold—but at this distance of years I hardly am sure), his ship's name, and a few other particulars of that sort, in the manner of a criminal making a reluctant and doleful confession. He had had terrible weather on the passage out—terrible —terrible—wife aboard, too.

By this time we were seated in the cabin and the steward brought in a tray with a bottle and glasses. "Thanks! No." Never took liquor. Would have some water, though. He drank two tumblerfuls. Terrible thirsty work. Ever since daylight had been exploring the islands round his ship.

"What was that for—fun?" I asked, with an appearance of polite interest.

"No!" He sighed. "Painful duty."

As he persisted in his mumbling and I wanted my double to hear every word, I hit upon the notion of informing him that I regretted to say I was hard of hearing.

"Such a young man, too!" he nodded, keeping his smeary blue, unintelligent eyes fastened upon me. "What was the cause of it—some disease?" he inquired, without the least sympathy and as if he thought that, if so, I'd got no more than I deserved.

"Yes; disease," I admitted in a cheerful tone which seemed to shock him. But my point was gained, because he had to raise his voice to give me his tale. It is not worth while to record that version. It was just over two months since all this had happened, and he had thought so much

about it that he seemed completely muddled as to its bearings, but still immensely impressed.

"What would you think of such a thing happening on board your own ship? I've had the *Sephora* for these fifteen years. I am a well-known shipmaster."

He was densely distressed—and perhaps I should have sympathized with him if I had been able to detach my mental vision from the unsuspected sharer of my cabin as though he were my second self. There he was on the other side of the bulkhead, four or five feet from us, no more, as we sat in the saloon. I looked politely at Captain Archbold (if that was his name), but it was the other I saw, in a gray sleeping-suit, seated on a low stool, his bare feet close together, his arms folded, and every word said between us falling into the ears of his dark head bowed on his chest.

"I have been at sea now, man and boy, for seven-and-thirty years, and I've never heard of such a thing happening in an English ship. And that it should be my ship. Wife on board, too."

I was hardly listening to him.

"Don't you think," I said, "that the heavy sea which, you told me, came aboard just then might have killed the man? I have seen the sheer weight of a sea kill a man very neatly, by simply breaking his neck."

"Good God!" he uttered, impressively, fixing his smeary blue eyes on me. "The sea! No man killed by the sea ever looked like that." He seemed positively scandalized at my suggestion. And as I gazed at him, certainly not prepared for anything original on his part, he advanced his head close to mine and thrust his tongue out at me so suddenly that I couldn't help starting back.

After scoring over my calmness in this graphic way he nodded wisely. If I had seen the sight, he assured me, I would never forget it as long as I lived. The weather was too bad to give the corpse a proper sea burial. So next day at dawn they took it up on the poop, covering its face with a bit of bunting; he read a short prayer, and then, just as it was, in its oil-skins and long boots, they launched it amongst those mountainous seas that seemed ready every moment to swallow up the ship herself and the terrified lives on board of her.

"That reefed foresail saved you," I threw in.

"Under God—it did," he exclaimed fervently. "It was by a special mercy, I firmly believe, that it stood some of those hurricane squalls."

"It was the setting of that sail which—" I began.

"God's own hand in it," he interrupted me. "Nothing less could have done it. I don't mind telling you that I hardly dared give the order. It seemed impossible that we could touch anything without losing it, and then our last hope would have been gone."

The terror of that gale was on him yet. I let him go on for a bit, then said, casually —as if returning to a minor subject:

"You were very anxious to give up your mate to the shore people, I believe?"

He was. To the law. His obscure tenacity on that point had in it something incomprehensible and a little awful; something, as it were, mystical, quite apart from his anxiety that he should not be suspected of "countenancing any doings of that sort." Seven-and-thirty virtuous years at sea, of which over twenty of immaculate command, and the last fifteen in the *Sephora,* seemed to have laid him under some pitiless obligation.

"And you know," he went on, groping shamefacedly amongst his feelings, "I did not engage that young fellow. His people had some interest with my owners. I was in a way forced to take him on. He looked very smart, very gentlemanly, and all that. But do you know—I never liked him, somehow. I am a plain man. You see, he wasn't exactly the sort for the chief mate of a ship like the *Sephora.*"

I had become so connected in thoughts and impressions with the secret sharer of my cabin that I felt as if I, personally, were being given to understand that I, too, was not the sort that would have done for the chief mate of a ship like the *Sephora.* I had no doubt of it in my mind.

"Not at all the style of man. You understand," he insisted, superfluously, looking hard at me.

I smiled urbanely. He seemed at a loss for a while.

"I suppose I must report a suicide."

"Beg pardon?"

"Sui-cide! That's what I'll have to write to my owners directly I get in."

"Unless you manage to recover him before tomorrow," I assented, dispassionately. . . . "I mean, alive."

He mumbled something which I really did not catch, and I turned my ear to him in a puzzled manner. He fairly bawled:

"The land—I say, the mainland is at least seven miles off my anchorage."

"About that."

My lack of excitement, of curiosity, of surprise, of any sort of pronounced interest, began to arouse his distrust. But except for the felicitous pretense of deafness I had not tried to pretend anything. I had felt utterly incapable of playing the part of ignorance properly, and therefore was afraid to try. It is also certain that he had brought some ready-made suspicions with him, and that he viewed my politeness as a strange and unnatural phenomenon. And yet how else could I have received him? Not heartily! That was impossible for psychological reasons, which I need not state here. My only object was to keep off his inquiries. Surlily? Yes, but surliness might have provoked a point-blank question. From its novelty to him and from its nature, punctilious courtesy was the manner best calculated to restrain the man. But there was the danger of his breaking through my defense bluntly. I could not, I think, have met him by a direct lie, also for psychological (not moral) reasons. If he had only known how afraid I was of his putting my feeling of identity with the other to the test! But, strangely enough—(I thought of it only afterwards)—I believe that he was not a little disconcerted by the reverse side of that weird situation, by something in me that reminded him of the man he was seeking—suggested a mysterious similitude to the young fellow he had distrusted and disliked from the first.

However that might have been, the silence was not very prolonged. He took another oblique step.

"I reckon I had no more than a two-mile pull to your ship. Not a bit more."

"And quite enough, too, in this awful heat," I said.

Another pause full of mistrust followed. Necessity, they say, is mother of invention, but fear, too, is not barren of ingenious suggestions. And I was afraid he would ask me point-blank for news of my other self.

"Nice little saloon, isn't it?" I remarked, as if noticing for the first time the way his eyes roamed from one closed door to the other. "And very well fitted out, too. Here, for instance," I continued, reaching over the back of my seat negligently and flinging the door open, "is my bath-room."

He made an eager movement, but hardly gave it a glance. I got up, shut the door of the bath-room, and invited him to have a look round, as if I were very proud of my accommodation. He had to rise and be shown round, but he went through the business without any raptures whatever.

"And now we'll have a look at my state-room," I declared, in a voice as loud as I dared to make it, crossing the cabin to the starboard side with purposely heavy steps.

He followed me in and gazed around. My intelligent double had vanished. I played my part.

"Very convenient—isn't it?"

"Very nice. Very comf . . ." He didn't finish and went out brusquely as if to escape from some unrighteous wiles of mine. But it was not to be. I had been too frightened not to feel vengeful; I felt I had him on the run, and I meant to keep him on the run. My polite insistence must have had something menacing in it, because he gave in suddenly. And I did not let him off a single item; mate's room, pantry, storerooms, the very sail-locker which was also under the poop—he had to look into them all. When at last I showed him out on the quarter-deck he drew a long, spiritless sigh, and mumbled dismally that he must really be going back to his ship now. I desired my mate, who had joined us, to see to the captain's boat.

The man of whiskers gave a blast on the whistle which he used to wear hanging round his neck, and yelled, "*Sephora's* away!" My double down there in my cabin must have heard, and certainly could not feel more relieved than I. Four fellows came running out from somewhere forward and went over the side, while my own men, appearing on deck too, lined the rail. I escorted my visitor to the gangway ceremoniously, and nearly overdid it. He was a tenacious beast. On the very ladder he lingered, and in that unique, guiltily conscientious manner of sticking to the point:

"I say . . . you . . . you don't think that—"

I covered his voice loudly:

"Certainly not. . . . I am delighted. Good-by."

I had an idea of what he meant to say, and just saved myself by the privilege of defective hearing. He was too shaken generally to insist, but my mate, close witness of that parting, looked mystified and his face took on a thoughtful cast. As I did not want to appear as if I wished to avoid all communication with my officers, he had the opportunity to address me.

"Seems a very nice man. His boat's crew told our chaps a very extraordinary story, if what I am told by the steward is true. I suppose you had it from the captain, sir?"

"Yes. I had a story from the captain."

"A very horrible affair—isn't it, sir?"

"It is."

"Beats all these tales we hear about murders in Yankee ships."

"I don't think it beats them. I don't think it resembled them in the least."

"Bless my soul—you don't say so! But of course I've no acquaintance whatever with American ships, not I, so I couldn't go against your knowledge. It's horrible enough for me. . . . But the queerest part is that those fellows seemed to have some idea the man was hidden aboard here.

They had really. Did you ever hear of such a thing?"

"Preposterous—isn't is?"

We were walking to and fro athwart the quarter-deck. No one of the crew forward could be seen (the day was Sunday), and the mate pursued:

"There was some little dispute about it. Our chaps took offense. 'As if we would harbor a thing like that,' they said. 'Wouldn't you like to look for him in our coal-hole?' Quite a tiff. But they made it up in the end. I suppose he did drown himself. Don't you, sir?"

"I don't suppose anything."

"You have no doubt in the matter, sir?"

"None whatever."

I left him suddenly. I felt I was producing a bad impression, but with my double down there it was most trying to be on deck. And it was almost as trying to be below. Altogether a nerve-trying situation. But on the whole I felt less torn in two when I was with him. There was no one in the whole ship whom I dared take into my confidence. Since the hands had got to know his story, it would have been impossible to pass him off for anyone else, and an accidental discovery was to be dreaded now more than ever. . . .

The steward being engaged in laying the table for dinner, we could talk only with our eyes when I first went down. Later in the afternoon we had a cautious try at whispering. The Sunday quietness of the ship was against us; the stillness of air and water around her was against us; the elements, the men were against us —everything was against us in our secret partnership; time itself—for this could not go on forever. The very trust in Providence was, I suppose, denied to his guilt. Shall I confess that this thought cast me down very much? And as to the chapter of accidents which counts for so much in the book of success, I could only hope that it was closed. For what favorable accident could be expected?

"Did you hear everything?" were my first words as soon as we took up our position side by side, leaning over my bed-place.

He had. And the proof of it was his earnest whisper, "The man told you he hardly dared to give the order."

I understood the reference to be to that saving foresail.

"Yes. He was afraid of it being lost in the setting."

"I assure you he never gave the order. He may think he did, but he never gave it. He stood there with me on the break of the poop after the maintopsail blew away, and whimpered about our last hope—positively whimpered about it and nothing else—and the night coming on! To hear one's skipper go on like that in such weather was enough to drive any fellow out of his mind. It worked me up into a sort of desperation. I just took it into my own hands and went away from him, boiling, and— But what's the use telling you? *You* know! . . . Do you think that if I had not been pretty fierce with them I should have got the men to do anything? Not it! The bo's'n perhaps? Perhaps! It wasn't a heavy sea—it was a sea gone mad! I suppose the end of the world will be something like that; and a man may have the heart to see it coming once and be done with it—but to have to face it day after day— I don't blame anybody. I was precious little better than the rest. Only—I was an officer of that old coal-wagon, anyhow—"

"I quite understand," I conveyed that sincere assurance into his ear. He was out of breath with whispering; I could hear him

pant slightly. It was all very simple. The same strung-up force which had given twenty-four men a chance, at least, for their lives, had, in a sort of recoil, crushed an unworthy mutinous existence.

But I had no leisure to weigh the merits of the matter—footsteps in the saloon, a heavy knock. "There's enough wind to get under way with, sir." Here was the call of a new claim upon my thoughts and even upon my feelings.

"Turn the hands up," I cried through the door. "I'll be on deck directly."

I was going out to make the acquaintance of my ship. Before I left the cabin our eyes met—the eyes of the only two strangers on board. I pointed to the recessed part where the little camp-stool awaited him and laid my finger on my lips. He made a gesture—somewhat vague—a little mysterious, accompanied by a faint smile, as if of regret.

This is not the place to enlarge upon the sensations of a man who feels for the first time a ship move under his feet to his own independent word. In my case they were not unalloyed. I was not wholly alone with my command; for there was that stranger in my cabin. Or rather, I was not completely and wholly with her. Part of me was absent. That mental feeling of being in two places at once affected me physically as if the mood of secrecy had penetrated my very soul. Before an hour had elapsed since the ship had begun to move, having occasion to ask the mate (he stood by my side) to take a compass bearing of the Pagoda, I caught myself reaching up to his ear in whispers. I say I caught myself, but enough had escaped to startle the man. I can't describe it otherwise than by saying that he shied. A grave, preoccupied manner, as though he were in possession of some perplexing intelligence, did not leave him henceforth. A little later I moved away from the rail to look at the compass with such a stealthy gait that the helmsman noticed it—and I could not help noticing the unusual roundness of his eyes. These are trifling instances, though it's to no commander's advantage to be suspected of ludicrous eccentricities. But I was also more seriously affected. There are to a seaman certain words, gestures, that should in given conditions come as naturally, as instinctively as the winking of a menaced eye. A certain order should spring onto his lips without thinking; a certain sign should get itself made, so to speak, without reflection. But all unconscious alertness had abandoned me. I had to make an effort of will to recall myself back (from the cabin) to the conditions of the moment. I felt that I was appearing an irresolute commander to those people who were watching me more or less critically.

And, besides, there were the scares. On the second day out, for instance, coming off the deck in the afternoon (I had straw slippers on my bare feet) I stopped at the open pantry door and spoke to the steward. He was doing something there with his back to me. At the sound of my voice he nearly jumped out of his skin, as the saying is, and incidentally broke a cup.

"What on earth's the matter with you?" I asked, astonished.

He was extremely confused. "Beg your pardon, sir. I made sure you were in your cabin."

"You see I wasn't."

"No, sir. I could have sworn I had heard you moving in there not a moment ago. It's most extraordinary . . . very sorry, sir."

I passed on with an inward shudder. I was so identified with my secret double that I did not even mention the fact in those scanty, fearful whispers we exchanged. I suppose he had made some slight noise of some kind or other. It would have been miraculous if he hadn't at one time or another. And yet, haggard as he appeared, he looked always perfectly self-controlled, more than calm—almost invulnerable. On my suggestion he remained almost entirely in the bath-room, which, upon the whole, was the safest place. There could be really no shadow of an excuse for anyone ever wanting to go in there, once the steward had done with it. It was a very tiny place. Sometimes he reclined on the floor, his legs bent, his head sustained on one elbow. At others I would find him on the camp-stool, sitting in his gray sleeping-suit and with his cropped dark hair like a patient, unmoved convict. At night I would smuggle him into my bed-place, and we would whisper together, with the regular footfalls of the officer of the watch passing and repassing over our heads. It was an infinitely miserable time. It was lucky that some tins of fine preserves were stowed in a locker in my stateroom; hard bread I could always get hold of; and so he lived on stewed chicken, pâté de foie gras, asparagus, cooked oysters, sardines—on all sorts of abominable sham delicacies out of tins. My early morning coffee he always drank; and it was all I dared do for him in that respect.

Every day there was the horrible maneuvering to go through so that my room and then the bath-room should be done in the usual way. I came to hate the sight of the steward, to abhor the voice of that harmless man. I felt that it was he who would bring on the disaster of discovery. It hung like a sword over our heads.

The fourth day out, I think (we were

then working down the east side of the Gulf of Siam, tack for tack, in light winds and smooth water)—the fourth day, I say, of this miserable juggling with the unavoidable, as we sat at our evening meal, that man, whose slightest movement I dreaded, after putting down the dishes ran up on deck busily. This could not be dangerous. Presently he came down again; and then it appeared that he had remembered a coat of mine which I had thrown over a rail to dry after having been wetted in a shower which had passed over the ship in the afternoon. Sitting stolidly at the head of the table I became terrified at the sight of the garment on his arm. Of course he made for my door. There was no time to lose.

"Steward," I thundered. My nerves were so shaken that I could not govern my voice and conceal my agitation. This was the sort of thing that made my terrifically whiskered mate tap his forehead with his forefinger. I had detected him using that gesture while talking on deck with a confidential air to the carpenter. It was too far to hear a word, but I had no doubt that this pantomime could only refer to the strange new captain.

"Yes, sir," the pale-faced steward turned resignedly to me. It was this maddening course of being shouted at, checked without rhyme or reason, arbitrarily chased out of my cabin, suddenly called into it, sent flying out of his pantry on incomprehensible errands, that accounted for the growing wretchedness of his expression.

"Where are you going with that coat?"

"To your room, sir."

"Is there another shower coming?"

"I'm sure I don't know, sir. Shall I go up again and see, sir?"

"No! never mind."

My object was attained, as of course my other self in there would have heard everything that passed. During this interlude my two officers never raised their eyes off their respective plates; but the lip of that confounded cub, the second mate, quivered visibly.

I expected the steward to hook my coat on and come out at once. He was very slow about it; but I dominated my nervousness sufficiently not to shout after him. Suddenly I became aware (it could be heard plainly enough) that the fellow for some reason or other was opening the door of the bath-room. It was the end. The place was literally not big enough to swing a cat in. My voice died in my throat and I went stony all over. I expected to hear a yell of surprise and terror, and made a movement, but had not the strength to get on my legs. Everything remained still. Had my second self taken the poor wretch by the throat? I don't know what I could have done next moment if I had not seen the steward come out of my room, close the door, and then stand quietly by the sideboard.

"Saved," I thought. "But, no! Lost! Gone! He was gone!"

I laid my knife and fork down and leaned back in my chair. My head swam. After a while, when sufficiently recovered to speak in a steady voice, I instructed my mate to put the ship round at eight o'clock himself.

"I won't come on deck," I went on. "I think I'll turn in, and unless the wind shifts I don't want to be disturbed before midnight. I feel a bit seedy."

"You did look middling bad a little while ago," the chief mate remarked without showing any great concern.

They both went out, and I stared at the steward clearing the table. There was nothing to be read on that wretched man's face. But why did he avoid my eyes I asked myself. Then I thought I should like to hear the sound of his voice.

"Steward!"

"Sir!" Startled as usual.

"Where did you hang up that coat?"

"In the bath-room, sir." The usual anxious tone. "It's not quite dry yet, sir."

For some time longer I sat in the cuddy. Had my double vanished as he had come? But of his coming there was an explanation, whereas his disappearance would be inexplicable. . . . I went slowly into my dark room, shut the door, lighted the lamp, and for a time dared not turn round. When at last I did I saw him standing bolt-upright in the narrow recessed part. It would not be true to say I had a shock, but an irresistible doubt of his bodily existence flitted through my mind. Can it be, I asked myself, that he is not visible to other eyes than mine? It was like being haunted. Motionless, with a grave face, he raised his hands slightly at me in a gesture which meant clearly, "Heavens! what a narrow escape!" Narrow indeed. I think I had come creeping quietly as near insanity as any man who has not actually gone over the border. That gesture restrained me, so to speak.

The mate with the terrific whiskers was now putting the ship on the other tack. In the moment of profound silence which follows upon the hands going to their stations I heard on the poop his raised voice: "Hard alee!" and the distant shout of the order repeated on the main-deck. The sails, in that light breeze, made but a faint fluttering noise. It ceased. The ship was coming round slowly; I held my breath in the renewed stillness of expectation; one wouldn't have thought that there was a single living soul on her decks. A sudden brisk shout, "Mainsail haul!" broke the

spell, and in the noisy cries and rush overhead of the men running away with the main-brace we two, down in my cabin, came together in our usual position by the bed-place.

He did not wait for my question. "I heard him fumbling here and just managed to squat myself down in the bath," he whispered to me. "The fellow only opened the door and put his arm in to hang the coat up. All the same—"

"I never thought of that," I whispered back, even more appalled than before at the closeness of the shave, and marveling at that something unyielding in his character which was carrying him through so finely. There was no agitation in his whisper. Whoever was being driven distracted, it was not he. He was sane. And the proof of his sanity was continued when he took up the whispering again.

"It would never do for me to come to life again."

It was something that a ghost might have said. But what he was alluding to was his old captain's reluctant admission of the theory of suicide. It would obviously serve his turn—if I had understood at all the view which seemed to govern the unalterable purpose of his action.

"You must maroon me as soon as ever you can get amongst these islands off the Cambodge shore," he went on.

"Maroon you! We are not living in a boy's adventure tale," I protested. His scornful whispering took me up.

"We aren't indeed! There's nothing of a boy's tale in this. But there's nothing else for it. I want no more. You don't suppose I am afraid of what can be done to me? Prison or gallows or whatever they may please. But you don't see me coming back to explain such things to an old fellow in a wig and twelve respectable tradesmen, do you? What can they know whether I am guilty or not—or of *what* I am guilty, either? That's my affair. What does the Bible say? 'Driven off the face of the earth.' Very well. I am off the face of the earth now. As I came at night so I shall go."

"Impossible!" I murmured. "You can't."

"Can't? . . . Not naked like a soul on the Day of Judgment. I shall freeze on to this sleeping-suit. The Last Day is not yet—and . . . you have understood thoroughly. Didn't you?"

I felt suddenly ashamed of myself. I may say truly that I understood—and my hesitation in letting that man swim away from my ship's side had been a mere sham sentiment, a sort of cowardice.

"It can't be done now till next night," I breathed out. "The ship is on the off-shore tack and the wind may fail us."

"As long as I know that you understand," he whispered. "But of course you do. It's a great satisfaction to have got somebody to understand. You seem to have been there on purpose." And in the same whisper, as if we two whenever we talked had to say things to each other which were not fit for the world to hear, he added, "It's very wonderful."

We remained side by side talking in our secret way—but sometimes silent or just exchanging a whispered word or two at long intervals. And as usual he stared through the port. A breath of wind came now and again into our faces. The ship might have been moored in dock, so gently and on an even keel she slipped through the water, that did not murmur even at our passage, shadowy and silent like a phantom sea.

At midnight I went on deck, and to my mate's great surprise put the ship round on the other tack. His terrible whiskers flitted round me in silent criticism. I certainly should not have done it if it had been only a question of getting out of that sleepy gulf as quickly as possible. I believe he told the second mate, who relieved him, that it was a great want of judgment. The other only yawned. That intolerable cub shuffled about so sleepily and lolled against the rails in such a slack, improper fashion that I came down on him sharply.

"Aren't you properly awake yet?"

"Yes, sir! I am awake."

"Well, then, be good enough to hold yourself as if you were. And keep a look-out. If there's any current we'll be closing with some islands before daylight."

The east side of the gulf is fringed with islands, some solitary, others in groups. On the blue background of the high coast they seem to float on silvery patches of calm water, arid and gray, or dark green and rounded like clumps of evergreen bushes, with the larges ones, a mile or two long, showing the outlines of ridges, ribs of gray rock under the dank mantle of matted leafage. Unknown to trade, to travel, almost to geography, the manner of life they harbor is an unsolved secret. There must be villages—settlements of fishermen at least—on the largest of them, and some communication with the world is probably kept up by native craft. But all that forenoon, as we headed for them, fanned along by the faintest of breezes, I saw no sign of man or canoe in the field of the telescope I kept on pointing at the scattered group.

At noon I gave no orders for a change of course, and the mate's whiskers became much concerned and seemed to be offering themselves unduly to my notice. At last I said:

"I am going to stand right in. Quite in—as far as I can take her."

The stare of extreme surprise imparted an air of ferocity also to his eyes, and he looked truly terrific for a moment.

"We're not doing well in the middle of the gulf," I continued, casually. "I am going to look for the land breezes tonight."

"Bless my soul! Do you mean, sir, in the dark amongst the lot of all them islands and reefs and shoals?"

"Well—if there are any regular land breezes at all on this coast one must get close inshore to find them, mustn't one?"

"Bless my soul!" he exclaimed again under his breath. All that afternoon he wore a dreamy, contemplative appearance which in him was a mark of perplexity. After dinner I went into my stateroom as if I mean to take some rest. There we two bent our dark heads over a half-unrolled chart lying on my bed.

"There," I said. "It's got to be Koh-ring. I've been looking at it ever since sunrise. It has got two hills and a low point. It must be inhabited. And on the coast opposite there is what looks like the mouth of a biggish river—with some town, no doubt, not far up. It's the best chance for you that I can see."

"Anything. Koh-ring let it be."

He looked thoughtfully at the chart as if surveying chances and distances from a lofty height—and following with his eyes his own figure wandering on the blank land of Cochin-China, and then passing off that piece of paper clean out of sight into uncharted regions. And it was as if the ship had two captains to plan her course for her. I had been so worried and restless running up and down that I had not had the patience to dress that day. I had remained in my sleeping-suit, with straw slippers and a soft floppy hat. The closeness of the heat in the gulf had been most oppressive, and the crew were used to see me wandering in that airy attire.

"She will clear the south point as she heads now," I whispered into his ear. "Goodness only knows when, though, but certainly after dark. I'll edge her in to half a mile, as far as I may be able to judge in the dark—"

"Be careful," he murmured, warningly —and I realized suddenly that all my future, the only future for which I was fit, would perhaps go irretrievably to pieces in any mishap to my first command.

I could not stop a moment longer in the room. I motioned him to get out of sight and made my way on the poop. That unplayful cub had the watch. I walked up and down for a while thinking things out, then beckoned him over.

"Send a couple of hands to open the two quarter-deck ports," I said, mildly.

He actually had the impudence, or else so forgot himself in his wonder at such an incomprehensible order, as to repeat:

"Open the quarter-deck ports! What for, sir?"

"The only reason you need concern yourself about is because I tell you to do so. Have them opened wide and fastened properly."

He reddened and went off, but I believe made some jeering remark to the carpenter as to the sensible practice of ventilating a ship's quarter-deck. I know he popped into the mate's cabin to impart the fact to him because the whiskers came on deck, as it were by chance, and stole glances at me from below—for signs of lunacy or drunkenness, I suppose.

A little before supper, feeling more restless than ever, I rejoined, for a moment, my second self. And to find him sitting so quietly was surprising, like something against nature, inhuman.

I developed my plan in a hurried whisper.

"I shall stand in as close as I dare and then put her round. I will presently find means to smuggle you out of here into the sail-locker, which communicates with the lobby. But there is an opening, a sort of square for hauling the sails out, which gives straight on the quarter-deck and which is never closed in fine weather, so as to give air to the sails. When the ship's way is deadened in stays and all the hands are aft at the main-braces you will have a clear road to slip out and get overboard through the open quarter-deck port. I've had them both fastened up. Use a rope's end to lower yourself into the water so as to avoid a splash—you know. It could be heard and cause some beastly complication."

He kept silent for a while, then whispered, "I understand."

"I won't be there to see you go," I began with an effort. "The rest . . . I only hope I have understood, too."

"You have. From first to last"—and for the first time there seemed to be a faltering, something strained in his whisper. He caught hold of my arm, but the ringing of the supper bell made me start. He didn't, though; he only released his grip.

After supper I didn't come below again till well past eight o'clock. The faint, steady breeze was loaded with dew; and the wet, darkened sails held all there was of propelling power in it. The night, clear and starry, sparkled darkly, and the opaque, lightless patches shifting slowly against the low stars were the drifting islets. On the port bow there was a big one more distant and shadowily imposing by the great space of sky it eclipsed.

On opening the door I had a back view of my very own self looking at a chart.

He had come out of the recess and was standing near the table.

"Quite dark enough," I whispered.

He stepped back and leaned against my bed with a level, quiet glance. I sat on the couch. We had nothing to say to each other. Over our heads the officer of the watch moved here and there. Then I heard him move quickly. I knew what that meant. He was making for the companion; and presently his voice was outside my door.

"We are drawing in pretty fast, sir. Land looks rather close."

"Very well," I answered. "I am coming on deck directly."

I waited till he was gone out of the cuddy, then rose. My double moved too. The time had come to exchange our last whispers, for neither of us was ever to hear each other's natural vocie.

"Look here!" I opened a drawer and took out three sovereigns. "Take this anyhow. I've got six and I'd give you the lot, only I must keep a little money to buy some fruit and vegetables for the crew from native boats as we go through Sunda Straits."

He shook his head.

"Take it," I urged him, whispering desperately. "No one can tell what—"

He smiled and slapped meaningly the only pocket of the sleeping-jacket. It was not safe, certainly. But I produced a large old silk handkerchief of mine, and tying the three pieces of gold in a corner, pressed it on him. He was touched, I suppose, because he took it at last and tied it quickly round his waist under the jacket, on his bare skin.

Our eyes met; several seconds elapsed, till, our glances still mingled, I extended my hand and turned the lamp out. Then I passed through the cuddy, leaving the door of my room wide open. . . . "Steward!"

He was still lingering in the pantry in the greatness of his zeal, giving a rub-up to a plated cruet stand the last thing before going to bed. Being careful not to wake up the mate, whose room was opposite, I spoke in an undertone.

He looked round anxiously. "Sir!"

"Can you get me a little hot water from the galley?"

"I am afraid, sir, the galley fire's been out for some time now."

"Go and see."

He flew up the stairs.

"Now," I whispered, loudly, into the saloon—too loudly, perhaps, but I was afraid I couldn't make a sound. He was by my side in an instant—the double captain slipped past the stairs—through a tiny dark passage . . . a sliding door. We were in the sail-locker, scrambling on our knees over the sails. A sudden thought struck me. I saw myself wandering barefooted, bareheaded, the sun beating on my dark poll. I snatched off my floppy hat and tried hurriedly in the dark to ram it on my other self. He dodged and fended off silently. I wonder what he thought had come to me before he understood and suddenly desisted. Our hands met gropingly, lingered united in a steady, motionless clasp for a second. . . . No word was breathed by either of us when they separated.

I was standing quietly by the pantry door when the steward returned.

"Sorry, sir. Kettle barely warm. Shall I light the spirit-lamp?"

"Never mind."

I came out on deck slowly. It was now a matter of conscience to shave the land as close as possible—for now he must go overboard whenever the ship was put in stays. Must! There could be no going back for him. After a moment I walked over to leeward and my heart flew into my mouth at the nearness of the land on the bow. Under any other circumstances I would not have held on a minute longer. The second mate had followed me anxiously.

I looked on till I felt I could command my voice.

"She will weather," I said then in a quiet tone.

"Are you going to try that, sir?" he stammered out incredulously.

I took no notice of him and raised my tone just enough to be heard by the helmsman.

"Keep her good full."

"Good full, sir."

The wind fanned my cheek, the sails slept, the world was silent. The strain of watching the dark loom of the land grow bigger and denser was too much for me. I had shut my eyes—because the ship must go closer. She must! The stillness was intolerable. Were we standing still?

When I opened my eyes the second view started my heart with a thump. The black southern hill of Koh-ring seemed to hang right over the ship like a towering fragment of the everlasting night. On that enormous mass of blackness there was not a gleam to be seen, not a sound to be heard. It was gliding irresistibly towards us and yet seemed already within reach of the hand. I saw the vague figures of the watch grouped in the waist, gazing in awed silence.

"Are you going on, sir?" inquired an unsteady voice at my elbow.

I ignored it. I had to go on.

"Keep her full. Don't check her way. That won't do now," I said, warningly.

"I can't see the sails very well," the

helmsman answered me, in strange, quavering tones.

Was she close enough? Already she was, I won't say in the shadow of the land, but in the very blackness of it, already swallowed up as it were, gone too close to be recalled, gone from me altogether.

"Give the mate a call," I said to the young man who stood at my elbow as still as death. "And turn all hands up."

My tone had a borrowed loudness reverberated from the height of the land. Several voices cried out together: "We are all on deck, sir."

Then stillness again, with the great shadow gliding closer, towering higher, without a light, without a sound. Such a hush had fallen on the ship that she might have been a bark of the dead floating in slowly under the very gate of Erebus.

"My God! Where are we?"

It was the mate moaning at my elbow. He was thunderstruck, and as it were deprived of the moral support of his whiskers. He clapped his hands and absolutely cried out, "Lost!"

"Be quiet," I said, sternly.

He lowered his tone, but I saw the shadowy gesture of his despair. "What are we doing here?"

"Looking for the land wind."

He made as if to tear his hair, and addressed me recklessly.

"She will never get out. You have done it, sir. I knew it'd end in something like this. She will never weather, and you are too close now to stay. She'll drift ashore before she's round. O my God!"

I caught his arm as he was raising it to batter his poor devoted head, and shook it violently.

"She's ashore already," he wailed, trying to tear himself away.

"Is she? . . . Keep good full there!"

"Good full, sir," cried the helmsman in a frightened, thin, child-like voice.

I hadn't let go the mate's arm and went on shaking it. "Ready about, do you hear? You go forward"—shake—"and stop there"—shake—"and hold your noise"—shake—"and see these head-sheets properly overhauled"—shake, shake—shake.

And all the time I dared not look towards the land lest my heart should fail me. I released my grip at last and he ran forward as if fleeing for dear life.

I wondered what my double there in the sail-locker thought of this commotion. He was able to hear everything—and perhaps he was able to understand why, on my conscience, it had to be thus close—no less. My first order "Hard alee!" re-echoed ominously under the towering shadow of Koh-ring as if I had shouted in a mountain gorge. And then I watched the land intently. In that smooth water and light wind it was impossible to feel the ship coming-to. No! I could not feel her. And my second self was making now ready to slip out and lower himself overboard. Perhaps he was gone already . . . ?

The great black mass brooding over our very mastheads began to pivot away from the ship's side silently. And now I forgot the secret stranger ready to depart, and remembered only that I was a total stranger to the ship. I did not know her. Would she do it? How was she to be handled?

I swung the mainyard and waited helplessly. She was perhaps stopped, and her very fate hung in the balance, with the black mass of Koh-ring like the gate of the everlasting night towering over her taffrail. What would she do now? Had she way on her yet? I stepped to the side swiftly, and on the shadowy water I could see nothing except a faint phosphorescent flash revealing the glassy smoothness of the sleeping surface. It was impossible to tell—and I had not learned yet the feel of my ship. Was she moving? What I needed was something easily seen, a piece of paper, which I could throw overboard and watch. I had nothing on me. To run down for it I didn't dare. There was no time. All at once my strained, yearning stare distinguished a white object floating within a yard of the ship's side. White on the black water. A phosphorescent flash passed under it. What was that thing? . . . I recognized my own floppy hat. It must have fallen off his head . . . and he didn't bother. Now I had what I wanted—the saving mark for my eyes. But I hardly thought of my other self, now gone from the ship, to be hidden forever from all friendly faces, to be a fugitive and a vagabond on the earth, with no brand of the curse on his sane forehead to stay a slaying hand . . . too proud to explain.

And I watched the hat—the expression of my sudden pity for his mere flesh. It had been meant to save his homeless head from the dangers of the sun. And now—behold—it was saving the ship, by serving me for a mark to help out the ignorance of my strangeness. Ha! It was drifting forward, warning me just in time that the ship had gathered sternway.

"Shift the helm," I said in a low voice to the seaman standing still like a statue.

The man's eyes glistened wildly in the binnacle light as he jumped round to the other side and spun round the wheel.

I walked to the break of the poop. On the overshadowed deck all hands stood by the forebraces waiting for my order. The stars ahead seemed to be gliding from right to left. And all was so still in the world that I heard the quiet remark, "She's round," passed in a tone of intense relief between two seamen.

"Let go and haul."

The foreyards ran round with a great noise, amidst cheery cries. And now the frightful whiskers made themselves heard giving various orders. Already the ship was drawing ahead. And I was alone with her. Nothing! no one in the world should stand now between us, throwing a shadow on the way of silent knowledge and mute affection, the perfect communion of a seaman with his first command.

Walking to the taffrail, I was in time to make out, on the very edge of a darkness thrown by a towering black mass like the very gateway of Erebus—yes, I was in time to catch an evanescent glimpse of my white hat left behind to mark the spot where the secret sharer of my cabin and of my thoughts, as though he were my second self, had lowered himself into the water to take his punishment: a free man, a proud swimmer striking out for a new destiny.

PART IV · DRAMA

THE FOLLOWING PLAYS will suggest the range of dramatic forms in the twentieth-century theater, and provide material for thoughtful discussion of numerous problems of our day.

In *The Philadelphia Story* and *Biography* will be found the wit, satire, and social criticism characteristic of modern comedy. *Winterset* (in Part I) is written as poetic tragedy. It may be profitably considered in relation to the essays on tragedy by Anderson, Miller, and in *Life* (in Part II), as well as with the whole problem of tragedy and poetry on the contemporary stage.

"*The Hairy Ape*" is an example of the dramatic expressionism introduced to the American theater by O'Neill in the early 1920s. At that time uninfluenced by German expressionist techniques, O'Neill found in August Strindberg, and in his own imagination, a dramatic form which broke sharply with contemporary realism and naturalism. As O'Neill said, "The old 'naturalism'—or 'realism,' if you prefer— . . . no longer applies. It represents our fathers' daring aspirations toward self-recognition by holding the family kodak up to ill-nature. . . . We have endured too much from the banality of surfaces."

The Glass Menagerie is a successful blend of several techniques. Basically a "memory play," as the author has said, it uses the expressionist device of "projecting the mind onto stage." The individual scenes are realistic, but are enhanced by the use of symbolism, thematic music, and "movie" slides.

The Fall of the City is a poetic drama written for radio presentation. It too is a blend: the chorus and messenger are drawn from Greek drama, the announcer and themes from the networks of the 1930s.

The themes of the plays have universality, as well as special pertinence to our time: the cry of Yank Smith in *The Hairy Ape*, "I ain't on 'oith and I ain't in heaven . . . I'm in de middle tryin' to separate 'em, takin' all de woist punches from bot' of 'em," the search for self-realization in *The Glass Menagerie,* the revenge and love motif in *Winterset* as well as the problem of justice, the question of individualism in *The Philadelphia Story,* the conservative-liberal-radical conflict in *Biography,* and the specter of totalitarianism in *The Fall of the City.*

THE PHILADELPHIA STORY

by PHILIP BARRY

CHARACTERS

SETH LORD	MACAULAY CONNOR
MARGARET LORD	GEORGE KITTREDGE
ALEXANDER LORD	DR. PARSONS
TRACY LORD	THOMAS
DINAH LORD	EDWARD
WILLIAM TRACY	ELSIE
C. K. DEXTER HAVEN	MAY
ELIZABETH IMBRIE	MAC

ACTION AND SCENE: *The play takes place in the course of twenty-four hours at the Seth Lords' house in the country near Philadelphia. The Time is the present, late June, and the Scenes are as follows:*

ACT I. *The Sitting Room. Late morning, Friday*

ACT II. *Scene 1: The Porch. Late evening, Friday*

       Scene 2: The Porch. Early morning, Saturday

ACT III. *The Sitting Room. Late morning, Saturday*

ACT I

[*The Sitting Room of the Lords' house in the country near Philadelphia is a large, comfortably furnished room of a somewhat faded elegance containing a number of very good Victorian pieces. The entrance from the Hall is at Right, upstage, down two broad, shallow steps. The entrance into what the family still call "the Parlor" is through double doors downstage Right. At Left are two glass doors leading to the Porch. A writing desk stands between them. There is a large marble fireplace in the back wall and a grand piano in the corner at Left. Chairs and a table are at downstage Right and at downstage Left another table, an easy chair and a sofa. There is a large and fine portrait over the fireplace and other paintings here and there. A wall cabinet contains a quantity of bric-a-brac and there is more of it, together with a number of signed photographs in silver frames, upon the tables and piano. There are also several cardboard boxes strewn about. It is late on a Friday morning, in June, an overcast day.* DINAH, *who is all of thirteen years old, is stretched out on the sofa reading a set of printers' galley proofs.* TRACY, *a strikingly lovely girl of 24, sits in the chair at Left, a leather writing set upon her knees, scribbling notes. She wears slacks and a blouse.* MARGARET LORD, *their mother, a young and smart 47, comes in from the Hall with three more boxes in her arms. She places them upon the table near* TRACY.]

MARGARET. I'm terribly afraid that some of the cards for these last-minute presents have got themselves mixed. Look at them, Tracy—perhaps you can tell.

TRACY. In a minute, Mother. I'm up to my neck in these blank thank-you notes. [DINAH *folds one of the proof sheets she is reading under another.*]

DINAH. This stinks.

MARGARET. Not "stinks," darling. If absolutely necessary, "smells"—but only if absolutely necessary. What is it?

DINAH. I found it in Sandy's room. It's something that's going to be in a magazine. It certainly stinks, all right.

MARGARET. Keep out of your brother's things, dear—and his house. [*She studies a list of names.*] Ninety-four for the ceremony, five hundred and six for the reception—I don't know where we'll put them all, if it should rain.

DINAH. It won't rain.

MARGARET. Uncle Willie wanted to insure against it with Lloyd's but I wouldn't let him. If I was God and someone bet I wouldn't let it rain, I'd show him fast enough. This second page is solid Cadwalader. Twenty-six.

DINAH. That's a lot of Cadwalader.

MARGARET. One, my child, is a lot of Cadwalader.

TRACY. How do you spell omelet?

MARGARET. O-m-m-e-l-e-t.

TRACY. I thought there was another "l."

MARGARET. The omelet dish from the—?

TRACY. You said it was an omelet dish.

MARGARET. It might be for fish.

TRACY. "Fish dish"? Sounds idiotic.

MARGARET. I should simply say "Thank you so much for your lovely silver dish."

TRACY. Here's the tag. "Old Dutch Muffin Ear, Circa 1810." What the—? [*She drops the card.*] I am simply enchanted with your old Dutch Muffin Ear—with which my husband and I will certainly hear any muffin coming a mile away.

DINAH. Lookit, Tracy: don't you think you've done enough notes for one day?

TRACY. Don't disturb me. [*She examines another card.*] From Cousin Horace Macomber, one pair of game shears, looking like hell. [*Picks up shears.*]

DINAH. He's so awful. What did he send the other time?

TRACY. No one to speak of sent anything the other time.

MARGARET. It's such a pity your brother Junius can't be here for your wedding. London's so far away.

DINAH. I miss old Junius: you did a good job when you had him, Mother.

MARGARET. The first is always the best. They deteriorate as you go on.

TRACY. There was no occasion to send anything the other time.

DINAH [*Reading the proof sheets.*] This is certainly pretty rooty-tooty all right.

TRACY. It could scarcely be considered a wedding at all, the other time. When you run off to Maryland, on a sudden impulse, the way Dexter and I did—

DINAH. Ten months is quite long to be married, though. You can have a baby in nine, can't you?

TRACY. I guess—if you put your mind to it.

DINAH. Why didn't you?

TRACY. Mother, don't you think it's time for her nap?

DINAH. I imagine you and George'll have slews of 'em.

TRACY. I hope so—all like you, dear, with the same wild grace. [*She rises from her chair with a box of envelopes, which she places upon the desk.*]

DINAH. Lookit: "the other time"—he's back from wherever he's been.

MARGARET. What do you mean?

DINAH. Dexter, of course. I saw his car in front of his house: the roadster. It must be him.

MARGARET. When? When did you?

DINAH. This morning, early, when I was out exercising The Hoofer.

MARGARET. Why didn't you tell us? [TRACY *moves to her unconcernedly.*]

TRACY. I'm not worried, Mother. The only trouble Mr. C. K. Dexter Haven ever gave me was when he married me.—*You* might say the same for one Seth Lord. If you'd just face it squarely as I did—

MARGARET. That will do! I will allow none of you to criticize your father.

TRACY. What are we expected to do when he treats you—

MARGARET. Did you hear me, Tracy?

TRACY. All right, I give up.

MARGARET.—And in view of this second attempt of yours, it might pay you to remind yourself that neither of us has proved to be a very great success as a wife.

TRACY. We just picked the wrong first husbands, that's all.

MARGARET. That is an extremely vulgar remark.

TRACY. Oh, who cares about either of them any more— [*She leans over the back of* MARGARET's *chair and hugs her.*] Golly Moses, I'm going to be happy now!

MARGARET. Darling.

TRACY. Isn't George an angel?

MARGARET. George is an angel.

TRACY. Is he handsome, or is he not?

MARGARET. George is handsome.

TRACY. Suds. I'm a lucky girl. [*She gathers up her boxes and writing case.*]

DINAH. *I* like Dexter. [TRACY *moves toward the Hall doorway.*]

TRACY. Really? Why don't you ask him to lunch, or something? [*And goes out.*]

DINAH [*looking after her*]. She's awfully mean about him, isn't she?

MARGARET. He was rather mean to her, my dear.

DINAH. Did he really sock her?

MARGARET. Don't say "sock," darling. "Strike" is quite an ugly enough word.

DINAH. But did he really?

MARGARET. I'm afraid I don't know the details.

DINAH. Cruelty and drunkenness, it said.

MARGARET. Dinah!

DINAH. It was right in the papers.

MARGARET. You read too much. You'll spoil your eyes.

DINAH. I think it's an awful thing to say about a man. I don't think they like things like that said about them.

MARGARET. I'm sure they don't. [DINAH *picks up the proof sheets again.*]

DINAH. Father's going to be hopping when he reads all this about himself in that magazine, *Destiny,* when it comes out.

MARGARET. All what? *About whom?*

DINAH. Father—that they're going to publish.

MARGARET. Dinah, what *are* you talking about?

DINAH. It's what they call proof sheets for some article they're going to call "Broadway and Finance," and Father's in it, and so they just sent it on to Sandy— sort of you know, on approval. It was just there on the table in his room, and so I—

MARGARET. But the article! What does the article say? [*She takes the proof sheets and examines them.*]

DINAH. Oh, it's partly about Father backing three shows for that dancer—what's her name—Tina Mara—and his early history—and about the stables—and why he's living in New York, instead of with us any more, and—

MARGARET. Great heaven—what on earth can we do?

DINAH. Couldn't Father sue them for—for liable?

MARGARET. But it's true—it's all— [*She glances at* DINAH.] That is, I mean to say—

DINAH. I don't think the part about Tina Mara is, the way they put it. It's simply full of innundo.

MARGARET. Of what?

DINAH. Of innundo. [*She rests her chin on her hand and stares into space.*] Oh, I do wish something would happen here. Nothing ever possibly in the least ever happens. [*Then suddenly hops up and goes to her mother.*] Next year can I go to the Conservatory in New York? They teach you to sing and dance and act and everything at once. *Can* I, Mother?

MARGARET. Save your dramatics, Dinah. [*She folds the proof sheets and puts them down.*] Oh, why didn't Sandy tell me!

DINAH. Mother, why won't Tracy at least *ask* her own *father* to her *wedding?*

MARGARET. Your sister has very definite opinions about certain things. [*She moves toward the desk at Left.*]

DINAH. [*following her*]. She's sort of—you know—hard, isn't she?

MARGARET. Not hard—none of my children is that, I hope. Tracy sets exceptionally high standards for herself, that's all—and although she lives up to them, other people aren't always quite able to. If your Uncle Willie Tracy comes in, tell him to wait. I want to see him. [*Having put the desk in order, she moves toward the Porch door.*]

DINAH. Tell me one thing: don't you think it's stinking not at least to *want* Father? [MARGARET *stops in the doorway and turns to her.*]

MARGARET. Yes, darling, between ourselves I think it's good and stinking. [*And goes out.*]

DINAH.—And I bet if Dexter knew what she— [*She waits a moment, then goes to the telephone and dials four numbers.*] Hello, may I please speak to Mr. Dexter Haven—what?—Dexter! It's you! [*Then affectedly.*] A very great pleasure to have you back.—Dinah, you goat, Dinah Lord. What?—You bet!—Lookit, Dexter, Tracy says why don't you come right over for lunch? What? But she told me to ask you.—Listen, though, maybe it would be better if you'd—Hello!—Hello! [*She replaces the telephone as* TRACY *comes in from the Hall with a large roll of paper.*]

TRACY. Who was that?

DINAH. Wrong number. [TRACY *spreads the roll of paper out on the table.*]

TRACY. Listen, darling, give me a hand with this cockeyed seating arrangement, will you? At least hold it down.—George doesn't want the Grants at the bridal table. [ALEXANDER (SANDY) LORD, 26, *comes in from the Hall.*] He says they're fast. He—

SANDY. Hello, kids.

TRACY. Sandy! [*She reaches up to him, hugs him.*]

SANDY. Where's Mother?

TRACY. She's around. How's New York? How's Sue?—How's the baby?

SANDY. Blooming. They sent their love, sorry they can't make the wedding. Is there a party tonight, of course?

TRACY. Aunt Geneva's throwing a monster.

SANDY. Boy, am I going to get plastered. [*To* DINAH.] Hello, little fellah.

DINAH. Hello, yourself. [*He gives her a small, flat box.*]

SANDY. This is for you, Mug. Get the three race horses into the paddock. It's tough. Work it out.

DINAH. Oh, thanks! [*She begins to work at the puzzle.*]

SANDY [*to* TRACY]. Sue's and my wedding present comes by registered mail, Tracy—and a pretty penny it set me back.

TRACY. You're a bonny boy, Sandy. I love you.

SANDY. Mutual. [MARGARET *re-enters from the Porch.*]

MARGARET. I was wondering about you. [SANDY *goes to her and embraces her.*]

SANDY. Give us a kiss.—You look fine.—Imagine this, a *grand*mother! How's everything?

MARGARET. Absolute chaos.

SANDY. Just how you like it, eh? Just when you function best!

MARGARET. How's my precious grandchild?

SANDY. Couldn't be better, Sue too. Ten more days in the hospital, and back home they'll be.

MARGARET. I broke into your house and did up the nursery.

SANDY. Good girl. Where's George, Tracy?

TRACY. He's staying in the Gatehouse. He still had business things to clear up and I thought he'd be quieter there.

SANDY. Did he see his picture in *Dime?* Was he sore at the "Former Coal Miner" caption? [MARGARET *picks up the proof sheets once more.*]

MARGARET. What about this absurd article about your father and—er—Tina Mara in *Destiny,* Sandy? Can't it be stopped?

TRACY. About Father and—? Let me see! [*She takes the proof sheets.*]

SANDY. Where'd you get hold of that? [*He tries unsuccessfully to recover them.*]

MARGARET. Get ready for lunch, Dinah.

DINAH. In a minute. I'm busy. [*She flops down on the Hall step and continues to work at her puzzle.*]

TRACY [*reading*]. Oh, the absolute devils!—Who publishes *Destiny?*

SANDY. Sidney Kidd.—Also *Dime,* also *Spy,* the picture sheet. I worked on *Dime* for two summers. You know that.

TRACY. Stopped? It's got to be! I'll go to him myself.

SANDY. A fat lot of good that would do. You're too much alike. God save us from the strong. [*He seats himself.*] I saw Kidd the day before yesterday. It took about three hours, but I finally got through to him.

TRACY. What happened?

SANDY. I think I fixed things.

TRACY. How?

SANDY. That would be telling.

MARGARET. Just so long as your father never hears of it.

SANDY. I had a copy of the piece made, and sent it around to his flat, with a little note saying, "How do you like it?" [TRACY *laughs shortly.*]

TRACY. You are a fellah.

MARGARET. Sandy!

SANDY. Why not? Let him worry a little.

TRACY. Let him worry a lot! [THOMAS *enters from Hall.*]

SANDY. Yes, Thomas?

THOMAS. Mr. Connor and the lady say they will be down directly, sir.

SANDY. Thanks, that's fine. Tell May or Elsie to look after Miss Imbrie, will you?

THOMAS. Very good, sir. [*He goes out.*]

MARGARET. What's all this?

TRACY. "Mr. Connor and—?"

SANDY. Mike Connor—Macaulay Connor, his name is.—And—er—Elizabeth Imbrie. I'm putting them up for over the wedding. They're quite nice, you'll like them.

TRACY. You asked people to stay in this house without even asking us?

MARGARET. I think it's very queer indeed.

TRACY. I think it's queerer than that—*I* think it's paranoiac.

SANDY. Keep your shirt on.—I just sort of drifted into them and we sort of got to talking about what riots weddings are as a rule, and they'd never been to a Philadelphia one, and—

TRACY. You're lying, Sandy.—I can always tell.

SANDY. Now look here, Tracy—

TRACY. Look where? "Elizabeth Imbrie"—I know that name! She's a—wait—damn your eyes, Sandy, she's a photographer!

SANDY. For a fact?

TRACY. For a couple of facts—and a famous one!

SANDY. Well, it might be nice to have some good shots of the wedding.

TRACY. What are they doing here?

SANDY. Just now I suppose they're brushing up and going to the bathroom. They're very interesting people. [*He moves uneasily about the room.*] She's practically an artist, and he's written a couple of books—and—and I thought you liked interesting people. [DINAH *rises from her step.*]

DINAH. *I* do!

TRACY [*suddenly*]. I know—now I know! They're from *Destiny.—Destiny* sent them!

MARGARET. *Destiny?*

SANDY. You're just a mass of intuition, Tray.

TRACY. Well, they can go right back again.

SANDY. No, they can't. Not till they get their story.

TRACY. Story? What story?

SANDY. The Philadelphia story.

MARGARET. And what on earth's that?

SANDY. Well, it seems Kidd has had Connor and Imbrie and a couple of others down here for two months doing the town: I mean writing it up. It's to come out in three parts in the Autumn. "Industrial Philadelphia," "Historical Philadelphia"—and then the third—

TRACY. I'm going to be sick.

SANDY. Yes, dear: "Fashionable Philadelphia."

TRACY. I *am* sick.

MARGARET. But why us? Surely there are other families who—

TRACY. Yes—why not the Drexels or the Biddles or the *qu'est-ce-que-c'est* Cassatts? [SANDY *seats himself again.*]

SANDY. We go even further back: it's those Quakers.—And of course there's your former marriage and your looks and your general prowess in golf and foxhunting, with a little big game on the side, and your impending second marriage into the coal fields—

TRACY. Never mind that!

SANDY. I don't, but they do. It's news, darling, news.

MARGARET. Is there no such thing as privacy any more?

TRACY. Only in bed, Mother, and not always there.

SANDY. Anyhow, I thought I was licked—and what else could I do?

TRACY. A trade, eh? So we're to let them publish the inside story of my wedding in order to keep Father's wretched little affair quiet!

MARGARET. It's utterly and completely disgusting.

SANDY. It was my suggestion, not Kidd's. I may have been put in the way of making it, I don't know. It's hard to tell, with a future President of the United States.

TRACY. What's the writer's name again?

SANDY. Connor, Macaulay Connor. I don't think he likes the assignment any more than we do—the gal either. They were handling the Industrial end. [TRACY *goes to the telephone, and dials.*]

TRACY. My heart's breaking for them.

MARGARET. I don't know what the world is coming to. It's an absolute invasion: two strange people tramping through the house, prying and investigating—

TRACY. Maybe we're going through a revolution without knowing it. [*To the telephone.*] Hello, is Mr. Briggs there?—This is Tracy Lord, Mr. Briggs.—Look, I wonder if you happen to have on hand any books by Macaulay Connor? [SANDY *rises.*]—You have? Could you surely send them out this afternoon?—Thanks, Mr. Briggs, you're sweet. [*She replaces the telephone, raging.*]—If they've got to have a story, I'll give them a story—I'll give them one they can't get through the mails!

SANDY. Oh—oh—I was afraid of this.

TRACY. Who the hell do they think they are, barging in on peaceful people—watching every little mannerism—jotting down notes on how we sit, and stand, and eat and move—

DINAH [*eagerly*]. Will they do that?

TRACY.—And all in the horrible, snide corkscrew English! Well, if we have to submit to it to save Father's face—which incidentally doesn't deserve it—I'm for giving them a picture of home life that will stand their hair on end.

MARGARET. You will do nothing of the sort, Tracy.

SANDY. She thinks she'll be the outrageous Miss Lord. The fact is, she'll probably be Sweetness and Light to the neck.

TRACY. Oh, will I!

SANDY. You don't know yet what being under the microscope does to people. I felt it a little coming out in the car. It's a funny feeling.

MARGARET. It's odd how self-conscious we've all become over the worldly possessions that once made us so confident.

SANDY. I know: you catch yourself explaining away your dough, the way you would a black eye: you've just run into it in the dark or something.

MARGARET. We shall be ourselves with them, very much ourselves.

DINAH. But, Mother, you want us to create a good impression, don't you?

MARGARET [*to* SANDY]. They don't know that *we* know what they're here for, I hope?

SANDY. No: that was understood.

DINAH. I should think it would look awfully funny to them, Father's not being here for his own daughter's wedding.

TRACY. Would you, now?

SANDY. That's all right; I fixed that, too.

TRACY. How do you mean you did?

SANDY. I told Sue to send a telegram before dinner. "Confined to bed with a cold, unable to attend nuptials, oceans of love, Father."

MARGARET. Not just in those words!

SANDY. Not exactly.—It'll come on the telephone and Thomas will take it and you won't have your glasses and he'll read it aloud to you.

MARGARET. Tracy, will you promise to behave like a lady, if only for my sake?

TRACY. I'll do my best, Mrs. Lord. I don't know how good that is.

MARGARET. Go put a dress on.

TRACY. Yes, Mother.

MARGARET. There are too many legs around here.

TRACY. Suds! I'll be pure Victorian, all frills and ruffles, conversationally chaste as an egg. [WILLIAM (UNCLE WILLIE) TRACY, *62, enters from the Parlor.*] Hello, Uncle Willie. Where did you come from?

UNCLE WILLIE. Your Great-aunt Geneva has requested my absence from the house until dinner time. Can you give me lunch, Margaret?

MARGARET. But of course! With pleasure.

DINAH. Hello, Uncle Willie.

SANDY. How are you, Uncle Willie?

UNCLE WILLIE. Alexander and Dinah, good morning. [*To* TRACY.]—My esteemed wife, the old war horse, is certainly spreading herself for your party. *I* seriously question the propriety of any such display in such times, but she—why aren't you being married in church, Tracy?

TRACY. I like the parlor here so much better. Didn't you think it looked pretty as you came through?

UNCLE WILLIE. That is not the point. The point is that I've sunk thousands in that church, and I'd like to get some use of it.—Give me a glass of sherry, Margaret.

MARGARET. Not until lunch time, my dear.

UNCLE WILLIE. These women.

DINAH. You're really a wicked old man, aren't you? [*He points beyond her, to the Porch.*]

UNCLE WILLIE. What's that out there? [DINAH *turns to look. He vigorously pinches her behind.*]

DINAH. Ouch!

UNCLE WILLIE. Never play with fire, child. [*He looks at the others.*] What's a-lack here? What's a-stirrin'? What's amiss?

SANDY. Uncle Willie, do you know anything about the laws of libel? [UNCLE WILLIE *seats himself.*]

UNCLE WILLIE. Certainly, I know about the laws of libel. Why shouldn't I? I know all about them. In 1916, I, Willie Q. Tracy, successfully defended the *Post,* and George Lorimer personally, against one of the cleverest, one of the subtlest—why? What do you want to say?

SANDY. It isn't what *I* want to say—

TRACY. Is it enough if they can simply prove that it is true?

UNCLE WILLIE. Certainly not! Take me: if I was totally bald and wore a toupee, if I had flat feet, with these damnable metal arches, false teeth, and a case of double—

DINAH. Poor Uncle Willie.

UNCLE WILLIE. I said *"If* I had"—And if such facts were presented in the public prints in such a manner as to hold me up to public ridicule, I could collect substantial damages—and would, if it took me all winter.

TRACY. Suppose the other way around. Suppose they printed things that weren't true.

UNCLE WILLIE. Suppose they did? Suppose it was erroneously stated, that during my travels as a young man I was married in a native ceremony to a dusky maiden in British Guinea, I doubt if I could collect a cent. [*He looks past her, toward the Hall door.*] Who are these two strange people coming down the hall? [*The entire family rises.*]

MARGARET. Oh, good gracious! [TRACY *takes* UNCLE WILLIE *by the arm.*]

TRACY. Come on—out! [*She leads him toward the Parlor at Right.*] What was she like, Uncle Willie?

UNCLE WILLIE. Who?

TRACY. British Guinea?

UNCLE WILLIE. So very unlike your Aunt Geneva, my dear. [*They go out.*]

MARGARET. Dinah—

DINAH. But, Mother, oughtn't we—?

MARGARET. Come! Sandy can entertain them until we—until we collect ourselves. [*She directs* DINAH *into the Parlor.*]

SANDY. What'll I say?

MARGARET. I wish I could tell you—in a few very well-chosen words. [*She goes out.* SANDY *is alone for a moment. He hunches his shoulders uncomfortably and clears his throat.* MACAULAY (MIKE), *30, and* ELIZABETH (LIZ) IMBRIE, *28, come in from the Hall.* LIZ *has a small and important camera hanging from a leather strap around her neck.*]

LIZ.—In here?

MIKE. He said the sitting room. I suppose that's contrasted to the living room, the ballroom, the drawing room, the morning room, the—[*He sees* SANDY.] Oh, hello again. Here you are.

SANDY. Here I am.

MIKE. It's quite a place.

SANDY. It is, isn't it?—I couldn't help overhearing you as you came in. Do you mind if I say something?

MIKE. Not at all. What?

SANDY. Your approach to your job seems definitely antagonistic. I don't think it's fair. I think you ought to give us a break.

MIKE. It's not a job I asked for.

SANDY. I know it's not. But in spite of it, and in spite of certain of our regrettable inherited characteristics, we just might be fairly decent. Why not wait and see? [MIKE *and* LIZ *seat themselves.*]

MIKE. You have quite a style yourself.— You're on the *Saturday Evening Post,* did you say? [SANDY *seats himself, facing* MIKE *and* LIZ.]

SANDY. I work for it.

MIKE. Which end?

SANDY. Editorial.

MIKE. I have to tell you, in all honesty, that I'm opposed to everything you represent.

SANDY. *Destiny* is hardly a radical sheet: what is it you're doing—boring from within?

MIKE.—And I'm not a communist, not by a long shot.

LIZ. Just a small pin-feather in the Left Wing. [MIKE *looks at her.*]—Sorry.

SANDY. Jeffersonian Democrat?

MIKE. That's more like it.

SANDY. Have you ever seen his house at Monticello? *It's* quite a place too.

LIZ. Home Team One; Visitors Nothing. [*She rises and looks about her.*] Is this house very old, Mr. Lord?

SANDY. No, there are a very few old ones on the Main Line.—The Gatehouse is, of course. Father's grandfather built that for a summer place when they all lived on Rittenhouse Square. Father and Mother did this about 1910—the spring before my brother Junius was born. He's the eldest. You won't meet him, he's in the diplomatic service in London.

MIKE [*to* LIZ]. Wouldn't you know?

SANDY. *I* worked for Sidney Kidd once. What do you make of him?

MIKE [*after a moment*]. A brilliant editor, and a very wonderful man.

LIZ. Also, our bread and butter.

SANDY. Sorry to have been rude. [MIKE *takes a sheaf of typewritten cards from his pocket and begins to glance through them.*]

MIKE. I suppose you're all opposed to the Administration?

SANDY. The present one? No—as a matter of fact we're Loyalists.

MIKE. Surprise, surprise.—The Research Department didn't give us much data.— Your sister's fiancé—George Kittredge—

aged 32.—Since last year General Manager Quaker State Coal, in charge of operation.—Is that right?

SANDY. That's right.—And brilliant at it.

MIKE. So I've heard tell. I seem to have read about him first back in '35 or '36.—Up from the bottom, wasn't he?

SANDY. Just exactly—and of the mines.

MIKE. Reorganized the entire works?

SANDY. He did.

MIKE. National hero, new model: makes drooping family incomes to revive again. Anthracite, sweet anthracite.—How did your sister happen to meet him?

SANDY. She and I went up a month ago to look things over.

MIKE. I see. And was it instant?

SANDY. Immediate.

MIKE. Good for her. He must be quite a guy.—Which side of this—er—fine aboriginal family does she resemble most, would you say? [SANDY *looks at him, rises.*]

SANDY. The histories of both are in the library: I'll get them out for you. I'll also see if I can round up some of the Living Members.

LIZ. They don't know about us, do they? [SANDY, *in the doorway, stops and turns.*]

SANDY.—Pleasanter not, don't you think?

LIZ. Much.

SANDY. That's what *I* thought—also what Kidd thought. [*Suddenly* MIKE *rises.*]

MIKE. Look here, Lord—

SANDY. Yes—?

MIKE. Why don't you throw us out? [SANDY *laughs shortly, then goes out.*]

SANDY. I hope you'll never know!

LIZ. Meaning what?

MIKE. Search me.

LIZ. Maybe Der Kidder has been up to his little tricks.

MIKE. If only I could get away from his damned paper—

LIZ. It's Sidney himself you can't get away from, dear. [*She begins to tour the room with her camera.*]

MIKE. I tried to resign again on the phone this morning.

LIZ.—Knickknacks—gimcracks—signed photographs! Wouldn't you know you'd have to be as rich as the Lords to live in a dump like this? [*Sees the portrait over the mantel.*] Save me—it's a Gilbert Stuart!

MIKE. A what?

LIZ. Catch me, Mike!

MIKE. Faint to the left, will you? [*He returns to the typewritten cards.*] "First husband, C. K.—"—Can you imagine what a guy named "C. K. Dexter Haven" must be like?

LIZ. "Macaulay Connor" is not such a homespun tag, my pet.

MIKE. I've been called Mike ever since I can remember.

LIZ. Well, maybe Dexter is "Ducky" to his friends.

MIKE. I wouldn't doubt it.—But I wonder what the "C. K." is for—

LIZ. Maybe it's Pennsylvania Dutch for "William Penn."

MIKE. "C. K. Dexter Haven"—God!

LIZ. I knew a plain Joe Smith once. He was only a clerk in a hardware store, but he was an absolute louse.

MIKE.—Also he plays polo. Also designs and races sailboats. "Class" boats, I think they call them. Very upper class, of course.

LIZ. Don't despair. He's out, and Kittredge, man of the people, is in.

MIKE. From all reports, quite a comer too. Political timber.—Poor fellow, I wonder how he fell for it.

Liz. I imagine she's a young lady who knows what she wants when she wants it.

Mike. The young, rich, rapacious American female—there's no other country where she exists.

Liz. I'll admit the idea of *her* scares even me.—Would I change places with her, for all her wealth and beauty? Boy! Just ask me!

Mike. I know how I'm going to begin. [*He leans back on the sofa, closes his eyes, and declaims.*] "—So much for Historical Philadelphia, so much for Industrial. Now, Gentle Reader, consider an entire section of American Society which, closely following the English tradition, lives on the land, but in a new sense. It is not the land that provides the living, it is—"

Liz. You're ahead of yourself. Wait till you do your documentation.

Mike. I'm tired. Kidd is a slave driver. I wish I was home in bed. Also I'm hungry. Tell four footmen to call me in time for lunch. [Dinah *re-enters from the Porch, her manner now very much that of a woman of the world. She rises upon her toes like a ballet dancer and advances toward them.*]

Dinah. Oh—how do you do?—Friends of Alexander's, are you not? [Mike *rises.*]

Mike. How do you do.—Why yes, we—

Dinah. I am Dinah Lord. My real name is Diana, but my sister changed it.

Liz. I'm Elizabeth Imbrie and this is Macaulay Connor. It's awfully nice of— [Dinah *extends an arched hand to each.*]

Dinah. *Enchantée de vous voir. Enchantée de faire votre connaisance.*—I spoke French before I spoke English. My early childhood was spent in Paris, where my father worked in a bank—the House of Morgan.

Liz. Really?

Dinah. *C'est vrai—absolument!* [*She runs up to the piano, leaping a low stool as she goes.*] Can you play the piano? I can. And sing at the same time. Listen— [*She plays and sings.*] "Pepper Sauce Woman, Pepper Sauce Woman—" [Liz *speaks lowly to* Mike.]

Liz. What is this?

Mike. An idiot, probably. They happen in the best of families, especially in the best.

Dinah.

"—Oh, what a shame; she has lost her name

Don't know who to blame, walkin' along in Shango Batchelor."

[*She stops singing and continues in a dreamy voice:*] The Bahamas—how well I remember them.—Those perfumed nights—the flowers—the native wines. I was there, once, on a little trip with Leopold Stokowski. [Tracy *comes in from the Porch. She has changed into a rather demure dress, high in neck and ample in skirt.*]

Tracy. You were there with your governess, after the whooping cough. [Dinah *gestures airily.*]

Dinah.—My sister Tracy. Greetings, Sister.

Tracy. Mother wants to see you at once. At once! [Dinah *rises from the piano.*]

Dinah. You've got on my hair ribbon.

Tracy. Your face is still dirty. [*As* Dinah *passes her,* Tracy *gives her one, deft, smart spank, then, as* Dinah *goes out into the Hall, comes up to* Mike *and* Liz, *cool, collected and charming, all Sweetness and Light.*] It's awfully nice having you here. [*She shakes hands with them.*] I do hope you'll stay for my wedding.

Liz. We'd like to very much.

Mike. In fact, that was our idea.

TRACY. I'm so pleased that it occurred to you. [*She indicates the sofa. They seat themselves there and* TRACY *takes a chair facing them.*] The house is in rather a mess, of course. We all have to huddle here, and overflow onto the porch.—I hope your rooms are comfortable. [MIKE *takes out a pack of cigarettes.*]

LIZ. Oh, very, thanks.

TRACY. Anything you want, ask Mary or Elsie. They're magic. [*She holds a cigarette box out to them. Each takes one.* LIZ's *camera catches her eye.*] What a cunning little camera. [MIKE *has struck a match. He sees that* TRACY *is holding an automatic lighter toward him as she talks to* LIZ.—*He slowly bends forward to accept a light for his cigarette, then blows his match out.* TRACY *graciously smiles at him.*]

LIZ. It's a Contax. I'm afraid I'm rather a nuisance with it. [*She accepts a light from the lighter.*]

TRACY. But, you couldn't be: I hope you'll take loads. Dear Papá and Mamá aren't allowing any reporters in—that is, except for little Mr. Grace, who does the social news. [*To* MIKE.] Can you imagine a grown-up man, having to sink so low?

MIKE. It does seem pretty bad.

TRACY. People have always been so kind about letting us live our simple and uneventful little life here unmolested. Of course, after my divorce last year—but I expect that always happens, and is more or less deserved. Dear Papá was quite angry, though, and swore he'd never let another reporter inside the gate. He thought some of their methods were a trifle underhanded.—You're a writer, aren't you, Mr. Connor?

MIKE. In a manner of speaking.

TRACY. Sandy told me. I've sent for your books. "Macaulay Connor"—What's the "Macaulay" for?

MIKE. My father taught English history. I'm "Mike" to my friends.

TRACY.—Of whom you have many, I'm sure. English history has always fascinated me. Cromwell—Bloody Mary, John the Bastard.—Where did he teach? I mean your father—

MIKE. In the high school in South Bend, Indiana.

TRACY. "South Bend"! It sounds like dancing, doesn't it? You must have had a most happy childhood there.

MIKE. It was terrific.

TRACY. I'm so glad.

MIKE. I don't mean it that way.

TRACY. I'm so sorry. Why?

MIKE. Largely due to the lack of the wherewithal, I guess.

TRACY. But that doesn't always cause unhappiness, does it?—not if you're the right kind of man. George Kittredge, my fiancé, never had anything either, but he—. Are either of you married?

MIKE. No.

LIZ. I—er—that is, no.

TRACY. You mean *you* were, but now you're divorced?

LIZ. Well, the fact is—

TRACY. Suds—you can't mean you're ashamed of it!

LIZ. Of course I'm not ashamed of it. [MIKE *is staring at her.*]

MIKE. Wha-at?

LIZ. It was ages ago, when I was a mere kid, in Duluth.

MIKE. Good Lord, Liz—you never told me you were—

LIZ. You never asked.

MIKE. I know, but—

LIZ. Joe Smith. Hardware.

MIKE. Liz, you're the damnedest girl.

LIZ. *I* think I'm sweet. [MIKE *rises,*

turns once around the sofa and seats himself again.]

TRACY. Duluth—that must be a lovely spot. It's west of here, isn't it?

LIZ. Sort of.—But occasionally we get the breezes.

TRACY. Is this your first visit in Philadelphia?

LIZ. Just about.

TRACY. It's a quaint old place, don't you think? I suppose it's affected somewhat by being the only really big city that's near New York.

LIZ. I think that's a very good point to make about it.

TRACY.—Though I suppose you consider us somewhat provincial.

LIZ. Not at all, I assure you.

TRACY. Odd customs, and such. Where the scrapples eat Biddle on Sunday. Of course it *is* very old—Philadelphia, I mean; the scrapple is fresh weekly. How old are *you*, Mr. Connor?

MIKE. I was thirty last month.

TRACY. Two books isn't much for a man of thirty. I don't mean to criticize. You probably have other interests outside your work.

MIKE. None.—Unless— [*He looks at* LIZ *and smiles.*]

TRACY. How sweet! Are you living together?

MIKE. Why, er—that is—

LIZ. That's an odd question, I must say!

TRACY. Why?

LIZ. Well—it just is.

TRACY. I don't see why. I think it's very interesting. [*She leans forward seriously, elbow on knee, chin on hand.*] Miss Imbrie—don't you agree that all this marrying and giving in marriage is the damnedest gyp that's ever been put over on an unsuspecting public?

MIKE [*to* LIZ]. Can she be human?

TRACY. Please, Mr. Connor!—I asked Miss Imbrie a question.

LIZ. No. The fact is, I don't.

TRACY. Good. Nor do I. That's why I'm putting my chin out for the second time tomorrow. [GEORGE, *off stage, Left, calls* "Tracy." *She rises and moves toward the Porch.*] Here's the lucky man now. I'll bring him right in and put him on view— a one-man exhibition.—In here, George! In here, my dear! [*She goes out,* LIZ *rises and turns to* MIKE.]

LIZ. My God—who's doing the interviewing here?

MIKE. She's a lot more than I counted on.

LIZ. Do you suppose she's caught on somehow?

MIKE. No. She's just a hellion.

LIZ. I'm beginning to feel the size of a pinhead.

MIKE. Don't let her throw you.

LIZ. Do you want to take over?

MIKE. I want to go home. [TRACY *re-enters with* GEORGE KITTREDGE, *aged 32, and brings him up to them.*]

TRACY. Miss Imbrie—Mr. Connor—Mr. Kittredge, my beau.—Friends of Sandy's, George.

GEORGE. Any friend of Sandy's— [*He shakes hands with them.*]

LIZ. How do you do?

MIKE. How are you?

GEORGE. Fine as silk, thanks.

LIZ. You certainly look it.

GEORGE. Thanks! I've shaken quite a lot of coal dust from my feet in the last day or two.

TRACY. Isn't he beautiful? Isn't it wonderful what a little soap and water will do?

MIKE. Didn't I read a piece about you in the *Nation* a while ago?

GEORGE. Quite a while ago: I've been

[416]

resting on my laurels since that—and a couple of others.

MIKE. Quite a neat piece of work—anticipating the Guffey Coal Act the way you did.—Or do I remember straight?

GEORGE. Anyone should have foreseen that. I was just lucky.

LIZ. A becoming modesty.

GEORGE. That's nothing to what's yet to be done with Labor relations.

TRACY. You ought to see him with the men—they simply adore him.

GEORGE. Oh—come on, Tracy!

TRACY. Oh, but they do! Never in my life will I forget that first night I saw you: all those wonderful faces, and the torch lights, and the way his voice boomed—

GEORGE. You see, I'm really a spellbinder. That's the way I got her.

TRACY. Except it was me who got you! —I'm going to put these two at the bridal table, in place of the Grants.

GEORGE. That's a good idea.

TRACY. George, it won't rain, will it?— Promise me it won't rain.

GEORGE. Tracy, I'll see to that personally.

TRACY. I almost believe you could.

MIKE. I guess this must be love.

GEORGE. Your guess is correct, Mr. Connor.

TRACY. I'm just his faithful Old Dog Tray.

GEORGE. Give me your paw. [*She presents her hand.*]

TRACY. You've got it. [*He takes it and kisses it.* MARGARET *enters from the Parlor, followed by* DINAH. DINAH *remains in the doorway.* MARGARET *goes directly to* LIZ *and* MIKE.]

MARGARET. How do you do? We're so happy to have you. Forgive me for not coming in sooner, but things are in such a state. I'd no idea that a simple country wedding could involve so much. [*She crosses to* TRACY *and* TRACY *to her. They beam fatuously upon one another.*] My little girl—[*She pats her face, then turns back to* LIZ.]—I do hope you'll be comfortable. Those rooms are inclined to be hot in this weather.—Aren't you pretty, my dear! [SANDY *comes in from the Hall.*] Look at the way she wears her hair, Tracy. Isn't it pretty?

TRACY. Mighty fine.

MARGARET. I do wish my husband might be here to greet you, but we expect him presently. He's been detained in New York on business for that lovely Tina Mara. You know her work?

LIZ. Only vaguely!

MARGARET. So talented—and such a lovely person! But like so many artists— no business head, none whatever. [*She gives* TRACY *a knowing smile.* TRACY *and* SANDY *smile.* SANDY *then smirks for* TRACY's *sole benefit.* EDWARD *comes in from the Hall, carrying a tray with a carafe of sherry and several glasses.* THOMAS *follows him.* EDWARD *pours,* THOMAS *serves.* MARGARET *beams upon* GEORGE.] Good morning, George!

GEORGE. Good morning, Mrs. Lord.

MARGARET. And this is my youngest daughter, Diana— [DINAH *curtseys.*]

MIKE. I think we've met. [THOMAS *gives* MARGARET *a glass of sherry.*]

MARGARET. Thank you, Thomas. [SANDY *stretches himself out in an easy chair.*]

SANDY. Now let's all relax, and throw ourselves into things. Hi, George!

GEORGE. Hello, Sandy—Welcome home! [*All take sherry, with the exception of* TRACY *and* DINAH.]

MARGARET. After lunch Sandy must show you some of the sights—the model dairy, and the stables, and the chicken farm—and perhaps there'll be time to run you out to some other places on the Main Line—Devon, St. Davids, Bryn Mawr, where my daughter Tracy went to college—

DINAH. Till she got bounced out on her—

MARGARET.—Dinah! [UNCLE WILLIE reenters from the Parlor.]

UNCLE WILLIE. It's a pretty kettle of fish when a man has to wait two mortal hours— [*Suddenly* TRACY *runs to him with her arms out.*]

TRACY. Papá!—Dear Papá— [*She embraces him warmly.*] Didn't the car meet you? [UNCLE WILLIE *is completely bewildered.*]

WILLIE. The car?

TRACY. You angel—to drop everything and get here in time for lunch!—Isn't he, Mamá?

MARGARET. In—indeed he is. [UNCLE WILLIE *stares at them.*]

UNCLE WILLIE. I'm not one to jump at conclusions, but—

TRACY. These are our friends, Mr. Connor and Miss Imbrie, Father.—They're here for the wedding.

MIKE *and* LIZ. How do you do, Mr. Lord?

UNCLE WILLIE. Dashed fine. How are you?

SANDY. Hi, Pops!

UNCLE WILLIE.—Alexander.

DINAH. Welcome back, Daddy!

UNCLE WILLIE. Dinah—Kittredge— [*He turns to* MARGARET *and bows.*] Margaret, my sweet. [THOMAS *comes down to his Left with a glass of sherry.* UNCLE WILLIE *tosses it off and returns the glass.*]

TRACY. Mother, don't you think you ought to explain the new arrangement to Father before lunch?

MARGARET. Why—yes—I think I'd best. [*She slips her arm through* UNCLE WILLIE's *and leads him to the desk which stands between the Porch doors.*] See here —here is the list now—Seth. [*In from the Porch comes* DEXTER HAVEN, *28.* SANDY *sees him and exclaims.*]

SANDY. Holy Cats! [MARGARET *turns quickly.*]

MARGARET. Dexter Haven!

DEXTER. Hello, friends and enemies. I came the short way, across the fields.

MARGARET. Well, this *is* a surprise.

GEORGE. I should think it is. [DEXTER *kisses* MARGARET *lightly upon the cheek.*]

DEXTER. Hello, you sweet thing.

MARGARET. Now you go right home at once!

UNCLE WILLIE. Remove yourself, young man!

DEXTER. But I've been invited. [*He shakes* UNCLE WILLIE's *hand.*] How are you, sir?

UNCLE WILLIE. No better, no worse. Get along.

DEXTER. Hello, Sandy. [*They shake hands.*]

SANDY. How are you, boy?

DEXTER. Never better. In fact, it's immoral how good I feel.

DINAH. What—what brings you here, Mr. Haven?

DEXTER. Dinah, my angel! [*He kisses her cheek.*] Why, she's turned into a raving beauty! [*He turns to* TRACY.]—Awfully sweet and thoughtful of you to ask me to lunch, Tray.

TRACY. Not at all.—Extra place, Thomas.

THOMAS. Yes, Miss Tracy. [*He and* EDWARD *go out, into the Hall.* UNCLE WILLIE *and* MARGARET *talk inaudibly at the desk.* TRACY *gestures toward* MIKE *and* LIZ.]

TRACY. Miss Imbrie—Mr. Connor—my former husband, whose name for the moment escapes me.

DEXTER. How do you do?

LIZ. How do you do?

MIKE. How do you do?

DEXTER.—Of course I intended to come anyway, but it did make it pleasanter.— Hello, Kittredge.

GEORGE. How are you, Haven? [*DEXTER peers at him.*]

DEXTER. What's the matter? You don't look as well as when I last saw you. [*He pats his arm sympathetically.*] Poor fellow —I know just how you feel. [*He turns to* TRACY, *gazes at her fondly.*] Redhead— isn't *she* in the pink, though!—*You* don't look old enough to marry anyone, even for the first time—you never did! She needs trouble to mature her, Kittredge. Give her lots of it.

GEORGE. I'm afraid she can't count on me for that.

DEXTER. No? Too bad.—Sometimes, for your own sake, I think you should have stuck to me longer, Red. [*TRACY goes to* GEORGE *and takes his arm.*]

TRACY. I thought it was for life, but the nice Judge gave me a full pardon.

DEXTER. That's the kind of talk I like to hear: no bitterness, no recrimination— just a good quick left to the jaw.

GEORGE. Very funny. [*THOMAS reappears in the Hall doorway.*]

THOMAS. Luncheon is served, Madam.

MARGARET. Thank you, Thomas. [*He goes out.* UNCLE WILLIE *advances from the desk.*]

UNCLE WILLIE. I don't suppose a man ever had a better or finer family. [*He turns and takes* MARGARET's *arm.*] I wake in the night and say to myself—"Seth, you lucky dog. What have you done to deserve it?"

MARGARET. And what *have* you? [*Arm in arm they go out into the Hall.*]

TRACY. Do you mind if I go in with Mr. Connor, Miss Imbrie?

LIZ. Why, not in the least. [*SANDY offers* LIZ *his arm.*]

SANDY. Sandy's your boy.

TRACY [*takes* MIKE's *arm*]—Because I think he's such an interesting man.

GEORGE. Come on, Dinah, I draw you, I guess.

DINAH. Dexter—

DEXTER [*to* GEORGE]. Isn't snatching one of my girls enough, you cad?

GEORGE. You're a very bright fellow, Haven. I'll hire you.

MIKE [*to* TRACY]. No wonder you want to get away from all this.

TRACY. That's very insulting—but consistently interesting. We must talk more. [*They are all approaching the Hall when* SETH LORD, *50, appears in the Porch doorway, hat in hand, a light topcoat over his arm.*]

SETH. I don't know how welcome I am, but after Sandy's note, I thought the least I could do was to— [*DINAH starts down the Hall steps to him but is stopped by* TRACY, *who suddenly cries out to* SETH.]

TRACY. Uncle Willie! [*She turns to others.*] Please go on in to lunch, everyone, I want a word with Uncle Willie. [*They go out.* TRACY *crosses the room and faces her father.*]

SETH. Well, daughter?

TRACY. Well?

SETH. Still Justice, with her shining sword—eh? Who's on the spot?

TRACY. We are; thanks to you—Uncle Willie.

CURTAIN

[419]

ACT II

SCENE I

[*The Porch, which is more like a room than a porch. Entrance from the Sitting Room is through the glass doors at back and to the Library, through glass doors at Stage Left; to the Garden, down broad stone steps from the Porch and along a gravel path past shrubbery to Left and Right. The open side of the Porch is shielded with latticework, and there are pots of geraniums on the steps. Early evening, Friday. The sky has cleared.* MIKE *is in a chair on the Porch, making additional notes.* LIZ *is seated on the steps, reloading her camera.*]

LIZ. I may need more film.

MIKE. I may need more paper.

LIZ. There's a cousin Joanna who's definitely crazy.

MIKE. Who told you?

LIZ. Dinah.

MIKE. Dinah should know.

LIZ. Where is she now? I want some more shots of her, while it's still light.

MIKE. She's out schooling a horse somewhere. It's the horses that get the schooling hereabouts. Did you shoot the old Tycoon milking his cows?

LIZ. Several times. He shot one at me, but he missed.

MIKE. Caption: "Seventy Times Seven Fat Kine Has He." [*He consults his notes.*] "George Kittredge, Important Official, Important Company. Controlling interest owned by Seth Lord."

LIZ. What a coincidence and will wonders never cease?

MIKE. I'm inclined to like Kittredge— I can see how she fell for him. I think he's in a tough spot, with Haven prowling around, though.

LIZ. Is a sinister fellow, Dexter.

MIKE. Is very.—But George is interesting. Get him on coal some time.

LIZ. I'd rather have him on toast.

MIKE. Answer me honestly, Liz: What right has a girl like Tracy Lord to exist?

LIZ. Politically, socially, or economically?

MIKE. But what place has she got in the world today? Come the Revolution and she'd be the first to go.

LIZ. Sure: right out under the Red General's arm.

MIKE. She's a new one on me. Maybe Philadelphia produces a different brand of monkey. [LIZ *looks at him keenly.*]

LIZ. You're a funny one, Mike.

MIKE. Why?

LIZ. Use the name "Wanamaker" in a sentence.

MIKE. I bite.

LIZ. I met a girl this morning. I hate her, but I—

MIKE. I get you, but you're wrong. You couldn't be wronger. Women like that bore the pants off me.

LIZ. For a writer, you use your figures of speech most ineptly. You know, I wish they knew why we were here. They're all such sweet innocents, it makes me feel like— [UNCLE WILLIE *and* SETH *enter from the Garden down Right.*]

UNCLE WILLIE. Would you accept this perfect rose, Miss Imbrie?

LIZ. Why, thank you, Mr. Lord. It's a beauty.

SETH. Miss Imbrie is amused at something.

LIZ. I'm sorry, Mr. Tracy, but it's so funny, you being uncle and nephew. Could I have a picture of you together?

UNCLE WILLIE. Certainly! [*He slips his arm through* SETH's.] Now then, stand up straight, Uncle Willie. He *is* younger than I. It was a matter of half-sisters marrying stepbrothers.

LIZ. I see. That is, I think I do. [*She snaps a picture.*]

UNCLE WILLIE. No incest, however.

LIZ. Of course not. [*And snaps another.*]

UNCLE WILLIE. There have been other things, however. [*He looks at* SETH.] Uncle Willie—I'm thinking of asking that little dancer, Tina Mara, to come down and dance for the wedding guests tomorrow. Do you think it's a good idea?

SETH. Excellent. It might put an end to the ridiculous gossip about you and her.

UNCLE WILLIE. Is there gossip?

SETH. There seems to be.

UNCLE WILLIE. Is it ridiculous?

SETH. All gossip is ridiculous. [SANDY *comes from the Library at Left and crosses the Porch to the Sitting-Room door.*]

SANDY. Look alive, men! Time to dress!

SETH. Right you are. Thanks, Sandy— [*He goes up the steps and over the Porch into the Sitting Room.* SANDY *follows him.*]

UNCLE WILLIE. Miss Imbrie, as a camera-fiend, I think I have another interesting subject for you.

LIZ. Will I have time?

UNCLE WILLIE. Time is an illusion. Come with me, please. [*He offers his arm, which she takes gingerly.*] It's part of the old house, a little removed from it.

LIZ. But what?

UNCLE WILLIE. An ancient granite privy, of superb design—a dream of loveliness.

LIZ.—At sunset—idyllic! [LIZ *and* UNCLE WILLIE *go out into the Garden.* MIKE *pockets his notebook and moves toward the Sitting Room. Suddenly* TRACY *appears in the Library doorway. She wears a bright-colored dressing gown over the foundation for a white evening dress and*

has a book in her hand, her finger marking a place toward the end of it.*]

TRACY. Please wait a minute.

MIKE. With pleasure. [*He stops where he is. She goes to him, turns him about and looks at him wonderingly.*] What's the matter?

TRACY. I've been reading these stories. They're so damned beautiful.

MIKE. You like? Thanks—

TRACY. Why, Connor, they're almost poetry. [*He laughs shortly.*]

MIKE. Don't fool yourself: they *are!*

TRACY. I can't make you out at all, now.

MIKE. Really? I thought I was easy.

TRACY. So did I, but you're not. You talk so big and tough—and then you write like this. Which is which?

MIKE. I guess I'm both.

TRACY. No—I believe you put the toughness on, to save your skin.

MIKE. You think?

TRACY. Yes. *I* know a little about that—

MIKE. Do you?

TRACY. Quite a lot. [*They look at each other for a moment. Then* TRACY *laughs a little embarrassedly and glances away.*] It—the book—it was just such a complete —hell of a surprise, that's all.

MIKE. Yes—it seems you do.

TRACY. What?

MIKE. Know about it.

TRACY. The one called "With The Rich and Mighty"—I think I liked *it* best.

MIKE. I got it from a Spanish peasant's proverb—"With The Rich and Mighty, always a little patience." [TRACY *laughs.*]

TRACY. Good! [*She seats herself, gazes again at the book.*] Tell me something, will you? When you can do a thing like this, how can you possibly do anything else?

MIKE. Such as what?

TRACY. You said after lunch—what was it you said? "Cheap stuff for expensive magazines."

MIKE. Did I?

TRACY. Yes. You did. You said you spent most of your time that way. [MIKE *seats himself, facing her.*]

MIKE. Practically all. Why? What about it?

TRACY. I can't understand it. And I like to understand things.

MIKE. You'll never believe it, but there are people in this world who have to earn their living.

TRACY. Of course! But people buy books, don't they?

MIKE. Sure they do: they even read them.

TRACY. Well, then!

MIKE. That one represents two solid years' work. It netted Connor something under six hundred dollars.

TRACY. But that shouldn't *be!*

MIKE.—Only unhappily it is. [*There is a pause.*]

TRACY. And what about your Miss Imbrie?

MIKE. Miss Imbrie is in somewhat the same fix. She's a born painter, and might be an important one. But Miss Imbrie must eat. Also, she prefers a roof over her head to being constantly out in the rain and snow. [TRACY *ponders this.*]

TRACY. Food and a roof—food and a roof—

MIKE. Those charming essentials.

TRACY [*suddenly*]. Listen: I've got an idea! [*She rises, goes to him, stands over him.*] Listen: I've got the most marvelous little house in Unionville. It's up on a hill, with a view that would knock you silly. I'm never there except in the hunting season, and not much then, and I'd be so happy to know it was of some use to someone. [*She moves swiftly across the Porch and back again.*] There's a brook and a small lake, no size really, and a patch of woods, and in any kind of weather, it's the— [*She is down the steps now, looking up at the sky.*] —And look at that sky now, will you! Suddenly it's clear as clear! It's going to be fine tomorrow! It's going to be fair! Good for you, God! [*She glances down the path.*] Hell! [*And quickly returns to the Porch.*] Someone's coming—someone I don't want to be alone with. Stand by for a couple of minutes, will you?

MIKE. Certainly—if you like.

TRACY.—You *will* think about the house, won't you?

MIKE. Why, it's terribly nice of you, but—

TRACY. Don't think I'd come trooping in every minute, because I wouldn't. I'd never come, except when expressly asked to.

MIKE. It isn't that.

TRACY. What is it?

MIKE. Well, you see—er—you see the idea of artists having a patron has more or less gone out, and— [*She looks at him steadily.*]

TRACY. I see. [*Then waits a moment.*] That wasn't especially kind of you, Mr. Connor. There's no need to rub our general uselessness in.

MIKE. I'm afraid I don't get you.

TRACY. Don't bother. I'm sorry to have seemed—patronizing.

MIKE. I didn't quite mean—

TRACY. Please don't bother, really. [DEXTER *comes in down the Garden path. He carries a small picture, wrapped in tissue paper.*]

DEXTER. Hello.

TRACY. Hello. Fancy seeing you here.

[*He mounts the Porch and goes to the table.*]

DEXTER. Orange juice? Certainly!—

TRACY. You're sure you don't want something stronger? I'll ring if you like. [*He pours himself a glass of orange juice from a pitcher.*]

DEXTER. Not now, thanks. This is fine.

TRACY. Don't tell me you've forsaken your beloved whisky-and-whiskies—

DEXTER. No, indeed. I've just changed their color, that's all. I go in for the pale pastel shades now. I find they're more becoming. [*He looks at* MIKE *over his glass.*] We met at lunch, didn't we?

MIKE. Yes, I seem to remember. Connor's my name.

DEXTER.—The writer—of course! Do you drink, Mr. Connor?

MIKE. A little. Why?

DEXTER. Not to excess?

MIKE. Not often.

DEXTER.—And a writer! It's extraordinary. I thought all writers drank to excess, and beat their wives. I expect that at one time *I* secretly wanted to be a writer.

TRACY. Dexter, would you mind doing something for me? [*He replaces the glass upon the table and puts the picture beside it.*]

DEXTER. Anything. What?

TRACY. Get the hell out of here.

DEXTER. Oh, no, I couldn't do that. That wouldn't be fair to you. You need me too much.

TRACY. Would you mind telling me just what it is you're hanging around for? [MIKE *moves toward the Library door.*] No—please don't go! I'd honestly much prefer it if you wouldn't. [*Reluctantly* MIKE *seats himself near the door.*]

DEXTER. So should I. Do stay, Mr. Connor. As a writer this ought to be right up your street.

TRACY [*to* MIKE]. Miss not a word! [DEXTER *gazes at her.*]

DEXTER. Honestly, you never looked better in your life. You're getting a fine tawny look.

TRACY. Oh, we're going to talk about me, are we? Goody.

DEXTER.—It's astonishing what money can do for people, don't you agree, Mr. Connor? Not too much, you know—just more than enough. Particularly for girls. Look at Tracy: there's never been a blow that hasn't been softened for her. There'll never be one that won't be softened. Why, it even changed her shape—she was a dumpy little thing originally.

TRACY.—Only as it happens, I'm not interested in myself, for the moment. What interests me now, is what, if any, your real point is, in—

DEXTER. Not interested in yourself? My dear, you're fascinated! You're far and away your favorite person in the world.

TRACY. Dexter, in case you don't know it, I—!

DEXTER. Shall I go on—?

TRACY. Oh, yes, please do, by all means— [*She seats herself.*]

DEXTER. Of course, she is kindness itself, Mr. Connor—

TRACY.—Itself, Mr. Connor.

DEXTER. She is generous to a fault—that is, except to other people's faults. For instance, she never had the slightest sympathy toward nor understanding of what used to be known as my deep and gorgeous thirst.

TRACY. That was your problem!

DEXTER. It was the problem of a young man of exceptionally high spirit, who drank to slow down that damned engine he'd found nothing yet to do with.—I refer to my mind. You took on that problem with me, when you took me.—You were no helpmate there, Tracy—you were a scold.

TRACY. It was disgusting. It made you so unattractive.

DEXTER. A weakness—sure. And strength is her religion, Mr. Connor. She is a goddess, without patience for any kind of human imperfection. And when I gradually discovered that my relation to her was expected to be not that of a loving husband and a good companion, but— [*He turns away from her.*] Oh—never mind—

TRACY. Say it!

DEXTER.—But that of a kind of high priest to a virgin goddess, then my drinks grew more frequent and deeper in hue, that's all.

TRACY. I never considered you as that, nor myself!

DEXTER. You did without knowing it. And the night that *you* got drunk on champagne, and climbed out on the roof and stood there naked, with your arms out to the moon, wailing like a banshee— [MIKE, *with a startled expression, moves sideways out into the Library.*]

TRACY. I told you I never had the slightest recollection of doing any such thing!

DEXTER. I know; you drew a blank. You wanted to.—Mr. Connor, what would you say in the case of— [*He turns and sees that* MIKE *has gone.*]

TRACY. He's a reporter, incidentally. He's doing us for *Destiny*.

DEXTER. Sandy told me. A pity we can't supply photographs of you on the roof.

TRACY. Honestly, the fuss you made over that silly, childish—!

DEXTER. It was enormously important, and most revealing. The moon is also a goddess, chaste and virginal.

TRACY. Stop using those foul words! We were married nearly a year, weren't we?

DEXTER. Marriage doesn't change a true case like yours, my dear. It's an affair of the spirit—not of the flesh.

TRACY. Dexter, what are you trying to make me out as?

DEXTER. Tracy, what do you fancy yourself as?

TRACY. I don't know that I fancy myself as anything.

DEXTER. When I read you were going to marry Kittredge, I couldn't believe it. How in the world can you even think of it? [*She turns on him.*]

TRACY. I love him, that's why! As I never even began to love you!

DEXTER. It may be true, but I doubt it. *I* think it's just a swing from me, and what I represent—but I think it's too violent a swing. That's why I came on. Kittredge is no great tower of strength, you know, Tracy. He's just a tower.

TRACY. You've known him how long? —half a day.

DEXTER. I knew him for two days two years ago, the time I went up to the fields with your father, but half a day would have done, I think.

TRACY. It's just personal, then—

DEXTER. Purely and completely.

TRACY. You couldn't possibly understand him or his qualities. I shouldn't expect you to.

DEXTER. I suppose when you come right down to it, Tray, it just offends my vanity to have anyone who was even remotely my wife, marry so obviously beneath her.

TRACY. "Beneath" me! How dare you —any of you—in this day and age, use such a—?

DEXTER. I'm talking about differences in mind and imagination. You could marry Mac, the night watchman, and I'd cheer for you.

TRACY. And what's wrong with George?

DEXTER. Nothing—utterly nothing. He's a wizard at his job, and I'm sure he is honest, sober, and industrious. He's just not for you.

TRACY. He *is* for me—he's a great man and a good man: already he's of national importance.

DEXTER. Good Lord—you sound like *Destiny* talking.—Well, whatever he is, you'll have to stick, Tray. He'll give you no out as I did.

TRACY. I won't require one.

DEXTER. I suppose you'd still be attractive to any man of spirit, though. There's something engaging about it, this virgin goddess business, something more challenging to the male than the more obvious charms.

TRACY. Really?

DEXTER. Oh, yes! We're very vain, you know—"This citadel can and shall be taken—and I'm just the boy to do it."

TRACY. You seem quite contemptuous of me, all of a sudden.

DEXTER. Not of you, Red, never of you. You could be the damnedest, finest woman on this earth. If I'm contemptuous of anything, it's of something in you you either can't help, or make no attempt to: your so-called "strength"—your prejudice against weakness—your blank intolerance—

TRACY. Is that all?

DEXTER. That's the gist of it; because you'll never be a first-class woman or a first-class human being, till you have learned to have some small regard for human frailty. It's a pity your own foot can't slip a little some time—but no, your sense of inner divinity won't allow it. The goddess must and shall remain intact.— You know, I think there are more of you around than people realize. You're a special class of American Female now—the

Married Maidens.—And of Type Philadelphiaensis, you're the absolute tops, my dear.

TRACY. Damn your soul, Dext, if you say another—! [*He sees* GEORGE *coming in from the Library at Left.*]

DEXTER. I'm through, Tracy—for the moment I've said my say. [GEORGE *smiles at them with a great attempt at good humor.*]

GEORGE. I suppose I ought to object to this twosome.

DEXTER. That would be most objectionable. Well, any time either of you wants more advice from me— [*He moves toward the steps.*]

GEORGE. When we do, we'll give you a ring, Haven.

DEXTER. Do that, will you? You'll find that I have a most sympathetic and understanding ear— [*He turns to* TRACY.] I left you a little wedding present there on the table, Red—I'm sorry I hadn't any ribbon to tie it up with. [*Then goes out down the path.*]

GEORGE. You see—it's no use even attempting to be friendly.

TRACY. Certainly not. You were a dear to try. Please don't mind him. [DINAH *comes in from the Garden, down the opposite path. She mounts the Porch and crosses to the Sitting-Room door.*]

DINAH [*to* TRACY]. You got taken when you bought that roan. She's parrot-jawed.

TRACY. Get into a tub. You're revolting.

DINAH. What's more, she swallows wind by the bucket.

TRACY. Where's Miss Imbrie? Wasn't she with you?

DINAH. No. She's gone to the privy with Uncle Willie. [*She goes out, into the Sitting Room.* TRACY *picks up the package left by* DEXTER, *scrutinizes it, shakes it.*]

TRACY. It's anyone's guess what this

might be. [*She unwraps it.*] It's—why it's a photograph of the "True Love."

GEORGE.—The?—What's that?

TRACY. A boat he designed—and built, practically. We sailed her down the coast of Maine and back, the summer we were married. My, she was yare.

GEORGE. "Yare?" What does that mean?

TRACY. It means—oh, what does it mean?—Easy to handle—quick to the helm—fast—bright—everything a boat should be. [*She gazes at the photograph for a moment without speaking, then drops it upon the table.*] —And the hell with it.

GEORGE. Rather bad taste, I'd say, giving you that.

TRACY. Dexter never concerns himself much with taste.

GEORGE. How'd you ever happen to marry a fellow like that, Tracy?

TRACY. Oh, I don't know—I expect it was kind of a hangover from childhood days. We grew up together, you know.

GEORGE. I see—propinquity.

TRACY. Oh, George—to get away—to get away—! Somehow to feel useful in the world—

GEORGE. Useful?—I'm going to build you an ivory tower with my own two hands.

TRACY. Like fun you are.

GEORGE. You mean you've been in one too long?

TRACY. I mean that, and a lot of things.

GEORGE. I'm going to make a grand life for us, dear—and you can help, all right.

TRACY. I hope I can.

GEORGE. From now on we'll both stop wasting time on unimportant people.

TRACY. That's all right with me.

GEORGE. Our little house on the river up there—I'd like people to consider it an honor to be asked there.

TRACY. Why an honor, especially?

GEORGE. We're going to represent something, Tracy—something straight and sound and fine.—And then perhaps young Mr. Haven may be somewhat less condescending. [*She looks at him.*]

TRACY. George—you don't really mind him, do you? I mean the fact of him—

GEORGE. The—? I don't see what you mean, Tracy.

TRACY. I mean that—you know—that he ever was—was my lord and master— That we ever were—

GEORGE. I don't believe he ever was—not really. I don't believe anyone ever was, or ever will be. That's the wonderful thing about you, Tracy. [*She looks at him startled.*]

TRACY. What? How—?

GEORGE. You're like some marvelous, distant—oh, queen, I guess. You're so cool and fine and—and always so much your own. That's the wonderful *you* in you—that no one can ever really possess—that no one can touch, hardly. It's—it's a kind of beautiful purity, Tracy, that's the only word for it. [*She is now really frightened.*]

TRACY. George—

GEORGE. Oh, it's grand, Tracy—it's just grand! Everyone feels it about you. It's what I first worshiped you for, Tracy, from afar.

TRACY. George, listen—

GEORGE. First, now, and always! [*He leans toward her.*] Only from a little nearer, now—eh, darling?

TRACY. I don't want to be worshiped! I want to be loved!

GEORGE. You're that, too. You're that, all right.

TRACY. I mean really loved.

GEORGE. But that goes without saying, Tracy.

TRACY. And now it's you—who doesn't see what *I* mean. [EDWARD, *carrying a tray with cocktail things and a bottle of champagne enters from the Sitting Room, followed by* ELSIE. ELSIE *picks up the orange-juice tray from the table.*] You can just leave them, Edward. [EDWARD *places the tray.* ELSIE *looks down at* DEXTER'S *present.*]

ELSIE. Shall I put this picture with the other presents, Miss Tracy?

TRACY. No—just leave it there, please.

ELSIE. Yes, Miss. [*They go out, into the Sitting Room.*]

GEORGE [*to* TRACY]. Don't let Miss Imbrie get hold of it.

TRACY. I should say not. [*She rewraps the picture.*]

GEORGE. I hope they'll soft pedal the first-marriage angle.

TRACY. I wish they'd pedal themselves right out of here.

GEORGE [*after a moment*]. They've got a job to do. And it's an honor, you know, Tracy.

TRACY. What is?

GEORGE. Why—to be done by *Destiny.* [TRACY *frowns at him.*]

TRACY. Are you joking?

GEORGE. Joking—?

TRACY. But you can't seriously mean that you think—!

GEORGE. I think *Destiny* fills a very definite place, Tracy. [TRACY *stares at him uncomprehendingly.* MARGARET *comes in from the Library, followed by* SETH. *Both are in evening clothes.*]

MARGARET. George, you aren't dressed! —And Tracy, you're guests of honor—you mustn't be late. [GEORGE *moves swiftly to the steps.*]

GEORGE. Right on my way, Ma'am! [*He stops and turns to* TRACY.] Wait for me, Tracy! I make the Gatehouse in nothing

flat, now! [*He is away, down the path, practically at a run.*]

SETH. Does he by any chance ever walk anywhere?

TRACY. When he likes, I expect.

SETH. I have a feeling he's going to take the ring tomorrow and go through center with it. [MARGARET *laughs and seats herself.*]

MARGARET. Seth, you idiot.

TRACY. That's very amusing, I'm sure.

SETH. Oh, don't take things to heart so, Tracy. You'll wear yourself out. [LIZ *hurries in from the Garden.*]

LIZ. I won't be a minute!

MARGARET. There's no hurry, Miss Imbrie. [LIZ *smiles, and goes out, into the Sitting Room.* SETH *is preparing cocktails.*]

SETH. What bothers me at the moment, is the spectacle we're all making of ourselves for the benefit of the young man and woman from *Destiny.*

TRACY. Whose fault is it?

SETH. That's beside the point.

MARGARET. Never in my life have I felt so self-conscious. It's all simply dreadful.

SETH. It's worse: it's stupid and childish and completely undignified.

TRACY. So are other things.

SETH. They can publish what they like about me, but—

TRACY.—My idea is, they'll publish nothing about any of us.

SETH. How do you propose to stop them?

TRACY. I don't quite know yet.

SETH. Well, at present the least we can do is to inform Connor and the camera-lady that we are all quite aware of their purpose here. I insist on that.

TRACY. All right! I'll tell them myself.

SETH. I think it will come better from me, don't you—as, at least, titular head of the family? [*He gives* Margaret *a cocktail. A moment, then* Tracy *speaks deliberately harshly.*]

Tracy. Of course—inasmuch as you let us in for it in the first place.

Seth. Do keep that note out of your voice, Tracy. It's most unattractive.

Tracy. Oh? How does Miss Mara talk? Or does she purr?

Margaret. Tracy!

Seth. It's all right, Margaret.

Tracy. Sweet and low, I suppose. Dulcet. Very ladylike.—You've got a fine right, you have—after the way you've treated Mother—after the way you've treated us all—a magnificent right you've got to come back here in your best county manner and strike attitudes and make stands and criticize my fiancé and give orders and mess things up generally, just as if you'd done—

Margaret. Stop it instantly, Tracy! [Tracy *rises abruptly.*]

Tracy. I can't help it. It's sickening.— As if he'd done nothing at all!

Margaret. It is no concern of yours. If it concerns anyone, it concerns—well, actually, I don't know whom it concerns, except your father.

Seth. That's very wise of you, Margaret. What most wives won't seem to realize, is that their husband's philandering—particularly the middle-aged kind—has nothing whatever to do with them.

Tracy. Oh? Then what has it to do with? [Seth *reseats himself.*]

Seth. A reluctance to grow old, I think. I suppose the best mainstay a man can have as he gets along in years is a daughter—the right kind of daughter.

Tracy. That's interesting, to say the least.

Seth.—One who loves him blindly—as no good wife ever should, of course.— One for whom he can do no wrong—

Tracy. How sweet.

Seth. I'm talking seriously about something I've thought out thoroughly. I've had to. I think a devoted young daughter gives a man the illusion that youth is still his.

Tracy. Very important, I suppose.

Seth. Very—and without her, he's inclined to go in search of it again, because it's as precious to him as it is to any woman.—But with a girl of his own full of warmth for him, full of foolish, unquestioning, uncritical affection—

Tracy.—None of which I've got.

Seth. None. You have a good mind, a pretty face and a disciplined body that does what you tell it. You have more wealth than any of us, thanks to one grandfather's name and another's red hair, and a shameless play for both of them since about age three. In fact—

Tracy. I never! I loved them!

Seth.—In fact, you have everything it takes to make a lovely woman except the one essential—an understanding heart. Without it, you might just as well be made of bronze.

Tracy [*after a moment*]. That's an awful thing to say to anyone.

Seth. Indeed it is.

Tracy. So I'm to blame for Tina Mara, am I?

Seth. If any blame attaches, to some extent I expect you are.

Tracy. You coward.

Seth. No.—But better to be one than a prig—and a perennial spinster, however many marriages.

Margaret. Seth! That's too much.

Seth. I'm afraid it's not enough [Tracy *is staring at him.*]

Tracy. Wha-what did you say I was?

SETH. Do you want me to repeat it?

MARGARET. Seth—now I understand a great deal that I didn't. [*He goes to her.*]

SETH. It's all past now, Margaret. It has been for some time. Forgive me. You won't have to again. *I* understand a lot more than I did, as well. [MARGARET *touches his hand understandingly. Still* TRACY *stares.*]

TRACY. "A prig and a—?" You mean—you mean you think *I* think I'm some kind of a virgin goddess or something?

SETH. If your ego wishes to call it that, yes.—Also, you've been talking like a jealous woman.

TRACY. A—? [*She turns away, her face a study.*] What's the matter with everyone all at once, anyhow? [UNCLE WILLIE *comes in from the Garden.*]

UNCLE WILLIE. Miss Imbrie preferred dressing, to my company. [*To* SETH.] What do you make of that, Uncle Willie?

SETH. We're going to drop all this. From now on you're yourself again—and so am I. I shall tell Connor and Miss Imbrie we know what their tender mission is, and at the first opportunity. [SANDY *and* DINAH, *in evening clothes, come in from the house.*]

UNCLE WILLIE. It's a pity. It was jolly good fun. Let's have a drink—

SANDY. Damme, let's do that. [*He pours cocktails.*]

DINAH. We're all so completely commonplace. *I* don't see how we interest anyone. [MARGARET *frowns over* DINAH'S *costume.*]

MARGARET. I think that dress hikes up a little behind. [DINAH *sighs.*]

DINAH. No—it's me that does. [TRACY *speaks briefly, out of her preoccupation.*]

TRACY. You look adorable, Dinah.

DINAH. Oh, thanks, Tracy! Thanks ever so much!

SANDY. A wedding without ushers and bridesmaids. Peace! It's wonderful—

DINAH. *I'm* the bridesmaid!—So can I have a cocktail at last? Can I?

MARGARET. Certainly not.

DINAH. It's a dirty gyp. [*She throws herself down in a chair.* SANDY *offers* TRACY *a cocktail.*]

SANDY. Tracy? [*She shakes her head.*] Champagne, instead?

TRACY. No, thanks.

SANDY. Excuse, please. I forgot, you never.

UNCLE WILLIE. Never? The girl's demented.

TRACY.—But prigs don't.

UNCLE WILLIE. What's that?

TRACY. Nor spinsters.

SANDY. We don't get you.

TRACY. Nor goddesses, virgin or otherwise.

SANDY [*to* UNCLE WILLIE].—Not completely: just a borderline case. [MIKE *and* LIZ, *dressed for dinner, enter from the house.* MIKE *wears a soft shirt.* SANDY *greets them.*] Hello! You were quick. [TRACY *is now standing away from them, leaning against a column of the Porch, noticing nothing.*]

UNCLE WILLIE. Miss Imbrie, you are a dream of loveliness. A cocktail or champagne?

LIZ. Thanks, champagne. I've never had enough.

SANDY. You will tonight. [UNCLE WILLIE *gives* LIZ *and* MIKE *a glass.*]

MIKE. Champagne flew. [*He clears his throat, straightens his tie and begins, to* UNCLE WILLIE.] Mr. Lord—er—that is to say— [SETH *speaks simultaneously.*]

SETH. Mr. Connor—oh—excuse me.

MIKE [*again to* UNCLE WILLIE]. Mr. Lord, Miss Imbrie and I have something on our minds—

UNCLE WILLIE. That's splendid; just the place for it. What?

MIKE. Well—er—it's sort of hard to explain—it's—er—about the reason we're here and so forth.

SETH. I think perhaps there's something I ought to explain too—

MIKE.—But did you ever hear of a man named Sidney Kidd? [THOMAS *enters with a tray and note.*]

SETH.—And did you ever hear of a man named Seth—er—? What is it, Thomas?

THOMAS. They've just phoned a telegram, Mr. Lord—

UNCLE WILLIE. Give it here.

THOMAS [*turns to him*]. It's for Mrs. Lord, Mr. Tracy. [LIZ and MIKE *exchange glances.*]

UNCLE WILLIE. Then why didn't you say so?

THOMAS.—Mrs. Lord and Miss Lord, that is. [MARGARET, *with a half-smile, glances at* SANDY.]

MARGARET. Read it, Thomas. I haven't my glasses.

SANDY. Hey! Wait a minute!

MARGARET. Read it, Thomas.

THOMAS. "Most frightfully sorry will not be able to get down for the wedding as am confined to my bed with everything wrong. Baby better. It was only gas. Love, Father." Is there any answer, Madam?

MARGARET. No, Thomas—none in this world. [*He goes out.*]

LIZ [*to* UNCLE WILLIE]. He got you a little mixed up, didn't he?

UNCLE WILLIE. A common mistake.

SETH. Now do you understand, Mr. Connor?

MIKE. I think we do.

LIZ. It's wonderful! Lord only knows where we go from here.

SANDY. To Aunt Geneva's!—Come on, everybody.

DINAH. My first party, and about time. [UNCLE WILLIE *moves to* LIZ, *speaks invitingly.*]

UNCLE WILLIE. Who'll come in my little car with me? [MARGARET *moves between them, separating them.*]

MARGARET. Seth and Dinah and I.—Sandy, will you bring Miss Imbrie and Mr. Connor?

SANDY. Like a shot.

DINAH. The evening is pregnant with possibilities. [MARGARET *takes her gently by the shoulders and ushers her out the Library door.*]

MARGARET. "Full of" is better, dear. [UNCLE WILLIE *passes behind* LIZ, *on his way out. She exclaims suddenly.*]

LIZ. Ouch! [SETH *moves to her solicitously.*]

SETH. What was it?

LIZ. N-nothing. [SETH *goes out. She turns to* SANDY.] You know, I felt exactly as if I'd been pinched.

SANDY. Don't think you weren't! [*He and* LIZ *go out.* MIKE *turns to follow them, then stops as he sees* TRACY *still standing motionless against the column.*]

MIKE. Aren't you coming?

TRACY. I'll follow along with George.

MIKE [*after a moment*]. What's the matter with you, Tracy?

TRACY. You tell *me*, will you? [*He looks at her intently.*]

MIKE. Damn if I know. I'd like to. [*She smiles uncertainly.*]

TRACY. Well, if you ever happen to find out—

MIKE.—I'll tell you. Sure. [*After another moment, she speaks again.*]

TRACY.—And remember, Mike—"With the Rich and Mighty—"

MIKE. "—Always a Little Patience"— Yes, Highness, I will.

TRACY. Do that. Please do. [*He looks*

at her for an instant longer, then turns abruptly and goes out. She is alone. She brushes her hair back from her brow. She sees the champagne upon the table before her. She takes up a glass, lifts it to her lips, drinks it deliberately, then thoughtfully reaches for another.]

CURTAIN

SCENE 2

[*The Porch. About half-past five on Saturday morning. It is going to be a clear day, and throughout the scene the light increases.* MAC, *the night watchman, about 30, crosses the path from Left to Right smoking a pipe and swinging a lighted lantern. He goes out, Right.* SANDY *enters from the house. He is carrying a tray with two bottles of champagne, one already opened, a pitcher of milk and glasses. He is followed by* TRACY. *Both are in evening dress.*]

SANDY. The question is, can we get away with it?

TRACY. You've got to get away with it! You must, Sandy!

SANDY. It's your idea, not mine.

TRACY. What difference does that make? [*She pours herself a glass of champagne.*]

SANDY. You get the ideas and I do all the work.

TRACY. Sandy!

SANDY. Okay.

TRACY. What you don't already know about the great Sidney Kidd, you can certainly fill in from Mike's ravings tonight.

SANDY. I used to have that *Dime* lingo down pretty pat.

TRACY. It's a chance to write a beauty: you know it is.

SANDY. Then I swap it with Kidd for Connor's piece on us—and where am I?

TRACY. You'll have the satisfaction of knowing you saved the lot of us single-handed.

SANDY. And if he won't swap?

TRACY. I'm not worried about that.

SANDY. I suppose there's a fair chance the *Post* would go for it.

TRACY. Of course! You can't possibly lose. Quick—they'll be here! How long will it take you?

SANDY. Three thousand words—all night —what there's left of it. [*He looks at his watch.*] Holy cats! You get to bed.

TRACY. Have you got a typewriter?

SANDY. My old Corona is upstairs, I think.

TRACY. Make it smoke.

SANDY. You bet.

TRACY. Suds. I can't stand it. You won't fall asleep?

SANDY. I've drunk nothing but black coffee since Connor began his lecture.

TRACY. "Sidney Kidd—his habits—his habitat—and how to hunt him."

SANDY. Poor Connor! It must have been bottled up in him for years.

TRACY. Waiter, another bottle.

SANDY. No. I've got enough for three articles now: profile, full-face—

TRACY.—Also rear elevation.—Mike and Liz—they mustn't suspect, Sandy.

SANDY. Oh, no—oh, my, no!

TRACY. They have simply stepped in their own chewing gum.—I suppose Kidd has one of those private numbers the rich and the mighty hide behind in New York.

SANDY. I'll dig it out of Liz and give him a buzz.

TRACY. What will you say?

SANDY. I'll be brief, bluff, belligerent. [TRACY *laughs and pours herself another glass of champagne.*] Here—lay off that!

TRACY. Why?

SANDY. You are already in wine, sister.

TRACY. Me? You lie. It never affects me, not in the slightest.

SANDY. That's because you never take it.

TRACY. Even if I did, it wouldn't.

SANDY. Don't say that: it's unlucky. [*She drains the glass.* SANDY *shakes his head over her.*] I have seen people fly in the face of Pommery before.

TRACY. I've just got a good head, I guess.

SANDY. Don't say it, don't say it! [TRACY *seats herself upon the steps.*]

TRACY. Sandy, you fool.

SANDY. George will spank.

TRACY. I could spank George for the way he behaved. [SANDY *seats himself beside her.*]

SANDY. He had a right to be sore. You and Mike disappeared for two hours, at least.

TRACY. You were along.

SANDY. All the same, tongues were wagging like tails. George said—

TRACY. George wanted to leave sharp at twelve—how could we?

SANDY. They need a lot of sleep, those big fellows.

TRACY. They must.—Then at one, with Father and Mother and Dinah.—Then at two, then at three—every hour on the hour. We fought like wolves in the car coming home.

SANDY. I hope you explained.

TRACY. Certainly not. He should have known. He was extremely rude. You'd have thought I had been out with Dexter, or something.—[*She thinks for a moment.*] I wonder where Dext was? I half expected him to— I don't like the look behind Dexter's eyes, Sandy. It makes me sad.

SANDY. Don't be sad, Tracy. [*He puts* an arm about her and for an instant she rests her head against his shoulder.*]

TRACY. Oh, Sandy, if you knew how I envy you and Sue that darling fat little creature you've just produced—

SANDY. You'll probably have four or five of your own any day now.

TRACY. Six! Oh, I hope—I do hope!—I hope I'm good for something besides knocking out golf balls and putting horses over fences.

SANDY. You're good for my money any day.

TRACY. Thanks! [*She gets up from the step and moves again to the table.*] Was I really mean to George I wonder? I don't want to be.

SANDY. You're in an odd mood, little fellah. What's amiss—what's afoot?

TRACY. I guess it's just that—a lot of things I always thought were terribly important, I find now are—and the other way around—and—oh, what the hell. [*She refills her glass, looks at it and puts it down upon the table.*]

SANDY. I don't think I'd spend much more time with Connor tonight, if I were you.

TRACY. Why not?

SANDY. Writers with wine sauce intoxicate little girls. [*She laughs uncertainly.*]

TRACY. They sort of do, don't they?— He fascinates me. He's so violent, Sandy.

SANDY. He's fallen, Tray. I could hear him bump.

TRACY. Mind your own beeswax, old Nosey Parker.

SANDY. Get thee to bed. [*She reaches for her glass—he stops her hand.*]

TRACY. No!

SANDY.—Before you have to be carried.

TRACY. No! No! No! [*She throws up her arms, her head back.*] I feel too delicious!—Sandy, I feel just elegant. [*Then cocks her head, listening.*] Is that my bedroom telephone?

SANDY. Now you're hearing things.

TRACY. It couldn't be anyone but George. I *was* sort of swinish to him. Perhaps I'd better— [*She starts toward the Sitting Room.*] As for you—get to work, you dog. Stop leaning on your shovel. [*She stops, as* MIKE *comes out upon the Porch from the Library. He is in fine fettle, coatless, his soft shirt open at the neck. He goes directly to the table.*]

MIKE. Listen! Now I'm really under way. Miss not an inflection.

TRACY. Is it Connor the poet, or Connor the conspirator?

MIKE. Both! [*He pours himself a glass of wine and begins to declaim.*] "No lightweight is balding, beetlebrowed Sidney Kidd, no mean displacement, his: for windy bias, bicarbonate." [*He drinks the wine, looks at the glass.*] This is funny stuff. I'm used to whisky. Whisky is a clap on the back. Champagne, entwining arms.

TRACY. That's pretty. Is it poetry?

MIKE. *Dime* will tell.

SANDY. "None before him but Writer Wolfgang Goethe has known all about all. Gigantic was Goethe's output, bigger already is Kidd's. Sample from his own pen: 'Pittsburgh is a gentle city.'"

TRACY. Sidney is a gentle man. [MIKE *points a finger at* SANDY.)

MIKE. Potent, able, beady-eyed scion of great wealth in Quakertown, why don't you do a piece on our great and good friend?

SANDY. On Kidd?

MIKE. On none other.

SANDY. Nimble scrivener, it's an idea.

TRACY. Brilliant. I wish *I'd* thought of it. [MIKE *turns and points a finger at her.*]

MIKE. Baby Giant Tycooness.

TRACY. But would it not be a low, dirty deed?

MIKE. *He'd* print a scandal about his best friend: he's said he would.

SANDY. Who is his best friend?

MIKE. I guess Santa Claus. [*He passes his hand vaguely over his face.*] What is this mist before my eyes? [TRACY *rises suddenly and goes to the table.*]

TRACY. *I* tell you what! Let's all have a quick swim to brighten us up. Go get Liz, Sandy. [*She strips off her bracelets and rings and leaves them on table.*]

SANDY. Not me: It's too cold this early.

TRACY. It's the best hour of the day! Dexter and I always swam after parties.

MIKE. I haven't got any bathing suit.

TRACY. But we won't need any! It's just ourselves. [*He looks at her uncertainly for an instant, then quickly fills two glasses, moves one gingerly toward her, and raises the other.*]

MIKE. Let's dip into this instead.

TRACY. [*after a brief pause, to* SANDY]. No takers.—Get Liz anyway, Sandy.

SANDY. If she's not in bed. [*He goes out into the Sitting Room.*]—Or even if she is.

TRACY [*to* MIKE, *after a moment*]. That was an odd thing you just did—

MIKE. Me?

TRACY [*turning away*]. You. For a moment you made me—self-conscious.

MIKE. How? About what?

TRACY. Never mind. [*She raises her glass.*] Hello, you. [*He raises his.*]

MIKE. Hello.

TRACY. You look fine.

MIKE. I *feel* fine.

TRACY. Quite a fellah.

MIKE. They say. [*They drink.*]

TRACY. Did you enjoy the party?

MIKE. Sure. The prettiest sight in this fine pretty world is the Privileged Class enjoying its privileges.

TRACY.—Also somewhat of a snob.

MIKE. How do you mean?

TRACY. I'm wondering.

MIKE. Consider, Gentle Reader: they toil not, neither do they spin.

TRACY. Oh, yes, they do! They spin in circles. [*She spins once and seats herself upon the step at Left.* MIKE *goes to her.*]

MIKE. Nicely put. "Awash with champagne was Mrs. Willie Q. Tracy (born Geneva Biddle)'s stately pleasure dome on a hilltop in smart Radnor, Pa., on a Saturday night late in June, the eve of her great-niece's—" [*He sits beside her.*] Tracy, you can't marry that guy.

TRACY. George?—I'm going to. Why not?

MIKE. I don't know. I'd have thought I'd be for it. But somehow you just don't seem to match up.

TRACY. Then the fault's with me.

MIKE. Maybe so: all the same, you can't do it. [TRACY *rises and moves a little way along the path.*]

TRACY. No? Come around about noon tomorrow—I mean today. [*After a moment he rises and faces her.*]

MIKE. Tracy—

TRACY. Yes, Mr. Connor?

MIKE. How do you mean, I'm "a snob"?

TRACY. You're the worst kind there is: an intellectual snob. You've made up your mind awfully young, it seems to me. [MIKE *goes to her.*]

MIKE. Thirty's about time to make up your mind.—And I'm nothing of the sort, not Mr. Connor.

TRACY. The time to make up your mind about people is never. Yes, you are—and a complete one.

MIKE. You're quite a girl.

TRACY. You think?

MIKE. I know.

TRACY. Thank you, Professor. I don't think I'm exceptional.

MIKE. You are, though.

TRACY. I know any number like me. You ought to get around more.

MIKE. In the Upper Clahss? No, thanks.

TRACY. You're just a mass of prejudices, aren't you? You're so much thought and so little feeling, Professor. [*She moves Right, further away from him.*]

MIKE. Oh, I am, am I? [*She wheels about on him.*]

TRACY. Yes, you am, are you!—Your damned intolerance furiates me. I mean *in*furiates me! I should think, of all people, a writer would need tolerance. The fact is, you'll never—you can't be a first-rate writer or a first-rate human being until you learn to have some small regard for— [*Suddenly she stops. Her eyes widen, remembering. She turns from him.*] Aren't the geraniums pretty, Professor? Is it not a handsome day that begins? [MIKE *mounts the Porch, looks down upon her.*]

MIKE. Lay off that "Professor."

TRACY. Yes, Professor. [*She mounts the Porch, faces him.*]

MIKE. You've got all the arrogance of your class all right, haven't you?

TRACY. Holy suds, what have "classes" to do with it!

MIKE. Quite a lot.

TRACY. Why? What do they matter—except for the people in them? George comes from the so-called "lower" class, Dexter comes from the upper. Well?

MIKE. Well?

TRACY.—Though there's a great deal to be said for Dexter—and don't you forget it!

MIKE. I'll try not to. [TRACY *moves to the table.*]

TRACY. Mac, the night watchman, is a prince among men and Joey, the stable boy, is a rat. Uncle Hugh is a saint. Uncle Willie's a pincher. [*She fills her glass again.*]

MIKE. So what?

TRACY. There aren't any rules about human beings, that's all!—You're teaching me things, Professor: this is new to me. Thanks, I am beholden to you. [*She raises her glass to him.*]

MIKE. Not at all.

TRACY. "Upper" and "lower" my eye! I'll take the lower, thanks. [*She brings the glass to her lips.*]

MIKE.—If you can't get a drawing-room. [*She puts the glass down, untasted, and turns on him.*]

TRACY. What do you mean by that?

MIKE. My mistake.

TRACY. Decidedly.

MIKE. Okay.

TRACY. You're insulting.

MIKE. I'm sorry.

TRACY. Oh, don't apologize!

MIKE. Who the hell's apologizing?

TRACY. I never knew such a man.

MIKE. You wouldn't be likely to, dear—not from where *you* sit.

TRACY. Talk about arrogance!

MIKE [*after a moment*]. Tracy—

TRACY. What do you want?

MIKE. You're wonderful. [*She laughs.*]

TRACY. Professor—may I go out?

MIKE. Class is dismissed. [*She moves Left.*] Miss Lord will please wait. [*She stops, turns and meets his gaze steadily.*]

TRACY. Miss Lord is privileged. [MIKE *speaks in a lower voice.*]

MIKE. There's magnificence in you, Tracy. I'm telling you.

TRACY. I'm—! [*A moment.*] Now I'm getting self-conscious again. I—it's funny— [*Another moment. Then she moves toward him, impulsively.*] Mike, let's— [*She stops herself.*]

MIKE. What?

TRACY. I—I don't know—go up, I guess. It's late.

MIKE.—A magnificence that comes out of your eyes, that's in your voice, in the way you stand there, in the way you walk. You're lit from within, bright, bright, bright. There are fires banked down in you, hearth-fires and holocausts— [*She moves another step toward him, stands before him.*]

TRACY. You—I don't seem to you—made of bronze, then—

MIKE. You're made of flesh and blood—that's the blank, unholy surprise of it. You're the golden girl, Tracy, full of love and warmth and delight— What the hell's this? You've got tears in your eyes.

TRACY. Shut up, shut up!—Oh, Mike—keep talking—keep talking! *Talk,* will you?

MIKE. I've stopped. [*For a long moment they look at each other. Then* TRACY *speaks, deliberately, harshly.*]

TRACY. Why? Has your mind taken hold again, dear Professor?

MIKE. You think so? [*She moves Right, away from him.*]

TRACY. Yes, Professor.

MIKE. A good thing, don't you agree? [*She leans against the column of the Porch, facing him.*]

TRACY. No, Professor.

MIKE. Drop that Professor—you hear me?

TRACY. Yes, Professor. [*He moves to her slowly, stands almost against her.*]

MIKE. That's really all I am to you, is it?

TRACY. Of course, Professor.

MIKE. Are you sure? [*She looks up at him.*]

TRACY. Why, why yes—yes, of course, Profess— [*His kiss stops the word. The*

[435]

kiss is taken and returned. After it she exclaims softly.] Golly. [*She gazes at him wonderingly, then raises her face to receive another. Then she stands in his arms, her cheek against his breast, amazement in her eyes.*] Golly Moses.

MIKE. Tracy dear—

TRACY. Mr. Connor—Mr. Connor—

MIKE. Let me tell you something—

TRACY. No, don't— All of a sudden I've got the shakes.

MIKE. I have, too.

TRACY. What *is* it?

MIKE. It must be something like love.

TRACY. No, no! It mustn't be. It can't—

MIKE. Why? Would it be inconvenient?

TRACY. Terribly. Anyway, it isn't. I know it's not. Oh, Mike, I'm a bad girl—

MIKE. Not you.

TRACY. We're out of our minds.

MIKE.—Right into our hearts.

TRACY. That ought to have music.

MIKE. It has, hasn't it?—Tracy, you lovely— [*She hears something, looks quickly toward the door, whispers.*]

TRACY. They're coming.

MIKE. The hell. [*She holds a hand out to him.*]

TRACY. It's—it's not far to the pool. It's only over the lawn, in the birch-grove— it'll be lovely now.

MIKE. Come on—

TRACY. Oh, it's as—it's as if my insteps —were melting away.—What is it? Have I—have I got feet of clay, or something?

MIKE.—Quick! Here they are— [*He takes her hand and hurries her down the steps.*]

TRACY. I—I feel so small all at once.

MIKE. You're immense—you're tremendous.

TRACY. Not me—oh, not me! Put me in your pocket, Mike— [*They are gone. A moment, then* SANDY *comes quickly in*

from the house, a sheaf of photographs in his hand. He is followed by LIZ, *in pajamas and wrapper.*]

LIZ. You give those back!

SANDY. Look, Tracy— [*He sees that the Porch is empty.*]

LIZ. May I have them, please?

SANDY. Did Kidd *know* you took these shots of him?

LIZ. Some of them.

SANDY. Sit down. Have a drink.

LIZ. I should say not. A drink would be redundant, tautological, and a mistake. [*Wearily she drops into a chair and eyes the pitcher on the table.*] Is that milk?

SANDY. That is milk.

LIZ. Gimme. Milk, I will accept. [*He pours and gives her a glass.*] I met this cow this afternoon. Nice Bossy.

SANDY. Let me keep just these three shots.

LIZ. What for?

SANDY. A low purpose.

LIZ. Sufficiently low?

SANDY. Nefarious.

LIZ. You won't reproduce them?

SANDY. Nope.

LIZ. Nor cause them to be reproduced?

SANDY. Honest.

LIZ.—In any way, shape, or manner, without permission?

SANDY. So help me, Sidney Kidd.

LIZ. Amen.

SANDY. What's his private number?

LIZ. You mean his private number or his sacred private number?

SANDY. The one by the bed and the bathtub.

LIZ. Regent 4-1416— [*She settles lower in the chair.* SANDY *goes to the telephone just inside the near Sitting-Room door.*] I won't tell you. [*She listens a moment, as he dials. Then.*] Is Mr. Kittredge pure gold, Lord? [SANDY *comes into the doorway, the telephone in hand.*]

SANDY. We must never doubt that, Missy. [*He stands behind her chair, looking down upon her.*]

LIZ [*sleepily*]. *Lèse majesté*—excuse it, please.

SANDY [*to the telephone*]. Regent 4-1416 New York.—Wayne 22-23. [*To* LIZ.]—And Mr. Connor—what of him?

LIZ. Percentage of base metal. Alloy.

SANDY. So.

LIZ.—Which imparts a certain shape and firmness.

SANDY [*to the telephone*]. Hello?—Mr. Kidd? This is Alexander Lord. [LIZ *listens intently.*]

LIZ. I know nothing about this.

SANDY. No, I'm in Philadelphia.—Yes, I know it is. It's early here, too. Look, Mr. Kidd, I think you'd better get over here as fast as you can. What?—I'm sorry to have to tell you, sir, but Connor has had an accident—yes, pretty bad—he had a pretty bad fall.—No, it's his heart we're worried about now.—Yes, I'm afraid so: He keeps talking about you, calling you names—I mean calling your name.— How's that?—No, the eleven o'clock's time enough. We don't expect him to regain consciousness much before then.

LIZ. His only hope is to get fired—I know it is.

SANDY. Sorry, Miss Imbrie's sleeping. Shock.—The newspapers? No, they don't know a thing about it. I understand. What? I said I understood, didn't I?— Twelve-twenty North Philadelphia—I'll have you met. [*He disappears briefly into the Sitting Room and returns without the telephone.*] He wants no publicity. [LIZ *has suppressed her broadening grin. She stirs lazily in her chair and inquires.*]

LIZ. Who was that?

SANDY. God. [*She looks toward the Garden path.*]

LIZ. Do I hear someone?

SANDY. It's Mac, the night watchman.— Liz—you're in love with Connor, aren't you?

LIZ. People ask the oddest questions.

SANDY. Why don't you marry him?

LIZ. I can't hear you.

SANDY. I say, why don't you—? [DEXTER *comes along the path and stops at the steps. He wears flannels and an old jacket.*] Hello, here's an early one!

DEXTER. Hello. I saw quite a full day ahead, and got myself up. [*He seats himself on the steps.*]—A good party?

SANDY. Fine.

DEXTER. Good. [*He lights a cigarette.* LIZ *rises from her chair.*]

LIZ.—And sufficient. Hell or high water, I'm going to bed. [*She moves toward the far Sitting-Room door.*]

SANDY [*following her*]. Why don't you, Liz—*you* know—what I asked?

LIZ. He's still got a lot to learn, and I don't want to get in his way yet a while. Okay?

SANDY. Okay.—Risky, though. Suppose another girl came along in the meantime?

LIZ. Oh, I'd just scratch her eyes out, I guess.—That is, unless she was going to marry someone else the next day.

SANDY. You're a good number, Liz.

LIZ. No, I just photograph well. [*She goes out.*]

DEXTER. Complications? [SANDY *re-examines the photographs.*]

SANDY. There might be.

DEXTER. Where are they?

SANDY. Who?

DEXTER. The complications.

SANDY. They went up—at least I hope and pray that they did.

DEXTER. Well, well. [SANDY *waves the photographs at him and moves toward the Library door.*]

SANDY. Make yourself comfortable, Dext. I've got a little blackmailing to do. [SANDY *goes out.* DEXTER *smokes quietly for a moment, then rises and stamps out his cigarette as he hears someone coming along the path.* GEORGE *enters, still in evening clothes. He stops in surprise at the sight of* DEXTER.]

GEORGE. What are you doing here?

DEXTER. Oh, I'm a friend of the family's —just dropped in for a chat.

GEORGE. Don't try to be funny. I asked you a question.

DEXTER. I might ask you the same one.

GEORGE. I telephoned Tracy and her phone didn't answer.

DEXTER. I didn't telephone. I just came right over.

GEORGE. I was worried, so I—

DEXTER. Yes, I was worried, too.

GEORGE. About what?

DEXTER. What do you think of this Connor—or do you?

GEORGE. What about him?

DEXTER. I just wondered. [*He moves away from him, toward the table.*]

GEORGE. Listen: If you're trying to insinuate some—

DEXTER. My dear fellow, I wouldn't dream of it! I was only— [*He stops suddenly as* TRACY's *rings and bracelets upon the table catch his eye.* GEORGE *looks down the Garden path.*]

GEORGE. Who's that I hear? [DEXTER *glances quickly down the path in the direction of the swimming pool, then pockets the rings and bracelets. He turns to* GEORGE.]

DEXTER. Look, Kittredge: I advise you to go to bed.

GEORGE. Oh, you do, do you?

DEXTER. Yes. I strongly urge you to do so at once.

GEORGE. I'm staying right here. [DEXTER *looks at him.*]

DEXTER. You're making a mistake. Somehow I don't think you'll understand.

GEORGE. You'd better leave that to—! I hear someone walking—

DEXTER. Yes?—Must be Mac. [*He calls out down the path, making every word clear.*] It's all right, Mac—it's only us! [*He turns to* GEORGE—*comes down to him.*] Come on—I'll walk along with you.

GEORGE. I'm staying right here—so are you.

DEXTER. All right, then: take the works, and may God be with you. [*He retires into a corner of the Porch. Heavy steps on the gravel path draw nearer. Finally,* MIKE *appears, carrying* TRACY *in his arms. Both are in bathrobes and slippers and there is a jumble of clothes, his and hers, slung over* MIKE's *shoulder. He stops with her for a moment at the top of the steps. She stirs in his arms, speaks lowly, as if from a long way away.*]

TRACY. Take me upstairs, Mike—

MIKE. Yes, dear. Here we go. [GEORGE *looms up.*]

GEORGE. What the—! [DEXTER *comes swiftly in between him and* MIKE.]

DEXTER. Easy, old boy! [*To* MIKE.] She's not hurt?

MIKE. No. She's just— [TRACY *murmurs dreamily.*]

TRACY. Not wounded, sire—but dead.

GEORGE. She—she hasn't any clothes on!

TRACY [*into* MIKE's *shoulder*]. Not a stitch—it's delicious. [MIKE *speaks lowly.*]

MIKE. It seems the minute she hit the water, the wine— [DEXTER *glances at* GEORGE, *who can only stare.*]

DEXTER. A likely story, Connor.

MIKE. What did you say?

DEXTER. I said, a likely story!

MIKE. Listen: if—!

DEXTER. You'll come down again directly?

MIKE. Yes, if you want.

DEXTER. I want. [TRACY *lifts her head limply and looks at them.*]

TRACY. Hello, Dexter. Hello, George. [*She crooks her head around and looks vaguely up at* MIKE.] Hello, Mike. [DEXTER *goes and opens the screen door for them.*]

DEXTER. The second door on the right at the top of the stairs. Mind you don't wake Dinah. [MIKE *moves toward the door with* TRACY.]

TRACY. My feet are of clay—made of clay—did you know it? [*She drops her head again and tightens her arms around* MIKE's *neck.*] Goo' nigh'—sleep well, little man. [MIKE *carries her out, past* DEXTER.]

DEXTER [*calling after them*]. Look out for Dinah! [*He comes forward.*] How are the mighty fallen!—But if I know Tracy—and I know her very well—she'll remember very little of this. For the second time in her life, she may draw quite a tidy blank.—Of course she may worry, though—

GEORGE. Good God! [DEXTER *turns on him swiftly.*]

DEXTER. You believe it, then?

GEORGE. Believe what?

DEXTER. The—er—the implications of what you've seen, let's say.

GEORGE. What else is there to believe?

DEXTER. Why, I suppose that's entirely up to you.

GEORGE. I've got eyes, and I've got imagination, haven't I?

DEXTER. I don't know. Have you?

GEORGE. So you pretend not to believe it—

DEXTER. Yes, I pretend not to.

GEORGE. Then you don't know women.

DEXTER. Possibly not.

GEORGE. You're a blind fool!

DEXTER. Oh, quite possibly!

GEORGE.—God! [DEXTER *studies him.*]

DEXTER. You won't be too hard on her, will you?

GEORGE. I'll make up my own mind what I'll be!

DEXTER. But we're all only human, you know.

GEORGE. You—all of you—with your damned sophisticated ideas!

DEXTER. Isn't it hell? [MIKE *comes swiftly through the door and up to* DEXTER.]

MIKE. Well? [GEORGE *advances.*]

GEORGE. Why, you lowdown—!

DEXTER [*quickly*]. The lady is my wife, Mr. Connor. [*His uppercut to* MIKE's *jaw sends him across the Porch and to the floor.*]

GEORGE. You!—What right have—?

DEXTER.—A husband's, till tomorrow, Kittredge.

GEORGE. I'll make up my mind, all right! [*He turns, and storms out down the Garden path.* DEXTER *bends over* MIKE.]

DEXTER. Okay, old man? [MIKE *sits up, nursing his chin.*]

MIKE. Listen: if you think—!

DEXTER. I know—I'm sorry. But I thought I'd better hit you before he did. [MAC, *the night watchman, comes along the Garden path from the opposite direction taken by* GEORGE. *He is putting his lantern out.* DEXTER *straightens up.*] Hello, Mac. How are you?

MAC. Hello, Dexter! Anything wrong?

DEXTER. Not a thing, Mac.—Just as quiet as a church.

MAC. Who is it? [MIKE *turns his face to him.*] Hell!—I thought it might be Kittredge.

DEXTER. We can't have everything, Mac. [MAC *laughs, shakes his head, and continues along the path.*]

CURTAIN

ACT III

[*The Sitting Room. Late morning, Saturday. The room is full of bright noonday sun and there are flowers everywhere.* UNCLE WILLIE, *in a morning coat, fancy waistcoat, and Ascot, stands in the center of the room facing* THOMAS.]

THOMAS. I am trying to think, Mr. Tracy. [*A moment, then* UNCLE WILLIE *demands impatiently.*]

UNCLE WILLIE. Well? Well?

THOMAS. She wakened late, sir, and had a tray in her room. I believe May and Elsie are just now dressing her.

UNCLE WILLIE. It's not the bride I'm asking about—it's her sister.

THOMAS. I haven't seen Miss Dinah since breakfast, sir. She came down rather early.

UNCLE WILLIE. Is there anything wrong with her?

THOMAS. I did notice that she seemed a trifle silent, took only one egg and neglected to finish her cereal. The hot cakes and bacon, however, went much as usual.

UNCLE WILLIE. She was telephoning me like a mad woman before I was out of my tub. [DINAH, *in blue-jeans, tiptoes in from the Porch and up behind him.*] I expected at least two bodies, hacked beyond recognition, the house stiff with police, and— [DINAH *tugs at his coattail. He starts and turns.*] Good God, child—don't do that! I drank champagne last night.

DINAH. Hello, Uncle Willie.

UNCLE WILLIE. *Why* must I come on ahead of your Aunt Geneva? Why must I waste not one minute? What's amiss? What's about? Speak up! Don't stand there with your big eyes like a stuffed owl. [DINAH *glances significantly at* THOMAS.]

THOMAS. Is there anything else, sir? If not—

UNCLE WILLIE. Thanks, Thomas, nothing. [THOMAS *goes out. Again* DINAH *tugs at* UNCLE WILLIE's *coattail, drawing him to an armchair.*]

DINAH. Come over here—and speak very low. Nobody's allowed to come in here this morning but Tracy—and speak terribly low.

UNCLE WILLIE. What the Sam Hill for? What's alack? What's afoot?

DINAH. I had no one to turn to but you, Uncle Willie.

UNCLE WILLIE. People are always turning to me. I wish they'd stop. [*She kneels on another chair, leaning over the table to him.*]

DINAH. It's desperate. It's about Tracy.

UNCLE WILLIE. Tracy? What's she up to now? Tracy this, and Tracy that. Upstairs and downstairs and in my lady's chamber.

DINAH. How did you know?

UNCLE WILLIE. Know what?

DINAH. It seems to me you know just about everything.

UNCLE WILLIE. I have a fund of information accumulated through the years. I am old, seasoned, and full of instruction.

[440]

But there are gaps in my knowledge. Ask me about falconry, say, or ballistics, and you will get nowhere.

DINAH. I meant more about people and —and sin.

UNCLE WILLIE. I know only that they are inseparable. I also know that the one consolation for being old is the realization that, however you live, you will never die young.—Get to the point, child. What do you want of me?

DINAH. Advice.

UNCLE WILLIE. On what subject or subjects?

DINAH [*after a moment*]. Well, lookit: you don't like George, do you?

UNCLE WILLIE. Kittredge? I deplore him.

DINAH. And you'd like it if Tracy didn't go ahead and have married him after all—or would you?

UNCLE WILLIE. Where do you go to school?

DINAH. I don't, yet. I'm going some place next fall.

UNCLE WILLIE. And high time.—Like it? I would cheer. I would raise my voice in song.

DINAH. Well, I think I know a way to stop her from, but I need advice on how.

UNCLE WILLIE. Proceed, child—proceed cautiously.

DINAH. Well, suppose she all of a sudden developed an illikit passion for someone—

UNCLE WILLIE. Can you arrange it?

DINAH. It doesn't need to be. It is already.

UNCLE WILLIE. Ah? Since when?

DINAH. Last night—and well into the morning.

UNCLE WILLIE. You surprise me, Dinah.

DINAH. Imagine what *I* was—and just imagine what *George* would be.

UNCLE WILLIE. And—er—the object of this—er—illikit passion—

DINAH. Let him be nameless.—Only tell me, should I tell George?—It's getting late. [*Unnoticed by them* DEXTER *has come in from the Porch.*]

UNCLE WILLIE. Maybe he'll want to marry her anyway.

DINAH. But she can't! If she marries anyone, it's got to be Mr. Connor!

UNCLE WILLIE. Connor? Why Connor?

DINAH. She's just got to, that's all! [DEXTER *comes forward.*]

DEXTER. Why, Dinah? What makes you think she should? [DINAH *looks at him, appalled.*]

DINAH. Dexter!

DEXTER. Isn't that a pretty big order to swing at this late date?

DINAH. I—I didn't say anything. What did *I* say?

DEXTER. Of course, you might talk it over with her.—But maybe you have.

DINAH. Certainly not, I haven't!

UNCLE WILLIE. Apparently the little cherub has seen or heard something.

DEXTER. That's Dexter's own Dinah.

UNCLE WILLIE. I must say *you* show a certain amount of cheek, walking in here on this, of all mornings.

DEXTER. Tracy just did a very sweet thing: she telephoned and asked me what to do for a feeling of fright accompanied by headache.

DINAH. I should think it would be bad luck for a first husband to see the bride before the wedding.

DEXTER. That's what I figured.—Why all this about Connor, Dinah? Did the party give you bad dreams?

DINAH. It wasn't any dream.

DEXTER. I wouldn't be too sure. Once you've gone to bed it's pretty hard to tell, isn't it? [DINAH *ponders this.*]

DINAH. Is it?

DEXTER. You bet your hat it is. It's practically impossible.

DINAH. I thought it was Sandy's typewriter woke me up. [TRACY *comes in from the Hall, in the dress in which she is to be married. A leather-strapped wrist watch dangles from her hand. She moves to the sofa.*]

TRACY. Hello! Isn't it a fine day, though! Is everyone fine? That's fine! [*She seats herself uncertainly.*] My, I'm hearty.

DEXTER. How are you otherwise?

TRACY. I don't know what's the matter with me. I must have had too much sun yesterday.

DEXTER. It's awfully easy to get too much. [*She picks up a silver cigarette box and looks at herself in it.*]

TRACY. My eyes don't open properly. [*She blinks up at* DEXTER.] Please go home, Dext.

DEXTER. Not till we get those eyes open. [*He seats himself beside her upon the sofa. She notices* UNCLE WILLIE.]

TRACY. Uncle Willie, good morning.

UNCLE WILLIE. That remains to be seen.

TRACY. Aren't you here early?

UNCLE WILLIE. Weddings get me out like nothing else.

DINAH. It's nearly half-past twelve.

TRACY. It can't be!

DINAH. Maybe it can't, but it is.

TRACY. Where—where's Mother? [DINAH *springs up.*]

DINAH. Do you want her?

TRACY. No, I just wondered. [DINAH *reseats herself.*]

DINAH. She's talking with the orchestra, and Father with the minister, and—

TRACY. Dr. Parsons—already?

DINAH.—And Miss Imbrie's gone with her camera to shoot the horses, and San-dy's in his room and—and Mr. Connor, he hasn't come down yet.

DEXTER. And it's Saturday.

TRACY. Thanks loads. It's nice to have things accounted for. [*She passes the hand with the wrist watch across her brow, then looks at the watch.*]—Only I wonder what this might be?

DEXTER. It looks terribly like a wrist watch.

TRACY. But whose? I found it in my room. I nearly stepped on it.

DINAH. Getting out of bed?

TRACY. Yes. Why?

DINAH. I just wondered. [TRACY *puts the watch on the table before her.*]

TRACY. There's another mystery, Uncle Willie.

UNCLE WILLIE. Mysteries irritate me.

TRACY. I was robbed at your house last night.

UNCLE WILLIE. You don't say.

TRACY. Yes—my bracelets and my engagement ring are missing everywhere.

UNCLE WILLIE. Probably someone's house guest from New York. [DEXTER *brings them out of his pocket.*]

DEXTER. Here you are. [*She takes them, stares at them, then at him.*]

TRACY.—But you weren't at the party!

DEXTER. Wasn't I?

TRACY. Were you?

DEXTER. Don't tell me you don't remember!

TRACY. I—I do now, sort of—but there were such a lot of people. [DEXTER *rises.*]

DEXTER. You should have taken a quick swim to shake them off. There's nothing like a swim after a late night.

TRACY.—A swim. [*And her eyes grow rounder.* DEXTER *laughs.*]

DEXTER. There! Now they're open!

DINAH. That was just the beginning—

and it was no dream. [DEXTER *glances at her, then moves to* UNCLE WILLIE.]

DEXTER. Don't you think, sir, that if you and I went to the pantry at this point—you know: speaking of eye-openers? [UNCLE WILLIE *rises and precedes him toward the Porch.*]

UNCLE WILLIE. The only sane remark I've heard this morning. I know a formula that is said to pop the pennies off the eyelids of dead Irishmen. [*He goes out.* DEXTER *stops beside* DINAH.]

DEXTER. Oh, Dinah—if conversation drags, you might tell Tracy your dream. [*He goes out.* DINAH *turns and gazes reflectively at* TRACY.]

TRACY. What did he say?

DINAH. Oh, nothing. [*She goes to* TRACY *and puts an arm around her shoulder.*] Tray—I hate you to get married and go away.

TRACY. I'll miss you, darling. I'll miss all of you.

DINAH. We'll miss you, too.—It—it isn't like when you married Dexter, and just moved down the road a ways.

TRACY. I'll come back often. It's only Wilkes-Barre.

DINAH. It gripes me.

TRACY [*fondly*]. Baby— [*There is another silence.* DINAH *gazes at her intently, then gathers her forces and speaks.*]

DINAH. You know, I did have the funniest dream about you last night.

TRACY [*without interest*]. Did you? What was it?

DINAH. It was terribly interesting, and —and awfully scary, sort of— [TRACY *rises from the sofa.*]

TRACY. Do you like my dress, Dinah?

DINAH. Yes, ever so much. [TRACY *has risen too quickly. She wavers a moment, steadies herself, then moves to the Porch door.*]

TRACY. It feels awfully heavy.—You'd better rush and get ready yourself.

DINAH. You know me: I don't take a minute. [MARGARET, *dressed for the wedding, comes in from the Parlor, from whence violins are now heard, tuning up.*]

MARGARET. Turn around, Tracy. [TRACY *turns.*] Yes, it looks lovely.

TRACY. What's that—that scratching sound I hear?

MARGARET. The orchestra tuning. Yes— I'm glad we decided against the blue one. [*She moves to the Hall door.*] Where's your father? You know, I feel completely impersonal about all this. I can't quite grasp it. Get dressed, Dinah. [*She goes out into the Hall.* TRACY *turns and blinks into the sunlight, blazing in from the Porch.*]

TRACY. That sun is certainly bright all right, isn't it?

DINAH. It was up awfully early.

TRACY. Was it?

DINAH. Unless I dreamed that, too.—It's supposed to be the longest day of the year or something, isn't it?

TRACY. I wouldn't doubt it for a minute.

DINAH. It was all certainly pretty rooty-tooty.

TRACY. What was?

DINAH. My dream. [TRACY *moves back from the Porch door.*]

TRACY. Dinah, you'll have to learn sooner or later that no one is interested in anyone else's dreams.

DINAH.—I thought I got up and went over to the window and looked out across the lawn. And guess what I thought I saw coming over out of the woods?

TRACY. I haven't the faintest idea. A skunk?

DINAH. Well, sort of.—It was Mr. Connor.

TRACY. Mr. Connor?

DINAH. Yes—with his both arms full of something. And guess what it turned out to be?

TRACY. What?

DINAH. You—and some clothes. [TRACY *turns slowly and looks at her.*] Wasn't it funny? It was sort of like as if you were coming from the pool— [TRACY *closes her eyes.*]

TRACY. The pool.—I'm going crazy. I'm standing here solidly on my own two hands going crazy.—And then what?

DINAH. Then I thought I heard something outside in the hall, and I went and opened my door a crack and there he was, still coming along with you, puffing like a steam engine. His wind can't be very good.

TRACY. And then what?—

DINAH. And you were sort of crooning—

TRACY. I never crooned in my life!

DINAH. I guess it just sort of sounded like you were. Then he—guess what?

TRACY. I—couldn't possibly.

DINAH. Then he just sailed right into your room with you and—and that scared me so, that I just flew back to bed—or thought I did—and pulled the covers up over my head and laid there shaking and thinking: if *that's* the way it is, why doesn't she marry him, instead of old George? And then I must have fallen even faster asleep, because the next thing I knew it was eight o'clock, and the typewriter still going.

TRACY. Sandy—the typewriter—

DINAH. So in a minute I got up and went to your door and peeked in, to make sure you were all right—and guess what?

TRACY [*agonized*]. What?

DINAH. You were. He was gone by then. [TRACY *assumes a high indignation.*]

TRACY. Gone? Of course he was gone— he was never there!

DINAH. I know, Tracy.

TRACY. Well! I should hope you did! [*She seats herself firmly in an armchair.*]

DINAH. I'm certainly glad I do, because if I didn't and if in a little while I heard Dr. Parsons saying, "If anyone knows any just cause or reason why these two should not be united in holy matrimony"—I just wouldn't know what to do. [*She sighs profoundly.*]—And it was all only a dream.

TRACY. Naturally!

DINAH. I know. Dexter said so, straight off.—But isn't it funny, how—

TRACY. Dexter!

DINAH. Yes.—He said— [TRACY *rises and seizes her by the arm.*]

TRACY. You told Dexter all that?

DINAH. Not a word. Not a single word. —But you know how quick he is.

TRACY. Dinah Lord—you little fiend, how can you stand here and—! [SETH *comes in from the Hall, in morning coat and striped trousers.*]

SETH. Tracy, the next time you marry, choose a different Man of God, will you? This one wears me out. [*He goes to the Parlor doors, opens them, glances in, and closes them again.*] Good heavens!—Dinah! Get into your clothes! You look like a tramp.

DINAH. I'm going. [SETH *is about to go out again into the Hall, when* TRACY's *voice stops him.*]

TRACY. Father. [*He turns to her.*]

SETH. Yes, Tracy?

TRACY. I'm glad you came back. I'm glad you're here. [*He comes to her.*]

SETH. Thank you, child.

TRACY. I'm sorry—I'm truly sorry I'm a disappointment to you.

SETH. I never said that, daughter—and I never will. [*He looks at her fondly for a moment, touches her arm, then turns abruptly and goes out into the Hall.*]

Where's your mother? Where's George?
[MIKE, *in a blue suit, comes in from the Porch. He goes to the table and puts a cigarette out there.*]

MIKE. Good morning.

TRACY. Oh, hello!

MIKE. I was taking the air. I like it, but it doesn't like me.—Hello, Dinah.

DINAH [*replies with great dignity*]. How do you do?

TRACY. Did—did you have a good sleep?

MIKE. Wonderful. How about you?

TRACY. Marvelous. Have you ever seen a handsomer day?

MIKE. Never. What did it set you back?

TRACY. I got it for nothing, for being a good girl.

MIKE. Good. [*There is a brief silence. They look at DINAH, who is regarding them fixedly.*]

DINAH. I'm going, don't worry. [*She moves toward the Parlor doors.*]

TRACY. Why should you?

DINAH. I guess you must have things you wish to discuss.

TRACY. "Things to"—? What are you talking about!

DINAH. Only remember, it's getting late. [*Gingerly she opens the Parlor doors a crack, and peers in.*] Some of them are in already. My, they look solemn. [*She moves toward the Hall.*] I'll be ready when you are! [*And goes out.*]

TRACY. She's always trying to make situations.—How's your work coming—are you doing us up brown?

MIKE. I've—somehow I've lost my angle.

TRACY. How do you mean, Mike?

MIKE. I've just got so damn tolerant all at once, I doubt if I'll ever be able to write another line. [TRACY *laughs uncertainly.*]

TRACY. You are a fellah, Mike.

MIKE. Or the mug of this world: I don't know.

TRACY. When you're at the work you ought to be doing, you'll soon see that tolerance— What's the matter with your chin?

MIKE. Does it show?

TRACY. A little. What happened?

MIKE. I guess I just stuck it out too far.

TRACY.—Into a door, in the dark?

MIKE. That's it. [*His voice lowers solicitously.*] Are you—are *you* all right, Tracy? [*The startled look comes back into her eyes. She laughs, to cover it.*]

TRACY. Me? Of course! Why shouldn't I be?

MIKE. That was a flock of wine we put away.

TRACY. I never felt better in my life. [*She moves away from him.*]

MIKE. That's fine. That's just daisy.

TRACY. I—I guess we're lucky both to have such good heads.

MIKE. Yes, I guess. [*He moves toward her.*]

TRACY. It must be awful for people who —you know—get up and make speeches or—or try to start a fight—or, you know, misbehave in general.

MIKE. It certainly must.

TRACY. It must be—some sort of hidden weakness coming out.

MIKE. Weakness? I'm not so sure of that. [*Again she moves away from him.*]

TRACY. Anyhow, I had a simply wonderful evening. I hope you enjoyed it too.

MIKE. I enjoyed the last part of it. [*She turns to him uncertainly.*]

TRACY. Really? Why—why especially the last?

MIKE. Are you asking me, Tracy?

TRACY. Oh, you mean the swim!—We did swim, and so forth, didn't we?

MIKE. We swam, and so forth. [*She advances to him suddenly.*]

TRACY. Mike—

MIKE [*gazing*]. You darling, darling girl—

TRACY. Mike!

MIKE. What can I say to you? Tell me, darling— [*She recovers herself and again moves away.*]

TRACY. Not anything—don't say anything. And especially not "Darling."

MIKE. Never in this world will I ever forget you.

TRACY.—Not anything, I said.

MIKE. You're going to go through with it, then—

TRACY. Through with what?

MIKE. The wedding.

TRACY. Why—why shouldn't I?

MIKE. Well, you see, I've made a funny discovery: that in spite of the fact that someone's up from the bottom, he may be quite a heel. And that even though someone else is born to the purple, he still may be quite a guy.—Hell, I'm only saying what you said last night!

TRACY. I said a lot of things last night, it seems.

MIKE [*after a moment*]. All right, no dice. But understand: also no regrets about last night.

TRACY. Why should I have?

MIKE. That's it! That's the stuff; you're wonderful. You're aces, Tracy. [*Now she is in full retreat.*]

TRACY. You don't know what I mean! I'm asking you—tell me straight out—tell me the reason why I should have any— [*But she cannot finish. Her head drops.*] No—don't.—Just tell me—what time is it?

MIKE [*glancing at his wrist*]. It's— what's happened to my wrist watch? [TRACY *stops, frozen, speaks without turning.*]

TRACY. Why? Is it broken?

MIKE. It's gone. I've lost it somewhere.

TRACY [*after a moment*]. I can't tell you how extremely ·sorry I am to hear that.

MIKE. Oh, well—I'd always just as soon not know the time.

TRACY [*her back to him*]. There on the table—

MIKE.—What is? [*He goes to the table, finds the watch.*] Well, for the love of—! Who found it? I'll give a reward, or something. [*He straps the watch on his wrist.*]

TRACY. I don't think any reward will be expected. [*She drops miserably down into an armchair.* DEXTER *comes in from the Porch, a small glass in hand.*]

DEXTER. Now then! This medicine indicated in cases of— [*He stops at the sight of* MIKE.] Hello, Connor. How are you?

MIKE. About as you'd think.—Is that for me?

DEXTER. For Tracy.—Why? Would you like one?

MIKE. I would sell my grandmother for a drink—and you know how I love my grandmother.

DEXTER. Uncle Willie's around in the pantry, doing weird and wonderful things. Just say I said, One of the same. [MIKE *moves toward the Porch.*]

MIKE. Is it all right if I say Two?

DEXTER. That's between you and your grandmother. [MIKE *goes out.* DEXTER *calls after him.*]—And find Liz! [DEXTER *goes to* TRACY *with the drink.*] Doctor's orders, Tray.

TRACY. What is it?

DEXTER. Just the juice of a few flowers. [TRACY *takes the glass and looks at it, and tastes it.*]

TRACY. Peppermint— [DEXTER *smiles.*]

DEXTER.—White.—And one other simple ingredient. It's called a stinger. It removes the sting. [TRACY *sets the glass down and looks away.*]

TRACY. Oh, Dext—don't say that!

Dexter. Why not, Tray?

Tracy.—Nothing will—nothing ever can! [*She rises from the chair.*] Oh, Dexter—I've done the most terrible thing to you!

Dexter [*after a moment*]. To *me*, did you say? [*She nods vigorously.*] I doubt that, Red. I doubt it very much.

Tracy. You don't know, you don't know!

Dexter. Well, maybe I shouldn't.

Tracy. You've got to—you must! I couldn't stand it, if you didn't! Oh, Dext—what am I going to do?

Dexter.—But why to *me*, Darling? [*She looks at him.*] Where do I come into it any more? [*Still she looks.*] Aren't you confusing me with someone else?—A fellow named Kittredge, or something?

Tracy [*a sudden, awful thought*]. George—

Dexter. That's right; George Kittredge. A splendid chap—very high morals—very broad shoulders.— [Tracy *goes to the telephone.*]

Tracy. I've got to tell him. [Dexter *follows her.*]

Dexter. Tell him what?

Tracy. I've got to tell him! [*She dials a number.*]

Dexter. But if he's got any brain at all, he'll have realized by this time what a fool he made of himself, when he—

Tracy.—When he what? [*To the telephone.*] Hello? Hello, George—this is Tracy. Look—I don't care whether it's bad luck or not, but I've got to see you for a minute before the wedding.—What? *What* note? I didn't get any note.—When? Well, why didn't someone tell me?— Right! Come on the run. [*She replaces the telephone, goes up to the fireplace, finds the wall bell and rings it.*] He sent a note over at ten o'clock.

Dexter. I told you he'd come to his senses. [Tracy *turns slowly.*]

Tracy. Was—was he here, too?

Dexter. Sure.

Tracy. My God—why didn't you sell tickets? [Dexter *brings her her drink.*]

Dexter. Finish your drink.

Tracy. Will it help?

Dexter. There's always the hope. [Edward *comes into the Hall doorway.*]

Edward. You rang, Miss?

Tracy. Isn't there a note for me from Mr. Kittredge somewhere?

Edward. I believe it was put on the hall table upstairs. Mrs. Lord said not to disturb you.

Tracy. I'd like to have it, if I may.

Edward. Very well, Miss. [*He goes out,* Tracy *finishes her drink and gives* Dexter *the empty glass.*]

Tracy. Say something, Dext—anything.

Dexter. No—you do.

Tracy. Oh, Dext—I'm wicked! [*She moves away from him.*] I'm such an unholy mess of a girl.

Dexter. That's no good. That's not even conversation.

Tracy. But never in all my life—not if I live to be a hundred—will I ever forget the way you tried to—to stand me on my feet again this morning.

Dexter. You—you're in grand shape. Tell me: what did you think of my wedding present? I like my presents at least to be acknowledged.

Tracy. It was beautiful and sweet, Dext.

Dexter. She was quite a boat, the "True Love."

Tracy. Was, and is.

Dexter. She had the same initials as yours—did you ever realize that? [Tracy *seats herself in the armchair at Left of the table.*]

Tracy. No, I never did.

DEXTER. Nor did I, till I last saw her.—Funny we missed it. My, she was yare.

TRACY. She was yare, all right. [*A moment.*] I wasn't, was I?

DEXTER. Wasn't what?

TRACY. Yare. [DEXTER *laughs shortly and seats himself in the chair across the table from her.*]

DEXTER. Not very!—You were good at the bright-work, though. I'll never forget you down on your knees on the deck every morning, with your little can of polish. [*They speak without looking at each other, straight out in front of them.*]

TRACY. I wouldn't let even you help, would I?

DEXTER. Not even me.

TRACY. I made her shine.—Where is she now?

DEXTER. In the yard at Seven Hundred Acre, getting gone over. I'm going to sell her to Rufe Watriss at Oyster Bay. [*There is a silence. Then she speaks, incredulously.*]

TRACY. You're going to sell the "True Love"?

DEXTER. Why not?

TRACY. For money?

DEXTER. He wired an offer yesterday.

TRACY.—To *that* fat old rum pot?

DEXTER. What the hell does it matter?

TRACY. She's too clean, she's too yare!

DEXTER. I know—but when you're through with a boat, you're— [*He looks at her.*] That is, of course, unless *you* want her. [*She turns away, without replying.*] Of course she's good for nothing but racing—and only really comfortable for two people—and not so damned so, for them. So I naturally thought— But of course, if *you* should want her—

TRACY. No—I don't want her.

DEXTER. I'm going to design another for myself, along a little more practical lines.

TRACY. Are you?

DEXTER. I started on the drawings a couple of weeks ago.

TRACY. What will you call her?

DEXTER. I thought the "True Love II."—What do you think? [TRACY *rises abruptly.*]

TRACY. Dexter, if you call any boat that, I promise you I'll blow you and it right out of the water!

DEXTER. I know it's not very imaginative, but—

TRACY. Just try it, that's all! [*She moves away from him.*] I'll tell you what you can call it, if you like—

DEXTER. What?

TRACY. In fond remembrance of me—

DEXTER. What?

TRACY. The "Easy Virtue." [DEXTER *goes to her.*]

DEXTER. Tray, I'll be damned if I'll have you thinking such things of yourself!

TRACY. What would you like me to think?

DEXTER. I don't know. But I do know that virtue, so-called, is no matter of a single misstep or two.

TRACY. You don't think so?

DEXTER. I know so. It's something inherent, it's something regardless of anything.

TRACY. Like fun it is.

DEXTER. You're wrong. The occasional misdeeds are often as good for a person as—as the more persistent virtues.—That is, if the person is there. Maybe you haven't committed enough, Tray. Maybe this is your coming-of-age.

TRACY. I don't know.—Oh, I don't know anything any more!

DEXTER. That sounds very hopeful. That's just fine, Tray.

TRACY. Oh, be still, you! [EDWARD *comes in with a note on a tray.*] Thanks, Edward.

EDWARD. They are practically all in, Miss —and quite a number standing in the back. [MIKE *and* LIZ *comes in from the Porch*.] All our best wishes, Miss.

TRACY. Thanks, Edward. Thanks, very much.

LIZ.—And all ours, Tracy.

TRACY. Thank you, thank everybody. [EDWARD *goes out, into the Hall, passing* SANDY, *who rushes in and up to* TRACY. *He wears a short morning coat*.]

SANDY. Tray—he's here! He's arrived!

TRACY [*opening the note*]. Who has?

SANDY. Kidd—Sidney Kidd.

TRACY. What for? What does *he* want?

LIZ. May I scream?

MIKE. What the—!

TRACY. Oh, now I remember!

SANDY. Well, I should hope you did. I haven't been to bed at all. I gave him the Profile. He's reading it now. I couldn't stand the suspense, so I—

MIKE. Profile, did you say? What profile?

SANDY. The Kidd himself, complete with photographs. Do you want to see a copy?

MIKE. Holy St. Rose of South Bend!

SANDY.—Offered in exchange for yours of us. I told him what a help you've both been to me.

LIZ. I don't think you'll find it so hard to resign now, Mike. Me neither.

MIKE. That's all right with me.

LIZ. Belts will be worn tighter this winter.

SANDY. I'll see how he's bearing up. [*He moves toward the Hall, meeting* DR. PARSONS, *a middle-aged clergyman, in surplice and stole, as he comes in*.] Good morning, Dr. Parsons. How's everything?

DR. PARSONS. Where is your sister? [SANDY *points to her and goes out.* TRACY *is now reading the note.* DR. PARSONS *calls*

to her.] Tracy? Tracy! [*She looks up startled*.]

TRACY. Yes? [*He smiles, and beckons engagingly*.]

DEXTER. One minute, Dr. Parsons, Mr. Kittredge is on his way. [DR. PARSONS *smiles again, and goes out into the Parlor, carefully closing the door behind him.* DEXTER *turns to* TRACY.] I'm afraid it's the deadline, Tracy.

TRACY. So is this. Listen—"My dear Tracy: Your conduct last night was so shocking to my ideals of womanhood, that my attitude toward you and the prospects of a happy and useful life together, has changed materially. Your, to me, totally unexpected breach of common decency, not to mention the moral aspect—" [GEORGE *comes in from the Porch*.]

GEORGE. Tracy!

TRACY. Hello, George.

GEORGE. Tracy—all these people!

TRACY. It's only a letter from a friend. They're my friends, too. "—not to mention the moral aspect, certainly entitles me to a full explanation, before going through with our proposed marriage. In the light of day, I am sure that you will agree with me. Otherwise, with profound regrets and all best wishes, yours very sincerely—" [*She folds the note and returns it to its envelope*.] Yes, George, I quite agree with you—in the light of day or the dark of night, for richer, for poorer, for better, for worse, in sickness and in health—and thank you so very much for your good wishes at this time.

GEORGE. That's all you've got to say?

TRACY. What else? I wish for your sake, as well as mine, I had an explanation. But unfortunately, I've none. You'd better just say "good riddance," George.

GEORGE. It isn't easy, you know.

TRACY. I don't see why.

Liz [*to* Mike]. Say something, Stupid.

Mike. Wait a minute. [*Preparatory music—Debussy—is now faintly heard from the Parlor.*]

George. You'll grant I had a right to be angry, and very angry.

Tracy. You certainly had, you certainly have.

George. "For your sake, as well," you said—

Tracy. Yes—it would be nice to know.

Liz [*to* Mike]. Will you say something?

Mike. Wait!

Liz. What for?

Mike. Enough rope.

George.—On the very eve of your wedding, an affair with another man—

Tracy. I told you I agreed, George— and I tell you again: good riddance to me.

George. That's for me to decide.

Tracy. Well, I wish you would a—a— little more quickly.

Mike. Look, Kittredge—

Tracy. If there was some way to make you see that—that regardless of it—or even because of it—I'm—somehow I feel more of a person, George.

George. That's a little difficult to understand. [Tracy *lets herself down into an armchair.*]

Tracy. Yes, I can see that it would be.

Dexter. Not necessarily.

George. You keep out of it!

Dexter. You forget: I am out of it. [*He seats himself upon the sofa, away from them all.*]

Mike [*advancing*]. Kittredge, it just might interest you to know that the so-called "affair" consisted of exactly two kisses and one rather late swim.

Tracy [*unwilling to accept the gallant gesture*]. Thanks, Mike, but there's no need to— [Mike *turns to her.*]

Mike. All of which I thoroughly en-joyed, and the memory of which I wouldn't part with for anything.

Tracy. It's no use, Mike.

Mike [*again to* George].—After which, I accompanied her to her room, deposited her on her bed, and promptly returned to you two on the porch—as you will doubt-less remember.

Dexter. Doubtless without a doubt.

George. You mean to say that was all there was to it?

Mike. I do. [George *ponders.* Tracy *is looking at* Mike *in astonishment. Sud-denly she rises and demands indignantly of him.*]

Tracy. Why? Was I so damned unat-tractive—so distant, so forbidding, or some-thing, that—?

George. This is fine talk, too!

Tracy. I'm asking a question! [*The music has stopped now.*]

Mike. You were extremely attractive— and as for "distant and forbidding," on the contrary. But you were also somewhat the worse—or the better—for wine, and there are rules about that, damn it.

Tracy [*after a moment*]. Thank you, Mike. I think men are wonderful.

Liz. The little dears.

George. Well, that's a relief, I'll admit. Still—

Tracy. Why? Where's the difference? If my wonderful, marvelous, beautiful virtue is still intact, it's no thanks to me, I assure you.

George. I don't think you—

Tracy.—It's purely by courtesy of the gentleman from South Bend.

Liz. Local papers, please copy.

George. I fail to see the humor in this situation, Miss Imbrie.

Liz. I appreciate that. It was a little hard for me too, at first—

TRACY. Oh, Liz— [*She goes to her, gropes for her hand.*]

LIZ. It's all right, Tracy. We all go a little haywire at times—and if we don't, maybe we ought to.

TRACY. Liz.

LIZ. You see, it really wasn't Tracy at all, Mr. Kittredge. It was another girl: a Miss Pommery, '28.

GEORGE. You'd had too much to drink—

TRACY. That seems to be the consensus of opinion.

GEORGE. Will you promise me never to touch the stuff again? [*She looks at him, speaking slowly.*]

TRACY. No, George, I don't believe I will. There are certain things about that other girl I rather like.

GEORGE. But a man expects his wife to—

TRACY.—To behave herself. Naturally.

DEXTER. To behave herself naturally. [GEORGE *glances angrily at him.*] Sorry.

GEORGE [*to* TRACY]. But if it hadn't been for the drink last night, all this might not have happened.

TRACY. But apparently nothing did. What made you think it had?

GEORGE. It didn't take much imagination, I can tell you that.

TRACY. Not much, perhaps—but just of a certain kind.

GEORGE. It seems *you* didn't think any too well of yourself.

TRACY. That's the odd thing, George: somehow I'd have hoped you'd think better of me than I did.

GEORGE. I'm not going to quibble, Tracy: all the evidence was there.

TRACY. And I was guilty straight off— that is, until I was proved innocent.

GEORGE. Well?

DEXTER. Downright un-American, if you ask me.

GEORGE. No one is asking you! [SANDY comes into the Hall doorway, consternation on his face.]

SANDY. Listen—he's read it—and holy cats, guess what?

LIZ. What?

SANDY. He loves it! He says it's brilliant— He wants it for *Destiny!*

MIKE. I give up.

GEORGE. Who wants what?

LIZ. Sidney Kidd—Sidney Kidd.

GEORGE [*hardly believing the good news.*] Sidney Kidd is here himself?!

SANDY. Big as life, and twice as handsome. Boy, is this wedding a National Affair now! [*He goes out.*]

GEORGE [*after a moment*]. It's extremely kind and thoughtful of him. [*Another moment. Then.*] Come on, Tracy—it must be late. Let's let bygones be bygones—what do you say?

TRACY. Yes—and good-by, George.

GEORGE. I don't understand you.

TRACY. Please—good-by.

GEORGE. But what on earth—?

LIZ. I imagine she means that your explanation is inadequate.

GEORGE. Look here, Tracy—

TRACY. You're too good for me, George. You're a hundred times too good.

GEORGE. I never said I—

TRACY. And I'd make you most unhappy, most.—That is, I'd do my best to. [GEORGE *looks at her.*]

GEORGE. Well, if that's the way you want it—

TRACY. That is the way it is.

GEORGE. All right. Possibly it's just as well. [*He starts toward the Hall.*]

DEXTER. I thought you'd eventually think so. [GEORGE *turns and confronts him.*]

GEORGE. I've got a feeling you've had more to do with this than anyone.

DEXTER. A novel and interesting idea, I'm sure.

GEORGE. You and your whole rotten class.

DEXTER. Oh, class my—! [*But he stops himself.*]

MIKE. Funny—I heard a truck driver say that yesterday—only with a short "a."

GEORGE. Listen: you're all on your way out—the lot of you—and don't think you aren't.—Yes, and good riddance! [*He goes out.*]

MIKE. Well, there goes George. [*Again the orchestra is heard. This time it is "Oh Promise Me." TRACY moves swiftly to the Parlor doors, opens them slightly, peers in, and exclaims.*]

TRACY. Oh, my sainted aunt—that welter of faces! [*She closes the doors and returns.*] What in the name of all that's holy am I to do? [MAY, *the housemaid, comes in with* TRACY's *hat and gloves.*]

MAY. You forgot your hat, Miss Tracy. [TRACY *takes the broad-brimmed hat, the immaculate gloves, and gazes at them helplessly.*]

TRACY. Oh, God— Oh, dear God—have mercy on Tracy! [MIKE *rises and goes to her.*]

MIKE. Tracy—

TRACY. Yes, Mike?

MIKE. Forget the license!

TRACY. License? [DEXTER *fumbles in his pocket.*]

DEXTER. I've got an old one here that we never used, Maryland being quicker—

MIKE. Forget it! [*To* TRACY.] Old Parson Parsons—he's never seen Kittredge, has he? Nor have most of the others. I got you into this, I'll get you out.—Will you marry me, Tracy? [*She looks at him for a long, grateful moment before speaking. Then.*]

TRACY. No, Mike.—Thanks, but no.

MIKE. But listen: I've never asked a girl to marry me before in my life!—I've avoided it!—You've got me all confused— why not—?

TRACY.—Because I don't think Liz would like it—and I'm not sure that you would—and I'm even a little doubtful about myself.—But I'm beholden to you, Mike, I'm most beholden. [MIKE *gestures impatiently.*]

MIKE. They're in there! They're waiting!

LIZ. Don't get too conventional all at once, will you?—There'll be a reaction.

MIKE [*an appeal*]. Liz—

LIZ. I count on your sustaining the mood. [*She beckons to him and he joins her.* DEXTER *rises.*]

DEXTER. It'll be all right, Tracy: you've been got out of jams before.

TRACY.—Been *got out* of them, did you say?

DEXTER. That's what I said, Tracy. Don't worry, you always are. [MARGARET *and* SETH *come in from the Hall.*]

MARGARET. Tracy, we met George in the hall—it's all right, dear: your father will make a very simple announcement.

SETH. Is there anything special you want me to say?

TRACY. No! I'll say it, whatever it is.— I won't be got out of anything more, thanks. [*She moves to the Parlor door.* UNCLE WILLIE *and* DINAH *enter from the Hall.*]

UNCLE WILLIE. What's alack? What's amiss?

MARGARET. Oh, this just can't be happening—it can't! [TRACY *throws open the Parlor doors and stands in the doorway gazing into the Parlor. She addresses her wedding guests.*]

TRACY. I'm—I'm—hello! Good morning. —I'm—that is to say—I'm terribly sorry to have kept you waiting, but—but there's been a little hitch in the proceedings. I've made a terrible fool of myself—which isn't unusual—and my fiancé—my fiancé— [*She stops and swallows.*]

MARGARET. Seth!

SETH. Wait, my dear.

TRACY.—my fiancé, that was, that is—he thinks we'd better call it a day and I quite agree with him. [*She half turns and whispers.*] Dexter—Dexter—what the hell next?

DEXTER. "Two years ago you were invited to a wedding in this house and I did you out of it by eloping to Maryland—" [*He moves swiftly to* MARGARET.]

TRACY. "Two years ago you were invited to a wedding in this house and I did you out of it by eloping to Maryland—" [*Then, desperately.*] Dexter, Dexter, where are you?

DEXTER [*simultaneously, to* MARGARET.] May I? Just as a loan? [*He takes a ring from her finger and goes to* MIKE *with it.*] Here, put this in your vest pocket.

MIKE. But I haven't got a vest.

DEXTER. Then hold it in your hand! [*He goes quickly to* TRACY.]

DEXTER. "Which was very bad manners—"

TRACY [*into the Parlor*]. "—Which was very bad manners—"

DEXTER. "But I hope to make it up to you by going through with it now, as originally planned."

TRACY. "But I hope to make it up to you by—by going—" [*Suddenly she realizes what she is saying and turns to* DEXTER *with blank wonder in her eyes. He gestures, and she turns again and continues.*] —by going beautifully through with it

now—as originally and—most beautifully —planned. [DEXTER *moves to* MIKE.]

DEXTER. I'd like you to be my best man, if you will, because I think you're one hell of a guy, Mike.

MIKE. I'd be honored, C. K.

UNCLE WILLIE. Ladies, follow me! No rushing please! [LIZ *and* MARGARET *go out with him into the Hall.*]

TRACY [*simultaneously, into the Parlor*]. —Because there's something awfully nice about a wedding—I don't know—they're so gay and attractive—and I've always wanted one, and—

DEXTER. "So if you'll just keep your seats a minute—"

TRACY. "So if you'll just keep your seats a minute—"

DEXTER. That's all.

TRACY. "That's all!" [*She closes the doors and turns breathlessly to* DEXTER.] Dexter—are you sure?

DEXTER. Not in the least.—But I'll risk it—will you?

TRACY. You bet!—And you didn't do it just to soften the blow?

DEXTER. No, Tray.

TRACY. Nor to save my face?

DEXTER. It's a nice little face.

TRACY. Oh—I'll be yare now—I'll promise to be yare!

DEXTER. Be whatever you like, you're my Redhead.—All set?

TRACY. All set! [*She runs and snatches her hat from a chair, puts it on before a mirror.*]—Oh, how did this ever happen?

SETH. Don't inquire.—Go on, Dinah: tell Mr. Dutton to start the music. [DINAH *goes out into the Hall, exclaiming triumphantly.*]

DINAH. I did it—I did it all! [DEXTER *and* MIKE *go to the Hall doorway, wait there for the signal;* SETH *turns to* TRACY.]

SETH. Daughter— [*She moves to him.*]

TRACY. I love you, Father.

SETH. And I love you, daughter.

TRACY. Never in my life have I been so full of love before.—[*The Wedding March begins to be heard from the Parlor.*]

DEXTER. See you soon, Red!

TRACY. See you soon, Dext! [DEXTER *and* MIKE *go out.* TRACY *stands before* SETH.] How do I look?

SETH. Like a queen—like a goddess.

TRACY. Do you know how I feel?

SETH. How?

TRACY. Like a human—like a human being! [SETH *smiles.*]

SETH.—And is that all right? [*She tightens her arm in his. They start to move slowly across the room in the direction of the Parlor.*]

TRACY. All right? Oh, Father, it's Heaven!

CURTAIN

BIOGRAPHY

A Comedy

by S. N. Behrman

CHARACTERS

RICHARD KURT   LEANDER NOLAN

MINNIE   WARWICK WILSON

MELCHIOR FEYDAK   ORRIN KINNICOTT

MARION FROUDE   SLADE KINNICOTT

SCENES: *The entire action takes place in Marion Froude's studio in New York City. The time is now.*

ACT I. *About five o'clock of an afternoon in November.*

ACT II. *Afternoon, three weeks later.*

ACT III. *Late afternoon, two weeks later.*

The curtain will be lowered during the act to denote a lapse of time.

ACT I

[SCENE: *The studio-apartment of* MARION FROUDE *in an old-fashioned studio-building in West 57th St., New York. A great, cavernous room expressing in its polyglot furnishings the artistic patois of the various landlords who have sublet this apartment to wandering tenants like* MARION FROUDE. *The styles range from medieval Florence to contemporary Grand Rapids; on a movable raised platform in the center is a papal throne chair in red velvet and gold fringes. Not far from it is an ordinary American kitchen chair. The hanging lamp which sheds a mellow light over a French Empire sofa is filigreed copper Byzantine. Another and longer sofa across the room against the grand piano is in soft green velvet and has the gentility of a polite Park Avenue drawing room. Under the stairs, rear, which go up to* MARION'S *bedroom, are stacks of her canvases. There is a quite fine wood carving of a Madonna which seems to be centuries old and in the* wall spaces looking at audience are great, dim canvases—copies by some former tenant left probably in lieu of rent—of Sargent's Lord Ribblesdale and Mme. X.

Whether it is due to the amenable spirit of the present incumbent or because they are relaxed in the democracy of art, these oddments of the creative spirit do not suggest disharmony. The room is warm, musty, with restful shadows and limpid lights. The enormous leaded window on the right, though some of its members are patched and cracked, gleams in the descending twilight with an opalescent light; even the copper cylinder of the fire extinguisher and its attendant ax, visible in the hall, seem to be not so much implements against calamity, as amusing museum-bits cherished from an earlier time. Every school is represented here except the modern. The studio has the mellowness of anachronism.

There is a door up-stage left leading to

[455]

the kitchen and MINNIE's *bedroom door,
center, under the stairs leads into hall-way.
A door on the stair landing, center, leads
to* MINNIE's *bedroom.*

TIME: *About five o'clock of an afternoon in November.*

AT RISE: RICHARD KURT *is finishing a
nervous cigarette. He has the essential audacity which comes from having seen the
worst happen, from having endured the
keenest pain. He has the hardness of one
who knows that he can be devastated by
pity, the bitterness which comes from having seen, in early youth, justice thwarted
and tears unavailing, the self reliance
which comes from having seen everything
go in a disordered world save one, stubborn, unyielding core of belief—at everything else he laughs, in this alone he trusts.
He has the intensity of the fanatic and the
carelessness of the vagabond. He goes to
the door from the hall and calls.*]

KURT. Say, you, hello there—what's
your name? [MINNIE, MARION FROUDE's
*inseparable maid, a German woman of
about fifty, comes in. She is indignant at
being thus summarily summoned, and by
a stranger.*]

MINNIE [*with dignity*]. My name iss
Minnie if you please.

KURT. What time did Miss Froude go
out?

MINNIE. About two o'clock.

KURT. It's nearly five now. She should
be home, shouldn't she?

MINNIE. She said she vas coming home
to tea and that is all I know.

KURT [*grimly*]. I know. She invited me
to tea. . . . Where did she go to lunch?

MINNIE [*acidly*]. That I do not know.

KURT. Did someone call for her or did
she go out alone? I have a reason for
asking.

MINNIE. She went out alone. Any more
questions?

KURT. No. I see there's no point in asking you questions.

MINNIE. Denn vy do you ask dem?
[*The doorbell rings.* MINNIE *throws up
her hands in despair. She goes out muttering:* "Ach Gott." KURT *is rather amused
at her. He lights another cigarette. Sounds
of vociferous greeting outside.* "Ach mein
lieber Herr Feydak. . . ." MELCHIOR FEY-
DAK, *the Austrian composer, comes in. He
is forty-five, tall, hook-nosed, thin-faced, a
humorist with a rather sad face.*]

FEYDAK. Nun, Minnie, und vo is die
schlechte . . . ? [MINNIE *makes a sign to
him not to disclose their free-masonry in
the presence of strangers. She is cautious. . . .*] Not home yet, eh, Minnie?
Where is she? Well—well. How do they
say—gallivanting—I love that word—gallivanting as usual. Well, I'll wait. It's hu-
miliating—but I'll wait. Chilly! Brr! I
don't mind so much being cold in London or Vienna. I expect it. But I can't
stand it in New York. [*He warms himself
before fire.*] And who is this young man?

MINNIE [*shortly*]. 'Ich weiss nicht! . . .
Er hat alle fünf minuten gefragt wo sie
ist— [*She goes out.*]

FEYDAK. You've offended Minnie I can
see that.

KURT. That's just too bad!

FEYDAK. We all tremble before Minnie.
. . . Been waiting long?

KURT. Over half an hour!

FEYDAK. Extraordinary thing—ever since
I've known Marion there's always been
someone waiting for her. There are two
kinds of people in one's life—people whom
one keeps waiting—and the people for
whom one waits. . . .

KURT. Is that an epigram?

FEYDAK. Do you object to epigrams?

KURT [*with some pride*]. I despise epigrams.

FEYDAK [*tolerantly sizing* KURT *up*]. Hm! Friend of Miss Froude's?

KURT. Not at all.

FEYDAK. That at least is no cause for pride.

KURT. I just don't happen to be that's all.

FEYDAK. I commiserate you.

KURT. I despise gallantry also.

FEYDAK [*lightly*]. And I thought Americans were so sentimental. . . .

KURT. And, together with other forms of glibness, I loathe generalization. . . .

FEYDAK [*drily*]. Young man, we have a great deal in common.

KURT. Also, there is a faint flavor of condescension in the way you say "young man" for which I don't really care. . . .

FEYDAK [*delighted and encouraging him to go on*]. What about me do you like? There must be something.

KURT. If I were that kind your question would embarrass me.

FEYDAK [*very pleased*]. Good for Marion!

KURT. Why do you say that?

FEYDAK. She always had a knack for picking up originals!

KURT. You are under a misapprehension. Miss Froude did not pick me up. I picked her up. [FEYDAK *stares at him. This does shock him.*] I wrote Miss Froude a letter—a business-letter. She answered and gave me an appointment for four-thirty. It is now after five. She has taken a half-hour out of my life. . . .

FEYDAK. I gather that fragment of time has great value. . . .

KURT. She has shortened my life by thirty minutes. God, how I hate Bohemians!

FEYDAK [*innocently*]. Are you by any chance—an Evangelist?

KURT. I am—for the moment—a business-man. I'm not here to hold hands or drink tea. I'm here on business. My presence here is a favor to Miss Froude and likely to bring her a handsome profit. . . .

FEYDAK. Profit! Ah! That accounts for her being late. . . .

KURT [*skeptically*]. You despise profit I suppose! Are you—by any chance—old-world?

FEYDAK. Young man, your technique is entirely wasted on me. . . .

KURT. Technique! What are you talking about?

FEYDAK. When I was a young man—before I achieved any sort of success—I was rude on principle. Deliberately rude and extravagantly bitter in order to make impression. When it is no longer necessary for you to wait around for people in order to do them favors you'll mellow down I assure you.

KURT [*fiercely, he has been touched*]. You think so, do you! That's where you're mistaken! I'm rude now. When I'm successful I'll be murderous!

FEYDAK [*genially*]. More power to you! But I've never seen it happen yet. Success is the great muffler! Not an epigram I hope. If it is—forgive me. [*A moment's pause.* KURT *studies him while* FEYDAK *crosses to stove and warms his hands.*]

KURT. I know you from somewhere. It's very tantalizing.

FEYDAK. I don't think so. I have only just arrived in this country. . . .

KURT. Still I know you—I'm sure—I've seen you somewhere. . . .

FEYDAK [*understanding the familiarity*]. Maybe you know Miss Froude's portrait of me. . . .

KURT [*doubtfully*]. Yes—maybe that's it . . . may I ask . . . ?

FEYDAK. Certainly. My name is Feydak.

KURT. The composer?

FEYDAK [*drily*]. Yes. . . .

KURT. I thought he was dead. . . .

FEYDAK. That is true. But I hope you won't tell anyone—for I am his ghost. . . .

KURT [*putting this down for Continental humor and genuinely contrite*]. Forgive me. . . .

FEYDAK. But why?

KURT. If you really are Feydak the composer—I have the most enormous admiration for you. I worship music above everything.

FEYDAK. [*slightly bored*]. Go on . . .

KURT. I read in the paper—you're on your way to Hollywood. . . .

FEYDAK. Yes. I am on my way to Hollywood. . . .

KURT. In the new state men like you won't have to prostitute themselves in Hollywood. . . .

FEYDAK. Ah! A Utopian!

KURT. Yes. You use the word as a term of contempt. Why? Every artist is a Utopian. You must be very tired or you wouldn't be so contemptuous of Utopians.

FEYDAK [*with a charming smile*]. I am rather tired. Old-world you would call it.

KURT. You can be anything you like. . . .

FEYDAK [*satirically*]. Thank you. . . .

KURT. You've written lovely music—I have a friend who plays every note of it. I didn't see your operetta when it was done here. . . . I didn't have the price . . . it was very badly done though, I heard. . . .

FEYDAK. I must explain to you—you are under a misapprehension. . . .

KURT. It was done here, wasn't it?

FEYDAK. Not about the operetta. You are under a misapprehension—about me. I am a composer—but I didn't write "Danubia." That was my brother, Victor Feydak. You are right. He is dead. You

are the first person I have met in New York who even suspected it.

KURT. I'm sorry.

FEYDAK. Not at all. I am flattered. At home our identities were never confused. Is this the well-known American hospitality? It is, in some sort, compensation for his death. . . . [KURT *is embarrassed and uncomfortable. It is part of his essential insecurity; he is only really at home in protest. He wants to get out.*]

KURT. I'm sorry—I. . . .

FEYDAK [*easily*]. But why?

KURT. I think I'll leave a note for Miss Froude—get that girl in here, will you?

FEYDAK. Let's have some tea—she's sure to be in any minute. . . .

KURT. No, thanks. And you might tell her for me that if she wants to see me about the matter I wrote her about she can come to my office. . . . [MARION FROUDE *comes in. She is one of those women, the sight of whom on Fifth Avenue where she has just been walking, causes foreigners to exclaim enthusiastically that American women are the most radiant in the world. She is tall, lithe, indomitably alive. Unlike* KURT, *the tears in things have warmed without scalding her; she floats life like a dancer's scarf in perpetual enjoyment of its colors and contours.*]

MARION [*to* KURT]. I'm *so* sorry!

FEYDAK [*coming toward her*]. I don't believe a word of it! [*She is overjoyed at seeing* FEYDAK. *She can't believe for a second that it is he. Then she flies into his arms.*]

MARION. Feydie! Oh, Feydie, I've been trying everywhere to reach you—I can't believe it. . . . Feydie darling!

FEYDAK [*severely*]. Is this how you keep a business appointment, Miss Froude?

MARION. How long have you waited? If

I'd only known. . . . [*Suddenly conscious that* Kurt *had waited too.*] Oh, I'm so sorry, Mr. —— Mr. —— . . . ?

Kurt. Kurt. Richard Kurt.

Marion. Oh, of course, Mr. Kurt. I say—could you possibly—would it be too much trouble—could you come back?

Feydak [*same tone*]. This young man is here on business. It is more important. I can wait. I'll come back.

Marion. No, no, Feydie—no, no. I can't wait for that. I'm sure Mr. Kurt will understand. Mr. Feydak is an old friend whom I haven't seen in ever so long. It isn't as if Mr. Kurt were a regular businessman. . . .

Feydak [*amused*]. How do you know he isn't?

Marion [*breathless with excitement*]. I can tell. He's not a bit like his letter. When I got your letter I was sure you were jowley and you know—[*She makes a gesture.*] convex. I'm sure, Feydie—whatever the business is—[*To* Kurt] you did say you had some, didn't you?—I'm sure it can wait. A half hour anyway. Can't it wait a half hour? You see Feydie and I haven't seen each other since. . . .

Kurt. Vienna!

Marion [*astonished*]. Yes. How did you know?

Kurt. It's always since Vienna that Bohemians haven't seen each other, isn't it? I'll be back in thirty minutes. [*He goes.*]

Marion. What a singular young man!

Feydak. I've been having a very amusing talk with him. Professional rebel, I think. Well, my dear—you look marvelous! [*They take each other in.*]

Marion. Isn't it wonderful. . . .

Feydak. It *is* nice! [*They sit on sofa,* Marion *left of* Feydak.]

Marion. How long is it?

Feydak. Well, it's since. . . .

Marion [*firmly*]. Since Vicki died.

Feydak. That's right. I haven't seen you since.

Marion. Since that day—we walked behind him.

Feydak. Yes.

Marion. I felt I couldn't bear to stay on. I left for London that night.

Feydak. Yes.

Marion. It's six years, isn't it?

Feydak. Yes. Six years last June. [*A pause.*]

Marion. What's happened since then? Nothing. . . .

Feydak. How long have you been here?

Marion. Two weeks.

Feydak. Busy?

Marion. Not professionally, I'm afraid. People are charming—they ask me to lunch and dinner and they're—"oh, so interested"—but no commissions so far. And God, how I need it. . . .

Feydak. I'm surprised. I gathered you'd been very successful.

Marion. It's always sounded like it, hasn't it? The impression, I believe, is due to the extreme notoriety of some of my sitters. Oh, I've managed well enough up to now—if I'd been more provident I dare say I could have put a tidy bit by—but at the moment people don't seem in a mood to have their portraits done. Are they less vain than they used to be? Or just poorer?

Feydak. Both, I think. . . .

Marion. Last time I came here I was awfully busy. Had great réclame because I'd been in Russia doing leading Communists. Obeying some subtle paradox the big financiers flocked to me. Pittsburgh manufacturers wanted to be done by the same brush that had tackled Lenin. Now they seem less eager. Must be some reason, Feydie. But what about you? Let me hear about you. How's Kathie?

FEYDAK. Well. She's here with me.

MARION. And Sadye?

FEYDAK. Splendid.

MARION. She must be a big girl now.

FEYDAK. As tall as you are.

MARION. Kathie used to hate me, didn't she? Frightened to death of me. Was afraid I was after Vicki's money. . . .

FEYDAK. Yes. She was afraid you'd marry him and that we should have less from him. When we knew he was dying she was in a panic.

MARION. Poor dear—I could have spared her all that worry if she'd been half-way civil to me.

FEYDAK. Kathie is practical. And she is a good mother. Those are attributes which make women avaricious. . . .

MARION. Did Vicki leave you very much?

FEYDAK. Not very much. Half to you.

MARION. Really? How sweet of him! How dear of him!

FEYDAK. We've spent it. . . .

MARION. Of course you should.

FEYDAK. But I'll soon be in position to repay you your share. I'm on my way to Hollywood.

MARION. Are you really? How wonderful for you, Feydie! I'm so glad. . . .

FEYDAK. You've been there, haven't you?

MARION. Yes. Last time I was in America.

FEYDAK. Did you like it?

MARION. Well, it's the new Eldorado—art on the gold-rush.

FEYDAK [*with a kind of ironic bitterness*]. Vicki left me an inheritance subject, it appears, to perpetual renewal.

MARION. How do you mean?

FEYDAK. Things have been going from bad to worse in Vienna—you haven't been there since '25 so you don't know. The theater's pretty well dead—even the first-rate fellows have had a hard time making their way. I managed to get several scores to do—but they were not—except that they were failures—up to my usual standard. . . .

MARION [*laughing, reproachful*]. Oh, Feydie . . . !

FEYDAK. If it weren't for the money Vicki left me—and you!—I don't know how we should have got through at all these six years. About a month ago we reached the end of our rope—we were hopelessly in debt—no means of getting out—when the miracle happened. . . . [MARION *is excited, touches his knee with her hand.*]

MARION [*murmuring*]. I can't bear it. . . .

FEYDAK. It was my dramatic agent on the phone. A great American film magnate was in town and wanted to see me. Ausgerechnet me and no other. Even my agent couldn't keep the surprise out of his voice. "Why me?" I asked. "God knows," says the agent. Well, we went around to the Bristol to see the magnate. And, as we talked to him, it gradually became apparent. He thought I was Vicki. He didn't know Vicki was dead! He thought I had written "Danubia."

MARION. Did he say so?

FEYDAK. No—not at all. But as we shook hands at the end he said to me: "Any man that can write a tune like this is the kind of man we want." And he whistled, so out of tune that I could hardly recognize it myself, the waltz from "Danubia." Do you remember it? [*He starts to hum the waltz and* MARION *joins him. They hum together, then* FEYDAK *continues to talk as* MARION *continues to hum a few more measures.*] He was so innocent, so affable that I had an impulse to say to him: "Look here, old fellow, you don't want me, you want my brother and, in order to get him, you'll have to resurrect him!" But noble impulses are luxury impulses. You have to be well off to gratify them. I kept quiet. We shook hands and here I am. Tonight they're giving me a dinner at the Waldorf Astoria for the press to meet my brother! Irony if you like, eh, Marion? [*There is a pause.*]

MARION. Feydie . . . [*A moment. He does not answer.*] Feydie—do you mind if I say something to you—very frankly?

FEYDAK. I doubt whether you can say anything to me more penetrating than the remarks I habitually address to myself.

MARION. You know Vicki was very fond of you. He used to say you put too high a valuation on genius.

FEYDAK. Because he had it he could afford to deprecate it.

MARION. Over and over again he used to say to me: "You know, Marion," he would say, "as a human being Feydie's far superior to me, more amiable, more witty, more talented, more patient. . . ."

FEYDAK [*shakes his head*]. Not true. I simply give the impression of these things. . . .

MARION. You under-rate yourself, Feydie. . . . How this would have amused him—this incident with the Hollywood man!

FEYDAK [*smiling bitterly*]. It would rather. . . .

MARION. Why do you grudge him a laugh somewhere? I never had a chance to tell you in Vienna—things were so—so close and terrible—at the end—but he had the greatest tenderness for you. He used to speak of you—I can't tell you how much. "Because of this sixth sense for making tunes which I have and he hasn't," he said to me one day—not a week before he died—"he thinks himself

less than me." He used to tell me that everything he had he owed to you—to the sacrifices you made to send him to the Conservatory when he was a boy. . . . The extent to which he had outstripped you hurt him—hurt him. I felt he would have given anything to dip into the golden bowl of his genius and pour it over you. And do you know what was the terror of his life, the obsessing terror of his life—his fear of your resenting him. . . .

FEYDAK [*moved, deeply ashamed*]. Marion. . . .

MARION. Don't resent him now, Feydie. . . . Why, it's such fun—don't you see? It's such a curious, marginal survival for him—that a badly remembered waltz-tune, five years after his death, should be the means of helping you at a moment when you need it so badly. . . . It's delicious, Feydie. It's such fun! The only awful thing is the possibility that he is unaware of it. It would have pleased him so, Feydie. Must you grudge him it?

FEYDAK. You make me horribly ashamed.

MARION [*brightly*]. Nonsense. . . .

FEYDAK. Because I did grudge him it—yes—I won't, though—I see now that it never occurred to me how . . . [*Bursts out laughing suddenly.*] God, it is funny, isn't it. . . .

MARION [*joining in his laughter*]. Of course—it's delightful. . . . [*They both laugh heartily and long.*] And the funny thing is—you'll be much better for them out there than he would have been.

FEYDAK. Surely! They'll be able to whistle *my* tunes!

MARION. Don't you see!

FEYDAK. Oh, Lieber Schatzel, come out there with me.

MARION. Can't!

FEYDAK. I wish, Marion, you would

come. I never feel life so warm and good as when you are in the neighborhood.

MARION. Dear Feydie, you're very comforting.

FEYDAK. Is there someone that keeps you here?

MARION. No, there's no one. I'm quite alone.

FEYDAK. Well then . . . !

MARION. No, this isn't the moment for me, Feydie. Besides, I can't afford the journey. I'm frightfuly hard up at the moment.

FEYDAK. Well, look here, I . . .

MARION. No, that's sweet of you but I couldn't.

FEYDAK. I don't see why—it's too silly. . . .

MARION. Vanity. A kind of vanity.

FEYDAK. But I owe it to you!

MARION. I suppose it is foolish in a way—but I've a kind of pride in maneuvering on my own. I always have done it—in that way at least I've been genuinely independent. I'm a little proud of my ingenuity. And do you know, Feydie, no matter how hard up I've been at different times something's always turned up for me. I have a kind of curiosity to know what it will be this time. It would spoil the fun for me to take money from my friends. Nothing—so much as that would make me doubtful of my own—shall we say—marketability?

FEYDAK. Paradoxical, isn't it?

MARION. Why not? Anyway it's a pet idée fixe of mine, so be a darling and let me indulge it, will you, Feydie, and don't offer me money. Anyway, I've a business proposition on. . . .

FEYDAK. Have you?

MARION. That young man who was just here. Do you suppose he'll come back? Now I think of it we were a bit short with

him, weren't we? I was so glad to see you I couldn't be bothered with him! [*Sound of doorbell.*] Ah! You see! [*Calls outside.*] Show him in, Minnie! [MINNIE *comes in and exits hall-door to admit the visitor.*]

FEYDAK. What are you doing for dinner?

MARION. There's a young man who attached himself to me on the boat. . . .

FEYDAK. Oh, Marion!

MARION. I seem to attract youth, Feydie. What shall I do about it?

FEYDAK. Where are you dining?

MARION. I don't know. . . . Which speakeasy? Tell me which one and I'll . . . [MINNIE *ushers in* MR. LEANDER NOLAN. *He is middle-aged, ample, handsome. Looks like the late Warren Gamaliel Harding. Soberly dressed and wears a waistcoat with white piping on it. The façade is impeccable but in* NOLAN's *eye you may discern, at odd moments, an uncertainty, an almost boyish anxiety to please, to be right, that is rather engaging.* MARION, *who expected the young man, is rather startled.* MR. NOLAN *regards her with satisfaction.*]

NOLAN. Hello, Marion.

MARION [*doubtfully, feels she should remember him*]. How do you do? Er—will you excuse me—just a second . . . ?

NOLAN [*genially*]. Certainly. [*He moves right.* MARION *walks* FEYDIE *to the hall-door.*]

FEYDAK [*under his breath to her*]. Looks like a commission. . . . [*She makes a gesture of silent prayer.*]

MARION [*out loud*]. Telephone me in an hour, will you, Feydie, and let me know which speakeasy. . . .

FEYDAK [*once he has her in the hall-way out of* NOLAN's *hearing*]. Also, du kommst ganz sicher?

MARION. Vielleicht später. 'Bye, Feydie

dear. [FEYDIE *goes out.* MARION *turns to face* NOLAN *who is standing with his arms behind his back rather enjoying the surprise he is about to give her.*]

NOLAN. How are you, Marion?

MARION [*delicately*]. Er—do I know you?

NOLAN. Yes. You know me.

MARION. Oh, yes—of course!

NOLAN. About time!

MARION [*brightly insecure*]. Lady Winchester's garden-party at Ascot—two summers ago. . . .

NOLAN. Guess again!

MARION. No—I know you perfectly well—it's just that—no, don't tell me. . . . [*She covers her eyes with her hand, trying to conjure him out of the past.*]

NOLAN. This is astonishing. If someone had said to me that I could walk into a room in front of Marion Froude and she not know me I'd have told 'em they were crazy . . . !

MARION [*desperate*]. I do know you. I know you perfectly well—it's just that . . .

NOLAN. You'll be awful sore at yourself—I warn you . . .

MARION. I can't forgive myself now—I know!

NOLAN. I don't believe it!

MARION. The American Embassy dinner in Rome on the Fourth of July—last year—you sat on my right. . . .

NOLAN. I did not!

MARION [*miserably*]. Well, you sat somewhere. Where did you sit?

NOLAN. I wasn't there.

MARION. Well, I think it's very unkind of you to keep me in suspense like this. I can't bear it another second!

NOLAN. I wouldn't have believed it!

MARION. Well, give me some hint, will you?

NOLAN. Think of home—think of Tennessee!

MARION. Oh . . . !

NOLAN. Little Mary Froude. . . .

MARION [*a light breaking in on her*]. No! Oh, no!

NOLAN. Well, it's about time. . . .

MARION. But . . . ! You were . . .

NOLAN. Well, so were you!

MARION. But—Bunny—you aren't Bunny Nolan, are you? You're his brother!

NOLAN. I have no brother.

MARION. But Bunny—Bunny dear—how important you've become!

NOLAN. I haven't done badly—no. . . .

MARION. Here, give me your coat and hat—[MARION, *taking his coat and hat, crosses up-stage to piano, and leaves them there. Laughing, a little hysterical.*] You should have warned me. It's not fair of you. Bunny! Of all people—I can scarcely believe it. . . . [*A moment's pause. He doesn't quite like her calling him Bunny but he doesn't know how to stop it. She sits on model-stand looking up at him as she says.*] You look wonderful. You look like a—like a—Senator or something monumental like that.

NOLAN [*sits on sofa below piano*]. That's a good omen. I'll have to tell Orrin.

MARION. What's a good omen? And who is Orrin?

NOLAN. Your saying I look like a Senator. Because—I don't want to be premature—but in a few months I may be one.

MARION. A Senator!

NOLAN [*smiling*]. Senator. Washington. Not Nashville.

MARION. Do you want to be a Senator or can't you help it?

NOLAN [*to whom this point of view is incomprehensible*]. What do you mean?

MARION. I'll paint you, Bunny. Toga Ferrule. Tribune of the people.

NOLAN. Not a bad idea. Not a bad idea at all. I remember now—you were always sketching me. Sketching everything. Say, you've done pretty well yourself, haven't you?

MARION. Not as well as you have, Bunny. Imagine. Bunny Nolan—a Senator at Washington. Well, well! And tell me—how do I seem to you? You knew me at once, didn't you?

NOLAN. Sure I did. You haven't changed so much—a little perhaps. . . .

MARION [*delicately*]. Ampler?

NOLAN [*inspecting her*]. No . . . not that I can notice. . . .

MARION [*with a sigh of relief*]. That's wonderful. . . .

NOLAN. You look just the same. You are just the same.

MARION. Oh, you don't know, Bunny. I'm artful. How long is it since we've seen each other? Twelve years anyway. More than that—fifteen . . .

NOLAN. Just about—hadn't even begun to practice law yet. . . .

MARION. We were just kids . . . children. . . . And now look at you! I can see how successful you are, Bunny.

NOLAN. How?

MARION. White piping on your vest. That suggests directorates to me. Multiple control. Vertical corporations. Are you vertical or horizontal, Bunny?

NOLAN. I'm both.

MARION. Good for you! Married?

NOLAN. Not yet . . .

MARION. How did you escape? You're going to be, though.

NOLAN. I'm engaged.

MARION. Who's the lucky girl?

NOLAN. Slade Kinnicott. Daughter of Orrin Kinnicott.

MARION. Orrin Kinnicott. The newspaper publisher?

NOLAN. Yes. He's backing me for the Senate.

MARION. Well, if he's backing you you ought to get in. All that circulation—not very good circulation, is it? Still, one vote's as good as another, I suppose. . . .

NOLAN [*hurt*]. In my own State the Kinnicott papers are as good as any. . . .

MARION. Well, I wish you luck. I'm sure you'll have it. My! Senator Nolan!

NOLAN. If I get in I'll be the youngest Senator . . .

MARION. And the best-looking too, Bunny . . .

NOLAN [*embarrassed*]. Well . . .

MARION. You're fussed! How charming of you! [*She sits beside him.*] Oh, Bunny, I'm very proud of you, really.

NOLAN. You see, Marion, I've been pretty successful in the law. Tremendously successful I may say. I've organized some of the biggest mergers of recent years. I've made a fortune—a sizeable fortune. Well, one day I woke up and I said to myself: Look here, Nolan, you've got to take stock. You've got to ask yourself where you're heading. I'd been so busy I'd never had a chance to ask myself these fundamental questions before. And I decided to call a halt. You've got enough, more than enough for life, I said to myself. It's time you quit piling up money for yourself and began thinking about your fellow-man. I've always been ambitious, Marion. You know that. You shared all my early dreams . . .

MARION. Of course I did. . . .

NOLAN. Remember I always told you I didn't want money and power for their own sakes—I always wanted to be a big man in a real sense—to do something for my country and my time . . .

MARION. Yes. Sometimes you sounded

like Daniel Webster, darling. I'm not a bit surprised you're going in the Senate.

NOLAN. I never thought—even in my wildest dreams . . .

MARION. Well, you see you under-estimated yourself. You may go even higher —the White House—why not?

NOLAN. I never let myself think of that.

MARION. Why not? It's no more wonderful than what's happened already, is it?

NOLAN [*Napoleon at Saint Helena*]. Destiny!

MARION. Exactly. Destiny!

NOLAN [*kind, richly human, patronizing*]. And you, my dear . . . ?

MARION. As you see. Obscure. Uncertain. Alone. Nowhere at all. Not the remotest chance of my getting into the Senate— unless I marry into it. Oh, Bunny, after you get to Washington will you introduce me to some Senators?

NOLAN. Well, that's premature . . . Naturally if the people should favor me I'd do what I could. I never forget a friend. Whatever faults I may have, disloyalty, I hope, is not one of them.

MARION. Of course it isn't. You're a dear. You always were. [*A moment's pause.*]

NOLAN. Who was that fellow I found you with when I came in?

MARION. An old friend of mine from Vienna—a composer.

NOLAN. You've been a lot with foreigners, haven't you?

MARION. A good deal . . .

NOLAN. Funny, I don't understand that.

MARION. Foreigners are people, you know, Bunny. Some of 'em are rather nice.

NOLAN. When I'm abroad a few weeks home begins to look pretty good to me.

MARION. I love New York but I can't say I feel an acute nostalgia for Tennessee. [*Another pause. He stares at her suddenly —still incredulous that he should be seeing her at all, and that, after all these years and quite without him, she should be radiant still.*]

NOLAN. Little Marion Froude! I can't believe it somehow. . . .

MARION. Oh, Bunny! You're sweet! You're so—ingenuous. That's what I always liked about you.

NOLAN. What do you mean?

MARION. The way you look at me, the incredulity, the surprise. What did you expect to see? A hulk, a remnant, a whitened sepulchre . . . what?

NOLAN [*uncomfortable at being caught*]. Not—not at all. . . .

MARION. Tell me, Bunny, what . . . ? I won't be hurt . . .

NOLAN [*miserably, stumbling*]. Well, naturally, after what I'd heard . . .

MARION. What have you heard? Oh, do tell me, Bunny.

NOLAN. Well, I mean—about your life. . . .

MARION. Racy, Bunny? Racy?

NOLAN. No use going into that. You chose your own way. Everybody has a right to live their own life I guess.

MARION [*pats his arm*]. That's very handsome of you, Bunny. I hope you take that liberal point of view when you reach the Senate.

NOLAN. I came here, Marion, in a perfectly sincere mood to say something to you, something that's been on my mind ever since we parted but if you're going to be flippant I suppose there's no use my saying anything—I might as well go, in fact. [*But he makes no attempt to do so.*]

MARION [*seriously*]. Do forgive me, Bunny. One gets into an idiom that passes for banter but really I'm not so changed. I'm not flippant. I'm awfully glad to see you, Bunny. [*An undertone of sadness creeps into her voice.*] After all, one makes very few real friends in life—and you are part of my youth—we are part of each other's youth . . .

NOLAN. You didn't even know me!

MARION. Complete surprise! After all I've been in New York many times during these years and never once—never once have you come near me. You've dropped me all these years. [*With a sigh.*] I'm afraid, Bunny, your career has been too much with you.

NOLAN [*grimly*]. So has yours!

MARION. I detect an overtone—faint but unmistakable—of moral censure.

NOLAN [*same tone*]. Well, I suppose it's impossible to live one's life in art without being sexually promiscuous! [*He looks at her accusingly.*]

MARION. Oh, dear me, Bunny! What shall I do? Shall I blush? Shall I hang my head in shame? What shall I do? How does one react in the face of an appalling accusation of this sort? I didn't know the news had got around so widely . . .

NOLAN. Well, so many of your lovers have been famous men. . . .

MARION. Well, you were obscure . . . But you're famous now, aren't you? I seem to be stimulating if nothing else . . .

NOLAN. If I had then some of the fame I have now you probably wouldn't have walked out on me at the last minute the way you did . . .

MARION. Dear, dear Bunny, that's not quite—

NOLAN [*irritated beyond control*]. I wish you wouldn't call me Bunny. . . .

MARION. Well, I always did. What is your real name?

NOLAN. You know perfectly well . . .

MARION. I swear I don't. . . .

NOLAN. My name is Leander. . . .

MARION. Bunny, really. . . .

NOLAN. That is my name.

MARION. Really I'd forgotten that. Leander! Who was he—he did something in the Hellespont, didn't he? What did he do in the Hellespont?

NOLAN [*sharply*]. Beside the point. . . .

MARION. Sorry! You say you wanted to tell me something—

NOLAN [*grimly*]. Yes!

MARION. I love to be told things.

NOLAN. That night you left me—

MARION. We'd quarrelled about something, hadn't we?

NOLAN. I realized after you left me how much I'd grown to depend on you—

MARION. Dear Bunny!

NOLAN. I plunged into work. I worked fiercely to forget you. I did forget you— [*He looks away from her.*] And yet—

MARION. And yet—?

NOLAN. The way we'd separated and I never heard from you—it left something bitter in my mind—something— [*He hesitates for a word.*]

MARION [*supplying it*]. Unresolved?

NOLAN [*quickly—relieved that she understands so exactly*]. Yes. All these years I've wanted to see you, to get it off my mind—

MARION. Did you want the last word, Bunny dear?

NOLAN [*fiercely*]. I wanted to see you, to stand before you, to tell myself—"Here she is and—and what of it!"

MARION. Well, can you?

NOLAN [*heatedly, with transparent overemphasis*]. Yes! Yes!

MARION. Good for you, Bunny. I know just how you feel—like having a tooth out, isn't it? [*Sincerely.*] In justice to myself— I must tell you this—that the reason I walked out on you in the summary way I did was not as you've just suggested because I doubted your future—it was obvious to me, even then, that you were destined for mighty things—but the reason was that I felt a disparity in our characters not conducive to matrimonial contentment. You see how right I was. I suspected in myself a—a tendency to explore, a spiritual and physical wanderlust—that I knew would horrify you once you found it out. It horrifies you now when we are no longer anything to each other. Imagine, Leander dear, if we were married how much more difficult it would be— If there is any one thing you have to be grateful to me for it is that instant's clear vision I had which made me see, which made me look ahead, which made me tear myself away from you. Why, everything you have now—your future, your prospects,—even your fiancée, Leander dear—you owe to me—no, I won't say to me—to that instinct—to that premonition. . . .

NOLAN [*nostalgic*]. We might have done it together. . . .

MARION. I wouldn't have stood for a fiancée, Bunny dear—not even I am as promiscuous as that. . . .

NOLAN. Don't use that word!

MARION. But, Leander! It's your own!

NOLAN. Do you think it hasn't been on my conscience ever since, do you think it hasn't tortured me . . . !

MARION. What, dear?

NOLAN. That thought!

MARION. Which thought?

NOLAN. Every time I heard about you— all the notoriety that's attended you in the American papers . . . painting pictures of Communist statesmen, running around California with movie comedians!

MARION. I have to practice my profession, Bunny. One must live, you know. Besides, I've done Capitalist statesmen too. And at Geneva. . . .

NOLAN [*darkly*]. You know what I mean . . . !

MARION. You mean . . . [*She whispers through her cupped hand.*] you mean promiscuous? Has that gotten around, Bunny? Is it whispered in the sewing-circles of Nashville? Will I be burned for a witch if I go back home? Will they have a trial over me? Will you defend me?

NOLAN [*quite literally, with sincere and disarming simplicity*]. I should be forced, as an honest man, to stand before the multitude and say: In condemning this woman you are condemning me who am asking your suffrages to represent you. For it was I with whom this woman first sinned before God. As an honorable man that is what I should have to do.

MARION. And has this worried you— actually . . . !

NOLAN. It's tortured me . . . !

MARION. You're the holy man and I'm Thaïs! That gives me an idea for the portrait which I hope you will commission me to do. I'll do you in a hair-shirt. Savonarola. He was a Senator too, wasn't he? Or was he?

NOLAN [*gloomily contemplating her*]. I can't forget that it was I who . . .

MARION. Did you think you were the first, Bunny? Was I so unscrupulously coquettish as to lead you to believe that I— oh, I couldn't have been. It's not like me. [*She crosses to right of model-stand.*]

NOLAN [*fiercely*]. Don't lie to me!

MARION [*sitting on stand*]. Bunny, you frighten me!

NOLAN [*stands over her almost threateningly*]. You're lying to me to salve my conscience but I won't have it! I know my guilt and I'm going to bear it!

MARION. Well, I don't want to deprive you of your little pleasures but . . .

NOLAN. You're evil, Marion. You haven't the face of evil but you're evil—evil!

MARION. Oh, Bunny darling, now you can't mean that surely. What's come over you? You never were like that—or were you? You know perfectly well I'm not evil. Casual—maybe—but not evil. Good Heavens, Bunny, I might as well say you're evil because you're intolerant. These are differences in temperament, that's all—charming differences in temperament.

NOLAN [*shakes his head, unconvinced*]. Sophistry!

MARION. All right, Dean Inge. Sophistry. By the way I've met the Gloomy Dean and he's not gloomy at all—he's very jolly. [*Gets up from stand.*] Let's have a cup of tea, shall we? Will your constituents care if you have a cup of tea with a promiscuous woman? Will they have to know?

NOLAN. I'm afraid I can't, Marion. I have to be getting on. . . .

MARION. Oh, stay and have some tea—[*Makes him sit down.*] what do you have to do that can't wait for a cup of tea? . . . [*Calls off.*] Minnie—Minnie. . . .

MINNIE [*appears in doorway*]. Ja, Fräulein. . . .

MARION. Bitte—tee. . . .

MINNIE. Ja, Fräulein. . . . [*She goes out.* MARION *smiles at* NOLAN *and sits beside him. He is quite uncomfortable.*]

NOLAN [*slightly embarrassed*]. About the painting, Marion. . . .

MARION. Oh, I was only joking . . . don't let yourself be bullied into it . . .

NOLAN. I've never been painted in oils. It might do for campaign purposes. And, if I should be elected, it would be very helpful to you in Washington.

MARION. You're awfully kind, Bunny. I must tell you frankly though that the dignified Senatorial style isn't exactly my forte. However, I might try. Yes—I'll try . . . [*She gives him a long look.*] I'll go the limit on you, Bunny—when I get through with you you'll be a symbol of Dignity. Solid man. No nonsense. Safe and sane. Holds the middle course—a slogan in a frock-coat. I'll make you look like Warren G. Harding—even handsomer— Get you the women's votes.

NOLAN. Well, that'll be very nice of you. . . . [MARION *suddenly kisses him.*]

MARION. Thank you, darling! [*He is very uncomfortable, embarrassed and thrilled.*]

NOLAN. Marion . . . !

MARION. Just a rush of feeling, dear!

NOLAN. You understand that this—this commission . . .

MARION. Of course. Strictly business. Don't worry. I shan't kiss you again till it's finished.

NOLAN. I don't know whether I told you—I'm going to be married in a month.

MARION. I'll have the portrait ready for your wedding-day.

NOLAN. And I am devoted to Slade with every fibre of my being. . . .

MARION. Every fibre—how thorough!

NOLAN. I'm not a Bohemian, you know, Marion.

MARION. Don't tell me! You're a gypsy! [*She continues to study him, poses him, poses his hand.* MINNIE *enters from left with tea-tray containing tea-pot, cups and saucers, spoons, sugar and cream, and a plate of cakes. She puts tray on model-stand and exits left.*] Oh, Bunny, what fun it'll be to do you. Thank you, Minnie. Tell me—how do you see yourself?

NOLAN. What do you mean?

MARION. In your heart of hearts—how do you see yourself? Napoleon, Scipio, Mussolini . . . ?

NOLAN. Nonsense! Do you think I'm an actor?

MARION. Of course. Everybody is. Everybody has some secret vision of himself.

Do you know what mine is? Do you know how I see myself? [*The doorbell rings.*]

NOLAN [*ironically*]. More visitors!

MARION [*calls to* MINNIE]. See who it is, will you, Minnie? . . . Probably the young man I met on the boat coming to take me to dinner.

NOLAN. What's his name?

MARION. I've forgotten. He's just a boy I met on the boat.

NOLAN. How can anybody live the way you live!

MARION. It's a special talent, dear. [*Doorbell rings again.*] Minnie, go to the door. [MINNIE *comes in and exits hall-way.*] This is my lucky day, Bunny.

NOLAN. Would you mind, in front of strangers, not to call me Bunny?

MARION. Oh, of course, what is it?

NOLAN [*irritated*]. Leander.

MARION [*mnemonic*]. Leander—Hellespont—Leander. . . . [MINNIE *comes down stage a few feet from the door.*]

MINNIE [*just inside the room*]. It's the Junge who was here before—er sagt er ist ausgeschifft da—

MARION. Oh, show him in, Minnie, and bring a cup for him too.

MINNIE [*as she goes*]. Ja.

NOLAN. And don't use these extravagant terms of endearment—anybody who didn't know you would misunderstand it. . . .

MARION [*very happy*]. All right, darling. [MINNIE *ushers in* RICHARD KURT, *goes out, comes back again with more tea.* MARION *comes forward to greet him.*] I'm so glad to see you again, Mr.— . . .

KURT. Kurt.

MARION. Oh. . . .

KURT. With a K.

MARION [*reassured*]. Oh—I'll try to re-

member. This is Senator Nolan—Mr. Kurt. . . .

NOLAN [*glowering*]. I am not Senator Nolan.

MARION. But you will be. [*She offers him a cup of tea; he takes it.*] Can't I just call you that—between ourselves? It gives me such a sense of quiet power. And maybe it'll impress my visitor. Do have a cup of tea, Mr. Kurt. [*She gives him one.*]

KURT [*puts his hat on sofa left*]. I am not impressed by politicians. And I didn't come to drink tea. I am here on business. [*Nevertheless he takes a hearty sip.*]

MARION. Well, you can do both. They do in England. American business-men are so tense.

KURT. I'm not a business-man.

NOLAN. Well, whatever you are, you are very ill-mannered.

KURT [*pleased*]. That's true!

MARION [*delighted*]. Isn't it nice you agree. For a moment I thought you weren't going to hit it off. . . .

NOLAN. In my day if a boy came in and behaved like this before a lady he'd be horsewhipped.

KURT. Well, when you get into the Senate you can introduce a horsewhipping bill. Probably bring you great kudos.

NOLAN. You talk like a Bolshevik.

KURT. Thank you! You talk like a Senator! [MARION *wants to laugh but thinks better of it. She looks at* KURT *with a new eye.*]

MARION [*quickly offering him more tea*]. Another cup, Mr. Kurt. . . .

KURT [*taking it*]. Thank you.

MARION. And one of these cakes—they're very nice . . . Minnie made them—almost as good as lebkuchen. Minnie spoils me.

KURT [*taking it*]. Thank you. [*Eats cake.*] Having said, from our respective points of view, the worst thing we could say about each other, having uttered the ultimate insult, there's no reason we can't be friends, Senator. Damn good cake. No lunch as a matter of fact.

MARION. That's what's the matter with him—he was hungry—hungry boy. . . .

NOLAN [*puts tea-cup on piano*]. He probably wants to sell you some insurance. . . .

KURT. Not at all. I'm not here to sell. I'm here to buy.

MARION. A picture!

KURT. Do I look like a picture-buyer!

MARION. As a matter of fact you don't . . . but I haven't anything to sell except pictures.

KURT [*confidently*]. I think you have!

MARION [*to* NOLAN]. This young man is very tantalizing.

NOLAN. Well, why don't you ask him to state his proposition and have done with it?

MARION [*turns to* KURT *and repeats mechanically*]. State your proposition and have done with it.

KURT [*puts his cup down on table rear of sofa left*]. What a nuisance women are!

NOLAN [*starting toward him*]. Why, you insolent young whelp—I've half a mind to . . .

KURT [*pleasantly*]. That's an impulse you'd better control. I wrote to this lady a business letter asking for an appointment. She granted it to me at four o'clock. It is now six. In that interval I've climbed these five flights of stairs three times. I've lost over an hour of my life going away and coming back. An hour in which I might have read a first-class book or made love to a girl or had an idea—an irreparable hour. That's rudeness if you like. It's unbusinesslike. It's sloppy. [*To* MARION.] Now will you see me alone or will you

keep me here fencing with this inadequate antagonist?

MARION. You are unquestionably the most impossible young man I've ever met. Go away!

KURT. Right! [*He turns to go and means it and she knows that he means it. And she is consumed with curiosity. As he goes.*] So long, Senator— Yours for the Revolution.

MARION [*as he reaches door, goes after him—pleads pitifully*]. Young man! Mr. Nolan is an old friend of mine. I should consult him in any case about whatever business you may suggest. Can't you speak in front of him? [*At the same time she shakes her head to him not to go away.*]

KURT. I cannot!

MARION. Please wait a minute. . . .

KURT. All right—one. [*He picks up a magazine and leafs through it negligently.*]

MARION [*to* LEANDER]. After all, Leander, I can't afford—it may be something. . . . [*She takes his arm and starts walking him to the door, whispering.*] I'm just curious to hear what he's got to say for himself. . . .

NOLAN. I'm not sure it's safe to leave you alone with a character like that. . . .

MARION. Minnie's in her room . . . with a bow and arrow!

NOLAN [*going up to hall-door*]. I have to go in any case—I'm late now.

MARION. When will I see you, Bunny? [*She is at door with him.*]

NOLAN [*taking up his hat and coat*]. I don't know. I'm very busy. I'll telephone you.

MARION. Do. Telephone me tonight. I'll tell you what he said. It'll probably be funny.

NOLAN [*out loud at* KURT]. It pains me, Marion, that you are so unprotected that

[470]

any hooligan—[KURT *turns page of magazine*] can write you and come to see you in your apartment. However, that is the way you have chosen. Good night.

MARION. Good night, dear. Are you in the book? I'll telephone you . . .

NOLAN [*hastily*]. No—no—you'd better not. I shall communicate with you. Good-by.

KURT. Good-by, Sir Galahad. [NOLAN *starts to retort, changes his mind and, in a very choleric mood, he goes out. There is a pause.*]

MARION. Well, I'm afraid you didn't make a very good impression on him!

KURT [*putting magazine away*]. That's just too bad!

MARION. That's no way for a young man to get on in the world—he's a very important person.

KURT. That's what passes for importance. You're not taken in by him, are you? Stuffed shirt—flatulent and pompous—perfect legislator!

MARION. As a matter of fact he's a very nice man—simple and kindly. [*Gets cigarettes and offers one to* KURT *who takes it and lights it. She takes one too but he forgets to light hers.*]

KURT. I bet he isn't simple and he isn't kindly. I bet he's greedy and vicious. Anyway he's a hypocrite. When a man starts worrying out loud about unprotected women you may know he's a hypocritical sensualist.

MARION. You're a violent young man, aren't you? [*Not getting light from* KURT *she lights her own. Throwing match to floor.*]

KURT. Yes. The world is full of things and people that make me see red. . . . Why do you keep calling me youth and young man? I'm twenty-five.

MARION. Well, you seem to have the lurid and uncorrected imagination of the adolescent.

KURT. Imagination! That's where you're wrong. I may tell you, Miss Froude, that I'm as realistic as anybody you've ever met.

MARION [*sitting on up-stage arm of sofa, right*]. Anybody who'd be so unreasonable over a nice fellow like Bunny Nolan . . . if you only knew—if only you'd been present at the interview I had with him just before you came. You'd have seen how wrong you are about him. Why, he was—he was awfully funny—but he was also touching.

KURT. You're one of those tolerant people, aren't you—see the best in people?

MARION. You say that as if tolerance were a crime.

KURT. Your kind is. It's criminal because it encourages dishonesty, incompetence, weakness and all kinds of knavery. What you call tolerance I call sloppy laziness. You're like those book-reviewers who find something to praise in every mediocre book.

MARION. You are a fanatical young man.

KURT. Having said that you think you dispose of me. Well, so be it. I'm disposed of. Now, let's get down to business. [*His manner plainly says: "Well, why should I bother to convince you? What importance can it possibly have what you think of me?" It is not wasted on* MARION.]

MARION. You are also a little patronizing . . .

KURT [*pleased*]. Am I?

MARION. However, I don't mind being patronized. That's where my tolerance comes in. It even amuses me a little bit. [*Crossing to piano-seat.*] But as I have to change for dinner perhaps you'd better . . .

KURT. Exactly.

MARION. Please sit down . . . [*A moment . . . She sits on piano-bench facing him.*]

KURT [*goes to piano and talks to her across it*]. I am the editor of a magazine called Every Week. Do you know it?

MARION. It seems to me I've seen it on news-stands. . . .

KURT. You've never read it?

MARION. I'm afraid I haven't.

KURT. That is a tribute to your discrimination. We have an immense circulation. Three millions, I believe. With a circulation of that size you may imagine that the average of our readers' intelligence cannot be very high. Yet occasionally we flatter them by printing the highbrows—in discreet doses we give them, at intervals, Shaw and Wells and Chesterton. So you'll be in good company anyway. . . .

MARION [*amazed*]. *I* will?

KURT. Yes. I want you to write your biography to run serially in Every Week. Later of course you can bring it out as a book.

MARION. My biography!

KURT. Yes. The story of your life.

MARION [*with dignity*]. I know the meaning of the word.

KURT. The money is pretty good. I am prepared to give you an advance of two thousand dollars.

MARION. Good Heavens, am I as old as that—that people want my biography!

KURT. We proceed on the theory that nothing exciting happens to people after they are forty. . . .

MARION. What a cruel idea!

KURT. Why wait till you're eighty. Your impressions will be dimmed by time. Most autobiographies are written by corpses. Why not do yours while you are still young, vital, in the thick of life?

MARION. But I'm not a writer. I shouldn't know how to begin.

KURT. You were born, weren't you? Begin with that.

MARION. I write pleasant letters, my friends tell me. . . . But look here, why should you want this story from me—why should anybody be interested?—I'm not a first-rate artist you know—not by far—I'm just clever. . . .

KURT [*bluntly*]. It's not you—it's the celebrity of your subjects. . . .

MARION [*amused*]. You're a brutal young man—I rather like you . . .

KURT. Well, you've been courageous. You've been forthright. For an American woman you've had a rather extraordinary career—you've done pretty well what you wanted. . . .

MARION. The Woman Who Dared sort-of-thing. . . . Isn't that passé?

KURT. I think your life will make good copy. You might have stayed here and settled down and done Pictorial Review covers of mothers hovering fondly over babies. Instead you went to Europe and managed to get the most inaccessible people to sit for you. How did you do it?

MARION. You'd be surprised how accessible some of these inaccessible people are!

KURT. Well, that's just what I want to get from your story. Just that. Tell what happened to you, that's all. The impulse that made you leave home, that made you go, for instance, to Russia, before the popular emigration set in, that's made you wander ever since, that's kept you from settling down in any of the places where you had a chance to get established.

MARION [*quite seriously*]. But supposing I don't know that. . . .

KURT. Well, that's interesting. That enigma is interesting. Maybe, while writing, you can solve it. It's a form of clarification. The more I talk to you the more I feel there's a great story in you and that you'll have great fun telling it.

MARION. Young man, you make me feel like an institution!

KURT. Should do you a lot of good in your professional career too—we'll reprint the portraits you've made of Lenin, Mussolini, Shaw—anything you like. . . . [*She begins to laugh, quietly at first, then heartily.*]

MARION. Forgive me. . . .

KURT [*unperturbed*]. What's the matter?

MARION. Something I remembered—the funniest thing—isn't it funny how the oddest things pop into your mind?

KURT. What was it?

MARION. Something that happened years ago. . . .

KURT. What?

MARION. Oh, I couldn't possibly tell you. It wouldn't be fair!

KURT. In that case it'll probably be great for the magazine. Save it!

MARION [*frightened*]. You won't do anything lurid, will you?

KURT. Just print the story—just as you write it—practically as you write it.

MARION. I'm scared! [*She puts out her cigarette in ash-tray on the piano.*]

KURT. Nonsense. Here's your first check. Two thousand dollars. [*He puts the check down on the table in front of her.*]

MARION [*wretched suddenly, picks up check, rises, looks at check*]. I can't tell you how old this makes me feel!

KURT. Suppose I asked you to write a novel! That wouldn't make you feel old, would it? Well, I'm simply asking you to write a novel of your life. The only lively reading these days is biography. People are bored with fiction. It's too tame. The fiction-writers haven't the audacity to put down what actually happens to people.

MARION. You may be disappointed, you know. You probably see headlines in your mind. The Woman of a Hundred Affairs, The Last of the Great Adventuresses, The Magda Who Wouldn't Go Home. I promise you—it won't be a bit like that.

KURT. We'll announce it next month—first installment the following month. O.K.?

MARION [*puts down check, paces down right*]. Oh, dear! I can't promise a thing like that—I really can't. . . .

KURT. Why not?

MARION. It'll worry me too much.

KURT. Well, don't promise. Just get to work.

MARION [*faces him*]. But what'll I do first?

KURT [*getting up*]. Well, if I were you I'd sit down. [*She does so helplessly on piano-bench.* KURT *then gives her paper, one of his own pencils.*] There now! You're all set!

MARION [*wailing*]. How can I go out to dinner—how can I ever do anything—with a chapter to write?

KURT. After all you don't have to make up anything. Just tell what happened to you. [*He lights a fresh cigarette.*]

MARION. Can I use names?

KURT. When they're prominent, yes. The obscure ones you can fake if you want to. Nobody'll know 'em anyway.

MARION [*looks at him*]. Oh . . . what's your name?

KURT [*looks at her*]. I told you—my name's Kurt.

MARION. I know—with a K—I can't call you Kurt! What's your *name*?

KURT [*sulkily*]. Richard.

MARION. That's better. I tell you, Dickie, when I think—when I think—of the funny men I've known . . . they're pretty nearly all brothers under the skin you know, Dickie.

KURT. Well, that, as they say in the office, is an angle. [*Suddenly her fear vanishes and she is overcome with the marvelous possibilities.*]

MARION [*jumps up and leans toward him as if to kiss him, but quickly thinks better of it*]. Dickie, I think it'll be marvelous! it'll be a knockout. And imagine— [*Picking up check*] I'm going to be paid for it! Dickie, you're an angel!

KURT [*sardonically*]. That's me! Angel Kurt! Well, so long. I'll be seeing you. [*Starts up-stage toward hall-door.*]

MARION [*suddenly panicky*]. Oh, don't go!

KURT. You don't think I'm going to sit here and hold your hand while you're remembering your conquests, do you?

MARION. Well, you can't go away and leave me like this—alone with my life. . . .

KURT. Perhaps it's time you got a good, straight, clear-eyed look at it—alone by yourself, without anybody around to hold your hand. . . .

MARION [*suddenly*]. No. I don't want to. [*Shrugs her shoulders as if she were cold.*] I think it would worry me. Besides, I feel superstitious about it.

KURT [*following her down stage*]. Superstitious!

MARION. Yes. A kind of—ultimate act. After you've written your biography, what else could there possibly be left for you to do?

KURT. Collect material for another!

MARION. What could you do over again —that wouldn't be repetitious? [*Sits right arm of sofa right.*]

KURT. It's repetitious to eat or to make love, isn't it? You keep on doing it.

MARION. You're cynical!

KURT [*almost spits it out*]. You're sentimental.

MARION. I am—Sentimental Journey— no, that's been used, hasn't it?

KURT. Don't worry about a title—I'll get that from the story after you've finished it.

MARION. There's something about it— I don't know—

KURT. What?

MARION. Vulgar. *Everybody* spouting memoirs. Who cares?

KURT. Well, wrong hunch! Sorry to have taken your valuable time. Good-by.

MARION [*the finality frightens her*]. What do you mean?

KURT [*he is withering—crosses to her*]. I'm prepared to admit I was mistaken— that's all. In your desire to escape vulgarity you would probably be—thin. You might even achieve refinement. I'm not interested. Padded episodes hovering on the edge of amour—

MARION [*turns on him*]. Young man, you're insufferable!

KURT. And you're a false alarm!

MARION [*after a moment*]. I congratulate you! You've brought me to the verge of losing my temper! But I tell you this —you're quite mistaken about the character of my life—and about my relations with my friends. My story won't be thin and episodic because my life hasn't been thin and episodic. And I won't have to pad—the problem will be to select. I'm going to write the damn thing just to show you. Come in tomorrow afternoon for a cocktail.

KURT. Whose memoirs are these going to be, yours or mine?

MARION. Well, you're an editor, aren't you? [*She smiles at him.*] Come in and edit.

KURT. All right, I'll come. But if you

aren't here I'll go away. I won't wait a minute. [*He goes out quickly.* MARION *stands looking after him, inclined to laugh, and yet affected. This is a new type even for her.*]

MARION [*she speaks to herself*]. What an extraordinary young man! [*In a moment* KURT *comes back in.* MARION *is very glad to see him, greets him as if there had been a long separation.*] Oh, hello!

KURT [*embarrassed*]. I forgot my hat! [*He can't see it at once.*]

MARION [*without moving nor looking away from him, she indicates the hat on the sofa left*]. There it is! Right next to mine.

KURT [*crosses for it*]. Oh, yes. [*Picks up the hat.*] Thanks. [*For a moment he stands uncertainly, hat in hand, looking at* MARION *who has not taken her eyes off him. He is embarrassed.*] Well, so long!

MARION. So long. [KURT *leaves again. She stands as before looking after him. She turns toward the piano—sees the check—picks it up and reads it to make sure it's true. The whole thing has a slightly fantastic quality to her. She is very happy and excited. She waves the check in her hand like a pennant and humming she crosses to the piano seat and sits and plays the waltz from "Danubia." She sees the pad and pencil on the piano and stops playing and picking up the pencil and the pad she crosses to the small arm-chair in the up-stage end of the window and sits with her feet on the window seat. She repeats the first words of the first chapter aloud to herself as she writes them down.*]

I am born . . . [MINNIE *enters from door left to get the tea things she had left on the model-stand.* MARION *taps the pencil on the pad as she repeats the words.*] I am born . . . [*The time seems remote to her.*] I am born—I meet Richard Kurt—Well, Minnie, here's the outline—I am born . . . I meet Richard Kurt—now all I have to do is to fill in. . . . [MINNIE, *used to having irrelevancies addressed to her, takes this program rather stolidly.*]

MINNIE. Was, Marion?

MARION [*trying to get rid of her*]. Fix something light, will you, Minnie . . . I'm not going out.

MINNIE. Aber der Junge kommt!

MARION. What Junge?

MINNIE. Der Junge dem sie . . .

MARION. Oh, yes! The Junge I met on the boat. You'll have to send him away. I can't go out tonight. From now on, Minnie, no more frivolous engagements!

MINNIE [*astonished*]. Sie bleiben ganzen abend zu Hause!

MARION. Yes, Minnie. I'm spending the evening alone with my life . . . [*She remembers* KURT'S *words and repeats them as if, after all, they have made a profound impression on her.*] get a good, straight, clear-eyed look at it . . .

MINNIE [*picks up the tea tray and bustles toward the kitchen, promising delights*]. Ein fleisch brühe und pfannkuchen! . . . [MINNIE *exits door left.*]

MARION [*already brooding over her past*]. I am born. . . .

[*Slowly the curtain falls.*]

ACT II

[SCENE: *The same. About three weeks later. Afternoon.*

AT RISE: MARION *is putting some* touches on the full length portrait of LEANDER NOLAN *which stands away from the audience. She is wearing her working* costume, baggy red corduroy trousers, a sash and a worn blue smock over a kind of sweater-jacket. She is very happy. . . . On the piano nearby are her writing things. While touching up LEANDER she is struck by an idea for her book. Puts down her brush and palette and goes to the piano to jot down some notes. The idea pleases her. She giggles to herself. Then she returns to her easel. MINNIE comes in and stands watching her a moment before MARION sees her.]

MARION [sees MINNIE at last]. Oh, yes, Minnie—do you want anything?

MINNIE. You asked me to come right away, Marion.

MARION. Did I?

MINNIE. Ja. [Sitting on sofa right.] Zo! You have left a note on the kitchen I should come in right away I am back from the market.

MARION [studying the portrait]. Of course I did. That's right, Minnie.

MINNIE. Well, what did you want, Marion?

MARION [washing paint brush in turpentine jar]. Did I tell you there'd be two for dinner?

MINNIE. Ja. Gewiss! Das ist vy I vent to the market.

MARION. Well, I've changed my plans. I'm dining out with Feydie after all.

MINNIE [rising and looking at picture]. Ach, Gott! [She studies the portrait.]

MARION [looks humorously at MINNIE and puts her arm about MINNIE's shoulders]. Gut?

MINNIE. Ziemlich gut—

MARION. Do you know who it is?

MINNIE. Oh, das sieht man ja gleich. Das ist Herr Nolan!

MARION [shaking her hand in gratitude].

Thank you, Minnie! [Doorbell rings.] See who that is, will you, Minnie?

MINNIE. Fräulein ist zu Hause?

MARION. Ich erwarte Herr Feydak. Für ihn bin ich immer zu Hause.

MINNIE [agreeing heartily as she crosses to the door]. Ja, Ja, der Herr Feydak. . . . [MINNIE goes out. MARION jots down a note on the pad which is on the piano. FEYDAK enters. MINNIE closes the door and exits left.]

MARION [at piano]. Hello, Feydie! Sit down!

FEYDAK. Well, my dear, which career do I interrupt?

MARION [laughing]. I don't know!

FEYDAK. One comes to see you with diffidence nowadays. [FEYDAK removes coat and hat and places them on the up-stage end of the sofa right, and sits on the left side of the sofa.]

MARION. While I'm painting I think of funny things to say, funny phrases. It won't be a serious biography, thank God. I'm dedicating it to Vicki: "To Vicki—the gayest person I have ever known!" By the way, have you got any little snapshots of Vicki—all I've got are formal photographs with his orders. I'd like to get something a little more intimate.

FEYDAK. I'll hunt some up for you.

MARION. Have you heard from the Powers yet, when you are to leave?

FEYDAK. Tomorrow.

MARION [stricken—sits right of him]. Feydie!

FEYDAK [fatalistically]. Tomorrow. [They sit.] I shall leave you with sorrow, Marion.

MARION. I'll have no one to laugh with.

FEYDAK. For me it's an exile.

MARION. You'll have a wonderful time. I shall miss you terribly.

FEYDAK. Perhaps you'll come out.

MARION. Perhaps I will. I've always wanted to go to China. If I have enough money left from all my labors I'll stop in on you—en route to China.

FEYDAK. That would be marvelous.

MARION. You know writing one's life has a sobering effect on one—you get it together and you think: "Well! look at the damn thing . . ."

FEYDAK. Do you want to be impressive?

MARION. Well, I don't want to be trivial . . .

FEYDAK. I think *you* escape that.

MARION. My friendships haven't been trivial. . . . [*She gives his hand a squeeze.*]

FEYDAK. Have you seen that bombastic young man?

MARION. Oh, yes. He comes in every once in a while to see how I'm getting on. He's quite insulting. Underneath his arrogance I suspect he's very uncertain.

FEYDAK. Oh, now, don't tell me he has an inferiority complex!

MARION. Well, I think he has!

FEYDAK. The new psychology is very confusing. In my simple day you said: "That young man is bumptious and insufferable" and you dismissed him. Now you say: "He has an inferiority complex" and you encourage him to be more bumptious and more insufferable. It's very confusing.

MARION. There's a kind of honesty about him that I like.

FEYDAK [*instantly putting two and two together*]. Oh!

MARION. Nothing like that, Feydie! As a matter of fact—I don't mind telling you . . . I like him very much—

FEYDAK. I think he is destined . . .

MARION. He's not interested. He's some kind of fanatic. Social, I think. I've met that kind in Russia—quite unassailable.

But I'm optimistic. . . . [*They laugh.*] Well, one must never despair, must one. Life is so much more resourceful and resilient than one is oneself. Three weeks ago when you came to see me I felt quite at the end of my rope. I didn't tell you quite but I actually didn't know which way to turn. I felt tired too—which troubled me. Well, now I find myself, quite suddenly [*She indicates portrait*] doing Leander and— [*She indicates manuscript on piano*] doing myself. New Vista. Very exciting.

FEYDAK. All this enthusiasm for art alone?

MARION [*laughing*]. Of course!—Feydie, what did you think?

FEYDAK. I don't believe it.

MARION. Come here and have a look at Leander!

FEYDAK [*he rises—walks to the canvas on the easel*]. Hm! Formal!

MARION. It's to hang in the White House. [*She winks at him, he laughs, puts his arm around her shoulder.*]

FEYDAK. Marion, you're adorable! [*They walk down stage together, their arms around each other's shoulders, very affectionately.*]

MARION. Oh, Feydie, I'm having a wonderful time. Quiet too. Writing *enforces* silence and solitude on one. I've always lived in such a rush—a kind of interminable scherzo. . . . .

FEYDAK. Good title! . . .

MARION. Think so? I'll put it down. . . . [*Writes on pad on piano. FEYDAK sits on right arm of sofa left facing her.*] Interminable scherzo. . . . How do you spell it? A little affected. Might do for a chapter heading maybe. . . . [*Returns to him—sitting on model-stand—facing him.*] But I realize now I haven't in years had time to stop and think. I sit here for hours,

Feydie, and nothing comes to me. Then, suddenly, the past will come in on me with such a rush—odd, remote, semi-forgotten things of the past. Are they true? How much is true? One can never be sure, can one? I remember certain griefs and fears. I remember their existence without recalling at all their intensity—their special anguish. Why? What was the matter with me? What made them so acute? It is like recalling a landscape without color, a kind of color-blindness of the memory. [*Doorbell rings. She calls out to her factotum.*] Minnie! [MINNIE *enters left and crosses rapidly to hall door.* MARION *arranges the model-stand on which stands the papal arm-chair in red and gold.*] This is probably the Hon. Nolan. He's due for a sitting. He pretends he doesn't like to have his picture painted, but I know he does. [MINNIE *enters from hall-way. She is flustered and giggly.*]

MINNIE [*very high-pitched voice*]. Herr Varvick Vilson!

MARION. Tympi Wilson!

MINNIE [*to* FEYDAK]. Der *film star!*

FEYDAK. So?

MINNIE [*radiant*]. Ja! Ja!

MARION. Oh, Feydie, you'll adore this. Ask him in, Minnie.

MINNIE [*as she goes out to admit* WILSON]. Gott, ist er schön!

MARION. Warwick's public.

FEYDAK. And mine!

MARION [*in a quick whisper*]. Whatever you do—outstay him! [MINNIE *has opened the door and* WARWICK WILSON *enters. He is very handsome, explosively emotional, and given to cosmic generalization. He is in evening clothes.*]

WILSON [*with a red carnation in his buttonhole, crossing to* MARION *and kissing her hand.*] Marion!

MARION. Warwick!

WILSON. Darling! How are you?

MARION. I'm splendid. Been up all night?

WILSON. No, no! This is business. [MINNIE *has crossed to kitchen door upper-left, never taking her eyes from* WILSON.]

MARION. This is Mr. Feydak. Mr. Warwick Wilson, the famous film star.

WILSON [*crosses to sofa and shakes hands with* FEYDAK—*dramatically*]. Feydak! *The* Mr. Feydak?

FEYDAK [*again mistaken for his brother*]. Ja.

WILSON. I've heard of you indeed!

FEYDAK. Have you? Thanks.

MARION. Mr. Feydak is on his way to Hollywood. He is to write the music for . . .

WILSON [*sits on the model-stand—facing front*]. Of course! I am honored, Mr. Feydak—deeply honored. That unforgettable waltz—how does it go? . . . [*He starts to hum with a swaying gesture the waltz from the "Merry Widow."*] Music's my one passion!

MARION. Once you said it was me.

WILSON. A lot of good it did me!

MARION [*to* WILSON]. Well, tell me . . . [*She sees* MINNIE *who is still staring at* WILSON.] Look at Minnie. The mere sight of you has upset her so that she's speechless.

MINNIE. Aber, Fräulein! [WILSON *rises graciously and gives* MINNIE *a friendly wave of the hand. He's no snob.* MINNIE, *speechless with delight, exits left.* WILSON *returns to his position on the model-stand.*]

MARION. All right, Minnie! Warwick, Warwick! You mustn't do things like that to Minnie, at her age!

WILSON [*tragically*]. There you are!

This face! This cursed face! I should go masked really. One has no private life!

MARION [*sits in throne chair on model-stand*]. What would you do with it if you had it, eh, Tympi?

WILSON [*delighted*]. That nickname!

MARION. It just rolled off my tongue. Did I call you that?

WILSON. You did! You invented it. No one's called me that since you left Hollywood. And you promised to explain the significance to me, but you never did.

MARION. Did it have a significance?

FEYDAK. Marion has a knack for nicknames.

MARION. I love 'em. I'd like to do a chapter on nicknames.

WILSON [*highly pleased*]. Tympi! Tympi! [*Very patronizing to* FEYDAK.] You are an intuitive person, Mr. Feydak. I can see that. [FEYDAK *ad libs: "Danke schön."*] Can you imagine what she meant?

FEYDAK. Her vagaries are beyond me, Mr. Wilson.

WILSON [*leaning back toward* MARION]. Speak, Oracle! No! Don't tell me now. Put it into that book you're writing.

MARION [MARION *and* FEYDAK *exchange glances*]. How things get around.

WILSON. It's been in the back of my mind for years, Marion . . . to have you paint me. Now that we're both in town together . . .

MARION. Well, I'd *love* to . . .

WILSON. In the costume of the Dane. [MARION *and* FEYDAK *exchange a look.*] [*Strikes a pose.*] I'd like to be done in *his* costume. I hope, Mr. Feydak, that they won't break your spirit in Hollywood as they've almost broken mine!

FEYDAK [*with a smile*]. My spirit is indestructible!

WILSON [*rises and crosses to rear of sofa*

and pats FEYDAK *on the back*]. I'm glad to hear it. [*Returns to left of model-stand and stands with his right foot on it.*] You know, for years I've been begging them to do Shakespeare. [*Gesticulates.*]

MARION [*interrupting him*]. Sit down and be comfortable.

WILSON. They simply won't listen. But I'm going to give up acting and produce!

MARION. Oh, good God! Don't do that!

WILSON. Why not!

MARION. What would Minnie do with her night off?

WILSON [*smiles*]. My public, eh?

MARION. Yes!

WILSON. Quite so! [*Patronizingly.*] You artists who work in media like painting or literature— [*To* FEYDAK.] Or music, that too is a beautiful art, Mr. Feydak—transcends speech—transcends everything, by saying nothing it says all.

FEYDAK. Ja! [*The doorbell rings.*]

WILSON. You are certainly lucky compared to us poor actors. We— [MINNIE *enters and crosses to hall-door upper center.*] Wouldn't it be ironic if all that remained of me after I am gone were your painting of me. That is why I want it perhaps—my poor grasp on immortality.

FEYDAK. You see, Marion, you confer immortality!

MARION. I think immortality is an over-rated commodity. But tell me, Tympi, what are you doing away from Hollywood?

MINNIE [*comes in announcing:*] Der Herr Nolan! [MINNIE *then looks at* WILSON. WILSON *stands—looks at* MINNIE.]

MARION. Show him in. Show him in. [*With a lingering look at* WILSON, MINNIE *goes back. To others, after watching* MINNIE *exit.*] You see!

FEYDAK. The effect is instantaneous— like music . . . [NOLAN *enters.* MINNIE *follows* NOLAN *in and exits into kitchen, murmuring ecstatically,* "Gott! Ist er schön!" *looking at* WILSON.]

MARION. Hello, Bunny! [*Introducing* NOLAN.] You know Mr. Feydak. Mr. Nolan, this is Warwick Wilson, you've heard of him. [FEYDAK *bows to* NOLAN, *who returns the bow.*]

WILSON. It's a pleasure, Mr. Nolan. I've heard of *you* indeed! [*They shake hands.*]

MARION. You're late for your sitting, Bunny. Will the presence of these gentlemen embarrass you? I don't mind if you don't.

NOLAN [*has entered rather worried and angry. He has a magazine rolled in his hand. He nows speaks very irritatedly*]. As a matter of fact, Marion . . .

MARION [*putting him in throne chair on model-stand*]. Oh, sit down like a good fellow. The light is getting bad. [NOLAN *sits.* WILSON *sits on the right arm of the sofa left on which* FEYDAK *is sitting.* MARION *gets to work on* BUNNY.] How did you find me, Tympi?

WILSON. I read in a magazine that you were barging into literature . . .

NOLAN [*half rising, showing magazine*]. This is true then!

MARION. Don't get up, Bunny . . . [*Nevertheless she takes the magazine and looks at it.*] Well, Dickie has gone and spread himself, hasn't he? [*She sits on sofa left between* WILSON *and* FEYDAK.] Look here, Feydie! [*Shows him the full-page announcement of her book in magazine.*]

FEYDAK [*looking*]. Do you think you can live up to this?

MARION. Why will they write this sort of thing! [*Rises and goes back.*] Makes me out a kind of female Casanova. [*She drops the magazine on the stand at* NOLAN's *feet.*] Well, they'll be disappointed.

NOLAN [*bitterly*]. Will they?

MARION. Bunny! [*But she thinks nothing of it—merely pushes him into a better light.*]

FEYDAK [*tactfully—he senses danger*]. May I ask, Mr. Wilson—are you making a picture at the moment?

WILSON. No, I'm in New York making some personal appearances.

MARION. Personal appearances. I love that phrase. Has such an air of magnanimity about it. [*Crosses to painting.*]

WILSON. Pretty boring, I can tell you! I've got writer's cramp signing autograph books. It's a perfect martyrdom I assure you. It's no fun at all. [WILSON *crosses to stand—puts his right foot on it, leans on his knee with his right arm and studies* NOLAN, *his face not six inches away from* NOLAN's. NOLAN *fidgets.*]

MARION. I can imagine! What's the matter, Bunny? You seem under a strain today . . . not relaxed.

NOLAN [*bursting out and glaring at all of them*]. It's like being watched while you're taking a bath!

MARION. Oh, I'm so sorry, Bunny!

FEYDAK [*rising*]. I quite sympathize with Mr. Nolan.

WILSON [*moves away*]. Supposing I were so shy, eh, Mr. Nolan?

FEYDAK [*crosses to* MARION *who is above her easel, right*]. I'm off, Marion. [*Kisses her hand.*] Auf wiedersehen!

MARION [*meaningfully*]. You'll have to go—[WILSON *sits again on arm of sofa left.*] both of you . . .

WILSON [*rises*]. I was just going myself. My next appearance is at 6:45. [*Speaks to others.*]

FEYDAK [*to help her*]. Perhaps I can drop you, Mr. Wilson.

WILSON [*faces* FEYDAK]. No, I'll drop you . . . [*Turns to* MARION] I say, Marion . . . [FEYDAK, *helpless, goes up-stage putting on coat.*]

MARION. Yes, Tympi?

WILSON. If you started my portrait right away and it turns out—I am sure it will turn out—you might put it in your book, mightn't you? I'm frankly sick of just appearing in fan-magazines.

MARION. We'll see. Why not?

WILSON. Splendid! *Don't fail to come to-night.* Good-by, dearest Marion. Good-by again, Mr. Nolan. [*He starts to shake* NO-LAN's *hand but is interrupted by* MARION, *almost screaming.*]

MARION. No, no, no! Don't do *that*—don't touch him.

WILSON. Most happy! See you later . . . [*He waves himself off at last—*MARION *returns to her easel.*]

MARION [*to* FEYDAK]. Don't forget—I'm dining with you.

FEYDAK [*like the player in Hamlet who burlesques Polonius*]. Most happy—see you later. [FEYDAK *leaves.*]

MARION [*with relief*]. Now then . . .

NOLAN [*muttering to himself*]. Silly ass!

MARION [*working on painting*]. That young man is one of the most famous people in the world, do you realize that, Bunny? His profile follows you all over Europe—*and* Asia. Ubiquitous profile. Have you ever seen him?

NOLAN [*unswerved*]. He's a silly ass!

MARION. I admit he's somewhat on that side—but that other one—that Feydie—he's the darling of the world!

NOLAN [*very short—bitterly*]. Evidently!

MARION [*surprised*]. Bunny!

NOLAN [*savage now*]. Who isn't a darling! Everyone's a darling as far as I can see! The world's full of darlings. Your world at any rate.

MARION. But, darling . . . [*She sud-denly stops—sits right end of sofa right.*] Oh, Bunny, I remember now!

NOLAN. You remember what!

MARION. Tympi! Why I nicknamed him Tympi. Don't you see?

NOLAN. No, I don't see . . .

MARION. For tympanum—a large instrument in the orchestra producing a hollow sound. [*She beats an imaginary drum with her paint brush.*] Boom! [*Suddenly* NOLAN *quits the pose.*] What is it?

NOLAN. I can't sit today. I'm not in the mood.

MARION. I could tell there was something worrying you.

NOLAN. There is something worrying me!

MARION. Well, what is it?

NOLAN. This confounded story! Are you really writing it?

MARION. Well, yes—I am.

NOLAN. What do you intend to tell?

MARION. Well, that's a rather difficult question to answer—it's like asking me what I've been doing all my life.

NOLAN. When does this biography start?

MARION [*beginning to wonder about this questioning*]. With my birth—coincidence, isn't it?

NOLAN. All the time back home—when you were a girl in Knoxville?

MARION. Yes, of course. I've had a wonderful time going back over it all.

NOLAN. Everything?

MARION. Everything I can remember.

NOLAN. Do I come into it?

MARION [*smiling to herself*]. You do! You certainly do!

NOLAN. You must leave me out of that story!

MARION. But, Bunny, how can I possibly leave you out?

NOLAN. You must, that's all!

MARION. But how can I? You were too

[481]

important—think of the role you played in my life. By your own confession, Bunny darling, you—you started me. That's a good idea for a chapter-heading, isn't it? "Bunny Starts Me." I must put that down.

NOLAN. This is no joke, Marion. [*With menace.*] I warn you . . .

MARION. Warn me! Let me understand you. Are you seriously asking me to give up an opportunity like this just because . . .

NOLAN [*rises and gets down from the model-stand. Speaks with brutal command*]. Opportunity! Cheap exhibitionism! A chance to flaunt your affairs in a rag like this. [*Indicating magazine on piano.*] I won't be drawn into it. I can tell you that! [*He is in a towering rage.*]

MARION [*after a pause*]. I know that by your standards, Bunny, I'm a loose character. But there are other standards, there just are.

NOLAN [*crosses to center—drops magazine on model-stand*]. Not in Tennessee!

MARION [*rises*]. I'm afraid you're provincial, Bunny.

NOLAN. I'm sorry.

MARION [*takes off her smock, crosses to small table down right, gets her notes, then crosses to desk upper right*]. I don't care what the advertisements say about my story—I know what I'm writing . . .

NOLAN. I'm sorry.

MARION. That's all right. [*But this has gone pretty deep.*]

NOLAN [*after a pause*]. If you're doing this for money— [*She turns and watches him.*] I know you've been pretty hard up —I promise you I'll get you commissions enough to more than make up for this story. I was talking about you only the other day to my prospective father-in-law. He's a big man, you know. I am sure I can get him to sit for you . . .

MARION. The tip isn't big enough.

NOLAN [*scared now that he sees the extent to which he has hurt her*]. Marion! . . .

MARION. It amuses me to write my life. I am pleasure-loving—you know that—I will therefore pass up the opportunity of painting your big father-in-law. I will even give up the pleasure of painting you. And we can part friends, then, can't we? [*She reaches out her hand to him.*] Good-by, Bunny.

NOLAN [*devastated*]. Marion—you can't do this to me—you can't send me away like this . . .

MARION. I don't think ever in my life that I've had a vulgar quarrel with anyone. This is the nearest I've come to it. I'm a little annoyed with you for that. I think it's better we part now while we can still do so with some—dignity. Shall we?

NOLAN. You don't realize what's involved—or you wouldn't talk like that . . .

MARION. What *is* involved?

NOLAN. My entire career. That's what's involved.

MARION. Oh!

NOLAN. This is the most critical moment of my life. My fiancée's father is the most powerful leader of opinion in my state. Frankly, I depend on him for support. To have this kind of thing bandied about now might cause a permanent rift between him and me—might seriously interfere not only with my candidacy for the Senate, but with my marriage.

MARION. They are interlocking—I quite understand.

NOLAN. A revelation of this kind—coming at this moment—might be fatal . . .

MARION. Revelation! You make me feel like—I can't tell you what you make me feel like . . . [*She laughs—semi-hysterically.*]

NOLAN [*sepulchral*]. You must give this up, Marion.

MARION. I've met distinguished men abroad—politicians, statesmen—a Prime Minister even—and this kind of "revelation"—as you so luridly call it, is no more to them than a theme for after-dinner banter. They take it in their stride. My God, Bunny, you take it so big!

NOLAN. These people I'm depending on to elect me aren't sophisticated like you or me. [MARION *looks at* NOLAN *with some surprise.*] What I mean is—they're country people essentially—my future father-in-law is sympathetic to their point of view.

MARION. Tell me—your father-in-law, is he the man with the chest-expansion?

NOLAN. He's a fine sturdy man—as you perhaps know, he makes a fetish of exercise.

MARION [*bubbling again*]. You see his pictures in shorts in Health Magazines.

NOLAN. There's no disgrace in that.

MARION [*sits right arm of sofa left*]. It doesn't shock me, Bunny. I was just identifying him, that's all.

NOLAN. I owe everything to Kinnicott—I wouldn't be running for the Senate right now if not for him. I can't risk offending him.

MARION. What the devil's happened to you anyway? You used to be quite a nice boy—even fun occasionally . . .

NOLAN [*wistful—turns away*]. Maybe—if you had stuck to me . . .

MARION. Ts! Ts! Ts! Poor Bunny. I'm sorry for you. Really I am! [*She strokes his arm.*]

NOLAN [*suddenly passionate—faces her*]. Don't touch me!

MARION [*amazed*]. Bunny!

NOLAN. Do you think I'm not human!

MARION. Well, if you aren't the most contradictory . . .

NOLAN. I realized the moment I came in here the other day—the moment I saw you . . .

MARION [*interrupting*]. But Bunny! You're engaged and you're going to be a Senator.

NOLAN [*walks away from her*]. Forget it! Forget I ever said it. . . .

MARION. You bewilder me . . .

NOLAN [*bitterly*]. I'm not surprised I bewilder you. You've spent your life among a lot of foreign counts. It's well known that foreigners are more immoral than we are.

MARION. I'm very touched. I am really. [*She kisses him in a friendly way.*]

NOLAN. Don't do that! I forbid you!

MARION. All right. I'll never attack you again, I promise.

NOLAN. I wish I had never come back into your life—it was a terrible mistake—you'd forgotten me.

MARION [*seriously*]. Oh, you're wrong. First love—one doesn't forget that.

NOLAN [*passionately*]. But you did! You forgot me! And if you got the chance again, you'd humiliate me again.

MARION. Humiliate! What queer notions you have— Is it a question of pride or vanity between us? We're old friends—friends.

NOLAN [*moves a step right*]. Please forget this—I don't know what came over me—I . . .

MARION. Of course. There's nothing to forget. [*Moves a step toward him.*] It's quite all right, dear . . . [*She pats him on his hand.*] Oh, excuse me . . .

NOLAN. I warn you, Marion—I solemnly warn you—if you persist in this—

MARION. Never in my life have I seen a

man vacillate so between passion and threat . . .

NOLAN. I shall find ways to stop you. Mr. Kinnicott, my future father-in-law, is a powerful man.

MARION. I know. Extraordinary biceps.

NOLAN. I warn you, Marion. This matter is beyond flippancy.

MARION [*sits*]. There'll be some very distinguished people in my biography. You needn't be ashamed.

NOLAN. That movie-actor!

MARION. Tympi in Hamlet costume— you in a toga. I'll print your portraits on opposite pages—my two men!

NOLAN. You are malicious!

MARION. I must admit, Bunny, that you provoke in me all my malicious impulses. You come here suddenly and you convey to me what I've missed in not marrying you. [*The back doorbell rings.* MINNIE *crosses to answer it during* MARION'S *speech.*] You dangle before me the inventory of your felicities—a career, a fortune, a fabulous bride—and then, because I get a chance to chronicle my own adventures —you object—you tell me I mustn't! I have a nice nature, Bunny, or I should be angry—I should be indignant. [KURT *enters.*]

NOLAN [*sharply and with threat*]. Now, Marion, I've warned you . . . You'll regret this.

MARION. Hello, Dickie, do talk to Bunny for a minute, will you? [*Crosses to the stairs and starts up them to her bedroom.*] I've simply got to change. [MINNIE *enters up center and exits left.*] Feydie's coming to take me out to dinner.

NOLAN. But, Marion . . .

MARION. I couldn't do anything about this in any case, Bunny dear, because I've promised Dickie. In fact, I signed something, didn't I, Dickie? Don't go away

either of you. . . . [MARION *blows them a kiss and exits into her bedroom. A pause between the two men.* KURT *crosses down stage to above the model-stand. Suddenly,* NOLAN *goes to* KURT *and reaches out his hand to him.*]

NOLAN. How do you do, young man?

KURT [*very much surprised*]. How do *you* do? [*He looks at him narrowly, his head a little on one side, a terrier appraising a mastiff.*]

NOLAN. I am very glad to see you.

KURT. Isn't that nice . . . ?

NOLAN. You may be surprised to learn that on the one occasion when we met you made quite an impression on me.

KURT. Did I?

NOLAN [*sits sofa right*]. You did. Sit down. In fact—I hope you don't mind— if you will allow me as a prerogative of seniority—to ask you a few questions. I have a purpose in mind and not—I trust— an idle purpose.

KURT. Shoot! [*Sits.*] Anything to enlighten the professor! [*He knows he is going to be pumped and has decided to be casual, naive and even respectful.*]

NOLAN [*clearing his throat*]. Now then —your present position on the magazine you represent—have you been on it long?

KURT. About two years.

NOLAN. And before that?

KURT. Newspaper work.

NOLAN. And before that?

KURT. Tramping around the world. Odd jobs. Quite a variety.

NOLAN. College?

KURT. Believe it or not—Yale—two years . . . worked my way through— washed dishes.

NOLAN. Very interesting preparation . . . very interesting . . . Tell me now— your present work—do you find it interesting? Is the remuneration satisfactory?

KURT. Two hundred smackers a week. That's twice what I've ever earned in my life before.

NOLAN. Now then—to come to the point—no doubt you've heard of my prospective father-in-law, Mr. Orrin Kinnicott?

KURT. Heard of him! We pay him the compliment of imitation. He is our model, our criterion, our guiding star!

NOLAN. As you know, Mr. Kinnicott's interests are varied. He owns some powerful newspapers in my state. The other day I heard him say that he wanted a new man in Washington.

KURT [*playing naively excited*]. Now that's to give one's eye-teeth for!

NOLAN [*pleased at the result*]. I think it might be possible to swing it—very possible.

KURT. God, what a break!

NOLAN. As it happens Mr. Kinnicott is at present in town. I shall arrange an appointment for you in the next few days. Naturally, I expect you to keep the matter entirely confidential.

KURT. Naturally! You needn't worry on that score, Senator, I assure you.

NOLAN. Thank you, Mr. Kurt. That is all I ask. [*A pause.*]

KURT. Mr. Nolan—do you mind if I ask *you* something?

NOLAN. Certainly not . . .

KURT. You won't consider me impertinent?

NOLAN [*with a smile*]. I don't object to impertinence, Mr. Kurt. I was often considered impertinent myself when I was your age.

KURT. Why are you making me this offer?

NOLAN. I am not making you an offer. I shall merely attempt to expedite . . .

KURT. Why? The first time we met we didn't exactly hit it off, now, did we?

Why then are you going to all this trouble?

NOLAN. I have discussed you with Miss Froude who is an old friend of mine and whose opinion I greatly respect. She thinks very highly of you, Mr. Kurt. My own impression . . .

KURT [*inexorably*]. Why? What, as they say, is the pay-off?

NOLAN. I'll tell you. I'll tell you quite frankly. I don't want Miss Froude's autobiography, which you have persuaded her to write, to appear in your magazine. I want it killed!

KURT. Oh! You want it killed?

NOLAN. Exactly.

KURT. Why?

NOLAN. Marion knows why. We needn't go into that.

KURT [*wounded by a sudden and devastating jealousy*]. Good God! You! You too! [MARION *enters from balcony. She is wearing a dove-colored evening-dress—the gamine transformed into lady-of-the-world.*]

MARION. Well! How have you two boys been getting on? What do you think?

KURT [*seething. Crosses to foot of stairs*]. I'll tell you what I think. . . .

MARION. About the dress I mean . . . [*She does a turn for them.*]

NOLAN [*without looking up at her or the dress. He is watching* KURT]. It's charming.

MARION. Thank you, Bunny. With all his faults Bunny is much more satisfactory than you are, Dickie.

KURT [*at boiling point*]. He's chivalrous he is! His chivalry is so exquisite that he has just been attempting to bribe me to keep your story from being published. His gallantry is so delicate that he's terrified about being mentioned in it.

MARION [*comes down stairs during*

KURT's *speech*]. Don't be so worked up about it, Dickie. You're another one who takes it big. It's catching!

KURT [*flaring at her*]. You're not very sensitive. . . .

MARION. Why should I be? You misapprehend Bunny. If he doesn't want to be in the same story with me that's his business. And it's nothing to do with chivalry or gallantry or nonsense like that.

NOLAN. Marion—this young man . . .

KURT [*taunting him*]. What about Washington, Mr. Nolan? Mr. Nolan, a prospective Senator offers to bribe me with a post in Washington controlled by his prospective father-in-law. . . .

MARION. If it's a good job take it, Dickie, by all means. . . .

KURT. I am afraid, Marion, that your code is more relaxed than mine . . .

MARION. Code, nonsense! I gave up codes long ago. I'm a big laissez-faire girl!

NOLAN. If this young man is an example of the distinguished company you've come to associate with, Marion . . .

MARION. Don't quarrel, children—please. It distresses me.

NOLAN. He's extremely objectionable.

KURT. What about Washington, now, *Senator?* Are you still to expedite . . . ! [KURT and NOLAN *stand glaring at each other.* MARION *tries to calm the troubled waters. Crosses to* NOLAN.]

MARION. Really, Dickie, you're very naughty. Don't mind him, Bunny. He's very young.

KURT. And incorruptible!

NOLAN. Marion, I claim the privilege of a friendship that antedates Mr. Kurt's by some years to beg you, very solemnly, not to prostitute your talents to his contemptible, sensation-mongering rag.

KURT [*faces them*]. There's a Senatorial sentence!

MARION. Hush, Dickie, hush! Bunny darling, it's true that Dickie's magazine isn't the Edinburgh Review. On the other hand your assumption that my story will be vulgar and sensational is a little gratuitous, isn't it?

NOLAN. You *refuse* then?

MARION [*gently but with a serious overtone*]. Yes. This—censorship before publication seems to me, shall we say, unfair. It is—even in an old friend—dictatorial.

NOLAN [*with an air of finality*]. You leave me then no alternative. I am very sorry.

KURT. Don't let him frighten you, Marion, he can't do anything.

NOLAN. I can forgive you anything, Marion, but the fact that you value my wishes below those of this insolent young man.

MARION. But this insolent young man hasn't anything to do with it! Can't you see, Bunny—it's my own wish that is involved.

NOLAN. I have explained to you the special circumstances. If you would consent to delay publication till after election. . . . [*She turns to* KURT *to ask him to make this concession but can't get a word in. She is wedged between both of them.*]

KURT. She has nothing to do with the publication-date. That's my province. Gosh, what a chance for the circulation-manager in Tennessee! [*He rubs his palms together in mock anticipation of profits.*]

NOLAN [*losing his temper at last*]. You are tampering with more than you bargain for Mr.—Mr. . . .

KURT. Kurt.

MARION. With a "K."

NOLAN. There are ways of dealing with a young man like this and you'll soon find out what they are!

KURT. Them's harsh words, Senator!

NOLAN. You wait and see.

MARION. Bunny!

NOLAN. Don't speak to me! I never want to see you again! [*He goes out.*]

MARION [*really distressed*]. This is awful!

KURT [*highly elated*]. It's wonderful!

MARION. But I'm very fond of Bunny. Oh, dear! I'll telephone him tonight . . .

KURT [*grimly*]. Over my dead body!

MARION. Can it be, Dickie, that I control the election of Senators from Tennessee? [*Sits right end of sofa left.*]

KURT [*after a moment*]. How could you ever have loved a stuffed-shirt like that!

MARION. He wasn't a stuffed-shirt. That's the funny part. He was charming. He was a charming boy. Rather thin. Rather reticent. He was much nicer than you as a matter of fact. . . .

KURT. I'm sure he was!

MARION. He was much less violent!

KURT [*sits*]. Hypocritical old buccaneer!

MARION. He used to work hard all day and at night he studied law. We used to walk the country lanes and dream about the future. He was scared—he was wistful. How did he emerge into this successful, ambitious, over-cautious—mediocrity? How do we all emerge into what we are? How did I emerge into what I am? I've dug up some of my old diaries. I was a tremulous young girl. I was eager.. I believe I was naive. Look at me now! Time, Dickie . . . What will you be at forty? A bond-holder and a commuter . . . Oh, Dickie!

KURT [*tensely*]. I'll never be forty!

MARION [*laughing*]. How will you avoid it?

KURT [*same tone*]. I'll use myself up before I'm forty.

MARION. Do you think so? I don't think so. [*Rises.*] I sometimes wake up on certain mornings feeling absolutely—immortal! Indestructible! One is perpetually reborn I think, Dickie. Everyone should write one's life I think—but not for publication. For oneself. A kind of spiritual Spring-cleaning!

KURT. The Ego preening . . . !

MARION [*sitting right arm of sofa left*]. Well, why not? After all, one's ego is all one really has.

KURT. Reminiscence is easy. So is anticipation. It's the *present* that's difficult and most people are too lazy or too indifferent to cope with it.

MARION. It's natural for you to say that —at your age one has no past and no future either because the intimation of the future comes only with the sense of the past . . .

KURT [*with sudden bitterness*]. I see the past as an *evil thing*—to be extirpated.

MARION. How awful! [*Pause.*] Why?

KURT. That's not important.

MARION [*rises*]. You freeze up so whenever I try to find out anything about you. I'm not used to that. Usually people open up to me—I'm a born confidante. But not you. . . . I'm interested too, because in an odd way I've become very fond of you.

KURT. My life's very dull, I assure you. *My* past lacks completely what you would call *glamor*.

MARION. No, Dickie. I don't believe that. I don't believe that's true of anybody's life.

KURT. Well, it's true. Moreover it's true of most people's lives. It's easy for anyone who's lived as you have to make romantic generalizations. It's very pleasant for you to believe them. Well, I shan't disillusion you. [*Turns away from her.*] Why should I? It's not important. [*She is sitting down, smoking a cigarette in a holder, watching him. He becomes conscious that she is studying him.*]

MARION. I had no idea you felt this way about me—you despise me, don't you? [*He doesn't answer.*] Don't you?

KURT. Yes.

MARION. Why?

KURT [*rises; walks away*]. Why did we start this?

MARION. You're annoyed at having even momentarily revealed yourself, aren't you? I'll have your secret, Dickie—I'll pluck out the heart of your mystery.

KURT. Secret! Mystery! More romantic nonsense. I have no secret. Nobody has a secret. There are different kinds of greed, different kinds of ambition—that's all!

MARION. Oh, you simplify too much—really I'm afraid you do. Tell me—why do you disapprove of me? Is it—as Bunny does—on moral grounds?

KURT [*right end of sofa left—angrily*]. You're superficial and casual and irresponsible. You take life, which is a tragic thing, as though it were a trivial bed-room farce. You're a second-rate artist who's acquired a reputation through vamping celebrities to sit for you.

MARION [*quietly, she continues smoking*]. Go on . . .

KURT. As an unglamorous upstart who has been forced to make my way I resent parasitism, that's all!

MARION. Isn't there in biology something about benevolent parasites, Dickie? Many great men, I believe, owe a debt of gratitude to their parasites, as many plants do . . . There are varieties. Again, Dickie, you simplify unduly. It is a defect of the radical and the young.

KURT. To return to the Honorable Nolan . . .

MARION. I return to him with relief . . .

KURT. He may exert pressure on us, you know . . .

MARION. How? I'm very interested. . . .

KURT. Well, for one thing, his future father-in-law might get me fired.

MARION. Could he do that?

KURT. He might. He might easily. [MARION *sits upright and looks at him.*] Some form of bribery. He might go to my chief and offer him a bigger job—anything.

MARION. All on account of my poor little biography,—it seems incredible that anyone would take all this trouble. . . .

KURT. I'd just like to see them try—I'd just like to, that's all . . .

MARION. What would you do?

KURT. Do? I'd make the Honorable Nolan the laughing stock of the country and his athletic father-in-law too. I'd just plaster them, that's what I'd do.

MARION. You sound vindictive.

KURT. Baby, I am vindictive!

MARION. Funny, I'm just amused . . .

KURT. Well, everything's a spectacle to you! [*Turns away from her.*] God, how I hate detachment!

MARION. Your desire to break up Bunny is quite impersonal then.

KURT. Surgical. Just as impersonal as that.

MARION. You're a funny boy, Dickie.

KURT [*turns away from her*]. I'm not funny and I'm not a boy. You've been around with dilettantes so long you don't recognize seriousness when you see it.

MARION. But it's the serious people who are funny, Dickie! Look at Bunny.

KURT [*faces her*]. Yes, look at him! An epitome of the brainless muddle of contemporary life, of all the self-seeking, second-raters who rise to power and wield power. That's why I'm going to do him in. [*The phone rings—for a moment they pay no attention to it.*] It's the most beautiful chance anybody ever had and I'd just like to see them try and stop me. [*Phone keeps ringing.* MARION *answers it.*]

MARION. Yes . . . yes . . . certainly. [*To* KURT—*a bit surprised.*] It's for you . . . [*She hands him hand-receiver.*]

KURT [*takes phone and talks from rear of sofa*]. Yes. Hello . . . sure. Well, what about it? . . . Oh, you want to talk to me about it, do you? . . . I thought you would . . . I'll be around . . . sure . . . so long. [*He hangs up.*] They've begun! [*He is almost gay with the heady scent of battle.*]

MARION. What do you mean?

KURT. That was my chief. He wants to talk to me about your story. Kinnicott's begun to put the screws on him. He's going to ask me to kill it. All right—I'll kill it!

MARION [*faintly*]. I can't believe it. . . .

KURT. Neff's had a call from the father-in-law . . .

MARION. Did he say so?

KURT. No, but you can bet he has!

MARION. I must say this puts my back up . . .

KURT. I'll make a fight for it to keep my job. But if he's stubborn I'll tell him to go to Hell—and go to a publisher with your manuscript. And if I don't get quick action that way I'll publish it myself—I'll put every penny I've saved into it . . .

MARION. But why should you? Why does it mean so much to you?

KURT. Do you think I'd miss a chance like this?—It'll test the calibre of our magazines, of our press, our Senators, our morality . . .

MARION. All on account of my poor little story—how Vicki would have laughed!

KURT [*a spasm of jealousy again*]. Who's Vicki?

MARION [*aware of it*]. An old friend to whom I'm dedicating the biography.

KURT. Yeah! [*Sits beside her, then speaks.*] Where is he now?

MARION. He's dead. [*A pause. She gets up and crosses to center.*] I've always rather despised these contemporary women who publicize their emotions. [*Another moment. She walks up-stage. She is thinking aloud.*] And here I am doing it myself. Too much self-revelation these days. Loud speakers in the confessional. Why should I add to the noise? I think, as far as this story is concerned, I'll call it a day, Dickie.

KURT. What!

MARION. Let's forget all about it, shall we?

KURT. If you let me down now, I'll hate you.

MARION. Will you? Why won't you take me into your confidence then? Why won't you tell me about yourself? What are you after?

KURT [*after a moment of inhibition decides to reveal his secret dream*]. My ambition is to be critic-at-large of things-as-they-are. I want to find out everything there is to know about the intimate structure of things. I want to reduce the whole system to absurdity. I want to laugh the powers that be out of existence in a great winnowing gale of laughter.

MARION. That's an interesting research. Of course it strikes me it's vitiated by one thing—you have a preconceived idea of what you will find. In a research biased like that from the start you are apt to overlook much that is noble and generous and gentle.

KURT [*challenging and bitter*]. Have you found generosity and gentleness and nobility?

MARION. A good deal—yes.

KURT. Well, I haven't!

MARION. I'm sorry for you.

KURT. You needn't be. Reserve your pity for weaklings. I don't need it!

MARION. Are you so strong? [*A pause.* KURT *doesn't answer.*] How old are you, Dickie?

KURT [*turns away*]. What difference does that make?

MARION. Who do you live with?

KURT. I live alone.

MARION. Are you in love with anybody?

KURT. No.

MARION. Where are your parents?

KURT. They're dead.

MARION. Long?

KURT. My mother is. I hardly remember her. Just barely remember her.

MARION. Your father? [*He doesn't answer.*] Do you remember your father?

KURT [*in a strange voice*]. Yes. I remember him all right.

MARION. What did your father do?

KURT. He was a coal miner.

MARION. Oh! Won't you tell me about him? I'd like to know.

KURT. I was a kid of fourteen. There was a strike. One day my father took me out for a walk. Sunny spring morning. We stopped to listen to an organizer. My father was a mild little man with kind of faded, tired blue eyes. We stood on the outskirts of the crowd. My father was holding me by the hand. Suddenly some-body shouted: The militia! There was a shot. Everybody scattered. My father was bewildered—he didn't know which way to turn. A second later he crumpled down beside me. He was bleeding. He was still holding my hand. He died like that. . . . [*A moment. He concludes harshly—coldly —like steel.*] Are there any other glamorous facts of my existence you would like to know?

MARION [*stirred to her heart*]. You poor boy . . . I knew there was something . . . I knew . . . !

KURT [*hard and ironic*]. It's trivial really. People exaggerate the importance of human life. One has to die. [*Turns to her.*] The point is to have fun while you're alive, isn't it? Well, you've managed. I congratulate you!

MARION [*her heart full*]. Dickie darling —why are you so bitter against me? Why against me . . . ?

KURT. Do you want to know that too? Well, it's because . . . [*His voice rises. She suddenly doesn't want him to speak.*]

MARION. Hush dearest—hush—don't say any more—I understand—not any more . . . [*His defenses vanish suddenly. He sinks to his knees beside her, his arms around her.*]

KURT. Marion, my angel!

MARION [*infinitely compassionate, stroking his hair*]. Dickie—Dickie—Dickie . . . Why have you been afraid to love me?

ACT III

[SCENE: *The same.*

TIME: *Late afternoon. Two weeks later. The telephone is ringing as the curtain rises. There is a moment and* MINNIE *enters and crosses to rear of the table rear of the sofa left. She picks up the receiver.*]

MINNIE [*speaking into the phone*]. Hello.—No, Mr. Kurt, she's not yet back. Vot. You're not coming home to dinner?! —But I've made the pfannkuchen you like —Vot?—You're tired of my damn pfannkuchen—[*She shouts angrily.*] Every night I make dinner and you and Marion go out!—I'm *not* yelling—Vot? Vot shall I tell Marion?—Vot— [*Doorbell rings.*] Wait—wait a minute.—Someone's ringing. [*She puts the receiver on the table and goes to the door.* Minnie *shows in* Leander Nolan *who is followed by* Orrin Kinnicott, *who is a big, well-developed Southerner, about fifty-five, with a high-pitched voice. He is a superbly built man with a magnificent chest development. He is aware that he is a fine figure of a man, impeccably dressed in formal afternoon clothes.*]

Nolan [*to* Minnie, *who has preceded him into the room*]. Did Miss Froude say she was expecting us for tea, Minnie?

Minnie. No, Mr. Nolan. She didn't say nothing to me.

Nolan. Not even when she'd be back?

Minnie [*hangs up coats*]. No. She just went out.

Nolan. All right, Minnie. We'll wait.

Minnie. Yes, Mr. Nolan. [*She is about to go out into kitchen when she remembers that* Kurt *is on the telephone. She picks up the receiver and says*] Hello—Mr. Kurt—you dere?—Good-by! [*She then hangs up the receiver and exits left.*]

Kinnicott [*querulously. Sits sofa right*]. Did you tell her four o'clock?

Nolan. Yes. I told her. [Nolan's *manner with his father-in-law-to-be in this scene conveys the beginnings of a secret irritation, an inner rebellion.*]

Kinnicott. Does she know I'm a busy man?

Nolan [*gloomily*]. She's not impressed much by busy men.

Kinnicott. I know these fly-by-night characters. I've dealt with 'em before . . . Bad— [*He sniffs the air of the room*] bad air. [*Rises—tries to open window, fails,*

sits on window seat.] Bet she's under-exercised.

Nolan. On the contrary—she's radiantly healthy!

Kinnicott. Cosmetics, I bet! These fly-by-night characters . . .

Nolan [*very irritated*]. Why do you keep calling her a fly-by-night character? She's nothing of the sort!

Kinnicott [*crosses to* Nolan]. Look here, Leander. . . .

Nolan. Well?

Kinnicott. Have you been entirely frank with me, in this matter?

Nolan. Of course I have. . . .

Kinnicott [*cryptic*]. About the past— yes. But I refer to the present.

Nolan. I don't know what you mean.

Kinnicott. I think you do know what I mean. Sometimes the way you talk I suspect—I suspect, Leander—that you are still in love with this woman.

Nolan. Nonsense! I simply tell you that she's not a fly-by-night character. That doesn't mean I'm in love with her!

Kinnicott. My daughter feels the same thing.

Nolan. Slade! You've discussed this with Slade!

Kinnicott. She's discussed it with me. She's no fool—that girl. She's noticed things lately.

Nolan. What things?

Kinnicott. She says she talks to you and that you're off somewhere else— dreaming. I tried to put her on another scent—but she was positive. She said: "Come on now, dad—don't stall me— come clean!" So I told her!

Nolan. You did!

Kinnicott. Yes.

Nolan. When?

Kinnicott. Yesterday. Told her it happened fifteen years ago, that you were a naive young feller, didn't know anything about women, were just naturally taken in . . .

NOLAN. That's not true though. I was not taken in.

KINNICOTT. There you go again—defending the woman that's endangering your entire career and using up my energies and yours when you ought to be home right now getting together with folks and thinking how to cinch this here election. Not going to be a walk-over, you know. [*Again trying the window.*] How do you open this thing to get some air? [*Sits on window seat.*]

NOLAN. I don't know. What did Slade say when you told her?

KINNICOTT. Nothin'. You know Slade's not the talkin' kind.

NOLAN. Funny she didn't mention it to me last night.

KINNICOTT. Didn't want to worry yer probably . . . all wool and a yard wide that girl is. I warn you, Leander, don't tamper with the most precious and rare thing . . .

NOLAN [*impatient of oratory*]. I know—I know. The point is—what are we going to do?

KINNICOTT. Course I can get that young fellow—what's his name?

NOLAN. Kurt.

KINNICOTT. I can get him fired all right. From what you've told me, Leander, he's got something else up his sleeve. . . .

NOLAN. I'm afraid so.

KINNICOTT. That's what I want to find out from your lady friend. And I've got a pretty sure idea right now what it is.

NOLAN. What do you mean?

KINNICOTT. Money!

NOLAN [*still not understanding*]. Money . . . ?

KINNICOTT. Blackmail!

NOLAN. You're crazy!

KINNICOTT. You don't know much about women, Leander; when you know the sex as well as I do you'll know that every woman has blackmail up her sleeve.

NOLAN. Look here, Orrin . . . !

KINNICOTT [*rises, confronts* NOLAN]. Now, you listen to me for a moment, son . . . This situation's gone about far enough right now. You'd better make up your mind whether you want this blackmailing female or whether you want my daughter . . . and you'd better make it up right quick.

NOLAN [*flaring up*]. I resent your tone, Orrin, and I won't be ordered around as if I were a high-grade servant!

KINNICOTT. Now, son, when you get control of your temper, and cool down a little bit, you'll see that my ordering hasn't been so bad for you. I'll acknowledge you were mighty successful as a lawyer, but in politics you're nothing but a novice.

NOLAN [*resentful*]. Am I! [*Doorbell.*]

KINNICOTT. Just look back a bit, that's all—I've had to push and bolster you to get you where you are.

NOLAN [*desperately*]. I know—I have every reason to be grateful to you—that's the worst of it. [MINNIE *enters and crosses to hall door. Both men turn and watch to see who it is that is calling.*]

MINNIE [*speaking to someone at the door*]. Ja, Fräulein?

SLADE [*off stage*]. Is Miss Froude in?

MINNIE. Nein, Fräulein.

SLADE [*entering*]. Well, I'll just wait. [SLADE KINNICOTT *is a good-looking, dark, high-spirited girl, a rather inspiring and healthy example of the generation growing up on D. H. Lawrence. To her father and* NOLAN *as she crosses down stage between them.*] Hello.

NOLAN. Slade!

KINNICOTT [*severely*]. Daughter! What are you doing here?

SLADE. Came to have my picture painted. What are you?

KINNICOTT. Your coming here at this time is most inopportune, daughter. We are here on business.

SLADE [*mischievously*]. I can imagine!

NOLAN. I'm very glad you came, Slade. I want you to meet the woman whom your father has just been accusing of the most reprehensible crimes!

SLADE. I'm pretty anxious to get a load of her myself. [*Looks about the room taking it in and then sits on the left end of the sofa below the piano.*] Nice lay-out. Gee, I wish I were artistic. What a lucky gal she is! A paint-brush and an easel and she can set up shop anywhere in the world. That's independence for you! Gosh! [*She looks about, admiring and envious.*]

KINNICOTT. Why must you come here to get your picture painted? We have tolerable good artists in Knoxville.

SLADE. Well, if you *must* know I'm very keen to have a heart-to-heart talk with my fiancé's old girl. Natural, isn't it?

KINNICOTT. No, it isn't natural!

NOLAN [*crosses angrily to window and back toward KINNICOTT and sits on stool down right near sofa on which SLADE and her father are sitting*]. This is what you get for telling her, Orrin.

SLADE. If you think I didn't suspect something was up ever since Froude arrived here, you don't know your little bride. Maybe I haven't been watching the clouds gather on that classic brow! Where is my rival? Don't tell me she's holding up two big shots like you two boys.

KINNICOTT. Slade, this is no time . . . please leave us before she comes.

SLADE. Not I! Just my luck when a story is going to come out which has something in it *I* want to read you two killjoys are going to suppress it!

NOLAN. This isn't exactly a joke, you know, Slade. . . .

SLADE. I mean it. . . .

KINNICOTT [*sadly*]. I've spoiled you, Slade—I've been too easy with you. . . .

SLADE. At least I hope you'll buy the *manuscript*. My God, father, I'm curious. Can't you understand that? I want to find out what Leander was like before he became ambitious. I've a right to know! This story might hurt you with the voters in Tennessee, Leander, but it's given me a kick out of you I didn't know was there! How did she make you, Leander—that's what I'd like to know. You've been pretty unapproachable to me but I sort of took it for granted National Figures were like that. Also I'd gotten to the point when I was going to suggest that we break our engagement, but this little incident revives my interest.

NOLAN [*furious*]. Indeed!

SLADE. Yes, indeed. Where is this woman? What is that secret? How to Make National Figures . . . there's a title for you!

KINNICOTT. Slade, you're talking too much! Shut up!

NOLAN [*rises and moves stool toward them a bit*]. No, she isn't at all. . . . [*To SLADE.*] If your interest in me requires the artificial stimulus of an episode that happened twenty years ago . . .

SLADE [*leaning toward him.*] It requires something. . . .

NOLAN [*leaning closer toward her. The three heads are now close together, KINNICOTT's in the center.*] Does it!

SLADE. It does. We were getting so that conversation, when we were alone, was rather difficult. [NOLAN *starts to argue.*]

KINNICOTT [*pushes them apart*]. Children! Children!

NOLAN. We're not children! [*To* SLADE.] If our relationship is so—

SLADE. Tenuous . . . ?

NOLAN. . . . That it requires artificial . . .

SLADE. Respiration . . . ?

NOLAN. If it's as bad as that then I think perhaps we'd both better . . .

SLADE. Call it a day? . . . You'll need me in the Senate, Leander, to fill in the gaps when you get hung up in a speech. Consider carefully what you are discarding. . . .

NOLAN. If that is the case I tell you solemnly we'd better separate now.

SLADE [*mock tragedy*]. Father, Leander is giving your daughter the air. Do something!

KINNICOTT. I don't blame him for being irritated. You should not be here. Please go home.

SLADE [*lights cigarette*]. Don't worry, dad. I'll get him back.

KINNICOTT. This is a bad mess, Leander. And I must tell you frankly that I don't altogether approve of your attitude . . .

NOLAN. And I must tell you frankly that I don't approve of *yours*. . . .

KINNICOTT. Is that so!

NOLAN. I don't like your tone in speaking of a woman with whom at one time I had a relation of the tenderest emotion— for whom I still have a high regard. . . .

KINNICOTT. That's evident anyway!

NOLAN. When you apply to such a woman the terms you used before Slade came in, when you impute to her motives so base, you cast an equal reflection on my judgment and my character. . . .

SLADE. And that, pop, is lèse-majesté.

NOLAN. And it may be perfectly true, Slade, that knowing Miss Froude has spoiled me for the flippant modernisms with which you study. . . .

SLADE. I'm dying to ask her one thing: when you made love to her in the old days did it always sound like a prepared speech on tariff schedules?

KINNICOTT. This is getting us nowhere. . . .

SLADE. Well, dad, what do you expect? Leander and I have broken our engagement since I came into this room. That's progress, isn't it?

KINNICOTT. Your coming here at this time was most unfortunate.

SLADE. Leander doesn't think so. [*Ironically.*] He's free now to pursue the lady for whom he still has a high regard. [*Rises.*] Are we no longer engaged, Leander?

NOLAN. That's not for me to say.

SLADE [*rises and shakes hands with* NOLAN]. Gentleman to the last! And at the very moment—

KINNICOTT [*in despair—speaks as* SLADE *starts to speak*]. Slade, if you would only go home!

SLADE [*crosses left*]. *Just* at the very moment when I was saying to myself: Well, if a brilliant and beautiful woman who has played footie with royalty in the capitols of the world loved him, maybe there's a secret charm in him that I've overlooked—just when I was saying that and preparing to probe and discover, [*Lightly*] he gives me the air. [*Sits on sofa left.*] By God, Orrin, there's life for you. [*Bell rings.*] Ah, that must be my rival! [NOLAN *gets up and fixes his tie expecting* MARION. *But it is* KURT *who comes in. He faces them. He is in a white heat of anger.*]

KURT. Well, gentlemen, I'm not surprised to find you here! [*Drops hat on model-stand and comes down stage left.*]

NOLAN [*about to introduce* KINNICOTT].
How do you do, Mr. Kurt . . . this . . .

KURT. I can guess who it is. I can guess
why you're here. Having failed to intimidate *me* you are here to intimidate Miss
Froude. [SLADE *rises, excited by this tem-
pest.*] Well, I can advise you that you will
fail with her too.

NOLAN. This is his usual style, Orrin.
Don't mind him.

KURT. I have just come from my office
where I have been informed by Mr. Neff—
[SLADE *stands below* KURT—*just behind
him—watching him.*] whom *you* doubtless know, Mr. Kinnicott—that I could decide between publishing Miss Froude's
story or giving up my job. I invited him
to go to Hell. That invitation I now cor-
dially extend to you two gentlemen.

SLADE. Why doesn't somebody introduce
me to this interesting young man? [*She
comes toward him.* KURT *is embarrassed,
but covers it in a gruff manner. He has
actually not been aware of her in the
room.*]

KURT. I'm sorry—I—I didn't know. . . .

SLADE. Why are you sorry? I'm Slade
Kinnicott. [*She gives him her hand. He
takes it, limply.*]

KURT. All right—all right. [*He is dis-
armed and feels, suddenly, rather foolish.*]

SLADE. Leander, why have you kept me
apart from this young man?

KURT. I'm sorry—I . . .

SLADE. Nonsense. What's your name?

KURT. Richard Kurt.

SLADE. Go to it— [*Turns him toward
others.*]

KINNICOTT [*impressively—interposing
between them*]. You're being very foolish,
young man.

KURT [*crosses toward them—to right of
model-stand*]. Possibly.

NOLAN. You can't argue with him. I've
tried it. He's a fanatic.

KURT. But if you ask me I think *you're*
being very foolish.

KINNICOTT [*who wants to find out
what's in* KURT's *mind*]. Are we? How
do you figure that, young man?

SLADE [*parroting—crosses and sits on
model-stand. She is having a wonderful
time*]. Yes, how!

KINNICOTT. Oh, hush your mouth.

KURT. Because I'm going to publish Miss
Froude's book myself. And I promise you
that it'll be the best-advertised first book
that's come out in a long time.

SLADE. Thank God! Will you send me
the advance sheets? I'll make it worth
your while, Mr. Kurt.

KINNICOTT. I can see you are an extremely impulsive young man. Have you
ever inquired, may I ask . . . ?

SLADE [*edges a bit closer to* KURT]. This
is going to be dangerous! Look out, Richard. . . . [NOLAN *sits on stool, disgusted
with* SLADE.]

KINNICOTT [*smoothly*]. Have you inquired into the penalties for libel, Mr.
Kurt?

KURT. Libel! You're going to sue me
for libel, are you!

KINNICOTT [*same voice*]. Yes. You and
Miss Froude both . . . yes . . .

KURT. Well, you just go ahead and try
it, that's all I can tell you. Go ahead and
sue. [*Crosses to above* NOLAN.] It'll put
Mr. Nolan in a charming position before
those *moral* constituents of his, won't it?
[*Includes both* NOLAN *and* KINNICOTT.]
Go ahead and sue, both of you—sue your
heads off . . . ! I promise the two of you
I'll give you the fight of your lives!

SLADE [*delighted*]. Good for you, Richard! [MARION *comes in. She wears a long
red velvet coat, and a little red cap stuck*

on the side of her golden head—she looks a little like Portia. She is at the top of her form.]

MARION [*beaming with hospitality*]. Well! How nice! Minnie!

KURT [*goes up-stage to right of* MARION]. This chivalrous gentleman has just been proposing to sue you for libel—he considers . . .

SLADE [*who rises and stands just below the model-stand*]. I'm Slade Kinnicott.

MARION [*crosses down stage to her and they shake hands over the model-stand*]. How very nice of you to come! [*Turns and faces* KINNICOTT.] Is this Mr. Kinnicott? [*He bows.*] I'm so glad to see you. [*They shake hands.*] I'm so sorry to be late. [*Waves hello to* NOLAN.] Hello, Bunny.

SLADE [*this is too much for her*]. Oh, my God—BUNNY! [*She sits, overcome.*]

MARION [*to* NOLAN]. I'm so sorry . . .

NOLAN [*glaring at* SLADE]. It's all right, Marion!

MARION. Has Minnie given you tea? I'll just . . . Minnie! [MINNIE *enters.*] Tea, Minnie, please. . . . [*To the men.*] Or cocktails—highball . . . ?

KINNICOTT. I never drink alcoholic mixtures.

NOLAN [*asserting his independence*]. I'll have a highball!

KINNICOTT. I must tell you, Leander, that I do not approve—

NOLAN. I'll have *two* whiskies straight!

MARION. Good! Highball for you, Miss Kinnicott?

SLADE. Thanks.

MARION. I'll fix them myself, Minnie. Just bring us some tea, Minnie.

KINNICOTT. Nor do I wish any tea.

KURT [*crosses down left*]. Nor do I.

MARION. Do you mind if I have a cup? Do sit down, Miss Kinnicott. A tiring day. . . . [SLADE *sits on model-stand.* MARION *goes up to rear of piano.*] Minnie, please bring me a cup of tea—

MINNIE. Ja, Fräulein. [*Remembering.*] A telegram for you, Fräulein.

MARION. Oh, thank you, Minnie. Just put it there on the table. [MINNIE *leaves the telegram on the table rear of the sofa left and then exits left.* MARION *removes her coat, crosses to rear of piano and starts to mix the highballs.*] Now then! What is all this nice cheerful talk about a libel suit? That's what they're always having in England, isn't it, on the least provocation? It's when you've circulated a lie about someone—defamed someone—maliciously—isn't it? Bunny! [*She gives* NOLAN *his two drinks. He takes them and returns to his position.* MARION *picks up the other glass and crosses with it to* SLADE.] Now then—whom have I defamed?

KURT. You've defamed the Honorable Mr. Nolan!

MARION [*hands drink to* SLADE]. Have I? Oh, I am tired. . . . [*She sits on sofa.*] Sit by me, won't you, Miss Kinnicott?

SLADE [*sauntering over*]. Thanks. [*She sits by* MARION *on the sofa.*]

MARION. You're very pretty. . . .

SLADE [*more warmly*]. Thanks!

MARION. Bunny, I congratulate you. I've heard so much about you, Miss Kinnicott. And I think it's very gracious of you to come and see me. If Bunny lets me I'd like to paint you—[MINNIE *enters*] and give you the portrait for a wedding-present. [*She rises and crosses to above model-stand to get cup of tea from* MINNIE. MINNIE *exits left.*] Thank you, Minnie.

SLADE. You're very lovely.

MARION. Thank you, my dear.

SLADE. I can't tell you how curious I've been about you—I—

KINNICOTT. This is all very well—but I'm a busy man . . .

MARION [*looks at* KINNICOTT *as she crosses and sits right of* SLADE. *A moment —then* MARION *speaks*]. It seems so strange to see you with all your clothes on. It seems a pity—as an artist I must say it seems a pity—to conceal that wonderful chest-development that I've admired so often in The Body Beautiful.

KINNICOTT. That's neither here nor there.

MARION [*this is almost an aside to* SLADE]. It seems to me that it's decidedly *there*. [MARION *and* SLADE *laugh quietly together*.]

KINNICOTT. Slade, you've upset everything by coming here. . . . [KURT *comes forward. He has been eaten up with irritation because the superb indignation he felt should have been so dissipated by this cascade of small talk. He can stand it no longer*.]

KURT [*crosses to right of model-stand*]. If you understand better what these gentlemen mean to do . . . !

NOLAN [*protests*]. It wasn't my idea!

KURT. You wouldn't be quite so friendly, Marion. . . .

MARION. I couldn't possibly be unfriendly to anyone so frank—and—and gladiatorial—as Mr. Kinnicott.

KURT [*furious at her for not letting him launch into it*]. A libel suit . . . !

MARION. Oh, yes! A libel suit! It sounds so cozy. Sit down, won't you? [KINNICOTT *sits on stool*.] A libel suit. Now then— what shall it be about?

KURT. The Honorable Nolan is going to sue you for libel. . . .

NOLAN. I'll punch your head if you say that again. . . .

KURT. On the assumption that when you say in your story that you and he were lovers you are lying and defaming his character!

MARION. Dear Bunny, you must want to be a Senator very very badly!

NOLAN [*in despair*]. I never said it, I tell you!

MARION. As a matter of fact how could I prove it? Come to think of it, are there any letters? Did you ever write to me, Bunny?

NOLAN. I don't remember.

MARION. I don't think you ever did. You see—we were always—during that dim brief period of your youth—we were always so close—letters were hardly necessary, were they? Did I ever send you any letters, Bunny?

NOLAN. I don't remember, I tell you.

MARION. Neither do I. You might look around in old trunks and places and see if you can find some old letters of an affectionate nature—I'd love to read them— they'd probably make wonderful reading now. Why is it that the things one writes when one's young always sound so foolish afterwards? Has that ever occurred to you, Mr. Kinnicott?

KINNICOTT. I don't admit the fact.

MARION. No?

KINNICOTT. No. I was looking over some old editorials of mine written in the depression of 1907 and they're just as apropos today. I haven't changed my ideas in twenty-five years.

MARION. Haven't you really? How very steadfast. Now if the world were equally changeless, how consistent that would make you. [*To* KURT.] Well, there isn't any documentary evidence.

KURT. It doesn't matter. . . .

KINNICOTT. As I said before, this is getting us nowhere. Don't you think, Miss Froude, that the only way we can settle this is by ourselves? [*She smiles at him.*] I can see you're a sensible woman.

MARION. I am very sensible.

KINNICOTT. And you and I can settle this matter in short order.

KURT. You don't have to talk to him at all if you don't want to.

MARION [*smiling at* KINNICOTT]. But I'd love to. I've always wanted to meet Mr. Kinnicott. There are some questions I want very much to ask him. [*To the others.*] You can all wait in my bedroom. It's fairly tidy, I think.

SLADE [*to* KURT—*rises, crosses to him*]. Why don't you take me for a walk, Richard?

MARION [*as* KURT *hesitates*]. Do that, Dickie. A walk'll do you good.

NOLAN. What'll I do?

MARION [*as if it were another dilemma*]. You wait in my bedroom. [*Aware suddenly of the proprieties.*] No—in Minnie's bedroom. It's just next to the kitchen.

NOLAN [*defiantly*]. I will! [*He exits into bedroom.*]

KURT [*sulky—he doesn't quite like the turn affairs have taken*]. We'll be back in ten minutes.

SLADE [*as they go out*]. You can't tell, Richard. [MARION *draws a deep breath. She assumes at once with* KINNICOTT *the air of two equals, mature people talking freely to each other after they've gotten rid of the children.*]

MARION [*they cross to sofa left*]. Now we can talk! It's funny—I feel we've put the children to bed and can have a quiet talk after a lot of chatter.

KINNICOTT. Same here!

MARION. Please sit down. [*They do.*]

KINNICOTT. I feel sure you and I can come to an understanding.

MARION. I'm sure we can.

KINNICOTT. Now then about this little

matter of the story—You won't mind if I speak very frankly to you . . . ?

MARION. Not at all.

KINNICOTT. You see, Miss Froude . . .

MARION. Oh, call me Marion. Everybody does.

KINNICOTT. Thanks. Call me Orrin.

MARION. All right, I'll try. Not a very usual name. Orrin. Fits you. Strong. Rugged strength.

KINNICOTT. Thank you.

MARION. You're welcome. What were you going to say when I interrupted you? You were going to say something. . . .

KINNICOTT. I was going to say—you're not at all what I expected to meet.

MARION. No? What did you think I'd be like? Tell me—I'd love to know.

KINNICOTT. Well, you're kind of homey —you know—folksey . . .

MARION. Folksey. [*Smiles.*] After all there's no reason I shouldn't be, is there? I'm just a small-town girl from Tennessee. I sometimes wonder at myself—how I ever got so far away. . . .

KINNICOTT [*positively*]. Metabolism!

MARION. I beg your pardon. . . .

KINNICOTT. I always say—take most of the bad men and most of the loose women —and correct their metabolism and you'll correct them.

MARION. Really?

KINNICOTT [*seriously*]. Absolutely. Trouble with our penology experts—so-called —is that they're psychologists—so-called— when they should be physiologists.

MARION. That is very interesting indeed. Have you ever written anything about that?

KINNICOTT. Off and on.

MARION. Any definitive work I mean?

KINNICOTT. I'm considering doing that right now.

MARION. Oh, I do wish you would! It's

extraordinary how little one knows about one's own body, isn't it? I get so impatient of myself sometimes—of my physical limitations. My mind is seething with ideas but I haven't the physical energy to go on working. I tire so quickly—and often for no apparent reason. Why is that, Mr. Kinnicott?

KINNICOTT. Defective— [*She says at same time with him.*]

MARION—KINNICOTT. Metabolism.

KINNICOTT. Tell me—

MARION. What?

KINNICOTT. Do you eat enough roughage?

MARION. I don't know, off-hand.

KINNICOTT [*firmly*]. Well, you should know!

MARION. As I say, Orrin—one is so ignorant of these fundamental things.

KINNICOTT [*definitely aware now of* MARION *as a personal possibility*]. I can see this, Marion—if you'd met me—instead of Leander—when you were a young girl—you'd have been a different woman.

MARION. I'm sure I would. Imagine—with one's metabolism disciplined early in life—how far one could go.

KINNICOTT [*confidentially offering her hope*]. It's not too late!

MARION. Isn't it?

KINNICOTT. Er. . . . [*He drops his voice still lower.*] What are you doing tomorrow evenin'?

MARION. I—I'm free.

KINNICOTT [*same voice*]. Will you have dinner with me?

MARION. I'd be delighted.

KINNICOTT. Fine! Then we can go over this little matter of the story and Leander quietly. Leander isn't strong on tact. . . .

MARION. You know, some men aren't.

KINNICOTT. You and I can make a friendly adjustment.

MARION. What fun! [*They chuckle.*]

KINNICOTT. What time shall we meet? Say seven-thirty?

MARION. Let's say eight . . . do you mind?

KINNICOTT. My apartment?

MARION. If you like.

KINNICOTT. Here's my card with the address. It's a roof apartment. I'm a widower.

MARION. Irresistible combination!

KINNICOTT. By the way—

MARION. What?

KINNICOTT. Don't mention our little date for tomorrow evenin' to Leander.

MARION [*rising*]. No, I agree with you. I don't think that would be wise.

KINNICOTT [*nodding trustingly—rises*]. Fine! At seven-thirty?

MARION. No—no. Eight.

KINNICOTT. Oh, yes . . . eight. [*A moment's pause. He visibly preens before her, buttoning his beautifully fitting frock-coat across his heroic chest.*]

MARION [*approving*]. Wonderful! Wonderful!

KINNICOTT [*going toward bedroom. To her*]. Do you mind if I . . . Leander . . .

MARION. Not at all.

KINNICOTT. It'll take the load off his mind. [*He goes out. She can't believe it. The whole situation is so fantastic. She flings off her little red cap and shaking with laughter collapses on the couch.* MINNIE *comes in to clear up the tea-things.*]

MARION [*as* MINNIE *enters*]. It's too good to be true, Minnie. . . .

MINNIE. Vat is too good to be true?

MARION. I must write some of it down before I forget it . . . [*The bell again.* MARION *gets up to make notes on her script.*] A widower's penthouse— [*With an irritated sigh* MINNIE *goes out to answer bell.* MARION *sits at desk jotting notes very fast.* SLADE *and* KURT *come in.* KURT *is morose.* MARION *gets up to greet them.*] Well, children?

SLADE. That walk was a total loss.

MARION [*laughing*]. What did you expect?

SLADE. Well, a little encouragement—just a soupçon . . .

MARION. Dickie's very serious.

SLADE. How did you come out with dad?

MARION. Wonderful! I'm crazy about him!

SLADE. Bet he got you to renig on the story . . .

MARION. Well, he thinks so. However, we're going to discuss it tomorrow evenin'.

SLADE. Thought he'd date you up—could tell by the way he eyed you. . . .

MARION. He's going to teach me how to live in a state of virtuous metabolism.

SLADE. Oh! Don't you believe it! Dad's an awful old chaser!

MARION [*rather shocked*]. Slade!

SLADE [*amused*]. Are you shocked?

MARION. You make me feel a little old-fashioned. [KURT *is intensely irritated by this conversation.*]

KURT. Where are they?

MARION. They're in there sitting on Minnie's bed. Orrin is probably telling Bunny that everything'll be all right.

SLADE [*sits left of* MARION]. Marion. . . .

MARION. Yes. . . .

SLADE. What is there about Bunny you can't help liking? [*Utterly disgusted,* KURT *goes to sofa down left and sits staring moodily into a gloomily tinted future.*]

MARION. He's a dear—there's something very touching about Bunny—sweet . . .

SLADE. Were you in love with him once?

MARION. Yes.

SLADE. Are you in love with him now?

MARION. No.

SLADE [*in a whisper*]. Are you in love with—someone else?

MARION [*a moment's pause*]. Yes.

SLADE. I thought you were. He's mad about you.—I envy you, Marion.

MARION. Do you? Why?

SLADE. You're independent. You're—yourself. You can do anything you like.

MARION. Yes, I know. But it's possible one can pay too much for independence. I'm adrift. Sometimes—you know what seems to me the most heavenly thing—the only thing—for a woman? Marriage, children—the dear boundaries of routine . . .

SLADE. If you had married Bunny he would've given 'em to you. He's still in love with you, but he doesn't quite know it. Shall I tell him?

MARION [*parrying*]. What are you talking about?

SLADE. I wish we could change places, Marion. You can with me but I can't with you. [KINNICOTT *and* NOLAN *come in from the bedroom.* KINNICOTT *is at his most oleaginous.*]

KINNICOTT [*to* KURT]. Well, young man! Over your little temper?

KURT. No, I'm not over it! What makes you think I'm over it?

KINNICOTT. Well, well, well! As far as I'm concerned there are no hard feelings. I'm going to call up your employer myself when I get home and tell him, that as far as you are concerned, to let by-gones be by-gones. Can't do more than that, can I?

KURT. To what do I owe this generosity?

KINNICOTT. To the fact that in Miss Froude you have a most gracious friend and intercepter. [*He gives* MARION *a gallant, old-South bow.*] Miss Froude—this has been a very great pleasure.

MARION [*rises—with an answering bow*]. Thank you! [SLADE *also rises*.]

KINNICOTT [*giving her his hand*]. Auf wiedersehen.

MARION. Auf wiedersehen. Ich kann es kaum erwarten!

KINNICOTT [*pretending to understand*]. Yes, oh, yes, yes, of course! [*To* SLADE.] Come, Slade. [*He goes to hall-door*.]

SLADE. All right, dad. [*To* NOLAN.] Coming—Bunny?

NOLAN. Well, yes—I'm coming.

SLADE [*to* NOLAN]. You want to stay. Why don't you?

KINNICOTT [*quickly marshaling his little following with a military precision*]. I think Leander had better come with us—

SLADE [*to* MARION]. Good-by, Marion.

MARION [*to* SLADE]. Good-by, Slade. [*They shake hands*.] Come to see me.

SLADE. Thanks, I will.

KINNICOTT [*smiles at* MARION]. Miss Froude! [*Bows to* MARION *who returns his bow*.] Come, daughter. Come, Leander. [*To* KURT.] Good-by, young man. No hard feelings. [KURT *glares at him*. KINNICOTT *again bows to* MARION.] Miss Froude! [MARION *is startled into still a third bow. He calls without looking back*.] Come, Slade! Leander!!

SLADE. Bunny! [*As she exits*.]

NOLAN [*lingers an instant then crosses to* MARION]. I'll be back.

MARION. When?

NOLAN. In a few minutes. All right?

MARION. I'll be in. [*He goes out quickly*. MARION *is in wonderful spirits. She runs to* KURT *and throws her arms around him*.] Oh, Dickie. That Orrin! That Orrin!

KURT. What did you say to him that put him in such good spirits?

MARION. Everything I said put him in good spirits. I can't wait for tomorrow evenin'. I can't wait for that dinner. It'll

probably consist entirely of roughage—just imagine! He's the quaintest man I ever met in my life. He's too good to be true. [*Sits right of* KURT.]

KURT. Well, he may be quaint to you but to me he's a putrescent old hypocrite and I don't see how you can bear to have him come near you, say less go to dinner with him!

MARION [*sobered by his intensity*.] You're so merciless in your judgments, Dickie. You quite frighten me sometimes —you do really.

KURT. And so do you me.

MARION. I do! That's absurd!

KURT. You do. It's like thinking a person fastidious and exacting and finding her suddenly . . .

MARION. Gross—indiscriminating?

KURT [*bluntly*]. Yes!

MARION. You know, Dickie, I adore you and I'm touched by you and I love you but I'd hate to live in a country where you were Dictator. It would be all right while you loved me but when you stopped. . . .

KURT. It wouldn't make any difference if I stopped—I shouldn't be that kind of a Dictator . . .

MARION [*glances at him. Almost sadly*]. I see you've thought of it. . . .

KURT [*inexorably*]. What did you say to Kinnicott?

MARION. Your manner is so—inquisitorial. I haven't been able to get used to it.

KURT [*angry and jealous*]. I heard you tell Nolan to come back too . . . How do you think I feel?

MARION. Dickie!

KURT. When Nolan sat there and told me he had been your lover, I felt like socking him. Even when we're alone together, I can't forget that . . . yet you encourage him, and Kinnicott— My God, Marion, you seem to like these people!

MARION. I certainly like Slade.

KURT. Well, I don't. She's conceited and over-bearing. Thinks she can have anything she likes because she's Orrin Kinnicott's daughter.

MARION. That's where you're wrong. She's a nice girl—and she's unhappy.

KURT [*bitterly*]. Maladjusted, I suppose!

MARION. Dickie, Dickie, Dickie! Studying you, I can see why so many movements against injustice become such absolute—tyrannies.

KURT. That beautiful detachment again. . . . [*He is white with fury. He hates her at this moment.*]

MARION [*with a little laugh*]. You hate me, don't you . . . ?

KURT. Yes! Temporizing with these . . . ! Yes . . . ! I hate you. [*She says nothing, sits there looking at him.*] These people flout you, they insult you in the most flagrant way. God knows I'm not a gentleman, but it horrifies me to think of the insufferable arrogance of their attitude toward you . . . as if the final insult to their pride and their honor could only come from the discovery that this stuffed shirt Nolan had once been your lover! The blot on the immaculate Tennessee scutcheon! Why, it's the God-damnedest insolence I ever heard of. And yet you flirt and curry favor and bandy with them. And you're amused—always amused!

MARION. Yes. I am amused.

KURT. I can't understand such . . . !

MARION. Of course you can't. That's the difference—one of the differences—between 25 and 35!

KURT. If the time ever comes when I'm amused by what I should hate, I hope somebody shoots me. What did you tell Kinnicott?

MARION. Nothing. Simply nothing. I saw no point in having a scene with him

so I inquired into his favorite subject. He gave me health hints. He thinks tomorrow night he will cajole me—through the exercise of his great personal charm—into giving up my plan to publish.

KURT. Well, why didn't you tell him right out that you wouldn't?

MARION. Because I wanted to avoid a scene.

KURT. You can't always avoid scenes. That's the trouble with you—you expect to go through life as if it were a beautifully lit drawing-room with modulated voices making polite chatter. Life isn't a drawing-room . . . !

MARION. I have—once or twice—suspected it.

KURT [*rises*]. What the devil are you afraid of, anyway? I had a scene today in the office and I was prepared for one here —until you let me down—

MARION [*lightly*]. Prepared? I think you were eager. . . .

KURT. What if I was! It's in your behalf, isn't it?

MARION. Is it? But you forget, Dickie. You're a born martyr. I'm not. I think the most uncomfortable thing about martyrs is that they look down on people who aren't. [*Thinks—looks at him.*] As a matter of fact, Dickie, I don't really understand. Why do you insist so on this story? Why is it so important—now wouldn't it be better to give it up?

KURT. Give it up!

MARION. Yes.

KURT. You'd give it up!

MARION. Why not?

KURT [*obeying a sudden manic impulse*]. After all this—after all I've—! Oh, yes, of course! Then you could marry Nolan and live happily forever after. And be amused. Good-by! [*He rushes up center,* grabs his hat from the stand as he passes it, and continues on out the door.]

MARION [*rises and runs after him*]. Dickie!

KURT [*going out the door*]. Good-by!

MARION. Dickie! Dickie! [*The door slams.* MARION *walks back into the room. A pause. She stands still for a moment; she shakes her head. . . . She is very distressed and saddened and a deep unhappiness is gnawing in her heart, an awareness of the vast, uncrossable deserts between the souls of human beings. She makes a little helpless gesture with her hands, murmuring to herself.*] Poor Dickie! Poor boy! [*In its Italian folder the manuscript of her book is lying on the piano before her. She picks it up—she gives the effect of weighing the script in her hand. Slowly, as if in a trance, she walks with the script to the Franklin stove downstage left and sits before it on a little stool. She opens the manuscript and then the isinglass door of the stove. The light from behind it glows on her face. She looks again down on her manuscript, at this morsel of her recorded past. She tears out a page or two and puts them into the fire. A moment and she has put the entire script into the stove and she sits there watching its cremation. The doorbell rings. As* MINNIE *comes in to answer it, she shuts the door of the stove quickly.*]

MARION. It's probably Mr. Nolan. [MINNIE *goes out.* MARION *makes a visible effort to shake herself out of her mood.* NOLAN *comes in followed by* MINNIE *who crosses stage and goes in the bedroom left.* NOLAN *is excited and distrait.*]

NOLAN. Hello, Marion. . . .

MARION. Hello, Bunny dear.

NOLAN [*sparring for time*]. Excuse me for rushing in on you like this . . . I . . .

MARION. I've been expecting you.

NOLAN. That's right! I told you I was coming back, didn't I? . . .

MARION. You did—yes.

NOLAN. I must have known—I must have felt it—what would happen. . . . Marion . . .

MARION. Bunny dear, you're all worked up. Won't you have a highball?

NOLAN. No, thanks. Marion. . . .

MARION. Yes, Bunny . . .

NOLAN. I've done it!

MARION. You've done what?

NOLAN. I've broken with Slade. I've broken with Kinnicott. I've broken with all of them.

MARION. You haven't!

NOLAN. Yes! I have!

MARION. Oh—oh, Bunny!

NOLAN [*sits*]. When Orrin told me what you'd done—that you were going to give up the story. . . .

MARION. But I—

NOLAN. He said he was sure he could get you to do it. It all came over me—your generosity—your wonderful generosity.

MARION [*beyond words*]. Oh, Bunny! [*Sits. She is in a sort of laughing despair. He hardly notices her attitude. He rushes on.*]

NOLAN. I realized in that moment that in all this time—since I'd been seeing you—I'd been hoping you wouldn't give up the story, that you would go through with it, that my career would go to smash. . . .

MARION [*faintly*]. Bunny. . . .

NOLAN. I saw then that all this—which I'd been telling myself I wanted—Slade, a career, Washington, public life—all of it—that I didn't want it, that I was sick at the prospect of it—that I wasn't up to it, that I was scared to death of it. I saw all that—and I told her—I told Slade. . . .

MARION. You did!

NOLAN. Yes.

MARION. What did she say?

NOLAN. She said she knew it. She's clever that girl. She's cleverer than I am. She's cleverer than you are. I'm afraid of her cleverness. I'm uncomfortable with it. Marion, I know I seem stupid and ridiculous to you—just a Babbitt—clumsy—but I love you, Marion. I always have—never anyone else. Let me go with you wherever you go— [*Lest she think it a "proposition."*] I mean—I want to marry you.

MARION. I'm terribly touched by this, Bunny darling, but I can't marry you.

NOLAN. Why not?

MARION. If I married you it would be for the wrong reasons. And it wouldn't be in character really—neither for me—nor for you. Besides that, I think you're wrong about Slade. She's very nice, you know. I like her very much.

NOLAN. I don't understand her. I never will.

MARION. If you did you'd like her. You better have another try. Really, Bunny, I wish you would.

NOLAN. Letting me down easy, aren't you?

MARION. It's Slade's manner that shocks you—her modern—gestures. If you really understood me—as you think you do—I'd really shock you very much, Bunny.

NOLAN. I'll risk it. Marion, my dearest Marion, won't you give me some hope? . . .

MARION [*sees she must tell him*]. Besides —I'm in love.

NOLAN [*stunned*]. Really! With whom?

MARION. Dickie . . . You see, Bunny . . . [*He can't get over this. There is a considerable pause.*] You see, Bunny . . .

NOLAN [*slowly*]. Do you mean that you and he—you don't mean that . . . ?

MARION. Yes, Bunny.

NOLAN [*dazed*]. Are you going to marry him?

MARION. No.

NOLAN [*he passes his hand over his forehead*]. This is a shock to me, Marion.

MARION [*gently*]. I thought it only fair to tell you.

NOLAN [*in a sudden passion*]. You— you. . . . [*He feels like striking her, controls himself with difficulty.*] Anybody else but him . . . !

MARION. You see, Bunny.

NOLAN [*after a moment—rises*]. Sorry! Funny, isn't it? Joke, isn't it?

MARION. I'm terribly fond of you, Bunny. [*Takes his hand.*] I always will be. That kind of tenderness outlasts many things.

NOLAN [*blindly*]. I'll go on, I suppose.

MARION. Of course you will! [NOLAN *crosses to model-stand and gets his hat.* KURT *comes in. There is a silence.* NOLAN *forces himself to look at him.* KURT *does not meet his glance.* KURT *is white and shaken—not in the least truculent.*] Good-by, Bunny dear. Bunny!

NOLAN. Yes, Marion.

MARION. Will you do me a favor?

NOLAN. Yes.

MARION. Will you please tell Mr. Kinnicott for me—that as I've been called out of town suddenly—I can't dine with him tomorrow night. You *will* see him, won't you, and you'll tell him?

NOLAN. Yes. [NOLAN *leaves. A silence again. . . . Suddenly* KURT *goes to her, embraces her with a kind of hopeless intensity.*]

KURT [*in a whisper, like a child*]. Please forgive me. . . .

MARION. Yes.

KURT. These moods come over me—I can't control myself—afterwards I hate myself—it's because I love you so much—I can't bear to . . .

MARION. I know, dear—I know. . . .

KURT. I'm torn up all the time—torn to bits.

MARION. I know, dear . . .

KURT. When this is all blown over—could we—do you think . . .

MARION. What, dear?

KURT. If we could only go away together, the two of us—somewhere away from people, by ourselves?

MARION. Why not, Dickie? We can go now, if you want to. . . .

KURT. Now? But you're crazy. How can we possibly leave now—with the book . . .

MARION. Dickie—I must tell you. . . .

KURT. You must tell me what?

MARION. You must be patient—you must hear me out for once—you must try to understand my point of view. [*She leads him to sofa left and sits beside him.*]

KURT. What do you mean?

MARION. You know, Dickie, I've been very troubled about you. I've been sad. I've been sad.

KURT. I was angry . . . I didn't mean . . . It was just that . . .

MARION. No, you don't understand—it wasn't your anger that troubled me. It was ourselves—the difference between us—not the years alone but the immutable difference in temperament. Your hates frighten me, Dickie. These people—poor Bunny, that ridiculous fellow Kinnicott—to you these rather ineffectual, blundering people symbolize the forces that have hurt you and you hate them. But I don't hate them. I can't hate them. Without feeling it, I can understand your hate but I can't bring myself to foster it. To you, this book has become a crusade. It couldn't be to me. Do you know, Dickie dear—and this has

made me laugh so to myself—that there was nothing in the book about Bunny that would ever have been recognized by anybody. It was an idyllic chapter of first-love—that's all—and there was nothing in it that could remotely have been connected with the Bunny that is now. . . .

KURT. So much the better—! Think of the spectacle they'll make of themselves—destroyed by laughter. . . .

MARION. I don't believe in destructive campaigns, Dickie . . . outside of the shocking vulgarity of it all—I couldn't do it—for the distress it would cause. . . .

KURT. You've decided not to publish then. . . .

MARION. I've destroyed the book, Dickie.

KURT. You've destroyed it!

MARION. Yes. I'm sorry.

KURT. You traitor!

MARION. It seemed the simple thing to do—the inevitable thing.

KURT. What about *me*? You might have consulted me—after what I've . . .

MARION. I'm terribly sorry—but I couldn't possibly have published that book.

KURT [*in a queer voice*]. I see now why everything is this way. . . .

MARION. I couldn't . . . !

KURT. Why the injustice and the cruelty go on—year after year—century after century—without change—because—as they grow older—people become—*tolerant!* Things amuse them. I hate you and I hate your tolerance. I always did.

MARION. I know you do. You hate my essential quality—the thing that is me. That's what I was thinking just now and that's what made me sad.

KURT. Nothing to be said, is there? [*Rises.*] Good-by.

MARION [*rises*]. All right! [KURT *starts to go. She calls after him, pitifully.*] Won't you kiss me good-by?

KURT. All right. [MARION *goes up after him. They kiss each other passionately.*]

MARION [*whispering to him*]. I would try to change you. I know I would. And if I changed you I should destroy what makes me love you. Good-by, my darling. Good-by, my dearest. Go quickly. [KURT *goes up-stage and exits without a word. He is blinded by pain.*] Dickie . . . ! [MARION *is left alone. She is trembling a little. She feels cold. She goes to the stove and sits in front of it, her back to it, try-ing to get warm. She becomes aware that her eyes are full of tears. As* MINNIE *comes in, she brushes them away.*]

MINNIE. Are you worried from any-thing, Marion?

MARION. No, Minnie. I'm all right.

MINNIE. I tink maybe dot telegram bring you bad news.

MARION. Telegram? What telegram?

MINNIE. Dot telegram I bring you.

MARION. Of course—I haven't even—where is it?

MINNIE [*gets telegram from table rear of sofa left and hands it to* MARION]. There it is!

MARION. Thank you, Minnie. [*Opens telegram and reads it.*] This is from heaven! Minnie, I want you to pack right away. We've leaving! [*She springs up.*]

MINNIE. Leaving? Ven?

MARION. Right away. Tonight! This is from Feydie! Listen! [*Reads telegram aloud to* MINNIE.] "Can get you commis-sion to paint prize-winners Motion Pic-ture Academy—wire answer at once. Feydie." [*Hysterically grateful for the mercy of having something to do at once, of being busy, of not having time to think.*] Something always turns up for me! Pack everything, Minnie. I want to get out right away. [*She rushes up-stage right, picks up her hat and coat and then runs to the stairs left.*]

MINNIE. Don't you tink you better vait till tomorrow?

MARION. No, Minnie. Once the tempta-tion to a journey comes into my head I can't bear it till I'm on my way! This time, Minnie, we'll have a real trip. From Hol-lywood we'll go to Honolulu and from Honolulu to China. How would you like that, Minnie? [*She starts up the stairs.*]

MINNIE [*for her, enthusiastic*]. Fine, Marion! [*Calls after her as she runs up-stairs.*] Dot crazy Kurt he goes vit us?

MARION [*as she disappears into her bed-room*]. No, Minnie—no one—we travel alone!

THE END

"THE HAIRY APE"

A Comedy of Ancient and Modern Life in Eight Scenes

by EUGENE O'NEILL

CHARACTERS

ROBERT SMITH, "YANK" SECOND ENGINEER
PADDY A GUARD
LONG A SECRETARY OF AN ORGANIZATION
MILDRED DOUGLAS *Stokers, Ladies, Gentlemen, etc.*
HER AUNT

SCENES

SCENE I: *The firemen's forecastle of an ocean liner
—an hour after sailing from New York.*
SCENE II: *Section of promenade deck, two days out—morning*
SCENE III: *The stokehole. A few minutes later.*
SCENE IV: *Same as Scene I. Half an hour later.*
SCENE V: *Fifth Avenue, New York. Three weeks later.*
SCENE VI: *An island near the city. The next night.*
SCENE VII: *In the city. About a month later.*
SCENE VIII: *In the city. Twilight of the next day.*

SCENE I

[*The firemen's forecastle of a transatlantic liner an hour after sailing from New York for the voyage across. Tiers of narrow, steel bunks, three deep, on all sides. An entrance in rear. Benches on the floor before the bunks. The room is crowded with men, shouting, cursing, laughing, singing—a confused, inchoate uproar swelling into a sort of unity, a meaning—the bewildered, furious, baffled defiance of a beast in a cage. Nearly all the men are drunk. Many bottles are passed from hand to hand. All are dressed in dungaree pants, heavy ugly shoes. Some wear singlets, but the majority are stripped to the waist.*

The treatment of this scene, or of any other scene in the play, should by no means be naturalistic. The effect sought after is a cramped space in the bowels of a ship, imprisoned by white steel. The lines of bunks, the uprights supporting them, cross each other like the steel framework of a cage. The ceiling crushes down upon the men's heads. They cannot stand upright. This accentuates the natural stooping posture which' shoveling coal and the resultant over-development of back and shoulder muscles have given them. The men themselves should resemble those pictures in which the appearance of Neanderthal Man is guessed at. All are

*hairy-chested, with long arms of tremen-
dous power, and low, receding brows
above their small, fierce, resentful eyes. All
the civilized white races are represented,
but except for the slight differentiation in
color of hair, skin, eyes, all these men are
alike.*

The curtain rises on a tumult of sound.
YANK *is seated in the foreground. He
seems broader, fiercer, more truculent,
more powerful, more sure of himself than
the rest. They respect his superior strength
—the grudging respect of fear. Then,
too, he represents to them a self-expression, the very last word in what they are,
their most highly developed individual.]*

VOICES. Gif me trink dere, you!
'Ave a wet!
Salute!
Gesundheit!
Skoal!
Drunk as a lord, God stiffen you!
Here's how!
Luck!
Pass back that bottle, damn you!
Pourin' it down his neck!
Ho, Froggy! Where the devil have you
   been?
La Touraine.
I hit him smash in yaw, py Gott!
Jenkins—the First—he's a rotten swine—
And the coppers nabbed him—and I run—
I like peer better. It don't pig head gif
   you.
A slut, I'm sayin'! She robbed me aslape—
To hell with 'em all!
You're a bloody liar!
Say dot again! [*Commotion. Two men
   about to fight are pulled apart.*]
No scrappin' now!
Tonight—
See who's the best man!
Bloody Dutchman!

Tonight on the for'ard square.
I'll bet on Dutchy.
He packa da wallop, I tella you!
Shut up, Wop!
No fightin', maties. We're all chums, ain't
   we?
[*A voice starts bawling a song.*]

"Beer, beer, glorious beer!
Fill yourselves right up to here."

YANK [*for the first time seeming to take
notice of the uproar about him, turns
around threateningly—in a tone of contemptuous authority*]. Choke off dat noise!
Where d'yuh get dat beer stuff? Beer,
hell! Beer's for goils—and Dutchmen. Me
for somep'n wit a kick to it! Gimme a
drink, one of youse guys. [*Several bottles
are eagerly offered. He takes a tremendous gulp at one of them; then, keeping
the bottle in his hand, glares belligerently
at the owner, who hastens to acquiesce in
this robbery by saying*] All righto, Yank.
Keep it and have another. [YANK *con-
temptuously turns his back on the crowd
again. For a second there is an embar-
rassed silence. Then—*]
VOICES. We must be passing the Hook.
She's beginning to roll to it.
Six days in hell—and then Southampton.
Py Yesus, I vish somepody take my first
   vatch for me!
Gittin' seasick, Square-head?
Drink up and forget it!
What's in your bottle?
Gin.
Dot's nigger trink.
Absinthe? It's doped. You'll go off your
   chump, Froggy!
Cochon!
Whisky, that's the ticket!
Where's Paddy?
Going asleep.

Sing us that whisky song, Paddy. [*They all turn to an old, wizened Irishman who is dozing, very drunk, on the benches forward. His face is extremely monkey-like with all the sad, patient pathos of that animal in his small eyes.*]

Singa da song, Caruso Pat!

He's gettin' old. The drink is too much for him.

He's too drunk.

PADDY [*blinking about him, starts to his feet resentfully, swaying, holding on to the edge of a bunk*]. I'm never too drunk to sing. 'Tis only when I'm dead to the world I'd be wishful to sing at all. [*With a sort of sad contempt.*] "Whisky Johnny," ye want? A chanty, ye want? Now that's a queer wish from the ugly like of you, God help you. But no matther. [*He starts to sing in a thin, nasal, doleful tone.*]

Oh, whisky is the life of man!
　Whisky! O Johnny! [*They all join in on this.*]
Oh, whisky is the life of man!
　Whisky for my Johnny! [*Again chorus.*]

Oh, whisky drove my old man mad!
　Whisky! O Johnny!
Oh, whisky drove my old man mad!
　Whisky for my Johnny!

YANK [*again turning around scornfully*]. Aw hell! Nix on dat old sailing ship stuff! All dat bull's dead, see? And you're dead, too, yuh damned old Harp, on'y yuh don't know it. Take it easy, see. Give us a rest. Nix on de loud noise. [*With a cynical grin*] Can't youse see I'm tryin' to t'ink?

ALL [*repeating the word after him as one with the same cynical amused mock-ery*]. Think! [*The chorused word has a brazen metallic quality as if their throats were phonograph horns. It is followed by a general uproar of hard, barking laughter*].

VOICES. Don't be cracking your head wit ut, Yank.

You gat headache, py yingo!

One thing about it—it rhymes with drink!

Ha, ha, ha!

Drink, don't think!

Drink, don't think!

Drink, don't think!

[*A whole chorus of voices has taken up this refrain, stamping on the floor, pounding on the benches with fists.*]

YANK [*taking a gulp from his bottle—good-naturedly*]. Aw right. Can de noise. I got yuh de foist time. [*The uproar subsides. A very drunken sentimental tenor begins to sing.*]

"Far away in Canada,
　Far across the sea,
There's a lass who fondly waits
　Making a home for me—"

YANK [*fiercely contemptuous*]. Shut up, yuh lousy boob! Where d'yuh get dat tripe? Home? Home, hell! I'll make a home for yuh! I'll knock yuh dead. Home! T'hell wit home! Where d'yuh get dat tripe? Dis is home, see? What d'yuh want wit home? [*Proudly.*] I runned away from mine when I was a kid. On'y too glad to beat it, dat was me. Home was lickings for me, dat's all. But yuh can bet your shoit no one ain't never licked me since! Wanter try it, any of youse? Huh! I guess not. [*In a more placated but still contemptuous tone.*] Goils waitin' for yuh, huh? Aw, hell! Dat's all tripe. Dey don't wait for no one. Dey'd double-cross yuh for a nickel. Dey're all tarts, get me? Treat 'em rough, dat's me. To hell wit 'em. Tarts, dat's what, de whole bunch of 'em.

LONG [*very drunk, jumps on a bench excitedly, gesticulating with a bottle in his hand*]. Listen 'ere, Comrades! Yank 'ere is right. 'E says this 'ere stinkin' ship is our 'ome. And 'e says as 'ome is 'ell. And 'e's right! This is 'ell. We lives in 'ell, Comrades—and right enough we'll die in it. [*Raging.*] And who's ter blame, I arsks yer? We ain't. We wasn't born this rotten way. All men is born free and ekal. That's in the bleedin' Bible, maties. But what d'they care for the Bible—them lazy, bloated swine what travels first cabin? Them's the ones. They dragged us down 'til we're on'y wage slaves in the bowels of a bloody ship, sweatin', burnin' up, eatin' coal dust! Hit's them's ter blame— the damned Capitalist clarss! [*There had been a gradual murmur of contemptuous resentment rising among the men until now he is interrupted by a storm of cat-calls, hisses, boos, hard laughter.*]

VOICES. Turn it off!
Shut up!
Sit down!
Closa da face!
Tamn fool! [*Etc.*]

YANK [*standing up and glaring at* LONG]. Sit down before I knock yuh down! [LONG *makes haste to efface himself.* YANK *goes on contemptuously.*] De Bible, huh? De Cap'tlist class, huh? Aw nix on dat Salvation Army-Socialist bull. Git a soapbox! Hire a hall! Come and be saved, huh? Jerk us to Jesus, huh? Aw g'wan! I've listened to lots of guys like you, see. Yuh're all wrong. Wanter know what I t'ink? Yuh ain't no good for no one. Yuh're de bunk. Yuh ain't got no' noive, get me? Yuh're yellow, dat's what.

Yellow, dat's you. Say! What's dem slobs in de foist cabin got to do wit us? We're better men dan dey are, ain't we? Sure! One of us guys could clean up de whole mob wit one mit. Put one of 'em down here for one watch in de stokehole, what'd happen? Dey'd carry him off on a stretcher. Dem boids don't amount to nothin'. Dey're just baggage. Who makes dis old tub run? Ain't it us guys? Well den, we belong, don't we? We belong and dey don't. Dat's all. [*A loud chorus of approval.* YANK *goes on.*] As for dis bein' hell—aw, nuts! Yuh lost your noive, dat's what. Dis is a man's job, get me? It belongs. It runs dis tub. No stiffs need apply. But yuh're a stiff, see? Yuh're yellow, dat's you.

VOICES [*with a great hard pride in them*].
Righto!
A man's job!
Talk is cheap, Long.
He never could hold up his end.
Divil take him!
Yank's right. We make it go.
Py Gott, Yank say right ting!
We don't need no one cryin' over us.
Makin' speeches.
Throw him out!
Yellow!
Chuck him overboard!
I'll break his jaw for him!
[*They crowd around* LONG *threateningly.*]

YANK [*half good-natured again—contemptuously*]. Aw, take it easy. Leave him alone. He ain't woith a punch. Drink up. Here's how, whoever owns dis. [*He takes a long swallow from his bottle. All drink with him. In a flash all is hilarious amiability again, backslapping, loud talk, etc.*]

PADDY [*who has been sitting in a blinking, melancholy daze—suddenly cries out in a voice full of old sorrow*]. We belong to this, you're saying? We make the ship to go, you're saying? Yerra then, that Almighty God have pity on us! [*His voice runs into the wail of a keen, he rocks back and forth on his bench. The men stare at him, startled and impressed in spite of themselves.*] Oh, to be back in the fine days of my youth, ochone! Oh, there was fine beautiful ships them days—clippers wid tall masts touching the sky—fine strong men in them—men that was sons of the sea as if 'twas the mother that bore them. Oh, the clean skins of them, and the clear eyes, the straight backs and full chests of them! Brave men they was, and bold men surely! We'd be sailing out, bound down round the Horn maybe. We'd be making sail in the dawn, with a fair breeze, singing a chanty song wid no care to it. And astern the land would be sinking low and dying out, but we'd give it no heed but a laugh, and never a look behind. For the day that was, was enough, for we was free men—and I'm thinking 'tis only slaves do be giving heed to the day that's gone or the day to come—until they're old like me. [*With a sort of religious exaltation.*] Oh, to be scudding south again wid the power of the Trade Wind driving her on steady through the nights and the days! Full sail on her! Nights and days! Nights when the foam of the wake would be flaming wid fire, when the sky'd be blazing and winking wid stars. Or the full of the moon maybe. Then you'd see her driving through the gray night, her sails stretching aloft all silver and white, not a sound on the deck, the lot of us dreaming dreams, till you'd believe 'twas no real ship at all you was on but a ghost ship like the *Flying Dutchman* they say does be roaming the seas forevermore widout touching a port. And there was the days, too. A warm sun on the clean decks.

Sun warming the blood of you, and wind over the miles of shiny green ocean like strong drink to your lungs. Work—aye, hard work—but who'd mind that at all? Sure, you worked under the sky and 'twas work wid skill and daring to it. And wid the day done, in the dog watch, smoking me pipe at ease, the lookout would be raising land maybe, and we'd see the mountains of South Americy wid the red fire of the setting sun painting their white tops and the clouds floating by them! [*His tone of exaltation ceases. He goes on mournfully.*] Yerra, what's the use of talking? 'Tis a dead man's whisper. [*To* YANK *resentfully.*] 'Twas them days men belonged to ships, not now. 'Twas them days a ship was part of the sea, and a man was part of a ship, and the sea joined all together and made it one. [*Scornfully.*] Is it one wid this you'd be, Yank—black smoke from the funnels smudging the sea, smudging the decks—the bloody engines pounding and throbbing and shaking— wid divil a sight of sun or a breath of clean air—choking our lungs wid coal dust—breaking our backs and hearts in the hell of the stokehole—feeding the bloody furnace—feeding our lives along wid the coal, I'm thinking—caged in by steel from a sight of the sky like bloody apes in the Zoo! [*With a harsh laugh.*] Ho-ho, divil mend you! Is it to belong to that you're wishing? Is it a flesh and blood wheel of the engines you'd be?

YANK [*who has been listening with a contemptuous sneer, barks out the answer*]. Sure ting! Dat's me. What about it?

PADDY [*as if to himself—with great sorrow*]. Me time is past due. That a great wave wid sun in the heart of it may sweep me over the side sometime I'd be dreaming of the days that's gone!

[511]

YANK. Aw, yuh crazy Mick! [*He springs to his feet and advances on* PADDY *threateningly—then stops, fighting some queer struggle within himself—lets his hands fall to his sides—contemptuously.*] Aw, take it easy. Yuh're aw right, at dat. Yuh're bugs, dat's all—nutty as a cuckoo. All dat tripe yuh been pullin'— Aw, dat's all right. On'y it's dead, get me? Yuh don't belong no more, see. Yuh don't get de stuff. Yuh're too old. [*Disgustedly.*] But aw say, come up for air onct in a while, can't yuh? See what's happened since yuh croaked. [*He suddenly bursts forth vehemently, growing more and more excited.*] Say! Sure! Sure I meant it! What de hell— Say, lemme talk! Hey! Hey, you old Harp! Hey, youse guys! Say, listen to me—wait a moment—I gotter talk, see. I belong and he don't. He's dead but I'm livin'. Listen to me! Sure I'm part of de engines! Why de hell not! Dey move, don't dey? Dey're speed, ain't dey? Dey smash trou, don't dey? Twenty-five knots a hour! Dat's goin' some! Dat's new stuff! Dat belongs! But him, he's too old. He gets dizzy. Say, listen. All dat crazy tripe about nights and days; all dat crazy tripe about stars and moons; all dat crazy tripe about suns and winds, fresh air and de rest of it— Aw hell, dat's all a dope dream! Hittin' de pipe of de past, dat's what he's doin'. He's old and don't belong no more. But me, I'm young! I'm in de pink! I move wit it! It, get me! I mean de ting dat's de guts of all dis. It ploughs trou all de tripe he's been sayin'. It blows dat up! It knocks dat dead! It slams dat offen de face of de oith! It, get me! De engines and de coal and de smoke and all de rest of it! He can't breathe and swallow coal dust, but I kin, see? Dat's fresh air for me! Dat's food for me! I'm new, get me? Hell in de stoke-hole? Sure! It takes a man to work in hell. Hell, sure, dat's my fav'rite climate. I eat it up! I git fat on it! It's me makes it hot! It's me makes it roar! It's me makes it move! Sure, on'y for me everyting stops. It all goes dead, get me? De noise and smoke and all de engines movin' de woild, dey stop. Dere ain't nothin' no more! Dat's what I'm sayin'. Everyting else dat makes de woild move, somep'n makes it move. It can't move witout somep'n else, see? Den yuh get down to me. I'm at de bottom, get me! Dere ain't nothin' foither. I'm de end! I'm de start! I start somep'n and de woild moves! It—dat's me!—de new dat's moiderin' de old! I'm de ting in coal dat makes it boin; I'm steam and oil for de engines; I'm de ting in noise dat makes yuh hear it; I'm smoke and express trains and steamers and factory whistles; I'm de ting in gold dat makes it money! And I'm what makes iron into steel! Steel, dat stands for de whole ting! And I'm steel—steel—steel! I'm de muscles in steel, de punch behind it! [*As he says this he pounds with his fist against the steel bunks. All the men, roused to a pitch of frenzied self-glorification by his speech, do likewise. There is a deafening metallic roar, through which* YANK's *voice can be heard bellowing.*] Slaves, hell! We run de whole woiks. All de rich guys dat tink dey're somep'n, dey ain't nothin'! Dey don't belong. But us guys, we're in de move, we're at de bottom, de whole ting is us! [PADDY *from the start of* YANK's *speech has been taking one gulp after another from his bottle, at first frightenedly, as if he were afraid to listen, then desperately, as if to drown his senses, but finally has achieved complete indifferent, even amused, drunkenness.* YANK *sees his lips moving. He quells the uproar with a shout.*] Hey, youse guys, take it easy!

Wait a moment! De nutty Harp is sayin' somep'n.

PADDY [*is heard now—throws his head back with a mocking burst of laughter*]. Ho-ho-ho-ho-ho—

YANK [*drawing back his fist, with a snarl*]. Aw! Look out who yuh're givin' the bark!

PADDY [*begins to sing the "Miller of Dee" with enormous good nature*].

> "I care for nobody, no, not I,
> And nobody cares for me."

YANK [*good-natured himself in a flash, interrupts* PADDY *with a slap on the bare back like a report*]. Dat's de stuff! Now yuh're gettin' wise to somep'n. Care for nobody, dat's de dope! To hell wit 'em all! And nix on nobody else carin'. I kin care for myself, get me! [*Eight bells sound, muffled, vibrating through the steel walls as if some enormous brazen gong were imbedded in the heart of the ship. All the men jump up mechanically, file through the door silently close upon each* other's heels in what is very like a prisoners' lockstep. YANK *slaps* PADDY *on the back.*] Our watch, yuh old Harp! [*Mockingly.*] Come on down in hell. Eat up de coal dust. Drink in de heat. It's it, see! Act like yuh liked it, yuh better—or croak yuhself.

PADDY [*with jovial defiance*]. To the divil wid it! I'll not report this watch. Let them log me and be damned. I'm no slave the like of you. I'll be sittin' here at me ease, and drinking, and thinking, and dreaming dreams.

YANK [*contemptuously*]. Tinkin' and dreamin', what'll that get yuh? What's tinkin' got to do with it? We move, don't we? Speed, ain't it? Fog, dat's all you stand for. But we drive trou dat, don't we? We split dat up and smash trou—twenty-five knots a hour! [*Turns his back on* PADDY *scornfully.*] Aw, yuh make me sick! Yuh don't belong! [*He strides out the door in rear.* PADDY *hums to himself, blinking drowsily.*]

CURTAIN

SCENE II

[*Two days out. A section of the promenade deck.* MILDRED DOUGLAS *and her aunt are discovered reclining in deck chairs. The former is a girl of twenty, slender, delicate, with a pale, pretty face marred by a self-conscious expression of disdainful superiority. She looks fretful, nervous and discontented, bored by her own anemia. Her aunt is a pompous and proud—and fat—old lady. She is a type even to the point of a double chin and lorgnettes. She is dressed pretentiously, as if afraid her face alone would never indicate her position in life.* MILDRED *is dressed all in white.*

The impression to be conveyed by this scene is one of the beautiful, vivid life of the sea all about—sunshine on the deck in a great flood, the fresh sea wind blowing across it. In the midst of this, these two incongruous, artificial figures, inert and disharmonious, the elder like a gray lump of dough touched up with rouge, the younger looking as if the vitality of her stock had been sapped before she was conceived, so that she is the expression not of its life energy but merely of the artificialities that energy had won for itself in the spending.]

[513]

MILDRED [*looking up with affected dreaminess*]. How the black smoke swirls back against the sky! Is it not beautiful?

AUNT [*without looking up*]. I dislike smoke of any kind.

MILDRED. My great-grandmother smoked a pipe—a clay pipe.

AUNT [*ruffling*]. Vulgar!

MILDRED. She was too distant a relative to be vulgar. Time mellows pipes.

AUNT [*pretending boredom but irritated*]. Did the sociology you took up at college teach you that—to play the ghoul on every possible occasion, excavating old bones? Why not let your great-grandmother rest in her grave?

MILDRED [*dreamily*]. With her pipe beside her—puffing in Paradise.

AUNT [*with spite*]. Yes, you are a natural born ghoul. You are even getting to look like one, my dear.

MILDRED [*in a passionless tone*]. I detest you, Aunt. [*Looking at her critically.*] Do you know what you remind me of? Of a cold pork pudding against a background of linoleum tablecloth in the kitchen of a—but the possibilities are wearisome. [*She closes her eyes.*]

AUNT [*with a bitter laugh*]. Merci for your candor. But since I am and must be your chaperon—in appearance, at least— let us patch up some sort of armed truce. For my part you are quite free to indulge any pose of eccentricity that beguiles you —as long as you observe the amenities—

MILDRED [*drawling*]. The inanities?

AUNT [*going on as if she hadn't heard*]. After exhausting the morbid thrills of social service work on New York's East Side—how they must have hated you, by the way, the poor that you made so much poorer in their own eyes!—you are now bent on making your slumming international. Well, I hope Whitechapel will pro-

vide the needed nerve tonic. Do not ask me to chaperon you there, however. I told your father I would not. I loathe deformity. We will hire an army of detectives and you may investigate everything—they allow you to see.

MILDRED [*protesting with a trace of genuine earnestness*]. Please do not mock at my attempts to discover how the other half lives. Give me credit for some sort of groping sincerity in that at least. I would like to help them. I would like to be some use in the world. Is it my fault I don't know how? I would like to be sincere, to touch life somewhere. [*With weary bitterness.*] But I'm afraid I have neither the vitality nor integrity. All that was burnt out in our stock before I was born. Grandfather's blast furnaces, flaming to the sky, melting steel, making millions—then father keeping those home fires burning, making more millions—and little me at the tail-end of it all. I'm a waste product in the Bessemer process— like the millions. Or rather, I inherit the acquired trait of the by-product, wealth, but none of the energy, none of the strength of the steel that made it. I am sired by gold and damned by it, as they say at the race track—damned in more ways than one. [*She laughs mirthlessly.*]

AUNT [*unimpressed — superciliously*]. You seem to be going in for sincerity today. It isn't becoming to you, really—except as an obvious pose. Be as artificial as you are, I advise. There's a sort of sincerity in that, you know. And, after all, you must confess you like that better.

MILDRED [*again affected and bored*]. Yes, I suppose I do. Pardon me for my outburst. When a leopard complains of its spots, it must sound rather grotesque. [*In a mocking tone.*] Purr, little leopard. Purr, scratch, tear, kill, gorge yourself and be happy—only stay in the jungle where your spots are camouflage. In a cage they make you conspicuous.

AUNT. I don't know what you are talking about.

MILDRED. It would be rude to talk about anything to you. Let's just talk. [*She looks at her wrist watch.*] Well, thank goodness, it's about time for them to come for me. That ought to give me a new thrill, Aunt.

AUNT [*affectedly troubled*]. You don't mean to say you're really going? The dirt —the heat must be frightful—

MILDRED. Grandfather started as a puddler. I should have inherited an immunity to heat that would make a salamander shiver. It will be fun to put it to the test.

AUNT. But don't you have to have the captain's—or someone's—permission to visit the stokehole?

MILDRED [*with a triumphant smile*]. I have it—both his and the chief engineer's. Oh, they didn't want to at first, in spite of my social service credentials. They didn't seem a bit anxious that I should investigate how the other half lives and works on a ship. So I had to tell them that my father, the president of Nazareth Steel, chairman of the board of directors of this line, had told me it would be all right.

AUNT. He didn't.

MILDRED. How naïve age makes one! But I said he did, Aunt. I even said he had given me a letter to them—which I had lost. And they were afraid to take the chance that I might be lying. [*Excitedly.*] So it's ho! for the stokehole. The second engineer is to escort me. [*Looking at her watch again.*] It's time. And here he comes, I think. [*The SECOND ENGINEER enters. He is a husky, fine-looking man of thirty-five or so. He stops before the two and tips his cap, visibly embarrassed and ill-at-ease.*]

SECOND ENGINEER. Miss Douglas?

MILDRED. Yes. [*Throwing off her rugs and getting to her feet.*] Are we all ready to start?

SECOND ENGINEER. In just a second, ma'am. I'm waiting for the Fourth. He's coming along.

MILDRED [*with a scornful smile*]. You don't care to shoulder this responsibility alone, is that it?

SECOND ENGINEER [*forcing a smile*]. Two are better than one. [*Disturbed by her eyes, glances out to sea—blurts out.*] A fine day we're having.

MILDRED. Is it?

SECOND ENGINEER. A nice warm breeze—

MILDRED. It feels cold to me.

SECOND ENGINEER. But it's hot enough in the sun—

MILDRED. Not hot enough for me. I don't like Nature. I was never athletic.

SECOND ENGINEER [*forcing a smile*]. Well, you'll find it hot enough where you're going.

MILDRED. Do you mean hell?

SECOND ENGINEER [*flabbergasted, decides to laugh*]. Ho-ho! No, I mean the stokehole.

MILDRED. My grandfather was a puddler. He played with boiling steel.

SECOND ENGINEER [*all at sea—uneasily*]. Is that so? Hum, you'll excuse me, ma'am, but are you intending to wear that dress?

MILDRED. Why not?

SECOND ENGINEER. You'll likely rub against oil and dirt. It can't be helped.

MILDRED. It doesn't matter. I have lots of white dresses.

SECOND ENGINEER. I have an old coat you might throw over—

MILDRED. I have fifty dresses like this. I will throw this one into the sea when I come back. That ought to wash it clean, don't you think?

SECOND ENGINEER [*doggedly*]. There's ladders to climb down that are none too clean—and dark alleyways—

MILDRED. I will wear this very dress and none other.

SECOND ENGINEER. No offense meant. It's none of my business. I was only warning you—

MILDRED. Warning? That sounds thrilling.

SECOND ENGINEER [*looking down the deck—with a sigh of relief*]. There's the Fourth now. He's waiting for us. If you'll come—

MILDRED. Go on. I'll follow you. [*He goes.* MILDRED *turns a mocking smile on her aunt.*] An oaf—but a handsome, virile oaf.

AUNT [*scornfully*]. Poser!

MILDRED. Take care. He said there were dark alleyways—

AUNT [*in the same tone*]. Poser!

MILDRED [*biting her lips angrily*]. You are right. But would that my millions were not so anemically chaste!

AUNT. Yes, for a fresh pose I have no doubt you would drag the name of Douglas in the gutter!

MILDRED. From which it sprang. Good-by, Aunt. Don't pray too hard that I may fall into the fiery furnace.

AUNT. Poser!

MILDRED [*viciously*]. Old hag. [*She slaps her aunt insultingly across the face and walks off, laughingly gaily.*]

AUNT [*screams after her*]. I said poser!

CURTAIN

SCENE III

[*The stokehole. In the rear, the dimly-outlined bulks of the furnaces and boilers. High overhead one hanging electric bulb sheds just enough light through the murky air laden with coal dust to pile up masses of shadows everywhere. A line of men, stripped to the waist, is before the furnace doors. They bend over, looking neither to right nor left, handling their shovels as if they were part of their bodies, with a strange, awkward, swinging rhythm. They use the shovels to throw open the furnace doors. Then from these fiery round holes in the black a flood of terrific light and heat pours full upon the men who are outlined in silhouette in the crouching, inhuman attitudes of chained gorillas. The men shovel with a rhythmic motion, swinging as on a pivot from the coal which lies in heaps on the floor behind to hurl it into the flaming mouths before them. There is a tumult of noise— the brazen clang of the furnace doors as they are flung open or slammed shut, the grating, teeth-gritting grind of steel against steel, of crunching coal. This clash of sounds stuns one's ears with its rending dissonance. But there is order in it, rhythm, a mechanical regulated recurrence, a tempo. And rising above all, making the air hum with the quiver of liberated energy, the roar of leaping flames in the furnaces, the monotonous throbbing beat of the engines.*

As the curtain rises, the furnace doors are shut. The men are taking a breathing spell. One or two are arranging the coal behind them, pulling it into more accessible heaps. The others can be dimly made out leaning on their shovels in relaxed attitudes of exhaustion.]

PADDY [*from somewhere in the line— plaintively*]. Yerra, will this divil's own watch nivir end? Me back is broke. I'm destroyed entirely.

YANK [*from the center of the line—with exuberant scorn*]. Aw, yuh make me sick! Lie down and croak, why don't yuh? Always beefin', dat's you! Say, dis is a cinch! Dis was made for me! It's my meat, get me! [*A whistle is blown—a thin, shrill note from somewhere overhead in the darkness. YANK curses without resentment.*] Dere's de damn engineer crackin' de whip. He tinks we're loafin'.

PADDY [*vindictively*]. God stiffen him!

YANK [*in an exultant tone of command*]. Come on, youse guys! Git into de game! She's gittin' hungry! Pile some grub in her. Trow it into her belly! Come on now, all of youse! Open her up! [*At this last all the men, who have followed his movements of getting into position, throw open their furnace doors with a deafening clang. The fiery light floods over their shoulders as they bend round for the coal. Rivulets of sooty sweat have traced maps on their backs. The enlarged muscles form bunches of high light and shadow.*]

YANK [*chanting a count as he shovels without seeming effort*]. One—two—tree— [*His voice rising exultantly in the joy of battle.*] Dat's de stuff! Let her have it! All togedder now! Sling it into her! Let her ride! Shoot de piece now! Call de toin on her! Drive her into it! Feel her move! Watch her smoke! Speed, dat's her middle name! Give her coal, youse guys! Coal, dat's her booze! Drink it up, baby! Let's see yuh sprint! Dig in and gain a lap! Dere she go-o-es. [*This last in the chanting formula of the gallery gods at the six-day bike race. He slams his furnace door shut. The others do likewise with as much unison as their wearied bodies will permit. The effect is of one fiery eye after another being blotted out with a series of accompanying bangs.*]

PADDY [*groaning*]. Me back is broke. I'm bate out—bate— [*There is a pause. Then the inexorable whistle sounds again from the dim regions above the electric light. There is a growl of cursing rage from all sides.*]

YANK [*shaking his fist upward—contemptuously*]. Take it easy dere, you! Who d'yuh tink's runnin' dis game, me or you? When I git ready, we move. Not before! When I git ready, get me!

VOICES [*approvingly*].
That's the stuff!
Yank tal him, py golly!
Yank ain't affeerd.
Goot poy, Yank!
Give him hell!
Tell 'im 'e's a bloody swine!
Bloody slave-driver!

YANK [*contemptuously*]. He ain't got no noive. He's yellow, get me? All de engineers is yellow. Dey got streaks a mile wide. Aw, to hell wit him! Let's move, youse guys. We had a rest. Come on, she needs it! Give her pep! It ain't for him. Him and his whistle, dey don't belong. But we belong, see! We gotter feed de baby! Come on! [*He turns and flings his furnace door open. They all follow his lead. At this instant the SECOND and FOURTH ENGINEERS enter from the darkness on the left with MILDRED between them. She starts, turns paler, her pose is crumbling, she shivers with fright in spite of the blazing heat, but forces herself to leave the ENGINEERS and take a few steps nearer the men. She is right behind YANK. All this happens quickly while the men have their backs turned.*]

YANK. Come on, youse guys! [*He is turning to get coal when the whistle sounds again in a peremptory, irritating note. This drives YANK into a sudden fury. While the other men have turned full*] *around and stopped dumfounded by the spectacle of* MILDRED *standing there in her white dress,* YANK *does not turn far enough to see her. Besides, his head is thrown back, he blinks upward through the murk trying to find the owner of the whistle, he brandishes his shovel murderously over his head in one hand, pounding on his chest, gorilla-like, with the other, shouting.*] Toin off dat whistle! Come down outa dere, yuh yellow, brass-buttoned, Belfast bum, yuh! Come down and I'll knock yer brains out! Yuh lousy, stinkin', yellow mut of a Catholic-moiderin' bastard! Come down and I'll moider yuh! Pullin' dat whistle on me, huh? I'll show yuh! I'll crash yer skull in! I'll drive yer teet' down yer troat! I'll slam yer nose trou de back of yer head! I'll cut yer guts out for a nickel, yuh lousy boob, yuh dirty, crummy, muck-eatin' son of a— [*Suddenly he becomes conscious of all the other men staring at something directly behind his back. He whirls defensively with a snarling, murderous growl, crouching to spring, his lips drawn back over his teeth, his small eyes gleaming ferociously. He sees* MILDRED, *like a white apparition in the full light from the open furnace doors. He glares into her eyes, turned to stone. As for her,*

during his speech she has listened, paralyzed with horror, terror, her whole personality crushed, beaten in, collapsed, by the terrific impact of this unknown, abysmal brutality, naked and shameless. As she looks at his gorilla face, as his eyes bore into hers, she utters a low, choking cry and shrinks away from him, putting both hands up before her eyes to shut out the sight of his face, to protect her own. This startles YANK *to a reaction. His mouth falls open, his eyes grow bewildered.*]

MILDRED [*about to faint—to the* ENGINEERS, *who now have her one by each arm—whimperingly*]. Take me away! Oh, the filthy beast! [*She faints. They carry her quickly back, disappearing in the darkness at the left, rear. An iron door clangs shut. Rage and bewildered fury rush back on* YANK. *He feels himself insulted in some unknown fashion in the very heart of his pride. He roars*]: God damn yuh! [*And hurls his shovel after them at the door which has just closed. It hits the steel bulkhead with a clang and falls clattering on the steel floor. From overhead the whistle sounds again in a long, angry, insistent command.*]

CURTAIN

SCENE IV

[*The firemen's forecastle.* YANK'S *watch has just come off duty and had dinner. Their faces and bodies shine from a soap and water scrubbing but around their eyes, where a hasty dousing does not touch, the coal dust sticks like black make-up, giving them a queer, sinister expression.* YANK *has not washed either face or body. He stands out in contrast to them, a blackened, brooding figure. He is seated for-*

ward on a bench in the exact attitude of Rodin's "The Thinker." The others, most of them smoking pipes, are staring at YANK *half-apprehensively, as if fearing an outburst; half-amusedly, as if they saw a joke somewhere that tickled them.*]

VOICES. He ain't ate nothin'.
Py golly, a fallar gat to gat grub in him.
Divil a lie.

Yank feeda da fire, no feeda da face.
Ha-ha.
He ain't even washed hisself.
He's forgot.
Hey, Yank, you forgot to wash.

YANK [*sullenly*]. Forgot nothin'! To hell wit washin'.

VOICES. It'll stick to you.
It'll get under your skin.
Give yer the bleedin' itch, that's wot.
It makes spots on you—like a leopard.
Like a piebald nigger, you mean.
Better wash up, Yank.
You sleep better.
Wash up, Yank.
Wash up! Wash up!

YANK [*resentfully*]. Aw say, youse guys. Lemme alone. Can't youse see I'm tryin' to tink?

ALL [*repeating the word after him as one with cynical mockery*]. Think! [*The word has a brazen, metallic quality as if their throats were phonograph horns. It is followed by a chorus of hard, barking laughter.*]

YANK [*springing to his feet and glaring at them belligerently*]. Yes, tink! Tink, dat's what I said! What about it? [*They are silent, puzzled by his sudden resentment at what used to be one of his jokes. YANK sits down again in the same attitude of "The Thinker".*]

VOICES. Leave him alone.
He's got a grouch on.
Why wouldn't he?

PADDY [*with a wink at the others*]. Sure I know what's the matther. 'Tis aisy to see. He's fallen in love, I'm telling you.

ALL [*repeating the word after him as one with cynical mockery*]. Love! [*The word has a brazen, metallic quality as if their throats were phonograph horns. It is followed by a chorus of hard, barking laughter.*]

YANK [*with a contemptuous snort*]. Love, hell! Hate, dat's what. I've fallen in hate, get me?

PADDY [*philosophically*]. 'Twould take a wise man to tell one from the other. [*With a bitter, ironical scorn, increasing as he goes on.*] But I'm telling you it's love that's in it. Sure what else but love for us poor bastes in the stokehole would be bringing a fine lady, dressed like a white quane, down a mile of ladders and steps to be havin' a look at us? [*A growl of anger goes up from all sides.*]

LONG [*jumping on a bench—hecticly*]. Hinsultin' us! Hinsultin' us, the bloody cow! And them bloody engineers! What right 'as they got to be exhibitin' us 's if we was bleedin' monkeys in a menagerie? Did we sign for hinsults to our dignity as 'onest workers? Is that in the ship's articles? You kin bloody well bet it ain't! But I knows why they done it. I arsked a deck steward 'o she was and 'e told me. 'Er old man's a bleedin' millionaire, a bloody Capitalist! 'E's got enuf bloody gold to sink this bleedin' ship! 'E makes arf the bloody steel in the world! 'E owns this bloody boat! And you and me, Comrades, we're 'is slaves! And the skipper and mates and engineers, they're 'is slaves! And she's 'is bloody daughter and we're all 'er slaves, too! And she gives 'er orders as 'ow she wants to see the bloody animals below decks and down they takes 'er! [*There is a roar of rage from all sides.*]

YANK [*blinking at him bewilderedly*]. Say! Wait a moment! Is all dat straight goods?

LONG. Straight as string! The bleedin' steward as waits on 'em, 'e told me about 'er. And what're we goin' ter do, I arsks yer? 'Ave we got ter swaller 'er hinsults like dogs? It ain't in the ship's articles. I tell yer we got a case. We kin go to law—

YANK [*with abysmal contempt*]. Hell! Law!

ALL [*repeating the word after him as one with cynical mockery*]. Law! [*The word has a brazen metallic quality as if their throats were phonograph horns. It is followed by a chorus of hard, barking laughter.*]

LONG [*feeling the ground slipping from under his feet—desperately*]. As voters and citizens we kin force the bloody governments—

YANK [*with abysmal contempt*]. Hell! Governments!

ALL [*repeating the word after him as one with cynical mockery*]. Governments! [*The word has a brazen metallic quality as if their throats were phonograph horns. It is followed by a chorus of hard, barking laughter.*]

LONG [*hysterically*]. We're free and equal in the sight of God—

YANK [*with abysmal contempt*]. Hell! God!

ALL [*repeating the word after him as one with cynical mockery*]. God! [*The word has a brazen metallic quality as if their throats were phonograph horns. It is followed by a chorus of hard, barking laughter.*]

YANK [*witheringly*]. Aw, join de Salvation Army!

ALL. Sit down! Shut up! Damn fool! Sea-lawyer! [LONG *slinks back out of sight.*]

PADDY [*continuing the trend of his thoughts as if he had never been interrupted—bitterly*]. And there she was standing behind us, and the Second pointing at us like a man you'd hear in a circus would be saying: In this cage is a queerer kind of baboon than ever you'd find in darkest Africy. We roast them in their own sweat—and be damned if you won't

hear some of them saying they like it! [*He glances scornfully at* YANK.]

YANK [*with a bewildered uncertain growl*]. Aw!

PADDY. And there was Yank roarin' curses and turning round wid his shovel to brain her—and she looked at him, and him at her—

YANK [*slowly*]. She was all white. I tought she was a ghost. Sure.

PADDY [*with heavy, biting sarcasm*]. 'Twas love at first sight, divil a doubt of it! If you'd seen the endearin' look on her pale mug when she shriveled away with her hands over her eyes to shut out the sight of him! Sure, 'twas as if she'd seen a great hairy ape escaped from the Zoo!

YANK [*stung—with a growl of rage*]. Aw!

PADDY. And the loving way Yank heaved his shovel at the skull of her, only she was out the door! [*A grin breaking over his face.*] 'Twas touching, I'm telling you! It put the touch of home, swate home in the stokehole. [*There is a roar of laughter from all.*]

YANK [*glaring at* PADDY *menacingly*]. Aw, choke dat off, see!

PADDY [*not heeding him—to the others*]. And her grabbin' at the Second's arm for protection. [*With a grotesque imitation of a woman's voice.*] Kiss me, Engineer dear, for it's dark down here and me old man's in Wall Street making money! Hug me tight, darlin', for I'm afeerd in the dark and me mother's on deck makin' eyes at the skipper! [*Another roar of laughter.*]

YANK [*threateningly*]. Say! What yuh tryin' to do, kid me, yuh old Harp?

PADDY. Divil a bit! Ain't I wishin' myself you'd brained her?

YANK [*fiercely*]. I'll brain her! I'll brain her yet, wait 'n' see! [*Coming over to*

PADDY—*slowly.*] Say, is dat what she called me—a hairy ape?

PADDY. She looked it at you if she didn't say the word itself.

YANK [*grinning horribly*]. Hairy ape, huh? Sure! Dat's de way she looked at me, aw right. Hairy ape! So dat's me, huh? [*Bursting into rage—as if she were still in front of him.*] Yuh skinny tart! Yuh white-faced bum, yuh! I'll show yuh who's a ape! [*Turning to the others, bewilderment seizing him again.*] Say, youse guys. I was bawlin' him out for pullin' de whistle on us. You heard me. And den I seen youse lookin' at somep'n and I tought he'd sneaked down to come up in back of me, and I hopped round to knock him dead wit de shovel. And dere she was wit de light on her! Christ, yuh coulda pushed me over with a finger! I was scared, get me? Sure! I tought she was a ghost, see? She was all in white like dey wrap around stiffs. You seen her. Kin yuh blame me? She didn't belong, dat's what. And den when I come to and seen it was a real skoit and seen de way she was lookin' at me—like Paddy said—Christ, I was sore, get me? I don't stand for dat stuff from nobody. And I flung de shovel —on'y she'd beat it. [*Furiously.*] I wished it'd banged her! I wished it'd knocked her block off!

LONG. And be 'anged for murder or 'lectrocuted? She ain't bleedin' well worth it.

YANK. I don't give a damn what! I'd be square wit her, wouldn't I? Tink I wanter let her put somep'n over on me? Tink I'm goin' to let her git away wit dat stuff? Yuh don't know me! No one ain't never put nothin' over on me and got away wit it, see!—not dat kind of stuff—no guy and no skoit neither! I'll fix her! Maybe she'll come down again—

VOICE. No chance, Yank. You scared her out of a year's growth.

YANK. I scared her? Why de hell should I scare her? Who de hell is she? Ain't she de same as me? Hairy ape, huh? [*With his old confident bravado.*] I'll show her I'm better'n her, if she on'y knew it. I belong and she don't, see! I move and she's dead! Twenty-five knots a hour, dat's me! Dat carries her but I make dat. She's on'y baggage. Sure! [*Again bewilderedly.*] But, Christ, she was funny lookin'! Did yuh pipe her hands? White and skinny. Yuh could see de bones through 'em. And her mush, dat was dead white, too. And her eyes, dey was like dey'd seen a ghost. Me, dat was! Sure! Hairy ape! Ghost, huh? Look at dat arm! [*He extends his right arm, swelling out the great muscles.*] I coulda took her wit dat, wit just my little finger even, and broke her in two. [*Again bewilderedly.*] Say, who is dat skoit, huh? What is she? What's she come from? Who made her? Who give her de noive to look at me like dat? Dis ting's got my goat right. I don't get her. She's new to me. What does a skoit like her mean, huh? She don't belong, get me! I can't see her. [*With growing anger.*] But one ting I'm wise to, aw right, aw right! Youse all kin bet your shoits I'll git even wit her. I'll show her if she tinks she— She grinds de organ and I'm on de string, huh? I'll fix her! Let her come down again and I'll fling her in de furnace! She'll move den! She won't shiver at nothin', den! Speed, dat'll be her! She'll belong den! [*He grins horribly.*]

PADDY. She'll never come. She's had her belly-full, I'm telling you. She'll be in bed now, I'm thinking, wid ten doctors and nurses feedin' her salts to clean the fear out of her.

YANK [*enraged*]. Yuh tink I made her sick, too, do yuh? Just lookin' at me, huh? Hairy ape, huh? [*In a frenzy of rage.*] I'll fix her! I'll tell her where to git off! She'll git down on her knees and take it back or I'll bust de face offen her! [*Shaking one fist upward and beating on his chest with the other.*] I'll find yuh! I'm comin', d'yuh hear? I'll fix yuh, God damn yuh! [*He makes a rush for the door.*]

VOICES. Stop him!
He'll get shot!
He'll murder her!
Trip him up!
Hold him!
He's gone crazy!
Gott, he's strong!
Hold him down!
Look out for a kick!
Pin his arms!

[*They have all piled on him and, after a fierce struggle, by sheer weight of numbers have borne him to the floor just inside the door.*]

PADDY [*who has remained detached*]. Kape him down till he's cooled off. [*Scornfully.*] Yerra, Yank, you're a great fool. Is it payin' attention at all you are to the like of that skinny sow widout one drop of rale blood in her?

YANK [*frenziedly, from the bottom of the heap*]. She done me doit! She done me doit, didn't she? I'll git square wit her! I'll get her some way! Git offen me, youse guys! Lemme up! I'll show her who's a ape!

CURTAIN

SCENE V

[*Three weeks later. A corner of Fifth Avenue in the Fifties on a fine Sunday morning. A general atmosphere of clean, well-tidied, wide street; a flood of mellow, tempered sunshine; gentle, genteel breezes. In the rear, the show windows of two shops, a jewelry establishment on the corner, a furrier's next to it. Here the adornments of extreme wealth are tantalizingly displayed. The jeweler's window is gaudy with glittering diamonds, emeralds, rubies, pearls, etc., fashioned in ornate tiaras, crowns, necklaces, collars, etc. From each piece hangs an enormous tag from which a dollar sign and numerals in intermittent electric lights wink out the incredible prices. The same in the furrier's. Rich furs of all varieties hang there bathed in a downpour of artificial light. The general effect is of a background of magnificence cheapened and made grotesque by commercialism, a background in tawdry disharmony with the clear light and sunshine on the street itself.*]

Up the side street YANK and LONG come swaggering. LONG *is dressed in shore clothes, wears a black Windsor tie, cloth cap.* YANK *is in his dirty dungarees. A fireman's cap with black peak is cocked defiantly on the side of his head. He has not shaved for days and around his fierce, resentful eyes—as around those of* LONG *to a lesser degree—the black smudge of coal dust still sticks like make-up. They hesitate and stand together at the corner, swaggering, looking about them with a forced, defiant contempt.*]

LONG [*indicating it all with an oratorical gesture*]. Well, 'ere we are. Fif' Avenoo. This 'ere's their bleedin' private lane, as yer might say. [*Bitterly.*] We're trespassers 'ere. Proletarians keep orf the grass!

YANK [*dully*]. I don't see no grass, yuh boob. [*Staring at the sidewalk.*] Clean, ain't it? Yuh could eat a fried egg offen it. The white wings got some job sweepin' dis up. [*Looking up and down the avenue —surlily.*] Where's all de white-collar stiffs yuh said was here—and de skoits—*her* kind?

LONG. In church, blarst 'em! Arskin' Jesus to give 'em more money.

YANK. Choich, huh? I useter go to choich onct—sure—when I was a kid. Me old man and woman, dey made me. Dey never went demselves, dough. Always got too big a head on Sunday mornin', dat was dem. [*With a grin.*] Dey was scrappers for fair, bot' of dem. On Satiday nights when dey bot' got a skinful dey could put up a bout oughter been staged at de Garden. When dey got trough dere wasn't a chair or table wit a leg under it. Or else dey bot' jumped on me for somep'n. Dat was where I loined to take punishment. [*With a grin and a swagger.*] I'm a chip offen de old block, get me?

LONG. Did yer old man follow the sea?

YANK. Naw. Worked along shore. I runned away when me old lady croaked wit de tremens. I helped at truckin' and in de market. Den I shipped in de stokehole. Sure. Dat belongs. De rest was nothin'. [*Looking around him.*] I ain't never seen dis before. De Brooklyn waterfront, dat was where I was dragged up. [*Taking a deep breath.*] Dis ain't so bad at dat, huh?

LONG. Not bad? Well, we pays for it wiv our bloody sweat, if yer wants to know!

YANK [*with sudden angry disgust*]. Aw, hell! I don't see no one, see—like her. All dis gives me a pain. It don't belong. Say, ain't dere a back room around dis dump? Let's go shoot a ball. All dis is too clean and quiet and dolled up, get me! It gives me a pain.

LONG. Wait and yer'll bloody well see—

YANK. I don't wait for no one. I keep on de move. Say, what yuh drag me up here for, anyway? Tryin' to kid me, yuh simp, yuh?

LONG. Yer wants to get back at 'er, don't yer? That's what yer been sayin' every bloomin' hour since she hinsulted yer.

YANK [*vehemently*]. Sure ting I do! Didn't I try to get even wit her in Southampton? Didn't I sneak on de dock and wait for her by de gangplank? I was goin' to spit in her pale mug, see! Sure, right in her pop-eyes! Dat woulda made me even, see? But no chanct. Dere was a whole army of plainclothes bulls around. Dey spotted me and gimme de bum's rush. I never seen her. But I'll git square wit her yet, you watch! [*Furiously.*] De lousy tart! She tinks she kin get away wit moider—but not wit me! I'll fix her! I'll tink of a way!

LONG [*as disgusted as he dares to be*]. Ain't that why I brought yer up 'ere—to show yer? Yer been lookin' at this 'ere 'ole affair wrong. Yer been actin' an' talkin' 's if it was all a bleedin' personal matter between yer and that bloody cow. I wants to convince yer she was on'y a representative of 'er clarss. I wants to awaken yer bloody clarss consciousness. Then yer'll see it's 'er clarss yer've got to fight, not 'er alone. There's a 'ole mob of 'em like 'er, Gawd blind 'em!

YANK [*spitting on his hands—belligerently*]. De more de merrier when I gits started. Bring on de gang!

LONG. Yer'll see 'em in arf a mo', when that church lets out. [*He turns and sees the window display in the two stores for the first time.*] Blimey! Look at that, will yer? [*They both walk back and stand looking in the jeweler's. LONG flies into a fury.*] Just look at this 'ere bloomin' mess! Just look at it! Look at the bleedin' prices on 'em—more'n our 'ole bloody stokehole makes in ten voyages sweatin' in 'ell! And they—'er and 'er bloody clarss —buys 'em for toys to dangle on 'em! One of these 'ere would buy scoff for a starvin' family for a year!

YANK. Aw, cut de sob stuff! T' hell wit de starvin' family! Yuh'll be passin' de hat to me next. [*With naïve admiration.*] Say, dem tings is pretty, huh? Bet yuh dey'd hock for a piece of change aw right. [*Then turning away, bored.*] But, aw hell, what good are dey? Let her have 'em. Dey don't belong no more'n she does. [*With a gesture of sweeping the jewelers into oblivion.*] All dat don't count, get me?

LONG [*who has moved to the furrier's— indignantly*]. And I s'pose this 'ere don't count neither—skins of poor, 'armless animals slaughtered so as 'er and 'ers can keep their bleedin' noses warm!

YANK [*who has been staring at something inside—with queer excitement*]. Take a slant at dat! Give it de once-over! Monkey fur—two t'ousand bucks! [*Bewilderedly.*] Is dat straight goods—monkey fur? What de hell—?

LONG [*bitterly*]. It's straight enuf. [*With grim humor.*] They wouldn't bloody well pay that for a 'airy ape's skin—no, nor for the 'ole livin' ape with all 'is 'ead, and body, and soul thrown in!

YANK [*clenching his fists, his face growing pale with rage as if the skin in the window were a personal insult*]. Trowin' it up in my face! Christ! I'll fix her!

LONG [*excitedly*]. Church is out. 'Ere they come, the bleedin' swine. [*After a glance at YANK's lowering face—uneasily.*] Easy goes, Comrade. Keep yer bloomin' temper. Remember force defeats itself. It ain't our weapon. We must impress our demands through peaceful means—the votes of the on-marching proletarians of the bloody world!

YANK [*with abysmal contempt*]. Votes, hell! Votes is a joke, see. Votes for women! Let dem do it!

LONG [*still more uneasily*]. Calm, now. Treat 'em wiv the proper contempt. Observe the bleedin' parasites but 'old yer 'orses.

YANK [*angrily*]. Git away from me! Yuh're yellow, dat's what. Force, dat's me! De punch, dat's me every time, see! [*The crowd from church enter from the right, sauntering slowly and affectedly, their heads held stiffly up, looking neither to right nor left, talking in toneless, simpering voices. The women are rouged, calcimined, dyed, overdressed to the nth degree. The men are in Prince Alberts, high hats, spats, canes, etc. A procession of gaudy marionettes, yet with something of the relentless horror of Frankensteins in their detached, mechanical unawareness.*]

VOICES. Dear Doctor Caiaphas! He is so sincere!

What was the sermon? I dozed off.

About the radicals, my dear—and the false doctrines that are being preached.

We must organize a hundred per cent American bazaar.

And let everyone contribute one one-hundredth per cent of their income tax.

What an original idea!

We can devote the proceeds to rehabilitating the veil of the temple.

But that has been done so many times.

YANK [*glaring from one to the other of them—with an insulting snort of scorn*]. Huh! Huh! [*Without seeming to see him, they make wide detours to avoid the spot where he stands in the middle of the sidewalk.*]

LONG [*frightenedly*]. Keep yer bloomin' mouth shut, I tells yer.

YANK [*viciously*]. G'wan! Tell it to Sweeney! [*He swaggers away and delib-*

erately lurches into a top-hatted gentle-
man, then glares at him pugnaciously.]
Say, who d'yuh tink yuh're bumpin'?
Tink yuh own de oith?

GENTLEMAN [coldly and affectedly]. I
beg your pardon. [He has not looked at
YANK and passes on without a glance,
leaving him bewildered.]

LONG [rushing up and grabbing YANK's
arm]. 'Ere! Come away! This wasn't what
I meant. Yer'll 'ave the bloody coppers
down on us.

YANK [savagely—giving him a push that
sends him sprawling]. G'wan!

LONG [picks himself up—hysterically].
I'll pop orf then. This ain't what I meant.
And whatever 'appens, yer can't blame
me. [He slinks off left.]

YANK. T' hell wit youse! [He approaches
a lady—with a vicious grin and a smirking
wink.] Hello, Kiddo. How's every little
ting? Got anyting on for tonight? I know
an old boiler down to de docks we kin
crawl into. [The lady stalks by without a
look, without a change of pace. YANK
turns to others—insultingly.] Holy smokes,
what a mug! Go hide yuhself before de
horses shy at yuh. Gee, pipe de heine on
dat one! Say, youse, yuh look like de stoin
of a ferryboat. Paint and powder! All
dolled up to kill! Yuh look like stiffs laid
out for de boneyard! Aw, g'wan, de lot
of youse! Yuh give me de eye-ache. Yuh
don't belong, get me! Look at me, why
don't youse dare? I belong, dat's me!
[Pointing to a skyscraper across the street
which is in process of construction—with
bravado.] See dat building goin' up dere?
See de steel work? Steel, dat's me! Youse
guys live on it and tink yuh're somep'n.
But I'm *in* it, see! I'm de hoistin' engine
dat makes it go up! I'm it—de inside and
bottom of it! Sure! I'm steel and steam
and smoke and de rest of it! It moves—
speed—twenty-five stories up—and me at

de top and bottom—movin'! Youse simps
don't move. Yuh're on'y dolls I winds
up to see 'm spin. Yuh're de garbage, get
me—de leavins—de ashes we dump over
de side! Now, what 'a' yuh gotta say?
[But as they seem neither to see nor hear
him, he flies into a fury.] Bums! Pigs!
Tarts! Bitches! [He turns in a rage on
the men, bumping viciously into them but
not jarring them the least bit. Rather it
is he who recoils after each collision. He
keeps growling.] Git off de oith! G'wan,
yuh bum! Look where yuh're goin', can't
yuh? Git outa here! Fight, why don't
yuh? Put up yer mits! Don't be a dog!
Fight or I'll knock yuh dead! [But, without seeming to see him, they all answer
with mechanical affected politeness]: I
beg your pardon. [Then at a cry from one
of the women, they all scurry to the furrier's window.]

THE WOMAN [ecstatically, with a gasp
of delight]. Monkey fur! [The whole
crowd of men and women chorus after
her in the same tone of affected delight]:
Monkey fur!

YANK [with a jerk of his head back on
his shoulders, as if he had received a punch
full in the face—raging]. I see yuh, all in
white! I see yuh, yuh white-faced tart,
yuh! Hairy ape, huh? I'll hairy ape yuh!
[He bends down and grips at the street
curbing as if to pluck it out and hurl it.
Foiled in this, snarling with passion, he
leaps to the lamp-post on the corner and
tries to pull it up for a club. Just at that
moment a bus is heard rumbling up. A
fat, high-hatted, spatted gentleman runs
out from the side street. He calls out
plaintively]: Bus! Bus! Stop there! [and
runs full tilt into the bending, straining
YANK, who is bowled off his balance.]

YANK [seeing a fight—with a roar of
joy as he springs to his feet]. At last! Bus,
huh? I'll bust yuh! [He lets drive a ter-

rific swing, his fist landing full on the fat gentleman's face. But the gentleman stands unmoved as if nothing had happened.]

GENTLEMAN. I beg your pardon. [*Then irritably.*] You have made me lose my bus. [*He claps his hands and begins to scream.*] Officer! Officer! [*Many police whistles shrill out on the instant and a whole* platoon of policemen rush in on YANK from all sides. He tries to fight but is clubbed to the pavement and fallen upon. The crowd at the window have not moved or noticed this disturbance. The clanging gong of the patrol wagon approaches with a clamoring din.]

CURTAIN

SCENE VI

[*Night of the following day. A row of cells in the prison on Blackwells Island. The cells extend back diagonally from right front to left rear. They do not stop, but disappear in the dark background as if they ran on, numberless, into infinity. One electric bulb from the low ceiling of the narrow corridor sheds its light through the heavy steel bars of the cell at the extreme front and reveals part of the interior. YANK can be seen within, crouched on the edge of his cot in the attitude of Rodin's "The Thinker." His face is spotted with black and blue bruises. A blood-stained bandage is wrapped around his head.*]

YANK [*suddenly starting as if awakening from a dream, reaches out and shakes the bars—aloud to himself, wonderingly*]. Steel. Dis is de Zoo, huh? [*A burst of hard, barking laughter comes from the unseen occupants of the cells, runs back down the tier, and abruptly ceases.*]

VOICES [*mockingly*]. The Zoo? That's a new name for this coop—a damn good name!

Steel, eh? You said a mouthful. This is the old iron house.

Who is that boob talkin'?

He's the bloke they brung in out of his head. The bulls had beat him up fierce.

YANK [*dully*]. I musta been dreamin'. I tought I was in a cage at de Zoo—but de apes don't talk, do dey?

VOICES [*with mocking laughter*]. You're in a cage aw right.

A coop!

A pen!

A sty!

A kennel! [*Hard laughter—a pause.*]

Say, guy! Who are you? No, never mind lying. What are you?

Yes, tell us your sad story. What's your game?

What did they jug yuh for?

YANK [*dully*]. I was a fireman—stokin' on de liners. [*Then with sudden rage, rattling his cell bars.*] I'm a hairy ape, get me? And I'll bust youse all in de jaw if yuh don't lay off kiddin' me.

VOICES. Huh! You're a hard boiled duck, ain't you!

When you spit, it bounces! [*Laughter.*]

Aw, can it. He's a regular guy. Ain't you?

What did he say he was—a ape?

YANK [*defiantly*]. Sure ting! Ain't dat what youse all are—apes? [*A silence. Then a furious rattling of bars from down the corridor.*]

A VOICE [*thick with rage*]. I'll show yuh who's a ape, yuh bum!

VOICES. Ssshh! Nix!

Can de noise!

Piano!

You'll have the guard down on us!

YANK [*scornfully*]. De guard? Yuh mean de keeper, don't yuh? [*Angry exclamations from all the cells.*]

VOICE [*placatingly*]. Aw, don't pay no attention to him. He's off his nut from the beatin'-up he got. Say, you guy! We're waitin' to hear what they landed you for —or ain't yuh tellin'?

YANK. Sure, I'll tell youse. Sure! Why de hell not? On'y—youse won't get me. Nobody gets me but me, see? I started to tell de Judge and all he says was: "Toity days to tink it over." Tink it over! Christ, dat's all I been doin' for weeks! [*After a pause.*] I was tryin' to git even wit someone, see?—someone dat done me doit.

VOICES [*cynically*]. De old stuff, I bet. Your goil, huh?
Give yuh the double-cross, huh?
That's them every time!
Did yuh beat up de odder guy?

YANK [*disgustedly*]. Aw, yuh're all wrong! Sure dere was a skoit in it—but not what youse mean, not dat old tripe. Dis was a new kind of skoit. She was dolled up all in white—in de stokehole. I tought she was a ghost. Sure. [*A pause.*]

VOICES [*whispering*]. Gee, he's still nutty.
Let him rave. It's fun listenin'.

YANK [*unheeding—groping in his thoughts*]. Her hands—dey was skinny and white like dey wasn't real but painted on somep'n. Dere was a million miles from me to her—twenty-five knots a hour. She was like some dead ting de cat brung in. Sure, dat's what. She didn't belong. She belonged in de window of a toy store, or on de top of a garbage can, see! Sure! [*He breaks out angrily.*] But would yuh believe it, she had de noive to do me doit. She lamped me like she was seein' somep'n broke loose from de menagerie. Christ, yuh'd oughter seen her eyes! [*He rattles the bars of his cell furiously.*] But I'll get back at her yet, you watch! And if I can't find her I'll take it out on de gang she runs wit. I'm wise to where dey hangs out now. I'll show her who belongs! I'll show her who's in de move and who ain't. You watch my smoke!

VOICES [*serious and joking*]. Dat's de talkin'!
Take her for all she's got!
What was this dame, anyway? Who was she, eh?

YANK. I dunno. First cabin stiff. Her old man's a millionaire, dey says—name of Douglas.

VOICES. Douglas? That's the president of the Steel Trust, I bet.
Sure. I seen his mug in de papers.
He's filthy with dough.

VOICE. Hey, feller, take a tip from me. If you want to get back at that dame, you better join the Wobblies. You'll get some action then.

YANK. Wobblies? What de hell's dat?

VOICE. Ain't you ever heard of the I. W. W.?

YANK. Naw. What is it?

VOICE. A gang of blokes—a tough gang. I been readin' about 'em today in the paper. The guard give me the *Sunday Times*. There's a long spiel about 'em. It's from a speech made in the Senate by a guy named Senator Queen. [*He is in the cell next to* YANK'S. *There is a rustling of paper.*] Wait'll I see if I got light enough and I'll read you. Listen. [*He reads.*] "There is a menace existing in this country today which threatens the vitals of our fair Republic—as foul a menace against the very life-blood of the American Eagle as was the foul conspiracy of Catiline against the eagles of ancient Rome!"

VOICE [*disgustedly*]. Aw, hell! Tell him to salt de tail of dat eagle!

Voice [*reading*]. "I refer to that devil's brew of rascals, jailbirds, murderers and cutthroats who libel all honest working men by calling themselves the Industrial Workers of the World; but in the light of their nefarious plots, I call them the Industrious *Wreckers* of the World!"

Yank [*with vengeful satisfaction*]. Wreckers, dat's de right dope! Dat belongs! Me for dem!

Voice. Ssshh! [*Reading.*] "This fiendish organization is a foul ulcer on the fair body of our Democracy—"

Voice. Democracy, hell! Give him the boid, fellers— the raspberry! [*They do.*]

Voice. Ssshh! [*Reading.*] "Like Cato I say to this Senate, the I. W. W. must be destroyed! For they represent an ever-present dagger pointed at the heart of the greatest nation the world has ever known, where all men are born free and equal, with equal opportunities to all, where the Founding Fathers have guaranteed to each one happiness, where Truth, Honor, Liberty, Justice, and the Brotherhood of Man are a religion absorbed with one's mother's milk, taught at our father's knee, sealed, signed, and stamped upon in the glorious Constitution of these United States!" [*A perfect storm of hisses, catcalls, boos, and hard laughter.*]

Voices [*scornfully*]. Hurrah for de Fort' of July!
Pass de hat!
Liberty!
Justice!
Honor!
Opportunity!
Brotherhood!

All [*with abysmal scorn*]. Aw, hell!

Voice. Give that Queen Senator guy the bark. All togedder now—one—two—tree— [*A terrific chorus of barking and yapping.*]

Guard [*from a distance*]. Quiet there, youse—or I'll git the hose. [*The noise subsides.*]

Yank [*with growling rage*]. I'd like to catch dat senator guy alone for a second. I'd loin him some trute!

Voice. Ssshh! Here's where he gits down to cases on the Wobblies. [*Reads.*] "They plot with fire in one hand and dynamite in the other. They stop not before murder to gain their ends, nor at the outraging of defenseless womanhood. They would tear down society, put the lowest scum in the seats of the mighty, turn Almighty God's revealed plan for the world topsy-turvy, and make of our sweet and lovely civilization a shambles, a desolation where man, God's masterpiece, would soon degenerate back to the ape!"

Voice [*to* Yank]. Hey, you guy. There's your ape stuff again.

Yank [*with a growl of fury*]. I got him. So dey blow up tings, do dey? Dey turn tings round, do dey? Hey, lend me dat paper, will yuh?

Voice. Sure. Give it to him. On'y keep it to yourself, see. We don't wanter listen to no more of that slop.

Voice. Here you are. Hide it under your mattress.

Yank [*reaching out*]. Tanks. I can't read much but I kin manage. [*He sits, the paper in the hand at his side, in the attitude of Rodin's "The Thinker." A pause. Several snores from down the corridor. Suddenly* Yank *jumps to his feet with a furious groan as if some appalling thought had crashed on him—bewilderedly.*] Sure—her old man—president of de Steel Trust—makes half de steel in de world—steel—where I tought I belonged—drivin' trou—movin'—in dat—to make her—and cage me in for her to spit on!

Christ! [*He shakes the bars of his cell door till the whole tier trembles. Irritated, protesting exclamations from those awakened or trying to get to sleep.*] He made dis— dis cage! Steel! *It* don't belong, dat's what! Cages, cells, locks, bolts, bars—dat's what it means!—holdin' me down with him at de top! But I'll drive trou! Fire, dat melts it! I'll be fire—under de heap—fire dat never goes out—hot as hell—breakin' out in de night—[*While he has been saying this last he has shaken his cell door to a clanging accompaniment. As he comes to the "breakin' out" he seizes one bar with both hands and, putting his two feet up against the others so that his position is parallel to the floor like a monkey's, he gives a great wrench backwards. The bar bends like a licorice stick under his tremendous strength. Just at this moment the* PRISON GUARD *rushes in, dragging a hose behind him.*]

GUARD [*angrily*]. I'll loin youse bums to wake me up! [*Sees* YANK.] Hello, it's you, huh? Got the D. Ts., hey? Well, I'll cure 'em. I'll drown your snakes for yuh! [*Noticing the bar.*] Hell, look at dat bar bended! On'y a bug is strong enough for dat!

YANK [*glaring at him*]. Or a hairy ape, yuh big yellow bum! Look out! Here I come! [*He grabs another bar.*]

GUARD [*scared now—yelling off left*]. Toin de hose on, Ben!—full pressure! And call de others—and a straitjacket! [*The curtain is falling. As it hides* YANK *from view, there is a splattering smash as the stream of water hits the steel of* YANK's *cell.*]

CURTAIN

SCENE VII

[*Nearly a month later. An I. W. W. local near the waterfront, showing the interior of a front room on the ground floor, and the street outside. Moonlight on the narrow street, buildings massed in black shadow. The interior of the room, which is general assembly room, office, and reading room, resembles some dingy settlement boys' club. A desk and high stool are in one corner. A table with papers, stacks of pamphlets, chairs about it, is at center. The whole is decidedly cheap, banal, commonplace and unmysterious as a room could well be. The secretary is perched on the stool making entries in a large ledger. An eye shade casts his face into shadows. Eight or ten men, longshoremen, iron workers, and the like, are grouped about the table. Two are playing checkers. One is writing a letter. Most of them are smoking pipes. A big signboard is on the wall at the rear, "Industrial Workers of the World—Local No. 57."*]

YANK [*comes down the street outside. He is dressed as in Scene Five. He moves cautiously, mysteriously. He comes to a point opposite the door; tiptoes softly up to it, listens, is impressed by the silence within, knocks carefully, as if he were guessing at the password to some secret rite. Listens. No answer. Knocks again a bit louder. No answer. Knocks impatiently, much louder.*]

SECRETARY [*turning around on his stool*]. What the hell is that—someone knocking? [*Shouts.*] Come in, why don't you? [*All the men in the room look up.* YANK *opens the door slowly, gingerly, as if afraid of an ambush. He looks around for secret doors, mystery, is taken aback by the commonplaceness of the room and the men in it, thinks he may have gotten in the wrong place, then sees the signboard on the wall and is reassured.*]

YANK [*blurts out*]. Hello.

MEN [*reservedly*]. Hello.

YANK [*more easily*]. I tought I'd bumped into de wrong dump.

SECRETARY [*scrutinizing him carefully*]. Maybe you have. Are you a member?

YANK. Naw, not yet. Dat's what I come for—to join.

SECRETARY. That's easy. What's your job —longshore?

YANK. Naw. Fireman—stoker on de liners.

SECRETARY [*with satisfaction*]. Welcome to our city. Glad to know you people are waking up at last. We haven't got many members in your line.

YANK. Naw. Dey're all dead to de woild.

SECRETARY. Well, you can help to wake 'em. What's your name? I'll make out your card.

YANK [*confused*]. Name? Lemme tink.

SECRETARY [*sharply*]. Don't you know your own name?

YANK. Sure; but I been just Yank for so long—Bob, dat's it—Bob Smith.

SECRETARY [*writing*]. Robert Smith. [*Fills out the rest of card.*] Here you are. Cost you half a dollar.

YANK. Is dat all—four bits? Dat's easy. [*Gives the Secretary the money.*]

SECRETARY [*throwing it in drawer*]. Thanks. Well, make yourself at home. No introductions needed. There's literature on the table. Take some of those pamphlets with you to distribute aboard ship. They may bring results. Sow the seed, only go about it right. Don't get caught and fired. We got plenty out of work. What we need is men who can hold their jobs—and work for us at the same time.

YANK. Sure. [*But he still stands, embarrassed and uneasy.*]

SECRETARY [*looking at him—curiously*]. What did you knock for? Think we had a coon in uniform to open doors?

YANK. Naw. I tought it was locked— and dat yuh'd wanter give me the once-over trou a peep-hole or somep'n to see if I was right.

SECRETARY [*alert and suspicious but with an easy laugh*]. Think we were running a crap game? That door is never locked. What put that in your nut?

YANK [*with a knowing grin, convinced that this is all camouflage, a part of the secrecy*]. Dis burg is full of bulls, ain't it?

SECRETARY [*sharply*]. What have the cops got to do with us? We're breaking no laws.

YANK [*with a knowing wink*]. Sure. Youse wouldn't for woilds. Sure. I'm wise to dat.

SECRETARY. You seem to be wise to a lot of stuff none of us knows about.

YANK [*with another wink*]. Aw, dat's aw right, see. [*Then made a bit resentful by the suspicious glances from all sides.*] Aw, can it! Youse needn't put me trou de toid degree. Can't youse see I belong? Sure! I'm reg'lar. I'll stick, get me? I'll shoot de woiks for youse. Dat's why I wanted to join in.

SECRETARY [*breezily, feeling him out*]. That's the right spirit. Only are you sure you understand what you've joined? It's all plain and above board; still, some guys get a wrong slant on us. [*Sharply.*] What's your notion of the purpose of the I. W. W.?

YANK. Aw, I know all about it.

SECRETARY [*sarcastically*]. Well, give us some of your valuable information.

YANK [*cunningly*]. I know enough not to speak outa my toin. [*Then resentfully again.*] Aw, say! I'm reg'lar. I'm wise to de game. I know yuh got to watch your step wit a stranger. For all youse know, I might be a plain-clothes dick, or somep'n, dat's what yuh're tinkin', huh? Aw, forget it! I belong, see? Ask any guy down to de docks if I don't.

Secretary. Who said you didn't?

Yank. After I'm 'nitiated, I'll show yuh.

Secretary [*astounded*]. Initiated? There's no initiation.

Yank [*disappointed*]. Ain't there no password—no grip nor nothin'?

Secretary. What'd you think this is—the Elks—or the Black Hand?

Yank. De Elks, hell! De Black Hand, dey're a lot of yellow back-stickin' Ginees. Naw. Dis is a man's gang, ain't it?

Secretary. You said it! That's why we stand on our two feet in the open. We got no secrets.

Yank [*surprised but admiringly*]. Yuh mean to say yuh always run wide open—like dis?

Secretary. Exactly.

Yank. Den yuh sure got your noive wit youse!

Secretary [*sharply*]. Just what was it made you want to join us? Come out with that straight.

Yank. Yuh call me? Well, I got noive, too! Here's my hand. Yuh wanter blow tings up, don't yuh? Well, dat's me! I belong!

Secretary [*with pretended carelessness*]. You mean change the unequal conditions of society by legitimate direct action—or with dynamite?

Yank. Dynamite! Blow it offen de oith—steel—all de cages—all de factories, steamers, buildings, jails—de Steel Trust and all dat makes it go.

Secretary. So—that's your idea, eh? And did you have any special job in that line you wanted to propose to us? [*He makes a sign to the men, who get up cautiously one by one and group behind Yank.*]

Yank [*boldly*]. Sure, I'll come out wit it. I'll show youse I'm one of de gang. Dere's dat millionaire guy, Douglas—

Secretary. President of the Steel Trust, you mean? Do you want to assassinate him?

Yank. Naw, dat don't get yuh nothin'. I mean blow up de factory, de woiks, where he makes de steel. Dat's what I'm after—to blow up de steel, knock all de steel in de woild up to de moon. Dat'll fix tings! [*Eagerly, with a touch of bravado.*] I'll do it by me lonesome! I'll show yuh! Tell me where his woiks is, how to git there, all de dope. Gimme de stuff, de old butter—and watch me do de rest! Watch de smoke and see it move! I don't give a damn if dey nab me—long as it's done! I'll soive life for it—and give 'em de laugh! [*Half to himself.*] And I'll write her a letter and tell her de hairy ape done it. Dat'll square tings.

Secretary [*stepping away from Yank*]. Very interesting. [*He gives a signal. The men, huskies all, throw themselves on Yank and before he knows it they have his legs and arms pinioned. But he is too flabbergasted to make a struggle, anyway. They feel him over for weapons.*]

Man. No gat, no knife. Shall we give him what's what and put the boots to him?

Secretary. No. He isn't worth the trouble we'd get into. He's too stupid. [*He comes closer and laughs mockingly in Yank's face.*] Ho-ho! By God, this is the biggest joke they've put up on us yet. Hey, you Joke! Who sent you—Burns or Pinkerton? No, by God, you're such a bonehead I'll bet you're in the Secret Service! Well, you dirty spy, you rotten agent provocator, you can go back and tell whatever skunk is paying you blood-money for betraying your brothers that he's wasting his coin. You couldn't catch a cold. And tell him that all he'll ever get on us, or ever has got, is just his own sneaking plots that he's framed up to put us in jail. We are what our manifesto says we are, neither more nor less—and we'll give him a copy of that any time he calls. And as for you— [*He glares scornfully at* YANK, *who is sunk in an oblivious stupor.*] Oh, hell, what's the use of talking? You're a brainless ape.

YANK [*aroused by the word to fierce but futile struggles*]. What's dat, yuh Sheeny bum, yuh!

SECRETARY. Throw him out, boys. [*In spite of his struggles, this is done with gusto and éclat. Propelled by several parting kicks,* YANK *lands sprawling in the middle of the narrow cobbled street. With a growl he starts to get up and storm the closed door, but stops bewildered by the confusion in his brain, pathetically impotent. He sits there, brooding, in as near to the attitude of Rodin's "Thinker" as he can get in his position.*]

YANK [*bitterly*]. So dem boids don't tink I belong, neider. Aw, to hell wit 'em! Dey're in de wrong pew—de same old bull—soapboxes and Salvation Army —no guts! Cut out an hour offen de job a day and make me happy! Gimme a dollar more a day and make me happy! Tree square a day, and cauliflowers in de front yard—ekal rights—a woman and kids—a lousy vote—and I'm all fixed for Jesus, huh? Aw, hell! What does dat get yuh? Dis ting's in your inside, but it ain't your belly. Feedin' your face—sinkers and coffee—dat don't touch it. It's way down—at de bottom. Yuh can't grab it, and yuh can't stop it. It moves, and everything moves. It stops and de whole woild stops. Dat's me now—I don't tick, see?— I'm a busted Ingersoll, dat's what. Steel was me, and I owned de woild. Now I ain't steel, and de woild owns me. Aw, hell! I can't see—it's all dark, get me? It's all wrong! [*He turns a bitter mocking face up like an ape gibbering at the moon.*] Say, youse up dere, Man in de Moon, yuh look so wise, gimme de answer, huh? Slip me de inside dope, de information right from de stable—where do I get off at, huh?

A POLICEMAN [*who has come up the street in time to hear this last—with grim humor*]. You'll get off at the station, you boob, if you don't get up out of that and keep movin'.

YANK [*looking up at him—with a hard, bitter laugh*]. Sure! Lock me up! Put me in a cage! Dat's de on'y answer yuh know. G'wan, lock me up!

POLICEMAN. What you been doin'?

YANK. Enuf to gimme life for! I was born, see? Sure, dat's de charge. Write it in de blotter. I was born, get me!

POLICEMAN [*jocosely*]. God pity your old woman! [*Then matter-of-fact.*] But I've no time for kidding. You're soused. I'd run you in but it's too long a walk to the station. Come on now, get up, or I'll fan your ears with this club. Beat it now! [*He hauls* YANK *to his feet.*]

YANK [*in a vague mocking tone*]. Say, where do I go from here?

POLICEMAN [*giving him a push—with a grin, indifferently*]. Go to hell.

CURTAIN

SCENE VIII

[*Twilight of the next day. The monkey house at the Zoo. One spot of clear gray light falls on the front of one cage so that the interior can be seen. The other cages are vague, shrouded in shadow from which chatterings pitched in a conversational tone can be heard. On the one cage a sign from which the word "gorilla" stands out. The gigantic animal himself is seen squatting on his haunches on a bench in much the same attitude as Rodin's "Thinker." YANK enters from the left. Immediately a chorus of angry chattering and screeching breaks out. The gorilla turns his eyes but makes no sound or move.*]

YANK [*with a hard, bitter laugh*]. Welcome to your city, huh? Hail, hail, de gang's all here! [*At the sound of his voice the chattering dies away into an attentive silence. YANK walks up to the gorilla's cage and, leaning over the railing, stares in at its occupant, who stares back at him, silent and motionless. There is a pause of dead stillness. Then YANK begins to talk in a friendly confidential tone, half-mockingly, but with a deep undercurrent of sympathy.*] Say, yuh're some hard-lookin' guy, ain't yuh? I seen lots of tough nuts dat de gang called gorillas, but yuh're de foist real one I ever seen. Some chest yuh got, and shoulders, and dem arms and mits! I bet yuh got a punch in eider fist dat'd knock 'em all silly! [*This with genuine admiration. The gorilla, as if he understood, stands upright, swelling out his chest and pounding on it with his fist. YANK grins sympathetically.*] Sure, I get yuh. Yuh challenge de whole woild, huh? Yuh got what I was sayin' even if yuh muffed de woids. [*Then bitterness creeping in.*] And why wouldn't yuh get me?

Ain't we both members of de same club —de Hairy Apes? [*They stare at each other—a pause—then* YANK *goes on slowly and bitterly.*] So yuh're what she seen when she looked at me, de white-faced tart! I was you to her, get me? On'y outa de cage—broke out—free to moider her, see? Sure! Dat's what she tought. She wasn't wise dat I was in a cage, too— worser'n yours—sure—a damn sight— 'cause you got some chanct to bust loose —but me— [*He grows confused.*] Aw, hell! It's all wrong, ain't it? [*A pause.*] I s'pose yuh wanter know what I'm doin' here, huh? I been warmin' a bench down to de Battery—ever since last night. Sure. I seen de sun come up. Dat was pretty, too—all red and pink and green. I was lookin' at de skyscrapers—steel—and all de ships comin' in, sailin' out, all over de oith—and dey was steel, too. De sun was warm, dey wasn't no clouds, and dere was a breeze blowin'. Sure, it was great stuff. I got it aw right—what Paddy said about dat bein' de right dope—on'y I couldn't get *in* it, see? I couldn't belong in dat. It was over my head. And I kept tinkin'—and den I beat it up here to see what youse was like. And I waited till dey was all gone to git yuh alone. Say, how d'yuh feel sittin' in dat pen all de time, havin' to stand for 'em comin' and starin' at yuh—de white-faced, skinny tarts and de boobs what marry 'em— makin' fun of yuh, laughin' at yuh, gittin' scared of yuh—damn 'em! [*He pounds on the rail with his fist. The gorilla rattles the bars of his cage and snarls. All the other monkeys set up an angry chattering in the darkness.* YANK *goes on excitedly.*] Sure! Dat's de way it hits me, too. On'y yuh're lucky, see? Yuh don't belong wit

[533]

'em and yuh know it. But me, I belong wit 'em—but I don't, see? Dey don't belong wit me, dat's what. Get me? Tinkin' is hard— [*He passes one hand across his forehead with a painful gesture. The gorilla growls impatiently.* YANK *goes on groping.*] It's dis way, what I'm drivin' at. Youse can sit and dope dream in de past, green woods, de jungle and de rest of it. Den yuh belong and dey don't. Den yuh kin laugh at 'em, see? Yuh're de champ of de woild. But me—I ain't got no past to tink in, nor nothin' dat's comin', on'y what's now—and dat don't belong. Sure, yuh're de best off! Yuh can't tink, can yuh? Yuh can't talk neider. But I kin make a bluff at talkin' and tinkin'—a'most git away wit it—a'most!—and dat's where de joker comes in. [*He laughs.*] I ain't on oith and I ain't in heaven, get me? I'm in de middle tryin' to separate 'em, takin' all de woist punches from bot' of 'em. Maybe dat's what dey call hell, huh? But you, yuh're at de bottom. You belong! Sure! Yuh're de on'y one in de woild dat does, yuh lucky stiff! [*The gorilla growls proudly.*] And dat's why dey gotter put yuh in a cage, see? [*The gorilla roars angrily.*] Sure! Yuh get me. It beats it when you try to tink it or talk it—it's way down—deep—behind—you 'n' me we feel it. Sure! Bot' members of dis club! [*He laughs—then in a savage tone.*] What de hell! T' hell wit it! A little action, dat's our meat! Dat belongs! Knock 'em down and keep bustin' 'em till dey croaks yuh wit a gat—wit steel; Sure! Are yuh game? Dey've looked at youse, ain't dey—in a cage? Wanter git even? Wanter wind up like a sport 'stead of croakin' slow in dere? [*The gorilla roars an emphatic affirmative.* YANK *goes on with a sort of furious exaltation.*] Sure! Yuh're reg'lar! Yuh'll stick to de finish! Me 'n' you, huh?—bot' members of this club! We'll put up one last star bout dat'll knock 'em offen deir seats! Dey'll have to make de cages stronger after we're trou! [*The gorilla is straining at his bars, growling, hopping from one foot to the other.* YANK *takes a jimmy from under his coat and forces the lock on the cage door. He throws this open.*] Pardon from de governor! Step out and shake hands. I'll take yuh for a walk down Fif' Avenoo. We'll knock 'em offen de oith and croak wit de band playin'. Come on, Brother. [*The gorilla scrambles gingerly out of his cage. Goes to* YANK *and stands looking at him.* YANK *keeps his mocking tone—holds out his hand.*] Shake—de secret grip of our order. [*Something, the tone of mockery, perhaps, suddenly enrages the animal. With a spring he wraps his huge arms around* YANK *in a murderous hug. There is a crackling snap of crushed ribs—a gasping cry, still mocking, from* YANK.] Hey, I didn't say kiss me! [*The gorilla lets the crushed body slip to the floor; stands over it uncertainly, considering; then picks it up, throws it in the cage, shuts the door, and shuffles off menacingly into the darkness at left. A great uproar of frightened chattering and whimpering comes from the other cages. Then* YANK *moves, groaning, opening his eyes, and there is silence. He mutters painfully.*] Say—dey oughter match him—wit Zybszko. He got me, aw right. I'm trou. Even him didn't tink I belonged. [*Then, with sudden passionate despair.*] Christ, where do I get off at? Where do I fit in? [*Checking himself as suddenly.*] Aw, what de hell! No squawkin', see! No quittin', get me! Croak wit your boots on! [*He grabs hold of the bars of the cage and hauls himself painfully to his feet—*

looks around him bewilderedly—forces a mocking laugh.] In de cage, huh? [*In the strident tones of a circus barker.*] Ladies and gents, step forward and take a slant at de one and only— [*His voice weakening.*]—one and original—Hairy Ape from de wilds of— [*He slips in a heap on the floor and dies. The monkeys set up a chattering, whimpering wail. And, perhaps, the Hairy Ape at last belongs.*]

CURTAIN

THE GLASS MENAGERIE

A Play

by TENNESSEE WILLIAMS

THE GLASS MENAGERIE *was first produced by Eddie Dowling and Louis J. Singer at the Civic Theatre, Chicago, Ill., on December 26, 1944, and at the Playhouse Theatre, New York City, on March 31, 1945, with the following cast:*

THE MOTHER	Laurette Taylor
HER SON	Eddie Dowling
HER DAUGHTER	Julie Haydon
THE GENTLEMAN CALLER	Anthony Ross

SETTING DESIGNED AND LIGHTED by Jo Mielziner
ORIGINAL MUSIC COMPOSED by Paul Bowles
STAGED by Eddie Dowling and Margo Jones

THE CHARACTERS

AMANDA WINGFIELD (*the mother*)..............................Laurette Taylor
  A little woman of great but confused vitality clinging frantically to another time and place. Her characterization must be carefully created, not copied from type. She is not paranoiac, but her life is paranoia. There is much to admire in Amanda, and as much to love and pity as there is to laugh at. Certainly she has endurance and a kind of heroism, and though her foolishness makes her unwittingly cruel at times, there is tenderness in her slight person.

LAURA WINGFIELD (*her daughter*)..............................Julie Haydon
  Amanda, having failed to establish contact with reality, continues to live vitally in her illusions, but Laura's situation is even graver. A childhood illness has left her

crippled, one leg slightly shorter than the other, and held in a brace. This defect need not be more than suggested on the stage. Stemming from this, Laura's separation increases till she is like a piece of her own glass collection, too exquisitely fragile to move from the shelf.

Tom Wingfield (*her son*) . . . . Eddie Dowling
  And the narrator of the play. A poet with a job in a warehouse. His nature is not remorseless, but to escape from a trap he has to act without pity.

Jim O'Connor (*the gentleman caller*) . . . . Anthony Ross
  A nice, ordinary, young man.

SCENE

An Alley in St. Louis

PART I. *Preparation for a Gentleman Caller.*
PART II. *The Gentleman calls.*

Time: Now and the Past.

PRODUCTION NOTES

Being a "memory play," *The Glass Menagerie* can be presented with unusual freedom of convention. Because of its considerably delicate or tenuous material, atmospheric touches and subtleties of direction play a particularly important part. Expressionism and all other unconventional techniques in drama have only one valid aim, and that is a closer approach to truth. When a play employs unconventional techniques, it is not, or certainly shouldn't be, trying to escape its responsibility of dealing with reality, or interpreting experience, but is actually or should be attempting to find a closer approach, a more penetrating and vivid expression of things as they are. The straight realistic play with its genuine frigidaire and authentic ice-cubes, its characters that speak exactly as its audience speaks, corresponds to the academic landscape and has the same virtue of a photographic likeness. Everyone should know nowadays the unimportance of the photographic in art: that truth, life, or reality is an organic thing which the poetic imagination can represent or suggest, in essence, only through transformation, through changing into other forms than those which were merely present in appearance.

These remarks are not meant as a preface only to this particular play. They have to do with a conception of a new, plastic theatre which must take the place of the exhausted theatre of realistic conventions if the theatre is to resume vitality as a part of our culture.

The Screen Device. There is *only one important difference between the original and acting version of the play* and that is the *omission* in the latter of the device which I tentatively included in my *original* script. This device was the use of a screen on which were projected magic-lantern slides bearing images or titles. I do not regret the omission of this device from the present Broadway production. The extraordinary power of Miss Taylor's performance made it suitable to have the utmost simplicity in the physical production. But I think it may be interesting to some readers to see how this device was conceived. So I am putting it into the published manuscript. These images and legends, projected from behind, were cast on a section of wall between the front-room and dining-room areas, which should be indistinguishable from the rest when not in use.

The purpose of this will probably be apparent. It is to give accent to certain values in each scene. Each scene contains a particular point (or several) which is structurally the most important. In an episodic play, such as this, the basic structure or narrative line may be obscured from the audience; the effect may seem fragmentary rather than architectural. This may not be the fault of the play so much as a lack of attention in the audience. The legend or image upon the screen will strengthen the effect of what is merely allusion in the writing and allow the primary point to be made more simply and lightly than if the entire responsibility were on the spoken lines. Aside from this structural value, I think the screen will have a definite emotional appeal, less definable but just as important. An imaginative producer or director may invent many other uses for this device than those indicated in the present script. In fact the possibilities of the device seem much larger to me than the instance of this play can possibly utilize.

The Music. Another extra-literary accent in this play is provided by the use of music. A single recurring tune, "The Glass Menagerie," is used to give emotional emphasis to suitable passages. This tune is like circus music, not when you are on the grounds or in the immediate vicinity of the parade, but when you are at some distance and very likely thinking of something else. It seems under those circumstances to continue almost interminably and it weaves in and out of your preoccupied consciousness; then it is the lightest, most delicate music in the world and perhaps the saddest. It expresses the surface vivacity of life with the underlying strain of immutable and inexpressible sorrow. When you look at a piece of delicately spun glass you think of two things: how beautiful it is and how easily it can be broken. Both of those ideas should be woven into the recurring tune, which dips in and out of the play as if it were carried on a wind that changes. It serves as a thread of connection and allusion between the narrator with his separate point in time and space and the subject of his story. Between each episode it returns as reference to the emotion, nostalgia, which is the first condition of the play. It is primarily Laura's music and therefore comes out most clearly when the play focuses upon her and the lovely fragility of glass which is her image.

The Lighting. The lighting in the play is not realistic. In keeping with the atmosphere of memory, the stage is dim. Shafts of light are focused on selected areas or actors, sometimes in contradistinction to what is the apparent center. For instance, in the quarrel scene between Tom and Amanda, in which Laura has no active part, the clearest pool of light is on her figure. This is also true of the supper scene, when her silent figure on the sofa should remain the visual center. The light upon Laura should be distinct from the others, having a peculiar pristine clarity such as

light used in early religious portraits of female saints or madonnas. A certain correspondence to light in religious paintings, such as El Greco's, where the figures are
radiant in atmosphere that is relatively dusky, could be effectively used throughout
the play. (It will also permit a more effective use of the screen.) A free, imaginative
use of light can be of enormous value in giving a mobile, plastic quality to plays
of a more or less static nature.

T. W.

SCENE I

*[The Wingfield apartment is in the rear
of the building, one of those vast hive-like
conglomerations of cellular living-units
that flower as warty growths in over-
crowded urban centers of lower middle-
class population and are symptomatic of
the impulse of this largest and fundamentally enslaved section of American society to avoid fluidity and differentiation
and to exist and function as one interfused
mass of automatism.*

*The apartment faces an alley and is
entered by a fire-escape, a structure whose
name is a touch of accidental poetic truth,
for all of these huge buildings are always
burning with the slow and implacable fires
of human desperation. The fire-escape is
included in the set—that is, the landing of
it and steps descending from it.*

*The scene is memory and is therefore
nonrealistic. Memory takes a lot of poetic
license. It omits some details; others are
exaggerated, according to the emotional
value of the articles it touches, for memory
is seated predominantly in the heart. The
interior is therefore rather dim and poetic.*

*At the rise of the curtain, the audience
is faced with the dark, grim rear wall of
the Wingfield tenement. This building,
which runs parallel to the footlights, is
flanked on both sides by dark, narrow
alleys which run into murky canyons of
tangled clotheslines, garbage cans and the
sinister latticework of neighboring fire-*

*escapes. It is up and down these side alleys
that exterior entrances and exits are made,
during the play. At the end of* Tom's *opening commentary, the dark tenement wall
slowly reveals (by means of a transpar-
ency) the interior of the ground floor
Wingfield apartment.*

*Downstage is the living room, which
also serves as a sleeping room for* Laura,
*the sofa unfolding to make her bed. Up-
stage, center, and divided by a wide arch
or second proscenium with transparent
faded portieres (or second curtain), is the
dining room. In an old-fashioned what-not
in the living room are seen scores of transparent glass animals. A blown-up photograph of the father hangs on the wall of
the living room, facing the audience, to the
left of the archway. It is the face of a very
handsome young man in a doughboy's
First World War cap. He is gallantly smiling, ineluctably smiling, as if to say, "I
will be smiling forever."*

*The audience hears and sees the opening
scene in the dining room through both the
transparent fourth wall of the building
and the transparent gauze portieres of the
dining-room arch. It is during this revealing scene that the fourth wall slowly as-
cends, out of sight. This transparent exterior wall is not brought down again until the very end of the play, during* Tom's
final speech.

*The narrator is an undisguised conven-
tion of the play. He takes whatever license*

with dramatic convention as is convenient to his purposes.

TOM *enters dressed as a merchant sailor from alley, stage left, and strolls across the front of the stage to the fire-escape. There he stops and lights a cigarette. He addresses the audience.*]

TOM. Yes, I have tricks in my pocket, I have things up my sleeve. But I am the opposite of a stage magician. He gives you illusion that has the appearance of truth. I give you truth in the pleasant disguise of illusion.

To begin with, I turn back time. I reverse it to that quaint period, the thirties, when the huge middle class of America was matriculating in a school for the blind. Their eyes had failed them, or they had failed their eyes, and so they were having their fingers pressed forcibly down on the fiery Braille alphabet of a dissolving economy.

In Spain there was revolution. Here there was only shouting and confusion.

In Spain there was Guernica. Here there were disturbances of labor, sometimes pretty violent, in otherwise peaceful cities such as Chicago, Cleveland, Saint Louis . . .

This is the social background of the play. [MUSIC.]

The play is memory.

Being a memory play, it is dimly lighted, it is sentimental, it is not realistic.

In memory everything seems to happen to music. That explains the fiddle in the wings.

I am the narrator of the play, and also a character in it.

The other characters are my mother, Amanda, my sister, Laura, and a gentleman caller who appears in the final scenes.

He is the most realistic character in the play, being an emissary from a world of reality that we were somehow set apart from.

But since I have a poet's weakness for symbols, I am using this character also as a symbol; he is the long delayed but always expected something that we live for.

There is a fifth character in the play who doesn't appear except in this larger-than-life-size photograph over the mantel.

This is our father who left us a long time 'ago.

He was a telephone man who fell in love with long distances; he gave up his job with the telephone company and skipped the light fantastic out of town . . .

The last we heard of him was a picture post-card from Mazátlan, on the Pacific coast of Mexico, containing a message of two words—

"Hello— Good-bye!" and no address.

I think the rest of the play will explain itself. . . . [AMANDA's *voice becomes audible through the portieres.* LEGEND ON SCREEN: "OÙ SONT LES NEIGES." *He divides the portieres and enters the upstage area.* AMANDA *and* LAURA *are seated at a drop-leaf table. Eating is indicated by gestures without food or utensils.* AMANDA *faces the audience.* TOM *and* LAURA *are seated in profile. The interior has lit up softly and through the scrim we see* AMANDA *and* LAURA *seated at the table in the upstage area.*]

AMANDA [*calling*]. Tom?

TOM. Yes, Mother.

AMANDA. We can't say grace until you come to the table!

TOM. Coming, Mother. [*He bows slightly and withdraws, reappearing a few moments later in his place at the table.*]

AMANDA [*to her son*]. Honey, don't *push* with your *fingers*. If you have to push with something, the thing to push with is a crust of bread. And chew—chew! Animals have sections in their stomachs which enable them to digest food without mastication, but human beings are supposed to chew their food before they swallow it down. Eat food leisurely, son, and really enjoy it. A well-cooked meal has lots of delicate flavors that have to be held in the mouth for appreciation. So chew your food and give your salivary glands a chance to function! [Tom *deliberately lays his imaginary fork down and pushes his chair back from the table.*]

Tom. I haven't enjoyed one bite of this dinner because of your constant directions on how to eat it. It's you that make me rush through meals with your hawk-like attention to every bite I take. Sickening— spoils my appetite—all this discussion of— animals' secretion—salivary glands—mastication!

Amanda [*lightly*]. Temperament like a Metropolitan star! [*He rises and crosses downstage.*] You're not excused from the table.

Tom. I'm getting a cigarette.

Amanda. You smoke too much. [Laura *rises.*]

Laura. I'll bring in the blanc mange. [*He remains standing with his cigarette by the portieres during the following.*]

Amanda [*rising*]. No, sister, no, sister— you be the lady this time and I'll be the darky.

Laura. I'm already up.

Amanda. Resume your seat, little sister —I want you to stay fresh and pretty— for gentlemen callers!

Laura. I'm not expecting any gentlemen callers.

Amanda [*crossing out to kitchenette. Airily*]. Sometimes they come when they are least expected! Why, I remember one Sunday afternoon in Blue Mountain— [*Enters kitchenette.*]

Tom. I know what's coming!

Laura. Yes. But let her tell it.

Tom. Again?

Laura. She loves to tell it. [Amanda *returns with bowl of dessert.*]

Amanda. One Sunday afternoon in Blue Mountain—your mother received—*seventeen!*—gentlemen callers! Why, sometimes there weren't chairs enough to accommodate them all. We had to send the nigger over to bring in folding chairs from the parish house.

Tom [*remaining at portieres*]. How did you entertain those gentlemen callers?

Amanda. I understood the art of conversation!

Tom. I bet you could talk.

Amanda. Girls in those days *knew* how to talk, I can tell you.

Tom. Yes? [Image: Amanda as a girl on a porch, greeting callers.]

Amanda. They knew how to entertain their gentlemen callers. It wasn't enough for a girl to be possessed of a pretty face and a graceful figure—although I wasn't slighted in either respect. She also needed to have a nimble wit and a tongue to meet all occasions.

Tom. What did you talk about?

Amanda. Things of importance going on in the world! Never anything coarse or common or vulgar. [*She addresses* Tom *as though he were seated in the vacant chair at the table though he remains by portieres. He plays this scene as though he held the book.*] My callers were gentlemen—all! Among my callers were some of the most prominent young planters of the Mississippi Delta—planters and sons of planters! [Tom *motions for music and a spot of light on* Amanda. *Her eyes lift, her face glows, her voice becomes rich and elegiac.* Screen legend: "où sont les neiges."]

There was young Champ Laughlin who later became vice-president of the Delta Planters Bank.

Hadley Stevenson who was drowned in Moon Lake and left his widow one hundred and fifty thousand in Government bonds.

There were the Cutrere brothers, Wesley and Bates. Bates was one of my bright particular beaux! He got in a quarrel with that wild Wainwright boy. They shot it out on the floor of Moon Lake Casino. Bates was shot through the stomach. Died in the ambulance on his way to Memphis. His widow was also well-provided for, came into eight or ten thousand acres, that's all. She married him on the rebound —never loved her—carried my picture on him the night he died!

And there was that boy that every girl in the Delta had set her cap for! That beautiful, brilliant young Fitzhugh boy from Greene County!

TOM. What did he leave his widow?

AMANDA. He never married! Gracious, you talk as though all of my old admirers had turned up their toes to the daisies!

TOM. Isn't this the first you've mentioned that still survives?

AMANDA. That Fitzhugh boy went North and made a fortune—came to be known as the Wolf of Wall Street! He had the Midas touch, whatever he touched turned to gold!

And I could have been Mrs. Duncan J. Fitzhugh, mind you! But—I picked your father!

LAURA [*rising*]. Mother, let me clear the table.

AMANDA. No, dear, you go in front and study your typewriter chart. Or practice your shorthand a little. Stay fresh and pretty!—It's almost time for our gentlemen callers to start arriving. [*She flounces girlishly toward the kitchenette.*] How many do you suppose we're going to entertain this afternoon? [TOM *throws down the paper and jumps up with a groan.*]

LAURA [*alone in the dining room*]. I don't believe we're going to receive any, Mother.

AMANDA [*reappearing, airily*]. What? No one—not one? You must be joking! [LAURA *nervously echoes her laugh. She slips in a fugitive manner through the half-open portieres and draws them gently behind her. A shaft of very clear light is thrown on her face against the faded tapestry of the curtains.* MUSIC: "THE GLASS MENAGERIE" UNDER FAINTLY. *Lightly.*] Not one gentleman caller? It can't be true! There must be a flood, there must have been a tornado!

LAURA. It isn't a flood, it's not a tornado, Mother. I'm just not popular like you were in Blue Mountain. . . . [TOM *utters another groan.* LAURA *glances at him with a faint, apologetic smile. Her voice catching a little.*] Mother's afraid I'm going to be an old maid.

[THE SCENE DIMS OUT WITH "GLASS MENAGERIE" MUSIC.]

SCENE II

["*Laura, Haven't You Ever Liked Some Boy?*"

On the dark stage the screen is lighted with the image of blue roses.

Gradually LAURA's figure becomes apparent and the screen goes out.

The music subsides.

LAURA *is seated in the delicate ivory chair at the small claw-foot table.*

She wears a dress of soft violet material for a kimono—her hair tied back from her forehead with a ribbon.

She is washing and polishing her collection of glass.

AMANDA *appears on the fire-escape steps. At the sound of her ascent,* LAURA *catches her breath, thrusts the bowl of ornaments away and seats herself stiffly before the diagram of the typewriter keyboard as though it held her spellbound.*

Something has happened to AMANDA. *It is written in her face as she climbs to the landing: a look that is grim and hopeless and a little absurd.*

She has on one of those cheap or imitation velvety-looking cloth coats with imitation fur collar. Her hat is five or six years old, one of those dreadful cloche hats that were worn in the late twenties and she is clasping an enormous black patent-leather pocketbook with nickel clasps and initials. This is her full-dress outfit, the one she usually wears to the D.A.R.

Before entering she looks through the door.

She purses her lips, opens her eyes very wide, rolls them upward and shakes her head.

Then she slowly lets herself in the door. Seeing her mother's expression LAURA *touches her lips with a nervous gesture.*]

LAURA. Hello, Mother, I was— [*She makes a nervous gesture toward the chart on the wall.* AMANDA *leans against the shut door and stares at* LAURA *with a martyred look.*]

AMANDA. Deception? Deception? [*She slowly removes her hat and gloves, continuing the sweet suffering stare. She lets the hat and gloves fall on the floor—a bit of acting.*]

LAURA [*shakily*]. How was the D.A.R. meeting? [AMANDA *slowly opens her purse and removes a dainty white handkerchief which she shakes out delicately and delicately touches to her lips and nostrils.*]

Didn't you go to the D.A.R. meeting, Mother?

AMANDA [*faintly, almost inaudibly*]. —No.—No. [*Then more forcibly.*] I did not have the strength—to go to the D.A.R. In fact, I did not have the courage! I wanted to find a hole in the ground and hide myself in it forever! [*She crosses slowly to the wall and removes the diagram of the typewriter keyboard. She holds it in front of her for a second, staring at it sweetly and sorrowfully—then bites her lips and tears it in two pieces.*]

LAURA [*faintly*]. Why did you do that, Mother? [AMANDA *repeats the same procedure with the chart of the Gregg Alphabet.*] Why are you—

AMANDA. Why? Why? How old are you, Laura?

LAURA. Mother, you know my age.

AMANDA. I thought that you were an adult; it seems that I was mistaken. [*She crosses slowly to the sofa and sinks down and stares at* LAURA.]

LAURA. Please don't stare at me, Mother. [AMANDA *closes her eyes and lowers her head. Count ten.*]

AMANDA. What are we going to do, what is going to become of us, what is the future? [*Count ten.*]

LAURA. Has something happened, Mother? [AMANDA *draws a long breath and takes out the handkerchief again. Dabbing process.*] Mother, has—something happened?

AMANDA. I'll be all right in a minute, I'm just bewildered—[*Count five.*]—by life. . . .

LAURA. Mother, I wish that you would tell me what's happened!

AMANDA. As you know, I was supposed to be inducted into my office at the D.A.R. this afternoon. [IMAGE: A SWARM OF TYPEWRITERS.] But I stopped off at Rubicam's business college to speak to your teachers about your having a cold and ask them what progress they thought you were making down there.

LAURA. Oh. . . .

AMANDA. I went to the typing instructor and introduced myself as your mother. She didn't know who you were. Wingfield, she said. We don't have any such student enrolled at the school!

I assured her she did, that you had been going to classes since early in January.

"I wonder," she said, "if you could be talking about that terribly shy little girl who dropped out of school after only a few days' attendance?"

"No," I said, "Laura, my daughter, has been going to school every day for the past six weeks!"

"Excuse me," she said. She took the attendance book out and there was your name, unmistakably printed, and all the dates you were absent until they decided that you had dropped out of school.

I still said, "No, there must have been some mistake! There must have been some mix-up in the records!"

And she said, "No—I remember her perfectly now. Her hands shook so that she couldn't hit the right keys! The first time we gave a speed-test, she broke down completely—was sick at the stomach and almost had to be carried into the washroom! After that morning she never showed up any more. We phoned the house but never got any answer—while I was working at Famous and Barr, I suppose, demonstrating those— Oh!"

I felt so weak I could barely keep on my feet!

I had to sit down while they got me a glass of water!

Fifty dollars' tuition, all of our plans— my hopes and ambitions for you—just gone up the spout, just gone up the spout like that. [LAURA *draws a long breath and gets awkwardly to her feet. She crosses to the victrola and winds it up.*]

What are you doing?

LAURA. Oh! [*She releases the handle and returns to her seat.*]

AMANDA. Laura, where have you been going when you've gone out pretending that you were going to business college?

LAURA. I've just been going out walking.

AMANDA. That's not true.

LAURA. It is. I just went walking.

AMANDA. Walking? Walking? In winter? Deliberately courting pneumonia in that light coat? Where did you walk to, Laura?

LAURA. All sorts of places—mostly in the park.

AMANDA. Even after you'd started catching that cold?

LAURA. It was the lesser of two evils, Mother. [IMAGE: WINTER SCENE IN PARK.] I couldn't go back up. I—threw up—on the floor!

AMANDA. From half past seven till after five every day you mean to tell me you walked around in the park, because you wanted to make me think that you were still going to Rubicam's Business College?

LAURA. It wasn't as bad as it sounds. I went inside places to get warmed up.

AMANDA. Inside where?

LAURA. I went in the art museum and the bird-houses at the Zoo. I visited the penguins every day! Sometimes I did without lunch and went to the movies. Lately I've been spending most of my afternoons in the Jewel-box, that big glass house where they raise the tropical flowers.

AMANDA. You did all this to deceive me, just for deception? [LAURA *looks down.*] Why?

LAURA. Mother, when you're disappointed, you get that awful suffering look on your face, like the picture of Jesus' mother in the museum!

AMANDA. Hush!

LAURA. I couldn't face it. [*Pause. A whisper of strings.* LEGEND: "THE CRUST OF HUMILITY."]

AMANDA [*hopelessly fingering the huge pocketbook*]. So what are we going to do the rest of our lives? Stay home and watch the parades go by? Amuse ourselves with the glass menagerie, darling? Eternally play those worn-out phonograph records your father left as a painful reminder of him?

We won't have a business career—we've given that up because it gave us nervous indigestion! [*Laughs wearily.*] What is there left but dependency all our lives? I know so well what becomes of unmarried women who aren't prepared to occupy a position. I've seen such pitiful cases in the South—barely tolerated spinsters living upon the grudging patronage of sister's husband or brother's wife!—stuck away in some little mouse-trap of a room —encouraged by one in-law to visit another—little birdlike women without any nest—eating the crust of humility all their life!

Is that the future that we've mapped out for ourselves?

I swear it's the only alternative I can think of!

It isn't a very pleasant alternative, is it?

Of course—some girls *do marry*. [LAURA *twists her hands nervously.*]

Haven't you ever liked some boy?

LAURA. Yes. I liked one once. [*Rises.*] I came across his picture a while ago.

AMANDA [*with some interest*]. He gave you his picture?

LAURA. No, it's in the year-book.

AMANDA [*disappointed*]. Oh—a high-school boy. [SCREEN IMAGE: JIM AS HIGH-SCHOOL HERO BEARING A SILVER CUP.]

LAURA. Yes. His name was Jim. [LAURA *lifts the heavy annual from the claw-foot table.*] Here he is in *The Pirates of Penzance*.

AMANDA [*absently*]. The what?

LAURA. The operetta the senior class put on. He had a wonderful voice and we sat across the aisle from each other Mondays, Wednesdays and Fridays in the Aud. Here he is with the silver cup for debating! See his grin?

AMANDA [*absently*]. He must have had a jolly disposition.

LAURA. He used to call me—Blue Roses. [IMAGE: BLUE ROSES.]

AMANDA. Why did he call you such a name as that?

LAURA. When I had that attack of pleurosis—he asked me what was the matter when I came back. I said pleurosis—he thought that I said Blue Roses! So that's what he always called me after that. Whenever he saw me, he'd holler, "Hello, Blue Roses!" I didn't care for the girl that he went out with. Emily Meisenbach. Emily was the best-dressed girl at Soldan. She never struck me, though, as being sincere . . . It says in the Personal Section—they're engaged. That's—six years ago! They must be married by now.

AMANDA. Girls that aren't cut out for business careers usually wind up married to some nice man. [*Gets up with a spark of revival.*] Sister, that's what you'll do! [LAURA *utters a startled, doubtful laugh. She reaches quickly for a piece of glass.*]

LAURA. But, Mother—

AMANDA. Yes? [*Crossing to photograph.*]

LAURA [*in a tone of frightened apology*]. I'm—crippled! [IMAGE: SCREEN.]

AMANDA. Nonsense! Laura, I've told you never, never to use that word. Why, you're not crippled, you just have a little defect—hardly noticeable, even! When people have some slight disadvantage like that, they cultivate other things to make up for it—develop charm—and vivacity—

and—*charm!* That's all you have to do! [*She turns again to the photograph.*] One thing your father had *plenty of*—was *charm!* [TOM *motions to the fiddle in the wings.*]

[THE SCENE FADES OUT WITH MUSIC.]

SCENE III

[LEGEND ON SCREEN: "AFTER THE FIASCO—" TOM *speaks from the fire-escape landing.*]

TOM. After the fiasco at Rubicam's Business College, the idea of getting a gentleman caller for Laura began to play a more and more important part in Mother's calculations.

It became an obsession. Like some archetype of the universal unconscious, the image of the gentleman caller haunted our small apartment. . . . [IMAGE: YOUNG MAN AT DOOR WITH FLOWERS.]

An evening at home rarely passed without some allusion to this image, this specter, this hope. . . .

Even when he wasn't mentioned, his presence hung in Mother's preoccupied look and in my sister's frightened, apologetic manner—hung like a sentence passed upon the Wingfields!

Mother was a woman of action as well as words.

She began to take logical steps in the planned direction.

Late that winter and in the early spring —realizing that extra money would be needed to properly feather the nest and plume the bird—she conducted a vigorous campaign on the telephone, roping in subscribers to one of those magazines for matrons called *The Home-maker's Companion,* the type of journal that features the serialized sublimations of ladies of letters who think in terms of delicate cup-

like breasts, slim, tapering waists, rich, creamy thighs, eyes like wood-smoke in autumn, fingers that soothe and caress like strains of music, bodies as powerful as Etruscan sculpture.

[SCREEN IMAGE: GLAMOR MAGAZINE COVER. AMANDA *enters with phone on long extension cord. She is spotted in the dim stage.*]

AMANDA. Ida Scott? This is Amanda Wingfield!

We *missed* you at the D.A.R. last Monday!

I said to myself: She's probably suffering with that sinus condition! How is that sinus condition?

Horrors! Heaven have mercy!—You're a Christian martyr, yes, that's what you are, a Christian martyr!

Well, I just now happened to notice that your subscription to the *Companion's* about to expire! Yes, it expires with the next issue, honey!—just when that wonderful new serial by Bessie Mae Hopper is getting off to such an exciting start. Oh, honey, it's something that you can't miss! You remember how *Gone With the Wind* took everybody by storm? You simply couldn't go out if you hadn't read it. All everybody *talked* was Scarlett O'Hara. Well, this is a book that critics already compare to *Gone With the Wind.* It's the *Gone With the Wind* of the post-World War generation!—What?—Burning?—Oh, honey, don't let them burn, go take a look in the oven and I'll hold the wire! Heavens—I think she's hung up!

[*DIM OUT*]

[LEGEND ON SCREEN: "YOU THINK I'M IN LOVE WITH CONTINENTAL SHOEMAKERS?" *Before the stage is lighted, the violent voices of* TOM *and* AMANDA *are heard. They are quarreling behind the portieres. In front of them stands* LAURA *with clenched hands and panicky expression. A clear pool of light on her figure throughout this scene.*]

TOM. What in Christ's name am I—

AMANDA [*shrilly*]. Don't you use that—

TOM. Supposed to do!

AMANDA. Expression! Not in my—

TOM. Ohhh!

AMANDA. Presence! Have you gone out of your senses?

TOM. I have, that's true, *driven* out!

AMANDA. What is the matter with you, you—big—big—IDIOT!

TOM. Look!—I've got *no thing,* no single thing—

AMANDA. Lower your voice!

TOM. In my life here that I can call my OWN! Everything is—

AMANDA. Stop that shouting!

TOM. Yesterday you confiscated my books! You had the nerve to—

AMANDA. I took that horrible novel back to the library—yes! That hideous book by that insane Mr. Lawrence. [TOM *laughs wildly.*] I cannot control the output of diseased minds or people who cater to them— [TOM *laughs still more wildly.*] BUT I WON'T ALLOW SUCH FILTH BROUGHT INTO MY HOUSE! No, no, no, no, no!

TOM. House, house! Who pays rent on it, who makes a slave of himself to—

AMANDA [*fairly screeching*]. Don't you DARE to—

TOM. No, no, *I* mustn't say things! *I've* got to just—

AMANDA. Let me tell you—

TOM. I don't want to hear any more! [*He tears the portieres open. The upstage area is lit with a turgid smoky red glow.* AMANDA's *hair is in metal curlers and she wears a very old bathrobe, much too large for her slight figure, a relic of the faithless Mr. Wingfield. An upright typewriter and a wild disarray of manuscripts is on the drop-leaf table. The quarrel was probably precipitated by* AMANDA's *interruption of his creative labor. A chair lying overthrown on the floor. Their gesticulating shadows are cast on the ceiling by the fiery glow.*]

AMANDA. You *will* hear more, you—

TOM. No, I won't hear more, I'm going out!

AMANDA. You come right back in—

TOM. Out, out, out! Because I'm—

AMANDA. Come back here, Tom Wingfield! I'm not through talking to you!

TOM. Oh, go— ·

LAURA [*desperately*]. —Tom!

AMANDA. You're going to listen, and no more insolence from you! I'm at the end of my patience! [*He comes back toward her.*]

TOM. What do you think I'm at? Aren't I supposed to have any patience to reach the end of, Mother? I know, I know. It seems unimportant to you, what I'm *doing*—what I *want* to do—having a little *difference* between them! You don't think that—

AMANDA. I think you've been doing things that you're ashamed of. That's why you act like this. I don't believe that you go every night to the movies. Nobody goes to the movies night after night. Nobody in their right minds goes to the movies as often as you pretend to. People don't go to the movies at nearly midnight, and movies don't let out at two A.M. Come in stumbling. Muttering to yourself like a maniac! You get three hours' sleep and then go to work. Oh, I can picture the way you're doing down there. Moping, doping, because you're in no condition.

TOM [*wildly*]. No, I'm in no condition!

AMANDA. What right have you got to jeopardize your job? Jeopardize the security of us all? How do you think we'd manage if you were—

TOM. Listen! You think I'm crazy *about* the *warehouse*? [*He bends fiercely toward her slight figure.*] You think I'm in love with the Continental Shoemakers? You think I want to spend fifty-five *years* down there in that—*celotex interior!* with—*fluorescent—tubes!* Look! I'd rather somebody picked up a crowbar and battered out my brains—than go back mornings! I *go!* Every time you come in yelling that God damn "*Rise and Shine!*" "*Rise and Shine!*" I say to myself, "How *lucky dead* people are!" But I get up. I *go!* For sixty-five dollars a month I give up all that I dream of doing and being *ever!* And you say self—*self's* all I ever think of. Why, listen, if self is what I thought of, Mother, I'd be where he is—GONE! [*Pointing to father's picture.*] As far as the system of transportation reaches! [*He starts past her. She grabs his arm.*] Don't grab at me, Mother!

AMANDA. Where are you going?

TOM. I'm going to the *movies!*

AMANDA. I don't believe that lie!

TOM [*crouching toward her, overtowering her tiny figure. She backs away, gasping.*] I'm going to opium dens! Yes, opium dens, dens of vice and criminals' hangouts, Mother. I've joined the Hogan gang, I'm a hired assassin, I carry a tommy gun in a violin case! I run a string of cathouses in the Valley! They call me Killer, Killer Wingfield, I'm leading a double-life, a simple, honest warehouse worker by day, by night a dynamic *czar* of the *underworld, Mother.* I go to gambling casinos, I spin away fortunes on the roulette table! I wear a patch over one eye and a false mustache, sometimes I put on green whiskers. On those occasions they call me—*El Diablo!* Oh, I could tell you things to make you sleepless! My enemies plan to dynamite this place. They're going to blow us all sky-high some night! I'll be glad, very happy, and so will you! You'll go up, up on a broomstick, over Blue Mountain with seventeen gentlemen callers! You ugly—babbling old—*witch.* . . . [*He goes through a series of violent, clumsy movements, seizing his overcoat, lunging to the door, pulling it fiercely open. The women watch him, aghast. His arm catches in the sleeve of the coat as he struggles to pull it on. For a moment he is pinioned by the bulky garment. With an outraged groan he tears the coat off again, splitting the shoulder of it, and hurls it across the room. It strikes against the shelf of LAURA's glass collection, there is a tinkle of shattering glass. LAURA cries out as if wounded. MUSIC. LEGEND: "THE GLASS MENAGERIE."*]

LAURA [*shrilly*]. My glass!—menagerie. . . . [*She covers her face and turns away. But AMANDA is still stunned and stupefied by the "ugly witch" so that she barely notices this occurrence. Now she recovers her speech.*]

AMANDA [*in an awful voice*]. I won't speak to you—until you apologize! [*She crosses through portieres and draws them together behind her. TOM is left with*]

LAURA. LAURA *clings weakly to the mantel with her face averted.* TOM *stares at her stupidly for a moment. Then he crosses to shelf. Drops awkwardly on his knees to collect the fallen glass, glancing at* LAURA *as if he would speak but couldn't.*]

[*"The Glass Menagerie" steals in as* THE SCENE DIMS OUT.]

SCENE IV

[*The interior is dark. Faint light in the alley.*

A deep-voiced bell in a church is tolling the hour of five as the scene commences.

TOM *appears at the top of the alley. After each solemn boom of the bell in the tower, he shakes a little noise-maker or rattle as if to express the tiny spasm of man in contrast to the sustained power and dignity of the Almighty. This and the unsteadiness of his advance make it evident that he has been drinking.*

As he climbs the few steps to the fire-escape landing light steals up inside. LAURA *appears in night-dress, observing* TOM'S *empty bed in the front room.*

TOM *fishes in his pockets for door-key, removing a motley assortment of articles in the search, including a perfect shower of movie-ticket stubs and an empty bottle. At last he finds the key, but just as he is about to insert it, it slips from his fingers. He strikes a match and crouches below the door.*]

TOM [*bitterly*]. One crack—and it falls through! [LAURA *opens the door.*]

LAURA. Tom! Tom, what are you doing?

TOM. Looking for a door-key.

LAURA. Where have you been all this time?

TOM. I have been to the movies.

LAURA. All this time at the movies?

TOM. There was a very long program. There was a Garbo picture and a Mickey Mouse and a travelogue and a newsreel and a preview of coming attractions. And there was an organ solo and a collection for the milk-fund—simultaneously—which ended up in a terrible fight between a fat lady and an usher!

LAURA [*innocently*.] Did you have to stay through everything?

TOM. Of course! And, oh, I forgot! There was a big stage show! The headliner on this stage show was Malvolio the Magician. He performed wonderful tricks, many of them, such as pouring water back and forth between pitchers. First it turned to wine and then it turned to beer and then it turned to whiskey. I know it was whiskey it finally turned into because he needed somebody to come up out of the audience to help him, and I came up—both shows! It was Kentucky Straight Bourbon. A very generous fellow, he gave souvenirs. [*He pulls from his back pocket a shimmering rainbow-colored scarf.*] He gave me this. This is his magic scarf. You can have it, Laura. You wave it over a canary cage and you get a bowl of gold-fish. You wave it over the gold-fish bowl and they fly away canaries. . . . But the wonderfullest trick of all was the coffin trick. We nailed him into a coffin and he got out of the coffin without removing one nail. [*He has come inside.*] There is a trick that would come in handy for me—get me out of this 2 by 4 situation! [*Flops onto bed and starts removing shoes.*]

LAURA. Tom—Shhh!

TOM. What're you shushing me for?

LAURA. You'll wake up Mother.

TOM. Goody, goody! Pay 'er back for all those "Rise an' Shines." [*Lies down, groaning.*] You know it don't take much intelligence to get yourself into a nailed-up coffin, Laura. But who in hell ever got himself out of one without removing one nail? [*As if in answer, the father's grinning photograph lights up.*]

[*SCENE DIMS OUT*]

[*Immediately following: The church bell is heard striking six. At the sixth stroke the alarm clock goes off in AMANDA's room, and after a few moments we hear her calling: "Rise and Shine! Rise and Shine! Laura, go tell your brother to rise and shine!"*]

TOM [*sitting up slowly*]. I'll rise—but I won't shine. [*The light increases.*]

AMANDA. Laura, tell your brother his coffee is ready. [*LAURA slips into front room.*]

LAURA. Tom!—It's nearly seven. Don't make Mother nervous. [*He stares at her stupidly. Beseechingly.*] Tom, speak to Mother this morning. Make up with her, apologize, speak to her!

TOM. She won't to me. It's her that started not speaking.

LAURA. If you just say you're sorry she'll start speaking.

TOM. Her not speaking—is that such a tragedy?

LAURA. Please—please!

AMANDA [*calling from kitchenette*]. Laura, are you going to do what I asked you to do, or do I have to get dressed and go out myself?

LAURA. Going, going—soon as I get on my coat! [*She pulls on a shapeless felt hat with nervous, jerky movement, pleadingly glancing at TOM. Rushes awkwardly for coat. The coat is one of AMANDA's, inaccurately made-over, the sleeves too short for LAURA.*] Butter and what else?

AMANDA [*entering upstage*]. Just butter. Tell them to charge it.

LAURA. Mother, they make such faces when I do that.

AMANDA. Sticks and stones can break our bones, but the expression on Mr. Garfinkel's face won't harm us! Tell your brother his coffee is getting cold.

LAURA [*at door*]. Do what I asked you, will you, will you, Tom? [*He looks sullenly away.*]

AMANDA. Laura, go now or just don't go at all!

LAURA [*rushing out*]. Going—going! [*A second later she cries out. TOM springs up and crosses to door. AMANDA rushes anxiously in. TOM opens the door.*]

TOM. Laura?

LAURA. I'm all right. I slipped, but I'm all right.

AMANDA [*peering anxiously after her*]. If anyone breaks a leg on those fire-escape steps, the landlord ought to be sued for every cent he possesses! [*She shuts door. Remembers she isn't speaking and returns to other room. As TOM enters listlessly for his coffee, she turns her back to him and stands rigidly facing the window on the gloomy gray vault of the areaway. Its light on her face with its aged but childish features is cruelly sharp, satirical as a Daumier print. MUSIC UNDER: "AVE MARIA." TOM glances sheepishly but sullenly at her averted figure and slumps at the table. The coffee is scalding hot; he sips it and gasps and spits it back in the cup. At his gasp, AMANDA catches her breath and half turns. Then catches herself and turns back to window. TOM blows on his coffee, glancing sidewise at his mother. She clears her throat. TOM clears his. He starts to rise. Sinks back down again, scratches his head, clears his throat again. AMANDA coughs. TOM raises his cup in both hands to blow on it, his eyes staring over the rim of it at his mother for several moments. Then he slowly sets the cup down*] *and awkwardly and hesitantly rises from the chair.*]

Tom [*hoarsely*]. Mother. I—I apologize, Mother. [Amanda *draws a quick, shuddering breath. Her face works grotesquely. She breaks into childlike tears.*] I'm sorry for what I said, for everything that I said, I didn't mean it.

Amanda [*sobbingly*]. My devotion has made me a witch and so I make myself hateful to my children!

Tom. *No, you don't.*

Amanda. I worry so much, don't sleep, it makes me nervous!

Tom [*gently*]. I understand that.

Amanda. I've had to put up a solitary battle all these years. But you're my right-hand bower! Don't fall down, don't fail!

Tom [*gently*]. I try, Mother.

Amanda [*with great enthusiasm*]. Try and you will succeed! [*The notion makes her breathless.*] Why, you—you're just *full* of natural endowments! Both of my children—they're *unusual* children! Don't you think I know it? I'm so—*proud!* Happy and—feel I've—so much to be thankful for but— Promise me one thing, Son!

Tom. What, Mother?

Amanda. Promise, son, you'll—never be a drunkard!

Tom [*turns to her grinning*]. I will never be a drunkard, Mother.

Amanda. That's what frightened me so, that you'd be drinking! Eat a bowl of Purina!

Tom. Just coffee, Mother.

Amanda. Shredded wheat biscuit?

Tom. No. No, Mother, just coffee.

Amanda. You can't put in a day's work on an empty stomach. You've got ten minutes—don't gulp! Drinking too-hot liquids makes cancer of the stomach. . . . Put cream in.

Tom. No, thank you.

Amanda. To cool it.

Tom. No! No, thank you, I want it black.

Amanda. I know, but it's not good for you. We have to do all that we can to build ourselves up. In these trying times we live in, all that we have to cling to is—each other. . . . That's why it's so important to— Tom, I— I sent out your sister so I could discuss something with you. If you hadn't spoken I would have spoken to you. [*Sits down.*]

Tom [*gently*]. What is it, Mother, that you want to discuss?

Amanda. *Laura!* [Tom *puts his cup down slowly.* Legend on screen: "laura." Music: "the glass menagerie."]

Tom.—Oh.—Laura . . .

Amanda [*touching his sleeve*]. You know how Laura is. So quiet but—still water runs deep! She notices things and I think she—broods about them. [Tom *looks up.*] A few days ago I came in and she was crying.

Tom. What about?

Amanda. You.

Tom. Me?

Amanda. She has an idea that you're not happy here.

Tom. What gave her that idea?

Amanda. What gives her any idea? However, you do act strangely. I—I'm not criticizing, understand *that!* I know your ambitions do not lie in the warehouse, that like everybody in the whole wide world—you've had to—make sacrifices, but —Tom—Tom—life's not easy, it calls for —Spartan endurance! There's so many things in my heart that I cannot describe to you! I've never told you but I—*loved* your father. . . .

Tom [*gently*]. I know that, Mother.

Amanda. And you—when I see you taking after his ways! Staying out late—and —well, you *had* been drinking the night you were in that—terrifying condition! Laura says that you hate the apartment and that you go out nights to get away from it! Is that true, Tom?

TOM. No. You say there's so much in your heart that you can't describe to me. That's true of me, too. There's so much in my heart that I can't describe to *you!* So let's respect each other's—

AMANDA. But, why—*why,* Tom—are you always so *restless?* Where do you *go* to, nights?

TOM. I—go to the movies.

AMANDA. Why do you go to the movies so much, Tom?

TOM. I go to the movies because—I like adventure. Adventure is something I don't have much of at work, so I go to the movies.

AMANDA. But, Tom, you go to the movies *entirely* too *much!*

TOM. I like a lot of adventure. [AMANDA *looks baffled, then hurt. As the familiar inquisition resumes he becomes hard and impatient again.* AMANDA *slips back into her querulous attitude toward him.* IMAGE ON SCREEN: SAILING VESSEL WITH JOLLY ROGER.]

AMANDA. Most young men find adventure in their careers.

TOM. Then most young men are not employed in a warehouse.

AMANDA. The world is full of young men employed in warehouses and offices and factories.

TOM. Do all of them find adventure in their careers?

AMANDA. They do or they do without it! Not everybody has a craze for adventure.

TOM. Man is by instinct a lover, a hunter, a fighter, and none of those instincts are given much play at the warehouse!

AMANDA. Man is by instinct! Don't quote instinct to me! Instinct is something that people have got away from! It belongs to animals! Christian adults don't want it!

TOM. What do Christian adults want, then, Mother?

AMANDA. Superior things! Things of the mind and the spirit! Only animals have to satisfy instincts! Surely your aims are somewhat higher than theirs! Than monkeys—pigs—

TOM. I reckon they're not.

AMANDA. You're joking. However, that isn't what I wanted to discuss.

TOM [*rising*]. I haven't much time.

AMANDA [*pushing his shoulders*]. Sit down.

TOM. You want me to punch in red at the warehouse, Mother?

AMANDA. You have five minutes. I want to talk about Laura. [LEGEND: "PLANS AND PROVISIONS."]

TOM. All right! What about Laura?

AMANDA. We have to be making some plans and provisions for her. She's older than you, two years, and nothing has happened. She just drifts along doing nothing. It frightens me terribly how she just drifts along.

TOM. I guess she's the type that people call home girls.

AMANDA. There's no such type, and if there is, it's a pity! That is unless the home is hers, with a husband!

TOM. What?

AMANDA. Oh, I can see the handwriting on the wall as plain as I see the nose in front of my face! It's terrifying!
More and more you remind me of your

father! He was out all hours without explanation!—Then *left! Good-bye!*

And me with the bag to hold. I saw that letter you got from the Merchant Marine. I know what you're dreaming of. I'm not standing here blindfolded.

Very well, then. Then *do* it!

But not till there's somebody to take your place.

Toм. What do you mean?

Amanda. I mean that as soon as Laura has got somebody to take care of her, married, a home of her own, independent— why, then you'll be free to go wherever you please, on land, on sea, whichever way the wind blows you!

But until that time you've got to look out for your sister. I don't say me because I'm old and don't matter! I say for your sister because she's young and dependent.

I put her in business college—a dismal failure! Frightened her so it made her sick at the stomach.

I took her over to the Young People's League at the church. Another fiasco. She spoke to nobody, nobody spoke to her. Now all she does is fool with those pieces of glass and play those worn-out records. What kind of a life is that for a girl to lead?

Toм. What can I do about it?

Amanda. Overcome selfishness!

Self, self, self is all that you ever think of! [Toм *springs up and crosses to get his coat. It is ugly and bulky. He pulls on a cap with earmuffs.*] Where is your muffler? Put your wool muffler on! [*He snatches it angrily from the closet and tosses it around his neck and pulls both ends tight.*] Tom! I haven't said what I had in mind to ask you.

Toм. I'm too late to—

Amanda [*catching his arm—very importunately. Then shyly*]. Down at the

warehouse, aren't there some—nice young men?

Toм. No!

Amanda. There *must* be—*some* . . .

Toм. Mother— [*Gesture.*]

Amanda. Find out one that's clean-living—doesn't drink and—ask him out for sister!

Toм. What?

Amanda. For *sister!* To *meet!* Get *acquainted!*

Toм [*stamping to door*]. Oh, my gosh!

Amanda. Will you? [*He opens door. Imploringly.*] Will you? [*He starts down.*] Will you? *Will* you, dear?

Toм [*calling back*]. yes! [Amanda *closes the door hesitantly and with a troubled but faintly hopeful expression.* SCREEN IMAGE: GLAMOR MAGAZINE COVER. *Spot* Amanda *at phone.*]

Amanda. Ella Cartwright? This is Amanda Wingfield!

How are you, honey?

How is that kidney condition? [*Count five.*] Horrors! [*Count five.*]

You're a Christian martyr, yes, honey, that's what you are, a Christian martyr!

Well, I just now happened to notice in my little red book that your subscription to the *Companion* has just run out! I knew that you wouldn't want to miss out on the wonderful serial starting in this new issue. It's by Bessie Mae Hopper, the first thing she's written since *Honeymoon for Three.*

Wasn't that a strange and interesting story? Well, this one is even lovelier, I believe. It has a sophisticated, society background. It's all about the horsey set on Long Island!

[FADE OUT]

SCENE V

[LEGEND ON SCREEN: "ANNUNCIATION." *Fade with music. It is early dusk of a spring evening. Supper has just been finished in the Wingfield apartment.* AMANDA *and* LAURA *in light-colored dresses are removing dishes from the table, in the upstage area, which is shadowy, their movements formalized almost as a dance or ritual, their moving forms as pale and silent as moths.* TOM, *in white shirt and trousers, rises from the table and crosses toward the fire-escape.*]

AMANDA [*as he passes her*]. Son, will you do me a favor?

TOM. What?

AMANDA. Comb your hair! You look so pretty when your hair is combed! [TOM *slouches on sofa with evening paper. Enormous caption "Franco Triumphs."*] There is only one respect in which I would like you to emulate your father.

TOM. What respect is that?

AMANDA. The care he always took of his appearance. He never allowed himself to look untidy. [*He throws down the paper and crosses to fire-escape.*] Where are you going?

TOM. I'm going out to smoke.

AMANDA. You smoke too much. A pack a day at fifteen cents a pack. How much would that amount to in a month? Thirty times fifteen is how much, Tom? Figure it out and you will be astounded at what you could save. Enough to give you a night-school course in accounting at Washington U! Just think what a wonderful thing that would be for you, Son! [TOM *is unmoved by the thought.*]

TOM. I'd rather smoke. [*He steps out on landing, letting the screen door slam.*]

AMANDA [*sharply*]. I know! That's the tragedy of it. . . . [*Alone, she turns to look at her husband's picture.* DANCE MUSIC: "ALL THE WORLD IS WAITING FOR THE SUNRISE!"]

TOM [*to the audience*]. Across the alley from us was the Paradise Dance Hall. On evenings in spring the windows and doors were open and the music came outdoors. Sometimes the lights were turned out except for a large glass sphere that hung from the ceiling. It would turn slowly about and filter the dusk with delicate rainbow colors. Then the orchestra played a waltz or a tango, something that had a slow and sensuous rhythm. Couples would come outside, to the relative privacy of the alley. You could see them kissing behind ash-pits and telephone poles.

This was the compensation for lives that passed like mine, without any change or adventure.

Adventure and change were imminent in this year. They were waiting around the corner for all these kids.

Suspended in the mist over Berchtesgaden, caught in the folds of Chamberlain's umbrella—

In Spain there was Guernica!

But here there was only hot swing music and liquor, dance halls, bars, and movies, and sex that hung in the gloom like a chandelier and flooded the world with brief, deceptive rainbows. . . .

All the world was waiting for bombardments! [AMANDA *turns from the picture and comes outside.*]

AMANDA [*sighing*]. A fire-escape landing's a poor excuse for a porch. [*She spreads a newspaper on a step and sits down, gracefully and demurely as if she were settling into a swing on a Mississippi veranda.*] What are you looking at?

TOM. The moon.

AMANDA. Is there a moon this evening?

TOM. It's rising over Garfinkel's Delicatessen.

AMANDA. So it is! A little silver slipper of a moon. Have you made a wish on it yet?

TOM. Um-hum.

AMANDA. What did you wish for?

TOM. That's a secret.

AMANDA. A secret, huh? Well, I won't tell mine either. I will be just as mysterious as you.

TOM. I bet I can guess what yours is.

AMANDA. Is my head so transparent?

TOM. You're not a sphinx.

AMANDA. No, I don't have secrets. I'll tell you what I wished for on the moon. Success and happiness for my precious children! I wish for that whenever there's a moon, and when there isn't a moon, I wish for it, too.

TOM. I thought perhaps you wished for a gentleman caller.

AMANDA. Why do you say that?

TOM. Don't you remember asking me to fetch one?

AMANDA. I remember suggesting that it would be nice for your sister if you brought home some nice young man from the warehouse. I think that I've made that suggestion more than once.

TOM. Yes, you have made it repeatedly.

AMANDA. Well?

TOM. We are going to have one.

AMANDA. *What?*

TOM. A gentleman caller! [THE ANNUNCIATION IS CELEBRATED WITH MUSIC. AMANDA *rises*. IMAGE ON SCREEN: CALLER WITH BOUQUET.]

AMANDA. You mean you have asked some nice young man to come over?

TOM. Yep. I've asked him to dinner.

AMANDA. You really did?

TOM. I did!

AMANDA. You did, and did he—*accept?*

TOM. He did!

AMANDA. Well, well—well, well! That's —lovely!

TOM. I thought that you would be pleased.

AMANDA. It's definite, then?

TOM. Very definite.

AMANDA. Soon?

TOM. Very soon.

AMANDA. For heaven's sake, stop putting on and tell me some things, will you?

TOM. What things do you want me to tell you?

AMANDA. *Naturally* I would like to know when he's *coming!*

TOM. He's coming tomorrow.

AMANDA. *Tomorrow?*

TOM. Yep. Tomorrow.

AMANDA. But, Tom!

TOM. Yes, Mother?

AMANDA. Tomorrow gives me no time!

TOM. Time for what?

AMANDA. Preparations! Why didn't you phone me at once, as soon as you asked him, the minute that he accepted? Then, don't you see, I could have been getting ready!

TOM. You don't have to make any fuss.

AMANDA. Oh, Tom, Tom, 'Tom, of course I have to make a fuss! I want things nice, not sloppy! Not thrown together. I'll certainly have to do some fast thinking, won't I?

TOM. I don't see why you have to think at all.

AMANDA. You just don't know. We can't have a gentleman caller in a pig-sty! All my wedding silver has to be polished, the monogrammed table linen ought to be laundered! The windows have to be washed and fresh curtains put up. And how about clothes? We have to *wear* something, don't we?

TOM. Mother, this boy is no one to make a fuss over!

AMANDA. Do you realize he's the first young man we've introduced to your sister?

It's terrible, dreadful, disgraceful that poor little sister has never received a single gentleman caller! Tom, come inside! [*She opens the screen door.*]

TOM. What for?

AMANDA. I want to ask you some things.

TOM. If you're going to make such a fuss, I'll call it off, I'll tell him not to come!

AMANDA. You certainly won't do anything of the kind. Nothing offends people worse than broken engagements. It simply means I'll have to work like a Turk! We won't be brilliant, but we will pass inspection. Come on inside. [TOM *follows, groaning.*] Sit down.

TOM. Any particular place you would like me to sit?

AMANDA. Thank heavens I've got that new sofa! I'm also making payments on a floor lamp I'll have sent out! And put the chintz covers on, they'll brighten things up! Of course I'd hoped to have these walls re-papered. . . . What is the young man's name?

TOM. His name is O'Connor.

AMANDA. That, of course, means fish—tomorrow is Friday! I'll have that salmon loaf—with Durkee's dressing! What does he do? He works at the warehouse?

TOM. Of course! How else would I—

AMANDA. Tom, he—doesn't drink?

TOM. Why do you ask me that?

AMANDA. Your father *did*!

TOM. Don't get started on that!

AMANDA. He *does* drink, then?

TOM. Not that I know of!

AMANDA. Make sure, be certain! The last thing I want for my daughter's a boy who drinks!

TOM. Aren't you being a little bit premature? Mr. O'Connor has not yet appeared on the scene!

AMANDA. But will tomorrow. To meet your sister, and what do I know about his character? Nothing! Old maids are better off than wives of drunkards!

TOM. Oh, my God!

AMANDA. Be still!

TOM [*leaning forward to whisper*]. Lots of fellows meet girls whom they don't marry!

AMANDA. Oh, talk sensibly, Tom—and don't be sarcastic! [*She has gotten a hairbrush.*]

TOM. What are you doing?

AMANDA. I'm brushing that cow-lick down!

What is this young man's position at the warehouse?

TOM [*submitting grimly to the brush and the interrogation*]. This young man's position is that of a shipping clerk, Mother.

AMANDA. Sounds to me like a fairly responsible job, the sort of a job *you* would be in if you just had more *get-up*.

What is his salary? Have you any idea?

TOM. I would judge it to be approximately eighty-five dollars a month.

AMANDA. Well—not princely, but—

TOM. Twenty more than I make.

AMANDA. Yes, how well I know! But for a family man, eighty-five dollars a month is not much more than you can just get by on. . . .

TOM. Yes, but Mr. O'Connor is not a family man.

AMANDA. He might be, mightn't he? Some time in the future?

TOM. I see. Plans and provisions.

AMANDA. You are the only young man that I know of who ignores the fact that the future becomes the present, the present the past, and the past turns into everlasting regret if you don't plan for it!

TOM. I will think that over and see what I can make of it.

AMANDA. Don't be supercilious with your mother! Tell me some more about this—what do you call him?

TOM. James D. O'Connor. The D. is for Delaney.

AMANDA. Irish on *both* sides! *Gracious!* And doesn't drink?

TOM. Shall I call him up and ask him right this minute?

AMANDA. The only way to find out about those things is to make discreet inquiries at the proper moment. When I was a girl in Blue Mountain and it was suspected that a young man drank, the girl whose attentions he had been receiving, if any girl *was,* would sometimes speak to the minister of his church, or rather her father would if her father was living, and sort of feel him out on the young man's character. That is the way such things are discreetly handled to keep a young woman from making a tragic mistake!

TOM. Then how did you happen to make a tragic mistake?

AMANDA. That innocent look of your father's had everyone fooled!

He *smiled*—the world was *enchanted!*

No girl can do worse than put herself at the mercy of a handsome appearance!

I hope that Mr. O'Connor is not too good-looking.

TOM. No, he's not too good-looking. He's covered with freckles and hasn't too much of a nose.

AMANDA. He's not right-down homely, though?

TOM. Not right-down homely. Just medium homely, I'd say.

AMANDA. Character's what to look for in a man.

TOM. That's what I've always said, Mother.

AMANDA. You've never said anything of the kind and I suspect you would never give it a thought.

TOM. Don't be so suspicious of me.

AMANDA. At least I hope he's the type that's up and coming.

TOM. I think he really goes in for self-improvement.

AMANDA. What reason have you to think so?

TOM. He goes to night school.

AMANDA [*beaming*]. Splendid! What does he do, I mean study?

TOM. Radio engineering and public speaking!

AMANDA. Then he has visions of being advanced in the world!

Any young man who studies public speaking is aiming to have an executive job some day!

And radio engineering? A thing for the future!

Both of these facts are very illuminating. Those are the sort of things that a mother should know concerning any young man who comes to call on her daughter. Seriously or—not.

TOM. One little warning. He doesn't know about Laura. I didn't let on that we had dark ulterior motives. I just said, why don't you come and have dinner with us? He said okay and that was the whole conversation.

AMANDA. I bet it was! You're eloquent as an oyster.

However, he'll know about Laura when he gets here. When he sees how lovely and sweet and pretty she is, he'll thank his lucky stars he was asked to dinner.

TOM. Mother, you mustn't expect too much of Laura.

AMANDA. What do you mean?

TOM. Laura seems all those things to you and me because she's ours and we love her. We don't even notice she's crippled any more.

AMANDA. Don't say crippled! You know that I never allow that word to be used!

TOM. But face facts, Mother. She is and —that's not all—

AMANDA. What do you mean "not all"?

TOM. Laura is very different from other girls.

AMANDA. I think the difference is all to her advantage.

TOM. Not quite all—in the eyes of others—strangers—she's terribly shy and lives in a world of her own and those things make her seem a little peculiar to people outside the house.

AMANDA. Don't say peculiar.

TOM. Face the facts. She is. [THE DANCE-HALL MUSIC CHANGES TO A TANGO THAT HAS A MINOR AND SOMEWHAT OMINOUS TONE.]

AMANDA. In what way is she peculiar—may I ask?

TOM [gently]. She lives in a world of her own—a world of—little glass ornaments, Mother. . . . [Gets up. AMANDA remains holding brush, looking at him, troubled.] She plays old phonograph records and—that's about all— [He glances at himself in the mirror and crosses to door.]

AMANDA [sharply]. Where are you going?

TOM. I'm going to the movies. [Out screen door.]

AMANDA. Not to the movies, every night to the movies! [Follows quickly to screen door.] I don't believe you always go to the movies! [He is gone. AMANDA looks worriedly after him for a moment. Then vitality and optimism return and she turns from the door. Crossing to portieres.] Laura! Laura! [LAURA answers from kitchenette.]

LAURA. Yes, Mother.

AMANDA. Let those dishes go and come in front! [LAURA appears with dish towel. Gaily.] Laura, come here and make a wish on the moon! [SCREEN IMAGE: MOON.]

LAURA [entering]. Moon—moon?

AMANDA. A little silver slipper of a moon. Look over your left shoulder, Laura, and make a wish! [LAURA looks faintly puzzled as if called out of sleep. AMANDA seizes her shoulders and turns her at an angle by the door.] Now! Now, darling, wish!

LAURA. What shall I wish for, Mother?

AMANDA [her voice trembling and her eyes suddenly filling with tears.] Happiness! Good fortune! [The violin rises and the stage dims out.]

[CURTAIN]

SCENE VI

[IMAGE: HIGH SCHOOL HERO.]

And so the following evening I brought Jim home to dinner. I had known Jim slightly in high school. In high school Jim was a hero. He had tremendous Irish good nature and vitality with the scrubbed and polished look of white chinaware. He seemed to move in a continual spotlight. He was a star in basketball, captain of the debating club, president of the senior class and the glee club and he sang the male lead in the annual light operas. He was always running or bounding, never just walking. He seemed always at the point of defeating the law of gravity. He was shooting with such velocity through his adolescence that you would logically expect him to arrive at nothing short of the

White House by the time he was thirty. But Jim apparently ran into more interference after his graduation from Soldan. His speed had definitely slowed. Six years after he left high school he was holding a job that wasn't much better than mine. [IMAGE: CLERK.]

He was the only one at the warehouse with whom I was on friendly terms. I was valuable to him as someone who could remember his former glory, who had seen him win basketball games and the silver cup in debating. He knew of my secret practice of retiring to a cabinet of the wash-room to work on poems when business was slack in the warehouse. He called me Shakespeare. And while the other boys in the warehouse regarded me with suspicious hostility, Jim took a humorous attitude toward me. Gradually his attitude affected the others, their hostility wore off and they also began to smile at me as people smile at an oddly fashioned dog who trots across their path at some distance.

I knew that Jim and Laura had known each other at Soldan, and I had heard Laura speak admiringly of his voice. I didn't know if Jim remembered her or not. In high school Laura had been as unobtrusive as Jim had been astonishing. If he did remember Laura, it was not as my sister, for when I asked him to dinner, he grinned and said, "You know, Shakespeare, I never thought of you as having folks!"

He was about to discover that I did. . . .

[LIGHT UPSTAGE. LEGEND ON SCREEN: "THE ACCENT OF A COMING FOOT." *Friday evening. It is about five o'clock of a late spring evening which comes "scattering poems in the sky." A delicate lemony light is in the Wingfield apartment.* AMANDA *has worked like a Turk in preparation for the gentleman caller. The results are astonishing. The new floor lamp with its rose-silk shade is in place, a colored paper lantern conceals the broken light fixture in the ceiling, new billowing white curtains are at the windows, chintz covers are on chairs and sofa, a pair of new sofa pillows make their initial appearance. Open boxes and tissue paper are scattered on the floor.* LAURA *stands in the middle with lifted arms while* AMANDA *crouches before her, adjusting the hem of the new dress, devout and ritualistic. The dress is colored and designed by memory. The arrangement of* LAURA's *hair is changed; it is softer and more becoming. A fragile, unearthly prettiness has come out in* LAURA: *she is like a piece of translucent glass touched by light, given a momentary radiance, not actual, not lasting.*]

AMANDA [*impatiently*]. Why are you trembling?

LAURA. Mother, you've made me so nervous!

AMANDA. How have I made you nervous?

LAURA. By all this fuss! You make it seem so important!

AMANDA. I don't understand you, Laura. You couldn't be satisfied with just sitting home, and yet whenever I try to arrange something for you, you seem to resist it. [*She gets up.*] Now take a look at yourself. No, wait! Wait just a moment—I have an idea!

LAURA. What is it now? [AMANDA *produces two powder puffs which she wraps in handkerchiefs and stuffs in* LAURA's *bosom.*] Mother, what are you doing?

AMANDA. They call them "Gay Deceivers"!

LAURA. I won't wear them!

AMANDA. You will!

LAURA. Why should I?

AMANDA. Because, to be painfully honest, your chest is flat.

LAURA. You make it seem like we were setting a trap.

AMANDA. All pretty girls are a trap, a pretty trap, and men expect them to be. [LEGEND: "A PRETTY TRAP."] Now look at yourself, young lady. This is the prettiest you will ever be!

I've got to fix myself now! You're going to be surprised by your mother's appearance! [*She crosses through portieres, humming gaily.* LAURA *moves slowly to the long mirror and stares solemnly at herself. A wind blows the white curtains inward in a slow, graceful motion and with a faint, sorrowful sighing.*]

AMANDA [*off stage*]. It isn't dark enough yet. [*She turns slowly before the mirror with a troubled look.*]

[LEGEND ON SCREEN: "THIS IS MY SISTER: CELEBRATE HER WITH STRINGS!" MUSIC.]

AMANDA [*laughing, off*]. I'm going to show you something. I'm going to make a spectacular appearance!

LAURA. What is it, Mother?

AMANDA. Possess your soul in patience—you will see!

Something I've resurrected from that old trunk! Styles haven't changed so terribly much after all. . . . [*She parts the portieres.*] Now just look at your mother! [*She wears a girlish frock of yellowed voile with a blue silk sash. She carries a bunch of jonquils—the legend of her youth is nearly revived. Feverishly.*] This is the dress in which I led the cotillion. Won the cakewalk twice at Sunset Hill, wore one spring to the Governor's ball in Jackson!

See how I sashayed around the ballroom, Laura? [*She raises her skirt and does a mincing step around the room.*] I wore it on Sundays for my gentlemen callers! I had it on the day I met your father—

I had malaria fever all that spring. The change of climate from East Tennessee to the Delta—weakened resistance—I had a little temperature all the time—not enough to be serious—just enough to make me restless and giddy!—Invitations poured in—parties all over the Delta!—"Stay in bed," said Mother, "you have fever!"—but I just wouldn't.—I took quinine but kept on going, going!—Evenings, dances!—Afternoons, long, long rides! Picnics—lovely!—So lovely, that country in May.—All lacy with dogwood, literally flooded with jonquils!—That was the spring I had the craze for jonquils. Jonquils became an absolute obsession. Mother said, "Honey, there's no more room for jonquils." And still I kept on bringing in more jonquils. Whenever, wherever I saw them, I'd say, "Stop! Stop! I see jonquils!" I made the young men help me gather the jonquils! It was a joke, Amanda and her jonquils! Finally there were no more vases to hold them, every available space was filled with jonquils. No vases to hold them? All right, I'll hold them myself! And then I—[*She stops in front of the picture.* MUSIC.] met your father!

Malaria fever and jonquils and then—this—boy. . . . [*She switches on the rose-colored lamp.*] I hope they get here before it starts to rain. [*She crosses upstage and places the jonquils in bowl on table.*] I gave your brother a little extra change so he and Mr. O'Connor could take the service car home.

LAURA [*with altered look*]. What did you say his name was?

AMANDA. O'Connor.

LAURA. What is his first name?

AMANDA. I don't remember. Oh, yes, I do. It was—Jim! [LAURA *sways slightly and catches hold of a chair.* LEGEND ON SCREEN: "NOT JIM!"]

LAURA [*faintly*]. Not—Jim!

AMANDA. Yes, that was it, it was Jim! I've never known a Jim that wasn't nice! [MUSIC: OMINOUS.]

LAURA. Are you sure his name is Jim O'Connor?

AMANDA. Yes. Why?

LAURA. Is he the one that Tom used to know in high school?

AMANDA. He didn't say so. I think he just got to know him at the warehouse.

LAURA. There was a Jim O'Connor we both knew in high school— [*Then, with effort.*] If that is the one that Tom is bringing to dinner—you'll have to excuse me, I won't come to the table.

AMANDA. What sort of nonsense is this?

LAURA. You asked me once if I'd ever liked a boy. Don't you remember I showed you this boy's picture?

AMANDA. You mean the boy you showed me in the year book?

LAURA. Yes, that boy.

AMANDA. Laura, Laura, were you in love with that boy?

LAURA. I don't know, Mother. All I know is I couldn't sit at the table if it was him!

AMANDA. It won't be him! It isn't the least bit likely. But whether it is or not, you will come to the table. You will not be excused.

LAURA. I'll have to be, Mother.

AMANDA. I don't intend to humor your silliness, Laura. I've had too much from you and your brother, both!

So just sit down and compose yourself till they come. Tom has forgotten his key so you'll have to let them in, when they arrive.

LAURA [*panicky*]. Oh, Mother—*you* answer the door!

AMANDA [*lightly*]. I'll be in the kitchen —busy!

LAURA. Oh, Mother, please answer the door, don't make me do it!

AMANDA [*crossing into kitchenette*]. I've got to fix the dressing for the salmon. Fuss, fuss—silliness!—over a gentleman caller!

[*Door swings shut.* LAURA *is left alone.* LEGEND: "TERROR!" *She utters a low moan and turns off the lamp—sits stiffly on the edge of the sofa, knotting her fingers together.* LEGEND ON SCREEN: "THE OPENING OF A DOOR!" TOM *and* JIM *appear on the fire-escape steps and climb to landing. Hearing their approach,* LAURA *rises with a panicky gesture. She retreats to the portieres. The doorbell.* LAURA *catches her breath and touches her throat. Low drums.*]

AMANDA [*calling*]. Laura, sweetheart! The door! [LAURA *stares at it without moving.*]

JIM. I think we just beat the rain.

TOM. Uh-huh. [*He rings again, nervously.* JIM *whistles and fishes for a cigarette.*]

AMANDA [*very, very gaily*]. Laura, that is your brother and Mr. O'Connor! Will you let them in, darling? [LAURA *crosses toward kitchenette door.*]

LAURA [*breathlessly*]. Mother—you go to the door! [AMANDA *steps out of kitchenette and stares furiously at* LAURA. *She points imperiously at the door.*]

LAURA. Please, please!

AMANDA [*in a fierce whisper*]. What is the matter with you, you silly thing?

LAURA [*desperately*]. Please, you answer it, *please!*

AMANDA. I told you I wasn't going to humor you, Laura. Why have you chosen this moment to lose your mind?

LAURA. Please, please, please, you go!

AMANDA. You'll have to go to the door because I can't!

LAURA [*despairingly*]. I can't either!

AMANDA. *Why?*

LAURA. I'm *sick!*

AMANDA. I'm sick, too—of your nonsense! Why can't you and your brother be normal people? Fantastic whims and behavior! [TOM *gives a long ring.*] Preposterous goings on! Can you give me one reason— [*Calls out lyrically.*] COMING! JUST ONE SECOND!—why you should be afraid to open a door? Now you answer it, Laura!

LAURA. Oh, oh, oh . . . [*She returns through the portieres. Darts to the victrola and winds it frantically and turns it on.*]

AMANDA. Laura Wingfield, you march right to that door!

LAURA. Yes—yes, Mother! [*A faraway, scratchy rendition of "Dardanella" softens the air and gives her strength to move through it. She slips to the door and draws it cautiously open.* TOM *enters with the caller,* JIM O'CONNOR.]

TOM. Laura, this is Jim. Jim, this is my sister, Laura.

JIM [*stepping inside*]. I didn't know that Shakespeare had a sister!

LAURA [*retreating stiff and trembling from the door*]. How—how do you do?

JIM [*heartily extending his hand*]. Okay! [LAURA *touches it hesitantly with hers.*]

JIM. Your hand's *cold,* Laura!

LAURA. Yes, well—I've been playing the victrola. . . .

JIM. Must have been playing classical music on it! You ought to play a little hot swing music to warm you up!

LAURA. Excuse me—I haven't finished playing the victrola. . . . [*She turns awkwardly and hurries into the front room. She pauses a second by the victrola. Then*

catches her breath and darts through the portieres like a frightened deer.]

JIM [*grinning*]. What was the matter?

TOM. Oh,—with Laura? Laura is—terribly shy.

JIM. Shy, huh? It's unusual to meet a shy girl nowadays. I don't believe you ever mentioned you had a sister.

TOM. Well, now you know. I have one. Here is the *Post Dispatch.* You want a piece of it?

JIM. Uh-huh.

TOM. What piece? The comics?

JIM. Sports! [*Glances at it.*] Ole Dizzy Dean is on his bad behavior.

TOM [*disinterest*]. Yeah? [*Lights cigarette and crosses back to fire-escape door.*]

JIM. Where are *you* going?

TOM. I'm going out on the terrace.

JIM [*goes after him*]. You know, Shakespeare—I'm going to sell you a bill of goods!

TOM. What goods?

JIM. A course I'm taking.

TOM. Huh?

JIM. In public speaking! You and me, we're not the warehouse type.

TOM. Thanks—that's good news. But what has public speaking got to do with it?

JIM. It fits you for—executive positions!

TOM. Awww.

JIM. I tell you it's done a helluva lot for me. [IMAGE: EXECUTIVE AT DESK.]

TOM. In what respect?

JIM. In every! Ask yourself what is the difference between you an' me and men in the office down front? Brains?—No!—Ability?—No! Then what? Just one little thing—

TOM. What is that one little thing?

JIM. Primarily it amounts to—social poise! Being able to square up to people and hold your own on any social level!

AMANDA [*off stage*]. Tom?

TOM. Yes, Mother?

AMANDA. Is that you and Mr. O'Connor?

TOM. Yes, Mother.

AMANDA. Well, you just make yourselves comfortable in there.

TOM. Yes, Mother.

AMANDA. Ask Mr. O'Connor if he would like to wash his hands.

JIM. Aw, no—no—thank you—I took care of that at the warehouse. Tom—

TOM. Yes?

JIM. Mr. Mendoza was speaking to me about you.

TOM. Favorably?

JIM. What do you think?

TOM. Well—

JIM. You're going to be out of a job if you don't wake up.

TOM. I am waking up—

JIM. You show no signs.

TOM. The signs are interior. [IMAGE ON SCREEN: THE SAILING VESSEL WITH JOLLY ROGER AGAIN.] I'm planning to change. [*He leans over the rail speaking with quiet exhilaration. The incandescent marquees and signs of the first-run movie houses light his face from across the alley. He looks like a voyager.*] I'm right at the point of committing myself to a future that doesn't include the warehouse and Mr. Mendoza or even a night-school course in public speaking.

JIM. What are you gassing about?

TOM. I'm tired of the movies.

JIM. Movies!

TOM. Yes, movies! Look at them— [*A wave toward the marvels of Grand Avenue.*] All of those glamorous people—having adventures—hogging it all, gobbling the whole thing up! You know what happens? People go to the *movies* instead of *moving!* Hollywood characters are sup-

posed to have all the adventures for everybody in America, while everybody in America sits in a dark room and watches them have them! Yes, until there's a war. That's when adventure becomes available to the masses! *Everyone's* dish, not only Gable's! Then the people in the dark room come out of the dark room to have some adventures themselves— Goody, goody!— It's our turn now, to go to the South Sea Island—to make a safari—to be exotic, far-off!—But I'm not patient. I don't want to wait till then. I'm tired of the *movies* and I am *about* to *move!*

JIM [*incredulously*]. Move?

TOM. Yes.

JIM. When?

TOM. Soon!

JIM. Where? Where? [THEME THREE MUSIC SEEMS TO ANSWER THE QUESTION, WHILE TOM THINKS IT OVER. HE SEARCHES AMONG HIS POCKETS.]

TOM. I'm starting to boil inside. I know I seem dreamy, but inside—well, I'm boiling!—Whenever I pick up a shoe, I shudder a little thinking how short life is and what I am doing!—Whatever that means, I know it doesn't mean shoes—except as something to wear on a traveler's feet! [*Finds paper.*] Look—

JIM. What?

TOM. I'm a member.

JIM [*reading*]. The Union of Merchant Seamen.

TOM. I paid my dues this month, instead of the light bill.

JIM. You will regret it when they turn the lights off.

TOM. I won't be here.

JIM. How about your mother?

TOM. I'm like my father. The bastard son of a bastard! See how he grins? And he's been absent going on sixteen years!

JIM. You're just talking, you drip. How does your mother feel about it?

TOM. Shhh!—Here comes Mother! Mother is not acquainted with my plans!

AMANDA [*enters portieres*]. Where are you all?

TOM. On the terrace, Mother. [*They start inside. She advances to them. TOM is distinctly shocked at her appearance. Even JIM blinks a little. He is making his first contact with girlish Southern vivacity and in spite of the night-school course in public speaking is somewhat thrown off the beam by the unexpected outlay of social charm. Certain responses are attempted by JIM but are swept aside by AMANDA's gay laughter and chatter. TOM is embarrassed but after the first shock JIM reacts very warmly. Grins and chuckles, is altogether won over. IMAGE: AMANDA AS A GIRL.*]

AMANDA [*coyly smiling, shaking her girlish ringlets*]. Well, well, well, so this is Mr. O'Connor. Introductions entirely unnecessary. I've heard so much about you from my boy. I finally said to him, Tom—good gracious!—why don't you bring this paragon to supper? I'd like to meet this nice young man at the warehouse!—Instead of just hearing him sing your praises so much!

I don't know why my son is so stand-offish—that's not Southern behavior!

Let's sit down and—I think we could stand a little more air in here! Tom, leave the door open. I felt a nice fresh breeze a moment ago. Where has it gone to?

Mmm, so warm already! And not quite summer, even. We're going to burn up when summer really gets started.

However, we're having—we're having a very light supper. I think light things are better fo' this time of year. The same as light clothes are. Light clothes an' light food are what warm weather calls fo'.

You know our blood gets so thick during th' winter—it takes a while fo' us to *adjust* ou'selves!—when the season changes . . .

It's come so quick this year. I wasn't prepared. All of a sudden—heavens! Already summer!—I ran to the trunk an' pulled out this light dress— Terribly old! Historical almost! But feels so good—so good an' co-ol, y' know. . . .

TOM. Mother—

AMANDA. Yes, honey?

TOM. How about—supper?

AMANDA. Honey, you go ask Sister if supper is ready! You know that Sister is in full charge of supper!

Tell her you hungry boys are waiting for it. [*To JIM.*] Have you met Laura?

JIM. She—

AMANDA. Let you in? Oh, good, you've met already! It's rare for a girl as sweet an' pretty as Laura to be domestic! But Laura is, thank heavens, not only pretty but also very domestic. I'm not at all. I never was a bit. I never could make a thing but angel-food cake. Well, in the South we had so many servants. Gone, gone, gone. All vestige of gracious living! Gone completely! I wasn't prepared for what the future brought me. All of my gentlemen callers were sons of planters and so of course I assumed that I would be married to one and raise my family on a large piece of land with plenty of servants. But man proposes—and woman accepts the proposal!—To vary that old, old saying a little bit—I married no planter! I married a man who worked for the telephone company!—That gallantly smiling gentleman over there! [*Points to the picture.*] A telephone man who—fell in love with long-distance!—Now he travels and I don't even know where!—But what am I going on for about my—tribulations?

Tell me yours—I hope you don't have any! Tom?

Tom [*returning*]. Yes, Mother?

Amanda. Is supper nearly ready?

Tom. It looks to me like supper is on the table.

Amanda. Let me look— [*She rises prettily and looks through portieres.*] Oh, lovely!—But where is Sister?

Tom. Laura is not feeling well and she says that she thinks she'd better not come to the table.

Amanda. What?—Nonsense!—Laura? Oh, Laura!

Laura [*off stage, faintly*]. Yes, Mother.

Amanda. You really must come to the table. We won't be seated until you come to the table!

Come in, Mr. O'Connor. You sit over there, and I'll—

Laura? Laura Wingfield!

You're keeping us waiting, honey! We can't say grace until you come to the table! [*The back door is pushed weakly open and* Laura *comes in. She is obviously quite faint, her lips trembling, her eyes wide and staring. She moves unsteadily toward the table.* Legend: "terror!" *Outside a summer storm is coming abruptly. The white curtains billow inward at the windows and there is a sor-* rowful *murmur and deep blue dusk.* Laura *suddenly stumbles—she catches at a chair with a faint moan.*]

Tom. Laura!

Amanda. Laura! [*There is a clap of thunder.* Legend: "ah!" *Despairingly.*]

Why, Laura, you *are* sick, darling! Tom, help your sister into the living room, dear!

Sit in the living room, Laura—rest on the sofa.

Well! [*To the gentleman caller.*] Standing over the hot stove made her ill!—I told her that it was just too warm this evening, but— [*Tom comes back in.* Laura *is on the sofa.*] Is Laura all right now?

Tom. Yes.

Amanda. What *is* that? Rain? A nice cool rain has come up! [*She gives the gentleman caller a frightened look.*] I think we may—have grace—now . . . [*Tom looks at her stupidly.*] Tom, honey—you say grace!

Tom. Oh . . . "For these and all thy mercies—" [*They bow their heads,* Amanda *stealing a nervous glance at* Jim. *In the living room* Laura, *stretched on the sofa, clenches her hand to her lips, to hold back a shuddering sob.*] God's Holy Name be praised—

[The scene dims out]

SCENE VII

[A Souvenir.

Half an hour later. Dinner is just being finished in the upstage area which is concealed by the drawn portieres.

As the curtain rises Laura *is still huddled upon the sofa, her feet drawn under her, her head resting on a pale blue pillow, her eyes wide and mysteriously watchful. The new floor lamp with its shade of rose-colored silk gives a soft, becoming light* to her face, bringing out the fragile, unearthly prettiness which usually escapes attention. There is a steady murmur of rain, but it is slackening and stops soon after the scene begins; the air outside becomes pale and luminous as the moon breaks out.

A moment after the curtain rises, the lights in both rooms flicker and go out.]

JIM. Hey, there, Mr. Light Bulb! [AMANDA *laughs nervously.* LEGEND: "SUS-PENSION OF A PUBLIC SERVICE."]

AMANDA. Where was Moses when the lights went out? Ha-ha. Do you know the answer to that one, Mr. O'Connor?

JIM. No, Ma'am, what's the answer?

AMANDA. In the dark! [JIM *laughs appreciatively.*] Everybody sit still. I'll light the candles. Isn't it lucky we have them on the table? Where's a match? Which of you gentlemen can provide a match?

JIM. Here.

AMANDA. Thank you, sir.

JIM. Not at all, Ma'am!

AMANDA. I guess the fuse has burnt out. Mr. O'Connor, can you tell a burnt-out fuse? I know I can't and Tom is a total loss when it comes to mechanics. [SOUND: GETTING UP: VOICES RECEDE A LITTLE TO KITCHENETTE.] Oh, be careful you don't bump into something. We don't want our gentleman caller to break his neck. Now wouldn't that be a fine howdy-do?

JIM. Ha-ha! Where is the fuse-box?

AMANDA. Right here next to the stove. Can you see anything?

JIM. Just a minute.

AMANDA. Isn't electricity a mysterious thing?

Wasn't it Benjamin Franklin who tied a key to a kite?

We live in such a mysterious universe, don't we? Some people say that science clears up all the mysteries for us. In my opinion it only creates more!

Have you found it yet?

JIM. No, Ma'am. All these fuses look okay to me.

AMANDA. Tom!

TOM. Yes, Mother?

AMANDA. That light bill I gave you several days ago. The one I told you we got the notices about? [LEGEND: "HA!"]

TOM. Oh.—Yeah.

AMANDA. You didn't neglect to pay it by any chance?

TOM. Why, I—

AMANDA. Didn't! I might have known it!

JIM. Shakespeare probably wrote a poem on that light bill, Mrs. Wingfield.

AMANDA. I might have known better than to trust him with it! There's such a high price for negligence in this world!

JIM. Maybe the poem will win a ten-dollar prize.

AMANDA. We'll just have to spend the remainder of the evening in the nineteenth century, before Mr. Edison made the Mazda lamp!

JIM. Candlelight is my favorite kind of light.

AMANDA. That shows you're romantic! But that's no excuse for Tom.

Well, we got through dinner. Very considerate of them to let us get through dinner before they plunged us into everlasting darkness, wasn't it, Mr. O'Connor?

JIM. Ha-ha!

AMANDA. Tom, as a penalty for your carelessness you can help me with the dishes.

JIM. Let me give you a hand.

AMANDA. Indeed you will not!

JIM. I ought to be good for something.

AMANDA. Good for something? [*Her tone is rhapsodic.*] You? Why, Mr. O'Connor, nobody, *nobody's* given me this much entertainment in years—as you have!

JIM. Aw, now, Mrs. Wingfield!

AMANDA. I'm not exaggerating, not one bit! But Sister is all by her lonesome. You go keep her company in the parlor!

I'll give you this lovely old candelabrum that used to be on the altar at the church of the Heavenly Rest. It was melted a little out of shape when the church burnt down. Lightning struck it one spring. Gypsy

Jones was holding a revival at the time and he intimated that the church was destroyed because the Episcopalians gave card parties.

JIM. Ha-ha.

AMANDA. And how about you coaxing Sister to drink a little wine? I think it would be good for her! Can you carry both at once?

JIM. Sure. I'm Superman!

AMANDA. Now, Thomas, get into this apron! [*The door of kitchenette swings closed on* AMANDA's *gay laughter; the flickering light approaches the portieres.* LAURA *sits up nervously as he enters. Her speech at first is low and breathless from the almost intolerable strain of being alone with a stranger.* THE LEGEND: "I DON'T SUPPOSE YOU REMEMBER ME AT ALL!" *In her first speeches in this scene, before* JIM's *warmth overcomes her paralyzing shyness,* LAURA's *voice is thin and breathless as though she has just run up a steep flight of stairs.* JIM's *attitude is gently humorous. In playing this scene it should be stressed that while the incident is apparently unimportant, it is to* LAURA *the climax of her secret life.*]

JIM. Hello, there, Laura.

LAURA [*faintly*]. Hello. [*She clears her throat.*]

JIM. How are you feeling now? Better?

LAURA. Yes. Yes, thank you.

JIM. This is for you. A little dandelion wine. [*He extends it toward her with extravagant gallantry.*]

LAURA. Thank you.

JIM. Drink it—but don't get drunk! [*He laughs heartily.* LAURA *takes the glass uncertainly; laughs shyly.*] Where shall I set the candles?

LAURA. Oh—oh, anywhere . . .

JIM. How about here on the floor? Any objections?

LAURA. No.

JIM. I'll spread a newspaper under to catch the drippings. I like to sit on the floor. Mind if I do?

LAURA. Oh, no.

JIM. Give me a pillow?

LAURA. What?

JIM. A pillow!

LAURA. Oh . . . [*Hands him one quickly.*]

JIM. How about you? Don't you like to sit on the floor?

LAURA. Oh—yes.

JIM. Why don't you, then?

LAURA. I—will.

JIM. Take a pillow! [LAURA *does. Sits on the other side of the candelabrum.* JIM *crosses his legs and smiles engagingly at her.*] I can't hardly see you sitting way over there.

LAURA. I can—see you.

JIM. I know, but that's not fair, I'm in the limelight. [LAURA *moves her pillow closer.*] Good! Now I can see you! Comfortable?

LAURA. Yes.

JIM. So am I. Comfortable as a cow! Will you have some gum?

LAURA. No, thank you.

JIM. I think that I will indulge, with your permission. [*Musingly unwraps it and holds it up.*] Think of the fortune made by the guy that invented the first piece of chewing gum. Amazing, huh? The Wrigley Building is one of the sights of Chicago.—I saw it summer before last when I went up to the Century of Progress. Did you take in the Century of Progress?

LAURA. No, I didn't.

JIM. Well, it was quite a wonderful exposition. What impressed me most was the Hall of Science. Gives you an idea of what the future will be in America, even more wonderful than the present time is!

[*Pause. Smiling at her.*] Your brother tells me you're shy. Is that right, Laura?

LAURA. I—don't know.

JIM. I judge you to be an old-fashioned type of girl. Well, I think that's a pretty good type to be. Hope you don't think I'm being too personal—do you?

LAURA [*hastily, out of embarrassment*]. I believe I *will* take a piece of gum, if you —don't mind. [*Clearing her throat.*] Mr. O'Connor, have you—kept up with your singing?

JIM. Singing? Me?

LAURA. Yes. I remember what a beautiful voice you had.

JIM. When did you hear me sing?

[VOICE OFF STAGE IN THE PAUSE.]

VOICE [*off stage*].

O blow, ye winds, heigh-ho,
A-roving I will go!
  I'm off to my love
  With a boxing glove—
Ten thousand miles away!

JIM. You say you've heard me sing?

LAURA. Oh, yes! Yes, very often . . . I —don't suppose—you remember me—at all?

JIM [*smiling doubtfully*]. You know I have an idea I've seen you before. I had that idea soon as you opened the door. It seemed almost like I was about to remember your name. But the name that I started to call you—wasn't a name! And so I stopped myself before I said it.

LAURA. Wasn't it—Blue Roses?

JIM [*springs up. Grinning*]. Blue Roses! —My gosh, yes—Blue Roses!

That's what I had on my tongue when you opened the door!

Isn't it funny what tricks your memory plays? I didn't connect you with high school somehow or other.

But that's where it was; it was high school. I didn't even know you were Shakespeare's sister! Gosh, I'm sorry.

LAURA. I didn't expect you to. You— barely knew me!

JIM. But we did have a speaking acquaintance, huh?

LAURA. Yes, we—spoke to each other.

JIM. When did you recognize me?

LAURA. Oh, right away!

JIM. Soon as I came in the door?

LAURA. When I heard your name I thought it was probably you. I knew that Tom used to know you a little in high school. So when you came in the door— Well, then I was—sure.

JIM. Why didn't you *say* something, then?

LAURA [*breathlessly*]. I didn't know what to say, I was—too surprised!

JIM. For goodness' sakes! You know, this sure is funny!

LAURA. Yes! Yes, isn't it, though . . .

JIM. Didn't we have a class in something together?

LAURA. Yes, we did.

JIM. What class was that?

LAURA. It was—singing—Chorus!

JIM. Aw!

LAURA. I sat across the aisle from you in the Aud.

JIM. Aw.

LAURA. Mondays, Wednesdays and Fridays.

JIM. Now I remember—you always came in late.

LAURA. Yes, it was so hard for me, getting upstairs. I had that brace on my leg— it clumped so loud!

JIM. I never heard any clumping.

LAURA [*wincing at the recollection*]. To me it sounded like—thunder!

JIM. Well, well, well, I never even noticed.

LAURA. And everybody was seated before I came in. I had to walk in front of all those people. My seat was in the back row. I had to go clumping all the way up the aisle with everyone watching!

JIM. You shouldn't have been self-conscious.

LAURA. I know, but I was. It was always such a relief when the singing started.

JIM. Aw, yes, I've placed you now! I used to call you Blue Roses. How was it that I got started calling you that?

LAURA. I was out of school a little while with pleurosis. When I came back you asked me what was the matter. I said I had pleurosis—you thought I said Blue Roses. That's what you always called me after that!

JIM. I hope you didn't mind.

LAURA. Oh, no—I liked it. You see, I wasn't acquainted with many—people. . . .

JIM. As I remember you sort of stuck by yourself.

LAURA. I—I—never have had much luck at—making friends.

JIM. I don't see why you wouldn't.

LAURA. Well, I—started out badly.

JIM. You mean being—

LAURA. Yes, it sort of—stood between me—

JIM. You shouldn't have let it!

LAURA. I know, but it did, and—

JIM. You were shy with people!

LAURA. I tried not to be but never could—

JIM. Overcome it?

LAURA. No, I—I never could!

JIM. I guess being shy is something you have to work out of kind of gradually.

LAURA [sorrowfully]. Yes—I guess it—

JIM. Takes time!

LAURA. Yes—

JIM. People are not so dreadful when you know them. That's what you have to remember! And everybody has problems, not just you, but practically everybody has got some problem.

You think of yourself as having the only problems, as being the only one who is disappointed. But just look around you and you will see lots of people as disappointed as you are. For instance, I hoped when I was going to high school that I would be further along at this time, six years later, than I am now— You remember that wonderful write-up I had in *The Torch?*

LAURA. Yes! [*She rises and crosses to table.*]

JIM. It said I was bound to succeed in anything I went into! [LAURA *returns with the annual.*] Holy Jeez! *The Torch!* [*He accepts it reverently. They smile across it with mutual wonder.* LAURA *crouches beside him and they begin to turn through it.* LAURA's *shyness is dissolving in his warmth.*]

LAURA. Here you are in *The Pirates of Penzance!*

JIM [*wistfully*]. I sang the baritone lead in that operetta.

LAURA [*raptly*]. So—*beautifully!*

JIM [*protesting*]. Aw—

LAURA. Yes, yes—beautifully—beautifully!

JIM. You heard me?

LAURA. All three times!

JIM. No!

LAURA. Yes!

JIM. All three performances?

LAURA [*looking down*]. Yes.

JIM. Why?

LAURA. I—wanted to ask you to—autograph my program.

JIM. Why didn't you ask me to?

LAURA. You were always surrounded by your own friends so much that I never had a chance to.

JIM. You should have just—

LAURA. Well, I—thought you might think I was—

JIM. Thought I might think you was— what?

LAURA. Oh—

JIM [*with reflective relish*]. I was beleaguered by females in those days.

LAURA. You were terribly popular!

JIM. Yeah—

LAURA. You had such a—friendly way—

JIM. I was spoiled in high school.

LAURA. Everybody—liked you!

JIM. Including you?

LAURA. I—yes, I—I did, too— [*She gently closes the book in her lap.*]

JIM. Well, well, well!—Give me that program, Laura. [*She hands it to him. He signs it with a flourish.*] There you are—better late than never!

LAURA. Oh, I—what a—surprise!

JIM. My signature isn't worth very much right now. But some day—maybe—it will increase in value! Being disappointed is one thing and being discouraged is something else. I am disappointed but I am not discouraged. I'm twenty-three years old. How old are you?

LAURA. I'll be twenty-four in June.

JIM. That's not old age!

LAURA. No, but—

JIM. You finished high school?

LAURA [*with difficulty*]. I didn't go back.

JIM. You mean you dropped out?

LAURA. I made bad grades in my final examinations. [*She rises and replaces the book and the program. Her voice strained.*] How is—Emily Meisenbach getting along?

JIM. Oh, that kraut-head!

LAURA. Why do you call her that?

JIM. That's what she was.

LAURA. You're not still—going with her?

JIM. I never see her.

LAURA. It said in the Personal Section that you were—engaged!

JIM. I know, but I wasn't impressed by that—propaganda!

LAURA. It wasn't—the truth?

JIM. Only in Emily's optimistic opinion!

LAURA. Oh— [LEGEND: "WHAT HAVE YOU DONE SINCE HIGH SCHOOL?" JIM *lights a cigarette and leans indolently back on his elbows smiling at* LAURA *with a warmth and charm which lights her inwardly with altar candles. She remains by the table and turns in her hands a piece of glass to cover her tumult.*]

JIM [*after several reflective puffs on a cigarette*]. What have you done since high school? [*She seems not to hear him.*] Huh? [LAURA *looks up.*] I said what have you done since high school, Laura?

LAURA. Nothing much.

JIM. You must have been doing something these six long years.

LAURA. Yes.

JIM. Well, then, such as what?

LAURA. I took a business course at business college—

JIM. How did that work out?

LAURA. Well, not very—well—I had to drop out, it gave me—indigestion— [JIM *laughs gently.*]

JIM. What are you doing now?

LAURA. I don't do anything—much. Oh, please don't think I sit around doing nothing! My glass collection takes up a good deal of time. Glass is something you have to take good care of.

JIM. What did you say—about glass?

LAURA. Collection I said—I have one— [*She clears her throat and turns away again, acutely shy.*]

JIM [*abruptly*]. You know what I judge to be the trouble with you?

Inferiority complex! Know what that is? That's what they call it when someone low-rates himself!

I understand it because I had it, too. Although my case was not so aggravated as yours seems to be. I had it until I took up public speaking, developed my voice, and learned that I had an aptitude for science. Before that time I never thought of myself as being outstanding in any way whatsoever!

Now I've never made a regular study of it, but I have a friend who says I can analyze people better than doctors that make a profession of it. I don't claim that to be necessarily true, but I can sure guess a person's psychology, Laura! [*Takes out his gum.*] Excuse me, Laura. I always take it out when the flavor is gone. I'll use this scrap of paper to wrap it in. I know how it is to get it stuck on a shoe.

Yep—that's what I judge to be your principal trouble. A lack of confidence in yourself as a person. You don't have the proper amount of faith in yourself. I'm basing that fact on a number of your remarks and also on certain observations I've made. For instance that clumping you thought was so awful in high school. You say that you even dreaded to walk into class. You see what you did? You dropped out of school, you gave up an education because of a clump, which as far as I know was practically non-existent! A little physical defect is what you have. Hardly noticeable even! Magnified thousands of times by imagination!

You know what my strong advice to you is? Think of yourself as *superior* in some way!

LAURA. In what way would I think?

JIM. Why, man alive, Laura! Just look about you a little. What do you see? A world full of common people! All of 'em born and all of 'em going to die!

Which of them has one-tenth of your good points! Or mine! Or anyone else's, as far as that goes— Gosh!

Everybody excels in some one thing. Some in many! [*Unconsciously glances at himself in the mirror.*] All you've got to do is discover in *what!*

Take me, for instance. [*He adjusts his tie at the mirror.*]

My interest happens to lie in electrodynamics. I'm taking a course in radio engineering at night school, Laura, on top of a fairly responsible job at the warehouse. I'm taking that course and studying public speaking.

LAURA. Ohhhh.

JIM. Because I believe in the future of television! [*Turning back to her.*]

I wish to be ready to go up right along with it. Therefore I'm planning to get in on the ground floor. In fact I've already made the right connections and all that remains is for the industry itself to get under way! Full steam— [*His eyes are starry.*] *Knowledge*—Zzzzzp! *Money*—Zzzzzzp!—*Power!* That's the cycle democracy is built on! [*His attitude is convincingly dynamic.* LAURA *stares at him, even her shyness eclipsed in her absolute wonder. He suddenly grins.*] I guess you think I think a lot of myself!

LAURA. No—o-o-o, I—

JIM. Now how about you? Isn't there something you take more interest in than anything else?

LAURA. Well, I do—as I said—have my— glass collection— [*A peal of girlish laughter from the kitchen.*]

JIM. I'm not right sure I know what you're talking about. What kind of glass is it?

LAURA. Little articles of it, they're ornaments mostly!

Most of them are little animals made out of glass, the tiniest little animals in the world. Mother calls them a glass menagerie!

Here's an example of one, if you'd like to see it!

This one is one of the oldest. It's nearly thirteen. [MUSIC: "THE GLASS MENAGERIE." *He stretches out his hand.*] Oh, be careful —if you breathe, it breaks!

JIM. I'd better not take it. I'm pretty clumsy with things.

LAURA. Go on, I trust you with him! [*Places it in his palm.*] There now—you're holding him gently!

Hold him over the light, he loves the light! You see how the light shines through him?

JIM. It sure does shine!

LAURA. I shouldn't be partial, but he is my favorite one.

JIM. What kind of a thing is this one supposed to be?

LAURA. Haven't you noticed the single horn on his forehead?

JIM. A unicorn, huh?

LAURA. Mmm-hmmm!

JIM. Unicorns, aren't they extinct in the modern world?

LAURA. I know!

JIM. Poor little fellow, he must feel sort of lonesome.

LAURA [*smiling*]. Well, if he does he doesn't complain about it. He stays on a shelf with some horses that don't have horns and all of them seem to get along nicely together.

JIM. How do you know?

LAURA [*lightly*]. I haven't heard any arguments among them!

JIM [*grinning*]. No arguments, huh? Well, that's a pretty good sign! Where shall I set him?

LAURA. Put him on the table. They all like a change of scenery once in a while!

JIM [*stretching*]. Well, well, well, well—Look how big my shadow is when I stretch!

LAURA. Oh, oh, yes—it stretches across the ceiling!

JIM [*crossing to door*]. I think it's stopped raining. [*Opens fire-escape door.*] Where does the music come from?

LAURA. From the Paradise Dance Hall across the alley.

JIM. How about cutting the rug a little, Miss Wingfield?

LAURA. Oh, I—

JIM. Or is your program filled up? Let me have a look at it. [*Grasps imaginary card.*] Why, every dance is taken! I'll just have to scratch some out. [WALTZ MUSIC: "LA GOLONDRINA."] Ahhh, a waltz! [*He executes some sweeping turns by himself then holds his arms toward* LAURA.]

LAURA [*breathlessly*]. I—can't dance!

JIM. There you go, that inferiority stuff!

LAURA. I've never danced in my life!

JIM. Come on, try!

LAURA. Oh, but I'd step on you!

JIM. I'm not made out of glass.

LAURA. How—how—how do we start?

JIM. Just leave it to me. You hold your arms out a little.

LAURA. Like this?

JIM. A little bit higher. Right. Now don't tighten up, that's the main thing about it—relax.

LAURA [*laughing breathlessly*]. It's hard not to.

JIM. Okay.

LAURA. I'm afraid you can't budge me.

JIM. What do you bet I can't? [*He swings her into motion.*]

LAURA. Goodness, yes, you can!

JIM. Let yourself go, now, Laura, just let yourself go.

LAURA. I'm—

JIM. Come on!

LAURA. Trying!

JIM. Not so stiff— Easy does it!

LAURA. I know but I'm—

JIM. Loosen th' backbone! There now, that's a lot better.

LAURA. Am I?

JIM. Lots, lots better! [*He moves her about the room in a clumsy waltz.*]

LAURA. Oh, my!

JIM. Ha-ha!

LAURA. Oh, my goodness!

JIM. Ha-ha-ha! [*They suddenly bump into the table.* JIM *stops.*] What did we hit on?

LAURA. Table.

JIM. Did something fall off it? I think—

LAURA. Yes.

JIM. I hope that it wasn't the little glass horse with the horn!

LAURA. Yes.

JIM. Aw, aw, aw. Is it broken?

LAURA. Now it is just like all the other horses.

JIM. It's lost its—

LAURA. Horn! It doesn't matter. Maybe it's a blessing in disguise.

JIM. You'll never forgive me. I bet that that was your favorite piece of glass.

LAURA. I don't have favorites much. It's no tragedy, Freckles. Glass breaks so easily. No matter how careful you are. The traffic jars the shelves and things fall off them.

JIM. Still I'm awfully sorry that I was the cause.

LAURA [*smiling*]. I'll just imagine he had an operation. The horn was removed to make him feel less—freakish! [*They both laugh.*] Now he will feel more at home with the other horses, the ones that don't have horns. . .

JIM. Ha-ha, that's very funny! [*Suddenly serious.*] I'm glad to see that you have a sense of humor. You know—you're—well —very different!

Surprisingly different from anyone else I know! [*His voice becomes soft and hesitant with a genuine feeling.*] Do you mind me telling you that? [LAURA *is abashed beyond speech.*] I mean it in a nice way . . . [LAURA *nods shyly, looking away.*] You make me feel sort of—I don't know how to put it! I'm usually pretty good at expressing things, but— This is something that I don't know how to say! [LAURA *touches her throat and clears it—turns the broken unicorn in her hands. Even softer.*]

Has anyone ever told you that you were pretty? [*Pause*: MUSIC. LAURA *looks up slowly, with wonder, and shakes her head.*] Well, you are! In a very different way from anyone else. And all the nicer because of the difference, too. [*His voice becomes low and husky.* LAURA *turns away, nearly faint with the novelty of her emotions.*]

I wish that you were my sister. I'd teach you to have some confidence in yourself. The different people are not like other people, but being different is nothing to be ashamed of. Because other people are not such wonderful people. They're one hundred times one thousand. You're one times one! They walk all over the earth. You just stay here. They're common as —weeds, but—you—well, you're—*Blue Roses!* [IMAGE ON SCREEN: BLUE ROSES. MUSIC CHANGES.]

LAURA. But blue is wrong for—roses . . .

JIM. It's right for you!—You're—pretty!

LAURA. In what respect am I pretty?

JIM. In all respects—believe me! Your eyes—your hair—are pretty! Your hands are pretty! [*He catches hold of her hand.*]

You think I'm making this up because I'm invited to dinner and have to be nice. Oh, I could do that! I could put on an act for you, Laura, and say lots of things without being very sincere. But this time I am. I'm talking to you sincerely. I happened to notice you had this inferiority complex that keeps you from feeling comfortable with people. Somebody needs to build your confidence up and make you proud instead of shy and turning away and—blushing—

Somebody—ought to—

Ought to—*kiss* you, Laura! [*His hand slips slowly up her arm to her shoulder.* MUSIC SWELLS TUMULTUOUSLY. *He suddenly turns her about and kisses her on the lips. When he releases her,* LAURA *sinks on the sofa with a bright, dazed look.* JIM *backs away and fishes in his pocket for a cigarette.* LEGEND ON SCREEN: "SOUVENIR."] Stumble-john! [*He lights the cigarette, avoiding her look. There is a peal of girlish laughter from* AMANDA *in the kitchen.* LAURA *slowly raises and opens her hand. It still contains the little broken glass animal. She looks at it with a tender, bewildered expression.*] Stumble-john! I shouldn't have done that— That was way off the beam. You don't smoke, do you? [*She looks up, smiling, not hearing the question. He sits beside her a little gingerly. She looks at him speechlessly— waiting. He coughs decorously and moves a little further aside as he considers the situation and senses her feelings, dimly, with perturbation. Gently.*] Would you—care for a—mint? [*She doesn't seem to hear him but her look grows brighter even.*] Peppermint—Life-Saver? My pocket's a regular drug store—wherever I go . . . [*He pops a mint in his mouth. Then gulps and decides to make a clean breast of it. He speaks slowly and gingerly.*] Laura, you know, if I had a sister like you, I'd do the same thing as Tom. I'd bring out fellows and—introduce her to them. The right type of boys of a type to—appreciate her.

Only—well—he made a mistake about me.

Maybe I've got no call to be saying this. That may not have been the idea in having me over. But what if it was?

There's nothing wrong about that. The only trouble is that in my case—I'm not in a situation to—do the right thing.

I can't take down your number and say I'll phone.

I can't call up next week and—ask for a date.

I thought I had better explain the situation in case you—misunderstood it and—

hurt your feelings. . . . [*Pause. Slowly, very slowly,* LAURA'S *look changes, her eyes returning slowly from his to the ornament in her palm.* AMANDA *utters another gay laugh in the kitchen.*]

LAURA [*faintly*]. You—won't—call again?

JIM. No, Laura, I can't. [*He rises from the sofa.*] As I was just explaining, I've—got strings on me. Laura, I've—been going steady! I go out all of the time with a girl named Betty. She's a home-girl like you, and Catholic, and Irish, and in a great many ways we—get along fine. I met her last summer on a moonlight boat trip up the river to Alton, on the *Majestic*. Well—right away from the start it was—love! [LEGEND: LOVE! LAURA *sways slightly forward and grips the arm of the sofa. He fails to notice, now enrapt in his own comfortable being.*] Being in love has made a new man of me! [*Leaning stiffly forward, clutching the arm of the sofa,* LAURA *struggles visibly with her storm. But* JIM *is oblivious, she is a long way off.*] The power of love is really pretty tremendous!

Love is something that—changes the whole world, Laura! [*The storm abates a little and* LAURA *leans back. He notices her again.*]

It happened that Betty's aunt took sick, she got a wire and had to go to Centralia. So Tom—when he asked me to dinner—I naturally just accepted the invitation, not knowing that you—that he—that I— [*He stops awkwardly.*] Huh—I'm a stumble-john! [*He flops back on the sofa. The holy candles in the altar of* LAURA'S *face have been snuffed out. There is a look of almost infinite desolation.* JIM *glances at her uneasily.*]

I wish that you would—say something. [*She bites her lip which was trembling and then bravely smiles. She opens her hand again on the broken glass ornament. Then she gently takes his hand and raises it level with her own. She carefully places the unicorn in the palm of his hand, then pushes his fingers closed upon it.*] What are you—doing that for? You want me to have him?—Laura? [*She nods.*] What for?

LAURA. A—souvenir . . . [*She rises unsteadily and crouches beside the victrola to wind it up.* LEGEND ON SCREEN: "THINGS HAVE A WAY OF TURNING OUT SO BADLY!" OR IMAGE: "GENTLEMAN CALLER WAVING GOOD-BYE!—GAILY." *At this moment* AMANDA *rushes brightly back in the front room. She bears a pitcher of fruit punch in an old-fashioned cut-glass pitcher and a plate of macaroons. The plate has a gold border and poppies painted on it.*]

AMANDA. Well, well, well! Isn't the air delightful after the shower? I've made you children a little liquid refreshment. [*Turns gaily to the gentleman caller.*] Jim, do you know that song about lemonade?

"Lemonade, lemonade
Made in the shade and stirred with a
spade—
Good enough for any old maid!"

JIM [*uneasily*]. Ha-ha! No—I never heard it.

AMANDA. Why, Laura! You look so serious!

JIM. We were having a serious conversation.

AMANDA. Good! Now you're better acquainted!

JIM [*uncertainly*]. Ha-ha! Yes.

AMANDA. You modern young people are much more serious-minded than my generation. I was so gay as a girl!

JIM. You haven't changed, Mrs. Wingfield.

AMANDA. Tonight I'm rejuvenated! The gaiety of the occasion, Mr. O'Connor! [*She tosses her head with a peal of laugh-*

ter. Spills lemonade.] Oooo! I'm baptizing myself!

JIM. Here—let me—

AMANDA [*setting the pitcher down*]. There now. I discovered we had some maraschino cherries. I dumped them in, juice and all!

JIM. You shouldn't have gone to that trouble, Mrs. Wingfield.

AMANDA. Trouble, trouble? Why, it was loads of fun!

Didn't you hear me cutting up in the kitchen? I bet your ears were burning! I told Tom how outdone with him I was for keeping you to himself so long a time! He should have brought you over much, much sooner! Well, now that you've found your way, I want you to be a very frequent caller! Not just occasional but all the time.

Oh, we're going to have a lot of gay times together! I see them coming!

Mmm, just breathe that air! So fresh, and the moon's so pretty!

I'll skip back out—I know where my place is when young folks are having a—serious conversation!

JIM. Oh, don't go out, Mrs. Wingfield. The fact of the matter is I've got to be going.

AMANDA. Going, now? You're joking! Why, it's only the shank of the evening, Mr. O'Connor!

JIM. Well, you know how it is.

AMANDA. You mean you're a young workingman and have to keep working-men's hours. We'll let you off early tonight. But only on the condition that next time you stay later.

What's the best night for you? Isn't Saturday night the best night for you work-ingmen?

JIM. I have a couple of time-clocks to punch, Mrs. Wingfield. One at morning, another one at night!

AMANDA. My, but you *are* ambitious! You work at night, too?

JIM. No, Ma'am, not work but—Betty! [*He crosses deliberately to pick up his hat. The band at the Paradise Dance Hall goes into a tender waltz.*]

AMANDA. Betty? Betty? Who's—Betty! [*There is an ominous cracking sound in the sky.*]

JIM. Oh, just a girl. The girl I go steady with! [*He smiles charmingly. The sky falls.* LEGEND: "THE SKY FALLS."]

AMANDA [*a long-drawn exhalation*]. Ohhhh . . . Is it a serious romance, Mr. O'Connor?

JIM. We're going to be married the second Sunday in June.

AMANDA. Ohhhh—how nice! Tom didn't mention that you were engaged to be married.

JIM. The cat's not out of the bag at the warehouse yet.

You know how they are. They call you Romeo and stuff like that. [*He stops at the oval mirror to put on his hat. He carefully shapes the brim and the crown to give a discreetly dashing effect.*] It's been a wonderful evening, Mrs. Wingfield. I guess this is what they mean by Southern hospitality.

AMANDA. It really wasn't anything at all.

JIM. I hope it don't seem like I'm rushing off. But I promised Betty I'd pick her up at the Wabash depot, an' by the time I get my jalopy down there her train'll be in. Some women are pretty upset if you keep 'em waiting.

AMANDA. Yes, I know— The tyranny of women! [*Extends her hand.*] Good-bye, Mr. O'Connor. I wish you luck—and happiness—and success! All three of them, and so does Laura!—Don't you, Laura?

LAURA. Yes!

JIM [*taking her hand*]. Good-bye, Laura. I'm certainly going to treasure that sou-

venir. And don't you forget the good advice I gave you. [*Raises his voice to a cheery shout.*] So long, Shakespeare! Thanks again, ladies— Good night! [*He grins and ducks jauntily out. Still bravely grimacing,* AMANDA *closes the door on the gentleman caller. Then she turns back to the room with a puzzled expression. She and* LAURA *don't dare to face each other.* LAURA *crouches beside the victrola to wind it.*]

AMANDA [*faintly*]. Things have a way of turning out so badly. I don't believe that I would play the victrola. Well, well —well— Our gentleman caller was engaged to be married! Tom!

TOM [*from back*]. Yes, Mother?

AMANDA. Come in here a minute. I want to tell you something awfully funny.

TOM [*enters with macaroon and a glass of the lemonade*]. Has the gentleman caller gotten away already?

AMANDA. The gentleman caller has made an early departure. What a wonderful joke you played on us!

TOM. How do you mean?

AMANDA. You didn't mention that he was engaged to be married.

TOM. Jim? Engaged?

AMANDA. That's what he just informed us.

TOM. I'll be jiggered! I didn't know about that.

AMANDA. That seems very peculiar.

TOM. What's peculiar about it?

AMANDA. Didn't you call him your best friend down at the warehouse?

TOM. He is, but how did I know?

AMANDA. It seems extremely peculiar that you wouldn't know your best friend was going to be married!

TOM. The warehouse is where I work, not where I know things about people!

AMANDA. You don't know things anywhere! You live in a dream; you manufacture illusions! [*He crosses to door.*] Where are you going?

TOM. I'm going to the movies.

AMANDA. That's right, now that you've had us make such fools of ourselves. The effort, the preparations, all the expense! The new floor lamp, the rug, the clothes for Laura! All for what? To entertain some other girl's fiancé!

Go to the movies, go! Don't think about us, a mother deserted, an unmarried sister who's crippled and has no job! Don't let anything interfere with your selfish pleasure!

Just go, go, go—to the movies!

TOM. All right, I will! The more you shout about my selfishness to me the quicker I'll go, and I won't go to the movies!

AMANDA. Go, then! Then go to the moon—you selfish dreamer!

[TOM *smashes his glass on the floor. He plunges out on the fire-escape, slamming the door.* LAURA *screams—cut by door. Dance-hall music up.* TOM *goes to the rail and grips it desperately, lifting his face in the chill white moonlight penetrating the narrow abyss of the alley.* LEGEND ON SCREEN: "AND SO GOOD-BYE . . ." TOM'S *closing speech is timed with the interior pantomime. The interior scene is played as though viewed through soundproof glass.* AMANDA *appears to be making a comforting speech to* LAURA *who is huddled upon the sofa. Now that we cannot hear the mother's speech, her silliness is gone and she has dignity and tragic beauty.* LAURA'S *dark hair hides her face until at the end of the speech she lifts it to smile at her mother.* AMANDA'S *gestures are slow and graceful, almost dance-like, as she comforts the daughter. At the end of her speech she glances a moment at the father's picture—then withdraws through the por-*

tieres. At close of TOM's *speech,* LAURA *blows out the candles, ending the play.*]

TOM. I didn't go to the moon, I went much further—for time is the longest distance between two places—

Not long after that I was fired for writing a poem on the lid of a shoe-box.

I left Saint Louis. I descended the steps of this fire-escape for a last time and followed, from then on, in my father's footsteps, attempting to find in motion what was lost in space—

I traveled around a great deal. The cities swept about me like dead leaves, leaves that were brightly colored but torn away from the branches.

I would have stopped, but I was pursued by something.

It always came upon me unawares, taking me altogether by surprise. Perhaps it was a familiar bit of music. Perhaps it was only a piece of transparent glass—

Perhaps I am walking along a street at night, in some strange city, before I have found companions. I pass the lighted window of a shop where perfume is sold. The window is filled with pieces of colored glass, tiny transparent bottles in delicate colors, like bits of a shattered rainbow.

Then all at once my sister touches my shoulder. I turn around and look into her eyes . . .

Oh, Laura, Laura, I tried to leave you behind me, but I am more faithful than I intended to be!

I reach for a cigarette, I cross the street, I run into the movies or a bar, I buy a drink, I speak to the nearest stranger—anything that can blow your candles out! [LAURA *bends over the candles.*] —for nowadays the world is lit by lightning! Blow out your candles, Laura—and so good-bye. . . . [*She blows the candles out.*]

[THE SCENE DISSOLVES]

THE FALL OF THE CITY

A Verse Play for Radio

by ARCHIBALD MACLEISH

VOICE OF THE STUDIO DIRECTOR [*orotund and professional*]

Ladies and gentlemen:
This broadcast comes to you from the city
Listeners over the curving air have heard
From furthest-off frontiers of foreign
hours—
Mountain Time: Ocean Time: of the
islands:
Of waters after the islands—some of them
waking
Where noon here is the night there: some
Where noon is the first few stars they see
or the last one.

For three days the world has watched this
city—
Not for the common occasions of brutal
crime
Or the usual violence of one sort or another
Or coronations of kings or popular festi-
vals:
No: for stranger and disturbing reasons—
The resurrection from death and the tomb
of a dead woman.

Each day for three days there has come
To the door of her tomb at noon a woman
buried!

The terror that stands at the shoulder of
our time
Touches the cheek with this: the flesh
winces.

There have been other omens in other
cities
But never of this sort and never so credible.

In a time like ours seemings and portents
signify.
Ours is a generation when dogs howl and
the
Skin crawls on the skull with its beast's
foreboding.
All men now alive with us have feared.
We have smelled the wind in the street
that changes weather.
We have seen the familiar room grow unfamiliar:
The order of numbers alter: the expectation
Cheat the expectant eye. The appearance
defaults with us.

Here in this city the wall of the time
cracks.

We take you now to the great square of
this city.

[*The shuffle and hum of a vast, patient crowd gradually rises: swells:
fills the background.*]

VOICE OF THE ANNOUNCER [*matter-of-
fact*]

We are here on the central plaza.
We are well off to the eastward edge.

There is a kind of terrace over the crowd
here.
It is precisely four minutes to twelve.
The crowd is enormous: there might be
ten thousand:
There might be more: the whole square
is faces.
Opposite over the roofs are the mountains.
It is quite clear: there are birds circling.
We think they are kites by the look: they
are very high. . . .

The tomb is off to the right somewhere—
We can't see for the great crowd.
Close to us here are the cabinet ministers:
They stand on a raised platform with
awnings.
The farmers' wives are squatting on the
stones:
Their children have fallen asleep on their
shoulders.
The heat is harsh: the light dazzles like
metal.
It dazes the air as the clang of a gong
does. . . .

News travels in this nation:
There are people here from away off—
Horse-raisers out of the country with
brooks in it:
Herders of cattle from up where the snow
stays—
The kind that cook for themselves mostly:
They look at the girls with their eyes hard
And a hard grin and their teeth show-
ing. . . .

It is one minute to twelve now:
There is still no sign: they are still wait-
ing:
No one doubts that she will come:
No one doubts that she will speak too:
Three times she has not spoken.

[*The murmur of the crowd changes—not
louder but more intense: higher.*]

THE VOICE OF THE ANNOUNCER [*low
but with increasing excitement*]
Now it is twelve: now they are rising:
Now the whole plaza is rising:
Fathers are lifting their small children:
The plumed fans on the platform are mo-
tionless. . . .

There is no sound but the shuffle of shoe
leather. . . .

Now even the shoes are still. . . .

We can hear the hawks: it is quiet as that
now. . . .

It is strange to see such throngs so silent. . . .

Nothing yet: nothing has happened. . . .

Wait! There's a stir here to the right of us:
They're turning their heads: the crowd
turns:
The cabinet ministers lean from their bal-
cony:
There's no sound: only the turning. . . .

[*A woman's voice comes over the silence
of the crowd: it is a weak voice, but penetrating: it speaks slowly and as though
with difficulty.*]

THE VOICE OF THE DEAD WOMAN
First the waters rose with no wind. . . .

THE VOICE OF THE ANNOUNCER [*whispering*]
Listen: that is she! She's speaking!

THE VOICE OF THE DEAD WOMAN
Then the stones of the temple kindled
Without flame or tinder of maize-
leaves . . .

THE VOICE OF THE ANNOUNCER [*whispering*]
They see her beyond us: The crowd sees
   her. . . .

THE VOICE OF THE DEAD WOMAN
Then there were cries in the night haze:
Words in a once-heard tongue: the air
Rustling above us as at dawn with herons.

Now it is I who must bring fear:
I who am four days dead: the tears
Still unshed for me—all of them: I
For whom a child still calls at nightfall.

Death is young in me to fear!
My dress is kept still in the press in my
   bedchamber:
No one has broken the dish of the dead
   woman.

Nevertheless I must speak painfully:
I am to stand here in the sun and speak:

[*There is a pause. Then her voice comes
again loud, mechanical, speaking as
by rote.*]

The city of masterless men
Will take a master.
There will be shouting then:
Blood after!

[*The crowd stirs. Her voice goes on weak
and slow as before.*]

Do not ask what it means: I do not know:
Only sorrow and no hope for it.

THE VOICE OF THE ANNOUNCER
She has gone. . . . No, they are still
   looking.

THE VOICE OF THE DEAD WOMAN
It is hard to return from the time past.
   I have come

In the dream we must learn to dream
   where the crumbling of
Time like the ash from a burnt string has
Stopped for me. For you the thread still
   burns:
You take the feathery ash upon your
   fingers.
You bring yourselves from the time past
   as it pleases you.

It is hard to return to the old nearness . . .

Harder to go again. . . .

THE VOICE OF THE ANNOUNCER
She is gone.
We know because the crowd is closing.
All we can see is the crowd closing.
We hear the releasing of held breath—
The weight shifting: the lifting of shoe
   leather.
The stillness is broken as surface of water
   is broken—
The sound circling from in outward.

[*The murmur of the crowd rises.*]

Small wonder they feel fear.
Before the murders of the famous kings—
Before imperial cities burned and fell—
The dead were said to show themselves
   and speak.
When dead men came disaster came. Presentiments
That let the living on their beds sleep on
Woke dead men out of death and gave
   them voices.
All ancient men in every nation knew
   this.

A VOICE OVER THE CROWD
Masterless men . . .

A VOICE OVER THE CROWD
When shall it be . . .

[579]

A Voice over the Crowd
Masterless men
Will take a master . . .

A Voice over the Crowd
What has she said to us . . .

A Voice over the Crowd
When shall it be . . .

A Voice over the Crowd
Masterless men
Will take a master.
Blood after . . .

A Voice over the Crowd
What has she said to us . . .

Voices Together
Blood after!

[*The voices run together into the excited
    roar of the crowd. The Announcer's
    voice is loud over it.*]

The Voice of the Announcer
They are milling around us like cattle
    that smell death.
The whole square is whirling and turning
    and shouting.
One of the ministers raises his arms on the
    platform.
No one is listening: now they are sound-
    ing drums:
Trying to quiet them likely: No! No!
Something is happening: there in the far
    corner:
A runner: a messenger: staggering: people
    are helping him:
People are calling: he comes through the
    crowd: they are quieter.
Only those on the far edge are still
    shouting:
Listen! He's here by the ministers now!
He is speaking. . . .

The Voice of the Messenger
There has come the conqueror!
I am to tell you.
I have raced over sea land:
I have run over cane land:
I have climbed over cone land.
It was laid on my shoulders
By shall and by shan't
That standing by day
And staying by night
Were not for my lot
Till I came to the sight of you.
Now I have come.

Be warned of this conqueror!
This one is dangerous!
Word has out-oared him.
East over sea-cross has
All taken—
Every country.
No men are free there.
Ears overhear them.
Their words are their murderers.
Judged before judgment
Tried after trial
They die as do animals:—
Offer their throats
As the goat to her slaughterer.
Terror has taught them this!

Now he is here!

He was violent in his vessel:
He was steering in her stern:
He was watching in her waist:
He was peering in her prow:
And he dragged her up
Nine lengths
Till her keel lodged
On this nation.

Now he is here
Waylaying and night-lying.
If they hide before dark
He comes before sunup.

Where hunger is eaten
There he sits down:
Where fear sleeps
There he arises.

I tell you beware of him!
All doors are dangers.
The warders of wealth
Will admit him by stealth.
The lovers of men
Will invite him as friend.
The drinkers of blood
Will drum him in suddenly.
Hope will unlatch to him:
Hopelessness open.

I say and say truly
To all men in honesty
Such is this conqueror!
Shame is his people.
Lickers of spittle
Their lives are unspeakable:
Their dying indecent.

Be well warned!
He comes to you slightly
Slanting and sprinting
Hinting and shadowing:
Sly is his hiding:—
A hard lot:
A late rider:

Watch! I have said to you!

THE VOICE OF THE ANNOUNCER
They are leading him out: his legs give:
Now he is gone in the crowd: they are
    silent:
No one has spoken since his speaking:

They stand still circling the ministers.
No one has spoken or called out:—
There is no stir at all nor movement:
Even the farthest have stood patiently:

They wait trusting the old men:
They wait faithfully trusting the answer.
Now the huddle on the platform opens:
A minister turns to them raising his two
    arms.

THE VOICE OF THE ORATOR
Freemen of this nation!
The persuasion of your wills against your
    wisdom is not dreamed of.
We offer themes for your consideration.

What is the surest defender of liberty?
Is it not liberty?
A free people resists by freedom:
Not locks! Not blockhouses!

The future is a mirror where the past
Marches to meet itself. Go armed toward
    arms!
Peaceful toward peace! Free and with
    music toward freedom!
Face tomorrow with knives and tomor-
    row's a knife-blade.
Murder your foe and your foe will be
    murder!—
Even your friends suspected of false
    speaking:
Hands on the door at night and the floor
    boards squeaking.

Those who win by the spear are the spear
    toters.
And what do they win? Spears! What
    else is there?
If their hands let go they have nothing
    to hold by.
They are no more free than a paralytic
    propped against a tree is.

With the armored man the arm is upheld
    by the weapon:
The man is worn by the knife.

[581]

Once depend on iron for your freedom
and your
Freedom's iron!
Once overcome your resisters with force
and your
Force will resist you!—
You will never be free of force.
Never of arms unarmed
Will the father return home:
The lover to her loved:
The mature man to his fruit orchard
Walking at peace in that beauty—
The years of his trees to assure him.

Force is a greater enemy than this conqueror—
A treacherous weapon.

Nevertheless my friends there *is* a weapon!
Weakness conquers!

Against chainlessness who breaks?
Against wall-lessness who vaults?
Against forcelessness who forces?

Against the feather of the thistle
Is blunted sharpest metal.
No edge cuts seed-fluff.

This conqueror unresisted
Will conquer no longer: a posturer
Beating his blows upon burdocks—
Shifting his guard against shadows.
Snickers will sound among road-menders:
Titters be stifled by laundresses:
Coarse guffaws among chambermaids.
Reddened with rage he will roar.
He will sweat in his uniform foolishly.
He will disappear: no one hear of him!

There *is* a weapon my friends.
Scorn conquers!

VOICE OF THE ANNOUNCER [*the Orator's
voice unintelligible under it*]
I wish you could all see this as we do—
The whole plaza full of these people—
Their colorful garments—the harsh sun-
light—
The water-sellers swinging enormous
gourds—
The orator there on the stone platform—
The temple behind him: the high pyra-
mid—
The hawks overhead in the sky teetering
Slow to the windward: swift to the down-
wind—
The houses blind with the blank sun on
them. . . .

THE VOICE OF THE ORATOR
There is a weapon.
Reason and truth are that weapon.

Let this conqueror come!
Show him no hindrance!
Suffer his flag and his drum!
Words . . . win!

THE VOICE OF THE ANNOUNCER
There's the shout now: he's done:
He's climbing down: a great speech:
They're all smiling and pressing around
him:
The women are squatting in full sun-
light:
They're opening packages: bread we'd
say by the look—
Yes: bread: bread wrapped between corn
leaves:
They're squatting to eat: they're quite
contented and happy:
Women are calling their men from the
sunny stones:
There are flutes sounding away off:
We can't see for the shifting and mov-
ing—

Yes: there are flutes in the cool shadow:
Children are dancing in intricate figures.

[*A drum and flute are heard under the
voice.*]

Even a few old men are dancing.
You'd say they'd never feared to see them
    dancing.

A great speech! really great!
Men forget these truths in passion:
They oppose the oppressors with blind
    blows:
They make of their towns tombs: of their
    roofs burials:
They build memorial ruins to liberty:
But liberty is not built from ruins:
Only in peace is the work excellent. . . .

That's odd! The music has stopped.
There's something—
It's a man there on the far side: he's point-
    ing:
He seems to be pointing back through the
    farthest street:
The people are twisting and rising: bread
    in their fists. . .
We can't see what it is. . . . Wait! . . .
    it's a messenger.
It must be a messenger. Yes. It's a message
    —another.
Here he is at the turn of the street trot-
    ting:
His neck's back at the nape: he looks
    tired:
He winds through the crowd with his
    mouth open: laboring:
People are offering water: he pushes away
    from them:
Now he has come to the stone steps: to
    the ministers:
Stand by: we're edging in. . . .

[*There are sounds of people close by:
coughs: murmurs. The Announcer's
voice is lowered.*]

Listen: he's leaning on the stone: he's
    speaking.

THE VOICE OF THE MESSENGER
There has come . . . the Conqueror. . . .

I am to tell you. . .

I have run over corn land:
I have climbed over cone land:
I have crossed over mountains.

It was laid on my shoulders
By shall and by shan't
That standing by day
And staying by night
Were not for my lot
Till I came to the sight of you.

Now I have come.

I bear word:
Beware of this conqueror!

The fame of his story
Like flame in the winter grass
Widens before him.
Beached on our shore
With the dawn over shoulder
The lawns were still cold
When he came to the sheep meadows:—
Sun could not keep with him
So was he forward.

Fame is his sword.

No man opposing him
Still grows his glory.
He needs neither foeman nor
Thickset of blows to
Gather his victories—

[583]

Nor a foe's match
To earn him his battles.

He brings his own enemy!

He baggages with him
His closet antagonist—
His private opposer.
He's setting him up
At every road corner—
A figure of horror
With blood for his color:
Fist for his hand:
Reek where he stands:
Hate for his heat:
Sneers for his mouth:
Clouts for his clothes:
Oaths if he speak:—
And he's knocking him down
In every town square
Till hair's on his blade
And blood's all about
Like dust in a drought
And the people are shouting
Flowers him flinging
Music him singing
And bringing him gold
And holding his heels
And feeling his thighs
Till their eyes start
And their hearts swell
And they're telling his praises
Like lays of the heroes
And chiefs of antiquity.

Such are his victories!
So does he come:
So he approaches . . .

[*A whisper rustles through the crowd.*]

No man to conquer.
Yet as a conqueror
Marches he forward . . .

[*The whisper is louder.*]

Stands in your mountains . . .

[*A murmur of voices.*]

Soon to descend on you!

[*A swelling roar.*]

THE VOICE OF THE ANNOUNCER
That touched them! That frightened
    them!
Some of them point to the east hills:
Some of them mock at the ministers:
    "Freedom!"
"Freedom for what. To die in a rat trap?"
They're frantic with anger and plain fear.
They're sold out they say. You can hear
    them.
"Down with the government! Down with
    the orators!
"Down with liberal learned minds!
"Down with the mouths and the loose
    tongues in them!
"Down with the lazy lot! They've sold us!
"We're sold out! Talking has done for
    us!" . . .
They're boiling around us like mullet that
    smell shark.
We can't move for the mob: they're crazy
    with terror . . .

A LOUD VOICE [*distant*]
God-lovers!
Think of your gods!

Earth-masters!
Taste your disasters!

Men!
Remember!

The Fall of the City

THE VOICE OF THE ANNOUNCER
There's a voice over the crowd somewhere.
They hear it: they're quieting down. . . .
   It's the priests!
We see them now: it's the priests on the
   pyramid!
There might be ten of them: black with
   their hair tangled.
The smoke of their fire is flat in the quick
   wind:
They stand in the thick of the smoke by
   the stone of the victims:
Their knives catch in the steep sun: they
   are shouting:
Listen!—

VOICES OF PRIESTS
Turn to your gods rememberers!

A SINGLE VOICE
Let the world be saved by surrendering
   the world:
Not otherwise shall it be saved.

VOICES OF PRIESTS
Turn to your gods rememberers!

SINGLE VOICE
Let evil be overcome by the coming over
   of evil:
Your hearts shall be elsewhere.

VOICES OF THE PRIESTS
Turn to your gods rememberers!

VOICES OF THE PRIESTS [antiphonally]
Turn to your gods!
The conqueror cannot take you!

Turn to your gods!
The narrow dark will keep you!

Turn to your gods!
In god's house is no breaking!

Turn to your gods!
In god's silences sleep is!

Lay up your will with the gods!
Stones cannot still you!

Lay up your mind with the gods!
Blade cannot blind you!

Lay up your heart with the gods!
Danger departs from you!

THE VOICE OF THE ANNOUNCER
It's a wonderful thing to see this crowd
   responding.
Even the simplest citizens feel the emo-
   tion.
There's hardly a sound now in the square.
   It's wonderful:
Really impressive: the priests there on the
   pyramid:
The smoke blowing: the bright sun: the
   faces—

A SINGLE VOICE
In the day of confusion of reason when
   all is delusion:
In the day of the tyrants of tongues when
   the truth is for hire:
In the day of deceit when ends meet:
Turn to your gods!

In the day of division of nations when
   hope is derision:
In the day of the supping of hate when
   the soul is corrupted:
In the day of despair when the heart's
   bare:
Turn to your gods!

[A slow drum beat.]

THE VOICE OF THE ANNOUNCER
A kind of dance is beginning: a serpent
   of people:

[585]

A current of people coiling and curling
  through people:
A circling of people through people like
  water through water . . .

CHANTING VOICES [*to the drums*]
Out of the stir of the sun
Out of the shout of the thunder
Out of the hush of the star . . .
Withdraw the heart.

THE VOICE OF THE ANNOUNCER [*The
  chant and drums under*]
A very young girl is leading them:
They have torn the shawl from her bare
  breast:
They are giving her flowers: her mouth
  laughs:
Her eyes are not laughing. . . .

CHANTING VOICES
Leave now the lovely air
To the sword and the sword-wearer—
Leave to the marksman the mark—
Withdraw the heart.

THE VOICE OF THE ANNOUNCER [*The
  chant and drums louder*]
She's coming . . . the drums pound . . .
  the crowd
Shrieks . . . she's reaching the temple
  . . . she's climbing it. . . .
Others are following: five: ten . . .
Hundreds are following . . . crowding
  the stairway. . . .
She's almost there . . . her flowers have
  fallen. . . .
She looks back . . . the priests are surrounding her. . . .

[*The drums suddenly stop: there is an
  instant's silence: then an angry shout
  from the crowd.*]

THE VOICE OF THE ANNOUNCER
Wait! Wait! Something has happened!
One of the ministers: one of the oldest:
The general: the one in the feathered
  coat:—
He's driving them down with the staff of
  a banner:
He's climbed after them driving them
  down:
There's shouting and yelling enough but
  they're going:
He's telling them off too: you can hear
  him—

A DEEP VOICE [*chatter of the crowd
  under it*]
Men! Old men! Listen!
Twist your necks on your nape bones!
The knife will wait in the fist for you.

There is a time for everything—
Time to be thinking of heaven:
Time of your own skins!

Cock your eyes to the windward!

Do you see smoke on those mountains?
The smoke is the smoke of towns.
And who makes it? The conqueror!
And where will he march now? Onward!
The heel of the future descends on you!

THE VOICE OF THE ANNOUNCER
He has them now: even the priests have
  seen it:
They're all looking away here to the east.
There's smoke too: filling the valleys: like
  thunderheads! . . .

THE VOICE OF THE GENERAL
You are foolish old men.

You ought to be flogged for your foolishness.

Your grandfathers died to be free
And you—you juggle with freedom!
Do you think you're free by a law
Like the falling of apples in autumn?

You thought you were safe in your liber-
ties!
You thought you could always quibble!
You can't! You take my word for it.
Freedom's the rarest bird!
You risk your neck to snare it—
It's gone while your eyeballs stare!

Those who'd lodge with a tyrant
Thinking to feed at his fire
And leave him again when they're fed are
Plain fools or were bred to it—
Brood of the servile races
Born with the hang-dog face. . . .

THE VOICE OF THE ANNOUNCER
They're all pointing and pushing together:
The women are shouldering baskets:
    bread: children. . . .
They smell smoke in the air: they smell
    terror. . . .

THE VOICE OF THE GENERAL [*louder
    over the increasing sound*]
There's nothing in this world worse—
Empty belly or purse or the
Pitiful hunger of children—
Than doing the Strong Man's will!

The free will fight for their freedom.
They're free men first. They feed
Meager or fat but as free men.
Everything else comes after—
Food: roof: craft—
Even the sky and the light of it!

[*The voices of the crowd rise to a tumult
    of sounds—drums: shouts: cries.*]

THE VOICE OF THE ANNOUNCER
The sun is yellow with smoke . . . the
    town's burning. . . .
The war's at the broken bridge. . . .

THE VOICE OF THE GENERAL [*shouting*]
You! Are you free? Will you fight?

There are still inches for fighting!

There is still a niche in the streets!

You can stand on the stairs and meet him!

You can hold in the dark of a hall!

You can die!

    —or your children will crawl for it!

THE VOICE OF THE ANNOUNCER [*over
    the tumult*]
They won't listen. They're shouting and
    screaming and circling.
The square is full of deserters with more
    coming.
Every street from the bridge is full of de-
    serters.
They're rolling in with the smoke blowing
    behind them.
The plaza's choked with the smoke and
    the struggling of stragglers.
They're climbing the platform: driving
    the ministers: shouting—
One speaks and another:

THE VOICES OF CITIZENS
The city is doomed!
    There's no holding it!

Let the conqueror have it! It's his!

The age is his! It's his century!

Our institutions are obsolete.
He marches a mile while we sit in a meeting.

Opinions and talk!
Deliberative walks beneath the ivy and
the creepers!

The age demands a made-up mind.
The conqueror's mind is decided on everything.

His doubt comes after the deed or never.

He knows what he wants for his want's
what he knows.
He's gone before they say he's going.
He's come before you've barred your
house.

He's one man: we are but thousands!
Who can defend us from one man?

Bury your arms! Break your standards!
Give him the town while the town stands!

THE VOICE OF THE ANNOUNCER
They're throwing their arms away: their
bows are in bonfires.
The plaza is littered with torn plumes:
spear handles. . . .

THE VOICES OF CITIZENS
Masterless men! . . .

Masterless men
Must take a master! . . .

Order must master us! . . .

Freedom's for fools:
Force is the certainty!

Freedom has eaten our strength and corrupted our virtues!

Men must be ruled!

Fools must be mastered!

Rigor and fast
Will restore us our dignity!

Chains will be liberty!

THE VOICE OF THE ANNOUNCER
The last defenders are coming: they whirl
from the streets like
Wild leaves on a wind: the square scat-
ters them.
Now they are fewer—ten together or five:
They come with their heads turned: their
eyes back.

Now there are none. The street's empty
—in shadow.
The crowd is retreating—watching the
empty street:
The shouts die.

The voices are silent.

They're watching. . . .

They stand in the slant of the sunlight
silent and watching.
The silence after the drums echoes the
drum beat.

Now there's a sound. They see him. They
must see him!
They're shading their eyes from the sun:
there's a rustle of whispering:
We can't see for the glare of it. . . . Yes!
. . . Yes! . . .
He's there in the end of the street in the
shadow. We see him!
He looks huge—a head taller than any-
one:
Broad as a brass door: a hard hero:

[588]

Heavy of heel on the brick: clanking with metal:
The helm closed on his head: the eyeholes hollow.

He's coming! . . .
   He's clear of the shadow! . . .
    The sun takes him.

They cover their faces with fingers. They cower before him.
They fall: they sprawl on the stone. He's alone where he's walking.
He marches with rattle of metal. He tramples his shadow.
He mounts by the pyramid—stamps on the stairway—turns—
His arm rises— His visor is opening. . . .

[*There is an instant's breathless silence: then the Voice of the Announcer low —almost a whisper.*]

              There's no one! . . .
There's no one at all! . . .
  No one! . . .
   The helmet is hollow!
The metal is empty! The armor is empty!
  I tell you
There's no one at all there: there's only the metal:
The barrel of metal: the bundle of armor. It's empty!

The push of a stiff pole at the nipple would topple it.

They don't see! They lie on the paving.
  They lie in the

Burnt spears: the ashes of arrows. They lie there. . .
They don't see or they won't see. They are silent. . . .

The people invent their oppressors: they wish to believe in them.
They wish to be free of their freedom: released from their liberty:—
The long labor of liberty ended!
  They lie there!

[*There is a whisper of sound. The Announcer's voice is louder.*]

Look! It's his arm! It is rising! His arm's rising!
They're watching his arm as it rises. They stir. They cry.
They cry out. They are shouting. They're shouting with happiness.
Listen! They're shouting like troops in a victory. Listen—
"The city of masterless men has found a master!"
You'd say it was they were the conquerors: they that had conquered.

A ROAR OF VOICES
The city of masterless men has found a master!
The city has fallen!
The city has fallen!

The VOICE OF THE ANNOUNCER [*flat*]
The city has fallen. . . .

PART V · POETRY

THE CONTEMPORARY POET writes against, and draws from, a large background of American, English, and Continental literature. Because that English background is usually studied in a Survey course, and because the Continental (particularly the French) could not be adequately represented in this volume, we have chosen to introduce this section with selections from the work of three nineteenth-century American poets. The different patterns of thought and technique found in Emerson, Dickinson, and Whitman have done their share in shaping the contemporary poet and his poem.

Thomas Hardy and A. E. Housman are frequently thought of as the first of the "modern" poets. Certainly the ruggedness of Hardy's poetry and the precision of Housman's did much to rescue poetry from the sentimentality and rhetoric so frequently found in the early part of this century.

The fifteen poets who complete this section are for our time and, with the exception of Robinson and Yeats, of our time. They range in technique from the "traditional" structures of Robinson and Frost through the symbolist patterns of Eliot to the typographical tricks of Cummings. They deal with a large and diverse subject matter: such precise things as snow in a wood lot, an express train, a shooting-gallery, and such general problems as the rise of Fascism, the individual in a world society, the search for truth. The attitudes of the poets are also diverse: Frost's search for a "Vantage Point," Sandburg's determined optimism, Eliot's early despair, Jeffers' rejection of man and society, Spender's early call to action, Auden's insistence that "we must love one another or die."

The work of ten of these poets is preceded by excerpts from their own prose statements on the nature of poetry, the poetic process, or their attitudes toward the world. These comments can be most helpful to the reader in fully understanding the intentions of the individual poets. In the Appendix will be found a list of poems recorded by the poets. As we hear the poet read his own work, our understanding of and pleasure in the poem is almost always increased.

We have included only one commentary on a poem. The Friar-Brinnin analysis of Yeats' "Byzantium" is a clear explication of a difficult poem. The

[591]

interested student will find many similar analyses of poems in critical literature of recent years. We have provided no other commentaries or questions
on the poems, believing that they should be left to the individual reader. We
like to think of Robert Frost's reply to the question, "I understand the poem
all right, but won't you tell me what it *means*?" He said, "If I had wanted
you to know, I would have told you in the poem."

Lake Through the Locusts
Luigi Lucioni
Used with the permission
of J. Watson Webb, Jr.

THE SNOW-STORM[1]

by RALPH WALDO EMERSON

Announced by all the trumpets of the sky,
Arrives the snow, and, driving o'er the
    fields,
Seems nowhere to alight: the whited air
Hides hills and woods, the river, and the
    heaven,
And veils the farm-house at the garden's
    end.
The sled and traveller stopped, the cour-
    ier's feet
Delayed, all friends shut out, the house-
    mates sit
Around the radiant fireplace, enclosed
In a tumultuous privacy of storm.

    Come see the north wind's masonry.
Out of an unseen quarry evermore
Furnished with tile, the fierce artificer
Curves his white bastions with projected
    roof
Round every windward stake, or tree, or
    door.

Speeding, the myriad-handed, his wild
    work
So fanciful, so savage, nought cares he
For number or proportion. Mockingly,
On coop or kennel he hangs Parian
    wreaths;
A swan-like form invests the hidden thorn;
Fills up the farmer's lane from wall to
    wall,
Maugre the farmer's sighs; and at the gate
A tapering turret overtops the work.
And when his hours are numbered, and
    the world
Is all his own, retiring, as he were not,
Leaves, when the sun appears, astonished
    Art
To mimic in slow structures, stone by
    stone,
Built in an age, the mad wind's nightwork,
The frolic architecture of the snow.

[1] "I will draw a sketch of a winter's day. I will trace as I can a rude outline of the far-assembled influences, the contribution of the universe wherein this magical structure rises like an exhalation, the wonder and charm of the immeasurable deep."

        —Emerson, *Journal*, November 27, 1832.

QUATRAINS

by RALPH WALDO EMERSON

Orator
He who has no hands
Perforce must use his tongue;
Foxes are so cunning
Because they are not strong.

Poet
To clothe the fiery thought
In simple words succeeds,
For still the craft of genius is
To mask a king in weeds.

THE RHODORA:

ON BEING ASKED, WHENCE IS THE FLOWER?

by RALPH WALDO EMERSON

In May, when sea-winds pierced our soli-
tudes,
I found the fresh Rhodora in the woods,
Spreading its leafless blooms in a damp
nook,
To please the desert and the sluggish
brook.
The purple petals, fallen in the pool,
Made the black water with their beauty
gay;
Here might the red-bird come his plumes
to cool,
And court the flower that cheapens his
array.
Rhodora! if the sages ask thee why
This charm is wasted on the earth and sky,
Tell them, dear, that if eyes were made for
seeing,
Then Beauty is its own excuse for being:
Why thou wert there, O rival of the rose!
I never thought to ask, I never knew:
But, in my simple ignorance, suppose
The self-same Power that brought me
there brought you.

ODE

INSCRIBED TO W. H. CHANNING

by RALPH WALDO EMERSON

Though loath to grieve
The evil time's sole patriot,
I cannot leave
My honied thought
For the priest's cant,
Or statesman's rant.

If I refuse
My study for their politique,
Which at the best is trick,
The angry Muse
Puts confusion in my brain.

But who is he that prates
Of the culture of mankind,
Of better arts and life?
Go, blindworm, go,
Behold the famous States

Harrying Mexico
With rifle and with knife!

Or who, with accent bolder,
Dare praise the freedom-loving mountain-
eer?
I found by thee, O rushing Contoocook!
And in thy valleys, Agiochook!
The jackals of the negro-holder.

The God who made New Hampshire
Taunted the lofty land
With little men;—
Small bat and wren
House in the oak:—
If earth-fire cleave
The upheaved land, and bury the folk,
The southern crocodile would grieve.

Virtue palters; Right is hence;
Freedom praised, but hid;
Funeral eloquence
Rattles the coffin-lid.

What boots thy zeal,
O glowing friend,
That would indignant rend
The northland from the south?
Wherefore? To what good end?
Boston Bay and Bunker Hill
Would serve things still;—
Things are of the snake.
The horseman serves the horse,
The neatherd serves the neat,
The merchant serves the purse,
The eater serves his meat;
'Tis the day of the chattel,
Web to weave, and corn to grind;
Things are in the saddle,
And ride mankind.

There are two laws discrete,
Not reconciled,—
Law for man, and law for thing;
The last builds town and fleet,
But it runs wild,
And doth the man unking.
'Tis fit the forest fall,
The steep be graded,
The mountain tunnelled,
The sand shaded,
The orchard planted,
The glebe tilled,
The prairie granted,
The steamer built.

Let man serve law for man;
Live for friendship, live for love,
For truth's and harmony's behoof;
The state may follow how it can,
As Olympus follows Jove.

Yet do not I implore
The wrinkled shopman to my sounding
    woods,
Nor bid the unwilling senator
Ask votes of thrushes in the solitudes.
Every one to his chosen work;—
Foolish hands may mix and mar;
Wise and sure the issues are.
Round they roll till dark is light,
Sex to sex, and even to odd;—
The over-god
Who marries Right to Might,
Who peoples, unpeoples,—
He who exterminates
Races by stronger races,
Black by white faces,—
Knows to bring honey
Out of the lion;
Grafts gentlest scion
On pirate and Turk.

The Cossack eats Poland,
Like stolen fruit;
Her last noble is ruined,
Her last poet mute:
Straight, into double band
The victors divide;
Half for freedom strike and stand;—
The astonished Muse finds thousands at
    her side.

GIVE ALL TO LOVE

by RALPH WALDO EMERSON

Give all to love;
Obey thy heart;
Friends, kindred, days,
Estate, good-fame,
Plans, credit and the Muse,—
Nothing refuse.

'T is a brave master;
Let it have scope:
Follow it utterly,
Hope beyond hope:
High and more high
It dives into noon,
With wing unspent,
Untold intent;
But it is a god,
Knows its own path
And the outlets of the sky.

It was never for the mean;
It requireth courage stout.
Souls above doubt,
Valor unbending,
It will reward,—
They shall return
More than they were,
And ever ascending.

Leave all for love;
Yet, hear me, yet,
One word more thy heart behoved,
One pulse more of firm endeavor,—
Keep thee to-day,
To-morrow, forever,
Free as an Arab
Of thy beloved.

Cling with life to the maid;
But when the surprise,
First vague shadow of surmise
Flits across her bosom young,
Of a joy apart from thee,
Free be she, fancy-free;
Nor thou detain her vesture's hem,
Nor the palest rose she flung
From her summer diadem.

Though thou loved her as thyself,
As a self of purer clay,
Though her parting dims the day,
Stealing grace from all alive;
Heartily know,
When half-gods go,
The gods arrive.

DAYS[1]

by RALPH WALDO EMERSON

Daughters of Time, the hypocritic Days,
Muffled and dumb like barefoot dervishes,
And marching single in an endless file,
Bring diadems and fagots in their hands.
To each they offer gifts after his will,
Bread, kingdoms, stars, and sky that holds
them all.

I, in my pleached garden, watched the
pomp,
Forgot my morning wishes, hastily
Took a few herbs and apples, and the Day
Turned and departed silent. I, too late,
Under her solemn fillet saw the scorn.

[1] "The days are ever divine, as to the first Aryans. They come and go like muffled and veiled figures, sent from a distant friendly party; but they say nothing, and if we so not use the gifts they bring, they carry them as silently away."

—Emerson, "Works and Days."

BRAHMA[1]

by RALPH WALDO EMERSON

If the red slayer think he slays,
  Or if the slain think he is slain,
They know not well the subtle ways
  I keep, and pass, and turn again.

Far or forgot to me is near;
  Shadow and sunlight are the same;
The vanished gods to me appear;
  And one to me are shame and fame.

They reckon ill who leave me out;
  When me they fly, I am the wings;
I am the doubter and the doubt,
  And I the hymn the Brahmin sings.

The strong gods pine for my abode,
  And pine in vain the sacred Seven;
But thou, meek lover of the good!
  Find me, and turn thy back on heaven.

[1] "In all nations there are minds which incline to dwell in the conception of the fundamental Unity . . . This tendency finds its highest expression in the religious writings of the East, and chiefly in the Indian Scriptures."

        —Emerson, essay on Plato.

Brahma is the soul or essence of all creation. The strong gods are Indra, Agni, and Yama. Emerson, aware of the difficulty of the poem, suggested, "Say Jehovah instead of Brahma," and approved the interpretation by a girl of Concord: "It simply means God everywhere."

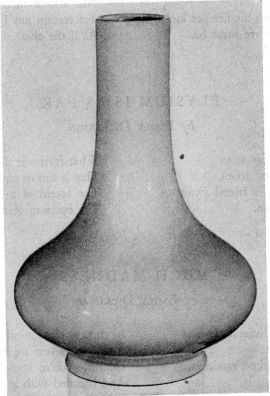

Courtesy, Museum
of Fine Arts, Boston

Chinese vase, Ch'ien-lung period.

THIS IS MY LETTER

by EMILY DICKINSON

This is my letter to the world,
　That never wrote to me,—
The simple news that Nature told,
　With tender majesty.

Her message is committed
　To hands I cannot see;
For love of her, sweet countrymen,
　Judge tenderly of me!

I NEVER SAW

by EMILY DICKINSON

I never saw a moor,
I never saw the sea;
Yet know I how the heather looks,
And what a wave must be.

I never spoke with God,
Nor visited in heaven;
Yet certain am I of the spot
As if the chart were given.

ELYSIUM IS AS FAR

by EMILY DICKINSON

Elysium is as far as to
The very nearest room,
If in that room a friend await
Felicity or doom.

What fortitude the soul contains,
That it can so endure
The accent of a coming foot,
The opening of a door!

MUCH MADNESS

by EMILY DICKINSON

Much madness is divinest sense
To a discerning eye;
Much sense the starkest madness.
'T is the majority

In this, as all, prevails.
Assent, and you are sane;
Demur,—you're straightway dangerous,
And handled with a chain.

All poems except "Although I put away" from *Poems by Emily Dickinson,* edited by Martha Dickinson Bianchi and Alfred Leete Hampson, Little, Brown and Company.

I CANNOT LIVE WITH YOU

by EMILY DICKINSON

I cannot live with you,
It would be life,
And life is over there
Behind the shelf

The sexton keeps the key to,
Putting up
Our life, his porcelain,
Like a cup

Discarded of the housewife,
Quaint or broken;
A newer Sèvres pleases,
Old ones crack.

I could not die with you,
For one must wait
To shut the other's gaze down,—
You could not.

And I, could I stand by
And see you freeze,
Without my right of frost,
Death's privilege?

Nor could I rise with you,
Because your face
Would put out Jesus',
That new grace

Glow plain and foreign
On my homesick eye,

Except that you, than he
Shone closer by.

They 'd judge us—how?
For you served Heaven, you know,
Or sought to;
I could not,

Because you saturated sight,
And I had no more eyes
For sordid excellence
As Paradise.

And were you lost, I would be,
Though my name
Rang loudest
On the heavenly fame.

And were you saved,
And I condemned to be
Where you were not,
That self were hell to me.

So we must keep apart,
You there, I here,
With just the door ajar
That oceans are,
And prayer,
And that pale sustenance,
Despair!

THERE'S A CERTAIN SLANT

by EMILY DICKINSON

There's a certain slant of light,
On winter afternoons,
That oppresses, like the weight
Of cathedral tunes.

Heavenly hurt it gives us;
We can find no scar,
But internal difference
Where the meanings are.

None may teach it anything,
'T is the seal, despair,—
An imperial affliction
Sent us of the air.

When it comes, the landscape listens,
Shadows hold their breath;
When it goes, 't is like the distance
On the look of death.

SUCCESS IS COUNTED

by EMILY DICKINSON

Success is counted sweetest
By those who ne'er succeed.
To comprehend a nectar
Requires sorest need.

Not one of all the purple host
Who took the flag to-day

Can tell the definition,
So clear, of victory,

As he, defeated, dying,
On whose forbidden ear
The distant strains of triumph
Break, agonized and clear.

THE SOUL SELECTS

by EMILY DICKINSON

The soul selects her own society,
Then shuts the door;
On her divine majority
Obtrude no more.

Unmoved, she notes the chariot's pausing
At her low gate;

Unmoved, an emperor is kneeling
Upon her mat.

I've known her from an ample nation
Choose one;
Then close the valves of her attention
Like stone.

TO FIGHT ALOUD

by EMILY DICKINSON

To fight aloud is very brave,
But gallanter, I know,
Who charge within the bosom,
The cavalry of woe.

Who win, and nations do not see,
Who fall, and none observe,

Whose dying eyes no country
Regards with patriot love.

We trust, in plumed procession,
For such the angels go,
Rank after rank, with even feet
And uniforms of snow.

ALTHOUGH I PUT AWAY*

by EMILY DICKINSON

Although I put away his life,
An ornament too grand
For forehead low as mine to wear,
This might have been the hand

That sowed the flowers he preferred,
Or smoothed a homely pain,
Or pushed a pebble from his path,
Or played his chosen tune

On lute the least, the latest,
But just his ear could know
That whatsoe'er delighted it
I never would let go.

The foot to bear his errand
A little boot I know
Would leap abroad like antelope
With just the grant to do.

His weariest commandment
A sweeter to obey
Than "Hide and Seek," or skip to flutes,
Or all day chase the bee.

Your servant, Sir, will weary,
The surgeon will not come,
The world will have its own to do,
The dust will vex your fame.

The cold will force your tightest door
Some February day,
But say my apron bring the sticks
To make your cottage gay,

That I may take that promise
To Paradise with me—
To teach the angels avarice
Your kiss first taught to me!

* Copyright 1929 by Martha Dickinson Bianchi.

MY LIFE CLOSED TWICE

by EMILY DICKINSON

My life closed twice before its close;
It yet remains to see
If Immortality unveil
A third event to me,

So huge, so hopeless to conceive,
As these that twice befell.
Parting is all we know of heaven,
And all we need of hell.

JUST LOST

by EMILY DICKINSON

Just lost when I was saved!
Just felt the world go by!
Just girt me for the onset with eternity,
When breath blew back,
And on the other side
I heard recede the disappointed tide!

Therefore, as one returned, I feel,
Odd secrets of the line to tell!
Some sailor, skirting foreign shores,
Some pale reporter from the awful doors
Before the seal!

Next time, to stay!
Next time, the things to see
By ear unheard,
Unscrutinized by eye.

Next time, to tarry,
While the ages steal,—
Slow tramp the centuries,
And the cycles wheel.

ONE'S-SELF I SING

by WALT WHITMAN

One's-self I sing, a simple separate person,
Yet utter the word Democratic, the word En-Masse.

Of physiology from top to toe I sing,
Not physiognomy alone nor brain alone is worthy for the Muse,
    I say the Form complete is worthier far,
The Female equally with the Male I sing.

Of Life immense in passion, pulse, and power,
Cheerful, for freest action form'd under the laws divine,
The Modern Man I sing.

from SONG OF MYSELF

by WALT WHITMAN

I

I celebrate myself, and sing myself,
And what I assume you shall assume,
For every atom belonging to me as good belongs to you.

I loafe and invite my soul,
I lean and loafe at my ease observing a spear of summer grass.

My tongue, every atom of my blood, form'd from this soil, this air,
Born here of parents born here from parents the same, and their parents the same,
I, now thirty-seven years old in perfect health begin,
Hoping to cease not till death.

Creeds and schools in abeyance,
Retiring back a while sufficed at what they are, but never forgotten,
I harbor for good or bad, I permit to speak at every hazard,
Nature without check with original energy.

.   .   .   .

3

I have heard what the talkers were talking, the talk of the beginning and the end,
But I do not talk of the beginning or the end.

There was never any more inception than there is now,
Nor any more youth or age than there is now,
And will never be any more perfection than there is now,
Nor any more heaven or hell than there is now.

Urge and urge and urge,
Always the procreant urge of the world.
Out of the dimness opposite equals advance, always substance and increase, always
    sex,
Always a knit of identity, always distinction, always a breed of life.

To elaborate is no avail, learn'd and unlearn'd feel that it is so.

Sure as the most certain sure, plumb in the uprights, well entretied, braced in the
    beams,
Stout as a horse, affectionate, haughty, electrical,
I and this mystery here we stand.

Clear and sweet is my soul, and clear and sweet is all that is not my soul.

Lack one lacks both, and the unseen is proved by the seen,
Till that becomes unseen and receives proof in its turn.

Showing the best and dividing it from the worst age vexes age,
Knowing the perfect fitness and equanimity of things, while they discuss I am silent,
    and go bathe and admire myself.
Welcome is every organ and attribute of me, and of any man hearty and clean,
Not an inch nor a particle of an inch is vile, and none shall be less familiar than
    the rest.

I am satisfied—I see, dance, laugh, sing;
As the hugging and loving bed-fellow sleeps at my side through the night, and
    withdraws at the peep of the day with stealthy tread,
Leaving me baskets cover'd with white towels swelling the house with their plenty,
Shall I postpone my acceptation and realization and scream at my eyes,
That they turn from gazing after and down the road,
And forthwith cipher and show me to a cent,
Exactly the value of one and exactly the value of two, and which is ahead? . . .

30

All truths wait in all things,
They neither hasten their own delivery nor resist it,

[6 0 4]

They do not need the obstetric forceps of the surgeon,
The insignificant is as big to me as any,
(What is less or more than a touch?)

Logic and sermons never convince,
The damp of the night drives deeper into my soul.

(Only what proves itself to every man and woman is so,
Only what nobody denies is so.)

A minute and a drop of me settle my brain,
I believe the soggy clods shall become lovers and lamps,
And a compend of compends is the meat of a man or woman,
And a summit and flower there is the feeling they have for each other,
And they are to branch boundlessly out of that lesson until it becomes omnific,
And until one and all shall delight us, and we them.

.   .   .   .   .   .

52

The spotted hawk swoops by and accuses me, he complains of my gab and my
   loitering.

I too am not a bit tamed, I too am untranslatable,
I sound my barbaric yawp over the roofs of the world.

The last scud of day holds back for me,
It flings my likeness after the rest and true as any on the shadow'd wilds,
It coaxes me to the vapor and the dusk.

I depart as air, I shake my white locks at the runaway sun,
I effuse my flesh in eddies, and drift it in lacy jags.

I bequeath myself to the dirt to grow from the grass I love,
If you want me again look for me under your boot-soles.

You will hardly know who I am or what I mean,
But I shall be good health to you nevertheless,
And filter and fibre your blood.

Failing to fetch me at first keep encouraged,
Missing me one place search another,
I stop somewhere waiting for you.

WHEN LILACS LAST IN THE DOORYARD BLOOM'D

by WALT WHITMAN

I

When lilacs last in the dooryard bloom'd,
And the great star early droop'd in the western sky in the night,
I mourn'd, and yet shall mourn with ever-returning spring.

Ever-returning spring, trinity sure to me you bring,
Lilac blooming perennial and drooping star in the west,
And thought of him I love.

2

O powerful western fallen star!
O shades of night—O moody, tearful night!
O great star disappear'd—O the black murk that hides the star!
O cruel hands that hold me powerless—O helpless soul of me!
O harsh surrrounding cloud that will not free my soul.

3

In the dooryard fronting an old farm-house near the white-wash'd palings,
Stands the lilac-bush tall-growing with heart-shaped leaves of rich green,
With many a pointed blossom rising delicate, with the perfume strong I love,
With every leaf a miracle—and from this bush in the dooryard,
With delicate-color'd blossoms and heart-shaped leaves of rich green,
A sprig with its flower I break.

4

In the swamp in secluded recesses,
A shy and hidden bird is warbling a song.
Solitary the thrush,
The hermit withdrawn to himself, avoiding the settlements,
Sings by himself a song.

Song of the bleeding throat,
Death's outlet song of life, (for well dear brother I know,
If thou wast not granted to sing thou would'st surely die.)

5

Over the breast of the spring, the land, amid cities,
Amid lanes and through old woods, where lately the violets peep'd from the ground,
    spotting the gray debris,
Amid the grass in the fields each side of the lanes, passing the endless grass,
Passing the yellow-spear'd wheat, every grain from its shroud in the dark-brown
    fields uprisen,
Passing the apple-tree blows of white and pink in the orchards,
Carrying a corpse to where it shall rest in the grave,
Night and day journeys a coffin.

6

Coffin that passes through lanes and streets,
Through day and night with the great cloud darkening the land,
With the pomp of the inloop'd flags with the cities draped in black,
With the show of the States themselves as of crape-veil'd women standing,
With processions long and winding and the flambeaus of the night,
With the countless torches lit, with the silent sea of faces and the unbared heads,
With the waiting depot, the arriving coffin, and the sombre faces,
With dirges through the night, with the thousand voices rising strong and solemn,
With all the mournful voices of the dirges pour'd around the coffin,
The dim-lit churches and the shuddering organs—where amid these you journey,
With the tolling tolling bells' perpetual clang,
Here, coffin that slowly passes,
I give you my sprig of lilac.

7

(Nor for you, for one alone,
Blossoms and branches green to coffins all I bring,
For fresh as the morning, thus would I chant a song for you O sane and sacred death.

All over bouquets of roses,
O death, I cover you over with roses and early lilies,
But mostly and now the lilac that blooms the first,
Copious I break, I break the sprigs from the bushes,
With loaded arms I come, pouring for you,
For you and the coffins all of you O death.)

8

O western orb sailing the heaven,
Now I know what you must have meant as a month since I walk'd,

As I walk'd in silence the transparent shadowy night,
As I saw you had something to tell as you bent to me night after night,
As you droop'd from the sky low down as if to my side, (while the other stars all
    look'd on,)
As we wander'd together the solemn night, (for something I know not what kept
    me from sleep,)
As the night advanced, and I saw on the rim of the west how full you were of woe,
As I stood on the rising ground in the breeze in the cool transparent night,
As I watch'd where you pass'd and was lost in the netherward black of the night,
As my soul in its trouble dissatisfied sank, as where you sad orb,
Concluded, dropt in the night, and was gone.

9

Sing on there in the swamp,
O singer bashful and tender, I hear your notes, I hear your call,
I hear, I come presently, I understand you,
But a moment I linger, for the lustrous star has detain'd me,
The star my departing comrade holds and detains me.

10

O how shall I warble myself for the dead one there I loved?
And how shall I deck my song for the large sweet soul that has gone?
And what shall my perfume be for the grave of him I love?

Sea-winds blown from east and west,
Blown from the Eastern sea and blown from the Western sea, till there on the
    prairies meeting,
These and with these and the breath of my chant,
I'll perfume the grave of him I love.

11

O what shall I hang on the chamber walls?
And what shall the pictures be that I hang on the walls,
To adorn the burial-house of him I love?

Pictures of growing spring and farms and homes,
With the Fourth-month eve at sundown, and the gray smoke lucid and bright,
With floods of the yellow gold of the gorgeous, indolent, sinking sun, burning,
    expanding the air,
With the fresh sweet herbage under foot, and the pale green leaves of the trees
    prolific,

[608]

In the distance the flowing glaze, the breast of the river, with a wind-dapple here
    and there,
With ranging hills on the banks, with many a line against the sky, and shadows,
And the city at hand with dwellings so dense, and stacks of chimneys,
And all the scenes of life and the workshops, and the workmen homeward returning.

12

Lo, body and soul—this land,
My own Manhattan with spires, and the sparkling and hurrying tides, and the ships,
The varied and ample land, the South and the North in the light, Ohio's shores and
    flashing Missouri,
And ever the far-spreading prairies cover'd with grass and corn.

Lo, the most excellent sun so calm and haughty,
The violet and purple morn with just-felt breezes,
The gentle soft-born measureless light,
The miracle spreading bathing all, the fulfill'd noon,
   The coming eve delicious, the welcome night and the stars,
Over my cities shining all, enveloping man and land.

13

Sing on, sing on you gray-brown bird,
Sing from the swamps, the recesses, pour your chant from the bushes,
Limitless out of the dusk, out of the cedars and pines.

Sing on dearest brother, warble your reedy song,
Loud human song, with voice of uttermost woe.

O liquid and free and tender!
O wild and loose to my soul—O wondrous singer!
You only I hear—yet the star holds me, (but will soon depart,)
Yet the lilac with mastering odor holds me.

14

Now while I sat in the day and look'd forth,
In the close of the day with its light and the fields of spring, and the farmers
    preparing their crops,
In the large unconscious scenery of my land with its lakes and forests,
In the heavenly aerial beauty, (after the perturb'd winds and the storms,)
Under the arching heavens of the afternoon swift passing, and the voices of children
    and women,

[609]

The many-moving sea-tides, and I saw the ships how they sail'd,
And the summer approaching with richness, and the fields all busy with labor,
And the infinite separate houses, how they all went on, each with its meals and
    minutia of daily usages,
And the streets how their throbbings throbb'd, and the cities pent—lo, then and
    there,
Falling upon them all and among them all, enveloping me with the rest,
Appear'd the cloud, appear'd the long black trail,
And I knew death, its thought, and the sacred knowledge of death.

Then with the knowledge of death as walking one side of me,
And the thought of death close-walking the other side of me,
And I in the middle as with companions, and as holding the hands of companions,
I fled forth to the hiding receiving night that talks not,
Down to the shores of the water, the path by the swamp in the dimness,
To the solemn shadowy cedars and ghostly pines so still.

And the singer so shy to the rest receiv'd me,
The gray-brown bird I know receiv'd us comrades three,
And he sang the carol of death, and a verse for him I love.

From deep secluded recesses,
From the fragrant cedars and the ghostly pines so still,
Came the carol of the bird.

And the charm of the carol rapt me,
As I held as if by their hands my comrades in the night,
And the voice of my spirit tallied the song of the bird.

Come lovely and soothing death,
Undulate round the world, serenely arriving, arriving,
In the day, in the night, to all, to each,
Sooner or later delicate death.

Prais'd be the fathomless universe,
For life and joy, and for objects and knowledge curious,
And for love, sweet love—but praise! praise! praise!
For the sure-enwinding arms of cool-enfolding death.

Dark mother always gliding near with soft feet,
Have none chanted for thee a chant of fullest welcome?

Then I chant it for thee, I glorify thee above all,
I bring thee a song that when thou must indeed come, come unfalteringly.

Approach strong deliveress,
When it is so, when thou hast taken them I joyously sing the dead,
Lost in the loving floating ocean of thee,
Laved in the flood of thy bliss O death.

From me to thee glad serenades,
Dances for thee I propose saluting thee, adornments and feastings for thee,
And the sights of the open landscape and the high-spread sky are fitting,
And life and the fields, and the huge and thoughtful night.

The night in silence under many a star,
The ocean shore and the husky whispering wave whose voice I know,
And the soul turning to thee O vast and well-veil'd death,
And the body gratefully nestling close to thee.

Over the tree-tops I float thee a song,
Over the rising and sinking waves, over the myriad fields and the prairies wide,
Over the dense-pack'd cities all and the teeming wharves and ways,
I float this carol with joy, with joy to thee O death.

15

To the tally of my soul,
Loud and strong kept up the gray-brown bird,
With pure deliberate notes spreading filling the night.

Loud in the pines and cedars dim,
Clear in the freshness moist and the swamp-perfume,
And I with my comrades there in the night.

While my sight that was bound in my eyes unclosed,
As to long panoramas of visions.

And I saw askant the armies,
I saw as in noiseless dreams hundreds of battle-flags,
Borne through the smoke of the battles and pierc'd with missiles I saw them,
And carried hither and yon through the smoke, and torn and bloody,
And at last but a few shreds left in the staffs, (and all in silence,)
And the staffs all splinter'd and broken.

I saw battle-corpses, myriads of them,
And the white skeletons of young men, I saw them,
I saw the debris and debris of all the slain soldiers of the war,
But I saw they were not as was thought,
They themselves were fully at rest, they suffer'd not,
The living remain'd and suffer'd, the mother suffer'd,
And the wife and the child and the musing comrade suffer'd,
And the armies that remain'd suffer'd.

16

Passing the visions, passing the night,
Passing, unloosing the hold of my comrades' hands,
Passing the song of the hermit bird and the tallying song of my soul,
Victorious song, death's outlet song, yet varying ever-altering song,
As low and wailing, yet clear the notes, rising and falling, flooding the night,
Sadly sinking and fainting, as warning and warning, and yet again bursting with joy,
Covering the earth and filling the spread of the heaven,
As that powerful psalm in the night I heard from recesses,
Passing, I leave thee lilac with heart-shaped leaves,
I leave thee there in the door-yard, blooming, returning with spring.

I cease from my song for thee,
From my gaze on thee in the west, fronting the west, communing with thee,
O comrade lustrous with silver face in the night.

Yet each to keep and all, retrievements out of the night,
The song, the wondrous chant of the gray-brown bird,
And the tallying chant, the echo arous'd in my soul,
With the lustrous and drooping star with the countenance full of woe,
With the holders holding my hand nearing the call of the bird,
Comrades mine and I in the midst, and their memory ever to keep, for the dead I
    loved so well,
For the sweetest, wisest soul of all my days and lands—and this for his dear sake,
Lilac and star and bird twined with the chant of my soul,
There in the fragrant pines and the cedars dusk and dim.

WHEN I HEARD THE LEARN'D ASTRONOMER

by WALT WHITMAN

When I heard the learn'd astronomer,
When the proofs, the figures, were ranged in columns before me,
When I was shown the charts and diagrams, to add, divide, and measure them,
When I sitting heard the astronomer where he lectured with much applause in the
    lecture-room,
How soon unaccountable I became tired and sick,
Till rising and gliding out I wander'd off by myself,
In the mystical moist night-air, and from time to time,
Look'd up in perfect silence at the stars.

"Preface" to LATE LYRICS AND EARLIER

by THOMAS HARDY

I believe that a good deal of the robustious, swaggering optimism of recent literature is at bottom cowardly and insincere . . . but my pessimism, if pessimism it be, does not involve the assumption that the world is going to the dogs. On the contrary, my practical philosophy is distinctly meliorist. What are my books but one plea against man's inhumanity to man—to woman—and to the lower animals. . . .

. . . while I am quite aware that a thinker is not expected, and, indeed, is scarcely allowed, now more than heretofore, to state all that crosses his mind concerning existence in this universe, in his attempts to explain or excuse the presence of evil and the incongruity of penalizing the irresponsible—it must be obvious to open intelligences that, without denying the beauty and faithful service of certain venerable cults, such disallowance of "obstinate questionings" and "blank misgivings" tends to a paralysed intellectual stalemate. Heine observed nearly a hundred years ago that the soul has her eternal rights; that she will not be darkened by statutes, nor lullabied by the music of bells. And what is to-day, in allusions to the present author's pages, alleged to be "pessimism" is, in truth, only such "questionings" in the exploration of reality and is the first step towards the soul's betterment, and the body's also.

If I may be forgiven for quoting my own old words, let me repeat what I printed in this relation more than twenty years ago, and wrote much earlier, in a poem entitled "In Tenebris":

"If way to the Better there be, it exacts a full look at the Worst": that is to say, by the exploration of reality, and its frank recognition stage by stage along the survey, with an eye to the best consummation possible: briefly, evolutionary meliorism. But it is called pessimism nevertheless; under which word, expressed with condemnatory emphasis, it is regarded by many as some pernicious new thing (though so old as to underlie the Gospel scheme, and even to permeate the Greek

The selections from Thomas Hardy, *Collected Poems,* copyright 1925, by The Macmillan Company and used with their permission.

drama); and the subject is charitably left to decent silence, as if further comment were needless.

Happily there are some who feel such Levitical passing-by to be, alas, by no means a permanent dismissal of the matter; that comment on where the world stands is very much the reverse of needless in these disordered years of our prematurely afflicted century: that amendment and not madness lies that way. And looking down the future these few hold fast to the same: that whether the human and kindred animal races survive till the exhaustion or destruction of the globe, or whether these races perish and are succeeded by others before that conclusion comes, pain to all upon it, tongued or dumb, shall be kept down to a minimum by loving-kindness, operating through scientific knowledge, and actuated by the modicum of free will conjecturally possessed by organic life when the mighty necessitating forces—unconscious or other —that have the "balancings of the clouds" happen to be in equilibrium, which may or may not be often.

.   .   .   .

Whether owing to the barbarizing of taste in the younger minds by the dark madness of the late war, the unabashed cultivation of selfishness in all classes, the plethoric growth of knowledge simultaneously with the stunting of wisdom, "a de-grading search after outrageous stimulation" (to quote Wordsworth again), or from any other cause we seem threatened with a new Dark Age. . . . In any event poetry, pure literature in general, religion —I include religion, in its essential and undogmatic sense, because poetry and religion touch each other, or rather modulate into each other; are, indeed, often but different names for the same thing—these, I say, the visible signs of mental and emotional life, must like all other things keep moving, becoming; even though at present . . . men's minds appear as above noted, to be moving backwards rather than on.

.   .   .   .

It may indeed be a forlorn hope, a mere dream, that of an alliance between religion which must be retained unless the world is to perish, and complete rationality, which must come, unless also the world is to perish, by means of the interfusing effect of poetry—"the breath and finer spirit of all knowledge; the impassioned expression of science," as it was defined by an English poet who was quite orthodox in his ideas. But if it be true, as Comte argued, that advance is never in a straight line, but in a looped orbit, we may, in the aforesaid ominous moving backward, be doing it *pour mieux sauter,* drawing back for a spring. I repeat that I forlornly hope so. . . . But one dares not prophesy.

HAP

by THOMAS HARDY

If but some vengeful god would call to me
From up the sky, and laugh: "Thou suffering thing,
Know that thy sorrow is my ecstasy,
That thy love's loss is my hate's profiting!"

Then would I bear it, clench myself, and die,
Steeled by the sense of ire unmerited;
Half-eased in that a Powerfuller than I
Had willed and meted me the tears I shed.

But not so. How arrives it joy lies slain,
And why unblooms the best hope ever sown?
—Crass Casualty obstructs the sun and rain,
And dicing Time for gladness casts a moan. . . .
These purblind Doomsters had as readily strown
Blisses about my pilgrimage as pain.

THE IMPERCIPIENT

(AT A CATHEDRAL SERVICE)

by THOMAS HARDY

That with this bright believing band
  I have no claim to be,
That faiths by which my comrades stand
  Seem fantasies to me,
And mirage-mists their Shining Land,
  Is a strange destiny.

Why thus my soul should be consigned
  To infelicity,
Why always I must feel as blind
  To sights my brethren see,
Why joys they've found I cannot find,
  Abides a mystery.

Since heart of mine knows not that ease
  Which they know; since it be
That He who breathes All's-Well to these
  Breathes no All's-Well to me,

My lack might move their sympathies
  And Christian charity!

I am like a gazer who should mark
  An inland company
Standing upfingered with, "Hark! hark!
  The glorious distant sea!"
And feel, "Alas, 'tis but yon dark
  And wind-swept pine to me!"

Yet I would bear my shortcomings
  With meet tranquillity,
But for the charge that blessed things
  I'd liefer not have be.
O, doth a bird deprived of wings
  Go earth-bound wilfully!

Enough. As yet disquiet clings
  About us. Rest shall we.

"AH, ARE YOU DIGGING ON MY GRAVE?"

by THOMAS HARDY

"Ah, are you digging on my grave,
　My loved one?—planting rue?"
—"No: yesterday he went to wed
One of the brightest wealth has bred.
'It cannot hurt her now,' he said,
　'That I should not be true.'"

"Then who is digging on my grave?
　My nearest dearest kin?"
—"Ah, no: they sit and think, 'What use!
What good will planting flowers produce?
No tendance of her mound can loose
　Her spirits from Death's gin.'"

"But some one digs upon my grave?
　My enemy?—prodding sly?"
—"Nay: when she heard you had passed
　the Gate
That shuts on all flesh soon or late,
She thought you no more worth her hate,
　And cares not where you lie."

"Then who is digging on my grave?
　Say—since I have not guessed!"
—"O it is I, my mistress dear,
Your little dog, who still lives near,
And much I hope my movements here
　Have not disturbed your rest?"

"Ah, yes! *You* dig upon my grave . . .
　Why flashed it not on me
That one true heart was left behind!
What feeling do we ever find
To equal among human kind
　A dog's fidelity!"

"Mistress, I dug upon your grave
　To bury a bone, in case
I should be hungry near this spot
When passing on my daily trot.
I am sorry, but I quite forgot
　It was your resting-place."

IN TENEBRIS

by THOMAS HARDY

"Considerabam ad dexteram, et videbam; et non erat qui cognosceret me . . . Non est qui requirat animam meam."—*Ps. cxlii.*

When the cloud's swoln bosoms echo back the shouts of the many and strong
That things are all as they best may be, save a few to be right ere long,
And my eyes have not the vision in them to discern what to these is so clear
The blot seems straightway in me alone; one better he were not here.

The stout upstanders say, All's well with us; ruers have nought to rue!
And what the potent say so oft, can it fail to be somewhat true?
Breezily go they, breezily come; their dust smokes around their career,
Till I think I am one born out of due time, who has no calling here.

Their dawns bring lusty joys it seems; their evenings all that is sweet;
Our times are blessed times, they cry: Life shapes it as is most meet,
And nothing is much the matter; there are many smiles to a tear;
Then what is the matter is I, I say. Why should such an one be here? . . .

Let him in whose ears the low-voiced Best is killed by the clash of the First,
Who holds that if way to the Better there be, it exacts a full look at the Worst,
Who feels that delight is a delicate growth cramped by crookedness, custom, and fear,
Get him up and be gone as one shaped awry; he disturbs the order here.

TO AN UNBORN PAUPER CHILD
by Thomas Hardy

I

Breathe not, hid Heart: cease silently,
And though thy birth-hour beckons thee,
    Sleep the long sleep:
    The Doomsters heap
Travails and teens around us here,
And Time-wraiths turn our songsingings to fear.

II

Hark, how the peoples surge and sigh,
And laughters fail, and greetings die:
    Hopes dwindle; yea,
    Faiths waste away,
Affections and enthusiasms numb;
Thou canst not mend these things if thou dost come.

III

Had I the ear of wombèd souls
Ere their terrestrial chart unrolls,
    And thou wert free
    To cease, or be,
Then would I tell thee all I know,
And put it to thee: wilt thou take Life so?

IV

Vain vow! No hint of mine may hence
To theeward fly; to thy locked sense

[617]

Explain none can
Life's pending plan:
Thou will thy ignorant entry make
Though skies spout fire and blood and nations quake.

V

Fain would I, dear, find some shut plot
Of earth's wide wold for thee, where not
 One tear, one qualm,
 Should break the calm.
But I am weak as thou and bare;
No man can change the common lot to rare.

VI

Must come and bide. And such are we—
Unreasoning, sanguine, visionary—
 That I can hope
 Health, love, friends, scope
In full for thee; can dream thou wilt find
Joys seldom yet attained by humankind!

THE OXEN

by THOMAS HARDY

Christmas Eve, and twelve of the clock.
 "Now they are all on their knees,"
An elder said as we sat in a flock
 By the embers in hearthside ease.

We pictured the meek mild creatures where
 They dwelt in their strawy pen,
Nor did it occur to one of us there
 To doubt they were kneeling then.

So fair a fancy few would weave
 In these years! Yet, I feel,
If someone said on Christmas Eve,
 "Come; see the oxen kneel,

Afterwards

"In the lonely barton by yonder coomb
Our childhood used to know,"
I should go with him in the gloom,
Hoping it might be so.

AFTERWARDS

by Thomas Hardy

When the Present has latched its postern behind my tremulous stay,
  And the May month flaps its glad green leaves like wings,
Delicate-filmed as new-spun silk, will the neighbors say,
  "He was a man who used to notice such things"?

If it be in the dusk when, like an eyelid's soundless blink,
  The dewfall-hawk comes crossing the shades to alight
Upon the wind-warped upland thorn, a gazer may think,
  "To him this must have been a familiar sight."

If I pass during some nocturnal blackness, mothy and warm,
  When the hedgehog travels furtively over the lawn,
One may say, "He strove that such innocent creatures should come to no harm,
  But he could do little for them; and now he is gone."

If, when hearing that I have been stilled at last, they stand at the door,
  Watching the full-starred heavens that winter sees,
Will this thought rise on those who will meet my face no more,
  "He was one who had an eye for such mysteries"?

And will any say when my bell of quittance is heard in the gloom,
  And a crossing breeze cuts a pause in its outrollings,
Till they rise again, as they were a new bell's boom,
  "He hears it not now, but used to notice such things"?

from THE NAME AND NATURE OF POETRY
by A. E. HOUSMAN

POETRY indeed seems to me more physical than intellectual. A year or two ago, in common with others, I received from America a request that I would define poetry. I replied that I could no more define poetry than a terrier can define a rat, but that I thought we both recognized the object by the symptoms it provokes in us. One of these symptoms was described in connection with another object by Eliphaz the Temanite: "A spirit passed before my face: the hair of my flesh stood up." Experience has taught me, while I am shaving of a morning, to keep watch over my thoughts, because, if a line of poetry strays into my memory, my skin bristles so that the razor ceases to act. This particular symptom is accompanied by a shiver down the spine; there is another which consists in a constriction of the throat and a precipitation of water to the eyes; and there is a third which I can only describe by borrowing a phrase from one of Keats's last letters, where he says, speaking of Fanny Brawne, "everything that reminds me of her goes through me like a spear." The seat of this sensation is the pit of the stomach.

My opinions on poetry are necessarily tinged, perhaps I should say tainted, by the circumstance that I have come into contact with it on two sides. We were saying a while ago that poetry is a very wide term, and inconveniently comprehensive: so comprehensive is it that it embraces two books, fortunately not large ones, of my own. I know how this stuff came into existence; and though I have no right to assume that any other poetry came into existence in the same way, yet I find reason to believe that some poetry, and quite good poetry, did. Wordsworth for instance says that poetry is the spontaneous overflow of powerful feelings, and Burns has left us this confession, "I have two or three times in my life composed from the wish rather than the impulse, but I never succeeded to any purpose." In short I think that the production of poetry, in its first stage, is less an active than a passive and involuntary process; and if I were obliged, not to define poetry, but to name the class of things to which it belongs, I should call it a secretion; whether a natural secretion, like turpentine in the fir, or a morbid secretion, like the pearl in the oyster, I think that my own case, though I may not deal with the material so cleverly as the oyster does, is the latter; because I have seldom written poetry unless I was rather out of health, and the experience, though pleasurable, was generally agitating and exhausting. If only that you may know what to avoid, I will give some account of the process.

Having drunk a pint of beer at luncheon—beer is a sedative to the brain, and my afternoons are the least intellectual portion of my life—I would go out for a walk of two or three hours. As I went along, thinking of nothing in particular, only looking at things around me and following the progress of the seasons, there would flow into my mind, with sudden and unaccountable emotion, sometimes a line or two of verse, sometimes a whole stanza at once, accompanied, not preceded, by a vague notion of the poem which they

From A. E. Housman, *The Name and Nature of Poetry*. By permission of The Macmillan Company, publishers.

were destined to form part of. Then there would usually be a lull of an hour or so, then perhaps the spring would bubble up again. I say bubble up because, so far as I could make out, the source of the suggestions thus proffered to the brain was an abyss which I have already had occasion to mention, the pit of the stomach. When I got home I wrote them down, leaving gaps, and hoping that further inspiration might be forthcoming another day. Sometimes it was, if I took my walks in a receptive and expectant frame of mind; but sometimes the poem had to be taken in hand and completed by the brain, which was apt to be a matter of trouble and anxiety, involving trial and disappointment, and sometimes ending in failure. I happen to remember distinctly the genesis of the piece which stands last in my first volume. Two of the stanzas, I do not say which, came into my head, just as they are printed, while I was crossing the corner of Hampstead Heath between the Spaniard's Inn and the footpath to Temple Fortune. A third stanza came with a little coaxing after tea. One more was needed, but it did not come: I had to turn to and compose it myself, and that was a laborious business. I wrote it thirteen times, and it was more than a twelvemonth before I got it right.

SOLDIER FROM THE WARS RETURNING

by A. E. HOUSMAN

Soldier from the wars returning,
  Spoiler of the taken town,
Here is ease that asks not earning;
  Turn you in and sit you down.

Peace is come and wars are over,
  Welcome you and welcome all,
While the charger crops the clover
  And his bridle hangs in stall.

Now no more of winters biting,
  Filth in trench from fall to spring,
Summers full of sweat and fighting
  For the Kesar or the King.

Rest you, charger, rust you, bridle;
  Kings and kesars, keep your pay;
Soldier, sit you down and idle
  At the inn of night for aye.

THE HALF-MOON WESTERS LOW, MY LOVE

by A. E. HOUSMAN

The half-moon westers low, my love,
  And the wind brings up the rain;
And wide apart lie we, my love,
  And seas between the twain.

I know not if it rains, my love,
  In the land where you do lie;
And oh, so sound you sleep, my love,
  You know no more than I.

Poems on pages 621-625 from A. E. Housman, *Collected Poems*, Henry Holt and Company, Inc.

THINK NO MORE, LAD

by A. E. HOUSMAN

Think no more, lad; laugh, be jolly:
  Why should men make haste to die?
Empty heads and tongues a-talking
Make the rough road easy walking,
And the feather pate of folly
  Bears the falling sky.

Oh, 'tis jesting, dancing, drinking
  Spins the heavy world around.
If young hearts were not so clever,
Oh, they would be young for ever:
Think no more; 'tis only thinking
  Lays lads underground.

THE LAWS OF GOD, THE LAWS OF MAN

by A. E. HOUSMAN

The laws of God, the laws of man,
He may keep that will and can;
Not I: let God and man decree
Laws for themselves and not for me;
And if my ways are not as theirs
Let them mind their own affairs.
Their deeds I judge and much condemn
Yet when did I make laws for them?
Please yourselves, say I, and they
Need only look the other way.
But no, they will not; they must still
Wrest their neighbour to their will,

And make me dance as they desire
With jail and gallows and hell-fire.
And how am I to face the odds
Of man's bedevilment and God's?
I, a stranger and afraid
In a world I never made.
They will be master, right or wrong;
Though both are foolish, both are strong.
And since, my soul, we cannot fly
To Saturn nor to Mercury,
Keep we must, if keep we can,
These foreign laws of God and man.

THE CHESTNUT CASTS HIS FLAMBEAUX

by A. E. HOUSMAN

The chestnut casts his flambeaux, and the flowers
  Stream from the hawthorn on the wind away,
The doors clap to, the pane is blind with showers.
  Pass me the can, lad; there's an end of May.

These poems from A. E. Housman, *Last Poems*, Henry Holt and Company, Inc.

There's one spoilt spring to scant our mortal lot,
    One season ruined of our little store.
May will be fine next year as like as not:
    Oh ay, but then we shall be twenty-four.

We for a certainty are not the first
    Have sat in taverns while the tempest hurled
Their hopeful plans to emptiness, and cursed
    Whatever brute and blackguard made the world.

It is in truth iniquity on high
    To cheat our sentenced souls of aught they crave,
And mar the merriment as you and I
    Fare on our long fool's-errand to the grave.

Iniquity it is; but pass the can.
    My lad, no pair of kings our mothers bore;
Our only portion is the estate of man:
    We want the moon, but we shall get no more.

If here to-day the cloud of thunder lours
    To-morrow it will hie on far behests;
The flesh will grieve on other bones than ours
    Soon, and the soul will mourn in other breasts.

The troubles of our proud and angry dust
    Are from eternity, and shall not fail.
Bear them we can, and if we can we must.
    Shoulder the sky, my lad, and drink your ale.

"TERENCE, THIS IS STUPID STUFF"

by A. E. Housman

"Terence, this is stupid stuff:
You eat your victuals fast enough;
There can't be much amiss, 'tis clear,
To see the rate you drink your beer.
But oh, good Lord, the verse you make,
It gives a chap the belly-ache.
The cow, the old cow, she is dead;
It sleeps well, the hornèd head:
We poor lads, 'tis our turn now
To hear such tunes as killed the cow.

Pretty friendship 'tis to rhyme
Your friends to death before their time
Moping melancholy mad:
Come, pipe a tune to dance to, lad."

    Why, if 'tis dancing you would be,
There's brisker pipes than poetry.
Say, for what were hop-yards meant,
Or why was Burton built on Trent?
Oh many a peer of England brews
Livelier liquor than the Muse,

From A. E. Housman, *A Shropshire Lad,* Henry Holt and Company, Inc.

And malt does more than Milton can
To justify God's ways to man.
Ale, man, ale's the stuff to drink
For fellows whom it hurts to think:
Look into the pewter pot
To see the world as the world's not.
And faith, 'tis pleasant till 'tis past:
The mischief is that 'twill not last.
Oh I have been to Ludlow fair
And left my necktie God knows where,
And carried half-way home, or near,
Pints and quarts of Ludlow beer:
Then the world seemed none so bad,
And I myself a sterling lad;
And down in lovely muck I've lain,
Happy till I woke again.
Then I saw the morning sky:
Heigho, the tale was all a lie;
The world, it was the old world yet,
I was I, my things were wet,
And nothing now remained to do
But begin the game anew.

Therefore, since the world has still
Much good, but much less good than ill,
And while the sun and moon endure
Luck's a chance, but trouble's sure,
I'd face it as a wise man would,
And train for ill and not for good.

'Tis true, the stuff I bring for sale
Is not so brisk a brew as ale:
Out of a stem that scored the hand
I wrung it in a weary land.
But take it: if the smack is sour,
The better for the embittered hour;
It should do good to heart and head
When your soul is in my soul's stead;
And I will friend you, if I may,
In the dark and cloudy day.

There was a king reigned in the East:
There, when kings will sit to feast,
They get their fill before they think
With poisoned meat and poisoned drink.
He gathered all that springs to birth
From the many-venomed earth;
First a little, thence to more,
He sampled all her killing store;
And easy, smiling, seasoned sound,
Sate the king when healths went round.
They put arsenic in his meat
And stared aghast to watch him eat;
They poured strychnine in his cup
And shook to see him drink it up:
They shook, they stared as white's their
 shirt:
Them it was their poison hurt.
—I tell the tale that I heard told.
Mithridates, he died old.

WHEN I WAS ONE-AND-TWENTY

by A. E. HOUSMAN

When I was one-and-twenty
  I heard a wise man say,
"Give crowns and pounds and guineas
  But not your heart away;
Give pearls away and rubies
  But keep your fancy free."
But I was one-and-twenty,
  No use to talk to me.

When I was one-and-twenty
  I heard him say again,
"The heart out of the bosom
  Was never given in vain;
'Tis paid with sighs aplenty
  And sold for endless rue."
And I am two-and-twenty,
  And oh, 'tis true, 'tis true.

REVEILLE

by A. E. HOUSMAN

Wake: the silver dusk returning
  Up the beach of darkness brims,
And the ship of sunrise burning
  Strands upon the eastern rims.

Wake: the vaulted shadow shatters,
  Trampled to the floor it spanned,
And the tent of night in tatters
  Straws the sky-pavilioned land.

Up, lad, up, 'tis late for lying:
  Hear the drums of morning play;
Hark, the empty highways crying
  "Who'll beyond the hills away?"

Towns and countries woo together,
  Forelands beacon, belfries call;
Never lad that trod on leather
  Lived to feast his heart with all.

Up, lad: thews that lie and cumber
  Sunlit pallets never thrive;
Morns abed and daylight slumber
  Were not meant for man alive.

Clay lies still, but blood's a rover;
  Breath's a ware that will not keep.
Up, lad: when the journey's over
  There'll be time enough to sleep.

LOVELIEST OF TREES, THE CHERRY NOW

by A. E. HOUSMAN

Loveliest of trees, the cherry now
Is hung with bloom along the bough,
And stands about the woodland ride
Wearing white for Eastertide.

Now, of my threescore years and ten,
Twenty will not come again,

And take from seventy springs a score
It only leaves me fifty more.

And since to look at things in bloom
Fifty springs are little room,
About the woodlands I will go
To see the cherry hung with snow.

These poems from A. E. Housman, *A Shropshire Lad,* Henry Holt and Company, Inc.

from SELECTED LETTERS

by EDWIN ARLINGTON ROBINSON

Not long ago I attempted . . . to define poetry as "a language that tells us, through a more or less emotional reaction, something that cannot be said." This might be an equally good, or bad, definition of music, but for the fact that the reader would balk instinctively at the qualifying "more or less" before "emotional"—the emotional reaction in the case of music that endures being unquestionably "more." And this, no doubt, is equally true of much of the best poetry . . . poetry is language and music at the same time.*

There is no "philosophy" in my poetry beyond an implication of an ordered universe and a sort of deterministic negation of the general futility that appears to be the basis of "rational" thought. So I suppose you will have to put me down as a mystic, if that means a man who cannot prove all his convictions to be true.*

The world is not a "prison house" but a kind of spiritual kindergarten, where millions of bewildered infants are trying to spell God with the wrong blocks.

—from The Bookman

CREDO

by EDWIN ARLINGTON ROBINSON

I cannot find my way: there is no star
In all the shrouded heavens anywhere;
And there is not a whisper in the air
Of any living voice but one so far
That I can hear it only as a bar
Of lost, imperial music, played when fair
And angel fingers wove, and unaware,
Dead leaves to garlands where no roses are.

No, there is not a glimmer, nor a call,
For one that welcomes, welcomes when he fears,
The black and awful chaos of the night;
For through it all—above, beyond it all—
I know the far-sent message of the years,
I feel the coming glory of the Light.

MR. FLOOD'S PARTY

by Edwin Arlington Robinson

Old Eben Flood, climbing alone one night
Over the hill between the town below
And the forsaken upland hermitage
That held as much as he should ever know
On earth again of home, paused warily.
The road was his with not a native near;
And Eben, having leisure, said aloud,
For no man else in Tilbury Town to hear:

"Well, Mr. Flood, we have the harvest
 moon
Again, and we may not have many more;
The bird is on the wing, the poet says,
And you and I have said it here before.
Drink to the bird." He raised up to the
 light
The jug that he had gone so far to fill,
And answered huskily: "Well, Mr. Flood,
Since you propose it, I believe I will."

Alone, as if enduring to the end
A valiant armor of scarred hopes outworn,
He stood there in the middle of the road
Like Roland's ghost winding a silent horn.
Below him, in the town among the trees,
Where friends of other days had honored
 him,
A phantom salutation of the dead
Rang thinly till old Eben's eyes were dim.

Then, as a mother lays her sleeping child
Down tenderly, fearing it may awake,
He set the jug down slowly at his feet
With trembling care, knowing that most
 things break;
And only when assured that on firm earth
It stood, as the uncertain lives of men

Assuredly did not, he paced away,
And with his hand extended paused again:

"Well, Mr. Flood, we have not met like
 this
In a long time; and many a change has
 come
To both of us, I fear, since last it was
We had a drop together. Welcome home!"
Convivially returning with himself,
Again he raised the jug up to the light;
And with an acquiescent quaver said:
"Well, Mr. Flood, if you insist, I might.

"Only a very little, Mr. Flood—
For auld lang syne. No more, sir; that
 will do."
So, for the time, apparently it did,
And Eben evidently thought so too;
For soon amid the silver loneliness
Of night he lifted up his voice and sang,
Secure, with only two moons listening,
Until the whole harmonious landscape
 rang—

"For auld lang syne." The weary throat
 gave out,
The last word wavered, and the song was
 done.
He raised again the jug regretfully
And shook his head, and was again alone.
There was not much that was ahead of
 him,
And there was nothing in the town be-
 low—
Where strangers would have shut the
 many doors
That many friends had opened long ago.

From E. A. Robinson, *Collected Poems*. By permission of The Macmillan Company, publishers.

SONNET

by EDWIN ARLINGTON ROBINSON

Never until our souls are strong enough
To plunge into the crater of the Scheme—
Triumphant in the flash there to redeem
Love's handsel and forevermore to slough,
Like cerements at a played-out masque, the rough
And reptile skins of us whereon we set
The stigma of scared years—are we to get
Where atoms and the ages are one stuff.

Nor ever shall we know the cursed waste
Of life in the beneficence divine
Of starlight and of sunlight and soul-shine
That we have squandered in sin's frail distress,
Till we have drunk, and trembled at the taste,
The mead of Thought's prophetic endlessness.

THE MILL

by EDWIN ARLINGTON ROBINSON

The miller's wife had waited long,
  The tea was cold, the fire was dead;
And there might yet be nothing wrong
  In how he went and what he said:
"There are no millers any more,"
  Was all that she had heard him say;
And he had lingered at the door
  So long that it seemed yesterday.

Sick with a fear that had no form
  She knew that she was there at last;
And in the mill there was a warm
  And mealy fragrance of the past.

What else there was would only seem
  To say again what he had meant;
And what was hanging from a beam
  Would not have heeded where she went.

And if she thought it followed her,
  She may have reasoned in the dark
That one way of the few there were
  Would hide her and would leave no
    mark:
Black water, smooth above the weir
  Like starry velvet in the night,
Though ruffled once, would soon appear
  The same as ever to the sight.

From E. A. Robinson, *Collected Poems.* By permission of The Macmillan Company, publishers.

RICHARD CORY

by Edwin Arlington Robinson

Whenever Richard Cory went down town,
　We people on the pavement looked at him:
He was a gentleman from sole to crown,
　Clean favored, and imperially slim.

And he was always quietly arrayed,
　And he was always human when he talked;
But still he fluttered pulses when he said,
　"Good-morning," and he glittered when he walked.

And he was rich—yes, richer than a king,
　And admirably schooled in every grace:
In fine, we thought that he was everything
　To make us wish that we were in his place.

So on we worked, and waited for the light,
　And went without the meat, and cursed the bread;
And Richard Cory, one calm summer night,
　Went home and put a bullet through his head.

From Edwin Arlington Robinson, *The Children of the Night;* used by permission of the publishers, Charles Scribner's Sons.

FLAMMONDE

by Edwin Arlington Robinson

The man Flammonde, from God knows
　where,
With firm address and foreign air,
With news of nations in his talk
And something royal in his walk,
With glint of iron in his eyes,
But never doubt, nor yet surprise,
Appeared, and stayed, and held his head
As one by kings accredited.

Erect, with his alert repose
About him, and about his clothes,
He pictured all tradition hears
Of what we owe to fifty years.
His cleansing heritage of taste
Paraded neither want nor waste;
And what he needed for his fee
To live, he borrowed graciously.

From E. A. Robinson, *Collected Poems.* By permission of The Macmillan Company, publishers.

He never told us what he was,
Or what mischance, or other cause,
Had banished him from better days
To play the Prince of Castaways.
Meanwhile he played surpassing well
A part, for most, unplayable;
In fine, one pauses, half afraid
To say for certain that he played.

For that, one may as well forego
Conviction as to yes or no;
Nor can I say just how intense
Would then have been the difference
To several, who, having striven
In vain to get what he was given,
Would see the stranger taken on
By friends not easy to be won.

Moreover, many a malcontent
He soothed and found munificent;
His courtesy beguiled and foiled
Suspicion that his years were soiled;
His mien distinguished any crowd,
His credit strengthened when he bowed;
And women, young and old, were fond
Of looking at the man Flammonde.

There was a woman in our town
On whom the fashion was to frown;
But while our talk renewed the tinge
Of a long-faded scarlet fringe,
The man Flammonde saw none of that,
And what he saw we wondered at—
That none of us, in her distress,
Could hide or find our littleness.

There was a boy that all agreed
Had shut within him the rare seed
Of learning. We could understand,
But none of us could lift a hand.
The man Flammonde appraised the youth,
And told a few of us the truth;
And thereby, for a little gold,
A flowered future was unrolled.

There were two citizens who fought
For years and years, and over nought;
They made life awkward for their friends,
And shortened their own dividends.
The man Flammonde said what was
   wrong
Should be made right; nor was it long
Before they were again in line,
And had each other in to dine.

And these I mention are but four
Of many out of many more.
So much for them. But what of him—
So firm in every look and limb?
What small satanic sort of kink
Was in his brain? What broken link
Withheld him from the destinies
That came so near to being his?

What was he, when we came to sift
His meaning, and to note the drift
Of incommunicable ways
That make us ponder while we praise?
Why was it that his charm revealed
Somehow the surface of a shield?
What was it that we never caught?
What was he, and what was he not?

How much it was of him we met
We cannot ever know; nor yet
Shall all he gave us quite atone
For what was his, and his alone;
Nor need we now, since he knew best,
Nourish an ethical unrest:
Rarely at once will nature give
The power to be Flammonde and live.

We cannot know how much we learn
From those who never will return,
Until a flash of unforeseen
Remembrance falls on what has been.
We've each a darkening hill to climb;
And this is why, from time to time
In Tilbury Town, we look beyond
Horizons for the man Flammonde.

THE MASTER

(LINCOLN)

by EDWIN ARLINGTON ROBINSON

A flying word from here and there
Had sown the name at which we sneered,
But soon the name was everywhere,
To be reviled and then revered—
A presence to be loved and feared,
We cannot hide it, or deny
That we, the gentlemen who jeered,
May be forgotten by and by.

He came when days were perilous
And hearts of men were sore beguiled;
And having made his note of us,
He pondered and was reconciled.
Was ever master yet so mild
As he, and so untamable?
We doubted, even when he smiled,
Not knowing what he knew so well.

He knew that undeceiving fate
Would shame us whom he served un-
    sought;
He knew that he must wince and wait—
The jest of those for whom he fought;
He knew devoutly what he thought
Of us and of our ridicule;
He knew that we must all be taught
Like little children in a school.

We gave a glamour to the task
That he encountered and saw through;
But little of us did he ask,
And little did we ever do.
And what appears if we review
The season when we railed and chaffed?—
It is the face of one who knew
That we were learning while we laughed.

The face that in our vision feels
Again the venom that we flung,
Transfigured to the world reveals
The vigilance to which we clung.
Shrewd, hallowed, harassed, and among
The mysteries that are untold—
The face we see was never young,
Nor could it wholly have been old.

For he, to whom we had applied
Our shopman's test of age and worth,
Was elemental when he died,
As he was ancient at his birth:
The saddest among kings of earth,
Bowed with a galling crown, this man
Met rancor with a cryptic mirth,
Laconic—and Olympian.

The love, the grandeur, and the fame
Are bounded by the world alone;
The calm, the smoldering, and the flame
Of awful patience were his own:
With him they are forever flown
Past all our fond self-shadowings,
Wherewith we cumber the Unknown
As with inept, Icarian wings.

For we were not as other men:
'Twas ours to soar and his to see;
But we are coming down again,
And we shall come down pleasantly;
Nor shall we longer disagree
On what it is to be sublime,
But flourish in our perigee
And have one Titan at a time.

Weary of the Truth   Marsden Hartley

CASSANDRA

by Edwin Arlington Robinson

I heard one who said: "Verily,
  What word have I for children here?
Your Dollar is your only Word,
  The wrath of it your only fear.

"You build it altars tall enough
  To make you see, but you are blind;
You cannot leave it long enough
  To look before you or behind.

"When Reason beckons you to pause,
  You laugh and say that you know best;
But what it is you know, you keep
  As dark as ingots in a chest.

"You laugh and answer, 'We are young;
  O leave us now, and let us grow.'—
Not asking how much more of this
  Will Time endure or Fate bestow.

"Because a few complacent years
  Have made your peril of your pride,
Think you that you are to go on
  Forever pampered and untried?

"What lost eclipse of history,
  What bivouac of the marching stars,
Has given the sign for you to see
  Millenniums and last great wars?

"What unrecorded overthrow
  Of all the world has ever known,
Or ever been, has made itself
  So plain to you, and you alone?

"Your Dollar, Dove, and Eagle make
  A Trinity that even you
Rate higher than you rate yourselves;
  It pays, it flatters, and it's new.

"And though your very flesh and blood
  Be what your Eagle eats and drinks,
You'll praise him for the best of birds,
  Not knowing what the Eagle thinks.

"The power is yours, but not the sight;
  You see not upon what you tread;
You have the ages for your guide,
  But not the wisdom to be led.

"Think you to tread forever down
  The merciless old verities?
And are you never to have eyes
  To see the world for what it is?

"Are you to pay for what you have
  With all you are?"—No other word
We caught, but with a laughing crowd
  Moved on. None heeded, and few heard.

From E. A. Robinson, *Collected Poems*. By permission of The Macmillan Company, publishers.

from CAPTAIN CRAIG

by Edwin Arlington Robinson

"I, Captain Craig, abhorred iconoclast,
Sage-errant, favored of the Mysteries,
And self-reputed humorist at large,
Do now, confessed of my world-worship-
  ing,
Time-questioning, sun-fearing, and heart-
  yielding,
Approve and unreservedly devise
To you and your assigns for evermore,
God's universe and yours. If I had won

From E. A. Robinson, *Collected Poems*. By permission of The Macmillan Company, publishers.

What first I sought, I might have made
you beam
By giving less; but now I make you laugh
By giving more than what had made you
beam,
And it is well. No man has ever done
The deed of humor that God promises,
But now and then we know tragedians
Reform, and in denial too divine
For sacrifice, too firm for ecstasy,
Record in letters, or in books they write,
What fragment of God's humor they have
caught,
What earnest of its rhythm; and I believe
That I, in having somewhat recognized
The formal measure of it, have endured
The discord of infirmity no less
Through fortune than by failure. What
men lose
Man gains; and what man gains reports
itself
In losses we but vaguely deprecate,
So they be not for us;—and this is right,
Except that when the devil in the sun
Misguides us we go darkly where the shine
Misleads us, and we know not what we
see:
We know not if we climb or if we fall;
And if we fly, we know not where we fly.

"And here do I insert an urging clause
For climbers and up-fliers of all sorts,
Cliff-climbers and high-fliers: Phaethon,
Bellerophon, and Icarus did each
Go gloriously up, and each in turn

Did famously come down—as you have
read
In poems and elsewhere; but other men
Have mounted where no fame has fol-
lowed them,
And we have had no sight, no news of
them,
And we have heard no crash. The crash
may count,
Undoubtedly, and earth be fairer for it;
Yet none save creatures out of harmony
Have ever, in their fealty to the flesh,
Made crashing an ideal. It is the flesh
That ails us, for the spirit knows no
qualm,
No failure, no down-falling: so climb
high,
And having set your steps regard not
much
The downward laughter clinging at your
feet,
Nor overmuch the warning; only know,
As well as you know dawn from lantern-
light,
That far above you, for you, and within
you,
There burns and shines and lives, un-
wavering
And always yours, the truth. Take on
yourself
But your sincerity, and you take on
Good promise for all climbing: fly for
truth,
And hell shall have no storm to crush your
flight,
No laughter to vex down your loyalty."

from "THE FIGURE A POEM MAKES"

by ROBERT FROST

The figure a poem makes. It begins in delight and ends in wisdom. The figure is the same as for love. No one can really hold that the ecstasy should be static and stand still in one place. It begins in delight, it inclines to the impulse, it assumes direction with the first line laid down, it runs a course of lucky events, and ends in a clarification of life—not necessarily a great clarification, such as sects and cults are founded on, but in a momentary stay against confusion. It has denouement. It has an outcome that though unforeseen was predestined from the first image of the original mood—and indeed from the very mood. It is but a trick poem and no poem at all if the best of it was thought of first and saved for the last. It finds its own name as it goes and discovers the best waiting for it in some final phrase at once wise and sad— the happy-sad blend of the drinking song.

No tears in the writer, no tears in the reader. No surprise for the writer, no surprise for the reader. For me the initial delight is in the surprise of remembering something I didn't know I knew. I am in a place, a situation, as if I had materialized from cloud or risen out of the ground. There is a glad recognition of the long lost and the rest follows. Step by step the wonder of unexpected supply keeps growing. The impressions most useful to my purpose seem always those I was unaware of and so made no note of at the time when taken, and the conclusion is come to that like giants we are always hurling experience ahead of us to pave the future with against the day when we may want to strike a line of purpose across it for somewhere. The line will have the more charm for not being mechanically straight. We enjoy the straight crookedness of a good walking stick. . . .

More than once I should have lost my soul to radicalism if it had been the originality it was mistaken for by its young converts. Originality and initiative are what I ask for my country. For myself, the originality need be no more than the freshness of a poem run in the way I have described: from delight to wisdom. The figure is the same as for love. Like a piece of ice on a hot stove the poem must ride on its own melting. A poem may be worked over once it is in being, but may not be worried into being. Its most precious quality will remain its having run itself and carried away the poet with it.

TWO TRAMPS IN MUD TIME

by ROBERT FROST

Out of the mud two strangers came
And caught me splitting wood in the yard.
And one of them put me off my aim
By hailing cheerily 'Hit them hard!'

I knew pretty well why he dropped behind
And let the other go on a way.
I knew pretty well what he had in mind:
He wanted to take my job for pay.

Good blocks of beech it was I split,
As large around as the chopping block;
And every piece I squarely hit
Fell splinterless as a cloven rock.
The blows that a life of self-control
Spares to strike for the common good
That day, giving a loose to my soul,
I spent on the unimportant wood.

The sun was warm but the wind was chill.
You know how it is with an April day
When the sun is out and the wind is still,
You're one month on in the middle of May.
But if you so much as dare to speak,
A cloud comes over the sunlit arch,
A wind comes off a frozen peak,
And you're two months back in the middle of March.

A bluebird comes tenderly up to alight
And fronts the wind to unruffle a plume,
His song so pitched as not to excite
A single flower as yet to bloom.
It is snowing a flake: and he half knew
Winter was only playing possum.
Except in color he isn't blue,
But he wouldn't advise a thing to blossom.

The water for which we may have to look
In summertime with a witching-wand,
In every wheelrut's now a brook,
In every print of a hoof a pond.
Be glad of water, but don't forget
The lurking frost in the earth beneath
That will steal forth after the sun is set
And show on the water its crystal teeth.

The time when most I loved my task
These two must make me love it more
By coming with what they came to ask.
You'd think I never had felt before
The weight of an ax-head poised aloft,
The grip on earth of outspread feet,
The life of muscles rocking soft
And smooth and moist in vernal heat.

Out of the woods two hulking tramps
(From sleeping God knows where last night,
But not long since in the lumber camps).
They thought all chopping was theirs of right.
Men of the woods and lumberjacks,
They judged me by their appropriate tool.
Except as a fellow handled an ax,
They had no way of knowing a fool.

Nothing on either side was said.
They knew they had but to stay their stay
And all their logic would fill my head:
As that I had no right to play
With what was another man's work for gain.
My right might be love but theirs was need.
And where the two exist in twain
Theirs was the better right—agreed.

But yield who will to their separation,
My object in living is to unite
My avocation and my vocation
As my two eyes make one in sight.
Only where love and need are one,
And the work is play for mortal stakes,
Is the deed ever really done
For Heaven and the future's sakes.

THE LOCKLESS DOOR

by ROBERT FROST

It went many years,
But at last came a knock,
And I thought of the door
With no lock to lock.

I blew out the light,
I tip-toed the floor,
And raised both hands
In prayer to the door.

But the knock came again.
My window was wide;

I climbed on the sill
And descended outside.

Back over the sill
I bade a 'Come in'
To whatever the knock
At the door may have been.

So at a knock
I emptied my cage
To hide in the world
And alter with age.

From *New Hampshire* by Robert Frost. Copyright, 1923, by Henry Holt and Company, Inc. Copyright, 1951, by Robert Frost.

THE STAR-SPLITTER

by ROBERT FROST

"You know Orion always comes up sideways.
Throwing a leg up over our fence of mountains,
And rising on his hands, he looks in on me
Busy outdoors by lantern-light with something
I should have done by daylight, and indeed,
After the ground is frozen, I should have done
Before it froze, and a gust flings a handful
Of waste leaves at my smoky lantern chimney
To make fun of my way of doing things,
Or else fun of Orion's having caught me.
Has a man, I should like to ask, no rights
These forces are obliged to pay respect to?"
So Brad McLaughlin mingled reckless talk
Of heavenly stars with hugger-mugger farming,
Till having failed at hugger-mugger farming,
He burned his house down for the fire insurance
And spent the proceeds on a telescope
To satisfy a life-long curiosity
About our place among the infinities.

From Robert Frost, *Collected Poems*, Henry Holt and Company, Inc.

"What do you want with one of those blame things?"
I asked him well beforehand. "Don't you get one!"
"Don't call it blamed; there isn't anything
More blameless in the sense of being less
A weapon in our human fight," he said.
"I'll have one if I sell my farm to buy it."
There where he moved the rocks to plow the ground
And plowed between the rocks he couldn't move,
Few farms changed hands; so rather than spend years
Trying to sell his farm and then not selling,
He burned his house down for the fire insurance
And bought the telescope with what it came to.
He had been heard to say by several:
"The best thing that we're put here for's to see;
The strongest thing that's given us to see with's
A telescope. Someone in every town
Seems to me owes it to the town to keep one.
In Littleton it may as well be me."
After such loose talk it was no surprise
When he did what he did and burned his house down.

Mean laughter went about the town that day
To let him know we weren't the least imposed on,
And he could wait—we'd see to him to-morrow.
But the first thing next morning we reflected
If one by one we counted people out
For the least sin, it wouldn't take us long
To get so we had no one left to live with.
For to be social is to be forgiving.
Our thief, the one who does our stealing from us,
We don't cut off from coming to church suppers,
But what we miss we go to him and ask for.
He promptly gives it back, that is if still
Uneaten, unworn out, or undisposed of.
It wouldn't do to be too hard on Brad
About his telescope. Beyond the age
Of being given one's gift for Christmas,
He had to take the best way he knew how
To find himself in one. Well, all we said was
He took a strange thing to be roguish over.
Some sympathy was wasted on the house,
A good old-timer dating back along;
But a house isn't sentient; the house
Didn't feel anything. And if it did,

The Star-Splitter

Why not regard it as a sacrifice,
And an old-fashioned sacrifice by fire,
Instead of a new-fashioned one at auction?

Out of a house and so out of a farm
At one stroke (of a match), Brad had to turn
To earn a living on the Concord railroad,
As under-ticket-agent at a station
Where his job, when he wasn't selling tickets,
Was setting out up track and down, not plants
As on a farm, but planets, evening stars
That varied in their hue from red to green.

He got a good glass for six hundred dollars.
His new job gave him leisure for star-gazing.
Often he bid me come and have a look
Up the brass barrel, velvet black inside,
At a star quaking in the other end.
I recollect a night of broken clouds
And underfoot snow melted down to ice,
And melting further in the wind to mud.
Bradford and I had out the telescope.
We spread our two legs as we spread its three,
Pointed our thoughts the way we pointed it,
And standing at our leisure till the day broke,
Said some of the best things we ever said.
That telescope was christened the Star-splitter,
Because it didn't do a thing but split
A star in two or three the way you split
A globule of quicksilver in your hand
With one stroke of your finger in the middle.
It's a star-splitter if there ever was one
And ought to do some good if splitting stars
'Sa thing to be compared with splitting wood.

We've looked and looked, but after all where are we?
Do we know any better where we are,
And how it stands between the night to-night
And a man with a smoky lantern chimney?
How different from the way it ever stood?

DEPARTMENTAL

by ROBERT FROST

An ant on the table cloth
Ran into a dormant moth
Of many times his size.
He showed not the least surprise.
His business wasn't with such.
He gave it scarcely a touch,
And was off on his duty run.
Yet if he encountered one
Of the hive's enquiry squad
Whose work is to find out God
And the nature of time and space,
He would put him onto the case.
Ants are a curious race;
One crossing with hurried tread
The body of one of their dead
Isn't given a moment's arrest—
Seems not even impressed.
But he no doubt reports to any
With whom he crosses antennae,
And they no doubt report
To the higher up at court.

Then word goes forth in Formic:
"Death's come to Jerry McCormic,
Our selfless forager Jerry.
Will the special Janizary
Whose office it is to bury
The dead of the commissary
Go bring him home to his people.
Lay him in state on a sepal.
Wrap him for shroud in a petal.
Embalm him with ichor of nettle.
This is the word of your Queen."
And presently on the scene
Appears a solemn mortician;
And taking formal position
With feelers calmly atwiddle,
Seizes the dead by the middle,
And heaving him high in the air,
Carries him out of there.
No one stands round to stare.
It is nobody else's affair.

It couldn't be called ungentle.
But how thoroughly departmental.

From Robert Frost, *Collected Poems*, Henry Holt and Company, Inc.

TO A THINKER

· *by* ROBERT FROST

The last step taken found your heft
Decidedly upon the left.
One more would throw you on the right.
Another still—you see your plight.

You call this thinking, but it's walking.
Not even that, it's only rocking,
Or weaving like a stabled horse:
From force to matter and back to force,

From form to content and back to form,
From norm to crazy and back to norm,
From bound to free and back to bound,
From sound to sense, and back to sound.
So back and forth. It almost scares
A man the way things come in pairs.
Just now you're off democracy
(With a polite regret to be),
And leaning on dictatorship;
But if you will accept the tip,
In less than no time, tongue and pen,
You'll be a democrat again.
A reasoner and good as such,
Don't let it bother you too much

If it makes you look helpless please
And a temptation to the tease.
Suppose you've no direction in you,
I don't see but you must continue
To use the gift you do possess,
And sway with reason more or less.
I own I never really warmed
To the reformer or reformed,
And yet conversion has its place
Not half way down the scale of grace.
So if you find you must repent
From side to side in argument,
At least don't use your mind too hard,
But trust my instinct—I'm a bard.

THE VANTAGE POINT

by Robert Frost

If tired of trees I seek again mankind,
   Well I know where to hie me—in the dawn,
   To a slope where the cattle keep the lawn.
There amid lolling juniper reclined,
Myself unseen, I see in white defined
   Far off the homes of men, and farther still,
   The graves of men on an opposing hill,
Living or dead, whichever are to mind.

And if by noon I have too much of these,
   I have but to turn on my arm, and lo,
   The sun-burned hillside sets my face aglow,
My breathing shakes the bluet like a breeze,
   I smell the earth, I smell the bruisèd plant,
   I look into the crater of the ant.

A DRUMLIN WOODCHUCK

by ROBERT FROST

One thing has a shelving bank,
Another a rotting plank,
To give it cozier skies
And make up for its lack of size.

My own strategic retreat
Is where two rocks almost meet,
And still more secure and snug,
A two-door burrow I dug.

With those in mind at my back
I can sit forth exposed to attack
As one who shrewdly pretends
That he and the world are friends.

All we who prefer to live
Have a little whistle we give,
And flash, at the least alarm
We dive down under the farm.

We allow some time for guile
And don't come out for a while
Either to eat or drink.
We take occasion to think.

And if after the hunt goes past
And the double-barrelled blast
(Like war and pestilence
And the loss of common sense),

If I can with confidence say
That still for another day,
Or even another year,
I will be there for you, my dear,

It will be because, though small
As measured against the All,
I have been so instinctively thorough
About my crevice and burrow.

STOPPING BY WOODS ON A SNOWY EVENING

by ROBERT FROST

Whose woods these are I think I know.
His house is in the village though;
He will not see me stopping here
To watch his woods fill up with snow.

My little horse must think it queer
To stop without a farmhouse near
Between the woods and frozen lake
The darkest evening of the year.

He gives his harness bells a shake
To ask if there is some mistake.
The only other sound's the sweep
Of easy wind and downy flake.

The woods are lovely, dark and deep.
But I have promises to keep,
And miles to go before I sleep,
And miles to go before I sleep.

NEITHER OUT FAR NOR IN DEEP

by ROBERT FROST

The people along the sand
All turn and look one way.
They turn their back on the land.
They look at the sea all day.

As long as it takes to pass
A ship keeps raising its hull;
The wetter ground like glass
Reflects a standing gull.

The land may vary more;
But wherever the truth may be—
The water comes ashore,
And the people look at the sea.

They cannot look out far.
They cannot look in deep.
But when was that ever a bar
To any watch they keep?

MENDING WALL

by ROBERT FROST

Something there is that doesn't love a wall,
That sends the frozen-ground-swell under it,
And spills the upper boulders in the sun;
And makes gaps even two can pass abreast.
The work of hunters is another thing:
I have come after them and made repair
Where they have left not one stone on a stone,
But they would have the rabbit out of hiding,
To please the yelping dogs. The gaps I mean,
No one has seen them made or heard them made,
But at spring mending-time we find them there.
I let my neighbour know beyond the hill;
And on a day we meet to walk the line
And set the wall between us once again.
We keep the wall between us as we go.
To each the boulders that have fallen to each.
And some are loaves and some so nearly balls
We have to use a spell to make them balance:
"Stay where you are until our backs are turned!"
We wear our fingers rough with handling them.
Oh, just another kind of out-door game,
One on a side. It comes to little more:
There where it is we do not need the wall:
He is all pine and I am apple orchard.

My apple trees will never get across
And eat the cones under his pines, I tell him.
He only says, "Good fences make good neighbours."
Spring is the mischief in me, and I wonder
If I could put a notion in his head:
"*Why* do they make good neighbours? Isn't it
Where there are cows? But here there are no cows.
Before I built a wall I'd ask to know
What I was walling in or walling out,
And to whom I was like to give offence.
Something there is that doesn't love a wall,
That wants it down." I could say "Elves" to him,
But it's not elves exactly, and I'd rather
He said it for himself. I see him there,
Bringing a stone grasped firmly by the top
In each hand, like an old-stone savage armed.
He moves in darkness as it seems to me,
Not of woods only and the shade of trees.
He will not go behind his father's saying,
And he likes having thought of it so well
He says again, "Good fences make good neighbours."

THERE ARE ROUGHLY ZONES

by ROBERT FROST

We sit indoors and talk of the cold outside.
And every gust that gathers strength and heaves
Is a threat to the house. But the house has long been tried.
We think of the tree. If it never again has leaves,
We'll know, we say, that this was the night it died.
It is very far north, we admit, to have brought the peach.
What comes over a man, is it soul or mind—
That to no limits and bounds he can stay confined?
You would say his ambition was to extend the reach
Clear to the Arctic of every living kind.
Why is his nature forever so hard to teach
That though there is no fixed line between wrong and right,
There are roughly zones whose laws must be obeyed.
There is nothing much we can do for the tree tonight,
But we can't help feeling more than a little betrayed

That the northwest wind should rise to such a height
Just when the cold went down so many below.
The tree has no leaves and may never have them again.
We must wait till some months hence in the spring to know.
But if it is destined never again to grow,
It can blame this limitless trait in the hearts of men.

ACQUAINTED WITH THE NIGHT

by ROBERT FROST

I have been one acquainted with the night.
I have walked out in rain—and back in rain.
I have outwalked the furthest city light.

I have looked down the saddest city lane.
I have passed by the watchman on his beat.
And dropped my eyes, unwilling to explain.

I have stood still and stopped the sound of feet
When far away an interrupted cry
Came over houses from another street,

But not to call me back or say good-bye;
And further still at an unearthly height,
One luminary clock against the sky

Proclaimed the time was neither wrong nor right.
I have been one acquainted with the night.

Courtesy Art Institute of Chicago

Nighthawks. Edward Hopper.

from THE PEOPLE, YES

by CARL SANDBURG

29

The people, yes—
Born with bones and heart fused in deep and violent secrets
Mixed from a bowl of sky blue dreams and sea slime facts—
A seething of saints and sinners, toilers, loafers, oxen, apes
In a womb of superstition, faith, genius, crime, sacrifice—
The one and only source of armies, navies, work-gangs,
The living flowing breath of the history of nations,
Of the little Family of Man hugging the little ball of Earth,
And a long hall of mirrors, straight, convex and concave,
Moving and endless with scrolls of the living,
Shimmering with phantoms flung from the past,
Shot over with lights of babies to come, not yet here.

The honorable orators, the gazettes of thunder,
The tycoons, big shots and dictators,
Flicker in the mirrors a few moments
And fade through the glass of death
For discussion in an autocracy of worms
While the rootholds of the earth nourish the majestic people
And the new generations with names never heard of
Plow deep in broken drums and shoot craps for old crowns,
Shouting unimagined shibboleths and slogans,
Tracing their heels in moth-eaten insignia of bawdy leaders—
Piling revolt on revolt across night valleys,
Letting loose insurrections, uprisings, strikes,
Marches, mass-meetings, banners, declared resolves,
Plodding in a somnambulism of fog and rain
Till a given moment exploded by long-prepared events—
Then again the overthrow of an old order
And the trials of another new authority
And death and taxes, crops and droughts,
Chinch bugs, grasshoppers, corn bores, boll weevils,
Top soil farms blown away in a dust and wind,
Inexorable rains carrying off rich loam,
And mortgages, house rent, groceries,
Jobs, pay cuts, layoffs, relief

And passion and poverty and crime
And the paradoxes not yet resolved
Of the shrewd and elusive proverbs,
The have-you-heard yarns,
The listen-to-this anecdote
Made by the people out of the roots of the earth,
Out of dirt, barns, workshops, time-tables,
Out of lumberjack payday jamborees,
Out of joybells and headaches the day after,
Out of births, weddings, accidents,
Out of wars, laws, promises, betrayals,
Out of mists of the lost and anonymous,
Out of plain living, early rising and spare belongings:

30

We'll see what we'll see.
Time is a great teacher.
Today me and tomorrow maybe you.
This old anvil laughs at many broken hammers.
What is bitter to stand against today may be sweet to remember tomorrow.
Fine words butter no parsnips. Moonlight dries no mittens.
Whether the stone bumps the jug or the jug bumps the stone it is bad for the jug.
One hand washes the other and both wash the face.
Better leave the child's nose dirty than wring it off.
We all belong to the same big family and have the same smell.
Handling honey, tar or dung some of it sticks to the fingers.
    The liar comes to believe his own lies.
He who burns himself must sit on the blisters.
    God alone understands fools.
The dumb mother understands the dumb child.
To work hard, to live hard, to die hard, and then to go to hell after all would be
    too damned hard.
You can fool all the people part of the time and part of the people all the time but
    you can't fool all of the people all of the time.
    It takes all kinds of people to make a world.
What is bred in the bone will tell.
Between the inbreds and the cross-breeds the argu-
    ment goes on.
You can breed them up as easy as you can breed
    them down.
"I don't know who my ancestors were," said a
    mongrel, "but we've been descending for a
    long time."

"My ancestors," said the Cherokee-blooded Okla-
homan, "didn't come over in the *Mayflower*
but we was there to meet the boat."
"Why," said the Denver Irish policeman as he
arrested a Pawnee Indian I.W.W. soapboxer,
"why don't you go back where you came from?"

An expert is only a damned fool a long ways from home.
You're either a thoroughbred, a scrub, or an in-between.
Speed is born with the foal—sometimes.
Always some dark horse never heard of before is coming under the wire a winner.
A thoroughbred always wins against a scrub, though you never know for sure: even
thoroughbreds have their off days: new blood tells: the wornout thoroughbreds
lose to the fast young scrubs.

> There is a luck of faces and bloods
> Comes to a child and touches it.
> It comes like a bird never seen.
> It goes like a bird never handled.
> There are little mothers hear the bird,
> Feel the flitting of wings never seen,
> And the touch of the givers of luck,
> The bringers of faces and bloods.

86

The people, yes, the people,
Until the people are taken care of one way or another,
Until the people are solved somehow for the day and hour,
Until then one hears "Yes but the people what about the people?"
Sometimes as though the people is a child to be pleased or fed
Or again a hoodlum you have to be tough with
And seldom as though the people is a caldron and a reservoir
Of the human reserves that shape history,
The river of welcome wherein the broken First Families fade,
The great pool wherein wornout breeds and clans drop for restorative silence.
Fire, chaos, shadows,
Events trickling from a thin line of flame
On into cries and combustions never expected:
The people have the element of surprise.
Where are the kings today?
What has become of their solid and fastened thrones?
Who are the temporary puppets holding sway while anything,

"God only knows what," waits around a corner, sits in the shadows and holds
    an ax, waiting for the appointed hour?

"The czar has eight million men with guns and bayonets.
"Nothing can happen to the czar.
"The czar is the voice of God and shall live forever.
"Turn and look at the forest of steel and cannon
"Where the czar is guarded by eight million soldiers.
"Nothing can happen to the czar."
They said that for years and in the summer of 1914
In the Year of Our Lord Nineteen Hundred and Fourteen
As a portent and an assurance they said with owl faces:
    "Nothing can happen to the czar."
Yet the czar and his bodyguard of eight million vanished
And the czar stood in a cellar before a little firing squad
And the command of fire was given
And the czar stepped into regions of mist and ice
The czar traveled into an ethereal uncharted siberia
While two kaisers also vanished from thrones
Ancient and established in blood and iron—
Two kaisers backed by ten million bayonets
Had their crowns in a gutter, their palaces mobbed.
    In fire, chaos, shadows,
In hurricanes beyond foretelling of probabilities,
In the shove and whirl of unforeseen combustions
    The people, yes, the people,
Move eternally in the elements of surprise,
Changing from hammer to bayonet and back to hammer,
The hallelujah chorus forever shifting its star soloists.

107

       The people will live on.
  The learning and blundering people will live on.
    They will be tricked and sold and again sold
And go back to the nourishing earth for rootholds,
    The people so peculiar in renewal and comeback,
    You can't laugh off their capacity to take it.
The mammoth rests between his cyclonic dramas.

The people so often sleepy, weary, enigmatic,
is a vast huddle with many units saying:
    "I earn my living.
    I make enough to get by

[649]

and it takes all my time.
If I had more time
I could do more for myself
and maybe for others.
I could read and study
and talk things over
and find out about things.
It takes time.
I wish I had the time."

The people is a tragic and comic two-face:
hero and hoodlum: phantom and gorilla twisting to moan with a gargoyle mouth: "They
buy me and sell me . . . it's a game . . .
sometime I'll break loose . . ."

Once having marched
Over the margins of animal necessity,
Over the grim line of sheer subsistence
Then man came
To the deeper rituals of his bones,
To the lights lighter than any bones,
To the time for thinking things over,
To the dance, the song, the story,
Or the hours given over to dreaming,
Once having so marched.

Between the finite limitations of the five senses
and the endless yearnings of man for the beyond
the people hold to the humdrum bidding of work and food
while reaching out when it comes their way
for lights beyond the prison of the five senses,
for keepsakes lasting beyond any hunger or death.
This reaching is alive.
The panderers and liars have violated and smutted it.
Yet this reaching is alive yet
for lights and keepsakes.

The people know the salt of the sea
and the strength of the winds
lashing the corners of the earth.
The people take the earth
as a tomb of rest and a cradle of hope.
Who else speaks for the Family of Man?

The People, Yes

They are in tune and step
with constellations of universal law.

The people is a polychrome,
a spectrum and a prism
held in a moving monolith,
a console organ of changing themes,
a clavilux of color poems
wherein the sea offers fog
and the fog moves off in rain
and the labrador sunset shortens
to a nocturne of clear stars
serene over the shot spray
of northern lights.

The steel mill sky is alive.
The fire breaks white and zigzag
shot on a gun-metal gloaming.
Man is a long time coming.
Man will yet win.
Brother may yet line up with brother:

> This old anvil laughs at many broken hammers.
> There are men who can't be bought.
> The fireborn are at home in fire.
> The stars make no noise.
> You can't hinder the wind from blowing.
> Time is a great teacher.
> Who can live without hope?

In the darkness with a great bundle of grief
the people march.
In the night, and overhead a shovel of stars for
keeps, the people march:
"Where to? what next?"

57

Lincoln?
He was a mystery in smoke and flags
saying yes to the smoke, yes to the flags,
yes to the paradoxes of democracy,
yes to the hopes of government
of the people by the people for the people,
no to debauchery of the public mind,
no to personal malice nursed and fed,
yes to the Constitution when a help,
no to the Constitution when a hindrance,
yes to man as a struggler amid illusions,
each man fated to answer for himself:
Which of the faiths and illusions of mankind
must I choose for my own sustaining light
to bring me beyond the present wilderness?

Lincoln? was he a poet?
and did he write verses?
"I have not willingly planted a thorn
in any man's bosom."
"I shall do nothing through malice; what
I deal with is too vast for malice."

Death was in the air.
So was birth.
What was dying few could say.
What was being born none could know.

He took the wheel in a lashing roaring
hurricane.
And by what compass did he steer the course
of the ship?
"My policy is to have no policy," he said in
the early months,
And three years later, "I have been controlled
by events."

From *The People, Yes* by Carl Sandburg. Copyright, 1936, by Harcourt, Brace and Company, Inc.

He could play with the wayward human mind, saying at Charleston, Illinois, September 18, 1858, it was no answer to an argument to call a man a liar.

"I assert that you [pointing a finger in the face of a man in the crowd] are here today, and you undertake to prove me a liar by showing that you were in Mattoon yesterday.

"I say that you took your hat off your head and you prove me a liar by putting it on your head."

He saw personal liberty across wide horizons.

"Our progress in degeneracy appears to me to be pretty rapid," he wrote Joshua F. Speed, August 24, 1855. "As a nation we began by declaring that 'all men are created equal, except Negroes.' When the Know-Nothings get control, it will read 'all men are created equal except Negroes and foreigners and Catholics.' When it comes to this, I shall prefer emigrating to some country where they make no pretense of loving liberty."

> Did he look deep into a crazy pool
> and see the strife and wrangling
> with a clear eye, writing the military
> head of a stormswept area:
> "If both factions, or neither, shall abuse
> you, you will probably be about right. Be-
> ware of being assailed by one and praised
> by the other"?

Lincoln? was he a historian?
did he know mass chaos?
did he have an answer for those
who asked him to organize chaos?

"Actual war coming, blood grows hot, and blood is spilled. Thought is forced from old channels into confusion. Deception breeds and thrives. Confidence dies and universal suspicion reigns.

"Each man feels an impulse to kill his neighbor, lest he be first killed by him. Revenge and retaliation follow. And all this, as before said, may be among honest men only; but this is not all.

"Every foul bird comes abroad and every dirty reptile rises up. These add crime to confusion.

"Strong measures, deemed indispensable, but harsh at best, such men make worse by maladministration. Murders for old grudges, and murders for pelf, proceed under any cloak that will best cover for the occasion. These causes amply account for what has happened in Missouri."

Early in '64 the Committee of the New York Workingman's Democratic Republican Association called on him with assurances and he meditated aloud for them, recalling race and draft riots:

"The most notable feature of a disturbance in your city last summer was the
hanging of some working people by other working people. It should never
be so.

"The strongest bond of human sympathy, outside of the family relation, should
be one uniting all working people, of all nations and tongues and kindreds.

"Let not him who is houseless pull down the house of another, but let him labor
diligently and build one for himself, thus by example assuring that his own
shall be safe from violence when built."

> Lincoln? did he gather
> the feel of the American dream
> and see its kindred over the earth?

"As labor is the common burden of our race,
so the effort of some to shift
their share of the burden
onto the shoulders of others
is the great durable curse of the race."

"I hold,
if the Almighty had ever made a set of men
that should do all of the eating
and none of the work,
he would have made them
with mouths only, and no hands;
and if he had ever made another class,
that he had intended should do all the work
and none of the eating,
he would have made them
without mouths and all hands."

"—the same spirit that says, 'You toil and
work and earn bread, and I'll eat it.' No
matter in what shape it comes, whether
from the mouth of a king who seeks to
bestride the people of his own nation
and live by the fruit of their labor, or
from one race of men as an apology for
enslaving another race, it is the same
tyrannical principle."

"As I would not be a *slave*, so I would not
be a *master*. This expresses my idea of
democracy. Whatever differs from this,
to the extent of the difference, is no democracy."

"I never knew a man who wished to be himself a slave. Consider if you know any
good thing that no man desires for himself."

"The sheep and the wolf
are not agreed upon a definition
of the word liberty."

"The whole people of this nation
will ever do well
if well done by."

"The plainest print cannot be read
through a gold eagle."

"How does it feel to be President?" an Illinois friend asked.
"Well, I'm like the man they rode out of
town on a rail. He said if it wasn't for
the honor of it he would just as soon
walk."

Lincoln? he was a dreamer.
He saw ships at sea,
he saw himself living and dead
in dreams that came.

Into a secretary's diary December 23, 1863,
went an entry: "The President tonight
had a dream. He was in a party of plain
people, and, as it became known who
he was, they began to comment on his
appearance. One of them said: 'He is a
very common-looking man.' The President replied: 'The Lord prefers common-looking people. That is the reason
he makes so many of them.'"

He spoke one verse for then and now:
"If we could first know where we are,
and whither we are tending,
we could better judge
what to do, and how to do it."

THE ROSE OF THE WORLD
by WILLIAM BUTLER YEATS

Who dreamed that beauty passes like a dream?
For these red lips with all their mournful pride,
Mournful that no new wonder may betide,
Troy passed away in one high funeral gleam,
And Usna's children died.

We and the laboring world are passing by:
Amid men's souls, that waver and give place,
Like the pale waters in their wintry race,
Under the passing stars, frame of the sky,
Lives on this lonely face.

Bow down, archangels, in your dim abode:
Before you were, or any hearts to beat,
Weary and kind, one lingered by His seat;
He made the world to be a grassy road
Before her wandering feet.

THE SECOND COMING
by WILLIAM BUTLER YEATS

Turning and turning in the widening gyre
The falcon cannot hear the falconer;
Things fall apart; the centre cannot hold;
Mere anarchy is loosed upon the world,
The blood-dimmed tide is loosed, and
  everywhere
The ceremony of innocence is drowned;
The best lack all conviction, while the
  worst
Are full of passionate intensity.

Surely some revelation is at hand;
Surely the Second Coming is at hand.
The Second Coming! Hardly are those
  words out
When a vast image out of *Spiritus Mundi*

Troubles my sight: somewhere in sands
  of the desert
A shape with lion body and the head of a
  man,
A gaze blank and pitiless as the sun,
Is moving its slow thighs, while all about
  it
Reel shadows of the indignant desert birds.
The darkness drops again; but now I
  know
That twenty centuries of stony sleep
Were vexed to nightmare by a rocking
  cradle,
And what rough beast, its hour come
  round at last,
Slouches towards Bethlehem to be born?

LEDA AND THE SWAN

by WILLIAM BUTLER YEATS

A sudden blow: the great wings beating still
Above the staggering girl, her thighs caressed
By the dark webs, her nape caught in his bill,
He holds her helpless breast upon his breast.

How can those terrified vague fingers push
The feathered glory from her loosening thighs?
And how can body, laid in that white rush,
But feel the strange heart beating where it lies?

A shudder in the loins engenders there
The broken wall, the burning roof and tower
And Agamemnon dead.
　　　　　　　　Being so caught up,
So mastered by the brute blood of the air,
Did she put on his knowledge with his power
Before the indifferent beak could let her drop?

I think if I could be given a month of Antiquity and leave to spend it where I chose, I would spend it in Byzantium a little before Justinian opened St. Sophia and closed the Academy of Plato. I think I could find in some little wine-shop some philosophical worker in mosaic who could answer all my questions, the supernatural descending nearer to him than to Plotinus even. . . . . I think that in early Byzantium, maybe never before or since in recorded history, religious, aesthetic and practical life were one . . .

　　　　　　　　　　　　　　　　　　—*A Vision*

SAILING TO BYZANTIUM

by WILLIAM BUTLER YEATS

That is no country for old men. The young
In one another's arm, birds in the trees,
—Those dying generations—at their song,
The salmon-falls, the mackerel-crowded seas,
Fish, flesh, or fowl, commend all summer long
Whatever is begotten, born, and dies.
Caught in that sensual music all neglect
Monuments of unageing intellect.

[657]

II

An aged man is but a paltry thing,
A tattered coat upon a stick, unless
Soul clap its hands and sing, and louder sing
For every tatter in its mortal dress,
Nor is there singing school but studying
Monuments of its own magnificence;
And therefore I have sailed the seas and come
To the holy city of Byzantium.

III

O sages standing in God's holy fire
As in the gold mosaic of a wall,
Come from the holy fire, perne in a gyre,
And be the singing-masters of my soul.
Consume my heart away; sick with desire
And fastened to a dying animal
It knows not what it is; and gather me
Into the artifice of eternity.

IV

Once out of nature I shall never take
My bodily form from any natural thing,
But such a form as Grecian goldsmiths make
Of hammered gold and gold enamelling
To keep a drowsy Emperor awake;
Or set upon a golden bough to sing
To lords and ladies of Byzantium
Of what is past, or passing, or to come.

BYZANTIUM

by WILLIAM BUTLER YEATS

The unpurged images of day recede;
The Emperor's drunken soldiery are abed;
Night resonance recedes, night-walkers' song
After great cathedral gong;
A starlit or a moonlit dome disdains

Byzantium

All that man is,
All mere complexities,
The fury and the mire of human veins.

Before me floats an image, man or shade,
Shade more than man, more image than a shade;
For Hades' bobbin bound in mummy-cloth
May unwind the winding path;
A mouth that has no moisture and no breath
Breathless mouths may summon;
I hail the superhuman;
I call it death-in-life and life-in-death.

Miracle, bird or golden handiwork,
More miracle than bird or handiwork,
Planted on the starlit golden bough,
Can like the cocks of Hades crow,
Or, by the moon embittered, scorn aloud
In glory of changeless metal
Common bird or petal
And all complexities of mire or blood.

At midnight on the Emperor's pavement flit
Flames that no faggot feeds, nor steel has lit,
Nor storm disturbs, flames begotten of flame,
Where blood-begotten spirits come
And all complexities of fury leave,
Dying into a dance,
An agony of trance,
An agony of flame that cannot singe a sleeve.

Astraddle on the dolphin's mire and blood,
Spirit after spirit! The smithies break the flood,
The golden smithies of the Emperor!
Marbles of the dancing floor
Break bitter furies of complexity,
Those images that yet
Fresh images beget,
That dolphin-torn, that gong-tormented sea.

A NOTE ON BYZANTIUM

In his Diary for April 30, 1930, Yeats wrote: "Subject for a poem . . . Describe Byzantium as it is in the system towards the end of the first Christian millennium. A walking mummy. Flames at the street corners where the soul is purified, birds of hammered gold singing in the golden trees, in the harbour [*sic*], offering their backs to the wailing dead that they may carry them to paradise." Yeats depicts the spirits of the dead purifying themselves from the impurities of the living. It is night in Byzantium. The impure and unpurged living have withdrawn. The sounds of night have receded, the songs of night-walkers and the sound of the cathedral gong, which is not only a symbol of religious ritual tolling out the living and tolling in the dead, but also of the sensual music of impurities which later torments the sea. A cathedral dome, as of Santa Sophia, is lit by the stars or the moon; that is, during Phase 1 at the dark of the moon, or during Phase 15 when the stars recede in the glare of the full moon. Both are supernatural phases where no human incarnation is possible, for Phase 1 "is a supernatural incarnation, like Phase 15, because there is complete objectivity, and human life cannot be completely objective. At Phase 15 mind was completely absorbed by being, but now body is completely absorbed in its supernatural environment . . . mind and body take whatever shape, accept whatever image is imprinted upon them . . . are indeed the instruments of supernatural manifestation, the final link between the living and more powerful beings."—*A Vision*, p. 183. In this great silence, the starlit or moonlit dome disdains the fury

and mire of human duality. The spirits now begin to float in from the realm of the dead.

Yeats describes various forms which the spirit may take during the second state: "In the *Meditation* it wears the form it had immediately before death; in the *Dreaming Back* and the *Phantasmagoria*, should it appear to the living, it has the form of the dream, in the *Return* the form worn during the event explored, in the *Shiftings* whatever form was most familiar to others during its life; in the *Purification* whatever form it fancies."—*A Vision*, p. 235. The spirits live in Hades; the bobbin, or spindle of Hades, symbolizes the revolving and gyrating motions of the dead undergoing their purifications, and the mummy-cloth is a symbol of their lives revolving on that spindle. Reliving their previous lives in memory, by *Dreaming Back* and in *Return*, they thus unwind a similar natural spindle or gyre of their lives upon earth called the "winding path" so that they may become freed of all natural attributes or memories. Caught in a limbo of air between the Condition of Fire and the terrestrial condition, they receive an inflowing from both directions and must continually shuttle between them. "The inflowing from their mirrored life, who themselves receive it from the Condition of Fire, falls upon the Winding Path called the Path of the Serpent, and that inflowing coming alike to men and to animals is called natural. . . . In so far as a man is like all other men, the inflow finds him upon the winding path, and in so far as he is a saint or sage, upon the straight path." The spirit's "descending power," however, "is neither the winding nor the straight line but zigzag . . . it is the sudden lightning, for all his acts of power are instantaneous. We perceive in the pulsation of the artery, and after slowly decline."—*Essays* (New York, Macmillan, 1924), pp. 528-529. Spirit now calls to spirit, and the poet, himself a spirit having neither the moisture nor the breath of the living, calls upon the superhuman in whom the dualities of life and death are being simultaneously resolved. The poet then turns to images of hammered golden birds wrought by human hands to such artifice that they seem inhuman and miraculous, identical in symbol to the spirits. In starlight these birds can crow like the cocks of Hades, a suggestion that if the spirits of the dead must recede before the crowing of a terrestrial cock, as legend has it, then the unpurged images of the living must recede before the cocks of Hades or the singing artificial birds of Byzantium. They sing of their singleness and changelessness, and scorn the passing, decaying birds and flowers of nature, the evil and passion of human complexity. The poet then turns again to the spirits of flame who in an agony of fire and trance are trying to die out of the complexities of human fury in a flaming dance which symbolizes the underlining rhythmic, gyrating pulse of creation. Since these spirits are composed of spiritual and not physical fire, no faggot can feed them, no flint can ignite them, no storm can disturb them, and they in turn cannot singe anything. They were once begotten out of the complexities of human blood which they must now purge away; also, like the bird who came out of the fire, spirit can beget spirit, flame beget flame "as one candle takes light from another."

In discussing that aspect of the second stage called *Phantasmagoria,* Yeats writes of those spirits that appear under the impulse of moral and emotional suffering, and recounts the story of a Japanese girl whose ghost tells a priest of a slight sin, which seems great to her because of her exaggerated conscience: "She is surrounded by flames, and though the priest explains that if she but ceased to believe in those flames they would cease to exist, believe she must, and the play ends in an elaborate dance, the dance of her agony." —*A Vision,* p. 231. Yeats reports the following conversation between himself and a spirit from the fifth state, that of *Purification:* " 'We have no power,' said an inhabitant of the state, 'except to purify our intention,' and when I asked of what, replied: 'Of complexity.' "—*A Vision,* p. 233. The poet finally turns to a vision of the spirits astraddle on the backs of dolphins plunging in an element of water and who carry them back and forth between the terrestrial condition of the living and the spiritual condition of fire and air. (According to Mrs. Arthur Strong's *Apotheosis and After-Life,* dolphins, in the art of the ancient world, were symbols of the soul and its transit.) The miraculous handiwork of the Byzantium goldsmiths, which are themselves now symbols of spirit, break in upon this spiritual flood, and also, in another sense of "break," transcend, overcome, or defeat the flood. The marble mosaics on the dancing floor of the Emperor's pavement (the Forum of Constantine known as "The Pavement" because of its marble floor), also break in upon and are involved in the dance. Thus the poem ends with a whirling dance broken into fragmented images, images begetting images of both symbol and spirit, and all tossed upon a dolphin-torn and gong-tormented sea of complexity, fury, and blood.

MEMOIR OF WILFRED OWEN (1893–Nov. 4, 1918)

by EDMUND BLUNDEN

THE SEED

[*by* WILFRED OWEN]

War broke. And now the winter of the world
With perishing great darkness closes in.
The cyclone of the pressure on Berlin
Is over all the width of Europe whirled,
Rending the sails of progress. Rent or furled
Are all art's ensigns. Verse moans. Now begin
Famines of thought and feeling. Love's wine's thin.
The grain of earth's great autumn rots, down-hurled.

For after Spring had bloomed in early Greece,
And Summer blazed to perfect strength in Rome,
There fell a slow grand age, a harvest-home,
Quietly ripening [rich with all increase].*
But now the exigent winter, and the need
Of sowings for new spring, and flesh for seed.

(* These words are deleted, but none substituted, in the ms.)

Such was his reading of the War as an abstract subject, and in 1915—the date of his enlistment was controlled by his tutorial engagement—he returned to England in order to take his share of its significances to the individual. He joined the Artist's Rifles. His view of the soldier as the victim began to appear in his verses. . . . Gazetted to the Manchester Regiment, Owen joined the 2nd Battalion in January 1917 on the Somme battle-field, where the last sharp fighting was in progress, in that hardest of winters, before the Germans withdrew to their new trench system. Letters home disclose something of his individual experience and of the general life—now so remote in its singularities—of British infantrymen in Flanders. Before leaving the Base Wilfred wrote: "I have just received Orders to take the train at Étaples to join the 2nd Manchesters. This is a Regular Regiment, so I have come off mighty well. . . . It is a huge satisfaction to be going among well-trained troops and genuine 'real-old' officers. . . . This morning I was hit! We were bombing, and a fragment from some where hit my thumb knuckle. I coaxed out one drop of blood. Alas! no more!! There is a fine heroic feeling about being in France, and I am in perfect spirits. A tinge of excitement is about me, but excitement is always necessary to my happiness."

Sunday, Jan. 7, 1917. "It is afternoon. We had an Inspection to make from 9 to 12 this morning. I have wandered into a village café where they gave me writing paper. We made a redoubtable march yesterday from the last Camp to this. The awful state of the roads, and the enormous weight carried, was too much for scores of men. Officers also carried full packs, but I had a horse part of the way. It was beginning to freeze through the rain when we arrived at our tents. We were at the mercy of the cold, and, being in health, I never suffered so terribly as yesterday afternoon. I am really quite well, but have sensations kindred to being seriously ill. As I was making my damp bed, I heard the guns for the first time. It was a sound not without a certain sublimity. They woke me again at 4 o'clock. We are two in a tent. I am with the Lewis Gun Officer. We begged stretchers from the doctor to sleep on. . . . This would not be so bad, but for lack of water and the intense damp cold. . . . This morning I have been reading Trench Standing Orders to my platoon (*verb. sap.*). Needless to say I show a cheerier face to them than I wear in writing this letter; but I must not disguise from you the fact that we are at one of the worst parts of the Line. . . . When we arrived at this deserted village last night, there had been no billets prepared for the battalion—owing to misunderstanding. Imagine the confusion! For my part I discovered, or rather my new-chosen and faithful servant discovered, a fine little hut, with a chair in it. A four-leggéd chair! The roof is waterproof, and there is a stove. There is only one slight disadvantage: there is a howitzer just 70 or 80 yards away, firing over the top every minute or so. I can't tell you how glad I am you got me the ear-defenders. I have to wear them at night. Every time No. 2 (the nearest gun) fires, all my pharmacopoeia, all my boots, candle, and nerves take a smart jump upwards. This phenomenon is immediately followed by a fine rain of particles from

the roof. I keep blowing them off the page. From time to time the village is shelled, but just now nothing is coming over. Anyhow there is a good cellar close to. . . . I spent an hour to-day behind the guns (to get used to them). The major commanding the battery was very pleasant indeed. He took me to his H.Q., and gave me a book of poems to read as if it were the natural thing to do!! But all night I shall be hearing the fellow's voice: 'Number Two—FIRE!' "

On January 16 he wrote: "I can see no excuse for deceiving you about these last 4 days. I have suffered seventh hell. I have not been at the front. I have been in front of it. I held an advanced post, that is, a 'dug-out' in the middle of No Man's Land. We had a march of 3 miles over shelled road, then nearly 3 along a flooded trench. After that we came to where the trenches had been blown flat out and had to go over the top. It was of course dark, too dark, and the ground was not mud, not sloppy mud, but an octopus of sucking clay, 3, 4 and 5 feet deep, relieved only by craters full of water. Men have been known to drown in them. Many stuck in the mud and only got out by leaving their waders, equipment, and in some cases their clothes. High explosives were dropping all around, and machine-guns spluttered every few minutes. But it was so dark that even the German flares did not reveal us. Three-quarters dead, I mean each of us ¾ dead, we reached the dug-out and relieved the wretches therein. I then had to go forth and find another dug-out for a still more advanced post where I left 18 bombers. I was responsible for other posts on the left, but there was a junior officer in charge. My dug-out held 25 men tight packed. Water filled it to a depth of 1 or 2 feet, leaving say 4 feet of air. One entrance had been blown in and blocked. So far, the other remained. The Germans knew we were staying there and decided we shouldn't. Those fifty hours were the agony of my happy life. Every ten minutes on Sunday afternoon seemed an hour. I nearly broke down and let myself drown in the water that was now slowly rising over my knees. Towards 6 o'clock, when, I suppose, you would be going to church, the shelling grew less intense and less accurate; so that I was mercifuly helped to do my duty and crawl, wade, climb and flounder over No Man's Land to visit my other post. It took me half an hour to move over 150 yards. I was chiefly annoyed by our own machine-guns from behind. The seeng-seeng-seeng of the bullets reminded me of Mary's canary. On the whole I can support the canary better. . . . I allow myself to tell you all these things because *I am never going back to this awful post.* It is the worst the Manchesters have ever held; and we are going back for a rest."

The winter of 1916-1917 will long be remembered for its scarcely tolerable cold. The 2nd Manchesters did ñot get the rest expected, and Owen was soon in the front line again. "In this place my platoon had no dug-outs, but had to lie in the snow under the deadly wind. By day it was impossible to stand up, or even crawl about, because we were behind only a little ridge screening us from the Boche's periscope. We had 5 Tommy's Cookers between the platoon, but they did not suffice to melt the ice in the water-cans. So we suffered cruelly from thirst. The marvel is that we did not all die of cold. As a matter of fact, only one of my party actually froze to death before he could be got back, but I am not able to tell how many have ended

in hospital. I have no real casualties from shelling, though for 10 minutes every hour whizzbangs fell a few yards short of us. Showers of soil rained on us but no fragment of shell could find us. . . . My feet ached until they could ache no more, and so they temporarily died. I was kept warm by the ardor of Life within me. I forgot hunger in the hunger for Life. . . . I cannot say I felt any fear. We were all half-crazed by the buffeting of the high explosives. I think the most unpleasant reflection that weighed on me was the impossibility of getting back any wounded, a total impossibility by day, and frightfully difficult by night. We were marooned on a frozen desert. There is not a sign of life on the horizon, and a thousand signs of death. Not a blade of grass, not an insect; once or twice a day the shadow of a big hawk, scenting carrion. . . ."

On March 1 he rejoined his battalion in the extreme south of the British trench line, recently taken over from the French. It was quiet—"so quiet that we have our meals in a shallow dug-out, and only go down deep to sleep." He was soon kept busy in charge of digging parties. On March 14 he reported an accident of a kind which might easily have been more frequent in the devastated area: "Last night I was going around through pitch darkness to see a man in a dangerous state of exhaustion. I fell into a kind of well, only about 15 ft., but I caught the back of my head on the way down. The doctors (not in consultation!) say I have a slight concussion. Of course I have a vile headache, but I don't feel at all fuddled." Five days later he wrote again of this mishap. "I am in a hospital bed (for the first time in life). After falling into that hole (which I believe was a shell-hole in a floor, laying open a deep cellar) I felt nothing more than a headache, for 3 days; and went up to the front in the usual way —or nearly the usual way, for I felt too weak to wrestle with the mud, and sneaked along the top, snapping my fingers at a clumsy sniper. When I got back I developed a high fever, vomited strenuously and long, and was seized with muscular pains. The night before last I was sent to a shanty a bit farther back, and yesterday motored on to this Field Hospital, called Casualty Clearing Station 13." He added that he felt better, and, on March 21, that he was getting up and expecting soon "to overtake my Battalion" again. . . . The battalion had been attacking, and he "caravanned" to them over unfamiliar territory. . . . He found his battalion, and was very welcome, for they had not made their successful attack without heavy losses. Then—"We stuck to our line four days (and four nights) without relief, in the open, and in the snow. Not an hour passed without a shell amongst us. I never went off to sleep on those days, because the others were far more fagged after several days of fighting than I fresh from bed. We lay in wet snow. I kept alive on brandy, the fear of death, and the glorious prospect of the cathedral town just below us.". . .

Almost three weeks passed before his next letter (April 25). He had been in attack in the period. "Never before has the Battalion encountered such intense shelling as rained upon us as we advanced in the open. . . . The reward we got for all this was to remain in the Line 12 days. For twelve days I did not wash my face, nor take off my boots, nor sleep a deep sleep. For twelve days we lay in holes, where at any moment a shell might put us out. I think the worst incident was one wet night when we lay up against a railway embankment. A big shell lit on the top of the bank, just 2 yards from my head. Before I awoke, I was blown in the air right away from the bank! I passed most of the following days in a railway cutting, in a hole just big enough to lie in, and covered with corrugated iron." . . .

"I think that the terribly long time we stayed unrelieved was unavoidable; yet it makes us feel bitterly toward those in England who might relieve us, and will not. We are now doing what is called a Rest, but we rise at 6.15 and work without break until about 10 p.m., for there is always a Pow-Wow for officers after dinner. And if I have not written yesterday, it is because I must have kept hundreds of letters uncensored, and inquiries about missing men unanswered."

On May 2 he wrote from the 13th Casualty Clearing Station: "Here again! The Doctor suddenly was moved to forbid me to go into action next time the Battalion go, which will be in a day or two. I did not go sick or anything, but he is nervous about my nerves, and sent me down yesterday—labeled Neurasthenia. I still of course suffer from the headaches traceable to my concussion. . . . Do not for a moment suppose I have had a 'breakdown'! I am simply avoiding one."

(May 14). "The sensations of going over the top are about as exhilarating as those dreams of falling over a precipice, when you see the rocks at the bottom surging up to you. I woke up without being squashed. Some didn't. There was an extraordinary exultation in the act of slowly walking forward, showing ourselves openly. There was no bugle and no drum, for which I was very sorry. I kept up a kind of chanting sing-song:

Keep the Line straight!
Not so fast on the left!
Steady on the left!
    Not so fast!

Then we were caught in a tornado of shells. The various 'waves' were all broken up, and we carried on like a crowd moving off a cricket-field. When I looked back and saw the ground all crawling and wormy with wounded bodies, I felt no horror at all, but only an immense exultation at having got through the barrage."

About June 10, after confused arrangements, Owen was at No. 1 General Hospital. . . . "At present," he wrote on August 8, clearly feeling the War's influence even more deeply than before, "I am a sick man in hospital, by night; a poet, for quarter of an hour after breakfast; I am whatever and whoever I see while going down to Edinburgh on the train: greengrocer, policeman, shopping lady, errand-boy, paper-boy, blind man, crippled Tommy, bank-clerk, carter, all of these in half an hour. . . ."

At Craiglockhart he was enterprising; he performed at concerts, he lectured, and he edited the hospital magazine called *The Hydra*. About the beginning of August, Captain Siegfried Sassoon arrived. Owen had been reading his *Old Huntsman*. "Nothing like his trench-life sketches has ever been written or ever will be written." One day he ventured to call at his hero's room and to show him some poems, which received some praise and some blame. On the evening of September 7, again, "Sassoon called me in to him; and having condemned some of my poems, amended others, and rejoiced over a few, he read me his very last works, which are superb beyond anything in his book. . . . I don't tell him so, or that I am not worthy to

light his pipe. I simply sit tight and tell him where I think he goes wrong."

Following an ancient custom of mankind, he reviewed the past on the last day of 1917, writing thus to his mother: "And so I have come to the true measure of man. I am not dissatisfied [with] my years. Everything has been done in bouts: Bouts of awful labor at Shrewsbury and Bordeaux; bouts of amazing pleasure in the Pyrenees, and play at Craiglockhart; bouts of religion at Dunsden; bouts of horrible danger on the Somme; bouts of poetry always; of your affection always; of sympathy for the oppressed always. I go out of this year a poet, my dear mother, as which I did not enter it. I am held peer by the Georgians; I am a poet's poet. I am started. The tugs have left me; I feel the great swelling of the open sea taking my galleon. Last year, at this time (it is just midnight, and now is the intolerable instant of the Change), last year I lay awake in a windy tent in the middle of a vast, dreadful encampment. It seemed neither France nor England, but a kind of paddock where the beasts are kept a few days before the shambles. I heard the revelling of the Scotch troops, who are now dead, and who knew they would be dead. I thought of this present night, and whether I should indeed—whether we should indeed—whether you would indeed —but I thought neither long nor deeply, for I am a master of elision. But chiefly I thought of the very strange look on all faces in that camp; an incomprehensible look, which a man will never see in England, though wars should be in England; nor can it be seen in any battle. But only in Étaples. It was not despair, or terror, it was more terrible than terror, for it was a blindfold look, and without expression, like a dead rabbit's. It will never be painted, and no actor will ever seize it. And to describe it, I think I must go back and be with them. We are sending seven officers straight out tomorrow. I have not said what I am thinking this night, but next December I will surely do so."

At the close of July he was preparing to go overseas. "Now must I throw my little candle on [Sassoon's] torch and go out again. There are rumors of a large draft of officers shortly." A few days later he reported that he was to attend for medical inspection, and would proceed to France. "I am glad. That is I am much gladder to be going out again than afraid. I shall be better able to cry my outcry, playing my part. The secondary annoyances and discomforts of France behind the line can be no worse than this Battalion." . . .

Owen was quickly with his old battalion, and he obtained the command of D Company. His new experiences, as he had anticipated, were terrible, but he maintained the serenity of which he spoke, and he continued to write poems on the war. He wrote to Mr. Sassoon on September 22: "You said it would be a good thing for my poetry if I went back. That is my consolation for feeling a fool. This is what shells scream at me every time: 'Haven't you got the wits to keep out of this?'" And on October 10: "Your letter reached me at the exact moment it was most needed—when we had come far enough out of the line to feel the misery of billets; and I had been seized with writer's cramp after making out my casualty reports. (I'm O.C. D. Coy.) The Battalion had a sheer time last week. I can find no better epithet; because I cannot say I suffered anything, having let my brain grow dull. That is to say, my nerves are in perfect order." . . .

A fellow-officer, Lieut. J. Foulkes, M.C., has obligingly written down his reminis-cences of the Owen who belonged to the trenches and billets of Flanders. "We traveled together. . . . The first real attack in which we took part was the one which followed the capture of the Hindenburg Line. We had to take what I think was then looked upon as a 2nd Hindenburg Line and which I remember was well wired. The attack was successful but costly —Owen and I were the only officers left in our Company and he became pro tem. Company Commander. It was for his work here that he received the M.C. Left with few men and lacking any means of cover save a German pill-box, which was really a death-trap because it was on this that the enemy concentrated his fire, Owen succeeded in holding the line until relieved by the Lancs. Fusiliers some time afterwards. This is where I admired his work—in leading his remnants, in the middle of the night, back to safety. I remember feeling how glad I was that it was not my job to know how to get out. I was content to follow him with the utmost confidence in his leadership."

October 31 . . . Writing to his mother, Owen repeated the words, "My nerves are in perfect order . . . I came out," he added, "in order to help these boys—directly by leading them as well as an officer can, indirectly by watching their sufferings that I may speak of them as well as a pleader can. I have done the first." He had, and he was to continue to the end, which came one week before the Armistice fell from heaven on those colorless and water-logged battle-fields. On November 4, 1918, in face of those resolute German machine-gunners who would not have yielded yet if they could have helped it, Wilfred Owen was endeavoring to pass his company over the Sambre Canal. "Zero," writes Mr. Foulkes, "was, I think, 6 A.M., and once more our Company was to lead. From the 'kicking-off' trench or road we reached the spot on the Canal which should have been temporarily bridged by the Engineers, but the plan had unfortunately failed owing to the heavy fire concentrated by machine-gunners and artillery at that particular spot. Instead of gaining the other side, we had therefore to take cover behind the Canal bank, which rose to a height of about four feet. Attempts were made to cross on rafts, but these were unsuccessful." Owen is remembered patting his men on the back as he moved about, with a "Well done!" and "You are doing very well, my boy." The Engineers who were trying to bridge the Canal almost all became casualties. Owen took a hand with some duckboards or planks, and was at the water's edge helping his men to fix them when he was hit and killed. "The battalion eventually crossed lower down by means of a bridge near the village of Ors, a few miles south of Landrécies."

Preface to A PROJECTED VOLUME OF POEMS
by WILFRED OWEN

THIS book is not about heroes. English Poetry is not yet fit to speak of them.

Nor is it about deeds, or lands, nor anything about glory, honor, might, majesty, dominion, or power, except War.

Above all I am not concerned with Poetry.

My subject is War, and the pity of War.

The Poetry is in the pity.

Yet these elegies are to this generation in no sense consolatory. They may be to the next. All a poet can do to-day is warn. That is why the true Poets must be truthful.

(If I thought the letter of this book would last, I might have used proper names; but if the spirit of it survives—survives Prussia—my ambition and those names will have achieved themselves fresher fields than Flanders. . . .)

APOLOGIA PRO POEMATE MEO
by WILFRED OWEN

I, too, saw God through mud—
    The mud that cracked on cheeks when wretches smiled.
    War brought more glory to their eyes than blood,
    And gave their laughs more glee than shakes a child.

Merry it was to laugh there—
    Where death becomes absurd and life absurder.
    For power was on us as we slashed bones bare
    Not to feel sickness or remorse of murder.

The poems on pages 668-672 from *Poems of Wilfred Owen,* by permission of the publishers, Chatto & Windus.

I, too, have dropped off fear—
    Behind the barrage, dead as my platoon,
    And sailed my spirit surging, light and clear
    Past the entanglement where hopes lay strewn;

And witnessed exaltation—
    Faces that used to curse me, scowl for scowl,
    Shine and lift up with passion of oblation,
    Seraphic for an hour; though they were foul.

I have made fellowships—
    Untold of happy lovers in old song.
    For love is not the binding of fair lips
    With the soft silk of eyes that look and long,

By Joy, whose ribbon slips,—
    But wound with war's hard wire whose stakes are strong;
    Bound with the bandage of the arm that drips;
    Knit in the webbing of the rifle-thong.

I have perceived much beauty
    In the hoarse oaths that kept our courage straight;
    Heard music in the silentness of duty;
    Found peace where shell-storms spouted reddest spate.

Nevertheless, except you share
    With them in hell the sorrowful dark of hell,
    Whose world is but the trembling of a flare,
    And heaven but as the highway for a shell,

You shall not hear their mirth:
    You shall not come to think them well content
    By any jest of mine. These men are worth
    Your tears. You are not worth their merriment.

ANTHEM FOR DOOMED YOUTH

by WILFRED OWEN

What passing-bells for these who die as cattle?
    Only the monstrous anger of the guns.
    Only the stuttering rifles' rapid rattle
Can patter out their hasty orisons.
No mockeries for them from prayers or bells,
Nor any voice of mourning save the choirs,—

The shrill, demented choirs of wailing shells;
And bugles calling for them from sad shires.

What candles may be held to speed them all?
    Not in the hands of boys, but in their eyes
Shall shine the holy glimmers of good-bys.
    The pallor of girls' brows shall be their pall;
Their flowers the tenderness of silent minds,
And each slow dusk a drawing-down of blinds.

GREATER LOVE

by Wilfred Owen

Red lips are not so red
    As the stained stones kissed by the
    English dead.
Kindness of wooed and wooer
Seems shame to their love pure.
O Love, your eyes lose lure
    When I behold eyes blinded in my
    stead!

Your slender attitude
    Trembles not exquisite like limbs
    knife-skewed,
Rolling and rolling there
Where God seems not to care;
Till the fierce Love they bear
    Cramps them in death's extreme de-
    crepitude.

Your voice sings not so soft,—
    Though even as wind murmuring
    through raftered loft,—
Your dear voice is not dear,
Gentle, and evening clear,
As theirs whom none now hear
    Now earth has stopped their piteous
    mouths that coughed.

Heart, you were never hot,
    Nor large, nor full like hearts made
    great with shot;
And though your hand be pale,
Paler are all which trail
Your cross through flame and hail:
    Weep, you may weep, for you may
    touch them not.

STRANGE MEETING

by Wilfred Owen

It seemed that out of the battle I escaped
Down some profound dull tunnel, long since scooped
Through granites which Titanic wars had groined.
Yet also there encumbered sleepers groaned,
Too fast in thought or death to be bestirred.
Then, as I probed them, one sprang up, and stared
With piteous recognition in fixed eyes,
Lifting distressful hands as if to bless.

And by his smile, I knew that sullen hall.
By his dead smile I knew we stood in Hell
With a thousand pains that vision's face was grained;
Yet no blood reached there from the upper ground,
And no guns thumped, or down the flues made moan.
"Strange friend," I said, "here is no cause to mourn."
"None," said the other, "save the undone years,
The hopelessness. Whatever hope is yours,
Was my life also; I went hunting wild
After the wildest beauty in the world,
Which lies not calm in eyes, or braided hair,
But mocks the steady running of the hour,
And if it grieves, grieves richlier than here.
For by my glee might many men have laughed,
And of my weeping something has been left,
Which must die now. I mean the truth untold,
The pity of war, the pity war distilled.
Now men will go content with what we spoiled,
Or, discontent, boil bloody, and be spilled.
They will be swift with swiftness of the tigress,
None will break ranks, though nations trek from progress.
Courage was mine, and I had mystery,
Wisdom was mine, and I had mastery;
To miss the march of this retreating world
Into vain citadels that are not walled.
Then when much blood had clogged their chariot-wheels
I would go up and wash them from sweet wells,
Even with truths that lie too deep for taint.
I would have poured my spirit without stint
But not through wounds; not on the cess of war.
Foreheads of men have bled where no wounds were.
I am the enemy you killed, my friend.
I knew you in this dark; for so you frowned
Yesterday through me as you jabbed and killed.
I parried; but my hands were loath and cold.
Let us sleep now. . . ."

DULCE ET DECORUM EST

by WILFRED OWEN

Bent double, like old beggars under sacks,
Knock-kneed, coughing like hags, we cursed through sludge,

Till on the haunting flares we turned our backs,
And towards our distant rest began to trudge.
Men marched asleep. Many had lost their boots,
But limped on, blood-shod. All went lame, all blind;
Drunk with fatigue; deaf even to the hoots
Of gas-shells dropping softly behind.

Gas! Gas! Quick, boys!—An ecstasy of fumbling,
Fitting the clumsy helmets just in time,
But some one still was yelling out and stumbling
And floundering like a man in fire or lime.—
Dim through the misty panes and thick green light,
As under a green sea, I saw him drowning.

In all my dreams before my helpless sight
He plunges at me, guttering, choking, drowning.

If in some smothering dreams, you too could pace
Behind the wagon that we flung him in,
And watch the white eyes writhing in his face,
His hanging face, like a devil's sick of sin,
If you could hear, at every jolt, the blood
Come gargling from the froth-corrupted lungs
Bitten as the cud
Of vile, incurable sores on innocent tongues,—
My friend, you would not tell with such high zest
To children ardent for some desperate glory,
The old Lie: Dulce et decorum est
Pro patria mori.

FUTILITY

by WILFRED OWEN

Move him into the sun—
Gently its touch awoke him once,
At home, whispering of fields unsown.
Always it woke him, even in France.
Until this morning and this snow.
If anything might rouse him now
The kind old sun will know.

Think how it wakes the seeds—
Woke, once, the clays of a cold star.
Are limbs so dear-achieved, are sides
Full-nerved,—still warm,—too hard to stir?
Was it for this the clay grew tall?
—Oh, what made fatuous sunbeams toil
To break earth's sleep at all?

from SELECTED ESSAYS
by T. S. Eliot

Dante

In my experience of the appreciation of poetry I have always found that the less I knew about the poet and his work, before I began to read it, the better.

Tradition and the Individual Talent

I am alive to a usual objection to what is clearly part of my programme for the *metier* of poetry. The objection is that the doctrine requires a ridiculous amount of erudition (pedantry), a claim which can be rejected by appeal to the lives of poets in any pantheon. It will even be affirmed that much learning deadens or perverts poetic sensibility.

The Metaphysical Poets

It is not a permanent necessity that poets should be interested in philosophy, or in any other subject. We can only say that it appears likely that poets in our civilization, as it exists at present, must be *difficult.* Our civilization comprehends great variety and complexity, and this variety and complexity, playing upon a refined sensibility, must produce various and complex results. The poet must become more and more comprehensive, more allusive, more indirect, in order to force, to dislocate if necessary, language into his meaning.

William Blake

Blake was endowed with a capacity for considerable understanding of human nature with a remarkable and original sense of language, and a gift of hallucinated vision. Had these been controlled by a respect for impersonal reason, for common sense, for the objectivity of science, it would have been better for him.

ANIMULA

by T. S. ELIOT

"Issues from the hand of God, the simple
  soul"
To a flat world of changing lights and
  noise,
To light, dark, dry or damp, chilly or
  warm;
Moving between the legs of tables and of
  chairs,
Rising or falling, grasping at kisses and
  toys,
Advancing boldly, sudden to take alarm,
Retreating to the corner of arm and knee,
Eager to be reassured, taking pleasure
In the fragrant brilliance of the Christmas
  tree,
Pleasure in the wind, the sunlight and the
  sea;
Studies the sunlit pattern on the floor
And running stags around a silver tray;
Confounds the actual and the fanciful,
Content with playing-cards and kings and
  queens,
What the fairies do and what the servants
  say.
The heavy burden of the growing soul
Perplexes and offends more, day by day;
Week by week, offends and perplexes
  more

With the imperatives of "is and seems"
And may and may not, desire and control
The pain of living and the drug of dreams
Curl up the small soul in the window seat
Behind the *Encylopædia Britannica.*
Issues from the hand of time the simple
  soul
Irresolute and selfish, misshapen, lame,
Unable to fare forward or retreat,
Fearing the warm reality, the offered
  good,
Denying the importunity of the blood,
Shadow of its own shadows, specter in its
  own gloom,
Leaving disordered papers in a dusty
  room;
Living first in the silence after the viati-
  cum.

Pray for Guiterriez, avid of speed and
  power,
For Boudin, blown to pieces,
For this one who made a great fortune,
And that one who went his own way.
Pray for Floret, by the boarhound slain
  between the yew trees,
Pray for us now and at the hour of our
  birth.

THE LOVE SONG OF J. ALFRED PRUFROCK
by T. S. ELIOT

S'io credesse che mia risposta fosse
A persona che mai tornasse al mondo,
Questa fiamma staria senza piu scosse.
Ma perciocche giammai di questo fondo
Non torno vivo alcun, s'i'odo il vero,
*Senza tema d'infamia ti rispondo.**

Let us go then, you and I,
When the evening is spread out against the sky
Like a patient etherized upon a table;
Let us go, through certain half-deserted streets,
The muttering retreats
Of restless nights in one-night cheap hotels
And sawdust restaurants with oyster-shells:
Streets that follow like a tedious argument
Of insidious intent
To lead you to an overwhelming question. . .
Oh, do not ask, "What is it?"
Let us go and make our visit.

In the room the women come and go
Talking of Michelangelo.

The yellow fog that rubs its back upon the window-panes,
The yellow smoke that rubs its muzzle on the window-panes
Licked its tongue into the corners of the evening,
Lingered upon the pools that stand in drains,

* If I thought my answer were to one who ever could return to the world, this flame should shake no more. But since none ever did return alive from this depth, if what I hear be true, without fear of infamy I answer thee.

Let fall upon its back the soot that falls from chimneys,
Slipped by the terrace, made a sudden leap,
And seeing that it was a soft October night,
Curled once about the house, and fell asleep.

And indeed there will be time
For the yellow smoke that slides along the street,
Rubbing its back upon the window-panes;
There will be time, there will be time
To prepare a face to meet the faces that you meet;
There will be time to murder and create,
And time for all the works and days of hands
That lift and drop a question on your plate;
Time for you and time for me,
And time yet for a hundred indecisions,
And for a hundred visions and revisions,
Before the taking of a toast and tea.

In the room the women come and go
Talking of Michelangelo.

And indeed there will be time
To wonder, "Do I dare?" and, "Do I dare?"
Time to turn back and descend the stair,
With a bald spot in the middle of my hair—
(They will say: "How his hair is growing thin!")
My morning coat, my collar mounting firmly to the chin,
My necktie rich and modest, but asserted by a simple pin—
(They will say: "But how his arms and legs are thin!")
Do I dare
Disturb the universe?
In a minute there is time
For decisions and revisions which a minute will reverse.

For I have known them all already, known them all:—
Have known the evenings, mornings, afternoons,
I have measured out my life with coffee spoons;
I know the voices dying with a dying fall
Beneath the music from a farther room.
　　So how should I presume?

And I have known the eyes already, known them all—
The eyes that fix you in a formulated phrase,
And when I am formulated, sprawling on a pin,

When I am pinned and wriggling on the wall,
Then how should I begin
To spit out all the butt-ends of my days and ways?
    And how should I presume?

And I have known the arms already, known them all—
Arms that are braceleted and white and bare
(But in the lamplight, downed with light brown hair!)
Is it perfume from a dress
That makes me so digress?
Arms that lie along a table, or wrap about a shawl.
    And should I then presume?
    And how should I begin?

.   .   .   .

Shall I say, I have gone at dusk through narrow streets
And watched the smoke that rises from the pipes
Of lonely men in shirt-sleeves, leaning out of windows? . . .

I should have been a pair of ragged claws
Scuttling across the floors of silent seas.

.   .   .   .

And the afternoon, the evening, sleeps so peacefully!
Smoothed by long fingers,
Asleep . . . tired . . . or it malingers,
Stretched on the floor, here beside you and me.
Should I, after tea and cakes and ices,
Have the strength to force the moment to its crisis?
But though I have wept and fasted, wept and prayed,
Though I have seen my head (grown slightly bald) brought in upon a platter
I am no prophet—and here's no great matter;
I have seen the moment of my greatness flicker,
And I have seen the eternal Footman hold my coat, and snicker,
And in short, I was afraid.

And would it have been worth it, after all,
After the cups, the marmalade, the tea,
Among the porcelain, among some talk of you and me,
Would it have been worth while,
To have bitten off the matter with a smile,
To have squeezed the universe into a ball
To roll it toward some overwhelming question,
To say: "I am Lazarus, come from the dead,

Come back to tell you all, I shall tell you all"—
If one, settling a pillow by her head,
    Should say: "That is not what I meant at all.
    That is not it, at all."

And would it have been worth it, after all,
Would it have been worth while,
After the sunsets and the dooryards and the sprinkled streets,
After the novels, after the teacups, after the skirts that trail along the floor—
And this, and so much more?—
It is impossible to say just what I mean!
But as if a magic lantern threw the nerves in patterns on a screen:
Would it have been worth while
If one, settling a pillow or throwing off a shawl,
And turning toward the window, should say:
    "That is not it at all,
    That is not what I meant, at all."

   .   .   .   .

No! I am not Prince Hamlet, nor was meant to be;
Am an attendant lord, one that will do
To swell a progress, start a scene or two,
Advise the prince; no doubt, an easy tool,
Deferential, glad to be of use,
Politic, cautious, and meticulous;
Full of high sentence, but a bit obtuse;
At times, indeed, almost ridiculous—
Almost, at times, the Fool.

I grow old . . . I grow old . . .
I shall wear the bottoms of my trousers rolled.

Shall I part my hair behind? Do I dare to eat a peach?
I shall wear white flannel trousers, and walk upon the beach.
I have heard the mermaids singing, each to each.

I do not think that they will sing to me.

I have seen them riding seaward on the waves
Combing the white hair of the waves blown back
When the wind blows the water white and black.

We have lingered in the chambers of the sea
By sea-girls wreathed with seaweed red and brown
Till human voices wake us, and we drown.

[678]

"*Promise you'll wait for me. I want something real to come back to.*"

PORTRAIT OF A LADY

by T. S. ELIOT

Thou hast committed—
Fornication: but that was in another country,
And besides, the wench is dead.
              —*The Jew of Malta.*

I

Among the smoke and fog of a December
    afternoon
You have the scene arrange itself—as it
    will seem to do—
With "I have saved this afternoon for
    you";
And four wax candles in the darkened
    room,
Four rings of light upon the ceiling over-
    head,
An atmosphere of Juliet's tomb
Prepared for all the things to be said, or
    left unsaid.
We have been, let us say, to hear the latest
    Pole
Transmit the Preludes, through his hair
    and finger-tips.
"So intimate, this Chopin, that I think his
    soul
Should be resurrected only among friends
Some two or three, who will not touch
    the bloom
That is rubbed and questioned in the con-
    cert room."
—And so the conversation slips
Among velleities and carefully caught re-
    grets
Through attenuated tones of violins
Mingled with remote cornets
And begins.
"You do not know how much they mean
    to me, my friends,

And how, how rare and strange it is, to
    find
In a life composed so much, so much of
    odds and ends,
(For indeed I do not love it . . . you
    knew? you are not blind!
How keen you are!)
To find a friend who has these qualities,
Who has, and gives
Those qualities upon which friendship
    lives.
How much it means that I say this to
    you—
Without these friendships—life, what
    cauchemar!"

Among the windings of the violins
And the ariettes
Of cracked cornets
Inside my brain a dull tom-tom begins
Absurdly hammering a prelude of its own,
Capricious monotone
That is at least one definite "false note."
—Let us take the air, in a tobacco trance,
Admire the monuments,
Discuss the late events,
Correct our watches by the public clocks.
Then sit for half an hour and drink our
    bocks.

II

Now that lilacs are in bloom
She has a bowl of lilacs in her room
And twists one in her fingers while she
    talks.
"Ah, my friend, you do not know, you
    do not know
What life is, you who hold it in your
    hands";

(Slowly twisting the lilac stalks)
"You let it flow from you, you let it flow,
And youth is cruel, and has no remorse
And smiles at situations which it cannot
see."
I smile, of course,
And go on drinking tea.
"Yet with these April sunsets, that some-
how recall
My buried life, and Paris in the Spring,
I feel immeasurably at peace, and find the
world
To be wonderful and youthful, after all."

The voice returns like the insistent out-of-
tune
Of a broken violin on an August after-
noon:
"I am always sure that you understand
My feelings, always sure that you feel,
Sure that across the gulf you reach your
hand.

You are invulnerable, you have no
Achilles' heel.
You will go on, and when you have pre-
vailed
You can say: at this point many a one has
failed.
But what have I, but what have I, my
friend,
To give you, what can you receive from
me?
Only the friendship and the sympathy
Of one about to reach her journey's end.

I shall sit here, serving tea to friends. . . ."

I take my hat: how can I make a cow-
ardly amends
For what she has said to me?
You will see me any morning in the park
Reading the comics and the sporting page.
Particularly I remark

An English countess goes upon the stage.
A Greek was murdered at a Polish dance,
Another bank defaulter has confessed.
I keep my countenance,
I remain self-possessed
Except when a street piano, mechanical
and tired
Reiterates some worn-out common song
With the smell of hyacinths across the
garden
Recalling things that other people have
desired.
Are these ideas right or wrong?

III

The October night comes down; returning as before
Except for a slight sensation of being ill
at ease
I mount the stairs and turn the handle
of the door
And feel as if I had mounted on my
hands and knees.

"And so you are going abroad; and when
do you return?
But that's a useless question.
You hardly know when you are coming
back,
You will find so much to learn."
My smile falls heavily among the bric-à-
brac.

"Perhaps you can write to me."
My self-possession flares up for a second;
This is as I had reckoned.
"I have been wondering frequently of late
(But our beginnings never know our
ends!)
Why we have not developed into friends."
I feel like one who smiles, and turning
shall remark
Suddenly, his expression in a glass.

My self-possession gutters; we are really in the dark.

"For everybody said so, all our friends,
They all were sure our feelings would re-
late
So closely! I myself can hardly under-
stand.
We must leave it now to fate.
You will write, at any rate.
Perhaps it is not too late.
I shall sit here, serving tea to friends."

And I must borrow every changing shape
To find expression . . . dance, dance
Like a dancing bear,
Cry like a parrot, chatter like an ape.
Let us take the air, in a tobacco trance—

Well! and what if she should die some afternoon,
Afternoon gray and smoky, evening yel-
low and rose;
Should die and leave me sitting pen in hand
With the smoke coming down above the housetops;
Doubtful, for a while
Not knowing what to feel or if I under-
stand
Or whether wise or foolish, tardy or too soon . . .
Would she not have the advantage, after all?
This music is successful with a "dying fall"
Now that we talk of dying—
And should I have the right to smile?

THE HOLLOW MEN

by T. S. ELIOT

A penny for the Old Guy.
MISTAH KURTZ—HE DEAD.

I

We are the hollow men
We are the stuffed men
Leaning together
Headpiece filled with straw. Alas!
Our dried voices, when
We whisper together
Are quiet and meaningless
As wind in dry grass
Or rats' feet over broken glass
In our dry cellar

Shape without form, shade without colour,
Paralysed force, gesture without motion;

Those who have crossed
With direct eyes, to death's other King-
dom
Remember us—if at all—not as lost
Violent souls, but only
As the hollow men
The stuffed men.

II

Eyes I dare not meet in dreams
In death's dream kingdom
These do not appear:
There, the eyes are
Sunlight on a broken column
There, is a tree swinging
And voices are
In the wind's singing

More distant and more solemn'
Than a fading star.

Let me be no nearer
In death's dream kingdom
Let me also wear
Such deliberate disguises
Rat's skin, crowskin, crossed staves
In a field
Behaving as the wind behaves
No nearer—

Not that final meeting
In the twilight kingdom

III

This is the dead land
This is cactus land
Here the stone images
Are raised, here they receive
The supplication of a dead man's hand
Under the twinkle of a fading star.

Is it like this
In death's other kingdom
Waking alone
At the hour when we are
Trembling with tenderness
Lips that would kiss
Form prayers to broken stone.

IV

The eyes are not here
There are no eyes here
In this valley of dying stars
In this hollow valley
This broken jaw of our lost kingdoms

In this last of meeting places
We grope together
And avoid speech
Gathered on this beach of the tumid river

Sightless, unless
The eyes reappear
As the perpetual star
Multifoliate rose
Of death's twilight kingdom
The hope only
Of empty men.

V

*Here we go round the prickly pear
Prickly pear prickly pear
Here we go round the prickly pear
At five o'clock in the morning.*

Between the idea
And the reality
Between the motion
And the act
Falls the Shadow
   For Thine is the Kingdom

Between the conception
And the creation
Between the emotion
And the response
Falls the Shadow
   Life is very long

Between the desire
And the spasm
Between the potency
And the existence
Between the essence
And the descent
Falls the Shadow
   For Thine is the Kingdom

For Thine is
Life is
For Thine is the

*This is the way the world ends
This is the way the world ends
This is the way the world ends
Not with a bang but a whimper.*

JOURNEY OF THE MAGI

by T. S. Eliot

'A cold coming we had of it,
Just the worst time of the year
For a journey, and such a long journey:
The ways deep and the weather sharp,
The very dead of winter.'
And the camels galled, sore-footed, refractory,
Lying down in the melting snow.
There were times we regretted
The summer palaces on slopes, the terraces,
And the silken girls bringing sherbet.
Then the camel men cursing and grumbling
And running away, and wanting their liquor and women,
And the night-fires going out, and the lack of shelters,
And the cities hostile and the towns unfriendly
And the villages dirty and charging high prices:
A hard time we had of it.
At the end we preferred to travel all night,
Sleeping in snatches,
With the voices singing in our ears, saying
That this was all folly.

Then at dawn we came down to a temperate valley,
Wet, below the snow line, smelling of vegetation;
With a running stream and a water-mill beating the darkness,
And three trees on the low sky,
And an old white horse galloped away in the meadow.
Then we came to a tavern with vine-leaves over the lintel,
Six hands at an open door dicing for pieces of silver,
And feet kicking the empty wine-skins.
But there was no information, and so we continued
And arrived at evening, not a moment too soon
Finding the place; it was (you may say) satisfactory.

All this was a long time ago, I remember,
And I would do it again, but set down
This set down
This: were we led all that way for
Birth or Death? There was a Birth, certainly,
We had evidence and no doubt. I had seen birth and death,

But had thought they were different; this Birth was
Hard and bitter agony for us, like Death, our death.
We returned to our places, these Kingdoms,
But no longer at ease here, in the old dispensation,
With an alien people clutching their gods.
I should be glad of another death.

TRIUMPHAL MARCH

by T. S. Eliot

Stone, bronze, stone, steel, stone, oakleaves horses' heels
Over the paving.
And the flags. And the trumpets. And so many eagles.
How many? Count them. And such a press of people.
We hardly knew ourselves that day, or knew the City.
This is the way to the temple, and we so many crowding the way.
So many waiting, how many waiting? what did it matter, on such a day?
Are they coming? No, not yet. You can see some eagles. And hear the trumpets.
Here they come. Is he coming?
The natural wakeful life of our Ego is a perceiving.
We can wait with our stools and our sausages.
What comes first? Can you see? Tell us. It is

       5,800,000 rifles and carbines,
         102,000 machine guns,
          28,000 trench mortars,
         53,000 field and heavy guns,
I cannot tell how many projectiles, mines and fuses,
         13,000 aeroplanes,
         24,000 aeroplane engines,
         50,000 ammunition waggons,
  now   55,000 army waggons,
         11,000 field kitchens,
          1,150 field bakeries.

What a time that took. Will it be he now? No,
Those are the golf club Captains, these the Scouts,
And now the *société gymnastique de Poissy*
And now come the Mayor and the Liverymen. Look
There he is now, look:
There is no interrogation in his eyes
Or in the hands, quiet over the horse's neck,
And the eyes watchful, waiting, perceiving, indifferent.

O hidden under the dove's wing, hidden in the turtle's breast,
Under the palmtree at noon, under the running water
At the still point of the turning world. O hidden.

Now they go up to the temple. Then the sacrifice.
Now come the virgins bearing urns, urns containing
Dust
Dust
Dust of dust, and now
Stone, bronze, stone, steel, stone, oakleaves, horses' heels
Over the paving.

That is all we could see. But how many eagles! and how many trumpets!
(And Easter Day, we didn't get to the country,
So we took young Cyril to church. And they rang a bell
And he said right out loud, *crumpets*.)
                    Don't throw away that sausage,
It'll come in handy. He's artful. Please, will you
Give us a light?
Light
Light
Et les soldats faisaient la haie? ILS LA FAISAIENT.

MACAVITY: THE MYSTERY CAT

by T. S. Eliot

Macavity's a Mystery Cat: he's called the Hidden Paw—
For he's the master criminal who can defy the Law.
He's the bafflement of Scotland Yard, the Flying Squad's despair:
For when they reach the scene of crime—*Macavity's not there!*

Macavity, Macavity, there's no one like Macavity,
He's broken every human law, he breaks the law of gravity.
His powers of levitation would make a fakir stare,
And when you reach the scene of crime—*Macavity's not there!*
You may seek him in the basement, you may look up in the air—
But I tell you once and once again, *Macavity's not there!*

Macavity's a ginger cat, he's very tall and thin;
You would know him if you saw him, for his eyes are sunken in.

Macavity: The Mystery Cat

His brow is deeply lined with thought, his head is highly domed;
His coat is dusty from neglect, his whiskers are uncombed.
He sways his head from side to side, with movements like a snake;
And when you think he's half asleep, he's always wide awake.

Macavity, Macavity, there's no one like Macavity,
For he's a fiend in feline shape, a monster of depravity.
You may meet him in a by-street, you may see him in the square—
But when a crime's discovered, then *Macavity's not there!*

He's outwardly respectable. (They say he cheats at cards.)
And his footprints are not found in any file of Scotland Yard's.
And when the larder's looted, or the jewel-case is rifled,
Or when the milk is missing, or another Peke's been stifled,
Or the greenhouse glass is broken, and the trellis past repair—
Ay, there's the wonder of the thing! *Macavity's not there!*

And when the Foreign Office find a Treaty's gone astray,
Or the Admiralty lose some plans and drawings by the way,
There may be a scrap of paper in the hall or on the stair—
But it's useless to investigate—*Macavity's not there!*
And when the loss has been disclosed, the Secret Service say:
"It *must* have been Macavity!"—but he's a mile away.
You'll be sure to find him resting, or a-licking of his thumbs,
Or engaged in doing complicated long division sums.

Macavity, Macavity, there's no one like Macavity,
There never was a Cat of such deceitfulness and suavity.
He always has an alibi, and one or two to spare:
At whatever time the deed took place—MACAVITY WASN'T THERE!
And they say that all the Cats whose wicked deeds are widely known
(I might mention Mungojerrie, I might mention Griddlebone)
Are nothing more than agents for the Cat who all the time
Just controls their operations: the Napoleon of Crime!

GUS: THE THEATRE CAT
by T. S. Eliot

Gus is the Cat at the Theatre Door.
His name, as I ought to have told you before,
Is really Asparagus. That's such a fuss
To pronounce, that we usually call him just Gus.
His coat's very shabby, he's thin as a rake,
And he suffers from palsy that makes his paw shake.
Yet he was, in his youth, quite the smartest of Cats—
But no longer a terror to mice and to rats.
For he isn't the Cat that he was in his prime;
Though his name was quite famous, he says, in its time.
And whenever he joins his friends at their club
(Which takes place at the back of the neighboring pub)
He loves to regale them, if someone else pays,
With anecdotes drawn from his palmiest days.
For he once was a Star of the highest degree—
He has acted with Irving, he's acted with Tree.
And he likes to relate his success on the Halls,
Where the Gallery once gave him seven cat-calls.
But his grandest creation, as he loves to tell,
Was Firefrorefiddle, the Fiend of the Fell.

"I have played," so he says, "every possible part,
And I used to know seventy speeches by heart.
I'd extemporize back-chat, I knew how to gag,
And I knew how to let the cat out of the bag.
I knew how to act with my back and my tail;
With an hour of rehearsal, I never could fail.
I'd a voice that would soften the hardest of hearts,
Whether I took the lead, or in character parts.
I have sat by the bedside of poor Little Nell;
When the Curfew was rung, then I swung on the bell.
In the Pantomime season I never fell flat,
And I once understudied Dick Whittington's Cat.
But my grandest creation, as history will tell,
Was Firefrorefiddle, the Fiend of the Fell."

Then, if someone will give him a toothful of gin,
He will tell how he once played a part in *East Lynne.*
At a Shakespeare performance he once walked on pat,
When some actor suggested the need for a cat.
He once played a Tiger—could do it again—
Which an Indian Colonel pursued down a drain.
And he thinks that he still can, much better than most,
Produce blood-curdling noises to bring on the Ghost.
And he once crossed the stage on a telegraph wire,
To rescue a child when a house was on fire.
And he says: "Now, these kittens, they do not get trained
As we did in the days when Victoria reigned.
They never get drilled in a regular troupe,
And they think they are smart, just to jump through a hoop."
And he'll say, as he scratches himself with his claws,
"Well, the Theatre's certainly not what it was.
These modern productions are all very well,
But there's nothing to equal, from what I hear tell,
 That moment of mystery
 When I made history
As Firefrorefiddle, the Fiend of the Fell."

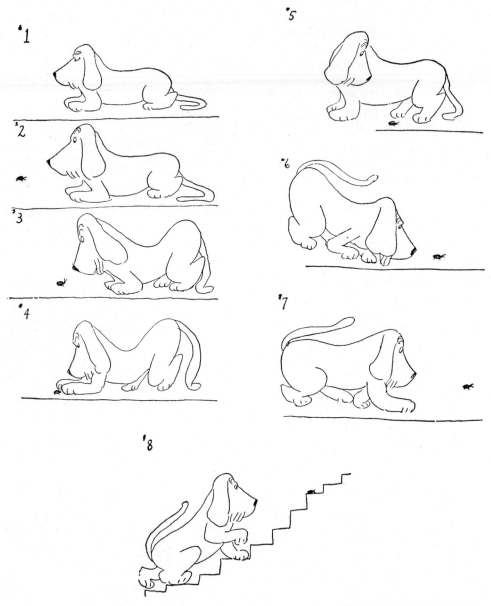

THE BLOODHOUND

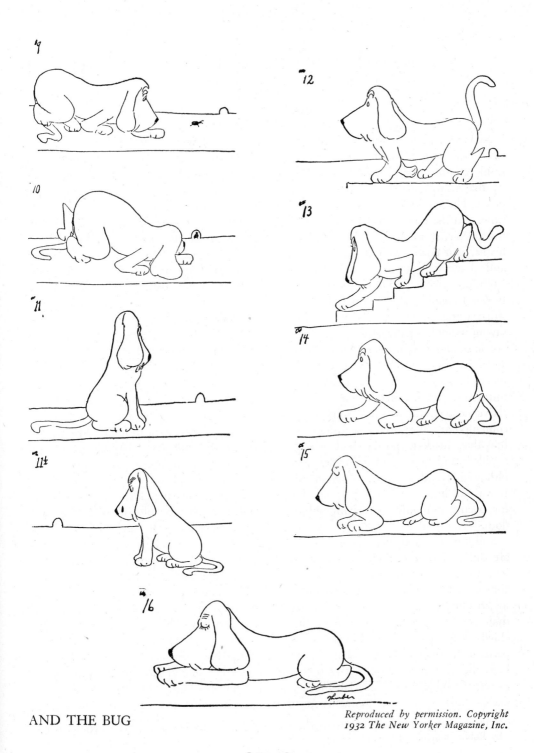

AND THE BUG

from Foreword to THE SELECTED POETRY OF ROBINSON JEFFERS

by ROBINSON JEFFERS

LONG AGO, . . . it became evident to me that poetry—if it was to survive at all—must reclaim some of the power and reality that it was so hastily surrendering to prose. The modern French poetry of that time, and the most "modern" of the English poetry, seemed to me thoroughly defeatist, as if poetry were in terror of prose, and desperately trying to save its soul from the victor by giving up its body. It was becoming slight and fantastic, abstract, unreal, eccentric; and was not even saving its soul, for these are generally antipoetic qualities. It must reclaim substance and sense, and physical and psychological reality. This feeling has been basic in my mind since then. It led me to write narrative poetry, and to draw subjects from contemporary life; to present aspects of life that modern poetry had generally avoided; and to attempt the expression of philosophic and scientific ideas in verse. It was not in my mind to open new fields for poetry, but only to reclaim old freedom.

Still it was obvious that poetry and prose are different things; their provinces overlap, but must not be confused. Prose, of course, is free of all fields; it seemed to me, reading poetry and trying to write it, that poetry is bound to concern itself chiefly with permanent things and the permanent aspects of life. That was perhaps the great distinction between them, as regards subject and material. Prose can discuss matters of the moment; poetry must deal with things that a reader two thousand years away could understand and be moved by. This excludes much of the circumstance of modern life, especially in the cities. Fashions, forms of machinery, the more complex social, financial, political adjustments, and so forth, are all ephemeral, exceptional; they exist but will never exist again. Poetry must concern itself with (relatively) permanent things. These have poetic value; the ephemeral has only news value.

Another formative principle came to me from a phrase of Nietzsche's: "The poets? The poets lie too much." I was nineteen when the phrase stuck in my mind; a dozen years passed before it worked effectively, and I decided not to tell lies in verse. Not to feign any emotion that I did not feel; not to pretend to believe in optimism or pessimism, or unreversible progress; not to say anything because it was popular, or generally accepted, or fashionable in intellectual circles, unless I myself believed it; and not to believe easily. These negatives limit the field; I am not recommending them but for my own occasions.

Here are the principles that conditioned the verse in this book before it was written; but it would not have been written at all except for certain accidents that changed and directed my life. (Some kind of verse I should have written, of course, but not this kind.) The first of these accidents was my meeting with the woman to whom this book is dedicated, and her influence, constant since that time. My nature is cold and undiscriminating; she excited and focused it, gave it eyes and nerves and sympathies. She never saw any of my poems until they were finished and typed, yet by her presence and conversation she has co-authored every one of them. Sometimes I think there must be some value in them, if only for that reason. She is more like a woman in a Scotch ballad, passionate, untamed and rather heroic—or like a falcon—than like any ordinary person.

A second piece of pure accident brought us to the Monterey coast mountains, where for the first time in my life I could see people living—amid magnificent unspoiled scenery—essentially as they did in the Idyls or the Sagas, or in Homer's Ithaca. Here was life purged of its ephemeral accretions. Men were riding after cattle, or plowing the headland, hovered by white sea-gulls, as they have done for thousands of years, and will for thousands of years to come. Here was contemporary life that was also permanent life; and not shut from the modern world but conscious of it and related to it; capable of expressing its spirit, but unencumbered by the mass of poetically irrelevant details and complexities that make a civilization.

By this time I was nearing thirty, and still a whole series of accidents was required to stir my lazy energies to the point of writing verse that seemed to be —whether good or bad—at least my own voice.

HURT HAWKS

by ROBINSON JEFFERS

I

The broken pillar of the wing jags from the clotted shoulder,
The wing trails like a banner in defeat,
No more to use the sky forever but live with famine
And pain a few days: cat nor coyote
Will shorten the week of waiting for death, there is game without talons.
He stands under the oak-bush and waits
The lame feet of salvation; at night he remembers freedom
And flies in a dream, the dawns ruin it.
He is strong and pain is worse to the strong, incapacity is worse.
The curs of the day come and torment him
At distance, no one but death the redeemer will humble that head,
The intrepid readiness, the terrible eyes.
The wild God of the world is sometimes merciful to those
That ask mercy, not often to the arrogant.
You do not know him, you communal people, or you have forgotten him;
Intemperate and savage, the hawk remembers him;
Beautiful and wild, the hawks, and men that are dying, remember him.

II

I'd sooner, except the penalties, kill a man than a hawk; but the great redtail
Had nothing left but unable misery
From the bone too shattered for mending, the wing that trailed under his talons
    when he moved.
We had fed him six weeks, I gave him freedom,
He wandered over the foreland hill and returned in the evening, asking for death,
Not like a beggar, still eyed with the old
Implacable arrogance. I gave him the lead gift in the twilight. What fell was relaxed,
Owl-downy, soft feminine feathers; but what
Soared: the fierce rush: the night-herons by the flooded river cried fear at its rising
Before it was quite unsheathed from reality.

TO THE STONE-CUTTERS

by ROBINSON JEFFERS

Stone-cutters fighting time with marble, you foredefeated
Challengers of oblivion,
Eat cynical earnings, knowing rock splits, records fall down,
The square-limbed Roman letters
Scale in the thaws, wear in the rain. The poet as well
Builds his monument mockingly;
For man will be blotted out, the blithe earth die, the brave sun
Die blind and blacken to the heart:
Yet stones have stood for a thousand years, and pained thoughts found
The honey of peace in old poems.

SHINE, PERISHING REPUBLIC

by ROBINSON JEFFERS

While this America settles in the mould of its vulgarity, heavily thickening to empire,
And protest, only a bubble in the molten mass, pops and sighs out, and the mass
    hardens,

I sadly smiling remember that the flower fades to make fruit, the fruit rots to make
    earth.
Out of the mother; and through the spring exultances, ripeness and decadence; and
    home to the mother.

You making haste haste on decay: not blameworthy; life is good, be it stubbornly
   long or suddenly
A mortal splendor: meteors are not needed less than mountains: shine, perishing
   republic.

But for my children, I would have them keep their distance from the thickening
   center; corruption
Never has been compulsory, when the cities lie at the monster's feet there are left
   the mountains.

And boys, be in nothing so moderate as in love of man, a clever servant, insufferable
   master.
There is the trap that catches noblest spirits, that caught—they say—God, when he
   walked on earth.

THE PURSE-SEINE

by ROBINSON JEFFERS

Our sardine fishermen work at night in the dark of the moon; daylight or moonlight
They could not tell where to spread the net, unable to see the phosphorescence of
   the shoals of fish.
They work northward from Monterey, coasting Santa Cruz; off New Year's Point
   or off Pigeon Point
The look-out man will see some lakes of milk-color light on the sea's night-purple;
   he points, and the helmsman
Turns the dark prow, the motorboat circles the gleaming shoal and drifts out her
   seine-net. They close the circle
And purse the bottom of the net, then with great labor haul it in.

I cannot tell you
How beautiful the scene is, and a little terrible, then, when the crowded fish
Know they are caught, and wildly beat from one wall to the other of their closing
   destiny the phosphorescent
Water to a pool of flame, each beautiful slender body sheeted with flame, like a live
   rocket
A comet's tail wake of clear yellow flame; while outside the narrowing
Floats and cordage of the net great sea-lions come up to watch, sighing in the dark;
   the vast walls of night
Stand erect to the stars.

Lately I was looking from a night mountain-top

On a wide city, the colored splendor, galaxies of light: how could I help but recall the seine-net

Gathering the luminous fish? I cannot tell you how beautiful the city appeared, and a little terrible.

I thought, We have geared the machines and locked all together into interdependence; we have built the great cities; now

There is no escape. We have gathered vast populations incapable of free survival, insulated

From the strong earth, each person in himself helpless, on all dependent. The circle is closed, and the net

Is being hauled in. They hardly feel the cords drawing, yet they shine already. The inevitable mass-disasters

Will not come in our time nor in our children's, but we and our children

Must watch the net draw narrower, government take all powers—or revolution, and the new government

Take more than all, add to kept bodies kept souls—or anarchy, the mass-disasters.

These things are Progress;

Do you marvel our verse is troubled or frowning, while it keeps its reason? Or it lets go, lets the mood flow

In the manner of the recent young men into mere hysteria, splintered gleams, crackled laughter. But they are quite wrong.

There is no reason for amazement: surely one always knew that cultures decay, and life's end is death.

THE ANSWER

by ROBINSON JEFFERS

Then what is the answer?—Not to be deluded by dreams.

To know that great civilizations have broken down into violence, and their tyrants come, many times before.

When open violence appears, to avoid it with honor or choose the least ugly faction; these evils are essential.

To keep one's own integrity, be merciful and uncorrupted and not wish for evil; and not be duped

By dreams of universal justice or happiness. These dreams will not be fulfilled.

To know this, and know that however ugly the parts appear the whole remains beautiful. A severed hand

Is an ugly thing, and man dissevered from the earth and stars and his history . . . for contemplation or in fact . . .

Often appears atrociously ugly. Integrity is wholeness, the greatest beauty is
Organic wholeness, the wholeness of life and things, the divine beauty of the universe. Love that, not man
Apart from that, or else you will share man's pitiful confusions, or drown in despair
when his days darken.

THE INQUISITORS

by ROBINSON JEFFERS

Coming around a corner of the dark trail . . . what was wrong with the valley?
Azevedo checked his horse and sat staring: it was all changed. It was occupied. There
were three hills
Where none had been: and firelight flickered red on their knees between them: if
they were hills:
They were more like Red Indians around a camp-fire, grave and dark, mountain-
high, hams on heels
Squatting around a little fire of hundred-foot logs. Azevedo remembers he felt an
ice-brook
Glide on his spine; he slipped down from the saddle and hid
In the brush by the trail, above the black redwood forest. This was the Little Sur
South Fork,
Its forest valley; the man had come in at nightfall over Bowcher's Gap, and a high
moon hunted
Through running clouds. He heard the rumble of a voice, heavy not loud, saying,
"I gathered some,
You can inspect them." One of the hills moved a huge hand
And poured its contents on a table-topped rock that stood in the firelight; men and
women fell out;
Some crawled and some lay quiet; the hills leaned to eye them. One said: "It seems
hardly possible
Such fragile creatures could be so noxious." Another answered,
"True, but we've seen. But it is only recently they have the power." The third
answered, "That bomb?"
"Oh," he said, "—and the rest." He reached across and picked up one of the mites
from the rock, and held it
Close to his eyes, and very carefully with finger and thumbnail peeled it: by chance
a young female

With long black hair: it was too helpless even to scream. He held it by one white
    leg and stared at it:
"I can see nothing strange: only so fragile." The third hill answered, "We suppose
    it is something
Inside the head." Then the other split the skull with his thumbnail, squinting his
    eyes and peering, and said,
"A drop of marrow. How could that spoil the earth?" "Nevertheless," he answered,
"They have that bomb. The blasts and the fires are nothing: freckles on the earth:
    the emanations
Might set the whole planet into a tricky fever
And destroy much." "Themselves," he answered. "Let them. Why not?" "No," he
    answered, "life."

Azevedo

Still watched in horror, and all three of the hills
Picked little animals from the rock, peeled them and cracked them, or toasted them
On the red coals, or split their bodies from the crotch upward
To stare inside. They said, "It remains a mystery. However," they said,
"It is not likely they can destroy all life: the planet is capacious. Life would surely
    grow up again
From grubs in the soil, or the newt and toad level, and be beautiful again. And
    again perhaps break its legs
On its own cleverness: who can forecast the future?" The speaker yawned, and with
    his flat hand
Brushed the rock clean; the three slowly stood up,
Taller than Pico Blanco into the sky, their Indian-beaked heads in the moon-cloud,
And trampled their watchfire out and went away southward, stepping across the
    Ventana mountains.

YOU, ANDREW MARVELL

by ARCHIBALD MacLEISH

And here face down beneath the sun
And here upon earth's noonward height
To feel the always coming on
The always rising of the night

To feel creep up the curving east
The earthy chill of dusk and slow
Upon those under lands the vast
And ever climbing shadow grow

And strange at Ecbatan the trees
Take leaf by leaf the evening strange
The flooding dark about their knees
The mountains over Persia change

And now at Kermanshah the gate
Dark empty and the withered grass
And through the twilight now the late
Few travelers in the westward pass

And Baghdad darken and the bridge
Across the silent river gone

And through Arabia the edge
Of evening widen and steal on

And deepen on Palmyra's street
The wheel rut in the ruined stone
And Lebanon fade out and Crete
High through the clouds and overblown

And over Sicily the air
Still flashing with the landward gulls
And loom and slowly disappear
The sails above the shadowy hulls

And Spain go under and the shore
Of Africa the gilded sand
And evening vanish and no more
The low pale light across that land

Nor now the long light on the sea

And here face downward in the sun
To feel how swift how secretly
The shadow of the night comes on . . .

from THE HAMLET OF A. MACLEISH

by ARCHIBALD MacLEISH

Night after night I lie like this listening.
Night after night I cannot sleep. I wake
Knowing something, thinking something has happened.
I have this feeling a great deal. I have
Sadness often. At night I have this feeling.
Waking I feel this pain as though I knew
Something not to be thought of, something unbearable.
I feel this pain at night as though some
Terrible thing had happened. At night the sky
Opens, the near things vanish, the bright walls
Fall, and the stars were always there, and the dark

The selections from Archibald MacLeish's *Poems 1924-1933* are used by permission of the publishers, Houghton Mifflin Company.

There and the cold and the stillness. I wake and stand
A long time by the window. I always think
The trees know the way they are silent. I always
Think some one has spoken, some one has told me.
Reading the books I always think so, reading
Words overheard in the books, reading the words
Like words in a strange language. I always hear
Music like that. I almost remember with music . . .
This is not what you think. It is not that. I swim
Every day at the beach under the fig tree.
I swim very well and far out. The smell
Of pine comes over the water. The wind blurs
Seaward. And afternoons I walk to the phare.
Much of the time I do not think anything;
Much of the time I do not even notice.
And then, speaking, closing a door, I see
Strangely as though I almost saw now, some
Shape of things I have always seen, the sun
White on a house and the windows open and swallows
In and out of the wallpaper, the moon's face
Faint by day in a mirror; I see some
Changed thing that is telling, something that almost
Tells—and this pain then, then this pain. And no
Words, only these shapes of things that seem
Ways of knowing what it is I am knowing.
I write these things in books, on pieces of paper.
I have written 'The wind rises . . .' I have written 'Bells
Plunged in the wind . . .' I have written 'Like
Doors . . .' 'Like evening . . .'
It is always the same: I cannot read what the words say.
It is always the same: there are signs and I cannot read them.
There are empty streets and the blinds drawn and the sky
Sliding in windows. There are lights before
Dawn in the yellow transoms over the doors.
There are steps that pass and pass all night that are always
One, always the same step passing . . .
I have traveled a great deal. I have seen at Homs
The cranes over the river and Isfahan
The fallen tiles in the empty garden, and Shiraz
Far off, the cypresses under the hill.
It is always the same. I have seen on the Kazvin road
On the moon grey desert the leafless wind,
The wind raging in moon-dusk. Or the light that comes
Seaward with slow oars from the mouth of the Euphrates.

I have heard the nightingales in the thickets of Gilan,
And at dawn, at Teheran, I have heard from the ancient
Westward greying face of the wandering planet
The voices calling the small new name of god,
The voices answered with cockcrow, answered at dusk
With the cry of jackals far away in the gardens.
I have heard the name of the moon beyond those mountains.
It is always the same. It is always as though some
Smell of leaves had made me not quite remember;
As though I had turned to look and there were no one.
It has always been secret like that with me.
Always something has not been said. Always
The stones were there, the trees were there, the motionless
Hills have appeared in the dusk to me, the moon
Has stood a long time white and still in the window.
Always the earth has been turned away from me hiding
The veiled eyes and the wind in the leaves has not spoken . . .

As now the night is still. As the night now
Stands at the farthest off of touch and like
A raised hand held upon the empty air
Means and is silent.
                    Look! It waves me still . . .
    I say Go on! Go on!

                              As the whole night now
Made visible behind this darkness seems
To beckon to me . . .

AMERICAN LETTER

for Gerald Murphy

by ARCHIBALD MACLEISH

The wind is east but the hot weather continues,
Blue and no clouds, the sound of the leaves thin,
Dry like the rustling of paper, scored across
With the slate-shrill screech of the locusts.
                              The tossing of
Pines is the low sound. In the wind's running
The wild carrots smell of the burning sun.
Why should I think of the dolphins at Capo di Mele?

Why should I see in my mind the taut sail
And the hill over St.-Tropez and your hand on the tiller?
Why should my heart be troubled with palms still?
I am neither a sold boy nor a Chinese official
Sent to sicken in Pa for some Lo-Yang dish.
This is my own land, my sky, my mountain:
This—not the humming pines and the surf and the sound
At the Ferme Blanche, nor Port Cros in the dusk and the harbor
Floating the motionless ship and the sea-drowned star.
I am neither Po Chü-i nor another after
Far from home, in a strange land, daft
For the talk of his own sort and the taste of his lettuces.
This land is my native land. And yet
I am sick for home for the red roofs and the olives,
And the foreign words and the smell of the sea fall.
How can a wise man have two countries?
How can a man have the earth and the wind and want
A land far off, alien, smelling of palm-trees
And the yellow gorse at noon in the long calms?

It is a strange thing—to be an American.
Neither an old house it is with the air
Tasting of hung herbs and the sun returning
Year after year to the same door and the churn
Making the same sound in the cool of the kitchen
Mother to son's wife, and the place to sit
Marked in the dusk by the worn stone at the wellhead—
That—nor the eyes like each other's eyes and the skull
Shaped to the same fault and the hands' sameness.
Neither a place it is nor a blood name.
America is West and the wind blowing.
America is a great word and the snow,
A way, a white bird, the rain falling,
A shining thing in the mind and the gulls' call.
America is neither a land nor a people,
A word's shape it is, a wind's sweep—
America is alone: many together,
Many of one mouth, of one breath,
Dressed as one—and none brothers among them:
Only the taught speech and the aped tongue.
America is alone and the gulls calling.

It is a strange thing to be an American.
It is strange to live on the high world in the stare
Of the naked sun and the stars as our bones live.
Men in the old lands housed by their rivers.

American Letter

They built their towns in the vales in the earth's shelter.
We first inhabit the world. We dwell
On the half earth, on the open curve of a continent.
Sea is divided from sea by the day-fall. The dawn
Rides the low east with us many hours;
First are the capes, then are the shorelands, now
The blue Appalachians faint at the day rise;
The willows shudder with light on the long Ohio:
The Lakes scatter the low sun: the prairies
Slide out of dark: in the eddy of clean air
The smoke goes up from the high plains of Wyoming:
The steep Sierras arise: the struck foam
Flames at the wind's heel on the far Pacific.
Already the noon leans to the eastern cliff:
The elms darken the door and the dust-heavy lilacs.

It is strange to sleep in the bare stars and to die
On an open land where few bury before us:
(From the new earth the dead return no more.)
It is strange to be born of no race and no people.
In the old lands they are many together. They keep
The wise past and the words spoken in common.
They remember the dead with their hands, their mouths dumb.
They answer each other with two words in their meeting.
They live together in small things. They eat
The same dish, their drink is the same and their proverbs.
Their youth is like. They are like in their ways of love.
They are many men. There are always others beside them.
Here it is one man and another and wide
On the darkening hills the faint smoke of the houses.
Here it is one man and the wind in the boughs.

Therefore our hearts are sick for the south water.
The smell of the gorse comes back to our night thought.
We are sick at heart for the red roofs and the olives;
We are sick at heart for the voice and the footfall. . .

Therefore we will not go though the sea call us.

This, this is our land, this is our people,
This that is neither a land nor a race. We must reap
The wind here in the grass for our soul's harvest:
Here we must eat our salt or our bones starve.
Here we must live or live only as shadows.
This is our race, we that have none, that have had
Neither the old walls nor the voices around us,

This is our land, this is our ancient ground—
The raw earth, the mixed bloods and the strangers,
The different eyes, the wind, and the heart's change.
These we will not leave though the old call us.
This is our country-earth, our blood, our kind.
Here we will live our years till the earth blind us—
The wind blows from the east. The leaves fall.
Far off in the pines a jay rises.
The wind smells of haze and the wild ripe apples.

I think of the masts at Cette and the sweet rain.

MEN

(*On a phrase of Apollinaire*)

by ARCHIBALD MACLEISH

Our history is grave noble and tragic
We trusted the look of the sun on the green leaves
We built our towns of stone with enduring ornaments
We worked the hard flint for basins of water

We believed in the feel of the earth under us
We planted corn grapes apple-trees rhubarb
Nevertheless we knew others had died
Everything we have done has been faithful and dangerous

We believed in the promises made by the brows of women
We begot children at night in the warm wool
We comforted those who wept in fear on our shoulders
Those who comforted us had themselves vanished

We fought at the dikes in the bright sun for the pride of it
We beat drums and marched with music and laughter
We were drunk and lay with our fine dreams in the straw
We saw the stars through the hair of lewd women

Our history is grave noble and tragic
Many of us have died and are not remembered
Many cities are gone and their channels broken
We have lived a long time in this land and with honor

The selection from Archibald MacLeish's *Poems 1924-1933* is used by permission of the publishers, Houghton Mifflin Company.

SPEECH TO THOSE WHO SAY COMRADE

by ARCHIBALD MacLEISH

The brotherhood is not by the blood certainly:
But neither are men brothers by speech—by saying so:
Men are brothers by life lived and are hurt for it:

Hunger and hurt are the great begetters of brotherhood:
Humiliation has gotten much love:
Danger I say is the nobler father and mother:

Those are as brothers whose bodies have shared fear
Or shared harm or shared hurt or indignity.
Why are the old soldiers brothers and nearest?

For this: with their minds they go over the sea a little
And find themselves in their youth again as they were in
Soissons and Meaux and at Ypres and those cities:

A French loaf and the girls with their eyelids painted
Bring back to aging and lonely men
Their twentieth year and the metal odor of danger:

It is this in life which of all things is tenderest—
To remember together with the unknown men the days
Common also to them and perils ended:

It is this which makes of many a generation—
A wave of men who having the same years
Have in common the same dead and the changes.

The solitary and unshared experience
Dies of itself like the violations of love
Or lives on as the dead live eerily.

The unshared and single man must cover his
Loneliness as a girl her shame for the way of
Life is neither by one man nor by suffering.

Who are the born brothers in truth? The puddlers
Scorched by the same flame in the same foundries:
Those who have spit on the same boards with the blood in it:

Ridden the same rivers with green logs:
Fought the police in the parks of the same cities:
Grinned for the same blows: the same flogging:

Veterans out of the same ships—factories—
Expeditions for fame: the founders of continents:
Those that hid in Geneva a time back:

Those that have hidden and hunted and all such—
Fought together: labored together: they carry the
Common look like a card and they pass touching.

Brotherhood! No word said can make you brothers!
Brotherhood only the brave earn and by danger or
Harm or by bearing hurt and by no other

Brotherhood here in the strange world is the rich and
Rarest giving of life and the most valued:
Not to be had for a word or a week's wishing.

AMERICA WAS PROMISES

by ARCHIBALD MACLEISH

Who is the voyager in these leaves?
Who is the traveler in this journey
Deciphers the revolving night: receives
The signal from the light returning?

America was promises to whom?

        East were the
Dead kings and the remembered sepulchres:
West was the grass.
        The groves of the oaks were at evening.

Eastward are the nights where we have slept.

And we move on: we move down:
With the first light we push forward:
We descend from the past as a wandering people from mountains.
We cross into the day to be discovered.
The dead are left where they fall—at dark
At night late under the coverlets.

We mark the place with the shape of our teeth on our fingers.
The room is left as it was: the love

Who is the traveler in these leaves these
Annual waters and beside the doors
Jonquils: then the rose: the eaves
Heaping the thunder up: the mornings
Opening on like great valleys
Never till now approached: the familiar trees
Far off: distant with the future:
The hollyhocks beyond the afternoons:
The butterflies over the ripening fruit on the balconies:
And all beautiful
All before us

America was always promises.
From the first voyage and the first ship there were promises—
'the tropic bird which does not sleep at sea'
'the great mass of dark heavy clouds which is a sign'
'the drizzle of rain without wind which is a sure sign'
'the whale which is an indication'
'the stick appearing to be carved with iron'
'the stalk loaded with roseberries'
'and all these signs were from the west'
'and all night heard birds passing.'

Who is the voyager on these coasts?
Who is the traveler in these waters
Expects the future as a shore: foresees
Like Indies to the west the ending—he
The rumor of the surf intends?

America was promises—to whom?

Jefferson knew:
Declared it before God and before history:
Declares it still in the remembering tomb.
The promises were Man's: the land was his—
Man endowed by his Creator:
Earnest in love: perfectible by reason:
Just and perceiving justice: his natural nature
Clear and sweet at the source as springs in trees are.
It was Man the promise contemplated.
The times had chosen Man: no other:

Bloom on his face of every future:
Brother of stars and of all travelers:
Brother of time and of all mysteries:
Brother of grass also: of fruit trees.
It was Man who had been promised: who should have.
Man was to ride from the Tidewater: over the Gap:
West and South with the water: taking the book with him:
Taking the wheat seed: corn seed: pip of apple:
Building liberty a farmyard wide
Breeding for useful labor: for good looks:
For husbandry: humanity: for pride—
Practising self-respect and common decency.

And Man turned into men in Philadelphia
Practising prudence on a long-term lease:
Building liberty to fit the parlor:
Bred for crystal on the frontroom shelves:
Just and perceiving justice by the dollar:
Patriotic with the bonds at par
(And their children's children brag of their deeds for the Colonies).
Man rode up from the Tidewater: over the Gap:
Turned into men: turned into two-day settlers:
Lawyers with the land-grants in their caps:
Coon-skin voters wanting theirs and getting it.

Turned the promises to capital: invested it.

America was always promises:
'the wheel like a sun as big as a cart wheel
    with many sorts of pictures on it
    the whole of fine gold'

'twenty golden ducks
    beautifully worked and very natural looking
    and some like dogs of the kind they keep'

And they waved us west from the dunes: they cried out
Colua! Colua!
Mexico! Mexico! . . . Colua!

America was promises to whom?

Old Man Adams knew. He told us—
An aristocracy of compound interest
Hereditary through the common stock!
We'd have one sure before the mare was older.
"The first want of every man was his dinner:

The second his girl." Kings were by the pocket.
Wealth made blood made wealth made blood made wealthy.
Enlightened selfishness gave lasting light.
Winners bred grandsons: losers only bred!

And the Aristocracy of politic selfishness
Bought the land up: bought the towns: the sites:
The goods: the government: the people. Bled them.
Sold them. Kept the profit. Lost itself.

The Aristocracy of Wealth and Talents
Turned its talents into wealth and lost them.
Turned enlightened selfishness to wealth.
Turned self-interest into bankbooks: balanced them.
Bred out: bred to fools: to hostlers:
Card sharps: well dressed women: dancefloor doublers.
The Aristocracy of Wealth and Talents
Sold its talents: bought the public notice:
Drank in public: went to bed in public:
Patronized the arts in public: pall'd with
Public authors public beauties: posed in
Public postures for the public page.
The Aristocracy of Wealth and Talents
Withered of talent and ashamed of wealth
Bred to sonsinlaw: insane relations:
Girls with open secrets: sailors' Galahads:
Prurient virgins with the tales to tell:
Women with dead wombs and living wishes.

The Aristocracy of Wealth and Talents
Moved out: settled on the Continent:
Sat beside the water at Rapallo:
Died in a rented house: unwept: unhonored.

And the child says I see the lightning on you.

The weed between the railroad tracks
Tasting of sweat: tasting of poverty:
The bitter and pure taste where the hawk hovers:
Native as the deer bone in the sand

O my America for whom?

For whom the promises? For whom the river
"It flows west! Look at the ripple of it!"

The grass "So that it was wonderful to see
And endless without end with wind wonderful!"
The Great Lakes: landless as oceans: their beaches
Coarse sand: clean gravel: pebbles:
Their bluffs smelling of sunflowers: smelling of surf:
Of fresh water: of wild sunflowers . . . wilderness.
For whom the evening mountains on the sky:
The night wind from the west: the moon descending?

Tom Paine knew.
Tom Paine knew the People.
The promises were spoken to the People.
History was voyages toward the People.
Americas were landfalls of the People.
Stars and expectations were the signals of the People.

Whatever was truly built the People had built it.
Whatever was taken down they had taken down.
Whatever was worn they had worn—ax-handles: fiddle-bows:
Sills of doorways: names for children: for mountains.
Whatever was long forgotten they had forgotten—
Fame of the great: names of the rich and their mottos.
The People had the promises: they'd keep them.
They waited their time in the world: they had wise sayings.
They counted out their time by day to day.
They counted it out day after day into history.
They had time and to spare in the spill of their big fists.
They had all the time there was like a handful of wheat seed.
When the time came they would speak and the rest would listen.

And the time came and the People did not speak.

The time came: the time comes: the speakers
Come and these who speak are not the People.

These who speak with gunstocks at the doors:
These the coarse ambitious priest
Leads by the bloody fingers forward:
These who reach with stiffened arm to touch
What none who took dared touch before:
These who touch the truth are not the People.

These the savage fables of the time
Lick at the fingers as a bitch will waked at morning:
These who teach the lie are not the People.

The time came: the time comes

Comes and to whom? To these? Was it for these
The surf was secret on the new-found shore?
Was it for these the branch was on the water?—
These whom all the years were toward
The golden images the clouds the mountains?

Never before: never in any summer:
Never were days so generous: stars so mild:
Even in old men's talk or in books or remembering
Far back in a gone childhood
Or farther still to the light where Homer wanders—
The air all lucid with the solemn blue
That hills take at the distance beyond change. . . .
That time takes also at the distances.

Never were there promises as now:
Never was green deeper: earth warmer:
Light more beautiful to see: the sound of
Water lovelier: the many forms of
Leaves: stones: clouds: beasts: shadows
Clearer more admirable or the faces
More like answering faces or the hands
Quicker: more brotherly:
                              the aching taste of
Time more salt upon the tongue: more human
Never in any summer: and to whom?

At dusk: by street lights: in the rooms we ask this.

We do not ask for Truth now from John Adams.
We do not ask for Tongues from Thomas Jefferson.
We do not ask for Justice from Tom Paine.
We ask for answers.

And there is an answer.

There is Spain Austria Poland China Bohemia.
There are dead men in the pits in all those countries.
Their mouths are silent but they speak. They say
"The promises are theirs who take them."

Listen! Brothers! Generation!
Listen! You have heard these words. Believe it!
Believe the promises are theirs who take them!

Believe unless we take them for ourselves
Others will take them for the use of others!

Believe unless we take them for ourselves
All of us: one here: another there:
Men not Man: people not the People:
Hands: mouths: arms: eyes: not syllables—
Believe unless we take them for ourselves
Others will take them: not for us: for others!

Believe unless we take them for ourselves
Now: soon: by the clock: before tomorrow:
Others will take them: not for now: for longer!

Listen! Brothers! Generation!
Companions of leaves: of the sun: of the slow evenings:
Companions of the many days: of all of them:
Listen! Believe the speaking dead! Believe
The journey is our journey. O believe
The signals were to us: the signs: the birds by
Night: the breaking surf.

> Believe
America is promises to
Take!

America is promises to
Us
To take them
Brutally
With love but
Take them.

O believe this!

MEMORIAL RAIN

by Archibald MacLeish

Ambassador Puser the ambassador
Reminds himself in French, felicitous tongue,
What these (young men no longer) lie here for
In rows that once, and somewhere else, were young—

The selections from Archibald MacLeish *Poems 1924-1933* are used by permission of the publishers, Houghton Mifflin Company.

Memorial Rain

All night in Brussels the wind had tugged at my door:
I had heard the wind at my door and the trees strung
Taut, and to me who had never been before
In that country it was a strange wind blowing
Steadily, stiffening the walls, the floor,
The roof of my room. I had not slept for knowing
He too, dead, was a stranger in that land
And felt beneath the earth in the wind's flowing
A tightening of roots and would not understand,
Remembering lake winds in Illinois,
That strange wind. I had felt his bones in the sand
Listening.

   —Reflects that these enjoy
Their country's gratitude, that deep repose,
That peace no pain can break, no hurt destroy,
That rest, that sleep—

    At Ghent the wind rose.
There was a smell of rain and a heavy drag
Of wind in the hedges but not as the wind blows
Over fresh water when the waves lag
Foaming and the willows huddle and it will rain:
I felt him waiting.

   —Indicates the flag
Which (may he say) enisles in Flanders' plain
This little field these happy, happy dead
Have made America—

    In the ripe grain
The wind coiled glistening, darted, fled,
Dragging its heavy body: at Waereghem
The wind coiled in the grass above his head:
Waiting—listening—

   —Dedicates to them
This earth their bones have hallowed, this last gift
A grateful country—

    Under the dry grass stem
The words are blurred, are thickened, the words sift
Confused by the rasp of the wind, by the thin grating

Of ants under the grass, the minute shift
And tumble of dusty sand separating
From dusty sand. The roots of the grass strain,
Tighten, the earth is rigid, waits—he is waiting—

And suddenly, and all at once, the rain!
The living scatter, they run into houses, the wind
Is trampled under the rain, shakes free, is again
Trampled. The rain gathers, running in thinned
Spurts of water that ravel in the dry sand
Seeping in the sand under the grass roots, seeping
Between cracked boards to the bones of a clenched hand:
The earth relaxes, loosens; he is sleeping,
He rests, he is quiet, he sleeps in a strange land.

EPISTLE TO BE LEFT IN THE EARTH

by ARCHIBALD MACLEISH

. . . It is colder now
     there are many stars
          we are drifting
North by the Great Bear
       the leaves are falling
The water is stone in the scooped rocks
         to southward
Red sun grey air
     the crows are
Slow on their crooked wings
        the jays have left us
Long since we passed the flares of Orion
Each man believes in his heart he will die
Many have written last thoughts and last letters
None know if our deaths are now or forever
None know if this wandering earth will be found

We lie down and the snow covers our garments
I pray you
    you (if any open this writing)
Make in your mouths the words that were our names

Geography of This Time

I will tell you all we have learned
                              I will tell you everything

The earth is round
                    there are springs under the orchards

The loam cuts with a blunt knife
                                   beware of

Elms in thunder
                  the lights in the sky are stars
We think they do not see
                          we think also
The trees do not know nor the leaves of the grasses
                                                    hear us

The birds too are ignorant
                            Do not listen
Do not stand at dark in the open windows
We before you have heard this
                               they are voices
They are not words at all but the wind rising
Also none among us has seen God
(. . . We have thought often
The flaws of sun in the late and driving weather
Pointed to one tree but it was not so)
As for the nights I warn you the nights are dangerous
The wind changes at night and the dreams come

It is very cold
                there are strange stars near Arcturus

Voices are crying an unknown name in the sky

GEOGRAPHY OF THIS TIME

by ARCHIBALD MACLEISH

What is required of us is the recognition of the frontiers between the centuries. And to take heart: to cross over.

Those who are killed in the place between out of ignorance, those who wander like cattle and are shot, those who are shot

From *The New Republic,* Oct. 28, 1942. Reprinted by permission of Mr. Archibald MacLeish and the editors.

and are left in the stone fields between the histories—these men may be pitied as the victims of accidents are pitied but their deaths do not signify. They are neither buried nor otherwise remembered but lie in the dead grass in the dry thorn in the worn light. Their years have no monuments.

There are many such in the sand here—many who did not perceive, who thought the time went on, the years went forward, the history was continuous—who thought tomorrow was of the same nation as today. There are many who came to the frontiers between the times and did not know them —who looked for the sentry-box at the stone bridge, for the barricade in the pines and the declaration in two languages—the warning and the opportunity to turn. They are dead there in the down light, in the sheep's barren.

What is required of us is the recognition

with no sign, with no word, with the

roads raveled out into ruts and the ruts into dust and the dust stirred by the wind —the roads from behind us ending in the dust.

What is required of us is the recognition of the frontiers where the roads end.

We are very far. We are past the place where the light lifts from us and farther on than the relinquishment of leaves—farther even than the persistence in the east of the green color. Beyond are the confused tracks, the guns, the watchers.

What is required of us, Companions, is the recognition of the frontiers across this history, and to take heart: to cross over

—to persist and to cross over and survive

But to survive

To cross over

SPACE BEING CURVED

by E. E. CUMMINGS

Space being(don't forget to remember)Curved
(and that reminds me who said o yes Frost
Something there is which isn't fond of walls)

an electromagnetic (now I've lost
the)Einstein expanded Newton's law preserved
conTinuum(but we read that beFore)

of Course life being just a Reflex you
know since Everything is Relative or

to sum it All Up god being Dead(not to

mention inTerred)
           LONG LIVE that Upwardlooking
Serene Illustrious and Beatific
Lord of Creation,MAN:
                at a least crooking
of Whose compassionate digit,earth's most terrific

quadruped swoons into billiardBalls!

O SWEET SPONTANEOUS

by E. E. CUMMINGS

O sweet spontaneous
earth how often have
the
doting
     fingers of
prurient philosophers pinched
and
poked
thee
, has the naughty thumb
of science prodded
thy
   beauty   . how
often have religions taken
thee upon their scraggy knees

squeezing and
buffeting thee that thou mightest
    conceive
gods
    (but
true

to the incomparable
couch of death thy
rhythmic
lover
    thou answerest

them only with

        spring)

"Well, it looks like a buttercup to me."

NOBODY LOSES ALL THE TIME

by E. E. CUMMINGS

nobody loses all the time

i had an uncle named
Sol who was a born failure and
nearly everybody said he should have gone
into vaudeville perhaps because my Uncle
    Sol could
sing McCann He Was A Diver on Xmas
    Eve like Hell Itself which
may or may not account for the fact that
    my Uncle

Sol indulged in that possibly most inex-
    cusable
of all to use a highfalootin phrase
luxuries that is or to
wit farming and be
it needlessly
added

my Uncle Sol's farm
failed because the chickens
ate the vegetables so
my Uncle Sol had a
chicken farm till the
skunks ate the chickens when

my Uncle Sol
had a skunk farm but
the skunks caught cold and
died so
my Uncle Sol imitated the
skunks in a subtle manner

or by drowning himself in the watertank
but somebody who'd given my Uncle Sol
    a Victor
Victrola and records while he lived pre-
    sented to
him upon the auspicious occasion of his
    decease a
scrumptious not to mention splendiferous
    funeral with
tall boys in black gloves and flowers and
    everything and

i remember we all cried like the Missouri
when my Uncle Sol's coffin lurched be-
    cause
somebody pressed a button
(and down went
my Uncle
Sol

and started a worm farm)

IF YOU CAN'T EAT YOU GOT TO

by E. E. CUMMINGS

If you can't eat you got to

smoke and we aint got
nothing to smoke:come on kid

let's go to sleep
if you can't smoke you got to

Sing and we aint got

nothing to sing;come on kid
let's go to sleep

if you can't sing you got to
die and we aint got

Nothing to die,come on kid

let's go to sleep
if you can't die you got to

dream and we aint got
nothing to dream(come on kid

Let's go to sleep)

Reprinted by permission of the publishers, Duell, Sloan & Pearce Inc.

SINCE FEELING IS FIRST

by E. E. CUMMINGS

since feeling is first
who pays any attention
to the syntax of things
will never wholly kiss you;

wholly to be a fool
while Spring is in the world

my blood approves,
and kisses are a better fate

than wisdom
lady i swear by all flowers. Don't cry
—the best gesture of my brain is less than
your eyelids' flutter which says

we are for each other: then
laugh, leaning back in my arms
for life's not a paragraph

And death i think is no parenthesis

Copyright, 1926, by Horace Liveright. From: *Collected Poems,* published by Harcourt, Brace and Company, Inc.

ANYONE LIVED IN A PRETTY HOW TOWN

by E. E. CUMMINGS

anyone lived in a pretty how town
(with up so floating many bells down)

spring summer autumn winter
he sang his didn't he danced his did.

Reprinted by permission of the publishers, Duell, Sloan & Pearce, Inc.

Women and men(both little and small)
cared for anyone not at all
they sowed their isn't they reaped their
   same
sun moon stars rain

children guessed(but only a few
and down they forgot as up they grew
autumn winter spring summer)
that noone loved him more by more

when by now and tree by leaf
she laughed his joy she cried his grief
bird by snow and stir by still
anyone's any was all to her

someones married their everyones
laughed their cryings and did their dance
(sleep wake hope and then)they
said their nevers they slept their dream

stars rain sun moon
(and only the snow can begin to explain
how children are apt to forget to remember
with up so floating many bells down)

one day anyone died i guess
(and noone stooped to kiss his face)
busy folk buried them side by side
little by little and was by was

all by all and deep by deep
and more by more they dream their sleep
noone and anyone earth by april
wish by spirit and if by yes.

Women and men(both dong and ding)
summer autumn winter spring
reaped their sowing and went their came
sun moon stars rain

THESE CHILDREN SINGING

by E. E. CUMMINGS

these children singing in stone a
silence of stone these
little children wound with stone
flowers opening for

ever these silently lit
tle children are petals
their song is a flower of
always their flowers

of stone are
silently singing
a song more silent
than silence these always

children forever
singing wreathed with singing
blossoms children of
stone with blossoming

eyes
know if a
lit tle
tree listens

forever to always children singing forever
a song made
of silent as stone silence of
song

Reprinted by permission of the publishers, Duell, Sloan & Pearce, Inc.

LOVE IS MORE THICKER

by E. E. Cummings

love is more thicker than forget
more thinner than recall
more seldom than a wave is wet
more frequent than to fail

it is most mad and moonly
and less it shall unbe
than all the sea which only
is deeper than the sea

love is less always than to win
less never than alive
less bigger than the least begin
less littler than forgive

it is most sane and sunly
and more it cannot die
than all the sky which only
is higher than the sky

Reprinted by permission of the publishers, Duell, Sloan & Pearce, Inc.

TRAVELOGUE IN A SHOOTING-GALLERY

by KENNETH FEARING

There is a jungle, there is a jungle, there is a vast, vivid, wild, wild, marvelous,
marvelous, marvelous jungle,
Open to the public during business hours,
A jungle not very far from an Automat, between a hat store there, and a radio shop.

There, there, whether it rains, or it snows, or it shines,
Under the hot, blazing, cloudless, tropical neon skies that the management always
arranges there,
Rows and rows of marching ducks, dozens and dozens and dozens of ducks, move
steadily along on smoothly-oiled ballbearing feet,
Ducks as big as telephone books, slow and fearless and out of this world,
While lines and lines of lions, lions, rabbits, panthers, elephants, crocodiles, zebras,
apes,
Filled with jungle hunger and jungle rage and jungle love,
Stalk their prey on endless, endless rotary belts through never-ending forests, and
burning deserts, and limitless veldts,
To the sound of tom-toms, equipped with silencers, beaten by thousands of savages
hidden there.

And there it is that all the big game hunters go, there the traders and the explorers
come,
Leanfaced men with windswept eyes who arrive by streetcar, auto or subway, taxi
or on foot, streetcar or bus,
And they nod, and they say, and they need no more:
"There . . . there . . .
There they come and there they go."

And weighing machines, in this civilized jungle, will read your soul like an open
book, for a penny at a time, and tell you all,
There, there, where smoking is permitted,
In a jungle that lies, like a rainbow's end, at the very end of every trail,
There, in the only jungle in the whole wide world where ducks are waiting for
streetcars,
And hunters can be psychoanalyzed, while they smoke and wait for ducks.

Return to Normal

RECEPTION GOOD

by KENNETH FEARING

Now, at a particular spot on the radio dial, "—in this corner, wearing purple trunks,"
Mingles, somehow, with the news that "—powerful enemy units have been sur-
    rounded in the drive—"
And both of these with the information that "—there is a way to avoid having
    chapped and roughened hands."

Such are the new and complex harmonies, it seems, of a strange and still more
    complex age;
It is not that the reception is confused or poor, but rather it is altogether too clear
    and good,

And no worse, in any case, than that other receiving set, the mind,
Forever faithfully transmitting the great and little impulses that arrive, however
    wavering or loud, from near and far:
"It is an ill wind—" it is apt to report, underscoring this with "—the bigger they
    are the harder they fall," and simultaneously reminding, darkly, that "Things
    are seldom as they seem,"

Reconciling, with ease, the irreconcilable,
Piecing together fragments of a flashing past with clouded snapshots of the present
    and the future,
("Something old, something new," its irrelevant announcer states. "Something bor-
    rowed, something blue.")

Fashioning a raw, wild symphony of a wedding march, a drinking song, and a dirge,
Multiplying enormous figures with precision, then raising the question: But after
    all, what is a man?
Somehow creating hope and fresh courage out of ancient doubt.

"Both boys are on their feet, they're going to it," the radio reports,
"—the sinking was attended by a heavy loss of life—"
"—this amazing cream for quick, miraculous results."

How many pieces are there, in a simple jigsaw puzzle?
How many phases of a man's life can crowd their way into a single moment?
How many angels, actually, can dance on the point of a pin?

NO CREDIT

by KENNETH FEARING

Whether dinner was pleasant, with the windows lit by gunfire, and no one disagreed; or whether, later, we argued in the park, and there was a touch of vomit-gas in the evening air;

Whether we found a greater, deeper, more perfect love, by courtesy of Camels, over NBC; whether the comics amused us, or the newspapers carried a hunger death and a White House prayer for mother's day;

Whether the bills were paid or not, whether or not we had our doubts, whether we spoke our minds at Joe's, and the receipt said "Not Returnable," and the cash-register rang up "No Sale,"

Whether the truth was then, or later, or whether the best had already gone—

Nevertheless, we know; as every turn is measured; as every unavoidable risk is known;

As nevertheless, the flesh grows old, dies, dies in its only life, is gone;

The reflection goes from the mirror; as the shadow, of even a rebel, is gone from the wall;

As nevertheless, the current is thrown and the wheels revolve; and nevertheless, as the word is spoken and the wheat grows tall and the ships sail on—

None but the fool is paid in full; none but the broker, none but the scab is certain of profit;

The sheriff alone may attend a third degree in formal attire; alone, the academy artists multiply in dignity as trooper's bayonet guards the door;

Only Steve, the side-show robot, knows content; only Steve, the mechanical man in love with a photo-electric beam, remains aloof; only Steve, who sits and smokes or stands in salute, is secure;

Steve, whose shoebutton eyes are blind to terror, whose painted ears are deaf to appeal, whose welded breast will never be slashed by bullets, whose armature soul can hold no fear.

PORTRAIT (2)

by KENNETH FEARING

The clear brown eyes, kindly and alert, with 12-20 vision, give confident regard to the passing world through R. K. Lampert & Company lenses framed in gold;

His soul, however, is all his own;

American Rhapsody

Arndt Brothers necktie and hat (with feather) supply a touch of youth.
With his soul his own, he drives, drives, chats and drives,
The first and second bicuspids, lower right, replaced by bridgework, while two in-
    cisors have porcelain crowns;

(Render unto Federal, state and city Caesar, but not unto time;
Render nothing unto time until Amalgamated Death serves final notice, in proper
    form;

   The vault is ready;
   The will has been drawn by Clagget, Clagget, Clagget & Brown;
   The policies are adequate, Confidential's best, reimbursing for disability, partial or
       complete, with double indemnity should the end be a pure and simple accident)

Nothing unto time,
Nothing unto change, nothing unto fate,
Nothing unto you, and nothing unto me, or to any other known or unknown party
    or parties, living or deceased;

But Mercury shoes, with special arch supports, take much of the wear and tear;
On the course, a custombuilt driver corrects a tendency to slice;
Love's ravages have been repaired (it was a textbook case) by Drs. Schultz, Light-
    ner, Mannheim, and Goode,
While all of it is enclosed in excellent tweed, with Mr. Baumer's personal attention
    to the shoulders and the waist;

And all of it now roving, chatting amiably through space in a Plymouth 6.
With his soul (his own) at peace, soothed by Walter Lippmann, and sustained by
    Haig & Haig.

AMERICAN RHAPSODY (4)

by KENNETH FEARING

First you bite your fingernails. And then you comb your hair again. And then you
    wait. And wait.
(They say, you know, that first you lie. And then you steal, they say. And then,
    they say, you kill.)

Then the doorbell rings. Then Peg drops in. And Bill. And Jane. And Doc.
And first you talk, and smoke, and hear the news and have a drink. Then you walk
    down the stairs.

And you dine, then, and go to a show after that, perhaps, and after that a night
  spot, and after that come home again, and climb the stairs again, and again go
  to bed.

But first Peg argues, and Doc replies. First you dance the same dance and you
  drink the same drink you always drank before.
And the piano builds a roof of notes above the world.
And the trumpet weaves a dome of music through space. And the drum makes a
  ceiling over space and time and night.
And then the table-wit. And then the check. Then home again to bed.
But first, the stairs

And do you now, baby, as you climb the stairs, do you still feel as you felt back
  there?
Do you feel again as you felt this morning? And the night before? And then the
  night before that?

(They say, you know, that first you hear voices. And then you have visions, they
  say. Then, they say, you kick and scream and rave.)
Or do you feel: What is one more night in a lifetime of nights?
What is one more death, or friendship, or divorce out of two, or three? Or four?
  Or five?
One more face among so many, many faces, one more life among so many million
  lives?

But first, baby, as you climb and count the stairs (and they total the same) did you,
  sometime or somewhere, have a different idea?
Is this, baby, what you were born to feel, and do, and be?

READINGS, FORECASTS, PERSONAL GUIDANCE

by KENNETH FEARING

It is not—I swear by every fiery omen to be seen these nights in every quarter of
  the heavens, I affirm it by all the monstrous portents of the earth and of the
  sea—
It is not that my belief in the true and mystic science is shaken, nor that I have
  lost faith in the magic of the cards, or in the augury of dreams, or in the great
  and good divinity of the stars.
No, I know still whose science fits the promise to the inquirer's need, invariably, for
  a change: Mine. My science foretells the wished-for journey, the business adjustment, the handsome stranger. (Each of these is considered a decided change.)

And I know whose skill weighs matrimony, risks a flyer in steel or wheat against
the vagaries of the moon.
(Planet of dreams, of mothers and of children, goddess of sailors and of all adventurers, forgive the liberty. But a man must eat.) My skill,
Mine, and the cunning and the patience. (Two dollars for the horoscope in brief
and five for a twelve months' forecast in detail.)

No, it is this: The wonders that I have seen with my own eyes.

It is this: That still these people know, as I do not, that what has never been on
earth before may still well come to pass,
That always, always there are new and brighter things beneath the sun,
That surely, in bargain basements or in walk-up flats, it must be so that still from
time to time they hear wild angel voices speak.
It is this: That I have known them for what they are,
Seen thievery written plainly in their planets, found greed and murder and worse
in their birth dates and their numbers, guilt etched in every line of every palm,
But still a light burns through the eyes they turn to me, a need more moving than
the damned and dirty dollars (which I must take) that form the pattern of
their larger hopes and deeper fears.

And it comes to this: That always I feel another hand, not mine, has drawn and
turned the card to find some incredible ace,
Always another word I did not write appears in the spirit parchment prepared by
me,
Always another face I do not know shows in the dream, the crystal globe, or the
flame.

And finally, this: Corrupt, in a world bankrupt and corrupt, what have I got to do
with these miracles?
If they want miracles, let them consult some one else.
Would they, in extremity, ask them of a physician? Or expect them, in desperation,
of an attorney? Or of a priest? Or of a poet?

Nevertheless, a man must eat.
Mrs. Raeburn is expected at five. She will communicate with a number of friends
and relatives long deceased.

DEVIL'S DREAM

by KENNETH FEARING

But it could never be true;
How could it ever happen, if it never did before, and it's not so now?

But suppose that the face behind those steel prison bars—
Why do you dream about a face lying cold in the trenches streaked with rain and
    dirt and blood?
Is it the very same face seen so often in the mirror?
Just as though it could be true—

But what if it is, what if it is, what if it is, what if the thing that cannot happen
    really happens just the same,
Suppose the fever goes a hundred, then a hundred and one,
What if Holy Savings Trust goes from 98 to 88 to 78 to 68, then drops down to
    28 and 8 and out of sight,
And the fever shoots a hundred two, a hundred three, a hundred four, then a hun-
    dred five and out?

But now there's only the wind and the sky and sunlight and the clouds,
With everyday people walking and talking as they always have before along the
    everyday street,
Doing ordinary things with ordinary faces and ordinary voices in the ordinary way,
Just as they always will—

Then why does it feel like a bomb, why does it feel like a target,
Like standing on the gallows with the trap about to drop,
Why does it feel like a thunderbolt the second before it strikes, why does it feel
    like a tight-rope walk high over hell?

Because it is not, will not, never could be true
That the whole wide, bright, green, warm, calm world goes:
CRASH.

TRAVELOGUE FOR EXILES
by KARL J. SHAPIRO

Look and remember. Look upon this sky;
Look deep and deep into the sea-clean air,
The unconfined, the terminus of prayer.
Speak now and speak into the hallowed dome.
What do you hear? What does the sky reply?
The heavens are taken: this is not your home.

Look and remember. Look upon this sea;
Look down and down into the tireless tide.
What of a life below, a life inside,
A tomb, a cradle in the curly foam?
The waves arise; sea-wind and sea agree
The waters are taken: this is not your home.

Look and remember. Look upon this land,
Far, far across the factories and the grass.
Surely, there, surely, they will let you pass.
Speak then and ask the forest and the loam.
What do you hear? What does the land command?
The earth is taken: this is not your home.

From *Poems: 1940-1952.* Copyright, 1942, by Karl J. Shapiro. Reprinted by permission of Random House, Inc.

ELEGY FOR A DEAD SOLDIER
by KARL J. SHAPIRO

I

A white sheet on the tail-gate of a truck
Becomes an altar; two small candlesticks
Sputter at each side of the crucifix
Laid round with flowers brighter than the
  blood,
Red as the red of our apocalypse,
Hibiscus that a marching man will pluck
To stick into his rifle or his hat,
And great blue morning-glories pale as lips
That shall no longer taste or kiss or swear.
The wind begins a low magnificat,
The chaplain chats, the palmtrees swirl
  their hair,
The columns come together through the
  mud.

II

We too are ashes as we watch and hear
The psalm, the sorrow, and the simple
  praise
Of one whose promised thoughts of other
  days
Were such as ours, but now wholly de-
  stroyed,
The service record of his youth wiped out,
His dream dispersed by shot, must dis-
  appear.
What can we feel but wonder at a loss
That seems to point at nothing but the
  doubt
Which flirts our sense of luck into the
  ditch?

From Karl Shapiro, *V-Letter and Other Poems,* Reynal and Hitchcock, Inc.

Reader of Paul who prays beside this fosse,
Shall we believe our eyes or legends rich
With glory and rebirth beyond the void?

III

For this comrade is dead, dead in the war,
A young man out of millions yet to live,
One cut away from all that war can give,
Freedom of self and peace to wander free.
Who mourns in all this sober multitude
Who did not feel the bite of it before
The bullet found its aim? This worthy
    flesh,
This boy laid in a coffin and reviewed—
Who has not wrapped himself in this same
    flag,
Heard the light fall of dirt, his wound still
    fresh,
Felt his eyes closed, and heard the distant
    brag
Of the last volley of humanity?

IV

By chance I saw him die, stretched on the
    ground,
A tattooed arm lifted to take the blood
Of someone else sealed in a tin. I stood
During the last delirium that stays
The intelligence a tiny moment more,
And then the strangulation, the last sound.
The end was sudden, like a foolish play,
A stupid fool slamming a foolish door,
The absurd catastrophe, half-prearranged,
And all the decisive things still left to say.
So we disbanded, angrier and unchanged,
Sick with the utter silence of dispraise.

V

We ask for no statistics of the killed,
For nothing political impinges on
This single casualty, or all those gone,
Missing or healing, sinking or dispersed,
Hundreds of thousands counted, millions
    lost.

More than an accident and less than willed
Is every fall, and this one like the rest.
However others calculate the cost,
To us the final aggregate is *one*,
One with a name, one transferred to the
    blest;
And though another stoops and takes the
    gun,
We cannot add the second to the first.

VI

I would not speak for him who could not
    speak
Unless my fear were true: he was not
    wronged,
He knew to which decision he belonged
But let it choose itself, Ripe in instinct,
Neither the victim nor the volunteer,
He followed, and the leaders could not
    seek
Beyond the followers. Much of this he
    knew;
The journey was a detour that would steer
Into the Lincoln Highway of a land
Remorselessly improved, excited, new,
And that was what he wanted. He had
    planned
To earn and drive. He and the world had
    winked.

VII

No history deceived him, for he knew
Little of times and armies not his own;
He never felt that peace was but a loan,
Had never questioned the idea of gain.
Beyond the headlines once or twice he saw
The gathering of a power by the few
But could not tell their names; he cast his
    vote,
Distrusting all the elected but not law.
He laughed at socialism; *on mourrait
Pour les industriels?* He shed his coat
And not for brotherhood, but for his pay.
To him the red flag marked the sewer
    main.

VIII

Above all else he loathed the homily,
The slogan and the ad. He paid his bill
But not for congressmen at Bunker Hill.
Ideals were few and those there were not
  made
For conversation. He belonged to church
But never spoke of God. The Christmas
  tree,
The Easter egg, baptism, he observed,
Never denied the preacher on his perch,
And would not sign Resolved That or
  Whereas.
Softness he had and hours and nights re-
  served
For thinking, dressing, dancing to the
  jazz.
His laugh was real, his manners were
  home-made.

IX

Of all men poverty pursued him least;
He was ashamed of all the down and out,
Spurned the panhandler like an uneasy
  doubt,
And saw the unemployed as a vague mass
Incapable of hunger or revolt.
He hated other races, south or east,
And shoved them to the margin of his
  mind.
He could recall the justice of the Colt,
Take interest in a gang-war like a game.
His ancestry was somewhere far behind
And left him only his peculiar name.
Doors opened, and he recognized no class.

X

His children would have known a heri-
  tage,
Just or unjust, the richest in the world,
The quantum of all art and science curled

In the horn of plenty, bursting from the
  horn,
A people bathed in honey, Paris come,
Vienna transferred with the highest wage,
A World's Fair spread to Phoenix, Jack-
  sonville,
Earth's capitol, the new Byzantium,
Kingdom of man—who knows? Hollow
  or firm,
No man can ever prophesy until
Out of our death some undiscovered germ,
Whole toleration or pure peace is born.

XI

The time to mourn is short that best be-
  comes
The military dead. We lift and fold the
  flag,
Lay bare the coffin with its written tag,
And march away. Behind, four others wait
To lift the box, the heaviest of loads.
The anesthetic afternoon benumbs,
Sickens our senses, forces back our talk.
We know that others on tomorrow's roads
Will fall, ourselves perhaps, the man be-
  side,
Over the world the threatened, all who
  walk;
And could we mark the grave of him who
  died
We would write this beneath his name
  and date—

EPITAPH

Underneath this wooden cross there lies
A Christian killed in battle. You who read,
Remember that this stranger died in pain;
And passing here, if you can lift your eyes
Upon a peace kept by the human creed,
Know that one soldier has not died in
  vain.

BUICK

by KARL J. SHAPIRO

As a sloop with a sweep of immaculate wing on her delicate spine
And a keel as steel as a root that holds in the sea as she leans,
Leaning and laughing, my warm-hearted beauty, you ride, you ride,
You tack on the curves with parabola speed and a kiss of goodbye,
Like a thoroughbred sloop, my new high-spirited spirit, my kiss.

As my foot suggests that you leap in the air with your hips of a girl,
My finger that praises your wheel and announces your voices of song,
Flouncing your skirts, you blueness of joy, you flirt of politeness,
You leap, you intelligence, essence of wheelness with silvery nose,
And your platinum clocks of excitement stir like the hairs of a fern.
But how alien you are from the booming belts of your birth and the smoke
Where you turned on the stinging lathes of Detroit and Lansing at night
And shrieked at the torch in your secret parts and the amorous tests,
But now with your eyes that enter the future of roads you forget;
You are all instinct with your phosphorus glow and your streaking hair.

And now when we stop it is not as the bird from the shell that I leave
Or the leatherly pilot who steps from his bird with a sneer of delight,
And not as the ignorant beast do you squat and watch me depart,
But with exquisite breathing you smile, with satisfaction of love,
And I touch you again as you tick in the silence and settle in sleep.

From Karl J. Shapiro, *Person, Place and Thing,* Reynal and Hitchcock, Inc.

from Foreword to THE STILL CENTRE

by STEPHEN SPENDER

POETRY does not state truth, it states the conditions within which something felt is true. Even while he is writing about the little portion of reality which is part of his experience, the poet may be conscious of a different reality outside. His problem is to relate the small truth to the sense of a wider, perhaps theoretically known, truth outside his experience. Poems exist within their own limits, they do not exclude the possibility of other things, which might also be subjects of poetry, being different. They remain true to experience and they establish the proportions of that experience. One day a poet will write truthfully about the heroism as well as the fears and anxiety of today; but such a poetry will be very different from the utilitarian heroics of the moment.

I think that there is a certain pressure of external events on poets today, making them tend to write about what is outside their own limited experience. The violence of the times we are living in, the necessity of sweeping and general and immediate action, tend to dwarf the experience of the individual, and to make his immediate environment and occupations perhaps something that he is even ashamed of. For this reason, in my most recent poems, I have deliberately turned back to a kind of writing which is more personal, and I have included within my subjects weakness and fantasy and illusion.

THE EXPRESS

by STEPHEN SPENDER

After the first powerful plain manifesto
The black statement of pistons, without more fuss
But gliding like a queen, she leaves the station.
Without bowing and with restrained unconcern
She passes the houses which humbly crowd outside,
The gasworks and at last the heavy page
Of death, printed by gravestones in the cemetery.
Beyond the town there lies the open country
Where, gathering speed, she acquires mystery,
The luminous self-possession of ships on ocean.
It is now she begins to sing—at first quite low
Then loud, and at last with a jazzy madness—

[735]

The song of her whistle screaming at curves,
Of deafening tunnels, brakes, innumerable bolts.
And always light, aerial, underneath
Goes the elate meter of her wheels.
Steaming through metal landscape on her lines
She plunges new eras of wild happiness
Where speed throws up strange shapes, broad curves
And parallels clean like the steel of guns.
At last, further than Edinburgh or Rome,
Beyond the crest of the world, she reaches night
Where only a low streamline brightness
Of phosphorus on the tossing hills is white.
Ah, like a comet through flames she moves entranced
Wrapt in her music no bird song, no, nor bough
Breaking with honey buds, shall ever equal.

NOT PALACES, AN ERA'S CROWN

by STEPHEN SPENDER

Not palaces, an era's crown
Where the mind dwells, intrigues, rests;
The architectural gold-leaved flower
From people ordered like a single mind,
I build. This only what I tell:
It is too late for rare accumulation
For family pride, for beauty's filtered
    dusts;
I say, stamping the words with emphasis,
Drink from here energy and only energy,
As from the electric charge of a battery,
To will this Time's change.
Eye, gazelle, delicate wanderer,
Drinker of horizon's fluid line;
Ear that suspends on a chord
The spirit drinking timelessness;
Touch, love, all senses;
Leave your gardens, your singing feasts,
Your dreams of suns circling before our
    sun,
Of heaven after our world.
Instead, watch images of flashing brass
That strike the outward sense, the pol-
    ished will
Flag of our purpose which the wind en-
    graves.
No spirit seek here rest. But this: No man
Shall hunger: Man shall spend equally.
Our goal which we compel: Man shall be
    man.

—That programme of the antique Satan
Bristling with guns on the indented page
With battleship towering from hilly
    waves:
For what? Drive of a ruining purpose
Destroying all but its age-long exploiters.
Our programme like this, yet opposite,
Death to the killers, bringing light to life.

THE LANDSCAPE NEAR AN AERODROME

by STEPHEN SPENDER

More beautiful and soft than any moth
With burring furred antennae feeling its huge path
Through dusk, the air-liner with shut-off engines
Glides over suburbs and the sleeves set trailing tall
To point the wind. Gently, broadly, she falls
Scarcely disturbing charted currents of air.

Lulled by descent, the travellers across sea
And across feminine land indulging its easy limbs
In miles of softness, now let their eyes trained by watching
Penetrate through dusk the outskirts of this town
Here where industry shows a fraying edge.
Here they may see what is being done.

Beyond the winking masthead light
And the landing-ground, they observe the outposts
Of work: chimneys like lank black fingers
Or figures frightening and mad: and squat buildings
With their strange air behind trees, like women's faces
Shattered by grief. Here where few houses
Moan with faint light behind their blinds
They remark the unhomely sense of complaint, like a dog
Shut out and shivering at the foreign moon.

In the last sweep of love, they pass over fields
Behind the aerodrome, where boys play all day
Hacking dead grass: whose cries, like wild birds,
Settle upon the nearest roofs
But soon are hid under the loud city.

Then, as they land, they hear the tolling bell
Reaching across the landscape of hysteria
To where, larger than all the charcoaled batteries
And imaged towers against that dying sky,
Religion stands, the church blocking the sun.

ULTIMA RATIO REGUM

by STEPHEN SPENDER

The guns spell money's ultimate reason
In letters of lead on the spring hillside.
But the boy lying dead under the olive trees
Was too young and too silly
To have been notable to their important eye.
He was a better target for a kiss.

When he lived, tall factory hooters never summoned him.
Nor did restaurant plate-glass doors revolve to wave him in.
His name never appeared in the papers.
The world maintained its traditional wall
Round the dead with their gold sunk deep as a well,
Whilst his life, intangible as a Stock Exchange rumour, drifted outside.

O too lightly he threw down his cap
One day when the breeze threw petals from the trees.
The unflowering wall sprouted with guns,
Machine-gun anger quickly scythed the grasses;
Flags and leaves fell from hands and branches;
The tweed cap rotted in the nettles.

Consider his life which was valueless
In terms of employment, hotel ledgers, news files.
Consider. One bullet in ten thousand kills a man.
Ask. Was so much expenditure justified
On the death of one so young and so silly
Lying under the olive trees, O world, O death?

from SPIRITUAL EXPLORATIONS

by STEPHEN SPENDER

VI

I am that witness through whom the whole
Knows it exists. Within the coils of blood,
Whispering under sleep, there moves the flood

Of stars, battles, dark and frozen pole.
All that I am I am not. The cold stone
Unfolds its angel for me. On my dreams ride
The racial legends. The stars outside
Glitter under my ribs. Being all, I am alone.
   I who say I call that eye I
Which is the mirror in which things see
Nothing except themselves. I die.
The things, the vision, still will be.
Upon this eye reflections of stars lie
And that which passes, passes away, is I.

I THINK CONTINUALLY OF THOSE WHO WERE
TRULY GREAT

by STEPHEN SPENDER

I think continually of those who were truly great.
Who, from the womb, remembered the soul's history
Through corridors of light where the hours are suns
Endless and singing. Whose lovely ambition
Was that their lips, still touched with fire,
Should tell of the Spirit clothed from head to foot in song.
And who hoarded from the Spring branches
The desires falling across their bodies like blossoms.

What is precious is never to forget
The essential delight of the blood drawn from ageless springs
Breaking through rocks in worlds before our earth.
Never to deny its pleasure in the morning simple light
Nor its grave evening demand for love.
Never to allow gradually the traffic to smother
With noise and fog the flowering of the spirit.

Near the snow, near the sun, in the highest fields
See how these names are fêted by the waving grass
And by the streamers of white cloud
And whispers of wind in the listening sky.
The names of those who in their lives fought for life
Who wore at their hearts the fire's centre.
Born of the sun they travelled a short while towards the sun,
And left the vivid air signed with their honour.

from "SQUARES AND OBLONGS" in POETS AT WORK

by W. H. AUDEN

A poet is, before anything else, a person who is passionately in love with language. Whether this love is a sign of his poetic gift or the gift itself—for falling in love is given not chosen—I don't know, but it is certainly the sign by which one recognizes whether a young man is potentially a poet or not.

Two theories of poetry. Poetry as a magical means for inducing desirable emotions and repelling undesirable emotions in oneself and others, or Poetry as a game of knowledge, a bringing to consciousness, by naming them, of emotions and their hidden relationships.

The first view was held by the Greeks, and is now held by MGM, Agit-Prop, and the collective public of the world. They are wrong.

The girl whose boy-friend starts writing her love poems should be on her guard. Perhaps he really does love her, but one thing is certain: while he was writing his poems he was not thinking of her but of his own feeling about her, and that is suspicious. Let her remember St. Augustine's confession of his feelings after the death of someone he loved very much: "I would rather have been deprived of my friend than of my grief."

How can I know what I think till I see what I say? A poet writes "The chestnut's comfortable root" and then changes this to "The chestnut's customary root." In this alteration there is no question of replacing one emotion by another, or of strengthening an emotion, but of discovering what the emotion is. The emotion is unchanged, but waiting to be identified like a telephone number one cannot remember. "8357. No, that's not it. 8557, 8457, no, it's on the tip of my tongue, wait a moment, I've got it, 8657. That's it."

The low-brow says: "I don't like poetry. It requires too much effort to understand and I'm afraid that if I learnt exactly what I feel, it would make me most uncomfortable." He is in the wrong, of course, but not so much in the wrong as the highbrow whose gifts make the effort to understand very little and who, having learned what he feels, is not at all uncomfortable, only interested.

NOW THROUGH NIGHT'S CARESSING GRIP

by W. H. AUDEN

Now through night's caressing grip
Earth and all her oceans slip,
Capes of China slide away
From her fingers into day,
And the Americas incline
Coasts toward her shadow line.
Now the ragged vagrants creep
Into crooked holes to sleep;
Just and unjust, worst and best,
Change their places as they rest;
Awkward lovers lie in fields
Where disdainful beauty yields;
While the splendid and the proud
Naked stand before the crowd,
And the losing gambler gains,
And the begger entertains.
May sleep's healing power extend
Through these hours to each friend;
Unpursued by hostile force
Traction engine bull or horse
Or revolting succubus;
Calmly till the morning break
Let them lie, then gently wake.

from LETTER TO LORD BYRON, Part IV

by W. H. AUDEN

The Great War had begun: but masters' scrutiny
  And fists of big boys were the war to us;
It was as harmless as the Indian Mutiny,
  A beating from the Head was dangerous.
  But once when half the form put down *Bellus*.
We were accused of that most deadly sin,
Wanting the Kaiser and the Huns to win.

The way in which we really were affected
   Was having such a varied lot to teach us.
The best were fighting, as the King expected,
   The remnant either elderly grey creatures,
   Or characters with most peculiar features.
Many were raggable, a few were waxy,
One had to leave abruptly in a taxi.

Surnames I must not write—O Reginald,
   You at least taught us that which fadeth not,
Our earliest visions of the great wide world;
   The beer and biscuits that your favourites got,
   Your tales revealing you a first-class shot,
Your riding breeks, your drama called *The Waves,*
A few of us will carry to our graves.

'Half a lunatic, half a knave.' No doubt
   A holy terror to the staff at tea;
A good headmaster must have soon found out
   Your moral character was all at sea;
   I question if you'd got a pass degree:
But little children bless your kind that knocks
Away the edifying stumbling blocks.

How can I thank you? For it only shows
   (Let me ride just this once my hobby-horse),
There're things a good headmaster never knows.
   There must be sober schoolmasters, of course,
   But what a prep school really puts across
Is knowledge of the world we'll soon be lost in:
To-day it's more like Dickens than Jane Austen.

I hate the modern trick, to tell the truth,
   Of straightening out the kinks in the young mind,
Our passion for the tender plant of youth,
   Our hatred for all weeds of any kind.
   Slogans are bad: the best that I can find
Is this: 'Let each child have that's in our care
As much neurosis as the child can bear.'

In this respect, at least, my bad old Adam is
   Pigheadedly against the general trend;
And has no use for all these new academies
   Where readers of the better weeklies send
   The child they probably did not intend,

Letter to Lord Byron

To paint a lampshade, marry, or keep pigeons,
Or make a study of the world religions.

Goddess of bossy underlings, Normality!
    What murders are committed in thy name!
Totalitarian is thy state Reality,
    Reeking of antiseptics and the shame
    Of faces that all look and feel the same.
Thy Muse is one unknown to classic histories,
The topping figure of the hockey mistress.

From thy dread Empire not a soul's exempted:
    More than the nursemaids pushing prams in parks,
By thee the intellectuals are tempted,
    O, to commit the treason of the clerks,
    Bewitched by thee to literary sharks.
But I must leave thee to thy office stool,
I must get on now to my public school.

Men had stopped throwing stones at one another,
    Butter and Father had come back again;
Gone were the holidays we spent with Mother
    In furnished rooms on mountain, moor, and fen;
    And gone those summer Sunday evenings, when
Along the seafronts fled a curious noise,
'Eternal Father,' sung by three young boys.

Nation spoke Peace, or said she did, with nation;
    The sexes tried their best to look the same;
Morals lost value during the inflation,
    The great Victorians kindly took the blame:
    Visions of Dada to the Post-War came,
Sitting in cafés, nostrils stuffed with bread,
Above the recent and the straight-laced dead.

I've said my say on public schools elsewhere:
    Romantic friendship, prefects, bullying,
I shall not deal with, c'est une autre affaire.
    Those who expect them, will get no such thing,
    It is the strictly relevant I sing.
Why should they grumble? They've the Greek Anthology,
And all the spicier bits of Anthropology.

[743]

Poetry

We all grow up the same way, more or less;
  Life is not known to give away her presents;
She only swops. The unself-consciousness
  That children share with animals and peasants
  Sinks in the 'stürm und drang' of Adolescence.
Like other boys I lost my taste for sweets,
Discovered sunsets, passion, God, and Keats.

I shall recall a single incident
  No more. I spoke of mining engineering
As the career on which my mind was bent,
  But for some time my fancies had been veering;
  Mirages of the future kept appearing;
Crazes had come and gone in short, sharp gales,
For motor-bikes, photography, and whales.

But indecision broke off with a clean-cut end
  One afternoon in March at half-past three
When walking in a ploughed field with a friend;
  Kicking a little stone, he turned to me
  And said, 'Tell me, do you write poetry?'
I never had, and said so, but I knew
That very moment what I wished to do.

Without a bridge passage this leads me straight
  Into the theme marked 'Oxford' on my score
From pages twenty-five to twenty-eight.
  Aesthetic trills I'd never heard before
  Rose from the strings, shrill poses from the cor;
The woodwind chattered like a pre-war Russian,
'Art' boomed the brass, and 'Life' thumped the percussion.

A raw provincial, my good taste was tardy,
  And Edward Thomas I as yet preferred;
I was still listening to Thomas Hardy
  Putting divinity about a bird;
  But Eliot spoke the still unspoken word;
For gasworks and dried tubers I forsook
The clock at Granchester, the English rook.

All youth's intolerant certainty was mine as
  I faced life in a double-breasted suit;
I bought and praised but did not read Aquinas,

At the *Criterion's* verdict I was mute,
　Though Arnold's I was ready to refute;
And through the quads dogmatic words rang clear,
'Good poetry is classic and austere.'

So much for Art. Of course Life had its passions too;
　The student's flesh like his imagination
Makes facts fit theories and has fashions too.
　We were the tail, a sort of poor relation
　To that debauched, eccentric generation
That grew up with their fathers at the War,
And made new glosses on the noun Amor.

Three years passed quickly while the Isis went
　Down to the sea for better or for worse;
Then to Berlin, not Carthage, I was sent
　With money from my parents in my purse,
　And ceased to see the world in terms of verse.
I met a chap called Layard and he fed
New doctrines into my receptive head.

Part came from Lane, and part from D. H. Lawrence;
　Gide, though I didn't know it then, gave part.
They taught me to express my deep abhorrence
　If I caught anyone preferring Art
　To Life and Love and being Pure-in-Heart.
I lived with crooks but seldom was molested;
The Pure-in-Heart can never be arrested.

He's gay; no bludgeonings of chance can spoil it,
　The Pure-in-Heart loves all men on a par,
And has no trouble with his private toilet;
　The Pure-in-Heart is never ill; catarrh
　Would be the yellow streak, the brush of tar;
Determined to be loving and forgiving,
I came back home to try and earn my living.

The only thing you never turned your hand to
　Was teaching English in a boarding school.
To-day it's a profession that seems grand to
　Those whose alternative's an office stool;
　For budding authors it's become the rule.
To many an unknown genius postmen bring
Typed notices from Rabbitarse and String.

[745]

The Head's M.A., a bishop is a patron,
    The assistant staff is highly qualified;
Health is the care of an experienced matron,
    The arts are taught by ladies from outside;
    The food is wholesome and the grounds are wide;
Their aim is training character and poise,
With special coaching for the backward boys.

I found the pay good and had time to spend it,   '
    Though others may not have the good luck I did:
For You I'd hesitate to recommend it;
    Several have told me that they can't abide it.
    Still, if one tends to get a bit one-sided,
It's pleasant as it's easy to secure
The hero worship of the immature.

More, it's a job, and jobs to-day are rare:
    All the ideals in the world won't feed us
Although they give our crimes a certain air.
    So barons of the press who know their readers
    Employ to write their more appalling leaders,
Instead of Satan's horned and hideous minions,
Clever young men of liberal opinions.

Which brings me up to nineteen-thirty-five;
    Six months of film work is another story
I can't tell now. But, here I am, alive
    Knowing the true source of that sense of glory
    That still surrounds the England of the Tory,
Come only to the rather tame conclusion
That no man by himself has life's solution.

MUSÉE DES BEAUX ARTS

by W. H. Auden

About suffering they were never wrong,
The Old Masters: how well they understood
Its human position; how it takes place
While someone else is eating or opening a window or just walking dully along;

How, when the aged are reverently, passionately waiting
For the miraculous birth, there always must be
Children who did not specially want it to happen, skating
On a pond at the edge of the wood:
They never forgot
That even the dreadful martyrdom must run its course
Anyhow in a corner, some untidy spot
Where the dogs go on with their doggy life and the torturer's horse
Scratches its innocent behind on a tree.

In Brueghel's *Icarus,* for instance: how everything turns away
Quite leisurely from the disaster; the ploughman may
Have heard the splash, the forsaken cry,
But for him it was not an important failure; the sun shone
As it had to on the white legs disappearing into the green
Water; and the expensive delicate ship that must have seen
Something amazing, a boy falling out of the sky,
Had somewhere to get to and sailed calmly on.

GET THERE IF YOU CAN

by W. H. Auden

Get there if you can and see the land you once were proud to own
Though the roads have almost vanished and the expresses never run:

Smokeless chimneys, damaged bridges, rotting wharves and choked canals,
Tramlines buckled, smashed trucks lying on their side across the rails;

Power-stations locked, deserted, since they drew the boiler fires;
Pylons fallen or subsiding, trailing dead high-tension wires;

Head-gears gaunt on grass-grown pit-banks, seams abandoned years ago;
Drop a stone and listen for its splash in flooded dark below.

Squeeze into the works through broken windows or through damp-sprung doors;
See the rotted shafting, see holes gaping in the upper floors;

Where the Sunday lads come talking motor bicycle and girl,
Smoking cigarettes in chains until their heads are in a whirl.

Far from there we spent the money, thinking we could well afford,
While they quietly undersold us with their cheaper trade abroad;

At the theatre, playing tennis, driving motor cars we had,
In our continental villas, mixing cocktails for a cad.

These were boon companions who devised the legends for our tombs,
Those who have betrayed us nicely while we took them to our rooms.

Newman, Ciddy, Plato, Fronny, Pascal, Bowdler, Baudelaire,
Doctor Frommer, Mrs. Allom, Freud, the Baron, and Flaubert.

Lured with their compelling logic, charmed with beauty of their verse,
With their loaded sideboards whispered 'Better join us, life is worse.'

Taught us at the annual camps arranged by the big business men
'Sunbathe, pretty till you're twenty. You shall be our servants then.'

Perfect pater. Marvellous mater. Knock the critic down who dares—
Very well, believe it, copy, till your hair is white as theirs.

Yours you say were parents to avoid, avoid then if you please
Do the reverse on all occasion till you catch the same disease.

When we asked the way to Heaven, these directed us ahead
To the padded room, the clinic and the hangman's little shed.

Intimate as war-time prisoners in an isolation camp,
Living month by month together, nervy, famished, lousy, damp.

On the sopping esplanade or from our dingy lodgings we
Stare out dully at the rain which falls for miles into the sea.

Lawrence, Blake and Homer Lane, once healers in our English land;
These are dead as iron for ever; these can never hold our hand.

Lawrence was brought down by smut-hounds, Blake went dotty as he sang,
Homer Lane was killed in action by the Twickenham Baptist gang.

Have things gone too far already? Are we done for? Must we wait
Hearing doom's approaching footsteps regular down miles of straight;

Run the whole night through in gumboots, stumble on and gasp for breath,
Terrors drawing close and closer, winter landscape, fox's death;

Or, in friendly fireside circle, sit and listen for the crash
Meaning that the mob has realized something's up, and start to smash;

Engine-drivers with their oil-cans, factory girls in overalls
Blowing sky-high monster stores, destroying intellectuals?

Hope and fear are neck and neck: which is it near the course's end
Crashes, having lost his nerve; is overtaken on the bend?

Shut up talking, charming in the best suits to be had in town,
Lecturing on navigation while the ship is going down.

Drop those priggish ways for ever, stop behaving like a stone:
Throw the bath-chairs right away, and learn to leave ourselves alone.

If we really want to live, we'd better start at once to try;
If we don't, it doesn't matter, but we'd better start to die.

LAW LIKE LOVE

by W. H. AUDEN

Law, say the gardeners, is the sun,
Law is the one
All gardeners obey
Tomorrow, yesterday, today.

Law is the wisdom of the old
The impotent grandfathers shrilly scold;
The grandchildren put out a treble tongue,
Law is the senses of the young.

Law, says the priest with a priestly look,
Expounding to an unpriestly people,
Law is the words in my priestly book,
Law is my pulpit and my steeple.

Law, says the judge as he looks down his
  nose,
Speaking clearly and most severely,
Law is as I've told you before,

Law is as you know I suppose,
Law is but let me explain it once more,
Law is the Law.

Yet law-abiding scholars write;
Law is neither wrong nor right,
Law is only crimes
Punished by places and by times,
Law is the clothes men wear
Anytime, anywhere,
Law is Good-morning and Good-night.

Others say, Law is our Fate;
Others say, Law is our State;
Others say, others say
Law is no more
Law has gone away.

And always the loud angry crowd
Very angry and very loud

Law is We,
And always the soft idiot softly Me.

If we, dear, know we know no more
Than they about the law,
If I no more than you
Know what we should and should not do
Except that all agree
Gladly or miserably
That the law is
And that all know this,
If therefore thinking it absurd
To identify Law with some other word.
Unlike so many men
I cannot say Law is again,

No more than they can we suppress
The universal wish to guess
Or slip out of our own position
Into an unconcerned condition.
Although I can at least confine
Your vanity and mine
To stating timidly
A timid similarity
We shall boast anyway:
Like love I say.

Like love we don't know where or why
Like love we can't compel or fly
Like love we often weep
Like love we seldom keep.

SEPTEMBER 1, 1939

by W. H. Auden

I sit in one of the dives
On Fifty-second Street
Uncertain and afraid
As the clever hopes expire
Of a low dishonest decade:
Waves of anger and fear
Circulate over the bright
And darkened lands of the earth,
Obsessing our private lives;
The unmentionable odour of death
Offends the September night.

Accurate scholarship can
Unearth the whole offence
From Luther until now
That has driven a culture mad,
Find what occurred at Linz,
What huge imago made
A psychopathic god:
I and the public know
What all schoolchildren learn,
Those to whom evil is done
Do evil in return.

Exiled Thucydides knew
All that a speech can say
About Democracy,
And what dictators do,
The elderly rubbish they talk
To an apathetic grave;
Analysed all in his book,
The enlightenment driven away,
The habit-forming pain,
Mismanagement and grief:
We must suffer them all again.

Into this neutral air
Where blind skyscrapers use
Their full height to proclaim
The strength of Collective Man,
Each language pours its vain
Competitive excuse:
But who can live for long
In an euphoric dream;
Out of the mirror they stare,
Imperialism's face
And the international wrong.

Faces along the bar
Cling to their average day:
The lights must never go out,
The music must always play,
All the conventions conspire
To make this fort assume
The furniture of home;
Lest we should see where we are,
Lost in a haunted wood,
Children afraid of the night
Who have never been happy or good.

The windiest militant trash
Important Persons shout
Is not so crude as our wish:
What mad Nijinsky wrote
About Diaghilev
Is true of the normal heart;
For the error bred in the bone
Of each woman and each man
Craves what it cannot have,
Not universal love
But to be loved alone.

From the conservative dark
Into the ethical life
The dense commuters come,
Repeating their morning vow;
"I *will* be true to the wife,
I'll concentrate more on my work,"
And helpless governors wake
To resume their compulsory game:
Who can release them now,
Who can reach the deaf,
Who can speak for the dumb?

Defenceless under the night
Our world in stupor lies;
Yet, dotted everywhere,
Ironic points of light
Flash out wherever the Just
Exchange their messages:
May I, composed like them
Of Eros and of dust,
Beleaguered by the same
Negation and despair,
Show an affirming flame.

REFUGEE BLUES

by W. H. Auden

Say this city has ten million souls,
Some are living in mansions, some are living in holes:
Yet there's no place for us, my dear, yet there's no place for us.

Once we had a country and we thought it fair,
Look in the atlas and you'll find it there:
We cannot go there now, my dear, we cannot go there now.

In the village churchyard there grows an old yew,
Every spring it blossoms anew:
Old passports can't do that, my dear, old passports can't do that.

The consul banged the table and said:
"If you've got no passport you're officially dead":
But we are still alive, my dear, but we are still alive.

Went to a committee; they offered me a chair;
Asked me politely to return next year:
But where shall we go today, my dear, but where shall we go today?

Came to a public meeting; the speaker got up and said:
"If we let them in, they will steal our daily bread";
He was talking of you and me, my dear, he was talking of you and me.

Thought I heard the thunder rumbling in the sky;
It was Hitler over Europe, saying: "They must die";
O we were in his mind, my dear, O we were in his mind.

Saw a poodle in a jacket fastened with a pin,
Saw a door opened and a cat let in:
But they weren't German Jews, my dear, but they weren't German Jews.

Went down the harbour and stood upon the quay,
Saw the fish swimming as if they were free:
Only ten feet away, my dear, only ten feet away.

Walked through a wood, saw the birds in the trees;
They had no politicians and sang at their ease:
They weren't the human race, my dear, they weren't the human race.

Dreamed I saw a building with a thousand floors,
A thousand windows and a thousand doors;
Not one of them was ours, my dear, not one of them was ours.

Stood on a great plain in the falling snow;
Ten thousand soldiers marched to and fro:
Looking for you and me, my dear, looking for you and me.

CASINO

by W. H. Auden

Only the hands are living; to the wheel attracted,
Are moved as deer trek desperately towards a creek
  Through the dust and scrub of the desert, or gently
  As sunflowers turn to the light.

And, as the night takes up the cries of feverish children,
The cravings of lions in dens, the loves of dons,
  Gathers them all and remains the night, the
  Great room is full of their prayers

To the last feast of isolation self-invited
They flock, and in the rite of disbelief are joined;
  From numbers all their stars are recreated,
  The enchanted, the world, the sad.

Without, the rivers flow among the wholly living,
Quite near their trysts; and the mountains part them; and the bird
  Deep in the greens and moistures of summer
  Sings towards their work.

But here no nymph comes naked to the youngest shepherd;
The fountain is deserted; the laurel will not grow;
  The labyrinth is safe but endless, and broken
  Is Ariadne's thread.

As deeper in these hands is grooved their fortune: "Lucky
Were few, and it is possible that none was loved;
  And what was godlike in this generation
  Was never to be born."

PRIME

by W. H. AUDEN

Simultaneously, as soundlessly,
  Spontaneously, suddenly
As, at the vaunt of the dawn, the kind
  Gates of the body fly open
To its world beyond, the gates of the mind,
  The horn gate and the ivory gate
Swing to, swing shut, instantaneously
  Quell the nocturnal rummage
Of its rebellious fronde, ill-favored,
  Ill-natured and second-rate,
Disenfranchised, widowed and orphaned
  By an historical mistake:
Recalled from the shades to be a seeing being,
  From absence to be on display,
Without a name or history I wake
  Between my body and the day.

Holy this moment, wholly in the right,
  As, in complete obedience
To the light's laconic outcry, next
  As a sheet, near as a wall,
Out there as a mountain's poise of stone,
  The world is present, about,
And I know that I am, here, not alone
  But with a world, and rejoice
Unvexed, for the will has still to claim
  This adjacent arm as my own.
The memory to name me, resume
  Its routine of praise and blame,
And smiling to me is this instant while
  Still the day is intact and I
The Adam sinless in our beginning,
  Adam still previous to any act.

I draw breath; that is of course to wish
  No matter what to be wise
To be different to die and the cost
  No matter how is Paradise

Lost of course and myself owing a death:
  The eager ridge, the steady sea,
The flat roofs of the fishing village
  Still asleep in its bunny,
Though as fresh and sunny still are not friends
  But things to hand, this ready flesh
No honest equal but my accomplice now
  My assassin to be and my name
Stands for my historical share of care
  For a lying self-made city,
Afraid of our living task, the dying
  Which the coming day will ask.

UNDER WHICH LYRE

A Reactionary Tract for the Times
(Phi Beta Kappa Poem. Harvard. 1946)

by W. H. AUDEN

Ares at last has quit the field,
The bloodstains on the bushes yield
    To seeping showers,
And in their convalescent state
The fractured towns associate
    With summer flowers.

Encamped upon the college plain
Raw veterans already train
    As freshman forces;
Instructors with sarcastic tongue
Shepherd the battle-weary young
    Through basic courses.

Among bewildering appliances
For mastering the arts and sciences
    They stroll or run,
And nerves that never flinched at slaughter
Are shot to pieces by the shorter
    Poems of Donne.

Professors back from secret missions
Resume their proper eruditions,
    Though some regret it;
They liked their dictaphones a lot,
They met some big wheels, and do not
    Let you forget it.

But Zeus' inscrutable decree
Permits the will-to-disagree
    To be pandemic,
Ordains that vaudeville shall preach
And every commencement speech
    Be a polemic.

Let Ares doze, that other war
Is instantly declared once more
    'Twixt those who follow
Precocious Hermes all the way
And those who without qualms obey
    Pompous Apollo.

Brutal like all Olympic games,
Though fought with smiles and Christian names
    And less dramatic,
This dialectic strife between
The civil gods is just as mean,
    And more fanatic.

What high immortals do in mirth
Is life and death on Middle Earth;
    Their a-historic
Antipathy forever gripes
All ages and somatic types,
    The sophomoric

Who face the future's darkest hints
With giggles or with prairie squints
    As stout as Cortez,
And those who like myself turn pale
As we approach with ragged sail
    The fattening forties.

The sons of Hermes love to play,
And only do their best when they
    Are told they oughtn't;

Under Which Lyre

Apollo's children never shrink
From boring jobs but have to think
    Their work important.

Related by antithesis,
A compromise between us is
    Impossible;
Respect perhaps but friendship never:
Falstaff the fool confronts forever
    The prig Prince Hal.

If he would leave the self alone,
Apollo's welcome to the throne,
    Fasces and falcons;
He loves to rule, has always done it;
The earth would soon, did Hermes run it,
    Be like the Balkans.

But jealous of our god of dreams,
His common-sense in secret schemes
    To rule the heart;
Unable to invent the lyre,
Creates with simulated fire
    Official art.

And when he occupies a college,
Truth is replaced by Useful Knowledge;
    He pays particular
Attention to Commercial Thought,
Public Relations, Hygiene, Sport,
    In his curricula

Athletic, extrovert and crude,
For him, to work in solitude
    Is the offence,
The goal a populous Nirvana:
His shield bears this device: *Mens sana*
    Qui mal y pense.

Today his arms, we must confess,
From Right to Left have met success,
    His banners wave
From Yale to Princeton, and the news
From Broadway to the Book Reviews
    Is very grave.

His radio Homers all day long
In over-Whitmanated song
    That does not scan,
With adjectives laid end to end,
Extol the doughnut and commend
    The Common Man.

His, too, each homely lyric thing
On sport or spousal love or spring
    Or dogs or dusters,
Invented by some court-house bard
For recitation by the yard
    In filibusters.

To him ascend the prize orations
And sets of fugal variations
    On some folk-ballad,
While dietitians sacrifice
A glass of prune-juice or a nice
    Marsh-mallow salad.

Charged with his compound of sensational
Sex plus some undenominational
    Religious matter,
Enormous novels by co-eds
Rain down on our defenceless heads
    Till our teeth chatter.

In fake Hermetic uniforms
Behind our battle-line, in swarms
    That keep alighting,
His existentialists declare
That they are in complete despair,
    Yet go on writing.

No matter; He shall be defied;
White Aphrodite is on our side:
    What though his threat
To organize us grow more critical?
Zeus willing, we, the unpolitical,
    Shall beat him yet.

Lone scholars, sniping from the walls
Of learned periodicals,
    Our facts defend,

Under Which Lyre

Our intellectual marines,
Landing in little magazines
    Capture a trend.

By night our student Underground
At cocktail parties whisper round
    From ear to ear;
Fat figures in the public eye
Collapse next morning, ambushed by
    Some witty sneer.

In our morale must lie our strength:
So, that we may behold at length
    Routed Apollo's
Battalions melt away like fog,
Keep well the Hermetic Decalogue,
    Which runs as follows:—

Thou shalt not do as the dean pleases,
Thou shalt not write thy doctor's thesis
    On education,
Thou shalt not worship projects nor
Shalt thou or thine bow down before
    Administration.

Thou shalt not answer questionnaires
Or quizzes upon World-Affairs,
    Nor with compliance
Take any test. Thou shalt not sit
With statisticians nor commit
    A social science.

Thou shalt not be on friendly terms
With guys in advertising firms,
    Nor speak with such
As read the Bible for its prose,
Nor, above all, make love to those
    Who wash too much.

Thou shalt not live within thy means
Nor on plain water and raw greens.
    If thou must choose
Between the chances, choose the odd;
Read *The New Yorker*, trust in God;
    And take short views.

from SELECTED WRITINGS

by DYLAN THOMAS

Poetry is the rhythmic, inevitably narrative, movement from an over-clothed blindness to a naked vision ... the physical and mental task of constructing a formally watertight compartment of words. ... Poetry must drag further into the clear nakedness of light more even of the hidden causes than Freud could realize.

IN MY CRAFT OR SULLEN ART

by DYLAN THOMAS

In my craft or sullen art
Exercised in the still night
When only the moon rages
And the lovers lie abed
With all their griefs in their arms,
I labour by singing light
Not for ambition or bread
Or the strut and trade of charms
On the ivory stages
But for the common wages

Of their most secret heart.
Not for the proud man apart
From the raging moon I write
On these spindrift pages
Not for the towering dead
With their nightingales and psalms
But for the lovers, their arms
Round the griefs of the ages,
Who pay no praise or wages
Nor heed my craft or art.

"THE HAND THAT SIGNED THE PAPER FELLED A CITY"

by DYLAN THOMAS

The hand that signed the paper felled a city;
Five sovereign fingers taxed the breath,
Doubled the globe of dead and halved a country;
These five kings did a king to death.

The mighty hand leads to a sloping shoulder,
The finger joints are cramped with chalk;
A goose's quill has put an end to murder
That put an end to talk.

The hand that signed the treaty bred a fever,
And famine grew, and locusts came;
Great is the hand that holds dominion over
Man by a scribbled name.

The five kings count the dead but do not soften
The crusted wound nor pat the brow;
A hand rules pity as a hand rules heaven;
Hands have no tears to flow.

POEM IN OCTOBER

by DYLAN THOMAS

It was my thirtieth year to heaven
Woke to my hearing from harbour and neighbour wood
  And the mussel pooled and the heron
     Priested shore
    The morning beckon
With water praying and call of seagull and rook
And the knock of sailing boats on the net webbed wall
    Myself to set foot
     That second
  In the still sleeping town and set forth.

  My birthday began with the water-
Birds and the birds of the winged trees flying my name
  Above the farms and the white horses
     And I rose
    In rainy autumn
And walked abroad in a shower of all my days.
High tide and the heron dived when I took the road
    Over the border
     And the gates
Of the town closed as the town awoke.

  A springful of larks in a rolling
Cloud and the roadside bushes brimming with whistling
  Blackbirds and the sun of October
     Summery
    On the hill's shoulder,
Here were fond climates and sweet singers suddenly
Come in the morning where I wandered and listened
    To the rain wringing
     Wind blow cold
  In the wood faraway under me.

  Pale rain over the dwindling harbour
And over the sea wet church the size of a snail
  With its horns through mist, and the castle
     Brown as owls,
    But all the gardens
Of spring and summer were blooming in the tall tales

Beyond the border and under the lark full cloud.
    There could I marvel
       My birthday
  Away but the weather turned around.

    It turned away from the blithe country
And down the other air and the blue altered sky
    Streamed again a wonder of summer
       With apples
      Pears and red currants
And I saw in the turning so clearly a child's
Forgotten mornings when he walked with his mother
      Through the parables
       Of sun light
    And the legends of the green chapels

    And the twice told fields of infancy
That his tears burned my cheeks and his heart moved in mine.
    These were the woods the river and sea
       Where a boy
     In the listening
Summertime of the dead whispered the truth of his joy
To the trees and the stones and the fish in the tide.
     And the mystery
      Sang alive
  Still in the water and singing birds.

    And there could I marvel my birthday
Away but the weather turned around. And the true
    Joy of the long dead child sang burning
      In the sun.
    It was my thirtieth
Year to heaven stood there then in the summer noon
Though the town below lay leaved with October blood.
    O may my heart's truth
     Still be sung
  On this high hill in a year's turning.

A WINTER'S TALE

by DYLAN THOMAS

It is a winter's tale
That the snow blind twilight ferries over the lakes
And floating fields from the farm in the cup of the vales,
Gliding windless through the hand folded flakes,
The pale breath of cattle at the stealthy sail,

And the stars falling cold,
And the smell of hay in the snow, and the far owl
Warning among the folds, and the frozen hold
Flocked with the sheep white smoke of the farm house cowl
In the river wended vales where the tale was told.

Once when the world turned old
On a star of faith pure as the drifting bread,
As the food and flames of the snow, a man unrolled
The scrolls of fire that burned in his heart and head,
Torn and alone in a farm house in a fold

Of fields. And burning then
In his firelit island ringed by the winged snow
And the dung hills white as wool and the hen
Roosts sleeping chill till the flame of the cock crow
Combs through the mantled yards and the morning men

Stumble out with their spades,
The cattle stirring, the mousing cat stepping shy,
The puffed birds hopping and hunting, the milk maids
Gentle in their clogs over the fallen sky,
And all the woken farm at its white trades,

He knelt, he wept, he prayed,
By the spit and the black pot in the log bright light
And the cup and the cut bread in the dancing shade,
In the muffled house, in the quick of night,
At the point of love, forsaken and afraid.

He knelt on the cold stones,
He wept from the crest of grief, he prayed to the veiled sky
May his hunger go howling on bare white bones

Past the statues of the stables and the sky roofed sties
And the duck pond glass and the blinding byres alone

  Into the home of prayers
And fires where he should prowl down the cloud
Of his snow blind love and rush in the white lairs.
His naked need struck him howling and bowed
Though no sound flowed down the hand folded air

  But only the wind strung
Hunger of birds in the fields of the bread of water, tossed
In high corn and the harvest melting on their tongues.
And his nameless need bound him burning and lost
When cold as snow he should run the wended vales among

  The rivers mouthed in night,
And drown in the drifts of his need, and lie curled caught
In the always desiring center of the white
Inhuman cradle and the bride bed forever sought
By the believer lost and the hurled outcast of light.

  Deliver him, he cried,
By losing him all in love, and cast his need
Alone and naked in the engulfing bride,
Never to flourish in the fields of the white seed
Or flower under the time dying flesh astride.

  Listen. The minstrels sing
In the departed villages. The nightingale,
Dust in the buried wood, flies on the grains of her wings
And spells on the winds of the dead his winter's tale.
The voice of the dust of water from the withered spring

  Is telling. The wizened
Stream with bells and baying water bounds. The dew rings
On the gristed leaves and the long gone glistening
Parish of snow. The carved mouths in the rock are wind swept strings.
Time sings through the intricately dead snow drop. Listen.

  It was a hand or sound
In the long ago land that glided the dark door wide
And there outside on the bread of the ground
A she bird rose and rayed like a burning bride.
A she bird dawned, and her breast with snow and scarlet downed.

A Winter's Tale

Look. And the dancers move
On the departed, snow bushed green, wanton in moon light
As a dust of pigeons. Exulting, the grave hooved
Horses, centaur dead, turn and tread the drenched white
Paddocks in the farms of birds. The dead oak walks for love.

The carved limbs in the rock
Leap, as to trumpets. Calligraphy of the old
Leaves is dancing. Lines of age on the stones weave in a flock.
And the harp shaped voice of the water's dust plucks in a fold
Of fields. For love, the long ago she bird rises. Look.

And the wild wings were raised
Above her folded head, and the soft feathered voice
Was flying through the house as though the she bird praised
And all the elements of the slow fall rejoiced
That a man knelt alone in the cup of the vales,

In the mantle and calm,
By the spit and the black pot in the log bright light.
And the sky of birds in the plumed voice charmed
Him up and he ran like a wind after the kindling flight
Past the blind barns and byres of the windless farm.

In the poles of the year
When black birds died like priests in the cloaked hedge row
And over the cloth of counties the far hills rode near,
Under the one leaved trees ran a scarecrow of snow
And fast through the drifts of the thickets antlered like deer,

Rags and prayers down the knee-
Deep hillocks and loud on the numbed lakes,
All night lost and long wading in the wake of the she-
Bird through the times and lands and tribes of the slow flakes.
Listen and look where she sails the goose plucked sea,

The sky, the bird, the bride,
The cloud, the need, the planted stars, the joy beyond
The fields of seed and the time dying flesh astride,
The heavens, the heaven, the grave, the burning font.
In the far ago land the door of his death glided wide,

And the bird descended.
On a bread white hill over the cupped farm

And the lakes and floating fields and the river wended
Vales where he prayed to come to the last harm
And the home of prayers and fires, the tale ended.

   The dancing perishes
On the white, no longer growing green, and, minstrel dead,
The singing breaks in the snow shoed villages of wishes
That once cut the figures of birds on the deep bread
And over the glazed lakes skated the shapes of fishes

   Flying. The rite is shorn
Of nightingale and centaur dead horse. The springs wither
Back. Lines of age sleep on the stones till trumpeting dawn.
Exultation lies down. Time buries the spring weather
That belled and bounded with the fossil and the dew reborn.

   For the bird lay bedded
In a choir of wings, as though she slept or died,
And the wings glided wide and he was hymned and wedded,
And through the thighs of the engulfing bride,
The woman breasted and the heaven headed

   Bird, he was brought low
Burning in the bride bed of love, in the whirl-
Pool at the wanting center, in the folds
Of paradise, in the spun bud of the world.
And she rose with him flowering in her melting snow.

PART VI · PROSE

URING THE LAST THIRTY-FIVE YEARS mankind has suffered a first
great war, a futile peace, a world-wide depression, mass unemployment, the fearful rise of political nationalisms, a second even greater
war, and a second even more doubtful peace. These were gigantic events, in a
troubled century. Before them the individual has often seemed to dwindle into
insignificance. Lonely and disillusioned, he has often felt helpless, as if his-
torically lost, and full of self-distrust. The essays in this section are intended
to present the human problems that arise in such a time, to explore causes and
effects, and to suggest ways out, even if only paths and not highways.

William Faulkner's recent remarks on "the old verities and truths of the
heart" would have sounded strange and irrelevant twenty years ago, but today
his words may well set us looking for a sense of the individual and society, as
earlier expressed by such men as Jefferson and Macaulay, a sense of the sort
we have lost and may wish again to possess. But Mitchell shows us what an
anomaly today is the once rugged individualist, of whole character and self-
contained. The solitude of Emerson and the wide-flung embrace of Whitman
only emphasize the extremes of this problem in a century during which, as
Turner insists, a simple geographical fact was changing radically the very terms
of the problem.

Though the difficulty of achieving, or even maintaining, freedom within
modern society was not confined to America, it appeared most dramatically
here, where a people and a nation came into being only after great social
and scientific changes in the Western World had made the new society possible.
The debate over causes and solutions sent writers like Adams and Soule deep
into the nature of change and tradition themselves. As White suggests that we
all are fond of the old, if known, and Sokolsky calls for a brake on change,
Beard raises the question whether anything has really changed and offers some
hope for believing that the old human forces are still strong, working under
new conditions.

World War II accentuated the existing problems for individual and society
while bringing men and nations together as never before to assert their desire
for freedom and to work for common goals. It solved few of the old problems
for long: *The Races of Mankind* indicates one of the oldest even as it per-

[767]

suades us that we ought to be able to solve it. But there was still war, though William James had earlier presented a cogent plea against it, and the war had become unlike any other men had seen, for it brought the atomic bomb. The methods of modern science, described by Barnett, had led, when pressed into military service, to the test over New Mexico and the bomber over Nagasaki. The implications for men and history, for science and civilization, are discussed by attackers and defenders in the succeeding essays.

The last three selections suggest that human belief is central to all the concerns of the writers in this section. Arnold's poem is the most famous of nineteenth-century statements of doubt, the terms of which Lippmann makes clear for our time. Forster, as a thinking wise man, represents the honesty and self-trust men must regain if they are to deserve any freedom within their society or earn the right to solve their own problems.

REMARKS UPON RECEIVING THE NOBEL PRIZE

by WILLIAM FAULKNER

I FEEL that this award was not made to me as a man but to my work—a life's work in the agony and sweat of the human spirit, not for glory and least of all for profit, but to create out of the materials of the human spirit something which did not exist before. So this award is only mine in trust. It will not be difficult to find a dedication for the money part of it commensurate with the purpose and significance of its origin. But I would like to do the same with the acclaim too, by using this moment as a pinnacle from which I might be listened to by the young men and women already dedicated to the same anguish and travail, among whom is already that one who will some day stand here where I am standing.

Our tragedy today is a general and universal physical fear so long sustained by now that we can even bear it. There are no longer problems of the spirit. There is only the question: when will I be blown up? Because of this, the young man or woman writing today has forgotten the problems of the human heart in conflict with itself which alone can make good writing because only that is worth writing about, worth the agony and the sweat.

He must learn them again. He must teach himself that the basest of all things is to be afraid; and, teaching himself that, forget it forever, leaving no room in his workshop for anything but the old verities and truths of the heart, the old universal truths lacking which any story is ephemeral and doomed—love and honor and pity and pride and compassion and sacrifice. Until he does so he labors under a curse. He writes not of love but of lust, of defeats in which nobody loses anything of value, of victories without hope and worst of all without pity or compassion. His griefs grieve on no universal bones, leaving no scars. He writes not of the heart but of the glands.

Until he relearns these things he will write as though he stood among and watched the end of man. I decline to accept the end of man. It is easy enough to say that man is immortal simply because he will endure; that when the last ding-dong of doom has clanged and faded from the last worthless rock hanging tideless in the last red and dying evening, that even then there will still be one more sound: that of his puny inexhaustible voice, still talking. I refuse to accept this. I believe that man will not merely endure: he will prevail. He is immortal, not because he alone among creatures has an inexhaustible voice, but because he has a soul, a spirit capable of compassion and sacrifice and endurance. The poet's, the writer's, duty is to write about these things. It is his privilege to help man endure by lifting his heart, by reminding him of the courage and honor and hope and pride and compassion and pity and sacrifice which have been the glory of his past. The poet's voice need not merely be the record of man, it can be one of the props, the pillars to help him endure and prevail.

William Faulkner, Nobel Prize Speech. Used with the permission of Random House, Inc.

ON NATURAL ARISTOCRACY

by THOMAS JEFFERSON

MONTICELLO, *October 28, 1813.*

[*To John Adams*]

. . . I agree with you that there is a natural aristocracy among men. The grounds of this are virtue and talents. Formerly, bodily powers gave place among the aristoi. But since the invention of gunpowder has armed the weak as well as the strong with missile death, bodily strength, like beauty, good humor, politeness and other accomplishments, has become but an auxiliary ground for distinction. There is also an artificial aristocracy, founded on wealth and birth, without either virtue or talents; for with these it would belong to the first class. The natural aristocracy I consider as the most precious gift of nature, for the instruction, the trusts, and government of society. And indeed, it would have been inconsistent in creation to have formed man for the social state, and not to have provided virtue and wisdom enough to manage the concerns of the society. May we not even say, that that form of government is the best, which provides the most effectually for a pure selection of these natural aristoi into the offices of government? The artificial aristocracy is a mischievous ingredient in government, and provision should be made to prevent its ascendancy. On the question, what is the best provision, you and I differ; but we differ as rational friends, using the free exercise of our own reason, and mutually indulging its errors. You think it best to put the pseudo-aristoi into a separate chamber of legislation, where they may be hindered from doing mischief by their co-ordinate branches, and where, also, they may be a protection to wealth against the Agrarian and plundering enterprises of the majority of the people. I think that to give them power in order to prevent them from doing mischief, is arming them for it, and increasing instead of remedying the evil. For if the co-ordinate branches can arrest their action, so may they that of the co-ordinates. Mischief may be done negatively as well as positively. Of this, a cabal in the Senate of the United States has furnished many proofs. Nor do I believe them necessary to protect the wealthy; because enough of these will find their way into every branch of the legislation, to protect themselves. From fifteen to twenty legislatures of our own, in action for thirty years past, have proved that no fears of an equalization of property are to be apprehended from them. I think the best remedy is exactly that provided by all our constitutions, to leave to the citizens the free election and separation of the aristoi from the pseudo-aristoi, of the wheat from the chaff. In general they will elect the really good and wise. In some instances, wealth may corrupt, and birth blind them; but not in sufficient degree to endanger the society.

It is probable that our difference of opinion may, in some measure, be produced by a difference of character in those among whom we live. From what I have seen of Massachusetts and Connecticut myself, and still more from what I have heard, and the character given of the former by yourself, who know them so much better, there seems to be in those two States a traditionary reverence for certain families, which has rendered the offices of the government nearly hereditary in those families. I presume that from an early period of your history, members of those families happening to possess virtue and talents, have honestly exercised them for the good of the people, and by their services have endeared their names to them. In coupling Connecticut with you, I mean it politically only, not morally. For having made the Bible the common law of their land, they seemed to have modeled their morality on the story of Jacob and Laban. But although this hereditary succession to office with you, may, in some degree, be founded in real family merit, yet in a much higher degree, it has proceeded from your strict alliance of Church and State. These families are canonized in the eyes of the people on common principles, "you tickle me, and I will tickle you." In Virginia we have nothing of this. Our clergy, before the revolution, having been secured against rivalship by fixed salaries, did not give themselves the trouble of acquiring influence over the people. Of wealth, there were great accumulations in particular families, handed down from generation to generation, under the English law of entails. But the only object of ambition for the wealthy was a seat in the King's Council. All their court then was paid to the crown and its creatures; and they Philipised in all collisions between the King and the people. Hence they were unpopular; and that unpopularity continues attached to their names. A Randolph, a Carter, or a Burwell must have great personal superiority over a common competitor to be elected by the people even at this day. At the first session of our legislature after the Declaration of Independence, we passed a law abolishing entails. And this was followed by one abolishing the privilege of primogeniture, and dividing the lands of intestates equally among all their children, or other representatives. These laws, drawn by myself, laid the ax to the foot of pseudo-aristocracy. And had another which I prepared been adopted by the legislature, our work would have been complete. It was a bill for the more general diffusion of learning. This proposed to divide every county into wards of five or six miles square, like your townships; to establish in each ward a free school for reading, writing and common arithmetic; to provide for the annual selection of the best subjects from these schools, who might receive, at the public expense, a higher degree of education at a district school; and from these district schools to select a certain number of the most promising subjects, to be completed at an University, where all the useful sciences should be taught. Worth and genius would thus have been sought out from every condition of life, and completely prepared by education for defeating the competition of wealth and birth for public trusts. My proposition had, for a further object, to impart to these wards those portions of self-government for which they are best qualified, by confiding to them the care of their poor, their roads, police, elections, the nomination of jurors, administration of justice in small cases, elementary exercises of militia; in short, to have made them little republics, with a warden at the head of each, for all those concerns which, being under their eye, they would better manage than the larger republics of the county or State. A general call of ward meetings by their wardens on the same day through the State, would at any time produce the genuine sense of the people on any required point, and would enable the State to act in mass, as your people have so often done, and with so much effect by their town meetings. The law for religious freedom, which made a part of this system, having put down the aristocracy of the clergy, and restored to the citizen the freedom of the mind, and those of entails and descents nurturing an equality of condition among them, this on education would have raised the mass of the people to the high ground of moral respectability necessary to their own safety, and to orderly government; and would have completed the great object of qualifying them to select the veritable aristoi, for the trusts of government, to the exclusion of the pseudalists; and the same Theognis who has furnished the epigraphs of your two letters, assures us that "Ουδεμιαν πω, Κυρν', αγαθοι πολιν ωλεσαν ανδρες." [Not any state, Curnus, have good men yet destroyed.] Although this law has not yet been acted on but in a small and inefficient degree, it is still considered as before the legislature, with other bills of the revised code, not yet taken up, and I have great hope that some patriotic spirit will, at a favorable moment, call it up, and make it the key-stone of the arch of our government.

With respect to aristocracy, we should further consider, that before the establishment of the American States, nothing was known to history but the man of the old world, crowded within limits either small or overcharged, and steeped in the vices which that situation generates. A government adapted to such men would be one thing; but a very different one, that for the man of these States. Here everyone may have land to labor for himself, if he chooses; or, preferring the exercise of any other industry, may exact for it such compensation as not only to afford a comfortable subsistence, but wherewith to provide for a cessation from labor in old age. Everyone, by his property, or by his satisfactory situation, is interested in the support of law and order. And such men may safely and advantageously reserve to themselves a wholesome control over their public affairs, and a degree of freedom, which, in the hands of the *canaille* of the cities of Europe, would be instantly perverted to the demolition and destruction of everything public and private. The history of the last twenty-five years of France, and of the last forty years in America, nay of its last two hundred years, proves the truth of both parts of this observation.

But even in Europe a change has sensibly taken place in the mind of man. Science had liberated the ideas of those who read and reflect, and the American example had kindled feelings of right in the people. An insurrection has consequently begun, of science, talents, and courage, against rank and birth, which have fallen into contempt. It has failed in its first effort, because the mobs of the cities, the instrument used for its accomplishment, debased by ignorance, poverty and vice, could not be restrained to rational action. But the world will recover from the panic of this first catastrophe. Science is progressive, and talents and enterprise on the alert. Resort may be had to the people of the country, a more governable power from their principles and subordination; and rank, and birth, and tinsel-aristocracy will finally shrink into insignificance, even there. This, however, we have no right to meddle with. It suffices for us, if the moral and physical condition of our own citizens qualifies them to select the able and good for the direction of their government, with a recurrence of elections at such short periods as will enable them to displace an unfaithful servant, before the mischief he meditates may be irremediable.

I have thus stated my opinion on a point on which we differ, not with a view to controversy, for we are both too old to change opinions which are the result of a long life of inquiry and reflection; but on the suggestions of a former letter of yours, that we ought not to die before we have explained ourselves to each other. We acted in perfect harmony, through a long and perilous contest for our liberty and independence. A constitution has been acquired, which, though neither of us thinks perfect, yet both consider as competent to render our fellow citizens the happiest and the securest on whom the sun has ever shone. If we do not think exactly alike as to its imperfections, it matters little to our country, which, after devoting to it long lives of disinterested labor, we have delivered over to our successors in life, who will be able to take care of it and of themselves.

Of the pamphlet on aristocracy which has been sent to you, or who may be its author, I have heard nothing but through your letter. If the person you suspect, it may be known from the quaint, mystical, and hyperbolical ideas, involved in affected, new-fangled and pedantic terms which stamp his writings. Whatever it be, I hope your quiet is not to be affected at this day by the rudeness or intemperance of scribblers; but that you may continue in tranquillity to live and to rejoice in the prosperity of our country, until it shall be your own wish to take your seat among the aristoi who have gone before you. Ever and affectionately yours.

LETTER TO A CORRESPONDENT IN AMERICA

by Thomas Babington Macaulay

Sir: The four volumes of the *Colonial History of New York* reached me safely. I assure you that I shall value them highly. They contain much to interest an English as well as an American reader. Pray, accept my thanks, and convey them to the Regents of the University.

You are surprised to learn that I have not a high opinion of Mr. Jefferson, and I am surprised at your surprise. I am certain that I never wrote a line, and that I never in Parliament, in conversation or even on the hustings—a place where it is the fashion to court the populace—uttered a word indicating an opinion that the supreme authority in a State ought to be entrusted to the majority of citizens, in other words, to the poorest and most ignorant part of society. I have long been convinced that institutions purely democratic must, sooner or later, destroy liberty or civilization, or both.

In Europe, where the population is dense, the effect of such institutions would be almost instantaneous. What happened lately in France is an example. In 1848 a pure democracy was established there. During a short time there was reason to expect a general spoliation, a national bankruptcy, a new partition of the soil, a maximum of prices, a ruinous load of taxation laid on the rich for the purpose of supporting the poor in idleness. Such a system would, in twenty years, have made France as poor and barbarous as the France of the Carlovingians. Happily, the danger was averted; and now there is a despotism, a silent tribune, an enslaved press. Liberty is gone, but civilization has been saved.

I have not the smallest doubt that, if we had a purely democratic government here, the effect would be the same. Either the poor would plunder the rich and civilization would perish, or order and property would be saved by a strong military government, and liberty would perish. You may think that your country enjoys an exemption from these evils. I will frankly own to you that I am of a very different opinion. Your fate I believe to be certain, though it is deferred by a physical cause. As long as you have a boundless extent of fertile and unoccupied land, your laboring population will be far more at ease than the laboring population of the old world, and, while that is the case, the Jeffersonian polity may continue to exist without causing any fatal calamity. But the time will come when New England will be as thickly populated as Old England. Wages will be as low, and will fluctuate as much with you as with us. You will have your Manchesters and Birminghams, and in those Manchesters and Birminghams hundreds of thousands of artisans will assuredly be sometimes out of work. Then your institutions will be fairly brought to the test. Distress everywhere makes the laborer mutinous and discontented, and inclines him to listen with eagerness to agitators who tell him that it is a monstrous iniquity that one man should have a million while another cannot get a full meal.

In bad years there is plenty of grumbling here, and sometimes a little rioting. But it matters little, for here the sufferers are not the rulers. The supreme power is in the hands of a class, numerous indeed, but select; of an educated class; of a class which is, and knows itself to be, deeply interested in the security of property and maintenance of order. Accordingly, the malcontents are firmly yet gently restrained. The bad time is got over without robbing the wealthy to relieve the indigent. The springs of national prosperity soon begin to flow again; work is plentiful, wages rise, and all is tranquillity and cheerfulness. I have seen England pass three or four times through such critical seasons as I have described.

Through such seasons, the United States will have to pass in the course of the next century, if not of this. How will you pass through them? I heartily wish you a good deliverance. But my reason and my wishes are at war, and I cannot help foreboding the worst. It is quite plain that your government will never be able to restrain a distressed and discontented majority. For with you the majority is the government, and has the rich, who are always a minority, absolutely at its mercy.

The day will come when, in the State of New York, a multitude of people, none of whom has had more than half a breakfast, or expects to have more than half a dinner, will choose a Legislature. Is it possible to doubt what sort of Legislature will be chosen? On one side is a statesman preaching patience, respect for vested rights, strict observance of public faith. On the other is a demagogue ranting about the tyranny of capitalists and usurers, and asking why anybody should be permitted to drink champagne and to ride in a carriage, while thousands of honest folks are in want of necessaries. Which of the two candidates is likely to be preferred by a workingman who hears his children cry for more bread? I seriously apprehend that you will in some such season of adversity as I have described, do things which will prevent prosperity from returning; that you will act like people who should in a year of scarcity devour all the seed corn, and thus make the next year a

year not of scarcity, but of absolute famine. There will be, I fear, spoliation. There is nothing to stop you. Your Constitution is all sail and no anchor.

As I said before, when a society has entered on this downward progress, either civilization or liberty must perish. Either some Caesar or Napoleon will seize the reins of government with a strong hand, or your Republic will be as fearfully plundered and laid waste by barbarians in the 20th Century as the Roman Empire was in the fifth—with this difference, that the Huns and Vandals who ravaged the Roman Empire came from without, and that your Huns and Vandals will have been engendered within your own country by your own institutions.

Thinking thus, of course, I cannot reckon Jefferson among the benefactors of mankind. I readily admit that his intentions were good and his abilities considerable. Odious stories have been circulated about his private life; but I do not know on what evidence those stories rest, and I think it probable that they are false or monstrously exaggerated. I have no doubt that I shall derive both pleasure and information from your account of him.

T. B. MACAULAY

Holly Lodge
May 23, 1857

PROFESSOR SEA GULL

by JOSEPH MITCHELL

JOE GOULD is a jaunty and emaciated little man who has been a notable in the cafeterias, diners, barrooms, and dumps of Greenwich Village for a quarter of a century. He sometimes brags rather wryly that he is the last of the bohemians. "All the others fell by the wayside," he says. "Some are in the grave, some are in the

From Joseph Mitchell, *McSorley's Wonderful Saloon*. Reprinted by permission of the publishers, Duell, Sloan & Pearce, Inc. Copyright 1942 by Joseph Mitchell. Originally appeared in *The New Yorker*.

loony bin, and some are in the advertising business." Gould's life is by no means carefree; he is constantly tormented by what he calls "the three H's"—homelessness, hunger, and hangovers. He sleeps on benches in subway stations, on the floor in the studios of friends, and in quarter-a-night flophouses. Once in a while he trudges up to one of Father Divine's Extension Heavens in lower Harlem and gets a night's lodging for fifteen cents. He is five feet four and he hardly ever weighs more than ninety-five pounds. Not long ago he told a friend that he hadn't eaten a square meal since June, 1936, when he bummed up to Cambridge and attended a banquet during a reunion of the Harvard class of 1911, of which he is a member. "I'm the foremost authority in the U. S. on the subject of doing without," he says. He tells people that he lives on "air, self-esteem, cigarette butts, cowboy coffee, fried-egg sandwiches, and ketchup." Cowboy coffee is black coffee without sugar. After finishing a sandwich, Gould customarily empties a bottle or two of ketchup on his plate and eats it with a spoon. The countermen in the Jefferson Diner, on Village Square, which is one of his hangouts, gather up the ketchup bottles and hide them the moment he puts his head in the door. "I don't particularly like the confounded stuff," he says, "but I make it a practice to eat all I can get. It's the only grub I know of that's free of charge."

Gould is a Yankee. His branch of the Goulds has been in New England since 1635, and he is related to the Lowell, Lawrence, Storer, and Vroom families. "There's nothing accidental about me," he once said. "I'll tell you what it took to make me what I am today. It took old Yankee blood, an overwhelming aversion to possessions, four years of Harvard, and twenty-five years of beating the living hell out of my insides with bad hooch and bad food. I'm out of joint with the rest of the human race because I don't want to own anything. If Mr. Chrysler tried to make me a present of the Chrysler Building, I'd damn near break my neck fleeing from him. I wouldn't own it; it'd own me. Back home in Massachusetts I'd be called an old Yankee crank. Here I'm called a bohemian. It's six of one, half a dozen of the other." Gould has a twangy voice and a Harvard accent. Bartenders and countermen in the Village refer to him as The Professor, Professor Bloomingdale, Professor Sea Gull, or The Mongoose. He dresses in the castoff clothes of his friends. His overcoat, suit, shirt, and even his shoes are all invariably two or three sizes too large, but he wears them with a forlorn-Chaplinlike rakishness. "Just look at me," he says. "The only thing that fits is the necktie." On bitter winter days he puts a layer of newspapers between his shirt and undershirt. "I'm snobbish," he says. "I only use the *Times*." He is fond of unusual headgear—a toboggan, a beret, or a yachting cap. One evening last summer he appeared at a party in a seersucker suit, a polo shirt, a scarlet cummerbund, sandals, and a yachting cap, all hand-me-downs. He uses a long ivory cigarette-holder, and a good deal of the time he smokes butts picked up off the sidewalks.

Bohemianism has aged Gould considerably beyond his years. He has got in the habit lately of asking people he has just met to guess his age. Their guesses range between sixty-five and seventy-five; he is fifty-three. He is never hurt by this; he looks upon it as proof of his superiority. "I get more living done in one year," he says, "than ordinary humans do in ten."

He is squint-eyed and toothless, his spectacles slip down to the end of his nose a moment after he puts them on, and his lower jaw swivels from side to side when he talks; sometimes, because of these things, he distinctly resembles Mahatma Gandhi. He is aware of this. Once, in Romany Marie's, a basement bohemian gathering place in the Village, he draped a tablecloth over his shoulders and sat cross-legged on the floor for half an hour or so, gabbling all the while in a weird, made-up language. People who came in were taken aback when they caught sight of him; one woman said she had no idea Mr. Gandhi was visiting the United States.

Gould is bald on top, but the hair at the back of his head is long and frizzly, and he has a bushy, cinnamon-colored beard, which he says he trims every other Easter. He doesn't wear his spectacles on the street and without them he has the wild, unfocussed stare of an old scholar who has strained his eyes on small print. Even in the Village many people turn and look at him. He is stooped and he moves rapidly, grumbling to himself, with his head thrust forward and held to one side. Under his left arm he usually totes a bulging, greasy, brown pasteboard portfolio, and he swings his right arm aggressively. As he hurries along, he seems to be warding off an imaginary enemy. Don Freeman, the artist, a friend of his, once made a sketch of him walking. Freeman called the sketch "Joe Gould versus the Elements." Gould is as restless and footloose as an alley cat, and he takes long hikes about the city, now and then disappearing from the Village for weeks at a time and mystifying his friends; they have never been able to figure out where he goes. When he returns, always looking pleased with himself, he makes a few cryptic remarks, giggles, and

then shuts up. "I went on a bird walk along the waterfront with an old countess," he said after his most recent absence. "The countess and I spent three weeks studying sea gulls."

Gould is almost never seen without his portfolio. He sits on it while he eats and he sleeps with it under his head. It usually contains a mass of manuscripts and notes, a dictionary, a bottle of ink, his extra shirts and socks, a cake of soap, a hairbrush, a paper bag of bread crumbs, and a paper bag of hard, round, dime-store candy of the type called sour balls. "I fight fatigue with sour balls," he says. The crumbs are for pigeons; like many other eccentrics, Gould is a pigeon feeder. He is devoted to a flock which makes its headquarters atop and around the statue of Garibaldi in Washington Square. These pigeons know him. When he comes up and takes a seat on the plinth of the statue, they flutter down and perch on his head and shoulders, waiting for him to bring out his bag of crumbs. He has given names to some of them. "Come here, Boss Tweed," he says. "A lady in Stewart's didn't finish her whole-wheat toast this morning and when she went out, bingo, I snatched it off her plate especially for you. Hello, Big Bosom. Hello, Popgut. Hello, Lady Astor. Hello, St. John the Baptist. Hello, Polly Adler. Hello, Fiorello, you old goat, how're you today?"

Although Gould strives to give the impression that he is a philosophical loafer, he has done an immense amount of work during his career as a bohemian. Every day, even when he is groggy as the result of hunger, he spends at least a couple of hours laboring on a formless, rather mysterious book which he calls "An Oral History of Our Time." He began this book twenty-six years ago, and it is nowhere

near finished. His preoccupation with it seems to be principally responsible for the way he lives; a steady job of any kind, he says, would interfere with his thinking. Depending on the weather, he writes in parks, in doorways, in flophouse lobbies, in cafeterias, on benches on "L" platforms, in subway trains, and in public libraries. When he is in the proper mood, he writes until he is exhausted, and he gets into the mood at peculiar times. He says that one night he sat for seven hours in a booth in a Third Avenue bar and grill, listening to a beery old Hungarian woman, once a madam and once a dealer in cocaine and now a soup cook in a hospital, tell the story of her life. Three days later, around four o'clock in the morning, on a cot in the Hotel Defender, at 300 Bowery, he was awakened by the foghorns of tugs on the East River and was unable to go back to sleep because he felt that he was in the exact mood to put the old soup cook's biography in his history. He has an abnormal memory; if he is sufficiently impressed by a conversation, he can keep it in his head, even if it is lengthy and senseless, for many days, much of it word for word. He had a bad cold, but he got up, dressed under a red exit light, and, tiptoeing so as not to disturb the men sleeping on cots all around him, went downstairs to the lobby.

He wrote in the lobby from 4:15 A.M. until noon. Then he left the Defender, drank some coffee in a Bowery diner, and walked up to the Public Library. He plugged away at a table in the genealogy room, which is one of his rainy-day hangouts and which he says he prefers to the main reading room because it is gloomier, until it closed at 6 P.M. Then he moved into the main reading room and stayed there, seldom taking his eyes off his work,

until the Library locked up for the night at 10 P.M. He ate a couple of egg sandwiches and a quantity of ketchup in a Times Square cafeteria. Then, not having two bits for a flophouse and being too engrossed to go to the Village and seek shelter, he hurried into the West Side subway and rode the balance of the night, scribbling ceaselessly while the train he was aboard made three round trips between the New Lots Avenue station in Brooklyn and the Van Cortlandt Park station in the Bronx. He kept his portfolio on his lap and used it as a desk. He has the endurance of the possessed. Whenever he got too sleepy to concentrate, he shook his head vigorously and then brought out his bag of sour balls and popped one in his mouth. People stared at him, and once he was interrupted by a drunk who asked him what in the name of God he was writing. Gould knows how to get rid of inquisitive drunks. He pointed at his left ear and said, "What? What's that? Deaf as a post. Can't hear a word." The drunk lost all interest in him. "Day was breaking when I left the subway," Gould says. "I was sneezing my head off, my eyes were sore, my knees were shaky, I was hungry as a bitch wolf, and I had exactly eight cents to my name. I didn't care. My history was longer by eleven thousand brand-new words, and at that moment I bet there wasn't a chairman of the board in all New York as happy as I."

Gould is haunted by the fear that he will die before he has the first draft of the Oral History finished. It is already eleven times as long as the Bible. He estimates that the manuscript contains 9,000,000 words, all in longhand. It may well be the lengthiest unpublished work in existence. Gould does his writing in nickel composition books, the kind that children use in

school, and the Oral History and the notes he has made for it fill two hundred and seventy of them, all of which are tattered and grimy and stained with coffee, grease, and beer. Using a fountain pen, he covers both sides of each page, leaving no margins anywhere, and his penmanship is poor; hundreds of thousands of words are legible only to him. He has never been able to interest a publisher in the Oral History. At one time or another he has lugged armfuls of it into fourteen publishing offices. "Half of them said it was obscene and outrageous and to get it out of there as quick as I could," he says, "and the others said they couldn't read my handwriting." Experiences of this nature do not dismay Gould; he keeps telling himself that it is posterity he is writing for, anyway. In his breast pocket, sealed in a dingy envelope, he always carries a will bequeathing two-thirds of the manuscript to the Harvard Library and the other third to the Smithsonian Institution. "A couple of generations after I'm dead and gone," he likes to say, "the Ph.D.'s will start lousing through my work. Just imagine their surprise. 'Why, I be damned,' they'll say, 'this fellow was the most brilliant historian of the century.' They'll give me my due. I don't claim that all of the Oral History is first-class, but some of it will live as long as the English language." Gould used to keep his composition books in a dusty pile on the floor of a closet in a friend's photography studio in the Village. Whenever he filled a book, he would come in and toss it on the pile. Several months ago, after hearing that the Metropolitan Museum had moved its most valuable paintings to a bombproof storage place somewhere inland, he became panicky. He made a huge, oilcloth-covered bale of the Oral History and entrusted it for the

duration to a woman he knows who owns a duck-and-chicken farm near Huntington, Long Island. The farmhouse has a stone cellar.

Gould puts into the Oral History only things he has seen or heard. At least half of it is made up of conversations taken down verbatim or summarized; hence the title. "What people say is history," Gould says. "What we used to think was history —all that chitty-chat about Caesar, Napoleon, treaties, inventions, big battles— is only formal history and largely false. I'll put down the informal history of the shirt-sleeved multitude—what they had to say about their jobs, love affairs, vittles, sprees, scrapes, and sorrows—or I'll perish in the attempt." The Oral History is a great hodgepodge and kitchen midden of hearsay, the fruit, according to Gould's estimate, of more than twenty thousand conversations. In it are the hopelessly incoherent biographies of hundreds of bums, accounts of the wanderings of seamen encountered in South Street barrooms, grisly descriptions of hospital and clinic experiences ("Did you ever have a painful operation or disease?" is one of the first questions that Gould, fountain pen and composition book in hand, asks a person he has just met), summaries of innumerable Union Square and Columbus Circle harangues, testimonies given by converts at Salvation Army street meetings, and the addled opinions of scores of park-bench oracles and gin-mill savants. For a time Gould haunted the all-night greasy spoons in the vicinity of Bellevue Hospital, eavesdropping on tired internes, nurses, ambulance-drivers, scrubwomen, embalming-school students, and morgue workers, and faithfully recording their talk. He scurries up and down Fifth Avenue during parades, feverishly taking notes. Gould writes with great candor, and the percentage of obscenity in the Oral History is high. He has a chapter called "Examples of the So-Called Dirty Story of Our Time," to which he makes almost daily additions. In another chapter are many rhymes and observations which he found scribbled on the walls of subway washrooms. He believes that such things are as truly historical as the strategy of General Robert E. Lee. Hundreds of thousands of words are devoted to the drunken behavior and the sexual adventures of various Greenwich Villagers in the twenties. There are hundreds of reports of ginny Village parties, including gossip about the guests and faithful reports of their arguments on such subjects as reincarnation, birth control, free love, psychoanalysis, Christian Science, Swedenborgianism, vegetarianism, alcoholism, and different political and art isms. "I have fully covered what might be termed the intellectual underworld of my time," Gould says. There are detailed descriptions of night life in the Village speakeasies, basement cabarets, and eating places which he frequented at one time or another and which are all now out of existence, such as the Little Quakeress, the Original Julius, Hubert's Cafeteria, the Troubadour Tavern, Alice McCollister's, and Eli Greifer's Last Oupost of Bohemia Tea Shoppe.

He is a night wanderer, and he has put down descriptions of dreadful things he has seen on dark New York streets—descriptions, for example, of the herds of big gray rats that come out in the hours before dawn in some neighborhoods of the lower East Side and Harlem and unconcernedly walk the sidewalks. "I sometimes believe that these rats are not rats at all," he says, "but the damned and aching souls of tenement landlords." A great deal of

the Oral History is in diary form. Gould is afflicted with total recall, and now and then he painstakingly writes down everything he did for a day, a week, or a month. Sometimes he writes a chapter in which he monotonously and hideously curses some person or institution. Here and there are rambling essays on such subjects as the flophouse flea, spaghetti, the zipper as a sign of the decay of civilization, false teeth, insanity, the jury system, remorse, cafeteria cooking, and the emasculating effect of the typewriter on literature. "William Shakespeare didn't sit around pecking on a dirty, damned, ninety-five-dollar dohicky," he wrote, "and Joe Gould doesn't, either." In his essay on insanity he wrote, "I suffer from a mild form of insanity. I have delusions of grandeur. I believe myself to be Joe Gould."

The Oral History is almost as discursive as *Tristram Shandy*. In one chapter, "The Good Men Are Dying Like Flies," Gould begins a biography of a diner proprietor and horse-race gambler named Side-Bet Benny Altschuler, who stuck a rusty icepick in his hand and died of lockjaw; and skips after a few paragraphs to a story a seaman told him about seeing a group of tipsy lepers on a beach in Port-of-Spain, Trinidad; and goes from that to an anecdote about a meeting held in Boston in 1915 to protest against the showing of "The Birth of a Nation," at which he kicked a policeman; and goes from that to a description of a trip he once made through the Central Islip insane asylum, in the course of which a woman pointed at him and screamed, "There he is! Thief! Thief! There's the man that picked my geraniums and stole my mama's mule and buggy"; and goes from that to an account an old stumblebum gave of glimpsing and feeling the blue-black flames of hell one night while sitting in a doorway on Great Jones Street and of seeing two mermaids playing in the East River just north of Fulton Fish Market later the same night; and goes from that to an explanation made by a priest of old St. Patrick's Cathedral on Mott Street of why Italian women are addicted to the wearing of black; and then returns at last to Side-Bet Benny, the lock-jawed diner proprietor.

Only a few of the hundreds of people who know Gould have read any of the Oral History, and most of them take it for granted that it is gibberish. Those who make the attempt usually bog down after a couple of chapters and give up. Gould says he can count on his hands and feet those who have read enough of it to be qualified to form an opinion. One is Horace Gregory, the poet and critic. "I look upon Gould as a sort of Samuel Pepys of the Bowery," Gregory says. "I once waded through twenty-odd composition books, and most of what I saw had the quality of a competent high-school theme, but some of it was written with the clear and wonderful veracity of a child, and here and there were flashes of hardbitten Yankee wit. If someone took the trouble to go through it and separate the good from the rubbish, as editors did with Thomas Wolfe's millions of words, it might be discovered that Gould actually has written a masterpiece. I can't imagine anyone with patience enough to tackle the job. It would require months and months, maybe years." Another is E. E. Cummings, the poet, who is a close friend of Gould's. Cummings once wrote a poem about Gould, No. 261 in his "Collected Poems," which contains the following description of the history:

. . . a myth is as good as a smile but little
   joe gould's quote oral
history unquote might (publishers note) be
   entitled a wraith's
progress or mainly awash while chiefly submerged or an amoral
morality   sort-of-aliveing   by   innumerable
   kind-of-deaths

Throughout the nineteen-twenties Gould haunted the office of *The Dial,* now dead, the most highbrow magazine of the time. Finally, in its April, 1929, issue, *The Dial* printed one of his shorter essays, "Civilization." In it he rambled along, referring to skyscrapers and steamships as "needless bric-a-brac," and remarking that "the auto is unnecessary. If all the perverted ingenuity which was put into making buzz-wagons had only gone into improving the breed of horses humanity would be better off." This essay had a curious effect on American literature. A copy of this issue of *The Dial* turned up three or four months later in a second-hand bookstore in Fresno, California, and was bought for a dime by William Saroyan, who then was twenty and floundering around, desperate to become a writer. He read Gould's essay and was deeply impressed and influenced by it. "It freed me from bothering about form," he says. Twelve years later, in the winter of 1941, in Don Freeman's studio on Columbus Circle, Saroyan saw some drawings Freeman had made of Gould for *Don Freeman's Newsstand,* a quarterly publication of pictures of odd New York scenes and personalities put out by the Associated American Artists. Saroyan became excited. He told Freeman about his indebtedness to Gould. "Who the hell is he, anyway?" Saroyan asked. "I've been trying to find out for years. Reading those few pages in *The Dial* was like going in the wrong direction and running into the right guy and then never seeing him again." Freeman told him about the Oral History. Saroyan sat down and wrote a commentary to accompany the drawings of Gould in *Newsstand*. "To this day," he wrote, in part, "I have not read anything else by Joe Gould. And yet to me he remains one of the few genuine and original American writers. He was easy and uncluttered, and almost all other American writing was uneasy and cluttered. It was not at home anywhere; it was trying too hard; it was miserable; it was a little sickly; it was literary; and it couldn't say anything simply. All other American writing was trying to get into one form or another, and no writer except Joe Gould seemed to understand that if the worst came to the worst you didn't need any form at all. All you had to do was say it." Not long after this issue of *Newsstand* came out, someone stopped Gould on Eighth Street and showed him Saroyan's endorsement of his work. Gould shrugged his shoulders. He had been on a spree and had lost his false teeth, and at the moment he was uninterested in literary matters. After thinking it over, however, he decided to call on Saroyan and ask him for help in getting some teeth. He found out somehow that Saroyan was living at the Hampshire House, on Central Park South. The doorman there followed Gould into the lobby and asked him what he wanted. Gould told him. "Do you know Mr. Saroyan?" the doorman asked. "Why, no," Gould said, "but that's all right. He's a disciple of mine." "What do you mean, disciple?" asked the doorman. "I mean," said Gould, "that he's a literary disciple of mine. I want to ask him to buy me some store teeth." "Come this way," said the doorman, gripping Gould's arm and ushering him to the street. Later Freeman arranged a meeting, and the pair spent several evenings together in bars. "Saroyan kept saying he wanted to hear all about the Oral History," Gould says, "but I never got a chance to tell him. He did all the talking. I couldn't get a word in edgewise."

Gould, ever since his childhood, has been perplexed by his own personality. There are scores of autobiographical essays in the Oral History, and he says that all of them are attempts to explain himself to himself. In one, "Why I Am Unable To Adjust Myself To Civilization, Such As It Is, or Do, Don't, Do, Don't, A Hell Of A Note," he came to the conclusion that his shyness was responsible for everything. "I am introvert and extrovert all rolled in one," he wrote, "a warring mixture of the recluse and the Sixth Avenue auctioneer. One foot says do, the other says don't. One foot says shut your mouth, the other says bellow like a bull. I am painfully shy, but try not to let people know it. They would take advantage of me." Gould keeps his shyness well hidden. It is evident only when he is cold sober. In that state he is silent, suspicious, and constrained, but a couple of beers or a single jigger of gin will untie his tongue and put a leer on his face. He is extraordinarily responsive to alcohol. "On a hot night," he says, "I can walk up and down in front of a gin mill for ten minutes, breathing real deep, and get a jag on."

Even though Gould requires only a few drinks, getting them is sometimes quite a task. Most evenings he prowls around the saloons and dives on the west side of the Village, on the lookout for curiosity-seeking tourists from whom he can cadge beers, sandwiches, and small sums of money. Such people are scarce nowadays. If he is unable to find anyone approachable in the tumultuous saloons around Sheridan Square, he goes over to Sixth Avenue and works north, hitting the Jericho Tavern, the Village Square Bar & Grill, the Belmar, Goody's, and the Rochambeau. He has a routine. He doesn't enter a place unless it is crowded. After he is in, he bustles over to the telephone booth and pretends to look up a number. While doing this, he scrutinizes the customers. If he sees a prospect, he goes over and says, "Let me introduce myself. The name is Joseph Ferdinand Gould, graduate of Harvard, *magna cum difficultate,* class of 1911, and chairman of the board of Weal and Woe, Incorporated. In exchange for a drink, I'll recite a poem, deliver a lecture, argue a point, or take off my shoes and imitate a sea gull. I prefer gin, but beer will do." Gould is by no means a bum. He feels that the entertainment he provides is well worth whatever he is able to cadge. He doesn't fawn, and he is never grateful. If he is turned down politely, he shrugs his shoulders and leaves the place. However, if the prospect passes a remark like "Get out of here, you bum," Gould turns on him, no matter how big he is, and gives him a frightening tongue-lashing. He is skilled in the use of the obscene epithet; he can curse for ten minutes, growing more shrill and scurrilous by the minute, without repeating himself. When aroused, he is fearless. He will drop his portfolio, put up his fists, and offer to fight men who could kill him with one halfhearted blow. If he doesn't find an audience on the trip up Sixth, he turns west on Eleventh and heads for the Village Vanguard, in a cellar on Seventh Avenue South. The Vanguard was once a sleazy rendezvous for arty people, but currently it is a thriving night club. Gould and the proprietor, a man named Max Gordon, have known each other for many years and are on fairly good terms much of the time. Gould always hits the Vanguard last. He is sure of it, and he keeps it in reserve. Since it became prosperous, the place annoys him. He goes down the stairs and says, "Hello, Max, you dirty capitalist. I want a bite to eat and a beer. If I don't get it, I'll walk right out on the dance floor and throw a fit." "Go argue with the cook," Gordon tells him. Gould goes into the kitchen, eats whatever the cook gives him, drinks a couple of beers, fills a bag with bread crumbs, and departs.

Despite his shyness, Gould has a great fondness for parties. He is acquainted with hundreds of artists, writers, sculptors, and actors in the Village, and whenever he learns that one of them is giving a party, he goes, friend or enemy, invited or not. Usually he keeps to himself for a while, uneasily smoking one cigarette after another and stiff as a board with tenseness. Sooner or later, however, impelled by a drink or two and by the desperation of the ill at ease, he begins to throw his weight around. He picks out the prettiest woman in the room, goes over, bows, and kisses her hand. He tells discreditable stories about himself. He becomes exuberant; suddenly, for no reason at all, he cackles with pleasure and jumps up and clicks his heels together. Presently he shouts, "All in favor of a one-man floor show, please say 'Aye'!" If he gets the slightest encouragement, he strips to the waist and does a hand-clapping, foot-stamping dance which he says he learned on a Chippewa reservation in North Dakota and which he calls the Joseph Ferdinand Gould Stomp. While dancing, he chants an old Salvation Army song, "There Are Flies on Me, There Are Flies on You, but There Are No Flies on Jesus."

Then he imitates a sea gull. He pulls off his shoes and socks and takes awkward, headlong skips about the room, flapping his arms and letting out a piercing caw with every skip. As a child he had several pet gulls, and he still spends many Sundays on the end of a fishing pier at Sheepshead Bay observing gulls; he claims he has such a thorough understanding of their cawing that he can translate poetry into it. "I have translated a number of Henry Wadsworth Longfellow's poems into sea gull," he says.

Inevitably, at every party Gould goes to, he gets up on a table and delivers some lectures. His lectures are brief, but he gives them lengthy titles, such as "Drunk as a Skunk, or How I Measured the Heads of Fifteen Hundred Indians in Zero Weather" and "The Dread Tomato Habit, or Watch Out! Watch Out! Down with Dr. Gallup!" For a reason he has never been able to make quite clear, statistics of any kind infuriate him. In the latter lecture, using statistics he maintains he has found in newspaper financial sections, he proves that the eating of tomatoes by railroad engineers was responsible for fifty-three per cent of the train wrecks in the United States during the last seven years. When Gould arrives at a party, people who have never seen him before usually take one look, snicker, and edge away. Before the evening is over, however, a few of them almost always develop a kind of puzzled respect for him; they get him in a corner, ask him questions, and try to determine what is wrong with him. Gould enjoys this. "When you came over and kissed my hand," a young woman told him once, "I said to myself, 'What a nice old gentleman.' A minute later I looked around and you were bouncing up and down with your shirt off, imitating a wild Indian. I was shocked. Why do you have to be such an exhibitionist?" "Madam," Gould said, "it is the duty of the bohemian to make a spectacle of himself. If my informality leads you to believe that I'm a rum-dumb, or that I belong in Bellevue, hold fast to that belief, hold fast, hold fast, and show your ignorance."

Gould is not particularly communicative about what he calls his pre-Oral History life. "I am the most recent black sheep in a family that can trace its ancestry right spang to William the Conqueror," he says. He is a native of Norwood, Massachusetts, a southwestern suburb of Boston. He comes from a family of physicians. His grandfather, Joseph Ferdinand Gould, for whom he was named, taught in the Harvard Medical School and had a practice in South Boston. His father, Clark Storer Gould, was a captain in the Army Medical Corps and died of blood poisoning in a camp in Ohio during the last war. The family was well-to-do until Gould was in his late teens, when his father invested unwisely in the stock of an Alaska land company. Gould says he went to Harvard only because it was a family custom. "I did not want to go," he wrote in one of his autobiographical essays. "It had been my plan to stay home and sit in a rocking chair on the back porch and brood." He says that he was an undistinguished student. Some of his classmates were Conrad Aiken, the poet; Howard Lindsay, the playwright and actor; Gluyas Williams, the cartoonist; and Richard F. Whitney, former president of the New York Stock Exchange. His best friends were three foreign students—a Chinese, a Siamese, and an Albanian.

Gould's mother had always taken it for granted that he would become a physician, but after getting his A.B. he told her he was through with formal education. She asked him what he intended to do. "I intend to stroll and ponder," he said. He passed most of the next three years strolling and pondering on the ranch of an uncle in Canada. In 1913, in an Albanian restaurant in Boston named the Scanderbeg, whose coffee he liked, he became acquainted with Theofan S. Noli, an archimandrite of the Albanian Orthodox Church, who interested him in Balkan politics. In February, 1914, Gould startled his family by announcing that he planned to devote the rest of his life to collecting funds to free Albania. He founded an organization in Boston called the Friends of Albanian Independence, enrolled a score or so of dues-paying members, and began telegraphing and calling on bewildered newspaper editors in Boston and Manhattan, trying to persuade them to print long treatises on Albanian affairs written by Noli. After about eight months of this, Gould was sitting in the Scanderbeg one night, drinking coffee and listening to a group of Albanian factory workers argue in their native tongue about Balkan politics, when he suddenly came to the conclusion that he was about to have a nervous breakdown. "I began to twitch uncontrollably and see double," he says. From that night on his interest in Albania slackened.

After another period of strolling and pondering, Gould took up eugenics. He has forgotten exactly how this came about. In any case, he spent the summer of 1915 as a student in eugenical field work at the Eugenics Record Office at Cold Spring Harbor. This organization, endowed by the Carnegie Institution, was engaged at that time in making studies of families of hereditary defectives, paupers, and town nuisances in several highly inbred com-

munities. Such people were too prosaic for Gould; he decided to specialize in Indians. That winter he went out to North Dakota and measured the heads of a thousand Chippewas on the Turtle Mountain Reservation and of five hundred Mandans on the Fort Berthold Reservation. Nowadays, when Gould is asked why he took these measurements, he changes the subject, saying, "The whole matter is a deep, scientific secret." He was happy in North Dakota. "It was the most rewarding period of my life," he says. "I'm a good horseman, if I do say so myself, and I like to dance and whoop, and the Indians seemed to enjoy having me around. I was afraid they'd think I was batty when I asked for permission to measure their noggins, but they didn't mind. It seemed to amuse them. Indians are the only true aristocrats I've ever known; nothing in God's world ever surprises them. They ought to run the country, and we ought to be put on the reservations." After seven months of reservation life, Gould ran out of money. He returned to Massachusetts and tried vainly to get funds for another head-measuring expedition. "At this juncture in my life," he says, "I decided to engage in literary work." He came to Manhattan and got a job as assistant Police Headquarters reporter for the *Evening Mail*. One morning in the summer of 1917, after he had been a reporter for about a year, he was basking in the sun on the back steps of Headquarters, trying to overcome a grappa hangover, when the idea for the Oral History blossomed in his mind. He promptly quit his job and began writing. "Since that fateful morning," he once said, in a moment of exaltation, "the Oral History has been my rope and my scaffold, my bed and my board, my wife and my floozy, my wound and the salt on it, my whiskey and my aspirin, and my rock and my salvation. It is the only thing that matters a damn to me. All else is dross."

Gould says that he rarely has more than a dollar at any one time, and that he doesn't particularly care. "As a rule," he says, "I despise money." However, there is a widely held belief in the Village that he is rich and that he receives an income from inherited property in New England. "Only an old millionaire could afford to go around as shabby as you," a bartender told him recently. "You're one of those fellows that die in doorways and when the cops search them their pockets are just busting with bankbooks. If you wanted to, I bet you could step over to the West Side Savings Bank right this minute and draw out twenty thousand dollars." After the death of his mother in 1939, Gould did come into some money. Close friends of his say that it was less than a thousand dollars and that he spent it in less than a month, wildly buying drinks all over the Village for people he had never seen before. "He seemed miserable with money in his pockets," Gordon, the proprietor of the Vanguard, says. "When it was all gone, it seemed to take a load off his mind." While Gould was spending his inheritance, he did one thing that satisfied him deeply. He bought a big, shiny radio and took it out on Sixth Avenue and kicked it to pieces. He has a low opinion of radio. "Five minutes of the idiot's babble that comes out of those machines," he says, "would turn the stomach of a goat."

During the twenties and the early thirties Gould occasionally interrupted his work on the Oral History to pose for classes at the Art Students' League and to do book-reviewing for newspapers and magazines. He says there were periods when he lived comfortably on the money he earned this way. Burton Rascoe, literary editor of the old *Tribune,* gave him a lot of work. In a notation in "A Bookman's Daybook," Rascoe told of an experience with Gould. "I once gave him a small book about the American Indians to review," Rascoe wrote, "and he brought me back enough manuscript to fill three complete editions of the Sunday *Tribune.* I especially honor him, because, unlike most reviewers, he has never dogged me with inquiries as to why I never ran it. He had his say, which was considerable, about the book, the author, and the subject, and there, for him, the matter ended." Gould says that he quit book-reviewing because he felt that it was beneath his dignity to compete with machines. "The Sunday *Times* and the Sunday *Herald Tribune* have machines that review books," he says. "You put a book in one of those machines and jerk down a couple of levers and a review drops out." In recent years Gould has got along on less than five dollars in actual money a week. He has a number of friends—Malcolm Cowley, the writer and editor; Aaron Siskind, the documentary photographer; Cummings, the poet; and Gordon, the night-club proprietor, are a few—who give him small sums of money regularly. No matter what they think of the Oral History, all these people greatly respect Gould's doggedness. . . .

Gould's opinion of contemporary writing other than the Oral History is low. Occasionally, at the Public Library, he takes out a recently published history and sits down with it at his favorite table in the genealogy room. Almost immediately he begins to grunt and groan and curse the author. "The hell you say," he is apt to exclaim, smacking the book with his palm and startling the other people at the table. "Who told you? It simply isn't true! Garbage, garbage, ten tons of garbage! And they saw down beautiful trees to make paper to print this stuff on! The awful waste! Oh! Oh! I just can't endure it!"

Gould's outspokenness has made him a lone wolf in the Village; he has never been allowed to join any of the art, poetry, or ism organizations. He has been trying for ten years to join the Raven Poetry Circle, which puts on the poetry exhibition in Washington Square each summer and is the most powerful organization of its kind in the Village, but he has been blackballed every time. However, the Ravens usually let him attend their readings. Francis Lambert McCrudden, a retired Telephone Company employee who is the head Raven, claims that Gould is not serious about poetry. "We serve wine at our readings, and that is the only reason Mr. Gould attends," he once said. "He sometimes insists on reading foolish poems of his own, and it gets on your nerves. At our religious-poetry night he demanded permission to recite a poem entitled 'My Religion.' I told him to go ahead, and this is what he recited:

> In winter I'm a Buddhist,
> And in summer I'm a nudist.

And at our nature-poetry night he begged to recite a poem entitled 'The Sea Gull.' I gave him permission, and he jumped out of his chair and began to wave his arms and leap about and scream, 'Scree-eek! Scree-eek!' It was upsetting. We are serious poets and we don't appreciate that sort of behavior." Last summer Gould picketed the Raven exhibition, which was held on the fence of a tennis court on Washington Square South. In one hand he carried his portfolio and in the other he held a placard on which he had printed: "JOSEPH FERDINAND GOULD, HOT SHOT POET FROM POETVILLE, A REFUGEE FROM THE RAVENS. POETS OF THE WORLD, IGNITE! YOU HAVE NOTHING TO LOSE BUT YOUR BRAINS!" Now and then, as he strutted back and forth, he would take a leap and then a skip and say to passers-by, "Would you like to hear what Joe Gould thinks of the world and all that's in it? Scree-eek! Scree-eek!"

Resettlement Administration photograph by Rothstein

SOCIETY AND SOLITUDE

by Ralph Waldo Emerson

I FELL in with a humorist on my travels, who had in his chamber a cast of the Rondanini Medusa, and who assured me that the name which that fine work of art bore in the catalogues was a misnomer, as he was convinced that the sculptor who carved it intended it for Memory, the mother of the Muses. In the conversation that followed, my new friend made some extraordinary confessions. "Do you not see," he said, "the penalty of learning, and that each of these scholars whom you have met at S——, though he were to be the last man, would, like the executioner in Hood's poem, guillotine the last but one?" He added many lively remarks, but his evident earnestness engaged my attention, and in the weeks that followed we became better acquainted. He had good abilities, a genial temper and no vices; but he had one defect—he could not speak in the tone of the people. There was some paralysis on his will, such that when he met men on common terms he spoke weakly and from the point, like a flighty girl. His consciousness of the fault made it worse. He envied every drover and lumberman in the tavern their manly speech. He coveted Mirabeau's *don terrible de la familiarité,* believing that he whose sympathy goes lowest is the man from whom kings have the most to fear. For himself he declared that he could not get enough alone to write a letter to a friend. He left the city; he hid himself in pastures. The solitary river was not solitary enough; the sun and moon put him out. When he bought a house, the first thing he did was to plant trees. He could not enough conceal himself. Set a hedge here; set oaks there—trees behind trees; above all, set evergreens, for they will keep a secret all the year round. The most agreeable compliment you could pay him was to imply that you had not observed him in a house or a street where you had met him. Whilst he suffered at being seen where he was, he consoled himself with the delicious thought of the inconceivable number of places where he was not. All he wished of his tailor was to provide that sober mean of color and cut which would never detain the eye for a moment. He went to Vienna, to Smyrna, to London. In all the variety of costumes, a carnival, a kaleidoscope of clothes, to his horror he could never discover a man in the street who wore anything like his own dress. He would have given his soul for the ring of Gyges. His dismay at his visibility had blunted the fears of mortality. "Do you think," he said, "I am in such great terror of being shot—I, who am only waiting to shuffle off my corporeal jacket to slip away into the back stars, and put diameters of the solar system and sidereal orbits between me and all souls—there to wear out ages in solitude, and forget memory itself, if it be possible?" He had a remorse running to despair of his social *gaucheries,* and walked miles and miles to get the twitchings out of his face, the starts and shrugs out of his arms and shoulders. God may forgive sins, he said, but awkwardness has no forgiveness in heaven or earth. He admired in Newton not so much his theory of the moon as his letter to Collins, in which he forbade him to insert his name with the solution of the problem in the Philosophical Transactions: "It would perhaps increase my acquaintance, the thing which I chiefly study to decline."

These conversations led me somewhat later to the knowledge of similar cases, and to the discovery that they are not of very infrequent occurrence. Few substances are found pure in nature. Those constitutions which can bear in open day the rough dealing of the world must be of that mean and average structure such as iron and salt, atmospheric air and water. But there are metals, like potassium and sodium, which, to be kept pure, must be kept under naphtha. Such are the talents determined on some specialty, which a culminating civilization fosters in the heart of great cities and in royal chambers. Nature protects her own work. To the culture of the world an Archimedes, a Newton is indispensable; so she guards them by a certain aridity. If these had been good fellows, fond of dancing, port and clubs, we should have had no Theory of the Sphere and no Principia. They had that necessity of isolation which genius feels. Each must stand on his glass tripod if he would keep his electricity. Even Swedenborg, whose theory of the universe is based on affection, and who reprobates to weariness the danger and vice of pure intellect, is constrained to make an extraordinary exception: "There are also angels who do not live consociated, but separate, house and house; these dwell in the midst of heaven, because they are the best of angels."

We have known many fine geniuses with that imperfection that they cannot do anything useful, not so much as write one clean sentence. 'T is worse, and tragic, that no man is fit for society who has fine traits. At a distance he is admired, but bring him hand to hand, he is a cripple. One protects himself by solitude, and one by courtesy, and one by an acid, worldly manner—each concealing how he can the thinness of his skin and his incapacity for strict association. But there is no remedy that can reach the heart of the disease but either habits of self-reliance that should go in practice to making the man independent of the human race, or else a religion of love. Now he hardly seems entitled to marry; for how can he protect a woman, who cannot protect himself?

We pray to be conventional. But the wary Heaven takes care you shall not be, if there is anything good in you. Dante was very bad company, and was never invited to dinner. Michael Angelo had a sad, sour time of it. The ministers of beauty are rarely beautiful in coaches and saloons. Columbus discovered no isle or key so lonely as himself. Yet each of these potentates saw well the reason of his exclusion. Solitary was he? Why, yes; but his society was limited only by the amount of brain nature appropriated in that age to carry on the government of the world. "If I stay," said Dante, when there was question of going to Rome, "who will go? and if I go, who will stay?"

But the necessity of solitude is deeper than we have said, and is organic. I have seen many a philosopher whose world is large enough for only one person. He affects to be a good companion; but we are still surprising his secret, that he means and needs to impose his system on all the rest. The determination of each is *from* all the others, like that of each tree up into free space. 'T is no wonder, when each has his whole head, our societies should be so small. Like President Tyler, our party falls from us every day, and we must ride in a sulky at last. Dear heart! take it sadly home to thee—there is no cooperation. We begin with friendships, and all our youth is a reconnoitring and recruiting of the holy fraternity they shall combine for the salvation of men. But so the remoter stars seem a nebula of united light, yet there is no group which a telescope will not resolve; and the dearest friends are separated by impassable gulfs. The cooperation is involuntary, and is put upon us by the Genius of Life, who reserves this as a part of his prerogative. 'T is fine for us to talk; we sit and muse and are serene and complete; but the moment we meet with anybody, each becomes a fraction.

Though the stuff of tragedy and of romances is in a moral union of two superior persons whose confidence in each other for long years, out of sight and in sight, and against all appearances, is at last justified by victorious proof of probity to gods and men, causing joyful emotions, tears and glory—though there be for heroes this *moral union,* yet they too are as far off as ever from an intellectual union, and the moral union is for comparatively low and external purposes, like the cooperation of a ship's company or of a fire-club. But how insular and pathetically solitary are all the people we know! Nor dare they tell what they think of each other when they meet in the street. We have a fine right, to be sure, to taunt men of the world with superficial and treacherous courtesies!

Such is the tragic necessity which strict science finds underneath our domestic and neighborly life, irresistibly driving each adult soul as with whips into the desert, and making our warm covenants sentimental and momentary. We must infer that the ends of thought were peremptory, if they were to be secured at such ruinous cost. They are deeper than can be told, and belong to the immensities and eternities. They reach down to that depth where society itself originates and disappears; where the question is, Which is first, man or men? where the individual is lost in his source.

But this banishment to the rocks and echoes no metaphysics can make right or tolerable. This result is so against nature, such a half-view, that it must be corrected by a common sense and experience. "A man is born by the side of his father, and there he remains." A man must be clothed with society, or we shall feel a certain bareness and poverty, as of a displaced and unfurnished member. He is to be dressed in arts and institutions, as well as in body garments. Now and then a man exquisitely made can live alone, and must; but coop up most men and you undo them. "The king lived and ate in his hall with men, and understood men," said Selden. When a young barrister said to the late Mr. Mason, "I keep my chamber to read law" —"Read law!" replied the veteran, "'t is in the court-room you must read law." Nor is the rule otherwise for literature. If you would learn to write, 't is in the street you must learn it. Both for the vehicle and for the aims of fine arts you must frequent the public square. The people, and not the college, is the writer's home. A scholar is a candle which the love and desire of all men will light. Never his lands or his rents, but the power to charm the disguised soul that sits veiled under this bearded and that rosy visage is his rent and ration. His products are as needful as those of the baker or the weaver. Society cannot do without cultivated men. As soon as the first wants are satisfied, the higher wants become imperative.

'T is hard to mesmerize ourselves, to whip our own top; but through sympathy we are capable of energy and endurance. Concert fires people to a certain fury of performance they can rarely reach alone. Here is the use of society: it is so easy with the great to be great; so easy to come up to an existing standard; as easy as it is to the lover to swim to his maiden through waves so grim before. The benefits of affection are immense; and the one event which never loses its romance is the encounter with superior persons on terms allowing the happiest intercourse.

It by no means follows that we are not fit for society, because *soirées* are tedious and because the *soirée* finds us tedious. A backwoodsman, who had been sent to the university, told me that when he heard the best-bred young men at the law-school talk together, he reckoned himself a boor; but whenever he caught them apart, and had one to himself alone, then they were the boors and he the better man. And if we recall the rare hours when we encountered the best persons, we then found ourselves, and then first society seemed to exist. That was society, though in the transom of a brig or on the Florida Keys.

A cold sluggish blood thinks it has not facts enough to the purpose, and must decline its turn in the conversation. But they who speak have no more—have less. 'T is not new facts that avail, but the heat to dissolve everybody's facts. Heat puts you in right relation with magazines of facts. The capital defect of cold, arid natures is the want of animal spirits. They seem a power incredible, as if God should raise the dead. The recluse witnesses what others perform by their aid, with a kind of fear. It is as much out of his possibility as the prowess of Cœur-de-Lion, or an Irishman's day's work on the railroad. 'T is said the present and the future are always rivals. Animal spirits constitute the power of the present, and their feats are like the structure of a pyramid. Their result is a lord, a general, or a boon companion. Before these what a base mendicant is Memory with his leathern badge! But this genial heat is latent in all constitutions, and is disengaged only by the fric-

tion of society. As Bacon said of manners, "To obtain them, it only needs not to despise them," so we say of animal spirits that they are the spontaneous product of health and of a social habit. "For behavior, men learn it, as they take diseases, one of another."

But the people are to be taken in very small doses. If solitude is proud, so is society vulgar. In society, high advantages are set down to the individual as disqualifications. We sink as easily as we rise, through sympathy. So many men whom I know are degraded by their sympathies; their native aims being high enough, but their relation all too tender to the gross people about them. Men cannot afford to live together on their merits, and they adjust themselves by their demerits—by their love of gossip, or by sheer tolerance and animal good nature. They untune and dissipate the brave aspirant.

The remedy is to reinforce each of these moods from the other. Conversation will not corrupt us if we come to the assembly in our own garb and speech and with the energy of health to select what is ours and reject what is not. Society we must have; but let it be society, and not exchanging news or eating from the same dish. Is it society to sit in one of your chairs? I cannot go to the houses of my nearest relatives, because I do not wish to be alone. Society exists by chemical affinity, and not otherwise.

Put any company of people together with freedom for conversation, and a rapid self-distribution takes place into sets and pairs. The best are accused of exclusiveness. It would be more true to say they separate as oil from water, as children from old people, without love or hatred in the matter, each seeking his like; and any interference with the affinities would produce constraint and suffocation. All conversation is a magnetic experiment. I know that my friend can talk eloquently; you know that he cannot articulate a sentence: we have seen him in different company. Assort your party, or invite none. Put Stubbs and Coleridge, Quintilian and Aunt Miriam, into pairs, and you make them all wretched. 'T is an extempore Sing-Sing built in a parlor. Leave them to seek their own mates, and they will be as merry as sparrows.

A higher civility will reëstablish in our customs a certain reverence which we have lost. What to do with these brisk young men who break through all fences, and make themselves at home in every house? I find out in an instant if my companion does not want me, and ropes cannot hold me when my welcome is gone. One would think that the affinities would pronounce themselves with a surer reciprocity.

Here again, as so often, nature delights to put us between extreme antagonisms, and our safety is in the skill with which we keep the diagonal line. Solitude is impracticable, and society fatal. We must keep our head in the one and our hands in the other. The conditions are met, if we keep our independence, yet do not lose our sympathy. These wonderful horses need to be driven by fine hands. We require such a solitude as shall hold us to its revelations when we are in the street and in palaces; for most men are cowed in society, and say good things to you in private, but will not stand to them in public. But let us not be the victims of words. Society and solitude are deceptive names. It is not the circumstance of seeing more or fewer people, but the readiness of sympathy, that imports; and a sound mind will derive its principles from insight, with ever a purer ascent to the sufficient and absolute right, and will accept society as the natural element in which they are to be applied.

from Preface to 1855 Edition of "LEAVES OF GRASS"
by WALT WHITMAN

AMERICA DOES NOT REPEL the past or what it has produced under its forms or amid other politics or the idea of castes or the old religions . . . accepts the lesson with calmness . . . is not so impatient as has been supposed that the slough still sticks to opinions and manners and literature while the life which served its requirements has passed into the new life of the new forms . . . perceives that the corpse is slowly borne from the eating and sleeping rooms of the house . . . perceives that it waits a little while in the door . . . that it was fittest for its days . . . that its action has descended to the stalwart and well-shaped heir who approaches . . . and that he shall be fittest for his days.

The Americans of all nations at any time upon the earth have probably the fullest poetical nature. The United States themselves are essentially the greatest poem. . . . Other states indicate themselves in their deputies . . . but the genius of the United States is not best or most in its executives or legislatures, nor in its ambassadors or authors or colleges or churches or parlors, nor even in its newspapers or inventors . . . but always most in the common people. Their manners, speech, dress, friendships—the freshness and candor of their physiognomy—the picturesque looseness of their carriage . . . their deathless attachment to freedom—their aversion to anything indecorous or soft or mean—the practical acknowledgment of the citizens of one state by the citizens of all other states—the fierceness of their roused resentment—their curiosity and welcome of novelty—their self-esteem and wonderful sympathy—their susceptibility to a slight —the air they have of persons who never knew how it felt to stand in the presence of superiors—the fluency of their speech—their delight in music, the sure symptom of manly tenderness and native elegance of soul . . . their good temper and openhandedness—the terrible significance of their elections—the President's taking off his hat to them not they to him—these too are unrhymed poetry. It awaits the gigantic and generous treatment worthy of it. . . .

The American poets are to enclose old and new, for America is the race of races. Of them a bard is to be commensurate with a people. To him the other continents arrive as contributions . . . he gives them reception for their sake and his own sake. His spirit responds to his country's spirit . . . he incarnates its geography and natural life and rivers and lakes. Mississippi with annual freshets and changing chutes, Missouri and Columbia and Ohio and Saint Lawrence with the falls and beautiful masculine Hudson, do not embouchure where they spend themselves more than they embouchure into him. The blue breadth over the inland sea of Virginia and Maryland and the sea off Massachusetts and Maine and over Manhattan bay and over Champlain and Erie and over Ontario and Huron and Michigan and Superior, and over the Texan and Mexican and Floridian and Cuban seas and over the seas off California and Oregon, is not tallied by the blue breadth of the

waters below more than the breadth of above and below is tallied by him. When the long Atlantic coast stretches longer and the Pacific coast stretches longer he easily stretches with them north or south. He spans between them also from east to west and reflects what is between them. On him rise solid growths that offset the growths of pine and cedar and hemlock and liveoak and locust and chestnut and cypress and hickory and limetree and cottonwood and tuliptree and cactus and wildvine and tamarind and persimmon . . . and tangles as tangled as any canebreak or swamp . . . and forests coated with transparent ice and icicles hanging from the boughs and crackling in the wind . . . and sides and peaks of mountains . . . and pasturage sweet and free as savannah or upland or prairie . . . with flights and songs and screams that answer those of the wildpigeon and highhold and orchard-oriole and coot and surf-duck and redshouldered-hawk and fish-hawk and white-ibis and indian-hen and cat-owl and water-pheasant and qua-bird and piedsheldrake and blackbird and mockingbird and buzzard and condor and night-heron and eagle. . . .

Of all nations the United States with veins full of poetical stuff most need poets and will doubtless have the greatest and use them the greatest. Their Presidents shall not be their common referee so much as their poets shall. Of all mankind the great poet is the equable man. Not in him but off from him things are grotesque or eccentric or fail of their sanity. Nothing out of its place is good and nothing in its place is bad. He bestows on every object or quality its fit proportions neither more nor less. He is the arbiter of the diverse and he is the key. He is the equalizer of his age and land . . . he supplies what wants supplying and checks what wants checking. . . .

The greatest poet hardly knows pettiness or triviality. If he breathes into any thing that was before thought small it dilates with the grandeur and life of the universe. He is a seer . . . he is individual . . . he is complete in himself . . . the others are as good as he, only he sees it and they do not. He is not one of the chorus . . . he does not stop for any regulations . . . he is the president of regulation. . . .

The land and sea, the animals, fishes and birds, the sky of heaven and the orbs, the forests mountains and rivers, are not small themes . . . but folks expect of the poet to indicate more than the beauty and dignity which always attach to dumb real objects . . . they expect him to indicate the path between reality and their souls. Men and women perceive the beauty well enough . . . probably as well as he. The passionate tenacity of hunters, woodmen, early risers, cultivators of gardens and orchards and fields, the love of healthy women for the manly form, seafaring persons, drivers of horses, the passion for light and the open air, all is an old varied sign of the unfailing perception of beauty and of a residence of the poetic in outdoor people. They can never be assisted by poets to perceive . . . some may but they never can. The poetic quality is not marshalled in rhyme or uniformity or abstract addresses to things nor in melancholy complaints or good precepts, but is the life of these and much else and is in the soul. . . . All beauty comes from beautiful blood and a beautiful brain. If the greatnesses are in conjunction in a man or woman it is enough . . . the fact will prevail through the universe . . . but the gaggery and gilt of a million years will not prevail. Who troubles himself about his orna-

ments or fluency is lost. This is what you shall do: Love the earth and sun and the animals, despise riches, give alms to every one that asks, stand up for the stupid and crazy, devote your income and labor to others, hate tyrants, argue not concerning God, have patience and indulgence toward the people, take off your hat to nothing known or unknown or to any man or number of men, go freely with powerful uneducated persons and with the young and with the mothers of families, read these leaves in the open air every season of every year of your life, re-examine all you have been told at school or church or in any book, dismiss whatever insults your own soul, and your very flesh shall be a great poem and have the richest fluency not only in its words but in the silent lines of its lips and face and between the lashes of your eyes and in every motion and joint of your body. . . . The poet shall not spend his time in unneeded work. He shall know that the ground is always ready plowed and manured . . . others may not know it but he shall. He shall go directly to the creation. His trust shall master the trust of everything he touches . . . and shall master all attachment. . . .

The art of art, the glory of expression and the sunshine of the light of letters is simplicity. Nothing is better than simplicity . . . nothing can make up for excess or for the lack of definiteness. To carry on the heave of impulse and pierce intellectual depths and give all subjects their articulations are powers neither common nor very uncommon. But to speak in literature with the perfect rectitude and insouciance of the movements of animals and the unimpeachableness of the sentiment of trees in the woods and grass by the roadside is the flawless triumph of art. If you have looked on him who has achieved it you have looked on one of the masters of the artists of all nations and times. . . . The greatest poet has less a marked style and is more the channel of thoughts and things without increase or diminution, and is the free channel of himself. He swears to his art, I will not be meddlesome, I will not have in my writing any elegance or effect or originality to hang in the way between me and the rest like curtains. I will have nothing hang in the way, not the richest curtains. What I tell I tell for precisely what it is. Let who may exalt or startle or fascinate or sooth I will have purposes as health or heat or snow has and be as regardless of observation. What I experience or portray shall go from my composition without a shred of my composition. You shall stand by my side and look in the mirror with me. . . .

The messages of great poets to each man and woman are, Come to us on equal terms, Only then can you understand us, We are no better than you, What we enclose you enclose, What we enjoy you may enjoy. Did you suppose there could be only one Supreme? We affirm there can be unnumbered Supremes, and that one does not countervail another any more than one eyesight countervails another . . . and that men can be good or grand only of the consciousness of their supremacy within them. What do you think is the grandeur of storms and dismemberments and the deadliest battles and wrecks and the wildest fury of the elements and the power of the sea and the motion of nature and of the throes of human desires and dignity and hate and love? It is that something in the soul which says, Rage on, Whirl on, I tread master here and everywhere, Master of the spasms of the sky and of the shatter of the sea, Master of nature and passion and death, And of all terror and all pain. . . .

Exact science and its practical movements are no checks on the greatest poet but always his encouragement and support. The outset and remembrance are there . . . there are the arms that lifted him first and brace him best . . . there he returns after all his goings and comings. The sailor and traveler . . . the anatomist chemist astronomer geologist phrenologist spiritualist mathematician historian and lexicographer are not poets, but they are the lawgivers of poets and their construction underlies the structure of every perfect poem. No matter what rises or is uttered they sent the seed of the conception of it . . . of them and by them stand the visible proofs of souls . . . always of their fatherstuff must be begotten the sinewy races of bards. If there shall be love and content between the father and the son and if the greatness of the son is the exuding of the greatness of the father there shall be love between the poet and the man of demonstrable science. In the beauty of poems are the tuft and final applause of science. . . .

In the make of the great masters the idea of political liberty is indispensable. Liberty takes the adherence of heroes wherever men and women exist . . . but never takes any adherence or welcome from the rest more than from poets. They are the voice and exposition of liberty. They out of ages are worthy the grand idea . . . to them it is confided and they must sustain it. Nothing has precedence of it and nothing can warp or degrade it. The attitude of great poets is to cheer up slaves and horrify despots. The turn of their necks, the sound of their feet, the motions of their wrists, are full of hazard to the one and hope to the other. Come nigh them awhile and though they neither speak nor advise you shall learn the faithful American lesson. Liberty is poorly served by men whose good intent is quelled from one failure or two failures or any number of failures, or from the casual indifference or ingratitude of the people, or from the sharp show of the tushes of power, or the bringing to bear soldiers and cannon or any penal statutes. Liberty relies upon itself, invites no one, promises nothing, sits in calmness and light, is positive and composed, and knows no discouragement. The battle rages with many a loud alarm and frequent advance and retreat . . . the enemy triumphs . . . the prison, the handcuffs, the iron necklace and anklet, the scaffold, garrote and leadballs do their work . . . the cause is asleep . . . the strong throats are choked with their own blood . . . the young men drop their eyelashes toward the ground when they pass each other . . . and is liberty gone out of that place? No never. When liberty goes it is not the first to go nor the second or third to go . . . it waits for all the rest to go . . . it is the last. . . . When the memories of the old martyrs are faded utterly away . . . when the large names of patriots are laughed at in the public halls from the lips of the orators . . . when the boys are no more christened after the same but christened after tyrants and traitors instead . . . when the laws of the free are grudgingly permitted and laws for informers and bloodmoney are sweet to the taste of the people . . . when I and you walk abroad upon the earth stung with compassion at the sight of numberless brothers answering our equal friendship and calling no man master— and when we are elated with noble joy at the sight of slaves . . . when the soul retires in the cool communion of the night and surveys its experience and has much extasy over the word and deed that put back a helpless innocent person into the

gripe of the gripers or into any cruel inferiority . . . when those in all parts of these states who could easier realize the true American character but do not yet— when the swarms of cringers, suckers, doughfaces, lice of politics, planners of sly involutions for their own preferment to city offices or state legislatures or the judiciary or congress or the presidency, obtain a response of love and natural deference from the people whether they get the offices or no . . . when it is better to be a bound booby and rogue in office at a high salary than the poorest free mechanic or farmer with his hat unmoved from his head and firm eyes and a candid and generous heart . . . and when servility by town or state or the federal government or any oppression on a large scale or small scale can be tried on without its own punishment following duly after in exact proportion against the smallest chance of escape . . . or rather when all life and all the souls of men and women are discharged from any part of the earth—then only shall the instinct of liberty be discharged from that part of the earth. . . .

. . . It has been thought that the prudent citizen was the citizen who applied himself to solid gains and did well for himself and his family and completed a lawful life without debt or crime. The greatest poet sees and admits these economies as he sees the economies of food and sleep, but has higher notions of prudence than to think he gives much when he gives a few slight attentions at the latch of the gate. The premises of the prudence of life are not the hospitality of it or the ripeness and harvest of it.

The direct trial of him who would be the greatest poet is today. If he does not flood himself with the immediate age as with vast oceanic tides . . . and if he does not attract his own land body and soul to himself and hang on its neck with incomparable love and plunge his semitic muscle into its merits and demerits . . . and if he be not himself the age transfigured . . . and if to him is not opened the eternity which gives similitude to all periods and locations and processes and animate and inanimate forms, and which is the bond of time, and rises up from its inconceivable vagueness and infiniteness in the swimming shape of today, and is held by the ductile anchors of life, and makes the present spot the passage from what was to what shall be, and commits itself to the representation of this wave of an hour and this one of the sixty beautiful children of the wave—let him merge in the general run and wait his development. . . . Still the final test of poems or any character or work remains. The prescient poet projects himself centuries ahead and judges performer or performance after the changes of time. . . .

A great poem is for ages and ages in common and for all degrees and complexions and all departments and sects and for a woman as much as a man and a man as much as a woman. A great poem is no finish to a man or woman but rather a beginning. Has any one fancied he could sit at last under some due authority and rest satisfied with explanations and realize and be content and full? To no such terminus does the greatest poet bring . . . he brings neither cessation nor sheltered fatness and ease. The touch of him tells in action. Whom he takes he takes with firm sure grasp into live regions previously unattained . . . thenceforward is no rest . . . they see the space and ineffable sheen that turn the old spots and lights into dead vacuums. The companion of him beholds the birth and progress of stars and learns one of the meanings. Now there shall be a man cohered out of tumult and chaos . . . the elder encourages the younger and shows him how . . . they two shall launch off fearlessly together till the new world fits an orbit for itself and looks unabashed on the lesser orbits of the stars and sweeps through the ceaseless rings and shall never be quiet again. . . .

The poems distilled from other poems will probably pass away. The coward will surely pass away. The expectation of the vital and great can only be satisfied by the demeanor of the vital and great. The swarms of the polished deprecating and reflectors and the polite float off and leave no remembrance. America prepares with composure and goodwill for the visitors that have sent word. It is not intellect that is to be their warrant and welcome. The talented, the artist, the ingenious, the editor, the statesman, the erudite . . . they are not unappreciated . . . they fall in their place and do their work. The soul of the nation also does its work. No disguise can pass on it . . . no disguise can conceal from it. It rejects none, it permits all. Only toward as good as itself and toward the like of itself will it advance half-way. An individual is as superb as a nation when he has the qualities which make a superb nation. The soul of the largest and wealthiest and proudest nation may well go half-way to meet that of its poets. The signs are effectual. There is no fear of mistake. If the one is true the other is true. The proof of a poet is that his country absorbs him as affectionately as he has absorbed it.

THE SIGNIFICANCE OF THE FRONTIER
IN AMERICAN HISTORY

by FREDERICK JACKSON TURNER

IN A RECENT BULLETIN of the Superintendent of the Census for 1890 appear these significant words: "Up to and including 1880 the country had a frontier of settlement, but at present the unsettled area has been so broken into by isolated bodies of settlement that there can hardly be said to be a frontier line. In the discussion of its extent, its westward movement, etc., it can not, therefore, any longer have a place in the census reports." This brief official statement marks the closing of a great historic movement. Up to our own day American history has been in a large degree the history of the colonization of the Great West. The existence of an area of free land, its continuous recession, and the advance of American settlement westward, explain American development.

Behind institutions, behind constitutional forms and modifications, lie the vital forces that call these organs into life and shape them to meet changing conditions. The peculiarity of American institutions is the fact that they have been compelled to adapt themselves to the changes of an expanding people—to the changes involved in crossing a continent, in winning a wilderness, and in developing at each area of this progress out of the primitive economic and political conditions of the frontier into the complexity of city life. Said Calhoun in 1817, "We are great, and rapidly—I was about to say fearfully—growing!" So saying, he touched the distinguishing feature of American life. All peoples show development; the germ theory of politics has been sufficiently emphasized. In the case of most nations, however, the development has occurred in a limited area; and if the nation has expanded, it has met other growing peoples whom it has conquered. But in the case of the United States we have a different phenomenon. Limiting our attention to the Atlantic coast, we have the familiar phenomenon of the evolution of institutions in a limited area, such as the rise of representative government; the differentiation of simple colonial governments into complex organs; the progress from primitive industrial society, without division of labor, up to manufacturing civilization. But we have in addition to this a recurrence of the process of evolution in each western area reached in the process of expansion. Thus American development has exhibited not merely advance along a single line, but a return to primitive conditions on a continually advancing frontier line, and a new development for that area. American social development has been continually beginning over again on the frontier. This perennial rebirth, this fluidity of American life, this expansion westward with its new opportunities, its continuous touch with the simplicity of primitive society, furnish the forces dominating American character. The true point of view in the history of this nation is not the Atlantic coast, it is the Great West. Even the slavery struggle, which is made so exclusive an object of attention by writers like Professor von Holst, occupies its important place in American history because of its relation to westward expansion.

In this advance, the frontier is the outer edge of the wave—the meeting point between savagery and civilization. Much has been written about the frontier from the point of view of border warfare and the chase, but as a field for the serious study of the economist and the historian it has been neglected.

The American frontier is sharply distinguished from the European frontier—a fortified boundary line running through dense populations. The most significant thing about the American frontier is, that it lies at the hither edge of free land. In the census reports it is treated as the margin of that settlement which has a density of two or more to the square mile. The term is an elastic one, and for our purposes does not need sharp definition. We shall consider the whole frontier belt, including the Indian country and the outer margin of the "settled area" of the census reports. This paper will make no attempt to treat the subject exhaustively; its aim is simply to call attention to the frontier as a fertile field for investigation, and to suggest some of the problems which arise in connection with it.

In the settlement of America we have to observe how European life entered the continent, and how America modified and developed that life and reacted on Europe. Our early history is the study of European germs developing in an American environment. Too exclusive attention has been paid by institutional students to the Germanic origins, too little to the American factors. The frontier is the line of most rapid and effective Americanization. The wilderness masters the colonist. It finds him a European in dress, industries, tools, modes of travel, and thought. It takes him from the railroad car and puts him in the birch canoe. It strips off the garments of civilization and arrays him in the hunting shirt and the moccasin. It puts him in the log cabin of the Cherokee and Iroquois and runs an Indian palisade around him. Before long he has gone to planting Indian corn and plowing with a sharp stick; he shouts the war cry and takes the scalp in orthodox Indian fashion. In short, at the frontier the environment is at first too strong for the man. He must accept the conditions which it furnishes, or perish, and so he fits himself into the Indian clearings and follows the Indian trails. Little by little he transforms the wilderness, but the outcome is not the old Europe, not simply the development of Germanic germs, any more than the first phenomenon was a case of reversion to the Germanic mark. The fact is, that here is a new product that is American. At first, the frontier was the Atlantic coast. It was the frontier of Europe in a very real sense. Moving westward, the frontier became more and more American. As successive terminal moraines result from successive glaciations, so each frontier leaves its traces behind it, and when it becomes a settled area the region still partakes of the frontier characteristics. Thus the advance of the frontier has meant a steady movement away from the influence of Europe, a steady growth of independence on American lines. And to study this advance, the men who grew up under these conditions, and the political, economic, and social results of it, is to study the really American part of our history.

In the course of the seventeenth century the frontier was advanced up the Atlantic river courses, just beyond the "fall line," and the tidewater region became the settled area. In the first half of the eighteenth century another advance occurred. Traders followed the Delaware and Shawnese Indians to the Ohio as early as the end of the first quarter of the century. Gov. Spotswood, of Virginia, made an expedition in 1714 across the Blue Ridge. The end of the first quarter of the century saw the advance of the Scotch-Irish and the Palatine Germans up the Shenandoah Valley into the western part of Virginia, and along the Piedmont region of the Carolinas. The Germans in New York pushed the frontier of settlement up the Mohawk to German Flats. In Pennsylvania the town of Bedford indicates the line of settlement. Settlements had begun on New River, a branch of the Kanawha, and on the sources of the Yadkin and French Broad. The King attempted to arrest the advance by his proclamation of 1763, forbidding settlements beyond the sources of the rivers flowing into the Atlantic; but in vain. In the period of the Revolution the frontier crossed the Alleghenies into Kentucky and Tennessee, and the upper waters of the Ohio were settled. When the first census was taken in 1790, the continuous settled area was bounded by a line which ran near the coast of Maine, and included New England except a portion of Vermont and New Hampshire, New York along the Hudson and up the Mohawk about Sche-

nectady, eastern and southern Pennsylvania, Virginia well across the Shenandoah Valley, and the Carolinas and eastern Georgia. Beyond this region of continuous settlement were the small settled areas of Kentucky and Tennessee, and the Ohio, with the mountains intervening between them and the Atlantic area, thus giving a new and important character to the frontier. The isolation of the region increased its peculiarly American tendencies, and the need of transportation facilities to connect it with the East called out important schemes of internal improvement, which will be noted farther on. The "West," as a self-conscious section, began to evolve.

From decade to decade distinct advances of the frontier occurred. By the census of 1820 the settled area included Ohio, southern Indiana and Illinois, southeastern Missouri, and about one-half of Louisiana. This settled area had surrounded Indian areas, and the management of these tribes became an object of political concern. The frontier region of the time lay along the Great Lakes, where Astor's American Fur Company operated in the Indian trade, and beyond the Mississippi, where Indian traders extended their activity even to the Rocky Mountains; Florida also furnished frontier conditions. The Mississippi River region was the scene of typical frontier settlements.

The rising steam navigation on western waters, the opening of the Erie Canal, and the westward extension of cotton culture added five frontier states to the Union in this period. Grund, writing in 1836, declares: "It appears then that the universal disposition of Americans to emigrate to the western wilderness, in order to enlarge their dominion over inanimate nature, is the actual result of an expansive power which is inherent in them, and which by continually agitating all classes of society is constantly throwing a large portion of the whole population on the extreme confines of the State, in order to gain space for its development. Hardly is a new State or Territory formed before the same principle manifests itself again and gives rise to a further emigration; and so is it destined to go on until a physical barrier must finally obstruct its progress."

In the middle of this century the line indicated by the present eastern boundary of Indian Territory, Nebraska, and Kansas marked the frontier of the Indian country. Minnesota and Wisconsin still exhibited frontier conditions, but the distinctive frontier of the period is found in California, where the gold discoveries had sent a sudden tide of adventurous miners, and in Oregon, and the settlements in Utah. As the frontier had leaped over the Alleghenies, so now it skipped the Great Plains and the Rocky Mountains; and in the same way that the advance of the frontiersmen beyond the Alleghenies had caused the rise of important questions of transportation and internal improvement, so now the settlers beyond the Rocky Mountains needed means of communication with the East, and in the furnishing of these arose the settlement of the Great Plains and the development of still another kind of frontier life. Railroads, fostered by land grants, sent an increasing tide of immigrants into the Far West. The United States Army fought a series of Indian wars in Minnesota, Dakota, and the Indian Territory.

By 1880 the settled area had been pushed into northern Michigan, Wisconsin, and Minnesota, along Dakota rivers, and in the Black Hills region, and was ascending the rivers of Kansas and Nebraska. The development of mines in Colorado had drawn isolated frontier settlements into

that region, and Montana and Idaho were receiving settlers. The frontier was found in these mining camps and the ranches of the Great Plains. The superintendent of the census for 1890 reports, as previously stated, that the settlements of the West lie so scattered over the region that there can no longer be said to be a frontier line.

In these successive frontiers we find natural boundary lines which have served to mark and to affect the characteristics of the frontiers, namely: the "fall line"; the Allegheny Mountains; the Mississippi; the Missouri where its direction approximates north and south; the line of the arid lands, approximately the ninety-ninth meridian; and the Rocky Mountains. The fall line marked the frontier of the seventeenth century; the Alleghenies that of the eighteenth; the Mississippi that of the first quarter of the nineteenth; the Missouri that of the middle of this century (omitting the California movement); and the belt of the Rocky Mountains and the arid tract, the present frontier. Each was won by a series of Indian wars.

At the Atlantic frontier one can study the germs of processes repeated at each successive frontier. We have the complex European life sharply precipitated by the wilderness into the simplicity of primitive conditions. The first frontier had to meet its Indian question, its question of the disposition of the public domain, of the means of intercourse with older settlements, of the extension of political organization, of religious and educational activity. And the settlement of these and similar questions for one frontier served as a guide for the next. The American student needs not to go to the "prim little townships of Sleswick" for illustrations of the law of continuity and development. For example, he may study the origin of our land policies in the colonial land policy; he may see how the system grew by adapting the statutes to the customs of the successive frontiers. He may see how the mining experience in the lead regions of Wisconsin, Illinois, and Iowa was applied to the mining laws of the Sierras, and how our Indian policy has been a series of experimentations on successive frontiers. Each tier of new States has found in the older ones material for its constitutions. Each frontier has made similar contributions to American characters, as will be discussed farther on.

But with all these similarities there are essential differences, due to the place element and the time element. It is evident that the farming frontier of the Mississippi Valley presents different conditions from the mining frontier of the Rocky Mountains. The frontier reached by the Pacific Railroad, surveyed into rectangles, guarded by the United States Army, and recruited by the daily immigrant ship, moves forward at a swifter pace and in a different way than the frontier reached by the birch canoe or the pack horse. The geologist traces patiently the shores of ancient seas, maps their areas, and compares the older and the newer. It would be a work worth the historian's labors to mark these various frontiers and in detail compare one with another. Not only would there result a more adequate conception of American development and characteristics, but invaluable additions would be made to the history of society.

Loria, the Italian economist, has urged the study of colonial life as an aid in understanding the stages of European development, affirming that colonial settlement is for economic science what the mountain is for geology, bringing to light primitive stratifications. "America," he says, "has the key to the historical enigma which Europe has sought for centuries in vain, and the land which has no history reveals luminously the course of universal history." There is much truth in this. The United States lies like a huge page in the history of society. Line by line as we read this continental page from West to East we find the record of social evolution. It begins with the Indian and the hunter; it goes on to tell of the disintegration of savagery by the entrance of the trader, the pathfinder of civilization; we read the annals of the pastoral stage in ranch life; the exploitation of the soil by the raising of unrotated crops of corn and wheat in sparsely settled farming communities; the intensive culture of the denser farm settlement; and finally the manufacturing organization with city and factory system. This page is familiar to the student of census statistics, but how little of it has been used by our historians. Particularly in eastern States this page is a palimpsest. What is now a manufacturing State was in an earlier decade an area of intensive farming. Earlier yet it had been a wheat area, and still earlier the "range" had attracted the cattle-herder. Thus Wisconsin, now developing manufacture, is a State with varied agricultural interests. But earlier it was given over to almost exclusive grain-raising, like North Dakota at the present time.

Each of these areas has had an influence in our economic and political history; the evolution of each into a higher stage has worked political transformations. But what constitutional historian has made any adequate attempt to interpret political facts by the light of these social areas and changes?

The Atlantic frontier was compounded of fisherman, fur-trader, miner, cattle-raiser, and farmer. Excepting the fisherman, each type of industry was on the march toward the West, impelled by an irresistible attraction. Each passed in successive waves across the continent. Stand at Cumberland Gap and watch the procession of civilization, marching single file —the buffalo following the trail to the salt springs, the Indian, the fur-trader and hunter, the cattle-raiser, the pioneer farmer—and the frontier has passed by. Stand at South Pass in the Rockies a century later and see the same procession with wider intervals between. The unequal rate of advance compels us to distinguish the frontier into the trader's frontier, the rancher's frontier, or the miner's frontier, and the farmer's frontier. When the mines and the cowpens were still near the fall line the traders' pack trains were tinkling across the Alleghenies, and the French on the Great Lakes were fortifying their posts, alarmed by the British trader's birch canoe. When the trappers scaled the Rockies, the farmer was still near the mouth of the Missouri.

Why was it that the Indian trader passed so rapidly across the continent? What effects followed from the trader's frontier? The trade was coeval with American discovery. The Norsemen, Vespuccius, Verrazani, Hudson, John Smith, all trafficked for furs. The Plymouth pilgrims settled in Indian cornfields, and their first return cargo was of beaver and lumber. The records of the various New England colonies show how steadily exploration was carried into the wilderness by this trade. What is true for New England is, as would be expected, even plainer for the rest of the colonies. All along the coast from Maine to Georgia the Indian trade opened up the river courses. Steadily the trader passed westward, utilizing the older lines of French trade. The Ohio, the Great Lakes, the Mississippi, the Missouri, and the Platte, the lines of western advance, were ascended by traders. They

found the passes in the Rocky Mountains and guided Lewis and Clark, Frémont, and Bidwell. The explanation of the rapidity of this advance is connected with the effects of the trader on the Indian. The trading post left the unarmed tribes at the mercy of those that had purchased firearms—a truth which the Iroquois Indians wrote in blood, and so the remote and unvisited tribes gave eager welcome to the trader. "The savages," wrote La Salle, "take better care of us French than of their own children; from us only can they get guns and goods." This accounts for the trader's power and the rapidity of his advance. Thus the disintegrating forces of civilization entered the wilderness. Every river valley and Indian trail became a fissure in Indian society, and so that society became honeycombed. Long before the pioneer farmer appeared on the scene, primitive Indian life had passed away. The farmers met Indians armed with guns. The trading frontier, while steadily undermining Indian power by making the tribes ultimately dependent on the whites, yet, through its sale of guns, gave to the Indian increased power of resistance to the farming frontier. French colonization was dominated by its trading frontier; English colonization by its farming frontier. There was an antagonism between the two frontiers as between the two nations. Said Duquesne to the Iroquois, "Are you ignorant of the difference between the king of England and the king of France? Go see the forts that our king has established and you will see that you can still hunt under their very walls. They have been placed for your advantage in places which you frequent. The English, on the contrary, are no sooner in possession of a place than the game is driven away. The forest falls before them as they advance, and the soil is laid bare so that you can scarce find the wherewithal to erect a shelter for the night."

And yet, in spite of this opposition of the interests of the trader and the farmer, the Indian trade pioneered the way for civilization. The buffalo trail became the Indian trail, and this became the trader's "trace"; the trails widened into roads, and the roads into turnpikes, and these in turn were transformed into railroads. The same origin can be shown for the railroads of the South, the Far West, and the Dominion of Canada. The trading posts reached by these trails were on the sites of Indian villages which had been placed in positions suggested by nature; and these trading posts, situated so as to command the water systems of the country, have grown into such cities as Albany, Pittsburgh, Detroit, Chicago, St. Louis, Council Bluffs, and Kansas City. Thus civilization in America has followed the arteries made by geology, pouring an ever richer tide through them, until at last the slender paths of aboriginal intercourse have been broadened and interwoven into the complex mazes of modern commercial lines; the wilderness has been interpenetrated by lines of civilization growing ever more numerous. It is like the steady growth of a complex nervous system for the originally simple, inert continent. If one would understand why we are to-day one nation, rather than a collection of isolated states, he must study this economic and social consolidation of the country. In this progress from savage conditions lie topics for the evolutionist.

The effect of the Indian frontier as a consolidating agent in our history is important. From the close of the seventeenth century various intercolonial congresses have been called to treat with Indians and establish common measures of defense. Particularism was strongest in colo-nies with no Indian frontier. This frontier stretched along the western border like a cord of union. The Indian was a common danger, demanding united action. Most celebrated of these conferences was the Albany congress of 1754, called to treat with the Six Nations, and to consider plans of union. Even a cursory reading of the plan proposed by the congress reveals the importance of the frontier. The powers of the general council and the officers were, chiefly, the determination of peace and war with the Indians, the regulation of Indian trade, the purchase of Indian lands, and the creation and government of new settlements as a security against the Indians. It is evident that the unifying tendencies of the Revolutionary period were facilitated by the previous cooperation in the regulation of the frontier. In this connection may be mentioned the importance of the frontier, from that day to this, as a military training school, keeping alive the power of resistance to aggression, and developing the stalwart and rugged qualities of the frontiersman.

It would not be possible in the limits of this paper to trace the other frontiers across the continent. Travelers of the eighteenth century found the "cowpens" among the canebrakes and peavine pastures of the South, and the "cow drivers" took their droves to Charleston, Philadelphia, and New York. Travelers at the close of the War of 1812 met droves of more than a thousand cattle and swine from the interior of Ohio going to Pennsylvania to fatten for the Philadelphia market. The ranges of the Great Plains, with ranch and cowboy and nomadic life, are things of yesterday and of to-day. The experience of the Carolina cowpens guided the ranchers of Texas. One element favoring the rapid extension of the rancher's frontier is the fact that in a remote country lacking transportation facilities the product must be in small bulk, or must be able to transport itself, and the cattle-raiser could easily drive his product to market. The effect of these great ranches on the subsequent agrarian history of the localities in which they existed should be studied.

The maps of the census reports show an uneven advance of the farmer's frontier, with tongues of settlement pushed forward and with indentations of wilderness. In part this is due to Indian resistance, in part to the location of river valleys and passes, in part to the unequal force of the centers of frontier attraction. Among the important centers of attraction may be mentioned the following: fertile and favorably situated soils, salt springs, mines, and army posts.

The frontier army post, serving to protect the settlers from the Indians, has also acted as a wedge to open the Indian country, and has been a nucleus for settlement. In this connection mention should also be made of the government military and exploring expeditions in determining the lines of settlement. But all the more important expeditions were greatly indebted to the earliest pathmakers, the Indian guides, the traders and trappers, and the French voyageurs, who were inevitable parts of governmental expeditions from the days of Lewis and Clark. Each expedition was an epitome of the previous factors in western advance.

In an interesting monograph, Victor Hehn has traced the effect of salt upon early European development, and has pointed out how it affected the lines of settlement and the form of administration. A similar study might be made for the salt springs of the United States. The early settlers were tied to the coast by the need of salt, without which they could not preserve their meats or live in comfort. Writ-

ing in 1752, Bishop Spangenburg says of a colony for which he was seeking lands in North Carolina, "They will require salt & other necessaries which they can neither manufacture nor raise. Either they must go to Charleston, which is 300 miles distant . . . Or else they must go to Boling's Point in V^a on a branch of the James & is also 300 miles from here . . . Or else they must go down the Roanoke—I know not how many miles—where salt is brought up from the Cape Fear." This may serve as a typical illustration. An annual pilgrimage to the coast for salt thus became essential. Taking flocks or furs and ginseng root, the early settlers sent their pack trains after seeding time each year to the coast. This proved to be an important educational influence, since it was almost the only way in which the pioneer learned what was going on in the East. But when discovery was made of the salt springs of the Kanawha, and the Holston, and Kentucky, and central New York, the West began to be freed from dependence on the coast. It was in part the effect of finding these salt springs that enabled settlement to cross the mountains.

From the time the mountains rose between the pioneer and the seaboard, a new order of Americanism arose. The West and the East began to get out of touch of each other. The settlements from the sea to the mountains kept connection with the rear and had a certain solidarity. But the over-mountain men grew more and more independent. The East took a narrow view of American advance, and nearly lost these men. Kentucky and Tennessee history bears abundant witness to the truth of this statement. The East began to try to hedge and limit westward expansion. Though Webster could declare that there were no Alleghenies in his politics, yet in politics in general they were a very solid factor.

The exploitation of the beasts took hunter and trader to the west, the exploitation of the grasses took the rancher west, and the exploitation of the virgin soil of the river valleys and prairies attracted the farmer. Good soils have been the most continuous attraction to the farmer's frontier. The land hunger of the Virginians drew them down the rivers into Carolina, in early colonial days; the search for soils took the Massachusetts men to Pennsylvania and to New York. As the eastern lands were taken up migration flowed across them to the west. Daniel Boone, the great backwoodsman, who combined the occupations of hunter, trader, cattle-raiser, farmer, and surveyor—learning, probably from the traders, of the fertility of the lands of the upper Yadkin, where the traders were wont to rest as they took their way to the Indians—left his Pennsylvania home with his father, and passed down the Great Valley road to that stream. Learning from a trader of the game and rich pastures of Kentucky, he pioneered the way for the farmers to that region. Thence he passed to the frontier of Missouri, where his settlement was long a landmark on the frontier. Here again he helped to open the way for civilization, finding salt licks, and trails, and land. His son was among the earliest trappers in the passes of the Rocky Mountains, and his party are said to have been the first to camp on the present site of Denver. His grandson, Col. A. J. Boone, of Colorado, was a power among the Indians of the Rocky Mountains, and was appointed an agent by the government. Kit Carson's mother was a Boone. Thus this family epitomizes the backwoodsman's advance across the continent.

The farmer's advance came in a distinct series of waves. In Peck's New Guide to the West, published in Boston in 1837, occurs this suggestive passage:

Generally, in all the western settlements, three classes, like the waves of the ocean, have rolled one after the other. First comes the pioneer, who depends for the subsistence of his family chiefly upon the natural growth of vegetation, called the "range," and the proceeds of hunting. His implements of agriculture are rude, chiefly of his own make, and his efforts directed mainly to a crop of corn and a "truck patch." The last is a rude garden for growing cabbage, beans, corn for roasting ears, cucumbers, and potatoes. A log cabin, and, occasionally, a stable and corn-crib, and a field of a dozen acres, the timber girdled or "deadened," and fenced, are enough for his occupancy. It is quite immaterial whether he ever becomes the owner of the soil. He is the occupant for the time being, pays no rent, and feels as independent as the "lord of the manor." With a horse, cow, and one or two breeders of swine, he strikes into the woods with his family, and becomes the founder of a new county, or perhaps state. He builds his cabin, gathers around him a few other families of similar tastes and habits, and occupies till the range is somewhat subdued, and hunting a little precarious, or, which is more frequently the case, till the neighbors crowd around, roads, bridges, and fields annoy him, and he lacks elbow room. The preemption law enables him to dispose of his cabin and cornfield to the next class of emigrants; and, to employ his own figures, he "breaks for the high timber," "clears out for the New Purchase," or migrates to Arkansas or Texas, to work the same process over.

The next class of emigrants purchase the lands, add field to field, clear out the roads, throw rough bridges over the streams, put up hewn log houses with glass windows and brick or stone chimneys, occasionally plant orchards, build mills, school-houses, courthouses, etc., and exhibit the picture and forms of plain, frugal, civilized life.

Another wave rolls on. The men of capital

and enterprise come. The settler is ready to sell out and take the advantage of the rise in property, push farther into the interior and become, himself, a man of capital and enterprise in turn. The small village rises to a spacious town or city; substantial edifices of brick, extensive fields, orchards, gardens, colleges, and churches are seen. Broadcloths, silks, leghorns, crapes, and all the refinements, luxuries, elegances, frivolities, and fashions are in vogue. Thus wave after wave is rolling westward; the real Eldorado is still farther on.

A portion of the two first classes remain stationary amidst the general movement, improve their habits and condition, and rise in the scale of society.

The writer has traveled much amongst the first class, the real pioneers. He has lived many years in connection with the second grade; and now the third wave is sweeping over large districts of Indiana, Illinois, and Missouri. Migration has become almost a habit in the West. Hundreds of men can be found, not over 50 years of age, who have settled for the fourth, fifth, or sixth time on a new spot. To sell out and remove only a few hundred miles makes up a portion of the variety of backwoods life and manners.

Omitting those of the pioneer farmers who move from the love of adventure, the advance of the more steady farmer is easy to understand. Obviously the immigrant was attracted by the cheap lands of the frontier, and even the native farmer felt their influence strongly. Year by year the farmers who lived on soil whose returns were diminished by unrotated crops were offered the virgin soil of the frontier at nominal prices. Their growing families demanded more lands, and these were dear. The competition of the unexhausted, cheap, and easily tilled prairie lands compelled the farmer either to go west and continue the exhaustion of the soil on a new frontier, or to adopt intensive culture. Thus the census of 1890 shows, in the Northwest, many counties in which there is an absolute or a relative decrease of population. These States have been sending farmers to advance the frontier on the plains, and have themselves begun to turn to intensive farming and to manufacture. A decade before this, Ohio had shown the same transition stage. Thus the demand for land and the love of wilderness freedom drew the frontier ever onward.

Having now roughly outlined the various kinds of frontiers, and their modes of advance, chiefly from the point of view of the frontier itself, we may next inquire what were the influences on the East and on the Old World. A rapid enumeration of some of the more noteworthy effects is all that I have time for.

First, we note that the frontier promoted the formation of a composite nationality for the American people. The coast was preponderantly English, but the later tides of continental immigration flowed across to the free lands. This was the case from the early colonial days. The Scotch-Irish and the Palatine Germans, or "Pennsylvania Dutch," furnished the dominant element in the stock of the colonial frontier. With these peoples were also the freed indented servants, or redemptioners, who at the expiration of their time of service passed to the frontier. Governor Spotswood of Virginia writes in 1717, "The inhabitants of our frontiers are composed generally of such as have been transported hither as servants, and, being out of their time, settle themselves where land is to be taken up and that will produce the necessarys of life with little labour." Very generally these redemptioners were of non-English stock. In the crucible of the frontier the immigrants were Americanized, liberated, and fused into a mixed race, English in neither nationality nor characteristics. The process has gone on from the early days to our own. Burke and other writers in the middle of the eighteenth century believed that Pennsylvania was "threatened with the danger of being wholly foreign in language, manners and perhaps even inclinations." The German and Scotch-Irish elements in the frontier of the South were only less great. In the middle of the present century the German element in Wisconsin was already so considerable that leading publicists looked to the creation of a German state out of the commonwealth by concentrating their colonization. Such examples teach us to beware of misinterpreting the fact that there is a common English speech in America into a belief that the stock is also English.

In another way the advance of the frontier decreased our dependence on England. The coast, particularly of the South, lacked diversified industries, and was dependent on England for the bulk of its supplies. In the South there was even a dependence on the Northern colonies for articles of food. Governor Glenn, of South Carolina, writes in the middle of the eighteenth century: "Our trade with New York and Philadelphia was of this sort, draining us of all the little money and bills we could gather from other places for their bread, flour, beer, hams, bacon, and other things of their produce, all which, except beer, our new townships begin to supply us with, which are settled with very industrious and thriving Germans. This no doubt diminishes the number of shipping and the appearance of our trade, but it is far from being a detriment to us." Before long the frontier created a demand for merchants. As it retreated from the coast it became less and less possible for England to bring her supplies directly to the consumer's wharfs, and carry away staple

crops, and staple crops began to give way to diversified agriculture for a time. The effect of this phase of the frontier action upon the northern section is perceived when we realize how the advance of the frontier aroused seaboard cities like Boston, New York, and Baltimore to engage in rivalry for what Washington called "the extensive and valuable trade of a rising empire."

The legislation which most developed the powers of the national government, and played the largest part in its activity, was conditioned on the frontier. Writers have discussed the subjects of tariff, land, and internal improvement, as subsidiary to the slavery question. But when American history comes to be rightly viewed it will be seen that the slavery question is an incident. In the period from the end of the first half of the present century to the close of the Civil War slavery rose to primary, but far from exclusive, importance. But this does not justify Dr. von Holst (to take an example) in treating our constitutional history in its formative period down to 1828 in a single volume, giving six volumes chiefly to the history of slavery from 1828 to 1861, under the title "Constitutional History of the United States." The growth of nationalism and the evolution of American political institutions were dependent on the advance of the frontier. Even so recent a writer as Rhodes, in his "History of the United States since the Compromise of 1850," has treated the legislation called out by the western advance as incidental to the slavery struggle.

This is a wrong perspective. The pioneer needed the goods of the coast, and so the grand series of internal improvement and railroad legislation began, with potent nationalizing effects. Over internal improvements occurred great debates, in which grave constitutional questions were discussed. Sectional groupings appear in the votes, profoundly significant for the historian. Loose construction increased as the nation marched westward. But the West was not content with bringing the farm to the factory. Under the lead of Clay—"Harry of the West"—protective tariffs were passed, with the cry of bringing the factory to the farm. The disposition of the public lands was a third important subject of national legislation influenced by the frontier.

The public domain has been a force of profound importance in the nationalization and development of the government. The effects of the struggle of the landed and the landless States, and of the Ordinance of 1787, need no discussion. Administratively the frontier called out some of the highest and most vitalizing activities of the general government. The purchase of Louisiana was perhaps the constitutional turning point in the history of the Republic, inasmuch as it afforded both a new area for national legislation and the occasion of the downfall of the policy of strict construction. But the purchase of Louisiana was called out by frontier needs and demands. As frontier States accrued to the Union the national power grew. In a speech on the dedication of the Calhoun monument Mr. Lamar explained: "In 1789 the States were the creators of the Federal Government; in 1861 the Federal Government was the creator of a large majority of the States."

When we consider the public domain from the point of view of the sale and disposal of the public lands we are again brought face to face with the frontier. The policy of the United States in dealing with its lands is in sharp contrast with the European system of scientific administration. Efforts to make this domain a source of revenue, and to withhold it from emi-

grants in order that settlement might be compact, were in vain. The jealousy and the fears of the East were powerless in the face of the demands of the frontiersmen. John Quincy Adams was obliged to confess: "My own system of administration, which was to make the national domain the inexhaustible fund for progressive and unceasing internal improvement, has failed." The reason is obvious: a system of administration was not what the West demanded; it wanted land. Adams states the situation as follows: "The slaveholders of the South have bought the cooperation of the western country by the bribe of the western lands, abandoning to the new Western States their own proportion of the public property and aiding them in the design of grasping all the lands into their own hands. Thomas H. Benton was the author of this system, which he brought forward as a substitute for the American system of Mr. Clay, and to supplant him as the leading statesman of the West. Mr. Clay, by his tariff compromise with Mr. Calhoun, abandoned his own American system. At the same time he brought forward a plan for distributing among all the States of the Union the proceeds of the sales of the public lands. His bill for that purpose passed both Houses of Congress, but was vetoed by President Jackson, who, in his annual message of December, 1832, formally recommended that all public lands should be gratuitously given away to individual adventurers and to the States in which the lands are situated."

"No subject," said Henry Clay, "which has presented itself to the present, or perhaps any preceding Congress, is of greater magnitude than that of the public lands." When we consider the far-reaching effects of the government's land policy upon political, economic, and social aspects of

American life, we are disposed to agree with him. But this legislation was framed under frontier influences, and under the lead of Western statesmen like Benton and Jackson. Said Senator Scott of Indiana in 1841: "I consider the preemption law merely declaratory of the custom or common law of the settlers."

It is safe to say that the legislation with regard to land, tariff, and internal improvements—the American system of the nationalizing Whig party—was conditioned on frontier ideas and needs. But it was not merely in legislative action that the frontier worked against the sectionalism of the coast. The economic and social characteristics of the frontier worked against sectionalism. The men of the frontier had closer resemblances to the Middle region than to either of the other sections. Pennsylvania had been the seed-plot of frontier emigration, and, although she passed on her settlers along the Great Valley into the west of Virginia and the Carolinas, yet the industrial society of these Southern frontiersmen was always more like that of the Middle region than like that of the tide-water portion of the South, which later came to spread its industrial type throughout the South.

The Middle region, entered by New York harbor, was an open door to all Europe. The tide-water part of the South represented typical Englishmen, modified by a warm climate and servile labor, and living in baronial fashion on great plantations; New England stood for a special English movement—Puritanism. The Middle region was less English than the other sections. It had a wide mixture of nationalities, a varied society, the mixed town and county system of local government, a varied economic life, many religious sects. In short, it was a region mediating between New England and the South, and

the East and the West. It represented that composite nationality which the contemporary United States exhibits, that juxtaposition of non-English groups, occupying a valley or a little settlement, and presenting reflections of the map of Europe in their variety. It was democratic and non-sectional, if not national; "easy, tolerant, and contented"; rooted strongly in material prosperity. It was typical of the modern United States. It was least sectional, not only because it lay between North and South, but also because with no barriers to shut out its frontiers from its settled region, and with a system of connecting waterways, the Middle region mediated between East and West as well as between North and South. Thus it became the typically American region. Even the New Englander, who was shut out from the frontier by the Middle region, tarrying in New York or Pennsylvania on his westward march, lost the acuteness of his sectionalism on the way.

The spread of cotton culture into the interior of the South finally broke down the contrast between the "tide-water" region and the rest of the State, and based Southern interests on slavery. Before this process revealed its results the western portion of the South, which was akin to Pennsylvania in stock, society, and industry, showed tendencies to fall away from the faith of the fathers into internal improvement legislation and nationalism. In the Virginia convention of 1829-30, called to revise the constitution, Mr. Leigh, of Chesterfield, one of the tide-water counties, declared:

One of the main causes of discontent which led to this convention, that which had the strongest influence in overcoming our veneration for the work of our fathers, which taught us to contemn the sentiments of Henry and Mason and Pendleton, which weaned us from our reverence for the constituted authorities of the State, was an overweening passion for internal improvement. I say this with perfect knowledge, for it has been avowed to me by gentlemen from the West over and over again. And let me tell the gentleman from Albemarle (Mr. Gordon) that it has been another principal object of those who set this ball of revolution in motion, to overturn the doctrine of State rights, of which Virginia has been the very pillar, and to remove the barrier she has interposed to the interference of the Federal Government in that same work of internal improvement, by so reorganizing the legislature that Virginia, too, may be hitched to the Federal car.

It was this nationalizing tendency of the West that transformed the democracy of Jefferson into the national republicanism of Monroe and the democracy of Andrew Jackson. The West of the War of 1812, the West of Clay, and Benton and Harrison, and Andrew Jackson, shut off by the Middle States and the mountains from the coast sections, had a solidarity of its own with national tendencies. On the tide of the Father of Waters, North and South met and mingled into a nation. Interstate migration went steadily on—a process of cross-fertilization of ideas and institutions. The fierce struggle of the sections over slavery on the western frontier does not diminish the truth of this statement; it proves the truth of it. Slavery was a sectional trait that would not down, but in the West it could not remain sectional. It was the greatest of frontiersmen who declared: "I believe this Government can not endure permanently half slave and half free. It will become all of one thing or all of the other." Nothing works for nationalism like intercourse within the nation. Mobility of population is death to

localism, and the western frontier worked irresistibly in unsettling population. The effect reached back from the frontier and affected profoundly the Atlantic coast and even the Old World.

But the most important effect of the frontier has been in the promotion of democracy here and in Europe. As has been indicated, the frontier is productive of individualism. Complex society is precipitated by the wilderness into a kind of primitive organization based on the family. The tendency is anti-social. It produces antipathy to control, and particularly to any direct control. The tax-gatherer is viewed as a representative of oppression. Prof. Osgood, in an able article, has pointed out that the frontier conditions prevalent in the colonies are important factors in the explanation of the American Revolution, where individual liberty was sometimes confused with absence of all effective government. The same conditions aid in explaining the difficulty of instituting a strong government in the period of the confederacy. The frontier individualism has from the beginning promoted democracy.

The frontier States that came into the Union in the first quarter of a century of its existence came in with democratic suffrage provisions, and had reactive effects of the highest importance upon the older States whose peoples were being attracted there. An extension of the franchise became essential. It was *western* New York that forced an extension of suffrage in the constitutional convention of that State in 1821; and it was *western* Virginia that compelled the tide-water region to put a more liberal suffrage provision in the constitution framed in 1830, and to give to the frontier region a more nearly proportionate representation with the tide-water aristocracy. The rise of democracy as an effective force in the nation came in with western preponderance under Jackson and William Henry Harrison, and it meant the triumph of the frontier—with all of its good and with all of its evil elements. An interesting illustration of the tone of frontier democracy in 1830 comes from the same debates in the Virginia convention already referred to. A representative from western Virginia declared:

But, sir, it is not the increase of population in the West which this gentleman ought to fear. It is the energy which the mountain breeze and western habits impart to those emigrants. They are regenerated, politically I mean, sir. They soon become *working politicians;* and the difference, sir, between a *talking* and a *working* politician is immense. The Old Dominion has long been celebrated for producing great orators; the ablest metaphysicians in policy; men that can split hairs in all abstruse questions of political economy. But at home, or when they return from Congress, they have Negroes to fan them asleep. But a Pennsylvania, a New York, an Ohio, or a western Virginia statesman, though far inferior in logic, metaphysics, and rhetoric to an old Virginia statesman, has this advantage, that when he returns home he takes off his coat and takes hold of the plow. This gives him bone and muscle, sir, and preserves his republican principles pure and uncontaminated.

So long as free land exists, the opportunity for a competency exists, and economic power secures political power. But the democracy born of free land, strong in selfishness and individualism, intolerant of administrative experience and education, and pressing individual liberty beyond its proper bounds, has its dangers as well as its benefits. Individualism in America has allowed a laxity in regard to governmental affairs which has rendered possible the spoils system and all the manifest evils that follow from the lack of a highly developed civic spirit. In this connection may be noted also the influence of frontier conditions in permitting lax business honor, inflated paper currency and wild-cat banking. The colonial and revolutionary frontier was the region whence emanated many of the worst forms of an evil currency. The West in the War of 1812 repeated the phenomenon on the frontier of that day, while the speculation and wild-cat banking of the period of the crisis of 1837 occurred on the new frontier belt of the next tier of States. Thus each one of the periods of lax financial integrity coincides with periods when a new set of frontier communities had arisen, and coincides in area with these successive frontiers, for the most part. The recent Populist agitation is a case in point. Many a State that now declines any connection with the tenets of the Populists, itself adhered to such ideas in an earlier stage of the development of the State. A primitive society can hardly be expected to show the intelligent appreciation of the complexity of business interests in a developed society. The continual recurrence of these areas of paper-money agitation is another evidence that the frontier can be isolated and studied as a factor in American history of the highest importance.

The East has always feared the result of an unregulated advance of the frontier, and has tried to check and guide it. The English authorities would have checked settlement at the headwaters of the Atlantic tributaries and allowed the "savages to enjoy their deserts in quiet lest the peltry trade should decrease." This called out Burke's splendid protest:

If you stopped your grants, what would be the consequence? The people would occupy without grants. They have already so occupied in many places. You can not station garrisons in every part of these deserts. If you drive the people from one place, they will carry on their annual tillage and remove with their flocks and herds to another. Many of the people in the back settlements are already little attached to particular situations. Already they have topped the Appalachian Mountains. From thence they behold before them an immense plain, one vast, rich level meadow; a square of five hundred miles. Over this they would wander without a possibility of restraint; they would change their manners with their habits of life; would soon forget a government by which they were disowned; would become hordes of English Tartars; and, pouring down upon your unfortified frontiers a fierce and irresistible cavalry, become masters of your governors and your counselers, your collectors and comptrollers, and of all the slaves that adhered to them. Such would, and in no long time must, be the effect of attempting to forbid as a crime and to suppress as an evil the command and blessing of Providence, "Increase and multiply." Such would be the happy result of an endeavor to keep as a lair of wild beasts that earth which God, by an express charter, has given to the children of men.

But the English Government was not alone in its desire to limit the advance of the frontier and guide its destinies. Tidewater Virginia and South Carolina gerrymandered those colonies to insure the dominance of the coast in their legislatures. Washington desired to settle a State at a time in the Northwest; Jefferson would reserve from settlement the territory of his Louisiana Purchase north of the thirty-second parallel, in order to offer it to the Indians in exchange for their settlements east of the Mississippi. "When we shall be full on this side," he writes, "we may lay off a range of States on the western bank from the head to the mouth, and

so range after range, advancing compactly as we multiply." Madison went so far as to argue to the French minister that the United States had no interest in seeing population extend itself on the right bank of the Mississippi, but should rather fear it. When the Oregon question was under debate, in 1824, Smyth, of Virginia, would draw an unchangeable line for the limits of the United States at the outer limit of two tiers of States beyond the Mississippi, complaining that the seaboard States were being drained of the flower of their population by the bringing of too much land into market. Even Thomas Benton, the man of widest views of the destiny of the West, at this stage of his career declared that along the ridge of the Rocky Mountains "the western limits of the Republic should be drawn, and the statue of the fabled god Terminus should be raised upon its highest peak, never to be thrown down." But the attempts to limit the boundaries, to restrict land sales and settlement, and to deprive the West of its share of political power were all in vain. Steadily the frontier of settlement advanced and carried with it individualism, democracy, and nationalism, and powerfully affected the East and the Old World.

The most effective efforts of the East to regulate the frontier came through its educational and religious activity, exerted by interstate migration and by organized societies. Speaking in 1835, Dr. Lyman Beecher declared: "It is equally plain that the religious and political destiny of our nation is to be decided in the West," and he pointed out that the population of the West "is assembled from all the States of the Union and from all the nations of Europe, and is rushing in like the waters of the flood, demanding for its moral preservation the immediate and universal action of those institutions which discipline the mind and arm the conscience and the heart. And so various are the opinions and habits, and so recent and imperfect is the acquaintance, and so sparse are the settlements of the West, that no homogeneous public sentiment can be formed to legislate immediately into being the requisite institutions. And yet they are all needed immediately in their utmost perfection and power. A nation is being 'born in a day.' . . . But what will become of the West if her prosperity rushes up to such a majesty of power, while those great institutions linger which are necessary to form the mind and the conscience and the heart of that vast world. It must not be permitted. . . . Let no man at the East quiet himself and dream of liberty, whatever may become of the West. . . . Her destiny is our destiny."

With the appeal to the conscience of New England, he adds appeals to her fears lest other religious sects anticipate her own. The New England preacher and school-teacher left their mark on the West. The dread of Western emancipation from New England's political and economic control was paralleled by her fears lest the West cut loose from her religion. Commenting in 1850 on reports that settlement was rapidly extending northward in Wisconsin, the editor of the *Home Missionary* writes: "We scarcely know whether to rejoice or mourn over this extension of our settlements. While we sympathize in whatever tends to increase the physical resources and prosperity of our country, we can not forget that with all these dispersions into remote and still remoter corners of the land the supply of the means of grace is becoming relatively less and less." Acting in accordance with such ideas, home missions were established and Western colleges were erected. As seaboard cities like Philadelphia, New York, and Baltimore strove for the mastery of Western trade, so the various denominations strove for the possession of the West. Thus an intellectual stream from New England sources fertilized the West. Other sections sent their missionaries; but the real struggle was between sects. The contest for power and the expansive tendency furnished to the various sects by the existence of a moving frontier must have had important results on the character of religious organization in the United States. The multiplication of rival churches in the little frontier towns had deep and lasting social effects. The religious aspects of the frontier make a chapter in our history which needs study.

From the conditions of frontier life came intellectual traits of profound importance. The works of travelers along each frontier from colonial days onward describe certain common traits, and these traits have, while softening down, still persisted as survivals in the place of their origin, even when a higher social organization succeeded. The result is that to the frontier the American intellect owes its striking characteristics. That coarseness and strength combined with acuteness and inquisitiveness; that practical, inventive turn of mind, quick to find expedients; that masterful grasp of material things, lacking in the artistic but powerful to effect great ends; that restless, nervous energy; that dominant individualism, working for good and for evil, and withal that buoyancy and exuberance which comes with freedom—these are traits of the frontier, or traits called out elsewhere because of the existence of the frontier. Since the days when the fleet of Columbus sailed into the waters of the New World, America has been another name for opportunity, and the people of the United States have

[815]

taken their tone from the incessant expansion which has not only been open but has even been forced upon them. He would be a rash prophet who should assert that the expansive character of American life has now entirely ceased. Movement has been its dominant fact, and, unless this training has no effect upon a people, the American energy will continually demand a wider field for its exercise. But never again will such gifts of free land offer themselves. For a moment, at the frontier, the bonds of custom are broken and unrestraint is triumphant. There is not *tabula rasa*. The stubborn American environment is there with its imperious summons to accept its conditions; the inherited ways of doing things are also there; and yet, in spite of environment, and in spite of cus-

tom, each frontier did indeed furnish a new field of opportunity, a gate of escape from the bondage of the past; and freshness, and confidence, and scorn of older society, impatience of its restraints and its ideas, and indifference to its lessons, have accompanied the frontier. What the Mediterranean Sea was to the Greeks, breaking the bond of custom, offering new experiences, calling out new institutions and activities, that, and more, the ever retreating frontier has been to the United States directly, and to the nations of Europe more remotely. And now, four centuries from the discovery of America, at the end of a hundred years of life under the Constitution, the frontier has gone, and with its going has closed the first period of American history.

FREDERICK JACKSON TURNER
by Carl L. Becker

I went to the University of Wisconsin (in 1893 it was) for the same reason that many boys go to one college rather than another—because a high school friend of mine, whose cousin or something had "been at Madison," was going there. As youth will, I at once endowed the place, which I had never seen and had only recently heard of, with a romantic glamour. Was not Madison a distant and large city? (I am speaking now of a prairie country boy who had never ventured from his small town into the world so wide.) And was it not located on a great body of water, a lake eight miles in diameter, no less? One other bit of knowledge contributed to the splendor that was Wisconsin. On the faculty of that University

there was a man whom a young lawyer in my town had belauded and bragged about, and familiarly referred to as "old Freddie Turner."

"Is he old?" I asked, picturing the long gray locks of a Faust before the devil comes in the spotlight.

"Oh, no, not *old*. We just called him that, I don't know why—just a rough way of showing boyish admiration without being sentimental about it, I suppose."

"What does he teach?"

"Well, he teaches American History. But it's not what he teaches, the subject I mean. The subject doesn't matter. It's what he is, the personality and all that sort of thing. It's something he gives you, inspiration, new ideas, a fresh light on

From *American Masters of Social Science,* edited by Howard W. Odum. By permission of Henry Holt and Company, Inc., copyright, 1927.

things in general. It's something he makes you want to do or be. I don't remember much American history, but I'll never forget that man Turner, old Freddie Turner."

So I went to the University of Wisconsin clear about one thing—I would take a course with old Freddie Turner. Unfortunately he taught history. The word held no blandishments for me. In high school I had studied (that isn't the word, but what word is there for it?) history, general history, Barnes' *General History,* or some such misdemeanor against youth; of which I remembered only one sentence: "Egypt has been called the gift of the Nile." That alone of all the history of the world I remembered; and even that I hadn't learned the meaning of, hadn't indeed supposed or ever been told that it was expected to have a meaning. A dull subject, history. And yet there I was at the University of Wisconsin determined to take a course in history because, unfortunately, that was the only "subject offered" by old Freddie Turner.

I was not many days in Madison before the man was pointed out to me, on the campus, going somewhere in a hurry, loaded down with an immense leather portfolio bulging with books and notes; belatedly hurrying up the hill to class I dare say, probably perspiring but certainly unbowed. Of course he wasn't old —thirty-three or thereabouts at that time. To a youth of eighteen, men of thirty-three, professors at all events, might more often that not *seem* old; were at least likely to convey the impression of having settled all disturbing questions, of having as it were astutely encased themselves in a neat armor of fixed defensive habit war-

ranted proof against the slings and arrows of whatever unusual experience or risky adventure the mischances of life, within cloistered academic walls, were likely to threaten them with. No such impression was conveyed by "that man Turner" beating it up the hill at 10:02 A.M. Even to a boy of eighteen there was something essentially youthful in the rounded lines of the short compact figure, in the free and unstudied swing of arms and legs; something gay and larky about the head ever so gallantly held, with ever so slight and so engaging a lifted backward tilt of valiant defiance to all the associated fates; something mischievously boyish even about the ruddy complexion, above all about the eyes and lips—eyes and lips that seemed always smiling even in repose, or always ready to smile, as if the world were so full of a number of things that odd chances and interesting episodes were to be momentarily expected. Expected and welcomed. Such was the impression. Serious indeed the man was, you never doubted that, but not solemn, above all not old, not professionally finished; just beginning rather, zestfully and buoyantly beginning, out for adventure, up to something, in the most casual friendly way inviting you to join in.

Inviting you to join in, yes. I don't mean (God forbid!) soliciting students to take his courses. Heaven knows he didn't need to make sly maneuvers to get you. Well I remember the opening day of the second year when I stood in line by his desk, waiting to ask him a question (totally unnecessary question, invented for the precise purpose of standing there and being spoken to). There I stood, and presently he turned to me with the quick upward flash of blue eyes that seemed to lift and throw over and through me a shaft of live light. I seemed, dumb shy youth that I was, to stand fully revealed in the light of those extraordinary eyes—cool, steady, challenging, yet friendly too, and hoping for the best. Haltingly I asked my foolish question, and was answered. The answer was nothing, the words were nothing, but the voice—the voice was everything: a voice not deep but full, rich, vibrant, and musically cadenced; such a voice as you would never grow weary of, so warm and intimate and human it was. I cannot describe the voice. I know only that it laid on me a kind of magic spell which I could never break, and have never wanted to. Well, there it was, the indefinable *charm*. An upward lift of the eyes, a few friendly words, and I, like I know not how many other lads of nineteen, was straightway a devoted disciple and questionless admirer of "old Freddie Turner." I didn't care *what* he offered. For him I would even study history.

Even then I didn't study history. I took courses in history, and in due time I took Turner's "junior course" in American history. But I didn't study history, not really; because I didn't know how to study it. Remembering what things happened at what times—that was what studying history meant to me then. Learning these things out of a book. Well, we had a book. To begin with Turner asked us to buy Thwaites' *Colonies,* and I bought it. I have it yet, with certain dates set down opposite the successive chapters in the table of contents; all these "assignments" having been given us once for all at the beginning of the term. Simple enough, I thought—each week I will learn a chapter. But after the second week we were behind the schedule, and after the fourth week we didn't know where we were, and never found out. Of course I read the book—I think I did; was expected to and, being an obedient boy, must have done so. But

the book was like all history books, dull, filled with uninteresting facts which I couldn't remember; and so it happened that when Turner sometimes for ten minutes asked us questions,—"Mr. Becker, what were the provisions of the Tariff Bill of 1816?"—I never could answer, or almost never. During the second term I did answer one question, a question which had just gone its weary round without eliciting any response. I forget what the question was. The answer was "1811." "Precisely," said Turner, in a tone implying that he now recognized me as of that select company of scholars who would see at once the peculiar significance of 1811.

But if I didn't study history that year, I was infected with the desire to do so. This of course was Turner's fault, not mine (Haskins' fault too, by the way; and if I were writing chiefly about myself instead of Turner, which it may be thought I am doing if I don't watch out, there would be much to be said about Haskins). For it was true, as my lawyer friend said, that Turner had a singular capacity for making you want to do and be something— to do, in short, what he was doing and to be, if possible, what he was. And what was he? And what was he doing? Fascinated by the man, I attended to his every gesture and expression, listened to everything he said, less at first for the content than for the voice, the intention, the implication. The implication of the whole performance was of something that had in itself only incidentally to do with students "taking a course." The implication was that we (all of us together, if *we* chose —that was our affair) were searching for something, ferreting out hidden secrets. Facts there were, plenty of them, and as a matter of course to be known; but that wasn't the end. There was something concealed there, in and behind the facts, some problem that concerned humanity at large waiting to be solved. The implication was that we might, on our own account, turn over the dead facts once more, on the chance of finding something, something the others had missed.

Inconceivable that Thwaites had missed anything, I couldn't suppose it! Yet so it appeared. For here was a "teacher," who at one moment confessed his ignorance and the next modestly questioned the textbook. Inviting us one day to consider the problem of sovereignty, he quoted Austin's definition; said he couldn't understand it; admitted he wasn't blessed with the logical mind; and drew two (or was it three?) overlapping circles on the blackboard illustrating the theory of "divided sovereignty," which he said seemed to fit the facts of American history better, but even of that he wasn't certain either. Well, a "teacher" was supposed to know everything, yet there was Turner not able to explain sovereignty. Supposed to know everything, a teacher was, but of course not more than the textbook. Yet there another day stood Turner saying, as casually as ever you please, "I do not agree with Thwaites on this point." What to make of a teacher who knew more than the textbook, but was still ignorant of something? After I know not how long it dawned on me, and with what a joyous sense of emancipation, that Turner wasn't, that no university professor need be, merely a teacher. Turner obviously hadn't just learned his history out of a book. The rash sceptic had gone out of his way to get the "facts" somewhere else, had "investigated"—that was the word—the documents on his own account, had taken his own notes from the "sources," was in short an "authority" in his own right, and might if he wishes write his own book of American history.

From the moment Turner ceased to figure in my mind as a teacher, I began to learn something from him. Not "teacher" but "historian" he was, better still "author," whose main occupation it was, not to teach us, but to be deeply engaged in researches preliminary to the writing of notable books. Obvious enough, once you got the idea. For surely no professor, coming somewhat distraitly into class at the last moment, ever spread about such a cheerful happy air of having been interrupted in preparatory studies, or ever more successfully conveyed the impression of going cheerfully on, during the brief hour, for our benefit, with the morning's labors. Material evidence of those labors there was a plenty in the stacks of notes deposited on the desk, notes on slips of paper 6 x 8, or some such size, filed in labeled manilla envelopes; more enveloped notes every day brought to class than could by any chance be looked into; as if the preoccupied scholar, leaving his study on the run, had hastily gathered together whatever he could conveniently lay his hands on, hoping to be prepared with illustrative material relevant to any one of a number of interesting topics which might, happily, turn up during the lecture.

The lecture itself, if that is the word for it, seemed never "prepared," never studiously "got up" under the lamp. It seemed rather the spontaneous result of preparations always going on and never finished. The lecture was just informal, intimately conversational talk, beginning as might happen with this interesting matter, and ending as might happen with that; always serious without ever being solemn; enlivened with humor and wholesome infectious laughter, yet never falling to the level of the sad professorial joke; running off into revelant digressions occasioned by some student query; coming back again to the main point; coming now and again to the full stop while "notes" were eagerly searched for and found (oh, well, usually found), if not in one manilla envelope perhaps in another, notes containing some desired quotation from the documents, with exact reference given, illustrating a point, clinching an argument. No, lecture isn't the word. Nothing *ex cathedra* here, no musty air of academic infallibility clouding the room, no laying down of the law and gospel according to Turner; but all compact of inquiry and novel ideas carelessly thrown out with more questions asked than were answered, more problems posed than solved. The professor seemed not at all concerned to ladle out the minimum dose of American history suitable to our complaint. He was just talking to us as a man might talk to men, about the problems that interested *him*, problems which he had apparently been thinking about after breakfast, and might very likely, one felt, think some more about after luncheon.

Such was the impression. But where then did we, poor dazed novices astray in the bright intellectual world, come in on this business? No doubt the method, or lack of it, was not well calculated to send the shining morning-faced student away rejoicing with neatly wrapped and labeled packets of "knowledge," to be held until called for, at examination time, and duly returned, unopened. No doubt the student often felt like asking, as students will, what precisely the "required work" was— "Professor, what are we expected to know for examination?" Well, one could trust to luck, would have to apparently. I at least knew that something (something about the bank was it?) happened in 1811. Curiously enough I didn't worry, timid and cautious youth that I was, I didn't worry much about the packets of

useful information; for you see I was getting, as failing students say, "a great deal out of the course." I was getting a great deal out of Turner. I was daily enjoying the inestimable privilege of watching an original and penetrating intelligence at work, playing freely with facts and ideas, handling with discrimination the problems of history, problems which so often turned out to be the problems of life itself. Unorganized the course was certainly; but the resulting impression was nevertheless not one of confusion. The impression always was that of a brilliant light being thrown on dark places. For the talk, however desultory it may have been, was never merely rambling, but went always winding in and through and round about the matter in hand at the behest of some fresh idea, suggestion, or tentative hypothesis. Something vital and significant in the facts these flashed ideas and hypotheses seemed always revealing. An ordered body of information I could get, and did afterwards get, for myself; but from no other man did I ever get in quite the same measure that sense of watching a first-class mind at work on its own account, and not merely rehearsing for the benefit of others; the most delightful sense in the world of sitting there waiting for ideas to be born; expectantly waiting for secret meanings, convenient explanatory hypotheses to be discovered, lurking as like as not under the dullest mass of drab facts ever seen.

In this happy way I got a new idea of history. It was after all no convention agreed upon to be learned by rote, but just the infinitely varied action and thought of men who in past times had lived and struggled and died for means or great objects. It was in short an aspect of life itself, and as such something to be probed into, thought about, written about. Who would not like to study history as Turner studied it? And write about it as he would write about it? Not possible of course to do it with his brilliant competence, not a chance; but still there was something to try for, a standard set, an ideal. And so in this eventful junior year I brought out my tiny little wagon and fumblingly hitched it to that bright particular star. Procuring quantities of paper and manilla envelopes, I began "pen in hand" to study history; with patient, plodding abandon pouring over such fascinating works as *Niles Register* and the *New York Colonial Documents,* or any other mouldy, crumbling old tome, provided only it contained those "original sources" which Turner, by some species of white magic, had invested with color and charm. What a joy it was in those days merely to turn the yellow pages of old books! With what a sense of solid work accomplished one extracted the substance of no matter what official document, always, with reverent piety, noting the "exact reference"—*Niles,* XII, 749. Still preserved they are, those stacks of notes in manilla envelopes, aging now undisturbed on upper shelves, long since covered with dust!

II

With the novitiate ended, one took the full vows. For three years I pursued my researches in Turner's seminary, a group of twelve or fifteen men, with a stray woman or two, meeting in the Law Building, or, better still, in the state Historical Society Library, then housed in the Capitol. Here we did our work, each man having a table, or part of one, in an alcove; and all of us assembling, on Mondays, Wednesdays, and Fridays, round one of the larger tables, with Turner in our midst. To be so commoded was to be in the very center of the temple of learning;

for we were here, all of us, professor and pupils, daily boxed about with walls of books, the books we needed and were currently using, those very collections of "documents" which exhaled the mothy odors of scholarship; so that just to sit motionless in the blest place breathing in the incensed atmosphere of research at its thickest enabled one to anticipate the illusions of the fully erudite.

Informal to a degree this seminary was, more informal even than the "junior course." Lectures there were none, or almost none, unless one prefers to say there were always lectures, or nearly always. For the engaging theory was that we were all scholars together, surveying broadly the field of American history, each man having his particular subject—the colonization of Virginia, Internal Improvements, or whatever—subjects large and unconfined, opening a career to talent. Each man was expected to master his subject as well as might be; to be responsible for it; to be ready like a cabinet minister to answer such questions, bearing upon it, as might be asked by the opposition; above all from time to time to make reports giving the matured results of his investigation. In this way each of us, including the professor, would lecture in turn, and all of the others, including the professor, would take notes. The Professor, such was the theory, was just one of us, the principal one no doubt, organizing and directing the whole performance, but still not professing to know too much, modestly deferring to any one of us where our particular topics were concerned, and himself taking notes, when we lectured, with an alert and convincing air of being instructed, of having old matter freshly examined and interpreted for him. I swear he did take notes, and he has since assured me, with just a trace of asperity I thought, that it was no frame-up, but that he did actually obtain from us valuable ideas and information which afterwards he sometimes made good use of. Well, I believe him. I do believe he did sometimes get from us some or other odd fact, such was his inordinate thirst for facts and his uncanny instinct for finding them in the most unlikely places, such his skill in disengaging what was significant from even the most confused jumble of the incompetent, the irrelevant, and the immaterial.

I took notes too, of course I did. It was part of the ritual, and I was nothing if not strong in the faith—in those old days. The notes I took are not such, I do confess, that one could reconstruct from them an adequate account of American history; but they had, and have had, for me at least, a high value nevertheless. Here before me, for example, are the notes, easily contained on one sheet of paper 6 x 8, of a two-days' report on the Mexican War.

Rogers' report—Mexican War. Polk. Taylor. Senate Bill. Biglow Papers frequently referred to. Turner asks: "By the way, Mr. Rogers, what exactly are the Biglow Papers?" Rogers says: "The Biglow Papers—" (Hesitates, seems a little dazed, has at last a happy inspiration) "Why, the Biglow Papers are— a well known work by—a famous author." Hilarious laughter, led by Turner, who then explains Biglow Papers. Don't myself know B. P. Remember look up and read B. P. Lowell, J. R.

Thus to my great regret I missed the significant points of the Mexican War, but at least read the Biglow Papers, and have always remembered that the work is well known and by a famous author. Another sheet lies before me.

Turner asks, why the unusual literary activity in generation following 1815? Vari-ous suggestions. Becker says perhaps on account of feeling of relief and freedom after War of 1812 and Napoleonic wars. Turner says, perhaps. Is that a fact or only a plausible inference? What is an historical fact? Can you prove an inference? May historian be satisfied with inference? Have all great wars been followed by intellectual and literary activity? What in general is cause of changes in character of thought? Fifteen minute talk, mostly questions, a cascade of questions. No one answers these questions. Why doesn't Turner tell us the answers? Something to think about.

Something to think about, sure enough! Well, I have thought about it, off and on, for twenty-five years; but I don't now wonder why Turner didn't tell us the answers.

As time passed I was made aware indeed that Turner very often didn't answer questions. Heaven knows he asked enough, was always handing out some riddle to be solved, always giving us something to think about and then serenely leaving us to think about it. But there were questions he neglected either to ask or to answer. For example, did the colonies or the British government have the right of it in the War of Independence? Should one properly sympathize with Jefferson or Marshall? Was the tariff a wise policy? Was Jacksonian democracy a good or a bad thing? Were the slave states justified in seceding from the Union? Important questions these were surely; questions which a teacher who had given his life to the study of American history might be supposed to answer for students who came to college expecting to be furnished with right opinions and convictions. But I don't recall that Turner ever answered these questions, or the like of them; so that to this day I don't know what his convictions are on the great issues. Is he protectionist or free trader? Democrat or republican? Baptist or infidel, or member of that great church which Lord Melbourne commended for never meddling with either politics or religion? Above all is he a conservative, satisfied with the evils we have? Or a liberal, willing to substitute for them others which formerly existed? Or a radical, eager for the shock of new ones never yet tried? I don't know. Turner never gave us answers to these questions. He never told us what to think.

I hope I am not conveying the impression that Turner appeared to his students in the somber light of a "strong silent man." Somber is the last word in the world to describe him, and silent isn't the word either. He talked freely enough, and he answered questions freely enough, questions of a certain sort. After I don't know how many months or years I learned that the answers he commonly neglected to give were answers which would have enabled me to borrow his opinions and judgments, and so save myself the trouble of thinking. He would do what he could to help me think, but he wouldn't if he knew it tell me what to think. He was not much given to handing down final judgments.

This is important, and I wish to emphasize it a little. Turner didn't pronounce final judgments. In those days it sometimes troubled me that he didn't. But I have long since forgiven him, blessed him indeed, for it, having seen quite enough of those complacent people who go about recreating the world in their own image and expecting others to see that it is good. Turner might have said, with Mr. Justice Holmes, that one important article of his creed as a scholar was that he was *not* God. Like Margaret Fuller, he "accepted the universe," although unlike that voluble lady, he did it silently. I am now speaking of Turner the scholar, not of Turner the man and citizen. As man and citizen he had, and always has had, convictions, knows what he thinks right and wise, and never leaves you in any doubt about it. As man and citizen he doesn't, I am sure, think this the best of conceivable worlds, or always find it a comfortable place to be in, as what intelligent or sensitive person does? He has indeed always met the reverses of life with serenity and high courage, no man I think ever more so; but I know not how many times he may in his heart have refreshingly damned the universe to extinction, as, on occasion, all good men do I hope. But I am now concerned with the scholar. As scholar, so it seems to me, Turner accepts men and things as given, the business of the scholar being not to *judge* but only to *understand* them.

To me at least it is a matter of no slight importance that he accepted us, graduate students, in that spirit. We, too, were apparently parts of the universe, to be accepted as given. He never made me feel that I was before the Judgment Seat. He was never the schoolmaster, standing behind me prodding, with sharp exclamation points pitchforking me up the steep path of learning. He criticized, and in the most honest friendly way, without leaving any after-taste of personal depravity in the mouth. He appeared to take me as the associated fates had made me, more or less intelligent, and to assume that I would willingly do the best I could. Amazing, to me at least, was the casual friendly way he had of treating us as equals, as serious scholars with whom it was a pleasure to be associated in common tasks. Even our work he didn't criticize much, condemning it by silence mainly, commending it on rare occasions by a few hearty words of approval. How the rash man gambled on us to be sure, professing to see in us qualities and virtues marking us out for future *savants*. Perhaps there was some method in this madness. To get the best out of graduate students, or any students, it is perhaps just as well not to assume to begin with that there isn't any best there to be got out. Often enough there isn't, but then it doesn't greatly matter. If there was any best in me, I at least needed, in order to get it out, just the freedom and friendly confidence which Turner gave me, having until then been for the most part "criticized" and "trained" quite sufficiently; oh, quite sufficiently told, by parents and uncles and aunts and teachers and pastors, what to do and what not to do; told in such an interesting variety of ways, and with such an implication of futility in the telling, as to leave me clutching the miserable little suspicion that I would probably never, all things considered, be much good at doing anything. Never having talked with my pastor, Turner didn't know this. He blandly assumed that I might amount to something, and at last one day told me that he thought I "had it in me" to become a scholar and a writer—seemed really to believe it. To be told by this admired master that I could probably do the very thing I most wanted to do released what little ability I had to do it. Released the ability, and intensified the desire to do it, because I then, and ever after, worked all the harder in order to justify Turner's faith in me.

This friendly method of dealing with graduate students (the honest ones, I mean; the occasional fakir got the full blaze of his hot scorn) might not have been the best method for another, but I am sure it was the best method for Turner. It was the best method precisely because there wasn't any method in it. When Turner came into class he didn't put on the teacher's manner because he didn't think of himself as a teacher. He thought of himself—or no, he didn't think of himself, that's just the point. He was just Turner, man and scholar, absorbed in his work, who met us because we were interested in the same thing he was; and who met us in the most casual democratic way in the world because it was perfectly natural for him to meet us in that way. The easy aristocratic grace and charm of this friendly democrat from Portage, Wisconsin, had about it neither a shade more nor less of any manner for his high placed colleagues than for the obscurest graduate student. It didn't, this unstudied friendly manner which at once put us at ease, seem to be even second nature. It seemed to be the instinctive expression of a lively and supple intelligence restrained and directed by some inexhaustible native fund of sincerity, integrity, and good will. This is after all one of the reasons, perhaps the chief reason, for his success with graduate students.

It is also, I think, one principal secret of his success as a scholar. For the scholar, the historian at all events, has to meet humanity in some fashion or other; and humanity will commonly reveal little to those who meet it with reticences and reservations and didactic motives. Even in those student days it seemed to me that Turner met humanity very much as he met us, graduate students; he didn't put on anything special for the occasion. Humanity, like graduate students, doubtless had virtues and qualities concealed somewhere about it, and might very well, such was the implication, stumble on, if you gave it rope enough, to some or other place worth going to. Best at all events to assume as much; for humanity is like graduate students in this too, that it will be more likely to do well if you trust it a little, if you have faith to gamble on its hidden capacities.

But who could tell us where poor old humanity is headed for, rope or no rope? I would not willingly charge a reputable historian with harboring a Philosophy of History. Yet I recall that one day Turner quoted Droysen, apparently with approval, to the effect that "history is the self-consciousness of humanity." And another day he said: "The question is not whether you have a Philosophy of History, but whether the philosophy you have is good for anything." In extenuation I feel moved to say that if Turner does indeed have a Philosophy of History, I can't imagine it taking the form of an answer. Much more likely to take the form of a question, thus: "If mankind could once really understand what it has done and thought in the past, is it not possible that it would stumble along now, and in the future, with more intelligence and a more conscious purpose?" I don't know whether this is a Philosophy of History or not. Whether, if it is, it is a good one, I know still less. But of one thing I feel quite sure: if Turner subscribes to it, whatever it is, it doesn't cost him much. It doesn't cost him anything in fact, for it doesn't burden him with any noticeable preoccupations or fixed ideas. He pursues his proper task, which is to find out what certain groups of men did and thought in past times, and to furnish the proximate explanation of their so acting and thinking; and this task he pursues as if he had no philosophy, as if it made no difference at all to him what they did and thought, or what the explanation might turn out to be. He pursues his task in short with detachment, with objectivity.

So at last we come to it, the inevitable word, objectivity. The word has many meanings. In those days I had myself got,

or at least got up, chiefly out of books, a notion of objectivity scarcely distinguishable from complete indifference, a sort of stiff solemnity or *rigor mortis* of the spirit; so that I sometimes wondered if Turner really was "objective and disinterested," so lively and interested he always seemed. Certainly indifference, such as Renan's Man in the Moon might be supposed to exhibit, couldn't by any stretch of the imagination be attributed to Turner. Here then was a dilemma; and not being willing to abandon either Turner or the ideal of objectivity, I ended by seeing that Turner was objective in some other fashion than the Man in the Moon. The objectivity of Turner's mind, I found, was a quality he enjoyed in his own right, and not something acquired by training. It wasn't something he had painfully got up in college out of Bernheim—a set of artificially induced and cultivated repressions such as would enable any careful historian to write, let us say, an account of the Battle of Cold Harbor without revealing the fact that his father was an ardent admirer of Grant. That kind of objectivity is common enough, and often pernicious enough, being the best substitute for ideas yet invented. Turner at least didn't need it, having always more ideas than he could perhaps well manage. The objectivity he had seemed rather to spring from that intense and sustained interest which an abundance of ideas can alone generate. A hard truth for me to learn, this was, since I hadn't too many ideas; but I couldn't help seeing that Turner was so wholly absorbed in his work that he hadn't time to think of anything else, not even of the necessity of being objective. He was "disinterested" because he was so interested in the object before him that he forgot, for the time being, to be interested in anything else; he was "objective" because he was so genuinely curious about that object, desired with such singleness of purpose to know it for the sake of knowing it, that his mind was empty, for the time being, of all other objects. This kind of objectivity doesn't come by willing (not that any sane man, living in a world of action, would will to have it); it is a quality of mind, like the sense of absolute pitch, which one is or isn't born with. No doubt it may, if one has it, be cultivated, but at any rate it is inseparable from genuine *intellectual curiosity,* the lively and irrepressible desire to know merely for the sake of knowing. A rare quality indeed that is, but I think Turner has it.

Another thing about Turner used in those days to strike me as a little odd. I don't know just what to call it. "Independence" isn't quite the word. Of course he was an independent scholar; but then most professors were independent scholars in the ordinary sense of the term. His was a peculiar kind of independence which struck me then, and still strikes me, as relatively uncommon among professors. I might call it a certain obliviousness to professional convention, an almost complete freedom from acadamic provincialism. I first noticed it indeed because it seemed to me then not quite the thing. For I was then doing what many college boys do—emancipating myself from one form of provincialism by taking on another. Coming fresh, or almost fresh, from the farm into an academic community, the professor's world seemed to me the last word in sophistication. The most obvious form which this sophistication took was a certain smart awareness on the professor's part of belonging to a larger and freer society than the one in which, geographically speaking, he perforce lived. Comfortable enough his ivory tower in Madison was no doubt; but he was likely to be often

looking out of it towards the more splendid towers of the east, over-anxiously concerned perhaps to know what the wise men there were thinking and doing. One gathered that there were decencies proper to the academic world, a minor one being that no professor should have too much confidence in himself until he received a call from Yale or Harvard, and even then a lively sense of the fitting, some hang over from colonial days perhaps, would keep him subtly servile and apologetic for being no more than an American scholar who must forever abandon hope of entering the sacred portals of Oxford, Paris, or Berlin. If all this was only a second provincialism worse than the first, I was not yet aware of the fact. It seemed to me then no more than the proper mark of those who had oriented themselves in the intellectual world, quite the attitude in short for a professor to have. Therefore it struck me as a little odd that my admired master Turner didn't have it.

For Turner didn't have it. There was no getting round the fact that he didn't have it at all. I got the distinct impression that he didn't mind living in Wisconsin, seemed to think Portage a jolly good place to come from, as if being born there, even if the fact became known, needn't seriously impair the quality of his scholarship. If he knew that Europe was infinitely richer than the United States in historic remains and traditions, I never heard him mention the fact, at least not with the appropriate air of regret for missed opportunities. He had, on the contrary, every appearance of being contented with his opportunities, seemed indeed to rejoice in his opportunities, quite as a man might who had just discovered a gold mine in his back yard. American history, he seemed to say, is a new lead, never yet properly uncovered, as rich and enticing a mine for the scholar as can anywhere be found, all the better for never having been worked by Waitz or von Ranke. It was as if some rank American flavor, some sturdy strain of backwoods independence, resisting every process of academic refinement, kept the man still proud to be an American citizen, contentedly dwelling in Madison, quite satisfied with the privilege of going every day to the State Historical Society Library where the Draper Manuscripts were.

Even in those days I felt, without quite understanding, this non-professional attitude on Turner's part. The time was to come when I found the professional attitude less engaging; and it was probably just because I saw Turner as "different" that these old student day impressions never faded, just because he was never quite the "professor" that his influence was more enduring than that of many professors. His influence was enduring I think because he himself didn't "date." Above all his ideas about American history didn't date, never struck one as being modeled upon any established authority or cribbed from any school of historians. Something personal there always was in his "point of view," in his "interpretations," as if the subject were being freshly looked at by a

mind washed clean of scholastic dust. Not that there was anything aggressive about his independence. He never gave one the impression that, having made up his mind to be original, he was somewhat bellicosely making good. His independence wasn't an achievement. And yet I wonder. Was there not about him too (or did I just imagine it?) some indefinable but quite jolly air of conscious insubordination, just a quick little gesture of the mind impatiently dismissing the solemn snobbery of all that is academically canonized and sacrosanct? I can't be sure, but I like to think so.

That is as it may be. But this I know, that three qualities of the man's mind made upon me a profound and indelible impression. These qualities were: a lively and irrepressible intellectual curiosity; a refreshing freedom from personal preoccupations and didactic motives; a quite unusual ability to look out upon the world in a humane, friendly way, in a fresh and strictly independent way, with a vision unobscured by academic inhibitions. These are also the qualities, I think, which have enabled him to make an "original contribution" (not so common a performance as is often supposed) to the study of American history.

---

from THE FUTURE OF AMERICAN LIBERALISM

by MORRIS R. COHEN

LIBERALISM is too often misconceived as a new set of dogmas taught by a newer and better set of priests called "liberals." Liberalism is an attitude rather than a set of dogmas—an attitude that insists upon questioning all plausible and self-evident

propositions, seeking not to reject them but to find out what evidence there is to support them rather than their possible alternatives. This open eye for possible alternatives which need to be scrutinized before we can determine which is the best grounded is profoundly disconcerting to all conservatives and to almost all revolutionaries. Conservatism clings to what has been established, fearing that, once we begin to question the beliefs that we have inherited, all the values of life will be destroyed. The revolutionary, impressed with the evil of the existing order or disorder, is prone to put his faith in some mighty-sounding principle without regard for the complications, compromises, dangers, and hardships that will be involved in the adjustment of this principle to other worthy principles. Revolutionaries and reactionaries alike are irritated and perhaps inwardly humiliated by the humane temper of liberalism, which reveals by contrast the common inhumanity of both violent parties to the social struggle. Liberalism, on the other hand, regards life as an adventure in which we must take risks in new situations, in which there is no guarantee that the new will always be the good or the true, in which progress is a precarious achievement rather than an inevitability.

OUR CHANGING CHARACTERISTICS
by JAMES TRUSLOW ADAMS

THERE ARE few things more difficult to generalize about without danger of valid objections than national character. The exceptions to any generalization at once begin to appear destructively numerous. A concept of a Frenchman must include not only such diverse types as the Gascon, the Parisian, and the Breton, but also the innumerable differences between individuals of these and other types in what is a rather small country which for long has been culturally and politically unified.

When we attempt the task in America it would seem to be hopeless. Who *is* an American? Is he the descendant of a Boston Brahman, of a Georgian cotton planter, or a newly arrived Armenian, Hungarian, or Italian? Is the typical American a clerk on the fifty-fourth story of a Wall Street office building or a farm hand of the machine age guiding in isolation a power plow along a furrow which stretches endlessly over the horizon? Is he a scientist working for pitiful pay and the love of science in some government bureau in Washington, or a one hundred per cent go-getter in a Chamber of Commerce whose ideas of progress are limited to increase of wealth and population? Is he Hamilton or Jefferson, Lincoln or Harding, Roosevelt or Coolidge, Emerson or Barnum?

The task of defining national character in such a conflicting welter of opposites is dismaying enough, and yet a fairly clear notion is of prime importance for any number of very practical purposes. The modern business man doing business on a national scale, making mass appeal to our whole hundred and twenty millions at once; the statesman, domestic or foreign, trying to forecast the success or failure of an idea or a policy; the genuine patriot interested in the highest development of his civilization—these and others must all take account of that real if vague concept which we call the national character. It is from the third point of view

From James Truslow Adams, *The Tempo of Modern Life,* Albert & Charles Boni, Inc., 1931.

that we are concerned with the topic in the present article.

There are many signs that our world is approaching a new and critical stage. Deeply embedded in the structure of the universe there is a power or force that is continually at work molding chaos into cosmos, formlessness into forms. These forms, or patterns, belong to the spiritual as well as to the physical plane of reality. A scale of values, an ethical system, a philosophy of life appear to be as "natural" and inevitable a part of the web and woof of that strange and inexplicable phantasmagoria that we call the universe as are crystals, corals, or living embodiments of the form-producing force in the plant or animal body.

For generations now we have been witnessing the gradual breakdown of old forms until we have reached the very nadir of formlessness in our whole spiritual life. But there are, as I have said, many indications that we are about to witness a new stage, the embryo stage of new forms.

For the most part this play of cosmic forces is independent of consciousness or will in individuals. The atoms know not and care not why or how they combine to make quartz crystals or a living cell of protoplasm. To a greater extent than we care to admit, perhaps, the higher forms —our scales of values, our philosophies— are also independent of conscious molding by ourselves. They are not wholly so, however, and if, as has recently been said, more and more of us here in America as elsewhere "are looking for a new set of controlling ideas capable of restoring value to human existence," it is evidence of the interplay between the blind form-making force of physical nature and the consciousness of man. What these ideas will be, will depend largely upon the soil in which

they will be rooted, the soil of our national character.

It is also clear that the form in which life, either physical or spiritual, is embodied is of transcendent importance for the individual. If living cells are arranged in the form of a bird, both the powers and limitations of the individual are wholly different from those of the individual when they are arranged in the form of a fish. Similarly in the spiritual world, powers and limitations depend largely upon the forms within which the spirit has its being. Because they are so largely intangible, we are likely to lose sight of the fact that these forms—scales of values, systems of thought, philosophies of life— all afford the spirit peculiar powers and impose peculiar limits.

What of the new forms? Arising from and in large part molded by the national character, are they likely to afford wider scope for man's highest aspirations, to enlarge the powers of the spirit, or to place limits and bind them closer to the earth? What of the national character itself?

Let us for the present discussion avoid the more difficult problem of a complete analysis and seek to establish a trend, often a simpler task, in the spiritual as in the physical world. Are our characteristics changing, and, if so, in what direction? Can we, in the first place, establish any definite points of reference which will be tangible and certain? I think we can.

Man expresses himself in his arts, and among these none is more illuminating than the earliest and most practical, that of architecture. It is one, moreover, in which we as Americans excel.

We need not greatly concern ourselves with the inchoate beginnings of our nationality in the first few generations of early settlement in the wilderness of the Atlantic seaboard. The physical tasks were almost overwhelmingly hard and there was little opportunity for a distinctly American expression of either old or new spiritual life. By the time there was, we find that the spirit of the colonies had expressed itself in an architectural form, characteristic with minor variations throughout all of them.

When we speak of "colonial architecture," what at once comes to our mind is the home, the dwelling house of Georgian type, modeled on the English but with a delicacy and refinement surpassing most of the models overseas. From New England to the Far South these homes had outwardly a perfection of form and inwardly a proportion, a refinement of detail, a simplicity that all clearly sprang from the spirit of the time.

We may note quickly, in passing, several points in regard to them. The high point of the architecture was domestic. They were homes. They had an air of spaciousness, of dignity. They were aristocratic in the best sense. They were restrained and disciplined. Display or vulgarity were unthinkable in connection with them. They evidenced an ordered and stratified society. They held peace and rest. They were simple, unostentatious, and profoundly satisfying. They were shelters for a quiet life, alien from haste.

Let us, using the same architectural measure, pass from this first flowering of the American spirit to the very instant of today. The great contribution of twentieth century America to the art of building is the skyscraper, of which we may take the office building as both the earliest and most typical example. What are some of its usual characteristics?

The buildings are commercial, not domestic. Their very *raison d'être* is financial, the desire to get the most money possible from a given plot of ground. Their bulk is huge but they are not spacious, save perhaps for their entrance halls in some instances. They are democratic in the physical sense of herding within their walls thousands of persons of every possible sort. In their primary insistence upon mere size and height regardless of every other element, they are undisciplined and unrestrained. Peace or rest is unthinkable within their walls with the incessant movement of thousands of hurrying individuals, and elevators moving at incredible speed.

They are lavish in their ostentation of expense on the ground floor, bare and unsatisfying above. A "front" of vulgar cost is built to hide the emptiness of the countless floors beyond the reach of the first casual glance from the street. Yet every small and growing community cries for them, and we hold them to the world as our characteristic achievement in art, as our most significant contribution in that most telltale of all arts, the housing of man's chief interest.

II

Here, then, we have two points of reference tangible enough to be noted by all men, because they are physical in structure, yet full of spiritual implications for our task. When we turn to other means of establishing our trend, such as literature, newspapers, our methods of living, the wants we create and strive to satisfy, our social ways of contact, our national ideals as expressed in political campaigns and policies, and other means less obvious than the buildings in which we live or work or express our spiritual aspirations, what do we find? I think we find the same trends indicated above, amplified and emphasized.

It is, if I may repeat myself to prevent misunderstanding, only with these trends and not with the whole complex national character that I am here concerned. As a historian, and with no wish to make a case but only to report what I find, certain trends in the past century appear to me to be clearly indicated. Let me note them just as from time to time I have jotted them down, without at first trying either to order or explain them.

These trends are the substitution of self-expression for self-discipline; of the concept of prosperity for that of liberty; of restlessness for rest; of spending for saving; of show for solidity; of desire for the new or novel in place of affection for the old and tried; of dependence for self-reliance; of gregariousness for solitude; of luxury for simplicity; of ostentation for restraint; of success for integrity; of national for local; of easy generosity for wise giving; of preferring impressions to thought, facts to ideas; of democracy for aristocracy; of the mediocre for the excellent.

For the most part I do not think any observer would quarrel with the validity of most of the above list. Discipline, self or other, has almost completely vanished from our life. In earlier days it was amply provided by school, family, and social life, by ideals and religious beliefs. Today it is not only absent in all these quarters but is preached against by psychologists and sociologists, decried by the new pedagogy, and even legislated against in school and prison.

Nothing is imposed any longer, from learning one's ABC's to honoring one's parents. Everything is elective, from college courses to marital fidelity. The man or woman who casts all discipline to the winds for the sake of transient gratifica-tion of selfish desires, who denies obligations and duties, is no longer considered a libertine or a cad but merely a modernist pursuing the legitimate end of self-expression.

For a considerable time evidence has been accumulating that the national rallying cry has become an economic balance sheet. Perhaps one of the chief values of the whole prohibition muddle has been to serve as a mirror for the American soul. In the arguments advanced for and against, in the spiritual tone of the discussion, we can see all too well reflected the moving ideals of the American people, and the argument that carries most weight would clearly appear to be that of prosperity. Balanced against this, the questions of personal liberty, class legislation, or constitutional propriety are but as straw weighed against iron.

Prohibition is only one of the many mirrors that reflect the same truth. In innumerable cases of business practice and of legislation it has become evident that when personal freedom and initiative have to be balanced against the prosperity of the moment according to the business methods of the moment, prosperity wins. The one liberty that is still valued is the liberty to exploit and to acquire. That liberty will be defended to the death, but other liberties, such as freedom of thought and speech, have become pale and unreal ghosts, academic questions of no interest to the practical man.

Who cares in the slightest about the innumerable cases of encroachment on personal liberties on the part of both state and federal governments in the past ten years so long as business is good? Who cares about the methods employed by our police? Who is willing to give thought to the treatment frequently meted out to foreigners by our immigration officials—treatment that could hardly be surpassed by the old Russian régime at its worst, treatment that we could not stand a moment if accorded to *our* citizens by any foreign government? No, personal liberty as a rallying cry today receives no answer. But we will elect any man President who will promise us prosperity.

There is as little question of our growing restlessness. By rail, boat, automobile, or plane we are as restless as a swarm of gnats in a summer sunbeam. "We don't know where we're going but we're on our way" is the cry of all. Even the babies get their rest by traveling at forty miles an hour swung in cradles in Ford cars. That much of the movement is mere restlessness and does not spring from a desire to see and learn may easily be observed by watching the speed of our new tourists when they travel, and by listening to their comments when they have to stop to look at anything. As for the "nature" they claim to go to see, they are ruining our whole countryside with appalling indifference.

The home itself has yielded and has ceased to afford any sense of permanence and security. In the old days a home was expected to serve for generations. In the South, frequently property was entailed and the family was assured of a continuing center where it could cluster. A year ago, on October first, a hundred thousand families in New York City moved from one apartment to another, in many instances for no better reason than that they were bored with the one they had occupied a twelvemonth. Our multimillionaires build palaces, and in a few years abandon them to country clubs or office buildings.

As for thrift and saving, with the entire complex of spiritual satisfactions that go with an assured future, they have not only notoriously been thrown overboard but are vigorously denounced by advertising experts like Bruce Barton and great industrial leaders like Henry Ford. "We should use, not save," the latter teaches the American people while they mortgage their homes, if they own them, to buy his cars. On every side we are being taught not to save but to borrow. The self-respect and satisfaction of the man of a generation ago who did not owe a penny in the world is being replaced by the social-respect and deep dissatisfaction of the man who has borrowed to the limit to live on the most expensive scale that hard cash and bank credit will allow.

With this has naturally come a preference for show to solidity. A witty and observing foreigner has said that Americans put all their goods in the shop window. In every vein the insidious poison is at work. A man who toiled and saved to own his home would see to it that it was well built and substantial. The man who expects to move every year cares for nothing more than that the roof will not fall until he gets out, provided the appearance is attractive. In an advertisement of houses for sale in a New York suburb recently one of the great advantages pointed out was that the roofs were guaranteed for three years.

The first thing that every business firm thinks of is show. Its office or shop must look as if there were unlimited resources behind it. Even a savings bank, whose real solidity should be seen in its list of investments and whose object is to encourage thrift, will squander hugely on marbles and bronze in its banking room to impress the depositor.

The same motive is at work in our intellectual life. One has only to glance at the advertisements of the classics, of language courses, of "five foot shelves" and note the motives that are appealed to for desiring culture. Nor are our schools and colleges exempt from the same poison. The insistence on degrees after a teacher's name, the regulating of wage scales in accordance with them, the insistence on a professor's publishing something which can be listed, are as much part of the same trend as is the clerk's wanting to be cultured so as to pass from a grilled window to an assistant-assistant executive's desk.

III

We could expand the above examples almost indefinitely and continue through the remainder of the list. But it is all obvious enough to anyone who will observe with fresh eyes, and ponder. Both for those who may agree or disagree with me, let us pass to some of the other questions that arise in connection with the trends I have noted. Do they in any way hang together? Do they make a unified whole or are they self-contradictory and hence probably mistaken? Do they derive from any conditions in our history that would make them natural and probable, or are they opposed to those conditions? If they are real, do they represent a transient phase or a permanent alteration in our character?

As we study them carefully, it seems to me that they do hang together remarkably and ominously well. A person, for example, who is restless, rather than one who cares for rest and permanence, would naturally prefer the new to the old, the novel for the tried, impressions instead of difficult and sustained thought. Both these characteristics, again, naturally cohere with the desire for show rather than solidity, and for self-expression rather than self-discipline.

With these same qualities would go the love of gregariousness rather than solitude, of luxury rather than simplicity, and, easily belonging to the same type of character, we would find the desire to spend ousting the desire to save, and the substitution of prosperity for liberty and of success for integrity. With such a succession of substitutions, that of dependence for self-reliance is not only natural but inevitable, and so with the other items in the trend. They all fit into a psychological whole. There is no self-contradiction to be found among them.

But is there any connection to be found between them and our history? Are they qualities that might be found to have developed with more or less logical and psychological necessity from the conditions of American life which have separated the period of the colonial home from that of the seventy-story office building? I think here again we find confirmation rather than contradiction.

I have no intention to rival Mr. Coolidge by writing the history of America in five hundred words. All I can do in my limited space is to point to certain facts and influences.

Until well into the eighteenth century, there had been no very great change in the character of the American to mark him off from his English cousin. The wilderness and remoteness had, indeed, had some effect, but this was small compared with the later effects of what we have come to call "the West." Leaving out a few minor strains—such as the Dutch, Swedes, and the earlier Germans—the settlers were almost wholly British, who sought, in a somewhat freer atmosphere and with somewhat wider economic opportunity, to reproduce the life they had left.

The continent open to them was of limited extent. Beyond a comparatively narrow strip lay the long barrier of the Appalachians and the claims of the French. The strip itself contained no great natural resources to arouse cupidity or feverish activity. The character of the colonists had become a little more democratic, a little more pliant, a little more rebellious and self-reliant than that of their cousins of similar social ranks at home. That was all. They might differ with the majority of both Englishmen and Parliament over questions of politics and economics, but those were differences of interest and policy, not of character.

There lay ahead, however, the operation of two factors that were to prove of enormous influence—the exploitation of the American continent, and the immigration from Europe. We cannot here trace this influence step by step chronologically, but we must summarize it. "The West"—there were successively many of them—unlike the colonial America, was of almost limitless extent and wealth. There were whole empires of farm land and forest, mines that made fortunes for the lucky almost overnight, reservoirs of gas and oil that spawned cities and millionaires.

All did not happen in a day, but it did happen within what might almost be the span of one long life. In ages past an Oriental conqueror might sack the riches of a rival's state, a king of Spain might draw gold from a Peruvian hoard, but never before had such boundless opportunities for sudden wealth been opened to the fortunate among a whole population which could join in the race unhampered.

In the rush for opportunity, old ties and loyalties were broken. A restlessness entered the American blood that has remained in it ever since. In American legend, the frontier has become the Land of Romance and we are bid to think of the pioneers as empire-builders. A very few may have dreamed of the future glory of America rather than of private gain, but it is well not to gild too much the plain truth, which is that in the vast majority of instances, the rush was for riches to be made as quickly as might be. In the killing of a million buffaloes a year, in the total destruction of forests without replanting, in the whole of the story in all its aspects there were few thoughts for a national destiny not linked with immediate personal gain at any expense to the nation. In this orgy of exploitation it is not difficult to discover the soil in which some of the elements of the changed trend in American character had its roots.

Another factor was also at work which combined with the above in its effects. The racial homogeneity of our earlier colonial days was broken by the millions of immigrants who came to us of racial stocks other than our own. Our first character had been that of seventeenth and eighteenth century Englishmen, not greatly altered until the Revolution. It was unified and stable, but the West and Europe both operated to undermine its stability.

On the one hand, the influence of the West, with the loosening of old bonds, its peculiar population, and its opportunities of limitless expansion and wealth greatly altered old ideals and standards of value. On the other, the steady infusion in large numbers of Germans, Irish, Swedes, Norwegians, Jews, Russians, Italians, Greeks, and other races also bore a conspicuous part in making the national character less uniform and stable. I am not concerned with their several contributions of value, but merely with the fact that the introduction of such foreign swarms tended to destroy a unified national character.

By the latter part of the nineteenth century, two things had thus happened. In the first place, the real America had become the West, and its traits were becoming dominant. One of these was restlessness, not only a willingness but a desire to try any new place or thing and make a complete break with the old. Moreover, although the frontier may breed some fine qualities, it is a good deal like the farm in the respect that although it may be a fine place to come from, it is a soul-killing place in which to remain. It bred emotion rather than thought, and to a considerable extent substituted new material values for the spiritual ones of the older America.

In the rush for wealth—whether won from forests or mines; farms tilled, raped, and abandoned for fresher soil; real estate values from fast-growing cities; lands fraudulently obtained from a complaisant government—restraint, self-discipline, thought for the future ceased to be virtues. With all this came a vast optimism, a belief that everything would become bigger and better, and, because the standards of success were economic, better because bigger. Wealth was the goal, and the faster things got bigger—towns, cities, the piles of slain buffaloes, the area of forests destroyed—the quicker one's personal wealth accumulated. Statistics took on a new significance and spelled the letters of one's private fate.

At the same time, by the latter half of the nineteenth century another thing had happened, as we have said. Partly from the effects of the West and partly from immigration, the old, stable American-English character had become unstable, soft, pliant, something which could be easily molded by new influences. It could readily take the impress of an emotion, a leader, a new invention. It was full of possibility, both of good and evil.

Suddenly this new, unformed, malleable national character, already warped to a large degree toward material values, was called upon to feel the full force of the influences flowing from the fruition of the industrial revolution. Invention followed invention with startling rapidity. Life itself became infinitely more mobile. Scientists, engineers, manufacturers threw at the public contrivance after contrivance of the most far-reaching influence upon man's personal and social life without a thought of what that influence might be beyond the profit of the moment to the individual manufacturer.

Choice became bewildering in its complexity. The national character had become unstable. It was in a real sense unformed and immature, far more so than it had been a century earlier. It had also lost belief in the necessity of restraint and discipline. It had accepted material standards and ideals. It was in far more danger of being overwhelmed by the ideals of a new, raw, and crude machine age than was perhaps any other nation of the civilized group.

With an ingenuity that would have been fiendish had it not been so unthinking and ignorant, the leaders of the new era used every resource of modern psychology to warp the unformed character of the people, to provide the greatest possible profit to the individuals and corporations that made and purveyed the new "goods." Our best and worst qualities, our love of wife and children, our national pride, our self-respect, our snobbery, our fear of social opinion, our neglect of the future, our lack of self-restraint and discipline, our love of mere physical comfort have all been played upon to make mush of our characters in order that big business might thrive. Even our national government, whether wittingly or not, undertook to inflame our American love of gambling and our desire to "get rich quick" regardless of effect on character.

IV

Taking all the molding influences of the past century and more into account, it is little wonder, perhaps, that our national characteristics exhibit the trend noted. The situation, serious as it is, might be less so had it occurred at a time when the spiritual forms in the world at large—its scales of values, its ethical systems, its philosophies of life—were intact. But as we have noted, they have been largely destroyed; and at the very time when new forms are in process of arising, largely to be molded by the national characters of the peoples among whom they arise, our own is in the state pictured above. The question whether our new characteristics are temporary or permanent thus becomes of acute significance.

"Race" is a word of such vague and undefined content as to be of slight help to us, but if we take the whole history of the Western nations from which we derive, I think we may say that the characteristics noted above may be classed as acquired and not inherited. Biologists consider such not to be permanent and heritable, though the analogy with biology again is so vague as to afford little comfort.

More hopeful, I think, is the fact that these new characteristics appear to have derived directly from circumstances, and that these circumstances themselves have been in large part such as have passed and will not recur again. Immigration and "the West" have ceased to be continuing factors in our development. Their effects remain and must be dealt with, but neither factor will continue to intensify them. The tides of immigration have been shut off. There is significance in the fact that "the Wests" which won under Jefferson, Jackson, and Lincoln were defeated in 1896 under Bryan.

"The West" of today is a new West in which conditions, and to a large extent ideals, are different. Yet its greatest contribution to our national life and character remains that broadening and deepening of the dream of a better and a richer life for all of every class which was the cause of its earlier victories and which goes far to redeem its less noble influences. The nation as a whole is entering upon a new era in which all the conditions will be different from any experienced heretofore. Territory, resources, opportunities are none of them any longer unexploited and boundless. What the future may hold, we cannot tell, but in fundamental influences it will be different from the past. The menacing factor that remains is that of mass production and the machine.

Also, we have spoken thus far only of the trend in characteristics, not of our character as a whole. In that there are certain noble traits which remain unaltered, or have matured and strengthened. It is possible, now the warping influences of the past century have to some extent disappeared, that the national character may develop around them as a core, that we shall forget in manhood the wild oats sown in our youth.

But age acquires no value save through thought and discipline. If we cannot reinstate those, we are in danger of hampering rather than aiding in that reconstruction of the spiritual life of man that is the inevitable and most vital task now before the nations. We must either forward or retard it. We are too great to live aloof. We could not if we would, and upon the trend of our character depends to a great extent the future of the world.

Nor let us forget that although fortune has poured her favors in our lap, there is a Nemesis that dogs the steps of all, and we cannot lightly scorn the growing enmity of half the world. Are we to treat the machine age and mass production only as a new and different "West," or are we at last, in growing up, to learn wisdom and restraint? Are we going to change the trend in our character, or is it to become fixed in its present form, a danger to ourselves and a menace to mankind?

"Has anybody ever thought of winning the Communists over to
<u>our</u> way of life?"

from FAREWELL ADDRESS TO THE PEOPLE OF THE UNITED STATES, SEPTEMBER 17th, 1796

by George Washington

TOWARDS the preservation of your Government and the permanency of your present happy state, it is requisite, not only that you steadily discountenance irregular oppositions to its acknowledged authority, but also that you resist with care the spirit of innovation upon its principles, however specious the pretexts.—One method of assault may be to effect, in the forms of the Constitution, alterations which will impair the energy of the system, and thus to undermine what cannot be directly overthrown.—In all the changes to which you may be invited, remember that time and habit are at least as necessary to fix the true character of Governments, as of other human institutions—that experience is the surest standard, by which to test the real tendency of the existing Constitution of a Country—that facility in changes upon the credit of mere hypothesis and opinion exposes to perpetual change, from the endless variety of hypothesis and opinion:—and remember, especially, that, for the efficient management of your common interests, in a country so extensive as ours, a Government of as much vigor as is consistent with the perfect security of Liberty is indispensable.—Liberty itself will find in such a Government, with powers properly distributed and adjusted, its surest Guardian.

CHANGE AND THE AMERICAN TRADITION

by George Soule

THE MINDS of Americans are deeply troubled nowadays by a conflict of ideas—the conflict between necessity for change and loyalty to American tradition.

We cannot look in any direction without observing perils threatening our society. The earlier promise of American life has been betrayed by the existence of millions of unemployed industrial workers, by the expropriation of farmers and other classes of property owners, by the disappearance of capital, and by the dependence of a large part of our population on governmental assistance. There is no assurance that similar disasters may not occur in the future. We have engaged in

From George Soule, *The Future of Liberty*. By permission of The Macmillan Company, publishers.

one world war, and are daily threatened by the suicide of another. There have been few periods in history when men and women were menaced by more confusion and peril. The ignominy of this situation is impressed upon us when we remember that it is not the outcome of an uncontrollable cataclysm of nature—except as man himself is regarded as part of nature. Though we have suffered earthquakes, droughts or floods, these have not brought us where we are. It is the result, almost exclusively, of human ways of acting and thinking. Somehow or other, the conceptions on which our action is supposed to be based, the forms of organization which we have built up, have either failed to control our behavior, or, if they have controlled it, have done so to little purpose.

The hope that we may blunder through to a temporary period of better fortune is enough to satisfy the more complacent; signs of "recovery" are continually cited to bring us courage. But it is axiomatic that if the modes of behavior that brought us to our recent misfortunes are continued unchanged, any better outcome in the future will give way in the end to a similar and possibly a worse calamity.

To change our fortune we must change our minds. General recognition of this fact has brought forth many suggestions for alteration in our institutions. Insistent pressure from the logic of events, working upon the deepest needs of the personality, forces us to consider new arrangements of society.

But here arises the conflict. Any suggestion of basic change offends our loyalty to the concepts on which we suppose our culture to have been founded. Assertion of the rights of life, liberty and the pursuit of happiness, belief in democracy and in its American constitutional expression,

faith in the perfectibility of the individual, trust in reason and science as the basis of assurance and in persuasion as a method of bringing about action in a free society, run deep in us. We are the inheritors of a powerful liberal tradition; it was in the period when these ideas were flowering most luxuriantly that this nation achieved its independence and adopted its form of government. We look abroad at the peoples that have made great changes in response to contemporary crises, and see that liberty and democracy in our sense of the words do not there exist. Both Fascism and Communism, though they are at opposite poles of doctrine in their major tenets, express contempt for liberalism. Many Americans, aroused by these challenges to old loyalties, forget the plight we ourselves are in, and talk as if the exclusive purpose of this nation were the negative one of avoiding what they conceive to be these new foreign dangers. Indeed, they are so moved by the call to protect our traditions that they attempt to avoid every change by exorcising it with one of the current vocabulary of bad names. William Randolph Hearst, for example, warns against "pestilent innovators." Even in more sober circles, relatively moderate innovations are suspect merely because they are innovations. New statutes have to pass the scrutiny of judges who examine them, not primarily to determine whether they will serve the social purposes that seemed good to the supposedly democratic agencies that enacted them, but rather to adjudicate their conformity to the constitutional framework of that democracy. The conflict between our need for change and our traditions gives us a national bad conscience and confuses our counsels.

This dilemma is not merely one of words, it is not one that begins and ends in ideas unconnected with the practical world. It appears again and again in problems of action. Let us take a common example. The citizen begins with the simple faith that the all-important task is to protect American liberty against those who desire to destroy it. An agitator comes into his community, helps to organize the workers and leads a strike for higher wages and better conditions. The local citizen is told that this agitator believes in Communism. The strike is conceived, both by him and by its leader, as in some sense a challenge to existing institutions. A court enjoins picketing. Police and troops are called out to suppress it. Public opinion is mobilized against the strikers by the newspapers. A band of vigilantes kidnaps the leaders and forces them out of the community by violence or threats of violence. Subsequently our good citizen supports so-called "criminal syndicalism" bills to punish mere membership in any organization that is supposed to teach the necessity of change in our form of government by violent means; possession of revolutionary literature is made a crime. What in fact has he done?

In the name of American liberty he has violated every one of its basic tenets. He has suppressed, in the interest of employers, an initial gesture toward democracy in industry. Not only is democracy denied, but equality also; even equal rights before the law are violated by the use of courts, police and military against the less fortunate party in an economic dispute. Further, he has himself broken the law and transgressed the principles of civil government by exercising private violence. He has abandoned reason and discarded persuasion by forceful suppression of the labor controversy, without any fair adjudication of the issues involved. He has also, by the laws he espouses, denied free speech and freedom of the press. He has made it

possible for the Communist agitator to prove to the workers through their own experience that liberalism is merely a mask for the dictatorship of capital, that the liberal, in a crisis, turns into a Fascist, and that the only real choice is between Fascism and Communism. The effort to protect a static conception of liberty has succeeded merely in making inevitable the destruction of liberty.

It is no answer to say that if we did not fight against revolutionaries, they would in the end destroy liberty anyway. If that is true, liberty is lost by either course. It is exposed as something that cannot be maintained in the modern world. If liberty cannot be protected without fighting enemies of liberty, and if fighting these enemies means abandoning liberty, then the conception of liberty is meaningless in fact, and cannot be a trustworthy guide to action.

Conflicts of liberties are not always so sharp and dramatic as this, and they occur continually throughout the warp and woof of our society. Shall the liberty of automobile drivers be restricted by traffic regulations, and if so, how far shall that restriction go? Shall the liberty of individual farmers to settle where they like, grow what they like, and manage their farms as they see fit, be restricted in the interest of higher prices for crops or in the effort to prevent loss of the nation's soil through erosion? Shall freedom of the press be restricted in the interest of discouraging immoral influence on the young? Shall the liberty of speculators on stock markets be restricted in the interest of innocent investors? Neither an abstract belief in liberty nor an abstract belief in regulation offers much help in the solution of such difficulties.

The examples to which we have referred are not irrelevant and isolated ones;

they are typical; they reveal a basic confusion in the symbols that determine our social behavior. The same issues arise whenever we try to deal with a practical situation which demands organization, regulation, or decision—and what situation does not? Some purpose must be sought, some compulsion must be exercised, someone must make a decision. But when purposes conflict—as they frequently do—the making of a decision obstructs the purpose against which the compulsion is exercised. Somebody's liberty to do something must be denied if any action is to be taken. This truth applies to all rules and all social institutions, from a baseball league to a national political government.

It is difficult to overestimate the importance of the problem that this conflict presents in a period of social crisis. Shall we abandon utterly our traditional conceptions in the interest of a new social order? Or shall we regard them as final, unquestionable dogmas, in the interest of which all thoughts of real change must be suppressed? Or do they contain a truth to which our actual development has been false, a truth that, reinterpreted, may guide our action?

At this point it is prudent to make a brief excursion to reveal the bias of the writer. Social questions are too often discussed without such frank revelation. For instance, the adherent of the economic principles of Adam Smith—a master propagandist if ever there was one—is likely to assume that while his attitude is calm, objective and scientific, any opposing point of view distorts the argument in behalf of a cause. No vulgarity is more common than to attack all "isms," as if the speaker himself were not defending, let us say, Americanism or liberalism, as if there were any ground for attacking anything whatever except on the basis of human desire and a system of thought that grows up about it. The most deceptive bias is that which is not acknowledged. Therefore it is an essential part of candor, indeed of the scientific method itself in the so-called social sciences, to acknowledge one's prejudice somewhere near the beginning.

My bias is democratic and liberal. The words of the Declaration of Independence have always aroused my enthusiastic loyalty. I take pride in the origin of this nation as the expression of a new faith in the destiny of mankind. I believe in the right of the individual to seek his own fulfillment, in equality of status, in the attempt of man to control his own destiny instead of having it controlled for him by some representative of hereditary right or superhuman revelation. I believe, not in blind submission, but in mutual respect among upstanding individuals. I believe in the right to question all creeds and institutions in the light of reason, in a continually recurring need to reject and build anew. I believe in the legitimacy of revolution: not merely the revolution that my forefathers helped to make in the eighteenth century, but any new revolution that may be justified by the interest and reason of the common man.

The Declaration of Independence begins with mention of "the course of human events" and the necessity for dissolution of traditional bonds. There is here an affirmation that human events move and that the movement sometimes demands fundamental change. It declares further:

We hold these truths to be self-evident, that all men are created equal, that they are endowed by their Creator with certain unalienable Rights, that among these are Life, Liberty and the pursuit of Happiness. That to secure these rights, Governments are instituted among Men, deriving their just powers from the consent of the governed, That whenever any Form of Government becomes destructive of these ends, it is the Right of the People to alter or to abolish it, and to institute new Government, laying its foundation on such principles and organizing its powers in such form, as to them shall seem most likely to effect their Safety and Happiness.

General as these words are, and difficult as they are to interpret in specific cases, they mean something that is precious even in the modern world. It is true that we do deprive men of life or liberty even in the literal sense every time we deal with a criminal. The pursuit of happiness is limited by a tangle of obligations and restrictions. We know that men are not equal in native gifts or in the rewards to which their activity entitles them. Nevertheless, there is something in the direction toward which these affirmations point that adds to the dignity and meaning of life. We could not enthusiastically assent to the contraries: that men have no rights, that they must be compelled to suffer death, slavery and pain, that inequality is natural and desirable.

The more sober statement of our civil liberties in the Bill of Rights embodied in amendments to the Federal Constitution is likewise worth repeating, as an expression of the safeguards against tyranny that are still of primary value. We must admit the tortured interpretation that courts have often given to the "due process" clauses, we must acknowledge that in practical application these generalities are often distorted beyond recognition by expansion in some cases and restriction in others. People are subjected to unfair trials, heavy bail, cruel punishments; freedom of speech and assembly is often forbidden. We can-

not forget Mooney and Billings, or Sacco and Vanzetti. Every year sees its long list of lynchings, of violent suppressions. Nevertheless the principles still mean something.

ARTICLE I

Congress shall make no law respecting an establishment of religion, or prohibiting the free exercise thereof; or abridging the freedom of speech, or of the press; or the right of the people peaceably to assemble, and to petition the Government for a redress of grievances.

ARTICLE IV

The right of the people to be secure in their persons, houses, papers, and effects, against unreasonable searches and seizures, shall not be violated, and no Warrants shall issue, but upon probable cause, supported by Oath or affirmation, and particularly describing the place to be searched, and the persons or things to be seized.

ARTICLE V

No person shall be held to answer for a capital or otherwise infamous crime, unless on a presentment or indictment of a Grand Jury, except in cases arising in the land or naval forces, or in the Militia, when in actual service in time of war or public danger; nor shall any person be subject for the same offense to be twice put in jeopardy of life or limb; nor shall be compelled in any criminal case to be a witness against himself, nor be deprived of life, liberty or property, without due process of law; nor shall private property be taken for public use, without just compensation.

ARTICLE VI

In all criminal prosecutions, the accused shall enjoy the right to a speedy and public trial, by an impartial jury of the State and district wherein the crime shall have been committed, which district shall have been previously ascertained by law, and to be informed of the nature and cause of the accusation; to be confronted with the witnesses against him; to have compulsory process for obtaining witnesses in his favor, and to have the Assistance of Counsel for his defense.

ARTICLE VIII

Excessive bail shall not be required, nor excessive fines imposed, nor cruel and unusual punishments inflicted.

ARTICLE XIV

All persons born or naturalized in the United States, and subject to the jurisdiction thereof, are citizens of the United States and of the State wherein they reside. No State shall make or enforce any law which shall abridge the privileges or immunities of citizens of the United States, nor shall any State deprive any person of life, liberty, or property without due process of law, nor deny to any person within its jurisdiction the equal protection of the laws.

Now it may be that these principles themselves are irrational or contradictory. As Carl Becker has told us in his "Heavenly City of the Eighteenth Century Philosophers," the founders of liberalism may have been performing a magician's trick in transferring divine sanction from the rule of kings and the lords of the church to the "unalienable" rights with which, in Thomas Jefferson's words, men have been "endowed by their creator." We have learned from candid historians like Charles A. Beard that the motives of the early Americans were not all pure and not all the same; economic interests played a large part both in their revolt against England and in the subsequent formation of the Constitution, a document that attempted the difficult and probably impossible compromise of protecting propertied interests while giving expression to Jeffersonian democracy. The history of the republic is in itself a most inadequate embodiment of the aspirations with which it began, and particularly so in recent years. In spite of all this, there is an ineradicable confidence that somehow or other such words are valid; that they provide, if properly defined and applied, an indispensable frame of reference and a standard of values. If the sort of faith that is embodied in these words is not a basis of social judgment, I do not know where to find another that I can accept.

This confession is important not just as the acknowledgment of a personal vagary that may have to be discounted in reading this book. It is also important because of acceptance among the generality of those who will have to act or lead action in the United States. Every personality, in order to find psychic security, has to organize itself about symbols of faith. When we drift along with a smooth current, these symbols may be submerged; the need of self-organization may be satisfied by the merest empty formula, seldom invoked and never examined. But when rough waters threaten to tear us apart; when external misfortunes create emotional disturbances, we seek ardently a set of beliefs about which we can integrate ourselves; we reject as vehemently those symbols that do not seem to fit this integration. As long as a man remains seriously divided within himself, he does not, he cannot act. Those who carry the day in a crisis are those whose minds have become crystallized, temporarily at least. This explains the importance, in revolutionary periods, of the leader or the leading idea. Regardless of the objective substance covered by the labels that we accept, we defend them as final and unquestionable truth. And the symbols to which we turn are likely to be, in some form or other, those that have aroused our loyalty in an impressionable

[844]

period. For better or for worse, the symbols that are most potent in this country are those that are found in our tradition. Whatever is done about them, they cannot be ignored by anyone who is long going to influence us as a people.

By the same token, however, it is equally important to attach these symbols to a kind of action that will satisfy continuing needs. If words like liberty and democracy are appropriated by the standard-bearers of opposition to all change, they may succeed for a period in freezing existing institutions. But if existing institutions will not feed us and clothe us, if they make us a nation of economic slaves and allow no room for the growth of the personality, we shall have suffered a false and superficial integration, which cannot endure. It is important, in an objective sense, what is done in the name of our faith, and what its effectiveness is. In 1917 we fought a war to make the world safe

for democracy, a war to end war. Let us be careful that a contemporary crusade for liberty does not lead us to an equally disastrous betrayal.

We proceed, then, on the following assumptions. Drastic change may be necessary for mere survival, to say nothing of more elaborate objectives. The conflict between the need for change and our traditional symbols of faith must somehow be allayed. An abolition of this conflict that involves a suppression of the faith is unlikely. Even if it occurred, the kind of change that resulted would be inferior because of its loss of whatever was valid in the faith. Abolition of the conflict by the victory of the faith over change would be a denial of needs as imperative as the faith itself. What we have to do is to re-examine and interpret the faith in such a way that it will allow room for the change, to do so, indeed, in a manner that will help to compel the change.

FAREWELL, MY LOVELY!

by LEE STROUT WHITE

I SEE by the new Sears Roebuck catalogue that it is still possible to buy an axle for a 1909 Model T Ford, but I am not deceived. The great days have faded, the end is in sight. Only one page in the current catalogue is devoted to parts and accessories for the Model T; yet everyone remembers springtimes when the Ford gadget section was larger than men's clothing, almost as large as household furnishings. The last Model T was built in 1927, and the car is fading from what scholars call the American scene—which is an understatement, because to a few million people who grew up with it, the old Ford practically *was* the American scene.

It was the miracle God had wrought. And it was patently the sort of thing that could only happen once. Mechanically uncanny, it was like nothing that had ever come to the world before. Flourishing industries rose and fell with it. As a vehicle, it was hard-working, commonplace, heroic; and it often seemed to transmit those qualities to the persons who rode in it. My own generation identifies it with Youth, with its gaudy, irretrievable excitements; before it fades into the mist, I would like to pay it the tribute of the sigh that is not a sob, and set down random entries in a shape somewhat less cumbersome than a Sears Roebuck catalogue.

The Model T was distinguished from all other makes of cars by the fact that its transmission was of a type known as planetary—which was half metaphysics, half sheer friction. Engineers accepted the word "planetary" in its epicyclic sense, but I was always conscious that it also meant "wandering," "erratic." Because of the peculiar nature of this planetary element, there was always, in Model T, a certain dull rapport between engine and wheels, and even when the car was in a state known as neutral, it trembled with a deep imperative and tended to inch forward. There was never a moment when the bands were not faintly egging the machine on. In this respect it was like a horse, rolling the bit on its tongue, and country people brought to it the same technique they used with draft animals.

Its most remarkable quality was its rate of acceleration. In its palmy days the Model T could take off faster than anything on the road. The reason was simple. To get under way, you simply hooked the third finger of the right hand around a lever on the steering column, pulled down hard, and shoved your left foot forcibly against the low-speed pedal. These were simple, positive motions; the car responded by lunging forward with a roar. After a few seconds of this turmoil, you took your toe off the pedal, eased up a mite on the throttle, and the car, possessed of only two forward speeds, catapulted directly into high with a series of ugly jerks and was off on its glorious errand. The abruptness of this departure was never equaled in other cars of the period. The human leg was (and still is) incapable of letting in a clutch with anything like the forthright abandon that used to send Model T on its way. Letting in a clutch is a negative, hesitant motion, depending on delicate nervous control; pushing down the Ford pedal was a simple, country motion—an expansive act, which came as natural as kicking an old door to make it budge.

The driver of the old Model T was a man enthroned. The car, with top up, stood seven feet high. The driver sat on top of the gas tank, brooding it with his own body. When he wanted gasoline, he alighted, along with everything else in the front seat; the seat was pulled off, the metal cap unscrewed, and a wooden stick thrust down to sound the liquid in the well. There were always a couple of these sounding sticks kicking around in the ratty sub-cushion regions of a flivver. Refueling was more of a social function then, because the driver had to unbend, whether he wanted to or not. Directly in front of the driver was the windshield—high, uncompromisingly erect. Nobody talked about air resistance, and the four cylinders pushed the car through the atmosphere with a simple disregard of physical law.

There was this about a Model T: the purchaser never regarded his purchase as a complete, finished product. When you bought a Ford, you figured you had a start—a vibrant, spirited framework to which could be screwed an almost limitless assortment of decorative and functional hardware. Driving away from the agency, hugging the new wheel between your knees, you were already full of creative worry. A Ford was born naked as a baby, and a flourishing industry grew up out of correcting its rare deficiencies and combating its fascinating diseases. Those were the great days of lily-painting. I have been looking at some old Sears Roebuck catalogues, and they bring everything back so clear.

First you bought a Ruby Safety Reflector for the rear, so that your posterior would glow in another car's brilliance. Then you invested thirty-nine cents in some radiator Moto Wings, a popular ornament which gave the Pegasus touch to the machine and did something godlike to the owner. For nine cents you bought a fan-belt guide to keep the belt from slipping off the pulley.

You bought a radiator compound to stop leaks. This was as much a part of everybody's equipment as aspirin tablets are of a medicine cabinet. You bought special oil to prevent chattering, a clamp-on dash light, a patching outfit, a tool box which you bolted to the running board, a sun visor, a steering-column brace to keep the column rigid, and a set of emergency containers for gas, oil, and water—three thin, disc-like cans which reposed in a case on the running board during long, important journeys—red for gas, gray for water, green for oil. It was only a beginning. After the car was about a year old, steps were taken to check the alarming disintegration. (Model T was full of tumors, but they were benign.) A set of anti-rattlers (98c) was a popular panacea. You hooked them on to the gas and spark rods, to the brake pull rod, and to the steering-rod connections. Hood silencers, of black rubber, were applied to the fluttering hood. Shock-absorbers and snubbers gave "complete relaxation." Some people bought rubber pedal pads, to fit over the standard metal pedals. (I didn't like these, I remember.) Persons of a suspicious or pugnacious turn of mind bought a rear-view mirror; but most Model T owners weren't worried by what was coming from behind because they would soon enough see it out in front. They rode in a state of cheerful catalepsy. Quite a large mutinous clique among Ford owners went over to a foot accelerator (you could buy one and screw it to the floor board), but there was a certain madness in these people, because the Model T, just as she stood, had a choice of three foot pedals to push, and there were plenty of moments when both feet were occupied in the routine performance of duty and when the only way to speed up the engine was with the hand throttle.

Gadget bred gadget. Owners not only bought ready made gadgets, they invented gadgets to meet special needs. I myself drove my car directly from the agency to the blacksmith's, and had the smith affix two enormous iron brackets to the port running board to support an army trunk.

People who owned closed models builded along different lines: they bought ball grip handles for opening doors, window anti-rattlers, and deluxe flower vases of the cut-glass anti-splash type. People with delicate sensibilities garnished their car with a device called the Donna Lee Automobile Disseminator—a porous vase guaranteed, according to Sears, to fill the car with a "faint clean odor of lavender." The gap between open cars and closed cars was not as great then as it is now: for $11.95, Sears Roebuck converted your touring car into a sedan and you went forth renewed. One agreeable quality of the old Fords was that they had no bumpers, and their fenders softened and wilted with the years and permitted the driver to squeeze in and out of tight places.

Tires were 30 x 3½, cost about twelve dollars, and punctured readily. Everybody carried a Jiffy patching set, with a nutmeg grater to roughen the tube before the goo was spread on. Everybody was capable of putting on a patch, expected to have to, and did have to.

During my association with Model T's, self-starters were not a prevalent accessory. They were expensive and under suspicion. Your car came equipped with a serviceable crank, and the first thing you learned was how to Get Results. It was a special trick, and until you learned it (usually from another Ford owner, but sometimes by a period of appalling experimentation) you might as well have been winding up an awning. The trick was to leave the ignition switch off, proceed to the animal's head, pull the choke (which was a little wire protruding through the radiator), and give the crank two or three nonchalant upward lifts. Then, whistling as though thinking about something else, you would saunter back to the driver's cabin, turn the ignition on, return to the crank, and this time, catching it on the down stroke, give it a quick spin with plenty of That. If this procedure was followed, the engine almost always responded—first with a few scattered explosions, then with a tumultuous gunfire, which you checked by racing around to the driver's seat and retarding the throttle. Often, if the emergency brake hadn't been pulled all the way back, the car advanced on you the instant the first explosion occurred and you would hold it back by leaning your weight against it. I can still feel my old Ford nuzzling me at the curb, as though looking for an apple in my pocket.

The lore and legend that governed the Ford were boundless. Owners had their own theories about everything; they discussed mutual problems in that wise, infinitely resourceful way old women discuss rheumatism. Exact knowledge was pretty scarce, and often proved less effective than superstition. Dropping a camphor ball into the gas tank was a popular expedient; it seemed to have a tonic effect on both man and machine. There wasn't much to base exact knowledge on. The Ford driver flew blind. He didn't know the temperature of his engine, the speed of his car, the amount of his fuel, or the pressure of his oil (the old Ford lubricated itself by what was amiably described as the "splash system"). A speedometer cost money and was an extra, like a windshield-wiper. The dashboard of the early models was bare save for an ignition key; later models, grown effete, boasted an ammeter which pulsated alarmingly with the throbbing of the car. Under the dash was a box of coils, with vibrators which you adjusted, or thought you adjusted. Whatever the driver learned of his motor, he learned not through instruments but through sudden developments. I remember that the timer was one of the vital organs about which there was ample doctrine. When everything else had been checked, you "had a look" at the timer. It was an extravagantly odd little device, simple in construction, mysterious in function. It contained a roller, held by a spring, and there were four contact points on the inside of the case against which, many people believed, the roller rolled. I have had a timer apart on a sick Ford many times, but I never really knew what I was up to—I was just showing off before God. There were almost as many schools of thought as there were timers. Some people, when things went wrong, just clenched their teeth and gave the timer a smart crack with a wrench. Other people opened it up and blew on it. There was a school that held that the timer needed large amounts of oil; they fixed it by frequent baptism. And there was a school that was positive it was meant to run dry as a bone; these people were continually taking it off and wiping it. I remember once spitting into a timer; not in anger, but in a spirit of research. You see, the Model T driver moved in the realm of metaphysics. He believed his car could be hexed.

One reason the Ford anatomy was never reduced to an exact science was that, having "fixed" it, the owner couldn't honestly claim that the treatment had brought about the cure. There were too many authenticated cases of Fords fixing themselves—restored naturally to health after a short rest. Farmers soon discovered this, and it fitted nicely with their draft-horse philosophy: "Let 'er cool off and she'll snap into it again."

A Ford owner had Number One Bearing constantly in mind. This bearing, being at the front end of the motor, was the one that always burned out, because the oil didn't reach it when the car was climbing hills. (That's what I was always told, anyway.) The oil used to recede and leave Number One dry as a clam flat; you had to watch that bearing like a hawk. It was like a weak heart—you could hear it start knocking, and that was when you stopped and let her cool off. Try as you would to keep the oil supply right, in the end Number One always went out. "Number One Bearing burned out on me and I had to have her replaced," you would say, wisely; and your companions always had a lot to tell about how to protect and pamper Number One to keep her alive.

Sprinkled not too liberally among the millions of amateur witch doctors who drove Fords and applied their own abominable cures were the heaven-sent mechanics who could really make the car talk. These professionals turned up in undreamed-of spots. One time, on the banks of the Columbia River in Washington, I heard the rear end go out of my Model T when I was trying to whip it up a steep incline onto the deck of a ferry. Something snapped; the car slid backward into the mud. It seemed to me like the end of the trail. But the captain of the ferry, observing the withered remnant, spoke up.

"What's got her?" he asked.

"I guess it's the rear end," I replied, listlessly. The captain leaned over the rail and stared. Then I saw that there was a hunger in his eyes that set him off from other men.

"Tell you what," he said, carelessly, trying to cover up his eagerness, "let's pull the son of a bitch up onto the boat, and I'll help you fix her while we're going back and forth on the river."

We did just this. All that day I plied between the towns of Pasco and Kennewick, while the skipper (who had once worked in a Ford garage) directed the amazing work of resetting the bones of my car.

Springtime in the heyday of the Model T was a delirious season. Owning a car was still a major excitement, roads were still wonderful and bad. The Fords were obviously conceived in madness: any car which was capable of going from forward into reverse without any perceptible mechanical hiatus was bound to be a mighty challenging thing to the human imagination. Boys used to veer them off the highway into a level pasture and run wild with them, as though they were cutting up with a girl. Most everybody used the reverse pedal quite as much as the regular foot brake—it distributed the wear over the bands and wore them all down evenly. That was the big trick, to wear all the bands down evenly, so that the final chattering would be total and the whole unit scream for renewal.

The days were golden, the nights were dim and strange. I still recall with trembling those loud, nocturnal crises when you drew up to a signpost and raced the engine so the lights would be bright enough to read destinations by. I have never been really planetary since. I suppose it's time to say good-by. Farewell, my lovely!

A CONSERVATIVE SPEAKS

by George E. Sokolsky

I speak as a conservative. In my youth I ran the gamut of revolutionary movements. Anarchist, pacifist, I.W.W. sympathizer, I have sought this path and that to a better, a more commodious life, not only for myself, but for all men.

In Russia, I witnessed the mass struggle of millions. I saw them try to move from pre-capitalism to Communism at one step. In China, I lived through the agonizing torture of man as he sought to free himself from the barbarities of feudalism— glamorous and luxurious for those on top, retching misery for those at the bottom. In Europe, I felt the pangs of instability and insecurity.

Therefore I speak as a Conservative. Let no man think of me as a Tory, as a Bourbon, as a heartless marauder in a predatory world. For I have nothing to defend—not even chains to lose. Like so many who have written for a living, I have nothing of the goods of this world but what I earn and consume today. And I can earn that and consume that no matter which cause I favor, for such is the way of my work.

Therefore I plead no personal cause. My tax bill will be not much higher or lower whichever way we go. The household servants I employ will be as few one way as the other and their loss would not seriously affect my personal life. All the property I own is an old farm which can sustain me on a low but comfortable standard of living one way or the other. Not a single personal interest—that is, not a single materialist consideration— moves me to hold or express my opinion.

If my current views associate me with similarly minded individuals who may be capitalists, manufacturers, merchants, other views would associate me with equally if not more interesting individuals. And if there is a monetary reward for defending my point of view I have long known that colleagues who defend other and opposite points of views are as well or even better paid. My income-tax statement, I am sure, cannot compare with that of such an opponent of Conservatism as Mr. Heywood Broun.

I go into these personalities to clear the decks. I want to say what I have to say without any consideration of praise or disdain. I want to project some ideas without having my presentation suffer from that personal equation which is whatever I am.

I

In terms of goods, poverty has been most general in non-capitalistic countries. For the immediate objective of capitalism is that standards of living shall ever be on the rise. More particularly, capitalism seeks that the purchasing capacity of a constantly increasing number of purchasers shall ever be on the rise.

Mass production, modern merchandising, advertising, the creation of new commodities, the popularization of old ones, have but one objective—namely, increased usage, increased consumption. And in pursuance of this single objective it has become altogether clear, beyond the barest shadow of a doubt, that not the expensiveness of a commodity but its cheapness

George E. Sokolsky, "A Conservative Speaks," *The Atlantic Monthly* (August, 1936). By permission of the author and *The Atlantic Monthly*.

[851]

makes it of greater value to its producer. The less it costs to buy an article, the more readily that article comes within the purchasing power of an increasingly large number of people.

The classical example is the motorcar. Ford makes more money selling $500 cars than anyone makes selling $10,000 cars. This is so obvious that anybody understands the rule who understands anything at all. But we need not limit ourselves to motorcars.

Oranges were once luxuries. Beef was a luxury and very expensive—that is to say, even hamburger was beyond the daily purchasing power of workers. Students of food consumption note the popular shift from a large consumption of starchy foods, such as oatmeal, white bread, and potatoes, to protein foods, like beef, eggs, and green vegetables. It is the cheapening of the price of the latter, in ratio to wages earned, that has increased the number of those to whom they are available.

Take such an item as fruit—always a great luxury to city dwellers. Fruit in many forms, as juices, cocktails, or salads, in tins and jars, fresh and preserved, for the table or at a soda fountain, has been made available to millions who in my childhood knew only sour apples and black bananas.

Women's clothes indicate most remarkably the workings of this theory. For today a woman can purchase within any price range better styles, more durable cloths, sturdier dyes, and more alluring patterns for very much less money than ever before. The mechanization of textile production, introduction of rayon and acetates, competitive improvements in undergarments, stimulation of the use of cosmetics, deodorants, hair removers, nail beautifiers, soaps and creams and whatnot, have served to give to the working woman the "tone" which formerly belonged only to those who regarded themselves as ultra-exclusive.

In every human activity, every walk of life, this rule is constantly in evidence. To repeat the rule: in the capitalist system the objective of production is to bring prices down so that more people come within the price range of a commodity.

This, then, is the only economic system in which it is possible to give practical application to the moral dictum of the greatest good for the greatest number without utilizing political disturbance as a means to that end. In this alone, if in nothing else, capitalism justifies itself.

It is evident from this statement of the situation that in capitalistic production it is essential for wealth, in the sense of purchasing power, to be widely diffused. Thus, contrary to Marxian theory, in the United States the ownership of wealth is more widely diffused than in any other country on earth.

Opponents of the capitalist system suffer a confusion between actual ownership of wealth and control of the agencies of production and distribution. For instance, it may be said for the sake of argument that control of the management of the United States Steel Corporation rests with J. P. Morgan and Company. But it is evident that the ownership of the wealth produced by this corporation is divided between about 200,000 investors and 200,000 employees. Both groups, up to 1929, found that the amount of wealth which they took out of this corporation steadily increased, and the indications are that, except as exorbitant taxes may intervene, the investor and the employee will continue to draw increasingly from this wealth-creating and wealth-diffusing agency.

In a country where more than one hundred billion dollars is invested in homes and farms, where one hundred and twenty billion dollars is in savings bank deposits and insurance policies, where the curve of wages is—over a period, say, of half a century—steadily moving upwards, it is evident that the diffusion of wealth is constant. No greater proof of that need be adduced than the volume of business done by chain and department stores even in a year like 1933—usually referred to as a depression year. The volume of business amounted to $25,037,225,000 or $208.64 for every man, woman, and child in the country. Such trade is impossible unless the diffusion of wealth is widespread.

Here, however, we face a difficulty. In this constant shift of population from one economic bracket to another, a residue of unshiftable people appears. These marginal human beings lag behind, and their economic status is often pitiful. In the rural regions they are termed hillbillies and share-croppers, and in the cities they dwell in slums.

The capitalist system has within itself no adequate solution for the welfare of these marginal peoples. They often represent a psychological as well as an economic deficiency. Frequently they are hostages to a changing mechanization of production. Sometimes they represent a geographical shift of an economic center with which they could not catch up, as, for instance, when a greater use is found for oil than for bituminous coal and miners get stuck in a profitless coal region.

These unfortunates often contrast with another and numerically smaller marginal group, the excessively rich. In the United States this group consists of a few individuals, principally women who inherit wealth which they themselves do not employ with any social usefulness. Their personal conduct is often so distressing as to bring shame upon the original producers of the wealth. For instance, the investment of a huge inherited fortune in tax-exempt government bonds is an outrageous withdrawal of wealth from productivity.

Both these groups bear unfortunate witness to the imperfections of the capitalist system. But numerically the two groups are small as compared with the total population which benefits from widespread diffusion of wealth and the enlarged availability of an increasing number of desirable commodities. The marginal poor should become the object of state aid, that they might be educated, trained, or reoriented to fit into the wage and price scales current for the whole population. The marginal rich should be taxed equably so that their wealth might be made available for productivity. For dead wealth—and nontaxable government bonds are dead wealth—serves no one beneficially.

Three specific characteristics mark the operations of the capitalist system at its best:—

(1) A higher return to the investor than he can receive from economic passivity, as when he invests in government bonds for security only.

(2) Wages so scientifically just that the purchasing power of the worker constantly increases.

(3) An adequate return to the farmer so that manufactured goods and the benefits of urban living are more generally available to him.

These three characteristics are normal in the United States.

II

The relationship between democracy and capitalism is not an inherent one, but this is a self-evident truth: democracy continues to flourish in countries where capitalism is most developed; it declines and disappears in those countries where the capitalist system is underdeveloped or does not exist.

The capitalist system is most perfectly developed in the United States, Great Britain, France, the Scandinavian countries, Holland, Switzerland, and Czechoslovakia. These are, in exact parallel, the most democratic countries in the world. (I could include certain South American parallels which would bear out the conclusion.) France, where the capitalist system has been forced to undergo the test of the war, inflation, depression, and the fear of future wars, witnesses at the moment a simultaneous attack on both capitalism and democracy.

In Communist, Fascist, and pre-capitalist countries, democracy does not exist. In such a land as Japan, where there is a confusion between capitalism and feudalism, there is also a confusion between democracy and military plutocracy. China differs from India only in this, that, whereas in India democracy does not even appear, in China its development is abortive because of the shift from an emerging capitalism to new projections of colonization on China's soil.

We return, then, to the phenomenon of the simultaneous growth and recession of capitalism and democracy in specific areas.

To those for whom political liberty as enunciated, for instance, in the Constitution of the United States has no significance, the preservation of democracy is futile. But the current view of the world forces the overwhelming conviction that for the individual man there can be no will, no personality, no character, almost no value in life, unless he enjoys that liberty.

It may be true, as opponents of capitalism will argue, that man cannot live by money incentive alone, and that in both Communist and Fascist countries men serve the state for no reward save the moral satisfactions which come from social service. That may or may not be true. Soviet Russia's admission of the theory of differentiated wages, Stakhanovism, the use of technical experts rather than ideologically correct party workers in management, and other evidences force the conclusion that Russia's experience is much the same as ours—namely, that men work best when their rewards include a greater purchasing power than their neighbors achieve with less notable work. In a word, in both countries it is not only a case of living up to the Joneses, but also of getting more than the Joneses.

If, then, social consciousness does not provide ample stimulation for productivity, why should the individual sacrifice his liberties for a cause which in the end brings him back to capitalism, under which he could enjoy his liberties? What motive should impel me lightly to trade away my rights under the Constitution of the United States?

It is at this point that the individual must choose for himself between a tried human experience and an asserted philosophic idealism. Admitting certain specific weaknesses and imperfections in the capitalist system, I yet retain political and social liberties under democratic institutions which are invaluable to me as a human being. If I sacrifice those liberties, will mankind be rid of the weaknesses and imperfections of our economic order? Do I envisage such results in Soviet Russia, Germany, Italy, Japan? Why should I assume that potentially their systems will restore human liberty when it is evident that the very persistence of these systems depends upon the destruction of human liberty? Stalin may authorize his people to smile or to use cosmetics, but there can be no liberty unless we can do either or neither without his interference.

Democracy, even in the well developed capitalist countries, is beginning to suffer from the expanding power of government. The Chief Justice of England, Lord Hewart of Bury, wrote a remarkable treatise, *The New Despotism,* against such expansion. We limit it here through the Supreme Court. Only in the United States is specific provision made in the organic law and in the machinery of government to limit the expanding power of government. Yet, when we analyze the provisions in our Constitution, we discover that many of them which in operation safeguard human personal rights were originally designed to safeguard property rights. In the American system, human rights and property rights are identical in theory and practice.

The interrelation between liberty and capitalism causes one to pause before any major revision of the capitalist system; for we have to measure the value of each reform by its possible effect upon democratic government and upon human liberty.

The question poses itself in this manner. Human beings can learn to live under any form of government. The Germans have lived under the semi-democracy of the Kaiser and under the sclerotic despotism of Hitler. The Russians built a subway in Moscow without utilizing the financial or engineering mechanism of capitalism. In China, during a twenty-year period of political and social revolution, when no one economic system applied to the entire country, remarkable progress was made in banking, manufacturing, communications, and every field of economic endeavor.

What, then, makes one system superior to another? Two factors, I think. One is the rising standard of living, the greater availability of useful and pleasant commodities and services; the other is human liberty.

Liberty is no God-given benefit to man. No Moses, no Solon, handed it down. Every evidence of human liberty is the product of an endless, vigilant struggle between the individual man and government. Whether it is trial by jury or freedom of the press, or the right to a writ of habeas corpus, each manifestation of liberty marks a successful struggle—and each right can be destroyed unless man is willing to struggle to maintain his rights to liberty.

Shall I, then, not judge the value of an economic system by its relationship to human liberty? And shall I not accept the evidence of history and the experience of the race? When I shall see the human liberty in Soviet Russia, in Italy, in Germany, in China, that I see in the United States and Great Britain, then, and only then, shall I feel justified in revising my view of the value of the capitalist system. Until then I am morally bound to conserve capitalism because I seek to conserve democracy.

III

The capitalist system is by no means perfect. It is an evolving, changing, flexible process of production and distribution. Like every dynamic human experience, it contains within itself the germs of its own destruction, and against the spread of these germs we who seek to conserve the benefits of the system must be eternally vigilant. These evils may be summarized as follows:—

(1) The principal weakness of capitalism is a tendency to monopoly. Large-scale production, the control of capital by banking groups, government price-fixing as under the NRA, control of operations during wars, the nationalistic stabilization of essential industries, are but a few of the causes which may result in monopoly.

There are instances when monopolies represent the most efficient and socially beneficial structure for the production and distribution of goods, and these instances are often cited to prove a rule.

The error, however, lies in this: the capitalistic-democratic system can only maintain itself by the elimination of decadent energy and the generation of new, vital energy. Thus, in the more highly developed capitalistic countries, new initiative, new capacity, comes to the top in every change from one commodity type to another. For instance, no wagon-trust monopoly could prevent the rise of the automobile; no ice trust could destroy electrical refrigeration; no theatrical trust could impede radio; no banking group interested in cereals could limit the consumption of citrous fruits.

Monopolies tend to rigidities in the production of goods: take what we give you, for there is nothing else. Competition forces ingenuity and inventiveness to curry the favor of the consumer. Without competition the capitalistic system breaks down in its every phase. Nevertheless, those that have achieved the top seek to hold it, and will permit themselves the momentary luxury of seeking to do business by monopolistic rather than by competitive processes. It is a short-sighted error. Sooner or later a brilliant competitor will rise to destroy the monopoly. This has been American economic history in all but two or three fields.

(2) The tendency to bureaucracy is not only evident in government, but in business as well. After the initial pioneering group has disappeared from an enterprise the organization tends to become stabilized into a more or less self-perpetuating bureaucracy in which seniority rather than capacity marks men off for advancement. In prosperous times such a tendency can do little harm, but during a depression or a competitive fight an enterprise may be utterly destroyed by a bureaucracy. And, unfortunately, psychological factors, nepotism, social relationships, often strengthen a bureaucratic group in its strangle hold upon an industry.

In the capitalist system there is no room for uncompetitive overhead, and that is what a bureaucracy represents. It destroys itself by the evidence of the balance sheet, and there comes a time when the most perfectly conceived alibis for unthinking management cease to be acceptable. The bureaucracy under capitalism is an error.

(3) Excessive wealth often defeats itself in Caligulan exhibitionism. Really the evil is limited to the individual. In fact his excesses, in economics, act as a means for a swifter redistribution of wealth.

Nevertheless, the picture of a grandson of a great pioneer with five or six concubines or the granddaughter of a great pioneer in quest of Sybaritic excitation, in contrast with that of the other marginal people, those who have nothing, those who perhaps never can have anything because they are residual tail-enders in a fierce struggle— these contrasting pictures ever before us stir such pity, such an emotional antagonism to all wealth, to all ownership of property, that an entirely false conception of the capitalist system replaces experience and knowledge.

In England the social system of royalty intervenes to save society from its fools. In the United States no such social mechanism is possible. Education, the church, breeding, have failed to safeguard society against the psychopathic rich. They are one of the major liabilities of our way of life, and a means must be found to curb them.

(4) Capitalism and democracy both recognize the individual as the center of power; under Communism and Fascism the center of power is the state. The individual in these systems possesses only such rights and powers as the state permits him to enjoy; under our system the state has only such powers as we delegate to it. Under these other systems the state can at its will completely destroy any individual or any class or group of individuals; under our system, at an election we can throw out of office all who control the state.

Herein lies the essential difference in point of view between our system and theirs. Under both Communism and Fascism, class distinctions are inevitable, whereas we seek to avoid class distinctions altogether.

As beneficial as this is to the individual in a democratic state, it has this essential weakness, that when an attack is made upon the capitalist system there are no capitalists to defend it, and when an attack is made on democracy there are no democrats to defend it. That sounds like a rhetorical inexactitude, but when we look at current literature, at current lecturing, even at the current drama, the emphasis is all in opposition and the defensive forces are weak. Even the so-called

free press, even the great capitalistic monthlies, publish vicious, unjustified, and badly conceived attacks on the very system which keeps them alive.

Why is this? Is there no conserving force in the country? Where are the conservatives to state their case? The answer is that they are producing and distributing goods and services. The men they hire to advertise their wares are specialists in the science of merchandising and are not designed by training to defend economic and social systems. That is why so many of the notable leaders in industry and banking appear so feeble in public life.

In England, men are trained for both business and public life. But we are only one generation from pioneering and our strong men are not philosophers. Nor do they think in terms of defending anything, because they are still building, still creating their world. It is not their function to study the whys and wherefores of their system. Theirs it is to create, produce, and distribute commodities, to arrange services, and to improve the purchasing power of their customers.

Yet the picture presents this weakness, that the non-producers are always flaw pickers. They can easily discover what is wrong with a system because they have nothing to do with its operations. The producers, on the other hand, have no time and less inclination to defend themselves. They are only capable of pouting against the injustice of an unappreciative world.

IV

Facing these situations, it is clear that capitalism and democracy in the United States must at the present stage fight a corrosive attack upon themselves, not by philosophic defense or by supine apologies, but by specific steps which are not to be remedies for some momentary distress or allurements designed to win an election. The objective should be the improvement of the capitalist system and the conserving of democracy.

First comes the whole problem of employment. In the United States unemployment and re-employment during the depression and the recovery have been considered politically. Both have become political weapons for the destruction and retention of political power.

The fact that no one in the United States knows how many unemployed there are as compared with the unemployed in 1929 is not only astonishing, but a self-evident criticism of government. Billions of dollars are available for all sorts of useful and useless projects, but not a cent for an employment census, scientifically conducted. Not a single figure used by anyone on the subject of employment or unemployment has any validity whatsoever. All are guesses—and it is clear from the variety of evidence that all the guesses are quite distant from the facts.

An employment census is the most essential economic step which can be taken in the United States today.

Yet certain facts are clear even without supporting figures. We know that a large number of people are unemployed. We do not know whether it is necessary for them to be permanently pauperized either by unemployment or by government relief. We must assume, however, that under the capitalist system there can be no general prosperity if a large part of the population is without consuming power earned by its own activity.

Herein lies a danger not only to capitalism but to democracy, because when human beings depend upon the state for their livelihood they are likely to become enslaved politically to those who at the moment control the state. It is not a question of their corruption by a vicious political machine; they would be corrupted by an angelic political machine.

Secondly, in the United States we face the specific task of restoring orderly processes of democratic government. These processes have become disorganized and confused by the depression and the assumption of emergency permissive powers. The American democratic scheme depends for its successful operation upon a strict adherence to the doctrine of limited powers and authority. Ultimate power must remain vested in the people, and this is possible only when all legislation and government authority are controlled by the limitations upon authority in the Constitution. Deviations from the essential structure, without orderly change, can only increase confusion and distress.

Thirdly, we have set up a form of relief to care for our marginal population. No matter how much this relief costs in money, it is justified by humane considerations. But it is now necessary to revalue the processes, for it is evident that relief has been so handled that a section of the population is being permanently pauperized and therefore being forced into a morally degraded condition. The problem is so to reorganize relief activities that they become focused on their own elimination. This can only be accomplished, except in certain specific instances, by making it possible for private enterprise to absorb an increasing number of employees.

Fourthly, restrictions placed upon economic activity, particularly state-imposed rigidities and exorbitant taxation, prevent private industry from expanding sufficiently to re-employ the total number of unemployed. These restrictions should be removed as rapidly as possible.

Finally, capitalism depends for its advance upon the stimulation and expansion of markets. In the United States this is always possible if prices are brought down so that increasingly numerous brackets of the population find that their purchasing power is available for greater consumption. Such stimulation and expansion must be left to the ingenuity and inventiveness of private enterprise and to the competitive process.

In a word, fundamentally our task, in conserving capitalism and democracy, is to restore freedom of action to the individual and to depend upon competition to achieve our main objective, which is to have our standard of living ever higher for a greater number of people.

WHITHER MANKIND?

by CHARLES A. BEARD

WHAT IS CALLED Western or modern civilization by way of contrast with the civilization of the Orient or medieval times is at bottom a civilization that rests upon machinery and science as distinguished from one founded on agriculture or handicraft commerce. It is in reality a technological civilization. It is only about two hundred years old, and, far from shrinking in its influence, is steadily extending its area into agriculture as well as handicrafts. If the records of patent offices, the statistics of production, and the reports of laboratories furnish evidence worthy of credence, technological civilization, instead of showing signs of contraction, threatens to overcome and transform the whole globe.

Considered with respect to its intrinsic nature, technological civilization presents certain precise characteristics. It rests fundamentally on power-driven machinery which transcends the physical limits of its human directors, multiplying indefinitely the capacity for the production of goods. Science in all its branches—physics, chemistry, biology, and psychology—is the servant and upholder of this system. The day of crude invention being almost over, continuous research in the natural sciences is absolutely necessary to the extension of the machine and its market, thus forcing continuously the creation of new goods, new processes, and new modes of life. As the money for learning comes in increasing proportions from taxes on industry and gifts by captains of capitalism, a steady growth in scientific endowments is to be expected, and the scientific curiosity thus aroused and stimulated will hardly fail to expand—and to invade all fields of thought with a technique of ever-refining subtlety. Affording the demand for the output of industry are the vast populations of the globe; hence mass production and marketing are inevitable concomitants of the machine routine.

For the present, machine civilization is associated with capitalism, under which large-scale production has risen to its present stage, but machine civilization is by no means synonymous with capitalism—that ever-changing scheme of exploitation. While the acquisitive instinct of the capitalist who builds factories and starts mass production is particularly emphasized by economists and is, no doubt, a factor of immense moment, it must not be forgotten that the acquisitive passion of the earth's multitudes for the goods, the comforts, and the securities of the classes is an equal, if not a more important, force, and in any case is likely to survive capitalism as we know it. Few choose nakedness when they can be clothed, the frosts of winter when they can be warm, or the misery of bacterial diseases when sanitation is offered to them. In fact, the ascetics and flagellants of the world belong nowhere in the main stream of civilization—and are of dubious utility and service in any civilization.

Though machine civilization has here been treated as if it were an order, it in fact differs from all others in that it is highly dynamic, containing within itself the seeds of constant reconstruction. Everywhere agricultural civilizations of the pre-

From Charles A. Beard, *Whither Mankind?*, Longmans, Green and Company, Inc.

machine age have changed only slowly with the fluctuations of markets, the fortunes of governments, and the vicissitudes of knowledge, keeping their basic institutions intact from century to century. Premachine urban civilizations have likewise retained their essential characteristics through long lapses of time. But machine civilization based on technology, science, invention, and expanding markets must of necessity change—and rapidly. The order of steam is hardly established before electricity invades it; electricity hardly gains a fair start before the internal combustion engine overtakes it. There has never been anywhere in the world any order comparable with it, and all analogies drawn from the Middle Ages, classical antiquity, and the Orient are utterly inapplicable to its potentialities, offering no revelations as to its future.

II

Granted that these essential characteristics of so-called Western civilization—namely, its mechanical and scientific foundations—are realistic, is it a mere "flash in the pan," an historical accident destined to give way to some other order based upon entirely different modes of life, lifting mankind "above the rudeness of the savage"? Now, if the term "decline" in this connection means anything concrete, it signifies the gradual or rapid abandonment of the material modes of production prevailing in any particular age and the habits and arts associated with them. Conceivably the Prussianism of the Hohenzollerns, described so well in Spengler's *Prussianism and Socialism,* may decline—is declining. It is highly probable that the petty tenure system of the French peasantry, the now sadly diluted aristocracy

inherited from the eighteenth century, the church of little mysteries and miracles may decline, but these things are not the peculiar characteristics of the West. They are the remnants of the agricultural complex which the machine is everywhere steadily subduing. The real question is this: Can and will machine society "decline"?

It is generally agreed among historians that the decay of agriculture, owing to the lack of scientific management and fertilization, was one of the chief causes for the breakdown of the Roman state. Is it to be supposed that the drive of the masses of mankind for machine-made goods will fail, that large-scale production will be abandoned, that the huge literature of natural science will disappear in the same fashion as most of the literature of ancient Egypt, that the ranks of scientific men will cease in time to be recruited, that the scientific power to meet new situations will fail? An affirmative answer requires a great deal of hardihood. The scientific order is not recruited from a class, such as the patricians of ancient Rome; nor is scientific knowledge the monopoly of a caste likely to dissolve. Unless all visible signs deceive us, there is no reason for supposing that either machinery or science will disappear or even dwindle to insignificance. And they are the basis of the modern civilization.

If Western civilization does not break down from such internal causes, is there good reason for supposing that any of the races now inhabiting Asia or Africa could overcome the machine order of the West by any process, peaceful or warlike, without themselves adopting the technical apparatus of that order? No doubt, some of them are already borrowing various features of machine society, but slowly and with indifferent success. The most efficient of them, the Japanese, still rely largely upon the West for a substantial part of their mechanical outfit—for inventiveness and creative mechanical skill. Unless there is a material decline in Western technology—and no evidence of such a slump is now in sight—then it may be safely contended that none of the agricultural civilizations of Asia or Africa will ever catch up with the scientific development of the West. As things stand at present, none of them gives any promise of being able to overrun the West as the conquerors of Rome overran the provinces of that empire. Certainly there is not likely to be, in any future that we can foresee, such an equality of armaments as existed between the best of the Roman legions and the forces of their conquerors. Hence the downfall of the West through conquest may fairly be ruled out of the possibilities of the coming centuries. If, in due time, the East smashes the West on the battlefield, it will be because the East has completely taken over the technology of the West, gone it one better, and thus become Western in civilization. In that case machine civilization will not disappear but will make a geographical shift.

Defining civilization narrowly in terms of letters and art, are the probabilities of a "decline" more numerous? Here we approach a more debatable, more intangible, topic. With reference to letters, taking into account the evidence of the last fifty years, there is no sign of a decay—at all events, a decay like that which occurred between the first and the sixth century in Roman history. Indeed, there are many cautious critics who tell us that the writers of the past hundred years, with the machine system at a high pitch, may be compared in number, competence, and power without fear with the writers of any century since the appearance of the Roman grand style. Granted that we have no Horace, Shakespeare, or Goethe, we may reasonably answer that literature of their manner has little meaning for a civilization founded on a different basis. Considered in relation to their environment rather than some fictitious absolute, the best of modern writers, it may well be argued, rank with the best of the Middle Ages and antiquity. If poetry sinks in the scale and tragedy becomes comical, it may be because the mythology upon which they feed is simply foreign to the spirit of the machine age—not because there has been a dissolution of inherited mental powers. The imagination of an Einstein, a Bohr, or a Millikan may well transcend that of a Milton or a Virgil. Who is to decide?

The case of the arts is on a similar footing. For the sake of the argument, it may be conceded that the machine age has produced nothing comparable with the best of the painting, sculpture, and architecture of antiquity and the Middle Ages. What does that signify? Anything more than a decline in the arts appropriate to an agricultural and market-city era? The machine age is young. As yet it can hardly be said to have created an art of its own, although there are signs of great competence, if not genius, about us—signs of a new art appropriate to speed, mechanics, motion, railway stations, factories, office buildings, and public institutions. Using the lowest common denominator in the reckoning, there is no evidence of a decay in artistic power such as appears in the contrast between the Pantheon of Agrippa and the rude churches of Saxon England. To say that the modern age has produced no ecclesiastical architecture comparable with that of the Middle Ages is to utter a judgment as relevant to our situation as a statement that the medieval times can show no aqueducts or baths equal to the noblest structures of pagan Rome. It may be that the machine age will finally prove to be poor in artistic genius—a debatable point—but it can hardly be said that it has produced its typical art, from which a decline may be expected.

Passing to a more tangible subject, is it possible that machine civilization may be destroyed by internal revolutions or civil wars such as have often wrecked great states in the past? That such disturbances will probably arise in the future from time to time cannot be denied, and the recent Bolshevik Revolution in Russia is often cited as a warning to contemporary statesmen. If the revolutions of antiquity be taken as illustrations, it must be pointed out that the analogies are to be used with extreme care in all applications to the machine age. When the worst has been said about the condition of the industrial proletariat, it must be conceded that as regards material welfare, knowledge, social consideration, and political power, it is far removed from the proletariat of Rome or the slaves of a more remote antiquity. The kind of servile revolt that was so often ruinous in Greece and Rome is hardly possible in a machine civilization, even if economic distress were to pass anything yet experienced since the eighteenth century. The most radical of the modern proletariat want more of the good things of civilization—not a destruction of technology. If the example of Russia be pressed as relevant, the reply is that Russia possessed not a machine, but an agricultural civilization of the crudest

sort; peasant soldiers supplied the storm troops of the November Revolution, and the Bolsheviki are straining every nerve to maintain their position by promising the peasants and urban dwellers that the benefits of a machine order will surely come. There will be upheavals in machine civilizations, no doubt, and occasional dictatorships like that in the United States between 1861 and 1865, but the triumph of a party dedicated to a deliberate return to pre-machine agriculture with its low standards of life, its diseases, and its illiteracy is beyond the imagination.

Finally, we must face the assertion that wars among the various nations of machine civilization may destroy the whole order. Probably terrible wars will arise and prove costly in blood and treasure, but it is a strain upon the speculative faculties to conceive of any conflict that could destroy the population and mechanical equipment of the Western world so extensively that human vitality and science could not restore economic prosperity and even improve upon the previous order. According to J. S. Mill, the whole mechanical outfit of a capitalistic country can be reproduced in about ten years. Hence the prospect of repeated and costly wars in the future need not lead us to the pessimistic view that suicide is to be the fate of machine civilization. We may admit the reality of the perils ahead without adopting the counsel of despair. If Europe and America were absolutely devastated, Japan with her present equipment in libraries, laboratories, and technology could begin the work of occupying the vacant areas, using the machine process in the operation.

For the reasons thus adduced it may be inferred: that modern civilization founded on science and the machine will not decline after the fashion of older agricultural civilizations; that analogies drawn from ages previous to technology are inapplicable; that according to signs on every hand technology promises to extend its area and intensify its characteristics; that it will afford the substance with which all who expect to lead and teach in the future must reckon.

III

Such appears to be the promise of the long future, if not the grand destiny of what we call modern civilization—the flexible framework in which the human spirit must operate during the coming centuries. Yet this view by no means precludes the idea that the machine system, as tested by its present results, presents shocking evils and indeed terrible menaces to the noblest faculties of the human race. By the use of material standards for measuring achievement, it is in danger of developing a kind of ignorant complacency that would make Phidias, Sophocles, Horace, St. Augustine, Dante, Michelangelo, Shakespeare, Lord Bacon, Newton, Goethe, Ruskin and Emerson appear to be mere trifling parasites as compared with Lord Beaverbrook, Hugo Stinnes, John Pierpont Morgan, and Henry Ford. To deny the peril that lies in any such numerical morality would be a work of supererogation. More perilous still is the concentration on the production of goods that will sell quickly at the best price the traffic will bear and fall to pieces quickly—mass production of cheap goods —rather than concentration on the manufacture and exchange of commodities with the finest intrinsic values capable of indefinite endurance. What the creed of "give as little as you can for as much as you can get" will do to the common honesty of

mankind, if followed blindly for centuries, can readily be imagined. Finally, it must be admitted that the dedication of the engines of state, supported by a passionate and uninformed chauvinism, to the promotion and sale of machine-made goods is creating zones of international rivalry likely to flame up in wars more vast and destructive than any yet witnessed.

To consider for the moment merely the domestic aspects of the question, the machine civilization is particularly open to attack from three sides.

On esthetic grounds, it has been assailed for nearly a hundred years, England, the classical home of the industrial revolution, being naturally enough the mother of the severest critics—Ruskin, Carlyle, Kingsley, and Matthew Arnold. The chief article in their indictment, perhaps, is the contention that men who work with machinery are not creative, joyous, or free, but are slaves to the monotonous routine of the inexorable wheel. In a sense it is true that, in the pre-machine age, each craftsman had a certain leeway in shaping his materials with his tools and that many a common artisan produced articles of great beauty.

Yet the point can be easily overworked. Doubtless the vast majority of medieval artisans merely followed designs made by master workmen. This is certainly true of artisans in the Orient today. With respect to the mass of mankind, it is safe to assume that the level of monotony on which labor is conducted under the machine régime is by and large not lower but higher than in the handicraft, servile, or slave systems of the past. Let anyone who has doubts on this matter compare the life of laborers on the latifundia of Rome or in the cities of modern China with that of the workers in by far the major portion of machine industries. Those who are prepared to sacrifice the standard of living for the millions to provide conditions presumably favorable to the creative arts must assume a responsibility of the first magnitude.

Indeed, it is not certain, so primitive as yet are the beginnings of machine civilization, that there can be no substitute for the handicrafts as esthetic stimulants, assuming that mechanical industry is not favorable to the creative life. The machine régime does not do away with the necessity for designing or reduce the opportunities for the practice of that craft: it transfers the operation from the shop to the laboratory; and it remains to be seen whether great esthetic powers will not flourish after the first storm of capitalism has passed. In any case, it must be admitted that the "cheap and nasty" character of machine-made goods, so marked everywhere, may really be due to the profit-making lust and the desire of the multitude to have imitations of the gewgaws loved by the patricians, not to the inherent nature of machine industry. Possibly what is lost in the merits of individual objects of beauty may be more than offset by city and community planning, realizing new types of esthetic ideals on a vast, democratic basis. Certainly the worst of the esthetic offenses created by the machine—the hideous factory town—can be avoided by intelligent coöperative action, as the garden-city movement faintly foreshadows. In a hundred years the coal-consuming engine may be as obsolete as the Dodo, and the Birminghams, Pittsburghs, and Essens of the modern world live only in the records of the historians. However this may be, the esthetes of the future will have to work within the limitations and opportunities created by science and the machine, directed, it may be hoped, by a more intelligent economy and nobler concepts of human values.

Frequently affiliated with esthetic criticism of the machine and science is the religious attack. With endless reiteration, the charge is made that industrial civilization is materialistic. In reply, the scornful might say, "Well, what of it?" But the issue deserves consideration on its merits, in spite of its illusive nature. As generally used, the term "materialistic" has some of the qualities of moonshine; it is difficult to grasp. It is the fashion of certain Catholic writers to call Protestantism materialistic, on account of its emphasis on thrift and business enterprise—a fashion which some radicals have adopted: Max Weber in Germany and R. H. Tawney in England, for example. With something akin to the same discrimination, Oswald Spengler calls all England materialistic, governed by pecuniary standards—as contrasted with old Prussia where "duty," "honor," and "simple piety" reigned supreme. More recently, André Siegfried, following a hundred English critics, with Matthew Arnold in the lead, has found materialism to be one of the chief characteristics of the United States, as contrasted with the richer and older civilizations of Europe, particularly France. And Gandhi consigns every one of them—England, Prussia, France, and America—to the same bottomless pit of industrial materialism. When all this verbiage is sifted, it usually means that the charge arises from emotions that have little or no relation to religion or philosophy—from the quarrels of races, sects, and nations.

If religion is taken in a crude, anthropomorphic sense, filling the universe with gods, spirits, and miraculous feats, then beyond question the machine and science are the foes of religion. If it is materialistic to disclose the influence of technology and environment in general upon humanity, then perhaps the machine and science are materialistic. But it is one of the ironies of history that science has shown the shallowness of the old battle between materialist and spiritist and through the mouths of physicists has confessed that it does not know what matter and force are. Matter is motion; motion is matter; both elude us, we are told. Doubtless science does make short shrift of a thousand little mysteries once deemed as essential to Christianity as were the thousand minor gods to the religion of old Japan, but for these little mysteries it has substituted a higher and sublimer mystery.

To descend to the concrete, is the prevention of disease by sanitation more materialistic than curing it by touching saints' bones? Is feeding the multitude by mass production more materialistic than feeding it by a miracle? Is the elimination of famines by a better distribution of goods more materialistic than prevention by the placation of the rain gods? At any rate, it is not likely that science and machinery will be abandoned because the theologian (who seldom refuses to partake of their benefits) wrings his hands and cries out against materialism. After all, how can he consistently maintain that Omnipotent God ruled the world wisely and well until the dawn of the modern age and abandoned it to the Evil One because Henry VIII or Martin Luther quarreled with the Pope and James Watt invented the steam engine?

Arising, perhaps, from the same emotional source as esthetic and religious criticism is the attack on the machine civilization as lacking in humanitarianism. Without commenting on man's inhumanity to man as an essential characteristic of the race, we may fairly ask on what grounds can anyone argue that the masses were more humanely treated in the agricultural civilization of antiquity or the Middle Ages than in the machine order of modern times. Tested by the mildness of its laws (brutal as many of them are), by its institutions of care and benevolence, by its death rate (that telltale measurement of human welfare), by its standards of life, and by every conceivable measure of human values, machine civilization, even in its present primitive stage, need fear no comparison with any other order on the score of general well-being.

Under the machine and science, the love of beauty, the sense of mystery, and the motive of compassion—sources of esthetics, religion, and humanism—are not destroyed. They remain essential parts of our nature. But the conditions under which they must operate, the channels they must take, the potentialities of their action are all changed. These ancient forces will become powerful in the modern age just in the proportion that men and women accept the inevitability of science and the machine, understand the nature of the civilization in which they must work, and turn their faces resolutely to the future.

THE FOUR FREEDOMS

by FRANKLIN D. ROOSEVELT

In the future days, which we seek to make secure, we look forward to a world founded upon four essential human freedoms.

The first is freedom of speech and expression—everywhere in the world.

The second is freedom of every person to worship God in his own way—everywhere in the world.

The third is freedom from want—which, translated into world terms, means economic understandings which will secure to every nation a healthy peace time life for its inhabitants—everywhere in the world.

The fourth is freedom from fear—which, translated into world terms, means a world-wide reduction of armaments to such a point and in such a thorough fashion that no nation will be in a position to commit an act of physical aggression against any neighbor—anywhere in the world.

That is no vision of a distant millennium. It is a definite basis for a kind of world attainable in our own time and generation.

—FRANKLIN D. ROOSEVELT, January 6, 1941

THE RACES OF MANKIND

by RUTH BENEDICT *and* GENE WELTFISH

THIRTY-FOUR NATIONS are now united in a common cause—victory over Axis aggression, the military destruction of fascism. This is the greatest fighting alliance of nations in history. These United Nations include the most different physical types of men, the most unlike beliefs, the most varied ways of life. White men, yellow men, black men, and the so-called "red men" of America, peoples of the East and the West, of the tropics and the arctic, are fighting together against one enemy.

Every morning in the newspapers and on the bulletin boards we read of yester-

From *The Races of Mankind,* by Ruth Benedict and Gene Weltfish, published by the Public Affairs Committee, Inc., New York 20, N. Y.

day's battles in Russia, in China, in Italy, in the Solomon Islands, and in New Guinea. One day's hop in a plane can carry us across the oceans. Our supply ships go to every corner of the globe. On the radio we hear men reporting on the spot from Cairo and Australia. Burma is much closer to us today than New Orleans was to Washington at the time of the War of 1812. Distance then was a hard fact; it had not been scaled down by the triumphs of human invention.

This war, for the first time, has brought home to Americans the fact that the whole world has been made one neighborhood. All races of man are shoulder to shoulder. Our armed forces are in North Africa with its Negro, Berber, and Near-East peoples. They are in India. They are in China. They are in the Solomons with its dark-skinned, "strong"-haired Melanesians. Our neighbors now are peoples of all the races of the earth.

For Americans this is not so new an experience as it is to people of most nations. In our country men of different color, hair texture, and head shape have lived together since the founding of our nation. They are citizens of the United States. Negroes and whites, Indians, Mexicans, Chinese, and people from the European nations are all taxable, subject to the draft and to the other laws of the land. They are part of our great national community. History today is only bringing together on a world scale races which have been brought together on a smaller scale here in America.

Americans know better than most how much hard feeling there can be when people of different races and nationalities have to live together and be part of one community. They know that there is often conflict. Today, when what we all want

more than anything else is to win this war, most Americans are confident that, whatever our origins, we shall be able to pull together to a final victory. Hitler, though, has always believed we were wrong; he has believed that hard feeling would break out and leave us defeated. He has been sure that he could "divide and conquer." He has believed that he could convince non-white races in Asia and Africa that this is a "white man's war." He has believed especially that America was a no man's land, where peoples of all origins were ready to fall to fighting among themselves. He believes that this is a front on which we are doomed to lose the battle. It is certainly a front no less important in this war than the Production Front and the Inflation Front.

In any great issue that concerns this war we turn to science. When we need new fuels, substitutes for rubber, lighter metals, or new plastics, we ask scientists to tell us what is possible and what is impossible. The chemists tell us how to make the plastics we need, and the physicists tell us how to detect and locate an approaching airplane, and the engineers tell us how to build a better fighting plane. When we are faced with war shortages, they tell us what essential materials we have been throwing out on the dump heap.

We need the scientist just as much on the race front. Scientists have studied race. Historians have studied the history of all nations and peoples. Sociologists have studied the way in which peoples band together. Biologists have studied how man's physical traits are passed down from one generation to the next. Anthropologists have studied man's bodily measurements and his cultural achievements. Psychologists have studied intelligence among different races. All that the scientists have learned is important to us at this crucial moment of history. They can tell us: "This is so," "This is not so," "This occurs under certain conditions," or "This occurs under opposite conditions."

This booklet cannot tell you all that science has learned about the races of mankind, but it states facts that have been learned and verified. We need them.

The Bible story of Adam and Eve, father and mother of the whole human race, told centuries ago the same truth that science has shown today: that all the peoples of the earth are a single family and have a common origin. Science describes the intricate make-up of the human body: all its different organs co-operating in keeping us alive, its curious anatomy that couldn't possibly have "just happened" to be the same in all men if they did not have a common origin. Take the structure of the human foot, for instance. When you list all the little bones and muscles and the joints of the toes, it is impossible to imagine that that would all have happened twice. Or take our teeth: so many front teeth, so many canines, so many molars. Who can imagine finding the same arrangements in two human species if they weren't one family?

The fact of the unity of the human race is proved, therefore, in its anatomy. It is proved also by the close similarity in what all races are physically fitted for. No difference among human races has affected limbs and teeth and relative strength so that one race is biologically outfitted like a lion and another biologically outfitted like a lamb. All races of men can either plow or fight, and all the racial differences among them are in non-essentials such as

texture of head hair, amount of body hair, shape of the nose or head, or color of the eyes and the skin. The white race is the hairiest, but a white man's hair isn't thick enough to keep him warm in cold climates. The Negro's dark skin gives him some protection against strong sunlight in the tropics, and white men often have to take precautions against sunstroke. But the war has shown that white men can work and fight even in a tropical desert. Today white men in hot countries wear sun helmets and protect themselves with clothes and rub their skin with sun-tan oil. Very dark-skinned people in the North, too, can add cod-liver oil and orange juice to their diet, and, if they need to, take a vitamin pill or two. The shape of the head, too, is a racial trait; but whether it is round or long, it can house a good brain.

The races of mankind are what the Bible says they are—brothers. In their bodies is the record of their brotherhood.

What Are Race Differences?

The greatest adventure story in the history of the world is the spread of early man to all corners of the globe. With crude tools, without agriculture, without domesticated animals except the dog, he pressed on, from somewhere in Asia to the tip of Africa, to the British Isles, across Bering Strait into America and down to Cape Horn. He occupied the islands of the Pacific and the continent of Australia. The world had a small population then, and many of these pioneers were for centuries as separated from other peoples as if they lived on another planet. Slowly they developed physical differences.

Those who settled nearer the equator, whether in Europe, Asia, or in the Americas, developed a darker skin color than those who settled to the north of them. People's hair is often the same over great areas: frizzly hair, lank hair, wavy hair. Europeans remained quite hairy, but in some parts of the world body hair almost disappeared. Blue eyes appeared in the north. In some places in Asia a fold of skin developed over the inner corner of the eye and produced what we call a slant eye.

All these distinctive traits made it easy to recognize people as belonging to different parts of the world. In each place the people got used to looking at one another. They said, "Our men are really men. Our women are beautiful. This is the way people should look." Sometimes they liked the appearance of their close neighbors. But strangers seemed odd and queer. Strangers wore funny clothes and their manners were bad. Even more important, strangers did not look the way people should. Their noses were too flat or too pointed. Their skin was "a sickly white" or "a dirty black." They were too fat or too short. Everywhere in the world men and women used the standard of their own people to judge others and thought that people who differed from this standard looked funny or ugly.

After the discovery of America by Columbus, Europeans began traveling to every quarter of the globe, and all the new peoples they met were complete strangers to them. For one thing, the Europeans couldn't understand their languages. They looked and acted strange. Europeans thought they were different creatures and named a lot of different "races." Gradually the Europeans described each one as having a skin color, kind of hair, kind of lips, height, and head shape that was

peculiar to that "race." Nowadays we know that this was a false impression.

Take height, for example. There are tall and short people almost everywhere in the world. Near the sources of the Nile the Shilluk Negroes are six feet two inches; their neighbors, the brown pygmies, are four feet eight inches. In Italy a six-footer and a five-footer could both be native Italians for generations back. Among the Arizona Indians the Hopi Pueblos are five feet four inches; their Mohave neighbors are nearly six feet.

A report of the Selective Service System of November 10, 1941, showed that registrants examined for the United States Army varied in height from four feet six inches to seven feet four inches. This represents the extremes of height anywhere in the world. The Army's limits for acceptance, from five feet to six feet six inches, would include most men the world over.

Take the shape of the head as another example. In West Africa there are more long heads; in the Congo, more round. Among the American Indians, as well as in the population of Europe, both the longest and the roundest heads are to be found, and in Asia Minor long heads and round heads appear among very close relatives.

Or let us take the brain itself. Because the brain is the thinking organ, some scientists have tried to find differences in the size and structure of the brain among different groups of people. In spite of these efforts, using the finest microscopes, the best scientists cannot tell from examining a brain to what group of people its owner belonged. The *average* size of the brain is different in different groups, but it has been proved over and over again that the size of the brain has nothing to do with intelligence. Some of the most brilliant men in the world have had very small brains. On the other hand, the world's largest brain belongs to an imbecile.

For ages men have spoken of "blood relations" as if different peoples had different blood. Some people have shouted that if we got into our veins the blood of someone with a different head shape, eye color, hair texture, or skin color, we should get some of that person's physical and mental characteristics.

Modern science has revealed this to be pure superstition. All human blood is the same, whether it is the blood of an Eskimo or a Frenchman, of the "purest" German "Aryan" or an African pygmy—except for one medically important difference. This medical difference was discovered when doctors first began to use blood transfusion in order to save life. In early attempts at transfusion it was discovered that "agglutination," or clumping together, of the red cells sometimes occurred and caused death. Gradually investigators learned that there are four types of blood, called O, A, B, and AB, and that although blood typed O can be mixed successfully with the other three, none of these can be mixed with one another without clumping.

These four types of blood are inherited by each child from its forebears. But whites, Negroes, Mongols, and all races of man have all these blood types. The color of their skin does not tell at all which blood type they have. You and an Australian bushman may have the same blood type. Because you inherit your bodily traits from your many different ancestors, you may have a different blood type from your mother or your father or your brothers and sisters. You may have eyes like your mother's, teeth and hair like your father's, feet like your grandfather's, and a blood type like your great-grandmother's.

Today doctors do not "type" blood for transfusion at all. The red and white cells or corpuscles are removed, and the remainder is the same whatever race it comes from. The Blood Bank calls it plasma. It is dried and kept indefinitely. When needed for emergency transfusions, it is mixed with water and can save the life of any man or woman in the world. The same blood plasma is used to restore any man of any color who has been wounded in battle.

Finally, let us take skin color, the most noticeable of the differences between peoples. Few traits have been used as widely to classify people. We all talk about black, white, and yellow races of man.

In the world today the darkest people are in West Africa, the lightest people in northwest Europe, while in southeast Asia are men with yellowish-tan skins. Most people in the world, however, are not of these extremes but are in-betweens. These in-betweens probably have the skin shades that were once most common, the white, yellow, and dark brown or black being extreme varieties.

Recently scientists found that skin color is determined by two special chemicals. One of these, *carotene,* gives a yellow tinge; the other, *melanin,* contributes the brown. These colors, along with the pinkish tinge that comes when the blood vessels show through, give various shades to the human skin. Every person, however light or dark his skin may appear, has some of each of these materials in his skin. The one exception is the albino, who lacks coloring substances—and albinos appear among dark- and light-skinned peoples alike. People of browner complexions simply have more *melanin* in their skin, people of yellowish color more *carotene.* It is not an all-or-nothing difference; it is a difference in proportion. Your skin color is due to the amount of these chemicals present in the skin.

How Are Races Classified?

The three primary races of the world are the Caucasian Race, the Mongoloid Race, and the Negroid Race.

The Caucasian Race inhabits Europe and a great part of the Near East and India. It is subdivided in broad bands that run east and west: Nordics (fair-skinned, blue-eyed, tall and long-headed) are most common in the north; Alpines (in-between skin color, often stocky, broad-headed) in the middle; Mediterraneans (slenderer, often darker than Alpines, long-headed) in the south. The distribution of racial subtypes is just about the same in Germany and in France; both are mostly Alpine and both have Nordics in their northern districts. Racially, France and Germany are made up of the same stocks in just about equal proportions.

American Indians are Mongoloid, though they differ physically both among themselves and from the Mongols of China.

The natives of Australia are sometimes called a fourth primary race. They are as hairy as Europeans, and yet they live in an area where other peoples have very little body hair.

Aryans, Jews, Italians are *not* races. Aryans are people who speak Indo-European, "Aryan" languages. Hitler uses the term in many ways—sometimes for blond Europeans, including the Scandinavians; sometimes for Germans, whether blond or brunet; sometimes for all who agree with him politically, including the Japanese. As Hitler uses it, the term "Aryan" has no meaning, racial, linguistic, or otherwise.

Jews are people who practice the Jewish religion. They are of all races, even Negro and Mongolian. European Jews are of many different biological types; physically they resemble the populations among whom they live. The so-called "Jewish type" is a Mediterranean type, and no more "Jewish" than the South Italian. Wherever Jews are persecuted or discriminated against, they cling to their old ways and keep apart from the rest of the population and develop so-called "Jewish" traits. But these are not racial or "Jewish"; they disappear under conditions where assimilation is easy.

Italians are a nationality. Italians are of many different racial strains; the "typical" South Italian is a Mediterranean, more like the Spaniard or the Greek or the Levantine Jew than the blond North Italian. The Germans, the Russians, and all other nations of Europe are *nations,* not races. They are bound together, not by their head shape and their coloring, but by their national pride, their love of their farms, their local customs, their language, and the like.

As far back in time as the scientist can go he finds proof that animals and men moved about in the world. There were different kinds of animals, and many of them went great distances. But wherever they went, the different kinds could not breed together. A tiger cannot mate with an elephant. Even a fox and a wolf cannot mate with each other. But whenever groups of people have traveled from one place to another and met other people, some of them have married and had children.

At first men had to travel by foot. It took them a long time, but they got almost all over the world that way. Long ago, when people knew only how to make tools out of stone, the Cro-Magnons lived in Europe. Waves of migration came in from the east and the southeast. These new people settled down, bred with the Cro-Magnons, and their children were the ancestors of modern Europeans. Since then there have been many migrations from Asia and northern Africa.

Later men tamed the horse. They built carts and rode horseback. They built great boats, which were rowed by hundreds of men. They could go faster and travel farther than ever before. The Phoenicians went on trading expeditions through the Mediterranean. The Romans went to Spain and up along the coast to the British Isles. Then the Huns swept in from Asia through central Europe and destroyed the Roman Empire. The Tartars came in from the east. They threatened to conquer all of Europe but were defeated in one of the greatest cavalry engagements of all time. The Mohammedans captured all of North Africa; they took Spain and went on up into France across the Pyrenees. Thousands of Negro slaves have been brought into Europe at various times. Where are they now? Peoples have come and gone in Europe for centuries. Wherever they went, some of them settled down and left children. Small groups were absorbed into the total population. Always the different races moved about and intermarried.

We are used to thinking of Americans as mixed. All of us have ancestors who came from regions far apart. But we think that the English are English and the French are French. This is true for their nationality, just as we are all Americans. But it is not true for their *race*. The Germans have claimed to be a pure German race, but no European is a pure anything. A country has a population. It does not have a race. If you go far enough back in the populations of Europe you are apt to find all kinds of ancestors: Cro-Mag-

nons, Slavs, Mongols, Africans, Celts, Saxons, and Teutons.

It is true, though, that people who live closer together intermarry more frequently. This is why there are places like Alsace-Lorraine, where Germans and French have intermarried so much that the children cannot tell whether they are German or French and so call themselves Alsatians. Czechoslovakia included old Bohemia, which had a population of Nordics and semi-Asiatics and Slavs. After World War I the Germans and the Czechs along the border between the two countries intermarried so often that the Germans of this section got to look like Czechs and the Czechs began to speak German. But this did not make the two countries love each other.

People of every European nation have racial brothers in other countries, often ones with which they are at war. If at any one moment you could sort into one camp all the people in the world who were most Mediterranean, no mystic sense of brotherhood would unite them. Neither camp would have language or nationality or mode of life to unite them. The old fights would break out again unless social conditions were changed—the old hatred between national groups, the old antagonisms between ruler and ruled and between the exploiter and the exploited.

The movements of peoples over the face of the earth inevitably produce race mixture and have produced it since before history began. No one has been able to show that this is necessarily bad. It has sometimes been a social advantage, sometimes a running sore threatening the health of the whole society. It can obviously be made a social evil, and, where it is so, sensible people will avoid contributing to it by grieving if their children make such alliances. We·must live in the world as it is. But, as far as we know, there are no immutable laws of nature that make racial intermixture harmful.

When they study racial differences, scientists investigate the way by which particular traits are passed on from parents to children. They measure head form and identify skin color on a color chart. They map out the distribution of different kinds of hair or noses in the world. Scientists recognize that these differences do not themselves show better or worse qualities in peoples, any more than bay horses are better than black ones. They knew that to prove that a bay horse is superior to a black one you have to do more than identify its skin color on a color chart; you have to test its abilities.

Science therefore treats human racial differences as facts to be studied and mapped. It treats racial superiorities as a separate field of investigation; it looks for evidence. When a Nazi says, "I am a blue-eyed Aryan and you are non-Aryan," he means, "I am superior and you are inferior." The scientist says: "Of course. You are a fair-haired, long-headed, tall North European (the anthropological term is Nordics, not Aryans), and I am a dark-haired, round-headed, less tall South European. But on what evidence do you base your claim to be superior? That is quite different."

Race prejudice turns on this point of inferiority and superiority. The man with race prejudice says of a man of another race, "No matter who he is, I don't have to compare myself with him. I'm superior anyway. I was born that way."

It is the study of racial superiorities and inferiorities, therefore, which is most important in race relations. This investiga-

tion, to have any meaning at all, must get evidence for and against the man who says, "I was *born* that way. My race is proof that I am the better man." It must be an investigation of what is better and what is worse in traits passed down by inheritance. Such traits are, by definition, racial. The first thing we want to know scientifically is what traits a man is born with and what things happen to him after he is born. If he is lucky after he is born, he will have good food, good care, good education, and a good start in life; these are not things of which he can boast: "I was *born* that way."

A man learns the language he speaks. If he'd been born of Nordic parents and brought up from infancy in China, he'd speak Chinese like a native and have as much difficulty learning Swedish when he was grown as if he'd been born of Chinese parents. He wasn't "born" to speak cockney English or to speak with a Brooklyn accent; he speaks the way people around him speak. It's not a racial trait; he didn't inherit it.

Differences in customs among peoples of the world are not a matter of race either. One race is not "born" to marry in church after a boy-and-girl courtship and another race to marry "blind" with a bride the groom has never seen carried veiled to his father's house. One race is not "born" equipped to build skyscrapers and put plumbing in their houses and another to run up flimsy shelters and carry their water from the river. All these things are "learned behavior," and even in the white race there are many millions who don't have our forms of courtship and marriage and who live in shacks. When a man boasts of his racial superiority and says that he was "born that way," perhaps what he's really saying is that he had a lot of luck after he was born. A man of another race might have been his equal if he'd had the same luck in his life. Science insists that race does not account for all human achievements.

The most careful investigations of intelligence have been made in America among Negroes and whites. The scientist realizes that every time he measures intelligence in any man, black or white, his results show the intelligence that man was born with *plus* what happened to him since he was born. The scientist has a lot of proof of this. For instance, in the First World War intelligence tests were given to the American Expeditionary Forces; they showed that Negroes made a lower score on intelligence tests than whites. But the tests also showed that Northerners, *black and white,* had higher scores than Southerners, *black and white.* Everyone knows that Southerners are inborn equals of Northerners, but in 1917 many Southern states' per capita expenditures for schools were only fractions of those in Northern states, and housing and diet and income were far below average too. Since the vast majority of Negroes lived in the South, their score on the intelligence test was a score they got not only as Negroes, but as Americans who had grown up under poor conditions in the South. Scientists therefore compared the scores of Southern whites and Northern Negroes.

MEDIAN SCORES ON A.E.F. INTELLIGENCE
TESTS

Southern Whites:
Mississippi 41.25
Kentucky 41.50
Arkansas 41.55

Northern Negroes:
New York 45.02
Illinois 47.35
Ohio 49.50

Negroes with better luck after they were born got higher scores than whites with less luck. The white race did badly where economic conditions were bad and schooling was not provided, and Negroes living under better conditions surpassed them. The differences did not arise because people were from the North or the South, or because they were white or black, but because of differences in income, education, cultural advantages, and other opportunities.

Scientists then studied gifted children. They found that children with top scores turn up among Negroes, Mexicans, and Orientals. Then they went to European countries to study the intelligence of children in homelands from which our immigrants come. Children from some of these countries got poor scores in America, but in their homeland children got good scores. Evidently the poor scores here were due to being uprooted, speaking a foreign language, and living in tenements; the children were not unintelligent *by heredity.*

The second superiority which a man claims when he says, "I was born a member of a superior race," is that his race has better *character.* The Nazis boast of their racial soul. But when they wanted to make a whole new generation into Nazis they didn't trust to "racial soul"; they made certain kinds of teaching compulsory in the schools, they broke up homes where the parents were anti-Nazi, they required boys to join certain Nazi youth organizations. By these means they got the kind of national character they wanted. But it was a planned and deliberately trained character, not an inborn "racial soul." In just the same way the Japanese have bred a generation of ruthless fighters. Fifty years ago Europeans who lived in Japan used to describe them as "butterflies flitting from flower to flower," incapable of "the stern drives" of Western civilization. Since 1900 the "butterflies" have fought six times overseas, and they are desperate and ruthless fighters. In a generation the butterflies have become gamecocks. But their *race* has not changed. The same blood still flows in their veins. But spiritually they are more like the Germans than they are like their racial brothers, the peace-loving Chinese.

It can go the other way too. In 1520 the ancient Mexicans were like the Germans. They talked like Nazis, thought like them, in many ways felt like them. They, too, believed war to be man's highest mission. They, too, trained their children for it, placing their boys in great state schools where they learned little else but the glories of battle and the rituals of their caste. They, too, believed themselves invincible, and against small, defenseless villages they were. But they were defeated in battle by the Spaniards with the help of the peoples whom the Aztecs had oppressed; their leaders were killed, their temples destroyed, their wealth pillaged, and their power broken. The Mexican peasant, who still speaks the Aztec language and in whose veins still runs the blood of Aztec conquerors, no longer dreams of glorious death in battle and eternal life in an Indian Valhalla. He no longer goes on the warpath, no longer provokes war with peaceful villages. He is a humble peon, wishing only to be left in peace to cultivate his little field, go to church, dance,

sing, and make love. These simple things endure.

Americans deny that the Nazis have produced a national character superior to that of Goethe's and Schiller's day, and that the ruthless Japanese of today are finer human beings than in those generations when they preferred to write poetry and paint pictures. Race prejudice is, after all, a determination to keep a people down, and it misuses the label "inferior" to justify unfairness and injustice. Race prejudice makes people ruthless; it invites violence. It is the opposite of "good character" as it is defined in the Christian religion—or in the Confucian religion, or in the Buddhist religion, or the Hindu religion, for that matter.

History proves that progress in civilization is not the monopoly of one race or subrace. When our white forebears in Europe were rude stone-age primitives, the civilizations of the Babylonians and the Egyptians had already flourished and been eclipsed. There were great Negro states in Africa when Europe was a sparsely settled forest. Negroes made iron tools and wove fine cloth for their clothing when fair-skinned Europeans wore skins and knew nothing of iron.

When Europe was just emerging from the Middle Ages, Marco Polo visited China and found there a great civilization, the like of which he had never imagined. Europe was a frontier country in those days compared with China.

Since the beginning of history an unusual collection of fortunate circumstances have been present among one race, sometimes among another. Up to now every great center of civilization has had its day and has given place to others. The proud rulers of yesterday become the simple peasants of another era. The crude people who once threatened the great cities become later the kings and emperors in the same country. The peoples change, but the old arts of life are, for the most part, not permanently lost. They pass into the common heritage of mankind.

Inventions pass, too, from one continent to another when people trade with each other. This has happened since the dawn of history. About five thousand years ago, when Europe was on the frontiers of the civilized world, Asiatics came to trade in Europe and North Africa in great caravans. They followed the main rivers—the Nile into North Africa, the Danube into Europe, and the Tigris and Euphrates rivers out of Asia. People from all over came in contact with one another and compared notes on what they knew. In this way they pooled their knowledge, and out of this combined knowledge came the great inventions of civilization—massive building and the arts of metallurgy, chemistry, writing, medicine, and mathematics; transportation on wheels. The idea of printing and the use of movable type is an old Chinese invention, and our power engines depend upon a knowledge of explosives that the Chinese worked out with firecrackers.

When Columbus discovered America, corn, "Irish" potatoes, tobacco, and "Boston" beans were unknown in Europe. They had been developed by American Indians. Within ten years corn was being planted in Central Asia and in the interior of Africa, and African tribes today think that corn was given them by their own gods "in the beginning."

All races have made their contributions to human knowledge. Those who have lived at the crossroads of the world have invented most; those who have lived isolated on islands or at the tip ends of continents have been content to earn their livelihoods by old traditional methods. There was, for them, no "necessity" to be "the mother of invention" after they had devised a way to live on the land.

Peoples who came into contact with strangers, however, gave what arts of life they had and took what the strangers had. These contributions to civilization accumulated over the centuries, and on this accumulation new discoveries are based. We are all the gainers.

The United States is the greatest crossroads of the world in all history. People have come here from every race and nation, and almost every race in the world is represented among our citizens. They have brought with them their own ways of cooking food, so that our "American" diet is indebted to a dozen peoples. Our turkey, corn, and cranberries come from the Indians. Our salads we borrowed from the French and Italians. Increasingly in recent years we have enriched our tables with soups from Russia, vegetables from Italy, appetizers from the Scandinavian countries, sea foods from the Mediterranean lands, chili and tortillas from Mexico, and so on almost endlessly. At the same time, everywhere we have gone in the world, we have popularized ice cream, beefsteak, breakfast cereals, corn on the cob, and other foods that are called "American."

Industry in the United States has taken the hand skills of our immigrants and made machines to do the work; without their skills we should not have known how. Our music, our buildings have developed from patterns brought to our shores or learned from every quarter of the world. Our country would be poorer in every phase of its culture if different cultures had not come together here, sharing and learning the special contributions each had to offer.

The Future of Race Prejudice

Nevertheless there is race prejudice in America and in the world. Race prejudice isn't an old universal "instinct." It is hardly a hundred years old. Before that, people persecuted Jews because of their religion—not their "blood"; they enslaved Negroes because they were pagans—not for being black.

Looking back now, moderns are horrified at all the blood that was shed for centuries in religious conflicts. It is not our custom any more to torture and kill a man because he has a different religion. The twenty-first century may well look back on our generation and be just as horrified. If that century builds its way of life on the Atlantic Charter—for the whole world—our era will seem a nightmare from which they have awakened. They will think we were crazy. "Why should race prejudice have swept the Western world," they will say, "where no nation was anything but a mixture of all kinds of racial groups? Why did nations just at that moment begin talking about 'the racial purity' of their blood? Why did they talk of their wars as racial wars? Why did they make people suffer, not because they were criminals or double-crossers, but because they were Jews or Negroes or non-Nordic?"

We who are living in these troubled times can tell them why. Today weak nations are afraid of the strong nations; the poor are afraid of the rich; the rich are afraid they will lose their riches. People are afraid of one another's political or economic power, they are afraid of revenge for past injuries, they are afraid of social rejection. Conflict grows fat on fear. And the slogans against "inferior races" lead us to pick on them as scapegoats. We pin on them the reason for all our fears.

Freedom from fear is the way to cure race prejudice. When aggressions like those of the Axis are made impossible by guarantees of collective security, those guarantees must cover countries of all races. Then Nazi race tactics will be outmoded. In any country every legal decision that upholds equal citizenship rights without regard to race or color, every labor decision that lessens the terror of being "laid off" and gives a man self-respect in his employment, every arrangement that secures the little farmer against losing his acres to the bank—all these and many more can free people from fear. They need not look for scapegoats.

The Russian nation has for a generation shown what can be done to outlaw race prejudice in a country with many kinds of people. They did not wait for people's minds to change. They made racial discrimination and persecution illegal. They welcomed and honored the different dress, different customs, different arts of the many tribes and countries that live as part of their nation. The more backward groups were given special aid to help them catch up with the more advanced. Each people was helped to develop its own cultural forms, its own written language, theater, music, dance, and so on. At the same time that each people was encouraged in its national self-development, the greatest possible interchange of customs was fostered, so that each group became more distinctively itself and at the same time more a part of the whole.

The Russians have welcomed cultural *differences* and they have refused to treat them as *inferiorities*. No part of the Russian program has had greater success than their racial program.

In the United States a considerable number of organizations are working for democratic race equality. To mention only a few: The East-West Association has done some splendid work in emphasizing the importance of racial understanding, especially between Asiatic and Western peoples. The China Institute is active in promoting the work of Chinese students in America, and the Phelps-Stokes Foundation has brought many African students here, cementing the relation between the two continents.

The Council Against Intolerance in America has a continuous program in the schools. The Council on Intercultural Relations has done much to emphasize the Negro's contribution to American culture. The Bureau for Intercultural Education interprets the contributions made to America by many different races and nationalities. The Rosenwald Foundation has sponsored Southern Negro schools, elementary, high school, and college, in order to make up for the deficiencies of Southern Negro education. They have also pressed for Negro housing and health projects in the North. The National Association for the Advancement of Colored People arranges publicity and fosters public education through periodicals, the radio, and special publications. It fights cases of discrimination in the courts and tries to get effective laws passed for the protection of Negro rights. The National Urban League helps Negroes who move from rural districts to the cities to find industrial work and proper living conditions.

Many church bodies have done much to help people realize that ideas of race superiority or inferiority are un-Christian. The Department of Race Relations of the Federal Council of the Churches of Christ in America and the National Conference of Christians and Jews have encouraged collaboration among church leaders interested in interracial co-operation. During World War II the Executive Committee of the Council called on all local churches to eliminate racial discrimination in their own practices. Church bodies of all faiths have encouraged education for tolerance.

For some twenty years white and Negro leaders of the South have co-operated actively through the Commission on Interracial Co-operation in establishing local committees of both whites and Negroes. This commission has promoted mutual respect and understanding. In many local areas small groups have worked patiently to increase interracial co-operation.

Among the unions we find that the National Maritime Union has fought and won the right of Negroes to serve as skilled workers instead of in menial jobs only. Today mixed crews on freighters, tankers, and merchant ships are doing a magnificent job without friction. The *Booker T. Washington,* with its Negro captain, Hugh Mulzac, is a notable example. The United Auto Workers has an interracial committee with Walter Hardin, a veteran Negro official, as its chairman. At first white workers resisted the right of Negroes to do more skilled kinds of work. For example, when Negroes were first placed on machines previously manned by white operators, a work stoppage shut down a whole section of the Packard plant. R. J. Thomas, the president of the union, ordered the white strikers to return to work or suffer loss of union membership and employment. Within a few hours the strikers were back, with the recently promoted Negroes still at their machines.

Besides the National Maritime Union and the Auto Workers, a number of other unions have taken the lead in promoting interracial understanding. They include the International Ladies Garment Workers, the Amalgamated Clothing Workers, the United Electrical Radio and Machine Workers, the Marine Shipbuilding Workers, and the United Rubber Workers. In the Birmingham, Alabama, area there are more than a hundred union locals with both white and Negro members, and the Southern Tenant Farmers Union has a mixed membership.

From the time of Lincoln's Emancipation Proclamation to the present day, the national and state governments have passed laws to carry forward the principles of our Declaration of Independence and our Constitution. In June 1941, President Roosevelt took direct action in his Executive Order No. 8802 toward eliminating discrimination in employment in plants with war contracts. The Fair Employment Practice Committee was set up and held public hearings in Los Angeles, Chicago, New York, and Birmingham. When an individual applied for a job in a plant doing war work and was refused for reasons of prejudice—because he was a Negro, a Jew, or a naturalized citizen—he could bring his case before the committee, who then called the company to a public hearing. This committee is now part of the War Manpower Commission.

The Negro Manpower Commission of this same body is headed by an able Negro economist and maintains a staff of Negro field representatives attached to the United States Employment Service. They also work through the regional offices of the Social Security Board to detect cases of racial discrimination.

The Bureau of Indian Affairs, under Commissioner Collier, should be mentioned here as a government bureau with a long record of successful effort for the adjustment of a racial minority.

But at best the government can act only as a policeman, finding a wrongdoer here and there. Only the people themselves can really end racial discrimination, through understanding, sympathy, and public action. But there is evidence that the American people as individuals are beginning to think and to act. One hundred thousand Americans have petitioned the War Department to have at least one division in the Army containing both Negroes and whites. A separate petition was signed by American white men of draft age who asked to be assigned to such a division— many of these were Southerners.

In Houston, Texas, the mayor and a group of prominent citizens advertised in the local papers that no disturbance would be tolerated that would blacken the reputation of Houston when the Negroes of that city celebrated Juneteenth Day in honor of the emancipation of the slaves. It began with the statement, "Don't do Hitler's work," and warned citizens not to repeat rumors. The celebration was peacefully carried out. It is unfortunate that in Beaumont, Texas, similar effective action was not undertaken and a serious riot occurred.

In the most disastrous of recent riots in Detroit, a number of obscure bystanders performed heroic actions.

A white passenger on a streetcar spoke to the mob and dissuaded them from searching the car.

Two women, a mother and daughter, realizing that the Negro passenger was in danger, sheltered him so that when the rioters looked into the car he was effectively hidden.

In a bus going South recently the white

passengers all remained standing rather than occupy the "white" seats of a Jim Crow bus.

During the recent disturbances in New York's Harlem, a group of Negroes stood in front of the restaurant of a white proprietor who had been their friend and in this way protected it from being broken into and destroyed by the mob.

In the last analysis these homely incidents tell the real story. They tell us that the conscience of America is aroused, that there is work to be done, and that some of us are already trying to do it.

With America's great tradition of democracy, the United States should clean its own house and get ready for a better twenty-first century. Then it could stand unashamed before the Nazis and condemn, without confusion, their doctrines of a Master Race. Then it could put its hand to the building of the United Nations, sure of support from all the yellow and the black races where the war is being fought, sure that victory in this war will be in the name, not of one race or of another, but of the universal Human Race.

from THE FAITH OF AN AMERICAN
by WALTER MILLIS

THE AMERICAN way of life has many faults and blemishes; it also has many things about it that one may hold up as worth fighting for and risking death for— its freedoms, its decencies, its strivings toward a better existence for greater numbers of its people, its effort to utilize as the springs of its social and political system the highest rather than the basest, the most advanced rather than the most primitive, instinctual drives in humanity. But great as these things are, and imminent though the present threat to them may be, I still do not think we can offer them as the sole, or even the primary, reason for again taking up the sword or again being prepared to do so. If our attitude is purely defensive, if we are merely sitting hoarding our liberties against threatened attack, those liberties are only too likely to atrophy anyway. If we try to make a bargain out of it, if we say to our countrymen, "you must be ready to fight in order to preserve your freedom, in order

to enjoy this or that benefit of a democratic as opposed to a totalitarian system, in order to safeguard the nation against invasion," we may always find that the reasons do not particularly appeal. Men's values inevitably differ, and in the last analysis are always irrational, beyond assessment by any form of cost accounting in which such-and-such an amount of pain or death can be equated to such-and-such a quantity of human or social advance. It is not, really, that kind of calculation at all. But suppose we say: "You must be ready to fight; if you are that; if the society of which you are a part has that much cohesion, conviction and energy as a social whole, then perhaps you will have a chance to make good your freedoms, to avoid the crimes of totalitarian retrogression, really to preserve your nation and whatever of its values seem best to you from foreign invasion—and to do all these things probably with far less cost in life and suffering than if you confess your social organization to be a weak and spineless thing, a mere collection of individual selfishnesses." Suppose we say that. I think we are much closer to the facts both of war and of social organization as a whole; I think we are much nearer to putting our hands upon the primary levers that operate the world we live in. We are then moving with, and not in puny revolt against, the main stream of human existence. We are not then merely kicking against the machinery which drives it; we are not, with the totalitarians, developing all the crudest, most primitive and most wasteful elements of that machinery in order easily to establish a barren power; but we are utilizing the basic mechanisms to produce, in time, better machinery, better results, a better ultimate life.

THE MORAL EQUIVALENT OF WAR
by WILLIAM JAMES

THE WAR against war is going to be no holiday excursion or camping party. The military feelings are too deeply grounded to abdicate their place among our ideals until better substitutes are offered than the glory and shame that come to nations as well as to individuals from the ups and downs of politics and the vicissitudes of trade. There is something highly paradoxical in the modern man's relation to war. Ask all our millions, north and south, whether they would vote now (were such a thing possible) to have our war for the Union expunged from history, and the record of a peaceful transition to the present time substituted for that of its marches and battles, and probably hardly a handful of eccentrics would say yes. Those ancestors, those efforts, those memories and legends, are the most ideal part of what we now own together, a sacred spiritual possession worth more than all the blood poured out. Yet ask those same people whether they would be willing in cold blood to start another civil war now to gain another similar possession, and not one man or woman would vote for the proposition. In modern eyes, precious though wars may be, they must not be waged solely for the sake of the ideal harvest. Only when forced upon one, only when an enemy's injustice leaves us no alternative, is a war now thought permissible.

It was not thus in ancient times. The earlier men were hunting men, and to hunt a neighboring tribe, kill the males, loot the village and possess the females, was the most profitable, as well as the most exciting, way of living. Thus were the more martial tribes selected, and in chiefs and peoples a pure pugnacity and love of glory came to mingle with the more fundamental appetite for plunder.

Modern war is so expensive that we feel trade to be a better avenue to plunder; but modern man inherits all the innate pugnacity and all the love of glory of his ancestors. Showing war's irrationality and horror is of no effect upon him. The horrors make the fascination. War is the *strong* life; it is life *in extremis;* war taxes are the only ones men never hesitate to pay, as the budgets of all nations show us.

History is a bath of blood. The *Iliad* is one long recital of how Diomedes and

From William James, *Memories and Studies,* Longmans, Green and Company, Inc.

Ajax, Sarpedon and Hector, *killed*. No detail of the wounds they made is spared us, and the Greek mind fed upon the story. Greek history is a panorama of jingoism and imperialism—war for war's sake, all the citizens being warriors. It is horrible reading, because of the irrationality of it all—save for the purpose of making "history"—and the history is that of the utter ruin of a civilization in intellectual respects perhaps the highest the earth has ever seen.

Those wars were purely piratical. Pride, gold, women, slaves, excitement, were their only motives. In the Peloponnesian War, for example, the Athenians asked the inhabitants of Melos (the island where the "Venus of Milo" was found), hitherto neutral, to own their lordship. The envoys meet, and hold a debate which Thucydides gives in full, and which, for sweet reasonableness of form, would have satisfied Matthew Arnold. "The powerful exact what they can," said the Athenians, "and the weak grant what they must." When the Meleans say that sooner than be slaves they will appeal to the gods, the Athenians reply: "Of the gods we believe and of men we know that, by a law of their nature, wherever they can rule they will. This law was not made by us, and we are not the first to have acted upon it; we did but inherit it, and we know that you and all mankind, if you were as strong as we are, would do as we do. So much for the gods; we have told you why we expect to stand as high in their good opinion as you." Well, the Meleans still refused, and their town was taken. "The Athenians," Thucydides quietly says, "thereupon put to death all who were of military age and made slaves of the women and children. They then colonized the is-land, sending thither five hundred settlers of their own."

Alexander's career was piracy pure and simple, nothing but an orgy of power and plunder, made romantic by the character of the hero. There was no rational principle in it, and the moment he died his generals and governors attacked one another. The cruelty of those times is incredible. When Rome finally conquered Greece, Paulus Aemilius was told by the Roman Senate to reward his soldiers for their toil by "giving" them the old kingdom of Epirus. They sacked seventy cities and carried off a hundred and fifty thousand inhabitants as slaves. How many they killed I know not; but in Etolia they killed all the senators, five hundred and fifty in number. Brutus was "the noblest Roman of them all," but to reanimate his soldiers on the eve of Philippi he similarly promises to give them the cities of Sparta and Thessalonica to ravage, if they win the fight.

Such was the gory nurse that trained societies to cohesiveness. We inherit the warlike type; and for most of the capacities of heroism that the human race is full of we have to thank this cruel history. Dead men tell no tales, and if there were any tribes of other type than this they have left no survivors. Our ancestors have bred pugnacity into our bone and marrow, and thousands of years of peace won't breed it out of us. The popular imagination fairly fattens on the thought of wars. Let public opinion once reach a certain fighting pitch, and no ruler can withstand it. In the Boer War both governments began with bluff, but couldn't stay there; the military tension was too much for them. In 1898 our people had read the word WAR in letters three inches high for three months in every newspaper. The pliant politician McKinley was swept away by their eagerness, and our squalid war with Spain became a necessity.

At the present day, civilized opinion is a curious mental mixture. The military instincts and ideals are as strong as ever, but are confronted by reflective criticisms which sorely curb their ancient freedom. Innumerable writers are showing up the bestial side of military service. Pure loot and mastery seem no longer morally avowable motives, and pretexts must be found for attributing them solely to the enemy. England and we, our army and navy authorities repeat without ceasing, arm solely for "peace"; Germany and Japan it is who are bent on loot and glory. "Peace" in military mouths today is a synonym for "war expected." The word has become a pure provocative, and no government wishing peace sincerely should allow it ever to be printed in a newspaper. Every up-to-date dictionary should say that "peace" and "war" mean the same thing, now *in posse,* now *in actu.* It may even reasonably be said that the intensely sharp competitive *preparation* for war by the nations *is the real war,* permanent, unceasing; and that the battles are only a sort of public verification of the mastery gained during the "peace" interval.

It is plain that on this subject civilized man has developed a sort of double personality. If we take European nations, no legitimate interest of any one of them would seem to justify the tremendous destructions which a war to compass it would necessarily entail. It would seem as though common sense and reason ought to find a way to reach agreement in every conflict of honest interests. I myself think it our bounden duty to believe in such international rationality as possible. But, as things stand, I see how desperately hard it is to bring the peace party and the war party together, and I believe that the difficulty is due to certain deficiencies in the program of pacificism which set the militarist imagination strongly, and to a certain extent justifiably, against it. In the whole discussion both sides are on imaginative and sentimental ground. It is but one utopia against another, and everything one says must be abstract and hypothetical. Subject to this criticism and caution, I will try to characterize in abstract strokes the opposite imaginative forces, and point out what to my own very fallible mind seems the best utopian hypothesis, the most promising line of conciliation.

In my remarks, pacifist though I am, I will refuse to speak of the bestial side of the war régime (already done justice to by many writers) and consider only the higher aspects of militaristic sentiment. Patriotism no one thinks discreditable; nor does anyone deny that war is the romance of history. But inordinate ambitions are the soul of every patriotism, and the possibility of violent death the soul of all romance. The militarily patriotic and romantic-minded everywhere, and especially the professional military class, refuse to admit for a moment that war may be a transitory phenomenon in social evolution. The notion of a sheep's paradise like that revolts, they say, our higher imagination. Where then would be the steeps of life? If war had ever stopped, we should have to reinvent it, on this view, to redeem life from flat degeneration.

Reflective apologists for war at the present day all take it religiously. It is a sort of sacrament. Its profits are to the vanquished as well as to the victor; and quite apart from any question of profit, it is an absolute good, we are told, for it is human nature at its highest dynamic. Its "horrors" are a cheap price to pay for rescue from the only alternative supposed, of a world of clerks and teachers, of co-education and zoophily, of "consumer's leagues" and "associated charities," of industrialism unlimited and feminism unabashed. No scorn, no hardness, no valor any more! Fie upon such a cattleyard of a planet!

So far as the central essence of this feeling goes, no healthy-minded person, it seems to me, can help to some degree partaking of it. Militarism is the great preserver of our ideals of hardihood, and human life with no use for hardihood would be contemptible. Without risks or prizes for the darer, history would be insipid indeed; and there is a type of military character which everyone feels that the race should never cease to breed, for everyone is sensitive to its superiority. The duty is incumbent on mankind, of keeping military characters in stock—of keeping them, if not for use, then as ends in themselves and as pure pieces of perfection —so that [Theodore] Roosevelt's weaklings and mollycoddles may not end by making everything else disappear from the face of nature.

This natural sort of feeling forms, I think, the innermost soul of army writings. Without any exception known to me, militarist authors take a highly mystical view of their subject, and regard war as a biological or sociological necessity, uncontrolled by ordinary psychological checks and motives. When the time of development is ripe the war must come, reason or no reason, for the justifications pleaded are invariably fictitious. War is, in short, a permanent human *obligation*. General Homer Lea, in his recent book, *The Valor of Ignorance,* plants himself squarely on this ground. Readiness for war is for him the essence of nationality,

and ability in it the supreme measure of the health of nations.

Nations, General Lea says, are never stationary—they must necessarily expand or shrink, according to their vitality or decrepitude. Japan now is culminating; and by the fatal law in question it is impossible that her statesmen should not long since have entered, with extraordinary foresight, upon a vast policy of conquest— the game in which the first moves were her wars with China and Russia and her treaty with England, and of which the final objective is the capture of the Philippines, the Hawaiian Islands, Alaska, and the whole of our coast west of the Sierra Passes. This will give Japan what her ineluctable vocation as a state absolutely forces her to claim, the possession of the entire Pacific Ocean; and to oppose these deep designs we Americans have, according to our author, nothing but our conceit, our ignorance, our commercialism, our corruption, and our feminism. General Lea makes a minute technical comparison of the military strength which we at present could oppose to the strength of Japan, and concludes that the islands, Alaska, Oregon, and Southern California, would fall almost without resistance, that San Francisco must surrender in a fortnight to a Japanese investment, that in three or four months the war would be over, and our Republic, unable to regain what it had heedlessly neglected to protect sufficiently, would then "disintegrate," until perhaps some Caesar should arise to weld us again into a nation.

A dismal forecast indeed! Yet not unplausible, if the mentality of Japan's statesmen be of the Caesarian type of which history shows so many examples, and which is all that General Lea seems able to imagine. But there is no reason to think that women can no longer be the mothers of Napoleonic or Alexandrian characters; and if these come in Japan and find their opportunity, just such surprises as *The Valor of Ignorance* paints may lurk in ambush for us. Ignorant as we still are of the innermost recesses of Japanese mentality, we may be foolhardy to disregard such possibilities.

Other militarists are more complex and more moral in their considerations. The *Philosophie des Krieges,* by S. R. Steinmetz, is a good example. War, according to this author, is an ordeal instituted by God, who weighs the nations in its balance. It is the essential form of the state, and the only function in which peoples can employ all their powers at once and convergently. No victory is possible save as the resultant of a totality of virtues, no defeat for which some vice or weakness is not responsible. Fidelity, cohesiveness, tenacity, heroism, conscience, education, inventiveness, economy, wealth, physical health and vigor—there isn't a moral or intellectual point of superiority that doesn't tell, when God holds his assizes and hurls the peoples upon one another. *Die Weltgeschichte ist das Weltgericht;*[1] and Dr. Steinmetz does not believe that in the long run chance and luck play any part in apportioning the issues.

The virtues that prevail, it must be noted, are virtues anyhow, superiorities that count in peaceful as well as in military competition; but the strain on them, being infinitely intenser in the latter case, makes war infinitely more searching as a trial. No ordeal is comparable to its winnowings. Its dread hammer is the welder of men into cohesive states, and nowhere but in such states can human nature adequately develop its capacity. The only alternative is "degeneration."

Dr. Steinmetz is a conscientious thinker, and his book, short as it is, takes much into account. Its upshot can, it seems to me, be summed up in Simon Patten's word, that mankind was nursed in pain and fear, and that the transition to a "pleasure economy" may be fatal to a being wielding no powers of defense against its disintegrative influences. If we speak of the *fear of emancipation from the fear régime,* we put the whole situation into a single phrase; fear regarding ourselves now taking the place of the ancient fear of the enemy.

Turn the fear over as I will in my mind, it all seems to lead back to two unwillingnesses of the imagination, one esthetic, and the other moral: unwillingness, first to envisage a future in which army life, with its many elements of charm, shall be forever impossible, and in which the destinies of peoples shall nevermore be decided quickly, thrillingly, and tragically, by force, but only gradually and insipidly by "evolution"; and, secondly, unwillingness to see the supreme theater of human strenuousness closed, and the splendid military aptitudes of men doomed to keep always in a state of latency and never show themselves in action. These insistent unwillingnesses, no less than other esthetic and ethical insistencies, have, it seems to me, to be listened to and respected. One cannot meet them effectively by mere counter-insistency on war's expensiveness and horror. The horror makes the thrill; and when the question is of getting the extremest and supremest out of human nature, talk of expense sounds ignominious. The weakness of so much merely negative criticism

[1] "The history of the world is the judgment of the world."

is evident—pacifism makes no converts from the military party. The military party denies neither the bestiality nor the horror, nor the expense; it only says that these things tell but half the story. It only says that war is *worth* them; that, taking human nature as a whole, its wars are its best protection against its weaker and more cowardly self, and that mankind cannot *afford* to adopt a peace economy.

Pacifists ought to enter more deeply into the esthetical and ethical point of view of their opponents. Do that first in any controversy, says J. J. Chapman; *then move the point,* and your opponent will follow. So long as anti-militarists propose no substitute for war's disciplinary function, no *moral equivalent* of war, analogous, as one might say, to the mechanical equivalent of heat, so long they fail to realize the full inwardness of the situation. And as a rule they do fail. The duties, penalties, and sanctions pictured in the utopias they paint are all too weak and tame to touch the military-minded. Tolstoi's pacificism is the only exception to this rule, for it is profoundly pessimistic as regards all this world's values, and makes the fear of the Lord furnish the moral spur provided elsewhere by the fear of the enemy. But our socialistic peace advocates all believe absolutely in this world's values; and instead of the fear of the Lord and the fear of the enemy, the only fear they reckon with is the fear of poverty if one be lazy. This weakness pervades all the socialistic literature with which I am acquainted. Even in Lowes Dickinson's exquisite dialogue,[2] high wages and short hours are the only forces invoked for overcoming man's distaste for repulsive kinds of labor. Meanwhile men at large still live as they always have lived, under a pain-and-fear economy —for those of us who live in an ease economy are but an island in the stormy ocean —and the whole atmosphere of present-day utopian literature tastes mawkish and dishwatery to people who still keep a sense for life's more bitter flavors. It suggests, in truth, ubiquitous inferiority.

Inferiority is always with us, and merciless scorn of it is the keynote of the military temper. "Dogs, would you live forever?" shouted Frederick the Great. "Yes," say our utopians, "let us live forever, and raise our level gradually." The best thing about our "inferiors" today is that they are as tough as nails, and physically and morally almost as insensitive. Utopianism would see them soft and squeamish, while militarism would keep their callousness, but transfigure it into a meritorious characteristic, needed by "the service," and redeemed by that from the suspicion of inferiority. All the qualities of a man acquire dignity when he knows that the service of the collectivity that owns him needs them. If proud of the collectivity, his own pride rises in proportion. No collectivity is like an army for nourishing such pride; but it has to be confessed that the only sentiment which the image of pacific cosmopolitan industrialism is capable of arousing in countless worthy breasts is shame at the idea of belonging to *such* a collectivity. It is obvious that the United States of America as they exist today impress a mind like General Lea's as so much human blubber. Where is the sharpness and precipitousness, the contempt for life, whether one's own or another's? Where is the savage "yes" and "no," the unconditional duty? Where is the conscription? Where is the blood tax?

[2] *Justice and Liberty,* New York, 1909.

Where is anything that one feels honored by belonging to?

Having said thus much in preparation, I will now confess my own utopia. I devoutly believe in the reign of peace and in the gradual advent of some sort of socialistic equilibrium. The fatalistic view of the war function is to me nonsense, for I know that war-making is due to definite motives and subject to prudential checks and reasonable criticisms, just like any other form of enterprise. And when whole nations are the armies, and the science of destruction vies in intellectual refinement with the sciences of production, I see that war becomes absurd and impossible from its own monstrosity. Extravagant ambitions will have to be replaced by reasonable claims, and nations must make common cause against them. I see no reason why all this should not apply to yellow as well as to white countries, and I look forward to a future when acts of war shall be formally outlawed as between civilized peoples.

All these beliefs of mine put me squarely into the anti-militarist party. But I do not believe that peace either ought to be or will be permanent on this globe, unless the states pacifically organized preserve some of the old elements of army discipline. A permanently successful peace economy cannot be a simple pleasure economy. In the more or less socialistic future toward which mankind seems drifting we must still subject ourselves collectively to these severities which answer to our real position upon this only partly hospitable globe. We must make new energies and hardihoods continue the manliness to which the military mind so faithfully clings. Martial virtues must be the enduring cement; intrepidity, contempt of softness, surrender of private interest, obedi-ence to command, must still remain the rock upon which states are built—unless, indeed, we wish for dangerous reactions against commonwealth fit only for contempt, and liable to invite attack whenever a center of crystallization for military-minded enterprise gets formed anywhere in their neighborhood.

The war party is assuredly right in affirming and reaffirming that the martial virtues, although originally gained by the race through war, are absolute and permanent human goods. Patriotic pride and ambition in their military form are, after all, only specifications of a more general competitive passion. They are its first form, but that is no reason for supposing them to be its last form. Men now are proud of belonging to a conquering nation, and without a murmur they lay down their persons and their wealth, if by so doing they may fend off subjection. But who can be sure that *other aspects of one's country* may not, with time and education and suggestion enough, come to be regarded with similarly effective feelings of pride and shame? Why should men not some day feel that it is worth a blood tax to belong to a collectivity superior in *any* ideal respect? Why should they not blush with indignant shame if the community that owns them is vile in any way whatsoever? Individuals, daily more numerous, now feel this civic passion. It is only a question of blowing on the spark till the whole population gets incandescent, and on the ruins of the old morals of military honor, a stable system of morals of civic honor builds itself up. What the whole community comes to believe in grasps the individual as in a vise. The war function has grasped us so far; but constructive interests may some day seem no less imperative, and impose on the individual a hardly lighter burden.

Let me illustrate my idea more concretely. There is nothing to make one indignant in the mere fact that life is hard, that men should toil and suffer pain. The planetary conditions once for all are such, and we can stand it. But that so many men, by mere accidents of birth and opportunity, should have a life of *nothing else* but toil and pain and hardness and inferiority imposed upon them, should have *no* vacation, while others natively no more deserving never get any taste of this campaigning life at all—*this* is capable of arousing indignation in reflective minds. It may end by seeming shameful to all of us that some of us have nothing but campaigning, and others nothing but unmanly ease. If now—and this is my idea—there were, instead of military conscription, a conscription of the whole youthful population to form for a certain number of years a part of the army enlisted against *Nature,* the injustice would tend to be evened out, and numerous other goods to the commonwealth would follow. The military ideals of hardihood and discipline would be wrought into the growing fiber of the people; no one would remain blind as the luxurious classes now are blind, to man's real relations to the globe he lives on, and to the permanently sour and hard foundations of his higher life. To coal and iron mines, to freight trains, to fishing fleets in December, to dish-washing, clothes-washing, and window-washing, to road-building and tunnel-making, to foundries and stokeholes, and to the frames of skyscrapers, would our gilded youths be drafted off, according to their choice, to get the childishness knocked out of them, and to come back into society with healthier sympathies and soberer

ideas. They would have paid their blood tax, done their own part in the immemorial human warfare against nature, they would tread the earth more proudly, the women would value them more highly, they would be better fathers and teachers of the following generation.

Such a conscription, with the state of public opinion that would have required it, and the many moral fruits it would bear, would preserve in the midst of a pacific civilization the manly virtues which the military party is so afraid of seeing disappear in peace. We should get toughness without callousness, authority with as little criminal cruelty as possible, and painful work done cheerily because the duty is temporary, and threatens not, as now, to degrade the whole remainder of one's life. I spoke of the "moral equivalent" of war. So far, war has been the only force that can discipline a whole community, and until an equivalent discipline is organized, I believe that war must have its way. But I have no serious doubt that the ordinary prides and shames of social man, once developed to a certain intensity, are capable of organizing such a moral equivalent as I have sketched, or some other just as effective for preserving manliness of type. It is but a question of time, of skillful propagandism, and of opinion-making men seizing historic opportunities.

The martial type of character can be bred without war. Strenuous honor and disinterestedness abound elsewhere. Priests and medical men are in a fashion educated to it, and we should all feel some degree of it imperative if we were conscious of our work as an obligatory service to the state. We should be *owned,* as soldiers are by the army, and our pride would rise accordingly. We could be poor, then, without humiliation, as army officers now are.

The only thing needed henceforward is to inflame the civic temper as past history has inflamed the military temper. H. G. Wells, as usual, sees the center of the situation. "In many ways," he says, "military organization is the most peaceful of activities. When the contemporary man steps from the street, of clamorous insincere advertisement, push, adulteration, underselling and intermittent employment, into the barrack yard, he steps on to a higher social plane, into an atmosphere of service and co-operation and of infinitely more honorable emulations. Here at least men are not flung out of employment to degenerate because there is no immediate work for them to do. They are fed and drilled and trained for better services. Here at least a man is supposed to win promotion by self-forgetfulness and not by self-seeking." [3] . . .

Wells adds that he thinks that the conceptions of order and discipline, the tradition of service and devotion, of physical fitness, unstinted exertion, and universal responsibility, which universal military duty is now teaching European nations, will remain a permanent acquisition, when the last ammunition has been used in the fireworks that celebrate the final peace. I believe as he does. It would be simply preposterous if the only force that could work ideals of honor and standards of efficiency into English or American natures should be the fear of being killed by the Germans or the Japanese. Great indeed is Fear; but it is not, as our military enthusiasts believe and try to make us believe, the only stimulus known for awakening the higher ranges of men's spiritual energy. The amount of alteration in public opinion which my utopia postulates is vastly less than the difference between the mentality of those black warriors who pursued Stanley's party on the Congo with their cannibal war cry of "Meat! Meat!" and that of the General Staff of any civilized nation. History has seen the latter interval bridged over: the former one can be bridged over much more easily.

[3] *First and Last Things*, 1908, p. 215.

THE UNIVERSE AND DR. EINSTEIN

by LINCOLN BARNETT

Part I

CARVED in the white walls of the Riverside Church in New York, the figures of six hundred great men of the ages—saints, philosophers, kings—stand in limestone immortality, surveying space and time with blank imperishable eyes. One panel enshrines the geniuses of science, fourteen of them, spanning the centuries from Hippocrates, who died around 370 B.C., to Albert Einstein, who was sixty-nine years old this March. It is noteworthy that Einstein is the only living man in this whole sculptured gallery of the illustrious dead.

It is equally noteworthy that of the thousands of people who worship weekly at Manhattan's most spectacular Protestant church, probably ninety-nine per cent would be hard pressed to explain why Einstein's image is there. It is there because a generation ago, when the iconography of the church was being planned, Dr. Harry Emerson Fosdick wrote letters to a group of the nation's leading scientists asking them to submit lists of the fourteen greatest names in scientific history. Their ballots varied. Most of them included Archimedes, Euclid, Galileo, and Newton. But on every list appeared the name of Albert Einstein.

The vast gap that has persisted for more than forty years—since 1905, when the Theory of Special Relativity was first published—between Einstein's scientific eminence and public understanding of it is the measure of a gap in American education. Today most newspaper readers know vaguely that Einstein had something to do with the atomic bomb; beyond that his name is simply a synonym for the abstruse. While his theories form part of the body of modern science, they are not yet part of the modern curriculum. It is not surprising therefore that many a college graduate still thinks of Einstein as a kind of mathematical surrealist rather than as the discoverer of certain cosmic laws of immense importance in man's slow struggle to understand physical reality. He does not know that Relativity, over and above its scientific import, comprises a major philosophical system which augments and illumines the reflections of the great theorists of knowledge—Locke, Berkeley, and Hume. Consequently he has very little notion of the vast, arcane, and mysteriously ordered universe in which he dwells.

Dr. Einstein, now professor emeritus at the Institute for Advanced Study at Princeton, is currently hard at work on a problem that has stumped him for more than a quarter-century and which he intends to solve before he dies. His ambition is to complete his "unified field theory," setting forth in one series of equations the laws governing the two fundamental forces of the universe, gravitation and electromagnetism. The significance of this task can be appreciated only when one realizes that virtually all the phenomena of nature are produced by these two primordial forces. Until a hundred years ago electricity and magnetism—while known and studied since early Greek times—were regarded as separate quantities. But the experiments of Oersted and Faraday in the nineteenth century showed that a current of electricity is always surrounded by a magnetic field, and conversely that under certain conditions magnetic forces can induce electrical currents. From these experiments came the discovery of the electromagnetic field which pervades all space and through which light waves, radio waves, and all other electromagnetic disturbances are propagated. Thus electricity and magnetism may be considered as a single force. Save for gravitation, nearly all other forces in the material universe—frictional forces, chemical forces which hold atoms together in molecules, cohesive forces which bind larger particles of matter, elastic forces which cause bodies to maintain their shape—are of electromagnetic origin; for all of these involve the interplay of matter, and all matter is composed of atoms which in turn are composed of electrical particles. Yet the similarities between gravitational and electromagnetic phenomena are very striking. The planets spin in the gravitational field of the sun; electrons swirl in the electromagnetic field of the atomic nucleus. The earth, moreover, is a big magnet—a peculiar fact which is apparent to anyone who has ever used a compass. The sun is also a magnet. And so are all the stars.

Although many attempts have been made to identify gravitational attraction as an electromagnetic effect, all have failed. Einstein himself thought he had succeeded in 1929 and published a unified field theory which he later scrapped as inadequate. His present objectives are more ambitious, for he is endeavoring now to formulate a set of universal laws that will encompass both the boundless gravitational and electromagnetic fields of interstellar space and the tiny, terrible field inside the atom. In this vast cosmic picture the abyss between macrocosmos and microcosmos—the very big and the very little—will be bridged,

and the whole complex of the universe will resolve into a homogeneous fabric in which matter and energy are indistinguishable and all forms of motion from the slow wheeling of the galaxies to the wild flight of electrons become simply changes in the structure and concentration of the primordial field.

Since the aim of science is to describe and explain the world we live in, Einstein would, by thus defining the manifold of nature within the terms of a single harmonious theory, attain its loftiest goal. The meaning of the word "explain," however, suffers a contraction with man's every step in quest of reality. Science cannot yet really "explain" electricity, magnetism, and gravitation; their effects can be measured and predicted, but of their ultimate nature no more is known to the modern scientist than to Thales of Miletus, who first speculated on the electrification of amber around 585 B.C. Most contemporary physicists reject the notion that man can ever discover what these mysterious forces "really" are. Electricity, Bertrand Russell says, "is not a thing, like St. Paul's Cathedral; it is a way in which things behave. When we have told how things behave when they are electrified, and under what circumstances they are electrified, we have told all there is to tell." Until recently scientists would have scorned such a thesis. Aristotle, whose natural science dominated Western thought for two thousand years, believed that man could arrive at an understanding of ultimate reality by reasoning from *self-evident principles*. It is, for example, a self-evident principle that everything in the universe has its proper place, hence one can deduce that objects fall to the ground because that's where they belong, and smoke goes up because that's where *it* belongs. The goal of Aristotelian science was to explain *why* things happen. Modern science was born when Galileo began trying to explain *how* things happen and thus originated the method of controlled experiment which now forms the basis of scientific investigation.

Out of Galileo's discoveries and those of Newton in the next generation there evolved a mechanical universe of forces, pressures, tensions, oscillations, and waves. There seemed to be no process of nature which could not be described in terms of ordinary experience, illustrated by a concrete model or predicted by Newton's amazingly accurate laws of mechanics. But before the turn of the past century certain deviations from these laws became apparent; and though these deviations were slight, they were of such a fundamental nature that the whole edifice of Newton's machine-like universe began to topple. The certainty that science can explain "how" things happen began to dim about twenty years ago. And right now it is a question whether scientific man is in touch with reality at all—or can ever hope to be.

II

The factors which first led physicists to distrust their faith in a smoothly functioning mechanical universe loomed on the inner and outer horizons of knowledge—in the unseen realm of the atom and in the fathomless depths of intergalactic space. To describe these phenomena quantitatively, two great theoretical systems were developed between 1900 and 1927. One was the Quantum Theory, dealing with the fundamental units of matter and energy. The other was Relativity, dealing with space, time, and the structure of the universe as a whole.

Both are now accepted pillars of modern physical thought. Both explain phenomena in their fields in terms of consistent, mathematical relationships. They do not answer the Newtonian "how" any more than Newton's laws answered the Aristotelian "why." They provide equations, for example, that define with great accuracy the laws governing the radiation and propagation of light. But the actual mechanism by which the atom radiates light and by which light is propagated through space remains one of nature's supreme mysteries. Similarly the laws governing the phenomenon of radioactivity enable scientists to predict that in a given quantity of uranium a certain number of atoms will disintegrate in a certain length of time. But just which atoms will decay and how they are selected for doom are questions that man cannot yet answer.

In accepting a mathematical description of nature, physicists have been forced to abandon the ordinary world of our experience, the world of sense perceptions. To understand the significance of this retreat it is necessary to step across the thin line that divides physics from metaphysics. Questions involving the relationship between observer and reality, subject and object, have haunted philosophical thinkers since the dawn of reason. Twenty-three centuries ago the Greek philosopher Democritus wrote: "Sweet and bitter, cold and warm as well as all the colors, all these things exist but in opinion and not in reality; what really exists are unchangeable particles, atoms, and their motions in empty space." Galileo also was aware of the purely subjective character of sense qualities like color, taste, smell, and sound and pointed out that "they can no more be ascribed to the external objects than can the tickling or the pain caused sometimes by touching such objects."

The English philosopher John Locke tried to penetrate to the "real essence of substances" by drawing a distinction between what he termed the primary and secondary qualities of matter. Thus he considered that shape, motion, solidity, and all geometrical properties were real or primary qualities, inherent in the object itself; while secondary qualities, like colors, sounds, tastes, were simply projections upon the organs of sense. The artificiality of this distinction was obvious to later thinkers.

"I am able to prove," wrote the great German mathematician, Leibnitz, "that not only light, color, heat, and the like, but motion, shape, and extension too are mere apparent qualities." Just as our visual sense, for example, tells us that a golf ball is white, so vision abetted by our sense of touch tells us that it is also round, smooth, and small—qualities that have no more reality, independent of our senses, than the quality which we define by convention as white.

Thus gradually philosophers and scientists arrived at the startling conclusion that the whole objective universe of matter and energy, atoms and stars, does not exist except as a construction of the consciousness, an edifice of conventional symbols shaped by the senses of man. As Berkeley, the archenemy of materialism, phrased it: "All the choir of heaven and furniture of earth, in a word all those bodies which compose the mighty frame of the world, have not any substance without the mind. . . . So long as they are not actually perceived by me, or do not exist in my mind, or that of any other created spirit, they must either have no existence at all, or else subsist in the mind of some Eternal Spirit." Einstein carried this train of logic to its ultimate limits by showing that even space and time are forms of intuition, which can no more be divorced from consciousness than can our concepts of color, shape, or size. Space has no objective reality except

as an order or arrangement of the objects we perceive in it, and time has no independent existence apart from the order of events by which we measure it.

These philosophical subtleties have a profound bearing on modern science. For with the philosophers' reduction of all objective reality to a shadow-world of perceptions, scientists became aware of the alarming limitations of man's senses. Anyone who has ever thrust a glass prism into a sunbeam and seen the rainbow colors of the solar spectrum refracted on a screen has looked upon the whole range of visible light. For the human eye is sensitive only to the narrow band of radiation that falls between the red and the violet. A difference of a few one hundred thousandths of a centimeter in wavelength makes the difference between visibility and invisibility. The wavelength of red light is .00007 cm. and that of violet light .00004 cm.

But the sun also emits other kinds of radiation. Infrared rays, for example, with a wavelength of .00008 to .032 cm. are just a little too long to excite the retina to an impression of light, though the skin detects their impact as heat. Similarly ultraviolet rays with a wavelength of .00003 to .000001 cm. are too short for the eye to perceive but can be recorded on a photographic plate. Photographs can also be made by the "light" of X-rays which are even shorter than ultraviolet rays. And there are other electromagnetic waves of lesser and greater frequency—the gamma rays of radium, radio waves, cosmic rays— which can be detected in various ways and differ from light only in wavelength. It is evident, therefore, that the human eye suppresses most of the "lights" in the world, and that what man can perceive of the reality around him is distorted and enfeebled by the limitations of his organ of vision. The world would appear far dif-

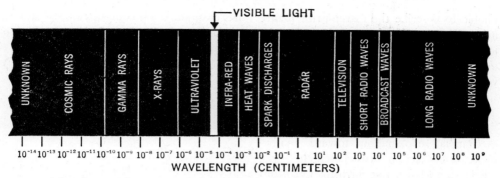

The electromagnetic spectrum reveals the narrow range of radiation visible to man's eye. From the standpoint of physics, the only difference between radio waves, visible light, and such high-frequency forms of radiation as X-rays and gamma rays lies in their wavelength. But out of this vast range of electromagnetic radiation, extending from cosmic rays with wavelengths of only one trillionth of a centimeter up to infinitely long radio waves, the human eye selects only the narrow band indicated in white on the above chart. Man's perceptions of the universe in which he dwells are thus restricted by the limitations of his visual sense. Wavelengths are indicated on the chart by the denary system; i.e. 10^3 centimeters equals $10 \times 10 \times 10$ equals 1,000; and 10^{-3} equals $1/10 \times 1/10 \times 1/10$ equals $1/1,000$.

ferent to him if his eye were sensitive, for example, to X-rays.

Realization that our whole knowledge of the universe is simply a residue of impressions clouded by our imperfect senses makes the quest for reality seem hopeless. If nothing has existence save in its being perceived, the world should dissolve into an anarchy of individual perceptions. But a curious order runs through our perceptions, as if indeed there might be an underlayer of objective reality which our senses translate. Although no man can ever know whether his sensation of red or of Middle C is the same as another man's, it is nevertheless possible to act on the assumption that everyone sees colors and hears tones more or less alike.

This functional harmony of nature Berkeley, Descartes, and Spinoza attributed to God. Modern physicists who prefer to solve their problems without recourse to God (although this seems to become

more difficult all the time) emphasize that nature mysteriously operates on mathematical principles. It is the mathematical orthodoxy of the universe that enables theorists like Einstein to predict and discover natural laws simply by the solution of equations. But the paradox of physics today is that with every improvement in its mathematical apparatus the gulf between man the observer and the objective world of scientific description becomes more profound.

It is perhaps significant that in terms of simple magnitude man is the mean between macrocosm and microcosm. Stated crudely this means that a supergiant red star (the largest material body in the universe) is just as much bigger than man as an electron (tiniest of physical entities) is smaller. It is not surprising, therefore, that the prime mysteries of nature dwell in those realms farthest removed from sense-imprisoned man, nor that science, unable to describe the extremes of reality in the homely metaphors of classical physics should content itself with noting such mathematical relationships as may be revealed.

III

The first step in science's retreat from mechanical explanation toward mathematical abstraction was taken in 1900, when Max Planck put forth his Quantum Theory to meet certain problems that had arisen in studies of radiation. It is common knowledge that when heated bodies become incandescent they emit a red glow that turns to orange, then yellow, then white as the temperature increases. Painstaking efforts were made during the past century to formulate a law stating how the amount of radiant energy given off by such heated bodies varied with wavelength and temperature. All attempts failed until Planck found by mathematical means an equation that satisfied the results of experiment. The extraordinary feature of his equation was that it rested on the assumption that radiant energy is emitted, not in an unbroken stream but in discontinuous bits or portions which he termed *quanta*.

Planck had no evidence for such an assumption, for no one knew anything (then or now) of the actual mechanism of radiation. But on purely theoretical grounds he concluded that each quantum carries an amount of energy given by the equation, $E = h v$, where v is the frequency of the radiation and h is Planck's Constant, a small but inexorable number (roughly .00000000000000000000000006624) which has since proved to be one of the most fundamental constants in nature. In any process of radiation the amount of emitted energy divided by the frequency is always equal to h. Although Planck's Constant

has dominated the computations of atomic physics for half a century, its magnitude

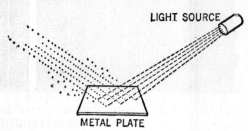

The photoelectric effect was interpreted by Einstein in 1905. When light falls on a metal plate, the plate ejects a shower of electrons. This phenomenon cannot be explained by the classic wave theory of light. Einstein deduced that light is not a continuous stream of energy but is composed of individual particles or bundles of energy which he called *photons*. When a photon strikes an electron the resulting action is analagous to the impact of billiard balls, as shown in the simplified conception above.

cannot be explained any more than the magnitude of the speed of light can be explained. Like other universal constants it is simply a mathematical fact for which no explanation can be given. Sir Arthur Eddington once observed that any true law of nature is likely to seem irrational to rational man; hence Planck's quantum principle, he thought, is one of the few real natural laws science has revealed.

The far-reaching implications of Planck's conjecture did not become apparent till 1905, when Einstein, who almost alone among contemporary physicists appreciated its significance, carried the quantum theory into a new domain. Planck had believed he was simply patching up the equations of radiation. But Einstein postulated that all forms of radiant energy—light, heat, X-rays—actually travel through space in separate and discontinuous quanta. Thus the sensation of warmth we experience when sitting in front of a fire results from the bombardment of our skin by innumerable quanta of radiant heat. Similarly sensations of color arise from the bombardment of our optic nerves by light quanta which differ from each other just as the frequency v varies in the equation $E = hv$.

Einstein substantiated this idea by working out a law accurately defining a puzzling phenomenon known as the photoelectric effect. Physicists had been at a loss to explain the fact that when a beam of pure violet light is allowed to shine upon a metal plate the plate ejects a shower of electrons. If light of lower frequency, say yellow or red, falls on the plate, electrons will again be ejected but at reduced velocities. The vehemence with which the electrons are torn from the metal depends only on the color of the light and not at all on its intensity. If the light source is removed to a considerable distance and dimmed to a faint glow the electrons that pop forth are fewer in number but their velocity is undiminished. The action is instantaneous even when the light fades to imperceptibility.

Einstein decided that these peculiar effects could be explained only by supposing that all light is composed of individual particles or grains of energy which he called *photons,* and that when one of them hits an electron the resulting action is comparable to the impact of two billiard balls. He reasoned further that photons of violet, ultraviolet, and other forms of high frequency radiation pack more energy than red and infrared photons, and that the velocity with which each electron flies from the metal plate is proportional to the energy content of the photon that strikes it. He expressed these principles in a series of historic equations which won him the

Nobel Prize and profoundly influenced later work in quantum physics and spectroscopy. Television and other applications of the photoelectric cell owe their existence to Einstein's Photoelectric Law.

In thus adducing an important new physical principle Einstein uncovered at the same time one of the deepest and most troubling enigmas of nature. No one doubts today that all matter is made up of atoms which in turn are composed of even smaller building blocks called electrons, neutrons, and protons. But Einstein's notion that light too may consist of discontinuous particles clashed with a far more venerable theory that light is made up of waves.

There are indeed certain phenomena involving light that can only be explained by the wave theory. For example, the shadows of ordinary objects like buildings, trees, and telegraph poles appear sharply defined; but when a very fine wire or hair is held between a light source and a screen it casts no distinct shadow whatsoever, suggesting that light rays have bent around it just as waves of water bend around a small rock. Similarly a beam of light passing through a round aperture projects a sharply-defined disk upon a screen; but if the aperture is reduced to the size of a pinhole, then the disk becomes ribbed with alternating concentric bands of light and darkness, somewhat like those of a conventional target. This phenomenon is known as diffraction and has been compared with the tendency of ocean waves to bend and diverge on passing through the narrow mouth of a harbor. If instead of one pinhole, two pinholes are employed very close together and side by side, the diffraction patterns merge in a series of parallel stripes. Just as two wave systems meeting in a swimming pool will reinforce each other when crest coincides with crest and annul each other when the crest of one wave meets the trough of another, so in the case of the adjacent pinholes the bright stripes occur where two light waves reinforce each other and the dark stripes where two waves have interfered. These phenomena—diffraction and interference—are strictly wave characteristics and would not occur if light were made up of individual corpuscles. More than two centuries of experiment and theory assert that light *must* consist of waves. Yet Einstein's Photoelectric Law shows that light *must* consist of photons.

This fundamental question—is light waves or is it particles?—has never been answered. The dual character of light is, however, only one aspect of a deeper and more remarkable duality which pervades all nature.

The first hint of this strange dualism came in 1925, when a young French physicist named Louis de Broglie suggested that phenomena involving the interplay of matter and radiation could best be understood by regarding electrons not as individual particles but as systems of waves. This audacious concept flouted two decades of quantum research in which physicists had built up rather specific ideas about the elementary particles of matter. The atom had come to be pictured as a kind of miniature solar system composed of a central nucleus surrounded by varying numbers of electrons (one for hydrogen, 92 for uranium) revolving in circular or elliptical orbits. The electron was less vivid. Experiments showed that all electrons had exactly the same mass and the same electrical charge, so it was natural to regard them as the ultimate foundation stones of the universe. It also seemed logical at first to picture them simply as hard elastic spheres. But little by little, as investigation

progressed, they became more capricious, defiant of observation and measurement. In many ways their behavior appeared too complex for any material particle. "The hard sphere," declared the British physicist, Sir James Jeans, "has always a definite position in space; the electron apparently has not. A hard sphere takes up a very definite amount of room; an electron— well it is probably as meaningless to discuss how much room an electron takes up as it is to discuss how much room a fear, an anxiety, or an uncertainty takes up."

Shortly after De Broglie had his vision of "matter waves" a Viennese physicist named Schrödinger developed the same idea in mathematical form, evolving a system that explained quantum phenomena by attributing specific wave functions to protons and electrons. This system, known as "wave mechanics," was corroborated in 1927 when two American scientists, Davisson and Germer, proved by experiment that electrons actually do exhibit wave characteristics. They directed a beam of electrons upon a metal crystal and obtained diffraction rings similar to those produced when light is passed through a pinhole. Their measurements indicated, moreover, that the wavelength of an electron is of the precise magnitude predicted by Schrödinger's equation, λ (lambda) $= h/mv$, where v is the velocity of the electron, m is its mass, and h is Planck's Constant. But further surprises were in store. For subsequent experiments showed that not only electrons but whole atoms and even molecules produce wave patterns when diffracted by a crystal surface, and that their wavelengths are exactly what de Broglie and Schrödinger forecast. And so all the basic units of matter—what J. Clerk Maxwell called "the imperishable foundation stones of the universe"—gradually shed their substance. The old-fashioned spherical electron was reduced to an undulating charge of electrical energy, the atom to a system of superimposed waves. One could only conclude that all matter is made of waves and we live in a universe of waves.

The paradox presented by waves of matter on the one hand and particles of light on the other was resolved by several developments in the decade before World War II. The German physicists, Heisenberg and Born, bridged the gap by developing a new mathematical apparatus that permitted accurate description of quantum phenomena either in terms of waves *or* in terms of particles as one wished. The idea behind their system had a profound influence on the philosophy of science. They maintained it is pointless for a physicist to worry about the properties of a single electron; in the laboratory he works with beams or showers of electrons, each containing billions of individual particles (or waves); he is concerned therefore only with mass behavior, with statistics and the laws of probability and chance. So it makes no practical difference whether individual electrons are particles or systems of waves—in aggregate they can be pictured either way. For example, if two physicists are at the seashore one may analyze a wave by saying, "Its properties and intensity are clearly indicated by the position of its crest and its trough"; while the other may observe with equal accuracy, "The section which you term a crest is significant simply because it contains more molecules of water than the area you call a trough." Analogously Heisenberg and Born took the mathematical expression used by Schrödinger in his equations to denote wave function and interpreted it as a "probability" in a statistical sense. That is to say they regarded the intensity of any part of a wave as a measure of the

probable distribution of particles at that point. And so "waves of matter" were reduced to "waves of probability." It no longer matters how we visualize an electron or an atom or a probability wave. The equations of Heisenberg and Born fit any picture. And we can, if we choose, imagine ourselves living in a universe of waves, a universe of particles, or as one facetious scientist has phrased it, a universe of "wavicles."

IV

While quantum physics thus defines with great accuracy the mathematical relationships governing the basic units of radiation and matter, it further obscures the true nature of both. Most modern physicists, however, consider it rather naïve to speculate about the true nature of anything. They are "positivists" who contend that a scientist can do no more than report his observations. And so if he performs two experiments with different instruments and one seems to reveal that light is made up of particles and the other that light is made up of waves, he must accept both results, regarding them not as contradictory but as complementary. By itself neither concept suffices to explain light, but together they do. Both are necessary to describe reality and it is meaningless to ask which is really true. For in the abstract lexicon of quantum physics there is no such word as "really."

It is futile, moreover, to hope that the invention of more delicate tools may enable man to penetrate much farther into the microcosm. There is an indeterminacy about all the events of the atomic universe which refinements of measurement and observation can never dispel. The element of caprice in atomic behavior cannot be

[899]

blamed on man's coarse-grained implements. It stems from the very nature of things, as shown by Heisenberg in 1927 in a famous statement of physical law known as the "Principle of Uncertainty." To illustrate his thesis Heisenberg pictured an imaginary experiment in which a physicist attempts to observe the position and velocity of a moving electron by using an immensely powerful supermicroscope. Inasmuch as an electron is smaller than a light wave, the physicist can "illuminate" his subject only by using radiation of shorter wavelength. Even X-rays are useless. The electron can be rendered visible only by the high-frequency gamma rays of radium. But the photoelectric effect, it will be recalled, showed that photons of ordinary light exert a violent force on electrons; and X-rays knock them about even more roughly. Hence the impact of a still more potent gamma ray would prove disastrous.

The Principle of Uncertainty asserts therefore that it is absolutely and forever impossible to determine the position and the velocity of an electron at the same time—to state confidently that an electron is "right here at this spot" and is moving at "such and such a speed." For by the very act of observing its position, its velocity is changed. And when the physicist computes the mathematical margin of uncertainty in his measurements of an electron's position and velocity he finds it is always a function of that mysterious quantity—Planck's Constant, h.

Quantum physics thus demolishes two more pillars of the old science, causality and determinism. For by dealing in terms of statistics and probabilities it abandons all idea that nature exhibits an inexorable sequence of cause and effect. And by its admission of margins of uncertainty it yields up the ancient hope that science, given the present condition and velocity of every material body in the universe, can forecast the history of the universe for all time. One byproduct of this surrender is a new argument for the existence of free will. For if physical events are indeterminate and the future is unpredictable, then perhaps the unknown quantity called "mind" may yet guide man's destiny among the infinite uncertainties of a capricious universe. But this notion invades a realm of thought with which the physicist is not concerned. Another conclusion of greater scientific importance is that in the evolution of quantum physics the barrier between man, peering dimly through the clouded windows of his senses, and whatever objective reality may exist has been rendered almost impassable. For whenever he attempts to penetrate and spy on the "real" objective world, he changes and distorts its workings by the very process of his observation. And when he tries to divorce this "real" world from his sense perceptions he is left with nothing but a mathematical scheme. He is indeed somewhat in the position of a blind man trying to discern the shape and texture of a snowflake. As soon as it touches his fingers or his tongue it dissolves. A wave electron, a photon, a wave of probability, cannot be visualized; they are simply symbols useful in expressing the mathematical relationships of the microcosm.

To the question, why does modern physics employ such abstract methods of description, the physicist answers: because the equations of quantum physics define more accurately than any mechanical model the fundamental phenomena beyond the range of vision. In short, *they work,* as the calculations which hatched the atomic bomb spectacularly proved. The aim of the practical physicist, therefore, is to enunciate the laws of nature in ever more precise mathematical terms. Where the nineteenth century physicist envisaged electricity as a fluid and, with this metaphor in mind, evolved the laws that generated our present electrical age, the twentieth century physicist tends to avoid metaphors. He knows that electricity is not a fluid, and he knows that such pictorial concepts as "waves" and "particles," while serving as guideposts to new discovery, must not be accepted as accurate representations of reality. In the abstract language of mathematics he can describe how things behave though he

does not know—or need to know—what they are.

Yet there are present-day physicists for whom the void between science and reality presents a challenge. Einstein has more than once expressed the hope that the statistical method of quantum physics would prove a temporary expedient. "I cannot believe," he says, "that God plays dice with the world." He repudiates the positivist doctrine that science can only report and correlate the results of observation. He believes in a universe of order and harmony. And he believes that questing man may yet attain a knowledge of ultimate reality. To this end he has looked not within the atom, but outward to the stars, and beyond them to the vast drowned depths of empty space and time.

$$_{92}U^{238} + {}_0n^1 \longrightarrow {}_{92}U^{239} + \text{gamma rays}$$

$$_{92}U^{239} \xrightarrow[\text{23 min.}]{} {}_{93}Np^{239} + {}_{-1}e^0$$

$$_{93}Np^{239} \xrightarrow[\text{2.3 days}]{} {}_{94}Pu^{239} + {}_{-1}e^0 + \text{gamma rays}$$

Nagasaki, Japan, under atomic bomb attack

UNITED STATES WAR DEPARTMENT RELEASE
ON NEW MEXICO TEST, JULY 16, 1945

MANKIND'S SUCCESSFUL TRANSITION to a new age, the Atomic Age, was ushered in July 16, 1945, before the eyes of a tense group of renowned scientists and military men gathered in the desertlands of New Mexico to witness the first end results of their $2,000,000,000 effort. Here in a remote section of the Alamogordo Air Base 120 miles southeast of Albuquerque the first man-made atomic explosion, the outstanding achievement of nuclear science, was achieved at 5:30 A.M. of that day. Darkening heavens, pouring forth rain and lightning immediately up to the zero hour, heightened the drama.

Mounted on a steel tower, a revolutionary weapon destined to change war as we know it, or which may even be the instrumentality to end all wars, was set off with an impact which signalized man's entrance into a new physical world. Success was greater than the most ambitious estimates. A small amount of matter, the product of a chain of huge specially constructed industrial plants, was made to release the energy of the universe locked up within the atom from the beginning of time. A fabulous achievement had been reached. Speculative theory, barely established in pre-war laboratories, had been projected into practicality.

This phase of the Atomic Bomb Project, which is headed by Major General Leslie R. Groves, was under the direction of Dr. J. R. Oppenheimer, theoretical physicist of the University of California. He is to be credited with achieving the implementation of atomic energy for military purposes.

Tension before the actual detonation was at a tremendous pitch. Failure was an ever-present possibility. Too great a success, envisoned by some of those present, might have meant an uncontrollable, unusable weapon.

Final assembly of the atomic bomb began on the night of July 12 in an old ranch house. As various component assemblies arrived from distant points, tension among the scientists rose to an increasing pitch. Coolest of all was the man charged with the actual assembly of the vital core, Dr. R. F. Bacher, in normal times a professor at Cornell University.

The entire cost of the project, representing the erection of whole cities and radically new plants spread over many miles of countryside, plus unprecedented experimentation, was represented in the pilot bomb and its parts. Here was the focal point of the venture. No other country in the world had been capable of such an outlay in brains and technical effort.

The full significance of these closing moments before the final factual test was *not* lost on these men of science. They fully knew their position as pioneers into another age. They also knew that one false move would blast them and their entire effort into eternity. Before the assembly started a receipt for the vital matter was signed by Brigadier General Thomas F. Farrell, General Groves' deputy. This signalized the formal transfer of the irreplaceable material from the scientists to the Army.

During final preliminary assembly, a bad few minutes developed when the assembly of an important section of the bomb was delayed. The entire unit was machine-tooled to the finest measurement. The insertion was partially completed

[903]

when it apparently wedged tightly and would go no farther. Dr. Bacher, however, was undismayed and reassured the group that time would solve the problem. In three minutes' time, Dr. Bacher's statement was verified and basic assembly was completed without further incident.

Specialty teams, comprised of the top men on specific phases of science, all of which were bound up in the whole, took over their specialized parts of the assembly. In each group was centralized months and even years of channelized endeavor.

On Saturday, July 14, the unit which was to determine the success or failure of the entire project was elevated to the top of the steel tower. All that day and the next, the job of preparation went on. In addition to the apparatus necessary to cause the detonation, complete instrumentation to determine the pulse beat and all reactions of the bomb was rigged on the tower.

The ominous weather which had dogged the assembly of the bomb had a very sobering effect on the assembled experts whose work was accomplished amid lightning flashes and peals of thunder. The weather, unusual and upsetting, blocked out aerial observation of the test. It even held up the actual explosion scheduled at 4:00 A.M. for an hour and a half. For many months the approximate date and time had been set and had been one of the high-level secrets of the best kept secret of the entire war.

Nearest observation point was set up 10,000 yards south of the tower where in a timber and earth shelter the controls for the test were located. At a point 17,000 yards from the tower at a point which would give the best observation the key figures in the atomic bomb project took their posts. These included General

Groves, Dr. Vannevar Bush, head of the Office of Scientific Research and Development and Dr. James B. Conant, president of Harvard University.

Actual detonation was in charge of Dr. K. T. Bainbridge of Massachusetts Institute of Technology. He and Lieutenant Bush, in charge of the Military Police Detachment, were the last men to inspect the tower with its cosmic bomb.

At three o'clock in the morning the party moved forward to the control station. General Groves and Dr. Oppenheimer consulted with the weathermen. The decision was made to go ahead with the test despite the lack of assurance of favorable weather. The time was set for 5:30 A.M.

General Groves rejoined Dr. Conant and Dr. Bush, and just before the test time they joined the many scientists gathered at the Base Camp. Here all present were ordered to lie on the ground, face downward, heads away from the blast direction.

Tension reached a tremendous pitch in the control room as the deadline approached. The several observation points in the area were tied in to the control room by radio and with twenty minutes to go, Dr. S. K. Allison of Chicago University took over the radio net and made periodic time announcements.

The time signals, "minus 20 minutes, minus fifteen minutes," and on and on increased the tension to the breaking point as the group in the control room which included Dr. Oppenheimer and General Farrell held their breaths, all praying with the intensity of the moment which will live forever with each man who was there. At "minus 45 seconds," robot mechanism took over and from that point on the whole great complicated mass of intricate mechanism was in operation without human control. Stationed at a reserve switch, however, was a soldier scientist ready to attempt to stop the explosion should the order be issued. The order never came.

At the appointed time there was a blinding flash lighting up the whole area brighter than the brightest daylight. A mountain range three miles from the observation point stood out in bold relief. Then came a tremendous sustained roar and a heavy pressure wave which knocked down two men outside the control center. Immediately thereafter, a huge multicolored surging cloud boiled to an altitude of over 40,000 feet. Clouds in its path disappeared. Soon the shifting substratosphere winds dispersed the now gray mass.

The test was over, the project a success.

The steel tower had been entirely vaporized. Where the tower had stood, there was a huge sloping crater. Dazed but relieved at the success of their tests, the scientists promptly marshaled their forces to estimate the strength of America's new weapon. To examine the nature of the crater, specially equipped tanks were wheeled into the area, one of which carried Dr. Enrico Fermi, noted nuclear scientist. Answer to their findings rests in the destruction effected in Japan today in the first military use of the atomic bomb.

Had it not been for the desolated area where the test was held and for the cooperation of the press in the area, it is certain that the test itself would have attracted far-reaching attention. As it was, many people in that area are still discussing the effect of the smash. A significant aspect, recorded by the press, was the experience of a blind girl near Albuquerque many miles from the scene, who, when the flash of the test lighted the sky before the explosion could be heard, exclaimed, "What was that?"

Interviews of General Groves and General Farrell give the following on-the-scene versions of the test. General Groves said: "My impressions of the night's high points follow: After about an hour's sleep I got up at 0100 and from that time on until about five I was with Dr. Oppenheimer constantly. Naturally he was tense, although his mind was working at its usual extraordinary efficiency. I attempted to shield him from the evident concern shown by many of his assistants who were disturbed by the uncertain weather conditions. By 0330 we decided that we could probably fire at 0530. By 0400 the rain had stopped but the sky was heavily overcast. Our decision became firmer as time went on.

"During most of these hours the two of us journeyed from the control house out into the darkness to look at the stars and to assure each other that the one or two visible stars were becoming brighter. At 0510 I left Dr. Oppenheimer and returned to the main observation point which was 17,000 yards from the point of explosion. In accordance with our orders I found all personnel not otherwise occupied massed on a bit of high ground.

"Two minutes before the scheduled firing time, all persons lay face down with their feet pointing towards the explosion. As the remaining time was called from the loud speaker from the 10,000-yard control station there was complete awesome silence. Dr. Conant said he had never imagined seconds could be so long. Most of the individuals in accordance with orders shielded their eyes in one way or another

"First came the burst of light of a brilliance beyond any comparison. We all rolled over and looked through dark glasses at the ball of fire. About forty seconds later came the shock wave followed by the sound, neither of which seemed startling after our complete astonishment at the extraordinary lighting intensity.

"A massive cloud was formed which surged and billowed upward with tremendous power, reaching the substratosphere in about five minutes.

"Two supplementary explosions of minor effect other than the lighting occurred in the cloud shortly after the main explosion.

"The cloud traveled to a great height first in the form of a ball, then mushroomed, then changed into a long trailing chimney-shaped column and finally was sent in several directions by the variable winds at the different elevations.

"Dr. Conant reached over and we shook hands in mutual congratulations. Dr. Bush, who was on the other side of me, did likewise. The feeling of the entire assembly, even the uninitiated, was of profound awe. Drs. Conant and Bush and myself were struck by an even stronger feeling that the faith of those who had been responsible for the initiation and the carrying on of this Herculean project had been justified."

General Farrell's impressions are: "The scene inside the shelter was dramatic beyond words. In and around the shelter were some twenty-odd people concerned with last-minute arrangements. Included were Dr. Oppenheimer, the Director who had borne the great scientific burden of developing the weapon from the raw materials made in Tennessee and Washington, and a dozen of his key assistants, Dr.

Kistiakowsky, Dr. Bainbridge, who supervised all the detailed arrangements for the test; the weather expert, and several others. Besides those, there were a handful of soldiers, two or three Army officers and one Naval officer. The shelter was filled with a great variety of instruments and radios.

"For some hectic two hours preceding the blast, General Groves stayed with the Director. Twenty minutes before the zero hour, General Groves left for his station at the base camp, first, because it provided a better observation point and, second, because of our rule that he and I must not be together in situations where there is an element of danger which existed at both points.

"Just after General Groves left, announcements began to be broadcast of the interval remaining before the blast to the other groups participating in and observing the test. As the time interval grew smaller and changed from minutes to seconds, the tension increased by leaps and bounds. Everyone in that room knew the awful potentialities of the thing that they thought was about to happen. The scientists felt that their figuring must be right and that the bomb had to go off but there was in everyone's mind a strong measure of doubt.

"We were reaching into the unknown and we did not know what might come of it. It can safely be said that most of those present were praying—and praying harder than they had ever prayed before. If the shot were successful, it was a justification of the several years of intensive effort of tens of thousands of people— statesmen, scientists, engineers, manufacturers, soldiers, and many others in every walk of life.

United States War Department Release on New Mexico Test, July 16, 1945

"In that brief instant in the remote New Mexico desert, the tremendous effort of the brains and brawn of all these people came suddenly and startlingly to the fullest fruition. Dr. Oppenheimer, on whom had rested a very heavy burden, grew tenser as the last seconds ticked off. He scarcely breathed. He held on to a post to steady himself. For the last few seconds, he stared directly ahead and then when the announcer shouted 'Now!' and there came this tremendous burst of light followed shortly thereafter by the deep growling roar of the explosion, his face relaxed into an expression of tremendous relief. Several of the observers standing back of the shelter to watch the lighting effects were knocked flat by the blast.

"The tension in the room let up and all started congratulating each other. Everyone sensed 'This is it!' No matter what might happen now all knew that the impossible scientific job had been done. Atomic fission would no longer be hidden in the cloisters of the theoretical physicists' dreams. It was almost full grown at birth. It was a great new force to be used for good or for evil. There was a feeling in that shelter that those concerned with its nativity should dedicate their lives to the mission that it would always be used for good and never for evil.

"Dr. Kistiakowsky threw his arms around Dr. Oppenheimer and embraced him with shouts of glee. Others were equally enthusiastic. All the pent-up emotions were released in those few minutes and all seemed to sense immediately that the explosion had far exceeded the most optimistic expectations and wildest hopes of the scientists. All seemed to feel that they had been present at the birth of a new age—The Age of Atomic Energy— and felt their profound responsibility to help in guiding into right channels the tremendous forces which had been unlocked for the first time in history.

"As to the present war, there was a feeling that no matter what else might happen, we now had the means to insure its speedy conclusion and save thousands of American lives. As to the future, there had been brought into being something big and something new that would prove to be immeasurably more important than the discovery of electricity or any of the other great discoveries which have so affected our existence.

"The effects could well be called unprecedented, magnificent, beautiful, stupendous and terrifying. No man-made phenomenon of such tremendous power had ever occurred before. The lighting effects beggared description. The whole country was lighted by a searing light with the intensity many times that of the midday sun. It was golden, purple, violet, gray and blue. It lighted every peak, crevasse and ridge of the near-by mountain range with a clarity and beauty that cannot be described but must be seen to be imagined. It was that beauty the great poets dream about but describe most poorly and inadequately. Thirty seconds after, the explosion came first, the air blast pressing hard against the people and things, to be followed almost immediately by the strong, sustained, awesome roar which warned of doomsday and made us feel that we puny things were blasphemous to dare tamper with the forces heretofore reserved to the Almighty. Words are inadequate tools for the job of acquainting those not present with the physical, mental and psychological effects. It had to be witnessed to be realized."

[907]

> What matters is not history as history, but human beings.
> ... What now matters is humanity and what will be-
> come of it.
>
> —DEMETRIOS CAPETANAKIS in *Heart of Europe*, p. 285

MODERN MAN IS OBSOLETE

by NORMAN COUSINS

WHATEVER ELATION there is in the world today because of final victory in the war is severely tempered by fear. It is a primitive fear, the fear of the unknown, the fear of forces man can neither channel nor comprehend. This fear is not new; in its classical form it is the fear of irrational death. But overnight it has become intensified, magnified. It has burst out of the sub-conscious and into the conscious, filling the mind with primordial apprehensions. It is thus that man stumbles fitfully into a new age of atomic energy for which he is as ill equipped to accept its potential blessings as he is to counteract or control its present dangers.

Where man can find no answer, he will find fear. While the dust was still settling over Hiroshima, he was asking himself questions and finding no answers. The biggest question of these concerns the nature of man. Is war in the nature of man? If so, how much time has he left before he employs the means he has already devised for the ultimate in self-destruction—extinction? And now that the science of warfare has reached the point where it threatens the planet itself, is it possible that man is destined to return the earth to its aboriginal incandescent mass blazing at fifty million degrees? If not—that is, if war is not in the nature of man—then how is he to interpret his own experience, which tells him that in all of recorded history there have been only 300 years in the aggregate during which he has been free of war?

Closely following upon these are other questions, flowing out endlessly from his fears and without prospect of definitive answer. Even assuming that he could hold destructive science in check, what changes would the new age bring or demand in his everyday life? What changes would it bring or demand in his culture, his education, his philosophy, his religion, his relationships with other human beings?

In speculating upon these questions, it should not be necessary to prove that on August 6, 1945, a new age was born. When on that day a parachute containing a small object floated to earth over Japan, it marked the violent death of one stage in man's history and the beginning of another. Nor should it be necessary to prove the saturating effect of the new age, permeating every aspect of man's activities, from machines to morals, from physics to philosophy, from politics to poetry; in sum, it is an effect creating a blanket of obsolescence not only over the methods and the products of man but over man himself.

It is a curious phenomenon of nature

"Modern Man Is Obsolete," by Norman Cousins, originally appeared as an editorial in *The Saturday Review of Literature*, August 18, 1945, and was later published in expanded, book form by The Viking Press, New York.

that only two species practice the art of war—men and ants, both of which, ironically, maintain complex social organizations. This does not mean that only men and ants engage in the murder of their own kind. Many animals of the same species kill each other, but only men and ants have practiced the science of organized destruction, employing their massed numbers in violent combat and relying on strategy and tactics to meet developing situations or, to capitalize on the weaknesses in the strategy and tactics of the other side. The longest continuous war ever fought between men lasted thirty years. The longest ant war ever recorded last six-and-a-half weeks, or whatever the corresponding units would be in ant reckoning.

It is encouraging to note that while all entomologists are agreed that war is instinctive with ants, not all anthropologists and biologists are agreed that war is instinctive with men. The strict empiricists, of course, find everything in man's history to indicate that war is locked up with his nature. But a broader and more generous, certainly more philosophical, view is held by those scientists who claim that the evidence to date is incomplete and misleading, and that man *does* have within him the power of abolishing war. Prominent among these is Julian Huxley, who draws a sharp distinction between human nature and the *expression* of human nature. Thus war is not a reflection but an expression of his nature. Moreover, the expression may change, as the factors which lead to war may change. "In man, as in ants, war in any serious sense is bound up with the existence of accumulations of property to fight about. . . . As for human nature, it contains no specific war instinct, as does the nature of harvester ants. There is in man's makeup a general aggressive tendency, but

this, like all other human urges, is not a specific and unvarying instinct; it can be molded into the most varied forms."

But even if this gives us a reassuring answer to the question—is war inevitable because of man's nature?—it still leaves unanswered the question concerning the causes leading up to war. The expression of man's nature will continue to be warlike if the same conditions are continued that have provoked warlike expressions in him in the past. And since man's survival on earth is now absolutely dependent on his ability to avoid a new war, he is faced with the so-far insoluble problem of eliminating those causes.

In the most primitive sense, war in man is an expression of his competitive impulses. Like everything else in nature, he has had to fight for existence; but the battle against other animals, once won, gave way in his evolution to battle against his own kind. Darwin called it the survival of the fittest, and its most overstretched interpretation is to be found in "Mein Kampf," with its naked glorification of brute force and the complete worship of might makes right. In the political and national sense, it has been the attempt of the "have-nots" to take from the "haves," or the attempt of the "haves" to add further to their lot at the expense of the "have-nots." Not always was property at stake; comparative advantages were measured in terms of power, and in terms of tribal or national superiority. The good luck of one nation became the hard luck of another. The good fortune of the Western powers in obtaining "concessions" in China at the turn of the century was the ill fortune of the Chinese. The power that Germany stripped from Austria, Czechoslovakia, Poland, and France at the beginning of World War II she added to her own.

What does it matter, then, if war is not in the nature of man so long as man continues through the expression of his nature to be a viciously competitive animal? The effect is the same, and therefore the result must be as conclusive—war being the effect, and complete obliteration of the human species being the result.

If this reasoning is correct, then modern man is obsolete, a self-made anachronism becoming more incongruous by the minute. He has exalted change in everything but himself. He has leaped centuries ahead in inventing a new world to live in, but he knows little or nothing about his own part in that world. He has surrounded and confounded himself with gaps—gaps between revolutionary science and evolutionary anthropology, between cosmic gadgets and human wisdom, between intellect and conscience. The struggle between science and morals that Henry Thomas Buckle foresaw a century ago has been all but won by science. Given time, man might be expected to bridge those gaps normally; but by his own hand, he is destroying even time. Communication, transportation, war no longer wait on time. Decision and execution in the modern world are becoming virtually synchronous. Thus, whatever bridges man has to build and cross he shall have to build and cross immediately.

This involves both biology and will. If he lacks the actual and potential biological equipment to build those bridges, then the birth certificate of the atomic age is in reality a *memento mori*. But even if he possesses the necessary biological equipment, he must still make the decision which says that he is to apply himself to the challenge. Capability without decision is inaction and inconsequence.

Man is left, then, with a crisis in decision. The main test before him involves his will to change rather than his ability to change. That he is capable of change is certain. For there is no more mutable or adaptable animal in the world. We have seen him migrate from one extreme clime to another. We have seen him step out of backward societies and join advanced groups. We have seen, within the space of a single generation, tribes of headhunters spurn their acephalous pastimes and rituals and become purveyors of the Western arts. This is not to imply that the change was necessarily for the better; only that change was possible. Changeability with the headhunters proceeded from external pressure and fear of punishment, true, and was only secondarily a matter of voluntary decision. But the stimulus was there; and mankind today need look no further for stimulus than its own desire to stay alive. The critical power of change, says Spengler, is directly linked to the survival drive. Once the instinct for survival is stimulated, the basic condition for change can be met.

That is why the quintessence of destruction as potentially represented by modern science must be dramatized and kept in the forefront of public opinion. The full dimensions of the peril must be seen and recognized. Then and only then will man realize that the first order of business is the question of continued existence. Then and only then will he be prepared to make the decisions necessary to assure that survival.

In making these decisions, there are two principal courses that are open to him. Both will keep him alive for an indefinite or at least a reasonably long period. These courses, however, are directly contradictory and represent polar extremes of approach.

The first course is the positive approach. It begins with a careful survey and appraisal of the obsolescences which constitute the afterbirth of the new age. The survey must begin with man himself. "The proper study of Mankind is Man," said Pope. No amount of tinkering with his institutions will be sufficient to insure his survival unless he can make the necessary adjustments in his own relationship to the world and to society.

The first adjustment or mutation needed in the expression of his nature, to use Huxley's words, is his savagely competitive impulses. In the pre-Atomic Age, those impulses were natural and occasionally justifiable, though they often led to war. But the rise of materialistic man had reasons behind it and must be viewed against its natural setting. Lyell, Spencer, Darwin, Lamarck, Malthus, and others have concerned themselves with various aspects of this natural setting, but its dominant feature was an insufficiency of the goods and the needs of life. From Biblical history right up through the present, there was never time when starvation and economic suffering were not acute somewhere in the world.

This is only part of the story, of course, for it is dangerous to apply an economic interpretation indiscriminately to all history. Politics, religion, force for force's sake, jealousy, ambition, love of conquest, love of reform—all these and others have figured in the equations of history and war. But the economic factor was seldom if ever absent, even when it was not the prime mover. Populations frequently increased more rapidly than available land, goods, or wealth. Malthus believed that they increased so rapidly at times that war or plague became nature's safety valve. This interpretation has undergone some revision, but it is not the interpretation but the circumstances that raises the problem.

Yet all this has been—or can be—changed by the new age. Man now has it within his grasp to emancipate himself economically. If he wills it, he is in a position to refine his competitive impulse; he can take the step from competitive man to co-operative man. He has at last unlocked enough of the earth's secrets to provide for his needs on a world scale. The same atomic and electrical energy that can destroy a city can also usher in an age of economic sufficiency. It need no longer be a question as to which peoples shall prosper and which shall be deprived. There is power enough and resources enough for all.

It is here that man's survey of himself needs the severest scrutiny, for he is his own greatest obstacle to the achievement of those attainable and necessary goals. While he is willing to mobilize all his scientific and intellectual energies for purposes of death, he is unwilling to undertake any comparable mobilization for purposes of life. He has shattered the atom and harnessed its fabulous power to a bomb, but he balks—or allows himself to be balked—when it comes to harnessing that power for human progress. Already, many representatives of industry have counseled words of synthetic caution, informing a puzzled public that we shall not see the practical application of atomic energy for general use in our lifetime. If it works out this way, it will not be because of any lack of knowledge or skill, but only because of the fear in certain quarters that atomic energy will mean a complete revamping of the economic structure, with the probability that it would be operated as a government utility or public service.

This is not a matter of urging a change

away from the present economic structure just for the sake of change; it is recognition of a hard new fact of life that has made that economic structure obsolete in an Atomic Age just as it has made practically all our other institutions obsolete.

The cry is certain to go up against further government experimentation with atomic energy for peacetime purposes, and industry will demand that government withdraw and give it the right to carry on its own experiments. These experiments, however, would most likely be no more consequential than the atomic bomb would have been if left to decentralized chance. Moreover, it takes enthusiasm to fertilize invention, and there is as yet little discernible enthusiasm for atomic energy in those quarters which are asking for the right to sponsor its peace-time uses. However understandable this lack of enthusiasm may be, it should not blind public opinion to the critical importance of having research for practical use carried on with the same urgency, the same fullness, the same scope and intensity as it has been for war ends thus far.

The size of the opportunity is exceeded only by the size of the promise. But even as man stands on the threshold of a new age, he is being pulled back by his coattails and told to look the other way, told that he must not allow his imagination to get out of hand—all this at a time when he should know almost instinctively that if he can put the same courage, daring, imagination, ingenuity, and skill that he demonstrated in winning the war into meeting the problems of the new age, he can win the peace as well.

He must believe, too, that mobilization of science and knowledge in peace should not be confined to cosmic forces, but must be extended to his other needs, principally health. What a fantastic irony that organized science knows the secret of the atom but as yet knows not a fig about the common cold! Who can tell what advances in medical knowledge might accrue to the welfare of mankind if as much mobilized effort were put into the study of man as there has been of matter! Cancer, heart disease, nephritis, leukemia, encephalitis, poliomyelitis, arteriosclerosis, aplastic anemia—all these are anomalies in the modern world; there is no reason why mobilized research should not be directed at their causes and cure. Nor is there any reason why even old age should not be regarded as a disease to be attacked by science in the same intensive fashion.

Surveying other adjustments he shall have to make if he chooses the positive course, man must consider himself in relation to his individual development. He can have the limitless opportunities that can come with time to think. The trend during the last fifty years towards shorter work weeks and shorter hours will not only be continued but sharply accelerated. Not more than half of each week will be spent earning a living. But a revolution is needed in his leisure-time activities—which so far have come to be associated almost entirely with the commodities of vended amusement. Once before, the world knew a Golden Age where the development of the individual—his mind and his body—was considered the first law of life. In Greece, it took the form of the revolution of awareness, the emancipation of the intellect from the limitations of corroding ignorance and prejudice.

Once again, if man wills it, he can be in a position to restore that first law of life. But he shall have to effect a radical transformation in his approach to and philosophy of education, which must prepare him for the opportunities and responsibilities not only of his chosen work but for the business of living itself. The primary aim should be the development of a critical intelligence. The futile war now going on between specialization and general study must be stopped. There need no longer be any conflict between the two. The individual will need both—specialization for the requirements of research, general knowledge for the requirements of living. As for the problem of time in which to accomplish these dual objectives, formalized education until the twenty-fifth or thirtieth year is doubtless indicated; but it should not abruptly end there. Education, like the capacity of the mind itself, has no rigid boundaries. Unlimited exploration should be the first imperative of any educational program.

We have saved for last the most crucial aspect of this general survey relating to the first course: the transformation or adjustment from national man to world man. Already he has become a world warrior; it is but one additional step—though a long one—for him to develop a world conscience. This is not vaporous idealism, but sheer driving necessity. It bears directly on the prospects of his own survival. He shall have to recognize the flat truth that the greatest obsolescence of all in the Atomic Age is national sovereignty. Even back in the old-fashioned rocket age before August 6, 1945, strict national sovereignty was an anomalous and preposterous hold-over from the tribal instinct in nations. If it was anomalous then, it is the quintessence of anomaly now. The world is a geographic entity. This is not only the basic requisite for world government but the basic reason behind the need. A common ground of destiny is not too large a site for the founding of any community.

Reject all other arguments for *real* world government—reject the economic, the ideological, the sociological, the humanitarian arguments, valid though they may be. Consider only the towering problem of policing the atom—the problem of keeping the smallest particle of matter from destroying all matter. We are building on soapbubbles if we expect this problem to be automatically solved by having America, Britain, and Canada keep the secret to themselves. That is not only highly improbable, but would in itself stimulate the other nations to undertake whatever additional research might be necessary over their present experimentation to yield the desired results. In all history, there is not a single instance of a new weapon being kept exclusively by any power or powers; sooner or later either the basic principles become generally known or parallel devices are invented. Before long, the atomic bomb will follow the jet plane, the rocket bomb, radar, and the flame thrower into general circulation. We must not forget that we were not the only horse in the atomic derby; we just happened to finish first. The others will be along in due time.

Nor can we rely on destructive atomic energy to take care of itself. Already there is the tempting but dangerous notion to the effect that the atomic bomb is so horrible and the terror of retaliation so great that we may have seen the last of war. This is quasi-logical, but war is no respecter of logic, relative or absolute. And if history teaches us anything, it is that the possibility of war increases in direct proportion to the effectiveness of the instruments of war.

Far from banishing war, the atomic bomb will in itself constitute a cause of war. In the absence of world control as part of world government, it will create universal fear and suspicion. Each nation will live nervously from one moment to the next, not knowing whether the designs or ambitions of other nations might prompt them to attempt a lightning blow of obliteration. The ordinary, the inevitable differences among nations which might in themselves be susceptible of solution might now become the signals for direct action, lest the other nation get in the first and decisive blow. Since the science of warfare will no longer be dependent upon armies but will be waged by push-buttons, releasing radio-controlled rocket planes carrying cargoes of atomic explosives, the slightest suspicion may start all the push-buttons going.

There is the argument, of course, that each nation will realize this; that is, that the first button might lead to universal catastrophe as all the other nations rush to their switchboards of annihilation. Here, too, there is the unwarranted presupposition of reason. In an atmosphere of high tension and suspicion, reason is an easy victim. Moreover, there will always be the feeling that one nation can escape though all the others may go down. What a temptation for the blitzkriegers!

No; there is no comfort to be derived from the war-is-now-too-horrible theory. There is one way and only one to achieve effective control of destructive atomic energy and that is through centralized world government. Not loose, informal organization. Not even through an international pool, or through an international policing agreement. A police force is no better than its laws, and there can be no laws without government. Finally, the potency of the weapon must dictate the potency of its control.

There is no need to discuss the historical reasons pointing to and arguing for world government. There is no need to talk of the difficulties in the way of world government. There is need only to ask whether we can afford to do without it. All other considerations become either secondary or inconsequential.

It would be comforting to know that the world had several generations in which it might be able to evolve naturally and progressively into a single governmental unit. In fact, even as late as August 5, 1945, it seemed that the Charter of the United Nations had made an adequate beginning in that direction, providing the machinery for revision which might lead within fifteen or twenty years to a real world structure. But the time factor has been shattered. We no longer have a leeway of fifteen or twenty years; whatever must be done must be done with an immediacy which is in keeping with the urgency. Once the basic peace settlements are arranged, the United Nations must convene again for an Atomic Age inventory, undertaking an overall examination of the revolutionary changes in the world since its conference in San Francisco in the long-ago spring of 1945.

If all this sounds like headlong argument, posing methods or solutions which seem above the reach of mortal man, the answer must be that mortal man's reach was long enough apparently to push science and invention ahead by at least five hundred years during five years of experimentation on atomic energy. His ability to do this not only indicates that he can extend or over-extend himself when pressed, but emphasizes the need to do the same with government.

In meeting this need, man need not be frightened by the enormity of the differences which shall have to be accommodated within the world structure. We can agree with Macneile Dixon in "The Human Situation," that "Many are the races and many the temperaments. There are vehement and hot-headed men, selfless and conciliatory men. They display, varying as they do in appearance, talents, behavior, every type of unpredictable reaction to their surroundings. There are sybarites and ascetics, dreamers and bustling active men of affairs, clever and stupid, worldly and religious, mockers and mystics, pugnacious, loyal, cunning, treacherous, cheerful and melancholy men. There are eagles among them, tigers, doves, and serpents. 'He was a comedian on the stage,' said the wife of a celebrated funny man, 'but a tragedian in the home.'" All these differences are in addition to those of ideology, politics, and geography.

And yet, it is not in spite of these variations but because of them that man is now in need of a general amalgam. If those variations did not exist, if man's actions were uniform and uniformly predictable, then man would be as free of war as the vegetable kingdom. The differences point up the problem, not the problem the differences. The important question is not how great an obstacle the differences may be to the setting up of a closely knit world structure, but whether man will be in a better position to reconcile those differences within world government than without it.

Man must decide, moreover, what is more important—his differences or his similarities. If he chooses the former, he embarks on a path that will, paradoxically, destroy the differences and himself as well. If he chooses the latter, he shows a willingness to meet the responsibilities that go with maturity and conscience. Though heterogeneity is the basic manifestation of nature. as Spencer observed, a still greater manifestation is the ability of nature to create larger areas of homogeneity which act as a sort of rim to the spokes of the human wheel.

True, in making the jump to world government, man is taking a big chance. Not only does he have to create the first world authority, but he shall have to make sure that this authority is wisely used. The world institution must be compatible with —indeed, must promote—free institutions. This challenge is not less important than the challenge to establish world government itself, for all through history there has been too great a contradiction between ideals and institutions and the forces which have taken over those ideals and institutions. Another way of saying this is that we have too often allowed the best ideas to fall into the hands of the worst men. There has not been a great ideal or idea which has not been perverted or exploited at one time or another by those who were looking for means to an end—the end being seldom compatible with the idea itself. The greatest idea ever to be taken up by the mind of man—Christianity—was for centuries violated and corrupted by its very administrators. Alexander's vision of a brotherhood of man fell victim to its own force—force based on might makes right. Mohammed dreamed of a universal religion based on the noblest of ethics, and taught that conversion by the sword was no conversion at all; yet his followers built an empire largely at the point of the sword. Passing from religion to politics, we have only to consider the immediate past. It was in the name of socialism and social progress that Fascism came to Italy and Nazism to Germany.

That is the double nature of the challenge: to bring about world government and to keep it pure. It is a large order, perhaps the largest order man has had to meet in his 50,000-odd years on earth, but he himself has set up the conditions which have made the order necessary.

All these are the various mutations and adjustments needed in the expression of man's nature, in his way of life, his thinking, his economics, his education, his conditioning and orientation, and his concept of government in an Atomic Age. But if he rejects this, the first course, there is yet another way, an alternative to world government. This is the second course. Preposterous as this second course may seem, we describe it in all seriousness, for it is possible that through it man may find a way to stay alive—which is the central problem under consideration in this paper.

The second course is relatively simple. It requires that man destroy, carefully and completely, everything relating to science and civilization. Let him destroy all machines and the knowledge which can build or operate those machines. Let him raze his cities, smash his laboratories, dismantle his factories, tear down his universities and schools, burn his libraries, rip apart his art. Let him murder his scientists, his doctors, his teachers, his lawmakers, his mechanics, his merchants, and anyone who has anything to do with the machinery of knowledge or progress. Let him punish literacy by death. Let him abolish nations and set up the tribe as sovereign. In short, let him revert to his condition in society in 10,000 B.C. Thus emancipated from science, from progress, from government, from knowledge, from thought, he can be reasonably certain of safeguarding his existence on this planet.

This is the alternative to world government—if modern man wishes an alternative.

THE PRIMITIVE AND THE TECHNICAL

by José Ortega y Gasset

IT IS MUCH to my purpose to recall that we are here engaged in the analysis of a situation—the actual one—which is of its essence ambiguous. Hence I suggested at the start that all the features of the present day, and in particular the rebellion of the masses, offer a double aspect. Any one of them not only admits of, but requires, a double interpretation, favorable and unfavorable. And this ambiguity lies, not in our minds, but in the reality itself. It is not that the present situation may appear to us good from one viewpoint, and evil from another, but that in itself it contains the twin potencies of triumph or of death.

There is no call to burden this essay with

From *The Revolt of the Masses* by José Ortega y Gasset. Published by W. W. Norton & Company, Inc.

a complete philosophy of history. But it is evident that I am basing it on the underlying foundation of my own philosophical convictions. I do not believe in the absolute determinism of history. On the contrary, I believe that all life, and consequently the life of history, is made up of simple moments, each of them relatively undetermined in respect of the previous one, so that in it reality hesitates, walks up and down, and is uncertain whether to decide for one or other of various possibilities. It is this metaphysical hesitancy which gives to everything living its unmistakable character of tremulous vibration. The rebellion of the masses *may,* in fact, be the transition to some new, unexampled organization of humanity, but it *may* also be a catastrophe of human destiny. There is no reason to deny the reality of progress, but there is to correct the notion that believes this progress secure. It is more in accordance with facts to hold that there is no certain progress, no evolution, without the threat of "involution," of retrogression. Everything is possible in history; triumphant, indefinite progress equally with periodic retrogression. For life, individual or collective, personal or historic, is the one entity in the universe whose substance is compact of danger, of adventure. It is, in the strict sense of the word, drama.[1]

This, which is true in general, acquires greater force in "moments of crisis" such as the present. And so, the symptoms of new conduct which are appearing under the actual dominion of the masses, and which we have grouped under the term "direct action," *may* also announce future perfections. It is evident that every old civilization drags with it in its advance worn-out tissues and no small load of callous matter, which form an obstacle to life, mere toxic dregs. There are dead institutions, valuations and estimates which still survive, though now meaningless, unnecessarily complicated solutions, standards whose lack of substance has been proved. All these constituents of "indirect action," of civilization, demand a period of feverish simplification. The tall hat and frock-coat of the romantic period are avenged by means of present-day *déshabillé* and "shirt-sleeves." Here, the simplification means hygiene and better taste, consequently a more perfect solution, as always happens when more is obtained by smaller means. The tree of romantic love also was badly in need of pruning in order to shed the abundance of imitation magnolias tacked on to its branches and the riot of creepers, spirals, and tortuous ramifications which deprived it of the sun.

In general, public life and above all politics, urgently needed to be brought back to reality, and European humanity could not turn the somersault which the optimist demands of it, without first taking off its

[1] Needless to say, hardly anyone will take seriously these expressions, and even the best-intentioned will understand them as mere metaphors, though perhaps striking ones. Only an odd reader, ingenuous enough not to believe that he already knows definitively what life is, or at least what it is not, will allow himself to be won over by the primary meaning of these phrases, and will be precisely the one who will *understand* them—be they true or false. Amongst the rest there will reign the most effusive unanimity, with this solitary difference: some will think that, *speaking seriously,* life is the process of existence of a soul, and others that it is a succession of chemical reactions. I do not conceive that it will improve my position with readers so hermetically sealed to resume my whole line of thought by saying that the *primary, radical* meaning of life appears when it is employed in the sense not of biology, but of biography. For the very strong reason that the whole of biology is quite definitely only a chapter in certain biographies, it is what biologists do in the portion of their lives open to biography. Anything else is abstraction, fantasy and myth.

clothes, getting down to its bare essence, returning to its real self. The enthusiasm which I feel for this discipline of stripping oneself bare, of being one's real self, the belief that it is indispensable in order to clear the way to a worthy future, leads me to claim full liberty of thought with regard to everything in the past. It is the future which must prevail over the past, and from it we take our orders regarding our attitude towards what has been.[2]

But it is necessary to avoid the great sin of those who directed the XIXth Century, the lack of recognition of their responsibilities which prevented them from keeping alert and on the watch. To let oneself slide down the easy slope offered by the course of events and to dull one's mind against the extent of the danger, the unpleasant features which characterize even the most joyous hour, that is precisely to fail in one's obligation of responsibility. Today it has become necessary to stir up an exaggerated sense of responsibility in those capable of feeling it, and it seems of supreme urgency to stress the evidently dangerous aspect of present-day symptoms.

There is no doubt that on striking a balance of our public life the adverse factors far outweigh the favorable ones, if the calculation be made not so much in regard to the present, as to what they announce and promise for the future.

All the increased material possibilities which life has experienced run the risk of being annulled when they are faced with the staggering problem that has come upon the destiny of Europe, and which I

once more formulate: the direction of society has been taken over by a type of man who is not interested in the principles of civilization. Not of this or that civilization but—from what we can judge today—of any civilization. Of course, he is interested in anesthetics, motor-cars, and a few other things. But this fact merely confirms his fundamental lack of interest in civilization. For those things are merely its products, and the fervor with which he greets them only brings into stronger relief his indifference to the principles from which they spring. It is sufficient to bring forward this fact: since the *nuove scienze,* the natural sciences, came into being—from the Renaissance on, that is to say—the enthusiasm for them had gone on increasing through the course of time. To put it more concretely, the proportionate number of people who devoted themselves to pure scientific research was in each generation greater. The first case of retrogression—relative, I repeat—has occurred in the generation of those between twenty and thirty at the present time. It is becoming difficult to attract students to the laboratories of pure science. And this is happening when industry is reaching its highest stage of development, and when people in general are showing still greater appetite for the use of the apparatus and the medicines created by science. If we did not wish to avoid prolixity, similar incongruity could be shown in politics, art, morals, religion, and in the everyday activities of life.

What is the significance to us of so paradoxical a situation? This essay is an at-

---

[2] This freedom of attitude towards the past is not, then, a peevish revolt, but, on the contrary, an evident obligation, on the part of every "period of criticism." If I defend the liberalism of the XIXth Century against the masses which rudely attack it, this does not mean that I renounce my full freedom of opinion as regards that same liberalism. And vice versa, the primitivism which in this essay appears in its worst aspect is in a certain sense a condition of every great historic advance. Compare what, a few years ago, I said on this matter in the essay "Biología y Pedagogía" (*El Espectador,* III, *La paradoja del salvajismo*).

tempt to prepare the answer to that question. The meaning is that the type of man dominant today is a primitive one, a *Naturmensch* rising up in the midst of a civilized world. The world is a civilized one, its inhabitant is not: he does not see the civilization of the world around him, but he uses it as if it were a natural force. The new man wants his motor-car, and enjoys it, but he believes that it is the spontaneous fruit of an Edenic tree. In the depths of his soul he is unaware of the artificial, almost incredible, character of civilization, and does not extend his enthusiasm for the instruments to the principles which make them possible. When some pages back, by a transposition of the words of Rathenau, I said that we are witnessing the "vertical invasion of the barbarians" it might be thought (it generally is) that it was only a matter of a "phrase." It is now clear that the expression may enshrine a truth or an error, but that it is the very opposite of a "phrase," namely: a formal definition which sums up a whole complicated analysis. The actual mass-man is, in fact, a primitive who has slipped through the wings onto the age-old stage of civilization.

There is continual talk today of the fabulous progress of technical knowledge; but I see no signs in this talk, even amongst the best, of a sufficiently dramatic realization of its future. Spengler himself, so subtle and profound—though so subject to mania—appears to me in this matter far too optimistic. For he believes that "culture" is to be succeeded by an era of "civilization," by which word he understands more especially technical efficiency. The idea that Spengler has of "culture" and of history in general is so remote from that underlying this essay, that it is not easy, even for the purpose of correction, to comment here upon his conclusions. It is only by taking great leaps and neglecting exact details, in order to bring both viewpoints under a common denominator, that it is possible to indicate the difference between us. Spengler believes that "technicism" can go on living when interest in the principles underlying culture are dead. I cannot bring myself to believe any such thing. Technicism and science are consubstantial, and science no longer exists when it ceases to interest for itself alone, and it cannot so interest unless men continue to feel enthusiasm for the general principles of culture. If this fervor is deadened—as appears to be happening—technicism can only survive for a time, for the duration of the inertia of the cultural impulse which started it. We live with our technical requirements, but not *by* them. These give neither nourishment nor breath to themselves, they are not *causae sui,* but a useful, practical precipitate of superfluous, unpractical activities.[3] I proceed, then, to the position that the actual interest in technical accomplishment guarantees nothing, less than nothing, for the progress or the duration of such accomplishment. It is quite right that technicism should be considered one of the characteristic features of "modern culture," that is to say, of a culture which comprises a species of science which proves materially profitable. Hence, when describing the newest aspect of the existence implanted by the XIXth Century, I was left with these two features: liberal democracy

[3] Hence, to my mind, a definition of North America by its "technicism" tells us nothing. One of the things that most seriously confuse the European mind is the mass of puerile judgments that one hears pronounced on North America even by the most cultured persons. This is one particular case of the disproportion which I indicate later on as existing between the complexity of present-day problems and the capacity of present-day minds.

and technicism. But I repeat that I am astonished at the ease with which when speaking of technicism it is forgotten that its vital center is pure science, and that the conditions for its continuance involve the same conditions that render possible pure scientific activity. Has any thought been given to the number of things that must remain active in men's souls in order that there may still continue to be "men of science" in real truth? Is it seriously thought that as long as there are dollars there will be science? This notion in which so many find rest is only a further proof of primitivism. As if there were not numberless ingredients, of most disparate nature, to be brought together and shaken up in order to obtain the cocktail of physico-chemical science! Under even the most perfunctory examination of this subject, the evident fact bursts into view that over the whole extent of space and time, physico-chemistry has succeeded in establishing itself completely only in the small quadrilateral enclosed by London, Berlin, Vienna, and Paris, and that only in the XIXth Century. This proves that experimental science is one of the most unlikely products of history. Seers, priests, warriors and shepherds have abounded in all times and places. But this fauna of experimental man apparently requires for its production a combination of circumstances more exceptional than those that engender the unicorn. Such a bare, sober fact should make us reflect a little on the supervolatile, evaporative character of scientific inspiration.[4] Blissful the man who believes that, were Europe to disappear, the North Americans could *continue* science! It would be of great value to treat the matter thoroughly and to specify in detail what are the historical presuppositions, vital to experimental science and, consequently, to technical accomplishment. But let no one hope that, even when this point was made clear, the mass-man would understand. The mass-man has no attention to spare for reasoning, he learns only in his own flesh.

There is one observation which bars me from deceiving myself as to the efficacy of such preachments, which by the fact of being based on reason would necessarily be subtle. Is it not altogether absurd that, under actual circumstances, the average man does not feel spontaneously, and without being preached at, an ardent enthusiasm for those sciences and the related ones of biology? For, just consider what the actual situation is. While evidently all the other constituents of culture—politics, art, social standards, morality itself—have become problematic, there is one which increasingly demonstrates, in a manner most indisputable and most suitable to impress the mass-man, its marvelous efficiency: and that one is empirical science. Every day furnishes a new invention which this average man utilizes. Every day produces a new anesthetic or vaccine from which this average man benefits. Everyone knows that, if scientific inspiration does not weaken and the laboratories are multiplied three times or ten times, there will be an automatic multiplication of wealth, comfort, health, prosperity. Can any more formidable, more convincing propaganda be imagined in favor of a vital principle? How is it, nevertheless, that there is no sign of the masses imposing on themselves any sacrifice of money or attention in order

---

[4] This, without speaking of more internal questions. The majority of the investigators themselves have not today the slightest suspicion of the very grave and dangerous internal crisis through which their science is passing.

to endow science more worthily? Far from this being the case, the post-war period has converted the man of science into a new social pariah. And note that I am referring to physicists, chemists, biologists, not to philosophers. Philosophy needs neither protection, attention nor sympathy from the masses. It maintains its character of complete inutility,[5] and thereby frees itself from all subservience to the average man. It recognizes itself as essentially problematic, and joyously accepts its free destiny as a bird of the air, without asking anybody to take it into account, without recommending or defending itself. If it does really turn out to the advantage of anyone, it rejoices from simple human sympathy; but does not live on the profit it brings to others, neither anticipating it nor hoping for it. How can it lay claim to being taken seriously by anyone if it starts off by doubting its own existence, if it lives only in the measure in which it combats itself, deprives itself of life? Let us, then, leave out of the question philosophy, which is an adventure of another order. But the experimental sciences do need the co-operation of the mass-man, just as he needs them, under pain of dissolution, inas much as in a planet without physico-chemistry the number of beings existing today cannot be sustained.

What arguments can bring about something which has not been brought about by the motor-car in which those men come and go, and the pantopon injection which destroys, *miraculously,* their pains? The disproportion between the constant, evident benefit which science procures them and the interest they show in it is such that it is impossible today to deceive oneself with illusory hopes and to expect anything but barbarism from those who so behave. *Especially if, as we shall see, this disregard of science as such appears, with possibly more evidence than elsewhere, in the mass of technicians themselves—doctors, engineers, etc.,* who are in the habit of exercising their profession in a state of mind identical in all essentials to that of the man who is content to use his motor-car or buy his tube of aspirin—without the slightest intimate solidarity with the future of science, of civilization.

There may be those who feel more disturbed by other symptoms of emergent barbarism which, being positive in quality, results of action and not of omission, strike the attention more, materialize into a spectacle. For myself, this matter of the disproportion between the profit which the average man draws from science and the gratitude which he returns—or, rather, does not return—to it; this is much more terrifying.[6] I can only succeed in explaining to myself this absence of adequate recognition by recalling that in Central Africa the Negroes also ride in motor-cars and dose themselves with aspirin. The European who is beginning to predominate—so runs my hypothesis—must then be, *in relation to the complex civilization into which he has been born,* a primitive man, a barbarian appearing on the stage through the trap-door, a "vertical invader."

[5] Aristotle, *Metaphysics,* 893*a*. 10.

[6] The monstrosity is increased a hundredfold by the fact that, as I have indicated, all the other vital principles, politics, law, art, morals, religion, are actually passing through a crisis, are at least temporarily bankrupt. Science alone is not bankrupt; rather does it every day pay out, with fabulous interest, all and more than it promises. It is, then, without a competitor; it is impossible to excuse the average man's disregard of it by considering him distracted from it by some other cultural enthusiasm.

AN OUTLINE OF SCIENTISTS

by JAMES THURBER

HAVING BEEN LAID UP by a bumblebee for a couple of weeks, I ran through the few old novels there were in the cottage I had rented in Bermuda and finally was reduced to reading "The Outline of Science, a Plain Story Simply Told," in four volumes. These books were published by Putnam's fifteen years ago and were edited by J. Arthur Thomson, Regius Professor of Natural History at the University of Aberdeen. The volumes contained hundreds of articles written by various scientists and over eight hundred illustrations, forty of which, the editor bragged on the flyleaf, were in color. A plain story simply told with a lot of illustrations, many of them in color, seemed just about the right mental fare for a man who had been laid up by a bee. Human nature being what it is, I suppose the morbid reader is more interested in how I happened to be laid up by a bee than in what I found in my scientific research, so I will dismiss that unfortunate matter in a few words. The bee stung me in the foot and I got an infection (staphylococcus, for short). It was the first time in my life that anything smaller than a turtle had ever got the best of me, and naturally I don't like to dwell on it. I prefer to go on to my studies in "The Outline of Science," if everybody is satisfied.

I happened to pick up Volume IV first, and was presently in the midst of a plain and simple explanation of the Einstein theory, a theory about which in my time I have done as much talking as the next man, although I admit now that I never understood it very clearly. I understood it even less clearly after I had tackled a little problem about a man running a hundred-yard dash and an aviator in a plane above him. Everything, from the roundness of the earth to the immortality of the soul, has been demonstrated by the figures of men in action, but here was a new proposition. It seems that if the aviator were traveling as fast as light, the stop watch held by the track judge would not, from the aviator's viewpoint, move at all. (You've got to make believe that the aviator could see the watch, which is going to be just as hard for you as it was for me.) You might think that this phenomenon of the unmoving watch hand would enable the runner to make a hundred yards in nothing flat, but, if so, you are living in a fool's paradise. To an aviator going as fast as light, the hundred-yard track would shrink to nothing at all. If the aviator were going *twice* as fast as light, the report of the track judge's gun would wake up the track judge, who would still be in bed in his pajamas, not yet having got up to go to the track meet. This last is my own private extension of the general theory, but it seems to me as sound as the rest of it.

I finally gave up the stop watch and the airplane, and went deeper into the chapter till I came to the author's summary of a scientific romance called "Lumen," by the celebrated French astronomer, M. Flammarion (in my youth, the Hearst Sunday feature sections leaned heavily on M. Flammarion's discoveries). The great man's lurid little romance deals, it seems, with a man who died in 1864 and whose soul

From *Let Your Mind Alone,* by James Thurber. Harper & Brothers. Reprinted by permission of Mr. Thurber.

flew with the speed of thought to one of the stars in the constellation Capella. This star was so far from the earth that it took light rays seventy-two years to get there, hence the man's soul kept catching up with light rays from old historical events and passing them. Thus the man's soul was able to see the battle of Waterloo, fought backward. First the man's soul— oh, let's call him Mr. Lumen—first Mr. Lumen saw a lot of dead soldiers and then he saw them get up and start fighting. "Two hundred thousand corpses, come to life, marched off the field in perfect order," wrote M. Flammarion. Perfect order, I should think, only backward.

I kept going over and over this section of the chapter on the Einstein theory. I even tried reading it backward, twice as fast as light, to see if I could capture Napoleon at Waterloo while he was still home in bed. If you are interested in the profound mathematical theory of the distinguished German scientist, you may care to glance at a diagram I drew for my own guidance, as follows:

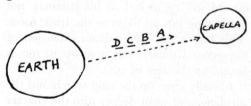

Now, A represents Napoleon entering the field at Waterloo and B represents his defeat there. The dotted line is, of course, Mr. Lumen, going hell-for-leather. C and D you need pay no particular attention to; the first represents the birth of Mr. George L. Snively, an obscure American engineer, in 1819, and the second the founding of the New England Glass Company, in

1826. I put them in to give the thing roundness and verisimilitude and to suggest that Mr. Lumen passed a lot of other events besides Waterloo.

In spite of my diagram and my careful reading and rereading of the chapter on the Einstein theory, I left it in the end with a feeling that my old grip on it, as weak as it may have been, was stronger than my new grip on it, and simpler, since it had not been mixed up with aviators, stop watches, Mr. Lumen, and Napoleon. The discouraging conviction crept over me that science was too much for me, that these brooding scientists, with their bewildering problems, many of which work backward, live on an intellectual level which I, who think of a hundred-yard dash as a hundred-yard dash, could never attain to. It was with relief that I drifted on to Chapter XXXVI, "The Story of Domesticated Animals." There wouldn't be anything in that going as fast as light or faster, and it was more the kind of thing that a man who has been put to bed by a bee should read for the alleviation of his humiliation. I picked out the section on dogs, and very shortly I came to this: "There are few dogs which do not inspire affection; many crave it. But there are some which seem to repel us, like the bloodhound. True, man has made him what he is. Terrible to look at and terrible to encounter, man has raised him up to hunt down his fellowman." Accompanying the article was a picture of a dignified and mournful-looking bloodhound, about as terrible to look at as Abraham Lincoln, about as terrible to encounter as Jimmy Durante.

Poor, frightened little scientist! I wondered who he was, this man whom Mr. J. Arthur Thomson, Regius Professor of Natural History at the University of Aberdeen, had selected to inform the world about dogs. Some of the chapters were signed, but this one wasn't, and neither was the one on the Einstein theory (you were given to understand that they had all been written by eminent scientists, however). I had the strange feeling that both of these articles had been written by the same man. I had the strange feeling that *all* scientists are the same man. Could it be possible that I had isolated here, as under a microscope, the true nature of the scientist? It pleased me to think so; it still pleases me to think so. I have never liked or trusted scientists very much, and I think now that I know why: they are afraid of bloodhounds. They must, therefore, be afraid of frogs, jack rabbits, and the larger pussycats. This must be the reason that most of them withdraw from the world and devote themselves to the study of the inanimate and the impalpable. Out of my analysis of those few sentences on the bloodhound, one of the gentlest of all breeds of dogs, I have arrived at what I call Thurber's Law, which is that scientists don't really know anything about anything. I doubt everything they have ever discovered. I don't think light has a speed of 7,000,000 miles per second at all (or whatever the legendary speed is). Scientists just think light is going that fast, because they are afraid of it. It's so terrible to look at. I have always suspected that light just plodded along, and now I am positive of it.

I can understand how that big baby dropped the subject of bloodhounds with those few shuddering sentences, but I propose to scare him and his fellow-scientists a little more about the huge and feral creatures. Bloodhounds are sometimes put on the trail of old lost ladies or little children who have wandered away from home. When a bloodhound finds an old lady or a little child, he instantly swallows the old lady or the little child whole, clothes and all. This is probably what happened to Charlie Ross, Judge Crater, Agnes Tufverson, and a man named Colonel Appel, who disappeared at the battle of Shiloh. God only knows how many thousands of people bloodhounds have swallowed, but it is probably twice as many as the Saint Bernards have swallowed. As everybody knows, the Saint Bernards, when they find travelers fainting in the snow, finish them off. Monks have notoriously little to eat and it stands to reason they couldn't feed a lot of big, full-grown Saint Bernards; hence they sick them on the lost travelers, who would never get anywhere, anyway. The brandy in the little kegs the dogs wear around their necks is used by the Saint Bernards in drunken orgies that follow the killings.

I guess that's all I have to say to the scientists right now, except *boo!*

SPACE BEING CURVED

by E. E. Cummings

Space being(don't forget to remember)Curved
(and that reminds me who said o yes Frost
Something there is which isn't fond of walls)

The Bright Young Men

From It's a long way to Heaven, *copyright, 1945, by Abner Dean, and reproduced by permission of Rinehart & Company, Inc., Publishers.*

IN DEFENSE OF MACHINES

by GEORGE BOAS

So MUCH has been written about machines and the Machine Age that the very words are taboo in polite conversation. The Machine Age, like Freudianism and War Guilt and Flaming Youth, is a topic of which everyone is sick and tired. But so much that has been said on the subject is muddled or beside the point or both, that one who is interested in the analysis of ideas may be pardoned perhaps for continuing the conversation, even though the audience gets up and leaves when he begins.

It is in a way absurd to discuss any great social movement in logical terms. Social movements are made by psychology, not logic. Yet it is barely possible that if everyone caught in the current would stop and think he might find a way of crawling out on dry land. But as a matter of fact no one to speak of is going to stop and think. Some people stop and scream, like the poor English weavers when the Industrial Revolution began concentrating production in factories or the conscientious objectors during the War. But such screaming is rarely effective because it is bad form. All the more difficult is it for people to stop and think. For thinking is not only bad form but hard. There is, moreover, the possibility that society as a whole, or even its major sub-divisions, gets what it wants, and when large sections of society find that what they want is illegal . . . they simply devise their own ways of nullifying laws or resisting change. Note the electoral status of the Negro in the South, the success of the Russian Revolution, the survival of Anglo-Saxon culture in England and, for that matter, the absorption of pagan divinities by institutionalized Christianity.

Thinking, therefore, may do no actual good in changing anything but men's minds, but it is at least harmless, which one cannot say of screaming.

To turn, then, to machines. We are first told that though man invented them to be his servants he has become theirs. The Frankenstein motif, as Mr. Stuart Chase pointed out in *Harper's* in March, 1929, seems to be the most prominent theme of the screamers. As Mr. Chase clearly indicated in that article, this argument is a gross exaggeration. Man is no more a slave of his machines now than he has ever been, or than he is to his body, of which they are—as I think Samuel Butler first suggested—an extension. A farmer is certainly as much of a slave to his primitive plow or sickle as a factory hand to his power loom or engine. Anyone who has ever lived on an old-fashioned farm knows how the farmer and his family get up at four in the morning to sharpen their instruments, filing, cutting, nailing, repairing, lest the machines on which their lives depend fall to pieces. I have lived closely enough to French peasants to observe them sweating and groaning over their tools. When they have no automatic binders and reapers they cut their wheat with sickles and bind it idyllically by hand. Are they who spend endless brutalizing hours in the fields because of the laziness and general inefficiency of their machines more free than our Western ranchmen with their tractors? I have seen milk be-

George Boas, "In Defense of Machines," *Harper's Magazine*, 165: 83-99 (June, 1932). By permission of the author.

come diseased and filthy because there was no ice or ice-machine and eggs wasted because there were no incubators and grain rotting because there were no reapers. The machines of primitive men, the hand-looms, the sickles, the wooden plows, the animals—which modern machines have often replaced—tyrannize over their owners not by their power but by their very weakness. Primitive men, with the possible exception of the Bushman who strangles his prey and eats it raw and goes naked and sleeps in the open and has no family life—if there be such a creature—are like the dutiful husbands of professional invalids.

In the second place, so far as I know, no clear definition of a machine has ever been given. A steamboat is a machine, according to Silas Bent—and in his opinion indeed the beginning of the steam age is the beginning of the machine age. But what makes a steamboat a machine and a sailboat a non-machine? The fact that condensed vapor instead of the wind makes it go? The fact that human beings had to freeze and half starve to catch the wind? But after all they roast and suffocate at least to boil the water to make the steam, if it is man-power one is thinking of. Steam undoubtedly produces much of the ugliness and dirt of our cities, but we are not for the moment discussing the aesthetic aspects of the question. Why steam is more mechanical than wind or falling water or muscle-driven hammers is somewhat obscure. A sailboat, a rowboat, an inflated goatskin, a log are all equally machines. A linotype, a hand-press, a pen, a reed, a charred stick are all machines. They are all mechanical supplements to man's corporeal inadequacies. They differ in quantity of output, in excellence of production, in speed, *i.e.,* in

what is usually called efficiency. A stone hurled from a sling at an insolent neighbor is as mechanical as shrapnel hurled from a cannon. It does not kill so many men; it is a worse machine. But man has always relied in part on mechanical devices, although he has dreamed of a time in the distant past when they were unnecessary because of the fertility of the earth, the simplicity of human desires, the general health of humanity, and its blissfully divine ignorance. No one would call the time of Nero a machine age; but read Seneca's Ninetieth Epistle. Machines are precisely what differentiate us from the brutes. Some people of course would prefer that the differentiation be less marked.

When I have pointed this out in conversation with primitivistic friends I have been invariably charged with sophistry. They have always insisted that my definition of "machine" was too broad. My answer is that the only alternative they offer arbitrarily identifies a machine with a bad machine. But any student of "Logic 1" knows that either all machines are bad because they are machines or because of something else. And if only some and not all machines are bad, then their badness is not the fact that they are machines. Take the case of the woman who calls a player-piano a machine but refuses to call a piano a machine. Yet a piano is a harp whose strings are struck, not plucked. This cannot be done by hand unless little hammers are attached to each finger. A harpsichord is a mechanical harp—that is a harp whose strings are plucked not by fingers but by little pieces of crow-quill or hard leather. The harpsichord does not do much more than could be done by hand. Does that put it in the class of player-pianos? The answer to this question does not lie in any principle of construction.

It lies in what you want to get out of the instrument. People who call player-pianos machines feel that it is better to play a piece of music inaccurately so long as one has maximum responsibility for what is played than to reproduce even the good playing of someone else. People who call all three instruments machines want above all an accurately rendered piece of music. One group thinks of the producing, the other of the product.

But that is not a question of machines *vs.* non-machines. It is a question of whether producing or consuming is better. Romanticists tend to think that activity, doing, originality are the greatest goods, regardless of what one does. Anti-romanticists are likely to think in terms of ends. The ungracious answer is that there is plenty of room in the world for both producers and consumers, and that no one can be exclusively one or the other. As a matter of fact, the present age furnishes amazing possibilities for the producers. There has probably never been a time when artists and scientists were freer to satisfy their desires for creation. Think of the universities and learned foundations which support men not to teach others, not to think of utilitarian ends, but simply to pursue research. The most absurd investigations are sanctified by the superstition that pure research is noble and deserves free maintenance. It is taken for granted nowadays that artists "be true to themselves," and few would dream of minutely prescribing what a painter or poet should produce.

II

In fact the real clash in opinion is probably ethical. We are—a great many of us —unhappy today and, following a long tradition, we attribute our unhappiness to the economic structure of our civilization. But one can find such outcries of woe as early as eight hundred years before Christ in the works of Hesiod. The crop of cynicism and despair which we uncritically think of as modern is simply human. There has often in the past been as profound and as general despair among the articulate members of society. We read more books and essays of our own time than we do of other times. But those of us who know anything about the history of ideas can find the most striking analogues to our contemporary attitude from Hesiod—if not from Homer—down: yearning for the past, which was of course better than the present; yearning for a society without arts, sciences, or crafts, where the earth bears spontaneously and there is neither money, trade, nor private property; yearning for happy islands beyond the seas, praise of noble savages. The Golden Age took the place of the Age of Handicraft, the Scythians and the Hyperboreans of American Indians, pre-Conquest Mexicans, or South Sea Islanders. This unhappiness of ours, which in its literary form expresses itself in tirades against steam, electricity, urban life, manufacturers, cannot, therefore, be attributed to machines.

Machines are not the cause either of happiness or unhappiness. They may be present or absent at the time when a man is miserable or blissful. They are irrelevant to what is called our spiritual welfare. Just because a man has a radio is no reason why a man should feel that he has been transported either to Heaven or Hell, unless a man wants to have or to brag of having what his fellows have. The same thing is true of our other possessions. Some of us snooty members of society feel a certain self-esteem in not having many of the right things to have. As for mechanized industry, it is simply not true that the farmer on his isolated farm in the old days in New England, without radio, telephone, automobile, tractor, reaper, and so on was any happier than the factory hand in Lowell or Lawrence—when there actually was industry in those cities. Some of them were probably happy; others were living a mean, stinted, swinish life, crabbed and thwarted, sickly in mind and body, full of the lowest motives that ever disgraced the human soul. If rustic life was so delightful, why did the rustic fly to the city as soon as he could find a city to fly to and the railroad fare? The pastoralist is usually either a genuine lover of rural things or a city dweller to whom the country means the spring gardens, the old swimming hole, barn dances, and corn husking, rather than winter, weeding and "cultivating," hauling water, the wood pile, drought, and insect pests.

To be sure factory hands can play a good second to farm hands so far as a dreary life goes. They are as a mass an unlovely lot. In my boyhood in Providence I used to see men, women, and children trudging to the mills at six-thirty in the morning, tin dinner pails in hand—and not so full at that, in spite of Mark Hanna—to return at six-thirty at night. They were pale and rickety, God knows, and nothing for the mill owners to look in the eyes. But that does not mean that their contemporaries on the farms were red-cheeked and stocky, effervescing with vitamines, sleeping late in the morning and going to bed early, delighting in robust rural pleasures.

Who has yet found the key to human happiness? Who knows whether there is a key to be found? We do know that it is not always produced by possessions—though it sometimes is. And, furthermore, we know that a man who has health is more likely to be capable of happiness than a man who is sickly. Can we attribute modern hygiene to anything other than our various 'scopes and 'graphs? Instruments of precision have been all important in producing modern longevity and health. For it was not unaided brains. The brains have always been there. But the brains could not see without lenses. I am no worshiper of mere hygiene nor am I extolling two-fistedness and red-bloodedness and he-manship. But it simply does not make sense to say that the millennium would set in if we could all relapse into dirt and disease. It would make no difference to some of us, I admit, and doubtless the human race would get used to it in time. But the fact that Occidentals have spent such effort to eliminate the combination is some evidence of its lack of charm. Unless it was done for self-mortification.

This point needs no emphasis, although many of the opponents of the machine seem to think that Oriental squalor is a help to the inner life. There are, to be sure, greater opportunities for a would-be saint in filth than in cleanliness, but that is precisely because human beings dislike it so. But the inner life is not entirely an affair of corporeal asceticism. I venture to suggest that the inner life of a Noguchi or an Einstein is as fine as that of a St. Simeon Stylites. I admit that I cannot prove it. Still one could point to dozens of men and women today whose works show as noble a perception of human values as those of their ancestors in a supposed machineless age. We still have mystics, devoted scientists, great artists. Religion, love, creative power, intelligence seem to be no less in evidence today than they ever were, and the lack of them no less bewailed in literature. A period which has produced a new religion (Christian Science), seen the increasing hold of an old one (Roman Catholicism), the rise of pacifism and internationalism, a new physical science, an artistic style in painting, sculpture, architecture, music, and literature has not been deprived of its inner life.

Machines are as indifferent to the inner life as they are to happiness. The inner life—if the term indicates the ability to think and to dream and all that is entailed in thinking and dreaming—is independent of the presence or absence of machines. Introverts have been and still are able to crawl into themselves in spite of factory whistles and automobile horns, and extroverts had no difficulty in finding trees to chop down and men to fight when they could not swat flies or pilot airplanes. One of the best proofs of the irrelevancy of machinery to the spirit is the flood of anti-machine literature. How in the world do these writers find the time to compose their essays and sermons in a breath-taking age dominated by a soul-gobbling Moloch? It is true that many of their productions seem to have required a minimum of reflection. But the Twentieth Century has no corner on unintelligence. If people would only read past as well as present literature, they would understand why President Eliot was able to house what was worth salvaging of three thousand years of writing on a five-foot shelf. But when we think of the past we forget the fools and remember the sages. We reverse the process for our own time.

III

One of the points especially emphasized by the enemies of machines is that they substitute something lifeless for something vital and human. Concretely, this means that a farmer cannot love a tractor or an incubator as he could a horse or a hen. This is very probable, particularly if the farmer started farming with horses and hens. But it is not absolutely certain otherwise. Machines can be as lovable as animals. Who has not known engineers who literally love their locomotives, or boys who care for their radios, speed boats, and automobiles as if they were alive? People are constantly personifying their machines as they do boats. They brag about their accomplishments as if the machines were able to accomplish things independently of their operators. One can always love that with which one can identify oneself, and a man can identify himself with a power loom or a turbine as well as with a football team, his family, or his wife. Think of a musician and his beloved violin or flute about which so many romantic stories are invented. Some machines are lovable and some aren't. As a boy I used to hate the old coal furnace which I was delegated to feed and water and clean, and it required all the attention that a voracious and diarrhoeic infant might demand. Today I worship my gas furnace with its exquisite little thermostat and its complete autonomy. It costs as much as a steam yacht, but love is blind. It can go the limit as far as this doting old fool is concerned. Another man might hate it and love the now abandoned coal furnace. The lovableness and hatefulness of these things is not entirely a function of their mechanical nature. It is in large measure a function of the person who owns or tends them. The old debate on the relative merits of cats and dogs as pets is very much like this—and no more sensible. For emotional qualities are in popular speech attributed to the things that arouse them and not to us in whom they are aroused.

So we say that a chair is comfortable, meaning that we are comfortable in the chair. And until human beings all react emotionally in the same way on all occasions to the same things—until women cease to ask, "What in the world could he see in her?"—there is no laying down the law about the inherent lovableness or hatefulness of anything.

Nor is it true that modern machines absorb us and make us part of them more than primitive machines did. A day laborer is as much part of his pick and shovel as the operator of a steam shovel is part of it. If a man is assumed to be his own boss, to be living on a small farm near the Equator, where we shall imagine that he can work or not without either starving or freezing, where there are no malevolent microorganisms, and food drops from the skies like manna, then of course he can lay down his tools at any time and pick them up at any time, as a woman can lay down and pick up a piece of embroidery. But such an earthly paradise has not existed since Adam ate the apple, and there is no sense in arguing as if it had or could. The Gloucester fisherman out for cod off the Grand Banks is probably living as non-mechanical and primitive a life as is possible for modern Americans. Is he less a part of his boat, sails, and tackle than the factory hand is of his levers and belts and spindles and presses? He makes more different motions and he may find them more interesting—though it is questionable whether the factory hand would—but he is no less absorbed into his tools.

It will be said that the old machines, actuated by human muscles rather than by steam or electricity, at least helped a man's creative power. Friends of the machine are constantly being told that hand-weaving is creative whereas machine-weaving is not. The old French artisan, we are told, lived a life of creativity; he stamped things with his own individuality; he projected his personality into his products. The modern American factory hand is passive; he makes nothing; his product is standardized. This, within limits, is true of the factory hand. But it was also true of the artisan. He had certain styles and patterns which he reproduced endlessly, as our great-grandmothers reproduced world without end the same old quilting patterns. That man's products have always been standardized is proved by archaeology, and the history of taste. If there had not been standardization, how could archaeologists date works of art by their style, material, and subject matter? There is no more individuality in the cave drawings at Les Eyzies—which are the most primitive works of art we have—than in the photographs of today. Yet drawing and painting are practically free of mechanical fetters. Peruvian pre-Columbian weaving is hardly the product of the machine age, yet we see running through it the same standardized weaves, the same colors, the same designs. Artists up to modern times almost always were working on commission; they executed orders; and it is a sheer falsification of history to think of their carrying out in matter the fancies of their dream-life. We have so much evidence of this that there is an embarrassment of choice.

One who knows history knows that the love of the individual, the different, the original is modern, wherever it exists at all. Where we find standardization of taste today we find not a product of the machine age but the survival of a long tradition. People in general have always wanted to be like everyone else in their social group—have we not books of etiquette running back to the fourteenth century at least? There are undeniably a great many people today—perhaps even the majority for all I know—who still want to be indistinguishable from their fellows. At the same time it is possible, if not always easy, for people even to think differently, whereas a century or so ago it was literally impossible if one wished to save one's skin.

As one digs into this discussion one finds the instinctive hatred that many people have always had for innovation. We do not hate machines, we hate new machines. A woman will object to buying a dress cut out by machine, but will not object to buying one sewn by machine. The very person who objected to the player-piano had no objections to a phonograph; she grew up with one and learned all the music she knows from it. I find myself fuming at automobiles and yearning for the old bicycles. I can remember old folks shaking their heads over telephones as their juniors now curse out the dial phones. I have heard a gardener in France inveighing against chemical fertilizers which "violent la terre," as if horse manure were non-chemical. Sailors in the windjammers railed against the steamboat, and steamboat crews think none too kindly of the johnnies who sail oil-burners. Greek and Roman literature is full of invective against any kind of navigation, for it takes the pine tree off its mountain top and sends men wandering.

Obviously a new machine, like an old one, must be judged on its merits, not on its novelty. But the fact that it is novel should not condemn it. Here are two stalwart platitudes. But think of the fools who objected to anaesthesia, to aeronautics, even to cooked foods, because they were not "natural." The question cannot be settled by the wild use of question-begging epithets. We must each establish a system of values for ourselves or absorb that of our social group, and judge machines by it as we do everything else. There is no other way of evaluating anything.

As we all know—we have certainly heard it frequently enough—the real question is what to do with our leisure. There is no doubt that we can have more of it now than we ever could in the past—if we want it. If it be true that movie palaces, dance halls, and speakeasies are crowded, that radios are going night and day, and automobiles are whizzing about like whirling atoms, it would seem as if most people had found the answer. It is an answer which displeases the magazine writers. That is because writers are by nature people who enjoy and need quiet and solitude and cannot understand other people's enjoying and needing noise and society. But can they point to a time when the leisure class as a mass was less ignobly amused? We happen to have a very large leisure class. It acts as idle human beings have always acted: the theater, the gaming table, the divan. Did anyone seriously think that it would take to improving its mind or sit cross-legged in rapt contemplation of its collective navel? Leisure is man's one opportunity to satisfy whatever appetites he happens to have. And no one can say that he is forced by lack of libraries, educational institutions, museums, and the like to spend it staring at films or boozing and petting. The fact is that most people are what their cultured fellows would call sots and always have been. And the probability is that in modern times—whether because or in spite of machines—they have more chance to rise from the sty than they have ever had. The machine has neither given them wings nor cloven hooves. In the very nature of the case it could do neither.

ATOMIC MEDICINE

The Great Search for Cures on a New Frontier

IN THE MUSHROOM-CLOUDED DAWN of the Atomic Age, dark as it was with fresh dangers for the human race, there shone a ray of brilliant promise; the sudden abundance of radioactive elements gave medical researchers their most important new tools since the invention of the microscope. For five years now, physicians and biochemists have been learning to handle them.

How much progress have they made?

The short answer is that they have wrought no miracles. Atomic medicine has cured no disease that cannot be cured without it. But in five years there has been time to explore only a fraction of the new frontier—and meanwhile there have come discoveries in three directions that are worth cheering about:

TREATMENT: radioactive iodine, phosphorus and gold are effective in half a dozen diseases, though in no more.

DIAGNOSIS: radioisotopes of iodine, sodium and potassium have already proved helpful in appraising several disorders of body chemistry, e.g., in cases of heart and kidney disease, to help establish the kind of treatment the patient can stand. Other isotopes are helpful in locating brain tumors.

STUDY OF BODY FUNCTION: with "tracer" doses of dozens of radioactive elements, medical researchers are beginning to learn things they never knew before about how the body, sick or well, performs some of its incredibly complex chemical processes.

Biochemists will be busy for many years in this field. Eventually their knowledge should lead to better ways of treating a host of diseases, and probably to new ways of curing some.

Iodine Is Unique

So far, about the only evident cure that atomic medicine can claim is with radioactive iodine in severe cases of Graves's disease (overactivity of the thyroid gland). For these, it is as good as other drugs or surgery, and probably better. Until radioisotopes began to be made (in cyclotrons) in the '30s, doctors were able to use only "external radiation"—X rays from an assortment of machines—or the closely related gamma rays given off by radium as it decays to lead. But the thyroid picks up any isotope of iodine in a greater concentration than any other part of the body by a factor of 100 or more to 1. So radioactive iodine (known as iodine-131 from its atomic weight) [1] was the answer to the radiologists' dream: it supplied internal radiation in a highly selective way. As the iodine crowded into the thyroid of a victim of Graves's disease, its disintegrating atoms destroyed the overactive tissue.

Nothing could have been neater—and nothing could have led to more disappointment. For, inevitably, researchers began to hunt for other elements which would localize equally well in a particular part of the body. They found none.

[1] The first radio-iodine used had an atomic weight of 128, but Dr. Joseph G. Hamilton, pioneering with it at the University of California, complained that it lost its radioactivity too fast. Physicist Glenn Seaborg nodded, said: "I'll see what I can find." He found iodine-131.

However, they found another valuable treatment use for radio-iodine. Cancer of the thyroid is not a common disease, and most cases do not yield to radio-iodine. But 15% to 20% of the time, the thyroid-cancer colonies which spread through the body behave like little thyroid glands and pick up radio-iodine. Such a case was that of Norman Bennett.

Norman is a lanky boy of 13 who has been playing basketball this season at Madisonville (Ky.) Junior High, and hopes to play football next fall. Two years ago, despite surgery and X rays, Norman was wasting away with a spreading cancer of the thyroid. Then his doctor got him into the little (30-bed) hospital at Oak Ridge, Tenn., which is set aside for atomic medicine. There, Norman had an "atomic cocktail"—radioactive sodium iodide dissolved in water. The cancer colonies soaked up the iodine; from each radioactive atom, beta particles and gamma rays shot out to destroy cancerous cells. Norman goes back to Oak Ridge regularly for checkups, and sometimes he gets another radioactive drink. He eats well and has gained 30 pounds.

Doctors cannot be sure how much they have done for Norman Bennett and others in his plight. They will not talk about a "cure," or even a "five-year cure" or a "ten-year cure." But they are confident that they have done a lot of good.

The benefits of radio-iodine extend to patients with chronic, congestive heart disease and angina pectoris. If, as is common in such cases, the healthy thyroid's activity is too high for a damaged heart, then a dose of iodine-131 can be used instead of the surgeon's knife to reduce the gland. Two-thirds of the heart cripples so treated at Boston's Beth Israel Hospital show worthwhile improvement, and half of these are so much better that they can lead nearly normal lives. Equally gratifying, the treatment releases many patients from the agonizing "tight" pains of angina.

A Shot of Phosphorus

After iodine, radioactive phosphorus is the isotope which has proved most useful in treatment. It seems to be as effective as any other means of combating two kinds of chronic leukemia (lymphatic and myeloid), and it is more convenient than others. It is useless against the acute leukemias of childhood.

Ten years ago a San Francisco shipping executive heard the bad news from his doctors: he had chronic lymphatic leukemia. X-ray treatment might have slowed down the disease enough to give the patient ten or even 20 years of useful life, but doctors have done the job more easily with an occasional injection of colorless fluid containing phosphorus-32.

The shipping man has his blood count checked regularly. About once a year the count shows that he needs another shot of atomic medicine. When he goes to a Gulf port on business, a local doctor watches his blood counts and reports back to San Francisco. If the white-cell count begins to go up ominously, there is still plenty of time for a dose of radiophosphorus to be flown to the Gulf Coast. The shipping man drives himself hard and feels fine.

If radiophosphorus is good for these leukemias, in which the white cells become predominant, it is even better for polycythemia vera, in which the red cells get too numerous. This is because the radioactive atoms act on the bone marrow, where both types of blood cells are made. If either red or white cells are increasing too fast, the radioactivity cuts down their birth rate. For simple polycythemia (uncomplicated by disease of the heart or lungs), radioactive phosphorus is the best medication known today. Some patients are still getting along well 15 years after beginning this treatment, and their number is growing daily.

Gold to Ease Pain

Ranking third among the isotopes used in the treatment of patients is radioactive gold. In a few U.S. medical centers, the gold is injected directly into the tumor mass in certain cases of cancer of the cervix or of the prostate gland. This work is still in its infancy; in the standard medical summary, "the results are encouraging but inconclusive." Far more widespread is the use of radiogold, with no thought of cure, but simply to ease the pain and inconvenience of excess fluid formation in cancers of the chest or abdominal cavity.

A typical case is that of Mrs. H., a storekeeper's wife, who was bloated and miserable when she first went to the women's clinic of Manhattan's Memorial Hospital. She had had an ovarian cancer removed, but not soon enough: its colonies were spread around the lining of her abdominal cavity, causing it to fill rapidly with fluid. She had constant pain, cramps and constipation; she could not keep house, and had to be "tapped" regularly. It got so the doctors had to drain off almost four quarts of fluid every ten days.

One day the doctors at Memorial drained off the fluid as usual, then injected ten cubic centimeters (two-thirds of a tablespoon) of purplish liquid containing 20 trillion particles of gold. It took a while for the doubly precious metal to work, and Mrs. H. soon had to be tapped again. But by then the radioactive gold had bombarded the cancer cells and checked their multiplication. For the first time in a year, Mrs. H. could enjoy a full meal. She has had to be tapped only once in the last six months. Mrs. H. is up and around, taking care of her teen-age children. She is not cured, and she knows it. But life is infinitely easier.

Several other radioisotopes offer marked advantages in treating some of the less dramatic (and usually nonfatal) forms of cancer. Example: blotting paper soaks up a solution containing phosphorus-32; the paper can then be cut to the exact shape of a skin cancer and held in place with adhesive tape. In a few days the cancer is arrested. Strontium-90, on the end of a probe, has been found to be even better than phosphorus-32 for treating malignant growths of the eye.

Atoms for Diagnosis

In the long run, atomic medicine may prove to be more important as a tool kit to help doctors in diagnosis than as a shelf of cures. Already, radio-sodium is extremely valuable as a treatment gauge in certain types of kidney disease of which children are most often the victims. It is all very well to keep these little patients, with their puffy eyes, on a diet from which salt is rigorously excluded. But doctors need to be sure that they are not going too far: if the system is really salt-starved (and hence, sodium-starved), the patient may die of kidney failure. With a tiny injection of radio-sodium, which mixes with the rest of the sodium in the body so that the dilution can be computed with the aid of a Geiger counter, doctors can tell when the danger point is approaching. Every day a dozen happy children banging around the playroom of the hospital at Long Island's Brookhaven Laboratory give testimony to the success of this technique.

It is often important for doctors to know how much water there is in a patient's body, especially if he has heart disease. Almost 20 years ago, Physicist George Hevesy worked out a way to use the stable isotope of hydrogen (deuterium or hydrogen-2) in heavy water for this purpose. But the technique is complicated and takes a long time. Now the University of California's Dr. John H. Lawrence, one of the first and most imaginative of the atomic medicine men, can do the job far faster with heavy-heavy water, the oxide of hydrogen-3 or tritium.[2] The radiant atoms of tritium reveal themselves (to the Geiger or scintillation counter); from the dilution of tritium oxide, it is a simple matter to calculate the total amount of water in the body.

Facts for the Surgeon

No less important is the mass of red blood cells in the body. Some researchers hold that the "count" of red cells in a droplet of blood is not precise enough. Lawrence now gets a more accurate estimate by tagging the red cells with phosphorus. Then there is the question of blood volume; a surgeon needs to know how much blood may have been lost by injury before he undertakes an amputation, and then how much is lost during the operation. With iodine-131 or phosphorus-32 and a Geiger counter, this, too, is relatively easy.

One of the most difficult problems facing cancer specialists and brain surgeons is the diagnosis and location of brain tumors. Now a team of doctors claims to have reached 95% accuracy in pinning down the tumor site with the aid of a dye tagged with iodine-131. Other doctors have not been able to get as good results, so the search goes on. Boston's Dr. Abra-

ham S. Freedberg is encouraged by the way radioactive rubidium (a rare trace element in the body) concentrates in the tumor more than in healthy brain tissue, making the cancer easier to spot.

Paths for Pioneers

The medical pioneers, advancing behind thick lead shields and armed with radiation counters, are striking out along two main paths: (1) experiments in actual treatment, where the benefit of new discoveries may be felt by the patient tomorrow, and (2) fundamental research into the most deeply hidden details of the chemistry of the body and its every cell—the results of which may not be apparent for years. Prime examples of experimental treatments:

Gold shows some tendency to concentrate in cancerous lymph nodes, but the metal stays in the body indefinitely after it has lost its radioactivity. Silver concentrates faster, and the body gets rid of most of it. However, radioactive silver is hard to make in a pile and therefore is hard to get. So in Nashville, Biochemist Paul F. Hahn is trying to fool the body by silver-plating his radiogold.

Bone cancers are hard to treat because if radioactive elements (such as calcium and phosphorus) settle in hard bone, they also affect the marrow and damage the blood-making cells. At Oak Ridge, doctors and radiologists have just eliminated gallium-72 as unsuitable for treatment, largely because it takes too long to settle in the bone (and meanwhile loses most of its radioactivity). Next on their list is gallium-67.

In scores of laboratories gadgeteering goes on. Atomic medicines are being put into capsules, safer and easier to handle than long "hot" drinks. To irradiate can-

[2] Which is also believed to be the vital element in the H-bomb.

cers in the stomach and bladder, balloons are inserted which can be filled with radioactive liquid or fitted with a solid, pinpoint source of radioactivity. Radioactive gold wire is built into hollow nylon sutures to be stitched into a tumor. For external radiation, frighteningly powerful amounts of atomic energy are being baked into little wafers of cobalt ("the poor man's radium").

Finally, in the most dramatic of all experiments in atomic medicine, Boston's Dr. William H. Sweet and Brookhaven's Dr. Lee E. Farr have developed something entirely new: internal, instantaneous radiation for treatment of brain tumors.

The first patient who received this treatment was almost unconscious when she went to Brookhaven. The woman could not talk and did not recognize her family. Into her bloodstream the doctors injected a solution containing boron, a common, stable element with an atomic weight of 10. But under neutron bombardment, boron-10 changes to an excited boron-11, which lives about one-hundredth of a trillionth of a second. In that infinitesimal fraction of time before it decays to stable lithium, it shoots out alpha particles.

When the boron had soaked through the woman's system, including the brain tumor that was killing her, the doctors placed her head near Brookhaven's high-flux pile. While the doctors watched from a platform, the pile operator threw the controls and a stream of neutrons from the pile shot through her skull, aimed at the tumor site. For 17 minutes the boron in the tumor was turned, atom by atom, into a source of instantaneous alpha radiation.

The patient lived only two months after the treatment, but in that interval she was up and about, talked almost normally, and enjoyed movies and baseball games. This epoch-making treatment has been used so far on only half a dozen patients. All that Drs. Sweet and Farr will say is that the results in the last two cases were most encouraging.

The Elementary Questions

It is in fundamental research that atomic medicine comes into its own. Here the frontiers of man's knowledge of how his body works, and how its every cell functions, are being extended day by day. To the men with their eyes on the future, the most elementary things, seemingly the simplest, are by far the most important. Certainly they have proved so far to be the most baffling.

What, for instance, happens to a relatively simple compound such as sugar when it is taken into the body in food or drink? What goes wrong with sugar metabolism in the diabetic patient? At what point does the normal metabolic chain snap? Now, at last, biochemists hope to find out. At Manhattan's Memorial Hospital and elsewhere, they have built common sugars such as sucrose and dextrose with one or more atoms of radioactive carbon-14. As the tagged sugar goes through the system and eventually escapes, its progress can be clocked. Doctors already know that there is more to diabetes than the body's inability to "burn" sugar. With tracers, they expect to find that the trouble lies in the body's failure to do a good job converting what it gets from sugar into fats or protein.

Because carbon occurs in nearly all the thousands of chemicals in the body, carbon-14 is the most widely useful tag in the isotope catalogue. Sometimes the tag can be hung on easily in the laboratory; sometimes nature has to be called in to help with "biosynthesis." In a fifth-floor laboratory atop a pseudo-Gothic building on the University of Chicago campus, intense researchers are growing common foxglove—in Pyrex cylinders filled with radioactive carbon dioxide. They harvest the leaves and make radioactive digitalis.

Foxglove tea was an old wives' remedy for heart cripples hundreds of years ago; 170 years have passed since Withering gave the treatment medical respectability. Doctors know that digitalis goes to the heart, but they want to know how long it stays there and how it is broken down into other compounds. The Chicago team has found out that digitalis stays in the system much longer than had been thought; next, they hope to learn in far greater detail how it works, and how the body ultimately disposes of it. They are also growing radioactive belladonna to make radioactive atropine, and white poppies to give morphine an atomic kick.

In the last analysis, it is vastly more important to know what goes on in the body's individual cells than in the body as a whole. One noted cancer researcher says that there is properly no such thing as "cancer-research"—only study of the life processes of cells. For, once the normal life processes are better understood, it should be but a step to find out wherein the life of a cancer cell differs from that of a normal cell, and another step or series of steps to find a way to eliminate the difference.

Throughout the U.S. (as in Canada and Britain and Western Europe), eager researchers are grasping for every usable tool they can find in the atomic kit. So far, of over a thousand known isotopes (many of them stable) of 98 elements, at least 60 radioactive forms have been tried in medicine and research. In the U.S., the Atomic Energy Commission is backing more than 300 research projects by private institutions in medicine and biochemistry, and there are many more, under security wraps, in AEC's own labs. And the nation's hospitals and universities themselves are sponsoring hundreds of projects.

The Elementary Precautions

Atomic medicine is far from the stage where a general practitioner down the block can look at a patient, reach into a lead-lined safe, pull out a shielded syringe and inject a radioactive isotope. Probably that stage will never be reached; even medically safe doses can be highly dangerous if carelessly handled. Wisely, the AEC has laid down strict rules to cover the distribution and use of its products. Before anyone may use an artificial radio-isotope,[3] he must tell the AEC what he wants to use it for, how he intends to use it, what he hopes to show, and give evidence that nobody in his laboratory will be endangered. If the applicant wants to work on humans, he cannot get his radiant atoms until his answers to these questions have been considered by the AEC's Subcommittee on Human Applications of Isotopes (known affectionately in the trade as the "Subhuman Committee").

Under this setup, atomic research is going ahead more rapidly than any other line of medical investigation. Louisiana's Dr. Jason P. Sanders was not exaggerating much when he told fellow general practitioners last week: "Work in this field is moving so fast that if a doctor is up-to-date one week, he may be behind the next."

[3] Thanks to the accident of prior discovery, radium has never been brought under similar control. Anyone can buy as much as he can afford and carry it home in his pocket. It might cost him $500,000 an ounce, but for a mere $3,000 he can get enough to burn through his pocket and flesh and well into his thigh bone.

THE VALUES OF SCIENCE

by J. W. N. SULLIVAN

I

SCIENCE is one of those human activities which has undergone a change of purpose or, at least, has come to serve different purposes, in the course of its development. The full wealth of values served by the major human activities are not apparent from the beginning. The cave drawings of primitive man, for example, are justly looked upon as the beginnings of pictorial art in the world. But it is very unlikely that primitive man conceived and executed them for purely artistic motives. They had, it is probable, a religious or magic significance. These representations of animals pierced with arrows were probably designed to secure a good kill on the morrow. And the early essays in science, as we have seen, were undertaken for purely practical reasons. Astronomy originated in the desire to construct a calendar for the benefit of an agricultural community, and the official reason given to-day for its support by civilized governments is that it aids navigation at sea.

Astronomy later developed into astrology, which had as its purpose the extremely practical one of foretelling human destiny. Biology began as medicine. Chemistry was for a long time alchemy, which was pursued chiefly because it was thought to hold the key to the discovery of the Philosopher's Stone and the Elixir of Life. Even mathematics was not always pursued for 'its own sake.' Certain mathematical relations were sought out for their supposed magical potencies, and others were valued for their usefulness in interpreting cabbalistic writings.

We have seen, however, that the sciences gradually lost their purely practical orientation and came to be pursued for the part they played in meeting man's curiosity about the external world. The 'search for truth' became the dominant motive in the prosecution of science. In the development of science it was often found, of course, that answers to questions of purely theoretic interest were also of great practical importance. But these practical applications were, very often, mere by-products of the scientific movement. Thus Maxwell's discovery of the electromagnetic theory of light was not prompted by the desire to provide every home with a wireless set.

Disinterested curiosity has been the great motive power of scientific research. Of the great 'Values' that condition our activities and make our lives worth living, Goodness, Beauty, Truth, science has been chiefly concerned with truth. But 'truth' does not seem to be a simple and unambiguous concept. We hear of 'higher' truths and 'deeper' truths. We may ask then, What sort of truth is science after? In what sense is a true scientific statement true?

This question, which the characteristically modern scientific researchers have raised to a position of supreme importance, has not yet received one clear, unequivocal answer. It will help us to understand the present position if we begin by considering what is meant by mathematical truth.

In the beginning, when man first became conscious of this curious mental power called mathematical reasoning, he regarded mathematical theorems as revelations of the fundamental principles on which the universe is constructed. And not only the exterior material universe, but also the universes of thought and emotion. Everything was regarded as being, essentially, an embodiment of number. Thus reason, whose great characteristic, according to the Pythagoreans, is its unchangeability, is a sort of embodiment of the number one. Mere opinion, as contrasted with reason, is an embodiment of the number two. The number two is also feminine, while three is masculine. Thus the essence of marriage is represented by the number five, which is a combination of the first feminine and the first masculine number. In this extreme form these ideas did not long survive. But, modified and debased, they persisted for centuries. We find traces of this outlook even in Kepler, and it persists to our own day, attenuated and incoherent, in superstitions about 'unlucky numbers.'

But even though Pythagorean extravagances had been abandoned, mathematics, until quite recent times, maintained the exalted position of acquainting us with 'necessary truths.' Descartes expresses this point of view in a famous passage from his Fifth Meditation:

I imagine a triangle, although perhaps such a figure does not exist and never has existed anywhere in the world outside my thought. Nevertheless this figure has a certain nature or form or determinate essence which is immutable and eternal, and which I have not invented, and which depends in no way on my mind. This is evident from the fact that I am able to demonstrate various properties of this triangle, for example, that its three interior angles are equal to two right angles, that the greatest angle is subtended by the greatest side, and so on. Whether I want to or not, I recognize very clearly and evidently that these properties are in the triangle although I have never thought about them before, and even if this is the first time I have imagined a triangle. Nevertheless, no one can say that I have invented or imagined them.

Thus the properties of a triangle, according to Descartes, in no way depend on the human mind. But the invention of the non-Euclidean geometries has taught us that these properties are necessary merely in the sense of being logical consequences of the axioms and postulates with which we start. And these axioms and postulates are arbitrary. They are not necessities of thought; they are matters of the mathematician's caprice. We can, if we like, start with the axioms assumed by Euclid, and then we get the properties that so impressed Descartes. Or we can start with Lobachevsky's axioms, and then we get quite different properties. Or we can start with Riemann's axioms, and get still different properties. And so on. None of these axioms are necessities of thought. Regarded logically, there is nothing to choose between them. Thus there is no reason to suppose that Descartes' triangle is a revelation of an eternally pre-existing truth—such as a thought in the mind of God. It is an arbitrary creation of the mathematician's mind, and did not exist until the mathematician thought of it.

Although the idea has been abandoned that mathematics gives us access to some external store of supersensible truths, there is still controversy as to its real nature. A school of Continental mathematicians holds that it is a sort of game, like noughts and crosses. Another school holds that it is a branch of formal logic. The arguments about this matter are extremely subtle and fatiguing, and the melancholy fact that they are not also convincing is sufficient testimony to the difficulty of the subject.

But the negative result of these investigations is sufficient for our present purpose; they have established the fact that mathematics has not the transcendental significance that was attributed to it by philosophers for about two thousand years. At the same time the precise nature of mathematical entities is still a difficult and controversial subject. Although the simple, primary mathematical ideas were doubtless originally suggested by experience, the mathematician's development of them has been very largely independent of the teachings of experience. He has been guided chiefly by considerations of form— a criterion which is probably, at bottom, aesthetic.

This development has, in fact, been so largely self-contained, so autonomous, that the fact that mathematical theorems can be applied to the happenings of the real world seems like a lucky accident. This lucky accident is so remarkable that it has led some modern speculators, as we have seen, to conclude that the universe had a mathematical designer. As against this we must remember the possibility that a mathematical web of some sort could be woven about any universe, and the extraordinary difficulties and incoherencies of modern mathematical physics suggest that, in spite of the extraordinary luxuriance of mathematical creation during the last few centuries, the universe is so odd an affair that we are not yet in a position to weave a satisfactory mathematical web about it. To sum up, we may say that even if mathematics be not purely subjective, it is not, in its nature, a body of truth about the objective, physical world. If it has an objective reference it is only in the sense that logic, according to some writers, has an objective reference.

When we come to science proper, as in the science of physics, we are obviously in a region where experience has played a much greater rôle. We have seen that all its primary concepts have been suggested by experience. In fact, to say that they have been 'suggested' by experience would seem to many an understatement. In their original intention, at any rate, the fundamental terms of physics were put forward as names for certain actual characteristics of nature. The physicist gave names to certain qualities that he observed just as Adam gave names to the animals in the Garden of Eden.

When Newton isolated the concept of 'mass,' for example, he thought he was singling out and naming an actual objective constituent of the external universe. Other properties of matter, such as size, shape, position, velocity, were also regarded as obviously objective existents. Force was a rather more mysterious notion. It was derived from our sensation of muscular effort. But it was not at all clear how we were to regard two distant bodies as pushing and pulling one another. It was hoped, however, to reduce all forces to impacts. It was hoped that, in the last analysis, all forces would reduce to the effects of little hard particles knocking against one another. Another way of dealing with the mystery was to declare the notion of force superfluous and attempts were made to construct systems of mechanics which would not employ this notion. Thus force came to be regarded as a semi-fictitious entity; it was a more abstract concept than the straightforward notions of mass, velocity, and so on. It became doubtful whether all these physical concepts are just names for objectively existing entities.

This doubt is heightened when we come to consider some of the entities that were later imported into physics. Thus the notion of energy is one of the most important of all physical concepts, and the principle of the Conservation of Energy one of its most important principles. But what is the precise status of this principle? Is it a fact of observation that there is some constituent of the external universe to which we have given the name Energy, and is it a fact of observation that this characteristic never increases and never diminishes?

Let us consider, for example, what happens when we let a stone fall from a height. The stone, on colliding with the ground, acquires heat, and the earth for a certain distance round the stone also acquires heat. Thus the universe, it appears, possesses more energy than it had at the moment before we let the stone fall. Where has this energy come from? It has come, we are told, from the energy of motion of the stone. Every moving body possesses energy in virtue of its motion. The stone has steadily been acquiring this sort of energy during its fall, and at the moment of impact, when its energy of motion is at its maximum, this energy is changed into heat energy.

But from what source has the stone been steadily acquiring its energy of motion? Here we come to the somewhat mysterious notion of 'potential' energy. A stone, or any other body, we are told, can possess energy purely in virtue of its position with respect to surrounding bodies. Thus a stone at the top of a mountain possesses more energy than an exactly similar stone at the foot of the mountain. Exactly similar stationary stones at different levels possess different energies. These energies are the potential energies of the stones. Potential energy, it must be admitted, is a somewhat mysterious notion. Other forms of energy, such as energy of motion and heat energy, are obviously 'energetic.' But potential energy is undetectable until it is transformed.

But it is only by importing this notion of potential energy that we can assert the conservation of energy. Otherwise, as in the case of the falling stone, we seem able to create energy. Similarly, by throwing a stone up in the air, we seem able to annihilate energy. At the moment of leaving the hand, the stone possesses energy of motion given to it by muscular exertion which has consumed energy from the body. But when the stone is at the top of its flight, its energy of motion, which has steadily been becoming less, becomes zero. It then begins again to acquire energy of motion, until it reaches the hand with the same energy with which it left it. The notion of potential energy comes in here to preserve the principle of the conservation of energy by saying that as the stone's energy of motion decreases in its upward flight its potential energy increases in such a way that, at the top of its flight, the potential energy is equal to the energy of motion with which the stone started.

Thus the notion of potential energy explains away apparent violations of the principle of the conservation of energy. But is not this the very reason for the importation of the notion of potential energy? Is it not a mathematical fiction, brought in for convenience? A quotation from a well-known Victorian text-book of physics [1] will show us the sort of attempts that were made to justify potential energy as a real physical quantity.

The question still remains, what becomes of the motion when the kinetic energy of a

[1] Preston's *Theory of Heat.*

system diminishes? Can motion ever be changed into anything else than motion? If we assume a fundamental medium whereby to explain all the phenomena of nature, then the properties of this medium ought to remain unchanged, and all other changes must be explained by motion of the medium. Such an assumption is quite philosophic, and the method of procedure is certainly scientific. An evident reply to the question of what becomes of the motion of a projectile rising upwards is that it passes into the ether. The first assumed property of the ether is that it can contain and convey energy. There is no *a priori* reason, then, why the energy of motion of a projectile as it rises upwards should not be stored up as energy of motion of the ether between the body and the earth, or elsewhere. The oscillation from kinetic to potential, and from potential to kinetic, in the case of the pendulum is then, from this point of view, merely an interchange of energy of motion going on between the mass of the pendulum and the ether around it. According to this view, all energy is energy of motion, and must be measured by the ordinary mechanical standard. The work we do in lifting a body from the earth is spent in generating motion in the ether, and as the body falls this motion passes from the ether to the body, which thus acquires velocity.

A rough mental picture of the process might be obtained as follows: We might suppose a body connected to the earth by vortex filaments in the ether, which would replace the lines of force. The ether is spinning round these lines, and when the body is lifted from the earth the work done is expended in increasing the length of the vortex filaments. The work is thus being stored up as energy of motion of the ether, and when the body falls to earth the vortex lines diminish in length, and their energy of motion passes into the body and is represented by the kinetic energy of the mass.

This quotation is sufficient to show that the author is uneasy at the apparently conventional character of potential energy,

and accordingly invokes unknown properties of the ether in order to give it standing as a physical quantity. This line of reasoning raises the principle of the conservation of energy to a position where it can no longer be either verified or disproved. Thus the author in question goes on to say that if a material system is found to be losing energy in some way that we cannot account for, then we must assume that the system is radiating energy into the ether in some unknown manner. Similarly, if the system is found to be gaining energy, we must assume that the ether is somehow conveying energy to it.

Thus the conservation of energy becomes an article of faith. It is no longer an observed characteristic of nature, based upon experimental evidence, but becomes, at best, a metaphysical doctrine. We see how difficult it is, in practice, for science to remain faithful to Newton's criterion. In modern relativity theory the notion of potential energy is not used, and the principle of the conservation of energy is somewhat modified. We find that the notion of potential energy was not an arbitrary creation; it arose from a sound mathematical intuition, but the problem it was invented to answer was not correctly formulated. The art of putting correct questions to nature is learned only gradually, and there can be no doubt that some of our present difficulties arise from the fact that this art is not yet completely mastered.

2

The examples of force and potential energy suffice to show that the naïve view of science is not correct, and that science does not construct its mathematical formulation of the world wholly in terms of directly observable physical quantities. There is, in science, a certain amount of useful myth. But the myths are useful because they are, as it were, pegs on which the mathematical formulation can be hung. It is very seldom, however, that myths have been introduced in full consciousness of their mythical character. Thus it can hardly be doubted that Newton believed in the reality of forces. Potential energy, as our quotation shows, was regarded as more than a mathematical device. Bohr's theory of the atom, with its circulating electrons, was at first taken to be a faithful picture of the objective reality. It was only later that it came to be realized that any other picture will do equally well provided it leads to the same mathematical equations. And the modern Schrödinger atom, with its waves in multi-dimensional space, presents us with a picture which is frankly incredible. Again all that matters is the mathematical formulation.

The reason for this apparently curious unconsciousness of the true nature of their task, on the part of men of science, is very simple and obvious. It is that men try to explain the unfamiliar in terms of the familiar. Scientific concepts were suggested by ordinary daily experience. It was only gradually discovered that natural processes cannot be accurately described in terms of these concepts. Whether man will ever be able to evolve concepts which are entirely adequate to nature is obviously a question which cannot yet be decided. The materials out of which he has built his theories have hitherto shown themselves to be not quite suitable. It is as if one were given the task of constructing a map of a country out of little straight sticks. It was impossible, for instance, for Newton to give a perfectly accurate picture of the solar system with his apparatus of forces and Euclidean geometry, just as the Ptolemaic apparatus of circular mo-

tions *could* not be made to fit the observed heavenly motions. Similarly, the motion of a little hard particle, however much it may be refined, cannot be made to account for the behaviour of an electron. Even such guiding principles of thought as continuity and causality are being found inappropriate for the scientific description of nature.

It is evident, even from this brief survey of scientific ideas, that a true scientific theory merely means a successful working hypothesis. It is highly probable that all scientific theories are wrong. Those that we accept are verifiable within our present limits of observation. Truth, then, in science, is a pragmatic affair. A good scientific theory accounts for known facts and enables us to predict new ones which are then verified by observation. Thus Newton's theory of gravitation accounted, within the then limits of observation, for the heavenly motions. Subsequently, in the hands of Adams and Leverrier, it enabled the existence of a hitherto unknown planet, Neptune, to be predicted. It did, in fact, lead a very successful career, and is as good an example of a scientific theory as can be found. But sufficiently precise observation showed that it did not perfectly account for the motion of the planet Mercury, and it was then seen that its account of the motions of the other planets only seemed complete because, in those cases, departures from the predicted motions were below the limits of observation.

The way in which scientific men attempted to remedy the defects in Newton's theory is instructive. Their method was to tinker with the details. They tried the effect of making the law of attraction just a little different from the exact inverse square law. They tried the effect of giving gravitation a finite velocity of propagation.

But no advance was made in this way. The difficulties could not be met by any extension of the theory. It was not until Einstein introduced an entirely new theory based on entirely new concepts, that the difficulties were cleared up. We now know that the apparatus of ideas with which Newton started, however deftly used, cannot be made to perform the task for which it was invented. It would probably be impossible to find another instance of a change as fundamental as this in the history of the sciences. Here we have no step-by-step modification of a theory, but the complete sweeping away of the very foundations of a scientific outlook. The one feature of the Newtonian outlook that is left is the insistence on a mathematical formulation of nature.

Another instance, although rather less marked, of a radical change of outlook, is provided by the fate of the ether theory. The universal medium called the ether was postulated chiefly in order to account for the propagation of light. Light takes eight minutes to reach us from the sun. How is it transmitted? The hypothesis that it consists of little corpuscles shot out of the sun was found to be unsatisfactory, and the theory was developed that light is a wave motion of some kind. But a wave motion implies, of course, a medium in which the waves travel. Thus there naturally arose the question as to the constitution of the medium. It was at first conceived, on the basis of previous experience of extended and not readily perceptible media, as a sort of gas. Certain experiments showed that this theory was inadmissible, and the notion of the ether as a sort of huge jelly was then developed. This fitted the observed facts much better—but the accordance was not perfect. Attempts to perfect the ether theory led to the amaz-ing developments that we have already described.

Then, by some obscure process of reason and intuition that cannot be clearly analysed, Maxwell developed his equations. He started with mechanical concepts not unlike those of his predecessors, but in developing them he made jumps—flashes of genius—that took him outside the mechanical scheme. He had arrived at the correct mathematical formulation of light-processes. He had thus, in a sense, reached the goal at which all the ether theorists had been aiming. But his mathematical formulation was not reducible to mechanical terms. Then what is Maxwell's Theory? Is it true, as Hertz said, that 'Maxwell's theory is Maxwell's system of equations'? In view of recent controversies this question conceals an ambiguity which it is desirable to make plain.

The issue raised divides physicists into two camps, and has an important bearing on our question as to what is meant by truth in science. The one group holds what is called the 'conventionalist' view, which has been expressed by a German writer as follows:

It has sometimes been supposed that a physical magnitude, such as time, for example, may have a meaning in itself, without any reference to the way in which it is to be measured, and that the method of measurement is a second question. As opposed to this view, it must be strongly emphasized that the meaning of every physical magnitude consists in certain numbers being ascribed to certain physical objects. Until it has been settled how this ascription is to take place, the magnitude itself is not settled and statements concerning it have no meaning.

Thus, on this view, there is no such thing as a physical quantity apart from a system of measurement. The other group holds that there are objective physical quantities which exist quite independently of our methods of measuring them. We may call this the 'realist' view. The conventionalist outlook is obviously an extension to physics of the outlook of the pure mathematician, for whom an entity exists purely in virtue of its definition. But the outlook seems to assign altogether too great a rôle to the subjective element in science. It may be true that the square root of 2 had no existence before the mathematician thought of it, but it certainly seems to be untrue that lapses of time, variations of light intensity, and so on, did not exist before the scientist devised ways of measuring them. We cannot say that the child and the savage have no knowledge whatever of such things simply because they cannot measure them. It seems, rather, that there are objective physical quantities of which they have a confused apprehension compared with the more precise apprehension of the scientific man.

And in the history of scientific measurement itself, the change from one system of measurement to another certainly does not appear to be a purely conventional change, but appears to be undertaken in the effort to obtain a more precise estimate of the magnitude of the physical quantity concerned. Thus, according to the conventionalist, the temperature of a body must be the reading on a thermometer. But scientific men, in their search for accuracy, have successively used different thermometers. Are there, then, as many temperatures as there are thermometers? Is there no objective physical quantity, *the* temperature of the body, that scientific men are trying to reach? According to the conventionalist it is meaningless to talk of any such quantity.

Another objection to the conventionalist outlook comes from the fact that, in the investigation of a physical quantity, entirely different methods, based on entirely different conventions, reach the same result. Unless it can be shown that the conventions have been specially designed so as to fit in with one another, we can explain the agreement only by supposing that there is an objective physical quantity that the measurements measure. But even if we assume that the world of physical quantities is a world that is investigated, but not created, by the physicist, it still remains true that the only knowledge of this world that science gives us is knowledge of its mathematical aspects.

The conventionalist view, we have given reason to suppose, goes too far. Nevertheless, there are physical quantities to which it can be plausibly applied. We have given instances in the notions of 'force' and 'potential energy.' These, it is evident, are not constituents of the external world in the sense that mass, temperature, electric charge, are constituents of the external world. But the basis of this difference is not to be found in our sense impressions. The earliest quantities isolated by physics are precisely those that directly affected our senses. Even 'heat' and 'cold,' as we have seen, were at one time regarded as distinct entities. But the degree of reality we now attach to a physical quantity seems to depend upon the part it plays in the coherent scheme of physics. And the history of physics shows that it is precisely in its search for reality that physics is led to its most abstract abstractions. And all that physics can tell us about these abstractions, we must repeat, is their mathematical specifications. Thus the 'real' world of physics is vastly different from the world of perception.

Owing to the lack of connection between quantum physics and field physics, it is impossible to say at present what are the fundamental physical quantities out of which physics proposes to build the world. Field physics, it is possible, can be based on 'point-events' and the relation called the 'interval.' This will not enable us to deduce quantum phenomena, which are at present based on different fundamental entities. But it is evident that, if we make an assumption similar to that of the old materialists, and regard the 'real' world of physics as the only objectively existing world, then it is not only the 'secondary qualities' of the old theorists that we must regard as illusory. Their fundamental realities must go too, for even space, time and matter are all derivative from more fundamental entities, according to the new physics.

The science of physics is concerned only with those aspects of the world which can be treated quantitatively. This imposes an immense restriction on the elements we select from the total elements of our experience. If we go further, and assume that only the elements of which physics treats are real, all the others being in some way illusory, then we are led to some such apparently fantastic conclusion as that 'point-events' are the only objective realities. But we may leave the philosophical issue involved here to the philosophers. Science itself does not assume that it alone is concerned with the real. The statements of science are true within the limited region it claims for itself—the region of mathematical structure. If you are curious about the mathematical structure of the material universe, then science can give you information on that point.

In pursuit of its aim science has shown itself to be accommodating and flexible. The science of physics has shown itself willing, at different times, to adopt quite different principles and concepts, provided they promised to be helpful in its one great aim of giving a mathematical description of nature. Where principles and concepts have persisted past their time of usefulness, this has been due to the inertia of mental habit. No scientific principles are sacrosanct; no scientific theory is held with religious conviction. Nevertheless, most scientific men believe that there is a final scientific truth about the universe to which successive scientific theories ever more closely approximate. But this is an article of faith. Science is still an adventure, and all its 'truths' are provisional.

3

This atmosphere of provisional hypothesis and practically verifiable statements constitutes what has been called the 'homely air' of science, and is one of its great charms. Science has adopted the pragmatic criterion of truth, namely, success, and as a result science has been successful. Indeed, it would not be too much to say that, judged by the criterion of general assent and practical efficacy, it is the most successful activity that man has yet hit upon. As Professor Levy [2] says:

Any such criterion of truth may not be one that commends itself to the professional philosopher. It may be that science ignores subtleties that appear vital to academic philosophy, that it skims easily over the surface of reality. The very principle that scientists must leave no differences behind may narrow the range to superficial agreement, and restrict the nature and number of the isolates it may form. Whether or not this be so, science can at any rate look upon itself as a united movement that has left in its wake a body of tested knowledge, while philosophy is still broken up into disunited schools of thought.

[2] *The Universe of Science.*

The criticism has, indeed, been made that science pays for its success by its superficiality. All the deepest problems of mankind, it has been pointed out, lie outside science. If neither philosophy nor religion can present any such 'body of tested knowledge,' it is because they have not been content with such cheap victories. There is doubtless some truth in this criticism, and it is probably true that the problems with which science deals are intrinsically inferior in human interest to those dealt with by either philosophy or religion.

Nevertheless, the actual atmosphere of science, the manner in which it goes about its work, is quite exceptionally agreeable. It is in the scientific attitude, as much as in the scientific results, that the true value of science is to be found. If the man of science has not aimed high, according to the philosopher, he has at least aimed with a single heart, with a docility in face of the facts, with an impersonal purpose to serve which is not always found amongst our prophets and philosophers, and which it is almost impossible to find elsewhere.

There is probably no other period in history, since modern science began, when the particular values it incorporates were so rarely to be encountered in other human activities. The human tendencies to prize certitude and fear knowledge, to indulge emotion at the expense of reason, were probably always as strong as they are to-day, but the circumstances of the time did not show them up in so pitiless a light. The mass of men were probably always as impatient of that careful, honest verification that is the very essence of science as they are to-day, but there was no huge popular press to bear daily witness to the fact.

If we are to judge from what seems the overwhelming evidence provided by such activities as politics, business, finance, we must conclude that the attention and respect accorded to science is directed wholly to its results, and that its spirit is the most unpopular thing in the modern world. Yet it could very reasonably be claimed that it is in its spirit that the chief value of science resides. This can be asserted without abating anything of our claim for the values of its results. Knowledge for the sake of knowledge, as the history of science proves, is an aim with an irresistible fascination for mankind, and which needs no defence. The mere fact that science does, to a great extent, gratify our intellectual curiosity, is a sufficient reason for its existence.

But it must be pointed out that this value is inextricably intertwined with another value—the aesthetic value of science. If scientific knowledge consisted of a mere inventory of facts, it might still be interesting and even useful, but it would not be one of the major activities of the mind. It would not be pursued with passion. It could, at best, only exert a somewhat more intensified form of the attraction we feel for a time-table. Indeed, the greatest single testimonial to the fact-gathering power of science, resting, as it does, on centuries of labour and ingenuity, is probably the *Nautical Almanac*—useful, but not entrancing, reading.

For science to have inspired such ardour and devotion in men it is obvious that it must meet one of the deepest needs of human nature. This need manifests itself as the desire for beauty. It is in its aesthetic aspect that the chief charm of science resides. This is true, be it noted, for scientific men themselves. To the majority of laymen, science is valuable chiefly for its practical applications. But to all the greatest men of science practical applications have emerged incidentally, as a sort of by-product. This is, perhaps, most obviously true of the men who have created the mathematical sciences. In the work of mathematicians, in particular, the aesthetic motive is very apparent. Many mathematicians have written about their work in a sort of prose poetry, and the satisfactions they get from it seem indistinguishable from those of an artist. The language of aesthetics is never far to seek in the writings of mathematicians. In their frequent references to the 'elegance,' 'beauty,' and so on of mathematical theorems they evidently imagine themselves to be appealing to sensibilities that all mathematicians share. Nearly all mathematicians show themselves uneasy in presence of a proof which is inelegant, however convincing—one which 'merely commands assent,' as Lord Rayleigh said—and sooner, or later, endeavour to replace it by one which approaches closer to their aesthetic ideal. Some of them, as the late Henri Poincaré, have gone so far as to remark that the actual solution of a problem interests them much less than the beauty of the methods by which they found that solution.

There can be little doubt that it is the aesthetic element in mathematics that has been chiefly responsible for the attention it has received. If mathematics is to be ranked as a science, then it is, of all the sciences, the one most akin to the arts. The history of its development bears out this assertion, for this development, in the main, has been a formal development. Certain branches of mathematics, it is true, have been created to deal with some actual physical problem but, for the most part, mathematics has been a remarkably autonomous activity. In this respect it greatly resembles the art of music, whose development also has been so largely conditioned by considerations springing from its own ground, and owing nothing, or almost nothing, to the external world.

But if the aesthetic element is most prominent in mathematics it is certainly not lacking in the physical sciences. The search for universal laws and comprehensive theories is indubitably a manifestation of the aesthetic impulse. It is sometimes said that scientific men, in their choice of one of two theories that equally well cover the facts, always choose the simpler. But simplicity is, at bottom, an aesthetic criterion. Fresnel said 'Nature takes no account of analytical difficulties.' If we interpret this to mean that there is no *a priori* reason to suppose that nature is simple, then the remark is doubtless true. But if nature was not simple, it is very doubtful if science would ever have been pursued. It would still be possible for science, of a kind, to exist. It is within the resources of mathematics to construct a formula for almost any sequence of changes, however arbitrary, but if this formula is of a kind from which no further deductions can be drawn, the whole investigation is regarded as being in a very unsatisfactory state. Where such formulae are used, as they often are in engineering, for example, it is solely for their immediate practical value. The exclusive construction of such empirical formulae is not an object that any scientific man would propose for himself.

It is because nature does seem to exhibit an order we can understand, because diverse phenomena can be grouped under general laws, that the pursuit of science is worth while. If nature did not possess a harmony that was beautiful to contemplate, said Poincaré, science would not be worth pursuing, and life would not be worth living. Life would not be worth living, that is to say, for Poincaré. But although most scientific men would doubtless find a scientifically unaesthetic universe quite worth living in, we may be confident that they would not devote themselves to science. 'You are young, I am old,' wrote Faraday to Tyndall, 'but then our subjects are so glorious, that to work at them rejoices and encourages the feeblest; delights and enchants the strongest.' And Einstein, writing on Max Planck, reveals himself when he says:

The longing to see this pre-established harmony is the source of the inexhaustible patience and persistence which we see in Planck's devotion to the most general problems of our science, undeflected by easier or more thankful tasks. I have often heard that colleagues sought to trace this characteristic to an extraordinary will-power; but I believe this to be wholly wrong. The emotional condition which renders possible such achievements is like that of the religious devotee or the lover; the daily striving is dictated by no principle or programme, but arises from an immediate personal need.

When we come to the sciences other than physics we find the same spirit. Whether it be Chemistry, Biology, or what not, we find that all the great advances have come from the desire to uncover what Einstein calls 'this pre-established harmony.' Science can, of course, content many appetites. It enables many more millions of lives to exist than would be possible without it. Also it enables many more millions of lives to be destroyed than was possible without it. It can give us marvels to gape at: the distance of the stars, the minuteness of the atom. It can stun us with figures. It can even help the dividend-hunter in his absorbing quest. But to the great man of science, science is an art, and he himself is an artist. And his creation is not the less a work of art because it is but a faint and imperfect copy of another—of the supreme work of art which is nature itself.

The aesthetic appeal of science is due to the fact that it bestows comprehension. Under the phrase 'aesthetic emotion' a number of elements are lumped together, and some only of them are present in any particular case. Our reaction to any great work of art is complex. But one of the most important of our reactions, in many cases, is that our desire for comprehension is gratified. To comprehend a thing is to see it in its relations, to see it in its place within a particular framework.

In the case of a work of literature this framework is provided by the artist's personal vision of life. This is, as it were, the unspoken context within which everything that the artist says acquires a meaning. And our lasting reaction to a work of art, the degree to which it works in us and modifies us when we have forgotten all its details, is dependent on the depth and comprehensiveness of this vision. This is the light which pervades the whole work, and bestows on it such harmony as it possesses, a harmony which lies much deeper than anything the artist may achieve by the technical dovetailing of the elements of his work. The chief function of art is to communicate this vision, and it is the mystery and miracle of art that it can do so.

The comprehension bestowed by a work of art is really the communication of the artist's personal vision. The comprehension bestowed by science is not so obviously personal. Indeed, it is generally supposed to be wholly impersonal. The frame of reference, or 'vision,' within which a scientific theory exists is the group of fundamental concepts and principles in terms of which that region of nature is to be described. These fundamental terms have often been regarded as necessary and unchangeable. We have seen that they are not. Theoretically they have alternatives, although their adoption at that particular time may seem to have been psychologically inevitable.

The Newtonian concepts, for instance, were the final formulation of ideas which, in a more or less vague state, had been 'in the air' for many years. Similarly, the biological theory of evolution has a long history. The Darwinian form of it, in fact, was independently hit upon by two different men. It was, as people say, 'bound to come.' Nevertheless, even if the impetus of the whole scientific movement was towards the Newtonian concepts, we see now that those concepts were not theoretically necessary. Einstein's utterly dissimilar way of looking at the same group of phenomena was a theoretically possible alternative. Not that Einstein could have produced his theory if he had lived at Newton's time. In the absence of the necessary mathematical technique that would have been impossible. In Newton's time it is probable that Einstein would either have developed Newton's theory or else have been the impotent prey of intuitions that he could not formulate. But this would have been merely an accident of history. Theoretically, the Newtonian concepts had alternatives. They were chosen although, as a mere matter of psychology, it may be, there was in fact no choice.

Einstein's theory is perhaps the clearest instance that can be given of our assertion that even a scientific theory may possess a personal element. Einstein's theory is so original that it is very difficult, even after the event, to provide it with an ancestry. It was not in the least a natural culmination of the ideas that preceded it. It was a bolt from the blue. The extraordinary lack of comprehension with which the scientific world at first greeted it was due not to its technical difficulties, but to the unfamiliarity of the outlook it assumed. It seemed to be the product of an alien mind.

We could say of this theory what Einstein said of some of the work of Gauss, that if its author had not thought of it, there is no reason to suppose that it would ever have been thought of. Science provides few instances of theories as original as this—indeed, perhaps there is no other scientific theory so intensely original as Einstein's theory. But there are other scientific theories which have a strong element of originality. Maxwell's electromagnetic theory, for example, was a very lonely achievement.

And it is precisely this quality of originality which is the personal element in science. The majority of men of science, including some of the greatest, impress us as journeying along the highroad. Newton, for instance, revealed nothing totally unsuspected by the best of his contemporaries. It is as if many converging lines of thought came to a focus in him. Newton's great quality was not a bewildering originality, but a bewildering and unequalled mastery of his material. Other men could see his problems; only Newton could solve them.

But the men who strike us as having branched away from the highroad, and having thereby given science an entirely new direction, have put to themselves entirely new problems. It is here, of course, that the personal element in the creation of a scientific theory is most clearly revealed. The history of science is not the history of some sort of automatic development. The actual course that science has pursued depends very largely on the types of mind which, as historical accidents, happen to have risen to the level of genius at favourable instants.

It is often said that the essential distinction between science and art consists in the fact that science makes appeal to universal assent, whereas art does not. A scientific statement, we are told, is open to verification by anybody, whereas a work of art appeals only to people with certain sensibilities. A work of music means nothing to a man who is stone-deaf. Science deals with a 'public' world, whereas art is concerned with a private world. A colour-blind man, for instance, would not appreciate painting, whereas a man born blind could master the whole theory of optics.

What are the primary judgments to which, according to this theory, science appeals? So far as the science of physics is concerned, they are judgments about the indications of measuring instruments. We have to say, for example, that a pointer coincides with a certain mark on a scale. We have to agree, also, about number judgments. We have to agree that an urn contains twelve balls, and not eleven or thirteen. These are the only judgments, we are told, that are involved in science, and about these we can secure unanimity. Two observers, with different colour perceptions, might disagree as to the colour of some particular bright line in the spectrum, but they would both agree as to its position on a numbered scale, that is, they would agree about its wave-length. And it is its wave-length, not its colour, that is dealt with by science. In any scientific statement where a colour is mentioned, the name of the colour could be deleted, and a figure for a wave-length substituted, without harming anything in the statement. The same is true about any scientific statement which seems to appeal to judgments about which men might differ. Two men might disagree as to whether one note was the octave of another, judging by sound only, but they would agree as to whether its rate of vibration, measured on a scale, was or was not double that of the other. And that, we are told, is all that is necessary for the purposes of science.

Now we may admit that universal agreement may be obtained about such things as the number of objects in a collection or coincidences in space without therefore concluding that science is potentially capable of securing universal assent. For science consists of a great deal more than such elementary judgments. The chief thing about science is its theories, and it is surely obvious that not all men are capable of assenting to its theories. A man may agree that a star crosses a wire in a transit telescope at the moment when the hands of a clock mark a certain time, but the theorem which enabled the astronomer to predict that occurrence may be for ever inaccessible to him. As a matter of fact, the upholders of this theory, which professes to be so realistic in the sense of dispensing with all 'subjective' elements, are not realistic at all.

A man may be blind, deaf, dumb, and paralysed—that, they cheerfully maintain, does not matter at all. But he must be a very fine reasoner. If we adopt this criterion that the truth of science is to be decided by an unanimous vote, then we must point out this unanimity, when it comes to actual science, and is not confined to such questions as the number of matches in a match-box, cannot be obtained. A large section of mankind, perhaps the majority, are congenitally incapable of understanding Einstein's theory, for example. If such people are to be ruled out as not affecting the unanimous vote, on what ground is the poet to be differentiated who rules out all those people who are insensitive to poetry? In both cases the claim could be made that *if* all people possessed the requisite sensibilities or faculties, the vote would be unanimous. And this is, in fact, the implied claim of those who preach the complete objectivity of science. For their criterion for objectivity is merely universal assent.

But even if we abandon the criterion of universal assent, and grant votes only to those capable of forming a judgment, we still do not get unanimity. It is notorious that theories that have been found convincing by some scientific men have been found unconvincing by others. Faraday, for instance, was opposed to the atomic theory at a time when, in the judgment of most of his contemporaries, it was well established.

At the present day we have an interesting example of the influence of purely 'subjective' factors in the creation of scientific theories in the methods adopted by Einstein and Eddington respectively in their attempts to reduce the laws of electromagnetism to geometry. Judged by the scientific criterion of accounting for phenomena, there seems nothing to choose between them. But Einstein has said that he dislikes Eddington's theory, although he is unable to disprove it, and Eddington has said of Einstein's theory that it is a matter of taste. Here we are in a region where the ordinary 'objective' criteria fail us. Our attitude towards these theories seems to depend on considerations which are, at bottom, aesthetic.

Other instances could be given, particularly from present-day quantum theory, where a chain of reasoning which is found quite convincing by one authority is found unconvincing by another. And the different judgments seem to depend on considerations which the authorities concerned find too elusive for expression. This dilemma sometimes becomes so acute, Professor Levy tells us, that a scientific society, in view of the conflicting reports of its referees, cannot decide whether to publish a certain paper or not. And Poincaré has told us that even in pure mathematics, where reason, one would think, is most pure and undefiled, a proof which is quite satisfactory to one mathematician is often not at all satisfactory to another. Indeed, Poincaré was led to divide mathematicians into psychological types, and to point out that a kind of reasoning which would convince one type would never convince another. These differences, in his opinion, are fundamental, and play a great part in the actual construction of science.

In view of these facts it is obviously misleading to present science as differing fundamentally from the arts by its 'impersonal' character. There is no absolute difference here, but only a difference of degree. Science is less personal than the arts, but it is a mistake to suppose that it is wholly impersonal. The reason for the difference lies in the fact that beauty and truth, in spite of Keats, are commonly distinguished. A work of art aims more consciously and deliberately at beauty than does a scientific theory. There are some works of art, indeed, where it is difficult to see that the criterion of truthfulness has any relevance at all. This is most obviously the case with some musical works. There are other works of art—e.g., in literature and painting—where truthfulness is relevant. And while it is probably true that no scientific theory has been constructed in complete independence of aesthetic considerations, it is nevertheless true that these alone are not sufficient.

Perhaps this is as far as the discussion can be carried on the common-sense level. A further analysis would have to distinguish between, for example, the 'truth' of mathematics and the 'truth' of physics. And we would have to question the complete independence of the quality called 'beauty.' We have already likened mathematics to music, and it could be objected that, since a mathematical development must be logical, any aesthetic charm it possesses must be incidental. But a musical development also obeys laws; it is not capricious. And although these laws are doubtless more various than those of logic and have not yet been isolated and given names, they nevertheless exist.

And in neither case is the beauty of the development some kind of extraneous quality mysteriously added on. It is in virtue of the fact that the development does obey laws that it is beautiful. Here, at any rate, we see some sense in Keats' remark that Truth is Beauty. When we come to an activity, such as physics, or a great part of literature, which is concerned with matters of fact, the notion of truth becomes somewhat different. Here we have the criterion of correspondence with an external world which need not have been as it is. But here, again, the truth is beautiful. Everywhere we encounter what Einstein calls 'pre-established harmonies,' and since the discovery and revelation of such harmonies is the concern, in their different regions, of both the artist and the man of science, we see once again that there is no essential distinction between the sciences and the arts.

In discussing the aesthetic aspect of science we have been discussing, perhaps at too great length, an aspect which appeals to the layman hardly at all. The layman is impressed, naturally enough, by the magnificent panorama of nature that science spreads before him, but the beauty of scientific theories is perhaps a consideration that appeals only to the scientific man.

The matter is different, however, when we come to what may be called the *moral* values incorporated in science. These have always been held, theoretically, in the greatest respect, especially the chief of them, namely, disinterested passion for the truth. But, as we have said, if we are to judge by its comparative rarity in the other activities of mankind, it is the most unpopular of virtues. How does it come about, then, that it plays so dominant a rôle in science? The first, and most obvious, reason is that science is an activity where success is not possible on any other terms. A business man, by concealment and misrepresentation, may become rich, that is, he may, by his standards, achieve success. A politician who was impatient with misleading catchwords, who really tried to think things out, would probably find his 'usefulness' destroyed, since he might become incapable even of stimulating that degree of conviction and moral fervour which is necessary to sway large audiences. And an advocate whose speeches should reflect the purely scientific attitude, giving every true fact its true weight, would not be likely to have a very successful career. Even those advocates who, we are told, never embrace a cause of whose justice they are not convinced, are hardly scientific, since they evidently have an extraordinary capacity for arriving at definite conclusions on matters which are obviously debatable.

Science is the activity where truthfulness is most obviously an essential condition for success. Its success, in fact, is measured by its truthfulness. Of hardly any other human activity can this be said. In nearly everything else truth is a means and not an end. And if it turns out to be an unsatisfactory means it is quite natural that it should be replaced by something else. But a scientific man who should misrepresent his observations, or deliberately concoct arguments in order to reach false conclusions, would merely be stultifying himself as a scientific man. He would not be prosecuting science. An advertisement may tell lies, but then telling the truth is not its object. Its object is to sell the stuff, which is an entirely different object. This is not to say, of course, that scientific men invariably tell the truth, or try to, even about their science. They have been known to lie, but they did not lie in order to serve science but, usually, religious or anti-religious prejudices. They were aiming at a different form of 'success.'

Such cases are, as it happens, very rare. Perhaps the reason is to be found in the fact that the success thereby achieved is very short-lived. Always the experiments are repeated, or the reasoning checked. The rigorous criticism, the complete lack of indulgence, that is shown by the scientific world, is one of its most agreeable characteristics. Its one simple but devastating criterion 'Is it true?' is perhaps the chief characteristic that makes it seem such an oasis for the spirit in the modern world.

One reason, then, for the embodiment of the disinterested passion for truth in science is that the activity is meaningless without it. But how did men come to pursue an object which can only be reached by what seems to be generally considered as a very painful discipline? The answer is that, owing to the nature of the subject-matter of science, the discipline was not felt to be painful. On all matters where their passions are strongly engaged, men prize certitude and fear knowledge. From certitude can come purpose and a feeling of strength. It breeds courage and action, and is a ready means of ensuring that most desired of all things, an increased sense of

vitality. Only the man of strong convictions can be a popular leader of mankind. For most men in most matters, whether it be the justice of a war, the rightness of a political creed, the guilt of a criminal, the wholesomeness of apples, certitude, in the entire absence of adequate evidence, is easily arrived at and passionately welcomed.

The scientific insistence on evidence, and the scientific absence of generosity in drawing conclusions from evidence, are resented in these matters. The scientific attitude, it is felt, with its promise of a long and very probably inconclusive investigation, would merely dam up the emotions that are clamouring for an outlet. But the matters with which science has hitherto been chiefly concerned are comparatively indifferent to us. For that reason science has been so successful. When Galileo investigated the law governing the motion of falling bodies, we cannot imagine that he cared in the least what the law would turn out to be. He could search for the truth with a single mind because none of his emotions could be outraged by the result. Similarly Newton's demonstration of the law of inverse squares roused no horror anywhere. Nobody had a strong emotional preference for the law of inverse cubes.

Towards most of the results of science we are indifferent. Their charm lies in the fact that they illustrate a harmony, but the results, in themselves, are matters of indifference. Any other results would do, provided they illustrated an equally beautiful harmony. The empirical fact that the velocity of light is nearer to 186,000 miles per second than it is to double that figure, excites no particular interest. But the fact that there must be an unsurpassable critical velocity in the sort of non-

Euclidean universe we live in, is a matter of great interest.

Our reaction to most scientific facts is one of indifference, and our reaction to most scientific theories is one of purely aesthetic appreciation. But when a scientific theory has a philosophic, religious, or briefly, a 'human' interest, we find at once that we are no longer content with our rôle of the disinterested seeker after truth. The opposition encountered by the Copernican theory and the Darwinian theory gives sufficient evidence of this. The splendid moral integrity manifested in scientific work, therefore, is due very largely to the nature of scientific material. It shows us the height to which man can rise, provided that a part only of his nature is involved. Science is truthful because it has practically no temptation to be anything else. In his work the scientific man is an artist, and his moral standard is superb, but the value of his example to the rest of mankind is limited by the fact that, in his work, the scientific man is not completely a man.

Conversation—Earth and Sky

Painting by Charles Sheeler, reproduced by permission
of the owner, the Downtown Gallery, and Fortune.

DOVER BEACH

by MATTHEW ARNOLD

The sea is calm to-night,
The tide is full, the moon lies fair
Upon the straits;—on the French coast the
  light
Gleams and is gone; the cliffs of England
  stand,
Glimmering and vast, out in the tranquil
  bay.
Come to the window, sweet is the night-
  air!
Only, from the long line of spray
Where the sea meets the moon-blanched
  land.
Listen! you hear the grating roar
Of pebbles which the waves draw back,
  and fling,
At their return, up the high strand,
Begin, and cease, and then again begin,
With tremulous cadence slow, and bring
The eternal note of sadness in.

Sophocles long ago
Heard it on the Aegaean, and it brought
Into his mind the turbid ebb and flow

Of human misery; we
Find also in the sound a thought,
Hearing it by this distant northern sea.

The Sea of Faith
Was once, too, at the full, and round
  earth's shore
Lay like the folds of a bright girdle furled.
But now I only hear
Its melancholy, long, withdrawing roar,
Retreating, to the breath
Of the night-wind, down the vast edges
  drear
And naked shingles of the world.
Ah, love, let us be true
To one another! for the world, which
  seems
To lie before us like a land of dreams,
So various, so beautiful, so new,
Hath really neither joy, nor love, nor light,
Nor certitude, nor peace, nor help for pain;
And we are here as on a darkling plain
Swept with confused alarms of struggle
  and flight,
Where ignorant armies clash by night.

THE PROBLEM OF UNBELIEF

by WALTER LIPPMANN

1. Whirl Is King

AMONG THOSE who no longer believe in the religion of their fathers, some are proudly defiant, and many are indifferent. But there are also a few, perhaps an increasing number, who feel that there is a vacancy in their lives. This inquiry deals with their problem. It is not intended to disturb the serenity of those who are unshaken in the faith they hold, and it is not concerned with those who are still exhilarated by their escape from some stale orthodoxy. It is concerned with those who are perplexed by the consequences of their own irreligion. It deals with the

From Walter Lippmann, *A Preface to Morals.* By permission of The Macmillan Company, publishers.

problem of unbelief, not as believers are accustomed to deal with it, in the spirit of men confidently calling the lost sheep back into the fold, but as unbelievers themselves must, I think, face the problem if they face it candidly and without presumption.

When such men put their feelings into words they are likely to say that, having lost their faith, they have lost the certainty that their lives are significant, and that it matters what they do with their lives. If they deal with young people they are likely to say that they know of no compelling reason which certifies the moral code they adhere to, and that, therefore, their own preferences, when tested by the ruthless curiosity of their children, seem to have no sure foundation of any kind. They are likely to point to the world about them, and to ask whether the modern man possesses any criterion by which he can measure the value of his own desires, whether there is any standard he really believes in which permits him to put a term upon that pursuit of money, of power, and of excitement which has created so much of the turmoil and the squalor and the explosiveness of modern civilization.

These are, perhaps, merely the rationalizations of the modern man's discontent. At the heart of it there are likely to be moments of blank misgiving in which he finds that the civilization of which he is a part leaves a dusty taste in his mouth. He may be very busy with many things, but he discovers one day that he is no longer sure they are worth doing. He has been much preoccupied; but he is no longer sure he knows why. He has become involved in an elaborate routine of pleasures; and they do not seem to amuse him very much. He finds it hard to believe that doing any one thing is better than doing any other thing, or, in fact, that it is better than doing nothing at all. It occurs to him that it is a great deal of trouble to live, and that even in the best of lives the thrills are few and far between. He begins more or less consciously to seek satisfactions, because he is no longer satisfied, and all the while he realizes that the pursuit of happiness was always a most unhappy quest. In the later stages of his woe he not only loses his appetite, but becomes excessively miserable trying to recover it. And then, surveying the flux of events and the giddiness of his own soul, he comes to feel that Aristophanes must have been thinking of him when he declared that "Whirl is King, having driven out Zeus."

2. False Prophecies

The modern age has been rich both in prophecies that men would at last inherit the kingdoms of this world, and in complaints at the kind of world they inherited. Thus Petrarch, who was an early victim of modernity, came to feel that he would "have preferred to be born in any other period" than his own; he tells us that he sought an escape by imagining that he lived in some other age. The Nineteenth Century, which begat us, was forever blowing the trumpets of freedom and providing asylums in which its most sensitive children could take refuge. Wordsworth fled from mankind to rejoice in nature. Chateaubriand fled from man to rejoice in savages. Byron fled to an imaginary Greece, and William Morris to the Middle Ages. A few tried an imaginary India. A few an equally imaginary China. Many fled to Bohemia, to Utopia, to the Golden West, and to the Latin

Quarter, and some, like James Thomson, to hell where they were

> gratified to gain
> That positive eternity of pain
> Instead of this insufferable inane.

They had all been disappointed by the failure of a great prophecy. The theme of this prophecy had been that man is a beautiful soul who in the course of history had somehow become enslaved by

Scepters, tiaras, swords, and chains, and tomes
Of reasoned wrong, glozed on by ignorance,

and they believed with Shelley that when "the loathsome mask has fallen," man, exempt from awe, worship, degree, the king over himself, would then be "free from guilt or pain." This was the orthodox liberalism to which men turned when they had lost the religion of their fathers. But the promises of liberalism have not been fulfilled. We are living in the midst of that vast dissolution of ancient habits which the emancipators believed would restore our birthright of happiness. We know now that they did not see very clearly beyond the evils against which they were rebelling. It is evident to us that their prophecies were pleasant fantasies which concealed the greater difficulties that confront men, when having won the freedom to do what they wish—that wish, as Byron said:

> which ages have not yet subdued
> In man—to have no master save his mood,

they are full of contrary moods and do not know what they wish to do. We have come to see that Huxley was right when he said that "a man's worst difficulties begin when he is able to do as he likes." The evidences of these greater difficulties lie all about us: in the brave and brilliant atheists who have defied the Methodist God, and have become very nervous; in the women who have emancipated themselves from the tyranny of fathers, husbands, and homes, and with the intermittent but expensive help of a psychoanalyst, are now enduring liberty as interior decorators; in the young men and women who are world-weary at twenty-two; in the multitudes who drug themselves with pleasure; in the crowds enfranchised by the blood of heroes who cannot be persuaded to take an interest in their destiny; in the millions, at last free to think without fear of priest or policeman, who have made the moving pictures and the popular newspapers what they are.

These are the prisoners who have been released. They ought to be very happy. They ought to be serene and composed. They are free to make their own lives. There are no conventions, no tabus, no gods, priests, princes, fathers, or revelations which they must accept. Yet the result is not so good as they thought it would be. The prison door is wide open. They stagger out into trackless space under a blinding sun. They find it nerve-racking. "My sensibility," said Flaubert, "is sharper than a razor's edge; the creaking of a door, the face of a bourgeois, an absurd statement set my heart to throbbing and completely upset me." They must find their own courage for battle and their own consolation in defeat. They complain, like Renan after he had broken with the Church, that the enchanted circle which embraced the whole of life is broken, and that they are left with a feeling of emptiness "like that which follows an attack of fever or an unhappy love affair." Where is my *home?* cried Nietzsche: "For it do I ask and seek, and have sought, but have not found it. O eternal everywhere, O eternal nowhere, O eternal in vain."

To more placid temperaments the pangs of freedom are no doubt less acute. It is possible for multitudes in time of peace and security to exist agreeably—somewhat incoherently, perhaps, but without convulsions—to dream a little and not unpleasantly, to have only now and then a nightmare, and only occasionally a rude awakening. It is possible to drift along not too discontentedly, somewhat nervously, somewhat anxiously, somewhat confusedly, hoping for the best, and believing in nothing very much. It is possible to be a passable citizen. But it is not possible to be wholly at peace. For serenity of soul requires some better organization of life than a man can attain by pursuing his casual ambitions, satisfying his hungers, and for the rest accepting destiny as an idiot's tale in which one dumb sensation succeeds another to no known end. And it is not possible for him to be wholly alive. For that depends upon his sense of being completely engaged with the world, with all his passions and all the faculties in rich harmonies with one other, and in deep rhythm with the nature of things.

These are the gifts of a vital religion which can bring the whole of a man into adjustment with the whole of his relevant experience. Our forefathers had such a religion. They quarreled a good deal about the details, but they had no doubt that there was an order in the universe which justified their lives because they were a part of it. The acids of modernity have dissolved that order for many of us, and there are some in consequence who think that the needs which religion fulfilled have also been dissolved. But however self-sufficient the eugenic and perfectly educated man of the distant future may be, our present experience is that the needs remain. In failing to meet them, it is plain that we have succeeded only in substitut-ing trivial illusions for majestic faiths. For while the modern emancipated man may wonder how anyone ever believed that in this universe of stars and atoms and multitudinous life, there is a drama in progress of which the principal event was enacted in Palestine nineteen hundred years ago, it is not really a stranger fable than many which he so readily accepts. He does not believe the words of the Gospel but he believes the best-advertised notion. The older fable may be incredible today, but when it was credible it bound together the whole of experience upon a stately and dignified theme. The modern man has ceased to believe in it but he has not ceased to be credulous, and the need to believe haunts him. It is no wonder that his impulse is to turn back from his freedom, and to find someone who says he knows the truth and can tell him what to do, to find the shrine of some new god, of any cult however newfangled, where he can kneel and be comforted, put on manacles to keep his hands from trembling, ensconce himself in some citadel where it is safe and warm.

For the modern man who has ceased to believe, without ceasing to be credulous, hangs, as it were, between heaven and earth, and is at rest nowhere. There is no theory of the meaning and value of events which he is compelled to accept, but he is none the less compelled to accept the events. There is no moral authority to which he must turn now, but there is coercion in opinions, fashions and fads. There is for him no inevitable purpose in the universe, but there are elaborate necessities, physical, political, economic. He does not feel himself to be an actor in a great and dramatic destiny, but he is subject to the massive powers of our civilization, forced to adopt their pace, bound to their routine, entangled in their conflicts. He can believe what he chooses about this civilization. He cannot, however, escape the compulsion of modern events. They compel his body and his senses as ruthlessly as ever did king or priest. They do not compel his mind. They have all the force of natural events, but not their majesty, all the tyrannical power of ancient institutions, but none of their moral certainty. Events are there, and they overpower him. But they do not convince him that they have that dignity which inheres in that which is necessary and in the nature of things.

In the old order the compulsions were often painful, but there was sense in the pain that was inflicted by the will of an all-knowing God. In the new order the compulsions are painful and, as it were, accidental, unnecessary, wanton, and full of mockery. The modern man does not make his peace with them. For in effect he has replaced natural piety with a grudging endurance of a series of unsanctified compulsions. When he believed that the unfolding of events was a manifestation of the will of God, he could say: Thy will be done. . . . In His will is our peace. But when he believes that events are determined by the votes of a majority, the orders of his bosses, the opinions of his neighbors, the laws of supply and demand, and the decisions of quite selfish men, he yields because he has to yield. He is conquered but unconvinced.

3. Sorties and Retreats

It might seem as if, in all this, men were merely going through once again what they have often gone through before. This is not the first age in which the orthodox religion has been in conflict with the science of the day. Plato was born into such an age. For two centuries the philosophers of Greece had been critical of Homer and of the popular gods, and when Socrates faced his accusers, his answer to the accusation of heresy must certainly have sounded unresponsive. "I do believe," he said, "that there are gods, and in a higher sense than that in which my accusers believe in them." That is all very well. But to believe in a "higher sense" is also to believe in a different sense.

There is nothing new in the fact that men have ceased to believe in the religion of their fathers. In the history of Catholic Christianity, there has always existed a tradition, extending from the author of the Fourth Gospel through Origen to the neo-Platonists of modern times, which rejects the popular idea of God as a power acting upon events, and of immortality as everlasting life, and translates the popular theology into a symbolic statement of a purely spiritual experience. In every civilized age there have been educated and discerning men who could not accept literally and simply the traditions of the ancient faith. We are told that during the Periclean Age "among educated men everything was in dispute: political sanctions, literary values, moral standards, religious convictions, even the possibility of reaching any truth about anything." When the educated classes of the Roman world accepted Christianity they had ceased to believe in the pagan gods, and were much too critical to accept the primitive Hebraic theories of the creation, the redemption, and the Messianic Kingdom which were so central in the popular religion. They had to do what Socrates had done; they had to take the popular theology in a "higher" and therefore in a different sense before they could use it. Indeed, it is so unusual to find an age of active-minded men in which the most highly educated are genuinely orthodox in the popular sense, that the Thirteenth Century, the age of Dante and St. Thomas Aquinas, when this phenomenon is reputed to have occurred, is regarded as a unique and wonderful period in the history of the world. It is not at all unlikely that there never was such an age in the history of civilized men.

And yet, the position of modern men who have broken with the religion of their fathers is in certain profound ways different from that of other men in other ages. This is the first age, I think, in the history of mankind when the circumstances of life have conspired with the intellectual habits of the time to render any fixed and authoritative belief incredible to large masses of men. The dissolution of the old modes of thought has gone so far, and is so cumulative in its effect, that the modern man is not able to sink back after a period of prophesying into a new but stable orthodoxy. The irreligion of the modern world is radical to a degree for which there is, I think, no counterpart. For always in the past it has been possible for new conventions to crystallize, and for men to find rest and surcease of effort in accepting them.

We often assume, therefore, that a period of dissolution will necessarily be followed by one of conformity, that the heterodoxy of one age will become the orthodoxy of the next, and that when this orthodoxy decays a new period of prophesying will begin. Thus we say that by the time of Hosea and Isaiah the religion of the Jews had become a system of rules for transacting business with Jehovah. The Prophets then revivified it by thundering against the conventional belief that religion was mere burnt offering and sacrifice. A few centuries passed and the religion based on the Law and the Prophets had in its turn become a set of mechanical rites manipu-lated by the Scribes and the Pharisees. As against this system Jesus and Paul preached a religion of grace, and against the "letter" of the synagogues the "spirit" of Christ. But the inner light which can perceive the spirit is rare, and so shortly after the death of Paul, the teaching gradually ceased to appeal to direct inspiration in the minds of the believers and became a body of dogma, a "sacred deposit" of the faith "once for all delivered to the saints." In the succeeding ages there appeared again many prophets who thought they had within them the revealing spirit. Though some of the prophets were burnt, much of the prophesying was absorbed into the canon. In Luther this sense of revelation appeared once more in a most confident form. He rejected the authority not only of the Pope and the clergy, but even of the Bible itself, except where in his opinion the Bible confirmed his faith. But in the establishment of a Lutheran Church the old difficulty reappeared: the inner light which had burned so fiercely in Luther did not burn brightly or steadily in all Lutherans, and so the right of private judgment, even in Luther's restricted use of the term, led to all kinds of heresies and abominations. Very soon there came to be an authoritative teaching backed by the power of the police. And in Calvinism the revolt of the Reformation became stabilized to the last degree. "Everything," said Calvin, "pertaining to the perfect rule of a good life the Lord has so comprehended in His law that there remains nothing for man to add to that summary."

Men fully as intelligent as the most emancipated among us once believed that, and I have no doubt that the successors of Mr. Darrow and Mr. Mencken would come to believe something very much like it if conditions permitted them to obey the instinct to retreat from the chaos of modernity into order and certainty. It is all very well to talk about being the captain of your soul. It is hard, and only a few heroes, saints, and geniuses have been the captains of their souls for any extended period of their lives. Most men, after a little freedom, have preferred authority with the consoling assurances and the economy of effort which it brings. "If, outside of Christ, you wish by your own thoughts to know your relation to God, you will break your neck. Thunder strikes him who examines." Thus spoke Martin Luther, and there is every reason to suppose that the German people thought he was talking the plainest common sense. "He who is gifted with the heavenly knowledge of faith," said the Council of Trent, "is free from an inquisitive curiosity." These words are rasping to our modern ears, but there is no occasion to doubt that the men who uttered them had made a shrewd appraisal of average human nature. The record of experience is one of sorties and retreats. The search for moral guidance which shall not depend upon external authority has invariably ended in the acknowledgment of some new authority.

4. Deep Dissolution

This same tendency manifests itself in the midst of our modern uneasiness. We have had a profusion of new cults, of revivals, and of essays in reconstruction. But there is reason for thinking that a new crystallization of an enduring and popular religion is unlikely in the modern world. For analogy drawn from the experience of the past is misleading.

When Luther, for example, rebelled against the authority of the Church, he did not suppose the way of life for the ordinary man would be radically altered. Luther supposed that men would continue to behave much as they had learned to behave under the Catholic discipline. The individual for whom he claimed the right of private judgment was one whose prejudgments had been well fixed in a Catholic society. The authority of the Pope was to be destroyed and certain evils abolished, but there was to remain that feeling for objective moral certainties which Catholicism had nurtured. When the Anabaptists carried the practice of his theory beyond this point, Luther denounced them violently. For what he believed in was Protestantism for good Catholics. The reformers of the Eighteenth Century made a similar assumption. They really believed in democracy for men who had an aristocratic training. Jefferson, for example, had an instinctive fear of the urban rabble, that most democratic part of the population. The society of free men which he dreamed about was composed of those who had the discipline, the standards of honor and the taste, without the privileges or the corruptions, that are to be found in a society of well-bred country gentlemen.

The more recent rebels frequently betray a somewhat similar inability to imagine the consequences of their own victories. For the smashing of idols is in itself such a preoccupation that it is almost impossible for the iconoclast to look clearly into a future when there will not be many idols left to smash. Yet that future is beginning to be our present, and it might be said that men are conscious of what modernity means insofar as they realize that they are confronted not so much with the necessity of promoting rebellion as of dealing with the consequences of it. The Nineteenth Century, roughly speaking the time between Voltaire and Mencken, was an age of terrific indictments and of feeble solutions. The Marxian indictment of capitalism is a case in point. The Nietzschean transvaluation of values is another; it is magnificent, but who can say, after he has shot his arrow of longing to the other shore, whether he will find Caesar Borgia, Henry Ford, or Isadora Duncan? Who knows, having read Mr. Mencken and Mr. Sinclair Lewis, what kind of world will be left when all the boobs and yokels have crawled back in their holes and have died of shame?

The rebel, while he is making his attack, is not likely to feel the need to answer such questions. For he moves in an unreal environment, one might almost say a parasitic environment. He goes forth to destroy Caesar, Mammon, George F. Babbitt, and Mrs. Grundy. As he wrestles with these demons, he leans upon them. By inversion they offer him much the same kind of support which the conformer enjoys. They provide him with an objective which enables him to know exactly what he thinks he wants to do. His energies are focused by his indignation. He does not suffer from emptiness, doubt, and division of soul. These are the maladies which come later when the struggle is over. While the rebel is in conflict with the established nuisances he has an aim in life which absorbs all his passions. He has his own sense of righteousness and his own feeling of communion with a grand purpose. For in attacking idols there is a kind of piety, in overthrowing tyrants a kind of loyalty, in ridiculing stupidities an imitation of wisdom. In the heat of battle the rebel is exalted by a wholehearted tension which is easily mistaken for a taste of the freedom that is to come. He is under the spell of an illusion. For what comes after the struggle is not the exaltation of freedom but a letting down of the tension that belongs solely to the struggle itself. The happiness of the rebel is as transient as the iconoclasm which produced it. When he has slain the dragon and rescued the beautiful maiden, there is usually nothing left for him to do but write his memoirs and dream of a time when the world was young.

What most distinguishes the generation who have approached maturity since the debacle of idealism at the end of the War is not their rebellion against the religion and the moral code of their parents, but their disillusionment with their own rebellion. It is common for young men and women to rebel, but that they should rebel sadly and without faith in their own rebellion, that they should distrust the new freedom no less than the old certainties—that is something of a novelty. As Mr. Canby once said, at the age of seven they saw through their parents and characterized them in a phrase. At fourteen they saw through education and dodged it. At eighteen they saw through morality and stepped over it. At twenty they lost respect for their home towns, and at twenty-one they discovered that our social system is ridiculous. At twenty-three the autobiography ends because the author has run through society to date and does not know what to do next. For, as Mr. Canby might have added, the idea of reforming that society makes no appeal to them. They have seen through all that. They cannot adopt any of the synthetic religions of the Nineteenth Century. They have seen through all of them.

They have seen through the religion of nature to which the early romantics turned for consolation. They have heard too much about the brutality of natural selection to feel, as Wordsworth did, that pleasant landscapes are divine. They have seen through the religion of beauty because, for one thing, they are too much oppressed by the ugliness of Main Street. They cannot take refuge in an ivory tower because the modern apartment house, with a radio loudspeaker on the floor above and on the floor below and just across the courtyard, will not permit it. They cannot, like Mazzini, make a religion of patriotism, because they have just been demobilized. They cannot make a religion of science like the post-Darwinians because they do not understand modern science. They never learned enough mathematics and physics. They do not like Bernard Shaw's religion of creative evolution because they have read enough to know that Mr. Shaw's biology is literary and evangelical. As for the religion of progress, that is pre-empted by George F. Babbitt and the Rotary Club, and the religion of humanity is utterly unacceptable to those who have to ride in the subways during the rush hour.

Yet the current attempts to modernize religious creeds are inspired by the hope that somehow it will be possible to construct a form of belief which will fit into this vacuum. It is evident that life soon becomes distracted and tiresome if it is not illuminated by communion with what William James called "a wider self through which saving experiences come." The eager search for new religions, the hasty adherence to cults, and the urgent appeals for a reconciliation between religion and science are confessions that to the modern man his activity seems to have no place in any rational order. His life seems mere restlessness and compulsion, rather than conduct lighted by luminous beliefs. He is possessed by a great deal of excitement amidst which, as Mr. Santayana once re-marked, he redoubles his effort when he has forgotten his aim.

For in the modern age, at first imperceptibly with the rise of the towns, and then catastrophically since the mechanical revolution, there have gone into dissolution not only the current orthodoxy, but the social order and the ways of living which supported it. Thus rebellion and emancipation have come to mean something far more drastic than they have ever meant before. The earlier rebels summoned men from one allegiance to another, but the feeling for certainty in religion and for decorum in society persisted. In the modern world it is this very feeling of certainty itself which is dissolving. It is dissolving not merely for an educated minority but for everyone who comes within the orbit of modernity.

Yet there remain the wants which orthodoxy of some sort satisfies. The natural man, when he is released from restraints, and has no substitute for them, is at sixes and sevens with himself and the world. For in the free play of his uninhabited instincts he does not find any natural substitute for those accumulated convictions which, however badly they did it, nevertheless organized his soul, economized his effort, consoled him, and gave him dignity in his own eyes because he was part of some greater whole. The acids of modernity are so powerful that they do not tolerate a crystallization of ideas which will serve as a new orthodoxy into which men can retreat. And so the modern world is haunted by a realization, which it becomes constantly less easy to ignore, that it is impossible to reconstruct an enduring orthodoxy, and impossible to live well without the satisfactions which an orthodoxy would provide.

WHAT I BELIEVE

by E. M. FORSTER

I DO NOT believe in belief. But this is an age of faith, in which one is surrounded by so many militant creeds that, in self-defense, one has to formulate a creed of one's own. Tolerance, good temper, and sympathy are no longer enough in a world which is rent by religious and racial persecution, in a world where ignorance rules, and science, which ought to have ruled, plays the subservient pimp. Tolerance, good temper, and sympathy—well, they are what matter really, and if the human race is not to collapse they must come to the front before long. But for the moment they don't seem enough; their action is no stronger than a flower battered beneath a military jack-boot. They want stiffening, even if the process coarsens them. Faith, to my mind, is a stiffening process, a sort of mental starch, which ought to be applied as sparingly as possible. I dislike the stuff. I do not believe in it, for its own sake, at all. My lawgivers are Erasmus and Montaigne, not Moses and St. Paul. My temple stands not upon Mount Moriah but in that Elysian Field where even the immoral are admitted.

I have, however, to live in an Age of Faith—the sort of thing I used to hear praised and recommended when I was a boy. It is damned unpleasant, really. It is bloody in every sense of the word. And I have to keep my end up in it. Where do I start?

With personal relationships. Here is something comparatively solid in a world full of violence and cruelty. Not absolutely solid, for psychology has split and shattered the idea of a "person" and has shown that there is something incalculable in each of us, which may at any moment rise to the surface and destroy our normal balance. We don't know what we're like. We can't know what we're like. We can't know what other people are like. How then can we put any trust in personal relationships, or cling to them in the gathering political storm? In theory we can't. But in practice we can and do. For the purpose of living one has to assume that the personality is solid, and the "self" is an entity, and to ignore all contrary evidence. And since to ignore evidence is one of the characteristics of faith, I certainly can proclaim that I believe in personal relationships.

Starting from them, I get a little order into the contemporary chaos. One must be fond of people and trust them if one isn't to make a mess of life, and it is therefore essential that they shouldn't let one down. They often do. The moral of which is that I must, myself, be as reliable as possible, and this I try to be. But reliability isn't a matter of contract. It is a matter for the heart, which signs no documents. In other words, reliability is impossible unless there is a natural warmth. Most men possess this warmth, though they often have bad luck and get chilled. Personal relationships are despised today. They are regarded as bourgeois luxuries, as products of a time of fair weather which has now passed, and we are urged to get rid of them, and to dedicate ourselves to some movement or cause instead. I hate the idea of dying for a cause, and if I had to choose between betraying my country and betraying my friend, I hope I should have the guts to betray my country. Such a choice may scandalize the modern reader, and he may stretch out his patriotic hand to the telephone at once, and ring up the police. It wouldn't have shocked Dante, though. Dante placed Brutus and Cassius in the lowest circle of Hell because they had chosen to betray their friend Julius Caesar, rather than their country, Rome.

This brings me along to democracy, "even Love, the Beloved Republic, which feeds upon Freedom and lives." Democracy isn't a beloved republic really, and never will be. But it is less hateful than other contemporary forms of government, and to that extent it deserves our support. It does start from the assumption that the individual is important, and that all types are needed to make a civilization. It doesn't divide its citizens into the bossers and the bossed, as an efficiency-regime tends to do. The people I admire most are those who are sensitive and want to create something or discover something, and don't see life in terms of power, and such people get more of a chance under a democracy than elsewhere. They found religions, great or small, or they produce literature and art, or they do disinterested scientific research, or they may be what are called "ordinary people," who are creative in their private lives, bring up their children decently, for instance, or help their neighbors. All these people need to express themselves, they can't do so unless society allows them liberty to do so, and the society which allows them most liberty is a democracy.

Democracy has another merit. It allows criticism, and if there isn't public criticism there are bound to be hushed-up scandals.

That is why I believe in the press, despite all its lies and vulgarity, and why I believe in Parliament. The British Parliament is often sneered at because it's a talking-shop. Well, I believe in it *because* it is a talking-shop. I believe in the Private Member who makes himself a nuisance. He gets snubbed and is told that he is cranky or ill-informed, but he exposes abuses which would otherwise never have been mentioned, and very often an abuse gets put right just by being mentioned. Occasionally, too, in my country, a well-meaning public official loses his head in the cause of efficiency, and thinks himself God Almighty. Such officials are particularly frequent in the Home Office. Well, there will be questions about them in Parliament sooner or later, and then they'll have to mend their ways. Whether Parliament is either a representative body or an efficient one is very doubtful, but I value it because it criticizes and talks, and because its chatter gets widely reported.

So two cheers for democracy: one because it admits variety and one because it permits criticism. Two cheers are quite enough: there is no occasion to give three. Only Love, the Beloved Republic, deserves that.

What about force, though? While we are trying to be sensitive and advanced and affectionate and tolerant, an unpleasant question pops up; doesn't all society rest upon force? If a government can't count upon the police and the army how can it hope to rule? And if an individual gets knocked on the head or sent to a labor camp, of what significance are his opinions?

This dilemma doesn't worry me as much as it does some. I realize that all society rests upon force. But all the great creative actions, all the decent human relations, occur during the intervals when force has not managed to come to the front. These intervals are what matter. I want them to be as frequent and as lengthy as possible, and I call them "civilization." Some people idealize force and pull it into the foreground and worship it, instead of keeping it in the background as long as possible. I think they make a mistake, and I think that their opposites, the mystics, err even more when they declare that force doesn't exist. I believe that it does exist, and that one of our jobs is to prevent it from getting out of its box. It gets out sooner or later, and then it destroys us and all the lovely things which we have made. But it isn't out all the time, for the fortunate reason that the strong are so stupid. Consider their conduct for a moment in the Niebelungs' Ring. The giants there have the gold, or in other words the guns; but they do nothing with it, they do not realize that they are all-powerful, with the result that the catastrophe is delayed and the castle of Valhalla, insecure but glorious, fronts the storms for generations. Fafnir, coiled round his hoard, grumbles and grunts; we can hear him under Europe today; the leaves of the wood already tremble, and the Bird calls its warnings uselessly. Fafnir will destroy us, but by a blessed dispensation he is stupid and slow, and creation goes on just outside the poisonous blast of his breath. The Nietzschean would hurry the monster up, the mystic would say he didn't exist, but Wotan, **wiser than** either, hastens to create warriors before doom declares itself. The Valkyries are symbols not only of courage but of intelligence; they represent the human spirit snatching its opportunity while the going is good, and one of them even finds time

to love. Brunhilde's last song hymns the recurrence of love, and since it is the privilege of art to exaggerate, she goes even further and proclaims the love which is eternally triumphant and feeds upon Freedom, and lives.

So that is what I feel about force and violence. I look the other way until fate strikes me. Whether this is due to courage or to cowardice in my own case I cannot be sure. But I know that if men hadn't looked the other way in the past nothing of any value would survive. The people I respect most behave as if they were immortal and as if society were eternal. Both assumptions are false: both of them must be accepted as true if we are to go on eating and working and loving, and are to keep open a few breathing holes for the human spirit. No millennium seems likely to descend upon humanity; no better and stronger League of Nations will be instituted; no form of Christianity and no alternative to Christianity will bring peace to the world or integrity to the individual; no "change of heart" will occur. And yet we needn't despair, indeed we cannot despair; the evidence of history shows us that men have always insisted on behaving creatively under the shadow of the sword, and that we had better follow their example under the shadow of the airplanes.

There is of course hero worship, fervently recommended as a panacea in some quarters. But here we shall get no help. Hero worship is a dangerous vice, and one of the minor merits of a democracy is that it does not encourage it, or produce that unmanageable type of citizen known as the Great Man. It produces instead different kinds of small men, and that's a much finer achievement. But people who can't get interested in the variety of life and can't make up their own minds get discontented over this, and they long for a hero to bow down before and to follow blindly. It's significant that a hero is an integral part of the authoritarian stock-in-trade today. An efficiency-regime can't be run without a few heroes stuck about to carry off the dullness—much as plums have to be put into a bad pudding to make it palatable. One hero at the top and a smaller one each side of him is a favorite arrangement, and the timid and the bored are comforted by such a trinity and, bowing down, feel exalted by it.

No, I distrust Great Men. They produce a desert of uniformity around them and often a pool of blood, too, and I always feel a little man's pleasure when they come a cropper. I believe in aristocracy though— if that's the right word, and if a democrat may use it. Not an aristocracy of power, based upon rank and influence, but an aristocracy of the sensitive, the considerate, and the plucky. Its members are to be found in all nations and classes, and all through the ages, and there is a secret understanding between them when they meet. They represent the true human tradition, the one permanent victory of our queer race over cruelty and chaos. Thousands of them perish in obscurity; a few are great names. They are sensitive for others as well as for themselves, they are considerate without being fussy, their pluck is not swankiness but the power to endure, and they can take a joke. I give no examples—it is risky to do that—but the reader may as well consider whether this is the type of person he would like to meet and to be, and whether (going further with me) he would prefer that the type should *not* be an ascetic one. I'm against asceticism myself. I'm with the old Scotchman who wanted less chastity and

more delicacy. I don't feel that my aristocrats are a real aristocracy if they thwart their bodies, since bodies are the instruments through which we register and enjoy the world. Still, I don't insist here. This isn't a major point. It's clearly possible to be sensitive, considerate, and plucky and yet be an ascetic too, and if anyone possesses the first three qualities, I'll let him in! On they go—an invincible army, yet not a victorious one. The aristocrats, the elect, the chosen, the best people—all the words that describe them are false, and all attempts to organize them fail. Again and again authority, seeing their value, has tried to net them and to utilize them as the Egyptian priesthood or the Christian church or the Chinese civil service or the Group Movement, or some other worthy stunt. But they slip through the net and are gone; when the door is shut they are no longer in the room; their temple, as one of them remarked, is the holiness of the heart's imagination, and their kingdom, though they never possess it, is the wide-open world.

With this type of person knocking about, and constantly crossing one's path if one has eyes to see or hands to feel, the experiment of earthly life cannot be dismissed as a failure. But it may well be hailed as a tragedy, the tragedy being that no device has been found by which these private decencies can be transferred to public affairs. As soon as people have power they go crooked and sometimes dotty, too, because the possession of power lifts them into a region where normal honesty never pays. For instance, the man who is selling newspapers outside the House of Parliament can safely leave his papers to go for a drink, and his cap beside them:

anyone who takes a paper is sure to drop a copper into the cap. But the men who are inside the houses of Parliament—they can't trust one another like that; still less can the government they compose trust other governments. No caps upon the pavement here, but suspicion, treachery, and armaments. The more highly public life is organized the lower does its morality sink; the nations of today behave to each other worse than they ever did in the past; they cheat, rob, bully, and bluff, make war without notice, and kill as many women and children as possible; whereas primitive tribes were at all events restrained by taboos.

The Savior of the future—if ever he comes—will not preach a new gospel. He will merely utilize my aristocracy; he will make effective the good will and the good temper which are already existing. In other words he will introduce a new technique. In economics, we are told that if there was a new technique of distribution, there need be no poverty, and people would not starve in one place while crops were dug under in another. A similar change is needed in the sphere of morals and politics. The desire for it is by no means new; it was expressed, for example, in theological terms by Jacopone da Todi over six hundred years ago. "Ordina questo amore, O tu che mi ami," he said. ("O thou who lovest me, set this love in order.") His prayer was not granted and I do not myself believe that it ever will be, but here, and not through a change of heart, is our probable route. Not by becoming better, but by ordering and distributing his native goodness, will man shut up force into its box, and so gain time to explore the universe and to set his mark upon it worthily.

Such a change, claim the orthodox, can only be made by Christianity, and will be made by it in God's good time: man always has failed and always will fail to organize his own goodness, and it is presumptuous of him to try. This claim leaves me cold. I cannot believe that Christianity will ever cope with the present world-wide mess, and I think that such influence as it retains in modern society is due to its financial backing rather than to its spiritual appeal. It was a spiritual force once, but the indwelling spirit will have to be restated if it is to calm the waters again, and probably in a non-Christian form.

These are the reflections of an individualist and a liberal who has found his liberalism crumbling beneath him and at first felt ashamed. Then, looking around, he decided there was no special reason for shame, since other people, whatever they felt, were equally insecure. And as for individualism—there seems no way out of this, even if one wants to find one. The dictator-hero can grind down his citizens till they are all alike, but he can't melt them into a single man. He can order them to merge, he can incite them to mass-antics, but they are obliged to be born separately and to die separately and, owing to these unavoidable termini, will always be running off the totalitarian rails. The memory of birth and the expectation of death always lurk within the human being, making him separate from his fellows and consequently capable of intercourse with them. Naked I came into the world, naked I shall go out of it! And a very good thing, too, for it reminds me that I am naked under my shirt. Until psychologists and biologists have done much more tinkering than seems likely, the individual remains firm and each of us must consent to be one, and to make the best of the difficult job.

APPENDICES

APPENDICES

SOME MODERN NOVELS

AIKEN, CONRAD: *Blue Voyage* (1927), *King Coffin* (1935)

ALGREN, NELSON: *The Man with the Golden Arm* (1949)

ANDERSON, SHERWOOD: *Winesburg, Ohio* (1919), *Poor White* (1920)

BENNETT, ARNOLD: *The Old Wives' Tale* (1908)

BOWEN, ELIZABETH: *The Death of the Heart* (1939), *The Heat of the Day* (1949)

BUCK, PEARL: *The Good Earth* (1931)

BURNS, JOHN HORNE: *The Gallery* (1947)

CABELL, JAMES BRANCH: *Jurgen* (1919)

CALDWELL, ERSKINE: *Tobacco Road* (1932)

CAMUS, ALBERT: *The Stranger* (1946), *The Plague* (1948)

CAPOTE, TRUMAN: *Other Voices, Other Rooms* (1948)

CATHER, WILLA: *My Ántonia* (1918), *A Lost Lady* (1923)

CLARK, WALTER VAN TILBURG: *The Ox-Bow Incident* (1940), *The Track of the Cat* (1949)

CONRAD, JOSEPH: *Lord Jim* (1900), *Victory* (1915), *Under Western Eyes* (1910)

CUMMINGS, E. E.: *The Enormous Room* (1922)

DOS PASSOS, JOHN: *Three Soldiers* (1921), *Manhattan Transfer* (1925), *U.S.A.* (1937), *District of Columbia* (1952)

DOUGLAS, NORMAN: *South Wind* (1917)

DREISER, THEODORE: *Sister Carrie* (1900), *An American Tragedy* (1925)

FARRELL, JAMES T.: *Studs Lonigan* (1935)

FAULKNER, WILLIAM: *The Sound and the Fury* (1929), *As I Lay Dying* (1930), *Sanctuary* (1931), *Light in August* (1932), *Absalom! Absalom!* (1936), *Intruder in the Dust* (1948)

FITZGERALD, F. SCOTT: *This Side of Paradise* (1920), *The Great Gatsby* (1925), *Tender is the Night* (1934), *The Last Tycoon* (1941)

FORD, FORD MADOX: *The Good Soldier* (1915), *Some Do Not* (1924), *The Last Post* (1928)

FORSTER, E. M.: *The Longest Journey* (1922), *A Passage to India* (1924)

GALSWORTHY, JOHN: *The Forsyte Saga* (1922), *A Modern Comedy* (1929)

GREEN, HENRY: *Living* (1925), *Party Going* (1939), *Loving* (1945), *Concluding* (1948)

GREENE, GRAHAM: *Brighton Rock* (1938), *The Power and the Glory* (1940), *The Heart of the Matter* (1948)

HEMINGWAY, ERNEST: *The Sun Also Rises* (1926), *A Farewell to Arms* (1929), *For Whom the Bell Tolls* (1940), *The Old Man and the Sea* (1952)

HERSEY, JOHN: *A Bell for Adano* (1944), *The Wall* (1950)

HEYWARD, DUBOSE: *Porgy* (1925)

HUDSON, W. H.: *Green Mansions* (1904)

HUXLEY, ALDOUS: *Antic Hay* (1923), *Point Counter Point* (1928), *Brave New World* (1932), *Time Must Have a Stop* (1944)

JOYCE, JAMES: *Portrait of the Artist as a Young Man* (1916), *Ulysses* (1922)

KAFKA, FRANZ: *The Trial* (1925), *The Castle* (1926)

KOESTLER, ARTHUR: *Darkness at Noon* (1942), *Arrival and Departure* (1943)

LAWRENCE, D. H.: *Sons and Lovers* (1913), *The Rainbow* (1915), *Women in Love* (1919), *Lady Chatterley's Lover* (1928)

LEWIS, SINCLAIR: *Main Street* (1920), *Babbitt* (1922), *Arrowsmith* (1925), *Dodsworth* (1929)

LOWRY, MALCOLM: *Under the Volcano* (1947)

MAILER, NORMAN: *The Naked and the Dead* (1948)

MALRAUX, ANDRÉ: *Man's Fate* (1934), *Man's Hope* (1938)

MANN, THOMAS: *Buddenbrooks* (1901), *The Magic Mountain* (1925), *Young Joseph* (1935), *The Transposed Heads* (1941), *The Holy Sinner* (1951)

MARQUAND, JOHN P.: *The Late George Apley* (1936), *So Little Time* (1943), *Point of No Return* (1949)

MAUGHAM, SOMERSET: *Of Human Bondage* (1915), *The Moon and Sixpence* (1919), *The Razor's Edge* (1945)

McCULLERS, CARSON: *The Heart is a Lonely Hunter* (1940), *Reflections in a Golden Eye* (1941), *The Member of the Wedding* (1946)

MOTLEY, WILLARD: *Knock on Any Door* (1947)

NORRIS, FRANK: *The Octopus* (1901), *The Pit* (1903)

RICHARDSON, DOROTHY: *Pilgrimage* (1932)

SANTAYANA, GEORGE: *The Last Puritan* (1935)

SAROYAN, WILLIAM: *The Human Comedy* (1943)

SCHULBERG, BUDD: *What Makes Sammy Run?* (1941), *The Disenchanted* (1950)

SHAW, IRWIN: *The Young Lions* (1948), *The Troubled Air* (1952)

SINCLAIR, UPTON: *The Jungle* (1906)

STAFFORD, JEAN: *Boston Adventure* (1944), *The Mountain Lion* (1947)

STEIN, GERTRUDE: *Three Lives* (1909)

STEINBECK, JOHN: *Tortilla Flat* (1935), *Of Mice and Men* (1937), *The Grapes of Wrath* (1939), *Cannery Row* (1945), *The Wayward Bus* (1947), *The Pearl* (1948), *East of Eden* (1952)

UNDSET, SIGRID: *Kristin Lavransdatter* (1929)

WARREN, ROBERT PENN: *Night Rider* (1939), *All the King's Men* (1946), *World Enough and Time* (1950)

WAUGH, EVELYN: *Decline and Fall* (1928), *A Handful of Dust* (1934), *The Loved One* (1948)

WELLS, H. G.: *Tono-Bungay* (1909), *The Shape of Things to Come* (1933)

WEST, NATHANAEL: *Miss Lonelyhearts* (1933), *The Day of the Locust* (1939)

WESTCOTT, GLENWAY: *The Grandmothers* (1927), *The Pilgrim Hawk* (1940)

WHARTON, EDITH: *The House of Mirth* (1905), *Ethan Frome* (1911), *The Age of Innocence* (1920)

WILDER, THORNTON: *The Bridge of San Luis Rey* (1927), *The Woman of Andros* (1930), *Heaven's My Destination* (1935)

WOLFE, THOMAS: *Look Homeward, Angel* (1929), *Of Time and the River* (1935), *You Can't Go Home Again* (1940).

WOOLF, VIRGINIA: *Mrs. Dalloway* (1925), *To the Lighthouse* (1927)

WRIGHT, RICHARD: *Native Son* (1940)

RECORDINGS OF POEMS

A NUMBER of modern poets can be heard reading their own poems on records. Various companies and services can supply these records, among them Columbia, Decca, Erpi Classroom Films, Inc., Harvard, HBC, HMV, Library of Congress, Linguaphone, Musicraft, National Council of Teachers of English, Timely, Victor, and Caedmon.

Among the poets who have recorded their poems are:

W. H. Auden	Linguaphone, NCTE, Columbia
George Barker	Harvard
S. V. Benét	NCTE
Elizabeth Bishop	Columbia
J. P. Bishop	NCTE
R. T. Coffin	Linguaphone, NCTE
E. E. Cummings	HBC, NCTE, Columbia
Walter de la Mare	HMV

Richard Eberhart	Harvard
T. S. Eliot	Harvard, Columbia, Library of Congress
J. G. Fletcher	Harvard
Robert Frost	Erpi, NCTE
Robert Hillyer	Harvard
John Holmes	Harvard
Robinson Jeffers	Harvard
Vachel Lindsay	Linguaphone, NCTE
Edwin Markham	Timely
Archibald MacLeish	Linguaphone, NCTE
Edna Millay	Victor
Marianne Moore	Columbia, NCTE
Ogden Nash	Columbia
Carl Sandburg	Decca, Musicraft
Stephen Spender	Harvard
Allen Tate	NCTE
Dylan Thomas	Columbia, Caedmon Publishers
W. C. Williams	Columbia, NCTE

BIOGRAPHICAL NOTES

FURTHER INFORMATION on the authors can be found in *Who's Who, Twentieth Century Authors,* edited by Kunitz and Haycroft, *Webster's Biographical Dictionary,* and in *Contemporary American Authors* and *Contemporary British Literature,* revised editions, both edited by Fred B. Millett.

JAMES TRUSLOW ADAMS (1878-1949) was born in Brooklyn. He received his B.A. from the Brooklyn Polytechnic and his M.A. from Yale. He became a partner in a stock exchange firm in Wall Street and exercised his interests in banking, manufacturing and railroading. During World War I he was a captain in military intelligence, and was later on the Colonel House Commission to prepare data for the peace conference. For ten years he was on the advisory council of the *Yale Review.* Among his writings are *The Founding of New England,* 1921, *Our Business Civilization,* 1929, *The March of Democracy,* 1932, and *America's Progress in Civilization* (with G. E. Freeland), 1940.

CHARLES ADDAMS (1912-   ) was born in New Jersey and studied at Colgate University, the University of Pennsylvania, and the Grand Central School of Art in New York. He is a contributor to *Collier's* and *The New Yorker,* where his cartoons have been appearing regularly since 1935. He has exhibited at museums, including the Metropolitan Museum of Art in New York, and published three collections, *Drawn and Quartered,* 1942, *Addams and Evil,* 1947, and *Monster Rally,* 1950.

MAXWELL ANDERSON (1888-   ) was born in Pennsylvania. After graduating from the University of North Dakota, where he studied drama under Frederick H. Koch, he taught English in North Dakota and California. Several years experience on newspapers in San Francisco and New York, during which time he wrote poetry and founded a poetry magazine, preceded his active work in drama. *White Desert* was a failure on the stage in 1923, but the success in 1924 of *What Price Glory?,* written with Laurence Stallings, turned him from editorial writing to the stage. His best known plays, besides *Winterset,* 1935, are *Elizabeth the Queen,* 1930, *Both Your Houses,* 1933, *Key Largo,* 1939, *The Eve of St. Mark,* 1942, *Joan of Lorraine,* 1946, and *Anne of the Thousand Days,* 1947.

SHERWOOD ANDERSON (1876-1941) was born in Camden, Ohio. He had little formal education after the age of fourteen, although he attended Wittenberg College briefly. After serving in the Spanish-American War, he managed a paint factory until one day when, according to legend, in the midst of dictating a letter he walked out of modern business into a literary career. In 1924 he settled in Marion, Virginia, where he edited both local papers, one Republican, one Democrat. His death interrupted a "good-will tour" of South America. His books include *Winesburg, Ohio,* 1919, *A Story Teller's Story,* 1924, *Dark Laughter,* 1925, *Home Town,* 1940, and *Memoirs,* 1942.

MATTHEW ARNOLD (1822-1888) was a graduate of Balliol College, Oxford, winning the Newdigate prize in poetry in 1843. He was inspector of schools from 1851 to 1886 and professor of poetry in Oxford from 1857 to 1867. He lectured widely and was in America in 1883-1884 and 1886. His critical works include two series of *Essays in Criticism,* 1865, 1888, *Culture and Anarchy,* 1869, and *Literature and Dogma,* 1873; his poems were collected in 1890.

W. H. AUDEN (1907-   ) was born at York, England, and educated at Christ Church College, Oxford. He taught for a time. In 1937 he served as an ambulance driver for the Loyalist forces in the Spanish Civil War. In 1939 he came to the United States and took out citizenship papers. He has taught at the New School for Social Research, the University of Michigan, and Swarthmore. His *Collected Poems* appeared in 1945. Later volumes are *The Age of Anxiety*, 1947, and *Nones*, 1951.

MARCH AVERY (1932-   ), born in New York City, has studied art from an early age. She spent a year at William Smith College and is at present a student of philosophy at Barnard College. Besides an ambition to write and paint, she is interested in ballet and children's book illustration. She is an associate editor of *The New Generation,* an intercollegiate quarterly of new writing and art.

LINCOLN BARNETT (1909-   ) was born in New York and attended Horace Mann School and Princeton University. He received his master's degree from Columbia University School of Journalism in 1932, the year after he became reporter on the city staff of the New York *Herald Tribune.* Later he joined *Life* as a staff writer and associate editor, where he remained until 1946. He now devotes all his time to writing.

PHILIP BARRY (1896-1949) was born in Rochester, New York, and educated at Yale. After graduation in 1919 he served as a clerk in embassy work in Washington and London, but resigned to enter the 47 Workshop at Harvard. For many years he wrote for both Broadway and Hollywood. His plays include *Hotel Universe,* 1930, *The Animal Kingdom,* 1932, and *The Philadelphia Story,* 1939.

CHARLES BEARD (1874-1948) was born in Indiana, and educated at DePauw, Oxford, Cornell and Columbia. He was professor of politics at Columbia from 1907 to 1917, after which he served for five years as director of the Training School for Public Service in New York. His later years have been devoted to writing and advisory work. His books include *Economic Interpretation of the Constitution,* 1913, *Economic Basis of Politics,* 1922, and, with his wife, *The Rise of American Civilization,* 1927, and *America in Midpassage,* 1939.

CARL BECKER (1873-1945) studied at Cornell College in Iowa, his native state, and at the University of Wisconsin. He held a fellowship in constitutional law at Columbia in 1898-1899 and taught at several universities and colleges, including Dartmouth, the University of Kansas and Cornell University, where he remained as professor of history from 1917 to his death. Some of his published books are *The Declaration of Independence—A Study in the History of Political Ideas,* 1922, *The Heavenly City of the Eighteenth Century Philosophers,* 1932, *Modern Democracy,* 1941, *How New Will the Better World Be?,* 1944, and *Freedom and Responsibility in the American Way of Life,* 1945.

S. N. BEHRMAN (1893-   ) was born in Massachusetts, and studied at Clark, Harvard and Columbia. He has contributed to various leading magazines and since 1927 has written for the stage and films. Among his plays are *Meteor,* 1929, *Brief Moment,* 1932, and *No Time for Comedy,* 1939. His scenarios include *Queen Christina* (Greta Garbo) and *The Tale of Two Cities* (Ronald Colman).

RUTH BENEDICT (1887-   ) was born in New York. After graduating from Vassar, she taught English, published poetry and studied anthropology under Franz Boas at Columbia, where she later became a member of the department. She has done field work among the Pueblo, Apache and Blackfoot Indians. Her books include *Patterns of Culture*, 1934, and *Race: Science and Politics*, 1940.

PETER BLUME (1906-   ) was born in Russia and came to the United States as a child. He was naturalized as a citizen in 1921. After attending public schools in New York City, he studied at the Art Students' Educational Alliance and the Art Students' League. He has held a Guggenheim Fellowship twice, in 1932 and 1936. Prominent among his honors are a first prize at the Carnegie International in 1934 and a purchase award in the Artists for Victory Exhibition at the Metropolitan Museum of Art in 1942.

EDMUND BLUNDEN (1896-   ) was born in Yalding, Kent. He interrupted his schooling in 1916 to enlist in World War I, became a lieutenant on active service, and was awarded the Military Cross. He completed his education at Oxford after the war, and has engaged in journalism, travel and teaching. Since 1931 he has been a Fellow and Tutor at Merton College, Oxford. He has edited the works of numerous English poets. His *Poems: 1930-1940* was issued in 1941.

GEORGE BOAS (1891-   ) studied at Brown, Harvard and Columbia. Beginning as an instructor in forensics at the University of California, he has taught at Johns Hopkins University since 1921, where he is professor of the history of philosophy. Author of *The Major Traditions of European Philosophy*, 1928, *Our New Ways of Thinking*, 1930, *Philosophy and Poetry*, 1933, *A Primer for Critics*, 1937, and contributor to *Harper's Magazine* and *The Atlantic Monthly*.

KENNETH BURKE (1897-   ) was born in Pittsburgh, and educated at Ohio State and Columbia. He was music critic of the *Dial*, 1927-1929, and of the *Nation*, 1934-1936. He won the *Dial* award in 1928 and was awarded a Guggenheim Fellowship in 1935. Among his books are *Permanence and Change: An Anatomy of Purpose*, 1935, *Attitudes Toward History*, 1937, *The Philosophy of Literary Form*, 1941, and *A Grammar of Motives*, 1945.

DEMETRIOS CAPETANAKIS (1913-1944) was born in Greece and studied at the universities of Athens, Heidelberg, and Cambridge. After the beginning of World War II, he remained in England to work for the Greek Ministry of Foreign Affairs in London. A number of his essays and poems, written in English, appeared in the British series, *Penguin New Writing* and *New Writing and Daylight*.

JOSEPH CONRAD (1857-1924) was born Jósef Teodor Konrad Korzeniowski in Russian Poland. He knew no English until he was twenty, learning it then laboriously from newspapers. At seventeen he shipped to sea on a French vessel, shifted later to English merchant ships and by 1880 had passed his examination as master. Failing health drove him from the sea in his late thirties, and settling in England, he became one of the greatest modern masters of prose fiction. His works include *The Nigger of the Narcissus*, 1897, *Lord Jim*, 1900, *Nostromo*, 1904, *Under Western Eyes*, 1911, and *Victory*, 1915.

NORMAN COUSINS was born in New Jersey, and studied at Columbia University. Writer and editor on various newspapers and magazines since 1934, he is now editor of *The Saturday Review of Literature*. He was publication consultant and editor for the Office of War Information's publication *U.S.A.* He is author of *The Good Inheritance*,

1941, and *The Democratic Chance,* 1942. *Modern Man Is Obsolete* has been issued in expanded book form by the Viking Press.

E. E. CUMMINGS (1894-) was born in Cambridge, Massachusetts, and graduated from Harvard in 1915. He received his M.A. the following year. He was a volunteer ambulance driver in France before the entry of the United States into World War I. After the war he lived in Paris for a time, then returned to New York. He made a trip to Russia in 1930. His novel, *The Enormous Room,* was published in 1922. His poetry includes *Collected Poems,* 1938, *Fifty Poems,* 1940, *1 × 1,* 1934, and *XAIPE: seventy-one poems,* 1950.

ROBERT DAY (1900-) was born in California and studied at the Otis Art Institute. He began work as a cartoonist for the Los Angeles *Times* and was later in the art departments of the Los Angeles *Examiner* and the New York *Herald Tribune.* In addition to drawings for advertisements, he has published *All Out for the Sack Race!* and illustrated *We Shook the Family Tree.* He is a contributor to *The New Yorker, Collier's,* and *The Saturday Evening Post.*

ABNER DEAN (1910-) was born in New York. After graduating from Dartmouth in 1931, he experimented with various art forms, published for some years cartoons and covers for *The New Yorker.* His work gained a wider notice with the publication of seven of his drawings in *Life* magazine and the consequent recognition given to his collections, *It's a long way to Heaven,* 1945, and *What am I doing here?,* 1947.

EMILY DICKINSON (1830-1886) was born in Amherst, Mass., into the quiet life and religious atmosphere of a very conservative town. She studied at the Academy founded by her grandfather, and for one year at the Mount Holyoke Female Seminary. When she was twenty-three years old, she journeyed to Washington to visit her father who was serving in Congress. After 1856 she virtually isolated herself in the family home for the rest of her life, and there wrote the poems which were neither known nor published until after her death. There has been much speculation over the reasons for this self-imposed isolation. Her 1862 letter to T. W. Higginson may provide a clue.

When a little girl, I had a friend who taught me Immortality; but venturing too near, himself, he never returned. Soon after, my tutor died, and for several years my lexicon was my only companion. Then I found one more, but he was not contented I be his scholar, so he left the land.

The majority of her poems are found in *Poems,* 1890, Second Series, 1891, Third Series, 1896, *Poems,* 1930, *Bolts of Melody,* 1945.

BONAMY DOBRÉE (1891-), British literary critic and scholar, has been professor of English literature at Leeds University since 1936. He was educated at the Royal Military Academy in Woolwich and at Cambridge University. His chief critical volumes are *Restoration Comedy,* 1924, *Restoration Tragedy,* 1929, *The Lamp and the Lute,* 1929, *John Wesley,* 1933, and *Alexander Pope,* 1951. With Herbert Read he edited *The London Book of English Prose,* 1931, and *The London Book of English Verse,* 1949; the former is an anthology-companion to his *Modern Prose Style.*

JOHN DOS PASSOS (1896-) was born in Chicago and graduated from Harvard. He was in the ambulance and medical services during World War I. Later he traveled widely as a newspaper correspondent and free-lance writer. Among his novels are *Three Soldiers,* 1921, *Manhattan Transfer,* 1925, the two trilogies, *U.S.A.,* 1937, and

District of Columbia, 1951, and *The Grand Design*, 1949. His volumes of discussion and reportage include *The Ground We Stand On*, 1941, and *Tour of Duty*, 1946.

HAROLD E. EDGERTON (1903-   ), electrical engineer and educator, was born in Fremont, Nebraska. After graduating from the University of Nebraska and employment with the Nebraska Light & Power Company and The General Electric Company, he studied at Massachusetts Institute of Technology for the degrees of Master and Doctor of Science. Now Professor of Electrical Engineering at M.I.T., he is the inventor of photographic apparatus for taking stroboscopic high-speed motion and still pictures. He is the winner of a medal from the Royal Photographic Society and author of *Flash!*, 1939.

T. S. ELIOT (1888-   ) was born in St. Louis, Missouri. He graduated with an M.A. in 1910 from Harvard, where his classmates included Heywood Broun, John Reed, Walter Lippmann and Stuart Chase. He has lived in England since 1915, and became a British subject in 1927. In 1928 he announced that he was "an Anglo-Catholic in religion, a classicist in literature, and a royalist in politics." His poetic works include *Collected Poems: 1909-1935*, *Four Quartets*, 1943, and the poetic plays, *Murder in the Cathedral*, 1935, *The Family Reunion*, 1939, and *The Cocktail Party*, 1950. Among his collections of essays are *Selected Essays: 1917-1932*, *Essays Ancient and Modern*, 1936, *The Idea of a Christian Society*, 1940, and *Notes towards the Definition of Culture*, 1949.

RALPH WALDO EMERSON (1803-1882) was born in Boston and educated at Harvard. Entering the ministry, he became pastor of the Second (Unitarian) Church of Boston, but personal and theological difficulties caused him to leave the ministry in 1832. Travel in America and Europe, where he met Coleridge, Wordsworth, Carlyle, and lecturing and writing occupied his later life.

Edwin Arlington Robinson regarded Emerson as America's greatest 19th Century poet, but Emerson was modest about his poetry, writing, "I feel it a hardship that—with something of a lover's passion for what is to me the most precious thing in life, poetry —I have no gift of fluency in it, only a rude and stammering utterance." Among his important works are *Nature*, 1836, *Essays*, First Series, 1841, *Poems*, 1847, *The Conduct of Life*, 1860, and *Society and Solitude*, 1870.

WILLIAM FAULKNER (1897-   ) was born in New Albany, Mississippi, of a family that had been reduced to genteel poverty by the Civil War. After the fifth grade his schooling was desultory. During World War I he flew with the Canadian Air Force, had two planes shot down over France, and was wounded. He returned to live in Oxford, Mississippi, and to write novels and stories about the inhabitants of mythical Yoknapatawpha County. When asked he describes his profession as "farmer." In 1950 he was awarded the Nobel prize for literature "for his forceful and independently artistic contribution to modern American fiction." Among his books are *The Sound and the Fury*, 1929, *As I Lay Dying*, 1930, *Sanctuary*, 1931, *Light in August*, 1932, *Absalom! Absalom!*, 1936, *Intruder in the Dust*, 1948, and *Collected Stories*, 1950. He prepared two versions of "The Bear": the shorter appears here, and the longer may be found in *Go Down, Moses, and Other Stories*, 1942.

KENNETH FEARING (1902-   ) was born in Oak Park, Illinois. He attended the University of Illinois, but transferred to and graduated from the University of Wisconsin in 1924. He worked at selling, free-lance writing, journalism, and for a time taught poetry at the League of American Writers in New York. He has said that poetry "must be exciting; otherwise it is valueless. . . . Besides being exciting, I think that poetry necessarily must be understandable." Among his books are *Collected Poems,* 1940, and *Afternoon of a Pawnbroker and Other Poems,* 1943.

F. SCOTT FITZGERALD (1896-1940) was born in St. Paul, Minnesota, and educated at Princeton. He left college in 1917 to serve as an infantry lieutenant and aide-de-camp until 1919. His first novel, *This Side of Paradise,* 1920, a reflection of the jazz age following World War I, was an instantaneous success. Thereafter he lived chiefly on Long Island or on the Riviera and in Rome. He spent his final three years in Hollywood and did some writing for motion pictures. Among his books are *The Great Gatsby,* 1925, *Tender Is the Night,* 1934, and the unfinished novel about Hollywood, *The Last Tycoon,* 1941.

E. M. FORSTER (1879-   ) was born in England and educated at Cambridge. He has spent much time in traveling, and turned the experiences of two years in India into his famous novel, *A Passage to India,* 1924. His other books include *A Room with a View,* 1908, *Howards End,* 1910, and a series of lectures, *Aspects of the Novel,* 1927.

ROBERT FROST (1875-   ) was born in San Francisco. After the death of his father in 1885, his mother took her children to Lawrence, Massachusetts. Eventually he attended Dartmouth for a few months, and Harvard for two years, but left college to teach and farm. He moved to England in 1912, where his first two books of poems were published—his first major recognition. In 1915 he returned to the United States. He has lectured and taught in various colleges, principally at Amherst. His work includes *Collected Poems,* 1939, *A Witness Tree,* 1942, *A Masque of Reason,* 1945, *A Masque of Mercy,* 1947, and *Steeple Bush,* 1947.

THOMAS HARDY (1840-1928) was born in Dorsetshire. After brief schooling he served as an architect's apprentice for several years. He became increasingly interested in creative writing, particularly in poetry but "necessity" turned him to the writing of novels. The first of his many novels appeared in 1871. His brilliant career as novelist was brought to a close by the critical attack on *Tess of the D'Urbervilles* and *Jude the Obscure.* "Cured of all interest in novel-writing," as he said, at the age of 58 he returned to poetry. He gradually won over an at first apathetic public, and his *Collected Poems* in 1919 showed his power as a poet. He continued to write until his death at the age of 88. In addition to his novels, short stories, and poems, he completed in 1908 an epic drama of the Napoleonic Wars, *The Dynasts.*

MARSDEN HARTLEY (1877-1943), painter and poet, was born in Lewiston, Maine, and spent his early years in Cleveland, Ohio. After study at the National Academy in New York and in Europe, he settled in New York City to paint the strongly colored, often symbolic and almost abstract landscapes and figures now in many American collections and museums. His first work, shown by Alfred Stieglitz in 1908, caused some critical controversy, but he continued to hold one-man exhibits for 30 years. In 1930 he won a Guggenheim Fellowship for study in Mexico. His poems and reproductions of some of his paintings are in *Selected Poems,* 1945.

S. I. HAYAKAWA (1906-   ) was born in Canada, and educated at the University of Manitoba, McGill and the University of Wisconsin. At present he is a professor of English at the Illinois Institute of Technology. His book, *Language in Action,* 1941, which grew primarily out of his research in semantics with the Polish semanticist Korzybski, has been revised as *Language in Thought and Action.* He is editor of *Etc.,* a journal of semantics.

ERNEST HEMINGWAY (1898-   ) was born in Oak Park, Illinois, ended his formal education with high school and became a Kansas City reporter. In World War I he served as volunteer ambulance driver in France and enlisted soldier in the Italian Army. While European correspondent for the Toronto *Star* and Paris correspondent for the Hearst newspapers, he began to write stories which brought him encouragement from Ezra Pound and Gertrude Stein. His subsequent writings have often been read less for their own qualities than for what they reveal about the skilled boxer, big-game hunter, ocean fisherman, and war correspondent who is their author. He reported on the Spanish Civil War, the Japanese invasion of northern China, and the Allied invasion of France in World War II, and he commanded his own yacht as a Q-boat hunting submarines off Cuba during the early years of World War II. *Death in the Afternoon*, 1932, and *Green Hills of Africa*, 1935, are stylized accounts of bullfighting and big-game hunting. His important novels are *The Sun Also Rises*, 1926, *A Farewell to Arms*, 1929, *For Whom the Bell Tolls*, 1940, *Across the River and into the Trees*, 1950, and *The Old Man and the Sea*, 1952. His stories are collected in *The Fifth Column and the First Forty-nine Stories*, 1938.

EDWARD HOPPER (1882-   ), American artist, has won many prizes and medals for his prints and paintings. He was born in Nyack, New York, and after attending public and private schools he studied at the New York School of Art under Chase and Henri. His works hang in a number of American museums, libraries, and private collections, and he is also a contributor to magazines.

A. E. HOUSMAN (1859-1936) was born in Worcestershire and attended St. John's College, Oxford. He failed his fourth-year honors examinations, but returned for one term of study to pass the degree. From 1882 to 1892 he was a clerk in the Government Patent Office in London. He continued his classical studies at night and won a reputation as a brilliant classical scholar. In 1892 he was appointed Professor of Latin in University College, London, and in 1911 received the same appointment in Trinity College, Cambridge, a position which he held until his death. He once said he was "not a pessimist but a pejorist." *A Shropshire Lad* was published in 1896, *Last Poems* in 1922. *More Poems*, a posthumous collection, appeared in 1936. His essay, *The Name and Nature of Poetry*, was printed in 1933.

ALDOUS HUXLEY (1894-   ) is the grandson of Thomas Henry Huxley and grand-nephew of Matthew Arnold. He was educated at Eton and Oxford. During 1919-1920 he was on the editorial staff of the *Athenaeum*, and during 1920-1921 served as dramatic critic on the *Westminster Gazette*. He has traveled widely and now lives in Hollywood, California. Among his novels are *Antic Hay*, 1923, *Point Counter Point*, 1928, *Brave New World*, 1932, *Eyeless in Gaza*, 1936, and *Time Must Have a Stop*, 1945. His other work includes *Proper Studies*, 1927, *Do What You Will*, 1929, *Texts and Pretexts*, 1932, *Ends and Means*, 1937, and *The Perennial Philosophy*, 1945.

WILLIAM JAMES (1842-1910), the American psychologist and philosopher, was the brother of Henry James the novelist. A graduate of Harvard Medical School, he taught anatomy, physiology and hygiene at Harvard from 1872, and was professor of philosophy there from 1881. He was the founder of Pragmatism and author of *Principles of Psychology*, 1890, *The Varieties of Religious Experience*, 1902, *Pragmatism*, 1907, *A Pluralistic Universe*, 1909, and *Essays in Radical Empiricism*, 1912.

ROBINSON JEFFERS (1887-   ) was born in Pittsburgh. He lived in Europe from 1899 until 1902. In 1905 he received his A.B. from Occidental College. He did some graduate work in forestry and medicine. In 1912 a legacy made him independent, and two years later he settled permanently at Carmel, California, where he built his famous stone tower. Among his books are *Selected Poetry*, 1938, *Be Angry at the Sun*, 1941, *Medea* (an adaptation of the Greek tragedy), 1946, and *The Double Axe*, 1948.

THOMAS JEFFERSON (1743-1826), third president of the United States, was born in Virginia and graduated from the College of William and Mary in 1762. Admitted to the bar in 1767, he was a member of Virginia House of Burgesses from 1769 to 1774, and at that time began the work that was to lead to American independence. A member of the Continental Congress, he wrote and presented the first draft of the Declaration of Independence to the Congress in 1776. Before his election as President in 1801, he was governor of Virginia, minister to France, Secretary of State, and Vice President. His election to the Presidency was by the House of Representatives after a tie with Aaron Burr in the popular vote. After his retirement in 1809, he helped found the University of Virginia and pursued his studies in agriculture, architecture, and literature. His chief writings, official and personal, are collected by S. K. Padover in *The Complete Jefferson*, 1942.

JAMES JOYCE (1882-1941) was born in Dublin and educated, at first with the intention of entering the priesthood, at Clongowes Wood College and Belvedere College in Ireland, and at the Royal University, Dublin, where he studied languages and literature. In 1904 he left Ireland, to return briefly only twice during the rest of his life. He studied medicine and music in Paris, taught languages in Italy and Switzerland, was in Zurich during World War I, and moved soon after to Paris, where he spent the remainder of his life. His first book, *Dubliners*, a group of short stories intended to portray the "paralysis" of Western civilization, was ready for publication in 1907, but was suppressed for

seven years because of references to Edward VII. *Ulysses* (1922) was at first banned in England and the United States, but was finally passed for publication in 1934. His last work, *Finnegans Wake*, an experiment in language and symbolism, was published in 1939.

D. H. LAWRENCE (1885-1930), British novelist and poet, struggled in his early years for an education and recognition of his gifts and in his later years against misunderstanding and prudish censorship of his work. Born in a small mining town in Nottinghamshire, he attended high school on a scholarship, worked as a clerk, and before he was twenty was an elementary school teacher. After two years in a Training College, he taught for five years until publication of some poems and his first novel gave him confidence in his talents. Rejected for war service because of his tubercular condition, he left England in 1919 in search of health and a simpler life than that allowed by what he considered the distorted values of modern civilization. Accompanied by his wife, the Baroness Frieda von Richtofen, he traveled in Australia, Sardinia, Sicily, and settled for longer periods in New Mexico and Mexico. When he died in 1930, at Vence, in southern France, he left nearly fifty volumes of novels, stories, plays, poems, essays and journals. Among his major novels are *Sons and Lovers*, 1913, *The Rainbow*, 1915, *Women in Love*, 1920, *The Plumed Serpent*, 1926, and *Lady Chatterley's Lover*, 1928. His poems were collected in 1929, his stories in 1934, and his letters (with an introduction by Aldous Huxley) in 1932. His other works include *Studies in Classic American Literature*, 1923, *Apocalypse* (collected essays), 1931, and *Etruscan Places*, 1932.

WALTER LIPPMANN (1889-   ) was born in New York and graduated from Harvard in 1910. In his last year he was assistant to George Santayana. After college he worked with Lincoln Steffens on *Everybody's Maga-*

zine. In 1914 he became one of the founding editors of the *New Republic*. For four months in 1917 he was assistant to Newton D. Baker, Secretary of War. He was a member of the American commission at the Versailles conference. In 1929 he became editor of the New York *World*, and when that daily ceased publication he went to the *Herald Tribune*. In 1936 he reversed his political position, announcing himself a Republican. He made a tour of Germany in 1946. His many books include *A Preface to Politics*, 1913, *A Preface to Morals*, 1929, *The Good Society*, 1937, *U. S. Foreign Policy*, 1944, and *U. S. War Aims*, 1944.

LUIGI LUCIONI (1900-   ) was born in Italy and came to the United States in 1911. He studied at the Cooper Union Art School (1916-1920) and the National Academy of Design (1920-1925). His work is represented by many paintings and etchings in American galleries and collections. He won the Tiffany medal in 1928, the first popular prize at the Carnegie International Exhibition in 1939 and in the same year the first popular prize at the Biennial Exhibition in Washington, D. C.

THOMAS MACAULAY (1800-1859) was born in Leicestershire and educated at Cambridge. A member of Parliament for four terms between 1830 and 1856, he was Secretary of War in 1839-1841, and was made the first Baron Macaulay in 1857. He was a contributor to the *Edinburgh Review* from 1825 on, and wrote five volumes of a *History of England*, covering the reigns of James II and William III, as well as numerous speeches, biographical and literary essays and *The Lays of Ancient Rome*, 1842.

ARCHIBALD MacLEISH (1892-   ) was born in Glencoe, Illinois. He received his B.A. from Yale in 1915, and his LL.B. from Harvard in 1919. He enlisted in the Field Artillery in 1917 and was discharged as a captain. From 1923 to 1928 he traveled abroad. On his return he worked on *Fortune*

magazine. In 1939 he was named Librarian of Congress, and in 1941 was appointed Director of Office of Facts and Figures (which later became the Office of War Information under Elmer Davis). For a while he served as Under-Secretary of State. Among his books are *Selected Poems: 1924-1933*, *Public Speech*, 1936, *America Was Promises*, 1939, the two radio plays, *The Fall of the City*, 1937, and *Air Raid*, 1938, and his essays, *The Irresponsibles*, 1940, *The American Cause*, 1941, and *A Time to Speak*, 1941. Since 1949 he has been Boylston Professor at Harvard University, and has contributed to many magazines. *Actfive and Other Poems* was published in 1948, and *Collected Poems* in 1952.

SOMERSET MAUGHAM (1874-   ) was born in Paris. Much of his early life is reflected in his novel, *Of Human Bondage*, 1915. He studied medicine, but never practiced, preferring writing instead. His first success came as a playwright in 1907. Since then he has traveled widely and lived in many parts of the world. His fiction includes *The Moon and Sixpence*, 1919, *The Razor's Edge*, 1945, and such collections of short stories as *The Trembling of a Leaf*, 1921, and *The Mixture as Before*, 1940. Among his plays are *The Circle*, 1921, and *Our Betters*, 1923. *The Summing Up*, 1938, is autobiography.

JO MIELZINER (1901-   ), born in Paris, has been a successful designer of stage settings for 24 years, working in all forms of theatrical presentation, plays, operas, ballets, and musical comedies. His work has been seen in *Strange Interlude, Pal Joey, The Glass Menagerie, Finian's Rainbow, Death of a Salesman, South Pacific,* and many others. He also designed the setting and lighting for the United Nations Conference at San Francisco in 1945 and has lectured on stage design at Fordham University.

ARTHUR MILLER (1915-   ), was born in New York City and graduated from the

University of Michigan in 1938, where he twice won the Avery Hopwood award for playwriting. In 1947 *All My Sons* received the Drama Critics Circle Award. He achieved nation-wide fame with *Death of a Salesman* in 1949, which won the Pulitzer Prize for drama. His most recent play, *The Crucible,* opened in New York in 1953.

JOSEPH MITCHELL (1908-   ) was born in North Carolina, and educated at the University of North Carolina. He began as a newspaper reporter in New York, and is now a staff member of *The New Yorker.* In an author's note to *McSorley's Wonderful Saloon,* 1944, from which "Professor Sea Gull" is reprinted, Mitchell says: "The people in a number of the stories are of the kind that many writers have recently got in the habit of referring to as 'the little people.' I regard this phrase as patronizing and repulsive. There are no little people in this book. They are as big as you are, whoever you are." He has also written *My Ears Are Bent.*

EUGENE O'NEILL (1888-   ) was born in New York City. His father was a popular actor. After one year at Princeton, O'Neill prospected for gold in Honduras, shipped for a year as a seaman, acted in his father's company and reported for the New London *Telegraph.* Sent to a sanatorium at twenty-three for tuberculosis, he there decided to become a playwright. He enrolled in 1914 in the 47 Workshop at Harvard, and in 1916 became associated with the Provincetown Theatre. His first full-length play, *Beyond the Horizon,* 1920, won the Pulitzer Prize. He has won it twice since, with *Anna Christie,* 1922, and *Strange Interlude,* 1928. In 1936 he was awarded the Nobel Prize. Other important plays are *The Emperor Jones,* 1921, *Desire Under the Elms,* 1925, *Mourning Becomes Electra,* 1931. Since 1935 he has been writing a cycle of nine plays tentatively titled *A Tale of Possessors Self-Dispossessed,* the saga of an American family, 1775-1932.

J. ORTEGA Y GASSET (1883-   ) is a Spanish philosopher, writer and statesman. A professor at the University of Madrid before the Spanish Civil War, he was also a member of the Cortes in 1931 and civil governor of Madrid. He lived in South America during the Spanish Civil War but has recently returned to Spain. He is the author of *Invertebrate Spain,* 1922, *The Revolt of the Masses,* 1932, *Concord and Liberty,* 1946, and *The Dehumanization of Art and Notes on the Novel,* 1948.

GEORGE ORWELL (1903-1950), whose real name was Eric Blair, was born in India of an Anglo-Indian family and attended Eton on scholarship. Five years of service with the India Imperial Police permanently injured his health and set his mind forever against the horrors of politics, particularly the imperialist kind, and he left India for Paris and England. Further political disillusionment came with the Spanish Civil War, in which he was wounded after four months of fighting for the Loyalists. He retired to a farm in England to become a prominent columnist and essayist for British and American periodicals, as well as to write the novels and personal accounts that have made him well known for insight into current affairs. Among his works are the satire on Russian Communism, *Animal Farm,* 1946, a novel of the future, *Nineteen Eighty-four,* 1949, a collection of essays, *Dickens, Dali, and Others,* 1946, and some volumes about his experiences in India, Paris, London, and Spain.

WILFRED OWEN (1893-1918) was born in Shropshire and educated at Birkenhead Institute, Liverpool. From 1913 to 1915 he tutored at Bordeaux. After England's entrance into World War I, he enlisted in the Artists' Rifles, saw much action, was wounded, and was awarded the Military Cross for gallantry. One week before the Armistice, he was killed trying to get his company across the Sambre Canal. *Poems,* 1920. Enlarged edition, 1931.

MARY PETTY lives in New York City and is married to Alan Dunn, the artist. In addition to drawing cartoons and covers for *The New Yorker*, she has illustrated *Goodbye, Mr. Chippendale* by T. H. Robsjohn-Gibbings and a new edition of Dickens' *Martin Chuzzlewit*. Of the people in her drawings she has said, "I'm afraid I am like the people I draw, of whom Harold Ross is reported to have once said, 'They look like something that lives under a rock.'"

PABLO PICASSO (1881-   ) was born in Spain and studied at the academies of Barcelona and Madrid. By the age of 17 he was winning prizes for his paintings. In 1901 he went to Paris, where he studied the moderns and formed strong friendships among writers and other painters. After trying several styles, his work began to earn notice about 1905, when he painted Gertrude Stein's portrait. He has continued to experiment in styles, cubist, classical, and surrealistic, and in many media, including stage settings for ballet, sculpture, collage, and ceramics. His "Guernica," a 250 foot square mural, was intended as a protest against Franco's bombing of Spanish villages. His works are in the major collections of modern art all over the world, notably in the Museum of Modern Art in New York.

KATHERINE ANNE PORTER (1894-   ) was born in Texas and educated at southern convent schools. She began writing when very young. In 1931 she was awarded a Guggenheim Fellowship. She has said of her writing: ". . . my one aim is to tell a straight story and to give true testimony." Her work includes *Flowering Judas*, 1930, *Pale Horse, Pale Rider*, 1939, and *The Leaning Tower*, 1943.

EDWIN ARLINGTON ROBINSON (1869-1935) was born in Head Tide, Maine. He spent two years at Harvard, then went to New York, where he worked on new subway construction, lived very frugally and continued his writing. In 1905 President Theodore Roosevelt, who had read and been impressed by his poems, had him appointed to the New York Customs House. After 1911 Robinson spent his summers at the MacDowell Colony in Peterboro, New Hampshire, and his winters in New York. His *Collected Poems* was printed in 1937.

CARL SANDBURG (1878-   ) was born in Galesburg, Illinois. He left school at thirteen and worked at miscellaneous jobs for several years. During the Spanish-American War he enlisted and served in Puerto Rico for eight months. After his discharge he worked his way at Lombard College but did not graduate. He then engaged in newspaper work, and for a time was secretary to the Socialist mayor of Milwaukee. After 1914, his poetry began to win him wide recognition. His poetry includes *Selected Poems*, 1926, *The People, Yes*, 1936, and *Home Front Memo*, 1943. He has also published a biography: *Abraham Lincoln, the Prairie Years*, 1926, and *Abraham Lincoln, the War Years*, 1939.

WILLIAM SAROYAN (1908-   ) was born in Fresno, California, of Armenian parentage. He began working very young and left school at the age of fifteen. He read widely, learned to use a typewriter, and started to write. Writing was easy for him, he says, because he wrote what he felt like writing and not what the world wished him to write. In 1934 his first volume of stories, *The Daring Young Man on the Flying Trapeze*, was published. Since then he has published several hundred stories, has had a number of plays produced and has written two novels, *The Human Comedy*, 1942, and *The Adventures of Wesley Jackson*, 1946. His play, *The Time of Your Life*, 1939, won the Pulitzer Prize, which Saroyan refused. He lives in California, where his life, as he says, is that of a loafer and natural-born writer.

ERIC SEVAREID (1912-   ), news analyst and radio correspondent, was born in Velva, North Dakota. He studied at the University of Minnesota and the Alliance Française in Paris. Beginning as copy boy, and later reporter, on Minneapolis newspapers, he continued reporting in France, where at one time he was both day city editor of the Paris *Herald* and night editor for United Press. Just before World War II he became European correspondent for the Columbia Broadcasting System at the insistence of Edward Murrow and with the help of H. V. Kaltenborn. He witnessed the disintegration of France, giving nightly broadcasts to America, and created what he modestly calls a "minor" legend in American radio by managing to report the capitulation of France from Tours and Bordeaux over a little known shortwave station still in French hands. He escaped to England and continued to report the war by radio from all parts of the world. He won the William Peabody Award for news reporting in 1950 and has published, in addition to his autobiographical volume, a children's book, *Canoeing with the Cree*, 1935, and a collection of broadcasts, *In One Ear*, 1952.

KARL SHAPIRO (1913-   ) was born in Baltimore, and attended the University of Virginia and Johns Hopkins briefly. He went into the army in March, 1941. He was in Australia, New Guinea and the Southwest Pacific Area from March, 1942, to the end of the war. His books are *Person, Place, and Thing*, 1942, *V-Letter and Other Poems*, 1944, *Essay on Rime*, 1945, and *Trial of a Poet*, 1947. He has been Consultant in Poetry for the Library of Congress, has taught at Johns Hopkins University, and is at present editor of *Poetry* magazine.

CHARLES SHEELER (1883-   ) was born in Philadelphia and studied at the School of Industrial Art, Philadelphia, and at the Pennsylvania Academy of The Fine Arts. After painting trips to Europe, while he took up photography as a means of livelihood, he began to exhibit his paintings. He has exhibited in many galleries and museums, the most complete showing being at the Museum of Modern Art in 1939. His work in both painting and photography is based, to use his own words, on "the concept of a picture as having an underlying architectural structure to support the elements in nature which comprise the picture."

GEORGE SOKOLSKY (1893-   ) was born in Utica, New York, and educated at Columbia. He was editor of the *Russian Daily News* in Petrograd in 1917, and spent the next dozen years in China, also in newspaper work. Later he became a contributor and columnist on American papers, and from 1937 to 1941 was a broadcaster for the National Association of Manufacturers. He is author of *Tinder Box of Asia*, 1932, *Labor Crisis in the United States*, 1938, and *The American Way of Life*, 1939.

GEORGE SOULE (1887-   ) was born in Stamford, Connecticut, and graduated from Yale in 1908. For a time he worked in a publishing house. During World War I he was in Washington for a while as a special writer on war organization, but in May, 1918, went into the coast artillery. Since 1923 he has been an editor of *The New Republic*. He has served on various national commissions on economic matters, and has taught at Yale and Columbia. His books include *A Planned Society*, 1932, *The Coming American Revolution*, 1934, *An Economic Constitution for Democracy*, 1939, and *The Strength of Nations*, 1942.

STEPHEN SPENDER (1909-   ) was born in London. He attended University College, Oxford, where he met and worked with W. H. Auden and Louis MacNeice. In 1937 he went to Spain to attend the International Writers Congress, and remained there for several months during the Civil War. His sympathies were with the Loyalists. During World War II he was in or near London, and served as a fireman through the blitz. His work includes *Poems*, 1933, *The Still Centre*, 1939, *Ruins and Visions*, 1942, *Poems of Dedication*, 1947, *The Edge of Being*, 1949, and the prose volumes, *The Destructive Element*, 1934, *European Witness*, 1946, and an autobiography, *World within World*, 1951.

GERTRUDE STEIN (1874-1946) was born in Allegheny, Pennsylvania. Part of her early life was spent in Europe, and after her college course at Radcliffe, where she studied under William James, and several years at the Johns Hopkins Medical School, she returned to France for residence. During World War I she drove an ambulance and increased the circle of her friends, which already included Picasso and Matisse. After the war she gave guidance and encouragement to many young writers, such as Ernest Hemingway, Glenway Westcott and F. Scott Fitzgerald. Her own writings include *Three Lives*, 1908, *Tender Buttons*, 1915, *The Making of Americans*, 1925, *The Autobiography of Alice B. Toklas*, 1933, *Four Saints in Three Acts* (with music by Virgil Thomson), 1934, *Lectures in America*, 1935, and *Picasso*, 1938. Her experiences during World War II were dealt with in *Wars I Have Seen*, 1945, and *Brewsie and Willie*, 1946.

JOHN STEINBECK (1902-   ) was born in Salinas, California, the scene of some of his fiction. He spent four years as a special student at Stanford, where his chief interest was in biology. Later he worked at many odd jobs. His first three books were failures. In 1935 *Tortilla Flat* was well received and was followed by *In Dubious Battle*, 1936, *Of Mice and Men*, 1937, and *The Long Valley* (short stories), 1938. His *Grapes of Wrath*, 1939, was a best-seller and was awarded the Pulitzer Prize in 1940. He also published

Sea of Cortez (with *E. F. Ricketts*), 1941, *The Moon Is Down*, 1942, *Cannery Row*, 1945, *The Wayward Bus*, 1947, *The Pearl*, 1948, *Burning Bright*, 1950, and *East of Eden*, 1952.

J. W. N. SULLIVAN (1886-1937), British mathematician, physicist, and philosopher, pursued his aptitude for mathematics at University College, London, and then turned to writing. Well known in England as an interpreter of modern science, he also wrote on philosophy and music and occasionally turned to fiction. Among his works are *Aspects of Science, Beethoven: His Spiritual Development, Three Men Discuss Relativity*, and *But for the Grace of God*.

DYLAN THOMAS (1914-   ) was born in Wales. After an early career in journalism and film scripting, he published *18 Poems* in 1934, saying that the poems were, "the record of my individual struggle from darkness towards some measure of light . . . My poetry is or should be useful to others for its individual recording of that same struggle with which they are necessarily acquainted." During the War he worked for the BBC. In 1950-52 he has traveled in the U. S. reading his poems at many colleges. His important collections are *The World I Breathe*, 1939, *Selected Writings*, 1946, *In Country Sleep*, 1952, and *Collected Poems*, 1953.

JAMES THURBER (1894-   ) was born in Columbus, Ohio, and educated at Ohio State University. For a time he was a reporter and writer on the Paris edition of the Chicago *Tribune*. He returned to New York in 1926, and began contributing humorous sketches, stories and drawings to *The New Yorker*. His books include *The Owl in the Attic and Other Perplexities*, 1931, *My Life and Hard Times*, 1933, *My World—and Welcome to It*, 1942, *The Thurber Carnival*, 1945, and *The Thurber Album*, 1952.

LIONEL TRILLING (1905-   ) was born and educated in New York City. His graduate study was at Columbia University, where he is now Professor of English. His editorial service on *The Kenyon Review* and *The Partisan Review* and for "The American Men of Letters Series" has made him well known among students of literature. Besides stories and criticism for leading magazines, he has published two critical biographies, *Matthew Arnold,* 1939, and *E. M. Forster,* 1943, a novel, *The Middle of the Journey,* 1949, and a collection of essays, *The Liberal Imagination,* 1950.

FREDERICK J. TURNER (1861-1932), American historian, was born in Portage, Wisconsin. He taught at the University of Wisconsin (1889-1910), as described here in Carl L. Becker's essay, and at Harvard University (1910-1924). His essay here, read before the American Historical Association in 1893, inaugurated a new theory concerning the influence of the West in American experience and has become a landmark for later historians. It was first included in *The Frontier in American History,* 1920. His *The Significance of Sections in American History,* 1932, received the Pulitzer Prize after his death.

GENE WELTFISH (1902-   ) studied at Barnard College, Columbia University. She has been an instructor in the Department of Anthropology at Columbia since 1936.

EUDORA WELTY (1909-   ) has lived all her life in her native Jackson, Mississippi, except for excursions to the University of Wisconsin, where she received a bachelor's degree in 1929, and to the School of Advertising at Columbia University. She has done publicity work, writing feature stories and radio scripts and taking photographs. Her stories have won a number of awards, the O. Henry Memorial Prize in 1942 and 1943 and the American Academy award, for "her artistry in the subtle portrayal of character,"

in 1944. Her first collection of short stories, *A Curtain of Green,* was introduced by Katherine Anne Porter in 1941. Other collections are *The Wide Net,* 1943, and *The Golden Apples,* 1949; her novels are *The Robber Bridegroom,* 1942, and *Delta Wedding,* 1946.

WALT WHITMAN (1819-1892), was born on Long Island. Brief schooling followed the family's removal to Brooklyn, and young Whitman went to work as a "printer's devil" and typesetter. Years of hack-work as a printer-journalist led to his editorship of the *Brooklyn Eagle.* After two years he left, and there followed years of unsuccessful journalism, of carpentry with his father, of lecturing. In 1855 his publication of *Leaves of Grass* brought high praise from Emerson, but abuse and incomprehension from others. He continued with his poetry, and the 3d Edition of *Leaves of Grass* in 1860 contained 157 poems. During the Civil War he worked as a volunteer nurse in army hospitals, and for some years after the War as a Government clerk. In 1873 he suffered a paralytic stroke which forced him to leave Washington. He settled in Camden, N. J., where he remained, a semi-invalid, for the rest of his life. In 1891 he was able to attend a dinner where he received the congratulations of some of the most distinguished Americans and Englishmen for his writing. His other works were *Drum Taps,* 1865, *Democratic Vistas,* 1871.

TENNESSEE WILLIAMS (1914-   ) was born in Columbus, Mississippi, and attended the University of Missouri, Washington University, and the University of Iowa. He has said that seeing a performance of Ibsen's *Ghosts* made him want to write for the theater. By 1939 his one-act plays had attracted attention. Scholarship awards from Theresa Helburn and John Gassner of the Theatre Guild, and awards from the American Academy and the Rockefeller Fellowship encouraged his writing. *The Glass Menagerie* in

1945 and *A Street Car Named Desire* in 1947 established him as one of our finest dramatists. *Summer and Smoke* in 1948 and *The Rose Tattoo* in 1951, while not so widely praised, show further development of his sensitive artistry.

THOMAS WOLFE (1900-1938) was born in Asheville, North Carolina. He graduated from the University of North Carolina in 1920, went on to Harvard, and after receiving his M.A. there was appointed instructor in English at Washington Square College, New York University. During the next six years he taught, traveled in Europe and worked at his writing. "A man must use the material and experience of his own life," he said, "if he is to create anything that has substantial value." The editor, Maxwell Perkins, helped him put his writing in publishable form, and in 1929 *Look Homeward, Angel* appeared. Its success was immediate. Among his other books are *Of Time and the River*, 1935, *From Death to Morning*, 1935, *The Story of a Novel*, 1936, and *You Can't Go Home Again*, 1940.

WILLIAM BUTLER YEATS (1865-1939) was born in Dublin. He first studied art, then turned to writing. He worked to encourage an Irish literary renaissance. For four years he was a Senator of the Irish Free State. He was awarded the Nobel Prize in 1923. His books include *Collected Poems*, 1933, *Collected Plays*, 1934, and *Last Poems and Plays*, 1940.

INDEX

Index

Index